Official

BASEBALL DOPE BOOK

1985 EDITION

Editor/Baseball Dope Book
CRAIG CARTER

Contributing Editor/Baseball Dope Book
DAVE SLOAN

President-Chief Executive Officer
RICHARD WATERS

Editor
DICK KAEGEL

Director of Books and Periodicals
RON SMITH

Published by

The Sporting News

1212 North Lindbergh Boulevard
P.O. Box 56 — St. Louis, MO 63166

Copyright © 1985
The Sporting News Publishing Company
a Times Mirror company

ISBN 0-89204-180-3   ISSN 0162-5411

TABLE OF CONTENTS

◆•◆

ON THE COVER: Boston slugger Tony Armas led the major leagues in home runs with 43 and runs batted in with 123 last season and was named an outfielder on both The Sporting News American League All-Star and Silver Slugger teams.

                                               —Photo by Richard Pilling

ROBERT W. BROWN
President
American League

PETER V. UEBERROTH
Commissioner
of Baseball

CHARLES S. FEENEY
President
National League

Major League Directory

Commissioner of Baseball—Peter V. Ueberroth
Secretary-Treasurer & General Counsel—Alexander H. Hadden
Office of Baseball—350 Park Avenue, New York, N. Y. 10022
Executive Council—Peter V. Ueberroth, Commissioner; Robert W. Brown, President of American League; Charles S. Feeney, President of National League; Roy Eisenhardt, Peter Hardy, Jerry Reinsdorf and Edward B. Williams, representatives of American League, and Charles Bronfman, Nelson Doubleday, Peter F. O'Malley and Ballard Smith, representatives of National League.

Administrative Officer—William A. Murray
Director of Broadcasting—Bryan L. Burns
Director of Information—Robert A. Wirz
Assistant to Administrative Officer—George E. Pfister,
Miguel A. Rodriguez (Winter League Baseball Coordinator)
Director of Security—Horace Gibbs

AMERICAN LEAGUE

President—Robert W. Brown, M.D.
Vice-Presidents—John E. Fetzer, Gene Autry
Executive Vice President—Robert O. Fishel
Director of Public Relations—Phyllis Merhige
League Office—350 Park Avenue, New York, N. Y. 10022

Umpires—Larry Barnett, Nick Bremigan, Joseph Brinkman, Alan Clark, Drew Coble, Terry Cooney, Derryl Cousins, Don Denkinger, James Evans, Dale Ford, Rich Garcia, Ted Hendry, John Hirschbeck, Mark Johnson, Ken Kaiser, Greg Kosc, Bill Kunkel, Tim McClelland, Larry McCoy, James McKean, Durwood Merrill, Dan Morrison, Jerry Neudecker, Steve Palermo, David Phillips, Rick Reed, Mike Reilly, John (Rocky) Roe, John Shulock, Marty Springstead, Vic Voltaggio, Tim Welke.

NATIONAL LEAGUE

President—Charles S. Feeney
Vice-President—John J. McHale
Secretary—Phyllis Collins
Administrator & Director of Public Relations—Blake Cullen
Business Manager—Louis H. Krems
League Office—350 Park Avenue, New York, N. Y. 10022

Umpires—Fred Brocklander, Jerry Crawford, Jerry Dale, Dave Davidson, Robert Davidson, Gerry Davis, Bob Engel, Bruce Froemming, Eric Gregg, Lanny Harris, Doug Harvey, John Kibler, Randy Marsh, John McSherry, Ed Montague, Dave Pallone, Frank Pulli, Jim Quick, Dutch Rennert, Steve Rippley, Paul Runge, Dick Stello, Terry Tata, Harry Wendelstedt, Joe West, Lee Weyer, Bill Williams, Charles Williams.

AMERICAN LEAGUE—Pennant Winners—1900-1984

1900—Chicago* .... .607	1929—Philadelphia .... .693	1958—New York................... .597
1901—Chicago..................... .610	1930—Philadelphia .... .662	1959—Chicago..................... .610
1902—Philadelphia .... .610	1931—Philadelphia .... .704	1960—New York................... .630
1903—Boston .... .659	1932—New York................... .695	1961—New York................... .673
1904—Boston .... .617	1933—Washington................ .651	1962—New York................... .593
1905—Philadelphia .... .622	1934—Detroit .... .656	1963—New York................... .646
1906—Chicago..................... .616	1935—Detroit .... .616	1964—New York................... .611
1907—Detroit .... .613	1936—New York................... .667	1965—Minnesota .... .630
1908—Detroit .... .588	1937—New York................... .662	1966—Baltimore.................. .606
1909—Detroit .... .645	1938—New York................... .651	1967—Boston .... .568
1910—Philadelphia .... .680	1939—New York................... .702	1968—Detroit .... .636
1911—Philadelphia .... .669	1940—Detroit .... .584	1969—Baltimore.................. .673
1912—Boston .... .691	1941—New York................... .656	1970—Baltimore.................. .667
1913—Philadelphia .... .627	1942—New York................... .669	1971—Baltimore.................. .639
1914—Philadelphia .... .651	1943—New York................... .636	1972—Oakland..................... .600
1915—Boston .... .669	1944—St. Louis .... .578	1973—Oakland..................... .580
1916—Boston .... .591	1945—Detroit .... .575	1974—Oakland..................... .556
1917—Chicago..................... .649	1946—Boston .... .675	1975—Boston .... .594
1918—Boston .... .595	1947—New York................... .630	1976—New York................... .610
1919—Chicago..................... .629	1948—Cleveland† .... .626	1977—New York................... .617
1920—Cleveland .... .636	1949—New York................... .630	1978—New York‡.................. .613
1921—New York................... .641	1950—New York................... .636	1979—Baltimore.................. .642
1922—New York................... .610	1951—New York................... .636	1980—Kansas City .... .599
1923—New York................... .645	1952—New York................... .617	1981—New York§.................. .551
1924—Washington................ .597	1953—New York................... .656	1982—Milwaukee................. .586
1925—Washington................ .636	1954—Cleveland .... .721	1983—Baltimore.................. .605
1926—New York................... .591	1955—New York................... .623	1984—Detroit .... .642
1927—New York................... .714	1956—New York................... .630	
1928—New York................... .656	1957—New York................... .636	

*Not recognized as major league in 1900. †Defeated Boston in one-game playoff for pennant. ‡Defeated Boston in one-game playoff for division championship. §Defeated Milwaukee in five-game playoff for division championship.

STANDING OF CLUBS AT CLOSE OF SEASON

EAST DIVISION

Club.	Det.	Tor.	N.Y.	Bos.	Bal.	Cle.	Mil.	Cal.	Chi.	K.C.	Min.	Oak.	Sea.	Tex.	W.	L.	Pct.	G.B.
Detroit	..	8	7	6	6	9	11	8	8	7	9	9	6	10	104	58	.642	....
Toronto	5	..	5	8	9	7	3	5	8	7	11	8	7	6	89	73	.549	15
New York.....	6	8	..	6	8	11	7	4	5	7	4	8	7	6	87	75	.537	17
Boston	7	5	7	..	7	10	9	9	7	3	6	7	4	5	86	76	.531	18
Baltimore	7	4	5	6	..	7	7	8	7	5	5	6	9	9	85	77	.525	19
Cleveland	4	6	2	3	6	..	9	4	4	6	7	7	8	9	75	87	.463	29
Milwaukee	2	10	6	4	6	4	..	4	5	6	5	4	6	5	67	94	.416	36½

WEST DIVISION

Club.	K.C.	Cal.	Min.	Oak.	Chi.	Sea.	Tex.	Bal.	Bos.	Cle.	Det.	Mil.	N.Y.	Tor.	W.	L.	Pct.	G.B.
Kan. City......	..	7	6	5	8	9	6	7	9	6	5	6	5	5	84	78	.519	....
California	6	..	4	7	8	9	5	4	3	8	4	8	8	7	81	81	.500	3
Minnesota.....	7	9	..	8	5	7	8	7	6	5	3	7	8	1	81	81	.500	3
Oakland	8	6	5	..	7	8	8	6	5	5	3	8	4	4	77	85	.475	7
Chicago........	5	5	8	6	..	5	5	5	5	8	4	7	7	4	74	88	.457	10
Seattle.........	4	4	6	5	8	..	10	3	8	4	6	6	5	5	74	88	.457	10
Texas............	7	8	5	5	8	3	..	3	7	3	2	6	6	6	69	92	.429	14½

Tie Game—Toronto vs. Cleveland.
Championship Series—Detroit defeated Kansas City, three games to none.

AMERICAN LEAGUE 1984 DEPARTMENTAL LEADERS

INDIVIDUAL BATTING

Average
Mattingly, New York	.343
Winfield, New York	.340
Boggs, Boston	.325

Doubles
Mattingly, New York	44
Parrish, Texas......................	42
Bell, Toronto	39

Triples
Collins, Toronto......................	15
Moseby, Toronto	15
Baines, Chicago.......................	10
Gibson, Detroit	10

Home Runs
Armas, Boston	43
Kingman, Oakland................	35
Murphy, Oak.; Parrish, Det.; Thornton, Clev....................	33

Runs Batted In
Armas, Boston	123
Rice, Boston	122
Kingman, Oakland................	118

Stolen Bases
Henderson, Oakland............	66
Collins, Toronto....................	60
Butler, Cleveland.................	52

INDIVIDUAL PITCHING

Earned-Run Average
Boddicker, Baltimore..........	2.79
Stieb, Toronto......................	2.83
Blyleven, Cleveland	2.87

Innings
Stieb, Toronto......................	267
Hough, Texas........................	266
Alexander, Toronto	261.2

Shutouts
Ojeda, Boston...........................	5
Zahn, California........................	5

Strikeouts
Langston, Seattle..................	204
Stieb, Toronto......................	198
Witt, California.....................	196

Complete Games
Hough, Texas........................	17
Boddicker, Baltimore...........	16
Dotson, Chicago	14

Victories
Boddicker, Baltimore...........	20
Blyleven, Cleveland	19
Morris, Detroit	19

BALTIMORE ORIOLES

Board Chairman—Edward Bennett Williams
Exec. V. P.-General Manager—Henry J. Peters
Vice-President-Stadium Operations—Jack Dunn, III
Vice-President-Finance—Joseph P. Hamper, Jr.
Director of Business Affairs—Bob Alyward
Traveling Secretary—Philip E. Itzoe
Public Relations Director—Robert W. Brown
Executive Director of Sales—Lou Michaelson
Scouting, Player Development—Thomas A. Giordano
Special Assistant to General Manager—Jim Russo
Offices—Memorial Stadium
Memorial Stadium Capacity—53,198.

Farm System: AAA—Rochester. AA—Charlotte. A—Daytona Beach (co-op), Hagerstown, Newark. Rookie—Bluefield.

Joe Altobelli

BALTIMORE ORIOLES' YEARLY STANDING

(Milwaukee Brewers, 1901; St. Louis Browns, 1902 to 1953, Inclusive)

Year—Position	W.	L.	Pct.	*G.B.	Manager	Attendance
1901—Eighth	48	89	.350	35½	Hugh Duffy	139,034
1902—Second	78	58	.574	5	James McAleer	272,283
1903—Sixth	65	74	.468	26½	James McAleer	380,405
1904—Sixth	65	87	.428	29	James McAleer	318,108
1905—Eighth	54	99	.354	40½	James McAleer	339,112
1906—Fifth	76	73	.510	16	James McAleer	389,157
1907—Sixth	69	83	.454	24	James McAleer	419,025
1908—Fourth	83	69	.546	6½	James McAleer	618,947
1909—Seventh	61	89	.407	36	James McAleer	366,274
1910—Eighth	47	107	.305	57	John O'Connor	249,889
1911—Eighth	45	107	.296	56½	Roderick Wallace	207,984
1912—Seventh	53	101	.344	53	Roderick Wallace, George Stovall	214,070
1913—Eighth	57	96	.373	39	George Stovall, Branch Rickey	250,330
1914—Fifth	71	82	.464	28½	Branch Rickey	244,714
1915—Sixth	63	91	.409	39½	Branch Rickey	150,358
1916—Fifth	79	75	.513	12	Fielder Jones	335,740
1917—Seventh	57	97	.370	43	Fielder Jones	210,486
1918—Fifth	58	64	.475	15	F. Jones, J. Austin, J. Burke	122,076
1919—Fifth	67	72	.482	20½	James Burke	349,350
1920—Fourth	76	77	.497	21½	James Burke	419,311
1921—Third	81	73	.526	17½	Lee Fohl	355,978
1922—Second	93	61	.604	1	Lee Fohl	712,918
1923—Fifth	74	78	.487	24	Lee Fohl, James Austin	430,296
1924—Fourth	74	78	.487	17	George Sisler	533,349
1925—Third	82	71	.536	15	George Sisler	462,898
1926—Seventh	62	92	.403	29	George Sisler	283,986
1927—Seventh	59	94	.336	50½	Dan Howley	247,879
1928—Third	82	72	.532	19	Dan Howley	339,497
1929—Fourth	79	73	.520	26	Dan Howley	280,697
1930—Sixth	64	90	.416	38	William Killefer	152,088
1931—Fifth	63	91	.409	45	William Killefer	179,126
1932—Sixth	63	91	.409	44	William Killefer	112,558
1933—Eighth	55	96	.364	43½	Killefer, Sothoron, Hornsby	88,113
1934—Sixth	67	85	.441	33	Rogers Hornsby	115,305
1935—Seventh	65	87	.428	28½	Rogers Hornsby	80,922
1936—Seventh	57	95	.375	44½	Rogers Hornsby	93,267
1937—Eighth	46	108	.299	56	Rogers Hornsby, J. Bottomley	123,121
1938—Seventh	55	97	.362	44	Charles (Gabby) Street	130,417
1939—Eighth	43	111	.279	64½	Fred Haney	109,159
1940—Sixth	67	87	.435	23	Fred Haney	239,591
1941—Sixth†	70	84	.455	31	Fred Haney, J. Luther Sewell	176,240
1942—Third	82	69	.543	19½	J. Luther (Luke) Sewell	255,617
1943—Sixth	72	80	.474	25	J. Luther (Luke) Sewell	214,392

BALTIMORE ORIOLES' YEARLY STANDING—Continued

Year—Position	W.	L.	Pct.	*G.B.	Manager	Attendance
1944—First............	89	65	.578	+ 1	J. Luther (Luke) Sewell.............................	508,644
1945—Third	81	70	.536	6	J. Luther (Luke) Sewell.............................	482,986
1946—Seventh.......	66	88	.429	38	J. Luther Sewell, Zack Taylor....................	526,435
1947—Eighth	59	95	.383	38	Herold (Muddy) Ruel................................	320,474
1948—Sixth............	59	94	.386	37	James (Zack) Taylor	335,546
1949—Seventh.......	53	101	.344	44	James (Zack) Taylor	270,936
1950—Seventh.......	58	96	.377	40	James (Zack) Taylor	247,131
1951—Eighth	52	102	.338	46	James (Zack) Taylor	293,790
1952—Seventh.......	64	90	.416	31	Rogers Hornsby, Martin Marion..............	518,796
1953—Eighth	54	100	.351	46½	Martin Marion..	297,238
1954—Seventh.......	54	100	.351	57	James Dykes...	1,060,910
1955—Seventh.......	57	97	.370	39	Paul Richards..	852,039
1956—Sixth............	69	85	.448	28	Paul Richards..	901,201
1957—Fifth............	76	76	.500	21	Paul Richards..	1,029,581
1958—Sixth............	74	79	.484	17½	Paul Richards..	829,991
1959—Sixth............	74	80	.481	20	Paul Richards..	891,926
1960—Second........	89	65	.578	8	Paul Richards..	1,187,849
1961—Third	95	67	.586	14	Paul Richards, C. Luman Harris..............	951,089
1962—Seventh.......	77	85	.475	19	William Hitchcock...................................	790,254
1963—Fourth	86	76	.531	18½	William Hitchcock...................................	774,343
1964—Third	97	65	.599	2	Henry Bauer...	1,116,215
1965—Third	94	68	.580	8	Henry Bauer...	781,649
1966—First............	97	63	.606	+ 9	Henry Bauer...	1,203,366
1967—Sixth†..........	76	85	.472	15½	Henry Bauer...	955,053
1968—Second........	91	71	.562	12	Henry Bauer, Earl Weaver.......................	943,977

EAST DIVISION

Year—Position	W.	L.	Pct.	*G.B.	Manager	Attendance
1969—First‡..........	109	53	.673	+19	Earl Weaver..	1,058,168
1970—First‡..........	108	54	.667	+15	Earl Weaver..	1,057,069
1971—First‡..........	101	57	.639	+12	Earl Weaver..	1,023,037
1972—Third	80	74	.519	5	Earl Weaver..	899,950
1973—First§..........	97	65	.599	+ 8	Earl Weaver..	958,667
1974—First§..........	91	71	.562	+ 2	Earl Weaver..	962,572
1975—Second........	90	69	.566	4½	Earl Weaver..	1,002,157
1976—Second........	88	74	.543	10½	Earl Weaver..	1,058,609
1977—Second†......	97	64	.602	2½	Earl Weaver..	1,195,769
1978—Fourth	90	71	.559	9	Earl Weaver..	1,051,724
1979—First‡..........	102	57	.642	+ 8	Earl Weaver..	1,681,009
1980—Second........	100	62	.617	3	Earl Weaver..	1,797,438
1981—2nd/2nd......	59	46	.562	x	Earl Weaver..	1,024,652
1982—Second........	94	68	.580	1	Earl Weaver..	1,613,031
1983—First‡..........	98	64	.605	+ 6	Joseph Altobelli......................................	2,042,071
1984—Fifth............	85	77	.525	19	Joseph Altobelli......................................	2,045,784

*Games behind winner.　†Tied for position.　‡Won Championship Series.　§Lost Championship Series.　xFirst half 31-23; second 28-23.

First Game Played at Memorial Stadium

Bringing major league baseball back to Baltimore after 52 years, the Orioles beat the Chicago White Sox, 3-1, on April 15, 1954, before 46,354 enthusiastic fans.

Bob Turley pitched the complete game for the Orioles, striking out nine. Clint Courtney and Vern Stephens homered off losing White Sox pitcher Virgil (Fire) Trucks.

BALTIMORE ORIOLES

(26) JOE ALTOBELLI—Manager

No. PITCHERS—	Bts.	Thrs.	Hgt.	Wgt.	Birth-date	1984 Club	IP.	W.	L.	ERA.
Aase, Don	R	R	6:03	210	9- 8-54	Redwood	12.1	0	1	5.11
						California	39.0	4	1	1.62
52 Boddicker, Mike	R	R	5:11	172	8-23-57	Baltimore	261.1	20	11	2.79
21 Brown, Mark	B	R	6:02	190	7-13-59	Rochester	77.0	4	4	3.74
						Baltimore	23.0	1	2	3.91
34 Davis, Storm	R	R	6:04	207	12-26-61	Baltimore	225.0	14	9	3.12
39 Dixon, Ken	B	R	5:11	166	10-17-60	Charlotte	240.0	16	8	2.85
						Baltimore	13.0	0	1	4.15
46 Flanagan, Mike	L	L	6:00	195	12-16-51	Baltimore	226.2	13	13	3.53
Habyan, John	R	R	6:01	195	1-29-64	Hagerstown	81.1	9	4	3.54
						Charlotte	77.0	4	7	4.44
Kucharski, Joe	R	R	6:03	222	2- 3-61	Rochester	148.0	7	13	4.99
30 Martinez, Dennis	R	R	6:01	185	5-14-55	Baltimore	141.2	6	9	5.02
23 Martinez, Tippy	L	L	5:10	175	5-31-50	Baltimore	89.2	4	9	3.91
16 McGregor, Scott	B	L	6:01	190	1-18-54	Baltimore	196.1	15	12	3.94
Ramirez, Allan	R	R	5:10	190	5- 1-57	Rochester	95.0	4	10	4.36
36 Snell, Nate	R	R	6:04	190	9- 2-55	Rochester	9.1	0	2	4.82
						Charlotte	81.2	9	4	2.42
						Baltimore	7.2	1	1	2.35
53 Stewart, Sammy	R	R	6:03	208	10-28-54	Baltimore	93.0	7	4	3.29
32 Swaggerty, Bill	R	R	6:02	186	12- 5-56	Rochester	64.1	6	2	2.66
						Baltimore	57.0	3	2	5.21
Welchel, Don	R	R	6:04	205	2- 3-57	Hagerstown	26.2	4	0	1.01
						Rochester	53.0	4	5	4.42

CATCHERS—						1984 Club	G.	HR.	RBI.	Avg.
24 Dempsey, Rick	R	R	6:00	184	9-13-49	Baltimore	109	11	34	.230
17 Nolan, Joe	L	R	6:00	190	5-21-51	Baltimore	35	1	9	.290
Pardo, Alberto	B	R	6:02	187	9- 8-62	Charlotte	138	13	81	.265

INFIELDERS—										
10 Cruz, Todd	R	R	6:00	175	11-23-55	Baltimore	96	3	9	.218
25 Dauer, Rich	R	R	6:00	180	7-27-52	Baltimore	127	2	24	.254
14 Gross, Wayne	L	R	6:02	205	1-14-52	Baltimore	127	22	64	.216
Hernandez, Leo	R	R	5:11	170	11- 6-59	Rochester	136	21	83	.275
33 Murray, Eddie	B	R	6:02	200	2-24-56	Baltimore	162	29	110	.306
6 Rayford, Floyd	R	R	5:10	195	7-27-57	Rochester	7	1	1	.056
						Baltimore	86	4	27	.256
8 Ripken, Cal	R	R	6:04	200	8-24-60	Baltimore	162	27	86	.304
2 Rodriguez, Victor	R	R	5:11	173	7-14-61	Rochester	132	6	46	.274
						Baltimore	11	0	2	.412
12 Sakata, Lenn	R	R	5:09	160	6- 8-53	Baltimore	81	3	11	.191
28 Traber, Jim	L	L	6:00	194	12-26-61	Hagerstown	48	2	29	.358
						Charlotte	75	16	56	.351
						Baltimore	10	0	2	.238

OUTFIELDERS—										
9 Dwyer, Jim	L	L	5:10	175	1- 3-50	Baltimore	76	2	21	.255
15 Ford, Dan	R	R	6:01	185	5-19-52	Baltimore	25	1	5	.231
Gerhart, Ken	R	R	6:00	190	5-19-61	Charlotte	85	13	40	.201
						Hagerstown	47	6	21	.321
Lacy, Lee	R	R	6:01	175	4-10-48	Pittsburgh	138	12	70	.321
38 Lowenstein, John	L	R	6:01	180	1-27-47	Baltimore	105	8	28	.237
19 Lynn, Fred	L	L	6:01	190	2- 3-52	California	142	23	79	.271
35 Roenicke, Gary	R	R	6:03	200	12- 5-54	Baltimore	121	10	44	.224
18 Sheets, Larry	L	R	6:03	217	12- 6-59	Rochester	134	13	67	.302
						Baltimore	8	1	2	.438
37 Shelby, John	B	R	6:01	175	2-23-58	Baltimore	128	6	30	.209
43 Young, Mike	B	R	6:02	194	3-20-60	Rochester	20	4	15	.333
						Baltimore	123	17	52	.252

ELROD HENDRICKS (44)—Coach CAL RIPKEN, SR. (47)—Coach
RAY MILLER (31)—Coach RALPH ROWE (54)—Coach
JIMMY WILLIAMS (40)—Coach

MEMORIAL STADIUM

	Seats	Prices
Sky Boxes	24	....
Lower Box Seats	7,475	$8.50
Terrace Box Seats	3,519	7.50
Mezzanine Box Seats	2,037	7.50
Upper Boxes	3,610	6.00
Lower Reserved	5,098	5.50
Upper Reserved	9,278	5.50
General Admission		
Lower	13,555	4.25
Upper	8,189	4.25

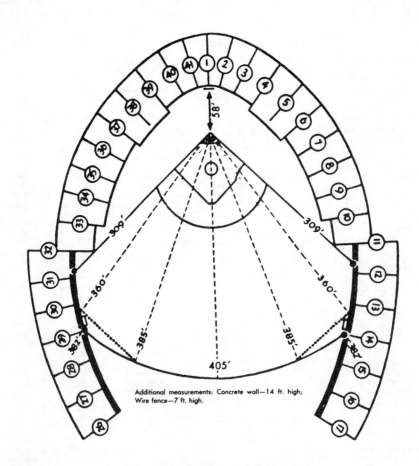

Additional measurements: Concrete wall—14 ft. high;
Wire fence—7 ft. high.

Memorial Stadium, Baltimore
First A.L. Game Played April 15, 1954

BOSTON RED SOX

President—Jean R. Yawkey
CEO/Chief Operating Officer—Haywood C. Sullivan
Executive Vice President, Administration—Edward G. LeRoux, Jr.
Vice President/General Manager—James L. Gorman
Vice President/Player Development Director—Edward F. Kenney
Scouting Director—Edward M. Kasko
Chief Financial Officer/Treasurer—Robert C. Furbush
Public Relations & Publicity Director—Richard L. Bresciani
Traveling Secretary—John J. Rogers
Controller—John J. Reilly
Offices—24 Yawkey Way
Fenway Park Seating Capacity—33,583

Farm System: AAA—Pawtucket. AA—New Britain, Conn. A—Winter Haven, Greensboro, Elmira.

John McNamara

BOSTON RED SOX' YEARLY STANDING

Year—Position	W.	L.	Pct.	*G.B.	Manager	Attendance
1901—Second	79	57	.581	4	James Collins	289,448
1902—Third	77	60	.562	6½	James Collins	348,567
1903—First	91	47	.659	+14½	James Collins	379,338
1904—First	95	59	.617	+ 1½	James Collins	623,295
1905—Fourth	78	74	.513	16	James Collins	468,828
1906—Eighth	49	105	.318	45½	James Collins, Charles Stahl	410,209
1907—Seventh	59	90	.396	32½	G. Huff, R. Unglaub, J. McGuire	436,777
1908—Fifth	75	79	.487	15½	James McGuire, Fred Lake	473,048
1909—Third	88	63	.583	9½	Fred Lake	668,965
1910—Fourth	81	72	.529	22½	Patrick Donovan	584,619
1911—Fifth	78	75	.510	24	Patrick Donovan	503,961
1912—First	105	47	.691	+14	J. Garland Stahl	597,096
1913—Fourth	79	71	.527	15½	J. Garland Stahl, W. Carrigan	437,194
1914—Second	91	62	.595	8½	William Carrigan	481,359
1915—First	101	50	.669	+ 2½	William Carrigan	539,885
1916—First	91	63	.591	+ 2	William Carrigan	496,397
1917—Second	90	62	.592	9	John Barry	387,856
1918—First	75	51	.595	+ 1½	Edward Barrow	249,513
1919—Sixth	66	71	.482	20½	Edward Barrow	417,291
1920—Fifth	72	81	.471	25½	Edward Barrow	402,445
1921—Fifth	75	79	.487	23½	Hugh Duffy	279,273
1922—Eighth	61	93	.396	33	Hugh Duffy	259,184
1923—Eighth	61	91	.401	37	Frank Chance	229,668
1924—Seventh	67	87	.435	25	Lee Fohl	448,556
1925—Eighth	47	105	.309	49½	Lee Fohl	267,782
1926—Eighth	46	107	.301	44½	Lee Fohl	285,155
1927—Eighth	51	103	.331	59	William Carrigan	305,275
1928—Eighth	57	96	.373	43½	William Carrigan	396,920
1929—Eighth	58	96	.377	48	William Carrigan	394,620
1930—Eighth	52	102	.338	50	Charles (Heinie) Wagner	444,045
1931—Sixth	62	90	.408	45	John Collins	350,975
1932—Eighth	43	111	.279	64	John Collins, Martin McManus	182,150
1933—Seventh	63	86	.423	34½	Martin McManus	268,715
1934—Fourth	76	76	.500	24	Stanley (Bucky) Harris	610,640
1935—Fourth	78	75	.510	16	Joseph Cronin	558,568
1936—Sixth	74	80	.481	28½	Joseph Cronin	626,895
1937—Fifth	80	72	.526	21	Joseph Cronin	559,659
1938—Second	88	61	.591	9½	Joseph Cronin	646,459
1939—Second	89	62	.589	17	Joseph Cronin	573,070
1940—Fourth	82	72	.532	8	Joseph Cronin	716,234
1941—Second	84	70	.545	17	Joseph Cronin	718,497
1942—Second	93	59	.612	9	Joseph Cronin	730,340
1943—Seventh	68	84	.447	29	Joseph Cronin	358,275
1944—Fourth	77	77	.500	12	Joseph Cronin	506,975

BOSTON RED SOX' YEARLY STANDING—Continued

Year—Position	W.	L.	Pct.	*G.B.	Manager	Attendance
1945—Seventh	71	83	.461	17½	Joseph Cronin	603,794
1946—First	104	50	.675	+12	Joseph Cronin	1,416,944
1947—Third	83	71	.539	14	Joseph Cronin	1,427,315
1948—Second‡	96	59	.619	1	Joseph McCarthy	1,558,798
1949—Second	96	58	.623	1	Joseph McCarthy	1,596,650
1950—Third	94	60	.610	4	Jos. McCarthy, Stephen O'Neill	1,344,080
1951—Third	87	67	.565	11	Stephen O'Neill	1,312,282
1952—Sixth	76	78	.494	19	Louis Boudreau	1,115,750
1953—Fourth	84	69	.549	16	Louis Boudreau	1,026,133
1954—Fourth	69	85	.448	42	Louis Boudreau	931,127
1955—Fourth	84	70	.545	12	Michael Higgins	1,203,200
1956—Fourth	84	70	.545	13	Michael Higgins	1,137,158
1957—Third	82	72	.532	16	Michael Higgins	1,181,087
1958—Third	79	75	.513	13	Michael Higgins	1,077,047
1959—Fifth	75	79	.487	19	Michael Higgins, William Jurges	984,102
1960—Seventh	65	89	.422	32	William Jurges, Michael Higgins	1,129,866
1961—Sixth	76	86	.469	33	Michael Higgins	850,589
1962—Eighth	76	84	.475	19	Michael Higgins	733,080
1963—Seventh	76	85	.472	28	John Pesky	942,642
1964—Eighth	72	90	.444	27	John Pesky, William Herman	883,276
1965—Ninth	62	100	.383	40	William Herman	652,201
1966—Ninth	72	90	.444	26	Wm. Herman, Jas. (Pete) Runnels	811,172
1967—First	92	70	.568	+ 1	Richard Williams	1,727,832
1968—Fourth	86	76	.531	17	Richard Williams	1,940,788

EAST DIVISION

Year—Position	W.	L.	Pct.	*G.B.	Manager	Attendance
1969—Third	87	75	.537	22	R. Williams, Edward Popowski	1,833,246
1970—Third	87	75	.537	21	Edward Kasko	1,595,278
1971—Third	85	77	.525	18	Edward Kasko	1,678,732
1972—Second	85	70	.548	½	Edward Kasko	1,441,718
1973—Second	89	73	.549	8	Edward Kasko	1,481,002
1974—Third	84	78	.519	7	Darrell D. Johnson	1,556,411
1975—First‡‡	95	65	.594	+ 4½	Darrell D. Johnson	1,748,587
1976—Third	83	79	.512	15½	Darrell D. Johnson, Don Zimmer	1,895,846
1977—Second†	97	64	.602	2½	Don Zimmer	2,074,549
1978—Second§	99	64	.607	1	Don Zimmer	2,320,643
1979—Third	91	69	.569	11½	Don Zimmer	2,353,114
1980—Fourth	83	77	.519	19	Don Zimmer, John Pesky	1,956,092
1981—5th/2nd	59	49	.546	x	Ralph Houk	1,060,379
1982—Third	89	73	.549	6	Ralph Houk	1,950,124
1983—Sixth	78	84	.481	20	Ralph Houk	1,782,285
1984—Fourth	86	76	.531	18	Ralph Houk	1,661,618

*Games behind winner. †Tied for position. ‡Lost to Cleveland in pennant playoff. ‡‡Won Championship Series. §Lost to New York in pennant playoff. xFirst half 30-26; second 29-23.

First Game Played at Fenway Park

The Red Sox won their Fenway Park debut, 7-6, in an exciting, 11-inning battle with the New York Highlanders on April 20, 1912.

Steve Yerkes scored the winner on Tris Speaker's two-out single in the 11th.

Yerkes was the batting star of the game, collecting hits in each of his first five times at the plate.

The game was scheduled to be played April 18, but rain caused a two-game cancellation.

BOSTON RED SOX

(1) JOHN McNAMARA—Manager

No. PITCHERS—	Bts.	Thrs.	Hgt.	Wgt.	Birth-date	1984 Club	IP.	W.	L.	ERA.
23 Boyd, Dennis	R	R	6:01	155	10- 6-59	Boston	197.2	12	12	4.37
						Pawtucket	37.1	3	1	2.89
27 Brown, Mike	R	R	6:02	195	3- 4-59	Boston	67.0	1	8	6.85
						Pawtucket	87.1	6	3	3.40
25 Clear, Mark	R	R	6:04	215	5-27-56	Boston	67.0	8	3	4.03
21 Clemens, Roger	R	R	6:04	205	8- 4-62	Pawtucket	46.2	2	3	1.93
						Boston	133.1	9	4	4.32
28 Crawford, Steve	R	R	6:05	225	4-29-58	Pawtucket	18.1	2	1	1.96
						Boston	62.0	5	0	3.34
44 Dorsey, Jim	R	R	6:02	200	8- 2-55	Pawtucket	105.1	6	4	2.91
						Boston	2.2	0	0	10.13
31 Glynn, Ed	R	L	6:02	180	6- 3-53	Maine	23.2	2	3	3.42
						Tidewater	31.1	0	1	2.01
47 Hurst, Bruce	L	L	6:03	215	3-24-58	Boston	218.0	12	12	3.92
48 Johnson, John Henry	L	L	6:02	210	8-21-56	Boston	63.2	1	2	3.53
40 Johnson, Mitch	R	R	6:05	218	8- 2-62	New Britain	174.1	11	10	2.89
Kison, Bruce	R	R	6:04	180	2-18-50	California	65.1	4	5	5.37
43 McCarthy, Tom	R	R	6:00	180	6-18-61	New Britain	79.1	8	5	3.06
38 Mitchell, Charlie	R	R	6:03	170	6-24-62	Pawtucket	59.2	10	4	2.11
						Boston	16.1	0	0	2.76
49 Nipper, Al	R	R	6:00	188	4- 2-59	Boston	182.2	11	6	3.89
19 Ojeda, Bob	L	L	6:01	190	12-17-57	Boston	216.2	12	12	3.99
46 Stanley, Bob	R	R	6:04	220	11-10-54	Boston	106.2	9	10	3.54
45 Trujillo, Mike	R	R	6:01	180	1-12-60	Glens Falls	121.2	13	3	2.37
						Denver	30.0	2	5	7.80
42 Woodward, Rob	R	R	6:03	185	9-28-62	New Britain	166.0	10	12	3.96

CATCHERS—						1984 Club	G.	HR.	RBI.	Avg.
10 Gedman, Rich	L	R	6:00	215	9-26-59	Boston	133	24	72	.269
5 Newman, Jeff	R	R	6:02	215	9-11-48	Boston	24	1	3	.222
15 Sullivan, Marc	R	R	6:04	205	7-25-58	Pawtucket	116	15	63	.204
						Boston	2	0	1	.500

INFIELDERS—										
17 Barrett, Marty	R	R	5:10	175	6-23-58	Boston	139	3	45	.303
26 Boggs, Wade	L	R	6:02	190	6-15-58	Boston	158	6	55	.325
16 Buckner, Bill	L	L	6:01	185	12-14-49	Chicago NL	21	0	2	.209
						Boston	114	11	67	.278
41 Gutierrez, Jackie	R	R	5:11	175	6-27-60	Boston	151	2	29	.263
18 Hoffman, Glenn	R	R	6:02	190	7- 7-58	Boston	64	0	4	.189
30 Horn, Sam	L	L	6:05	215	11- 2-63	Winston-Salem	127	21	89	.313
22 Jurak, Ed	R	R	6:02	185	10-24-57	Boston	47	1	7	.242
12 Lyons, Steve	L	R	6:03	190	6- 3-60	Pawtucket	131	17	62	.268
2 Remy, Jerry	L	R	5:09	165	11- 8-52	Boston	30	0	8	.250
11 Stapleton, Dave	R	R	6:01	185	1-16-54	Boston	13	0	1	.231

OUTFIELDERS—										
20 Armas, Tony	R	R	6:01	200	7- 2-53	Boston	157	43	123	.268
50 Burgess, Gus	L	L	5:11	189	12-18-61	Pawtucket	132	11	65	.272
7 Easler, Mike	L	R	6:01	196	11-29-50	Boston	156	27	91	.313
24 Evans, Dwight	R	R	6:03	205	11- 3-51	Boston	162	32	104	.295
34 Greenwell, Mike	L	R	6:00	170	7-18-63	Winston-Salem	130	16	84	.306
3 Miller, Rick	L	L	6:00	180	4-19-48	Boston	95	0	12	.260
13 Nichols, Reid	R	R	5:11	172	8- 5-58	Boston	73	1	14	.226
14 Rice, Jim	R	R	6:02	205	3- 8-53	Boston	159	28	122	.280
29 Romine, Kevin	R	R	5:11	185	5-23-61	Pawtucket	113	12	72	.253

BILL FISCHER (34)—Coach   RENE LACHEMANN (36)—Coach
WALT HRINIAK (33)—Coach   JOE MORGAN (35)—Coach

TONY TORCHIA (32)—Coach

FENWAY PARK

	Seats	Prices
Roof	1,568	$8.50
Box Seats	13,250	....
Upper Boxes		7.50-8.00
Lower Boxes		9.50
Reserved Grandstand....................	12,202	7.00
Bleachers	6,563	3.00

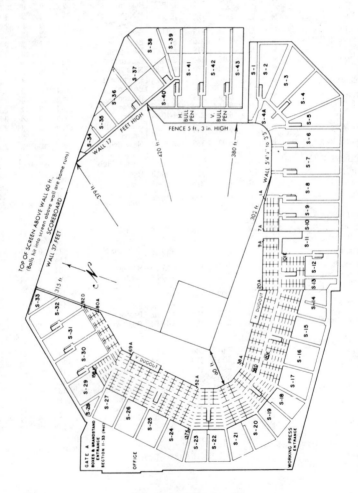

Fenway Park, Boston
First A.L. Game Played April 20, 1912

Gene Mauch

CALIFORNIA ANGELS

Chairman of the Board—Gene Autry
Vice-President-General Manager—Mike Port
Vice-President Marketing—John W. Hays
Vice-President Finance & Administration—James Wilson
Assistant to Chairman of the Board—Arthur E. Patterson
Director of Scouting—Larry Himes
Director of Public Relations—Tom Seeberg
Traveling Secretary—Frank Sims
Offices—Anaheim Stadium
Anaheim Stadium Capacity—65,158

Farm System: AAA—Edmonton. AA—Midland. A—Davenport, Redwood, Salem.

CALIFORNIA ANGELS' YEARLY STANDING

Year—Position	W.	L.	Pct.	*G.B.	Manager	Attendance
1961—Eighth	70	91	.435	38½	William Rigney	603,510
1962—Third	86	76	.531	10	William Rigney	1,144,063
1963—Ninth	70	91	.435	34	William Rigney	821,015
1964—Fifth	82	80	.506	17	William Rigney	760,439
1965—Seventh	75	87	.463	27	William Rigney	566,727
1966—Sixth	80	82	.494	18	William Rigney	1,400,321
1967—Fifth	84	77	.522	7½	William Rigney	1,317,713
1968—Eighth†	67	95	.414	36	William Rigney	1,025,956

WEST DIVISION

Year—Position	W.	L.	Pct.	*G.B.	Manager	Attendance
1969—Third	71	91	.438	26	William Rigney, Harold Phillips	758,388
1970—Third	86	76	.531	12	Harold (Lefty) Phillips	1,077,741
1971—Fourth	76	86	.469	25½	Harold (Lefty) Phillips	926,373
1972—Fifth	75	80	.484	18	Del Rice	744,190
1973—Fourth	79	83	.488	15	Bobby B. Winkles	1,058,206
1974—Sixth	68	94	.420	22	Bobby B. Winkles, Dick Williams	917,269
1975—Sixth	72	89	.447	25½	Dick Williams	1,058,163
1976—Fourth†	76	86	.469	14	Dick Williams, Norm Sherry	1,006,774
1977—Fifth	74	88	.457	28	Norm Sherry, David Garcia	1,432,633
1978—Second†	87	75	.537	5	David Garcia, James Fregosi	1,755,386
1979—First§	88	74	.543	+ 3	James Fregosi	2,523,575
1980—Sixth	65	95	.406	31	James Fregosi	2,297,327
1981—4th/7th	51	59	.464	x	James Fregosi, Gene Mauch	1,441,545
1982—First§	93	69	.574	+ 3	Gene Mauch	2,807,360
1983—Fifth†	70	92	.432	29	John McNamara	2,555,016
1984—Second†	81	81	.500	3	John McNamara	2,402,997

*Games behind winner. †Tied for position. §Lost Championship Series. xFirst half 31-29; second 20-30.

First Game Played at Anaheim Stadium

In the Angels' Anaheim Stadium debut, 31,660 saw the Chicago White Sox emerge victorious, 3-1, on April 19, 1966.

Rick Reichardt put the Angels on top, 1-0, with a second-inning home run, but Tommie Agee tied the game with a homer in the sixth.

Singles by Don Buford and Floyd Robinson scored the White Sox' winning runs in the eighth inning. Tommy John and Eddie Fisher combined for the White Sox' four-hit victory.

CALIFORNIA ANGELS

(3) GENE MAUCH—Manager

No. PITCHERS—	Bts.	Thrs.	Hgt.	Wgt.	Birth-date	1984 Club	IP.	W.	L.	ERA.
33 Cliburn, Stu	R	R	6:00	187	12-19-56	Edmonton	75.0	7	7	2.88
						California	2.0	0	0	13.50
23 Corbett, Doug	R	R	6:01	188	11- 4-52	Edmonton	4.2	1	0	0.00
						California	85.0	5	1	2.12
43 Forsch, Ken	R	R	6:04	215	9- 8-46	California	16.1	1	1	2.20
52 Gonzalez, Julian	R	R	6:04	198	8-20-64	Redwood	72.2	8	6	2.72
25 John, Tommy	R	L	6:03	200	5-22-43	California	181.1	7	13	4.52
48 Kaufman, Curt	R	R	6:02	175	7-19-57	California	69.0	2	3	4.57
36 Kipper, Bob	R	L	6:02	200	7- 8-64	Redwood	185.0	18	8	2.04
27 LaCorte, Frank	R	R	6:01	180	10-13-51	California	29.1	1	2	7.06
						Edmonton	9.2	0	1	11.17
18 Lugo, Rafael	R	R	6:00	185	8-12-62	Waterbury	164.1	13	8	2.79
15 Mack, Tony	R	R	5:10	177	4-30-61	Waterbury	171.1	11	8	3.26
27 McCaskill, Kirk	R	R	6:01	195	4- 9-61	Edmonton	143.0	7	11	5.73
37 Romanick, Ron	R	R	6:04	211	11- 6-60	California	229.2	12	12	3.76
40 Sanchez, Luis	R	R	6:02	215	8-24-53	California	83.2	9	7	3.33
41 Slaton, Jim	R	R	6:00	192	6-20-50	California	163.0	7	10	4.97
35 Smith, David W.	R	R	6:01	196	8-30-57	Edmonton	69.0	6	3	3.13
						California	1.0	0	0	18.00
42 Steirer, Rick	R	R	6:04	211	8-27-56	Edmonton	133.1	12	4	3.71
						California	2.2	0	1	16.88
45 Timberlake, Don	R	R	6:03	210	1-14-64	Redwood	156.2	15	5	3.04
39 Witt, Mike	R	R	6:07	192	7-20-60	California	246.2	15	11	3.47
38 Zahn, Geoff	L	L	6:01	175	12-19-46	California	199.1	13	10	3.12

CATCHERS—						1984 Club	G.	HR.	RBI.	Avg.
8 Boone, Bob	R	R	6:02	208	11-19-47	California	139	3	32	.202
16 Liddle, Steve	R	R	6:04	205	3- 4-59	Edmonton	92	6	51	.262
32 Miller, Darrell	R	R	6:02	200	2-26-59	Edmonton	92	12	67	.326
						California	17	0	1	.171
34 Narron, Jerry	L	R	6:03	195	1-15-56	California	69	3	17	.247

INFIELDERS—										
7 Burleson, Rick	R	R	5:10	160	4-29-51	California	7	0	0	.000
29 Carew, Rod	L	R	6:00	180	10- 1-45	California	93	3	31	.295
14 Carrasco, Norm	R	R	5:09	172	8- 6-62	Waterbury	134	9	64	.285
11 DeCinces, Doug	R	R	6:02	197	8-29-50	California	146	20	82	.269
2 Gerber, Craig	L	R	6:00	175	1- 8-59	Edmonton	113	1	40	.230
4 Grich, Bobby	R	R	6:02	194	1-15-49	California	116	18	58	.256
28 Lubratich, Steve	R	R	6:00	172	5- 1-55	Edmonton	127	9	85	.305
17 McLemore, Mark	B	R	5:11	175	10- 4-64	Redwood	134	0	45	.295
10 Picciolo, Rob	R	R	6:02	178	2- 4-53	California	87	1	9	.202
22 Schofield, Dick	R	R	5:10	176	11-21-62	California	140	4	21	.193
6 Sconiers, Daryl	L	L	6:02	199	10- 3-58	California	57	4	17	.244
9 Wilfong, Rob	L	R	6:01	185	9- 1-53	California	108	6	33	.248

OUTFIELDERS—										
12 Beniquez, Juan	R	R	5:11	178	5-13-50	California	110	8	39	.336
21 Brown, Mike	R	R	6:02	197	12-29-59	Edmonton	26	4	24	.343
						California	62	7	22	.284
5 Downing, Brian	R	R	5:10	198	10- 9-50	California	156	23	91	.275
44 Jackson, Reggie	L	L	6:00	206	5-18-46	California	143	25	81	.223
20 Pettis, Gary	B	R	6:01	159	4- 3-58	California	140	2	29	.227
30 White, Devon	B	R	6:01	170	12-29-62	Redwood	138	7	55	.283

BOB CLEAR (49)—Coach
BOBBY KNOOP (1)—Coach

MARCEL LACHEMANN (51)—Coach
JIMMIE REESE (50)—Coach

MOOSE STUBING (47)—Coach

ANAHEIM STADIUM

	Seats	Prices
Club Level Boxes	11,814	$7.00
Field Boxes	13,482	7.00
Terrace Level Boxes	12,827	6.00
View Level Reserved	7,863	4.50
View Level Unreserved	19,172	2.50

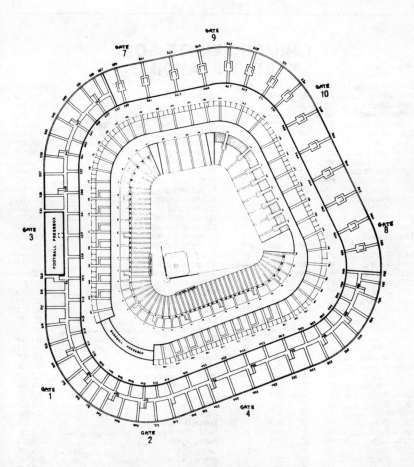

**Anaheim Stadium, Anaheim, Calif.
First A.L. Game Played April 19, 1966**

Tony LaRussa

CHICAGO WHITE SOX

Chairman of the Board—Jerry Reinsdorf
President—Edward M. Einhorn
Vice-President/General Manager—Roland Hemond
Executive Vice-President—Howard Pizer
Director, Public Relations—Paul Jensen
Traveling Secretary—Glen Rosenbaum
Director, Player Development—Bobby Winkles
Offices—Comiskey Park
Comiskey Park Capacity—44,432

Farm System: AAA—Buffalo. AA—Glens Falls. A—Appleton, Niag-
ara Falls. Rookie—Sarasota.

CHICAGO WHITE SOX' YEARLY STANDING

Year—Position	W.	L.	Pct.	*G.B.	Manager	Attendance
1901—First	83	53	.610	+ 4	Clark Griffith	354,350
1902—Fourth	74	60	.552	8	Clark Griffith	337,898
1903—Seventh	60	77	.438	30½	James Callahan	286,183
1904—Third	89	65	.578	6	James Callahan, Fielder Jones	557,123
1905—Second	92	60	.605	2	Fielder Jones	687,419
1906—First	93	58	.616	+ 3	Fielder Jones	585,202
1907—Third	87	64	.576	5½	Fielder Jones	666,307
1908—Third	88	64	.579	1½	Fielder Jones	636,096
1909—Fourth	78	74	.513	20	William Sullivan	478,400
1910—Sixth	68	85	.444	35½	Hugh Duffy	552,084
1911—Fourth	77	74	.510	24	Hugh Duffy	583,208
1912—Fourth	78	76	.506	28	James Callahan	602,241
1913—Fifth	78	74	.513	17½	James Callahan	644,501
1914—Sixth†	70	84	.455	30	James Callahan	469,290
1915—Third	93	61	.604	9½	Clarence Rowland	539,461
1916—Second	89	65	.578	2	Clarence Rowland	679,923
1917—First	100	54	.649	+ 9	Clarence Rowland	684,521
1918—Sixth	57	67	.460	17	Clarence Rowland	195,081
1919—First	88	52	.629	+ 3½	William Gleason	627,186
1920—Second	96	58	.623	2	William Gleason	833,492
1921—Seventh	62	92	.403	36½	William Gleason	543,650
1922—Fifth	77	77	.500	17	William Gleason	602,860
1923—Seventh	69	85	.448	30	William Gleason	573,778
1924—Eighth	66	87	.431	25½	Frank Chance, John Evers	606,658
1925—Fifth	79	75	.513	18½	Edward Collins	832,231
1926—Fifth	81	72	.529	9½	Edward Collins	710,339
1927—Fifth	70	83	.458	29½	Ray Schalk	614,423
1928—Fifth	72	82	.468	29	Ray Schalk, Russell Blackburne	494,152
1929—Seventh	59	93	.388	46	Russell Blackburne	426,795
1930—Seventh	62	92	.403	40	Owen (Donie) Bush	406,123
1931—Eighth	56	97	.366	51	Owen (Donie) Bush	403,550
1932—Seventh	49	102	.325	56½	Lewis Fonseca	233,198
1933—Sixth	67	83	.447	31	Lewis Fonseca	397,789
1934—Eighth	53	99	.349	47	Lewis Fonseca, James Dykes	236,559
1935—Fifth	74	78	.487	19½	James Dykes	470,281
1936—Third	81	70	.536	20	James Dykes	440,810
1937—Third	86	68	.558	16	James Dykes	589,245
1938—Sixth	65	83	.439	32	James Dykes	338,278
1939—Fourth	85	69	.552	22½	James Dykes	594,104
1940—Fourth†	82	72	.532	8	James Dykes	660,336
1941—Third	77	77	.500	24	James Dykes	677,077
1942—Sixth	66	82	.446	34	James Dykes	425,734
1943—Fourth	82	72	.532	16	James Dykes	508,962
1944—Seventh	71	83	.461	18	James Dykes	563,539

CHICAGO WHITE SOX' YEARLY STANDING—Continued

Year—Position	W.	L.	Pct.	*G.B.	Manager	Attendance
1945—Sixth	71	78	.477	15	James Dykes	657,981
1946—Fifth	74	80	.481	30	James Dykes, Theodore Lyons	983,403
1947—Sixth	70	84	.455	27	Theodore Lyons	876,948
1948—Eighth	51	101	.336	44½	Theodore Lyons	777,844
1949—Sixth	63	91	.409	34	Jack Onslow	937,151
1950—Sixth	60	94	.390	38	Jack Onslow, John Corriden	781,330
1951—Fourth	81	73	.526	17	Paul Richards	1,328,234
1952—Third	81	73	.526	14	Paul Richards	1,231,675
1953—Third	89	65	.578	11½	Paul Richards	1,191,353
1954—Third	94	60	.610	17	Paul Richards, Martin Marion	1,231,629
1955—Third	91	63	.591	5	Martin Marion	1,175,684
1956—Third	85	69	.552	12	Martin Marion	1,000,090
1957—Second	90	64	.584	8	Alfonso Lopez	1,135,668
1958—Second	82	72	.532	10	Alfonso Lopez	797,451
1959—First	94	60	.610	+ 5	Alfonso Lopez	1,423,144
1960—Third	87	67	.565	10	Alfonso Lopez	1,644,460
1961—Fourth	86	76	.531	23	Alfonso Lopez	1,146,019
1962—Fifth	85	77	.525	11	Alfonso Lopez	1,131,562
1963—Second	94	68	.580	10½	Alfonso Lopez	1,158,848
1964—Second	98	64	.605	1	Alfonso Lopez	1,250,053
1965—Second	95	67	.586	7	Alfonso Lopez	1,130,519
1966—Fourth	83	79	.512	15	Edward Stanky	990,016
1967—Fourth	89	73	.549	3	Edward Stanky	985,634
1968—Eighth†	67	95	.414	36	Edward Stanky, Alfonso Lopez	803,775

WEST DIVISION

Year—Position	W.	L.	Pct.	*G.B.	Manager	Attendance
1969—Fifth	68	94	.420	29	Al Lopez, Donald Gutteridge	589,546
1970—Sixth	56	106	.346	42	D. Gutteridge, Charles Tanner	495,355
1971—Third	79	83	.488	22½	Charles Tanner	833,891
1972—Second	87	67	.565	5½	Charles Tanner	1,177,318
1973—Fifth	77	85	.475	17	Charles Tanner	1,302,527
1974—Fourth	80	80	.500	9	Charles Tanner	1,149,596
1975—Fifth	75	86	.466	22½	Charles Tanner	750,802
1976—Sixth	64	97	.398	25½	Paul Richards	914,945
1977—Third	90	72	.556	12	Robert Lemon	1,657,135
1978—Fifth	71	90	.441	20½	Robert Lemon, Lawrence Doby	1,491,100
1979—Fifth	73	87	.456	14	Donald Kessinger, Anthony LaRussa	1,280,702
1980—Fifth	70	90	.438	26	Anthony LaRussa	1,200,365
1981—3rd/7th	54	52	.509	‡	Anthony LaRussa	946,651
1982—Third	87	75	.537	6	Anthony LaRussa	1,567,787
1983—First§	99	63	.611	+20	Anthony LaRussa	2,132,821
1984—Fifth†	74	88	.457	10	Anthony LaRussa	2,136,988

*Games behind winner. †Tied for position. ‡First half 31-22; second 23-30. §Lost Championship Series.

First Game Played at Comiskey Park

St. Louis Browns hurler Barney Pelty shut out the White Sox on five hits, 2-0, as Comiskey Park was unveiled for an estimated 28,000 Chicago fans on July 1, 1910.

George Stone was the batting star of the day, collecting three of the Browns' seven hits, including a single, double and triple.

CHICAGO WHITE SOX

(10) TONY LaRUSSA—Manager

No. PITCHERS—	Bts.	Thrs.	Hgt.	Wgt.	Birth-date	1984 Club	IP.	W.	L.	ERA.
50 Agosto, Juan	L	L	6:02	187	2-23-58	Chicago	55.1	2	1	3.09
24 Bannister, Floyd	L	L	6:01	193	6-10-55	Chicago	218.0	14	11	4.83
40 Burns, Britt	R	L	6:05	231	6- 8-59	Chicago	117.0	4	12	5.00
56 Correa, Ed	R	R	6:02	192	4-29-66	Appleton	149.1	10	6	3.44
34 Dotson, Richard	R	R	6:00	204	1-10-59	Chicago	245.2	14	15	3.59
27 Fallon, Bob	L	L	6:03	211	2-18-60	Denver	115.1	5	8	3.75
43 James, Bob	R	R	6:04	230	8-15-58	Montreal	96.0	6	6	3.66
49 Jones, Al	R	R	5:11	165	2-10-59	Chicago	20.1	1	1	4.43
						Denver	28.2	2	3	4.71
45 Landrum, Bill	R	R	6:02	180	8-17-57	Wichita	130.1	7	4	3.45
46 Lollar, Tim	L	L	6:03	195	3-17-56	San Diego	195.2	11	13	3.91
30 Nelson, Gene	R	R	6:00	175	12- 3-60	Salt Lake	112.0	6	8	5.63
						Chicago	74.2	3	5	4.46
48 Niemann, Randy	L	L	6:05	205	11-15-55	Denver	190.1	10	12	5.86
						Chicago	5.1	0	0	1.69
36 Reed, Ron	R	R	6:06	215	11- 2-42	Chicago	72.2	0	6	3.10
41 Seaver, Tom	R	R	6:01	210	11-17-44	Chicago	236.2	15	11	3.95
64 Speck, Cliff	R	R	6:04	210	8- 8-56	Denver	176.2	12	11	5.15
37 Spillner, Dan	R	R	6:01	190	11-27-51	Cleveland	51.0	0	5	5.65
						Chicago	48.1	1	0	4.10

CATCHERS—	Bts.	Thrs.	Hgt.	Wgt.	Birth-date	1984 Club	G.	HR.	RBI.	Avg.
72 Fisk, Carlton	R	R	6:02	215	12-26-47	Chicago	102	21	43	.231
7 Hill, Marc	R	R	6:03	240	2-18-52	Chicago	77	5	20	.233
33 Karkovice, Ron	R	R	6:01	200	8- 8-63	Glens Falls	88	13	39	.215
						Denver	31	2	10	.221
22 Skinner, Joel	R	R	6:04	208	2-21-61	Denver	42	10	27	.284
						Chicago	43	0	3	.213

INFIELDERS—	Bts.	Thrs.	Hgt.	Wgt.	Birth-date	1984 Club	G.	HR.	RBI.	Avg.
38 Castro, Jose	R	R	5:09	155	5- 5-58	Denver	129	12	67	.316
16 Cruz, Julio	B	R	5:09	180	12- 2-54	Chicago	143	5	43	.222
20 Dybzinski, Jerry	R	R	6:02	186	7- 7-55	Chicago	94	1	10	.235
1 Fletcher, Scott	R	R	5:11	170	7-30-58	Chicago	149	3	35	.250
5 Guillen, Ozzie	L	R	5:11	150	1-20-64	Las Vegas	122	5	53	.296
32 Hulett, Tim	R	R	6:00	185	1-12-60	Chicago	8	0	0	.000
						Denver	139	16	80	.263
26 O'Malley, Tom	L	R	6:00	180	12-25-60	San Francisco	13	0	0	.120
						Phoenix	105	5	72	.346
						Chicago	12	0	3	.125
44 Paciorek, Tom	R	R	6:04	204	11- 2-46	Chicago	111	4	29	.256
31 Salazar, Luis	R	R	6:00	185	5-19-56	San Diego	93	3	17	.241
12 Smalley, Roy	B	R	6:01	182	10-25-52	New York AL	67	7	46	.239
						Chicago	47	4	13	.170
25 Squires, Mike	L	L	5:10	194	3- 5-52	Chicago	104	0	6	.183
29 Walker, Greg	L	R	6:03	198	10- 6-59	Chicago	136	24	75	.294

OUTFIELDERS—	Bts.	Thrs.	Hgt.	Wgt.	Birth-date	1984 Club	G.	HR.	RBI.	Avg.
3 Baines, Harold	L	L	6:02	189	3-15-59	Chicago	147	29	94	.304
33 Boston, Daryl	L	L	6:03	185	1- 4-63	Denver	127	15	82	.312
						Chicago	35	0	3	.169
17 Hairston, Jerry	B	R	5:10	190	2-16-52	Chicago	115	5	19	.260
42 Kittle, Ron	R	R	6:04	212	1- 5-58	Chicago	139	32	74	.215
11 Law, Rudy	L	L	6:02	176	10- 7-56	Chicago	136	6	37	.251
70 Williams, Ken	R	R	6:01	180	4- 6-64	Appleton	38	5	26	.286
						Glens Falls	97	8	47	.246
52 Yobs, Dave	L	L	6:00	196	1-17-59	Denver	93	10	47	.249

ED BRINKMAN (35)—Coach
ART KUSNYER (15)—Coach
JOE NOSSEK (14)—Coach
DAVE DUNCAN (18)—Coach
JIM LEYLAND (21)—Coach

COMISKEY PARK

	Seats	Prices
Golden Boxes	4,432	$9.50
Loge Seats	1,018	8.50
Box Seats	11,611	7.50
Mezzanine	11,506	5.50
Reserved Grandstand	6,332	4.50
General Admission	7,734	3.00

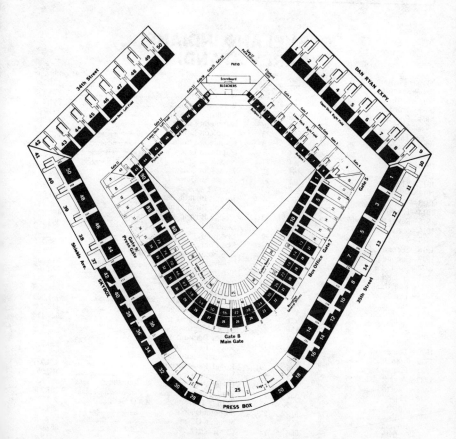

Comiskey Park, Chicago
First A.L. Game Played July 1, 1910

Pat Corrales

CLEVELAND INDIANS

President, Chief Executive Officer—Gabe Paul
Chairman of the Board—Patrick J. O'Neill
Vice-President-General Manager—Philip Seghi
V.P., Player Development & Scouting—Bob Quinn
Director of Stadium Operations—Daniel W. Zerbey
Traveling Secretary—Mike Seghi
Director of Public Relations—Bob DiBiasio
Offices—Municipal Stadium
Municipal Stadium Capacity—74,208

Farm System: AAA—Old Orchard Beach, Me. AA—Waterbury. A—
Waterloo, Batavia.

CLEVELAND INDIANS' YEARLY STANDING

Year—Position	W.	L.	Pct.	*G.B.	Manager	Attendance
1901—Seventh	54	82	.397	29	James McAleer	131,380
1902—Fifth	69	67	.507	14	William Armour	275,395
1903—Third	77	63	.550	15	William Armour	311,280
1904—Fourth	86	65	.570	7½	William Armour	264,749
1905—Fifth	76	78	.494	19	Napoleon Lajoie	316,306
1906—Third	89	64	.582	5	Napoleon Lajoie	325,733
1907—Fourth	85	67	.559	8	Napoleon Lajoie	382,046
1908—Second	90	64	.584	½	Napoleon Lajoie	422,242
1909—Sixth	71	82	.464	27½	Napoleon Lajoie, James McGuire	354,627
1910—Fifth	71	81	.467	32	James McGuire	293,456
1911—Third	80	73	.523	22	James McGuire, George Stovall	406,296
1912—Fifth	75	78	.490	30½	Harry Davis, Joseph Birmingham	336,844
1913—Third	86	66	.566	9½	Joseph Birmingham	541,000
1914—Eighth	51	102	.333	48½	Joseph Birmingham	185,997
1915—Seventh	57	95	.375	44½	Joseph Birmingham, Lee Fohl	159,285
1916—Sixth	77	77	.500	14	Lee Fohl	492,106
1917—Third	88	66	.571	12	Lee Fohl	477,298
1918—Second	73	54	.575	1½	Lee Fohl	295,515
1919—Second	84	55	.604	3½	Lee Fohl, Tristram Speaker	538,135
1920—First	98	56	.636	+ 2	Tristram Speaker	912,832
1921—Second	94	60	.610	4½	Tristram Speaker	748,705
1922—Fourth	78	76	.507	16	Tristram Speaker	528,145
1923—Third	82	71	.536	16½	Tristram Speaker	558,856
1924—Sixth	67	86	.438	24½	Tristram Speaker	481,905
1925—Sixth	70	84	.455	27½	Tristram Speaker	419,005
1926—Second	88	66	.571	3	Tristram Speaker	627,426
1927—Sixth	66	87	.431	43½	Jack McCallister	373,138
1928—Seventh	62	92	.403	39	Roger Peckinpaugh	375,907
1929—Third	81	71	.533	24	Roger Peckinpaugh	536,210
1930—Fourth	81	73	.536	21	Roger Peckinpaugh	528,657
1931—Fourth	78	76	.506	30	Roger Peckinpaugh	483,027
1932—Fourth	87	65	.572	19	Roger Peckinpaugh	468,953
1933—Fourth	75	76	.497	23½	Roger Peckinpaugh, W. Johnson	387,936
1934—Third	85	69	.552	16	Walter Johnson	391,338
1935—Third	82	71	.536	12	Walter Johnson, Stephen O'Neill	397,615
1936—Fifth	80	74	.519	22½	Stephen O'Neill	500,391
1937—Fourth	83	71	.539	19	Stephen O'Neill	564,849
1938—Third	86	66	.566	13	Oscar Vitt	652,006
1939—Third	87	67	.565	20½	Oscar Vitt	563,926
1940—Second	89	65	.578	1	Oscar Vitt	902,576
1941—Fourth†	75	79	.487	26	Roger Peckinpaugh	745,948
1942—Fourth	75	79	.487	28	Louis Boudreau	459,447

CLEVELAND INDIANS' YEARLY STANDING—Continued

Year—Position	W.	L.	Pct.	*G.B.	Manager	Attendance
1943—Third	82	71	.536	15½	Louis Boudreau	438,894
1944—Fifth†	72	82	.468	17	Louis Boudreau	475,272
1945—Fifth	73	72	.503	11	Louis Boudreau	558,182
1946—Sixth	68	86	.442	36	Louis Boudreau	1,057,289
1947—Fourth	80	74	.519	17	Louis Boudreau	1,521,978
1948—First‡	97	58	.626	+ 1	Louis Boudreau	2,620,627
1949—Third	89	65	.578	8	Louis Boudreau	2,233,771
1950—Fourth	92	62	.597	6	Louis Boudreau	1,727,464
1951—Second	93	61	.604	5	Alfonso Lopez	1,704,984
1952—Second	93	61	.604	2	Alfonso Lopez	1,444,607
1953—Second	92	62	.597	8½	Alfonso Lopez	1,069,176
1954—First	111	43	.721	+ 8	Alfonso Lopez	1,335,472
1955—Second	93	61	.604	3	Alfonso Lopez	1,221,780
1956—Sixth	88	66	.571	9	Alfonso Lopez	865,467
1957—Sixth	76	77	.497	21½	M. Kerby Farrell	722,256
1958—Fourth	77	76	.503	14½	Robert Bragan, Joseph Gordon	663,805
1959—Second	89	65	.578	5	Joseph Gordon	1,497,976
1960—Fourth	76	78	.494	21	Joseph Gordon, James Dykes	950,985
1961—Fifth	78	83	.484	30½	James Dykes	725,547
1962—Sixth	80	82	.494	16	F. Melvin McGaha	716,076
1963—Fifth†	79	83	.488	25½	George (Birdie) Tebbetts	562,507
1964—Sixth†	79	83	.488	20	George (Birdie) Tebbetts	653,293
1965—Fifth	87	75	.537	15	George (Birdie) Tebbetts	934,786
1966—Fifth	81	81	.500	17	Geo. Tebbetts, Geo. Strickland	903,359
1967—Eighth	75	87	.463	17	Joseph Adcock	662,980
1968—Third	86	75	.534	16½	Alvin Dark	857,994

EAST DIVISION

Year—Position	W.	L.	Pct.	*G.B.	Manager	Attendance
1969—Sixth	62	99	.385	46½	Alvin Dark	619,970
1970—Fifth	76	86	.469	32	Alvin Dark	729,752
1971—Sixth	60	102	.370	43	Alvin Dark, John Lipon	591,361
1972—Fifth	72	84	.462	14	Ken Aspromonte	626,354
1973—Sixth	71	91	.438	26	Ken Aspromonte	615,107
1974—Fourth	77	85	.475	14	Ken Aspromonte	1,114,262
1975—Fourth	79	80	.497	15½	Frank Robinson	977,039
1976—Fourth	81	78	.509	16	Frank Robinson	948,776
1977—Fifth	71	90	.441	28½	Frank Robinson, Jeffrey Torborg	900,365
1978—Sixth	69	90	.434	29	Jeffrey Torborg	800,584
1979—Sixth	81	80	.503	22	Jeffrey Torborg, David Garcia	1,011,644
1980—Sixth	79	81	.494	23	David Garcia	1,033,827
1981—6th/4th	52	51	.504	§	David Garcia	661,395
1982—Sixth†	78	84	.481	17	David Garcia	1,044,021
1983—Seventh	70	92	.432	28	Michael Ferraro, Patrick Corrales	768,941
1984—Sixth	75	87	.463	29	Pat Corrales	734,079

*Games behind winner. †Tied for position. ‡Defeated Boston in pennant playoff. §First half 26-24; second 26-27.

First Game Played at Municipal Stadium

The Philadelphia Athletics' Lefty Grove outdueled Mel Harder in a thrilling 1-0 contest on July 31, 1932, to open Municipal Stadium.

Mickey Cochrane drove in the only run in the eighth inning, while Grove shut out the Indians on four hits. A crowd of 76,979 fans witnessed the game.

BASEBALL DOPE BOOK

CLEVELAND INDIANS

(18) PAT CORRALES—Manager

No. PITCHERS—	Bts.	Thrs.	Hgt.	Wgt.	Birth-date	1984 Club	IP.	W.	L.	ERA.
41 Baller, Jay	R	R	6:06	215	10- 6-60	Buffalo	79.1	4	5	4.54
						Maine	83.2	9	4	5.38
49 Barkley, Jeff	B	R	6:03	178	11-21-60	Maine	85.1	5	6	2.85
						Cleveland	4.0	0	0	6.75
32 Behenna, Rick	R	R	6:02	170	3- 6-60	Cleveland	9.2	0	3	13.97
28 Blyleven, Bert	R	R	6:03	205	4- 6-51	Cleveland	245.0	19	7	2.87
13 Camacho, Ernie	R	R	6:01	180	2- 1-56	Cleveland	100.0	5	9	2.43
64 Doyle, Rich	R	R	6:05	205	2- 4-64	Buffalo	119.1	7	11	5.66
36 Easterly, Jamie	L	L	5:10	180	2-17-53	Cleveland	69.1	3	1	3.37
34 Farr, Steve	R	R	5:11	190	12-12-56	Maine	45.0	4	0	2.60
						Cleveland	116.0	3	11	4.58
44 Heaton, Neal	L	L	6:01	205	3- 3-60	Cleveland	198.2	12	15	5.21
46 Jeffcoat, Mike	L	L	6:02	187	8- 3-59	Cleveland	75.1	5	2	2.99
65 Roman, Jose	R	R	6:00	175	5-21-63	Buffalo	143.2	14	6	3.88
						Cleveland	6.0	0	2	18.00
50 Romero, Ramon	L	L	6:04	170	1- 8-59	Buffalo	51.1	3	4	5.61
						Maine	59.2	1	2	2.56
						Cleveland	3.0	0	0	0.00
Ruhle, Vern	R	R	6:01	195	1-25-51	Houston	90.1	1	9	4.58
						Iowa	74.1	5	4	4.26
37 Schulze, Don	R	R	6:03	225	9-27-62	Chicago NL	3.0	0	0	12.00
						Maine	9.1	1	1	8.68
						Cleveland	85.2	3	6	4.83
53 Siwy, Jim	R	R	6:04	200	9-20-58	Denver	96.0	4	5	5.25
						Maine	17.2	1	0	2.04
33 Smith, Roy	R	R	6:03	200	9- 6-61	Maine	80.2	5	4	4.35
						Cleveland	86.1	5	5	4.59
43 Ujdur, Jerry	R	R	6:01	205	3- 5-57	Maine	166.0	14	8	3.69
						Cleveland	14.1	1	2	6.91
54 Waddell, Tom	R	R	6:01	190	9-17-58	Cleveland	97.0	7	4	3.06

CATCHERS—	Bts.	Thrs.	Hgt.	Wgt.	Birth-date	1984 Club	G.	HR.	RBI.	Avg.
23 Bando, Chris	B	R	6:00	195	2- 4-56	Maine	29	3	13	.261
						Cleveland	75	12	41	.291
16 Willard, Jerry	L	R	6:02	195	3-14-60	Cleveland	87	10	37	.224

INFIELDERS—										
4 Bernazard, Tony	B	R	5:09	160	8-24-56	Cleveland	140	2	38	.221
22 Fischlin, Mike	R	R	6:01	165	9-13-55	Cleveland	85	1	14	.226
14 Franco, Julio	R	R	6:00	160	8-23-61	Cleveland	160	3	79	.286
21 Hargrove, Mike	L	L	6:00	195	10-26-49	Cleveland	133	2	44	.267
26 Jacoby, Brook	R	R	5:11	175	11-23-59	Cleveland	126	7	40	.264
11 Moronko, Jeff	R	R	6:02	190	8-17-59	Buffalo	131	13	95	.314
						Cleveland	7	0	3	.158
17 Noboa, Junior	R	R	5:10	155	11-10-64	Buffalo	117	1	45	.253
55 Quinones, Luis	B	R	6:00	165	4-28-62	Maine	131	8	60	.268
10 Tabler, Pat	R	R	6:02	198	2- 2-58	Cleveland	144	10	68	.290
29 Thornton, Andre	R	R	6:02	205	8-13-49	Cleveland	155	33	99	.271

OUTFIELDERS—										
63 Brito, Bernardo	R	R	6:00	190	12- 4-63	Batavia	76	19	57	.300
2 Butler, Brett	L	L	5:10	160	6-15-57	Cleveland	159	3	49	.269
30 Carter, Joe	R	R	6:03	215	3- 7-60	Iowa	59	14	66	.313
						Cleveland	66	13	41	.275
8 Castillo, Carmen	R	R	6:01	185	6- 8-58	Cleveland	87	10	36	.261
27 Hall, Mel	L	L	6:01	185	9-16-60	Chicago NL	48	4	22	.280
						Cleveland	83	7	30	.257
20 Nixon, Otis	B	R	6:02	180	1- 9-59	Cleveland	49	0	1	.154
						Maine	72	0	22	.277
69 Roman, Miguel	R	R	6:02	170	6-18-64	Batavia	70	16	53	.254
						Waterloo	32	2	10	.232
62 Taylor, Dwight	L	L	5:09	160	3-23-60	Maine	108	4	50	.271
24 Vukovich, George	L	L	6:00	198	6-24-56	Cleveland	134	9	60	.304
61 Washington, Randy	R	R	5:11	190	8- 7-63	Buffalo	120	9	63	.282

BOBBY BONDS (25)—Coach
JOHNNY GORYL (45)—Coach

DON McMAHON (47)—Coach
ED NAPOLEON (1)—Coach

DENNY SOMMERS (6)—Coach

MUNICIPAL STADIUM

	Seats	Prices
Field Boxes	1,880	$8.00
Box Seats in Lower Deck	14,104	8.00
Box Seats in Upper Deck	7,535	8.00
Reserved Seats in Lower Deck	15,425	6.00
Reserved Seats in Upper Deck	14,941	6.00
General Admission		
Lower Deck	7,397	3.50
Upper Deck	7,110	3.50
Bleachers	5,000	2.00
Loge	816	....

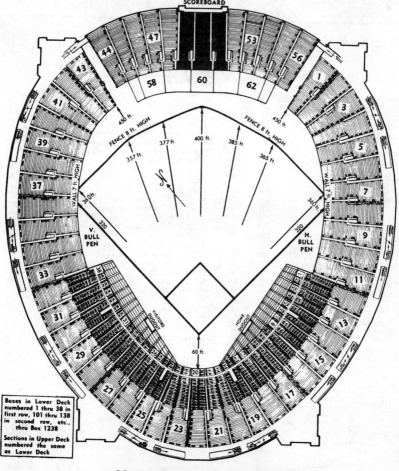

Boxes in Lower Deck numbered 1 thru 38 in first row, 101 thru 138 in second row, etc., thru Box 1238

Sections in Upper Deck numbered the same as Lower Deck

**Municipal Stadium, Cleveland
First A.L. Game Played July 31, 1932
(Indians' Permanent Home Since 1947)**

Sparky Anderson

DETROIT TIGERS

Chairman of the Board—John E. Fetzer
Vice Chairman—Thomas S. Monaghan
President-Chief Executive Officer—James A. Campbell
Executive Vice Pres.-Chief Operating Officer—William E. Haase
Vice President-General Manager—William R. Lajoie
Vice President-Secretary-Treasurer—Alex Callam
Director of Public Relations—Dan Ewald
Traveling Secretary—Bill Brown
Offices—Tiger Stadium
Tiger Stadium Capacity—52,806

Farm System: AAA—Nashville. AA—Birmingham. A—Lakeland.
Rookie—Bristol, Va.

DETROIT TIGERS' YEARLY STANDING

Year—Position	W.	L.	Pct.	*G.B.	Manager	Attendance
1901—Third	74	61	.548	8½	George Stallings	259,430
1902—Seventh	52	83	.385	30½	Frank Dwyer	189,469
1903—Fifth	65	71	.478	25	Edward Barrow	224,523
1904—Seventh	62	90	.408	32	Edward Barrow, Robert Lowe	177,796
1905—Third	79	74	.516	15½	William Armour	193,384
1906—Sixth	71	78	.477	21	William Armour	174,043
1907—First	92	58	.613	+ 1½	Hugh Jennings	297,079
1908—First	90	63	.588	+ ½	Hugh Jennings	436,199
1909—First	98	54	.645	+ 3½	Hugh Jennings	490,490
1910—Third	86	68	.558	18	Hugh Jennings	391,288
1911—Second	89	65	.578	13½	Hugh Jennings	484,988
1912—Sixth	69	84	.451	36½	Hugh Jennings	402,870
1913—Sixth	66	87	.431	30	Hugh Jennings	398,502
1914—Fourth	80	73	.523	19½	Hugh Jennings	416,225
1915—Second	100	54	.649	2½	Hugh Jennings	476,105
1916—Third	87	67	.565	5	Hugh Jennings	616,772
1917—Fourth	78	75	.510	21½	Hugh Jennings	457,289
1918—Seventh	55	71	.437	20	Hugh Jennings	203,719
1919—Fourth	80	60	.571	8	Hugh Jennings	643,805
1920—Seventh	61	93	.396	37	Hugh Jennings	579,650
1921—Sixth	71	82	.464	27	Tyrus Cobb	661,527
1922—Third	79	75	.513	15	Tyrus Cobb	861,206
1923—Second	83	71	.539	16	Tyrus Cobb	911,377
1924—Third	86	68	.558	6	Tyrus Cobb	1,015,136
1925—Fourth	81	73	.526	16½	Tyrus Cobb	820,766
1926—Sixth	79	75	.513	12	Tyrus Cobb	711,914
1927—Fourth	82	71	.536	27½	George Moriarty	773,716
1928—Sixth	68	86	.442	33	George Moriarty	474,323
1929—Sixth	70	84	.455	36	Stanley (Bucky) Harris	869,318
1930—Fifth	75	79	.487	27	Stanley (Bucky) Harris	649,450
1931—Seventh	61	93	.396	47	Stanley (Bucky) Harris	434,056
1932—Fifth	76	75	.503	29½	Stanley (Bucky) Harris	397,157
1933—Fifth	75	79	.487	25	Stanley Harris, Delmer Baker	320,972
1934—First	101	53	.656	+ 7	Gordon (Mickey) Cochrane	919,161
1935—First	93	58	.616	+ 3	Gordon (Mickey) Cochrane	1,034,929
1936—Second	83	71	.539	19½	Gordon (Mickey) Cochrane	875,948
1937—Second	89	65	.578	13	Gordon (Mickey) Cochrane	1,072,276
1938—Fourth	84	70	.545	16	Gordon Cochrane, Delmer Baker	799,557
1939—Fifth	81	73	.526	26½	Delmer Baker	836,279
1940—First	90	64	.584	+ 1	Delmer Baker	1,112,693
1941—Fourth†	75	79	.487	26	Delmer Baker	684,915
1942—Fifth	73	81	.474	30	Delmer Baker	580,087
1943—Fifth	78	76	.506	20	Stephen O'Neill	606,287
1944—Second	88	66	.571	1	Stephen O'Neill	923,176

DETROIT TIGERS' YEARLY STANDING—Continued

Year—Position	W.	L.	Pct.	*G.B.	Manager	Attendance
1945—First	88	65	.575	+ 1½	Stephen O'Neill	1,280,341
1946—Second	92	62	.597	12	Stephen O'Neill	1,722,590
1947—Second	85	69	.552	12	Stephen O'Neill	1,398,093
1948—Fifth	78	76	.506	18½	Stephen O'Neill	1,743,035
1949—Fourth	87	67	.565	10	Robert (Red) Rolfe	1,821,204
1950—Second	95	59	.617	3	Robert (Red) Rolfe	1,951,474
1951—Fifth	73	81	.474	25	Robert (Red) Rolfe	1,132,641
1952—Eighth	50	104	.325	45	Robert Rolfe, Fred Hutchinson	1,026,846
1953—Sixth	60	94	.390	40½	Fred Hutchinson	884,658
1954—Fifth	68	86	.442	43	Fred Hutchinson	1,079,847
1955—Fifth	79	75	.513	17	Stanley (Bucky) Harris	1,181,838
1956—Fifth	82	72	.532	15	Stanley (Bucky) Harris	1,051,182
1957—Fourth	78	76	.506	20	John Tighe	1,272,346
1958—Fifth	77	77	.500	15	John Tighe, Willis (Bill) Norman	1,098,924
1959—Fourth	76	78	.494	18	Willis Norman, James Dykes	1,221,221
1960—Sixth	71	83	.461	26	James Dykes, Joseph Gordon	1,167,669
1961—Second	101	61	.623	8	Robert Scheffing	1,600,710
1962—Fourth	85	76	.528	10½	Robert Scheffing	1,207,881
1963—Fifth†	79	83	.488	25½	Robert Scheffing, Charles Dressen	821,952
1964—Fourth	85	77	.525	14	Charles (Chuck) Dressen	816,139
1965—Fourth	89	73	.549	13	Charles (Chuck) Dressen	1,029,645
1966—Third	88	74	.543	10	C. Dressen, R. Swift, F. Skaff	1,124,293
1967—Second†	91	71	.562	1	Mayo Smith	1,447,143
1968—First	103	59	.636	+12	Mayo Smith	2,031,847

EAST DIVISION

Year—Position	W.	L.	Pct.	*G.B.	Manager	Attendance
1969—Second	90	72	.566	19	Mayo Smith	1,577,481
1970—Fourth	79	83	.488	29	Mayo Smith	1,501,293
1971—Second	91	71	.562	12	Alfred (Billy) Martin	1,591,073
1972—First‡	86	70	.551	+ ½	Alfred (Billy) Martin	1,892,386
1973—Third	85	77	.525	12	Alfred Martin, Joseph Schultz	1,724,146
1974—Sixth	72	90	.444	19	Ralph Houk	1,243,080
1975—Sixth	57	102	.358	37½	Ralph Houk	1,058,836
1976—Fifth	74	87	.460	24	Ralph Houk	1,467,020
1977—Fourth	74	88	.457	26	Ralph Houk	1,359,856
1978—Fifth	86	76	.531	13½	Ralph Houk	1,714,893
1979—Fifth	85	76	.528	18	J. Lester Moss, George Anderson	1,630,929
1980—Fifth	84	78	.519	19	George Anderson	1,785,293
1981—4th/2nd	60	49	.550	x	George Anderson	1,149,144
1982—Fourth	83	79	.512	12	George Anderson	1,636,058
1983—Second	92	70	.568	6	George Anderson	1,829,636
1984—First y	104	58	.642	+15	George Anderson	2,704,794

*Games behind winner. †Tied for position. ‡Lost Championship Series. xFirst half 31-26; second 29-23. yWon Championship Series.

First Game Played at Tiger Stadium

George Mullin singled with two out in the 11th inning to score Donie Bush with the winning tally as the Tigers defeated the Cleveland Naps, 6-5, in the opening of reconstructed Bennett Park on April 20, 1912.

The highlight of the game occurred in the first inning when Ty Cobb and Sam Crawford pulled a pair of double-steals, climaxed by Cobb's theft of home.

Rain had caused a two-day delay in the opening of the park.

DETROIT TIGERS

(11) SPARKY ANDERSON—Manager

No. PITCHERS—	Bts.	Thrs.	Hgt.	Wgt.	Birth-date	1984 Club	IP.	W.	L.	ERA.
40 Bair, Doug	R	R	6:00	180	8-22-49	Detroit	93.2	5	3	3.75
44 Berenguer, Juan	R	R	5:11	215	11-30-54	Detroit	168.1	11	10	3.48
43 Gumpert, Dave	R	R	6:01	190	5- 5-58	Evansville	87.1	7	4	4.95
21 Hernandez, Willie	L	L	6:02	185	11-14-54	Detroit	140.1	9	3	1.92
45 Kelly, Bryan	R	R	6:02	195	2-24-59	Birmingham	172.0	7	10	4.29
29 Lopez, Aurelio	R	R	6:00	225	10- 5-48	Detroit	137.2	10	1	2.94
48 Mason, Roger	R	R	6:06	215	9-18-58	Evansville	151.2	9	7	3.80
						Detroit	22.0	1	1	4.50
36 Monteleone, Rich	R	R	6:02	205	3-22-63	Birmingham	123.2	7	8	4.66
						Evansville	64.0	5	3	4.50
47 Morris, Jack	R	R	6:03	200	5-16-55	Detroit	240.1	19	11	3.60
49 O'Neal, Randy	R	R	6:02	195	8-30-60	Evansville	166.1	9	10	3.57
						Detroit	18.2	2	1	3.38
46 Petry, Dan	R	R	6:04	200	11-13-58	Detroit	233.1	18	8	3.24
17 Scherrer, Bill	L	L	6:04	170	1-20-58	Cincinnati	52.1	1	1	4.99
						Wichita	16.2	2	3	3.24
						Detroit	19.0	1	0	1.89
35 Terrell, Walt	L	R	6:02	205	5-11-58	New York NL	215.0	11	12	3.52
39 Wilcox, Milt	R	R	6:02	215	4-20-50	Detroit	193.2	17	8	4.00

CATCHERS—	Bts.	Thrs.	Hgt.	Wgt.	Birth-date	1984 Club	G.	HR.	RBI.	Avg.
8 Castillo, Marty	R	R	6:01	205	1-16-57	Detroit	70	4	17	.234
25 Lowry, Dwight	L	R	6:03	210	10-23-57	Detroit	32	2	7	.244
						Evansville	61	5	28	.220
18 Melvin, Bob	R	R	6:04	205	10-28-61	Evansville	44	0	11	.248
						Birmingham	69	2	33	.269
13 Parrish, Lance	R	R	6:03	220	6-15-56	Detroit	147	33	98	.237

INFIELDERS—	Bts.	Thrs.	Hgt.	Wgt.	Birth-date	1984 Club	G.	HR.	RBI.	Avg.
9 Baker, Doug	B	R	5:09	165	4- 3-61	Evansville	77	8	30	.259
						Detroit	43	0	12	.185
14 Bergman, Dave	L	L	6:02	180	6- 6-53	Detroit	120	7	44	.273
16 Brookens, Tom	R	R	5:10	170	8-10-53	Detroit	113	5	26	.246
22 Chavez, Pedro	R	R	5:11	160	2-23-62	Birmingham	60	1	25	.237
						Evansville	88	1	27	.269
24 Earl, Scott	R	R	5:11	165	9-18-60	Evansville	153	11	51	.251
						Detroit	14	0	1	.114
41 Evans, Darrell	L	R	6:02	205	5-26-47	Detroit	131	16	63	.232
27 Garbey, Barbaro	R	R	5:10	170	12- 4-56	Detroit	110	5	52	.287
4 Laga, Mike	L	L	6:02	210	6-14-60	Evansville	153	30	94	.265
						Detroit	9	0	1	.545
12 Pittaro, Chris	B	R	5:11	170	9-16-61	Birmingham	137	11	61	.284
3 Trammell, Alan	R	R	6:00	175	2-21-58	Detroit	139	14	69	.314
1 Whitaker, Lou	L	R	5:11	160	5-12-57	Detroit	143	13	56	.289

OUTFIELDERS—	Bts.	Thrs.	Hgt.	Wgt.	Birth-date	1984 Club	G.	HR.	RBI.	Avg.
23 Gibson, Kirk	L	L	6:03	215	5-28-57	Detroit	149	27	91	.282
30 Grubb, John	L	R	6:03	180	8- 4-48	Detroit	86	8	17	.267
31 Herndon, Larry	R	R	6:03	200	11- 3-53	Detroit	125	7	43	.280
15 Kuntz, Rusty	R	R	6:03	190	2- 4-55	Detroit	84	2	22	.286
						Evansville	10	0	0	.185
34 Lemon, Chet	R	R	6:00	190	2-12-55	Detroit	141	20	76	.287
37 Simmons, Nelson	B	R	6:01	195	6-27-63	Evansville	142	22	83	.307
						Detroit	9	0	3	.433
28 Weaver, James	L	L	6:03	190	10-10-59	Orlando	24	3	16	.259
						Toledo	111	15	64	.230

BILLY CONSOLO (50)—Coach
BILLY MUFFETT (52)—Coach

ALEX GRAMMAS (51)—Coach
DICK TRACEWSKI (53)—Coach

TIGER STADIUM

	Seats	Prices
Box Seats	11,718	$9.00
Reserved Grandstand	23,508	7.50
General Admission	6,269	5.00
Bleachers	11,192	3.50

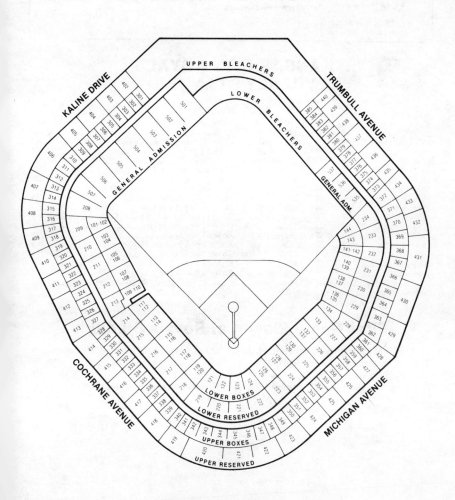

Tiger Stadium, Detroit
First A.L. Game Played April 20, 1912

KANSAS CITY ROYALS

Dick Howser

Co-owners—Ewing Kauffman, Avron Fogelman
President—Joe Burke
Executive Vice-Pres. & Gen. Manager—John Schuerholz
Vice-President-Administration—Spencer Robinson
Vice-President-Controller—Dale Rohr
Director of Public Relations—Dean Vogelaar
Traveling Secretary—Will Rudd
Assistant Director of Public Relations—Jeff Coy
Offices—Royals Stadium
Royals Stadium Capacity—40,625

Farm System: AAA—Omaha. AA—Memphis. A—Eugene, Fort Myers. Rookie—Sarasota.

KANSAS CITY ROYALS' YEARLY STANDING

WEST DIVISION

Year—Position	W.	L.	Pct.	*G.B.	Manager	Attendance
1969—Fourth	69	93	.426	28	Joseph Gordon	902,414
1970—Fourth†	65	97	.401	33	Charles Metro, Robert Lemon	693,047
1971—Second	85	76	.528	16	Robert Lemon	910,784
1972—Fourth	76	78	.494	16½	Robert Lemon	707,656
1973—Second	88	74	.543	6	John A. McKeon	1,345,341
1974—Fifth	77	85	.475	13	John A. McKeon	1,173,292
1975—Second	91	71	.562	7	J. A. McKeon, D. (Whitey) Herzog	1,151,836
1976—First‡	90	72	.556	+ 2½	Dorrel (Whitey) Herzog	1,680,265
1977—First‡	102	60	.630	+ 8	Dorrel (Whitey) Herzog	1,852,603
1978—First‡	92	70	.568	+ 5	Dorrel (Whitey) Herzog	2,255,493
1979—Second	85	77	.525	3	Dorrel (Whitey) Herzog	2,261,845
1980—First§	97	65	.599	+14	James Frey	2,288,714
1981—5th/1st	50	53	.485	x	James Frey, Richard Howser	1,279,403
1982—Second	90	72	.556	3	Richard Howser	2,284,464
1983—Second	79	83	.488	20	Richard Howser	1,963,875
1984—First‡	84	78	.519	+ 3	Richard Howser	1,810,018

*Games behind winner. †Tied for position. ‡Lost Championship Series. §Won Championship Series. xFirst half 20-30; second 30-23.

First Game Played at Royals Stadium

Despite 39-degree temperatures, 39,464 brave fans saw Kansas City trounce the Texas Rangers, 12-1, in the Royals' modern new palace on April 10, 1973.

John Mayberry led the attack with a single, a home run and four RBIs. Jeff Burroughs of the Rangers ruined Paul Splittorff's shutout with a ninth-inning home run.

KANSAS CITY ROYALS

(10) DICK HOWSER—Manager

No. PITCHERS—	Bts.	Thrs.	Hgt.	Wgt.	Birth-date	1984 Club	IP.	W.	L.	ERA.
27 Beckwith, Joe	L	R	6:02	200	1-28-55	Kansas City	100.2	8	4	3.40
40 Black, Bud	L	R	6:02	180	6-30-57	Kansas City	257.0	17	12	3.12
13 Cone, David	L	R	6:01	180	1- 2-63	Memphis	178.2	8	12	4.28
51 Ferreira, Tony	L	L	6:01	160	10- 4-62	Omaha	114.1	7	10	4.57
23 Gubicza, Mark	R	R	6:06	215	8-14-62	Kansas City	189.0	10	14	4.05
32 Gura, Larry	L	L	6:01	185	11-26-47	Kansas City	168.2	12	9	5.18
38 Huismann, Mark	R	R	6:03	195	5-11-58	Omaha	19.0	2	0	0.00
						Kansas City	75.0	3	3	4.20
25 Jackson, Danny	R	L	6:00	190	1- 5-62	Omaha	110.1	5	8	3.67
						Kansas City	76.0	2	6	4.26
17 Jones, Mike	L	L	6:05	230	7-30-59	Omaha	73.1	4	5	3.44
						Kansas City	81.0	2	3	4.89
37 Leibrandt, Charlie	R	L	6:03	200	10- 4-56	Omaha	72.2	7	1	1.24
						Kansas City	143.2	11	7	3.63
22 Leonard, Dennis	R	R	6:01	195	5- 8-51	Kansas City	(Did not play)			
29 Quisenberry, Dan	R	R	6:02	180	2- 7-53	Kansas City	129.1	6	3	2.64
31 Saberhagen, Bret	R	R	6:01	160	4-11-64	Kansas City	157.2	10	11	3.48
19 Wills, Frank	R	R	6:02	200	10-26-58	Omaha	89.2	7	4	2.81
						Kansas City	37.0	2	3	5.11

CATCHERS—						1984 Club	G.	HR.	RBI.	Avg.
7 Slaught, Don	R	R	6:00	185	9-11-58	Kansas City	124	4	42	.264
39 Stephans, Russ	R	R	6:00	190	5-20-59	Omaha	109	9	48	.290
12 Wathan, John	R	R	6:02	205	10- 4-49	Kansas City	97	2	10	.181

INFIELDERS—										
45 Balboni, Steve	R	R	6:03	225	1-16-57	Kansas City	126	28	77	.244
1 Biancalana, Buddy	B	R	5:11	160	2- 2-60	Omaha	58	7	25	.260
						Kansas City	66	2	9	.194
5 Brett, George	L	R	6:00	200	5-15-53	Kansas City	104	13	69	.284
2 Concepcion, Onix	R	R	5:06	180	10- 5-58	Kansas City	90	1	23	.282
4 Pryor, Greg	R	R	6:00	185	10- 2-49	Kansas City	123	4	25	.263
16 Scranton, Jim	R	R	6:00	175	5- 5-60	Omaha	136	3	37	.251
						Kansas City	2	0	0	.000
20 White, Frank	R	R	5:11	175	9- 4-50	Kansas City	129	17	56	.271

OUTFIELDERS—										
59 Allen, Ed	R	R	6:02	190	6-13-64	Fort Myers	136	0	42	.257
47 Brewer, Mike	R	R	6:05	190	10-24-59	Omaha	104	11	41	.203
						Memphis	35	2	23	.225
33 Davis, Butch	R	R	6:00	185	6-19-58	Kansas City	14	0	5	.191
						Omaha	83	7	43	.325
9 Iorg, Dane	L	R	6:00	180	5-11-50	St. Louis	15	0	3	.143
						Kansas City	78	5	30	.255
35 Jones, Lynn	R	R	5:09	170	1- 1-53	Kansas City	47	1	10	.301
						Omaha	17	1	3	.254
36 Leeper, Dave	L	L	5:11	170	10-30-59	Omaha	149	16	79	.257
						Kansas City	4	0	0	.000
11 McRae, Hal	R	R	5:11	185	7-10-46	Kansas City	106	3	42	.303
8 Morris, John	L	L	6:01	185	2-23-61	Omaha	148	15	60	.270
24 Motley, Darryl	R	R	5:09	196	1-21-60	Kansas City	146	15	70	.284
3 Orta, Jorge	L	R	5:10	175	11-26-50	Kansas City	122	9	50	.298
15 Sheridan, Pat	L	R	6:03	175	12- 4-57	Kansas City	138	8	53	.283
48 Snider, Van	L	R	6:03	180	8-11-63	Memphis	132	7	62	.246
6 Wilson, Willie	B	R	6:03	195	7- 9-55	Kansas City	128	2	44	.301

GARY BLAYLOCK (43)—Coach   MIKE FERRARO (41)—Coach
JOSE MARTINEZ (42)—Coach   LEE MAY (14)—Coach
                    JIM SCHAFFER (44)—Coach

ROYALS STADIUM

	Seats	Prices
Club Boxes	2,487	$9.00
Field Box Seats	7,605	8.00
View Box Seats	4,543	6.00
Plaza Reserved Seats	7,641	6.00
View Reserved Seats	13,279	5.00
General Admission	5,070	2.00

Note—There are no seating sections as such. Seating is controlled by aisle numbers. Even numbers start behind home plate and go in ascending order toward right field, odd numbers toward left field.

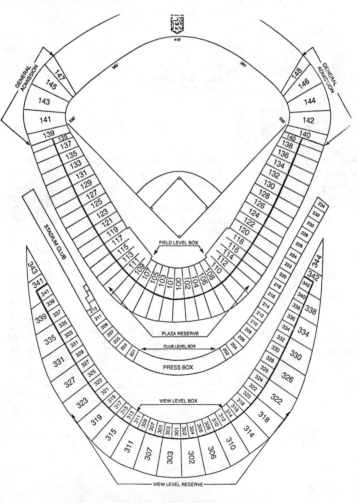

Royals Stadium, Kansas City
First A.L. Game Played April 10, 1973

MILWAUKEE BREWERS

President—Allan (Bud) Selig
Exec. Vice-President-General Manager—Harry Dalton
Traveling Secretary—Jimmy Bank
Vice-President Marketing—Richard Hackett
Coordinator of Player Procurement—Ray Poitevint
Director of Publicity—Tom Skibosh
Assistant Director, Publicity—Mario Ziino
Offices—County Stadium
County Stadium Seating Capacity—53,192

Farm System: AAA—Vancouver. AA—El Paso. A—Beloit, Stockton.
Rookie—Helena.

George Bamberger

MILWAUKEE BREWERS' YEARLY STANDING

(Seattle Pilots Prior To 1970)

WEST DIVISION

Year—Position	W.	L.	Pct.	*G.B.	Manager	Attendance
1969—Sixth	64	98	.395	33	Joseph Schultz	677,944
1970—Fourth†	65	97	.401	33	J. David Bristol	933,690
1971—Sixth	69	92	.429	32	J. David Bristol	731,531

EAST DIVISION

Year—Position	W.	L.	Pct.	*G.B.	Manager	Attendance
1972—Sixth	65	91	.417	21	J. David Bristol, Del Crandall	600,440
1973—Fifth	74	88	.457	23	Del Crandall	1,092,158
1974—Fifth	76	86	.469	15	Del Crandall	955,741
1975—Fifth	68	94	.420	28	Del Crandall	1,213,357
1976—Sixth	66	95	.410	32	Alexander Grammas	1,012,164
1977—Sixth	67	95	.414	33	Alexander Grammas	1,114,938
1978—Third	93	69	.574	6½	George Bamberger	1,601,406
1979—Second	95	66	.590	8	George Bamberger	1,918,343
1980—Third	86	76	.531	17	George Bamberger, Robert Rodgers	1,857,408
1981—3rd/1st	62	47	.569	‡	Robert Rodgers	878,432
1982—First§	95	67	.586	+ 1	Robert Rodgers, Harvey Kuenn	1,978,896
1983—Fifth	87	75	.537	11	Harvey Kuenn	2,397,131
1984—Seventh	67	94	.416	36½	Rene Lachemann	1,608,509

*Games behind winner. †Tied for position. ‡First half 31-25; second 31-22. §Won Championship Series.

First Games Played at County Stadium

County Stadium has been host to three home openers.

On April 14, 1953, a crowd of 34,357 greeted major league baseball's return to Milwaukee and saw the Braves edge out a 3-2 victory over St. Louis on a controversial home run by rookie Bill Bruton. Bruton's 10th-inning smash bounced off the glove of right fielder Enos Slaughter and over the fence, causing temporary indecision among the umpires.

On May 15, 1968, the Chicago White Sox played the first of 20 "home" games in Milwaukee, losing to the California Angels, 4-2. Despite rainy weather, 23,510 fans turned out.

The Brewers made their debut on April 7, 1970, losing to the Angels, 12-0. A crowd of 30,107 watched the Angels' Andy Messersmith limit the Brewers to four hits—three by Steve Hovley.

MILWAUKEE BREWERS

(31) GEORGE BAMBERGER—Manager

No.	PITCHERS—	Bts.	Thrs.	Hgt.	Wgt.	Birth-date	1984 Club	IP.	W.	L.	ERA.
	Bosio, Chris	R	R	6:03	210	4- 3-63	Beloit	181.0	17	6	2.73
	Burris, Ray	R	R	6:05	210	8-22-50	Oakland	211.2	13	10	3.15
47	Cocanower, Jaime	R	R	6:04	190	2-14-57	Milwaukee	174.2	8	16	4.02
	Crim, Chuck	R	R	6:00	170	7-23-61	El Paso	90.0	7	4	1.50
34	Fingers, Rollie	R	R	6:04	200	8-25-46	Milwaukee	46.0	1	2	1.96
40	Gibson, Bob	R	R	6:00	195	6-19-57	Milwaukee	69.0	2	5	4.96
							Vancouver	73.1	3	4	4.54
30	Haas, Moose	R	R	6:00	170	4-22-56	Milwaukee	189.1	9	11	3.99
	Higuera, Ted	B	L	5:10	178	11- 9-58	Vancouver	40.0	1	4	4.73
							El Paso	121.0	8	7	2.60
27	Ladd, Pete	R	R	6:03	235	7-17-56	Milwaukee	91.0	4	9	5.24
10	McClure, Bob	B	L	5:11	170	4-29-53	Milwaukee	139.2	4	8	4.38
43	Porter, Chuck	R	R	6:03	188	1-12-56	Milwaukee	81.1	6	4	3.87
	Roberts, Scott	R	R	6:04	200	10- 7-59	Vancouver	151.0	8	6	3.58
41	Searage, Ray	L	L	6:01	180	5- 1-55	Milwaukee	38.1	2	1	0.70
							Vancouver	76.1	6	3	3.07
42	Tellmann, Tom	R	R	6:04	184	3-29-54	Milwaukee	81.0	6	3	2.78
50	Vuckovich, Pete	R	R	6:04	220	10-27-52	Milwaukee	(Did not play)			
36	Waits, Rick	L	L	6:03	195	5-15-52	Milwaukee	73.0	2	4	3.58
18	Wegman, Bill	R	R	6:05	200	12-19-62	Vancouver	27.2	0	3	1.95
							El Paso	64.0	4	5	2.67

No.	CATCHERS—	Bts.	Thrs.	Hgt.	Wgt.	Birth-date	1984 Club	G.	HR.	RBI.	Avg.
21	Schroeder, Bill	R	R	6:02	200	9- 7-58	Milwaukee	61	14	25	.257
23	Simmons, Ted	B	R	6:00	200	8- 9-49	Milwaukee	132	4	52	.221
8	Sundberg, Jim	R	R	6:01	192	5-18-51	Milwaukee	110	7	43	.261

No.	INFIELDERS—	Bts.	Thrs.	Hgt.	Wgt.	Birth-date	1984 Club	G.	HR.	RBI.	Avg.
51	Castillo, Juan	B	R	5:11	155	1-25-62	Vancouver	8	0	2	.333
							El Paso	119	4	59	.288
15	Cooper, Cecil	L	L	6:02	190	12-20-49	Milwaukee	148	11	67	.275
17	Gantner, Jim	L	R	5:11	175	1- 5-54	Milwaukee	153	3	56	.282
	Giles, Brian	R	R	6:01	165	4-27-60	Tidewater	118	6	37	.242
4	Molitor, Paul	R	R	6:00	175	8-22-56	Milwaukee	13	0	6	.217
2	Ready, Randy	R	R	5:11	180	1- 8-60	Vancouver	43	3	18	.325
							Milwaukee	37	3	13	.189
58	Riles, Earnest	L	R	6:01	180	10- 2-60	Vancouver	123	3	54	.267
	Robidoux, Billy	L	R	6:01	200	1-13-64	Stockton	97	5	67	.279
11	Romero, Ed	R	R	5:11	150	12- 9-57	Milwaukee	116	1	31	.252
	Sveum, Dale	B	R	6:03	185	11-23-63	El Paso	131	9	83	.329
19	Yount, Robin	R	R	6:00	170	9-16-55	Milwaukee	160	16	80	.298

No.	OUTFIELDERS—	Bts.	Thrs.	Hgt.	Wgt.	Birth-date	1984 Club	G.	HR.	RBI.	Avg.
29	Brouhard, Mark	R	R	6:01	210	5-22-56	Milwaukee	66	6	22	.239
25	Clark, Bobby	R	R	6:00	190	6-13-55	Milwaukee	58	2	16	.260
53	Felder, Mike	B	R	5:08	160	11-18-62	El Paso	122	9	71	.290
7	Householder, Paul	B	R	6:00	185	9- 4-58	Cincinnati	14	0	0	.083
							Wichita	118	18	63	.248
							St. Louis	13	0	0	.143
14	James, Dion	L	L	6:00	170	11- 9-62	Milwaukee	128	1	30	.295
5	Loman, Doug	L	L	6:00	185	5- 9-58	Milwaukee	23	2	12	.276
							Vancouver	142	18	102	.324
28	Manning, Rick	L	R	6:01	180	9- 2-54	Milwaukee	119	7	31	.249
22	Moore, Charlie	R	R	5:11	180	6-21-53	Milwaukee	70	2	17	.234
24	Oglivie, Ben	L	L	6:02	170	2-11-49	Milwaukee	131	12	60	.262

ANDY ETCHEBARREN (45)—Coach　　　　　　　　LARRY HANEY (12)—Coach
FRANK HOWARD (33)—Coach　　　　　　　　　TONY MUSER (35)—Coach
HERM STARRETTE (38)—Coach

COUNTY STADIUM

	Seats	Prices
Deluxe Mezzanine	76	$9.00
Mezzanine	933	8.50
Box Seats	11,572	....
Lower	6,885	8.00
Upper	4,687	8.00
Lower Grandstand	21,231	7.00
Upper Grandstand	13,380	5.50
General Admission	*	5.50
Bleachers	6,000	3.00

*Variable

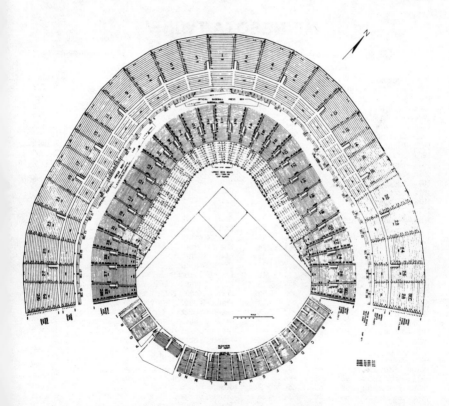

County Stadium, Milwaukee
First A.L. Game Played May 15, 1968

Billy Gardner

MINNESOTA TWINS

President—Howard T. Fox, Jr.
Executive Vice-President—Bruce G. Haynes
Vice-Pres.-Farm Director—George Brophy
Assistant Farm Director—Jim Rantz
Director of Public Relations—Tom Mee
Offices—Metrodome, Minneapolis
Metrodome Capacity—55,122

Farm System: AAA—Toledo. AA—Orlando. A—Kenosha, Visalia.
Rookie—Elizabethton.

MINNESOTA TWINS' YEARLY STANDING

(Original Washington Senators Prior to 1961)

Year—Position	W.	L.	Pct.	*G.B.	Manager	Attendance
1901—Sixth	61	72	.459	20½	James Manning	161,661
1902—Sixth	61	75	.449	22	Thomas Loftus	188,158
1903—Eighth	43	94	.314	47½	Thomas Loftus	128,878
1904—Eighth	38	113	.251	55½	Patrick Donovan	131,744
1905—Seventh	64	87	.421	29½	J. Garland Stahl	252,027
1906—Seventh	55	95	.367	37½	J. Garland Stahl	129,903
1907—Eighth	49	102	.325	43½	Joseph Cantillon	221,929
1908—Seventh	67	85	.441	22½	Joseph Cantillon	264,252
1909—Eighth	42	110	.276	56	Joseph Cantillon	205,199
1910—Seventh	66	85	.437	36½	James McAleer	254,591
1911—Seventh	64	90	.416	38½	James McAleer	244,884
1912—Second	91	61	.599	14	Clark Griffith	350,663
1913—Second	90	64	.584	6½	Clark Griffith	325,831
1914—Third	81	73	.526	19	Clark Griffith	243,888
1915—Fourth	85	68	.556	17	Clark Griffith	167,332
1916—Seventh	76	77	.497	14½	Clark Griffith	177,265
1917—Fifth	74	79	.484	25½	Clark Griffith	89,682
1918—Third	72	56	.563	4	Clark Griffith	182,122
1919—Seventh	56	84	.400	32	Clark Griffith	234,096
1920—Sixth	68	84	.447	29	Clark Griffith	359,260
1921—Fourth	80	73	.523	18	George McBride	456,069
1922—Sixth	69	85	.448	25	Clyde Milan	458,552
1923—Fourth	75	78	.490	23½	Owen (Donie) Bush	357,406
1924—First	92	62	.597	+ 2	Stanley (Bucky) Harris	534,310
1925—First	96	55	.636	+ 8½	Stanley (Bucky) Harris	817,199
1926—Fourth	81	69	.540	8	Stanley (Bucky) Harris	551,580
1927—Third	85	69	.552	25	Stanley (Bucky) Harris	528,976
1928—Fourth	75	79	.487	26	Stanley (Bucky) Harris	378,501
1929—Fifth	71	81	.467	34	Walter Johnson	355,506
1930—Second	94	60	.610	8	Walter Johnson	614,474
1931—Third	92	62	.597	16	Walter Johnson	492,657
1932—Third	93	61	.604	14	Walter Johnson	371,396
1933—First	99	53	.651	+ 7	Joseph Cronin	437,533
1934—Seventh	66	86	.434	34	Joseph Cronin	330,074
1935—Sixth	67	86	.438	27	Stanley (Bucky) Harris	255,011
1936—Fourth	82	71	.536	20	Stanley (Bucky) Harris	379,525
1937—Sixth	73	80	.477	28½	Stanley (Bucky) Harris	522,694
1939—Sixth	65	87	.428	41½	Stanley (Bucky) Harris	339,257
1940—Seventh	64	90	.416	26	Stanley (Bucky) Harris	381,241
1941—Sixth†	70	84	.455	31	Stanley (Bucky) Harris	415,663
1942—Seventh	62	89	.411	39½	Stanley (Bucky) Harris	403,493
1943—Second	84	69	.549	13½	Oswald Bluege	574,694
1944—Eighth	64	90	.416	25	Oswald Bluege	525,235

MINNESOTA TWINS' YEARLY STANDING—Continued

Year—Position	W.	L.	Pct.	*G.B.	Manager	Attendance
1945—Second	87	67	.565	1½	Oswald Bluege	652,660
1946—Fourth	76	78	.494	28	Oswald Bluege	1,027,216
1947—Seventh	64	90	.416	33	Oswald Bluege	850,758
1948—Seventh	56	97	.366	40	Joseph Kuhel	795,254
1949—Eighth	50	104	.325	47	Joseph Kuhel	770,745
1950—Fifth	67	87	.435	31	Stanley (Bucky) Harris	699,697
1951—Seventh	62	92	.403	36	Stanley (Bucky) Harris	695,167
1952—Fifth	78	76	.506	17	Stanley (Bucky) Harris	699,457
1953—Fifth	76	76	.500	23½	Stanley (Bucky) Harris	595,594
1954—Sixth	66	88	.429	45	Stanley (Bucky) Harris	503,542
1955—Eighth	53	101	.344	43	Charles (Chuck) Dressen	425,238
1956—Seventh	59	95	.383	38	Charles (Chuck) Dressen	431,647
1957—Eighth	55	99	.357	43	Chas. Dressen, Harry Lavagetto	457,079
1958—Eighth	61	93	.396	31	Harry (Cookie) Lavagetto	475,288
1959—Eighth	63	91	.409	31	Harry (Cookie) Lavagetto	615,372
1960—Fifth	73	81	.474	24	Harry (Cookie) Lavagetto	743,404
1961—Seventh	70	90	.438	38	Harry Lavagetto, Sam Mele	1,256,723
1962—Second	91	71	.562	5	Sabath (Sam) Mele	1,433,116
1963—Third	91	70	.565	13	Sabath (Sam) Mele	1,406,652
1964—Sixth†	79	83	.488	20	Sabath (Sam) Mele	1,207,514
1965—First	102	60	.630	+ 7	Sabath (Sam) Mele	1,463,258
1966—Second	89	73	.549	9	Sabath (Sam) Mele	1,259,374
1967—Second†	91	71	.562	1	Sabath (Sam) Mele, Calvin Ermer	1,483,547
1968—Seventh	79	83	.488	24	Calvin Ermer	1,143,257

WEST DIVISION

Year—Position	W.	L.	Pct.	*G.B.	Manager	Attendance
1969—First‡	97	65	.599	+ 9	Alfred (Billy) Martin	1,349,328
1970—First‡	98	64	.605	+ 9	William Rigney	1,261,887
1971—Fifth	74	86	.463	26½	William Rigney	940,858
1972—Third	77	77	.500	15½	William Rigney, Frank Quilici	797,901
1973—Third	81	81	.500	13	Frank Quilici	907,499
1974—Third	82	80	.506	8	Frank Quilici	662,401
1975—Fourth	76	83	.478	20½	Frank Quilici	737,156
1976—Third	85	77	.525	5	Gene Mauch	715,394
1977—Fourth	84	77	.522	17½	Gene Mauch	1,162,727
1978—Fourth	73	89	.451	19	Gene Mauch	787,878
1979—Fourth	82	80	.506	6	Gene Mauch	1,070,521
1980—Third	77	84	.478	19½	Gene Mauch, John Goryl	769,206
1981—7th/4th	41	68	.376	§	John Goryl, William Gardner	469,090
1982—Seventh	60	102	.370	33	William Gardner	921,186
1983—Fifth†	70	92	.432	29	William Gardner	858,939
1984—Second†	81	81	.500	3	William Gardner	1,598,422

*Games behind winner.   †Tied for position.   ‡First half 31-25; second 31-22. §Won Championship Series.

First Game Played at The Metrodome

In front of a crowd of 52,279—the largest crowd in Minnesota baseball history—Seattle's Jim Maler collected three hits and drove in five runs as the Mariners spoiled the Twins' home opener, 11-7, on April 6, 1982.

Twins third baseman Gary Gaetti drove in four runs and tied an opening-day record by hitting two home runs. He narrowly missed a third when he was tagged out at the plate trying for an inside-the-park homer.

MINNESOTA TWINS

(42) BILLY GARDNER—Manager

No. PITCHERS—	Bts.	Thrs.	Hgt.	Wgt.	Birth-date	1984 Club	IP.	W.	L.	ERA.
32 Butcher, John	R	R	6:04	190	3- 8-57	Minnesota	225.0	13	11	3.44
39 Davis, Ron	R	R	6:04	196	8- 6-55	Minnesota	83.0	7	11	4.55
23 Filson, Pete	B	L	6:02	195	9-28-58	Minnesota	118.2	6	5	4.10
27 Havens, Brad	L	L	6:01	192	11-17-59	Toledo	169.0	11	10	2.61
17 Hodge, Ed	L	L	6:02	192	4-19-58	Toledo	22.1	2	0	2.01
						Minnesota	100.0	4	3	4.77
19 Lysander, Rick	R	R	6:02	188	2-21-53	Toledo	37.0	3	2	3.41
						Minnesota	56.2	4	3	3.49
37 Oelkers, Bryan	L	L	6:03	192	3-11-61	Orlando	219.2	16	11	3.40
44 Portugal, Mark	R	R	6:00	170	10-30-62	Orlando	196.0	14	7	2.98
18 Schrom, Ken	R	R	6:02	195	11-23-54	Orlando	10.0	0	0	2.70
						Minnesota	137.0	5	11	4.47
48 Smithson, Mike	L	R	6:08	215	1-21-55	Minnesota	252.0	15	13	3.68
16 Viola, Frank	L	L	6:04	209	4-19-60	Minnesota	257.2	18	12	3.21
30 Walters, Mike	R	R	6:05	203	10-18-57	Toledo	4.0	0	0	4.50
						Minnesota	29.0	0	3	3.72
36 Wardle, Curt	L	L	6:05	220	11-16-60	Orlando	78.0	6	1	0.69
						Minnesota	4.0	0	0	4.50
22 Whitehouse, Len	L	L	5:09	174	9-10-57	Toledo	4.1	0	0	0.00
						Minnesota	31.1	2	2	3.16
28 Yett, Rich	R	R	6:02	187	10-6-62	Toledo	174.2	12	9	3.25

CATCHERS—	Bts.	Thrs.	Hgt.	Wgt.	Birth-date	1984 Club	G.	HR.	RBI.	Avg.
20 Engle, Dave	R	R	6:03	216	11-30-56	Minnesota	109	4	38	.266
15 Laudner, Tim	R	R	6:03	208	6- 7-58	Minnesota	87	10	35	.206
10 Reed, Jeff	L	R	6:02	185	11-12-62	Toledo	94	3	35	.266
						Minnesota	18	0	1	.143
12 Salas, Mark	L	R	6:00	180	3- 8-61	Louisville	95	12	48	.244
						St. Louis	14	0	1	.100

INFIELDERS—	Bts.	Thrs.	Hgt.	Wgt.	Birth-date	1984 Club	G.	HR.	RBI.	Avg.
2 Castino, John	R	R	5:11	178	10-23-54	Minnesota	8	0	3	.444
1 Espinoza, Alvaro	R	R	6:00	160	2-19-62	Toledo	104	0	30	.233
8 Gaetti, Gary	R	R	6:00	193	8-19-58	Minnesota	162	5	65	.262
31 Gagne, Greg	R	R	5:11	185	11-12-61	Toledo	70	9	27	.280
						Minnesota	2	0	0	.000
45 Holmes, Stan	R	R	6:00	206	2- 1-60	Orlando	142	25	101	.280
14 Hrbek, Kent	L	R	6:04	229	5-21-60	Minnesota	149	27	107	.311
5 Jimenez, Houston	R	R	5:07	144	10-30-57	Minnesota	108	0	19	.201
49 Lombardozzi, Steve	R	R	6:00	175	4-26-60	Toledo	119	9	31	.249
11 Teufel, Tim	R	R	6:00	175	7- 7-58	Minnesota	157	14	61	.262
38 Washington, Ron	R	R	5:11	163	4-29-52	Minnesota	88	3	23	.294

OUTFIELDERS—	Bts.	Thrs.	Hgt.	Wgt.	Birth-date	1984 Club	G.	HR.	RBI.	Avg.
26 Brown, Darrell	B	R	6:00	184	10-29-55	Minnesota	95	1	19	.273
24 Brunansky, Tom	R	R	6:04	211	8-20-60	Minnesota	155	32	85	.254
25 Bush, Randy	L	L	6:01	186	10- 5-58	Minnesota	113	11	43	.222
21 David, Andre	L	L	6:00	170	5-18-58	Toledo	61	7	24	.294
						Minnesota	33	1	5	.250
9 Hatcher, Mickey	R	R	6:02	199	3-15-55	Minnesota	152	5	69	.302
7 Meier, Dave	R	R	6:00	185	8- 8-59	Minnesota	59	0	13	.238
34 Puckett, Kirby	R	R	5:08	175	3-14-61	Toledo	21	1	5	.263
						Minnesota	128	0	31	.296
Stenhouse, Mike	L	R	6:01	195	5-29-58	Indianapolis	27	8	27	.333
						Montreal	80	4	16	.183

TOM KELLY (41)—Coach   TONY OLIVA (6)—Coach
JOHNNY PODRES (46)—Coach   RICK STELMASZEK (43)—Coach

THE METRODOME

	Seats	Prices
Private Boxes	1,074	$8.00
Lower Deck Reserved Seats	14,903	8.00
Upper Deck Reserved Seats	19,621	7.00
Lower Leftfield	6,600	4.00
General Admission	12,924	3.00

*Sold on season basis only.

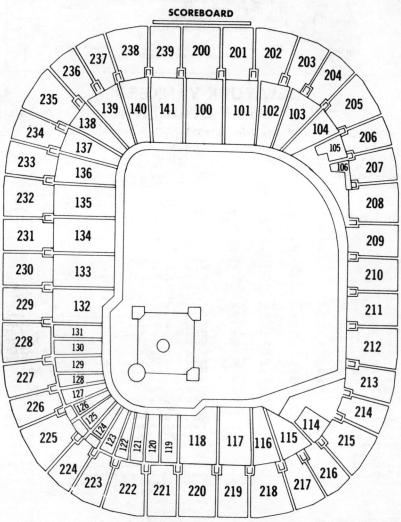

**The Metrodome, Minneapolis, Minn.
First A.L. Game Played April 6, 1982**

NEW YORK YANKEES

Principal Owner—George M. Steinbrenner III
President—Eugene J. McHale
V.P., General Manager—Clyde King
Administrative Vice-President, Treasurer—David Weidler
Vice-President, General Counsel—Mel Southard Jr.
Vice-President, Baseball Administration—Woody Woodward
Director of Minor League Operations—Bobby Hofman
Director of Scouting—Doug Melvin
Director of Media Relations—Joe Safety
Traveling Secretary—Bill Kane
Offices—Yankee Stadium
Yankee Stadium Capacity—57,545

Yogi Berra

Farm System: AAA—Columbus, O. AA—Albany-Colonie, N.Y. A—Fort Lauderdale, Oneonta. Rookie—Sarasota.

NEW YORK YANKEES' YEARLY STANDING

(Baltimore Orioles, 1901 to 1902, Inclusive)

Year—Position	W.	L.	Pct.	*G.B.	Manager	Attendance
1901—Fifth	68	65	.511	13½	John McGraw	141,952
1902—Eighth	50	88	.362	34	John McGraw, Wilbert Robinson	174,606
1903—Fourth	72	62	.537	17	Clark Griffith	211,808
1904—Second	92	59	.609	1½	Clark Griffith	438,919
1905—Sixth	71	78	.477	21½	Clark Griffith	309,100
1906—Second	90	61	.596	3	Clark Griffith	434,709
1907—Fifth	70	78	.473	21	Clark Griffith	350,020
1908—Eighth	51	103	.331	39½	Clark Griffith, Norman Elberfeld	305,500
1909—Fifth	74	77	.490	23½	George Stallings	501,000
1910—Second	88	63	.583	14½	George Stallings, Hal Chase	355,857
1911—Sixth	76	76	.500	25½	Hal Chase	302,444
1912—Eighth	50	102	.329	55	Harry Wolverton	242,194
1913—Seventh	57	94	.377	38	Frank Chance	357,551
1914—Sixth†	70	84	.455	30	F. Chance, Roger Peckinpaugh	359,477
1915—Fifth	69	83	.454	32½	William Donovan	256,035
1916—Fourth	80	74	.519	11	William Donovan	469,211
1917—Sixth	71	82	.464	28½	William Donovan	330,294
1918—Fourth	60	63	.488	13½	Miller Huggins	282,047
1919—Third	80	59	.576	7½	Miller Huggins	619,164
1920—Third	95	59	.617	3	Miller Huggins	1,289,422
1921—First	98	55	.641	+ 4½	Miller Huggins	1,230,696
1922—First	94	60	.610	+ 1	Miller Huggins	1,026,134
1923—First	98	54	.645	+16	Miller Huggins	1,007,066
1924—Second	89	63	.586	2	Miller Huggins	1,053,533
1925—Seventh	69	85	.448	30	Miller Huggins	697,267
1926—First	91	63	.591	+ 3	Miller Huggins	1,027,095
1927—First	110	44	.714	+19	Miller Huggins	1,164,015
1928—First	101	53	.656	+ 2½	Miller Huggins	1,072,132
1929—Second	88	66	.571	18	Miller Huggins, Arthur Fletcher	960,148
1930—Third	86	68	.558	16	J. Robert Shawkey	1,169,230
1931—Second	94	59	.614	13½	Joseph McCarthy	912,437
1932—First	107	47	.695	+13	Joseph McCarthy	962,320
1933—Second	91	59	.607	7	Joseph McCarthy	728,014
1934—Second	94	60	.610	7	Joseph McCarthy	854,682
1935—Second	89	60	.597	3	Joseph McCarthy	657,508
1936—First	102	51	.667	+19½	Joseph McCarthy	976,913
1937—First	102	52	.662	+13	Joseph McCarthy	998,148
1938—First	99	53	.651	+ 9½	Joseph McCarthy	970,916
1939—First	106	45	.702	+17	Joseph McCarthy	859,785
1940—Third	88	66	.571	2	Joseph McCarthy	988,975
1941—First	101	53	.656	+17	Joseph McCarthy	964,722
1942—First	103	51	.669	+ 9	Joseph McCarthy	988,251
1943—First	98	56	.636	+13½	Joseph McCarthy	645,006
1944—Third	83	71	.539	6	Joseph McCarthy	822,864

NEW YORK YANKEES' YEARLY STANDING—Continued

Year—Position	W.	L.	Pct.	*G.B.	Manager	Attendance
1945—Fourth	81	71	.533	6½	Joseph McCarthy	881,846
1946—Third	87	67	.565	17	J. McCarthy, W. Dickey, J. Neun	2,265,512
1947—First	97	57	.630	+12	Stanley (Bucky) Harris	2,178,937
1948—Third	94	60	.610	2½	Stanley (Bucky) Harris	2,373,901
1949—First	97	57	.630	+ 1	Chas. (Casey) Stengel	2,281,676
1950—First	98	56	.636	+ 3	Chas. (Casey) Stengel	2,081,380
1951—First	98	56	.636	+ 5	Chas. (Casey) Stengel	1,950,107
1952—First	95	59	.617	+ 2	Chas. (Casey) Stengel	1,629,665
1953—First	99	52	.656	+ 8½	Chas. (Casey) Stengel	1,537,811
1954—Second	103	51	.669	8	Chas. (Casey) Stengel	1,475,171
1955—First	96	58	.623	+ 3	Chas. (Casey) Stengel	1,490,138
1956—First	97	57	.630	+ 9	Chas. (Casey) Stengel	1,491,784
1957—First	98	56	.636	+ 8	Chas. (Casey) Stengel	1,497,134
1958—First	92	62	.597	+10	Chas. (Casey) Stengel	1,428,438
1959—Third	79	75	.513	15	Chas. (Casey) Stengel	1,552,030
1960—First	97	57	.630	+ 8	Chas. (Casey) Stengel	1,627,349
1961—First	109	53	.673	+ 8	Ralph Houk	1,747,725
1962—First	96	66	.593	+ 5	Ralph Houk	1,493,574
1963—First	104	57	.646	+10½	Ralph Houk	1,308,920
1964—First	99	63	.611	+ 1	Lawrence (Yogi) Berra	1,305,638
1965—Sixth	77	85	.475	25	John Keane	1,213,552
1966—Tenth	70	89	.440	26½	John Keane, Ralph Houk	1,124,648
1967—Ninth	72	90	.444	20	Ralph Houk	1,259,514
1968—Fifth	83	79	.512	20	Ralph Houk	1,185,666

EAST DIVISION

Year—Position	W.	L.	Pct.	*G.B.	Manager	Attendance
1969—Fifth	80	81	.497	28½	Ralph Houk	1,067,996
1970—Second	93	69	.574	15	Ralph Houk	1,136,879
1971—Fourth	82	80	.506	21	Ralph Houk	1,070,771
1972—Fourth	79	76	.510	6½	Ralph Houk	966,328
1973—Fourth	80	82	.494	17	Ralph Houk	1,262,103
1974—Second	89	73	.549	2	William Virdon	1,273,075
1975—Third	83	77	.519	12	William Virdon, Billy Martin	1,288,048
1976—First‡	97	62	.610	+10½	Billy Martin	2,012,434
1977—First‡	100	62	.617	+ 2½	Billy Martin	2,103,092
1978—First§‡	100	63	.613	+ 1	Billy Martin, Robert Lemon	2,335,871
1979—Fourth	89	71	.556	13½	R. Lemon, Billy Martin	2,537,765
1980—First a	103	59	.636	+ 3	Richard Howser	2,627,417
1981—1st/4th	59	48	.551	b	Eugene Michael, Robert Lemon	1,614,533
1982—Fifth	79	83	.488	16	Bob Lemon, Gene Michael, Clyde King	2,041,219
1983—Third	91	71	.562	7	Billy Martin	2,257,976
1984—Third	87	75	.537	17	Lawrence (Yogi) Berra	1,821,815

*Games behind winner. †Tied for position. ‡Won Championship Series. §Defeated Boston in pennant playoff. aLost Championship Series. bFirst half 34-22; second 25-26.

First Game Played at Yankee Stadium

Babe Ruth christened the "House That Ruth Built" with a three-run homer to lead the Yankees past the Boston Red Sox, 4-1, on April 18, 1923.

Yankee hurler Bob Shawkey scattered three Boston hits en route to his victory over Howard Ehmke. The announced attendance of the game was 74,217.

NEW YORK YANKEES

(8) YOGI BERRA—Manager

No. PITCHERS—	Bts.	Thrs.	Hgt.	Wgt.	Birth-date	1984 Club	IP.	W.	L.	ERA.
36 Armstrong, Mike	R	R	6:03	195	3-17-54	Fort Lauderdale	11.2	1	0	0.77
						New York	54.1	3	2	3.48
Bordi, Rich	R	R	6:07	220	4-18-59	Chicago NL	83.1	5	2	3.46
53 Bystrom, Marty	R	R	6:05	210	7-26-58	Philadelphia	56.2	4	4	5.08
						New York	39.1	2	2	2.97
67 Christiansen, Clay	R	R	6:04	220	6-28-58	Columbus	107.1	6	3	3.10
						New York	38.2	2	4	6.05
41 Cowley, Joe	R	R	6:05	210	8-15-58	Columbus	113.0	10	3	3.66
						New York	83.1	9	2	3.56
66 Deshaies, Jim	L	L	6:04	222	6-23-60	Nashville	45.0	3	2	2.80
						Columbus	135.2	10	5	2.39
						New York	7.0	0	1	11.57
49 Guidry, Ron	L	L	5:11	157	8-28-50	New York	195.2	10	11	4.51
24 Montefusco, John	R	R	6:01	192	5-25-50	Columbus	13.0	1	0	0.69
						New York	55.1	5	3	3.58
48 Murray, Dale	R	R	6:04	205	2- 2-50	Columbus	16.2	0	3	5.94
						New York	23.2	1	2	4.94
35 Niekro, Phil	R	R	6:01	193	4- 1-39	New York	215.2	16	8	3.09
Pulido, Alfonso	L	L	5:11	170	1-23-59	Hawaii	216.0	18	6	2.54
						Pittsburgh	2.0	0	0	9.00
45 Rasmussen, Dennis	L	L	6:07	225	4-18-59	Columbus	43.2	4	1	3.09
						New York	147.2	9	6	4.57
19 Righetti, Dave	L	L	6:03	198	11-28-58	New York	96.1	5	6	2.34
29 Shirley, Bob	R	L	6:00	180	6-25-54	New York	114.1	3	3	3.68
Whitson, Ed	R	R	6:03	200	5-19-55	San Diego	189.0	14	8	3.24

CATCHERS—						1984 Club	G.	HR.	RBI.	Avg.
34 Bradley, Scott	L	R	5:11	185	3-22-60	Columbus	138	6	84	.335
						New York	9	0	2	.286
Hassey, Ron	L	R	6:02	195	2-27-53	Cleveland	48	0	19	.255
						Chicago NL	19	2	5	.333
27 Wynegar, Butch	B	R	6:01	192	3-14-56	New York	129	6	45	.267

INFIELDERS—										
17 Berra, Dale	R	R	6:00	192	12-13-56	Pittsburgh	136	9	52	.222
33 Griffey, Ken	L	L	6:00	200	4-10-50	New York	120	7	56	.273
11 Harrah, Toby	R	R	6:00	190	10-26-48	New York	88	1	27	.217
56 Hudler, Rex	R	R	6:01	180	9- 2-60	Columbus	114	1	35	.292
						New York	9	0	0	.143
23 Mattingly, Don	L	L	6:00	175	4-20-61	New York	153	23	110	.343
20 Meacham, Bobby	B	R	6:01	180	8-25-60	Nashville	8	0	3	.290
						Columbus	46	2	13	.283
						New York	99	2	25	.253
46 Pagliarulo, Mike	L	R	6:02	195	3-15-60	Columbus	58	7	25	.212
						New York	67	7	34	.239
30 Randolph, Willie	R	R	5:11	166	7- 6-54	New York	142	2	31	.287
18 Robertson, Andre	R	R	5:10	162	10- 2-57	Columbus	69	6	19	.239
						New York	52	0	6	.214
13 Smith, Keith	B	R	6:01	185	10-20-61	Nashville	138	3	42	.278
						New York	2	0	0	.000

OUTFIELDERS—										
25 Baylor, Don	R	R	6:01	210	6-28-48	New York	134	27	89	.262
Henderson, Rickey	R	L	5:10	185	12-25-58	Oakland	142	16	58	.293
55 Mata, Vic	R	R	6:01	165	6-17-61	Columbus	87	10	49	.277
						New York	30	1	6	.329
22 Moreno, Omar	L	L	6:03	188	10-24-52	New York	117	4	38	.259
Pasqua, Dan	L	L	6:00	203	10-17-61	Nashville	136	33	91	.243
31 Winfield, Dave	R	R	6:06	220	10- 3-51	New York	141	19	100	.340
54 Winters, Matt	L	R	6:03	202	3-18-60	Columbus	130	10	54	.248

MARK CONNOR (52)—Coach   STUMP MERRILL (42)—Coach
GENE MICHAEL (40)—Coach   LOU PINIELLA (14)—Coach
JEFF TORBORG (44)—Coach

YANKEE STADIUM

	Seats	Prices
Luxury Boxes	NA	*
Field Boxes...	7,521	$9.75
Main Level Boxes.....................................	NA	9.75
Loge...	NA	9.75
Upper Boxes..	7,955	9.75
Main Level Reserved...............................	NA	8.25
Upper Reserved..	15,652	8.25
General Admission....................................		4.50
Bleachers	5,939	1.50

*Sold only on season basis.

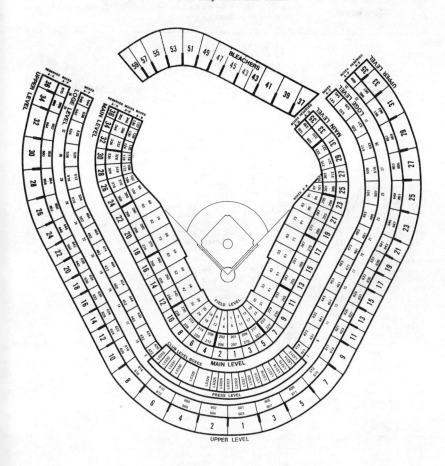

Yankee Stadium, New York
First A.L. Game Played April 18, 1923

OAKLAND A's

President—Roy Eisenhardt
Executive Vice-President—Walter J. Haas
Vice-President/Baseball Operations—Sandy Alderson
Vice-President/Business Operations—Andy Dolich
Vice-President/Finance—Kathleen McCracken
Director of Baseball Administration—Walt Jocketty
Director of Player Development—Karl Kuehl
Director of Scouting—Dick Bogard
Director of Team Travel, Press Relations—Mickey Morabito
Director of Stadium Operations—Jorge Costa
Offices—Oakland-Alameda County Coliseum
Coliseum Capacity—50,255.

Jackie Moore

Farm System: AAA—Tacoma. AA—Huntsville. A—Modesto, Medford, Madison. Rookie—Pocatello.

OAKLAND A's
YEARLY STANDING

(Philadelphia Athletics, 1901-54; Kansas City Athletics, 1955-67)

Year—Position	W.	L.	Pct.	*G.B.	Manager	Attendance
1901—Fourth	74	62	.544	9	Connie Mack	206,329
1902—First	83	53	.610	+ 5	Connie Mack	442,473
1903—Second	75	60	.556	14½	Connie Mack	420,078
1904—Fifth	81	70	.536	12½	Connie Mack	512,294
1905—First	92	56	.622	+ 2	Connie Mack	554,576
1906—Fourth	78	67	.538	12	Connie Mack	489,129
1907—Second	88	57	.607	1½	Connie Mack	625,581
1908—First	68	85	.444	22	Connie Mack	455,062
1909—Second	95	58	.621	3½	Connie Mack	674,915
1910—First	102	48	.680	+14½	Connie Mack	588,905
1911—First	101	50	.669	+13½	Connie Mack	605,749
1912—Third	90	62	.592	15	Connie Mack	517,653
1913—First	96	57	.627	+ 6½	Connie Mack	571,896
1914—First	99	53	.651	+ 8½	Connie Mack	346,641
1915—Eighth	43	109	.283	58½	Connie Mack	146,223
1916—Eighth	36	117	.235	54½	Connie Mack	184,471
1917—Eighth	55	98	.359	44½	Connie Mack	221,432
1918—Eighth	52	76	.402	24	Connie Mack	177,926
1919—Eighth	36	104	.257	52	Connie Mack	225,209
1920—Eighth	48	106	.312	50	Connie Mack	287,888
1921—Eighth	53	100	.346	45	Connie Mack	344,430
1922—Seventh	65	89	.422	29	Connie Mack	425,356
1923—Sixth	69	83	.454	29	Connie Mack	534,122
1924—Fifth	71	81	.467	20	Connie Mack	531,992
1925—Second	88	64	.579	8½	Connie Mack	869,703
1926—Third	83	67	.533	6	Connie Mack	714,308
1927—Second	91	63	.591	19	Connie Mack	605,529
1928—Second	98	55	.641	2½	Connie Mack	689,756
1929—First	104	46	.693	+18	Connie Mack	839,176
1930—First	102	52	.662	+ 8	Connie Mack	721,663
1931—First	107	45	.704	+13½	Connie Mack	627,464
1932—Second	94	60	.610	13	Connie Mack	405,500
1933—Third	79	72	.523	19½	Connie Mack	297,138
1934—Fifth	68	82	.453	31	Connie Mack	305,847
1935—Eighth	58	91	.389	34	Connie Mack	233,173
1936—Eighth	53	100	.346	49	Connie Mack	285,173
1937—Seventh	54	97	.358	46½	Connie Mack	430,733
1938—Eighth	53	99	.349	46	Connie Mack	385,357
1939—Seventh	55	97	.362	51½	Connie Mack	395,022
1940—Eighth	54	100	.351	36	Connie Mack	432,145
1941—Eighth	64	90	.416	37	Connie Mack	528,894
1942—Eighth	55	99	.357	48	Connie Mack	423,487
1943—Eighth†	49	105	.318	49	Connie Mack	376,735
1944—Fifth†	72	82	.468	17	Connie Mack	505,322

OAKLAND A's YEARLY STANDING—Continued

Year—Position	W.	L.	Pct.	*G.B.	Manager	Attendance
1945—Eighth	52	98	.347	34½	Connie Mack	462,631
1946—Eighth	49	105	.318	55	Connie Mack	621,793
1947—Fifth	78	76	.506	19	Connie Mack	911,566
1948—Fourth	84	70	.545	12½	Connie Mack	945,076
1949—Fifth	81	73	.526	16	Connie Mack	816,514
1950—Eighth	52	102	.338	46	Connie Mack	309,805
1951—Sixth	70	84	.455	28	James Dykes	465,469
1952—Fourth	79	75	.513	16	James Dykes	627,100
1953—Seventh	59	95	.383	41½	James Dykes	362,113
1954—Eighth	51	103	.331	60	Edwin Joost	304,666
1955—Sixth	63	91	.409	33	Louis Boudreau	1,393,054
1956—Eighth	52	102	.338	45	Louis Boudreau	1,015,154
1957—Seventh	59	94	.386	38½	Louis Boudreau, Harry Craft	901,067
1958—Seventh	73	81	.474	19	Harry Craft	925,090
1959—Seventh	66	88	.429	28	Harry Craft	963,683
1960—Eighth	58	96	.377	39	Robert Elliott	774,944
1961—Ninth†	61	100	.379	47½	Joseph Gordon, Henry Bauer	683,817
1962—Ninth	72	90	.444	24	Henry Bauer	635,675
1963—Eighth	73	89	.451	31½	Edmund Lopat	762,364
1964—Tenth	57	105	.352	42	E. Lopat, F. Melvin McGaha	642,478
1965—Tenth	59	103	.364	43	Mel McGaha, Haywood Sullivan	528,344
1966—Seventh	74	86	.463	23	Alvin Dark	773,929
1967—Tenth	62	99	.385	29½	Alvin Dark, Luke Appling	726,639
1968—Sixth	82	80	.506	21	Robert Kennedy	837,466

WEST DIVISION

Year—Position	W.	L.	Pct.	*G.B.	Manager	Attendance
1969—Second	88	74	.543	9	Henry Bauer, John McNamara	778,232
1970—Second	89	73	.549	9	John McNamara	778,355
1971—First‡	101	60	.627	+16	Richard Williams	914,993
1972—First‡‡	93	62	.600	+ 5½	Richard Williams	921,323
1973—First‡‡	94	68	.580	+ 6	Richard Williams	1,000,763
1974—First‡‡	90	72	.556	+ 5	Alvin Dark	845,693
1975—First‡	98	64	.605	+ 7	Alvin Dark	1,075,518
1976—Second	87	74	.540	2½	Charles Tanner	780,593
1977—Seventh	63	98	.391	38½	Jack McKeon, Bobby Winkles	495,599
1978—Sixth	69	93	.426	23	Bobby Winkles, Jack McKeon	526,999
1979—Seventh	54	108	.333	34	R. James Marshall	306,763
1980—Second	83	79	.512	14	Alfred (Billy) Martin	842,259
1981—1st/2nd	64	45	.587	§	Alfred (Billy) Martin	1,304,054
1982—Fifth	68	94	.420	25	Alfred (Billy) Martin	1,735,489
1983—Fourth	74	88	.457	25	Steven Boros	1,294,941
1984—Fourth	77	85	.475	7	Steven Boros, Jackie Moore	1,353,281

*Games behind winner. †Tied for position. ‡Lost Championship Series. ‡‡Won Championship Series. §First half 37-23; second 27-22.

First Game Played at the Oakland Coliseum

The A's managed only two hits off Baltimore's Dave McNally as the Orioles spoiled their Oakland debut, 4-1, on April 17, 1968.

The only hits collected by Oakland were Rick Monday's sixth-inning home run and a pinch-single by Tony LaRussa in the ninth.

The Orioles were powered by the home run bats of Boog Powell, Mark Belanger and Brooks Robinson.

OAKLAND A's

(42) JACKIE MOORE—Manager

No. PITCHERS—	Bts.	Thrs.	Hgt.	Wgt.	Birth-date	1984 Club	IP.	W.	L.	ERA.
55 Atherton, Keith	R	R	6:04	200	2-19-59	Oakland	104.0	7	6	4.33
48 Birtsas, Tim	L	L	6:06	235	9- 5-60	Fort Lauderdale	57.2	5	1	3.59
39 Burgmeier, Tom	L	L	5:11	180	8- 2-43	Oakland	23.0	3	0	2.35
23 Codiroli, Chris	R	R	6:01	160	3-26-58	Oakland	89.1	6	4	5.84
						Tacoma	57.0	2	1	3.79
24 Conroy, Tim	L	L	6:01	185	4- 3-60	Oakland	93.0	1	6	5.23
50 Howell, Jay	R	R	6:03	215	11-26-55	New York AL	103.2	9	4	2.69
40 Kaiser, Jeff	R	L	6:03	195	7-24-60	Tacoma	74.2	4	7	4.58
						Albany	47.2	5	1	1.89
32 Krueger, Bill	L	L	6:05	205	4-24-58	Oakland	142.0	10	10	4.75
						Tacoma	31.2	2	2	3.69
47 Kyles, Stan	R	R	6:01	165	2-26-61	Albany	64.1	4	4	3.50
22 Langford, Rick	R	R	6:00	180	3-20-52	Oakland	8.2	0	0	8.31
						Tacoma	15.0	0	2	6.00
52 Leiper, Dave	L	L	6:01	170	6-18-62	Oakland	7.0	1	0	9.00
						Tacoma	32.2	2	3	3.03
						Modesto	35.1	5	0	0.25
54 McCatty, Steve	R	R	6:03	210	3-20-54	Oakland	179.2	8	14	4.76
49 Myers, Ed	R	R	6:00	175	8-11-60	Tacoma	92.0	5	4	4.01
						Albany	86.2	8	2	1.35
17 Norris, Mike	R	R	6:02	170	3-19-55	Oakland	(Did not play)			
61 Ontiveros, Steve	R	R	6:00	180	3- 5-61	Tacoma	11.1	1	1	7.94
						Madison	30.2	3	1	2.05
51 Plunk, Eric	R	R	6:03	170	9- 3-63	Fort Lauderdale	176.1	12	12	2.86
30 Rainey, Chuck	R	R	5:11	195	7-14-54	Chicago NL	88.1	5	7	4.28
						Oakland	30.2	1	1	6.75
27 Sutton, Don	R	R	6:01	190	4- 2-45	Milwaukee	212.2	14	12	3.77
43 Warren, Mike	R	R	6:01	175	3-26-61	Oakland	90.0	3	6	4.90
						Tacoma	67.1	4	3	4.95
29 Young, Curt	R	L	6:01	175	10-18-59	Oakland	108.2	9	4	4.06
						Tacoma	95.1	6	4	3.78

CATCHERS—						1984 Club	G.	HR.	RBI.	Avg.
19 Essian, Jim	R	R	6:01	190	1- 2-51	Oakland	63	2	10	.235
2 Heath, Mike	R	R	5:11	180	2- 5-55	Oakland	140	13	64	.248
9 O'Brien, Charlie	R	R	6:02	195	5- 1-60	Tacoma	69	9	22	.226
						Modesto	9	1	5	.281
6 Tettleton, Mickey	B	R	6:02	200	9-16-60	Oakland	33	1	5	.263
						Albany	86	5	47	.231

INFIELDERS—										
20 Bochte, Bruce	L	L	6:03	200	11-12-50	Oakland	148	5	52	.264
3 Griffin, Alfredo	B	R	5:11	165	3- 6-57	Toronto	140	4	30	.241
25 Hill, Donnie	B	R	5:10	160	11-12-60	Oakland	73	2	16	.230
						Tacoma	42	2	24	.326
28 Kiefer, Steve	R	R	6:01	175	10-18-60	Oakland	23	0	2	.175
						Tacoma	125	16	54	.284
4 Lansford, Carney	R	R	6:02	195	2- 7-57	Oakland	151	14	74	.300
12 Meyer, Dan	L	R	5:11	180	8- 3-52	Tacoma	124	7	57	.293
						Oakland	20	0	4	.318
18 Phillips, Tony	B	R	5:10	160	11- 9-59	Oakland	154	4	37	.266
15 Reece, Thad	R	R	5:10	170	11-15-58	Albany	120	2	46	.331
14 Stephenson, Phil	L	L	6:01	190	9-19-60	Tacoma	124	10	69	.302

OUTFIELDERS—										
33 Canseco, Jose	R	R	6:03	195	7- 2-64	Modesto	116	15	73	.276
11 Collins, Dave	B	L	5:10	175	10-20-52	Toronto	128	2	44	.308
16 Davis, Mike	L	L	6:03	185	6-11-59	Oakland	134	9	46	.230
56 Harrison, Ron	L	R	6:02	170	10-15-60	Tacoma	55	2	24	.270
						Madison	19	0	9	.197
10 Kingman, Dave	R	R	6:06	210	12-21-48	Oakland	147	35	118	.268
21 Murphy, Dwayne	L	R	6:01	185	3-18-55	Oakland	153	33	88	.256
31 Romano, Tom	R	R	5:11	170	10-25-58	Tacoma	133	15	75	.280

CLETE BOYER (41)—Coach　　　　　　　　　　BOB DIDIER (45)—Coach
DAVE McKAY (46)—Coach　　　　　　　　　　WES STOCK (44)—Coach
BILLY WILLIAMS (26)—Coach

THE COLISEUM

	Seats	Prices
Loge Boxes	1,605	$8.00
Field Deck	16,856	8.00
Plaza Level	11,219	7.00
Upper Reserved	13,537	5.00
Bleachers	6,000	3.00

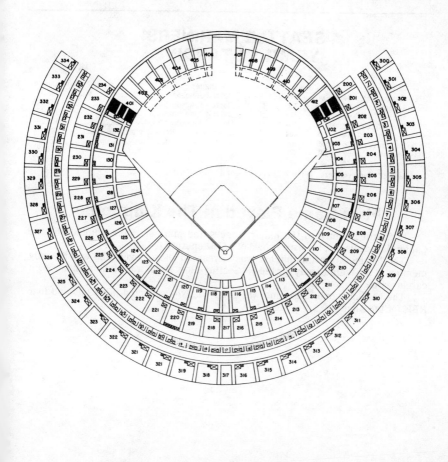

Oakland-Alameda Coliseum, Oakland
First A.L. Game Played April 17, 1968

Chuck Cottier

SEATTLE MARINERS

Principal Owner—George L. Argyros
President & Operating Officer—Chuck Armstrong
Vice-President Sales & Marketing—Bill Knudsen
V.-P., Baseball Operations and G.M.—Hal Keller
Traveling Secretary—Lee Pelekoudas
Public Relations Director—Bob Porter
Offices—P.O. Box 4100
Kingdome, King County Stadium Capacity—59,438

Farm System: AAA—Calgary. AA—Chattanooga. A—Bellingham, Salinas, Wausau.

SEATTLE MARINERS' YEARLY STANDING

Year—Position	W.	L.	Pct.	*G.B.	Manager	Attendance
1977—Sixth	64	98	.395	38	Darrell Johnson	1,338,511
1978—Seventh	56	104	.350	35	Darrell Johnson	877,440
1979—Sixth	67	95	.414	21	Darrell Johnson	844,447
1980—Seventh	59	103	.364	38	Darrell Johnson, Maurice Wills	836,204
1981—6th/5th	44	65	.404	†	Maurice Wills, Rene Lachemann	636,276
1982—Fourth	76	86	.469	17	Rene Lachemann	1,070,404
1983—Seventh	60	102	.370	39	Rene Lachemann, Del Crandall	813,537
1984—Fifth‡	74	88	.457	10	Del Crandall, Chuck Cottier	870,372

*Games behind winner.   †First half 21-36; second 23-29. ‡Tied for position.

First Game Played at The Kingdome

In Seattle's return to the major leagues, the Mariners were humbled by the California Angels, 7-0, before a crowd of 57,762 on April 6, 1977.

The Mariners' starting pitcher was 38-year-old Diego Segui, who was the only member of the team to play for the old Seattle Pilots. Segui was pitching in his 600th career game.

The batting star of the game was Joe Rudi, who collected three hits and four RBIs for the Angels.

SEATTLE MARINERS

(15) CHUCK COTTIER—Manager

No. PITCHERS—	Bts.	Thrs.	Hgt.	Wgt.	Birth-date	1984 Club	IP.	W.	L.	ERA.
31 Barojas, Salome	R	R	5:09	188	6-16-57	Chicago AL	39.1	3	2	4.58
						Denver	9.0	1	0	1.00
						Seattle	95.1	6	5	3.97
36 Beard, Dave	L	R	6:05	215	10- 2-59	Seattle	76.0	3	2	5.80
						Salt Lake City	9.2	0	1	5.79
45 Beattie, Jim	R	R	6:06	220	7- 4-54	Seattle	211.0	12	16	3.41
39 Best, Karl	R	R	6:04	200	3- 6-59	Salt Lake City	76.0	6	5	5.21
						Seattle	6.0	1	1	3.00
37 Geisel, Dave	L	L	6:03	210	1-18-55	Salt Lake City	72.0	4	2	4.88
						Seattle	43.1	1	1	4.15
36 Guetterman, Lee	L	L	6:08	225	11-22-58	Chattanooga	157.0	11	7	3.88
						Seattle	4.1	0	0	4.15
12 Langston, Mark	R	L	6:02	177	8-20-60	Seattle	225.0	17	10	3.40
52 Mirabella, Paul	L	L	6:02	196	3-20-54	Seattle	68.0	2	5	4.37
25 Moore, Mike	R	R	6:04	205	11-26-59	Seattle	212.0	7	17	4.97
Morgan, Mike	R	R	6:03	195	10- 8-59	Syracuse	185.2	13	11	4.07
30 Nunez, Edwin	R	R	6:05	235	5-27-63	Salt Lake City	27.2	3	2	3.58
						Seattle	67.2	2	1	3.19
46 Stanton, Mike	R	R	6:02	200	9-25-52	Seattle	61.0	4	4	3.54
56 Taylor, Terry	R	R	6:01	180	7-28-64	Salinas	104.1	7	6	2.93
32 Vande Berg, Ed	R	L	6:02	175	10-26-58	Seattle	130.1	6	12	4.76
40 Young, Matt	L	L	6:03	205	8- 9-58	Seattle	113.1	6	8	5.72

No. CATCHERS—	Bts.	Thrs.	Hgt.	Wgt.	Birth-date	1984 Club	G.	HR.	RBI.	Avg.
11 Kearney, Bob	R	R	6:00	180	10- 3-56	Seattle	133	7	43	.225
2 Mercado, Orlando	R	R	6:00	180	11- 7-61	Salt Lake City	29	6	22	.358
						Seattle	30	0	5	.218
41 Valle, Dave	R	R	6:02	200	10-30-61	Salt Lake City	86	12	54	.278
						Seattle	13	1	4	.296

No. INFIELDERS—	Bts.	Thrs.	Hgt.	Wgt.	Birth-date	1984 Club	G.	HR.	RBI.	Avg.
19 Coles, Darnell	R	R	6:01	170	6-22-62	Seattle	48	0	6	.161
						Salt Lake City	69	14	68	.318
21 Davis, Alvin	L	R	6:01	190	9- 9-60	Salt Lake City	1	0	1	.667
						Seattle	152	27	116	.284
8 Milbourne, Larry	B	R	6:00	165	2-14-51	Seattle	79	1	22	.265
7 Owen, Spike	B	R	5:10	160	4-19-61	Seattle	152	3	43	.245
14 Perconte, Jack	L	R	5:10	160	8-31-54	Seattle	155	0	31	.294
44 Phelps, Ken	L	L	6:01	205	8- 6-54	Seattle	101	24	51	.241
						Salt Lake City	12	3	13	.311
17 Presley, Jim	R	R	6:01	180	10-23-61	Salt Lake City	69	13	56	.317
						Seattle	70	10	36	.227
24 Reynolds, Harold	B	R	5:11	165	11-26-60	Salt Lake City	135	3	54	.296
						Seattle	9	0	0	.300
38 Tartabull, Danny	R	R	6:01	185	10-30-61	Salt Lake City	116	13	73	.309
						Seattle	10	2	7	.300

No. OUTFIELDERS—	Bts.	Thrs.	Hgt.	Wgt.	Birth-date	1984 Club	G.	HR.	RBI.	Avg.
9 Bonnell, Barry	R	R	6:03	205	10-27-53	Seattle	110	8	48	.264
29 Bradley, Phil	R	R	6:00	175	3-11-59	Seattle	124	0	24	.301
13 Calderon, Ivan	R	R	6:02	205	3-19-62	Salt Lake City	66	4	45	.365
						Seattle	11	1	1	.208
47 Chambers, Al	L	L	6:04	217	3-24-61	Salt Lake City	100	13	73	.291
						Seattle	22	1	4	.224
16 Cowens, Al	R	R	6:02	200	10-25-51	Seattle	139	15	78	.277
42 Henderson, Dave	R	R	6:02	210	7-21-58	Seattle	112	14	43	.280
26 Moses, John	B	L	5:10	165	8- 9-57	Chattanooga	53	0	12	.253
						Salt Lake City	70	0	27	.275
						Seattle	19	0	2	.343
10 Nelson, Ricky	L	R	6:00	200	5- 8-59	Salt Lake City	75	11	42	.294
						Seattle	9	1	2	.200
48 Nixon, Donell	R	R	6:01	185	12-31-61	Chattanooga	140	4	57	.269
20 Thomas, Gorman	R	R	6:02	210	12-12-50	Seattle	35	1	13	.157
22 Zisk, Richie	R	R	6:01	220	2- 6-49	Seattle	(Did not play)			

MARTY MARTINEZ (43)—Coach   PHIL REGAN (27)—Coach

PHIL ROOF (4)—Coach

THE KINGDOME

	Seats	Prices
Box Seats	11,467	$8.50
Reserved Seats..	11,926	7.50
View Bench Seats......................................	18,559	5.50
General Admission (lower)	14,902	4.00
General Admission (left field only)	2,584	2.00

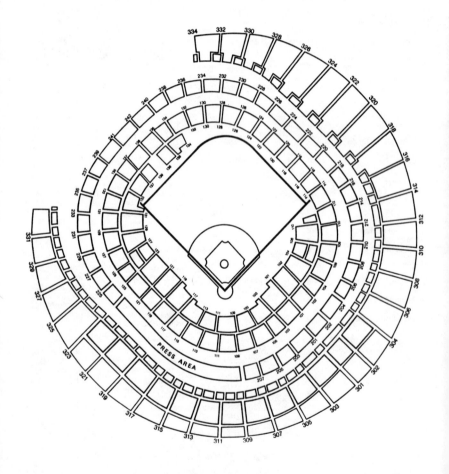

The Kingdome, Seattle
First A.L. Game Played April 6, 1977

TEXAS RANGERS

Chairman of the Board, Chief Executive Officer—Eddie Chiles
President, Chief Operating Officer—Michael H. Stone
Vice President, General Manager—Thomas A. Grieve
Vice President, Marketing and Administration—Larry Schmittou
Vice President, Finance/Treasurer—Charles F. Wangner
Asst. G.M., Player Personnel and Scouting—Sandy Johnson
Assistant General Manager—Wayne Krivsky
Director of Player Development—Marty Scott
Director of Media Relations—John Blake
Traveling Secretary—Dan Schimek
Offices—1200 Copeland Road, P.O. Box 1111, Arlington, Tex. 76010
Stadium—Arlington Stadium, Arlington, Tex. 76010
Capacity—43,508

Doug Rader

Farm System: AAA—Oklahoma City. AA—Tulsa. A—Burlington, Daytona Beach (co-op), Salem. Rookie—Sarasota.

TEXAS RANGERS' YEARLY STANDING

(Second Washington Senators Club prior to 1972)

Year—Position	W.	L.	Pct.	*G.B.	Manager	Attendance
1961—Ninth†	61	100	.379	47½	James (Mickey) Vernon	597,287
1962—Tenth	60	101	.373	35½	James (Mickey) Vernon	729,775
1963—Tenth	56	106	.346	48½	Mickey Vernon, Gilbert Hodges	535,604
1964—Ninth	62	100	.383	37	Gilbert Hodges	600,106
1965—Eighth	70	92	.432	32	Gilbert Hodges	560,083
1966—Eighth	71	88	.447	25½	Gilbert Hodges	576,260
1967—Sixth†	76	85	.472	15½	Gilbert Hodges	770,863
1968—Tenth	65	96	.404	37½	James Lemon	546,661

EAST DIVISION

Year—Position	W.	L.	Pct.	*G.B.	Manager	Attendance
1969—Fourth	86	76	.531	23	Theodore Williams	918,106
1970—Sixth	70	92	.432	38	Theodore Williams	824,789
1971—Fifth	63	96	.396	38½	Theodore Williams	655,156

WEST DIVISION

Year—Position	W.	L.	Pct.	*G.B.	Manager	Attendance
1972—Sixth	54	100	.351	38½	Theodore Williams	662,974
1973—Sixth	57	105	.352	37	D. (Whitey) Herzog, Billy Martin	686,085
1974—Second	84	76	.525	5	Alfred (Billy) Martin	1,193,902
1975—Third	79	83	.488	19	A. (Billy) Martin, Frank Lucchesi	1,127,924
1976—Fourth†	76	86	.469	14	Frank Lucchesi	1,164,982
1977—Second	94	68	.580	8	Frank Lucchesi, Ed Stanky, Connie Ryan, Billy Hunter	1,250,722
1978—Second†	87	75	.537	5	Billy Hunter, Patrick Corrales	1,447,963
1979—Third	83	79	.512	5	Patrick Corrales	1,519,671
1980—Fourth	76	85	.472	20½	Patrick Corrales	1,198,175
1981—2nd/3rd	57	48	.543	‡	Donald Zimmer	850,076
1982—Sixth	64	98	.395	29	Donald Zimmer, Darrell Johnson	1,154,432
1983—Third	77	85	.475	22	Doug Rader	1,363,469
1984—Seventh	69	92	.429	14½	Doug Rader	1,102,471

*Games behind winner. †Tied for position. ‡First half 33-22; second 24-26.

First Game Played at Arlington Stadium

In the Rangers' home debut, Texas defeated the California Angels, 7-6, on April 21, 1972.

Frank Howard's 400-foot homer highlighted the first inning and Dave Nelson hit a fifth-inning home run for the Rangers.

Lenny Randle provided most of the offense, however, collecting a double and two singles in his four-RBI effort.

TEXAS RANGERS

(11) DOUG RADER—Manager

No. PITCHERS—	Bts.	Thrs.	Hgt.	Wgt.	Birth-date	1984 Club	IP.	W.	L.	ERA.
33 Cook, Glen	R	R	5:11	180	9- 8-59	Oklahoma City	167.0	9	8	4.85
44 Darwin, Danny	R	R	6:03	190	10-25-55	Texas	223.2	8	12	3.94
29 Guzman, Jose	R	R	6:02	160	4- 9-63	Tulsa	140.1	7	9	4.17
35 Henke, Tom	R	R	6:05	215	12-21-57	Oklahoma City	64.2	6	2	2.64
						Texas	28.1	1	1	6.35
45 Henry, Dwayne	R	R	6:03	205	2-16-62	Tulsa	85.0	5	8	3.39
						Texas	4.1	0	1	8.31
46 Hooton, Burt	R	R	6:01	210	2- 7-50	Los Angeles	110.0	3	6	3.44
49 Hough, Charlie	R	R	6:02	190	1- 5-48	Texas	266.0	16	14	3.76
51 Lachowicz, Al	R	R	6:03	198	9- 6-60	Oklahoma City	116.1	2	11	4.18
16 Mason, Mike	L	L	6:02	205	12-21-58	Texas	184.1	9	13	3.61
36 Noles, Dickie	R	R	6:02	190	11-19-56	Chicago NL	50.2	2	2	5.15
						Texas	57.2	2	3	5.15
Rozema, Dave	R	R	6:04	200	8- 5-56	Detroit	101.0	7	6	3.74
24 Schmidt, Dave	R	R	6:01	185	4-22-57	Texas	70.1	6	6	2.56
48 Stewart, Dave	R	R	6:02	200	2-19-57	Texas	192.1	7	14	4.73
28 Tanana, Frank	L	L	6:03	195	7- 3-53	Texas	246.1	15	15	3.25
31 Taylor, Billy	B	R	6:08	200	10-16-61	Tulsa	80.0	5	3	3.83
Williams, Mitchell	L	L	6:03	180	11-17-64	Reno	164.0	9	8	4.99
38 Wright, Ricky	L	L	6:03	175	11-22-58	Oklahoma City	48.2	2	1	2.40
						Texas	14.2	0	2	6.14
34 Zwolensky, Mitch	R	R	6:02	200	12-29-59	Oklahoma City	138.1	7	8	4.36

CATCHERS—						1984 Club	G.	HR.	RBI.	Avg.
10 Buckley, Kevin	R	R	6:01	200	1-16-59	Oklahoma City	139	23	92	.261
						Texas	5	0	0	.286
12 Scott, Donnie	B	R	5:11	185	8-16-61	Oklahoma City	46	3	25	.327
						Texas	81	3	20	.221
7 Yost, Ned	R	R	6:01	185	8-19-55	Texas	80	6	25	.182

INFIELDERS—										
14 Anderson, Jim	R	R	6:00	180	2-23-57	Texas	39	0	1	.106
						Oklahoma City	36	1	9	.214
2 Bannister, Alan	R	R	5:11	175	9- 3-51	Houston	9	0	0	.200
						Texas	47	2	9	.300
25 Bell, Buddy	R	R	6:02	185	8-27-51	Texas	148	11	83	.315
58 Buechele, Steve	R	R	6:02	190	9-26-61	Oklahoma City	131	7	59	.264
Johnson, Cliff	R	R	6:04	225	7-22-47	Toronto	127	16	61	.304
20 Kunkel, Jeff	R	R	6:02	180	3-25-62	Tulsa	47	4	22	.316
						Texas	50	3	7	.204
9 O'Brien, Pete	L	L	6:01	198	2- 9-58	Texas	142	18	80	.287
1 Stein, Bill	R	R	5:10	170	1-21-47	Texas	27	0	3	.279
27 Tabor, Greg	R	R	6:00	165	5-21-61	Tulsa	123	6	53	.299
3 Tolleson, Wayne	B	R	5:09	160	11-22-55	Texas	118	0	9	.213
19 Wilkerson, Curtis	B	R	5:09	158	4-26-61	Texas	153	1	26	.248

OUTFIELDERS—										
13 Dunbar, Tommy	L	L	6:02	192	11-24-59	Oklahoma City	105	12	61	.337
						Texas	34	2	10	.258
6 Jones, Bobby	L	L	6:01	170	11-11-49	Texas	64	4	22	.259
15 Parrish, Larry	R	R	6:03	215	11-10-53	Texas	156	22	101	.285
17 Rivers, Mickey	L	L	5:10	162	10-30-48	Texas	102	4	33	.300
5 Sample, Billy	R	R	5:09	175	4- 2-55	Texas	130	5	33	.247
23 Stockstill, Dave	L	R	6:00	185	10- 4-57	Oklahoma City	102	16	55	.282
32 Ward, Gary	R	R	6:02	202	12- 6-53	Texas	155	21	79	.284
26 Wright, George	B	R	5:11	180	12-22-58	Texas	101	9	48	.243

RICH DONNELLY (37)—Coach   GLENN EZELL (18)—Coach
MERV RETTENMUND (22)—Coach   DICK SUCH (52)—Coach
WAYNE TERWILLIGER (42)—Coach

ARLINGTON STADIUM

	Seats	Prices
Field and Mezzanine Boxes	14,999	$8.50
Reserved	2,875	7.50
Plaza	5,021	6.50
Reserved Grandstand	3,649	5.00
General Admission	16,332	*3.75

*Children 13 and under $2.25.

Arlington Stadium, Arlington, Tex.
First A.L. Game Played April 21, 1972

TORONTO BLUE JAYS

Bobby Cox

Chairman of the Board—R. Howard Webster
Vice-Chairman, Chief Exec. Officer—N.E. Hardy
Exec. Vice-President, Business Operations—Paul Beeston
Exec. Vice-President, Baseball Operations—Pat Gillick
Player Personnel—Gord Ash
Director of Operations—Ken Erskine
Director of Team Travel—Ken Carson
Director of Public Relations—Howard Starkman
Offices—Exhibition Stadium, Box 7777
Exhibition Stadium Capacity—43,737

Farm System: AAA—Syracuse. AA—Knoxville. A—Kinston, Florence. Rookie—Bradenton, Medicine Hat.

TORONTO BLUE JAYS' YEARLY STANDING

Year—Position	W.	L.	Pct.	*G.B.	Manager	Attendance
1977—Seventh	54	107	.335	45½	Roy Hartsfield	1,701,052
1978—Seventh	59	102	.366	40	Roy Hartsfield	1,562,585
1979—Seventh	53	109	.327	50½	Roy Hartsfield	1,431,651
1980—Seventh	67	95	.414	36	Bobby Mattick	1,400,327
1981—7th/5th	37	69	.349	†	Bobby Mattick	755,083
1982—Sixth‡	78	84	.481	17	Robert Cox	1,275,978
1983—Fourth	89	73	.549	9	Robert Cox	1,930,415
1984—Second	89	73	.549	15	Robert Cox	2,110,009

*Games behind winner. †First half 16-42; second 21-27. ‡Tied for position.

First Game Played at Exhibition Stadium

The Blue Jays slugged their way to a 9-5 triumph over the Chicago White Sox in their April 7, 1977, debut.

Despite snow flurries before the game and near-freezing temperatures, 44,649 fans witnessed the exciting contest, which featured 16 hits by the Blue Jays and 15 by Chicago.

Doug Ault smacked two homers and a single and rookie Al Woods hit a pinch-homer in his first big-league at-bat for Toronto. Richie Zisk had four hits for the visitors.

BEST MAJOR LEAGUE ATTENDANCE MARKS

1. Los Angeles	3,608,881	1982		11. Detroit	2,704,794	1984
2. Los Angeles	3,510,313	1983		12. Philadelphia	2,700,070	1977
3. Los Angeles	3,347,845	1978		13. New York NL	2,697,479	1970
4. Los Angeles	3,249,287	1980		14. Philadelphia	2,651,650	1980
5. Los Angeles	3,134,824	1984		15. Los Angeles	2,632,474	1974
6. Los Angeles	2,955,087	1977		16. Cincinnati	2,629,708	1976
7. Los Angeles	2,860,954	1979		17. New York AL	2,627,417	1980
8. California	2,807,360	1982		18. Cleveland	2,620,627	1948
9. Philadelphia	2,775,011	1979		19. Los Angeles	2,617,029	1966
10. Los Angeles	2,755,184	1962		20. Philadelphia	2,583,389	1978

TORONTO BLUE JAYS

(6) BOBBY COX—Manager

No. PITCHERS—	Bts.	Thrs.	Hgt.	Wgt.	Birth-date	1984 Club	IP.	W.	L.	ERA.
31 Acker, Jim	R	R	6:02	212	9-24-58	Toronto	72.0	3	5	4.38
33 Alexander, Doyle	R	R	6:03	200	9- 4-50	Toronto	261.2	17	6	3.13
32 Aquino, Luis	R	R	6:00	155	5-19-65	Kinston	70.0	5	6	2.70
						Knoxville	4.0	0	0	9.00
36 Caudill, Bill	R	R	6:01	210	7-13-56	Oakland	96.1	9	7	2.71
55 Cerutti, John	L	L	6:02	195	4-28-60	Syracuse	148.0	7	13	4.44
18 Clancy, Jim	R	R	6:04	210	12-18-55	Toronto	219.2	13	15	5.12
35 Clark, Bryan	L	L	6:02	200	7-12-56	Syracuse	34.0	3	1	3.44
						Toronto	45.2	1	2	5.91
34 Clarke, Stan	R	L	6:01	180	8- 9-60	Syracuse	56.2	2	3	4.13
38 Gott, Jim	R	R	6:04	215	8- 3-59	Toronto	109.2	7	6	4.02
25 Jackson, Roy Lee	R	R	6:02	205	5- 1-54	Toronto	86.0	7	8	3.56
22 Key, Jimmy	R	L	6:01	175	4-22-61	Toronto	62.0	4	5	4.65
53 Lamp, Dennis	R	R	6:03	210	9-23-52	Toronto	85.0	8	8	4.55
48 Leal, Luis	R	R	6:03	215	3-21-57	Toronto	222.1	13	8	3.89
49 McKnight, Jack	R	R	6:02	185	6- 7-61	Knoxville	151.0	11	8	3.81
40 McLaughlin, Colin	B	R	6:06	205	6- 9-59	Syracuse	24.2	2	1	3.65
						Knoxville	63.2	1	5	6.22
30 Musselman, Ron	R	R	6:02	185	11-11-54	Oklahoma City	26.2	1	2	4.05
						Syracuse	31.0	1	2	2.90
						Toronto	21.1	0	2	2.11
37 Stieb, Dave	R	R	6:00	190	7-22-57	Toronto	267.0	16	8	2.83
45 Williams, Matt	R	R	6:01	200	7-25-59	Syracuse	178.0	9	12	3.34

CATCHERS—	Bts.	Thrs.	Hgt.	Wgt.	Birth-date	1984 Club	G.	HR.	RBI.	Avg.
13 Martinez, Buck	R	R	5:11	200	11- 7-48	Toronto	102	5	37	.220
12 Whitt, Ernie	L	R	6:02	200	6-13-52	Toronto	124	15	46	.238

INFIELDERS—	Bts.	Thrs.	Hgt.	Wgt.	Birth-date	1984 Club	G.	HR.	RBI.	Avg.
24 Aikens, Willie	L	R	6:02	220	10-14-54	Toronto	93	11	26	.205
1 Fernandez, Tony	B	R	6:02	165	8- 6-62	Syracuse	26	0	6	.255
						Toronto	88	3	19	.270
7 Garcia, Damaso	R	R	6:00	175	2- 7-57	Toronto	152	5	46	.284
17 Gruber, Kelly	R	R	6:00	175	2-26-56	Syracuse	97	21	55	.269
						Toronto	15	1	2	.063
14 Infante, Alexis	R	R	5:10	175	12- 4-62	Knoxville	67	2	29	.265
						Syracuse	72	0	7	.222
16 Iorg, Garth	R	R	5:11	170	10-12-54	Toronto	121	1	25	.227
4 Lee, Manny	B	R	5:10	145	6-17-65	Columbia	102	2	33	.329
2 Manrique, Fred	R	R	6:01	175	11- 5-61	Syracuse	129	6	45	.282
						Toronto	10	0	1	.333
19 McGriff, Fred	L	L	6:03	200	10-31-63	Knoxville	56	9	25	.249
						Syracuse	70	13	28	.235
5 Mulliniks, Rance	L	R	6:00	170	1-15-56	Toronto	125	3	42	.324
10 Sharperson, Mike	R	R	6:01	175	10- 4-61	Knoxville	140	4	48	.304
26 Upshaw, Willie	L	L	6:00	185	4-27-57	Toronto	152	19	84	.278

OUTFIELDERS—	Bts.	Thrs.	Hgt.	Wgt.	Birth-date	1984 Club	G.	HR.	RBI.	Avg.
29 Barfield, Jesse	R	R	6:01	200	10-29-59	Toronto	110	14	49	.284
20 Beauchamp, Kash	R	R	6:03	165	1- 8-63	Kinston	130	8	58	.266
						Knoxville	3	1	3	.400
11 Bell, George	R	R	6:01	185	10-21-59	Toronto	159	26	87	.292
Burroughs, Jeff	R	R	6:00	200	3- 7-51	Oakland	58	2	8	.211
15 Moseby, Lloyd	L	R	6:03	205	11- 5-59	Toronto	158	18	92	.280
21 Shepherd, Ron	R	R	6:04	175	10-27-60	Syracuse	113	12	50	.220
						Toronto	12	0	0	.000
28 Thornton, Louis	L	R	6:02	185	4-26-63	Lynchburg	131	6	67	.275
23 Webster, Mitch	B	L	6:01	185	5-16-59	Syracuse	95	3	25	.300
						Toronto	26	0	4	.227

CITO GASTON (43)—Coach   BILLY SMITH (42)—Coach
JOHN SULLIVAN (8)—Coach   AL WIDMAR (41)—Coach

JIMY WILLIAMS (3)—Coach

EXHIBITION STADIUM

	Seats	Prices
Field Level, Chair	11,300	$10.50
Upper Level, Chair	6,600	9.00
First Base Reserved, Bench	5,100	7.50
Right Field Reserved, Bench	6,700	5.00
General Admission	14,037	4.00

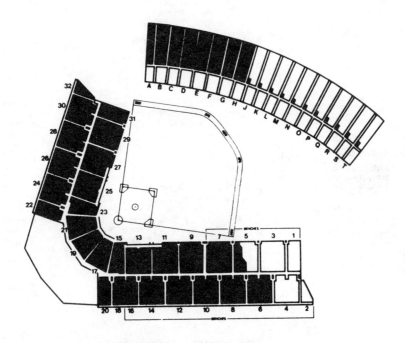

Exhibition Stadium, Toronto
First A.L. Game Played April 7, 1977

NATIONAL LEAGUE—Pennant Winners—1876-1984

1876—Chicago .... .788	1904—New York .... .693	1932—Chicago .... .584	1960—Pittsburgh ... .617
1877—Boston........... .646	1905—New York .... .686	1933—New York .... .599	1961—Cincinnati.... .604
1878—Boston........... .683	1906—Chicago .... .763	1934—St. Louis .... .621	1962—San Fran.§... .624
1879—Providence .. .705	1907—Chicago .... .704	1935—Chicago .... .649	1963—Los Angeles . .611
1880—Chicago .... .798	1908—Chicago .... .643	1936—New York .... .597	1964—St. Louis ...... .574
1881—Chicago .... .667	1909—Pittsburgh ... .724	1937—New York .... .625	1965—Los Angeles . .599
1882—Chicago .... .655	1910—Chicago .... .675	1938—Chicago .... .586	1966—Los Angeles . .586
1883—Boston........... .643	1911—New York .... .647	1939—Cincinnati..... .630	1967—St. Louis ...... .627
1884—Providence .. .750	1912—New York .... .682	1940—Cincinnati..... .654	1968—St. Louis ...... .599
1885—Chicago .... .777	1913—New York .... .664	1941—Brooklyn...... .649	1969—New York .... .617
1886—Chicago .... .726	1914—Boston.......... .614	1942—St. Louis ...... .688	1970—Cincinnati..... .630
1887—Detroit.......... .637	1915—Philadel........ .592	1943—St. Louis ...... .682	1971—Pittsburgh ... .599
1888—New York .... .641	1916—Brooklyn...... .610	1944—St. Louis ...... .682	1972—Cincinnati..... .617
1889—New York .... .659	1917—New York .... .636	1945—Chicago .... .636	1973—New York .... .509
1890—Brooklyn...... .667	1918—Chicago .... .651	1946—St. Louis*..... .628	1974—Los Angeles . .630
1891—Boston........... .630	1919—Cincinnati..... .686	1947—Brooklyn...... .610	1975—Cincinnati..... .667
1892—Boston........... .680	1920—Brooklyn...... .604	1948—Boston........... .595	1976—Cincinnati..... .630
1893—Boston........... .662	1921—New York .... .614	1949—Brooklyn...... .630	1977—Los Angeles . .605
1894—Baltimore .... .695	1922—New York .... .604	1950—Philadel........ .591	1978—Los Angeles . .586
1895—Baltimore .... .669	1923—New York .... .621	1951—New York†.... .624	1979—Pittsburgh.... .605
1896—Baltimore .... .698	1924—New York .... .608	1952—Brooklyn...... .627	1980—Philadelphia . .562
1897—Boston........... .705	1925—Pittsburgh ... .621	1953—Brooklyn...... .682	1981—L. Angelesx . .573
1898—Boston........... .685	1926—St. Louis ...... .578	1954—New York .... .630	1982—St. Louis....... .568
1899—Brooklyn...... .677	1927—Pittsburgh ... .610	1955—Brooklyn...... .641	1983—Philadelphia . .556
1900—Brooklyn...... .603	1928—St. Louis ...... .617	1956—Brooklyn...... .604	1984—San Diego..... .568
1901—Pittsburgh ... .647	1929—Chicago .... .645	1957—Milwaukee... .617	
1902—Pittsburgh ... .741	1930—St. Louis ...... .597	1958—Milwaukee... .597	
1903—Pittsburgh ... .650	1931—St. Louis .... .656	1959—Los Ang.‡ ..... .564	

*Defeated Brooklyn, two games to none, in playoff for pennant. †Defeated Brooklyn, two games to one, in playoff for pennant. ‡Defeated Milwaukee, two games to none, in playoff for pennant. §Defeated Los Angeles, two games to one, in playoff for pennant. xDefeated Houston in five-game playoff for division championship.

STANDING OF CLUBS AT CLOSE OF SEASON

EAST DIVISION

Club	Chi.	N.Y.	St.L.	Phil.	Mon.	Pitt.	Atl.	Cin.	Hou.	L.A.	S.D.	S.F.	W.	L.	Pct.	G.B.
Chicago.....................	..	12	13	9	10	8	9	7	6	7	6	9	96	65	.596	....
New York................	6	..	7	10	11	12	8	9	8	9	6	4	90	72	.556	6½
St. Louis..................	5	11	..	10	9	14	7	8	4	6	5	5	84	78	.519	12½
Philadelphia	9	8	8	..	7	7	5	7	6	9	7	8	81	81	.500	15½
Montreal..................	7	7	9	11	..	7	7	5	5	6	7	7	78	83	.484	18
Pittsburgh...............	10	6	4	11	11	..	4	5	6	8	4	6	75	87	.463	21½

WEST DIVISION

Club	S.D.	Atl.	Hou.	L.A.	Cin.	S.F.	Chi.	Mon.	N.Y.	Phil.	Pitt.	St.L.	W.	L.	Pct.	G.B.
San Diego	..	11	12	8	11	13	6	5	6	5	8	7	92	70	.568	....
Atlanta.....................	7	..	12	6	13	10	3	5	4	7	8	5	80	82	.494	12
Houston....................	6	6	..	9	10	12	6	7	4	6	6	8	80	82	.494	12
Los Angeles	10	12	9	..	11	10	5	6	3	3	4	6	79	83	.488	13
Cincinnati................	7	5	8	7	..	12	5	7	3	5	7	4	70	92	.432	22
San Francisco..........	5	8	6	8	6	..	3	5	8	4	6	7	66	96	.407	26

Championship Series—San Diego defeated Chicago, three games to two.

NATIONAL LEAGUE 1984 DEPARTMENTAL LEADERS

INDIVIDUAL BATTING

Average

Gwynn, San Diego...............	.351
Lacy, Pittsburgh..................	.321
C. Davis, San Francisco	.315

Doubles

Raines, Montreal	38
Ray, Pittsburgh.......................	38
Samuel, Philadelphia..............	36
Sandberg, Chicago..................	36

Triples

Samuel, Philadelphia..............	19
Sandberg, Chicago..................	19
Cruz, Houston..........................	13

Home Runs

Murphy, Atlanta.....................	36
Schmidt, Philadelphia	36
Carter, Montreal.....................	27

Runs Batted In

Carter, Montreal	106
Schmidt, Philadelphia	106
Murphy, Atlanta.....................	100

Stolen Bases

Raines, Montreal	75
Samuel, Philadelphia..............	72
Wiggins, San Diego.................	70

INDIVIDUAL PITCHING

Earned-Run Average

Pena, Los Angeles	2.48
Gooden, New York	2.60
Hershiser, Los Angeles	2.66

Complete Games

Soto, Cincinnati......................	13
Andujar, St. Louis...................	12
Valenzuela, Los Angeles........	12

Strikeouts

Gooden, New York	276
Valenzuela, Los Angeles......	240
Ryan, Houston	197

Shutouts

Andujar, St. Louis...................	4
Hershiser, Los Angeles.............	4
Pena, Los Angeles...................	4

Innings

Andujar, St. Louis....................	261.1
Valenzuela, Los Angeles..	260
Niekro, Houston.................	248.1

Victories

Andujar, St. Louis..................	20
Soto, Cincinnati......................	18
Gooden, New York	17

ATLANTA BRAVES

Chairman of the Board—William C. Bartholomay
President—R. E. (Ted) Turner III
Executive Vice-President—Al Thornwell
Vice-President-General Manager—John Mullen
Vice-President, Player Development—Hank Aaron
Dir. Public Relations-Promotions-Publications—Wayne Minshew
Offices—Atlanta Stadium
Atlanta Stadium Capacity—52,785

Farm System: AAA—Richmond. AA—Greenville. A—Anderson, Durham. Rookie—Bradenton, Pulaski.

Eddie Haas

ATLANTA BRAVES' YEARLY STANDING

(Boston Braves Prior to 1953; Milwaukee Braves 1953-65)

Year—Position	W.	L.	Pct.	*G.B.	Manager	Attendance
1901—Fifth	69	69	.500	20½	Frank Selee	146,502
1902—Third	73	64	.533	29	Albert Buckenberger	116,960
1903—Sixth	58	80	.420	32	Albert Buckenberger	143,155
1904—Seventh	55	98	.359	51	Albert Buckenberger	140,694
1905—Seventh	51	103	.331	54½	Fred Tenney	150,003
1906—Eighth	49	102	.325	66½	Fred Tenney	143,280
1907—Seventh	58	90	.392	47	Fred Tenney	203,221
1908—Sixth	63	91	.409	36	Joseph Kelley	253,750
1909—Eighth	45	108	.294	65½	Frank Bowerman, Harry Smith	195,188
1910—Eighth	53	100	.346	50½	Fred Lake	149,027
1911—Eighth	44	107	.291	54	Fred Tenney	116,000
1912—Eighth	52	101	.340	52	John Kling	121,000
1913—Fifth	69	82	.457	31½	George Stallings	208,000
1914—First	94	59	.614	+10½	George Stallings	382,913
1915—Second	83	69	.546	7	George Stallings	376,283
1916—Third	89	63	.586	4	George Stallings	313,495
1917—Sixth	72	81	.471	25½	George Stallings	174,253
1918—Seventh	53	71	.427	28½	George Stallings	84,938
1919—Sixth	57	82	.410	38½	George Stallings	167,401
1920—Seventh	62	90	.408	30	George Stallings	162,483
1921—Fourth	79	74	.516	15	Fred Mitchell	318,627
1922—Eighth	53	100	.346	39½	Fred Mitchell	167,965
1923—Seventh	54	100	.351	41½	Fred Mitchell	227,802
1924—Eighth	53	100	.346	40	David Bancroft	117,478
1925—Fifth	70	83	.458	25	David Bancroft	313,528
1926—Seventh	66	86	.434	22	David Bancroft	303,598
1927—Seventh	60	94	.390	34	David Bancroft	288,685
1928—Seventh	50	103	.327	44½	John Slattery, Rogers Hornsby	227,001
1929—Eighth	56	98	.364	43	Emil Fuchs, Walter Maranville	372,351
1930—Sixth	70	84	.455	22	William McKechnie	464,835
1931—Seventh	64	90	.416	37	William McKechnie	515,005
1932—Fifth	77	77	.500	13	William McKechnie	507,606
1933—Fourth	83	71	.539	9	William McKechnie	517,803
1934—Fourth	78	73	.517	16	William McKechnie	303,205
1935—Eighth	38	115	.248	61½	William McKechnie	232,754
1936—Sixth	71	83	.461	21	William McKechnie	340,585
1937—Fifth	79	73	.520	16	William McKechnie	385,339
1938—Fifth	77	75	.507	12	Charles (Casey) Stengel	341,149
1939—Seventh	63	88	.417	32½	Charles (Casey) Stengel	285,994
1940—Seventh	65	87	.428	34½	Charles (Casey) Stengel	241,616
1941—Seventh	62	92	.403	38	Charles (Casey) Stengel	263,680
1942—Seventh	59	89	.399	44	Charles (Casey) Stengel	285,332
1943—Sixth	68	85	.444	36½	Charles (Casey) Stengel	271,289
1944—Sixth	65	89	.422	40	Robert Coleman	208,691

ATLANTA BRAVES' YEARLY STANDING—Continued

Year—Position	W.	L.	Pct.	*G.B.	Manager	Attendance
1945—Sixth	67	85	.441	30	R. Coleman, Adelphia Bissonette	374,178
1946—Fourth	81	72	.529	15½	William Southworth	969,673
1947—Third	86	68	.558	8	William Southworth	1,277,361
1948—First	91	62	.595	+ 6½	William Southworth	1,455,439
1949—Fourth	75	79	.487	22	William Southworth	1,081,795
1950—Fourth	83	71	.539	8	William Southworth	944,391
1951—Fourth	76	78	.494	20½	W. Southworth, T. Holmes	487,475
1952—Seventh	64	89	.418	32	Thomas Holmes, Charles Grimm	281,278
1953—Second	92	62	.597	13	Charles Grimm	1,826,397
1954—Third	89	65	.578	8	Charles Grimm	2,131,388
1955—Second	85	69	.552	13½	Charles Grimm	2,005,836
1956—Second	92	62	.597	1	Charles Grimm, Fred Haney	2,046,331
1957—First	95	59	.617	+ 8	Fred Haney	2,215,404
1958—First	92	62	.597	+ 8	Fred Haney	1,971,101
1959—Second†	86	70	.551	2	Fred Haney	1,749,112
1960—Second	88	66	.571	7	Charles Dressen	1,497,799
1961—Fourth	83	71	.539	10	Chas. Dressen, Birdie Tebbetts	1,101,441
1962—Fifth	86	76	.531	15½	George (Birdie) Tebbetts	766,921
1963—Sixth	84	78	.519	15	Robert Bragan	773,018
1964—Fifth	88	74	.543	5	Robert Bragan	910,911
1965—Fifth	86	76	.531	11	Robert Bragan	555,584
1966—Fifth	85	77	.525	10	Robert Bragan, Wm. Hitchcock	1,539,801
1967—Seventh	77	85	.475	24½	Wm. Hitchcock, Ken Silvestri	1,389,222
1968—Fifth	81	81	.500	16	Luman Harris	1,126,540

WEST DIVISION

Year—Position	W.	L.	Pct.	*G.B.	Manager	Attendance
1969—First‡	93	69	.574	+ 3	Luman Harris	1,458,320
1970—Fifth	76	86	.469	26	Luman Harris	1,078,848
1971—Third	82	80	.506	8	Luman Harris	1,006,320
1972—Fourth	70	84	.455	25	Luman Harris, Edwin Mathews	752,973
1973—Fifth	76	85	.472	22½	Edwin Mathews	800,655
1974—Third	88	74	.543	14	Edwin Mathews, Clyde King	981,085
1975—Fifth	67	94	.416	40½	Clyde King, Connie Ryan	534,672
1976—Sixth	70	92	.432	32	J. David Bristol	818,179
1977—Sixth	61	101	.377	37	J. David Bristol, Ted Turner	872,464
1978—Sixth	69	93	.426	26	Robert Cox	904,494
1979—Sixth	66	94	.413	23½	Robert Cox	769,465
1980—Fourth	81	80	.503	11	Robert Cox	1,048,411
1981—4th/5th	50	56	.472	§	Robert Cox	535,418
1982—First‡	89	73	.549	+ 1	Joseph Torre	1,801,985
1983—Second	88	74	.543	3	Joseph Torre	2,119,935
1984—Second x	80	82	.494	12	Joseph Torre	1,724,892

*Games behind winner. †Lost to Los Angeles in pennant playoff. ‡Lost Championship Series. §First half 25-29; second 25-27. xTied for position.

First Game Played at Atlanta Stadium

The Braves made their debut in the new $18 million stadium, bowing to the Pittsburgh Pirates, 3-2, in 13 innings, before a crowd of 50,761 on April 12, 1966.

All runs were scored via the home run ball. Joe Torre put the Braves on the scoreboard in the fifth with a homer. Jim Pagliaroni tied the score at 1-1 with his eighth-inning clout.

Willie Stargell provided the winning margin with a two-run shot in the 13th. Torre hit his second homer of the game in the last of the 13th, but the Pirates held on to win.

Despite losing the game, Tony Cloninger pitched all 13 innings and struck out 12 batters.

ATLANTA BRAVES

(22) EDDIE HAAS—Manager

No. PITCHERS—	Bts.	Thrs.	Hgt.	Wgt.	Birth-date	1984 Club	IP.	W.	L.	ERA.
39 Barker, Len	R	R	6:04	230	7- 7-55	Atlanta	126.1	7	8	3.85
32 Bedrosian, Steve	R	R	6:03	195	12- 6-57	Atlanta	83.2	9	6	2.37
48 Brizzolara, Tony	R	R	6:05	217	1-14-57	Richmond	111.1	7	7	3.23
						Atlanta	29.0	1	2	5.28
37 Camp, Rick	R	R	6:01	198	6-10-53	Atlanta	148.2	8	6	3.27
49 Dedmon, Jeff	L	R	6:02	200	3- 4-60	Richmond	10.0	1	2	8.10
						Atlanta	81.0	4	3	3.78
51 Forster, Terry	L	L	6:04	220	1-14-52	Atlanta	26.2	2	0	2.70
26 Garber, Gene	R	R	5:10	172	11-13-47	Atlanta	106.0	3	6	3.06
55 Johnson, Joe	R	R	6:02	195	10-30-61	Greenville	151.0	8	10	3.75
						Richmond	20.1	0	2	5.75
42 Mahler, Rick	R	R	6:01	202	8- 5-53	Atlanta	222.0	13	10	3.12
29 McMurtry, Craig	R	R	6:05	195	11- 5-59	Atlanta	183.1	9	17	4.32
31 Moore, Donnie	L	R	6:00	185	2-13-54	Atlanta	64.1	4	5	2.94
47 Payne, Mike	R	R	5:11	167	11-15-61	Richmond	145.1	10	10	3.28
						Atlanta	5.2	0	1	6.35
27 Perez, Pascual	R	R	6:02	163	5-17-57	Atlanta	211.2	14	8	3.74
57 Shields, Steve	R	R	6:05	220	11-30-58	Richmond	110.0	9	4	4.75
34 Smith, Zane	L	L	6:02	195	12-28-60	Greenville	60.0	7	0	1.65
						Richmond	123.2	7	4	4.15
						Atlanta	20.0	1	0	2.25
Sutter, Bruce	R	R	6:02	190	1- 8-53	St. Louis	122.2	5	7	1.54
56 Ward, Duane	R	R	6:04	180	5-28-64	Greenville	104.2	4	9	4.99
45 West, Matt	B	R	6:04	195	1-13-60	Greenville	145.0	10	7	4.47

CATCHERS—	Bts.	Thrs.	Hgt.	Wgt.	Birth-date	1984 Club	G.	HR.	RBI.	Avg.
20 Benedict, Bruce	R	R	6:01	185	8-18-55	Atlanta	95	4	25	.223
Cerone, Rick	R	R	5:11	185	5-19-54	Columbus	8	0	1	.200
						New York AL	38	2	13	.208
8 Owen, Larry	R	R	5:11	185	5-31-55	Richmond	94	7	45	.242
25 Trevino, Alex	R	R	5:11	170	8-26-57	Cincinnati	6	0	0	.166
						Atlanta	79	3	28	.244

INFIELDERS—	Bts.	Thrs.	Hgt.	Wgt.	Birth-date	1984 Club	G.	HR.	RBI.	Avg.
10 Chambliss, Chris	L	R	6:01	221	12-26-48	Atlanta	135	9	44	.257
11 Horner, Bob	R	R	6:01	215	8- 6-57	Atlanta	32	3	19	.274
17 Hubbard, Glenn	R	R	5:08	169	9-25-57	Atlanta	120	9	43	.234
6 Johnson, Randy	R	R	6:01	190	6-10-56	Atlanta	91	5	30	.279
24 Oberkfell, Ken	L	R	6:01	210	5- 4-56	St. Louis	50	0	11	.309
						Atlanta	50	1	10	.233
28 Perry, Gerald	L	R	5:11	180	10-30-60	Atlanta	122	7	47	.265
16 Ramirez, Rafael	R	R	6:00	185	2-18-59	Atlanta	145	2	48	.266
12 Runge, Paul	R	R	6:00	175	5-21-58	Richmond	91	8	41	.239
						Atlanta	28	0	3	.267
1 Sosa, Miguel	R	R	5:10	165	5-15-60	Greenville	53	11	31	.294
						Richmond	64	15	41	.295
62 Thomas, Andres	R	R	6:01	170	11-10-63	Durham	114	7	44	.263
18 Zuvella, Paul	R	R	6:00	175	10-31-58	Richmond	127	6	55	.303
						Atlanta	11	0	1	.200

OUTFIELDERS—	Bts.	Thrs.	Hgt.	Wgt.	Birth-date	1984 Club	G.	HR.	RBI.	Avg.
2 Hall, Albert	B	R	5:11	155	3- 7-59	Atlanta	87	1	9	.261
19 Harper, Terry	R	R	6:01	202	8-19-55	Richmond	59	10	38	.324
						Atlanta	40	0	8	.157
7 Komminsk, Brad	R	R	6:02	205	4- 4-61	Richmond	42	5	28	.257
						Atlanta	90	8	36	.203
3 Murphy, Dale	R	R	6:05	215	3-12-56	Atlanta	162	36	100	.290
30 Thompson, Milt	L	R	5:11	160	1- 5-59	Richmond	134	4	40	.288
						Atlanta	25	2	4	.303
40 Vargas, Leo	R	R	6:01	180	9-12-57	Richmond	121	10	62	.260
15 Washington, Claudell	L	L	6:00	195	8-31-54	Atlanta	120	17	61	.286

DAL MAXVILL (53)—Coach   LEO MAZZONE (52)—Coach
JOHNNY SAIN (33)—Coach   BRIAN SNITKER (50)—Coach
BOBBY WINE (9)—Coach

ATLANTA STADIUM

	Seats	Prices
Club Level Box & Booths	196	**
Club Level Box Seats	2,790	$8.50
Dugout Level Box Seats	2,278	8.50
Field Level Seats	17,105	7.00
Upper Level Seats	17,262	5.00
Pavilion Level	4,676	4.00
General Admission	8,427	*3.00
Patio Boxes	200	9.00

*Children under 12 $1.00
**Sold only on season basis.

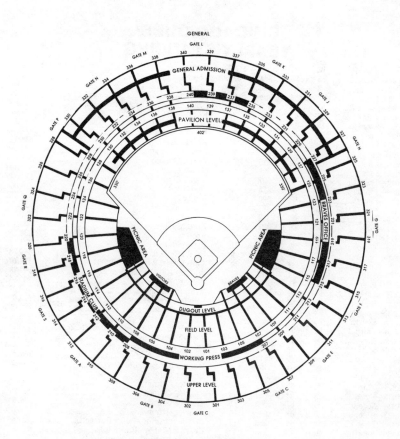

Atlanta Stadium, Atlanta
First N.L. Game Played April 12, 1966

CHICAGO CUBS

Jim Frey

President & General Manager—Dallas Green
Director of Park Operations—Thomas Cooper
Director of Minor Leagues & Scouting—Gordon Goldsberry
Director of Public Relations—Bob Ibach
Traveling Secretary—John Cox
Offices—Wrigley Field
Wrigley Field Capacity—37,272

Farm System: AAA—Iowa. AA—Pittsfield. A—Geneva, Peoria, Winston-Salem.

CHICAGO CUBS' YEARLY STANDING

Year—Position	W.	L.	Pct.	*G.B.	Manager	Attendance
1901—Sixth	53	86	.381	37	Thomas Loftus	205,071
1902—Fifth	68	69	.496	34	Frank Selee	263,700
1903—Third	82	56	.594	8	Frank Selee	386,205
1904—Second	93	60	.608	13	Frank Selee	439,100
1905—Third	92	61	.601	13	Frank Selee, Frank Chance	509,900
1906—First	116	36	.763	+20	Frank Chance	654,300
1907—First	107	45	.704	+17	Frank Chance	422,550
1908—First	99	55	.643	+ 1	Frank Chance	665,325
1909—Second	104	49	.680	6½	Frank Chance	633,480
1910—First	104	50	.675	+13	Frank Chance	526,152
1911—Second	92	62	.597	7½	Frank Chance	576,000
1912—Third	91	59	.607	11½	Frank Chance	514,000
1913—Third	88	65	.575	13½	John Evers	419,000
1914—Fourth	78	76	.506	16½	Henry (Hank) O'Day	202,516
1915—Fourth	73	80	.477	17½	Roger Bresnahan	217,058
1916—Fifth	67	86	.438	26½	Joseph Tinker	453,685
1917—Fifth	74	80	.481	24	Fred Mitchell	360,218
1918—First	84	45	.651	+10½	Fred Mitchell	337,256
1919—Third	75	65	.536	21	Fred Mitchell	424,430
1920—Fifth†	75	79	.487	18	Fred Mitchell	480,783
1921—Seventh	64	89	.418	30	John Evers, William Killefer	410,107
1922—Fifth	80	74	.519	13	William Killefer	542,283
1923—Fourth	83	71	.539	12½	William Killefer	703,705
1924—Fifth	81	72	.529	12	William Killefer	716,922
1925—Eighth	68	86	.442	27½	Killefer, W. Maranville, G. Gibson	622,610
1926—Fourth	82	72	.532	7	Joseph McCarthy	885,063
1927—Fourth	85	68	.556	8½	Joseph McCarthy	1,159,168
1928—Third	91	63	.591	4	Joseph McCarthy	1,143,740
1929—First	98	54	.645	+10½	Joseph McCarthy	1,485,166
1930—Second	90	64	.584	2	Jos. McCarthy, Rogers Hornsby	1,463,624
1931—Third	84	70	.545	17	Rogers Hornsby	1,086,422
1932—First	90	64	.584	+ 4	Rogers Hornsby, Charles Grimm	974,688
1933—Third	86	68	.558	6	Charles Grimm	594,112
1934—Third	86	65	.570	8	Charles Grimm	707,525
1935—First	100	54	.649	+ 4	Charles Grimm	692,604
1936—Second†	87	67	.565	5	Charles Grimm	699,370
1937—Second	93	61	.604	3	Charles Grimm	895,020
1938—First	89	63	.586	+ 2	Charles Grimm, Gabby Hartnett	951,640
1939—Fourth	84	70	.545	13	Charles (Gabby) Hartnett	726,663
1940—Fifth	75	79	.487	25½	Charles (Gabby) Hartnett	534,878
1941—Sixth	70	84	.455	30	James Wilson	545,159
1942—Sixth	68	86	.442	38	James Wilson	590,872
1943—Fifth	74	79	.484	30½	James Wilson	508,247
1944—Fourth	75	79	.487	30	James Wilson, Charles Grimm	640,110

CHICAGO CUBS' YEARLY STANDING—Continued

Year—Position	W.	L.	Pct.	*G.B.	Manager	Attendance
1945—First	98	56	.636	+ 3	Charles Grimm	1,036,386
1946—Third	82	71	.536	14½	Charles Grimm	1,342,970
1947—Sixth	69	85	.448	25	Charles Grimm	1,364,039
1948—Eighth	64	90	.416	27½	Charles Grimm	1,237,792
1949—Eighth	61	93	.396	36	Charles Grimm, Frank Frisch	1,143,139
1950—Seventh	64	89	.418	26½	Frank Frisch	1,165,944
1951—Eighth	62	92	.403	34½	Frank Frisch, Philip Cavarretta	894,415
1952—Fifth	77	77	.500	19½	Philip Cavarretta	1,024,826
1953—Seventh	65	89	.422	40	Philip Cavarretta	763,658
1954—Seventh	64	90	.416	33	Stanley Hack	748,183
1955—Sixth	72	81	.471	26	Stanley Hack	875,800
1956—Eighth	60	94	.390	33	Stanley Hack	720,118
1957—Seventh†	62	92	.403	33	Robert Scheffing	670,629
1958—Fifth†	72	82	.468	20	Robert Scheffing	979,904
1959—Fifth†	74	80	.481	13	Robert Scheffing	858,255
1960—Seventh	60	94	.390	35	Charles Grimm, Louis Boudreau	809,770
1961—Seventh	64	90	.416	29	H. Craft, A. Himsl, L. Klein, E. Tappe	673,057
1962—Ninth	59	103	.364	42½	E. Tappe, L. Klein, Chas. Metro	609,802
1963—Seventh	82	80	.506	17	Robert Kennedy	979,551
1964—Eighth	76	86	.469	17	Robert Kennedy	751,647
1965—Eighth	72	90	.444	25	Robert Kennedy, Louis Klein	641,361
1966—Tenth	59	103	.364	36	Leo Durocher	635,891
1967—Third	87	74	.540	14	Leo Durocher	977,226
1968—Third	84	78	.519	13	Leo Durocher	1,043,409

EAST DIVISION

Year—Position	W.	L.	Pct.	*G.B.	Manager	Attendance
1969—Second	92	70	.568	8	Leo Durocher	1,674,993
1970—Second	84	78	.519	5	Leo Durocher	1,642,705
1971—Third†	83	79	.512	14	Leo Durocher	1,653,007
1972—Second	85	70	.548	11	Leo Durocher, Whitey Lockman	1,299,163
1973—Fifth	77	84	.478	5	Carroll (Whitey) Lockman	1,351,705
1974—Sixth	66	96	.407	22	Whitey Lockman, James Marshall	1,015,378
1975—Fifth†	75	87	.463	17½	James Marshall	1,034,819
1976—Fourth	75	87	.463	26	James Marshall	1,026,217
1977—Fourth	81	81	.500	20	Herman Franks	1,439,834
1978—Third	79	83	.488	11	Herman Franks	1,525,311
1979—Fifth	80	82	.494	18	Herman Franks, Joe Amalfitano	1,648,587
1980—Sixth	64	98	.395	27	Preston Gomez, Joe Amalfitano	1,206,776
1981—6th/5th	38	65	.369	‡	Joe Amalfitano	565,637
1982—Fifth	73	89	.451	19	Lee Elia	1,249,278
1983—Fifth	71	91	.438	19	Lee Elia, Charles Fox	1,479,717
1984—First§	96	65	.596	+6½	James Frey	2,104,219

*Games behind winner. †Tied for position. ‡First half 15-37; second 23-28. §Lost Championship Series.

First Game Played at Wrigley Field

Vic Saier's 11th-inning single plated the winning run in the Cubs' 7-6 victory over Cincinnati at the Cubs' new North Side grounds on April 20, 1916.

The park, which was the home of the Federal League Whales the previous two seasons, was overflowing with people in the Cubs' opener. Each team collected 15 hits and each club used four pitchers.

Cubs catcher Bill Fischer was the batting star, going 4-for-5.

CHICAGO CUBS

(8) JIM FREY—Manager

No. PITCHERS—	Bts.	Thrs.	Hgt.	Wgt.	Birth-date	1984 Club	IP.	W.	L.	ERA.
32 Abrego, Johnny	R	R	6:01	185	7- 4-62	Lodi	150.1	9	9	2.10
						Iowa	26.2	1	1	5.06
47 Botelho, Derek	R	R	6:02	180	8- 2-56	Iowa	177.1	10	11	3.81
41 Brusstar, Warren	R	R	6:03	200	2- 2-52	Chicago	63.2	1	1	3.11
43 Eckersley, Dennis	R	R	6:02	195	10- 3-54	Boston	64.2	4	4	5.01
						Chicago	160.1	10	8	3.03
Fontenot, Ray	L	L	6:00	175	8- 8-57	New York AL	169.1	8	9	3.61
39 Frazier, George	R	R	6:05	200	10-13-54	Cleveland	44.1	3	2	3.65
						Chicago	63.2	6	3	4.10
37 Johnson, Bill	R	R	6:04	204	10- 6-60	Iowa	89.0	5	9	4.85
						Chicago	5.1	0	0	1.69
38 Meridith, Ron	L	L	6:00	175	11-26-55	Iowa	93.2	7	3	3.17
						Chicago	5.1	0	0	3.38
52 Patterson, Reggie	L	R	6:04	180	11- 7-58	Iowa	178.2	14	7	4.33
						Chicago	6.0	0	1	10.50
44 Ruthven, Dick	R	R	6:03	190	3-27-51	Lodi	9.0	1	0	4.00
						Chicago	126.2	6	10	5.04
21 Sanderson, Scott	R	R	6:05	200	7-22-56	Lodi	5.0	0	1	3.60
						Chicago	140.2	8	5	3.14
46 Smith, Lee	R	R	6:06	235	12- 4-57	Chicago	101.0	9	7	3.65
Sorensen, Lary	R	R	6:02	200	10- 4-55	Oakland	183.1	6	13	4.91
40 Sutcliffe, Rick	L	R	6:07	215	6-21-56	Cleveland	94.1	4	5	5.15
						Chicago	150.1	16	1	2.69
34 Trout, Steve	L	L	6:04	189	7-30-57	Chicago	190.0	13	7	3.41

CATCHERS—						1984 Club	G.	HR.	RBI.	Avg.
7 Davis, Jody	R	R	6:03	210	11-12-56	Chicago	150	19	94	.256
16 Lake, Steve	R	R	6:01	190	3-14-57	Midland	9	0	1	.160
						Chicago	25	2	7	.222

INFIELDERS—										
1 Bowa, Larry	B	R	5:10	155	12- 6-45	Chicago	133	0	17	.223
11 Cey, Ron	R	R	5:09	185	2-15-48	Chicago	146	25	97	.240
24 Dunston, Shawon	R	R	6:01	175	3-21-63	Iowa	61	7	27	.233
						Midland	73	3	34	.329
10 Durham, Leon	L	L	6:02	210	7-31-57	Chicago	137	23	96	.279
18 Hebner, Richie	L	R	6:01	200	11-26-47	Chicago	44	2	8	.333
12 Lopes, Davey	R	R	5:09	170	5- 3-46	Oakland	72	9	36	.257
						Chicago	16	0	0	.235
19 Owen, Dave	B	R	6:01	175	4-25-58	Iowa	43	1	9	.228
						Chicago	47	1	10	.194
17 Rohn, Dan	L	R	5:07	165	1-10-56	Iowa	109	8	46	.268
						Chicago	25	1	3	.129
23 Sandberg, Ryne	R	R	6:02	180	9-18-59	Chicago	156	19	84	.314
29 Veryzer, Tom	R	R	6:01	180	2-11-53	Midland	7	0	0	.182
						Chicago	44	0	4	.189
26 Woods, Tony	R	R	6:02	185	1- 6-62	Midland	73	7	29	.281

OUTFIELDERS—										
27 Bosley, Thad	L	L	6:03	175	9-17-56	Iowa	51	6	43	.358
						Chicago	55	2	14	.296
Dayett, Brian	R	R	5:10	185	1-22-57	Columbus	45	5	24	.301
						New York AL	64	4	23	.244
20 Dernier, Bob	R	R	6:00	165	1- 5-57	Chicago	143	3	32	.278
22 Hatcher, Billy	R	R	5:09	175	10- 4-60	Iowa	150	9	59	.276
						Chicago	8	0	0	.111
30 Jackson, Darrin	R	R	6:01	170	8-22-63	Midland	132	15	54	.270
36 Matthews, Gary	R	R	6:03	205	7- 5-50	Chicago	147	14	82	.291
6 Moreland, Keith	R	R	6:00	200	5- 2-54	Chicago	140	16	80	.279
25 Woods, Gary	R	R	6:02	190	7-20-53	Chicago	87	3	10	.235

REUBEN AMARO (5)—Coach   BILLY CONNORS (3)—Coach
JOHNNY OATES (9)—Coach   JOHN VUKOVICH (2)—Coach
DON ZIMMER (4)—Coach

WRIGLEY FIELD

	Seats	Prices
Club Box Seats—First 10 Rows Lower Deck	2,434	$9.50
Field Box Seats	7,120	9.50
Terrace Box Seats	2,394	7.50
Upper Box Seats	4,601	7.50
Terrace Reserved	12,133	6.00
General Admission	5,110	*5.00
Bleachers	3,260	3.50

*Children under 13 $2.50

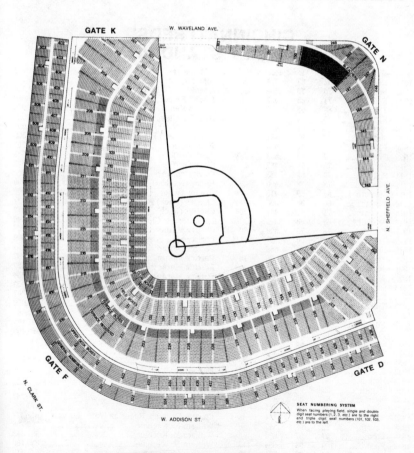

SEAT NUMBERING SYSTEM
When facing playing field, single and double digit seat numbers (1, 2, 3, etc.) are to the right and triple digit seat numbers (101, 102, 103, etc.) are to the left

Wrigley Field, Chicago
First N.L. Game Played April 20, 1916

CINCINNATI REDS

General Partner—Marge Schott
President, Chief Executive Officer—Robert L. Howsam Sr.
General Manager—Bill Bergesch
Vice-President, Marketing—Robert L. Howsam Jr.
Vice-President, Player Personnel—Sheldon Bender
Vice-President, Controller—D. L. Porco
Vice-President, Publicity—Jim Ferguson
Traveling Secretary—Steve Cobb
Offices—Riverfront Stadium
Riverfront Stadium Capacity—52,392

Farm System: AAA—Denver. AA—Burlington, Vt. A—Cedar Rapids, Tampa. Rookie—Billings, Sarasota.

Pete Rose

CINCINNATI REDS' YEARLY STANDING

Year—Position	W.	L.	Pct.	*G.B.	Manager	Attendance
1901—Eighth	52	87	.374	38	John McPhee	205,728
1902—Fourth	70	70	.500	33½	J. McPhee, F. Bancroft, J. Kelley	217,300
1903—Fourth	74	65	.532	16½	Joseph Kelley	351,680
1904—Third	88	65	.575	18	Joseph Kelley	391,915
1905—Fifth	79	74	.516	26	Joseph Kelley	313,927
1906—Sixth	64	87	.424	51½	Edward (Ned) Hanlon	330,056
1907—Sixth	66	87	.431	41½	Edward (Ned) Hanlon	317,500
1908—Fifth	73	81	.474	26	John Ganzel	399,200
1909—Fourth	77	76	.503	33½	Clark Griffith	424,643
1910—Fifth	75	79	.487	29	Clark Griffith	380,622
1911—Sixth	70	83	.458	29	Clark Griffith	300,000
1912—Fourth	75	78	.490	29	Henry (Hank) O'Day	344,000
1913—Seventh	64	89	.418	37½	Joseph Tinker	258,000
1914—Eighth	60	94	.390	34½	Charles (Buck) Herzog	100,791
1915—Seventh	71	83	.461	20	Charles (Buck) Herzog	218,878
1916—Seventh†	60	93	.392	33½	Buck Herzog, Christy Mathewson	255,846
1917—Fourth	78	76	.506	20	Christy Mathewson	269,056
1918—Third	68	60	.531	15½	Christy Mathewson, Henry Groh	163,009
1919—First	96	44	.686	+ 9	Patrick Moran	532,501
1920—Third	82	71	.536	10½	Patrick Moran	568,107
1921—Sixth	70	83	.458	24	Patrick Moran	311,227
1922—Second	86	68	.558	7	Patrick Moran	493,754
1923—Second	91	63	.591	4½	Patrick Moran	575,063
1924—Fourth	83	70	.542	10	John (Jack) Hendricks	437,707
1925—Third	80	73	.523	15	John (Jack) Hendricks	464,920
1926—Second	87	67	.565	2	John (Jack) Hendricks	672,987
1927—Fifth	75	78	.490	18½	John (Jack) Hendricks	442,164
1928—Fifth	78	74	.513	16	John (Jack) Hendricks	490,490
1929—Seventh	66	88	.429	33	John (Jack) Hendricks	295,040
1930—Seventh	59	95	.383	33	Daniel Howley	386,727
1931—Eighth	58	96	.377	43	Daniel Howley	263,316
1932—Eighth	60	94	.390	30	Daniel Howley	356,950
1933—Eighth	58	94	.382	33	Owen (Donie) Bush	218,281
1934—Eighth	52	99	.344	42	Robert O'Farrell, Charles Dressen	206,773
1935—Sixth	68	85	.444	31½	Charles Dressen	448,247
1936—Fifth	74	80	.481	18	Charles Dressen	466,245
1937—Eighth	56	98	.364	40	Charles Dressen, Roderick Wallace	411,221
1938—Fourth	82	68	.547	6	William McKechnie	706,756
1939—First	97	57	.630	+ 4½	William McKechnie	981,443
1940—First	100	53	.654	+12	William McKechnie	850,180
1941—Third	88	66	.571	12	William McKechnie	643,513
1942—Fourth	76	76	.500	29	William McKechnie	427,031
1943—Second	87	67	.565	18	William McKechnie	379,122
1944—Third	89	65	.578	16	William McKechnie	409,567

CINCINNATI REDS' YEARLY STANDING—Continued

Year—Position	W.	L.	Pct.	*G.B.	Manager	Attendance
1945—Seventh	61	93	.396	37	William McKechnie	290,070
1946—Sixth	67	87	.435	30	William McKechnie	715,751
1947—Fifth	73	81	.474	21	John Neun	899,975
1948—Seventh	64	89	.418	27	John Neun, William Walters	823,386
1949—Seventh	62	92	.403	35	William (Bucky) Walters	707,782
1950—Sixth	66	87	.431	24½	J. Luther Sewell	538,794
1951—Sixth	68	86	.442	28½	J. Luther Sewell	588,268
1952—Sixth	69	85	.448	27½	J. Luther Sewell, Rogers Hornsby	604,197
1953—Sixth	68	86	.442	37	Rogers Hornsby, C. Buster Mills	548,086
1954—Fifth	74	80	.481	23	George (Birdie) Tebbetts	704,167
1955—Fifth	75	79	.487	23½	George (Birdie) Tebbetts	693,662
1956—Third	91	63	.591	2	George (Birdie) Tebbetts	1,125,928
1957—Fourth	80	74	.519	15	George (Birdie) Tebbetts	1,070,850
1958—Fourth	76	78	.494	16	Birdie Tebbetts, James Dykes	788,582
1959—Fifth†	74	80	.481	13	E. Mayo Smith, Fred Hutchinson	801,289
1960—Sixth	67	87	.435	28	Fred Hutchinson	663,486
1961—First	93	61	.604	+ 4	Fred Hutchinson	1,117,603
1962—Third	98	64	.605	3½	Fred Hutchinson	982,085
1963—Fifth	86	76	.531	13	Fred Hutchinson	858,805
1964—Second†	92	70	.549	1	Fred Hutchinson, Richard Sisler	862,466
1965—Fourth	89	73	.549	8	Richard Sisler	1,047,824
1966—Seventh	76	84	.475	18	Donald Heffner, J. David Bristol	742,958
1967—Fourth	87	75	.537	14½	J. David Bristol	958,300
1968—Fourth	83	79	.512	14	J. David Bristol	733,354

WEST DIVISION

Year—Position	W.	L.	Pct.	*G.B.	Manager	Attendance
1969—Third	89	73	.549	4	J. David Bristol	987,991
1970—First‡	102	60	.630	+14½	George (Sparky) Anderson	1,803,568
1971—Fourth†	79	83	.488	11	George (Sparky) Anderson	1,501,122
1972—First‡	95	59	.617	+10½	George (Sparky) Anderson	1,611,459
1973—First§	99	63	.611	+ 3½	George (Sparky) Anderson	2,017,601
1974—Second	98	64	.605	4	George (Sparky) Anderson	2,164,307
1975—First‡	108	54	.667	+20	George (Sparky) Anderson	2,315,603
1976—First‡	102	60	.630	+10	George (Sparky) Anderson	2,629,708
1977—Second	88	74	.543	10	George (Sparky) Anderson	2,519,670
1978—Second	92	69	.571	2½	George (Sparky) Anderson	2,532,497
1979—First§	90	71	.559	+ 1½	John McNamara	2,356,933
1980—Third	89	73	.549	3½	John McNamara	2,022,450
1981—2nd/2nd	66	42	.611	x	John McNamara	1,093,730
1982—Sixth	61	101	.377	28	John McNamara, Russell Nixon	1,326,528
1983—Sixth	74	88	.457	17	Russell Nixon	1,190,419
1984—Fifth	70	92	.432	22	Vernon Rapp, Peter Rose	1,275,887

*Games behind winner. †Tied for position. ‡Won Championship Series. §Lost Championship Series. xFirst half 35-21; second 31-21.

First Game Played at Riverfront Stadium

The Atlanta Braves spoiled the Reds' debut in their new $48 million stadium, 8-2 on June 30, 1970.

The 51,050 fans had barely settled into their seats when Hank Aaron hit the first home run of the new park in the first inning. Rico Carty added a homer and four RBIs in the Braves' rout.

The Reds scored their only two runs in the fourth on singles by Tommy Helms, Woody Woodward, Angel Bravo and Pete Rose.

BASEBALL DOPE BOOK

CINCINNATI REDS

(14) PETE ROSE—Manager

No. PITCHERS—	Bts.	Thrs.	Hgt.	Wgt.	Birth-date	1984 Club	IP.	W.	L.	ERA.
32 Browning, Tom	L	L	6:01	190	4-28-60	Wichita	189.1	12	10	3.95
						Cincinnati	23.1	1	0	1.54
51 Buchanan, Bob	L	L	6:01	185	5- 3-61	Vermont	20.2	1	2	2.18
						Wichita	58.2	1	2	3.07
31 Franco, John	L	L	5:10	175	9-17-60	Wichita	9.1	1	0	5.79
						Cincinnati	79.1	6	2	2.61
58 Hawley, Billy	L	R	6:03	195	3-12-64	Tampa	178.0	18	5	1.87
47 Hume, Tom	R	R	6:01	185	3-29-53	Cincinnati	113.1	4	13	5.64
37 McGaffigan, Andy	R	R	6:03	195	10-25-56	Montreal	46.0	3	4	2.54
						Cincinnati	23.0	0	2	5.48
54 Murphy, Rob	L	L	6:02	200	5-26-60	Vermont	69.2	2	3	2.71
35 Pastore, Frank	R	R	6:03	215	8-21-57	Cincinnati	98.1	3	8	6.50
48 Power, Ted	R	R	6:04	225	1-31-55	Cincinnati	108.2	9	7	2.82
49 Price, Joe	R	L	6:04	215	11-29-56	Cincinnati	171.2	7	13	4.19
33 Robinson, Ron	R	R	6:04	215	3-24-62	Wichita	150.1	9	6	4.61
						Cincinnati	39.2	1	2	2.72
46 Russell, Jeff	R	R	6:04	195	9- 2-61	Cincinnati	181.2	6	18	4.26
53 Smith, Mike	R	R	6:00	195	2-23-61	Vermont	51.0	3	3	3.35
						Wichita	18.0	3	2	4.00
						Cincinnati	10.1	1	0	5.23
36 Soto, Mario	R	R	6:00	190	7-12-56	Cincinnati	237.1	18	7	3.53
42 Stuper, John	R	R	6:02	200	5- 9-57	Louisville	11.2	0	0	4.63
						Vancouver	63.0	2	3	3.86
						St. Louis	61.1	3	5	5.28
59 Terry, Scott	R	R	5:10	185	11-21-59	Vermont	144.0	14	3	1.50
						Wichita	9.1	0	0	5.79
38 Tibbs, Jay	R	R	6:01	180	4- 4-62	Jackson	37.1	1	2	3.13
						Tidewater	41.1	3	5	5.23
						Wichita	27.2	3	0	3.58
						Cincinnati	100.2	6	2	2.86
30 Toliver, Fred	R	R	6:01	170	2- 3-61	Wichita	164.0	11	6	4.83
						Cincinnati	10.0	0	0	0.90
40 Willis, Carl	L	R	6:04	210	12-28-60	Evansville	60.1	5	3	3.73
						Detroit	16.0	0	2	7.31
						Cincinnati	9.2	0	1	3.72

CATCHERS—	Bts.	Thrs.	Hgt.	Wgt.	Birth-date	1984 Club	G.	HR.	RBI.	Avg.
11 Bilardello, Dann	R	R	6:00	190	5-26-59	Wichita	49	5	17	.240
						Cincinnati	68	2	10	.209
4 Gulden, Brad	L	R	5:11	180	6- 5-56	Cincinnati	107	4	33	.226
34 Knicely, Alan	R	R	6:00	195	5-19-55	Wichita	152	33	126	.333
						Cincinnati	10	0	5	.138
52 McGriff, Terry	R	R	6:02	180	9-23-63	Tampa	110	7	41	.278
23 Van Gorder, Dave	R	R	6:02	205	3-27-57	Wichita	67	4	36	.263
						Cincinnati	38	0	6	.228

INFIELDERS—	Bts.	Thrs.	Hgt.	Wgt.	Birth-date	1984 Club	G.	HR.	RBI.	Avg.
21 Barnes, Skeeter	R	R	5:11	175	3- 7-57	Wichita	92	14	67	.328
						Cincinnati	32	1	3	.119
13 Concepcion, Dave	R	R	6:01	190	6-17-48	Cincinnati	154	4	58	.245
12 Esasky, Nick	R	R	6:03	200	2-24-60	Cincinnati	113	10	45	.193
10 Foley, Tom	L	R	6:01	175	9- 9-59	Cincinnati	106	5	27	.253
15 Krenchicki, Wayne	L	R	6:01	180	9-17-54	Wichita	18	2	5	.281
						Cincinnati	97	6	22	.298
16 Oester, Ron	R	R	6:02	190	5- 5-56	Cincinnati	150	3	38	.242
14 Rose, Pete	R	R	5:11	200	4-14-41	Montreal	95	0	23	.259
						Cincinnati	26	0	11	.365
56 Rowdon, Wade	R	R	6:02	175	9- 7-60	Wichita	144	16	72	.251
						Cincinnati	4	0	0	.286

OUTFIELDERS—	Bts.	Thrs.	Hgt.	Wgt.	Birth-date	1984 Club	G.	HR.	RBI.	Avg.
28 Cedeno, Cesar	R	R	6:02	200	2-25-51	Cincinnati	110	10	47	.276
55 Daniels, Kal	L	R	5:11	185	8-20-63	Vermont	122	17	62	.313
44 Davis, Eric	R	R	6:02	170	5-29-62	Wichita	52	14	34	.314
						Cincinnati	57	10	30	.224
20 Milner, Eddie	L	L	5:11	175	5-21-55	Cincinnati	117	7	29	.232

No. OUTFIELDERS—	Bts.	Thrs.	Hgt.	Wgt.	Birth-date	1984 Club	G.	HR.	RBI.	Avg.
57 O'Neill, Paul	L	L	6:04	200	2-25-63	Vermont	134	16	76	.265
39 Parker, Dave	L	R	6:05	230	6- 9-51	Cincinnati	156	16	94	.285
2 Redus, Gary	R	R	6:01	180	11- 1-56	Cincinnati	123	7	22	.254
26 Walker, Duane	L	L	6:00	185	3-13-57	Cincinnati	83	10	28	.292

BILLY DeMARS (7)—Coach   TOMMY HELMS (19)—Coach
JIM KAAT (45)—Coach   BRUCE KIMM (6)—Coach

GEORGE SCHERGER (3)—Coach

RIVERFRONT STADIUM

	Seats	Prices
Blue Level, Yellow Level Boxes	12,003	$8.00
Green Level Boxes	6,827	7.50
Red Level Boxes	3,224	7.00
Green Level Reserved	4,928	6.00
Red Level Reserved	18,010	5.50
"Top Six" Seats...	7,400	3.50

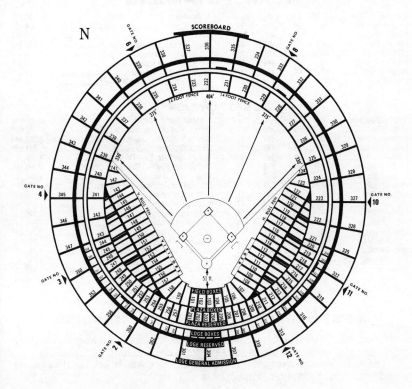

Riverfront Stadium, Cincinnati
First N.L. Game Played June 30, 1970

Bob Lillis

HOUSTON ASTROS

Chairman of the Board—Dr. John J. McMullen
President and General Manager—Al Rosen
Vice President-Baseball Operations—Bob Kennedy
Assistant to the President—Donald Davidson
Assistant General Manager—Andy MacPhail
Director of Minor League Operations—Bill Wood
Director of Scouting—Dan O'Brien Jr.
Director of Public Relations—Mike Ryan
Asst. Director of Public Relations—Rick Rivers
Offices—Astrodome
Astrodome Capacity—45,000

Farm System: AAA—Tucson. AA—Columbus, Ga. A—Asheville, Auburn, Osceola, Fla. Rookie—Sarasota.

HOUSTON ASTROS' YEARLY STANDING

Year—Position	W.	L.	Pct.	*G.B.	Manager	Attendance
1962—Eighth	64	96	.400	36½	Harry Craft	924,456
1963—Ninth	66	96	.407	33	Harry Craft	719,502
1964—Ninth	66	96	.407	27	Harry Craft, C. Luman Harris	725,773
1965—Ninth	65	97	.401	32	C. Luman Harris	2,151,470
1966—Eighth	72	90	.444	23	Grady Hatton	1,872,108
1967—Ninth	69	93	.426	32½	Grady Hatton	1,348,303
1968—Tenth	72	90	.444	25	Grady Hatton, Harry Walker	1,312,887

WEST DIVISION

Year—Position	W.	L.	Pct.	*G.B.	Manager	Attendance
1969—Fifth	81	81	.500	12	Harry Walker	1,442,995
1970—Fourth	79	83	.488	23	Harry Walker	1,253,444
1971—Fourth†	79	83	.488	11	Harry Walker	1,261,589
1972—Second	84	69	.549	10½	Harry Walker, Leo Durocher	1,469,247
1973—Fourth	82	80	.506	17	Durocher, Pedro (Preston) Gomez	1,394,004
1974—Fourth	81	81	.500	21	Pedro (Preston) Gomez	1,090,728
1975—Sixth	64	97	.398	43½	Pedro Gomez, William Virdon	858,002
1976—Third	80	82	.494	22	William Virdon	886,146
1977—Third	81	81	.500	17	William Virdon	1,109,560
1978—Fifth	74	88	.457	21	William Virdon	1,126,145
1979—Second	89	73	.549	1½	William Virdon	1,900,312
1980—First‡§	93	70	.571	+1	William Virdon	2,278,217
1981—3rd/1st	61	49	.555	x	William Virdon	1,321,282
1982—Fifth	77	85	.475	12	William Virdon, Robert Lillis	1,558,555
1983—Third	85	77	.525	6	Robert Lillis	1,351,962
1984—Second†	80	82	.494	12	Robert Lillis	1,229,862

*Games behind winner. †Tied for position. ‡Defeated Los Angeles in division playoff. §Lost Championship Series. xFirst half 28-29; second 33-20.

First Game Played at the Astrodome

Richie Allen's two-run homer for the Phillies in the third inning provided the only tallies in Houston's 2-0 loss in the Astrodome opener on April 12, 1965.

The Astros managed only four hits off Chris Short, who struck out 11 in gaining the complete-game victory for Philadelphia.

HOUSTON ASTROS

(5) BOB LILLIS—Manager

No. PITCHERS—	Bts.	Thrs.	Hgt.	Wgt.	Birth-date	1984 Club	IP.	W.	L.	ERA.
51 Acker, Larry	L	L	6:03	195	10- 4-60	Columbus	198.1	15	8	3.54
49 Calhoun, Jeff	L	L	6:02	190	4-11-58	Columbus	63.2	4	2	2.83
						Tucson	21.2	1	1	1.66
						Houston	15.1	0	1	1.17
46 Dawley, Bill	R	R	6:04	240	2- 6-58	Houston	98.0	11	4	1.93
11 DiPino, Frank	L	L	6:00	180	10-22-56	Houston	75.1	4	9	3.35
31 Heathcock, Jeff	R	R	6:04	195	11-18-59	Tucson	16.2	1	1	4.32
38 Hernandez, Manny	R	R	6:00	150	5- 7-61	Tucson	146.2	6	9	4.91
39 Knepper, Bob	L	L	6:02	210	5-25-54	Houston	233.2	15	10	3.20
37 Knudson, Mark	R	R	6:05	215	10-28-60	Columbus	101.0	4	5	2.23
						Tucson	84.0	4	6	3.64
53 Madden, Mike	L	L	6:01	190	1-13-58	Tucson	60.2	4	3	4.30
						Houston	40.2	2	3	5.53
36 Niekro, Joe	R	R	6:01	195	11- 7-44	Houston	248.1	16	12	3.04
47 Ross, Mark	R	R	6:00	195	8- 8-57	Tucson	92.0	5	6	2.93
						Houston	2.1	1	0	0.00
34 Ryan, Nolan	R	R	6:02	210	1-31-47	Houston	183.2	12	11	3.04
35 Sambito, Joe	L	L	6:01	190	6-28-52	Tucson	8.0	0	0	2.25
						Houston	47.2	0	0	3.02
33 Scott, Mike	R	R	6:03	215	4-26-55	Houston	154.0	5	11	4.68
45 Smith, Dave	R	R	6:01	195	1-21-55	Houston	77.1	5	4	2.21
52 Solano, Julio	R	R	6:01	160	1- 8-60	Tucson	80.2	3	5	2.57
						Houston	50.2	1	3	1.95

CATCHERS—	Bts.	Thrs.	Hgt.	Wgt.	Birth-date	1984 Club	G.	HR.	RBI.	Avg.
14 Ashby, Alan	R	R	6:02	195	7- 8-51	Houston	66	4	27	.262
6 Bailey, Mark	R	R	6:05	195	11- 4-61	Columbus	17	0	9	.283
						Houston	108	9	34	.212
4 Mizerock, John	L	R	5:11	190	12- 8-60	Columbus	61	4	23	.238

INFIELDERS—						1984 Club	G.	HR.	RBI.	Avg.
23 Cabell, Enos	R	R	6:05	185	10- 8-49	Houston	127	8	44	.310
27 Davis, Glenn	R	R	6:03	210	3-28-61	Tucson	131	16	94	.297
						Houston	18	2	8	.213
19 Doran, Bill	B	R	6:00	175	5-28-58	Houston	147	4	41	.261
3 Garner, Phil	R	R	5:10	175	4-30-49	Houston	128	4	45	.278
20 Pankovits, Jim	R	R	5:10	174	8- 6-55	Tucson	49	7	39	.332
						Houston	53	1	14	.284
1 Pena, Bert	R	R	5:11	165	7-11-59	Tucson	89	5	35	.260
						Houston	24	1	4	.205
12 Reynolds, Craig	L	R	6:01	175	12-27-52	Houston	146	6	60	.260
30 Richardt, Mike	R	R	6:00	170	5-24-58	Okla. City	17	1	5	.308
						Texas	7	0	0	.111
						Tucson	38	3	20	.295
						Houston	16	0	2	.267
16 Spilman, Harry	L	R	6:01	190	7-18-54	Houston	32	2	15	.264
10 Thon, Dickie	R	R	5:11	175	6-20-58	Houston	5	0	1	.353
29 Walling, Denny	L	R	6:01	185	4-17-54	Houston	87	3	31	.281

OUTFIELDERS—						1984 Club	G.	HR.	RBI.	Avg.
17 Bass, Kevin	B	R	6:00	180	5-12-59	Houston	121	2	29	.260
9 Bullock, Eric	L	L	5:11	185	2-16-60	Columbus	71	3	41	.291
						Tucson	60	1	16	.276
25 Cruz, Jose	L	L	6:00	185	8- 8-47	Houston	160	12	95	.312
24 Gainey, Ty	R	L	6:01	190	12-25-60	Columbus	133	13	78	.276
28 Mumphrey, Jerry	B	R	6:02	200	9- 9-52	Houston	151	9	83	.290
21 Puhl, Terry	L	R	6:02	200	7- 8-56	Houston	132	9	55	.301
38 Tolman, Tim	R	R	6:00	195	4-20-56	Tucson	102	9	54	.353
						Houston	14	0	0	.176

COT DEAL (2)—Coach   MATT GALANTE (48)—Coach
DON LEPPERT (43)—Coach   DENIS MENKE (15)—Coach
                      JERRY WALKER (54)—Coach

THE ASTRODOME

	Seats	Prices
Field Level	10,532	$8.50
Mezzanine Level	10,658	7.50
Loge Level	4,912	6.50
Gold Box	2,536	5.00
Gold Reserved	9,205	4.00
General Admission	3,910	*3.00

*Children under 14 $1.00

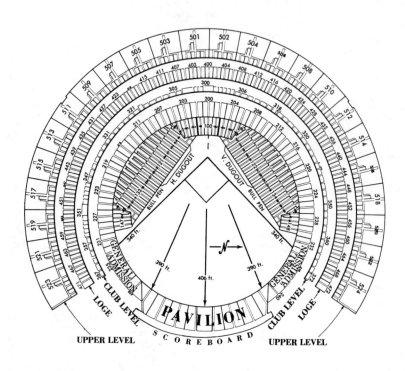

The Astrodome, Houston
First N.L. Game Played April 12, 1965

LOS ANGELES DODGERS

President—Peter O'Malley
Executive Vice President—Fred Claire
Vice-President, Player Personnel—Al Campanis
V-P, Minor League Operations—William P. Schweppe
Vice-President, Marketing—Merritt Willey
Publicity Director—Steve Brener
Traveling Secretary—Bill DeLury
Offices—Dodger Stadium
Dodger Stadium Capacity—56,000

Farm System: AAA—Albuquerque. AA—San Antonio. A—Bakersfield, Vero Beach. Rookie—Great Falls, Bradenton.

Tom Lasorda

LOS ANGELES DODGERS' YEARLY STANDING

(Brooklyn Dodgers Prior to 1958)

Year—Position	W.	L.	Pct.	*G.B.	Manager	Attendance
1901—Third	79	57	.581	9½	Edward (Ned) Hanlon	189,200
1902—Second	75	63	.543	27½	Edward (Ned) Hanlon	199,868
1903—Fifth	70	66	.515	19	Edward (Ned) Hanlon	224,670
1904—Sixth	56	97	.366	50	Edward (Ned) Hanlon	214,600
1905—Eighth	48	104	.316	56½	Edward (Ned) Hanlon	227,924
1906—Fifth	66	86	.434	50	Patrick (Patsy) Donovan	227,400
1907—Fifth	65	83	.439	40	Patrick (Patsy) Donovan	312,500
1908—Seventh	53	101	.344	46	Patrick (Patsy) Donovan	275,600
1909—Sixth	55	98	.359	55½	Harry Lumley	321,300
1910—Sixth	64	90	.416	40	William Dahlen	279,321
1911—Seventh	64	86	.427	33½	William Dahlen	269,000
1912—Seventh	58	95	.379	46	William Dahlen	243,000
1913—Sixth	65	84	.436	34½	William Dahlen	347,000
1914—Fifth	75	79	.487	19½	Wilbert Robinson	122,671
1915—Third	80	72	.526	10	Wilbert Robinson	297,766
1916—First	94	60	.610	+ 2½	Wilbert Robinson	447,747
1917—Seventh	70	81	.464	26½	Wilbert Robinson	221,619
1918—Fifth	57	69	.452	25½	Wilbert Robinson	83,831
1919—Fifth	69	71	.493	27	Wilbert Robinson	360,721
1920—First	93	61	.604	+ 7	Wilbert Robinson	808,722
1921—Fifth	77	75	.507	16½	Wilbert Robinson	613,245
1922—Sixth	76	78	.494	17	Wilbert Robinson	498,856
1923—Sixth	76	78	.494	19½	Wilbert Robinson	564,666
1924—Second	92	62	.597	1½	Wilbert Robinson	818,883
1925—Sixth†	68	85	.444	27	Wilbert Robinson	659,435
1926—Sixth	71	82	.464	17½	Wilbert Robinson	650,819
1927—Sixth	65	88	.425	28½	Wilbert Robinson	637,230
1928—Sixth	77	76	.503	17½	Wilbert Robinson	664,863
1929—Sixth	70	83	.458	28½	Wilbert Robinson	731,886
1930—Fourth	86	68	.558	6	Wilbert Robinson	1,097,339
1931—Fourth	79	73	.520	21	Wilbert Robinson	753,133
1932—Third	81	73	.526	9	Max Carey	681,827
1933—Sixth	65	88	.425	26½	Max Carey	526,815
1934—Sixth	71	81	.467	23½	Charles (Casey) Stengel	434,188
1935—Fifth	70	83	.458	29½	Charles (Casey) Stengel	470,517
1936—Seventh	67	87	.435	25	Charles (Casey) Stengel	489,618
1937—Sixth	62	91	.405	33½	Burleigh Grimes	482,481
1938—Seventh	69	80	.463	18½	Burleigh Grimes	663,087
1939—Third	84	69	.549	12½	Leo Durocher	955,668
1940—Second	88	65	.575	12	Leo Durocher	975,978
1941—First	100	54	.649	+ 2½	Leo Durocher	1,214,910
1942—Second	104	50	.675	2	Leo Durocher	1,037,765

LOS ANGELES DODGERS' YEARLY STANDING—Continued

Year—Position	W.	L.	Pct.	*G.B.	Manager	Attendance
1943—Third	81	72	.529	23½	Leo Durocher	661,739
1944—Seventh	63	91	.409	42	Leo Durocher	605,905
1945—Third	87	67	.565	11	Leo Durocher	1,059,220
1946—Second‡	96	60	.615	2	Leo Durocher	1,796,824
1947—First	94	60	.610	+ 5	Clyde Sukeforth, Burton Shotton	1,807,526
1948—Third	84	70	.545	7½	Leo Durocher, Burton Shotton	1,398,967
1949—First	97	57	.630	+ 1	Burton Shotton	1,633,747
1950—Second	89	65	.578	2	Burton Shotton	1,185,896
1951—Second‡	97	60	.618	1	Charles (Chuck) Dressen	1,282,628
1952—First	96	57	.627	+ 4½	Charles (Chuck) Dressen	1,088,704
1953—First	105	49	.682	+13	Charles (Chuck) Dressen	1,163,419
1954—Second	92	62	.597	2	Walter (Smokey) Alston	1,020,531
1955—First	98	55	.641	+13½	Walter (Smokey) Alston	1,033,589
1956—First	93	61	.604	+ 1	Walter (Smokey) Alston	1,213,562
1957—Third	84	70	.545	11	Walter (Smokey) Alston	1,028,258
1958—Seventh	71	83	.461	21	Walter (Smokey) Alston	1,845,556
1959—First§	88	68	.564	+ 2	Walter (Smokey) Alston	2,071,045
1960—Fourth	82	72	.532	13	Walter (Smokey) Alston	2,253,887
1961—Second	89	65	.578	4	Walter (Smokey) Alston	1,804,250
1962—Second‡	102	63	.618	1	Walter (Smokey) Alston	2,755,184
1963—First	99	63	.611	+ 6	Walter (Smokey) Alston	2,538,602
1964—Sixth†	80	82	.494	13	Walter (Smokey) Alston	2,228,751
1965—First	97	65	.599	+ 2	Walter (Smokey) Alston	2,553,577
1966—First	95	67	.586	+ 1½	Walter (Smokey) Alston	2,617,029
1967—Eighth	73	89	.451	28½	Walter (Smokey) Alston	1,664,362
1968—Seventh	76	86	.469	21	Walter (Smokey) Alston	1,581,093

WEST DIVISION

Year—Position	W.	L.	Pct.	*G.B.	Manager	Attendance
1969—Fourth	85	77	.525	8	Walter (Smokey) Alston	1,784,527
1970—Second	87	74	.540	14½	Walter (Smokey) Alston	1,697,142
1971—Second	89	73	.549	1	Walter (Smokey) Alston	2,064,594
1972—Third	85	70	.548	10½	Walter (Smokey) Alston	1,860,858
1973—Second	95	66	.590	3½	Walter (Smokey) Alston	2,136,192
1974—Firstx	102	60	.630	+ 4	Walter (Smokey) Alston	2,632,474
1975—Second	88	74	.543	20	Walter (Smokey) Alston	2,539,349
1976—Second	92	70	.568	10	Walter Alston, Thomas Lasorda	2,386,301
1977—Firstx	98	64	.605	+10	Thomas Lasorda	2,955,087
1978—First†x	95	67	.586	+ 2½	Thomas Lasorda	3,347,845
1979—Third	79	83	.488	11½	Thomas Lasorda	2,860,954
1980—Second y	92	71	.564	1	Thomas Lasorda	3,249,287
1981—1st/4th	63	47	.573	z	Thomas Lasorda	2,381,292
1982—Second	88	74	.543	1	Thomas Lasorda	3,608,881
1983—First a	91	71	.652	+ 3	Thomas Lasorda	3,510,313
1984—Fourth	79	83	.488	13	Thomas Lasorda	3,134,824

*Games behind winner. †Tied for position. ‡Lost pennant playoff. §Won pennant playoff. xWon Championship Series. yLost to Houston in division playoff. zFirst half 36-21; second 27-26. aLost Championship Series.

First Game Played at Dodger Stadium

Wally Post's three-run, seventh-inning home run broke a 2-2 tie, helping the Cincinnati Reds spoil the Dodgers' home debut, 6-3, on April 10, 1962.

The crowd of 52,564 fans saw the Reds pile up 14 hits, including four by Vada Pinson, while the home club managed only eight.

One week later, the Los Angeles Angels also lost their first game in their temporary home. The Kansas City A's beat the Angels, 5-3, before a crowd of 18,416.

After the Angels scored a first-inning run, the A's came back with run-scoring singles by Jerry Lumpe and Wayne Causey to take the lead in the third. The Angels, who managed only five hits, could never catch up.

LOS ANGELES DODGERS

(2) TOM LASORDA—Manager

No. PITCHERS—	Bts.	Thrs.	Hgt.	Wgt.	Birth-date	1984 Club	IP	W	L	ERA.
27 Diaz, Carlos	R	L	6:00	170	1- 7-58	Los Angeles	41.0	1	0	5.49
						Albuquerque	46.1	1	2	4.47
55 Hershiser, Orel	R	R	6:03	190	9-16-58	Los Angeles	189.2	11	8	2.66
40 Honeycutt, Rick	L	L	5:11	192	6-29-54	Los Angeles	183.2	10	9	2.84
57 Howe, Steve	L	L	5:11	190	3-10-58	Los Angeles	(Did not play)			
43 Howell, Ken	R	R	6:03	200	11-28-60	Albuquerque	72.1	8	2	4.60
						Los Angeles	51.1	5	5	3.33
49 Niedenfuer, Tom	R	R	6:05	225	8-13-59	Los Angeles	47.1	2	5	2.47
26 Pena, Alejandro	R	R	6:01	200	6-25-59	Los Angeles	199.1	12	6	2.48
41 Reuss, Jerry	L	L	6:05	225	6-19-49	Los Angeles	99.0	5	7	3.82
34 Valenzuela, Fernando	L	L	5:11	195	11- 1-60	Los Angeles	261.0	12	17	3.03
35 Welch, Bob	R	R	6:03	190	11- 3-56	Los Angeles	178.2	13	13	3.78
47 White, Larry	B	R	6:05	190	9-24-58	Albuquerque	159.2	7	12	6.09
						Los Angeles	12.0	0	1	3.00
38 Zachry, Pat	R	R	6:05	175	4-24-52	Los Angeles	82.2	5	6	3.81

CATCHERS—	Bts.	Thrs.	Hgt.	Wgt.	Birth-date	1984 Club	G	HR	RBI.	Avg.
31 Fimple, Jack	R	R	6:02	185	2-10-59	Albuquerque	107	11	60	.249
						Los Angeles	12	0	3	.192
15 Reyes, Gilberto	R	R	6:02	200	12-10-63	San Antonio	120	10	78	.303
						Los Angeles	4	0	0	.000
14 Scioscia, Mike	L	R	6:02	220	11-27-58	Los Angeles	114	5	38	.273
7 Yeager, Steve	R	R	6:00	200	11-24-48	Los Angeles	74	4	29	.228

INFIELDERS—	Bts.	Thrs.	Hgt.	Wgt.	Birth-date	1984 Club	G	HR	RBI.	Avg.
10 Anderson, Dave	R	R	6:02	185	8- 1-60	Los Angeles	121	3	34	.251
21 Bailor, Bob	R	R	5:10	160	7-10-51	Los Angeles	65	0	8	.275
33 Bream, Sid	L	L	6:04	215	8- 3-60	Albuquerque	114	20	90	.343
						Los Angeles	27	0	6	.184
9 Brock, Greg	L	R	6:03	205	6-14-57	Los Angeles	88	14	34	.225
						Albuquerque	24	6	15	.312
12 Duncan, Mariano	R	R	6:00	160	3-13-63	San Antonio	125	2	44	.253
25 Rivera, German	R	R	6:02	195	7- 6-59	Los Angeles	94	2	17	.260
						Albuquerque	51	4	39	.315
18 Russell, Bill	R	R	6:00	187	10-21-48	Los Angeles	89	0	19	.267
3 Sax, Steve	R	R	5:11	185	1-29-60	Los Angeles	145	1	35	.243
22 Stubbs, Franklin	L	L	6:02	215	10-21-60	Albuquerque	29	6	24	.324
						Los Angeles	87	8	17	.194

OUTFIELDERS—	Bts.	Thrs.	Hgt.	Wgt.	Birth-date	1984 Club	G	HR	RBI.	Avg.
17 Amelung, Ed	L	L	6:00	185	4-13-59	Albuquerque	107	15	63	.351
						Los Angeles	34	0	4	.217
50 Brewer, Tony	R	R	5:11	180	11-25-57	Albuquerque	104	19	83	.357
						Los Angeles	24	1	4	.108
29 Bryant, Ralph	L	R	6:02	200	5-20-61	San Antonio	115	31	86	.300
52 Espy, Cecil	B	R	6:03	195	1-20-63	San Antonio	133	8	60	.273
36 Gonzalez, Jose	R	R	6:02	190	11-23-64	Bakersfield	129	11	59	.221
28 Guerrero, Pedro	R	R	6:00	195	6-29-56	Los Angeles	144	16	72	.303
44 Landreaux, Ken	L	R	5:11	190	12-22-54	Los Angeles	134	11	47	.251
20 Maldonado, Candy	R	R	5:11	195	9- 5-60	Los Angeles	116	5	28	.268
5 Marshall, Mike	R	R	6:05	220	1-12-60	Los Angeles	134	21	65	.257
51 Miller, Lemmie	R	R	6:01	190	6- 2-60	Albuquerque	124	3	39	.311
						Los Angeles	8	0	0	.167
37 Ramsey, Mike	R	L	6:00	170	7- 8-60	Vero Beach	143	4	46	.263
23 Reynolds, Robert	B	R	6:00	190	4-19-60	Albuquerque	47	3	30	.347
						Los Angeles	73	2	24	.258
45 Whitfield, Terry	L	R	6:01	200	1-12-53	Los Angeles	87	4	18	.244

JOE AMALFITANO (8)—Coach   MONTY BASGALL (54)—Coach
MARK CRESSE (58)—Coach   MANNY MOTA (11)—Coach
RON PERRANOSKI (16)—Coach

DODGER STADIUM

	Seats	Prices
Dugout, Club Level Boxes	1,732	*
Field, Loge Box Seats	24,446	$6.00
Reserved Grandstand...................	19,322	5.00
General Admission (Top Deck)..........	4,266	3.00
General Admission (Pavilion)..........	6,234	3.00

*Sold only on season basis.

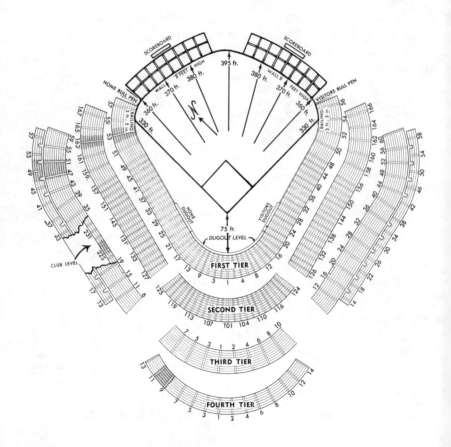

Dodger Stadium, Los Angeles
First N.L. Game Played April 10, 1962

Buck Rodgers

MONTREAL EXPOS

Chairman of the Board—Charles R. Bronfman
President & Chief Executive Officer—John J. McHale
Vice-President, Player Development, Scouting—Jim Fanning
Vice-President, Director of Business Operations—Gerry Trudeau
Group Vice-President—Pierre Gauvreau
V.P., Director of Marketing and Public Affairs—Rene Guimond
Vice-President, Baseball Operations—Bill Stoneman
Director of Minor League Operations—Bob Gebhard
Publicists—Monique Giroux, Richard Griffin
Traveling Secretary—Peter Durso
Offices—P. O. Box 500, Station M
Olympic Stadium Capacity—59,149

Farm System: AAA—Indianapolis. AA—Jacksonville. A—Jamestown, West Palm Beach.

MONTREAL EXPOS' YEARLY STANDING

EAST DIVISION

Year—Position	W.	L.	Pct.	*G.B.	Manager	Attendance
1969—Sixth	52	110	.321	48	Gene Mauch	1,212,608
1970—Sixth	73	89	.451	16	Gene Mauch	1,424,683
1971—Fifth	71	90	.441	25½	Gene Mauch	1,290,963
1972—Fifth	70	86	.449	26½	Gene Mauch	1,142,145
1973—Fourth	79	83	.488	3½	Gene Mauch	1,246,863
1974—Fourth	79	82	.491	8½	Gene Mauch	1,019,134
1975—Fifth†	75	87	.463	17½	Gene Mauch	908,292
1976—Sixth	55	107	.340	46	Karl Kuehl, Charlie Fox	646,704
1977—Fifth	75	87	.463	26	Richard Williams	1,433,757
1978—Fourth	76	86	.469	14	Richard Williams	1,427,007
1979—Second	95	65	.594	2	Richard Williams	2,102,173
1980—Second	90	72	.556	1	Richard Williams	2,208,175
1981—3rd/1st	60	48	.556	‡	Richard Williams, James Fanning	1,534,564
1982—Third	86	76	.531	6	James Fanning	2,318,292
1983—Third	82	80	.506	8	William Virdon	2,320,651
1984—Fifth	78	83	.484	18	William Virdon, James Fanning	1,606,531

*Games behind winner. †Tied for position. ‡First half 30-25; second 30-23.

First Game Played at Olympic Stadium

Before 57,592 fans, then the largest Expos' crowd in their history, Montreal lost to the Philadelphia Phillies, 7-2, on April 15, 1977.

Jay Johnstone and Greg Luzinski each knocked in two runs for the visitors. Ellis Valentine provided the only Expo run with a homer and an infield out.

MONTREAL EXPOS
(37) BUCK RODGERS—Manager

No.	PITCHERS—	Bts.	Thrs.	Hgt.	Wgt.	Birth-date	1984 Club	IP.	W.	L.	ERA.
39	Bargar, Greg	R	R	6:02	185	1-27-59	Indianapolis	180.1	9	8	4.64
							Montreal	8.0	0	1	7.88
48	Breining, Fred	R	R	6:04	185	11-15-55	Montreal	6.2	0	0	1.35
50	Cates, Tim	R	R	6:02	185	11-11-59	Jacksonville	69.2	5	3	2.45
							Indianapolis	92.2	6	6	4.76
54	Dopson, John	L	R	6:04	205	7-14-63	Jacksonville	170.2	10	8	3.69
47	Grapenthin, Dick	R	R	6:02	205	4-16-58	Indianapolis	91.0	6	7	3.07
							Montreal	23.0	1	2	3.52
34	Gullickson, Bill	R	R	6:03	215	2-20-59	Montreal	226.2	12	9	3.61
38	Hesketh, Joe	L	L	6:02	170	2-15-59	Indianapolis	147.2	12	3	3.05
							Montreal	45.0	2	2	1.80
53	Lea, Charlie	R	R	6:04	200	12-25-56	Montreal	224.1	15	10	2.89
25	Lucas, Gary	L	L	6:05	200	11- 8-54	Montreal	53.0	0	3	2.72
46	Palmer, David	R	R	6:01	205	10-19-57	Montreal	105.1	7	3	3.84
41	Reardon, Jeff	R	R	6:01	200	10- 1-55	Montreal	87.0	7	7	2.90
42	Roberge, Bert	R	R	6:04	190	10- 3-54	Denver	37.0	5	1	1.95
							Chicago AL	40.2	3	3	3.76
45	Rogers, Steve	R	R	6:01	185	10-26-49	Montreal	169.1	6	15	4.31
51	St. Claire, Randy	R	R	6:03	180	8-23-60	Jacksonville	75.0	10	7	2.88
							Indianapolis	17.2	1	1	1.02
							Montreal	8.0	0	0	4.50
43	Schatzeder, Dan	L	L	6:00	196	12- 1-54	Montreal	136.0	7	7	2.71
28	Smith, Bryn	R	R	6:02	210	8-11-55	Montreal	179.0	12	13	3.32
33	Youmans, Floyd	R	R	6:02	180	5-11-64	Lynchburg	39.2	5	2	3.63
							Jackson	86.0	6	7	4.60

No.	CATCHERS—	Bts.	Thrs.	Hgt.	Wgt.	Birth-date	1984 Club	G.	HR.	RBI.	Avg.
21	Fitzgerald, Mike	R	R	6:00	185	7-13-60	New York NL	112	2	33	.242
44	Ramos, Bobby	R	R	5:10	200	11- 5-55	Montreal	31	2	5	.193

No.	INFIELDERS—	Bts.	Thrs.	Hgt.	Wgt.	Birth-date	1984 Club	G.	HR.	RBI.	Avg.
11	Brooks, Hubie	R	R	6:00	188	9-24-56	New York NL	153	16	73	.283
22	Driessen, Dan	L	R	5:11	200	7-29-51	Cincinnati	81	7	28	.280
							Montreal	51	9	32	.254
23	Flynn, Doug	R	R	5:11	172	4-18-51	Montreal	124	0	17	.243
52	Galarraga, Andres	R	R	6:03	235	6-18-61	Jacksonville	143	27	87	.289
19	Gonzales, Rene	R	R	6:03	180	9- 3-61	Indianapolis	114	2	32	.234
							Montreal	29	0	2	.233
2	Law, Vance	R	R	6:02	190	10- 1-56	Chicago AL	151	17	59	.252
20	Lawless, Tom	R	R	5:11	170	12-19-56	Wichita	31	3	11	.233
							Cincinnati	43	1	2	.250
							Indianapolis	19	1	12	.329
							Montreal	11	0	0	.176
60	Newman, Al	B	R	5:09	175	6-30-60	Beaumont	88	0	23	.252
							Indianapolis	37	0	11	.301
4	Ramsey, Mike	B	R	6:01	175	3-29-54	St. Louis	21	0	0	.067
							Montreal	37	0	3	.214
57	Rivera, Luis	R	R	5:10	160	1- 3-64	W. Palm Beach	124	6	43	.288
6	Salazar, Argenis	R	R	6:00	170	11- 4-61	Indianapolis	50	1	14	.276
							Montreal	80	0	12	.155
31	Shines, Razor	B	R	6:01	210	7-18-56	Indianapolis	131	18	80	.282
							Montreal	12	0	2	.300
29	Wallach, Tim	R	R	6:03	200	9-14-58	Montreal	160	18	72	.246
	Washington, U.L.	B	R	5:11	175	10-27-53	Kansas City	63	1	10	.224

No.	OUTFIELDERS—	Bts.	Thrs.	Hgt.	Wgt.	Birth-date	1984 Club	G.	HR.	RBI.	Avg.
10	Dawson, Andre	R	R	6:03	195	7-10-54	Montreal	138	17	86	.248
16	Francona, Terry	L	L	6:01	175	4-22-59	Montreal	58	1	18	.346
15	Fuentes, Mike	R	R	6:03	190	7-11-58	Indianapolis	148	22	80	.251
							Montreal	3	0	0	.250
27	Johnson, Roy	L	L	6:04	205	6-27-59	Indianapolis	107	9	49	.270
							Montreal	16	1	2	.152
30	Raines, Tim	B	R	5:08	178	9-16-59	Montreal	160	8	60	.309
49	Venable, Max	L	R	5:10	185	6- 6-57	Indianapolis	99	9	47	.248
							Montreal	38	2	7	.239
3	Winningham, Herman	L	R	6:01	170	12- 1-61	Tidewater	115	3	47	.281
							New York NL	14	0	5	.407

LARRY BEARNARTH (36)—Coach　　　　　　　RON HANSEN (26)—Coach
JOE KERRIGAN (40)—Coach　　　　　　　　　RUSS NIXON (9)—Coach
　　　　　　　　　　RICK RENICK (35)—Coach

OLYMPIC STADIUM

	Seats	Prices
Level 200	5,532	$11.50
Level 300	11,337	9.50
Level 400	9,137	8.00
Level 600/700	23,780	5.25
General Admission	6,260	2.00

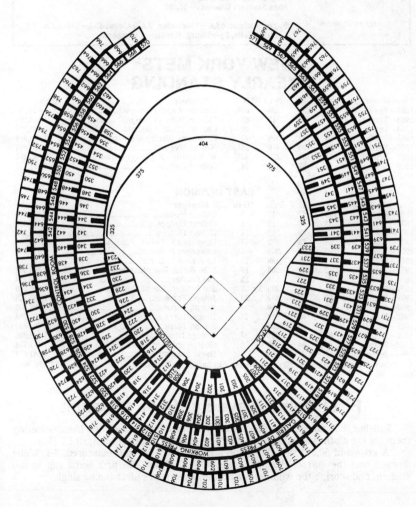

Olympic Stadium, Montreal
First N.L. Game Played April 15, 1977

NEW YORK METS

Chairman of the Board—Nelson Doubleday
President—Fred Wilpon
Executive V. P.-General Manager—Frank Cashen
Vice-President, Marketing—Michael Aronin
Vice-President, Baseball—Alan Harazin
V.P., Finance—Harry O'Shaughnessy
Vice-President, Operations—Robert Mandt
Asst. V.P., Director of Player Personnel—Joseph McIlvaine
Director of Minor Leagues—Steve Schryver
Asst. to G.M.-Traveling Secretary—Arthur Richman
Director of Public Relations—Jay Horwitz
Offices—Shea Stadium
Shea Stadium Capacity—55,300

Dave Johnson

Farm System: AAA—Tidewater. AA—Jackson. A—Columbia, S.C.,
Little Falls, Lynchburg. Rookie—Kingsport.

NEW YORK METS' YEARLY STANDING

Year—Position	W.	L.	Pct.	*G.B.	Manager	Attendance
1962—Tenth	40	120	.250	60½	Charles (Casey) Stengel	922,530
1963—Tenth	51	111	.315	48	Charles (Casey) Stengel	1,080,108
1964—Tenth	53	109	.327	40	Charles (Casey) Stengel	1,732,597
1965—Tenth	50	112	.309	47	C. Stengel, Wesley Westrum	1,768,389
1966—Ninth	66	95	.410	28½	Wesley Westrum	1,932,693
1967—Tenth	61	101	.377	40½	W. Westrum, F. (Salty) Parker	1,565,492
1968—Ninth	73	89	.451	24	Gilbert Hodges	1,781,657

EAST DIVISION

Year—Position	W.	L.	Pct.	*G.B.	Manager	Attendance
1969—First†	100	62	.617	+ 8	Gilbert Hodges	2,175,373
1970—Third	83	79	.512	6	Gilbert Hodges	2,697,479
1971—Third‡	83	79	.512	14	Gilbert Hodges	2,266,680
1972—Third	83	73	.532	13½	Lawrence P. Berra	2,134,185
1973—First†	82	79	.509	+ 1½	Lawrence P. Berra	1,912,390
1974—Fifth	71	91	.438	17	Lawrence P. Berra	1,722,209
1975—Third‡	82	80	.506	10½	L. P. Berra, Roy McMillan	1,730,566
1976—Third	86	76	.531	15	Joe Frazier	1,468,754
1977—Sixth	64	98	.395	37	Joe Frazier, Joseph Torre	1,066,825
1978—Sixth	66	96	.407	24	Joseph Torre	1,007,328
1979—Sixth	63	99	.389	35	Joseph Torre	788,905
1980—Fifth	67	95	.414	24	Joseph Torre	1,192,073
1981—5th/4th	41	62	.398	§	Joseph Torre	704,244
1982—Sixth	65	97	.401	27	George Bamberger	1,323,036
1983—Sixth	68	94	.420	22	George Bamberger, Frank Howard	1,112,774
1984—Second	90	72	.556	6½	David Johnson	1,842,695

*Games behind winner. †Won Championship Series. ‡Tied for position. §First half 17-34; second 24-28.

First Game Played at Shea Stadium

Pittsburgh Pirates hurler Bob Friend continued his hex over the Mets, defeating them for the ninth straight time in their Shea Stadium opener on April 17, 1964.

A crowd of 50,312 saw the home team outhit, 16-7, and outscored, 4-3. Willie Stargell was the star of the day, going 4-for-5, hitting the first home run in the stadium and scoring the winning run on Bill Mazeroski's ninth-inning single.

NEW YORK METS

(5) DAVEY JOHNSON—Manager

No. PITCHERS—	Bts.	Thrs.	Hgt.	Wgt.	Birth-date	1984 Club	IP.	W.	L.	ERA.
31 Berenyi, Bruce	R	R	6:03	215	8-21-54	Cincinnati	51.0	3	7	6.00
						New York	115.0	9	6	3.76
33 Bettendorf, Jeff	R	R	6:03	190	12-10-61	Oakland	9.2	0	0	4.66
						Jackson	45.0	5	0	2.20
						Tidewater	71.0	4	8	5.70
44 Darling, Ron	R	R	6:03	195	8-19-60	New York	205.2	12	9	3.81
50 Fernandez, Sid	L	L	6:01	220	10-12-62	Tidewater	105.2	6	5	2.56
						New York	90.0	6	6	3.50
45 Gaff, Brent	R	R	6:02	200	10- 5-58	Tidewater	25.1	3	1	4.26
						New York	84.1	3	2	3.63
27 Gardner, Wes	R	R	6:04	195	4-29-61	Tidewater	56.0	1	2	1.61
						New York	25.1	1	1	6.39
16 Gooden, Dwight	R	R	6:02	190	11-16-64	New York	218.0	17	9	2.60
29 Gorman, Tom	L	L	6:04	200	12-16-57	New York	18.0	1	2	3.00
						New York	57.2	6	0	2.97
64 Latham, Bill	L	L	6:02	190	8-29-60	Jackson	44.2	2	2	2.22
						Tidewater	132.1	11	3	3.06
38 Leary, Tim	R	R	6:03	190	12-23-58	New York	53.2	3	3	4.02
						Tidewater	53.1	4	4	4.05
36 Lynch, Ed	R	R	6:05	207	2-25-56	New York	124.0	9	8	4.50
42 McDowell, Roger	R	R	6:01	175	12-21-60	Jackson	7.1	0	0	3.68
63 Myers, Randy	L	L	6:01	190	9-19-62	Lynchburg	157.0	13	5	2.06
						Jackson	35.0	2	1	2.06
47 Orosco, Jesse	R	L	6:02	185	4-21-57	New York	87.0	10	6	2.59
40 Schiraldi, Calvin	R	R	6:04	200	6-16-62	Jackson	156.1	14	3	2.88
						Tidewater	31.1	3	1	1.15
						New York	17.1	0	2	5.71
39 Sisk, Doug	R	R	6:02	210	9-26-57	New York	77.2	1	3	2.09

CATCHERS—	Bts.	Thrs.	Hgt.	Wgt.	Birth-date	1984 Club	G.	HR.	RBI.	Avg.
8 Carter, Gary	R	R	6:02	210	4- 8-54	Montreal	159	27	106	.294
7 Gibbons, John	R	R	5:11	187	6- 8-62	New York	10	0	1	.065
						Tidewater	65	6	27	.256
9 Reynolds, Ronn	R	R	6:00	200	9-28-58	Tidewater	90	11	46	.261

INFIELDERS—	Bts.	Thrs.	Hgt.	Wgt.	Birth-date	1984 Club	G.	HR.	RBI.	Avg.
6 Backman, Wally	B	R	5:09	160	9-22-59	New York	128	1	26	.280
11 Chapman, Kelvin	R	R	5:11	172	6- 2-56	Tidewater	12	0	6	.275
						New York	75	3	23	.289
62 Cochrane, Dave	B	R	6:02	180	1-31-63	Jackson	129	22	77	.267
19 Gardenhire, Ron	R	R	6:00	174	10-24-57	New York	74	1	10	.246
17 Hernandez, Keith	L	L	6:00	195	10-20-53	New York	154	15	94	.311
20 Johnson, Howard	B	R	6:00	175	11-29-60	Detroit	116	12	50	.248
22 Knight, Ray	R	R	6:02	190	12-28-52	Houston	88	2	29	.223
						New York	27	1	6	.280
32 Mitchell, Kevin	R	R	5:11	210	1-13-62	Tidewater	120	10	54	.243
						New York	7	0	1	.214
2 Oquendo, Jose	R	R	5:10	156	7- 4-63	New York	81	0	10	.222
						Tidewater	38	1	8	.159
3 Santana, Rafael	R	R	6:01	160	1-31-58	Tidewater	77	1	23	.278
						New York	51	1	12	.276

OUTFIELDERS—	Bts.	Thrs.	Hgt.	Wgt.	Birth-date	1984 Club	G.	HR.	RBI.	Avg.
43 Beane, Billy	R	R	6:04	195	3-29-62	Jackson	123	20	72	.281
						New York	5	0	0	.100
61 Blocker, Terry	L	L	6:02	195	8-18-60	Tidewater	115	3	31	.220
35 Christensen, John	R	R	6:00	180	9- 5-60	Tidewater	129	15	71	.316
						New York	5	0	3	.273
4 Dykstra, Lenny	L	L	5:10	160	2-10-63	Jackson	131	6	52	.275
15 Foster, George	R	R	6:01	198	12- 1-48	New York	146	24	86	.269
25 Heep, Danny	L	L	5:11	185	7- 3-57	New York	99	1	12	.231
10 Staub, Rusty	L	R	6:02	225	4- 1-44	New York	78	1	18	.264
18 Strawberry, Darryl	L	L	6:06	190	3-12-62	New York	147	26	97	.251
1 Wilson, Mookie	B	R	5:10	168	2- 9-56	New York	154	10	54	.276

VERN HOSCHEIT (51)—Coach   BILL ROBINSON (28)—Coach
MEL STOTTLEMYRE (30)—Coach   BOBBY VALENTINE (26)—Coach

SHEA STADIUM

	Seats	Prices
Field, Loge Level Boxes	12,792	$9.00
Mezzanine, Upper Level Boxes	7,680	7.50
Loge Level Reserved	6,582	7.50
Mezzanine Level Reserved	10,542	7.50
Upper Reserved		6.00
General Admission	17,704	4.00

Note—Proportion of reserved and general admission seats in loge, mezzanine and upper deck dependent upon anticipated size of crowd.

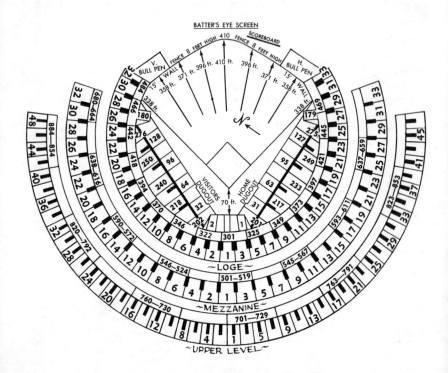

William A. Shea Stadium, New York
First N.L. Game Played April 17, 1964

PHILADELPHIA PHILLIES

President—Bill Giles
Partners—Taft Broadcasting Co., John Drew Betz, Tri-Play Associates, Fitz Eugene Dixon, Mrs. Rochelle Levy
Assistant to the President—Paul Owens
Executive Vice-President—Dave Montgomery
V.P., Baseball Administration—Tony Siegle
V.P., Director of Player Development—Jim Baumer
Vice-President, Finance—Jerry Clothier
Vice-President, Public Relations—Larry Shenk
Secretary & Counsel—William Y. Webb
Traveling Secretary—Eddie Ferenz
Offices—Veterans Stadium
Veterans Stadium Capacity—66,744

John Felske

Farm System: AAA—Portland. AA—Reading. A—Bend, Clearwater, Spartanburg, Peninsula.

PHILADELPHIA PHILLIES' YEARLY STANDING

Year—Position	W.	L.	Pct.	*G.B.	Manager	Attendance
1901—Second	83	57	.593	7½	William Shettsline	234,937
1902—Seventh	56	81	.409	46	William Shettsline	112,066
1903—Seventh	49	86	.363	39½	Charles (Chief) Zimmer	151,729
1904—Eighth	52	100	.342	53½	Hugh Duffy	140,771
1905—Fourth	83	69	.546	21½	Hugh Duffy	317,932
1906—Fourth	71	82	.464	45½	Hugh Duffy	294,680
1907—Third	83	64	.565	21½	William J. Murray	341,216
1908—Fourth	83	71	.539	16	William J. Murray	420,660
1909—Fifth	74	79	.484	36½	William J. Murray	303,177
1910—Fourth	78	75	.510	25½	Charles (Red) Dooin	296,597
1911—Fourth	79	73	.520	19½	Charles (Red) Dooin	416,000
1912—Fifth	73	79	.480	30½	Charles (Red) Dooin	250,000
1913—Second	88	63	.583	12½	Charles (Red) Dooin	470,000
1914—Sixth	74	80	.481	20½	Charles (Red) Dooin	138,474
1915—First	90	62	.592	+ 7	Patrick Moran	449,898
1916—Second	91	62	.595	2½	Patrick Moran	515,365
1917—Second	87	65	.572	10	Patrick Moran	354,428
1918—Sixth	55	68	.447	26	Patrick Moran	122,266
1919—Eighth	47	90	.343	47½	John Coombs, Clifford Cravath	240,424
1920—Eighth	62	91	.405	30½	Clifford (Gavvy) Cravath	330,998
1921—Eighth	51	103	.331	43½	William Donovan, Irvin Wilhelm	273,961
1922—Seventh	57	96	.373	35½	Irvin Wilhelm	232,471
1923—Eighth	50	104	.325	45½	Arthur Fletcher	228,168
1924—Seventh	55	96	.364	37	Arthur Fletcher	299,818
1925—Sixth†	68	85	.444	27	Arthur Fletcher	304,905
1926—Eighth	58	93	.384	29½	Arthur Fletcher	240,600
1927—Eighth	51	103	.331	43	John (Stuffy) McInnis	305,420
1928—Eighth	43	109	.283	51	Burton Shotton	182,168
1929—Fifth	71	82	.464	27½	Burton Shotton	281,200
1930—Eighth	52	102	.338	40	Burton Shotton	299,007
1931—Sixth	66	88	.429	35	Burton Shotton	284,849
1932—Fourth	78	76	.506	12	Burton Shotton	268,914
1933—Seventh	60	92	.395	31	Burton Shotton	156,421
1934—Seventh	56	93	.376	37	James Wilson	169,885
1935—Seventh	64	89	.418	35½	James Wilson	205,470
1936—Eighth	54	100	.351	38	James Wilson	249,219
1937—Seventh	61	92	.399	34½	James Wilson	212,790
1938—Eighth	45	105	.300	43	James Wilson, John Lobert	166,111
1939—Eighth	45	106	.298	50½	James (Doc) Prothro	277,973
1940—Eighth	50	103	.327	50	James (Doc) Prothro	207,177
1941—Eighth	43	111	.279	57	James (Doc) Prothro	231,401
1942—Eighth	42	109	.278	62½	John (Hans) Lobert	230,183
1943—Seventh	64	90	.416	41	Stanley Harris, Fred Fitzsimmons	466,975
1944—Eighth	61	92	.399	43½	Fred Fitzsimmons	369,586

PHILADELPHIA PHILLIES' YEARLY STANDING—Continued

Year—Position	W.	L.	Pct.	*G.B.	Manager	Attendance
1945—Eighth	46	108	.299	52	Fred Fitzsimmons, Ben Chapman	285,057
1946—Fifth.............	69	85	.448	28	W. Benjamin Chapman	1,045,247
1947—Seventh†	62	92	.403	32	W. Benjamin Chapman	907,332
1948—Sixth............	66	88	.429	25½	B. Chap'n, Al Cooke, Ed Sawyer	767,429
1949—Third	81	73	.526	16	Edwin Sawyer	819,698
1950—First.............	91	63	.591	+ 2	Edwin Sawyer	1,217,035
1951—Fifth.............	73	81	.474	23½	Edwin Sawyer	937,658
1952—Fourth..........	87	67	.565	9½	Edwin Sawyer, Stephen O'Neill	775,417
1953—Third†	83	71	.539	22	Stephen O'Neill..	853,644
1954—Fourth..........	75	79	.487	22	Stephen O'Neill, Terry Moore	738,991
1955—Fourth..........	77	77	.500	21½	E. Mayo Smith	922,886
1956—Fifth.............	71	83	.461	22	E. Mayo Smith	934,798
1957—Fifth.............	77	77	.500	19	E. Mayo Smith	1,146,230
1958—Eighth	69	85	.448	23	E. Mayo Smith, Edwin Sawyer....................	931,110
1959—Eighth	64	90	.416	23	Edwin Sawyer	802,815
1960—Eighth	59	95	.383	36	E. Sawyer, Andy Cohen, G. Mauch	862,205
1961—Eighth	47	107	.305	46	Gene Mauch	590,039
1962—Seventh	81	80	.503	20	Gene Mauch	762,034
1963—Fourth..........	87	75	.537	12	Gene Mauch	907,141
1964—Second†	92	70	.568	1	Gene Mauch	1,425,891
1965—Sixth............	85	76	.528	11½	Gene Mauch	1,166,376
1966—Fourth..........	87	75	.537	8	Gene Mauch	1,108,201
1967—Fifth.............	82	80	.506	19½	Gene Mauch	828,888
1968—Seventh†	76	86	.469	21	G. Mauch, George Myatt, Robert Skinner	664,546

EAST DIVISION

Year—Position	W.	L.	Pct.	*G.B.	Manager	Attendance
1969—Fifth.............	63	99	.389	37	Robert Skinner, George Myatt....................	519,414
1970—Fifth.............	73	88	.453	15½	Frank Lucchesi	708,247
1971—Sixth............	67	95	.414	30	Frank Lucchesi	1,511,223
1972—Sixth............	59	97	.378	37½	Frank Lucchesi, Paul Owens......................	1,343,329
1973—Sixth............	71	91	.438	11½	Daniel L. Ozark	1,475,934
1974—Third	80	82	.494	8	Daniel L. Ozark	1,808,648
1975—Second........	86	76	.531	6½	Daniel L. Ozark	1,909,233
1976—First‡..........	101	61	.623	+ 9	Daniel L. Ozark	2,480,150
1977—First‡..........	101	61	.623	+ 5	Daniel L. Ozark	2,700,070
1978—First‡..........	90	72	.556	+ 1½	Daniel L. Ozark	2,583,389
1979—Fourth..........	84	78	.519	14	Daniel L. Ozark, G. Dallas Green...............	2,775,011
1980—First§	91	71	.562	+ 1	G. Dallas Green...	2,651,650
1981—1st/3rd.........	59	48	.551	x	G. Dallas Green...	1,638,752
1982—Second........	89	73	.549	3	Patrick Corrales..	2,376,394
1983—First§	90	72	.556	+ 6	Pat Corrales, Paul Owens..........................	2,128,339
1984—Fourth..........	81	81	.500	15½	Paul Owens..	2.062,693

*Games behind winner. †Tied for position. ‡Lost Championship Series. §Won Championship Series. xFirst half 34-21; second 25-27.

First Game Played at Veterans Stadium

The Phillies made a successful debut in their $49.5-million stadium, beating the Expos, 4-1, on April 10, 1971.

Trailing, 1-0, in the sixth, Don Money treated the 55,352 fans in attendance to the stadium's first home run, tying the game. The Phillies went ahead in the same inning, getting RBIs from Roger Freed and Tim McCarver. Larry Bowa tripled and scored the final run in the seventh.

Although all 56,371 of the stadium's seats were sold, cold weather prevented many people from showing up.

PHILADELPHIA PHILLIES

(7) JOHN FELSKE—Manager

No. PITCHERS—	Bts.	Thrs.	Hgt.	Wgt.	Birth-date	1984 Club	IP.	W.	L.	ERA.
47 Andersen, Larry	R	R	6:03	205	5- 6-53	Philadelphia	90.2	3	7	2.38
39 Campbell, Bill	R	R	6:04	200	8- 9-48	Philadelphia	81.1	6	5	3.43
Caraballo, Ramon	R	R	6:04	200	8-20-62	Spartanburg	70.0	6	2	2.19
						Peninsula	1.0	0	0	0.00
32 Carlton, Steve	L	L	6:05	212	12-22-44	Philadelphia	229.0	13	7	3.58
42 Carman, Don	L	L	6:03	190	8-14-59	Portland	55.2	3	3	5.34
						Philadelphia	13.1	0	1	5.40
Childress, Rocky	R	R	6:02	195	2-18-62	Reading	103.1	7	6	2.96
Cole, Rodger	R	R	5:07	160	3-21-61	Portland	96.1	3	5	5.33
						Reading	63.2	3	4	1.98
40 Denny, John	R	R	6:03	190	11- 8-52	Philadelphia	154.1	7	7	2.45
46 Gross, Kevin	R	R	6:05	203	6- 8-61	Philadelphia	129.0	8	5	4.12
19 Holland, Al	R	L	5:11	210	8-16-52	Philadelphia	98.1	5	10	3.39
49 Hudson, Charles	R	R	6:03	185	3-16-59	Philadelphia	173.2	9	11	4.04
24 Koosman, Jerry	R	L	6:02	225	12-23-43	Philadelphia	224.0	14	15	3.25
Maddux, Mike	R	R	6:02	180	8-27-61	Portland	45.0	2	4	5.80
						Reading	116.0	3	12	5.04
Olwine, Ed	L	L	6:02	165	5-28-58	Tidewater	68.0	4	2	2.38
48 Rawley, Shane	R	L	6:00	180	7-27-55	New York AL	42.0	2	3	6.21
						Philadelphia	120.1	10	6	3.81

CATCHERS—						1984 Club	G.	HR.	RBI.	Avg.
Daulton, Darren	L	R	6:02	190	1- 3-62	Portland	80	7	38	.298
6 Diaz, Bo	R	R	5:11	200	3-23-53	Reading	3	1	3	.429
						Philadelphia	27	1	9	.213
Diaz, Mike	R	R	6:02	195	4-15-53	Portland	105	14	46	.270
17 Virgil, Ozzie	R	R	6:01	205	12- 7-56	Philadelphia	141	18	68	.261
15 Wockenfuss, John	R	R	6:00	190	2-27-49	Philadelphia	86	6	24	.289

INFIELDERS—										
16 Aguayo, Luis	R	R	5:09	185	3-13-59	Portland	3	1	2	.538
						Philadelphia	58	3	11	.278
22 Corcoran, Tim	L	L	5:11	175	4-19-53	Philadelphia	102	5	36	.341
11 DeJesus, Ivan	R	R	5:11	182	1- 9-53	Philadelphia	144	0	35	.257
Jackson, Ken	R	R	5:09	162	5-27-63	Reading	72	1	19	.240
						Peninsula	71	3	22	.225
James, Chris	R	R	6:01	190	10- 4-62	Reading	128	8	57	.256
30 Jeltz, Steve	R	R	5:11	170	5-28-59	Portland	134	2	46	.220
						Philadelphia	28	1	7	.206
12 Matuszek, Len	L	R	6:02	198	9-27-54	Philadelphia	101	12	43	.248
52 Melendez, Francisco	L	L	6:00	170	1-25-64	Portland	128	3	65	.315
						Philadelphia	21	0	2	.130
0 Oliver, Al	L	L	6:01	185	10-14-46	San Francisco	91	0	34	.298
						Philadelphia	28	0	14	.312
8 Samuel, Juan	R	R	5:11	168	12- 9-60	Philadelphia	160	15	69	.272
20 Schmidt, Mike	R	R	6:02	203	9-27-49	Philadelphia	151	36	106	.277
53 Schu, Rick	R	R	6:00	170	1-26-62	Portland	140	12	72	.301
						Philadelphia	17	2	5	.276

OUTFIELDERS—										
21 Gross, Greg	L	L	5:11	175	8- 1-52	Philadelphia	112	0	16	.322
9 Hayes, Von	L	R	6:05	185	8-31-58	Philadelphia	152	16	67	.292
23 Lefebvre, Joe	L	L	5:10	180	2-22-56	Reading	6	0	0	.333
						Philadelphia	52	3	18	.250
31 Maddox, Garry	R	R	6:03	190	9- 1-49	Philadelphia	77	5	19	.282
29 Russell, John	R	R	6:00	190	2- 5-61	Portland	93	19	77	.289
						Philadelphia	39	2	11	.283
Salava, Randy	L	R	6:01	190	7-18-59	Portland	110	11	69	.287
26 Stone, Jeff	L	R	6:00	175	12-26-60	Portland	82	7	34	.307
						Philadelphia	51	1	15	.362
27 Wilson, Glenn	R	R	6:01	190	12-22-58	Philadelphia	132	6	31	.240

DAVE BRISTOL (4)—Coach   LEE ELIA ( )—Coach
CLAUDE OSTEEN (3)—Coach   MIKE RYAN (25)—Coach
DEL UNSER ( )—Coach

VETERANS STADIUM

	Seats	Prices
Super Boxes—Fourth Level	890	*
Deluxe Boxes	1,276	*
Field Boxes................................	10,361	$8.50
Terrace Boxes..............................	10,870	7.50
Loge Boxes	5,711	7.50
Upper Reserved, 600 Level..............	11,367	6.00
Upper Reserved, 700 Level..............	9,383	5.00
General Admission.......................	15,147	3.00

*Sold only on season basis.

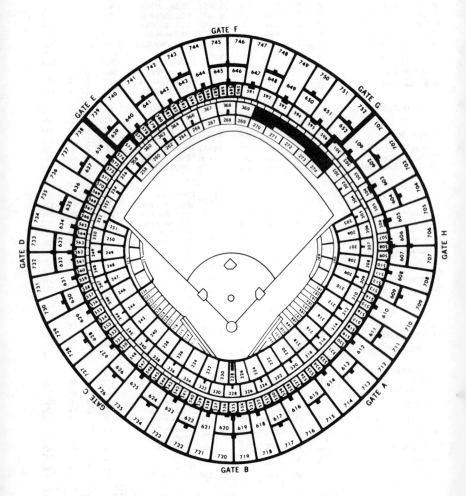

Veterans Stadium, Philadelphia
First N.L. Game Played April 10, 1971

Chuck Tanner

PITTSBURGH PIRATES

Chairman of the Board—John W. Galbreath
President—Daniel M. Galbreath
Executive Vice-President—Harding Peterson
Vice-President-Business—Joseph M. O'Toole
Vice-Pres.-P.R.-Marketing—Jack Schrom
Director of Publicity—Ed Wade
Assistant Directors of Publicity—Sally O'Leary, Greg Johnson
Publicity Assistant—James G. Bowden
Traveling Secretary—Charles Muse
Offices—Three Rivers Stadium
Three Rivers Stadium Capacity—58,429

Farm System: AAA—Hawaii. AA—Nashua. A—Prince William, Macon, Watertown. Rookie—Bradenton.

PITTSBURGH PIRATES' YEARLY STANDING

Year—Position	W.	L.	Pct.	*G.B.	Manager	Attendance
1901—First	90	49	.647	+ 7½	Fred Clarke	251,955
1902—First	103	36	.741	+27½	Fred Clarke	243,826
1903—First	91	49	.650	+ 6½	Fred Clarke	326,855
1904—Fourth	87	66	.569	19	Fred Clarke	340,615
1905—Second	96	57	.627	9	Fred Clarke	369,124
1906—Third	93	60	.608	23½	Fred Clarke	394,877
1907—Second	91	63	.591	17	Fred Clarke	319,506
1908—Second†	98	56	.636	1	Fred Clarke	382,444
1909—First	110	42	.724	+ 6½	Fred Clarke	534,950
1910—Third	86	67	.562	17½	Fred Clarke	436,586
1911—Third	85	69	.552	14½	Fred Clarke	432,000
1912—Second	93	58	.616	10	Fred Clarke	384,000
1913—Fourth	78	71	.523	21½	Fred Clarke	296,000
1914—Seventh	69	85	.448	25½	Fred Clarke	139,620
1915—Fifth	73	81	.474	18	Fred Clarke	225,743
1916—Sixth	65	89	.422	29	James Callahan	289,132
1917—Eighth	51	103	.331	47	J. Callahan, J. Wagner, H. Bezdek	192,807
1918—Fourth	65	60	.520	17	Hugo Bezdek	213,610
1919—Fourth	71	68	.511	24½	Hugo Bezdek	276,810
1920—Fourth	79	75	.513	14	George Gibson	429,037
1921—Second	90	63	.588	4	George Gibson	701,567
1922—Third†	85	69	.552	8	Geo. Gibson, William McKechnie	523,675
1923—Third	87	67	.565	8½	William McKechnie	611,082
1924—Third	90	63	.588	3	William McKechnie	736,883
1925—First	95	58	.621	+ 8½	William McKechnie	804,354
1926—Third	84	69	.549	4½	William McKechnie	798,542
1927—First	94	60	.610	+ 1½	Owen (Donie) Bush	869,720
1928—Fourth	85	67	.559	9	Owen (Donie) Bush	495,070
1929—Second	88	65	.575	10½	Owen (Donie) Bush, Jewel Ens	491,377
1930—Fifth	80	74	.519	12	Jewel Ens	357,795
1931—Fifth	75	79	.487	26	Jewel Ens	260,392
1932—Second	86	68	.558	4	George Gibson	287,262
1933—Second	87	67	.565	5	George Gibson	288,747
1934—Fifth	74	76	.493	19½	Geo. Gibson, Harold Traynor	322,622
1935—Fourth	86	67	.562	13½	Harold (Pie) Traynor	352,885
1936—Fourth	84	70	.545	8	Harold (Pie) Traynor	372,524
1937—Third	86	68	.558	10	Harold (Pie) Traynor	459,679
1938—Second	86	64	.573	2	Harold (Pie) Traynor	641,033
1939—Sixth	68	85	.444	28½	Harold (Pie) Traynor	376,734
1940—Fourth	78	76	.506	22½	Frank Frisch	507,934
1941—Fourth	81	73	.526	19	Frank Frisch	482,241
1942—Fifth	66	81	.449	36½	Frank Frisch	448,897
1943—Fourth	80	74	.519	25	Frank Frisch	604,278
1944—Second	90	63	.588	14½	Frank Frisch	498,740

PITTSBURGH PIRATES' YEARLY STANDING—Continued

Year—Position	W.	L.	Pct.	*G.B.	Manager	Attendance
1945—Fourth	82	72	.532	16	Frank Frisch	604,694
1946—Seventh	63	91	.409	34	Frank Frisch	749,962
1947—Seventh†	62	92	.403	32	William Herman, William Burwell	1,283,531
1948—Fourth	83	71	.539	8½	William Meyer	1,517,021
1949—Sixth	71	83	.461	26	William Meyer	1,499,435
1950—Eighth	57	96	.373	33½	William Meyer	1,166,267
1951—Seventh	64	90	.416	32½	William Meyer	980,590
1952—Eighth	42	112	.273	54½	William Meyer	686,673
1953—Eighth	50	104	.325	55	Fred Haney	572,757
1954—Eighth	53	101	.344	44	Fred Haney	475,494
1955—Eighth	60	94	.390	38½	Fred Haney	469,397
1956—Seventh	66	88	.429	27	Robert Bragan	949,878
1957—Seventh†	62	92	.403	33	Robert Bragan, Daniel Murtaugh	850,732
1958—Second	84	70	.545	8	Daniel Murtaugh	1,311,988
1959—Fourth	78	76	.506	9	Daniel Murtaugh	1,359,917
1960—First	95	59	.617	+ 7	Daniel Murtaugh	1,705,828
1961—Sixth	75	79	.487	18	Daniel Murtaugh	1,199,128
1962—Fourth	93	68	.578	8	Daniel Murtaugh	1,090,648
1963—Eighth	74	88	.457	25	Daniel Murtaugh	783,648
1964—Sixth†	80	82	.494	13	Daniel Murtaugh	759,496
1965—Third	90	72	.556	7	Harry Walker	909,279
1966—Third	92	70	.568	3	Harry Walker	1,196,618
1967—Sixth	81	81	.500	20½	Harry Walker, Daniel Murtaugh	907,012
1968—Sixth	80	82	.494	17	Lawrence Shepard	693,485

EAST DIVISION

Year—Position	W.	L.	Pct.	*G.B.	Manager	Attendance
1969—Third	88	74	.543	12	Law. Shepard, Alex Grammas	769,369
1970—First‡	89	73	.549	+ 5	Daniel Murtaugh	1,341,947
1971—First§	97	65	.599	+ 7	Daniel Murtaugh	1,501,132
1972—First‡	96	59	.619	+11	William Virdon	1,427,460
1973—Third	80	82	.494	2½	William Virdon, Daniel Murtaugh	1,319,913
1974—First‡	88	74	.543	+ 1½	Daniel Murtaugh	1,110,552
1975—First‡	92	69	.571	+ 6½	Daniel Murtaugh	1,270,018
1976—Second	92	70	.568	9	Daniel Murtaugh	1,025,945
1977—Second	96	66	.593	5	Charles Tanner	1,237,349
1978—Second	88	73	.547	1½	Charles Tanner	964,106
1979—First§	98	64	.605	+2	Charles Tanner	1,435,454
1980—Third	83	79	.512	8	Charles Tanner	1,646,757
1981—4th/6th	46	56	.451	x	Charles Tanner	541,789
1982—Fourth	84	78	.519	8	Charles Tanner	1,024,106
1983—Second	84	78	.519	6	Charles Tanner	1,225,916
1984—Sixth	75	87	.463	21½	Charles Tanner	773,500

*Games behind winner. †Tied for position. ‡Lost Championship Series. §Won Championship Series. xFirst half 25-23; second 21-33.

First Game Played at Three Rivers Stadium

Lee May's ninth-inning single drove in Tony Perez with the winning run as the Cincinnati Reds spoiled the Pirates' home opener, 3-2, on July 16, 1970.

Playing before 48,846, the largest crowd in Pittsburgh baseball history, the Pirates jumped on top in the first when Richie Hebner singled and scored the first run in the stadium.

Perez gave the Reds a brief 2-1 lead with a fifth-inning homer, but Willie Stargell tied the game with a homer in the sixth.

PITTSBURGH PIRATES

(7) CHUCK TANNER—Manager

No. PITCHERS—	Bts.	Thrs.	Hgt.	Wgt.	Birth-date	1984 Club	IP.	W.	L.	ERA.
34 Bielecki, Mike	R	R	6:03	200	7-31-59	Hawaii	187.2	19	3	2.97
						Pittsburgh	4.1	0	0	0.00
45 Candelaria, John	B	L	6:07	250	11- 6-53	Pittsburgh	185.1	12	11	2.72
25 DeLeon, Jose	R	R	6:03	219	12-20-60	Pittsburgh	192.1	7	13	3.74
35 Green, Chris	L	L	6:04	207	9- 5-60	Hawaii	16.2	2	2	5.94
						Pittsburgh	3.0	0	0	6.00
47 Guante, Cecilio	R	R	6:03	200	2- 2-60	Nashua	3.0	0	0	3.00
						Pittsburgh	41.1	2	3	2.61
46 Krawczyk, Ray	R	R	6:01	184	10- 9-59	Hawaii	72.0	4	5	2.13
						Pittsburgh	5.1	0	0	3.38
49 McWilliams, Larry	L	L	6:05	181	2-10-54	Pittsburgh	227.1	12	11	2.93
29 Rhoden, Rick	R	R	6:04	203	5-16-53	Pittsburgh	238.1	14	9	2.72
43 Robinson, Don	R	R	6:04	225	6- 8-57	Pittsburgh	122.0	5	6	3.02
38 Sarmiento, Manny	R	R	5:11	188	2- 2-56	Pittsburgh	(Did not play)			
19 Scurry, Rod	L	L	6:02	195	3-17-56	Pittsburgh	46.1	5	6	2.53
27 Tekulve, Kent	R	R	6:04	185	3- 5-47	Pittsburgh	88.0	3	9	2.66
22 Tunnell, Lee	R	R	6:01	180	10-30-60	Pittsburgh	68.1	1	7	5.27
18 Walk, Bob	R	R	6:04	208	11-26-56	Hawaii	127.1	9	5	2.26
						Pittsburgh	10.1	1	1	2.61
41 Winn, Jim	R	R	6:03	210	9-23-59	Hawaii	44.2	6	1	3.43
						Pittsburgh	18.2	1	0	3.86
44 Zaske, Jeff	R	R	6:05	193	10- 6-60	Hawaii	60.1	2	4	3.58
						Pittsburgh	5.0	0	0	0.00

CATCHERS—	Bts.	Thrs.	Hgt.	Wgt.	Birth-date	1984 Club	G.	HR.	RBI.	Avg.
14 Ortiz, Junior	R	R	5:10	170	10-24-59	New York NL	40	0	11	.198
6 Pena, Tony	R	R	6:00	181	6- 4-57	Pittsburgh	147	15	78	.286
57 Rodriguez, Ruben	R	R	6:00	163	8- 4-64	Nashua	87	4	32	.219

INFIELDERS—	Bts.	Thrs.	Hgt.	Wgt.	Birth-date	1984 Club	G.	HR.	RBI.	Avg.
37 Belliard, Rafael	R	R	5:06	150	10-24-61	Pittsburgh	20	0	0	.227
Foli, Tim	R	R	6:00	175	12- 8-50	New York AL	61	0	16	.252
28 Gonzalez, Denny	R	R	5:11	184	7-22-63	Hawaii	113	15	67	.300
						Pittsburgh	26	0	4	.183
58 Khalifa, Sam	R	R	5:11	170	12- 5-63	Nashua	91	1	36	.238
5 Madlock, Bill	R	R	5:11	206	1-12-51	Pittsburgh	103	4	44	.253
2 Morrison, Jim	R	R	5:11	185	9-23-52	Pittsburgh	100	11	45	.286
3 Ray, Johnny	B	R	5:11	185	3- 1-57	Pittsburgh	155	6	67	.312
60 Roberts, Leon	B	R	5:07	160	10-27-63	Prince William	134	8	77	.301
30 Thompson, Jason	L	L	6:03	218	7- 6-54	Pittsburgh	154	17	74	.254
50 Vargas, Hedi	R	R	6:04	212	2-23-59	Hawaii	43	9	30	.293
						Pittsburgh	18	0	2	.226
15 Wotus, Ron	R	R	6:01	180	3- 3-61	Hawaii	61	5	23	.254
						Pittsburgh	27	0	2	.218

OUTFIELDERS—	Bts.	Thrs.	Hgt.	Wgt.	Birth-date	1984 Club	G.	HR.	RBI.	Avg.
52 Bonilla, Bobby	B	R	6:03	210	2-23-63	Nashua	136	11	71	.264
13 Davis, Trench	L	L	6:03	171	9-12-60	Hawaii	141	1	39	.259
10 Distefano, Benny	L	L	6:01	205	1-23-62	Hawaii	66	6	33	.304
						Pittsburgh	45	3	9	.167
51 Frobel, Doug	L	R	6:04	193	6- 6-59	Pittsburgh	126	12	28	.203
17 Hendrick, George	R	R	6:05	195	10-18-49	St. Louis	120	9	69	.277
Kemp, Steve	L	L	6:00	190	8- 7-54	New York AL	94	7	41	.291
16 Mazzilli, Lee	B	R	6:01	190	3-25-55	Pittsburgh	111	4	21	.237
11 Orsulak, Joe	L	L	6:01	185	5-31-62	Hawaii	98	3	53	.284
						Pittsburgh	32	0	3	.254
36 Wynne, Marvell	L	L	5:11	169	12-17-59	Pittsburgh	154	0	39	.266

STEVE DEMETER (32)—Coach   MILT GRAFF (31)—Coach
GRANT JACKSON (23)—Coach   RICK PETERSON (55)—Coach
BOB SKINNER (48)—Coach

THREE RIVERS STADIUM

	Seats	Prices
Field Boxes	8,089	$8.50
Loge Boxes	8,731	8.50
Lounge Boxes	1,228	*
Special Boxes	150	*
Club Boxes	2,216	8.50
Club Reserved	2,612	4.00
Terrace Boxes	2,839	7.00
Terrace Reserved	13,794	6.00
Loge Reserved	2,243	4.00
General Admission	16,257	2.50

*Sold on season basis only.

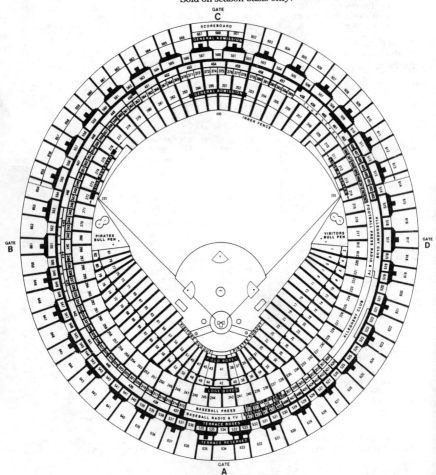

**Three Rivers Stadium, Pittsburgh
First N.L. Game Played July 16, 1970**

ST. LOUIS CARDINALS

Chairman of the Board-President-CEO—August A. Busch, Jr.
Executive Vice-President—Fred L. Kuhlmann
Vice-President—August A. Busch III
Manager—Whitey Herzog
Vice Pres.-Business Operations—Gary Blase
Director of Public Relations—Jim Toomey
Director of Player Development—Lee Thomas
Director of Scouting—Fred McAlister
Director of Minor League Operations—Paul Fauks
Director of Merchandising—Marty Hendin
Traveling Secretary—C. J. Cherre
Offices—Busch Stadium
Busch Stadium Capacity—50,222

Farm System: AAA—Louisville. AA—Arkansas. A—Erie, St. Petersburg, Savannah, Springfield, Ill. Rookie—Johnson City.

Whitey Herzog

ST. LOUIS CARDINALS' YEARLY STANDING

Year—Position	W.	L.	Pct.	*G.B.	Manager	Attendance
1901—Fourth	76	64	.543	14½	Patrick Donovan	379,988
1902—Sixth	56	78	.418	44½	Patrick Donovan	226,417
1903—Eighth	43	94	.314	46½	Patrick Donovan	226,538
1904—Fifth	75	79	.487	31½	Charles (Kid) Nichols	386,750
1905—Sixth	58	96	.377	47½	C. Nichols, J. Burke, Stan Robison	292,800
1906—Seventh	52	98	.347	63	John McCloskey	283,770
1907—Eighth	52	101	.340	55½	John McCloskey	185,377
1908—Eighth	49	105	.318	50	John McCloskey	205,129
1909—Seventh	54	98	.355	56	Roger Bresnahan	299,982
1910—Seventh	63	90	.412	40½	Roger Bresnahan	355,668
1911—Fifth	75	74	.503	22	Roger Bresnahan	447,768
1912—Sixth	63	90	.412	41	Roger Bresnahan	241,759
1913—Eighth	51	99	.340	49	Miller Huggins	203,531
1914—Third	81	72	.529	13	Miller Huggins	256,099
1915—Sixth	72	81	.471	18½	Miller Huggins	252,666
1916—Seventh†	60	93	.392	33½	Miller Huggins	224,308
1917—Third	82	70	.539	15	Miller Huggins	288,491
1918—Eighth	51	78	.395	33	John (Jack) Hendricks	110,599
1919—Seventh	54	83	.394	40½	Branch Rickey	167,059
1920—Fifth†	75	79	.487	18	Branch Rickey	326,836
1921—Third	87	66	.569	7	Branch Rickey	384,773
1922—Third†	85	69	.552	8	Branch Rickey	536,998
1923—Fifth	79	74	.516	16	Branch Rickey	338,551
1924—Sixth	65	89	.422	28½	Branch Rickey	272,885
1925—Fourth	77	76	.503	18	B. Rickey, Rogers Hornsby	404,959
1926—First	89	65	.578	+ 2	Rogers Hornsby	668,428
1927—Second	92	61	.601	1½	Robert O'Farrell	749,340
1928—First	95	59	.617	+ 2	William McKechnie	761,574
1929—Fourth	78	74	.513	20	Wm. McKechnie, Wm. Southworth	399,887
1930—First	92	62	.597	+ 2	Charles (Gabby) Street	508,501
1931—First	101	53	.656	+13	Charles (Gabby) Street	608,535
1932—Sixth†	72	82	.468	18	Charles (Gabby) Street	279,219
1933—Fifth	82	71	.536	9½	Gabby Street, Frank Frisch	256,171
1934—First	95	58	.621	+ 2	Frank Frisch	325,056
1935—Second	96	58	.623	4	Frank Frisch	506,084
1936—Second†	87	67	.565	5	Frank Frisch	448,078
1937—Fourth	81	73	.526	15	Frank Frisch	430,811
1938—Sixth	71	80	.470	17½	Frank Frisch, Mike Gonzalez	291,418
1939—Second	92	61	.601	4½	Raymond Blades	400,245
1940—Third	84	69	.549	16	R. Blades, M. Gonzalez, Southworth	324,078
1941—Second	97	56	.634	2½	William Southworth	633,645
1942—First	106	48	.688	+ 2	William Southworth	553,552
1943—First	105	49	.682	+18	William Southworth	517,135
1944—First	105	49	.682	+14½	William Southworth	461,968

ST. LOUIS CARDINALS' YEARLY STANDING—Continued

Year—Position	W.	L.	Pct.	*G.B.	Manager	Attendance
1945—Second........	95	59	.617	3	William Southworth..................................	594,630
1946—First‡.........	98	58	.628	+ 2	Edwin Dyer	1,061,807
1947—Second........	89	65	.578	5	Edwin Dyer	1,247,913
1948—Second........	85	69	.552	6½	Edwin Dyer	1,111,440
1949—Second........	96	58	.623	1	Edwin Dyer	1,430,676
1950—Fifth............	78	75	.510	12½	Edwin Dyer	1,093,411
1951—Third	81	73	.526	15½	Martin Marion	1,013,429
1952—Third	88	66	.571	8½	Edward Stanky	913,113
1953—Third†	83	71	.539	22	Edward Stanky	880,242
1954—Sixth...........	72	82	.468	25	Edward Stanky	1,039,698
1955—Seventh......	68	86	.442	30½	Edward Stanky, Harry Walker	849,130
1956—Fourth........	76	78	.494	17	Fred Hutchinson	1,029,773
1957—Second........	87	67	.565	8	Fred Hutchinson	1,183,575
1958—Fifth†..........	72	82	.468	20	Fred Hutchinson, Stanley Hack................	1,063,730
1959—Seventh......	71	83	.461	16	Solly Hemus	929,953
1960—Third	86	68	.558	9	Solly Hemus..	1,096,632
1961—Fifth............	80	74	.519	13	Solly Hemus, John Keane.......................	855,305
1962—Sixth...........	84	78	.519	17½	John Keane..	953,895
1963—Second........	93	69	.574	6	John Keane..	1,170,546
1964—First............	93	69	.574	+ 1	John Keane..	1,143,294
1965—Seventh......	80	81	.497	16½	Albert (Red) Schoendienst......................	1,241,201
1966—Sixth...........	83	79	.512	12	Albert (Red) Schoendienst......................	1,712,980
1967—First............	101	60	.627	+10½	Albert (Red) Schoendienst......................	2,090,145
1968—First............	97	65	.599	+ 9	Albert (Red) Schoendienst......................	2,011,167

EAST DIVISION

Year—Position	W.	L.	Pct.	*G.B.	Manager	Attendance
1969—Fourth........	87	75	.537	13	Albert (Red) Schoendienst......................	1,682,783
1970—Fourth........	76	86	.469	13	Albert (Red) Schoendienst......................	1,629,736
1971—Second........	90	72	.556	7	Albert (Red) Schoendienst......................	1,604,671
1972—Fourth........	75	81	.481	21½	Albert (Red) Schoendienst......................	1,196,894
1973—Second........	81	81	.500	1½	Albert (Red) Schoendienst......................	1,574,046
1974—Second........	86	75	.534	1½	Albert (Red) Schoendienst......................	1,838,413
1975—Third†	82	80	.506	10½	Albert (Red) Schoendienst......................	1,695,270
1976—Fifth............	72	90	.444	29	Albert (Red) Schoendienst......................	1,207,079
1977—Third	83	79	.512	18	Vernon Rapp..	1,659,287
1978—Fifth	69	93	.426	21	Vernon Rapp, Kenton Boyer....................	1,278,215
1979—Third...........	86	76	.531	12	Kenton Boyer..	1,627,256
1980—Fourth........	74	88	.457	17	K. Boyer, W. Herzog, A. Schoendienst	1,385,147
1981—2nd/2nd.......	59	43	.578	§	Dorrel (Whitey) Herzog............................	1,010,247
1982—First x.........	92	70	.568	+ 3	Dorrel (Whitey) Herzog............................	2,111,906
1983—Fourth........	79	83	.488	11	Dorrel (Whitey) Herzog............................	2,317,914
1984—Third...........	84	78	.519	12½	Dorrel (Whitey) Herzog............................	2,037,448

*Games behind winner. †Tied for position. ‡Defeated Brooklyn in pennant playoff. §First half 30-20; second 29-23. xWon Championship Series.

First Game Played at Busch Stadium

The Cardinals opened new Busch Stadium with a thrilling 4-3, 12-inning victory over the Atlanta Braves on May 12, 1966.

The winning marker came home in the 12th on Lou Brock's single. Jerry Buchek's ninth-inning single tied the game, 3-3, and sent it into extra innings. The Braves' Felipe Alou homered twice in a losing cause.

ST. LOUIS CARDINALS
(24) WHITEY HERZOG—Manager

No. PITCHERS—	Bts.	Thrs.	Hgt.	Wgt.	Birth-date	1984 Club	IP.	W.	L.	ERA.
13 Allen, Neil	R	R	6:02	190	1-24-58	St. Louis	119.0	9	6	3.55
47 Andujar, Joaquin	B	R	5:11	180	12-21-52	St. Louis	261.1	20	14	3.34
43 Citarella, Ralph	R	R	6:00	180	2- 7-58	Louisville	89.2	9	2	3.91
						St. Louis	22.1	0	1	3.63
34 Cox, Danny	R	R	6:04	230	9-21-59	Louisville	42.1	4	1	2.13
						St. Louis	156.1	9	11	4.04
46 Dayley, Ken	L	L	6:00	171	2-25-59	Richmond	62.1	5	1	4.04
						Atlanta	18.2	0	3	5.30
						St. Louis	5.0	0	2	18.00
31 Forsch, Bob	R	R	6:01	215	1-13-50	Louisville	96.1	4	6	3.27
						St. Louis	52.1	2	5	6.02
35 Hagen, Kevin	R	R	6:02	185	3- 8-60	Louisville	176.2	10	9	3.46
						St. Louis	7.1	1	0	2.45
44 Hassler, Andy	L	L	6:05	220	10-18-51	Arkansas	10.1	1	1	5.23
						Louisville	64.0	7	4	2.11
						St. Louis	2.1	1	0	11.57
49 Horton, Ricky	L	L	6:02	195	7-30-59	St. Louis	125.2	9	4	3.44
50 Kepshire, Kurt	L	R	6:01	180	7- 3-59	Louisville	107.2	7	5	4.60
						St. Louis	109.0	6	5	3.30
32 Lahti, Jeff	R	R	6:00	180	10- 8-56	St. Louis	84.2	4	2	3.72
39 LaPoint, Dave	L	L	6:03	215	7-29-59	St. Louis	193.0	12	10	3.96
40 Ownbey, Rick	R	R	6:03	185	10-20-57	Louisville	96.1	6	6	4.02
						St. Louis	19.0	0	3	4.74
37 Perry, Pat	L	L	6:01	170	2- 4-59	Arkansas	48.2	4	2	1.11
						Louisville	44.2	4	3	2.22
36 Rucker, Dave	L	L	6:01	190	9- 1-57	St. Louis	73.0	2	3	2.10
41 Shade, Mike	R	R	6:02	205	3- 7-61	St. Petersburg	45.2	0	2	1.38
						Arkansas	46.2	2	4	3.09
						Louisville	2.2	0	1	10.13
48 Tudor, John	L	L	6:00	185	2- 2-54	Pittsburgh	212.0	12	11	3.27
38 Worrell, Todd	R	R	6:05	200	9-28-59	Arkansas	100.1	3	10	4.49
						St. Petersburg	47.1	3	2	2.09
52 Young, John	R	L	6:02	175	12- 4-60	Arkansas	151.2	9	7	3.56

CATCHERS—	Bts.	Thrs.	Hgt.	Wgt.	Birth-date	1984 Club	G.	HR.	RBI.	Avg.
11 Brummer, Glenn	R	R	6:00	200	11-23-54	St. Louis	28	1	3	.207
						Louisville	16	1	4	.208
10 Hunt, Randy	R	R	6:00	185	1- 3-60	St. Petersburg	100	5	59	.274
						Arkansas	27	0	4	.222
23 Nieto, Tom	R	R	6:01	193	10-27-60	Louisville	77	7	34	.277
						St. Louis	33	3	12	.279
15 Porter, Darrell	L	R	6:01	202	1-17-52	St. Louis	127	11	68	.232

INFIELDERS—	Bts.	Thrs.	Hgt.	Wgt.	Birth-date	1984 Club	G.	HR.	RBI.	Avg.
5 Gonzalez, Jose	B	R	5:10	160	1-21-60	Louisville	145	3	46	.279
						St. Louis	8	0	3	.211
22 Green, David	R	R	6:01	165	12- 4-60	St. Louis	126	15	65	.268
28 Herr, Tom	B	R	6:00	185	4- 4-56	St. Louis	145	4	49	.276
7 Howe, Art	R	R	6:01	185	12-15-46	St. Louis	89	2	12	.216
19 Jorgensen, Mike	L	L	6:00	187	8-16-48	Atlanta	31	0	5	.269
						St. Louis	59	1	12	.245
53 Lozado, Willie	R	R	6:00	166	5-12-59	Milwaukee	43	1	20	.271
9 Pendleton, Terry	B	R	5:09	180	7-16-60	Louisville	91	4	44	.297
						St. Louis	67	1	33	.324
33 Rajsich, Gary	L	R	6:02	206	10-28-54	Louisville	117	29	95	.286
						St. Louis	7	0	2	.143
1 Smith, Ozzie	B	R	5:10	150	12-26-54	St. Louis	124	1	44	.257

OUTFIELDERS—	Bts.	Thrs.	Hgt.	Wgt.	Birth-date	1984 Club	G.	HR.	RBI.	Avg.
26 Braun, Steve	L	R	5:10	175	5- 8-48	St. Louis	86	0	16	.276
29 Coleman, Vince	B	R	6:00	170	9-22-61	Louisville	152	4	48	.257
12 Ford, Curt	L	R	5:10	150	10-11-60	Arkansas	118	10	78	.324
						Louisville	13	0	1	.263
25 Harper, Brian	R	R	6:02	195	10-16-59	Pittsburgh	46	2	11	.259
21 Landrum, Tito	R	R	5:11	175	10-25-54	St. Louis	105	3	26	.272
51 McGee, Willie	B	R	6:01	175	11- 2-58	St. Louis	145	6	50	.291
27 Smith, Lonnie	R	R	5:09	170	12-22-55	St. Louis	145	6	49	.250
18 Van Slyke, Andy	L	R	6:02	190	12-21-60	St. Louis	137	7	50	.244

HAL LANIER (8)—Coach   NICK LEYVA (16)—Coach
DAVE RICKETTS (3)—Coach   MIKE ROARKE (4)—Coach

RED SCHOENDIENST (2)—Coach

BUSCH MEMORIAL STADIUM

	Seats	Prices
Deluxe Boxes	390	*
Box Seats	14,643	$9.00
Reserved Seats	23,025	6.50
General Admission	8,082	4.00
Bleachers	4,082	3.00

*Sold only on season basis.

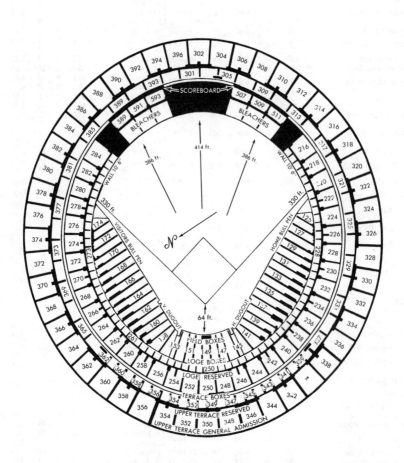

Busch Memorial Stadium, St. Louis
First N.L. Game Played May 12, 1966

Dick Williams

SAN DIEGO PADRES

Owner and Chairwoman—Joan Kroc
Directors—Ballard Smith, Anthony J. Zulfer, Jr.
President—Ballard Smith
Vice-Pres., Baseball Operations—Jack McKeon
Vice-Pres., Business Operations—Elten Schiller
Minor League Administrator—Tom Romenesko
Director of Media Relations—Bill Beck
Traveling Secretary—John Mattei
Offices—San Diego Stadium
San Diego Stadium Capacity—58,671

Farm System: AAA—Las Vegas. AA—Beaumont. A—Reno, Charleston, S.C., Spokane.

SAN DIEGO PADRES' YEARLY STANDING

WEST DIVISION

Year—Position	W.	L.	Pct.	*G.B.	Manager	Attendance
1969—Sixth	52	110	.321	41	Pedro (Preston) Gomez	512,970
1970—Sixth	63	99	.389	39	Pedro (Preston) Gomez	643,679
1971—Sixth	61	100	.379	28½	Pedro (Preston) Gomez	557,513
1972—Sixth	58	95	.379	36½	Preston Gomez, Donald Zimmer	644,273
1973—Sixth	60	102	.370	39	Donald Zimmer	611,826
1974—Sixth	60	102	.370	42	John McNamara	1,075,399
1975—Fourth	71	91	.438	37	John McNamara	1,281,747
1976—Fifth	73	89	.451	29	John McNamara	1,458,478
1977—Fifth	69	93	.426	29	John McNamara, Alvin Dark	1,376,269
1978—Fourth	84	78	.519	11	Roger Craig	1,670,107
1979—Fifth	68	93	.422	22	Roger Craig	1,456,967
1980—Sixth	73	89	.451	19½	Gerald Coleman	1,139,026
1981—6th/6th	41	69	.373	†	Frank Howard	519,161
1982—Fourth	81	81	.500	8	Richard Williams	1,607,516
1983—Fourth	81	81	.500	10	Richard Williams	1,539,815
1984—First‡	92	70	.568	+12	Richard Williams	1,983,904

*Games behind winner. †First half 23-33; second 18-36. ‡Won Championship Series.

First Game Played at San Diego Stadium

Before an opening-night crowd of 23,370, the Padres made their National League debut a success, beating the Houston Astros, 2-1, on April 8, 1969.

The Padres benefited from excellent pitching by Dick Selma, who allowed only five hits and struck out 12. San Diego managed only four hits off Don Wilson and Jack Billingham, but they were timely.

Ed Spiezio collected the Padres' first hit, a fifth-inning home run that tied the score.

SAN DIEGO PADRES

(23) DICK WILLIAMS—Manager

No. PITCHERS—	Bts.	Thrs.	Hgt.	Wgt.	Birth-date	1984 Club	IP.	W.	L.	ERA.
51 Booker, Greg	R	R	6:06	230	6-22-60	Las Vegas	55.2	4	3	5.50
						San Diego	57.1	1	1	3.30
35 DeLeon, Luis	R	R	6:01	153	8-19-58	San Diego	42.2	2	2	5.48
						Las Vegas	20.2	1	1	4.79
43 Dravecky, Dave	R	L	6:01	195	2-14-56	San Diego	156.2	9	8	2.93
54 Gossage, Rich	R	R	6:03	215	7- 5-51	San Diego	102.1	10	6	2.90
						Montreal	17.2	0	1	2.04
42 Harris, Greg	B	R	6:00	165	11- 2-55	Indianapolis	44.2	4	4	4.43
						San Diego	36.2	2	1	2.70
40 Hawkins, Andy	R	R	6:03	200	1-21-60	San Diego	146.0	8	9	4.68
31 Hoyt, LaMarr	R	R	6:03	244	1- 1-55	Chicago AL	235.2	13	18	4.47
45 Jones, Jimmy	R	R	6:02	175	4-20-64	Beaumont	85.2	7	2	2.10
37 Lefferts, Craig	L	L	6:01	180	9-29-57	San Diego	105.2	3	4	2.13
50 McCullers, Lance	L	R	6:01	185	3- 8-64	Miami	106.1	6	4	2.54
						Beaumont	55.1	4	1	2.11
46 Patterson, Bob	R	R	6:02	185	5-16-59	Las Vegas	143.1	8	9	3.27
30 Show, Eric	R	R	6:01	185	5-19-56	San Diego	206.2	15	9	3.40
Stoddard, Tim	R	R	6:07	250	1-24-53	Chicago NL	92.0	10	6	3.82
38 Thurmond, Mark	L	L	6:00	180	9-12-56	San Diego	178.2	14	8	2.97
49 Walter, Gene	L	L	6:04	200	11-22-60	Miami	59.0	3	5	2.29
						Beaumont	76.0	7	3	2.25
26 Wojna, Ed	R	R	6:01	185	8-20-60	Las Vegas	159.1	14	8	5.08

CATCHERS—						1984 Club	G.	HR.	RBI.	Avg.
15 Bochy, Bruce	R	R	6:04	210	3-16-55	Las Vegas	34	7	22	.264
						San Diego	37	4	15	.228
16 Kennedy, Terry	L	R	6:04	220	6- 4-56	San Diego	148	14	57	.240

INFIELDERS—										
7 Bevacqua, Kurt	R	R	6:02	194	1-23-47	San Diego	59	1	9	.200
11 Flannery, Tim	L	R	5:11	170	9-29-57	San Diego	86	2	10	.273
6 Garvey, Steve	R	R	5:10	190	12-22-48	San Diego	161	8	86	.284
21 Lansford, Joe	R	R	6:05	225	1-15-61	Las Vegas	131	20	80	.267
9 Nettles, Graig	L	R	6:00	187	8-20-44	San Diego	124	20	65	.228
12 Ramirez, Mario	R	R	5:09	159	9-12-57	San Diego	48	2	9	.119
Royster, Jerry	R	R	6:00	165	10-18-52	Atlanta	81	1	21	.207
1 Templeton, Garry	B	R	5:11	170	3-24-56	San Diego	148	2	35	.258
2 Wiggins, Alan	B	B	6:02	165	2-17-58	San Diego	158	3	34	.258

OUTFIELDERS—										
20 Brown, Bobby	B	R	6:01	225	5-24-54	San Diego	85	3	29	.251
28 Davis, Jerry	R	R	6:00	185	12-25-58	Las Vegas	129	9	64	.302
19 Gwynn, Tony	L	L	5:11	185	5- 9-60	San Diego	158	5	71	.351
22 Hinshaw, George	R	R	6:00	185	10-23-59	Las Vegas	121	12	53	.269
14 Martinez, Carmelo	R	R	6:02	185	7-28-60	San Diego	149	13	66	.250
18 McReynolds, Kevin	R	R	6:01	205	10-16-59	San Diego	147	20	75	.278
41 Roenicke, Ron	B	L	6:00	180	8-19-56	Las Vegas	90	8	45	.310
						San Diego	12	1	2	.300
52 Steels, James	L	L	5:10	180	5-30-61	Beaumont	127	12	81	.340

GALEN CISCO (　)—Coach　　　　　　　　　DEACON JONES (29)—Coach
HARRY DUNLOP (33)—Coach　　　　　　　　JACK KROL (34)—Coach
　　　　　　　OZZIE VIRGIL (32)—Coach

SAN DIEGO STADIUM

	Seats	Prices
Club-Press Box Seats	2,193	$7.50
Field Box Seats	6,394	7.50
Plaza Reserved Seats	11,945	7.50
Loge Reserved Seats	10,969	6.50
General Admission	16,445	3.50
Right Field Pavilion	3,373	3.50

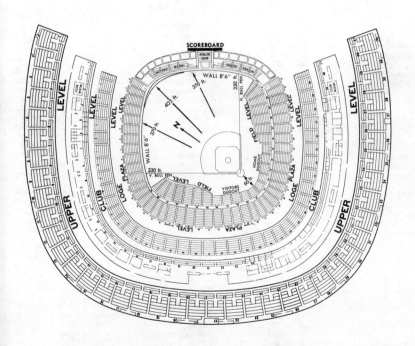

San Diego Stadium, San Diego
First N.L. Game Played April 8, 1969

SAN FRANCISCO GIANTS

President—Robert Lurie
Exec. Vice-Pres.-Administration—Corey Busch
Exec. Vice-President-Baseball Operations—Tom Haller
Vice-Pres.-Business—Pat Gallagher
Asst. VP-Baseball Operations—Ralph E. Nelson, Jr.
Minor League Consultant—John Schwarz
Director of Player Personnel/Scouting—Bob Fontaine
Field Director of Player Development—Jim Lefebvre
Publicity Director—Duffy Jennings
Traveling Secretary—Dirk Smith
Offices—Candlestick Park
Candlestick Park Capacity—58,000

Farm System: AAA—Phoenix. AA—Shreveport. A—Clinton, Fresno, Everett.

Jim Davenport

SAN FRANCISCO GIANTS' YEARLY STANDING

(New York Giants Prior to 1958)

Year—Position	W.	L.	Pct.	*G.B.	Manager	Attendance
1901—Seventh	52	85	.380	37	George S. Davis	297,650
1902—Eighth	48	88	.353	53½	H. Fogel, G. Smith, J. McGraw	302,875
1903—Second	84	55	.604	6½	John McGraw	579,530
1904—First	106	47	.693	+13	John McGraw	609,826
1905—First	105	48	.686	+9	John McGraw	552,700
1906—Second	96	56	.632	20	John McGraw	402,850
1907—Fourth	82	71	.536	25½	John McGraw	538,350
1908—Second†	98	56	.636	1	John McGraw	910,000
1909—Third	92	61	.601	18½	John McGraw	783,700
1910—Second	91	63	.591	13	John McGraw	511,785
1911—First	99	54	.647	+ 7½	John McGraw	675,000
1912—First	103	48	.682	+10	John McGraw	638,000
1913—First	101	51	.664	+12½	John McGraw	630,000
1914—Second	84	70	.545	10½	John McGraw	364,313
1915—Eighth	69	83	.454	21	John McGraw	391,850
1916—Fourth	86	66	.566	7	John McGraw	552,056
1917—First	98	56	.636	+10	John McGraw	500,264
1918—Second	71	53	.573	10½	John McGraw	256,618
1919—Second	87	53	.621	9	John McGraw	708,857
1920—Second	86	68	.558	7	John McGraw	929,609
1921—First	94	59	.614	+ 4	John McGraw	773,477
1922—First	93	61	.604	+ 7	John McGraw	945,809
1923—First	95	58	.621	+ 4½	John McGraw	820,780
1924—First	93	60	.608	+ 1½	John McGraw	844,068
1925—Second	86	66	.566	8½	John McGraw	778,993
1926—Fifth	74	77	.490	13½	John McGraw	700,362
1927—Third	92	62	.597	2	John McGraw	858,190
1928—Second	93	61	.604	2	John McGraw	916,191
1929—Third	84	67	.556	13½	John McGraw	868,806
1930—Third	87	67	.565	5	John McGraw	868,714
1931—Second	87	65	.572	13	John McGraw	812,163
1932—Sixth†	72	82	.468	18	John McGraw, William Terry	484,868
1933—First	91	61	.599	+ 5	William Terry	604,471
1934—Second	93	60	.608	2	William Terry	730,851
1935—Third	91	62	.595	8½	William Terry	748,748
1936—First	92	62	.597	+ 5	William Terry	837,952
1937—First	95	57	.625	+ 3	William Terry	926,887
1938—Third	83	67	.553	5	William Terry	799,633
1939—Fifth	77	74	.510	18½	William Terry	702,457
1940—Sixth	72	80	.474	27½	William Terry	747,852
1941—Fifth	74	79	.484	25½	William Terry	763,098
1942—Third	85	67	.559	20	Melvin Ott	779,621
1943—Eighth	55	98	.359	49½	Melvin Ott	466,095

SAN FRANCISCO GIANTS' YEARLY STANDING—Continued

Year—Position	W.	L.	Pct.	*G.B.	Manager	Attendance
1944—Fifth	67	87	.435	38	Melvin Ott	674,083
1945—Fifth	78	74	.513	19	Melvin Ott	1,016,468
1946—Eighth	61	93	.396	36	Melvin Ott	1,219,873
1947—Fourth	81	73	.526	13	Melvin Ott	1,600,793
1948—Fifth	78	76	.506	13½	Melvin Ott, Leo Durocher	1,459,269
1949—Fifth	73	81	.474	24	Leo Durocher	1,218,446
1950—Third	86	68	.558	5	Leo Durocher	1,008,876
1951—First‡	98	59	.624	+ 1	Leo Durocher	1,059,539
1952—Second	92	62	.597	4½	Leo Durocher	984,940
1953—Fifth	70	84	.455	35	Leo Durocher	811,518
1954—First	97	57	.630	+ 5	Leo Durocher	1,155,067
1955—Third	80	74	.519	18½	Leo Durocher	824,112
1956—Sixth	67	87	.435	26	William Rigney	629,179
1957—Sixth	69	85	.448	26	William Rigney	653,923
1958—Third	80	74	.519	12	William Rigney	1,272,625
1959—Third	83	71	.539	4	William Rigney	1,422,130
1960—Fifth	79	75	.513	16	William Rigney, Thomas Sheehan	1,795,356
1961—Third	85	69	.552	8	Alvin Dark	1,390,679
1962—First§	103	62	.624	+ 1	Alvin Dark	1,592,594
1963—Third	88	74	.543	11	Alvin Dark	1,571,306
1964—Fourth	90	72	.556	3	Alvin Dark	1,504,364
1965—Second	95	67	.586	2	Herman Franks	1,546,075
1966—Second	93	68	.578	1½	Herman Franks	1,657,192
1967—Second	91	71	.562	10½	Herman Franks	1,242,480
1968—Second	88	74	.543	9	Herman Franks	837,220

WEST DIVISION

Year—Position	W.	L.	Pct.	*G.B.	Manager	Attendance
1969—Second	90	72	.556	3	Clyde King	873,603
1970—Third	86	76	.531	16	Clyde King, Charles Fox	740,720
1971—Firstx	90	72	.556	+ 1	Charles Fox	1,106,043
1972—Fifth	69	86	.445	26½	Charles Fox	647,744
1973—Third	88	74	.543	11	Charles Fox	834,193
1974—Fifth	72	90	.444	30	Charles Fox, Wesley Westrum	519,987
1975—Third	80	81	.497	27½	Wesley Westrum	522,919
1976—Fourth	74	88	.457	28	William Rigney	626,868
1977—Fourth	75	87	.463	23	Joseph Altobelli	700,056
1978—Third	89	73	.549	6	Joseph Altobelli	1,740,477
1979—Fourth	71	91	.438	19½	Joseph Altobelli, J. David Bristol	1,456,402
1980—Fifth	75	86	.466	17	J. David Bristol	1,096,115
1981—5th/3rd	56	55	.505	y	Frank Robinson	632,274
1982—Third	87	75	.537	2	Frank Robinson	1,200,948
1983—Fifth	79	83	.488	12	Frank Robinson	1,251,530
1984—Sixth	66	96	.407	26	Frank Robinson, Daniel L. Ozark	1,001,545

*Games behind winner. †Tied for position. ‡Defeated Brooklyn in pennant playoff. §Defeated Los Angeles in pennant playoff. xLost Championship Series. yFirst half 27-32; second 29-23.

First Game Played at Candlestick Park

Willie Mays drove in all the Giants' runs in their 3-1 victory over the St. Louis Cardinals before a crowd of 42,269 on April 12, 1960.

Mays got the Giants on the winning track with his two-run triple in the first inning. He singled in another run in the third.

The Cardinals' only run came on Leon Wagner's fifth-inning homer. Sam Jones pitched the complete game for the Giants, defeating Larry Jackson.

SAN FRANCISCO GIANTS

(10) JIM DAVENPORT—Manager

No. PITCHERS—	Bts.	Thrs.	Hgt.	Wgt.	Birth-date	1984 Club	IP.	W.	L.	ERA.
32 Calvert, Mark	R	R	6:01	195	9-29-56	Phoenix	108.0	6	6	5.75
						San Francisco	32.0	2	4	5.06
31 Cornell, Jeff	R	R	5:11	170	2-10-57	Phoenix	62.2	5	5	3.45
						San Francisco	38.1	1	3	6.10
13 Davis, Mark	L	L	6:04	195	10-19-60	San Francisco	174.2	5	17	5.36
50 Garrelts, Scott	R	R	6:04	195	10-31-61	Phoenix	97.2	5	7	5.90
						San Francisco	43.0	2	3	5.65
34 Grant, Mark	R	R	6:02	195	10-24-63	Phoenix	111.1	5	7	3.96
						San Francisco	53.2	1	4	6.37
14 Hammaker, Atlee	L	L	6:02	195	1-24-58	Phoenix	8.0	0	1	4.50
						San Francisco	33.0	2	0	2.18
39 Krukow, Mike	R	R	6:04	205	1-21-52	San Francisco	199.1	11	12	4.56
17 Lacey, Bob	R	L	6:04	190	8-25-53	Phoenix	49.2	5	3	5.80
						San Francisco	51.0	1	3	3.88
19 Laskey, Bill	R	R	6:05	190	12-20-57	San Francisco	207.2	9	14	4.33
46 Lavelle, Gary	R	L	6:01	200	1- 3-49	San Francisco	101.0	5	4	2.76
38 Minton, Greg	B	R	6:02	190	7-29-51	San Francisco	124.1	4	9	3.76
28 Riley, George	L	L	6:04	200	10- 6-56	Portland	164.0	11	7	2.97
						San Francisco	29.1	1	0	3.99
49 Robinson, Jeff	R	R	6:04	200	12-13-60	San Francisco	171.2	7	15	4.56
53 Ward, Colin	L	L	6:03	190	11-22-60	Phoenix	126.2	7	8	5.26
47 Williams, Frank	R	R	6:01	180	2-13-58	San Francisco	106.1	9	4	3.55

CATCHERS—	Bts.	Thrs.	Hgt.	Wgt.	Birth-date	1984 Club	G.	HR.	RBI.	Avg.
15 Brenly, Bob	R	R	6:02	210	2-25-54	San Francisco	145	20	80	.291
Gwosdz, Doug	R	R	5:11	180	6-20-60	San Diego	7	0	1	.250
						Las Vegas	61	6	27	.228
51 Nokes, Matt	L	R	6:01	185	10-31-63	Shreveport	97	11	61	.289
37 Ouellette, Phil	B	R	6:00	190	10-10-61	Phoenix	70	7	29	.263

INFIELDERS—	Bts.	Thrs.	Hgt.	Wgt.	Birth-date	1984 Club	G.	HR.	RBI.	Avg.
52 Brown, Chris	R	R	6:00	185	8-15-61	Phoenix	84	9	64	.283
						San Francisco	23	1	11	.286
18 Kuiper, Duane	L	R	6:00	175	6-19-50	San Francisco	83	0	11	.200
10 LeMaster, Johnnie	R	R	6:02	180	6-19-54	San Francisco	132	4	32	.217
16 Mullins, Fran	R	R	6:00	180	5-14-57	San Francisco	57	2	10	.218
5 Rabb, John	R	R	6:01	180	6-23-60	San Francisco	54	3	9	.195
41 Thompson, Scot	L	L	6:03	195	12- 7-55	San Francisco	120	1	31	.306
9 Trillo, Manny	R	R	6:01	164	12-25-50	San Francisco	98	4	36	.254
36 Wellman, Brad	R	R	6:00	170	8-17-59	Phoenix	43	0	11	.296
						San Francisco	93	2	25	.226

OUTFIELDERS—	Bts.	Thrs.	Hgt.	Wgt.	Birth-date	1984 Club	G.	HR.	RBI.	Avg.
12 Baker, Dusty	R	R	6:02	200	6-15-49	San Francisco	100	3	32	.292
22 Clark, Jack	R	R	6:03	210	11-10-55	San Francisco	57	11	44	.320
30 Davis, Chili	B	R	6:03	195	1-17-60	San Francisco	137	21	81	.315
45 Deer, Rob	R	R	6:03	210	9-29-60	Phoenix	133	31	69	.227
						San Francisco	13	3	3	.167
25 Gladden, Dan	R	R	5:11	180	7- 7-57	Phoenix	59	3	27	.397
						San Francisco	86	4	31	.351
20 Leonard, Jeff	R	R	6:04	200	9-22-55	San Francisco	136	21	86	.302
33 Sanchez, Alex	R	R	6:00	185	2-26-59	Phoenix	135	26	108	.318
						San Francisco	13	0	2	.195
8 Youngblood, Joel	R	R	5:11	175	8-28-51	San Francisco	134	10	51	.254

ROCKY BRIDGES (6)—Coach   CHUCK HILLER (2)—Coach
TOM McCRAW (21)—Coach   BOB MILLER (48)—Coach
JACK MULL (42)—Coach

CANDLESTICK PARK

	Seats	Prices
Mezzanine Boxes	556	*
Box Seats (lower)	15,672	$8.00
(upper)		6.00
Reserved Seats (lower)	35,917	7.00
(upper)		5.00
General Admission	6,800	2.50

*Sold only on season basis.

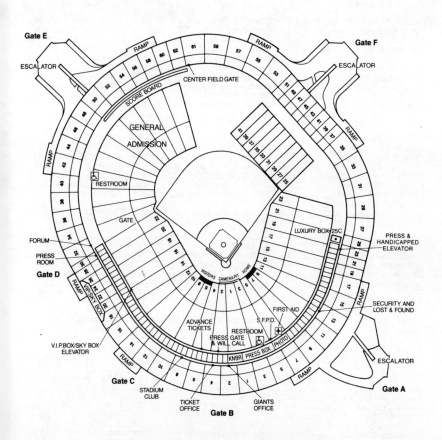

Candlestick Park, San Francisco
First N.L. Game Played April 12, 1960

The Sporting News

Major League All-Star Teams

1925

Bottomley, St. L. NL............ 1B
Hornsby, St. Louis NL......... 2B
Wright, Pittsburgh NL .... SS
Traynor, Pittsb'gh NL 3B
Cuyler, Pittsb'gh NL ....OF
Carey, Pittsb'gh NL ....OF
Goslin, Wash'ton AL ....OF
Cochrane, Phila. AL C
Johnson, Wash'ton AL......... P
Rommel, Phila. AL.............. P
Vance, Brooklyn NL............ P

1926

G. Burns, Cleve. AL
Hornsby, St. Louis NL
J. Sewell, Cleve. AL
Traynor, Pittsb'gh NL
Goslin, Wash'ton AL
Mostil, Chicago AL
Ruth, New York AL
O'Farrell, St. Louis NL
Pennock, N. York AL
Uhle, Cleveland AL
Alexander, St. L. NL

1927

1B—Gehrig, N. York AL
2B—Hornsby, N. York NL
SS—Jackson, N. York NL
3B—Traynor, Pitts. NL
OF—Ruth, New York AL
OF—Simmons, Phila. AL
OF—P. Waner, Pitts. NL
C—Hartnett, Chicago NL
P—Root, Chicago, NL
P—Lyons, Chicago AL

1928

Gehrig, New York AL 1B
Hornsby, Boston NL 2B
Jackson, N. York NL........... SS
Lindstrom, N. Y. NL............ 3B
Ruth, New York AL ....OF
Manush, St. Louis AL ....OF
P. Waner, Pitts. NL ....OF
Cochrane, Phila. AL C
Grove, Phila'phia AL........... P
Hoyt, New York AL.............. P

1929

Foxx, Phila'phia AL
Hornsby, Chicago NL
Jackson, N. York NL
Traynor, Pittsb'gh NL
Simmons, Phila. AL
L. Wilson, Chi. NL
Ruth, New York AL
Cochrane, Phila. AL
Grove, Phila'phia AL
Grimes, Pittsburgh NL

1930

1B—Terry, New York NL
2B—Frisch, St. Louis NL
SS—Cronin, Wash'ton, AL
3B—Lindstrom, N. Y. NL
OF—Simmons, Phila. AL
OF—L. Wilson, Chi. NL
OF—Ruth, New York AL
C—Cochrane, Phila. AL
P—Grove, Phila'phia AL
P—W. Ferrell, Cleve. AL

1931

Gehrig, New York AL 1B
Frisch, St. Louis NL 2B
Cronin, Wash'ton AL .... SS
Traynor, Pittsb'gh NL 3B
Simmons, Phila. AL.............OF
Averill, Cleve'd AL ....OF
Ruth, New York AL ....OF
Cochrane, Phila. AL C
Grove, Phila'phia AL........... P
Earnshaw, Phila. AL........... P

1932

Foxx, Phila'phia AL
Lazzeri, N. York AL
Cronin, Wash'ton AL
Traynor, Pittsb'gh NL
O'Doul, Brooklyn NL
Averill, Cleveland AL
Klein, Phila'phia NL
Dickey, New York AL
Grove, Phila'phia AL
Warneke, Chicago NL

1933

1B—Foxx, Phila'phia AL
2B—Gehringer, Det. AL
SS—Cronin, Wash'ton AL
3B—Traynor, Pitts. NL
OF—Simmons, Chi. AL
OF—Berger, Boston NL
OF—Klein, Phila'phia NL
C—Dickey, N. York AL
P—Crowder, Wash. AL
P—Hubbell, N. York NL

1934

Gehrig, New York AL 1B
Gehringer, Det. AL 2B
Cronin, Wash'ton AL .... SS
Higgins, Phil'phia AL........... 3B
Simmons, Chicago AL..........OF
Averill, Cleveland AL...........OF
Ott, New York NL ....OF
Cochrane, Detroit AL C
Gomez, New York AL .... P
Rowe, Detroit AL................. P
J. Dean, St. Louis NL .... P

1935

Greenberg, Det. AL
Gehringer, Det. AL
Vaughan, Pitts. NL
J. Martin, St. L. NL
Medwick, St. L. NL
Cramer, Phila. AL
Ott, New York NL
Cochrane, Detroit AL
Hubbell, N. York NL
J. Dean, St. Louis NL

1936

1B—Gehrig, New York AL
2B—Gehringer, Det. AL
SS—Appling, Chicago AL
3B—Higgins, Phila. AL
OF—Medwick, St. L. NL
OF—Averill, Cleve. AL
OF—Ott, New York NL
C—Dickey, N.Y. AL
P—Hubbell, N. York NL
P—J. Dean, St. Louis NL

1937

Gehrig, New York AL 1B
Gehringer, Det. AL 2B
Bartell, New York NL......... SS
Rolfe, New York AL............ 3B
Medwick, St. L. NL.............OF
J. DiMaggio, N.Y. AL..........OF
P. Waner, Pitts. NL ....OF
Hartnett, Chicago, NL C
Hubbell, New York NL......... P
Ruffing, New York AL........ P

1938

Foxx, Boston AL
Gehringer, Detroit AL
Cronin, Boston AL
Rolfe, New York AL
Medwick, St. Louis NL
J. DiMaggio, N. Y. AL
Ott, New York NL
Dickey, New York AL
Ruffing, New York AL
Gomez, New York AL
Vander Meer, Cin. NL

1939

1B—Foxx, Boston, AL
2B—Gordon, N. York AL
SS—Cronin, Boston AL
3B—Rolfe, New York AL
OF—Medwick, St. L. NL
OF—J. DiMaggio, N.Y. AL
OF—Williams, Boston AL
C—Dickey, N. York AL
P—Ruffing, N. York AL
P—Feller, Cleveland AL
P—Walters, Cinn. NL

1940

F. McCormick, Cin. NL	1B
Gordon, N. York AL	2B
Appling, Chicago AL	SS
Hack, Chicago NL	3B
Greenberg, Det. AL	OF
J. DiMaggio, N.Y. AL	OF
Williams, Boston AL	OF
Danning, N. York NL	C
Feller, Cleveland AL	P
Walters, Cinn. NL	P
Derringer, Cinn. NL	P

1941

Camilli, Brooklyn NL
Gordon, N. York AL
Travis, Wash'ton AL
Hack, Chicago NL
Williams, Boston AL
J. DiMaggio, N. Y. AL
Reiser, Brooklyn NL
Dickey, New York AL
Feller, Cleveland AL
Wyatt, Brooklyn NL
Lee, Chicago NL

1942

1B—Mize, New York NL
2B—Gordon, N. York AL
SS—Pesky, Boston AL
3B—Hack, Chicago NL
OF—Williams, Boston AL
OF—J. DiMaggio, N. Y. AL
OF—Slaughter, St. L. NL
C—Owen, Brooklyn NL
P—M. Cooper, St. L. NL
P—Bonham, N. York AL
P—Hughson, Boston AL

1943

York, Detroit AL	1B
Herman, Brooklyn NL	2B
Appling, Chicago AL	SS
Johnson, N. York AL	3B
Wakefield, Detroit AL	OF
Musial, St. Louis NL	OF
Nicholson, Chi. NL	OF
W. Cooper, St. L. NL	C
Chandler, N. Y. AL	P
M. Cooper, St. L. NL	P
Sewell, Pittsburgh NL	P

1944

Sanders, St. Louis NL
Doerr, Boston AL
Marion, St. Louis NL
Elliott, Pittsburgh NL
Musial, St. Louis NL
Wakefield, Detroit AL
F. Walker, Brkn. NL
W. Cooper, St. L. NL
Newhouser, Det. AL
M. Cooper, St. L. NL
Trout, Detroit AL

1945

1B—Cavarretta, Chi. NL
2B—Stirnweiss, N. Y. AL
SS—Marion, St. Louis NL
3B—Kurowski, St. L. NL
OF—Holmes, Boston NL
OF—Pafko, Chicago NL
OF—Rosen, Brooklyn, NL
C—Richards, Detroit AL
P—Newhouser, Det. AL
P—Ferriss, Boston AL
P—Borowy, Chicago NL

1946

Musial, St. Louis NL	1B
Doerr, Boston AL	2B
Pesky, Boston AL	SS
Kell, Detroit AL	3B
Williams, Boston AL	OF
D. DiMaggio, Bos. AL	OF
Slaughter, St. L. NL	OF
Robinson, N. York AL	C
Newhouser, Detroit AL	P
Feller, Cleveland AL	P
Ferriss, Boston AL	P

1947

Mize, New York NL
Gordon, Cleveland AL
Boudreau, Cleve. AL
Kell, Detroit AL
Williams, Boston AL
J. DiMaggio, N.Y. AL
Kiner, Pittsburgh NL
W. Cooper, N. Y. NL
Blackwell, Cinn. NL
Feller, Cleveland AL
Branca, Brooklyn NL

1948

1B—Mize, New York NL
2B—Gordon, Clevel'd AL
SS—Boudreau, Cleve. AL
3B—Elliott, Boston NL
OF—Williams, Boston AL
OF—J. DiMaggio, N.Y. AL
OF—Musial, St. Louis NL
C—Tebbetts, Boston AL
P—Sain, Boston NL
P—Lemon, Cleveland AL
P—Brecheen, St. L. NL

1949

Henrich, N. York AL	1B
Robinson, Brkn. NL	2B
Rizzuto, N. York AL	SS
Kell, Detroit AL	3B
Williams, Boston AL	OF
Musial, St. Louis NL	OF
Kiner, Pittsburgh NL	OF
Campanella, Brkn. NL	C
Parnell, Boston AL	P
Kinder, Boston AL	P
Page, New York AL	P

1950

Dropo, Boston AL
Robinson, Brkn. NL
Rizzuto, New York AL
Kell, Detroit AL
Musial, St. Louis NL
Kiner, Pittsburgh NL
Doby, Cleveland AL
Berra, New York AL
Raschi, New York AL
Lemon, Cleveland AL
Konstanty, Phila. NL

1951

1B—Fain, Phila. AL
2B—Robinson, Brkn. NL
SS—Rizzuto, N. York AL
3B—Kell, Detroit AL
OF—Musial, St. Louis NL
OF—Williams, Boston AL
OF—Kiner, Pittsburgh NL
C—Campanella, Brk. NL
P—Maglie, N.Y. NL
P—Roe, Brooklyn NL
P—Reynolds, N. York AL

1952

Fain, Phila'phia AL	1B
Robinson, Brkn. NL	2B
Rizzuto, New York AL	SS
Kell, Boston AL	3B
Musial, St. Louis NL	OF
Sauer, Chicago NL	OF
Mantle, N. York AL	OF
Berra, New York AL	C
Roberts, Phila'phia NL	P
Shantz, Phila'phia AL	P
Reynolds, N. York AL	P

1953

Vernon, Wash'ton AL
Schoendi'st, St. L. NL
Reese, Brooklyn NL
Rosen, Cleveland AL
Musial, St. Louis NL
Snider, Brooklyn NL
Furillo, Brooklyn NL
Campanella, Brkn. NL
Roberts, Phila'phia NL
Spahn, Milwaukee NL
Porterfield, Wash. AL

1954

1B—Kluszewski, Cinn. NL
2B—Avila, Cleveland AL
SS—Dark, New York NL
3B—Rosen, Cleveland AL
OF—Mays, New York NL
OF—Musial, St. Louis NL
OF—Snider, Brooklyn NL
C—Berra, New York AL
P—Lemon, Cleveland AL
P—Antonelli, N.Y. NL
P—Roberts, Phila. NL

The incomparable Babe Ruth appeared on six consecutive TSN major league all-star teams (1926 through 1931) during his slugging heydays with the Yankees.

1955

Kluszewski, Cinn. NL.......... 1B
Fox, Chicago AL 2B
Banks, Chicago NL .... SS
Mathews, Milw. NL............. 3B
Snider, Brooklyn NL ....OF
Williams, Boston AL............OF
Kaline, Detroit AL ....OF
Campanella, Brkn. NL........ C
Roberts, Phila. NL.............. P
Newcombe, Brkn. NL .... P
Ford, New York AL............. P

1956

Kluszewski, Cinn. NL
Fox, Chicago AL
Kuenn, Detroit AL
Boyer, St. Louis NL
Mantle, New York AL
Aaron, Milwaukee NL
Williams, Boston AL
Berra, New York AL
Newcombe, Brkn. NL
Ford, New York AL
Pierce, Chicago AL

1957

1B—Musial, St. Louis NL
2B—Scho'st, N.Y-Mil. NL
SS—McDougald, N.Y. AL
3B—Mathews, Milw. NL
OF—Mantle, N. Y. AL
OF—Williams, Boston AL
OF—Mays, New York NL
C—Berra, New York AL
P—Spahn, Milw. NL
P—Pierce, Chicago AL
P—Bunning, Detroit AL

1958

Musial, St. Louis NL............. 1B
Fox, Chicago AL 2B
Banks, Chicago NL .... SS
Thomas, Pitts. NL............... 3B
Williams, Boston AL............OF
Mays, San Fran. NL............OF
Aaron, Milwaukee NL ....OF
Crandall, Milw. NL.............. C
Turley, New York AL .... P
Spahn, Milwaukee NL .... P
Friend, Pittsburgh NL........ P

1959

Cepeda, San Fran. NL
Fox, Chicago AL
Banks, Chicago NL
Mathews, Milw. NL
Minoso, Cleveland AL
Mays, San Fran. NL
Aaron, Milwaukee NL
Lollar, Chicago AL
Wynn, Chicago AL
S. Jones, S. Fran. NL
Antonelli, S. Fran. NL

1960

1B—Skowron, N. Y. AL
2B—Mazeroski, Pitts. NL
SS—Banks, Chicago NL
3B—Mathews, Milw. NL
OF—Minoso, Chicago AL
OF—Mays, San Fran. NL
OF—Maris, New York AL
C—Crandall, Milw. NL
P—Law, Pittsburgh NL
P—Spahn, Milw. NL
P—Broglio, St. Louis NL

1961—American

1B—Norm Cash, Detroit
2B—Bobby Richardson, New York
SS—Tony Kubek, New York
3B—Brooks Robinson, Baltimore
OF—Mickey Mantle, New York
OF—Roger Maris, New York
OF—Rocky Colavito, Detroit
C—Elston Howard, New York
P—Whitey Ford, New York
P—Frank Lary, Detroit

1962—American

1B—Norm Siebern, Kansas City
2B—Bobby Richardson, New York
SS—Tom Tresh, New York
3B—Brooks Robinson, Baltimore
OF—Leon Wagner, Los Angeles
OF—Mickey Mantle, New York
OF—Al Kaline, Detroit
C—Earl Battey, Minnesota
P—Ralph Terry, New York
P—Dick Donovan, Cleveland

1963—American

1B—Joe Pepitone, New York
2B—Bobby Richardson, New York
SS—Luis Aparicio, Baltimore
3B—Frank Malzone, Boston
OF—Carl Yastrzemski, Boston
OF—Albie Pearson, Los Angeles
OF—Al Kaline, Detroit
C—Elston Howard, New York
P—Whitey Ford, New York
P—Gary Peters, Chicago

1964—American

1B—Dick Stuart, Boston
2B—Bobby Richardson, New York
SS—Jim Fregosi, Los Angeles
3B—Brooks Robinson, Baltimore
OF—Harmon Killebrew, Minnesota
OF—Mickey Mantle, New York
OF—Tony Oliva, Minnesota
C—Elston Howard, New York
P—Dean Chance, Los Angeles
P—Gary Peters, Chicago

1965—American

1B—Fred Whitfield, Cleveland
2B—Bobby Richardson, New York
SS—Zoilo Versalles, Minnesota
3B—Brooks Robinson, Baltimore
LF—Carl Yastrzemski, Boston
CF—Jimmie Hall, Minnesota
RF—Tony Oliva, Minnesota
C—Earl Battey, Minnesota
P—Jim Grant, Minnesota
P—Mel Stottlemyre, New York

1966—American

1B—Boog Powell, Baltimore
2B—Bobby Richardson, New York
SS—Luis Aparicio, Baltimore
3B—Brooks Robinson, Baltimore
LF—Frank Robinson, Baltimore
CF—Al Kaline, Detroit
RF—Tony Oliva, Minnesota
C—Paul Casanova, Washington
P—Jim Kaat, Minnesota
P—Earl Wilson, Detroit

1961—National

1B—Orlando Cepeda, San Francisco
2B—Frank Bolling, Milwaukee
SS—Maury Wills, Los Angeles
3B—Ken Boyer, St. Louis
OF—Willie Mays, San Francisco
OF—Frank Robinson, Cincinnati
OF—Roberto Clemente, Pittsburgh
C—Smoky Burgess, Pittsburgh
P—Joey Jay, Cincinnati
P—Warren Spahn, Milwaukee

1962—National

1B—Orlando Cepeda, San Francisco
2B—Bill Mazeroski, Pittsburgh
SS—Maury Wills, Los Angeles
3B—Ken Boyer, St. Louis
OF—Tommy Davis, Los Angeles
OF—Willie Mays, San Francisco
OF—Frank Robinson, Cincinnati
C—Del Crandall, Milwaukee
P—Don Drysdale, Los Angeles
P—Bob Purkey, Cincinnati

1963—National

1B—Bill White, St. Louis
2B—Jim Gilliam, Los Angeles
SS—Dick Groat, St. Louis
3B—Ken Boyer, St. Louis
OF—Tommy Davis, Los Angeles
OF—Willie Mays, San Francisco
OF—Hank Aaron, Milwaukee
C—John Edwards, Cincinnati
P—Sandy Koufax, Los Angeles
P—Juan Marichal, San Francisco

1964—National

1B—Bill White, St. Louis
2B—Ron Hunt, New York
SS—Dick Groat, St. Louis
3B—Ken Boyer, St. Louis
OF—Billy Williams, Chicago
OF—Willie Mays, San Francisco
OF—Roberto Clemente, Pittsburgh
C—Joe Torre, Milwaukee
P—Sandy Koufax, Los Angeles
P—Jim Bunning, Philadelphia

1965—National

1B—Willie McCovey, San Francisco
2B—Pete Rose, Cincinnati
SS—Maury Wills, Los Angeles
3B—Deron Johnson, Cincinnati
LF—Willie Stargell, Pittsburgh
CF—Willie Mays, San Francisco
RF—Hank Aaron, Milwaukee
C—Joe Torre, Milwaukee
P—Sandy Koufax, Los Angeles
P—Juan Marichal, San Francisco

1966—National

1B—Felipe Alou, Atlanta
2B—Pete Rose, Cincinnati
SS—Gene Alley, Pittsburgh
3B—Ron Santo, Chicago
LF—Willie Stargell, Pittsburgh
CF—Willie Mays, San Francisco
RF—Roberto Clemente, Pittsburgh
C—Joe Torre, Atlanta
P—Sandy Koufax, Los Angeles
P—Juan Marichal, San Francisco

1967—American

1B—Harmon Killebrew, Minnesota
2B—Rod Carew, Minnesota
SS—Jim Fregosi, California
3B—Brooks Robinson, Baltimore
LF—Carl Yastrzemski, Boston
CF—Al Kaline, Detroit
RF—Frank Robinson, Baltimore
C—Bill Freehan, Detroit
P—Jim Lonborg, Boston
P—Earl Wilson, Detroit

1967—National

1B—Orlando Cepeda, St. Louis
2B—Bill Mazeroski, Pittsburgh
SS—Gene Alley, Pittsburgh
3B—Ron Santo, Chicago
LF—Hank Aaron, Atlanta
CF—Jim Wynn, Houston
RF—Roberto Clemente, Pittsburgh
C—Tim McCarver, St. Louis
P—Mike McCormick, San Francisco
P—Ferguson Jenkins, Chicago

1968—American

1B—Boog Powell, Baltimore
2B—Rod Carew, Minnesota
SS—Luis Aparicio, Chicago
3B—Brooks Robinson, Baltimore
OF—Ken Harrelson, Boston
OF—Willie Horton, Detroit
OF—Frank Howard, Washington
C—Bill Freehan, Detroit
P—Dave McNally, Baltimore
P—Denny McLain, Detroit

1968—National

1B—Willie McCovey, San Francisco
2B—Tommy Helms, Cincinnati
SS—Don Kessinger, Chicago
3B—Ron Santo, Chicago
OF—Billy Williams, Chicago
OF—Curt Flood, St. Louis
OF—Pete Rose, Cincinnati
C—Johnny Bench, Cincinnati
P—Bob Gibson, St. Louis
P—Juan Marichal, San Francisco

1969—American

1B—Boog Powell, Baltimore
2B—Rod Carew, Minnesota
SS—Rico Petrocelli, Boston
3B—Harmon Killebrew, Minnesota
OF—Frank Howard, Washington
OF—Paul Blair, Baltimore
OF—Reggie Jackson, Oakland
C—Bill Freehan, Detroit
RHP—Denny McLain, Detroit
LHP—Mike Cuellar, Baltimore

1969—National

1B—Willie McCovey, San Francisco
2B—Glenn Beckert, Chicago
SS—Don Kessinger, Chicago
3B—Ron Santo, Chicago
OF—Cleon Jones, New York
OF—Matty Alou, Pittsburgh
OF—Hank Aaron, Atlanta
C—Johnny Bench, Cincinnati
RHP—Tom Seaver, New York
LHP—Steve Carlton, St. Louis

1970—American

1B—Boog Powell, Baltimore
2B—Dave Johnson, Baltimore
SS—Luis Aparicio, Chicago
3B—Harmon Killebrew, Minnesota
OF—Frank Howard, Washington
OF—Reggie Smith, Boston
OF—Tony Oliva, Minnesota
C—Ray Fosse, Cleveland
RHP—Jim Perry, Minnesota
LHP—Sam McDowell, Cleveland

1970—National

1B—Willie McCovey, San Francisco
2B—Glenn Beckert, Chicago
SS—Don Kessinger, Chicago
3B—Tony Perez, Cincinnati
OF—Billy Williams, Chicago
OF—Bobby Tolan, Cincinnati
OF—Hank Aaron, Atlanta
C—Johnny Bench, Cincinnati
RHP—Bob Gibson, St. Louis
LHP—Jim Merritt, Cincinnati

1971—American

1B—Norm Cash, Detroit
2B—Cookie Rojas, Kansas City
SS—Leo Cardenas, Minnesota
3B—Brooks Robinson, Baltimore
LF—Merv Rettenmund, Baltimore
CF—Bobby Murcer, New York
RF—Tony Oliva, Minnesota
C—Bill Freehan, Detroit
RHP—Jim Palmer, Baltimore
LHP—Vida Blue, Oakland

1971—National

1B—Lee May, Cincinnati
2B—Glenn Beckert, Chicago
SS—Bud Harrelson, New York
3B—Joe Torre, St. Louis
LF—Willie Stargell, Pittsburgh
CF—Willie Davis, Los Angeles
RF—Hank Aaron, Atlanta
C—Manny Sanguillen, Pittsburgh
RHP—Ferguson Jenkins, Chicago
LHP—Steve Carlton, St. Louis

1972—American

1B—Dick Allen, Chicago
2B—Rod Carew, Minnesota
SS—Luis Aparicio, Boston
3B—Brooks Robinson, Baltimore
LF—Joe Rudi, Oakland
CF—Bobby Murcer, New York
RF—Richie Scheinblum, Kan. City
C—Carlton Fisk, Boston
RHP—Gaylord Perry, Cleveland
LHP—Wilbur Wood, Chicago

1972—National

1B—Willie Stargell, Pittsburgh
2B—Joe Morgan, Cincinnati
SS—Chris Speier, San Francisco
3B—Ron Santo, Chicago
LF—Billy Williams, Chicago
CF—Cesar Cedeno, Houston
RF—Roberto Clemente, Pittsburgh
C—Johnny Bench, Cincinnati
RHP—Ferguson Jenkins, Chicago
LHP—Steve Carlton, Philadelphia

1973—American

1B—John Mayberry, Kansas City
2B—Rod Carew, Minnesota
SS—Bert Campaneris, Oakland
3B—Sal Bando, Oakland
LF—Reggie Jackson, Oakland
CF—Amos Otis, Kansas City
RF—Bobby Murcer, New York
 C—Thurman Munson, New York
RHP—Jim Palmer, Baltimore
LHP—Ken Holtzman, Oakland

1973—National

1B—Tony Perez, Cincinnati
2B—Dave Johnson, Atlanta
SS—Bill Russell, Los Angeles
3B—Darrell Evans, Atlanta
LF—Bobby Bonds, San Francisco
CF—Cesar Cedeno, Houston
RF—Pete Rose, Cincinnati
 C—Johnny Bench, Cincinnati
RHP—Tom Seaver, New York
LHP—Ron Bryant, San Francisco

1974—American

1B—Dick Allen, Chicago
2B—Rod Carew, Minnesota
SS—Bert Campaneris, Oakland
3B—Sal Bando, Oakland
LF—Joe Rudi, Oakland
CF—Paul Blair, Baltimore
RF—Jeff Burroughs, Texas
 C—Thurman Munson, New York
DH—Tommy Davis, Baltimore
RHP—Jim Hunter, Oakland
LHP—Mike Cuellar, Baltimore

1974—National

1B—Steve Garvey, Los Angeles
2B—Joe Morgan, Cincinnati
SS—Dave Concepcion, Cincinnati
3B—Mike Schmidt, Philadelphia
LF—Lou Brock, St. Louis
CF—Jim Wynn, Los Angeles
RF—Richie Zisk, Pittsburgh
 C—Johnny Bench, Cincinnati
RHP—Andy Messersmith, Los Angeles
LHP—Don Gullett, Cincinnati

1975—American

1B—John Mayberry, Kansas City
2B—Rod Carew, Minnesota
SS—Toby Harrah, Texas
3B—Graig Nettles, New York
LF—Jim Rice, Boston
CF—Fred Lynn, Boston
RF—Reggie Jackson, Oakland
 C—Thurman Munson, New York
DH—Willie Horton, Detroit
RHP—Jim Palmer, Baltimore
LHP—Jim Kaat, Chicago

1975—National

1B—Steve Garvey, Los Angeles
2B—Joe Morgan, Cincinnati
SS—Larry Bowa, Philadelphia
3B—Bill Madlock, Chicago
LF—Greg Luzinski, Philadelphia
CF—Al Oliver, Pittsburgh
RF—Dave Parker, Pittsburgh
 C—Johnny Bench, Cincinnati
RHP—Tom Seaver, New York
LHP—Randy Jones, San Diego

1976—American

1B—Chris Chambliss, New York
2B—Bobby Grich, Baltimore
3B—George Brett, Kansas City
SS—Mark Belanger, Baltimore
LF—Joe Rudi, Oakland
CF—Mickey Rivers, New York
RF—Reggie Jackson, Baltimore
 C—Thurman Munson, New York
DH—Hal McRae, Kansas City
RHP—Jim Palmer, Baltimore
LHP—Frank Tanana, California

1976—National

1B—Willie Montanez, San Fran.-Atlanta
2B—Joe Morgan, Cincinnati
3B—Mike Schmidt, Philadelphia
SS—Dave Concepcion, Cincinnati
LF—George Foster, Cincinnati
CF—Cesar Cedeno, Houston
RF—Ken Griffey, Cincinnati
 C—Bob Boone, Philadelphia
RHP—Don Sutton, Los Angeles
LHP—Randy Jones, San Diego

1977—American

1B—Rod Carew, Minnesota
2B—Willie Randolph, New York
3B—Graig Nettles, New York
SS—Rick Burleson, Boston
OF—Jim Rice, Boston
OF—Larry Hisle, Minnesota
OF—Bobby Bonds, California
 C—Carlton Fisk, Boston
DH—Hal McRae, Kansas City
RHP—Nolan Ryan, California
LHP—Frank Tanana, California

1977—National

1B—Steve Garvey, Los Angeles
2B—Joe Morgan, Cincinnati
3B—Mike Schmidt, Philadelphia
SS—Garry Templeton, St. Louis
OF—George Foster, Cincinnati
OF—Dave Parker, Pittsburgh
OF—Greg Luzinski, Philadelphia
 C—Ted Simmons, St. Louis
RHP—Rick Reuschel, Chicago
LHP—Steve Carlton, Philadelphia

1978—American

1B—Rod Carew, Minnesota
2B—Frank White, Kansas City
3B—Graig Nettles, New York
SS—Robin Yount, Milwaukee
OF—Jim Rice, Boston
OF—Larry Hisle, Milwaukee
OF—Fred Lynn, Boston
C—Jim Sundberg, Texas
DH—Rusty Staub, Detroit
RHP—Jim Palmer, Baltimore
LHP—Ron Guidry, New York

1978—National

1B—Steve Garvey, Los Angeles
2B—Dave Lopes, Los Angeles
3B—Pete Rose, Cincinnati
SS—Larry Bowa, Philadelphia
OF—George Foster, Cincinnati
OF—Dave Parker, Pittsburgh
OF—Jack Clark, San Francisco
C—Ted Simmons, St. Louis
RHP—Gaylord Perry, San Diego
LHP—Vida Blue, San Francisco

1979—American

1B—Cecil Cooper, Milwaukee
2B—Bobby Grich, California
3B—George Brett, Kansas City
SS—Roy Smalley, Minnesota
LF—Jim Rice, Boston
CF—Fred Lynn, Boston
RF—Ken Singleton, Baltimore
C—Darrell Porter, Kansas City
DH—Don Baylor, California
RHP—Jim Kern, Texas
LHP—Mike Flanagan, Baltimore

1979—National

1B—Keith Hernandez, St. Louis
2B—Dave Lopes, Los Angeles
3B—Mike Schmidt, Philadelphia
SS—Garry Templeton, St. Louis
LF—Dave Kingman, Chicago
CF—Omar Moreno, Pittsburgh
RF—Dave Winfield, San Diego
C—Ted Simmons, St. Louis
RHP—Joe Niekro, Houston
LHP—Steve Carlton, Philadelphia

1980—American

1B—Cecil Cooper, Milwaukee
2B—Willie Randolph, New York
3B—George Brett, Kansas City
SS—Robin Yount, Milwaukee
LF—Ben Oglivie, Milwaukee
CF—Al Bumbry, Baltimore
RF-DH—Reggie Jackson, New York
C—Rick Cerone, New York
RHP—Steve Stone, Baltimore
LHP—Tommy John, New York

1980—National

1B—Keith Hernandez, St. Louis
2B—Manny Trillo, Philadelphia
3B—Mike Schmidt, Philadelphia
SS—Garry Templeton, St. Louis
LF—Dusty Baker, Los Angeles
CF—Cesar Cedeno, Houston
RF—George Hendrick, St. Louis
C—Gary Carter, Montreal
RHP—Jim Bibby, Pittsburgh
LHP—Steve Carlton, Philadelphia

1981—American

1B—Cecil Cooper, Milwaukee
2B—Bobby Grich, California
3B—Buddy Bell, Texas
SS—Rick Burleson, California
LF—Rickey Henderson, Oakland
CF—Dwayne Murphy, Oakland
RF—Tony Armas, Oakland
C—Jim Sundberg, Texas
DH—Richie Zisk, Seattle
RHP—Jack Morris, Detroit
LHP—Ron Guidry, New York

1981—National

1B—Pete Rose, Philadelphia
2B—Manny Trillo, Philadelphia
3B—Mike Schmidt, Philadelphia
SS—Dave Concepcion, Cincinnati
LF—George Foster, Cincinnati
CF—Andre Dawson, Montreal
RF—Pedro Guerrero, Los Angeles
C—Gary Carter, Montreal
RHP—Tom Seaver, Cincinnati
LHP—Fernando Valenzuela, Los Angeles

1982—American

1B—Cecil Cooper, Milwaukee
2B—Damaso Garcia, Toronto
3B—Doug DeCinces, California
SS—Robin Yount, Milwaukee
LF—Dave Winfield, New York
CF—Gorman Thomas, Milwaukee
RF—Dwight Evans, Boston
C—Lance Parrish, Detroit
DH—Hal McRae, Kansas City
RHP—Dave Stieb, Toronto
LHP—Geoff Zahn, California

1982—National

1B—Al Oliver, Montreal
2B—Manny Trillo, Philadelphia
3B—Mike Schmidt, Philadelphia
SS—Ozzie Smith, St. Louis
LF—Lonnie Smith, St. Louis
CF—Dale Murphy, Atlanta
RF—Pedro Guerrero, Los Angeles
C—Gary Carter, Montreal
RHP—Steve Rogers, Montreal
LHP—Steve Carlton, Philadelphia

Cubs second baseman Ryne Sandberg, the National League MVP and The Sporting News' Major League Player of the Year, is making his first appearance on a TSN all-star team.

1983—American

1B—Eddie Murray, Baltimore
2B—Lou Whitaker, Detroit
3B—Wade Boggs, Boston
SS—Cal Ripken, Baltimore
OF—Jim Rice, Boston
OF—Dave Winfield, New York
OF—Lloyd Moseby, Toronto
C—Carlton Fisk, Chicago
DH—Greg Luzinski, Chicago
RHP—LaMarr Hoyt, Chicago
LHP—Ron Guidry, New York

1983—National

1B—George Hendrick, St. Louis
2B—Glenn Hubbard, Atlanta
3B—Mike Schmidt, Philadelphia
SS—Dickie Thon, Houston
OF—Dale Murphy, Atlanta
OF—Andre Dawson, Montreal
OF—Tim Raines, Montreal
C—Tony Pena, Pittsburgh
RHP—John Denny, Philadelphia
LHP—Larry McWilliams, Pittsburgh

1984—American

1B—Don Mattingly, New York
2B—Lou Whitaker, Detroit
3B—Buddy Bell, Texas
SS—Cal Ripken, Baltimore
OF—Tony Armas, Boston
OF—Dwight Evans, Boston
OF—Dave Winfield, New York
C—Lance Parrish, Detroit
DH—Dave Kingman, Oakland
RHP—Mike Boddicker, Baltimore
LHP—Willie Hernandez, Detroit

1984—National

1B—Keith Hernandez, New York
2B—Ryne Sandberg, Chicago
3B—Mike Schmidt, Philadelphia
SS—Ozzie Smith, St. Louis
OF—Dale Murphy, Atlanta
OF—Jose Cruz, Houston
OF—Tony Gwynn, San Diego
C—Gary Carter, Montreal
RHP—Rick Sutcliffe, Chicago
LHP—Mark Thurmond, San Diego

The Sporting News
Gold Glove Fielding Teams

1957 Majors	1958 American	1958 National
P—Shantz, N. Y. AL	P—Shantz, New York	P—Haddix, Cincinnati
C—Lollar, Chicago AL	C—Lollar, Chicago	C—Crandall, Milwaukee
1B—Hodges, Brooklyn	1B—Power, Cleveland	1B—Hodges, Los Angeles
2B—Fox, Chicago AL	2B—Bolling, Detroit	2B—Mazeroski, Pitt.
3B—Malzone, Boston	3B—Malzone, Boston	3B—Boyer, St. Louis
SS—McMillan, Cin.	SS—Aparicio, Chicago	SS—McMillan, Cin.
LF—Minoso, Chicago AL	LF—Siebern, New York	LF—Robinson, Cin.
CF—Mays, N. Y. NL	CF—Piersall, Boston	CF—Mays, S. Francisco
RF—Kaline, Detroit	RF—Kaline, Detroit	RF—Aaron, Milwaukee

1959 American	1959 National
P—Shantz, New York	P—Haddix, Pittsburgh
C—Lollar, Chicago	C—Crandall, Milwaukee
1B—Power, Cleveland	1B—Hodges, Los Angeles
2B—Fox, Chicago	2B—Neal, Los Angeles
3B—Malzone, Boston	3B—Boyer, St. Louis
SS—Aparicio, Chicago	SS—McMillan, Cincinnati
LF—Minoso, Cleveland	LF—Brandt, St. Louis
CF—Kaline, Detroit	CF—Mays, San Francisco
RF—Jensen, Boston	RF—Aaron, Milwaukee

1960 American	1960 National
P—Shantz, New York	P—Haddix, Pittsburgh
C—Battey, Washington	C—Crandall, Milwaukee
1B—Power, Cleveland	1B—White, St. Louis
2B—Fox, Chicago	2B—Mazeroski, Pittsburgh
3B—Robinson, Baltimore	3B—Boyer, St. Louis
SS—Aparicio, Chicago	SS—Banks, Chicago
LF—Minoso, Chicago	LF—Moon, Los Angeles
CF—Landis, Chicago	CF—Mays, San Francisco
RF—Maris, New York	RF—Aaron, Milwaukee

1961 American	1961 National
P—Lary, Detroit	P—Shantz, Pittsburgh
C—Battey, Chicago	C—Roseboro, Los Angeles
1B—Power, Cleveland	1B—White, St. Louis
2B—Richardson, New York	2B—Mazeroski, Pittsburgh
3B—Robinson, Baltimore	3B—Boyer, St. Louis
SS—Aparicio, Chicago	SS—Wills, Los Angeles
OF—Kaline, Detroit	OF—Mays, San Francisco
OF—Piersall, Cleveland	OF—Clemente, Pittsburgh
OF—Landis, Chicago	OF—Pinson, Cincinnati

1962 American	1962 National
P—Kaat, Minnesota	P—Shantz, St. Louis
C—Battey, Minnesota	C—Crandall, Milwaukee
1B—Power, Minnesota	1B—White, St. Louis
2B—Richardson, New York	2B—Hubbs, Chicago
3B—Robinson, Baltimore	3B—Davenport, San Francisco
SS—Aparicio, Chicago	SS—Wills, Los Angeles
OF—Landis, Chicago	OF—Mays, San Francisco
OF—Mantle, New York	OF—Clemente, Pittsburgh
OF—Kaline, Detroit	OF—Virdon, Pittsburgh

1963 American	1963 National
P—Kaat, Minnesota	P—Shantz, St. Louis
C—Howard, New York	C—Edwards, Cincinnati
1B—Power, Minnesota	1B—White, St. Louis
2B—Richardson, New York	2B—Mazeroski, Pittsburgh
3B—Robinson, Baltimore	3B—Boyer, St. Louis
SS—Versalles, Minnesota	SS—Wine, Philadelphia
OF—Kaline, Detroit	OF—Mays, San Francisco
OF—Yastrzemski, Boston	OF—Clemente, Pittsburgh
OF—Landis, Chicago	OF—Flood, St. Louis

1964 American

P—Kaat, Minnesota
C—Howard, New York
1B—Power, Los Angeles
2B—Richardson, New York
3B—Robinson, Baltimore
SS—Aparicio, Baltimore
OF—Kaline, Detroit
OF—Landis, Chicago
OF—Davalillo, Cleveland

1964 National

P—Shantz, Philadelphia
C—Edwards, Cincinnati
1B—White, St. Louis
2B—Mazeroski, Pittsburgh
3B—Santo, Chicago
SS—Amaro, Philadelphia
OF—Mays, San Francisco
OF—Clemente, Pittsburgh
OF—Flood, St. Louis

1965 American

P—Kaat, Minnesota
C—Freehan, Detroit
1B—Pepitone, New York
2B—Richardson, New York
3B—Robinson, Baltimore
SS—Versalles, Minnesota
OF—Kaline, Detroit
OF—Tresh, New York
OF—Yastrzemski, Boston

1965 National

P—Gibson, St. Louis
C—Torre, Atlanta
1B—White, St. Louis
2B—Mazeroski, Pittsburgh
3B—Santo, Chicago
SS—Cardenas, Cincinnati
OF—Mays, San Francisco
OF—Clemente, Pittsburgh
OF—Flood, St. Louis

1966 American

P—Kaat, Minnesota
C—Freehan, Detroit
1B—Pepitone, New York
2B—Knoop, California
3B—B. Robinson, Baltimore
SS—Aparicio, Baltimore
OF—Kaline, Detroit
OF—Agee, Chicago
OF—Oliva, Minnesota

1966 National

P—Gibson, St. Louis
C—Roseboro, Los Angeles
1B—White, Philadelphia
2B—Mazeroski, Pittsburgh
3B—Santo, Chicago
SS—Alley, Pittsburgh
OF—Mays, San Francisco
OF—Flood, St. Louis
OF—Clemente, Pittsburgh

1967 American

P—Kaat, Minnesota
C—Freehan, Detroit
1B—Scott, Boston
2B—Knoop, California
3B—B. Robinson, Baltimore
SS—Fregosi, California
OF—Yastrzemski, Boston
OF—Blair, Baltimore
OF—Kaline, Detroit

1967 National

P—Gibson, St. Louis
C—Hundley, Chicago
1B—Parker, Los Angeles
2B—Mazeroski, Pittsburgh
3B—Santo, Chicago
SS—Alley, Pittsburgh
OF—Clemente, Pittsburgh
OF—Flood, St. Louis
OF—Mays, San Francisco

1968 American

P—Kaat, Minnesota
C—Freehan, Detroit
1B—Scott, Boston
2B—Knoop, California
3B—B. Robinson, Baltimore
SS—Aparicio, Chicago
OF—Stanley, Detroit
OF—Yastrzemski, Boston
OF—Smith, Boston

1968 National

P—Gibson, St. Louis
C—Bench, Cincinnati
1B—Parker, Los Angeles
2B—Beckert, Chicago
3B—Santo, Chicago
SS—Maxvill, St. Louis
OF—Mays, San Francisco
OF—Clemente, Pittsburgh
OF—Flood, St. Louis

1969 American

P—Kaat, Minnesota
C—Freehan, Detroit
1B—Pepitone, New York
2B—Johnson, Baltimore
3B—B. Robinson, Baltimore
SS—Belanger, Baltimore
OF—Blair, Baltimore
OF—Stanley, Detroit
OF—Yastrzemski, Boston

1969 National

P—Gibson, St. Louis
C—Bench, Cincinnati
1B—Parker, Los Angeles
2B—Millan, Atlanta
3B—Boyer, Atlanta
SS—Kessinger, Chicago
OF—Clemente, Pittsburgh
OF—Flood, St. Louis
OF—Rose, Cincinnati

1970 American

P—Kaat, Minnesota
C—Fosse, Cleveland
1B—Spencer, California
2B—Johnson, Baltimore
3B—B. Robinson, Baltimore
SS—Aparicio, Chicago
OF—Stanley, Detroit
OF—Blair, Baltimore
OF—Berry, Chicago

1970 National

P—Gibson, St. Louis
C—Bench, Cincinnati
1B—Parker, Los Angeles
2B—Helms, Cincinnati
3B—Rader, Houston
SS—Kessinger, Chicago
OF—Clemente, Pittsburgh
OF—Agee, New York
OF—Rose, Cincinnati

1971 American

P—Kaat, Minnesota
C—Fosse, Cleveland
1B—Scott, Boston
2B—Johnson, Baltimore
3B—B. Robinson, Baltimore
SS—Belanger, Baltimore
OF—Blair, Baltimore
OF—Otis, Kansas City
OF—Yastrzemski, Boston

1971 National

P—Gibson, St. Louis
C—Bench, Cincinnati
1B—Parker, Los Angeles
2B—Helms, Cincinnati
3B—Rader, Houston
SS—Harrelson, New York
OF—Clemente, Pittsburgh
OF—Bonds, San Francisco
OF—Davis, Los Angeles

1972 American

P—Kaat, Minnesota
C—Fisk, Boston
1B—Scott, Milwaukee
2B—Griffin, Boston
3B—Robinson, Baltimore
SS—Brinkman, Detroit
OF—Blair, Baltimore
OF—Murcer, New York
OF—Berry, California

1972 National

P—Gibson, St. Louis
C—Bench, Cincinnati
1B—Parker, Los Angeles
2B—Millan, Atlanta
3B—Rader, Houston
SS—Bowa, Philadelphia
OF—Clemente, Pittsburgh
OF—Cedeno, Houston
OF—Davis, Los Angeles

1973 American

P—Kaat, Chicago
C—Munson, New York
1B—Scott, Milwaukee
2B—Grich, Baltimore
3B—Robinson, Baltimore
SS—Belanger, Baltimore
OF—Blair, Baltimore
OF—Otis, Kansas City
OF—Stanley, Detroit

1973 National

P—Gibson, St. Louis
C—Bench, Cincinnati
1B—Jorgensen, Montreal
2B—Morgan, Cincinnati
3B—Rader, Houston
SS—Metzger, Houston
OF—Bonds, San Francisco
OF—Cedeno, Houston
OF—Davis, Los Angeles

1974 American

P—Kaat, Chicago
C—Munson, New York
1B—Scott, Milwaukee
2B—Grich, Baltimore
3B—Robinson, Baltimore
SS—Belanger, Baltimore
OF—Blair, Baltimore
OF—Otis, Kansas City
OF—Rudi, Oakland

1974 National

P—Messersmith, Los Angeles
C—Bench, Cincinnati
1B—Garvey, Los Angeles
2B—Morgan, Cincinnati
3B—Rader, Houston
SS—Concepcion, Cincinnati
OF—Cedeno, Houston
OF—Geronimo, Cincinnati
OF—Bonds, San Francisco

1975 American

P—Kaat, Chicago
C—Munson, New York
1B—Scott, Milwaukee
2B—Grich, Baltimore
3B—Robinson, Baltimore
SS—Belanger, Baltimore
OF—Blair, Baltimore
OF—Rudi, Oakland
OF—Lynn, Boston

1975 National

P—Messersmith, Los Angeles
C—Bench, Cincinnati
1B—Garvey, Los Angeles
2B—Morgan, Cincinnati
3B—Reitz, St. Louis
SS—Concepcion, Cincinnati
OF—Cedeno, Houston
OF—Geronimo, Cincinnati
OF—Maddox, Philadelphia

1976 American

P—Palmer, Baltimore
C—Sundberg, Texas
1B—Scott, Milwaukee
2B—Grich, Baltimore
3B—Rodriguez, Detroit
SS—Belanger, Baltimore
OF—Rudi, Oakland
OF—Evans, Boston
OF—Manning, Cleveland

1976 National

P—Kaat, Philadelphia
C—Bench, Cincinnati
1B—Garvey, Los Angeles
2B—Morgan, Cincinnati
3B—Schmidt, Philadelphia
SS—Concepcion, Cincinnati
OF—Cedeno, Houston
OF—Geronimo, Cincinnati
OF—Maddox, Philadelphia

1977 American

P—Palmer, Baltimore
C—Sundberg, Texas
1B—Spencer, Chicago
2B—White, Kansas City
3B—Nettles, New York
SS—Belanger, Baltimore
OF—Beniquez, Texas
OF—Yastrzemski, Boston
OF—Cowens, Kansas City

1977 National

P—Kaat, Philadelphia
C—Bench, Cincinnati
1B—Garvey, Los Angeles
2B—Morgan, Cincinnati
3B—Schmidt, Philadelphia
SS—Concepcion, Cincinnati
OF—Geronimo, Cincinnati
OF—Maddox, Philadelphia
OF—Parker, Pittsburgh

1978 American

P—Palmer, Baltimore
C—Sundberg, Texas
1B—Chambliss, New York
2B—White, Kansas City
3B—Nettles, New York
SS—Belanger, Baltimore
OF—Lynn, Boston
OF—Evans, Boston
OF—Miller, California

1978 National

P—Niekro, Atlanta
C—Boone, Philadelphia
1B—Hernandez, St. Louis
2B—Lopes, Los Angeles
3B—Schmidt, Philadelphia
SS—Bowa, Philadelphia
OF—Maddox, Philadelphia
OF—Parker, Pittsburgh
OF—Valentine, Montreal

1979 American

P—Palmer, Baltimore
C—Sundberg, Texas
1B—Cooper, Milwaukee
2B—White, Kansas City
3B—Bell, Texas
SS—Burleson, Boston
OF—Evans, Boston
OF—Lezcano, Milwaukee
OF—Lynn, Boston

1979 National

P—Niekro, Atlanta
C—Boone, Philadelphia
1B—Hernandez, St. Louis
2B—Trillo, Philadelphia
3B—Schmidt, Philadelphia
SS—Concepcion, Cincinnati
OF—Maddox, Philadelphia
OF—Parker, Pittsburgh
OF—Winfield, San Diego

1980 American

P—Norris, Oakland
C—Sundberg, Texas
1B—Cooper, Milwaukee
2B—White, Kansas City
3B—Bell, Texas
SS—Trammell, Detroit
OF—Lynn, Boston
OF—Murphy, Oakland
OF—Wilson, Kansas City

1980 National

P—Niekro, Atlanta
C—Carter, Montreal
1B—Hernandez, St. Louis
2B—Flynn, New York
3B—Schmidt, Philadelphia
SS—Smith, San Diego
OF—Dawson, Montreal
OF—Maddox, Philadelphia
OF—Winfield, San Diego

1981 American

P—Norris, Oakland
C—Sundberg, Texas
1B—Squires, Chicago
2B—White, Kansas City
3B—Bell, Texas
SS—Trammell, Detroit
OF—Murphy, Oakland
OF—Evans, Boston
OF—Henderson, Oakland

1981 National

P—Carlton, Philadelphia
C—Carter, Montreal
1B—Hernandez, St. Louis
2B—Trillo, Philadelphia
3B—Schmidt, Philadelphia
SS—Smith, San Diego
OF—Dawson, Montreal
OF—Maddox, Philadelphia
OF—Baker, Los Angeles

Texas third baseman Buddy Bell is making his sixth consecutive appearance on TSN's Gold Glove Fielding Team.

1982 American

P—Guidry, New York
C—Boone, California
1B—Murray, Baltimore
2B—White, Kansas City
3B—Bell, Texas
SS—Yount, Milwaukee
OF—Evans, Boston
OF—Winfield, New York
OF—Murphy, Oakland

1982 National

P—Niekro, Atlanta
C—Carter, Montreal
1B—Hernandez, St. Louis
2B—Trillo, Philadelphia
3B—Schmidt, Philadelphia
SS—O. Smith, St. Louis
OF—Dawson, Montreal
OF—Murphy, Atlanta
OF—Maddox, Philadelphia

1983 American

P—Guidry, New York
C—Parrish, Detroit
1B—Murray, Baltimore
2B—Whitaker, Detroit
3B—Bell, Texas
SS—Trammell, Detroit
OF—Evans, Boston
OF—Winfield, New York
OF—Murphy, Oakland

1983 National

P—Niekro, Atlanta
C—Pena, Pittsburgh
1B—Hernandez, St.L.-N.Y.
2B—Sandberg, Chicago
3B—Schmidt, Philadelphia
SS—O. Smith, St. Louis
OF—Dawson, Montreal
OF—Murphy, Atlanta
OF—McGee, St. Louis

1984 American

P—Guidry, New York
C—Parrish, Detroit
1B—Murray, Baltimore
2B—Whitaker, Detroit
3B—Bell, Texas
SS—Trammell, Detroit
OF—Evans, Boston
OF—Winfield, New York
OF—Murphy, Oakland

1984 National

P—Andujar, St. Louis
C—Pena, Pittsburgh
1B—Hernandez, New York
2B—Sandberg, Chicago
3B—Schmidt, Philadelphia
SS—O. Smith, St. Louis
OF—Murphy, Atlanta
OF—Dernier, Chicago
OF—Dawson, Montreal

The Sporting News
Silver Slugger Teams

1980 American
1B—Cecil Cooper, Milwaukee
2B—Willie Randolph, New York
3B—George Brett, Kansas City
SS—Robin Yount, Milwaukee
OF—Ben Oglivie, Milwaukee
OF—Al Oliver, Texas
OF—Willie Wilson, Kansas City
C—Lance Parrish, Detroit
DH—Reggie Jackson, New York

1980 National
1B—Keith Hernandez, St. Louis
2B—Manny Trillo, Philadelphia
3B—Mike Schmidt, Philadelphia
SS—Garry Templeton, St. Louis
OF—Dusty Baker, Los Angeles
OF—Andre Dawson, Montreal
OF—George Hendrick, St. Louis
C—Ted Simmons, St. Louis
P—Bob Forsch, St. Louis

1981 American
1B—Cecil Cooper, Milwaukee
2B—Bobby Grich, California
3B—Carney Lansford, Boston
SS—Rick Burleson, California
OF—Rickey Henderson, Oakland
OF—Dwight Evans, Boston
OF—Dave Winfield, New York
C—Carlton Fisk, Chicago
DH—Al Oliver, Texas

1981 National
1B—Pete Rose, Philadelphia
2B—Manny Trillo, Philadelphia
3B—Mike Schmidt, Philadelphia
SS—Dave Concepcion, Cincinnati
OF—Andre Dawson, Montreal
OF—George Foster, Cincinnati
OF—Dusty Baker, Los Angeles
C—Gary Carter, Montreal
P—Fernando Valenzuela, Los Angeles

1982 American
1B—Cecil Cooper, Milwaukee
2B—Damaso Garcia, Toronto
3B—Doug DeCinces, California
SS—Robin Yount, Milwaukee
OF—Dave Winfield, New York
OF—Willie Wilson, Kansas City
OF—Reggie Jackson, California
C—Lance Parrish, Detroit
DH—Hal McRae, Kansas City

1982 National
1B—Al Oliver, Montreal
2B—Joe Morgan, San Francisco
3B—Mike Schmidt, Philadelphia
SS—Dave Concepcion, Cincinnati
OF—Dale Murphy, Atlanta
OF—Pedro Guerrero, Los Angeles
OF—Leon Durham, Chicago
C—Gary Carter, Montreal
P—Don Robinson, Pittsburgh

1983 American
1B—Eddie Murray, Baltimore
2B—Lou Whitaker, Detroit
3B—Wade Boggs, Boston
SS—Cal Ripken, Baltimore
OF—Jim Rice, Boston
OF—Dave Winfield, New York
OF—Lloyd Moseby, Toronto
C—Lance Parrish, Detroit
DH—Don Baylor, New York

1983 National
1B—George Hendrick, St. Louis
2B—Johnny Ray, Pittsburgh
3B—Mike Schmidt, Philadelphia
SS—Dickie Thon, Houston
OF—Andre Dawson, Montreal
OF—Dale Murphy, Atlanta
OF—Jose Cruz, Houston
C—Terry Kennedy, San Diego
P—Fernando Valenzuela, Los Angeles

1984 American
1B—Eddie Murray, Baltimore
2B—Lou Whitaker, Detroit
3B—Buddy Bell, Texas
SS—Cal Ripken, Baltimore
OF—Tony Armas, Boston
OF—Jim Rice, Boston
OF—Dave Winfield, New York
C—Lance Parrish, Detroit
DH—Andre Thornton, Cleveland

1984 National
1B—Keith Hernandez, New York
2B—Ryne Sandberg, Chicago
3B—Mike Schmidt, Philadelphia
SS—Garry Templeton, San Diego
OF—Dale Murphy, Atlanta
OF—Jose Cruz, Houston
OF—Tony Gwynn, San Diego
C—Gary Carter, Montreal
P—Rick Rhoden, Pittsburgh

No-Hit Games Listed by Clubs

AMERICAN LEAGUE

BALTIMORE ORIOLES

Pitcher—Opponent	Score	Date
Hoyt Wilhelm, New York	1-0	9-20-58
Steve Barber (8⅔)-Stu Miller (⅓), Detroit	1-2	4-30-67
Tom Phoebus, Boston	6-0	4-27-68
Jim Palmer, Oakland	8-0	8-13-69

BOSTON RED SOX

Cy Young, Philadelphia	*3-0	5- 5-04
Jesse Tannehill, Chicago	6-0	8-17-04
Bill Dinneen, Chicago	2-0	9-27-05
Cy Young, New York	8-0	6-30-08
Joe Wood, St. Louis	5-0	7-29-11
George Foster, New York	2-0	6-21-16
Hub Leonard, St. Louis	4-0	8-30-16
Ernie Shore, Washington	*4-0	6-23-17
Hub Leonard, Detroit	5-0	6- 3-18
Howard Ehmke, Philadelphia	4-0	9- 7-23
Mel Parnell, Chicago	4-0	7-14-56
Earl Wilson, Los Angeles	2-0	6-26-62
Bill Monbouquette, Chicago	1-0	8- 1-62
Dave Morehead, Cleveland	2-0	9-16-65
*Perfect game.		

CALIFORNIA ANGELS

Bo Belinsky, Baltimore	2-0	5- 5-62
Clyde Wright, Oakland	4-0	7- 3-70
Nolan Ryan, Kansas City	3-0	5-15-73
Nolan Ryan, Detroit	6-0	7-15-73
Nolan Ryan, Minnesota	4-0	9-28-74
Nolan Ryan, Baltimore	1-0	6- 1-75
Mike Witt, Texas	*1-0	9-30-84
*Perfect game.		

CHICAGO WHITE SOX

Jim Callahan, Detroit	3-0	9-20-02
Frank Smith, Detroit	15-0	9- 6-05
Frank Smith, Philadelphia	1-0	9-20-08
Ed Walsh, Boston	5-0	8-27-11
Jim Scott, Washington	0-1	5-14-14
Lost on two hits in ten innings.		
Joe Benz, Cleveland	6-1	5-31-14
Ed Cicotte, St. Louis	11-0	4-14-17
Charles Robertson, Detroit	*2-0	4-30-22
Ted Lyons, Boston	6-0	8-21-26
Vern Kennedy, Cleveland	5-0	8-31-35
Bill Dietrich, St. Louis	8-0	6- 1-37
Bob Keegan, Washington	6-0	8-20-57
Joe Horlen, Detroit	6-0	9-10-67
Johnny Odom (5) and Francisco Barrios (4), Oakland	2-1	7-28-76
*Perfect game.		

CLEVELAND INDIANS

Earl Moore, Chicago	2-4	5- 9-01
Lost on two hits in ten innings.		
Bob Rhoades, Boston	2-1	9-18-08
Addie Joss, Chicago	*1-0	10- 2-08
Addie Joss, Chicago	1-0	4-20-10
Ray Caldwell, New York	3-0	9-10-19
Wes Ferrell, St. Louis	9-0	4-29-31
Bob Feller, Chicago	1-0	4-16-40
Bob Feller, New York	1-0	4-30-46
Don Black, Philadelphia	3-0	7-10-47
Bob Lemon, Detroit	2-0	6-30-48

Bob Feller, Detroit	2-1	7- 1-51
Sonny Siebert, Washington	2-0	6-10-66
Dick Bosman, Oakland	4-0	7-19-74
Dennis Eckersley, California	1-0	5-30-77
Leonard Barker, Toronto	*3-0	5-15-81
*Perfect game.		

DETROIT TIGERS

George Mullin, St. Louis	7-0	7- 4-12
Virgil Trucks, Washington	1-0	5-15-52
Virgil Trucks, New York	1-0	8-25-52
Jim Bunning, Boston	3-0	7-20-58
Jack Morris, Chicago	4-0	4- 7-84

KANSAS CITY ROYALS

Steve Busby, Detroit	3-0	4-27-73
Steve Busby, Milwaukee	2-0	6-19-74
Jim Colborn, Texas	6-0	5-14-77

MINNESOTA TWINS

Jack Kralick, Kansas City	1-0	8-26-62
Dean Chance, Cleveland	2-1	8-25-67

NEW YORK YANKEES

Tom Hughes, Cleveland	0-5	8-30-10
Yielded one hit in tenth; lost on seven hits in 11 innings.		
George Mogridge, Boston	2-1	4-24-17
Sam Jones, Philadelphia	2-0	9- 4-23
Monte Pearson, Cleveland	13-0	8-27-38
Allie Reynolds, Cleveland	1-0	7-12-51
Allie Reynolds, Boston	8-0	9-28-51
Don Larsen, Brooklyn	‡2-0	10- 8-56
Dave Righetti, Boston	4-0	7- 4-83
‡World Series perfect game.		

OAKLAND ATHLETICS

Jim Hunter, Minnesota	*4-0	5- 8-68
Vida Blue, Minnesota	6-0	9-21-70
Vida Blue (5), Glenn Abbott (1), Paul Lindblad (1), Rollie Fingers (2), California	5-0	9-28-75
Mike Warren, Chicago	3-0	9-29-83
*Perfect game.		

PHILADELPHIA ATHLETICS

Weldon Henley, St. Louis	6-0	7-22-05
Chief Bender, Cleveland	4-0	5-12-10
Joe Bush, Cleveland	5-0	8-26-16
Dick Fowler, St. Louis	1-0	9- 9-45
Bill McCahan, Washington	3-0	9- 3-47

ST. LOUIS BROWNS

Earl Hamilton, Detroit	5-1	8-30-12
Ernie Koob, Chicago	1-0	5- 5-17
Bob Groom, Chicago	3-0	5- 6-17
Buck Newsom, Boston	1-2	9-18-34
Lost on one hit in tenth inning.		
Bobo Holloman, Philadelphia	6-0	5- 6-53

TEXAS RANGERS

Jim Bibby, Oakland	6-0	7-30-73
Bert Blyleven, California	6-0	9-22-77

WASHINGTON SENATORS

Walter Johnson, Boston	1-0	7- 1-20
Bob Burke, Boston	*5-0	8- 8-31

NATIONAL LEAGUE
(PRESENT CLUBS)

ATLANTA BRAVES

Pitcher—Opponent	Score	Date
Phil Niekro, San Diego	9-0	8- 5-73

CHICAGO CUBS

Larry Corcoran, Boston	6-0	8-19-80
Larry Corcoran, Worcester	5-0	9-20-82
Larry Corcoran, Providence	6-0	6-27-84
John Clarkson, Providence	4-0	7-27-85
Walter Thornton, Brooklyn	2-0	8-21-98
Bob Wicker, New York	1-0	6-11-04

Yielded only hit in tenth; won in 12 innings.

Jimmy Lavender, New York	2-0	8-31-15
Hippo Vaughn, Cincinnati	0-1	5- 2-17

Lost on two hits in tenth inning; Fred Toney, Cincinnati, pitched ten hitless innings in same game.

Sam Jones, Pittsburgh	4-0	5-12-55
Don Cardwell, St. Louis	4-0	5-16-60
Ken Holtzman, Atlanta	3-0	8-19-69
Ken Holtzman, Cincinnati	1-0	6- 3-71
Burt Hooton, Philadelphia	4-0	4-16-72
Milt Pappas, San Diego	8-0	9- 2-72

CINCINNATI REDS

Bumpus Jones, Pittsburgh	7-1	10-15-92
Theo. Breitenstein, Pittsburgh	11-0	4-22-98
Noodles Hahn, Philadelphia	4-0	7-12-00
Fred Toney, Chicago	†1-0	5- 2-17

Toney's opponent, Hippo Vaughn, pitched nine hitless innings.

Hod Eller, St. Louis	6-0	5-11-19
John Vander Meer, Boston	3-0	6-11-38
John Vander Meer, Brooklyn	6-0	6-15-38
Clyde Shoun, Boston	1-0	5-15-44
Ewell Blackwell, Boston	6-0	6-18-47
John Klippstein (7), Hersh Freeman (1), Joe Black (2⅓), Milwaukee	1-2	5-26-56

Trio yielded no hits until tenth; lost on three hits in 11th inning.

Jim Maloney, New York	0-1	6-14-65

Lost on two hits in eleventh inning.

Jim Maloney, Chicago	†1-0	8-19-65
George Culver, Philadelphia	6-1	7-29-68
Jim Maloney, Houston	10-0	4-30-69
Tom Seaver, St. Louis	4-0	6-16-78

†Ten innings.

HOUSTON ASTROS

Don Nottebart, Philadelphia	4-1	5-17-63
Ken Johnson, Cincinnati	0-1	4-23-64
Don Wilson, Atlanta	2-0	6-18-67
Don Wilson, Cincinnati	4-0	5- 1-69

Larry Dierker, Montreal	6-0	7- 9-76
Ken Forsch, Atlanta	6-0	4-17-79
Nolan Ryan, Los Angeles	5-0	9-26-81

LOS ANGELES DODGERS

Sandy Koufax, New York	5-0	6-30-62
Sandy Koufax, San Francisco	8-0	5-11-63
Sandy Koufax, Philadelphia	3-0	6- 4-64
Sandy Koufax, Chicago	*1-0	9- 9-65
Bill Singer, Philadelphia	5-0	7-20-70
Jerry Reuss, San Francisco	8-0	6-27-80

*Perfect game.

MONTREAL EXPOS

Bill Stoneman, Philadelphia	7-0	4-17-69
Bill Stoneman, New York	7-0	10- 2-72
Charles Lea, San Francisco	4-0	5-10-81

PHILADELPHIA PHILLIES

Charles Ferguson, Providence	1-0	8-29-85
Frank Donohue, Boston	5-0	7- 8-98
Chic Fraser, Chicago	10-0	9-18-03
John Lush, Brooklyn	6-0	5- 1-06
Jim Bunning, New York	*6-0	6-21-64
Rick Wise, Cincinnati	4-0	6-23-71

*Perfect game.

PITTSBURGH PIRATES

Nick Maddox, Brooklyn	2-1	9-20-07
Cliff Chambers, Boston	3-0	5- 6-51
*Harvey Haddix, Milwaukee	0-1	5-26-59
Bob Moose, New York	4-0	9-20-69
Dock Ellis, San Diego	2-0	6-12-70
John Candelaria, Los Angeles	2-0	8- 9-76

*Pitched 12 perfect innings; lost on one hit in 13 innings.

ST. LOUIS CARDINALS

George Bradley, Hartford	2-0	7-15-76
Jess Haines, Boston	5-0	7-17-24
Paul Dean, Brooklyn	3-0	9-21-34
Lon Warneke, Cincinnati	2-0	8-30-41
Ray Washburn, San Francisco	2-0	9-18-68
Bob Gibson, Pittsburgh	11-0	8-14-71
Bob Forsch, Philadelphia	5-0	4-16-78
Bob Forsch, Montreal	3-0	9-26-83

SAN FRANCISCO GIANTS

Juan Marichal, Houston	1-0	6-15-63
Gaylord Perry, St. Louis	1-0	9-17-68
Ed Halicki, New York	6-0	8-24-74
John Montefusco, Atlanta	9-0	9-29-76

(FORMER CLUBS)

BALTIMORE ORIOLES

Pitcher—Opponent	Score	Date
Bill Hawke, Washington	5-0	8-16-93
Jim Hughes, Boston	8-0	4-22-98

BOSTON BRAVES

John Stivetts, Brooklyn	11-0	8- 6-92
Vic Willis, Washington	7-1	8- 7-99
Frank Pfeffer, Cincinnati	6-0	5- 8-07
George Davis, Philadelphia	7-0	9- 9-14
Tom Hughes, Pittsburgh	2-0	6-16-16
Jim Tobin, Brooklyn	2-0	4-27-44
Vern Bickford, Brooklyn	7-0	8-11-50

BROOKLYN DODGERS

Tom Lovett, New York	4-0	6-22-91

Mal Eason, St. Louis	2-0	7-20-06
Harry McIntire, Pittsburgh	0-1	8- 1-06

Yielded first hit in 11th inning; lost on four hits in 13th.

Nap Rucker, Boston	6-0	9- 5-08
Dazzy Vance, Philadelphia	10-1	9-13-25
Tex Carleton, Cincinnati	3-0	4-30-40
Ed Head, Boston	5-0	4-23-46
Rex Barney, New York	2-0	9- 9-48
Carl Erskine, Chicago	5-0	6-19-52
Carl Erskine, New York	3-0	5-12-56
Sal Maglie, Philadelphia	5-0	9-25-56

BUFFALO

Jim Galvin, Worcester	1-0	8-20-80
Jim Galvin, Detroit	18-0	8- 4-84

California's Mike Witt waited until the final day of the 1984 season to throw the first nine-inning major league perfect game since Cleveland's Len Barker accomplished the feat in 1981. Witt recorded a 1-0 victory over the Texas Rangers.

CLEVELAND

Hugh Dalley, Philadelphia	1-0	9-13-83
Cy Young, Cincinnati	6-0	9-18-97

LOUISVILLE

Alex Sanders, Baltimore	6-2	8-22-92
Deacon Phillippe, New York	7-0	5-25-99

MILWAUKEE BRAVES

Jim Wilson, Philadelphia	2-0	6-12-54
Lou Burdette, Philadelphia	1-0	8-18-60
Warren Spahn, Philadelphia	4-0	9-16-60
Warren Spahn, San Francisco	1-0	4-28-61

NEW YORK GIANTS

Amos Rusie, Brooklyn	6-0	7-31-91
Christy Mathewson, St. Louis	5-0	7-15-01
Christy Mathewson, Chicago	1-0	6-13-05
George Wiltse, Philadelphia	†1-0	7- 4-08

Leon Ames, Brooklyn	0-3	4-15-09

Yielded one hit in tenth; lost on seven hits in 13 innings.

Jeff Tesreau, Philadelphia	3-0	9- 6-12
Rube Marquard, Brooklyn	2-0	4-15-15
Jesse Barnes, Philadelphia	6-0	5- 7-22
Carl Hubbell, Pittsburgh	11-0	5- 8-29

†Ten innings.

PROVIDENCE

John Ward, Buffalo	*5-0	6-17-80
Charles Radbourn, Cleveland	8-0	7-25-83

*Perfect game.

WORCESTER

John Richmond, Cleveland	*1-0	6-12-80

*Perfect game.

NOTE—Present pitching distance of 60 feet, six inches was adopted effective with 1893 season.

All-Star Game History

The majors' annual All-Star Game was the brainchild of Arch Ward, late sports editor of the Chicago Tribune. Although the owners approved the first game in 1933 somewhat reluctantly, it has become as much a fixture of the baseball season as the World Series. Even those who at first were cool or indifferent to the idea have since agreed that the game gives baseball a decided midseason pickup.

While there had been talk of an All-Star Game for some years prior to 1933, it took Ward to sell the idea to Commissioner Kenesaw M. Landis and the major leagues as part of the sports program of Chicago's Century of Progress Exposition of that year. The first game was played at Comiskey Park, Chicago, July 6, 1933, and the mid-summer classic has been staged every year since except in 1945, when there was a one-year break because of the wartime curtailment on travel.

They have termed it the "Dream Game," and it has been all of that. The contests have produced some of the most dramatic moments in the history of the sport. The All-Star attractions have been featured by everything from Carl Hubbell striking out Babe Ruth, Lou Gehrig, Jimmie Foxx, Al Simmons and Joe Cronin in succession in the 1934 game to Ted Williams' two-out, two-on homer in the ninth inning to win the 1941 game.

Fortunately, the All-Star competition was started when such great players as Ruth, Gehrig, Hubbell, Simmons, Foxx, Frankie Frisch, Pie Traynor, Jimmie Dykes and others still were headliners. Playing in the first and second games at the age of 38 and 39, Ruth hit a homer and single in six times at bat.

The World Series pilots of the preceding fall usually draw the All-Star managerial nominations. However, in a touch of sentiment, League Presidents Will Harridge and John Heydler selected those grand leaders of the game, Connie Mack and John McGraw, as managers of the first game in 1933. McGraw had retired in midseason of 1932 and made the All-Star Game just in time, for he died the following February.

Of the 11 cities represented in the majors when the All-Star Game was originated, Brooklyn was the last to stage the game. The 1942 contest was awarded to Brooklyn, but because the proceeds were to go to war organizations, Lt.-Col. Larry MacPhail, then president of the Dodgers, permitted the game to be transferred to the Polo Grounds in New York so a larger crowd could be accommodated.

Unfortunately, afternoon showers and a hard downpour at game time held attendance to a disappointing 34,178. Ebbets Field finally was the scene of the mid-summer classic in 1949.

The largest crowd ever for an All-Star Game, 72,086, showed up to see the 1981 contest in Cleveland's Municipal Stadium. There had been speculation prior to the game that fan turnout might be low because the contest, already delayed almost a month, was the first baseball played after a 50-day strike. The N.L. won the game, played on August 9, 5-4.

The smallest crowd in All-Star history, 25,556, turned out for the 1936 game at Braves' Field in Boston.

When Ward first advanced the plan of the Dream Game, it was his idea that the fans should pick the players for the rival teams. This plan was followed more or less in 1933 and 1934, with the managers reserving the right to use other players as they deemed necessary.

Starting in 1935, the magnates turned selection of the teams over to the managers. In 1947, the system of naming the performers was changed again, with the eight starters for each team—all but the pitchers—being picked in a nationwide fan poll and the rival managers selecting the remainder of their squads.

Late in 1957 it was decided to abandon this plan in favor of having the leagues'

A crowd of 47,595 squeezed into Chicago's Comiskey Park for the first All-Star Game in 1933.

managers, coaches and players vote to choose the eight starters on each team with the rival managers picking the remainder of their squads. This plan was followed through 1969.

In 1970, Commissioner Bowie Kuhn returned the selection of the starting teams to the fans. Under the present system, ballots (computerized cards) are distributed in major and minor league ball parks throughout the month of June and voting is done by punching out a box next to the player preferred for each position.

There was considerable criticism in 1970 when Rico Carty, of the Atlanta Braves, was not listed among the nominees for outfielder on the National League team. He was leading the league in batting at the time and, indeed, he went on to win the National League batting championship for the season. However, the fans elected him through write-ins and he was in the starting lineup.

A radical change went into effect in 1959. At the request of the players, the owners agreed to an arrangement of two games each year to speed payment of pension fund indebtedness. Sixty percent of the All-Star gate receipts and radio-television money went into the pension fund. However, after playing two games each season for four years, the players approved a return to one game in December, 1962. The fans' interest was centered on one game and diminished with two.

The 1985 All-Star Game is scheduled to be played at night at the Metrodome in Minneapolis, July 16.

Game of 1933

Comiskey Park, Chicago, July 6

Babe Ruth, with his genius for stealing the thunder, was the hero of the first All-Star Game as the American Leaguers defeated the Nationals, 4-2. The Bambino's two-run homer in the third inning represented the margin of victory. In addition, Ruth made the game's best defensive play. He moved his 38-year-old legs fast over the turf to grab a steaming line drive by Chick Hafey in the eighth inning.

The American League players wore their regular home uniforms, but John Heydler, then National League president, dressed up the N.L. players in special uniforms for the occasion. They were steel gray with "National League" spelled out in blue letters across the blouses. The game yielded $52,000, of which $45,000 went to the Association of Professional Ball Players, the game's benevolent society.

Connie Mack stated that the American League was out to win rather than to see how many stars it could inject into the box score. He made only one change in his lineup apart from pitchers. By contrast, N.L. Manager John McGraw used 17 players.

McGraw started Bill Hallahan, Cardinal southpaw, in hopes of curbing Ruth and Lou Gehrig, but the selection was unfortunate for the National League. Hallahan was terribly wild, giving up five walks and three runs before he was derricked with none out in the third inning. All of the N.L. runs came off Alvin Crowder, Mack's middle pitcher.

Lefty Gomez was credited with the victory, but he still is prouder of the fact that he drove in the first run in All-Star competition. After Al Simmons flied out in the second inning, Jimmie Dykes coaxed a pass. Joe Cronin also worked Hallahan for a walk, but Rick Ferrell lined out. Gomez then surprised the N.L. contingent by lining a single over shortstop to plate Dykes. The box score:

American League 4, National League 2

(American League Leads Series, 1-0)

NATIONALS	AB.	R.	H.	PO.	A.	E.	AMERICANS	AB.	R.	H.	PO.	A.	E.
Martin (Cardinals), 3b	4	0	0	0	3	0	Chapman (Yankees), lf-rf	5	0	1	1	0	0
Frisch (Cardinals), 2b	4	1	2	5	3	0	Gehringer (Tigers), 2b	3	1	0	1	3	0
Klein (Phillies), rf	4	0	1	3	0	0	Ruth (Yankees), rf	4	1	2	1	0	0
P. Waner (Pirates), rf	0	0	0	0	0	0	West (Browns), cf	0	0	0	0	0	0
Hafey (Reds), lf	4	0	1	0	0	0	Gehrig (Yankees), 1b	2	0	0	12	0	1
Terry (Giants), 1b	4	0	2	7	2	0	Simmons (Wh. Sox), cf-lf	4	0	1	4	0	0
Berger (Braves), cf	4	0	0	4	0	0	Dykes (White Sox), 3b	3	1	2	2	4	0
Bartell (Phillies), ss	2	0	0	0	3	0	Cronin (Senators), ss	3	1	1	2	4	0
cTraynor (Pirates)	1	0	1	0	0	0	R. Ferrell (Red Sox), c	3	0	0	4	0	0
Hubbell (Giants), p	0	0	0	0	0	0	Gomez (Yankees), p	1	0	1	0	0	0
eCuccinello (Dodgers)	1	0	0	0	0	0	Crowder (Senators), p	1	0	0	0	0	0
Wilson (Cardinals), c	1	0	0	2	0	0	bAverill (Indians)	1	0	1	0	0	0
aO'Doul (Giants)	1	0	0	0	0	0	Grove (Athletics), p	1	0	0	0	0	0
Hartnett (Cubs), c	1	0	0	2	0	0	Totals	31	4	9	27	11	1
Hallahan (Cardinals), p	1	0	0	1	0	0							
Warneke (Cubs), p	1	1	1	0	0	0							
dEnglish (Cubs), ss	1	0	0	0	0	0							
Totals	34	2	8	24	11	0							

```
National League ..................................  0   0   0      0   0   2      0   0   0 — 2
American League ..................................  0   1   2      0   0   1      0   0   x — 4
```

Nationals	IP.	H.	R.	ER.	BB.	SO.	Americans	IP.	H.	R.	ER.	BB.	SO.
Hallahan (Cardinals)	2*	2	3	3	5	1	Gomez (Yankees)	3	2	0	0	0	1
Warneke (Cubs)	4	6	1	1	0	2	Crowder (Senators)	3	3	2	2	0	0
Hubbell (Giants)	2	1	0	0	1	1	Grove (Athletics)	3	3	0	0	0	3

*Pitched to three batters in third.

Winning pitcher—Gomez.   Losing pitcher—Hallahan.

aGrounded out for Wilson in sixth. bSingled for Crowder in sixth. cDoubled for Bartell in seventh. dFlied out for Warneke in seventh. eFanned for Hubbell in ninth. Runs batted in—Martin, Frisch, Ruth 2, Gomez, Averill. Two-base hit—Traynor. Three-base hit—Warneke. Home runs—Ruth, Frisch. Sacrifice hit—Ferrell. Stolen base—Gehringer. Double plays—Bartell, Frisch and Terry; Dykes and Gehrig. Left on bases—Americans 10, Nationals 5. Umpires—Dinneen and McGowan (A.L.), Klem and Rigler (N.L.). Time of game—2:05. Attendance—47,595.

Game of 1934

Polo Grounds, New York, July 10

For drama, excitement and a quick change in fortunes, the second All-Star Game was a real thriller. Victory again went to the American League, 9-7, but only after a titanic struggle. Despite the big score, the game saw some of the greatest All-Star pitching by Carl Hubbell and Mel Harder.

The N. L. had the better of it in the early going, grabbing a 4-0 lead as Hubbell performed his mound magic. After the first two A. L. stars reached base in the opening inning, the Giants' southpaw struck out Babe Ruth, Lou Gehrig and Jimmie Foxx in succession. In the second inning, he fanned Al Simmons and Joe Cronin to make it five strikeouts in succession. After Bill Dickey singled, Lefty Gomez became Hubbell's sixth whiff victim in two innings.

The Americans bounced back with a vengeance to score eight runs off Lon Warneke and Van Mungo in the fourth and fifth innings. The Nationals then kayoed Red Ruffing before he could retire a batter in their fifth turn, but Harder came on to perform his magic, holding the N. L. to one hit over the last five rounds.

Homers by Frank Frisch in the first inning and Joe Medwick with two aboard in the third staked the Nationals to their early 4-0 lead.

Earl Averill was the Americans' batting hero. He hammered a run-scoring triple as a pinch-hitter in the fourth inning and then doubled across two more runs in the fifth. The box score:

American League 9, National League 7

(American League Leads Series, 2-0)

AMERICAN	AB.	R.	H.	PO.	A.	E.
Gehringer (Tigers), 2b	3	0	2	2	1	0
Manush (Senators), lf	2	0	0	0	0	0
Ruffing (Yankees), p	1	0	1	0	0	0
Harder (Indians), p	2	0	0	1	0	0
Ruth (Yankees), rf	2	1	0	0	0	0
Chapman (Yankees), rf	2	0	1	0	1	0
Gehrig (Yankees), 1b	4	1	0	11	1	1
Foxx, (Athletics), 3b	5	1	2	1	2	0
Simmons (Wh. Sox), cf-lf	5	3	3	3	0	0
Cronin (Senators), ss	5	1	2	2	8	0
Dickey (Yankees), c	2	1	1	4	0	0
hCochrane (Tigers), c	1	0	0	1	1	0
Gomez (Yankees), p	1	0	0	0	0	0
bAverill (Indians), cf	4	1	2	1	0	0
West (Browns), cf	0	0	0	1	0	0
Totals	39	9	14	27	14	1

NATIONALS	AB.	R.	H.	PO.	A.	E.
Frisch (Cardinals), 2b	3	3	2	0	1	0
aHerman (Cubs), 2b	2	0	1	0	1	0
Traynor (Pirates), 3b	5	2	2	1	0	0
Medwick (Cardinals), lf	2	1	1	0	0	0
dKlein (Cubs), lf	3	0	1	1	0	0
Cuyler (Cubs), rf	2	0	0	2	0	0
eOtt (Giants), rf	2	0	0	0	1	0
Berger (Braves), cf	2	0	0	0	0	1
fP. Waner (Pirates), cf	2	0	0	1	0	0
Terry (Giants), 1b	3	0	1	4	0	0
Jackson (Giants), ss	2	0	0	1	0	0
gVaughan (Pirates), ss	2	0	0	4	0	0
Hartnett (Cubs), c	2	0	0	9	0	0
Lopez (Dodgers), c	2	0	0	5	1	0
Hubbell (Giants), p	0	0	0	0	0	0
Warneke (Cubs), p	0	0	0	0	0	0
Mungo (Dodgers), p	0	0	0	0	0	0
cMartin (Cardinals)	0	1	0	0	0	0
Dean (Cardinals), p	1	0	0	0	0	0
Frankhouse (Braves), p	1	0	0	0	0	0
Totals	36	7	8	27	5	1

American League	0	0	0	2	6	1	0	0	0	—9
National League	1	0	3	0	3	0	0	0	0	—7

Americans	IP.	H.	R.	ER.	BB.	SO.
Gomez (Yankees)	3	3	4	4	1	3
Ruffing (Yankees)	1†	4	3	3	1	0
Harder (Indians)	5	1	0	0	1	2

Nationals	IP.	H.	R.	ER.	BB.	SO.
Hubbell (Giants)	3	2	0	0	2	6
Warneke (Cubs)	1*	3	4	4	3	1
Mungo (Dodgers)	1	4	4	4	2	1
Dean (Cardinals)	3	5	1	1	1	4
Frankhouse (Braves)	1	0	0	0	1	0

*Pitched to two batters in fifth. †Pitched to four batters in fifth.

Winning pitcher—Harder. Losing pitcher—Mungo.

aPopped out for Hubbell in third but was permitted to replace Frisch in seventh. bTripled for Gomez in fourth. cWalked for Mungo in fifth. dSingled for Medwick in fifth. eForced runner for Cuyler in fifth. fFanned for Berger in fifth. gForced runner for Jackson in fifth. hRan for Dickey in sixth. Runs batted in—Frisch, Medwick 3, Cronin 2, Averill 3, Foxx, Simmons, Ruffing 2, Traynor, Klein. Two-base hits—Foxx, Simmons 2, Cronin, Averill, Herman. Three-base hits—Chapman, Averill. Home runs—Frisch, Medwick. Stolen bases—Gehringer, Manush, Traynor, Ott. Double play—Lopez and Vaughan. Left on bases—American 12, Nationals 5. Umpires—Pfirman and Stark (N. L.), Owens and Moriarty (A. L.). Time of game—2:44. Attendance—48,363.

Game of 1935
Municipal Stadium, Cleveland, July 8

A crowd of 69,831—the largest throng to see an All-Star Game—packed Cleveland's big lakefront stadium for the third contest and, being largely American League rooters, thrilled to the junior circuit's third successive victory, 4-1.

Cardinals' Manager Frank Frisch, who piloted the National League team, started his own southpaw, Bill Walker. After retiring the A. L.'s first batter of the game, Walker passed Charley Gehringer, but Lou Gehrig forced him. Jimmie Foxx then applied his broad shoulders to a pitch and rode it into the left-field stands for a homer and a 2-0 lead.

The Americans jumped on Walker for another run in the second inning on a triple by Rollie Hemsley and Joe Cronin's fly to Wally Berger. Hal Schumacher struck out five in his four-inning tour of duty for the Nationals, but yielded the Americans' final run in the fifth inning. With two out, Joe Vosmik singled and went to third on Gehringer's single. After Gehrig walked, filling the bases, Foxx singled Vosmik across.

Mickey Cochrane, American League manager, used just two pitchers, Lefty Gomez and Mel Harder. Gomez worked the first six innings, yielding three hits and the lone National League run. It came in the fourth inning when Arky Vaughan led off with a double to right and scored on Bill Terry's single.

Because Harder worked five innings in the 1934 game and Gomez went six in this contest, the National League had the All-Star rules changed so that no pitcher could hurl more than three innings unless a game went into overtime. Harder allowed only one hit in three innings this time, giving him a record of permitting only two hits in eight successive innings against the N. L.'s hardest hitters.

The box score:

American League 4, National League 1
(American League Leads Series, 3-0)

NATIONALS	AB.	R.	H.	PO.	A.	E.
Martin (Cardinals), 3b	4	0	1	0	0	1
Vaughan (Pirates), ss	3	1	1	2	2	0
Ott (Giants), rf	4	0	0	1	0	0
Medwick (Cardinals), lf	3	0	0	0	0	0
Terry (Giants), 1b	3	0	1	5	1	0
Collins (Cardinals), 1b	1	0	0	2	0	0
Berger (Braves), cf	2	0	0	1	0	0
bMoore (Giants), cf	2	0	0	1	0	0
Herman (Cubs), 2b	3	0	0	1	4	0
Wilson (Phillies), c	3	0	1	8	0	0
cWhitehead (Cardinals)	0	0	0	0	0	0
Hartnett (Cubs), c	0	0	0	3	0	0
Walker (Giants), p	0	0	0	0	0	0
aMancuso (Giants)	1	0	0	0	0	0
Schmuacher (Giants), p	1	0	0	0	1	0
dP. Waner (Pirates)	1	0	0	0	0	0
Derringer (Reds), p	0	0	0	0	0	0
Dean (Cardinals), p	0	0	0	0	0	0
Totals	31	1	4	24	8	1

AMERICANS	AB.	R.	H.	PO.	A.	E.
Vosmik (Indians), rf	4	1	1	1	0	0
Gehringer (Tigers), 2b	3	0	2	1	3	0
Gehrig (Yankees), 1b	3	1	0	12	0	0
Foxx (Athletics), 3b	3	1	2	0	0	0
Bluege (Senators), 3b	0	0	0	0	0	0
Johnson (Athletics), lf	4	0	0	4	0	0
Chapman (Yankees), lf	0	0	0	0	0	0
Simmons (Wh. Sox), cf	4	0	2	2	0	0
Cramer (Athletics), cf	0	0	0	0	0	0
Hemsley (Browns), c	4	1	1	6	0	0
Cronin (Red Sox), ss	4	0	1	1	4	0
Gomez (Yankees), p	2	0	0	0	2	0
Harder (Indians), p	1	0	0	0	1	0
Totals	32	4	8	27	10	0

National League	0	0	0	1	0	0	0	0	0—1
American League	2	1	0	0	1	0	0	0	x—4

Nationals	IP.	H.	R.	ER.	BB.	SO.
Walker (Cardinals)	2	2	3	3	1	2
Schumacher (Giants)	4	4	1	1	1	5
Derringer (Reds)	1	1	0	0	0	1
Dean (Cardinals)	1	1	0	0	1	1

Americans	IP.	H.	R.	ER.	BB.	SO.
Gomez (Yankees)	6	3	1	1	2	4
Harder (Indians)	3	1	0	0	0	1

Winning pitcher—Gomez. Losing pitcher—Walker.

aFlied out for Walker in third. bFlied out for Berger in seventh. cRan for Wilson in seventh. dGrounded out for Schumacher in seventh. Runs batted in—Foxx 3, Cronin, Terry. Two-base hits—Vaughan, Wilson, Gehringer, Simmons. Three-base hit—Hemsley. Home run—Foxx. Left on bases—Americans 7, Nationals 5. Umpires—Ormsby and Geisel (A. L.), Magerkurth and Sears (N. L.). Time of game—2:06. Attendance—69,831.

Game of 1936
Braves Field, Boston, July 7

After losing three straight, the National League gained its first All-Star victory, 4-3. An unfortunate mixup in the sale of unreserved seats resulted in only 25,556 fans attending, leaving some 10,000 empty seats.

Joe McCarthy, who went on to manage seven All-Star teams, got into his first game— as a pinch-manager for Mickey Cochrane. Cochrane, Detroit's fighting catcher-manager, was slated to be the American League manager, but he had a nervous breakdown in June and was sent to a Wyoming ranch to recuperate.

Joe DiMaggio, the Yankees' brilliant rookie center fielder, was the goat of the first A. L. defeat. Coming up repeatedly in the pinch, he failed to get a hit in five attempts, although one of his line drives almost spun Leo Durocher around.

DiMaggio, who played right field, also missed on an attempted shoestring catch on Gabby Hartnett in the second inning and the ball went for a triple. The hit helped the N. L. to a 2-0 lead. In the fifth frame, DiMag's fumble on a single by Billy Herman also proved costly, setting up the Nationals' final run. The error came just moments after Augie Galan smashed a drive that hit the right-field flagpole for a home run.

Dizzy Dean, Carl Hubbell, Curt Davis and Lon Warneke pitched the N. L. to its first victory, although Davis almost wrecked his team's chances in his brief turn on the mound in the seventh inning. Lou Gehrig greeted Davis with a homer. After he retired the next two batters, a pair of singles and a walk filled the bases and Luke Appling's ace plated two more A. L. runs. Warneke then came on and, after passing Charley Gehringer to fill the bases, he faced DiMaggio. With a chance to redeem himself, DiMag hit a terrific liner just a bit to Durocher's right, but Leo gloved the ball just as it was about to sail to the outfield. The box score:

National League 4, American League 3
(American League Leads Series, 3-1)

AMERICANS	AB.	R.	H.	PO.	A.	E.	NATIONALS	AB.	R.	H.	PO.	A.	E.
Appling (Wh. Sox), ss	4	0	1	2	2	0	Galan (Cubs), cf	4	1	1	1	0	0
Gehringer (Tigers), 2b	3	0	2	2	1	0	Herman (Cubs), 2b	3	1	2	3	4	0
DiMaggio (Yankees), rf	5	0	0	1	0	1	Collins (Cardinals), 1b	2	0	0	9	1	0
Gehrig (Yankees), 1b	2	1	1	7	0	0	Medwick (Cardinals), lf	4	0	1	0	0	0
Averill (Indians), cf	3	0	0	3	1	0	Demaree (Cubs), rf	3	1	1	1	0	0
Chapman (Senators), cf	0	0	0	0	0	0	dOtt (Giants), rf	1	0	1	0	0	0
Ferrell (Red Sox), c	2	0	0	4	0	0	Hartnett (Cubs), c	4	1	1	7	0	0
aDickey (Yankees), c	2	0	0	2	0	0	Whitney (Phillies), 3b	3	0	1	0	2	0
Radcliff (Wh. Sox), lf	2	0	1	2	0	0	eRiggs (Reds), 3b	1	0	0	0	0	0
Goslin (Tigers), lf	1	1	1	1	0	0	Durocher (Cardinals), ss	3	0	1	4	0	0
Higgins (Athletics), 3b	2	0	0	1	1	0	J. Dean (Cardinals), p	1	0	0	0	2	0
bFoxx (Red Sox), 3b	2	1	1	0	1	0	Hubbell (Giants), p	1	0	0	2	1	0
Grove (Red Sox), p	1	0	0	0	0	0	Davis (Cubs), p	0	0	0	0	1	0
Rowe (Tigers), p	1	0	0	0	0	0	Warneke (Cubs), p	1	0	0	0	0	0
cSelkirk (Yankees)	0	0	0	0	0	0	Totals	31	4	9	27	11	0
Harder (Indians), p	0	0	0	0	1	0							
fCrosetti (Yankees)	1	0	0	0	0	0							
Totals	32	3	7	24	7	1							

American League	0	0	0	0	0	0	3	0	0 — 3	
National League	0	2	0	0	2	0	0	0	x — 4	

Americans	IP.	H.	R.	ER.	BB.	SO.	Nationals	IP.	H.	R.	ER.	BB.	SO.
Grove (Red Sox)	3	3	2	2	2	2	J. Dean (Cardinals)	3	0	0	0	2	3
Rowe (Tigers)	3	4	2	1	1	2	Hubbell (Giants)	3	2	0	0	1	2
Harder (Indians)	2	2	0	0	0	2	Davis (Cubs)	⅔	4	3	3	1	0
							Warneke (Cubs)	2⅓	1	0	0	3	2

Winning pitcher—J. Dean. Losing pitcher—Grove.

aGrounded out for Ferrell in seventh. bSingled for Higgins in seventh. cWalked for Rowe in seventh. dSingled for Demaree in eighth. eFanned for Whitney in eighth. fFanned for Harder in ninth. Runs batted in—Hartnett, Whitney, Medwick, Galan, Appling 2, Gehrig. Two-base hit—Gehringer. Three-base hit—Hartnett. Home runs—Galan, Gehrig. Double plays—Whitney, Herman and Collins; Appling, Gehringer and Gehrig. Left on bases—Americans 9, Nationals 6. Wild pitch—Hubbell. Umpires—Reardon and Stewart (N. L.), Summers and Kolls (A. L.). Time of game—2:00. Attendance—25,556.

Game of 1937

Griffith Stadium, Washington, July 7

The American League All-Stars, made up largely of Yankees, really dazzled, pounding out an easy 8-3 victory before a crowd of 31,391. The turnout included President Franklin D. Roosevelt, who drove on the field in an open car, plus cabinet officers and members of Congress.

Joe McCarthy, A. L. manager, had five of his Yankees in the starting lineup—Lou Gehrig, Red Rolfe, Joe DiMaggio, Bill Dickey and Lefty Gomez. All but Gomez played the entire game. Gehrig, enjoying his last big season, was the winners' batting star, driving in four runs with a homer and double.

Dizzy Dean, the Nationals' starting pitcher, remembered this game to the day he died. He began the day as baseball's outstanding pitcher, but a toe fracture suffered in the third inning started him on the downgrade and he never was the same thereafter.

It all began when Diz shook off Gabby Hartnett on a 3-and-2 pitch to Gehrig. Throwing a smoking fast ball instead of a curve, Dean saw Gehrig send it high over the distant right-field wall for a two-run homer and a 2-0 lead. Earl Averill, next up, then hit a line drive back at Dean's foot with the force of a machine gun bullet. Dizzy managed to recover the ball and retire Averill, but when he reached the clubhouse, he discovered he had a broken toe on his left foot.

The Americans pretty well sewed up the game against Carl Hubbell in the fourth inning, tagging him for three runs on a walk, a single, Rolfe's triple and a single by Charley Gehringer. The box score:

American League 8, National League 3

(American League Leads Series, 4-1)

NATIONALS	AB.	R.	H.	PO.	A.	E.	AMERICANS	AB.	R.	H.	PO.	A.	E.
P. Waner (Pirates), rf	5	0	0	0	0	0	Rolfe, (Yankees), 3b	4	2	2	0	1	2
Herman (Cubs), 2b	5	1	2	1	4	0	Gehringer (Tigers), 2b	5	1	3	2	5	0
Vaughan (Pirates), 3b	5	0	2	3	0	0	DiMaggio (Yankees), rf	4	1	1	1	1	0
Medwick (Cardinals), lf	5	1	4	1	0	0	Gehrig (Yankees), 1b	4	1	2	10	1	0
Demaree (Cubs), cf	5	0	1	3	1	0	Averill (Indians), cf	3	0	1	2	0	0
Mize (Cardinals), 1b	4	0	0	7	0	0	Cronin (Red Sox), ss	4	1	1	4	3	0
Hartnett (Cubs), c	3	1	1	6	0	0	Dickey (Yankees), c	3	1	2	2	0	0
bWhitehead (Giants)	0	0	0	0	0	0	West (Browns), lf	4	1	1	5	0	0
Mancuso (Giants), c	1	0	0	1	0	0	Gomez (Yankees), p	1	0	0	0	0	0
Bartell (Giants), ss	4	0	1	2	3	0	Bridges (Tigers), p	1	0	0	0	1	0
J. Dean (Cardinals), p	1	0	0	0	1	0	dFoxx (Red Sox)	1	0	0	0	0	0
Hubbell (Giants), p	0	0	0	0	0	0	Harder (Indians), p	1	0	0	1	1	0
Blanton (Pirates), p	0	0	0	0	0	0	Totals	35	8	13	27	13	2
aOtt (Giants)	1	0	1	0	0	0							
Grissom (Reds), p	0	0	0	0	0	0							
cCollins (Cubs)	1	0	1	0	0	0							
Mungo (Dodgers), p	0	0	0	0	1	0							
eMoore (Giants)	1	0	0	0	0	0							
Walters (Phillies), p	0	0	0	0	1	0							
Totals	41	3	13	24	11	0							

National League	0	0	0	1	1	1	0	0	0 — 3			
American League	0	0	2	3	1	2	0	0	x — 8			

Nationals	IP.	H.	R.	ER.	BB.	SO.	Americans	IP.	H.	R.	ER.	BB.	SO.
J. Dean (Cardinals)	3	4	2	2	1	2	Gomez (Yankees)	3	1	0	0	0	0
Hubbell (Giants)	⅔	3	3	3	1	1	Bridges (Tigers)	3	7	3	3	0	0
Blanton (Pirates)	⅓	0	0	0	0	1	Harder (Indians)	3	5	0	0	0	0
Grissom (Reds)	1	2	1	1	0	2							
Mungo (Dodgers)	2	2	2	2	2	1							
Walters (Phillies)	1	2	0	0	0	0							

Winning pitcher—Gomez. Losing pitcher—J. Dean.

aDoubled for Blanton in fifth. bRan for Hartnett in sixth. cSingled for Grissom in sixth. dGrounded out for Bridges in sixth. eForced runner for Mungo in eighth. Runs batted in—Gehrig 4, Rolfe 2, Gehringer, Dickey, P. Waner, Medwick, Mize. Two-base hits—Gehrig, Dickey, Cronin, Ott, Medwick 2. Three-base hit—Rolfe. Home run—Gehrig. Double play—Bartell and Mize. Left on bases—Nationals 11, Americans 7. Umpires—McGowan and Quinn (A. L.), Barr and Pinelli (N. L.). Time of game—2:30. Attendance—31,391.

Game of 1938
Crosley Field, Cincinnati, July 6

The strong-armed pitching of Johnny Vander Meer, Bill Lee and Mace Brown led the National League to a 4-1 victory. The trio limited the A.L. All-Stars to seven hits.

This was the year of Vander Meer's successive no-hitters, and the white-haired boy of the Cincinnati team didn't disappoint his 27,067 hometown fans in the midsummer classic. Manager Bill Terry gave him the distinction of starting the game. Vandy turned back the A.L. stars with one hit in his three innings.

Unlike his course in the 1934 and 1937 games, Terry made no effort to turn the game into a parade of National League stars. Except for pitchers, he didn't make a single change in his lineup, using only 12 players.

Lefty Gomez opened on the mound for the A.L. and suffered his first defeat, but it wasn't his fault. An error by Joe Cronin—the first of four A.L. boots—set up a run in the opening inning. Johnny Allen yielded a second run in the fourth on Mel Ott's triple and a single by Ernie Lombardi.

The N.L. scored two more off Lefty Grove in the seventh on the most ludicrous of All-Star plays.

Frank McCormick greeted Grove with a single and Leo Durocher laid down a sacrifice bunt. It did as much damage as a home run because Jimmie Foxx, playing third base, threw the ball into right field. When Joe DiMaggio, after retrieving the ball, overthrew the plate trying for McCormick, Durocher continued running until he scored for a "bunt-home run."

The Americans pasted Mace Brown hard in the ninth inning, but he escaped with one run. A single by DiMaggio and Joe Cronin's long double produced the marker.

Two great catches by Joe Medwick and Ival Goodman spared Brown from further trouble. The box score:

National League 4, American League 1

(American League Leads Series, 4-2)

AMERICANS	AB.	R.	H.	PO.	A.	E.	NATIONALS	AB.	R.	H.	PO.	A.	E.
Kreevich (Wh. Sox), lf	2	0	0	1	0	0	Hack (Cubs), 3b	4	1	1	1	2	0
cCramer (Red Sox), lf	2	0	0	0	0	0	Herman (Cubs), 2b	4	0	1	3	4	0
Gehringer (Tigers), 2b	3	0	1	2	2	0	Goodman (Reds), rf	3	0	0	2	0	0
Averill (Indians), cf	4	0	0	5	0	0	Medwick (Cardinals), lf	4	0	1	2	0	0
Foxx (Red Sox), 1b-3b	4	0	1	5	1	1	Ott (Giants), cf	4	1	1	3	0	0
DiMaggio (Yankees), rf	4	1	1	2	0	1	Lombardi (Reds), c	4	0	2	5	0	0
Dickey (Yankees), c	4	0	1	8	0	1	McCormick (Reds), 1b	4	1	1	11	0	0
Cronin (Red Sox), ss	3	0	2	0	2	1	Durocher (Dodgers), ss	3	1	1	0	3	0
Lewis (Senators), 3b	1	0	0	0	1	0	Vander Meer (Reds), p	0	0	0	0	3	0
bGehrig (Yankees), 1b	3	0	1	1	0	0	aLeiber (Giants)	1	0	0	0	0	0
Gomez (Yankees), p	1	0	0	0	0	0	Lee (Cubs), p	1	0	0	0	0	0
Allen (Indians), p	1	0	0	0	0	0	Brown (Pirates) p	1	0	0	0	1	0
dYork (Tigers)	1	0	0	0	0	0	Totals	33	4	8	27	13	0
Grove (Red Sox), p	0	0	0	0	0	0							
eJohnson (Athletics)	1	0	0	0	0	0							
Totals	34	1	7	24	6	4							

American League	0	0	0	0	0	0	0	0	1 — 1
National League	1	0	0	1	0	0	2	0	x — 4

Americans	IP.	H.	R.	ER.	BB.	SO.	Nationals	IP.	H.	R.	ER.	BB.	SO.
Gomez (Yankees)	3	2	1	0	0	1	Vander Meer (Reds)	3	1	0	0	0	1
Allen (Indians)	3	2	1	1	0	3	Lee (Cubs)	3	1	0	0	1	2
Grove (Red Sox)	2	4	2	0	0	3	Brown (Pirates)	3	5	1	1	1	2

Winning pitcher—Vander Meer. Losing pitcher—Gomez.

aLined out for Vander Meer in third. bGrounded out for Lewis in fifth. cGrounded out for Kreevich in sixth. dFanned for Allen in seventh. eStruck out for Grove in ninth. Runs batted in—Medwick, Lombardi, Cronin. Two-base hits—Dickey, Cronin. Three-base hit—Ott. Stolen bases—Goodman, DiMaggio. Left on bases—Americans 8, Nationals 6. Hit by pitcher—By Allen—(Goodman). Umpires—Ballanfant and Klem (N. L.), Basil and Geisel (A. L.). Time of game—1:58. Attendance—27,067.

Game of 1939
Yankee Stadium, New York, July 11

With six Yankees in the starting lineup, the American League stars emerged victorious, 3-1. The game was the second to be played in New York and was awarded to the Big Town because it was World's Fair year there. A crowd of 62,892 attended.

The announcer's introduction of six Yankees in the starting lineup prompted an inebriated fan with N.L. sympathies to pull a famous quip. "That isn't fair," he remarked. "They ought to make Joe McCarthy play an All-Star American League team. We can beat them, but we can't beat the Yankees."

McCarthy opened with a New York battery of Red Ruffing and Bill Dickey. Other Yankees in the lineup were Joe DiMaggio, George Selkirk, Joe Gordon and Red Rolfe. And the only time Marse Joe called on a pinch-hitter he used Myril Hoag, a former Yankee.

The N.L. was the first to score, picking up its lone run off Ruffing in the third inning on singles by Arky Vaughan and Stan Hack plus Lonnie Frey's double.

The Americans gained the lead with two tallies in the fourth at the expense of Bill Lee.

With one out, Dickey walked and Hank Greenberg singled. Another ace by Selkirk plated one run and Greenberg subsequently scored when Vaughan bobbled Gordon's roller. DiMaggio closed the run-making with a homer in the fifth.

The A.L.'s big hero was Bob Feller. He took over in a ticklish situation in the sixth inning. The bases were full with one out and Vaughan at bat when Bob relieved Tommy Bridges.

Feller didn't waste any time, retiring the side on one pitch, which Vaughan hit into a double play. The Cleveland fireballer then checked the N.L. on one hit over the last three frames. The box score:

American League 3, National League 1

(American League Leads Series, 5-2)

NATIONALS	AB.	R.	H.	PO.	A.	E.
Hack (Cubs), 3b	4	0	1	1	1	0
Frey (Reds), 2b	4	0	1	0	4	0
Goodman (Reds), rf	1	0	0	0	0	0
cHerman (Cubs)	1	0	0	0	0	0
Moore (Cardinals), cf	1	0	0	0	0	0
McCormick (Reds), 1b	4	0	0	7	1	0
Lombardi (Reds), c	4	0	2	6	0	0
Medwick (Cardinals), lf	4	0	1	0	0	0
Ott (Giants), cf-rf	4	0	2	4	0	0
Vaughan (Pirates), ss	3	1	1	4	1	1
Derringer (Reds), p	1	0	0	0	0	0
bCamilli (Dodgers)	1	0	0	0	0	0
Lee (Cubs), p	0	0	0	0	0	0
dPhelps (Dodgers)	1	0	0	0	0	0
Fette (Braves), p	0	0	0	1	0	0
eMize (Cardinals)	1	0	0	0	0	0
Totals	34	1	7	24	7	1

AMERICANS	AB.	R.	H.	PO.	A.	E.
Cramer (Red Sox), rf	4	0	1	3	0	0
Rolfe (Yankees), 3b	4	0	1	0	0	0
DiMaggio (Yankees), cf	4	1	1	1	0	0
Dickey (Yankees), c	3	1	0	10	0	0
Greenberg (Tigers), 1b	3	1	1	7	1	0
Cronin (Red Sox), ss	4	0	1	2	3	1
Selkirk (Yankees), lf	2	0	1	0	0	0
Gordon (Yankees), 2b	4	0	0	2	5	0
Ruffing (Yankees), p	0	0	0	0	0	0
aHoag (Browns)	1	0	0	0	0	0
Bridges (Tigers), p	1	0	0	1	0	0
Feller (Indians), p	1	0	0	0	0	0
Totals	31	3	6	27	9	1

National League	0	0	1	0	0	0	0	0	0 — 1
American League	0	0	0	2	1	0	0	0	x — 3

Nationals	IP.	H.	R.	ER.	BB.	SO.
Derringer (Reds)	3	2	0	0	0	1
Lee (Cubs)	3	3	3	2	3	4
Fette (Braves)	2	1	0	0	1	1

Americans	IP.	H.	R.	ER.	BB.	SO.
Ruffing (Yankees)	3	4	1	1	1	4
Bridges (Tigers)	2⅓	2	0	0	1	3
Feller (Indians)	3⅔	1	0	0	1	2

Winning pitcher—Bridges. Losing pitcher—Lee.

aFanned for Ruffing in third. bStruck out for Derringer in fourth. cStruck out for Goodman in fifth. dGrounded out for Lee in seventh. eStruck out for Fette in ninth. Runs batted in—DiMaggio, Selkirk, Frey. Home run—DiMaggio. Double play—Gordon, Cronin and Greenberg. Left on bases—Nationals 9, Americans 8. Umpires—Hubbard and Rommel (A. L.), Goetz and Magerkurth (N. L.). Time of game—1:55. Attendance—62,892.

Game of 1940
Sportsman's Park, St. Louis, July 9

The National League scored the first shutout of the All-Star series when five hurlers combined to blank the A. L. on three hits, 4-0. Bill McKechnie, senior circuit skipper, worked Paul Derringer, Bucky Walters, Whit Wyatt and Larry French in two-inning shifts and then used Carl Hubbell to wrap it up in the ninth inning.

Reverting to an earlier N. L. practice, McKechnie tried to show all of his stars, using no fewer than 22 players.

Joe Cronin, who handled the Americans because the loop's magnates figured Joe McCarthy had had the honor often enough, took a cue from his senior circuit rival and employed 18 players himself.

The game was decided before many of the 32,373 fans had settled in their seats. Oddly enough, it was one of the lesser lights of the N. L. squad who was the hero. After Arky Vaughan and Billy Herman opened with singles off Red Ruffing in the first inning, Max West drove a home run into the stands in right-center, giving the Nationals a 3-0 lead before Ruffing retired a man.

In the very next inning, West crumpled in front of the right-field wall while trying to make a leaping catch of Luke Appling's liner. Max had to be assisted from the field, but the injury was not serious.

Following their first-inning burst, the Nationals went out as regularly against Ruffing, Buck Newsom and Bob Feller as the Americans until they scored a parting run off Feller in the eighth.

Mel Ott worked Feller for a walk, moved to second on a sacrifice and came home when Harry Danning singled. The box score:

National League 4, American League 0

(American League Leads Series, 5-3)

AMERICANS	AB.	R.	H.	PO.	A.	E.	NATIONALS	AB.	R.	H.	PO.	A.	E.
Travis (Senators), 3b	3	0	0	0	0	0	Vaughan (Pirates), ss	3	1	1	0	1	0
Keltner (Indians), 3b	1	0	0	2	1	0	Miller (Braves), ss	1	0	0	2	1	0
Williams (Red Sox), lf	2	0	0	3	0	0	Herman (Cubs), 2b	3	1	3	0	3	0
Finney (Red Sox), rf	0	0	0	0	0	0	Coscarart (Dodgers), 2b	1	0	0	0	2	0
Keller (Yankees), rf	2	0	0	4	0	0	West (Braves), rf	1	1	1	0	0	0
Greenberg (Tigers), lf	2	0	0	0	0	0	Nicholson (Cubs), rf	2	0	0	1	0	0
DiMaggio (Yankees), cf	4	0	0	1	0	0	Ott (Giants), rf	0	1	0	0	0	0
Foxx (Red Sox), 1b	3	0	0	4	2	0	Mize (Cardinals), 1b	2	0	0	8	0	0
Appling (White Sox), ss	3	0	2	0	0	0	F. McCormick (Reds), 1b	1	0	0	2	0	0
Boudreau (Indians), ss	0	0	0	0	0	0	Lombardi (Reds), c	2	0	1	3	0	0
Dickey (Yankees), c	1	0	0	2	0	0	Phelps (Dodgers), c	0	0	0	1	0	0
Hayes (Athletics), c	1	0	0	1	0	0	Danning (Giants), c	1	0	1	6	0	0
Hemsley (Indians), c	1	0	0	3	0	1	Medwick (Dodgers), lf	2	0	1	1	0	0
Gordon (Yankees), 2b	2	0	0	3	1	0	J. Moore (Giants), lf	2	0	0	1	0	0
aMack (Indians), 2b	1	0	0	0	0	0	Lavagetto (Dodgers), 3b	2	0	0	0	1	0
Ruffing (Yankees), p	1	0	0	0	0	0	May (Phillies), 3b	1	0	0	0	0	0
Newsom (Tigers), p	1	0	1	0	0	0	T. Moore (Cardinals), cf	3	0	0	2	0	0
Feller (Indians), p	1	0	0	1	0	0	Derringer (Reds), p	1	0	0	0	1	0
Totals	29	0	3	24	4	1	Walters (Reds), p	0	0	0	0	1	0
							Wyatt (Dodgers), p	1	0	0	0	0	0
							French (Cubs), p	0	0	0	0	0	0
							Hubbell (Giants), p	0	0	0	0	0	0
							Totals	29	4	7	27	10	0

American League	0	0	0	0	0	0	0	0	0 — 0
National League	3	0	0	0	0	0	0	1	x — 4

Americans	IP.	H.	R.	ER.	BB.	SO.	Nationals	IP.	H.	R.	ER.	BB.	SO.
Ruffing (Yankees)	3	5	3	3	0	2	Derringer (Reds)	2	1	0	0	1	3
Newsom (Tigers)	3	1	0	0	1	1	Walters (Reds)	2	0	0	0	0	0
Feller (Indians)	2	1	1	1	2	3	Wyatt (Dodgers)	2	1	0	0	0	1
							French (Cubs)	2	1	0	0	0	2
							Hubbell (Giants)	1	0	0	0	1	1

Winning pitcher—Derringer. Losing pitcher—Ruffing.

aStruck out for Gordon in eighth. Runs batted in—West 3, Danning. Two-base hit—Appling. Home run—West. Sacrifice hits—F. McCormick, French. Double play—Coscarart, Miller and F. McCormick. Left on bases—Nationals 7, Americans 4. Hit by pitcher—By Feller (May). Umpires—Reardon and Stewart (N. L.), Pipgras and Basil (A. L.). Time of game—1:53. Attendance—32,373.

Boston Braves outfielder Max West made a short but sweet appearance in the 1940 All-Star Game. After hitting a three-run, first-inning homer, West crashed into the right-field wall at St. Louis' Sportsman's Park while trying to make a catch in the second inning and had to be removed from the game.

Game of 1941
Briggs Stadium, Detroit, July 8

Few important games between the two leagues have left as many heartaches for the senior major as this contest. Leading by 5-4 with two out in the ninth inning, the Nationals seemed to have victory in the bag. But then Ted Williams, the Red Sox' great young hitter, sent a three-run homer into the upper right-field stands and the Americans won, 7-5.

Never before or since has the finish of an All-Star Game produced such an explosion of uninhibited joy as the emotional outpouring staged in the A. L. dressing room. Manager Del Baker, not an overly demonstrative man, hugged and kissed the tall, grinning Williams.

The tough luck player of the day was Arky Vaughan. The Pirate shortstop hit successive two-run homers for the National League in the seventh and eighth innings, one off righthander Sid Hudson and the second off lefty Edgar Smith. Vaughan looked like the big hero of the game until Williams' tremendous drive made Arky's two round-trippers just incidents in another N. L. defeat.

Vaughan's second smash made the score 5-2, but the A. L. came back with one run in its half of the eighth against Claude Passeau. Joe DiMaggio doubled and scored when brother Dom DiMaggio singled.

That set the stage for the dramatic ninth. With one out, pinch-hitter Ken Keltner singled. Joe Gordon also singled and when Passeau walked Cecil Travis, the bags were full. Joe DiMaggio hit into a force play, scoring Keltner, and then came Williams' payoff blow. The box score:

American League 7, National League 5

(American League Leads Series, 6-3)

NATIONALS	AB.	R.	H.	PO.	A.	E.	AMERICANS	AB.	R.	H.	PO.	A.	E.
Hack (Cubs), 3b	2	0	1	3	0	0	Doerr (Red Sox), 2b	3	0	0	0	0	0
fLavagetto (Dodgers), 3b	1	0	0	0	0	0	Gordon (Yankees), 2b	2	1	1	2	0	0
T. Moore (Cardinals), lf	5	0	0	0	0	0	Travis (Senators), 3b	4	1	1	1	2	0
Reiser (Dodgers), cf	4	0	0	6	0	2	J. DiMaggio (Yanks), cf	4	3	1	1	0	0
Mize (Cardinals), 1b	4	1	1	5	0	0	Williams (Red Sox), lf	4	1	2	3	0	1
F. McCormick (Reds), 1b	0	0	0	0	0	0	Heath (Indians), rf	2	0	0	1	0	1
Nicholson (Cubs), rf	1	0	0	1	0	0	D. DiMaggio (R. Sox), rf	1	0	1	1	0	0
Elliott (Pirates), rf	1	0	0	0	0	0	Cronin (Red Sox), ss	2	0	0	3	0	0
Slaughter (Cardinals), rf	2	1	1	0	0	0	Boudreau (Indians), ss	2	0	2	0	1	0
Vaughan (Pirates), ss	4	2	3	1	2	0	York (Tigers), 1b	3	0	1	6	2	0
Miller (Braves), ss	0	0	0	1	0	0	Foxx (Red Sox), 1b	1	0	0	2	2	0
Frey (Reds), 2b	1	0	1	1	3	0	Dickey (Yankees), c	3	0	1	4	2	0
cHerman (Dodgers), 2b	3	0	2	3	0	0	Hayes (Athletics), c	1	0	0	2	0	0
Owen (Dodgers), c	1	0	0	0	0	0	Feller (Indians), p	0	0	0	0	1	0
Lopez (Pirates), c	1	0	0	3	0	0	bCullenbine (Browns)	1	0	0	0	0	0
Danning (Giants), c	1	0	0	3	0	0	Lee (White Sox), p	1	0	0	0	1	0
Wyatt (Dodgers), p	0	0	0	0	0	0	Hudson (Senators), p	0	0	0	0	0	0
aOtt (Giants)	1	0	0	0	0	0	eKeller (Yankees)	1	0	0	0	0	0
Derringer (Reds), p	0	0	0	0	1	0	Smith (White Sox), p	0	0	0	1	0	1
Walters (Reds), p	1	1	1	0	0	0	gKeltner, (Indians)	1	1	1	0	0	0
dMedwick (Dodgers)	1	0	0	0	0	0	Totals	36	7	11	27	11	3
Passeau (Cubs), p	1	0	0	0	0	0							
Totals	35	5	10	26	7	2							

National League	0	0	0	0	0	1	2	2	0 — 5
American League	0	0	0	1	0	1	0	1	4 — 7

Two out when winning run scored.

Nationals	IP.	H.	R.	ER.	BB.	SO.	Americans	IP.	H.	R.	ER.	BB.	SO.
Wyatt (Dodgers)	2	0	0	0	1	0	Feller (Indians)	3	1	0	0	0	4
Derringer (Reds)	2	2	1	1	0	1	Lee (White Sox)	3	4	1	1	0	0
Walters (Reds)	2	3	1	1	2	2	Hudson (Senators)	1	3	2	2	1	1
Passeau (Cubs)	2⅔	6	5	5	1	3	Smith (White Sox)	2	2	2	2	0	2

Winning pitcher—Smith. Losing pitcher—Passeau.

aStruck out for Wyatt in third. bGrounded out for Feller in third. cSingled for Frey in fifth. dGrounded out for Walters in seventh. eStruck out for Hudson in seventh. fGrounded out for Hack in ninth. gSingled for Smith in ninth. Runs batted in—Williams 4, Moore, Boudreau, Vaughan 4, D. DiMaggio, J. DiMaggio. Two-base hits—Travis, Williams, Walters, Herman, Mize, J. DiMaggio. Home runs—Vaughan 2, Williams. Sacrifice hits—Hack, Lopez. Double plays—Frey, Vaughan and Mize; York and Cronin. Left on bases—Americans 7, Nationals 6. Umpires—Summers and Grieve (A. L.), Jorda and Pinelli (N. L.). Time of game—2:23. Attendance—54,674.

After hitting a dramatic two-out, three-run homer to win the 1941 All-Star Game for the American League, young Boston slugger Ted Williams received a warm handshake from A.L. President William Harridge.

Game of 1942
Polo Grounds, New York, July 6

A first-inning home-run barrage against Mort Cooper, Cardinal ace, enabled the Americans to win, 3-1. The game, a twilight affair, was originally scheduled for Brooklyn, but since the proceeds were to go to war charities, Larry MacPhail permitted the contest to be transferred to the Polo Grounds because of its larger capacity.

Even so, the crowd of 34,178 fell far below expectations. There were, however, extenuating circumstances. Afternoon showers fell in New York, and shortly before the scheduled 6 p.m. game time, a cloudburst struck the Polo Grounds. The downpour ruined the sale of unreserved seats.

Because the winning team was scheduled to play the Service All-Stars, recruited from top-notch big leaguers in the Army and Navy, in Cleveland the next night, the three-inning rule for pitchers was suspended. Instead, the managers were permitted to work their pitchers as many as five innings. Joe McCarthy took advantage of the rule, using Spud Chandler the first four innings and Alton Benton the last five.

Lou Boudreau hit Mort Cooper's second pitch of the game into the upper left-field stands for a home run. Tommy Henrich followed with a double. Cooper retired the next two batters, but then Rudy York sliced a drive into the lower right-field stands about five feet inside the foul line, giving the A.L. a 3-0 lead.

The only N.L. run came in the eighth when Mickey Owen hit a pinch-homer into the left-field stands. Ironically, he didn't sock a single home run in 133 league games that year. The box score:

American League 3, National League 1

(American League Leads Series, 7-3)

AMERICANS	AB.	R.	H.	PO.	A.	E.	NATIONALS	AB.	R.	H.	PO.	A.	E.
Boudreau (Indians), ss	4	1	1	4	5	0	Brown (Cardinals), 2b	2	0	0	1	0	1
Henrich (Yankees), rf	4	1	1	2	0	0	Herman (Dodgers), 2b	1	0	0	0	0	0
Williams (Red Sox), lf	4	0	1	0	0	0	Vaughan (Dodgers), 3b	2	0	0	2	2	0
J. DiMaggio (Yankees), cf	4	0	2	2	0	0	Elliott (Pirates), 3b	1	0	1	1	2	0
York (Tigers), 1b	4	1	1	11	3	0	Reiser (Dodgers), cf	3	0	1	3	0	0
Gordon (Yankees), 2b	4	0	0	1	4	0	Moore (Cardinals), cf	1	0	0	1	0	0
Keltner (Indians), 3b	4	0	0	0	1	0	Mize (Giants), 1b	2	0	0	3	0	0
Tebbetts (Tigers), c	4	0	0	4	1	0	F. McCormick (Reds), 1b	2	0	0	3	0	0
Chandler (Yankees), p	1	0	0	3	1	0	Ott (Giants), rf	4	0	0	1	0	0
bJohnson (Athletics)	1	0	1	0	0	0	Medwick (Dodgers), lf	2	0	0	1	0	0
Benton (Tigers), p	1	0	0	0	1	0	Slaughter (Cardinals), lf	2	0	1	1	0	0
Totals	35	3	7	27	16	0	W. Cooper (Cardinals), c	2	0	1	7	0	0
							Lombardi (Braves), c	1	0	0	2	0	0
							Miller (Braves), ss	2	0	0	2	1	0
							Reese (Dodgers), ss	1	0	0	0	1	0
							M. Cooper (Cardinals), p	0	0	0	0	0	0
							aMarshall (Giants)	1	0	0	0	0	0
							Vander Meer (Reds), p	0	0	0	0	1	0
							cLitwhiler (Phillies)	1	0	1	0	0	0
							Passeau (Cubs), p	0	0	0	0	0	0
							dOwen (Dodgers)	1	1	1	0	0	0
							Walters (Reds), p	0	0	0	0	0	0
							Totals	31	1	6	27	7	1

American League	3	0	0	0	0	0	0	0	0—3
National League	0	0	0	0	0	0	0	1	0—1

Americans	IP.	H.	R.	ER.	BB.	SO.	Nationals	IP.	H.	R.	ER.	BB.	SO.
Chandler (Yankees)	4	2	0	0	0	2	M. Cooper (Cardinals)	3	4	3	3	0	2
Benton (Tigers)	5	4	1	1	2	1	Vander Meer (Reds)	3	2	0	0	0	4
							Passeau (Cubs)	2	1	0	0	0	1
							Walters (Reds)	1	0	0	0	0	1

Winning pitcher—Chandler. Losing pitcher—M. Cooper.

aForced runner for M. Cooper in third. bSingled for Chandler in fifth. cSingled for Vander Meer in sixth. dHomered for Passeau in eighth. Runs batted in—Boudreau, York 2, Owen. Two-base hit—Henrich. Home runs—Boudreau, York, Owen. Double plays—Gordon, Boudreau and York; Boudreau and York. Hit by pitcher—By Chandler (Brown). Passed ball—Tebbetts. Left on bases—Nationals 6, Americans 5. Umpires—Ballanfant and Barlick (N. L.), Stewart and McGowan (A. L.). Time of game—2:07. Attendance—34,178.

Detroit first baseman Rudy York crosses the plate after connecting for a first-inning home run in the 1942 All-Star Game at the Polo Grounds in New York.

Game of 1943

Shibe Park, Philadelphia, July 13

In the first night game in All-Star history, the American Leaguers edged the Nationals, 5-3, for their eighth victory in 11 games. Mort Cooper, Cardinal ace, again was the victim, just as he had been the year before.

Although the Yankees qualified six players, more than any other team, Manager Joe McCarthy didn't use a single member of his club. The brazen move apparently stemmed from his resentment of accusations that he had favored his players in earlier games and a decision to prove that he could win without a single Yankee.

The fair-haired boy for the Americans was Bobby Doerr. The Red Sox second baseman tagged Mort Cooper for a three-run homer in the second inning. The blow, which erased a 1-0 lead the N.L. had taken against Dutch Leonard in the opening frame, followed a pair of walks.

Cooper still was wobbly in the third and the A.L. stars scored again on doubles by Ken Keltner and Dick Wakefield. After Vern Stephens sacrificed Wakefield to third, Manager Billy Southworth lifted Cooper in favor of Johnny Vander Meer, who struck out both Rudy York and Chet Laabs to end the inning.

Vander Meer fanned six in his two and two-thirds innings, but was on the mound when the Americans scored their fifth run in the fifth.

Vince DiMaggio, who entered the game in the fourth inning as a pinch-hitter, was the Nationals' batting hero. He was a one-man blitz with a single, triple and homer in three attempts. The box score:

American League 5, National League 3

(American League Leads Series, 8-3)

NATIONALS	AB.	R.	H.	PO.	A.	E.
Hack (Cubs), 3b	5	1	3	0	2	1
Herman (Dodgers), 2b	5	0	2	3	3	2
Musial (Cardinals), lf-rf	4	0	1	0	0	0
Nicholson (Cubs), rf	2	0	0	0	0	0
cGalan (Dodgers), lf	1	0	0	1	0	0
Fletcher (Pirates), 1b	2	0	0	3	0	0
dDahlgren (Phillies), 1b	2	0	0	3	0	0
W. Cooper (Cardinals), c	2	0	1	7	1	0
eLombardi (Giants), c	2	0	0	3	0	0
H. Walker (Cards), cf	1	0	0	1	0	0
bDiMaggio (Pirates), cf	3	2	3	1	0	0
Marion (Cardinals), ss	2	0	0	2	2	0
gOtt (Giants)	1	0	0	0	0	0
Miller (Reds), ss	1	0	0	1	0	0
M. Cooper (Cardinals), p	1	0	0	0	1	0
Vander Meer (Reds), p	1	0	0	0	1	0
Sewell (Pirates), p	0	0	0	0	1	0
hF. Walker (Dodgers)	1	0	0	0	0	0
Javery (Braves), p	0	0	0	0	0	0
iFrey (Reds)	1	0	0	0	0	0
Totals	37	3	10	24	12	3

AMERICANS	AB.	R.	H.	PO.	A.	E.
Case (Senators), rf	2	1	0	0	0	0
Keltner (Indians), 3b	4	1	1	2	2	0
Wakefield (Tigers), lf	4	0	2	3	0	0
R. Johnson (Senators), lf	0	0	0	1	0	0
Stephens (Browns), ss	3	0	1	1	3	1
Siebert (Athletics), 1b	1	0	0	3	1	0
aYork (Tigers), 1b	3	0	1	4	0	0
Laabs (Browns), cf	3	1	0	7	0	0
Early (Senators), c	2	1	0	3	0	0
Doerr (Red Sox), 2b	4	1	2	3	3	0
Leonard (Senators), p	1	0	1	0	1	0
Newhouser (Tigers), p	1	0	0	0	0	0
fHeath (Indians)	1	0	0	0	0	0
Hughson (Red Sox), p	0	0	0	0	0	0
Totals	29	5	8	27	10	1

	1								
National League	1	0	0	0	0	0	1	0	1 – 3
American League	0	3	1	0	1	0	0	0	x – 5

Nationals	IP.	H.	R.	ER.	BB.	SO.
M. Cooper (Cardinals)	2⅓	4	4	4	2	1
Vander Meer (Reds)	2⅔	2	1	0	1	6
Sewell (Pirates)	1	0	0	0	0	0
Javery (Braves)	2	2	0	0	0	3

Americans	IP.	H.	R.	ER.	BB.	SO.
Leonard (Senators)	3	2	1	1	0	0
Newhouser (Tigers)	3	3	0	0	1	1
Hughson (Red Sox)	3	5	2	2	0	2

Winning pitcher—Leonard. Losing pitcher—M. Cooper.

aStruck out for Siebert in third. bSingled for H. Walker in fourth. cWalked for Nicholson in sixth. dHit into double play for Fletcher in sixth. eFlied out for W. Cooper in sixth. fFlied out for Newhouser in sixth. gStruck out for Marion in seventh. hFlied out for Sewell in seventh. iFlied out for Javery in ninth. Runs batted in—Musial, F. Walker, DiMaggio, Doerr 3, Wakefield. Two-base hits—Musial, Keltner, Wakefield. Three-base hit—DiMaggio. Home runs—Doerr, DiMaggio. Sacrifice hits—Stephens, Early. Double plays—Hack, Herman and Fletcher; Vander Meer, Marion and Herman; Miller, Herman and Dahlgren; Stephens, Doerr and York. Hit by pitcher—By M. Cooper (Case). Left on bases—Nationals 8, Americans 6. Umpires—Rommel and Rue (A. L.), Conlan and Dunn (N. L.). Time of game—2:07. Attendance—31,938.

Game of 1944
Forbes Field, Pittsburgh, July 11

Erupting for 12 hits, the Nationals romped to an easy 7-1 victory before an arc-light turnout of 29,589. It was only the fourth win for the senior circuit in 12 All-Star clashes.

Joe McCarthy started Hank Borowy, and the Yankee righthander not only blanked the N.L. on three hits in his three-inning stint, but also drove in the A.L.'s only run. The tally came off Bucky Walters.

Tex Hughson's successor, breezed through the fourth inning, but blew up in the fifth. Connie Ryan opened the inning with a single and stole second. A pinch-double by Bill Nicholson drove in the tying run. Augie Galan followed with a single, scoring Nicholson. A pass and an error by George McQuinn filled the bases. Singles by Walker Cooper and Dixie Walker added two more runs.

In the seventh inning, with Hal Newhouser on duty, Whitey Kurowski doubled across a pair of N.L. runs to make the score 6-1. The final tally in the eighth came without the benefit of a hit. Marty Marion, leading off, struck out but reached base safely when Frank Hayes missed the third strike. Two walks subsequently filled the bases, and Marion counted on Musial's fly ball.

Phil Cavarretta set an All-Star Game record by reaching base safely five straight times on a triple, single and three walks. Each of the passes came from a different pitcher.

With $81,275 from gate receipts, $25,000 from Gillette Safety Razor Co. for broadcasting rights and a contribution by Sportservice from the concessions, the game produced net receipts of $100,999.39 to buy equipment for men in the armed forces. The box score:

National League 7, American League 1
(American League Leads Series, 8-4)

AMERICANS	AB.	R.	H.	PO.	A.	E.	NATIONALS	AB.	R.	H.	PO.	A.	E.
Tucker (White Sox), cf	4	0	0	4	0	0	Galan (Dodgers), lf	4	1	1	2	0	0
Spence (Senators), rf	4	0	2	2	1	0	Cavarretta, (Cubs), 1b	2	1	2	12	0	0
McQuinn (Browns), 1b	4	0	1	5	1	1	Musial (Cardinals), cf-rf	4	1	1	2	1	0
Stephens (Browns), ss	4	0	1	1	0	0	W. Cooper (Cardinals), c	5	1	2	5	2	0
Johnson (Red Sox), lf	3	0	0	2	1	0	Mueller (Reds), c	0	0	0	0	0	0
Keltner (Indians), 3b	4	1	1	0	4	0	Walker (Dodgers), rf	4	0	2	0	0	0
Doerr (Red Sox), 2b	3	0	0	4	1	1	DiMaggio (Pirates), cf	0	0	0	0	0	0
Hemsley (Yankees), c	2	0	0	2	0	0	Elliott (Pirates), 3b	3	0	0	3	0	0
Hayes (Athletics), c	1	0	0	3	0	1	Kurowski (Cardinals), 3b	1	0	1	0	1	0
Borowy (Yankees), p	1	0	1	0	0	0	Ryan (Braves), 2b	4	1	2	4	4	1
Hughson (Red Sox), p	1	0	0	0	0	0	Marion (Cardinals), ss	3	1	0	2	3	0
Muncrief (Browns), p	0	0	0	1	0	0	Walters (Reds), p	0	0	0	0	1	0
cHiggins (Tigers)	1	0	0	0	0	0	aOtt (Giants)	1	0	0	0	0	0
Newhouser (Tigers), p	0	0	0	0	1	0	Raffensberger (Phils), p	0	0	0	0	0	0
Newsom (Athletics), p	0	0	0	0	0	0	bNicholson (Cubs)	1	1	1	0	0	0
							Sewell (Pirates), p	1	0	0	0	0	0
Totals	32	1	6	24	9	3	dMedwick (Giants)	0	0	0	0	0	0
							Tobin (Braves) p	0	0	0	0	0	0
							Totals	33	7	12	27	15	1

```
American League.........................  0   1   0     0   0   0     0   0   0 — 1
National League.........................  0   0   0     0   4   0     2   1   x — 7
```

Americans	IP.	H.	R.	ER.	BB.	SO.	Nationals	IP.	H.	R.	ER.	BB.	SO.
Borowy (Yankees)	3	3	0	0	1	0	Walters (Reds)	3	5	1	1	0	1
Hughson (Red Sox)	1⅔	5	4	3	1	2	Raffensberger (Phillies)	2	1	0	0	0	2
Muncrief (Browns)	1⅓	1	0	0	0	1	Sewell (Pirates)	3	0	0	0	1	2
Newhouser (Tigers)	1⅔	3	3	2	2	1	Tobin (Braves)	1	0	0	0	0	0
Newsom (Athletics)	⅓	0	0	0	0	0							

Winning pitcher—Raffensberger. Losing pitcher—Hughson.

aFlied out for Walters in third. bDoubled for Raffensberger in fifth. cGrounded out for Muncrief in seventh. dSacrificed for Sewell in eighth. Runs batted in—Kurowski 2, Nicholson, Galan, W. Cooper, Walker, Musial, Borowy. Two-base hits—Nicholson. Kurowski. Three-base hit—Cavarretta. Sacrifice hits—Marion, Musial, Medwick. Stolen base —Ryan. Double plays—Spence and Hemsley; Marion, Ryan and Cavarretta. Wild pitch—Muncrief. Left on bases—Nationals 9, Americans 5. Umpires—Barr and Sears (N. L.), Berry and Hubbard (A. L.). Time of game—2:11. Attendance— 29,589.

Game of 1946
Fenway Park, Boston, July 9

After a one-year interruption because of war travel restrictions, the All-Star Game was resumed and the American League scored the most overwhelming triumph of the series, crushing the Nationals, 12-0.

Ted Williams, playing before his home fans, staged one of the most magnificent shows in the history of the midsummer classic. He hit two homers and two singles and drew a walk in five times at bat. In addition, he scored four runs and drove in five.

The Splendid Splinter's first homer was a terrific smash into the center-field bleachers off Kirby Higbe in the fourth inning. In the eighth, swinging against a blooper pitch by Rip Sewell, Williams supplied the power to drive the ball into the right-field bullpen for his second round-tripper.

The American League collected a total of 14 hits and gave an early intimation of the rout that followed when Charlie Keller bashed a homer off Claude Passeau following a walk to Williams in the first inning. Williams' first homer made it 3-0 in the fourth.

The Americans added three more runs in the fifth while kayoing Higbe. A double by Vern Stephens with the bags full and a single by Williams were the big blows.

Ewell Blackwell was nicked for two runs in the seventh and then Williams capped the scoring with a three-run blast off Sewell in the eighth after Sam Chapman plated a run earlier in the inning with a fly ball. The box score:

American League 12, National League 0

(American League Leads Series, 9-4)

NATIONALS	AB.	R.	H.	PO.	A.	E.	AMERICANS	AB.	R.	H.	PO.	A.	E.
Schoendienst (Cards), 2b	2	0	0	0	2	0	DiMaggio (R. Sox), cf	2	0	1	1	0	0
cGustine (Pirates), 2b	1	0	0	1	1	0	Spence (Senators), cf	0	1	0	1	0	0
Musial (Cardinals), lf	2	0	0	0	0	0	Chapman (Athletics), cf	2	0	0	1	0	0
dEnnis (Phillies), lf	2	0	0	0	0	0	Pesky (Red Sox), ss	2	0	0	1	0	1
Hopp (Braves), cf	2	0	1	0	0	0	Stephens (Browns), ss	3	1	2	0	4	0
eLowrey (Cubs), cf	2	0	1	3	0	0	Williams (Red Sox), lf	4	4	4	1	0	0
Walker (Dodgers), rf	3	0	0	1	0	0	Keller (Yankees), rf	4	2	1	1	0	0
Slaughter (Cardinals), rf	1	0	0	0	0	0	Doerr (Red Sox), 2b	2	0	0	1	1	0
Kurowski (Cardinals), 3b	3	0	0	2	1	0	Gordon (Yankees), 2b	2	0	1	0	1	0
iVerban (Phillies)	1	0	0	0	0	0	Vernon (Senators), 1b	2	0	0	2	1	0
Mize (Giants), 1b	1	0	0	7	0	0	York (Red Sox), 1b	2	0	1	5	0	0
bMcCormick (Phils), 1b	1	0	0	1	1	0	Keltner (Indians), 3b	0	0	0	0	0	0
gCavarretta (Cubs), 1b	1	0	0	1	0	0	Stirnweiss (Yankees), 3b	3	1	1	0	0	0
Cooper (Giants), c	1	0	1	0	0	0	Hayes (Indians), c	1	0	0	3	0	0
Masi (Braves), c	2	0	0	4	1	0	Rosar (Athletics), c	2	1	1	5	0	0
Marion (Cardinals), ss	3	0	0	4	6	0	Wagner (Red Sox), c	1	0	0	4	0	0
Passeau (Cubs), p	1	0	0	0	1	0	Feller (Indians), p	0	0	0	0	0	0
Higbe (Dodgers), p	1	0	0	0	0	0	aAppling (White Sox)	1	0	0	0	0	0
Blackwell (Reds), p	0	0	0	0	0	0	Newhouser (Tigers), p	1	1	1	1	0	0
hLamanno (Reds)	1	0	0	0	0	0	fDickey (Yankees)	1	0	0	0	0	0
Sewell (Pirates), p	0	0	0	0	0	0	Kramer (Browns), p	1	1	1	0	0	0
Totals	31	0	3	24	13	0	Totals	36	12	14	27	7	1

```
National League ................................... 0   0   0    0   0   0    0   0   0 — 0
American League ................................. 2   0   0    1   3   0    2   4   x — 12
```

Nationals	IP.	H.	R.	ER.	BB.	SO.	Americans	IP.	H.	R.	ER.	BB.	SO.
Passeau (Cubs)	3	2	2	2	0	2	Feller (Indians)	3	2	0	0	0	3
Higbe (Dodgers)	1⅓	5	4	4	1	2	Newhouser (Tigers)	3	1	0	0	0	4
Blackwell (Reds)	2⅔	3	2	2	1	1	Kramer (Browns)	3	0	0	0	1	3
Sewell (Pirates)	1	4	4	4	0	0							

Winning pitcher—Feller. Losing pitcher—Passeau.

aGrounded out for Feller in third. bFlied out for Mize in fourth. cStruck out for Schoendienst in sixth. dStruck out for Musial in sixth. eSingled for Hopp in sixth. fStruck out for Newhouser in sixth. gStruck out for McCormick in seventh. hGrounded out for Blackwell in eighth. iFouled out for Kurowski in ninth. Runs batted in—Keller 2, Williams 5, Stephens 2, Gordon 2, Chapman. Two-base hits—Stephens, Gordon. Home runs—Williams 2, Keller. Double plays—Marion and Mize; Schoendienst, Marion and Mize. Wild pitch—Blackwell. Left on bases—Nationals 5, Americans 4. Umpires—Summers and Rommel (A. L.), Boggess and Goetz (N. L.). Time of game—2:19. Attendance—34,906.

Game of 1947
Wrigley Field, Chicago, July 8

The ability of two pinch-hitters to deliver in the clutch provided the American League with a 2-1 victory in a dramatic contest. The triumph was credited to Frank Shea of the Yankees, the first rookie to earn this distinction in All-Star competition.

Luke Appling and Stan Spence supplied the pinch-blows that enabled the A. L. to come from behind. The junior loop collected eight hits to the five permitted by four pitchers employed by Manager Joe Cronin.

Johnny Mize broke a scoreless battle when he stroked a Shea pitch for a home run in the fourth inning.

The Americans knotted the game in the sixth against Harry Brecheen. Appling launched the rally with his pinch-single. Ted Williams followed with a single, sending Appling to third, and Luke then crossed the plate while the N. L. executed a double play on Joe DiMaggio's grounder to short.

Johnny Sain was on the mound in the seventh when the Americans tabbed their decisive run. Bobby Doerr singled and stole second. The A. L. got a break when Sain, attempting to pick Doerr off second, hit him with the ball, which bounced into center field, enabling the runner to go to third. He scored easily when Spence, batting for Shea, singled to right-center.

The Nationals threatened in the eighth, but reliever Joe Page came on to quell the threat, retiring St. Louis' Enos Slaughter with two runners on base. The box score:

American League 2, National League 1
(American League Leads Series, 10-4)

AMERICANS	AB.	R.	H.	PO.	A.	E.	NATIONALS	AB.	R.	H.	PO.	A.	E.
Kell (Tigers), 3b	4	0	0	0	0	0	H. Walker (Phillies), cf	2	0	0	1	0	0
Johnson (Yanks), 3b	0	0	0	0	0	0	Pafko (Cubs), cf	2	0	1	2	0	0
Lewis (Senators), rf	2	0	0	1	0	0	F. Walker (Dodgers), rf	2	0	0	1	0	0
bAppling (White Sox)	1	1	1	0	0	0	Marshall (Giants), rf	1	0	0	3	0	0
Henrich (Yankees), rf	1	0	0	3	0	0	W. Cooper (Giants), c	3	0	0	6	0	0
Williams (Red Sox), lf	4	0	2	3	0	0	Edwards (Giants), c	0	0	0	2	0	0
DiMaggio (Yanks), cf	3	0	1	1	0	0	eCavarretta (Cubs), 1b	1	0	0	1	0	0
Boudreau (Indians), ss	4	0	1	4	4	0	Mize (Giants), 1b	3	1	2	8	0	0
McQuinn (Yankees), 1b	4	0	0	9	1	0	fMasi (Braves), c	0	0	0	0	0	0
Gordon (Yankees), 2b	2	0	1	0	4	0	Slaughter (Cardinals), lf	3	0	0	1	0	0
Doerr (Red Sox), 2b	2	1	1	0	2	0	Gustine (Pirates), 3b	2	0	0	0	2	0
Rosar (Athletics), c	4	0	0	6	0	0	Kurowski (Cards), 3b	2	0	0	0	1	0
Newhouser (Tigers), p	1	0	0	0	0	0	Marion (Cardinals), ss	2	0	1	0	1	0
Shea (Yankees), p	1	0	0	0	0	0	Reese (Dodgers), ss	1	0	0	0	2	0
cSpence (Senators)	1	0	1	0	0	0	Verban (Phillies), 2b	2	0	0	0	0	0
Masterson (Senators), p	0	0	0	0	0	0	Stanky (Dodgers), 2b	2	0	0	2	2	0
Page (Yankees), p	0	0	0	0	0	0	Blackwell (Reds), p	0	0	0	0	0	0
Totals	34	2	8	27	11	0	aHaas (Reds)	1	0	1	0	0	0
							Brecheen (Cardinals), p	1	0	0	0	1	0
							Sain (Braves), p	0	0	0	0	0	1
							dMusial (Cardinals)	1	0	0	0	0	0
							Spahn (Braves), p	0	0	0	0	0	0
							gRowe (Phillies)	1	0	0	0	0	0
							Totals	32	1	5	27	9	1

American League	0	0	0	0	0	1	1	0	0 — 2
National League	0	0	0	1	0	0	0	0	0 — 1

Americans	IP.	H.	R.	ER.	BB.	SO.	Nationals	IP.	H.	R.	ER.	BB.	SO.
Newhouser (Tigers)	3	1	0	0	0	2	Blackwell (Reds)	3	1	0	0	0	4
Shea (Yankees)	3	3	1	1	2	2	Brecheen (Cardinals)	3	5	1	1	0	2
Masterson (Senators)	1⅔	0	0	0	1	2	Sain (Braves)	1	2	1	1	0	1
Page (Yankees)	1⅓	1	0	0	1	0	Spahn (Braves)	2	0	0	0	1	1

Winning pitcher—Shea. Losing pitcher—Sain.

aSingled for Blackwell in third. bSingled for Lewis in sixth. cSingled for Shea in seventh. dGrounded out for Sain in seventh. eStruck out for Edwards in eighth. fRan for Mize in eighth. gFlied out for Spahn in ninth. Runs batted in—Mize, Spence. Two-base hits—Williams, Gordon. Home run—Mize. Stolen base—Doerr. Double play—Reese, Stanky and Mize. Wild pitch—Blackwell. Passed ball—W. Cooper. Left on bases—Nationals 8, Americans 6. Umpires—Boyer and Passarella (A. L.), Conlan and Henline (N. L.). Time of game—2:19. Attendance—41,123.

Game of 1948
Sportsman's Park, St. Louis, July 13

Injuries prevented four of the American League's top performers—Ted Williams, Joe DiMaggio, George Kell and Hal Newhouser—from taking their regular places in the lineup, but the junior circuit still managed to win, 5-2, for its 11th victory in 15 games.

Three of the American League cripples made brief appearances. DiMaggio, hobbled by a swollen left knee, and Williams, handicapped by a torn rib cartilage, served as pinch-hitters, while Newhouser, suffering from bursitis in his left shoulder, was used as a pinch-runner. Kell, who had a sprained ankle, did not see action.

Walter Masterson was the Americans' starting pitcher and the N. L. cuffed the Senator hurler for two quick runs in the opening frame on an infield hit by Richie Ashburn and a homer by Stan Musial. A single by Johnny Mize and a walk to Enos Slaughter kept Masterson in hot water, but he bore down to end the inning without further damage.

Masterson followed with two shutout innings, after which Vic Raschi and Joe Coleman completed the job of holding the N. L. in check.

Hoot Evers opened the junior loop's scoring with a homer off Ralph Branca in the second inning.

Two walks, a double steal and Lou Boudreau's fly ball produced the tying run against Branca in the third.

With Johnny Schmitz on the hill, the A. L. filled the bases with one out in the fourth inning. Raschi then came through with a single, scoring two runs. Joe DiMaggio's long fly ball drove in another run. The box score:

American League 5, National League 2
(American League Leads Series, 11-4)

NATIONALS	AB.	R.	H.	PO.	A.	E.	AMERICANS	AB.	R.	H.	PO.	A.	E.
Ashburn (Phillies), cf	4	1	2	1	0	0	Mullin (Tigers), rf	1	0	0	0	0	0
Kiner (Pirates), lf	1	0	0	1	0	0	cDiMaggio (Yankees)	1	0	0	0	0	0
Schoendienst (Cards), 2b	4	0	0	0	1	0	Zarilla (Browns), rf	2	0	0	2	0	0
Rigney (Giants), 2b	0	0	0	2	0	0	Henrich (Yankees), lf	3	0	0	1	0	0
Musial (Cardinals), lf-cf	4	1	2	3	0	0	Boudreau (Indians), ss	2	0	0	2	0	0
Mize (Giants), 1b	4	0	1	4	1	0	Stephens (Red Sox), ss	2	0	1	0	0	0
Slaughter (Cardinals), rf	2	0	1	2	0	0	Gordon (Indians), 2b	2	0	0	1	2	0
Holmes (Braves), rf	1	0	0	1	0	0	Doerr (Red Sox), 2b	2	0	0	0	3	0
Pafko (Cubs), 3b	2	0	0	0	0	0	Evers (Tigers), cf	4	1	1	0	0	0
Elliott (Braves), 3b	2	0	1	0	0	0	Keltner (Indians), 3b	3	1	1	1	6	0
Cooper (Giants), c	2	0	0	3	0	0	McQuinn (Yankees), 1b	4	1	2	14	0	0
Masi (Braves), c	2	0	1	4	0	0	Rosar (Athletics), c	1	0	0	1	0	0
Reese (Dodgers), ss	2	0	0	2	2	0	Tebbetts (Red Sox), c	1	1	0	5	1	0
Kerr (Giants), ss	2	0	0	1	0	0	Masterson (Senators), p	0	0	0	0	0	0
Branca (Dodgers), p	1	0	0	0	0	0	aVernon (Senators)	0	1	0	0	0	0
bGustine (Pirates)	1	0	0	0	0	0	Raschi (Yankees), p	1	0	1	0	1	0
Schmitz (Cubs), p	0	0	0	0	0	0	eWilliams (Red Sox)	0	0	0	0	0	0
Sain (Braves), p	0	0	0	0	0	0	fNewhouser (Tigers)	0	0	0	0	0	0
dWaitkus (Cubs)	0	0	0	0	0	0	Coleman (Athletics), p	0	0	0	0	1	0
Blackwell (Reds), p	0	0	0	0	0	0	Totals	29	5	6	27	14	0
gThomson (Giants)	1	0	0	0	0	0							
Totals	35	2	8	24	4	0							

National League	2	0	0	0	0	0	0	0	0—2
American League	0	1	1	3	0	0	0	0	x—5

Nationals	IP.	H.	R.	ER.	BB.	SO.	Americans	IP.	H.	R.	ER.	BB.	SO.
Branca (Dodgers)	3	1	2	2	3	3	Masterson (Senators)	3	5	2	2	1	1
Schmitz (Cubs)	⅓	3	3	3	1	0	Raschi (Yankees)	3	3	0	0	1	3
Sain (Braves)	1⅔	0	0	0	0	3	Coleman (Athletics)	3	0	0	0	2	3
Blackwell (Reds)	3	2	0	0	3	1							

Winning pitcher—Raschi. Losing pitcher—Schmitz.

aWalked for Masterson in third. bStruck out for Branca in fourth. cFlied out for Mullin in fourth, scoring Tebbetts from third. dWalked for Sain in sixth. eWalked for Raschi in sixth. fRan for Williams in sixth. gStruck out for Blackwell in ninth. Runs batted in—Musial 2, Evers, Boudreau, Raschi 2, DiMaggio. Home runs—Musial, Evers. Stolen bases—Ashburn, Vernon, Mullin, McQuinn. Sacrifice hit—Coleman. Wild pitch—Masterson. Left on bases—Nationals 10, Americans 8. Umpires—Berry and Paparella (A. L.), Reardon and Stewart (N. L.). Time of game—2:27. Attendance—34,009.

Game of 1949
Ebbets Field, Brooklyn, July 12

In a loosely-played game marred by six errors, five of them by the National League, the Americans continued their mastery by pounding out an 11-7 triumph.

The contest marked the first appearance of Negro players in All-Star competition.

Jackie Robinson, Roy Campanella and Don Newcombe of the host Dodgers were named for the N.L. squad and Larry Doby of the Indians for the A.L. Newcombe, although charged with the defeat, came close to being the senior circuit's hero. With the bags full in the second inning, he smashed a long drive to the corner in left field. At first it looked like a home run, but the wind caught the ball and Ted Williams, racing over, speared it with one hand.

Manager Billy Southworth used seven of the eight pitchers on the N.L. team. Starter Warren Spahn was rapped for four runs, all unearned. Mel Parnell, the A.L.'s starter, also got his early bumps, being tagged for a two-run homer by Stan Musial in the opening frame.

Ralph Kiner's homer with a mate aboard in the sixth cut the Nationals' deficit to 8-7, but the A.L. jumped on Howie Pollet for three runs in the seventh to sew up the game. The box score:

American League 11, National League 7

(American League Leads Series, 12-4)

AMERICANS	AB.	R.	H.	PO.	A.	E.
D. DiM'gio (R. Sox), rf-cf	5	2	2	2	0	0
Raschi (Yankees), p	1	0	0	0	1	0
Kell (Tigers), 3b	3	2	2	0	1	0
dDillinger (Browns), 3b	1	2	1	0	2	0
Williams (Red Sox), lf	2	1	0	1	0	0
Mitchell (Indians), lf	1	0	1	1	0	1
J. DiMaggio (Yankees), cf	4	1	2	0	0	0
eDoby (Indians), rf-cf	1	0	0	2	0	0
Joost (Athletics), ss	2	1	1	2	2	0
Stephens (Red Sox), ss	2	0	0	2	0	0
E. Robinson (Senators), 1b	5	1	1	8	0	0
Goodman (Red Sox), 1b	0	0	0	1	1	0
Michaels (White Sox), 2b	2	0	0	1	3	0
J. Gordon (Indians), 2b	2	1	1	3	3	0
Tebbetts (Red Sox), c	2	0	2	2	0	0
Berra (Yankees), c	3	0	0	2	1	0
Parnell (Red Sox), p	1	0	0	0	1	0
Trucks (Tigers), p	1	0	0	0	0	0
Brissie (Athletics), p	1	0	0	0	0	0
gWertz (Tigers), rf	2	0	0	0	0	0
Totals	41	11	13	27	15	1

NATIONALS	AB.	R.	H.	PO.	A.	E.
Reese (Dodgers), ss	5	0	0	3	3	1
J. Robinson (Dodgers), 2b	4	3	1	1	1	0
Musial (Cardinals), cf-rf	4	1	3	2	0	0
Kiner (Pirates), lf	5	1	1	3	0	0
Mize (Giants), 1b	2	0	1	1	0	1
aHodges (Dodgers), 1b	3	1	1	8	2	0
Marshall (Phillies), rf	1	1	0	1	0	1
Bickford (Braves), p	0	0	0	0	0	0
fThomson (Giants)	1	0	0	0	0	0
Pollet (Cardinals), p	0	0	0	1	0	0
Blackwell (Reds), p	0	0	0	0	0	0
hSlaughter (Cardinals)	1	0	0	0	0	0
Roe (Dodgers), p	0	0	0	0	0	0
Kazak (Cardinals), 3b	2	0	2	0	1	0
S. Gordon (Giants), 3b	2	0	1	0	4	0
Seminick (Phillies), c	1	0	0	3	0	1
Campanella (Dodgers), c	2	0	0	2	0	1
Spahn (Braves), p	0	0	0	0	0	0
Newcombe (Dodgers), p	1	0	0	0	0	0
bSchoendienst (Cardinals)	1	0	1	0	0	0
Munger (Cardinals), p	0	0	0	0	0	0
cPafko (Cubs), cf	2	0	1	2	0	0
Totals	37	7	12	27	11	5

American League	4	0	0	2	0	2	3	0	0 —	11
National League	2	1	2	0	0	2	0	0	0 —	7

Americans	IP.	H.	R.	ER.	BB.	SO.
Parnell (Red Sox)	1*	3	3	3	1	1
Trucks (Tigers)	2	3	2	2	2	0
Brissie (Athletics)	3	5	2	2	2	1
Raschi (Yankees)	3	1	0	0	3	1

Nationals	IP.	H.	R.	ER.	BB.	SO.
Spahn (Braves)	1⅓	4	4	0	2	3
Newcombe (Dodgers)	2⅔	3	2	2	1	0
Munger (Cardinals)	1	0	0	0	1	0
Bickford (Braves)	1	2	2	2	1	0
Pollet (Cardinals)	1	4	3	3	0	0
Blackwell (Reds)	1	0	0	0	0	2
Roe (Dodgers)	1	0	0	0	0	0

*Pitched to three batters in second inning.

Winning pitcher—Trucks.   Losing pitcher—Newcombe.

aRan for Mize in third. bSingled for Newcombe in fourth. cStruck out for Munger in fifth. dRan for Kell in sixth. eRan for J. DiMaggio in sixth. fFlied out for Bickford in sixth. gFlied out for Brissie in seventh. hFlied out for Blackwell in eighth. Runs batted in—J. DiMaggio 3, E. Robinson, Tebbetts, Musial 2, Newcombe, Kazak, Joost 2, Kiner 2. D. DiMaggio, Dillinger, Mitchell. (Joost scored on Reese's error in first.) (J. Robinson scored when Kiner hit into double play in third.) Two-base hits—J. Robinson, Tebbetts, S. Gordon, D. DiMaggio, J. DiMaggio, J. Gordon, Mitchell. Home runs—Musial, Kiner. Stolen base—Kell. Double plays—Michaels, Joost and E. Robinson; Joost, Michaels and E. Robinson; J. Robinson, Reese and Hodges. Hit by pitcher—By Parnell (Seminick). Left on bases—Nationals 12, Americans 8. Umpires—Barlick, Gore and Ballanfant (N.L.), Hubbard, Summers and Grieve (A.L.). Time of game—3:04. Attendance —32,577.

Game of 1950
Comiskey Park, Chicago, July 11

Red Schoendienst's fourteenth-inning home run gave the National League a dramatic 4-3 victory, snapping a long-time jinx. The triumph marked the senior circuit's first in nine All-Star games played in American League parks and was the old loop's first win since 1944.

The game, one of the most thrilling in the series, was the first to go extra innings.

The Nationals gained the decision by employing the American Leaguers' old home-run weapon. Besides Schoendienst's winning wallop, Ralph Kiner smashed a ninth-inning homer off Art Houtteman to tie the score.

An injury to Ted Williams marred the contest, although the extent of the mishap wasn't known until the next day. In the first inning the Red Sox slugger bumped against the wall while pulling down a long drive by Kiner. Williams hurt his left elbow in the crash, but despite considerable pain he remained in the game until the ninth inning.

X-rays the next day showed a fracture, which sidelined Williams until late in the season.

Enos Slaughter helped the N.L. to a 2-0 lead in the second inning with a triple. The Americans picked up one run off Robin Roberts in the third and then tore into Don Newcombe two innings later for two runs and a 3-2 lead. Williams singled across the tie-breaking marker. The box score:

National League 4, American League 3

(American League Leads Series, 12-5)

NATIONALS	AB.	R.	H.	PO.	A.	E.	AMERICANS	AB.	R.	H.	PO.	A.	E.
Jones (Phillies), 3b	7	0	1	2	3	0	Rizzuto (Yankees), ss	6	0	2	2	2	0
Kiner (Pirates), lf	6	1	2	1	0	0	Doby (Indians), cf	6	1	2	9	0	0
Musial (Cardinals), 1b	5	0	0	11	1	0	Kell (Tigers), 3b	6	0	0	2	4	0
Robinson (Dodgers), 2b	4	1	1	3	2	0	Williams (Red Sox), lf	4	0	1	2	0	0
fWyrostek (Reds), rf	2	0	0	0	0	0	D. DiMaggio (R. Sox), lf	2	0	0	1	0	0
Slaughter (Cards), cf-rf	4	1	2	3	0	0	Dropo (Red Sox), 1b	3	0	1	8	1	0
Schoendienst (Cards), 2b	1	1	1	1	1	0	eFain (Athletics), 1b	3	0	1	2	1	0
Sauer (Cubs), rf	2	0	0	1	0	0	Evers (Tigers), rf	2	0	0	1	0	0
Pafko (Cubs), cf	4	0	2	4	0	0	J. DiMaggio (Yanks), rf	3	0	0	3	0	0
Campanella (Dodgers), c	6	0	0	13	2	0	Berra (Yankees), c	2	0	0	2	0	0
Marion (Cardinals), ss	2	0	0	0	2	0	bHegan (Indians), c	3	0	0	7	1	0
Konstanty (Phillies), p	0	0	0	0	0	0	Doerr (Red Sox), 2b	3	0	1	4	4	0
Jansen (Giants), p	2	0	0	1	0	0	Coleman (Yankees), 2b	2	0	0	0	0	1
gSnider (Dodgers)	1	0	0	0	0	0	Raschi (Yankees), p	0	0	0	0	0	0
Blackwell (Reds), p	1	0	0	0	1	0	aMichaels (Senators)	1	1	1	0	0	0
Roberts (Phillies), p	1	0	0	0	0	0	Lemon (Indians), p	0	1	0	1	0	0
Newcombe (Dodgers), p	0	0	0	0	1	0	Houtteman (Tigers), p	1	0	0	1	0	0
cSisler (Phillies)	1	0	1	0	0	0	Reynolds (Yankees), p	1	0	0	0	0	0
dReese (Dodgers), ss	3	0	0	2	4	0	hHenrich (Yankees)	1	0	0	0	0	0
							Gray (Tigers), p	0	0	0	0	0	0
							Feller (Indians), p	0	0	0	0	0	0
Totals	52	4	10	42	17	0	Totals	49	3	8	42	13	1

```
National League ................... 0  2  0   0  0  0   0  0  1   0  0  0   0  1—4
American League ................. 0  0  1   0  2  0   0  0  0   0  0  0   0  0—3
```

Nationals	IP.	H.	R.	ER.	BB.	SO.	Americans	IP.	H.	R.	ER.	BB.	SO.
Roberts (Phillies)	3	3	1	1	1	1	Raschi (Yankees)	3	2	2	2	0	1
Newcombe (Dodgers)	2	3	2	2	1	1	Lemon (Indians)	3	1	0	0	0	2
Konstanty (Phillies)	1	0	0	0	0	2	Houtteman (Tigers)	3	3	1	1	1	0
Jansen (Giants)	5	1	0	0	0	6	Reynolds (Yankees)	3	1	0	0	1	2
Blackwell (Reds)	3	1	0	0	1	0	Gray (Tigers)	1⅓	3	1	1	0	1
							Feller (Indians)	⅔	0	0	0	1	1

Winning pitcher—Blackwell. Losing pitcher—Gray.

aDoubled for Raschi in third. bRan for Berra in fourth. cSingled for Newcombe in sixth. dRan for Sisler in sixth. ePopped out for Dropo in eighth. fFlied out for Robinson in eleventh. gFlied out for Jansen in twelfth. hFlied out for Reynolds in twelfth. Two-base hits—Michaels, Doby, Kiner. Three-base hits—Slaughter, Dropo. Home runs—Kiner, Schoendienst. Double plays—Rizzuto, Doerr and Dropo; Jones, Schoendienst and Musial. Wild pitch—Roberts. Passed ball—Hegan. Left on bases—Nationals 9, Americans 6. Umpires—McGowan, Rommel and Stevens (A.L.); Pinelli, Conlan and Robb (N.L.). Time of game—3:19. Attendance—46,127.

Game of 1951
Briggs Stadium, Detroit, July 10

Exploding for a record total of four home runs, the National League trounced the American League, 8-3, in the 18th annual classic. The victory was the old loop's second in succession, marking the first time the N. L. had won in consecutive years.

The practice of having the two leagues alternate as host was broken when the game was played in the Motor City. Originally, it was slated for Philadelphia under the auspices of the Phillies, but the magnates agreed to switch it to Detroit as part of that city's 250th anniversary.

The four N. L. homers accounted for six runs. The senior circuit's siege guns went to work in the fourth inning. Stan Musial hit Ed Lopat's first pitch for a home run and Bob Elliott also connected later in the inning with a mate aboard for a 4-1 lead.

Gil Hodges unloaded a two-run homer off Fred Hutchinson in the sixth inning and Ralph Kiner connected against Mel Parnell in the eighth to climax the day's scoring.

American League hitters unloaded two homers, making a record total of six for the game. Both homers were hit by members of the host club—Vic Wertz and George Kell.

Joe DiMaggio, who announced his retirement at the close of the season, was a member of the A. L. squad, but a leg injury prevented The Yankee Clipper from seeing action. The box score:

National League 8, American League 3
(American League Leads Series, 12-6)

NATIONALS	AB.	R.	H.	PO.	A.	E.	AMERICANS	AB.	R.	H.	PO.	A.	E.
Ashburn (Phillies), cf	4	2	2	4	1	0	D. DiMaggio (R. Sox), cf	5	0	1	1	0	0
Snider (Dodgers), cf	0	0	0	0	0	0	Fox (White Sox), 2b	3	0	1	3	1	1
Dark (Giants), ss	5	0	1	0	3	0	eDoerr (Red Sox), 2b	1	0	1	1	0	0
Reese (Dodgers), ss	0	0	0	0	1	0	Kell (Tigers), 3b	3	1	1	4	2	0
Musial (Cards), lf-rf-lf	4	1	2	0	0	0	Williams (Red Sox), lf	3	0	1	3	0	0
Westlake (Cardinals), lf	0	0	0	0	0	0	Busby (White Sox), lf	0	0	0	0	0	0
J. Robinson (Dodgers), 2b	4	1	2	3	1	1	Berra (Yankees), c	4	1	1	4	2	1
Schoendienst (Cards), 2b	0	0	0	0	0	0	Wertz (Tigers), rf	3	1	1	2	0	0
Hodges (Dodgers), 1b	5	2	2	6	0	0	Rizzuto (Yankees), ss	1	0	0	1	2	0
Elliott (Braves), 3b	2	1	1	1	1	0	Fain (Athletics), 1b	3	0	1	5	0	0
Jones (Phillies), 3b	2	0	0	3	0	0	fE. Robin'n (W. Sox), 1b	1	0	0	0	1	0
Ennis (Phillies), rf	2	0	0	0	0	0	Carrasquel (Wh. Sox), ss	2	0	1	0	3	0
Kiner (Pirates), lf	2	1	1	1	0	0	cMinoso (White Sox), rf	2	0	0	2	0	0
Wyrostek (Reds), rf	1	0	0	0	0	0	Garver (Browns), p	1	0	0	0	0	0
Campanella (Dodgers), c	4	0	0	9	1	0	Lopat (Yankees), p	0	0	0	0	0	0
Roberts (Phillies), p	0	0	0	0	0	0	bDoby (Indians)	1	0	0	0	0	0
aSlaughter (Cardinals)	1	0	0	0	0	0	Hutchinson (Tigers), p	0	0	0	0	0	0
Maglie (Giants), p	1	0	0	0	0	0	dStephens (Red Sox)	1	0	0	0	0	0
Newcombe (Dodgers), p	2	0	1	0	1	0	Parnell (Red Sox), p	0	0	0	0	0	0
Blackwell (Reds), p	0	0	0	0	0	0	Lemon (Indians), p	0	0	0	1	0	0
							gHegan (Indians)	1	0	1	0	0	0
Totals	39	8	12	27	9	1	Totals	35	3	10	27	11	2

National League	1	0	0	3	0	2	1	1	0	—	8	
American League	0	1	0	1	1	0	0	0	0	—	3	

Americans	IP.	H.	R.	ER.	BB.	SO.	Nationals	IP.	H.	R.	ER.	BB.	SO.
Garver (Browns)	3	1	1	0	1	1	Roberts (Phillies)	2	4	1	1	1	1
Lopat (Yankees)	1	3	3	3	0	0	Maglie (Giants)	3	3	2	2	1	1
Hutchinson (Tigers)	3	3	3	3	2	0	Newcombe (Dodgers)	3	2	0	0	0	3
Parnell (Red Sox)	1	3	1	1	0	1	Blackwell (Reds)	1	1	0	0	1	2
Lemon (Indians)	1	2	0	0	1	1							

Winning pitcher—Maglie. Losing pitcher—Lopat.

aLined out for Roberts in third. bPopped out for Lopat in fourth. cGrounded out for Carrasquel in sixth. dStruck out for Hutchinson in seventh. eSingled for Fox in seventh. fGrounded out for Fain in eighth. gDoubled for Lemon in ninth. Runs batted in—Fain, Musial, Elliott 2, Wertz, Kell, Hodges 2, J. Robinson, Kiner. Two-base hits—Ashburn, Hegan. Three-base hits—Fain, Williams. Home runs—Musial, Elliott, Wertz, Kell, Hodges, Kiner. Sacrifice hit—Kell. Double play—Berra and Kell. Left on bases—Nationals 8, Americans 9. Passed ball—Campanella. Umpires—Passarella, Hurley and Honochick (A. L.), Robb, Jorda and Dascoli (N. L.). Time of game—2:41. Attendance—52,075.

Game of 1952
Shibe Park, Philadelphia, July 8

For the first time in All-Star history, rain cut short a game, halting play after five innings with the Nationals emerging victorious, 3-2. The defeat was the third straight for the American League.

The N. L. again employed the home-run punch. Jackie Robinson accounted for the game's initial run when he clouted a Vic Raschi pitch into the stands in the opening inning, and then Hank Sauer unloaded a two-run homer off Bob Lemon in the fourth for what proved to be the margin of victory.

Rain, which fell intermittently during the morning and almost steadily during the game, made footing insecure, but the crowd saw an exceptionally well-played game.

Because of the weather, both teams dispensed with pre-game drills, and the start of the contest was delayed nearly 20 minutes in the hope there might be a letup in the showers.

From a pitching standpoint, two southpaws from the home-town clubs—Curt Simmons of the host Phillies and Bobby Shantz of the Athletics—stole the show. Simmons blanked the Americans on one hit over the first three innings. Shantz was the last of three hurlers used by Casey Stengel, and rain limited him to one inning.

In that brief appearance, the A's diminutive portsider performed one of the top mound feats in All-Star history, fanning Whitey Lockman, Jackie Robinson and Stan Musial in succession.

Rain deprived Shantz of a chance to go after Carl Hubbell's record of whiffing five in succession in the 1934 game.

The Americans scored their two runs off Bob Rush in the fourth inning. Minnie Minoso led off with a pinch-double. Following a walk and an out, Eddie Robinson singled for one run and another scored when Bobby Avila beat out an infield hit. The box score:

National League 3, American League 2

(American League Leads Series, 12-7)

AMERICANS	AB.	R.	H.	PO.	A.	E.	NATIONALS	AB.	R.	H.	PO.	A.	E.
DiMaggio (Red Sox), cf	2	0	1	1	0	0	Lockman (Giants), 1b	3	0	0	5	0	0
Doby (Indians), cf	0	0	0	0	0	0	J. Robinson (Dodgers), 2b	3	1	1	2	2	0
Bauer (Yankees), rf	3	0	1	2	0	0	Musial (Cardinals), cf	2	1	0	1	0	0
Jensen (Senators), rf	0	0	0	0	0	0	Sauer (Cubs), lf	2	1	1	0	0	0
Mitchell (Indians), lf	1	0	0	1	0	0	Campanella (Dodgers), c	1	0	0	5	1	0
cMinoso (White Sox), lf	1	1	1	0	0	0	Slaughter (Cardinals), rf	2	0	1	0	0	0
Rosen (Indians), 3b	1	1	0	3	1	0	Thomson (Giants), 3b	2	0	0	1	1	0
Berra (Yankees), c	2	0	0	6	0	0	Hamner (Phillies), ss	1	0	0	1	3	0
E. Robin'n (W. Sox), 1b	2	0	1	1	0	0	Simmons (Phillies), p	0	0	0	0	0	0
Avila (Indians), 2b	2	0	1	0	0	0	bReese (Dodgers)	1	0	0	0	0	0
Rizzuto (Yankees), ss	2	0	0	1	0	0	Rush (Cubs), p	1	0	0	0	0	0
Raschi (Yankees), p	0	0	0	0	0	0	Totals	18	3	3	15	7	0
aMcDougald (Yankees)	1	0	0	0	0	0							
Lemon (Indians), p	1	0	0	0	0	0							
Shantz (Athletics), p	0	0	0	0	0	0							
Totals	18	2	5	15	1	0							

American League	0	0	0	2	0—2	
National League	1	0	0	2	0—3	

Stopped by rain.

Americans	IP.	H.	R.	ER.	BB.	SO.	Nationals	IP.	H.	R.	ER.	BB.	SO.
Raschi (Yankees)	2	1	1	1	0	3	Simmons (Phillies)	3	1	0	0	1	3
Lemon (Indians)	2	2	2	2	2	0	Rush (Cubs)	2	4	2	2	1	1
Shantz (Athletics)	1	0	0	0	0	3							

Winning pitcher—Rush. Losing pitcher—Lemon.

aGrounded out for Raschi in third. bFlied out for Simmons in third. cDoubled for Mitchell in fourth. Runs batted in—J. Robinson, E. Robinson, Avila, Sauer 2. Two-base hits—DiMaggio, Minoso, Slaughter. Home runs—J. Robinson, Sauer. Double play—Hamner, J. Robinson and Lockman. Left on bases—Americans 3, Nationals 3. Hit by pitcher—By Lemon (Musial). Umpires—Barlick, Boggess and Warneke (N. L.), Berry, Summers and Soar (A. L.). Time of game—1:29. Attendance—32,785.

Game of 1953
Crosley Field, Cincinnati, July 14

Combining a 10-hit attack with effective pitching, the National League gained its fourth straight victory, 5-1. By winning four years in a row, the N.L. matched the Americans' best run of victories. Curiously, the manager of the four-time A.L. losers was Casey Stengel, who went on to lead the Yankees to a fifth successive flag in 1953.

The game was more one-sided than the score would indicate. For eight innings the Americans were held to two hits. Only one runner reached second base during that time. In the ninth inning, Murry Dickson yielded three singles for the lone A.L. run.

Aside from the pitchers, the Nationals' top star was Enos Slaughter. The 37-year-old Cardinal outfielder collected two hits and a walk, drove in one, scored two and made a catch that compared with the best fielding plays ever seen in the midsummer classic.

It came in the sixth inning when Harvey Kuenn smashed a drive down the right-field line for what seemed a sure hit until Slaughter skidded on his left shoulder to grab the ball.

For the first time since 1944, there were no home runs. The N.L. scored twice off Allie Reynolds in the fifth inning and once off Mike Garcia in the seventh. Satchel Paige, ageless Negro pitcher, yielded the last two runs in the eighth, with Slaughter driving in one and Dickson the other. The box score:

National League 5, American League 1
(American League Leads Series, 12-8)

AMERICANS	AB.	R.	H.	PO.	A.	E.	NATIONALS	AB.	R.	H.	PO.	A.	E.
Goodman (Red Sox), 2b	2	0	0	1	1	0	Reese (Dodgers), ss	4	0	2	1	1	0
Fox (White Sox), 2b	1	0	0	1	0	0	Hamner (Phillies), ss	0	0	0	0	0	0
Vernon (Senators), 1b	3	0	0	6	0	0	Schoendienst (Cards), 2b	3	0	0	3	3	0
Fain (White Sox), 1b	1	1	1	1	1	0	Williams (Giants), 2b	0	0	0	2	0	0
Bauer (Yankees), rf	2	0	3	0	0	0	Musial (Cardinals), lf	4	0	2	3	0	0
jMize (Yankees)	1	0	1	0	0	0	Kluszewski (Reds), 1b	3	0	1	5	0	0
Mantle (Yankees), cf	2	0	0	0	0	0	dHodges (Dodgers), 1b	1	0	0	1	0	0
eHunter (Browns)	0	0	0	0	0	0	Campanella (Dodgers), c	4	1	1	6	2	0
Doby (Indians), cf	1	0	0	1	1	0	Mathews (Braves), 3b	3	1	0	0	0	0
Rosen (Indians), 3b	4	0	0	2	4	0	Bell (Reds), cf	3	0	0	4	0	0
Zernial (Athletics), lf	2	0	1	1	0	0	iSnider (Dodgers), cf	0	1	0	1	0	0
Minoso (White Sox), lf	2	0	2	0	0	0	Slaughter (Cardinals), rf	3	2	2	4	0	0
Berra (Yankees), c	4	0	0	4	0	0	Roberts (Phillies), p	0	0	0	0	1	0
Carrasquel (Wh. Sox), ss	2	0	0	2	1	0	aKiner (Cubs)	1	0	0	0	0	0
gKell (Red Sox)	1	0	0	0	0	0	Spahn (Braves), p	0	0	0	0	0	0
Rizzuto (Yankees), ss	0	0	0	1	0	0	bAshburn (Phillies)	1	0	1	0	0	0
Pierce (White Sox), p	1	0	0	0	0	0	Simmons (Phillies), p	0	0	0	0	0	0
Reynolds (Yankees), p	0	0	0	0	0	0	fJ. Robinson (Dodgers)	1	0	0	0	0	0
cKuenn (Tigers)	1	0	0	0	0	0	Dickson (Pirates), p	1	0	1	0	0	0
Garcia (Indians), p	0	0	0	1	0	0	Totals	32	5	10	27	7	0
hE. Robinson (Athletics)	1	0	0	0	0	0							
Paige (Browns) p	0	0	0	0	0	0							
Totals	31	1	5	24	8	0							

American League	0	0	0	0	0	0	0	0	1—1		
National League	0	0	0	0	2	0	1	2	x—5		

Americans	IP.	H.	R.	ER.	BB.	SO.	Nationals	IP.	H.	R.	ER.	BB.	SO.
Pierce (White Sox)	3	1	0	0	0	1	Roberts (Phillies)	3	1	0	0	1	2
Reynolds (Yankees)	2	2	2	2	1	0	Spahn (Braves)	2	0	0	0	1	2
Garcia (Indians)	2	4	1	1	1	2	Simmons (Phillies)	2	1	0	0	1	1
Paige (Browns)	1	3	2	2	1	0	Dickson (Pirates)	2	3	1	1	0	0

Winning pitcher—Spahn. Losing pitcher—Reynolds.

aStruck out for Roberts in third. bSingled for Spahn in fifth. cLined out for Reynolds in sixth. dRan for Kluszewski in sixth. eRan for Mantle in seventh. fPopped out for Simmons in seventh. gFlied out for Carrasquel in eighth. hLined out for Garcia in eighth. iWalked for Bell in eighth. jSingled for Bauer in ninth. Runs batted in—Ashburn, Reese 2, Slaughter, Dickson, Minoso. Two-base hit—Reese. Stolen base—Slaughter. Double play—Carrasquel and Vernon. Left on bases—Nationals 7, Americans 6. Hit by pitcher—By Reynolds (Mathews). Umpires—Conlan, Donatelli and Engeln (N. L.), Stevens, McKinley and Napp (A. L.). Time of game—2:19. Attendance—30,846.

Game of 1954
Municipal Stadium, Cleveland, July 13

In a spectacular slugfest that set All-Star marks for runs and hits by the two clubs, the American League edged the National, 11-9, before 68,751 fans—only 1,080 under the record set in the same park in 1935. With increased ticket prices, gross gate receipts were $292,678, topping the former high by more than $100,000.

The slugfest produced six home runs, including four by the A. L. Both were record-equalling totals. Ironically, the decisive hit was a blooper over second base by Nellie Fox with the bags loaded and the score 9-9 in the eighth inning. The bleeder, which barely eluded shortstop Alvin Dark, scored the winning runs.

Three Indians—Al Rosen, Larry Doby and Bobby Avila—starred before their home-town crowd. They drove in eight of the A. L. runs, with Rosen walloping two successive home runs and a single to bat in five runs. His two homers and five RBIs tied All-Star records.

A two-run pinch-homer by Gus Bell in the eighth put the Nationals ahead, 9-8. Later in the inning, immediately after Dean Stone took the mound, Red Schoendienst made a surprise attempt to steal home, but the A. L. hurler hurried his motion and nailed him. The National Leaguers argued that Stone had balked, but Plate Umpire Bill Stewart disagreed. Though Stone faced no other batter, he was the winner. The box score:

American League 11, National League 9

(American League Leads Series, 13-8)

NATIONALS	AB.	R.	H.	PO.	A.	E.
Hamner (Phillies), 2b	3	0	0	0	0	0
Schoendienst (Cards), 2b	2	0	0	1	0	0
Dark (Giants), ss	5	0	1	1	2	0
Snider (Dodgers), cf-rf	4	2	3	2	0	0
Musial (Cards), rf-lf	5	1	2	2	1	0
Kluszewski (Reds), 1b	4	2	2	5	0	0
Hodges (Dodgers), 1b	1	0	0	1	0	0
Jablonski (Cards), 3b	3	1	1	0	1	0
Jackson (Cubs), 3b	2	0	0	1	1	0
Robinson (Dodgers), lf	2	1	1	0	0	0
Mays (Giants), cf	2	1	1	1	0	0
Campanella (Dodgers), c	3	0	1	9	0	0
Burgess (Phillies), c	0	0	0	1	0	0
Roberts (Phillies), p	1	0	0	0	0	0
aMueller (Giants)	1	0	1	0	0	0
Antonelli (Giants), p	0	0	0	0	0	0
cThomas (Pirates)	1	0	0	0	0	0
Spahn (Braves), p	0	0	0	0	0	0
Grissom (Giants), p	0	0	0	0	0	0
eBell (Reds)	1	1	1	0	0	0
Conley (Braves), p	0	0	0	0	0	0
Erskine (Dodgers), p	0	0	0	0	0	0
Totals	40	9	14	24	5	0

AMERICANS	AB.	R.	H.	PO.	A.	E.
Minoso (White Sox), lf-rf	4	1	2	1	0	1
Piersall (Red Sox), rf	0	0	0	0	0	0
Avila (Indians), 2b	3	1	3	1	1	0
Keegan (White Sox), p	0	0	0	0	0	0
Stone (Senators), p	0	0	0	0	0	0
fDoby (Indians), cf	1	1	1	0	0	0
Mantle (Yankees), cf	5	1	2	2	0	0
Trucks (White Sox), p	0	0	0	0	0	0
Berra (Yankees), c	4	2	2	5	0	0
Rosen (Indians), 1b-3b	4	2	3	7	0	0
Boone (Tigers), 3b	4	1	1	1	3	0
gVernon (Senators), 1b	1	0	0	1	0	0
Bauer (Yankees), rf	2	0	1	1	0	0
Porterfield (Senators), p	1	0	0	0	0	0
dFox (White Sox), 2b	2	0	1	1	0	0
Carrasquel (Wh. Sox), ss	5	1	1	5	4	0
Ford (Yankees), p	1	0	0	0	0	0
Consuegra (White Sox), p	0	0	0	0	0	0
Lemon (Indians), p	0	0	0	0	0	0
bWilliams (Red Sox), lf	2	1	0	2	0	0
Noren (Yankees), lf	0	0	0	0	0	0
Totals	39	11	17	27	8	1

National League	0	0	0	5	2	0	0	2	0 —	9
American League	0	0	4	1	2	1	0	3	x —	11

Nationals	IP.	H.	R.	ER.	BB.	SO.
Roberts (Phillies)	3	5	4	4	2	5
Antonelli (Giants)	2	4	3	3	0	2
Spahn (Braves)	2/3	4	1	1	1	0
Grissom (Giants)	1 1/3	0	0	0	0	2
Conley (Braves)	1/3	3	3	3	1	0
Erskine (Dodgers)	2/3	1	0	0	0	1

Americans	IP.	H.	R.	ER.	BB.	SO.
Ford (Yankees)	3	1	0	0	1	0
Consuegra (White Sox)	1/3	5	5	5	0	1
Lemon (Indians)	2/3	1	0	0	0	0
Porterfield (Senators)	3	4	2	2	0	1
Keegan (White Sox)	2/3	3	2	2	0	1
Stone (Senators)	1/3	0	0	0	0	0
Trucks (White Sox)	1	0	0	0	1	0

Winning pitcher—Stone. Losing pitcher—Conley.

aDoubled for Roberts in fourth. bStruck out for Lemon in fourth. cStruck out for Antonelli in sixth. dStruck out for Porterfield in seventh. eHomered for Grissom in eighth. fHomered for Stone in eighth. gStruck out for Boone in eighth. Runs batted in—Rosen 5, Boone, Kluszewski 3, Jablonski, Robinson 2, Mueller, Avila 2, Bell 2, Doby, Fox 2. Two-base hits—Robinson, Mueller, Snider. Home runs—Rosen 2, Boone, Kluszewski, Bell, Doby. Sacrifice fly—Avila. Double play—Avila, Carrasquel and Rosen. Left on bases—Nationals 6, Americans 9. Umpires—Rommel, Honochick and Paparella (A. L.), Ballanfant, Stewart and Gorman (N. L.). Time of game—3:10. Attendance—68,751.

Indians slugger Al Rosen gave hometown fans a real treat when he connected for two home runs and drove in five runs to lead the American League to an 11-9 victory in the 1954 All-Star Game at Cleveland's Municipal Stadium.

Game of 1955

County Stadium, Milwaukee, July 12

Stan Musial's home run on the first pitch in the 12th inning climaxed a stirring uphill battle that enabled the Nationals to nose out a 6-5 victory. Victim of the blast was Frank Sullivan.

Moments before Musial broke up the game, the crowd of 45,643 gave Gene Conley, Braves' hurler, a standing ovation. He earned the plaudits by fanning three of the Americans' greatest hitters—Al Kaline, Mickey Vernon and Al Rosen—in succession in the top half of the frame.

Robin Roberts had another sad experience as the starting N. L. pitcher. Famed as a control pitcher, he uncorked a wild pitch that let in the first A. L. run in the opening inning and moments later saw Mickey Mantle smash a 430-foot homer over the center-field fence for three more runs.

Trailing by 5-0, the Nationals rallied for two runs off Whitey Ford in the seventh inning on a single by Willie Mays, a walk, another ace by Johnny Logan and Chico Carrasquel's error. After the Yankee lefty retired the first two batters in the eighth, the N. L. combined singles by Mays, Ted Kluszewski, Randy Jackson and Hank Aaron with Al Rosen's error for three runs to knot the score, paving the way for extra innings and the thrilling finish. The box score:

National League 6, American League 5

(American League Leads Series, 13-9)

AMERICANS	AB.	R.	H.	PO.	A.	E.	NATIONALS	AB.	R.	H.	PO.	A.	E.
Kuenn (Tigers), ss	3	1	1	1	0	0	Schoendienst (Cards), 2b	6	0	2	3	2	0
Carrasquel (Wh. Sox), ss	3	0	2	1	3	1	Ennis (Phillies), lf	1	0	0	1	0	0
Fox (White Sox), 2b	3	1	1	2	0	0	cMusial (Cardinals), lf	4	1	1	0	0	0
Avila (Indians), 2b	1	0	0	1	2	0	Snider (Dodgers), cf	2	0	0	3	0	0
Williams (Red Sox), lf	3	1	1	1	0	0	Mays (Giants), cf	3	2	2	3	0	0
Smith (Indians), lf	1	0	0	0	0	0	Kluszewski (Reds), 1b	5	1	2	9	1	0
Mantle (Yankees), cf	6	1	2	3	0	0	Mathews (Braves), 3b	2	0	0	0	3	1
Berra (Yankees), c	6	1	1	8	2	0	Jackson (Cubs), 3b	3	1	1	0	0	0
Kaline (Tigers), rf	4	0	1	6	0	0	Mueller (Giants), rf	2	0	1	0	0	0
Vernon (Senators), 1b	5	0	1	8	0	0	dAaron (Braves), rf	2	1	2	0	0	0
Finigan (Athletics), 3b	3	0	0	2	0	0	Banks (Cubs), ss	2	0	0	2	1	0
Rosen (Indians), 3b	2	0	0	0	0	1	Logan (Braves), ss	3	0	1	1	1	0
Pierce (White Sox), p	0	0	0	0	0	0	Crandall (Braves), c	1	0	0	1	0	0
bJensen (Red Sox)	1	0	0	0	0	0	eBurgess (Reds), c	1	0	0	2	0	0
Wynn (Indians), p	0	0	0	0	1	0	hLopata (Phillies), c	3	0	0	10	0	0
gPower (Athletics)	1	0	0	0	0	0	Roberts (Phillies), p	0	0	0	1	1	0
Ford (Yankees), p	1	0	0	0	1	0	aThomas (Pirates)	1	0	0	0	0	0
Sullivan (Red Sox), p	1	0	0	0	0	0	Haddix (Cardinals), p	0	0	0	0	2	0
Totals	44	5	10	33	9	2	fHodges (Dodgers)	1	0	1	0	0	0
							Newcombe (Dodgers), p	0	0	0	0	0	0
							iBaker (Cubs)	1	0	0	0	0	0
							Jones (Cubs), p	0	0	0	0	0	0
							Nuxhall (Reds), p	2	0	0	0	1	0
							Conley (Braves), p	0	0	0	0	0	0
							Totals	45	6	13	36	12	1

American League	4	0	0		0	0	1		0	0	0		0	0	0—5
National League	0	0	0		0	0	0		2	3	0		0	0	1—6

None out when winning run scored.

Americans	IP.	H.	R.	ER.	BB.	SO.	Nationals	IP.	H.	R.	ER.	BB.	SO.
Pierce (White Sox)	3	1	0	0	0	3	Roberts (Phillies)	3	4	4	4	1	0
Wynn (Indians)	3	3	0	0	0	1	Haddix (Cardinals)	3	3	1	1	0	2
Ford (Yankees)	1⅔	5	5	3	1	0	Newcombe (Dodgers)	1	1	0	0	0	1
Sullivan (Red Sox)	3⅓*	4	1	1	1	4	Jones (Cubs)	⅔	0	0	0	2	1
							Nuxhall (Reds)	3⅓	2	0	0	3	5
							Conley (Braves)	1	0	0	0	0	3

*Pitched to one batter in twelfth.

Winning pitcher—Conley. Losing pitcher—Sullivan.

aPopped out for Roberts in third. bPopped out for Pierce in fourth. cStruck out for Ennis in fourth. dRan for Mueller in fifth. eHit into force play for Crandall in fifth. fSingled for Haddix in sixth. gPopped out for Wynn in seventh. hSafe on error for Burgess in seventh. iFlied out for Newcombe in seventh. Runs batted in—Mantle 3, Vernon, Logan, Jackson, Aaron, Musial. Two-base hits—Kluszewski, Kaline. Home runs—Mantle, Musial. Sacrifice hits—Pierce, Avila. Double plays—Kluszewski, Banks and Roberts; Wynn, Carrasquel and Vernon. Left on bases—Americans 12, Nationals 8. Hit by pitcher—By Jones (Kaline). Wild pitch—Roberts. Passed ball—Crandall. Umpires—Barlick, Boggess and Secory (N. L.), Soar, Summers and Runge (A. L.). Time of game—3:17. Attendance—45,643.

Game of 1956
Griffith Stadium, Washington, July 10

Capitalizing on a power-packed lineup, the Nationals breezed to a 7-3 victory. The triumph was the senior circuit's sixth in the last seven contests and whittled the A. L.'s once-overwhelming edge to 13-10.

In a sense, the outcome vindicated the judgment of the fans, who again selected the starting lineups. Although Cincinnati was battling for first place, there was considerable criticism when, as the result of a campaign by a Cincinnati radio station, five Reds were named to the N. L. lineup and three other regulars were runners-up at their positions.

The Nationals had numerous standouts, but the real star was Ken Boyer. The Cardinal third baseman went 3-for-5 at bat and in the field broke the hearts of the American Leaguers with three fine plays.

The N. L. cracked the scoring ice with a run in the third and then made it 3-0 when Willie Mays tagged Whitey Ford for a two-run homer as a pinch-hitter in the fourth.

Down by 5-0, the Americans came to life in the sixth inning, routing Warren Spahn. Nellie Fox opened with a single and then Ted Williams and Mickey Mantle smashed successive homers. Johnny Antonelli replaced Spahn and blanked the A. L. the remainder of the way.

The Nationals added their final two runs in the seventh inning. Stan Musial homered into the left-center field bleachers. Later, Willie Mays walked and scored on Ted Kluszewski's two-bagger. The box score:

National League 7, American League 3

(American League Leads Series, 13-10)

NATIONALS	AB.	R.	H.	PO.	A.	E.	AMERICANS	AB.	R.	H.	PO.	A.	E.
Temple (Reds), 2b	4	1	2	2	3	0	Kuenn (Tigers), ss	5	0	1	2	3	0
Robinson (Reds), lf	2	0	0	1	0	0	Fox (White Sox), 2b	4	1	2	1	0	0
dSnider (Dodgers), cf	3	0	0	1	0	0	Williams (Red Sox), lf	4	1	1	2	0	0
Musial (Cardinals), rf-lf	4	1	1	2	0	0	Mantle (Yankees), cf	4	1	1	0	0	0
Aaron (Braves), lf	1	0	0	0	0	0	Berra (Yankees), c	2	0	2	10	1	0
Boyer (Cardinals), 3b	5	1	3	3	1	0	gLollar (White Sox), c	2	0	1	4	0	0
Bell (Reds), cf	1	0	0	2	0	0	Kaline (Tigers), rf	3	0	1	0	0	0
bMays (Giants), cf-rf	3	2	1	2	0	0	Piersall (Red Sox), rf	1	0	0	1	0	0
Long (Pirates), 1b	2	0	0	6	0	0	Vernon (Red Sox), 1b	2	0	0	4	0	0
fKluszewski (Reds), 1b	2	1	2	2	0	0	hPower (Athletics), 1b	2	0	1	3	0	0
Bailey (Reds), c	3	0	0	3	1	0	Kell (Orioles), 3b	4	0	1	0	1	0
Campanella (Dodgers), c	0	0	0	1	0	0	Pierce (White Sox), p	0	0	0	0	1	0
McMillan (Reds), ss	3	1	2	1	5	0	aSimpson (Athletics)	1	0	0	0	0	0
Friend (Pirates), p	0	0	0	0	0	0	Ford (Yankees), p	0	0	0	0	0	0
cRepulski (Cardinals)	1	0	0	0	0	0	Wilson (White Sox), p	0	0	0	0	1	0
Spahn (Braves), p	1	0	0	0	0	0	eMartin (Yankees)	1	0	0	0	0	0
Antonelli (Giants), p	1	0	0	1	0	0	Brewer (Red Sox), p	0	0	0	0	0	0
Totals	36	7	11	27	10	0	iBoone (Tigers)	1	0	0	0	0	0
							Score (Indians), p	0	0	0	0	0	0
							Wynn (Indians), p	0	0	0	0	0	0
							jSievers (Senators)	1	0	0	0	0	0
							Totals	37	3	11	27	7	0

National League	0	0	1	2	1	1	2	0	0 — 7
American League	0	0	0	0	0	3	0	0	0 — 3

Nationals	IP.	H.	R.	ER.	BB.	SO.	Americans	IP.	H.	R.	ER.	BB.	SO.
Friend (Pirates)	3	3	0	0	0	3	Pierce (White Sox)	3	2	1	1	1	5
Spahn (Braves)	2*	4	3	3	0	1	Ford (Yankees)	1	3	2	2	1	2
Antonelli (Giants)	4	4	0	0	0	1	Wilson (White Sox)	1	2	1	1	0	1
*Pitched to three batters in sixth.							Brewer (Red Sox)	2	4	3	3	1	2
							Score (Indians)	1	0	0	0	1	1
							Wynn (Indians)	1	0	0	0	0	1

Winning pitcher—Friend. Losing pitcher—Pierce.

aStruck out for Pierce in third. bHomered for Bell in fourth. cFouled out for Friend in fourth. dFlied out for Robinson in fifth. eGrounded out for Wilson in fifth. fDoubled for Long in sixth. gSingled for Berra in sixth. hFlied out for Vernon in sixth. iLined out for Brewer in seventh. jPopped out for Wynn in ninth. Runs batted in—Temple, Mays 2, Boyer, Williams 2, Mantle, Musial, Kluszewski. Two-base hits—Kluszewski 2. Home runs—Mays, Williams, Mantle, Musial. Stolen base—Temple. Sacrifice hit—Friend. Double play—McMillan, Temple and Kluszewski. Left on bases—Nationals 7, Americans 7. Wild pitches—Brewer 2. Umpires—Berry, Hurley and Flaherty (A. L.), Pinelli, Gore and Jackowski (N. L.). Time of game—2:45. Attendance—28,843.

Game of 1957

Busch Stadium, St. Louis, July 9

In a contest in which most of the action was packed into the ninth inning, the Americans emerged victorious, 6-5. The game produced almost everything except a home run.

A deluge of 500,000 late votes from Cincinnati resulted in all of the Reds' regulars except first baseman George Crowe being the leaders at their respective positions.

However, because of the over-balance of Cincinnati votes, Commissioner Ford Frick ordered outfielder Gus Bell and Wally Post dropped from consideration. Manager Walter Alston later added Bell to his squad.

The Americans jumped off to a 2-0 lead in the second inning against Curt Simmons and Lou Burdette on three walks and a pair of singles and added another run in the sixth.

The N.L. got back in the game in the seventh when a pinch-double by Bell plated two runs, but in the ninth the A.L. expanded its lead to 6-2. However, the Nationals gave the crowd a thrill in their final turn.

A walk to Stan Musial, Willie Mays' triple and a wild pitch produced two quick runs. When Hank Foiles followed with a single and Bell walked, Manager Casey Stengel rushed in Don Mossi. A single by Ernie Banks added the final run, but Bell was nailed trying to go from first to third. Gil Hodges then lined sharply to left field to end the game. The box score:

American League 6, National League 5

(American League Leads Series, 14-10)

AMERICANS	AB.	R.	H.	PO.	A.	E.	NATIONALS	AB.	R.	H.	PO.	A.	E.
Kuenn (Tigers), ss	2	0	0	0	1	0	Temple (Reds), 2b	2	0	0	3	0	0
McDougald (Yankees), ss	2	1	0	1	0	0	eSchoend'nst (Braves), 2b	2	0	0	0	0	1
Fox (White Sox), 2b	4	0	0	2	4	0	Aaron (Braves), rf	4	0	1	2	0	0
Kaline (Tigers), rf	5	1	2	1	1	0	Musial (Cardinals), 1b	3	1	1	9	0	0
Mantle (Yankees), cf	4	1	1	4	0	0	Mays (Giants), cf	4	2	2	2	0	0
Williams (Red Sox), lf	3	1	0	2	0	0	Bailey (Reds), c	3	1	1	2	0	0
Minoso (White Sox), lf	1	0	1	1	1	0	hFoiles (Pirates)	1	1	1	0	0	0
Wertz (Indians), 1b	2	0	1	3	0	0	Robinson (Reds), lf	2	0	1	5	0	0
Skowron (Yankees), 1b	3	1	2	5	1	0	fBell (Reds), lf	1	0	1	0	0	0
Berra (Yankees), c	3	0	1	6	0	0	Hoak (Reds), 3b	1	0	0	1	0	0
Kell (Orioles), 3b	2	0	0	0	1	0	bMathews (Braves), 3b	3	0	0	1	0	0
Malzone (Red Sox), 3b	2	0	0	1	1	0	McMillan (Reds), ss	1	0	0	2	0	0
Bunning (Tigers), p	1	0	0	0	0	0	cBanks (Cubs), ss	3	0	1	0	3	0
aMaxwell (Tigers)	1	0	1	0	0	0	Simmons (Phillies), p	0	0	0	0	0	0
Loes (Orioles), p	1	0	0	0	1	0	Burdette (Braves), p	1	0	0	0	0	0
Wynn (Indians), p	0	0	0	0	0	0	Sanford (Phillies), p	0	0	0	0	0	0
Pierce (White Sox), p	1	1	1	1	0	0	dMoon (Cardinals)	1	0	0	0	0	0
Mossi (Indians), p	0	0	0	0	0	0	Jackson (Cardinals), p	0	0	0	0	1	0
Grim (Yankees), p	0	0	0	0	0	0	gCimoli (Dodgers)	1	0	0	0	0	0
							Labine (Dodgers), p	0	0	0	0	1	0
							iHodges (Dodgers)	1	0	0	0	0	0
Totals	37	6	10	27	11	0	Totals	34	5	9	27	5	1

American League	0	2	0	0	0	1	0	0	3 — 6
National League	0	0	0	0	0	0	2	0	3 — 5

Americans	IP.	H.	R.	ER.	BB.	SO.	Nationals	IP.	H.	R.	ER.	BB.	SO.
Bunning (Tigers)	3	0	0	0	0	1	Simmons (Phillies)	1*	2	2	2	2	0
Loes (Orioles)	3	3	0	0	0	1	Burdette (Braves)	4	2	0	0	1	0
Wynn (Indians)	⅓	2	2	2	0	0	Sanford (Phillies)	1	2	1	1	0	0
Pierce (White Sox)	1⅔†	2	3	3	2	3	Jackson (Cardinals)	2	1	0	0	1	0
Mossi (Indians)	⅔	1	0	0	0	0	Labine (Dodgers)	1	3	3	1	0	1
Grim (Yankees)	⅓	0	0	0	0	1							

*Pitched to four batters in second. †Pitched to four batters in ninth.

Winning pitcher—Bunning. Losing pitcher—Simmons.

aSingled for Bunning in fourth. bHit into force play for Hoak in fifth. cHit into double play for McMillan in fifth. dGrounded out for Sanford in sixth. eFlied out for Temple in sixth. fDoubled for Robinson in seventh. gCalled out on strikes for Jackson in eighth. hSingled for Bailey in ninth. iFlied out for Labine in ninth. Runs batted in—Wertz, Kuenn, Berra, Bell 2, Kaline 2, Minoso, Mays, Banks. Two-base hits—Musial, Skowron, Bell, Minoso. Three-base hit—Mays. Sacrifice hit—Fox. Double play—Malzone, Fox and Skowron. Left on bases—Americans 9, Nationals 4. Wild pitches—Sanford, Pierce. Umpires—Dascoli, Dixon and Landes (N.L.); Napp, Stevens and Chylak (A.L.). Time of game—2:43. Attendance—30,693.

Game of 1958
Memorial Stadium, Baltimore, July 8

Pitchers stole the show as the American League stars edged their National League rivals, 4-3. The game produced only 13 hits, all of them singles. It marked the first time in the history of the midsummer classic that there were no extra-base blows.

Vice-President Richard Nixon was among the capacity crowd of 48,829. He came over from Washington to throw out the first ball.

Except for Bob Turley, who went on to win the Cy Young Award as the year's outstanding pitcher, American League hurlers enjoyed a banner afternoon. The Yankee ace gave up all three runs and three of the four hits collected by the Nationals.

Turley was in trouble right from the start. Willie Mays led off with a single; another ace by Stan Musial and Hank Aaron's sacrifice fly produced a quick run. After a hit batsman and walk filled the bases, Turley uncorked a wild pitch, scoring another run.

The Americans got one of these runs back in their turn, but the N.L. scored once in the second when Mays, after forcing Warren Spahn, stole second, continued to third on catcher Gus Triandos' throwing error and tallied when Bob Skinner singled.

The Americans counted once again in their half and then tied the score in the fifth. They tabbed the winning run in the sixth on singles by Frank Malzone and Gil McDougald sandwiched around an error.

While Early Wynn received credit for the victory, Billy O'Dell was the real mound hero for the A.L. The Baltimore southpaw blotted out nine successive batters over the last three innings to protect the one-run lead. The box score:

American League 4, National League 3

(American League Leads Series, 15-10)

NATIONALS	AB.	R.	H.	PO.	A.	E.	AMERICANS	AB.	R.	H.	PO.	A.	E.
Mays (Giants), cf	4	2	1	1	0	0	Fox (White Sox), 2b	4	1	2	5	3	1
Skinner (Pirates), lf	3	0	1	2	0	0	Mantle (Yankees), cf	2	0	1	3	0	0
gWalls (Cubs), lf	1	0	0	0	0	0	Jensen (Red Sox), rf	4	0	0	1	0	0
Musial (Cardinals), 1b	4	1	1	7	0	0	Cerv (Athletics), lf	2	0	1	4	0	0
Aaron (Braves), rf	2	0	0	2	0	0	O'Dell (Orioles), p	0	0	0	0	0	0
Banks, (Cubs), ss	3	0	0	2	3	1	Skowron (Yankees), 1b	4	0	0	8	0	0
Thomas (Pirates), 3b	3	0	1	1	3	1	Malzone (Red Sox), 3b	4	1	1	0	2	0
Mazeroski (Pirates), 2b	4	0	0	4	5	0	Triandos (Orioles), c	2	0	1	1	0	1
Crandall (Braves), c	4	0	0	5	0	0	cBerra (Yankees), c	2	0	0	3	0	0
Spahn (Braves), p	0	0	0	0	1	0	Aparicio (White Sox), ss	2	1	0	1	1	0
aBlasingame (Cardinals)	1	0	0	0	0	0	dWilliams (Red Sox), lf	2	0	0	1	0	0
Friend (Pirates), p	0	0	0	0	0	0	Kaline (Tigers), lf	0	0	0	0	0	0
Jackson (Cardinals), p	0	0	0	0	0	0	Turley (Yankees), p	0	0	0	0	0	0
fLogan (Braves)	1	0	0	0	0	0	Narleski (Indians), p	1	0	1	0	0	0
Farrell (Phillies), p	0	0	0	0	0	0	bVernon (Indians)	1	1	1	0	0	0
Totals	30	3	4	24	12	2	Wynn (White Sox), p	0	0	0	0	0	0
							eMcDougald (Yanks), ss	1	0	1	0	3	0
							Totals	31	4	9	27	9	2

National League	2	1	0	0	0	0	0	0	0 — 3
American League	1	1	0	0	1	1	0	0	x — 4

Nationals	IP.	H.	R.	ER.	BB.	SO.	Americans	IP.	H.	R.	ER.	BB.	SO.
Spahn (Braves)	3	5	2	1	0	0	Turley (Yankees)	1⅔	3	3	3	2	0
Friend (Pirates)	2⅓	4	2	1	2	0	Narleski (Indians)	3⅓	0	0	0	1	0
Jackson (Cardinals)	⅔	0	0	0	0	0	Wynn (White Sox)	1	0	0	0	0	0
Farrell (Phillies)	2	0	0	0	1	4	O'Dell (Orioles)	3	0	0	0	0	2

Winning pitcher—Wynn. Losing pitcher—Friend.

aFlied out for Spahn in fourth. bSingled for Narleski in fifth. cPopped out for Triandos in sixth. dSafe on error for Aparicio in sixth. eSingled for Wynn in sixth. fFlied out for Jackson in seventh. gGrounded out for Skinner in seventh. Runs batted in—Skinner, Aaron, Fox, Jensen, McDougald. Sacrifice hit—O'Dell. Sacrifice fly—Aaron. Stolen base—Mays. Left on bases—Nationals 5, Americans 7. Double plays—Thomas, Mazeroski and Musial; Malzone, Fox and Skowron; Banks, Mazeroski and Musial 2. Hit by pitcher—By Turley (Banks). Wild pitch—Turley. Umpires—Rommel, McKinley and Umont (A.L.); Gorman, Conlan and Secory (N.L.). Time of game—2:13. Attendance—48,829.

First Game of 1959

Forbes Field, Pittsburgh, July 7

Breaking with tradition, the owners and players agreed to expand the All-Star Game into a double feature in 1959. The regularly-scheduled contest was played in Pittsburgh as part of that city's bicentennial celebration and saw the Nationals return as victors, 5-4.

For six and one-half innings, the crowd of 35,277, which included Vice-President Richard Nixon, saw a tremendous pitching duel, but then the sluggers took charge.

Homers by Eddie Mathews in the first inning and Al Kaline in the fourth accounted for the only tallies as Don Drysdale and Lou Burdette, pitching for the Nationals, and Early Wynn and Ryne Duren, for the Americans, battled on even terms through the first six innings.

In the seventh, the N. L. rocked Jim Bunning for two runs on a double by Ernie Banks and singles by Del Crandall and Bill Mazeroski.

Roy Face, Pittsburgh relief ace who was 12-0 at the time, retired the first two A. L. batters in the eighth, but two singles, a walk and Gus Triandos' double scored three runs for a 4-3 lead. Johnny Antonelli relieved at that point and halted the threat.

The Nationals won the game in their turn. Whitey Ford was the victim. Singles by Ken Boyer and Hank Aaron sandwiched around a sacrifice accounted for the tying run and then Willie Mays tripled to score Aaron with the decisive marker. The box score:

National League 5, American League 4

(American League Leads Series, 15-11)

AMERICANS	AB.	R.	H.	PO.	A.	E.	NATIONALS	AB.	R.	H.	PO.	A.	E.
Minoso (Indians), lf	5	0	0	1	0	0	Temple (Reds), 2b	2	0	0	1	3	0
Fox (White Sox), 2b	5	1	2	2	0	0	aMusial (Cardinals)	1	0	0	0	0	0
Kaline (Tigers), cf	3	1	1	1	0	0	Face (Pirates), p	0	0	0	0	0	0
Kuenn (Tigers), cf	1	1	0	0	0	0	Antonelli (Giants), p	0	0	0	0	0	0
Skowron (Yankees), 1b	3	0	2	3	0	0	hBoyer, (Cardinals), 3b	1	1	1	1	0	0
Power (Indians), 1b	1	1	1	3	0	0	Mathews (Braves), 3b	3	1	1	2	1	1
Colavito (Indians), rf	3	0	1	1	0	0	iGroat (Pirates)	0	0	0	0	0	0
bWilliams (Red Sox)	0	0	0	0	0	0	Elston (Cubs), p	0	0	0	0	0	0
cMcDougald (Yanks), ss	0	0	0	0	0	0	Aaron (Braves), rf	4	1	2	2	0	0
Triandos (Orioles), c	4	0	1	8	0	0	Mays (Giants), cf	4	0	1	2	0	0
fMantle (Yankees), rf	0	0	0	0	0	0	Banks (Cubs), ss	3	1	2	1	2	0
Killebrew (Senators), 3b	3	0	0	0	1	0	Cepeda (Giants), 1b	4	0	0	6	0	0
Bunning (Tigers), p	0	0	0	0	0	0	Moon (Dodgers), lf	2	0	0	1	0	0
dRunnels (Red Sox)	0	0	0	0	0	0	Crandall (Braves), c	3	1	1	10	0	0
eSievers (Senators)	0	0	0	0	0	0	Drysdale (Dodgers), p	1	0	0	0	0	0
Ford (Yankees), p	0	0	0	0	0	0	Burdette (Braves), p	1	0	0	0	0	0
Daley (Athletics), p	0	0	0	0	1	0	Mazeroski (Pirates), 2b	1	0	1	1	0	0
Aparicio (White Sox), ss	3	0	0	4	2	0	Totals	30	5	9	27	6	1
gLollar (White Sox), c	1	0	0	1	0	0							
Wynn (White Sox), p	1	0	0	1	0	0							
Duren (Yankees), p	1	0	0	0	0	0							
Malzone (Red Sox), 3b	2	0	0	0	0	0							
Totals	36	4	8	24	5	0							

American League	0	0	0	1	0	0	0	3	0	—4
National League	1	0	0	0	0	0	2	2	x	—5

Americans	IP.	H.	R.	ER.	BB.	SO.	Nationals	IP.	H.	R.	ER.	BB.	SO.
Wynn (White Sox)	3	2	1	1	1	3	Drysdale (Dodgers)	3	0	0	0	0	4
Duren (Yankees)	3	1	0	0	1	4	Burdette (Braves)	3	4	1	1	0	2
Bunning (Tigers)	1	3	2	2	0	1	Face (Pirates)	1⅔	3	3	3	2	2
Ford (Yankees)	⅓	3	2	2	0	0	Antonelli (Giants)	⅓	0	0	0	1	0
Daley (Athletics)	⅔	0	0	0	0	0	Elston (Cubs)	1	1	0	0	0	1

Winning pitcher—Antonelli. Losing pitcher—Ford.

aPopped out for Temple in sixth. bWalked for Colavito in eighth. cRan for Williams in eighth. dAnnounced as batter for Bunning in eighth. eWalked for Runnels in eighth. fRan for Triandos in eighth. gHit into force play for Aparicio in eighth. hSingled for Antonelli in eighth. iSacrificed for Mathews in eighth. Runs batted in—Kaline, Power, Triandos 2, Mathews, Aaron, Mays, Crandall, Mazeroski. Two-base hits—Banks 2, Triandos. Three-base hit—Mays. Home runs—Mathews, Kaline. Sacrifice hit—Groat. Double play—Aparicio and Skowron. Left on bases—Americans 8, Nationals 4. Wild pitch—Elston. Umpires—Barlick, Donatelli and Crawford (N. L.), Runge, Paparella and Rice (A. L.). Time of game—2:33. Attendance—35,277.

San Francisco's Willie Mays pulls into third base with a game-winning triple in the National League's 5-4 victory in the 1959 All-Star Game at Pittsburgh's Forbes Field.

Second Game of 1959
Memorial Col., Los Angeles, Aug. 3

In the Dream Game encore, the Americans gained sweet revenge by winning, 5-3. To avoid the early-afternoon heat and also to permit more fans in the East and Midwest to view the telecast, the game began at 4 o'clock.

With 60 percent of the gate and radio-TV revenue going into the players' pension fund, the contest produced an extra $307,401 to meet back service obligations.

Unhampered by any restrictions on the use of players, Casey Stengel placed six lefthanded swingers at the head of the A. L. lineup to face Don Drysdale, Dodger right-hander, and the move paid off.

Home runs accounted for six of the game's eight runs. After the Nationals jumped on Jerry Walker for a tally in the opening frame, Frank Malzone lofted a Drysdale pitch just barely over the chummy left-field screen in the second to tie the score.

Yogi Berra's long smash over the right-field fence with one aboard in the third made it 3-1, but Frank Robinson narrowed the N. L. deficit when he homered deep into the left-field seats in the fifth.

After going hitless for three innings, the Americans reached Sam Jones for a run in the seventh on a walk, two errors and Nellie Fox' single. The Nationals got the run back in their turn on Jim Gilliam's homer over the left-field screen, but Rocky Colavito connected in the eighth inning for the game's final tally. The box score:

American League 5, National League 3
(American League Leads Series, 16-11)

AMERICANS	AB.	R.	H.	PO.	A.	E.	NATIONALS	AB.	R.	H.	PO.	A.	E.
Runnels (Red Sox), 1b	3	0	0	9	0	0	Temple (Reds), 2b	2	1	1	1	1	0
Power (Indians), 1b	1	0	0	4	0	0	dGilliam (Dodgers), 3b	2	1	1	0	0	0
Fox (White Sox), 2b	4	1	2	3	1	0	Boyer (Cardinals), 3b	2	0	0	0	1	0
Williams (Red Sox), lf	3	0	0	0	0	0	Neal (Dodgers), 2b	1	0	0	0	2	0
Kaline (Tigers), lf-cf	2	0	0	0	0	0	Aaron (Braves), rf	3	0	0	2	0	0
Berra (Yankees), c	3	1	1	2	0	0	Mays (Giants), cf	4	0	0	3	0	0
Lollar (White Sox), c	0	0	0	2	0	0	Banks (Cubs), ss	4	0	0	2	0	0
Mantle (Yankees), cf	3	0	1	3	0	0	Musial (Cardinals), 1b	0	0	0	3	1	0
O'Dell (Orioles), p	0	0	0	0	0	0	Robinson (Reds), 1b	3	1	3	3	0	1
McLish (Indians), p	0	0	0	0	0	0	Moon (Dodgers), lf	2	0	0	1	0	0
Maris (Athletics), rf	2	0	0	1	0	0	Crandall (Braves), c	2	0	1	7	1	0
Colavito (Indians), rf	2	1	1	0	0	0	Smith (Cardinals), c	2	0	0	5	0	0
Malzone (Red Sox), 3b	4	1	1	1	6	0	Drysdale (Dodgers), p	0	0	0	0	0	0
Aparicio (White Sox), ss	3	0	0	1	2	0	aMathews (Braves)	1	0	0	0	0	0
Walker (Orioles), p	1	0	0	0	0	0	Conley (Phillies), p	0	0	0	0	1	0
bWoodling (Orioles)	1	0	0	0	0	0	cCunningham (Cardinals)	1	0	0	0	0	0
Wynn (White Sox), p	0	0	0	1	0	0	ePinson (Reds)	0	0	0	0	0	0
Wilhelm (Orioles), p	0	0	0	0	0	0	Jones (Giants), p	0	0	0	0	0	1
fKubek (Yankees), lf	1	1	0	0	0	0	gGroat (Pirates)	1	0	0	0	0	0
Totals	33	5	6	27	9	0	Face (Pirates), p	0	0	0	0	0	0
							hBurgess (Pirates)	1	0	0	0	0	0
							Totals	31	3	6	27	7	3

American League	0	1	2	0	0	0	1	1	0 —	5
National League	1	0	0	0	1	0	1	0	0 —	3

Americans	IP.	H.	R.	ER.	BB.	SO.	Nationals	IP.	H.	R.	ER.	BB.	SO.
Walker (Orioles)	3	2	1	1	1	1	Drysdale (Dodgers)	3	4	3	3	3	5
Wynn (White Sox)	2	1	1	1	3	1	Conley (Phillies)	2	0	0	0	1	2
Wilhelm (Orioles)	1	1	0	0	0	0	Jones (Giants)	2	1	1	0	2	3
O'Dell (Orioles)	1	1	1	1	0	0	Face (Pirates)	2	1	1	1	0	2
McLish (Indians)	2	1	0	0	1	2							

Winning pitcher—Walker. Losing pitcher—Drysdale.

aStruck out for Drysdale in third. bGrounded out for Walker in fourth. cHit into force play for Conley in fifth. dWalked for Temple in fifth. eRan for Cunningham in fifth. fWalked for Wilhelm in seventh. gGrounded out for Jones in seventh. hGrounded out for Face in ninth. Runs batted in—Fox, Berra 2, Colavito, Malzone, Gilliam, Aaron, Robinson. Two-base hit—Temple. Home runs—Malzone, Berra, Robinson, Gilliam, Colavito. Sacrifice fly—Aaron. Stolen base—Aparicio. Double play—Runnels (unassisted). Left on bases—Americans 7, Nationals 7. Umpires—Jackowski, Venzon and Burkhart (N. L.), Berry, Summers and Soar (A. L.). Time of game—2:42. Attendance—55,105.

First Game of 1960
Municipal Stadium, Kansas City, July 11

Despite a heat wave that sent the temperature soaring to 101, a capacity crowd of 30,619 turned out for the first All-Star Game ever played in Kansas City and saw the Nationals nose out a 5-3 victory.

The N. L. wasted little time in spoiling the occasion for the American League partisans, jumping on Bill Monbouquette and Chuck Estrada for all of their runs in the first three innings.

Willie Mays opened the game with a triple and Bob Skinner followed with a single. Monbouquette retired the next two batters, but then Ernie Banks homered and it was 3-0.

Del Crandall also hit for the circuit in the second inning and Estrada yielded the final N. L. run in the third on a double by Banks and singles by Joe Adcock and Bill Mazeroski.

Blanked for five innings by Bob Friend and Mike McCormick, the Americans jumped on the Giant lefty for a run in the sixth, but with the bags full and one out, Roy Face snuffed out the threat.

Bob Buhl yielded the Americans' other runs in the eighth when he served up a home run to Al Kaline following Charlie Neal's error on a grounder by Kuenn. The box score:

National League 5, American League 4
(American League Leads Series, 16-12)

NATIONALS	AB.	R.	H.	PO.	A.	E.	AMERICANS	AB.	R.	H.	PO.	A.	E.
Mays (Giants), cf	4	1	3	4	0	0	Minoso (White Sox), lf	3	0	0	0	0	0
Pinson (Reds), cf	1	0	0	1	0	0	Lemon (Senators), lf	1	0	0	1	0	0
Skinner (Pirates), lf	4	1	1	1	0	0	Malzone (Red Sox), 3b	3	0	0	1	1	0
Cepeda (Giants), lf	1	0	0	0	0	0	Robinson (Orioles), 3b	2	0	0	0	0	0
Mathews (Braves), 3b	4	0	0	1	0	0	Maris (Yankees), rf	2	0	0	1	0	0
Boyer (Cardinals), 3b	0	0	0	0	2	0	Kuenn (Indians), rf	3	1	1	1	0	0
Aaron (Braves), rf	4	0	0	0	1	0	Mantle (Yankees), cf	0	0	0	2	0	0
Clemente (Pirates), rf	1	0	0	2	0	0	Kaline (Tigers), cf	2	2	1	1	0	0
Banks (Cubs), ss	4	2	2	2	2	0	Skowron (Yankees), 1b	3	0	1	9	0	0
Groat (Pirates), ss	0	0	0	0	1	0	Lary (Tigers), p	0	0	0	0	0	0
Adcock (Braves), 1b	3	0	2	3	0	0	hLollar (White Sox)	1	0	0	0	0	0
bWhite (Cardinals), 1b	1	0	0	4	0	0	B. Daley (Athletics), p	0	0	0	0	0	1
Mazeroski (Pirates), 2b	2	0	1	2	2	0	Berra (Yankees), c	2	0	0	5	0	0
eMusial (Cardinals)	1	0	1	0	0	0	Howard (Yankees), c	1	0	0	4	0	0
fTaylor (Phillies)	0	0	0	0	0	0	Runnels (Red Sox), 2b	1	0	0	1	0	0
Neal (Dodgers), 2b	0	0	0	0	0	1	Fox (White Sox), 2b	2	0	1	1	3	0
Crandall (Braves), c	3	1	2	4	0	0	Hansen (Orioles), ss	2	0	1	0	0	0
Burgess (Pirates), c	1	0	0	3	0	1	Aparicio (White Sox), ss	2	0	0	1	1	0
Friend (Pirates), p	2	0	0	0	0	0	Monbouquette (R. Sox), p	0	0	0	0	0	0
McCormick (Giants), p	1	0	0	0	0	0	aWilliams (Red Sox)	1	0	0	0	0	0
Face (Pirates), p	0	0	0	0	0	0	Estrada (Orioles), p	0	0	0	0	0	0
gLarker (Dodgers)	1	0	0	0	0	0	Coates (Yankees), p	0	0	0	0	1	0
Buhl (Braves), p	0	0	0	0	0	0	cSmith (White Sox)	1	0	0	0	0	0
Law (Pirates), p	0	0	0	0	0	0	Bell (Indians), p	0	0	0	0	1	0
							dGentile (Orioles), 1b	2	0	1	0	0	0
Totals	38	5	12	27	8	4	Totals	34	3	6	27	8	1

National League	3	1	1	0	0	0	0	0	0 — 5
American League	0	0	0	0	0	1	0	2	0 — 3

Nationals	IP.	H.	R.	ER.	BB.	SO.	Americans	IP.	H.	R.	ER.	BB.	SO.
Friend (Pirates)	3	1	0	0	1	2	Monbouquette (Red Sox)	2	5	4	4	0	2
McCormick (Giants)	2⅓	3	1	0	3	2	Estrada (Orioles)	1	4	1	1	0	1
Face (Pirates)	1⅔	0	0	0	0	2	Coates (Yankees)	2	2	0	0	0	0
Buhl (Braves)	1⅓	2	2	1	1	1	Bell (Indians)	2	0	0	0	0	0
Law (Pirates)	⅔	0	0	0	0	0	Lary (Tigers)	1	1	0	0	0	1
							B. Daley (Athletics)	1	0	0	0	1	2

Winning pitcher—Friend. Losing pitcher—Monbouquette.

aGrounded out for Monbouquette in second. bRan for Adcock in fifth. cFlied out for Coates in fifth. dStruck out for Bell in seventh. eSingled for Mazeroski in eighth. fRan for Musial in eighth. gGrounded into force play for Face in eighth. hGrounded out for Lary in eighth. Runs batted in—Skinner, Banks 2, Mazeroski, Crandall, Kaline 2, Fox. Two-base hits—Banks, Mays, Adcock. Three-base hit—Mays. Home runs—Banks, Crandall, Kaline. Stolen base—Skinner. Double plays—Malzone and Skowron; Banks, Mazeroski and White. Left on bases—Nationals 8, Americans 9. Hit by pitcher—By Coates (Mazeroski). Wild pitch—Friend. Balk—Friend. Umpires—Honochick, Chylak and Stevens (A. L.), Gorman, Boggess and Smith (N. L.). Time of game—2:39. Attendance—30,619.

Second Game of 1960
Yankee Stadium, New York, July 13

Displaying a blase approach to a second All-Star game, only 38,362 New York fans turned out for the 1960 encore. They saw the National League make a sweep of the two-game set by winning, 6-0.

Both squads were exactly the same as for the earlier game at Kansas City, even down to the coaches.

Led by Willie Mays, who made a triumphant return to New York, the N. L. stars banged four home runs. Meantime, Walter Alston's six-man pitching relay blanked the Americans on eight hits.

Mays repeated his heroics of the first clash at Kansas City, rapping three hits, including a homer. Eddie Mathews, Stan Musial and Ken Boyer delivered the other round-trippers.

Whitey Ford took another defeat when Mathews solved him for a two-run homer in the second inning and Mays connected in the third.

Musial walloped his four-bagger as a pinch-hitter against Gerry Staley in the seventh and then Boyer capped the N. L.'s explosive afternoon by homering against Gary Bell with a mate aboard in the ninth. The box score:

National League 6, American League 0
(American League Leads Series, 16-13)

NATIONALS	AB.	R.	H.	PO.	A.	E.	AMERICANS	AB.	R.	H.	PO.	A.	E.
Mays (Giants), cf	4	1	3	5	0	0	Minoso (White Sox), lf	2	0	0	1	0	0
Pinson (Reds), cf	0	0	0	0	0	0	eT. Williams (Red Sox)	1	0	1	0	0	0
Skinner (Pirates), lf	3	0	1	2	0	0	fRobinson (Orioles), 3b	1	0	0	0	0	0
Cepeda (Giants), lf	2	0	0	0	0	0	Runnels (Red Sox), 2b	2	0	0	0	1	0
Aaron (Braves), rf	3	0	0	1	0	0	Staley (White Sox), p	0	0	0	1	1	0
hClemente (Pirates), rf	0	0	0	0	0	0	gKaline (Tigers), lf	1	0	1	3	0	0
Banks (Cubs), ss	3	0	1	2	3	0	Maris (Yankees), rf	4	0	0	0	0	0
iGroat (Pirates), ss	1	0	0	0	1	0	Mantle (Yankees), cf	4	0	1	3	0	0
Adcock (Braves), 1b	2	1	1	3	0	0	Skowron (Yankees), 1b	1	0	1	6	0	0
White (Cardinals), 1b	1	0	0	2	0	0	Power (Indians), 1b	2	0	0	5	1	0
kLarker (Dodgers), 1b	0	1	0	3	0	0	Berra (Yankees), c	2	0	0	4	1	0
Mathews (Braves), 3b	3	1	1	0	1	0	Lollar (White Sox), c	2	0	1	0	0	0
Boyer (Cardinals), 3b	1	1	1	1	0	0	Malzone (Red Sox), 3b	2	0	0	2	2	0
Mazeroski (Pirates), 2b	2	0	0	0	0	0	Lary (Tigers), p	0	0	0	0	0	0
Neal (Dodgers), 2b	1	0	0	1	2	0	jSmith (White Sox)	1	0	0	0	0	0
Taylor (Phillies), 2b	1	0	1	2	1	0	Bell (Indians), p	0	0	0	0	1	0
Crandall (Braves), c	2	0	0	3	0	0	Hansen (Orioles), ss	4	0	2	2	4	0
S. Williams (Dodgers), p	0	0	0	0	0	0	Ford (Yankees), p	0	0	0	0	0	0
dMusial (Cardinals)	1	1	1	0	0	0	aKuenn (Indians)	1	0	0	0	0	0
Jackson (Cardinals), p	0	0	0	0	0	0	Wynn (White Sox), p	0	0	0	0	0	0
Bailey (Reds), c	1	0	0	0	0	0	cFox (White Sox), 2b	3	0	1	0	1	0
Law (Pirates), p	1	0	0	0	1	0	Totals	33	0	8	27	12	0
Podres (Dodgers), p	0	0	0	0	1	0							
bBurgess (Pirates), c	2	0	0	2	0	0							
Henry (Reds), p	0	0	0	0	0	0							
McDaniel (Cardinals), p	0	0	0	0	0	0							
Totals	34	6	10	27	10	0							

National League	0	2 1	0 0 0	1 0	2—6
American League	0	0 0	0 0 0	0 0	0—0

Nationals	IP.	H.	R.	ER.	BB.	SO.	Americans	IP.	H.	R.	ER.	BB.	SO.
Law (Pirates)	2	1	0	0	0	1	Ford (Yankees)	3	5	3	3	0	1
Podres (Dodgers)	2	1	0	0	3	1	Wynn (White Sox)	2	0	0	0	0	2
S. Williams (Dodgers)	2	2	0	0	1	2	Staley (White Sox)	2	2	1	1	0	0
Jackson (Cardinals)	1	1	0	0	2	0	Lary (Tigers)	1	1	0	0	1	0
Henry (Reds)	1	2	0	0	0	0	Bell (Indians)	1	2	2	2	2	0
McDaniel (Cardinals)	1	1	0	0	0	0							

Winning pitcher—Law. Losing pitcher—Ford.

aFlied out for Ford in third. bStruck out for Podres in fifth. cSingled for Wynn in fifth. dHomered for S. Williams in seventh. eSingled for Minoso in seventh. fRan for T. Williams in seventh. gWalked for Staley in seventh. hWalked for Aaron in eighth. iHit into double play for Banks in eighth. jPopped out for Lary in eighth. kWalked for White in ninth. Runs batted in—Mays, Mathews 2, Boyer 2, Musial. Two-base hit—Lollar. Home runs—Mathews, Mays, Musial, Boyer. Stolen base—Mays. Caught stealing—Mays. Sacrifice hit—Henry. Double plays—Law, Banks and Adcock; Banks, Neal and White; Fox, Hansen and Power. Left on bases—Nationals 5, Americans 12. Umpires—Chylak, Honochick and Stevens (A. L.), Boggess, Gorman and Smith (N. L.). Time of game—2:42. Attendance—38,362.

First Game of 1961
Candlestick Park, San Francisco, July 11

A near gale contributed to a wild climax as the Nationals came from behind in the 10th inning to win, 5-4, in a game marked by a record seven errors, five of them by the winning team.

The victory marked the first time either loop had pulled a game from the fire in overtime. It also gave the N.L. a 3-0 record in extra-inning All-Star encounters.

The gale-like winds that struck in the late innings were responsible for many of the errors. Ken Boyer, Cardinal third baseman, was guilty of two of the worst miscues. The game produced two homers, both by pinch-hitters—Harmon Killebrew and George Altman.

As the A.L. came to bat in the ninth, trailing 3-1, the wind began blowing and turned the game into a weird nightmare. With one run in and two runners on base, Stu Miller relieved and the near gale caused him to commit a costly balk, after which Boyer bobbled a grounder, permitting the tying run to score.

In the 10th, Boyer made a wild throw that allowed Nellie Fox to score all the way from first base. However, the Nationals came back with two runs in their turn when Hank Aaron singled, Willie Mays doubled and Roberto Clemente came through with a single. The box score:

National League 5, American League 4
(American League Leads Series, 16-14)

AMERICANS	AB	R	H	PO	A	E
Temple (Indians), 2b	3	0	0	1	2	0
fGentile (Orioles), 1b	2	0	0	2	0	1
Cash (Tigers), 1b	4	0	1	6	0	0
gFox (White Sox), 2b	0	2	0	1	0	0
Mantle (Yankees), cf	3	0	0	3	0	0
Kaline (Tigers), cf	2	1	1	1	0	0
Maris (Yankees), rf	4	0	1	3	0	0
Colavito (Tigers), lf	4	0	1	0	0	0
Kubek (Yankees), ss	4	0	0	1	2	1
Romano (Indians), c	3	0	0	7	0	0
hBerra (Yankees), c	1	0	0	0	0	0
Howard (Yankees), c	0	0	0	0	0	0
B. Robinson (Ori.), 3b	2	0	0	0	2	0
Bunning (Tigers), p	0	0	0	1	0	0
dBrandt (Orioles)	1	0	0	0	0	0
Fornieles (Red Sox), p	0	0	0	0	0	0
Wilhelm (Orioles), p	1	0	0	0	0	0
Ford (Yankees), p	1	0	0	0	0	0
Lary (Tigers), p	0	0	0	0	0	0
Donovan (Senators), p	0	0	0	0	0	0
cKillebrew (Twins), 3b	2	1	1	0	0	0
Howser (Athletics), 3b	1	0	0	0	1	0
Totals	38	4	4	27	8	2

NATIONALS	AB	R	H	PO	A	E
Wills (Dodgers), ss	5	0	1	0	2	0
Mathews (Braves), 3b	2	0	0	0	0	0
Purkey (Reds), p	0	0	0	1	0	0
bMusial (Cardinals)	1	0	0	0	0	0
McCormick (Giants), p	0	0	0	0	0	0
eAltman (Cubs)	1	1	1	0	0	0
Face (Pirates), p	0	0	0	0	0	0
Koufax (Dodgers), p	0	0	0	0	0	0
Miller (Giants), p	0	0	0	0	0	0
iAaron (Braves)	1	1	1	0	0	0
Mays (Giants), cf	5	2	2	3	0	0
Cepeda (Giants), lf	3	0	0	1	0	1
F. Robinson (Reds), lf	1	0	1	2	0	0
Clemente (Pirates), rf	4	1	2	2	0	0
White (Cardinals), 1b	3	0	1	7	1	0
Bolling (Braves), 2b	3	0	0	1	3	0
Zimmer (Cubs), 2b	1	0	0	0	0	1
Burgess (Pirates), c	4	0	1	13	0	1
Spahn (Braves), p	0	0	0	0	0	0
aStuart (Pirates)	1	0	1	0	0	0
Boyer (Cardinals), 3b	2	0	0	0	1	2
Totals	37	5	11	30	8	5

```
American League.............. 0  0  0  0  0  1  0  0  2   1—4
National League.............. 0  1  0  1  0  0  0  1  0   2—5
```

None out when winning run scored.

Americans	IP	H	R	ER	BB	SO
Ford (Yankees)	3	2	1	1	0	2
Lary (Tigers)	0*	1	0	0	0	0
Donovan (Senators)	2	4	0	0	0	1
Bunning (Tigers)	2	0	0	0	0	2
Fornieles (Red Sox)	⅓	2	1	1	0	0
Wilhelm (Orioles)	1⅔‡	3	2	2	1	1

Nationals	IP	H	R	ER	BB	SO
Spahn (Braves)	3	0	0	0	0	3
Purkey (Reds)	2	0	0	0	0	0
McCormick (Giants)	3	1	1	1	1	3
Face (Pirates)	⅓	2	2	2	0	1
Koufax (Dodgers)	0†	1	0	0	0	0
Miller (Giants)	1⅔	0	1	0	1	4

*Pitched to one batter in fourth. †Pitched to one batter in ninth. ‡Pitched to four batters in tenth.

Winning pitcher—Miller. Losing pitcher—Wilhelm.

aDoubled for Spahn in third. bFlied out for Purkey in fifth. cHomered for Donovan in sixth. dStruck out for Bunning in eighth. eHomered for McCormick in eighth. fStruck out for Temple in ninth. gRan for Cash in ninth. hSafe on error for Romano in ninth. iSingled for Miller in tenth. Runs batted in—Kaline, Colavito, Killebrew, Altman, Mays, Clemente 2, White. Two-base hits—Stuart, Cash, Mays. Three-base hit—Clemente. Home runs—Killebrew, Altman. Stolen base—F. Robinson. Sacrifice flies—Clemente, White. Left on bases—Americans 6, Nationals 9. Hit by pitcher—By Wilhelm (F. Robinson). Balk—Miller. Passed ball—Howard. Umpires—Landes, Crawford and Vargo (N. L.), Umont, Runge and Drummond (A. L.). Time of game—2:53. Attendance—44,115.

Second Game of 1961

Fenway Park, Boston, July 31

Just as in the year's first contest, the elements played a prominent role in the encore. A heavy downpour that fell just as the ninth inning ended forced the two clubs to settle for a 1-1 stalemate.

Except for a misplayed grounder, the game might have resulted in the first 1-0 decision in All-Star history. As it was, the crowd of 31,851 witnessed the best-pitched game in the long series.

A first-inning homer by Rocky Colavito off Bob Purkey accounted for the American League's lone score. The blow was the A. L.'s only hit off Purkey and Art Mahaffey in the first four innings.

Jim Bunning started for the junior loop and worked three hitless innings. Don Schwall was on the mound when the Nationals tied the score in the sixth. With one away, he walked Eddie Mathews; one out later, he nicked Orlando Cepeda with a pitch.

Luis Aparicio then was guilty of a mental lapse which helped the N.L. to its run. On Eddie Kasko's dribbler toward shortstop, Aparicio waited for the ball instead of moving in for it. The last bounce was a tricky one, and by the time the White Sox shortstop got the ball, it was too late for a play. The infield hit filled the bases.

A moment later, Aparicio made a great play which proved a game-saver for the Americans. Bill White slapped a sharp grounder toward the box, which Schwall barely deflected. Dashing behind second, Aparicio made a tremendous stop. One run scored on the hit, but Aparicio's play forced Cepeda to stop at third. Schwall then retired the next batter.

Rain began falling as the ninth inning ended, and after a 30-minute wait, the umpires called the game. The box score:

National League 1, American League 1

(American League Leads Series, 16-14-1)

NATIONALS	AB.	R.	H.	PO.	A.	E.	AMERICANS	AB.	R.	H.	PO.	A.	E.
Wills (Dodgers), ss	2	0	1	1	1	0	Cash (Tigers), 1b	4	0	0	11	0	0
Aaron (Braves), rf	2	0	0	1	0	0	Colavito (Tigers), lf	4	1	1	3	0	0
Miller (Giants), p	0	0	0	0	0	0	Kaline (Tigers), rf	4	0	2	1	0	0
Mathews (Braves), 3b	3	1	0	0	2	0	Mantle (Yankees), cf	3	0	0	2	0	0
Mays (Giants), cf	3	0	1	1	0	0	Romano (Indians), c	1	0	0	1	0	0
Cepeda (Giants), lf	3	0	0	0	0	0	bMaris (Yankees)	1	0	0	0	0	0
Clemente (Pirates), rf	2	0	0	0	0	0	Howard (Yankees), c	2	0	0	6	0	0
Kasko (Reds), ss	1	0	1	2	4	0	Aparicio (Wh. Sox), ss	2	0	0	1	3	0
eBanks (Cubs), ss	1	0	0	0	0	0	fSievers (White Sox)	1	0	0	0	0	0
White (Cardinals), 1b	4	0	2	11	1	0	Temple (Indians), 2b	2	0	0	2	3	0
Bolling (Braves), 2b	4	0	0	3	2	1	B. Robinson (Orioles), 3b	3	0	1	0	3	0
Burgess (Pirates), c	1	0	0	2	0	0	Bunning (Tigers), p	1	0	0	0	0	0
Roseboro (Dodgers), c	3	0	0	6	0	0	Schwall (Red Sox), p	1	0	0	0	0	0
Purkey (Reds), p	0	0	0	0	1	0	Pascual (Twins), p	1	0	0	0	0	0
aStuart (Pirates)	1	0	0	0	0	0	Totals	30	1	4	27	9	0
Mahaffey (Phillies), p	0	0	0	0	0	0							
cMusial (Cardinals)	1	0	0	0	0	0							
Koufax (Dodgers), p	0	0	0	0	0	0							
dAltman (Cubs), rf	1	0	0	0	0	0							
Totals	32	1	5	27	11	1							

```
National League ............ 0   0   0     0   0   1     0   0   0—1
American League ............ 1   0   0     0   0   0     0   0   0—1
```
Called because of rain.

Nationals	IP.	H.	R.	ER.	BB.	SO.	Americans	IP.	H.	R.	ER.	BB.	SO.
Purkey (Reds)	2	1	1	1	2	2	Bunning (Tigers)	3	0	0	0	0	1
Mahaffey (Phillies)	2	0	0	0	1	0	Schwall (Red Sox)	3	5	1	1	1	2
Koufax (Dodgers)	2	2	0	0	0	1	Pascual (Twins)	3	0	0	0	1	4
Miller (Giants)	3	1	0	0	0	5							

aGrounded out for Purkey in third. bPopped out for Romano in fourth. cFanned for Mahaffey in fifth. dFlied out for Koufax in seventh. eFanned for Kasko in eighth. fFanned for Aparicio in ninth. Runs batted in—White, Colavito. Two-base hit—White. Home run—Colavito. Stolen base—Kaline. Double plays—Bolling, Kasko and White; White, Kasko and Bolling. Left on bases—Nationals 7, Americans 5. Hit by pitcher—By Schwall (Cepeda). Passed ball—Burgess. Umpires—Napp, Flaherty and Smith (A. L.), Secory, Sudol and Pelekoudas (N. L.). Time of game—2:27. Attendance—31,851.

First Game of 1962

D. C. Stadium, Washington, July 10

The Nationals scored their 11th victory in the last 15 decisions by nipping the Americans, 3-1, in a sharply-pitched game. A capacity crowd of 45,480, including President John F. Kennedy and Vice-President Lyndon Johnson, jammed Washington's new stadium for the game. President Kennedy threw out the first ball.

Maury Wills shared the spotlight with the four-hit chucking of four N. L. pitchers. Although he didn't enter the game until the sixth inning—when it was still scoreless—Wills literally stole the show.

Veteran Stan Musial launched the first scoring drive when he singled as a pinch-hitter in the sixth. Wills ran for him and promptly stole second and scored on Dick Groat's single. Roberto Clemente followed with his third successive hit, and Groat subsequently scored on an infield out.

The Americans tallied their lone run in the bottom of the sixth on singles by Rich Rollins and Billy Moran plus a long fly ball by Roger Maris which Willie Mays caught against the wall in right-center.

Wills gave the crowd another thrill in the eighth. Leading off with a single, he daringly raced to third on Jim Davenport's single to left. When Felipe Alou followed with a foul fly to Leon Wagner in short right field, Wills tagged up and slid across the plate with the Nationals' third run.

The Americans made an abortive bid to tie the score in the ninth inning. With Bob Shaw on the hill, Rocky Colavito led off with a single. After Shaw retired the next two batters, John Romano singled and Luis Aparicio smashed a drive to deep right-center. For a moment, it looked like a triple, but Mays caught it to end the game. The box score:

National League 3, American League 1

(American League Leads Series, 16-15-1)

NATIONALS	AB.	R.	H.	PO.	A.	E.	AMERICANS	AB.	R.	H.	PO.	A.	E.
Groat (Pirates), ss	3	1	1	3	3	0	Rollins (Twins), 3b	2	1	1	1	3	0
Davenport (Giants), 3b	1	0	1	0	1	0	Robinson (Orioles), 3b	0	0	0	0	1	0
Clemente (Pirates), rf	3	0	3	2	0	0	Moran (Angels), 2b	3	0	1	0	0	0
F. Alou (Giants), rf	0	0	0	0	0	0	Richardson (Yankees), 2b	1	0	0	1	0	0
Mays (Giants), cf	3	0	0	3	0	0	Maris (Yankees), cf	2	0	0	2	0	0
Cepeda (Giants), 1b	3	0	0	2	2	0	Landis (White Sox), cf	1	0	0	2	0	0
Purkey (Reds), p	0	0	0	0	1	0	Mantle (Yankees), rf	1	0	0	0	0	0
eCallison (Phillies)	1	0	1	0	0	0	bColavito (Tigers), lf	1	0	1	0	0	0
Shaw (Braves), p	0	0	0	1	0	0	Gentile (Orioles), 1b	3	0	0	8	0	0
T. Davis (Dodgers), lf	4	0	0	2	0	0	Wagner (Angels), lf-rf	4	0	4	0	0	0
Boyer (Cardinals), 3b	2	0	0	1	0	0	Battey (Twins), c	2	0	0	4	1	0
Banks (Cubs), 1b	2	0	0	4	1	0	Romano (Indians), c	2	0	1	1	0	0
Crandall (Braves), c	4	0	0	5	0	0	Aparicio (White Sox), ss	4	0	1	3	2	0
Mazeroski (Pirates), 2b	2	0	0	1	0	0	Bunning (Tigers), p	0	0	0	0	0	0
Bolling (Braves), 2b	2	0	0	1	3	0	aL. Thomas (Angels)	1	0	0	0	0	0
Drysdale (Dodgers), p	1	0	0	1	0	0	Pascual (Twins), p	1	0	0	0	1	0
Marichal (Giants), p	0	0	0	0	0	0	Donovan (Indians), p	0	0	0	0	0	0
cMusial (Cardinals)	1	0	1	0	0	0	fSiebern (Athletics)	1	0	0	0	0	0
dWills (Dodgers), ss	1	2	1	1	1	0	Pappas (Orioles), p	0	0	0	0	0	0
Totals	33	3	8	27	12	0	Totals	29	1	4	27	8	0

```
National League .................................  0   0   0      0   0   2      0   1   0 — 3
American League .................................  0   0   0      0   0   1      0   0   0 — 1
```

Nationals	IP.	H.	R.	ER.	BB.	SO.	Americans	IP.	H.	R.	ER.	BB.	SO.
Drysdale (Dodgers)	3	1	0	0	1	3	Bunning (Tigers)	3	1	0	0	0	2
Marichal (Giants)	2	0	0	0	1	0	Pascual (Twins)	3	4	2	2	1	1
Purkey (Reds)	2	2	1	1	0	1	Donovan (Indians)	2	3	1	1	0	0
Shaw (Braves)	2	1	0	0	1	1	Pappas (Orioles)	1	0	0	0	0	0

Winning pitcher—Marichal. Losing pitcher—Pascual.

aPopped out for Bunning in third. bRan for Mantle in fourth. cSingled for Marichal in sixth. dRan for Musial in sixth. eSingled for Purkey in eighth. fGrounded out for Donovan in eighth. Runs batted in—Groat, Cepeda, Maris, F. Alou. Two-base hit—Clemente. Three-base hit—Aparicio. Stolen bases—Mays, Wills. Caught stealing—Clemente. Sacrifice flies—Maris, F. Alou. Double plays—Cepeda, Groat and Drysdale; Battey and Rollins. Left on bases—Nationals 5, Americans 7. Hit by pitcher—By Drysdale (Rollins), by Shaw (Robinson). Umpires—Hurley, Stewart and Schwarts (A. L.), Donatelli, Venzon and Steiner (N. L.). Time of game—2:33. Attendance—45,480.

Second Game of 1962

Wrigley Field, Chicago, July 30

The National League muffed an opportunity to deadlock the All-Star series when the Americans hauled out the lethal home-run weapon to hammer out an easy 9-4 victory.

Both teams collected 10 hits, but three A. L. homers spelled the difference. The first came from a surprise source, Pete Runnels. The Boston infielder, who had previously hit only 45 round-trippers in 12 years in the majors, connected against Art Mahaffey in the third inning.

Leon Wagner belted Mahaffey for a two-run homer in the fourth to make it 3-1. After the Americans picked up another run off Bob Gibson in the sixth, Rocky Colavito virtually iced the game by smashing a three-run homer off Dick Farrell in the seventh.

The Nationals got to Hank Aguirre for single tallies in the seventh and eighth, but the Americans added two insurance runs in the ninth off Juan Marichal on a double error by Eddie Mathews, Roger Maris' double, a wild pitch and a sacrifice fly by Colavito. For Colavito, it was his fourth RBI of the day.

John Roseboro wound up the afternoon's run making by socking the Nationals' lone homer—off Milt Pappas—in the ninth. The box score:

American League 9, National League 4

(American League Leads Series, 17-15-1)

AMERICANS	AB.	R.	H.	PO.	A.	E.	NATIONALS	AB.	R.	H.	PO.	A.	E.
Rollins (Twins), 3b	3	0	1	0	1	0	Groat (Pirates), ss	3	0	2	3	3	1
B. Robinson (Orioles), 3b	1	1	0	0	1	0	Wills (Dodgers), ss	1	0	0	0	1	0
Moran (Angels), 2b	4	0	1	1	4	0	Clemente (Pirates), rf	2	0	0	2	0	0
fBerra (Yankees)	1	0	0	0	0	0	F. Robinson (Reds), rf	3	0	0	1	0	0
gRich'dson (Yankees), 2b	0	1	0	2	0	0	Mays (Giants), cf	2	0	2	2	0	0
Maris (Yankees), cf	4	2	1	4	0	0	H. Aaron (Braves), cf	2	0	0	1	0	0
Colavito (Tigers), rf	4	1	1	2	0	0	Cepeda (Giants), 1b	1	0	0	2	0	0
Gentile (Orioles), 1b	4	0	1	10	0	0	Banks (Cubs), 1b	2	1	1	1	1	0
Battey (Twins), c	2	1	0	2	0	0	T. Davis (Dodgers), lf	1	0	0	0	1	1
dKaline (Tigers)	0	1	0	0	0	0	bMusial (Cardinals), lf	2	0	0	0	1	0
Howard (Yankees), c	2	0	0	2	0	0	Williams (Cubs), lf	1	0	0	2	0	0
Wagner (Angels), lf	4	1	3	1	0	0	Boyer (Cardinals), 3b	3	0	1	1	2	0
L. Thomas (Angels), lf	0	0	0	1	0	0	Mathews (Braves), 3b	1	0	0	0	0	2
Aparicio (White Sox), ss	2	0	0	2	3	0	Crandall (Braves), c	1	0	0	3	0	0
Tresh (Yankees), ss	2	0	1	0	4	0	Roseboro (Dodgers), c	3	1	1	6	0	0
Stenhouse (Senators), p	0	0	0	0	0	0	Mazeroski (Pirates), 2b	1	0	0	0	0	0
aRunnels (Red Sox)	1	1	1	0	0	0	cAltman (Cubs)	1	0	0	0	0	0
Herbert (White Sox), p	1	0	0	0	0	0	Gibson (Cardinals), p	0	0	0	0	0	0
Aguirre (Tigers), p	2	0	0	0	0	0	Farrell (Colts), p	0	0	0	0	0	0
Pappas (Orioles), p	0	0	0	0	0	0	eAshburn (Mets)	1	1	1	0	0	0
Totals	37	9	10	27	13	0	Marichal (Giants), p	0	0	0	0	0	0
							hCallison (Phillies)	0	0	0	0	0	0
							Podres (Dodgers), p	1	1	0	0	0	0
							Mahaffey (Phillies), p	0	0	0	0	0	0
							Bolling (Braves), 2b	3	0	1	3	1	0
							Totals	35	4	10	27	10	4

American League	0	0 1	2 0 1	3 0	2 — 9			
National League	0	1 0	0 0 0	1 1	— 4			

Americans	IP.	H.	R.	ER.	BB.	SO.	Nationals	IP.	H.	R.	ER.	BB.	SO.
Stenhouse (Senators)	2	3	1	1	1	1	Podres (Dodgers)	2	2	0	0	0	2
Herbert (White Sox)	3	3	0	0	0	0	Mahaffey (Phillies)	2	3	3	3	1	1
Aguirre (Tigers)	3	2	2	2	0	2	Gibson (Cardinals)	2	1	1	2	1	1
Pappas (Orioles)	1	1	1	1	1	0	Farrell (Colts)	1	3	3	3	1	2
							Marichal (Giants)	2	2	2	1	0	2

Winning pitcher—Herbert. Losing pitcher—Mahaffey.

aHomered for Stenhouse in third. bGrounded out for T. Davis in third. cFlied out for Mazeroski in fourth. dRan for Battey in sixth. eSingled for Farrell in seventh. fSafe on error for Moran in ninth. gRan for Berra in ninth. hWalked for Marichal in ninth. Runs batted in—Groat 2, Runnels, Wagner 2, Tresh, Colavito 4, Williams, Maris, Roseboro. Two-base hits—Podres, Tresh, Bolling, Maris. Three-base hit—Banks. Home runs—Runnels, Wagner, Colavito, Roseboro. Sacrifice fly—Colavito. Double plays—Aparicio, Moran and Gentile; Moran, Aparicio and Gentile. Left on bases—Americans 6, Nationals 7. Hit by pitcher—By Stenhouse (Groat). Wild pitches—Marichal 2, Stenhouse. Umpires—Conlan, Burkhart and Forman (N. L.), McKinley, Rice and Kinnamon (A. L.). Time of game—2:28. Attendance—38,359.

Willie Mays, the offensive star in the National League's 5-3 victory in the 1963 All-Star Game at Cleveland's Municipal Stadium, added icing to the cake when he made a remarkable catch on Joe Pepitone's long eighth-inning drive.

Game of 1963
Municipal Stadium, Cleveland, July 9

After four years as a double feature, the All-Star Game went back to a single performance and it found the National League utilizing its speed to run past the American League stars, 5-3. Only 44,160 fans—nearly 30,000 under capacity—attended.

Willie Mays was easily the standout performer. He collected only one hit, but drove in two runs, walked once, stole two bases, scored twice and contributed the game's most scintillating catch.

Oddly, the Americans outhit the Nationals, 11 to six, and had the only extra-base blow. However, Mays' two stolen bases and another by Bill White each set up a run for the senior circuit.

Mays started the N. L. on the road to victory when he walked in the second inning, swiped second and scored on Dick Groat's single. After the Americans knotted the score in their turn, the senior loop came up with two more runs in the third on a single by Tommy Davis, an infield out, a run-scoring ace by Mays, his theft and a hit by Ed Bailey.

The Americans got the two runs back in their turn against Larry Jackson. Albie Pearson doubled and tallied on Frank Malzone's single. An infield out and Earl Battey's single fetched in the tying marker.

The N. L. broke the deadlock against Jim Bunning in the fifth on a walk, an error by Bobby Richardson and Willie Mays' infield out. The Nationals added their final run in the eighth when White singled off Dick Radatz, stole second and scored on Ron Santo's ace. The box score:

National League 5, American League 3
(American League Leads Series, 17-16-1)

NATIONALS	AB.	R.	H.	PO.	A.	E.	AMERICANS	AB.	R.	H.	PO.	A.	E.
T. Davis (Dodgers), lf	3	1	1	2	1	0	Fox (White Sox), 2b	3	0	1	3	1	0
eSnider (Mets), lf	1	0	0	0	0	0	Richardson (Yankees), 2b	2	0	0	1	1	1
H. Aaron (Braves), rf	4	1	0	3	0	0	Pearson (Angels), cf	4	1	2	4	0	0
White (Cardinals), 1b	4	1	1	5	3	0	Tresh (Yankees), cf	0	0	0	0	0	0
Mays (Giants), cf	3	2	1	1	0	0	Kaline (Tigers), rf	3	0	0	2	0	0
Clemente (Pirates), cf	0	0	0	0	0	0	Allison (Twins), rf	1	0	0	0	0	0
Bailey (Giants), c	1	0	1	4	1	0	Malzone (Red Sox), 3b	3	1	1	1	3	0
aMusial (Cardinals)	1	0	0	0	0	0	Bouton (Yankees), p	0	0	0	0	0	0
Culp (Phillies), p	0	0	0	0	1	0	Pizarro (White Sox), p	0	0	0	0	0	0
Santo (Cubs), 3b	1	0	1	0	0	0	cKillebrew (Twins)	1	0	0	0	0	0
Boyer (Cardinals), 3b	3	0	0	0	0	0	Radatz (Red Sox), p	0	0	0	0	0	0
Woodeshick (Colts), p	0	0	0	0	1	0	Wagner (Angels), lf	3	1	2	1	0	0
dMcCovey (Giants)	1	0	0	0	0	0	Howard (Yankees), c	1	0	0	5	0	0
Drysdale (Dodgers), p	0	0	0	0	0	0	Battey (Twins), c	2	0	1	1	0	0
Groat (Cardinals), ss	4	0	1	2	2	0	bYastrzemski (R. Sox), lf	2	0	0	1	0	0
Javier (Cardinals), 2b	4	0	0	4	1	0	Pepitone (Yankees), 1b	4	0	0	8	0	0
O'Toole (Reds), p	1	0	0	0	0	0	Versalles (Twins), ss	1	0	1	0	2	0
Jackson (Cubs), p	1	0	0	1	0	0	Aparicio (Orioles), ss	1	0	0	0	0	0
Edwards (Reds), c	2	0	0	5	0	0	McBride (Angels), ss	1	0	1	0	0	0
							Bunning (Tigers), p	0	0	0	0	0	0
							Robinson (Orioles), 3b	2	0	2	1	1	0
Totals	34	5	6	27	10	0	Totals	34	3	11	27	8	1

National League	0	1	2	0	1	0	0	1	0—5	
American League	0	1	2	0	0	0	0	0	0—3	

Nationals	IP.	H.	R.	ER.	BB.	SO.	Americans	IP.	H.	R.	ER.	BB.	SO.
O'Toole (Reds)	2	4	1	1	0	1	McBride (Angels)	3	4	3	3	2	1
Jackson (Cubs)	2	4	2	2	0	3	Bunning (Tigers)	2	0	1	0	1	0
Culp (Phillies)	1	1	0	0	0	0	Bouton (Yankees)	1	0	0	0	0	0
Woodeshick (Colts)	2	1	0	0	1	3	Pizarro (White Sox)	1	0	0	0	0	0
Drysdale (Dodgers)	2	1	0	0	0	2	Radatz (Red Sox)	2	2	1	1	0	5

Winning pitcher—Jackson. Losing pitcher—Bunning.

aLined out for Bailey in fifth. bFouled out for Battey in fifth. cCalled out on strikes for Pizarro in seventh. dStruck out for Woodeshick in eighth. eCalled out on strikes for T. Davis in ninth. Runs batted in—Mays 2, Bailey, Santo, Groat, Malzone, Battey, McBride. Two-base hit—Pearson. Stolen bases—Mays 2, White. Sacrifice hit—Bunning. Double plays—T. Davis and Bailey; Groat, Javier and White; White, Groat and White. Left on bases—Nationals 5, Americans 7. Hit by pitcher—By O'Toole (Versalles). Umpires—Soar, Smith and Haller (A. L.), Jackowski, Pryor and Harvey (N. L.). Time of game—2:20. Attendance—44,160.

Game of 1964

Shea Stadium, New York, July 7

Staging a dramatic ninth-inning rally, the Nationals came from behind to win, 7-4, and knot the All-Star series at 17 victories each. It also was the N. L.'s sixth win in the last seven decisions.

The Americans led, 4-3, going into the bottom of the ninth. Dick Radatz, Red Sox relief ace, was on the mound and had already hurled two hitless innings. However, Willie Mays coaxed a walk to start the ninth. Then, in an unorthodox move, he stole second.

Orlando Cepeda followed with a bloop hit to short right field and Mays raced home with the tying run when first baseman Joe Pepitone, who retrieved the ball, made a bad throw to the plate. Following two outs sandwiched around a walk, Johnny Callison smashed the ball into the right-field seats to break up the game.

The Nationals' first two runs came in the fourth inning when Billy Williams and Ken Boyer tagged Johnny Wyatt for homers. The N. L. made it 3-1 with a run off Camilo Pascual with two out in the fifth on a single by Roberto Clemente and Dick Groat's double. However, Brooks Robinson tripled across two A. L. mates in the sixth to tie the score.

Dick Farrell was pitching when the Americans went ahead, 4-3, in the seventh inning. He hit Elston Howard with a pitch and Rocky Colavito then singled Howard to third. Jim Fregosi followed with a sacrifice fly that scored Howard. That set the stage for the N. L.'s thrilling rally in the ninth inning. The box score:

National League 7, American League 4

(Series Tied, 17-17-1)

AMERICANS	AB.	R.	H.	PO.	A.	E.	NATIONALS	AB.	R.	H.	PO.	A.	E.
Fregosi (Angels), ss	4	1	1	4	1	0	Clemente (Pirates), rf	3	1	1	1	0	0
Oliva (Twins), rf	4	0	0	0	0	0	Short (Phillies), p	0	0	0	0	1	0
Radatz (Red Sox), p	1	0	0	0	0	0	Farrell (Colts), p	0	0	0	0	0	0
Mantle (Yankees), cf	4	1	1	2	0	0	gWhite (Cardinals)	1	0	0	0	0	0
Hall (Twins), cf	0	0	0	0	0	0	Marichal (Giants), p	0	0	0	0	0	0
Killebrew (Twins), lf	4	1	3	1	0	0	Groat (Cardinals), ss	3	0	1	0	0	0
Hinton (Senators), lf	0	0	0	0	0	0	dCardenas (Reds), ss	1	0	0	1	0	0
Allison (Twins), 1b	3	0	0	9	0	0	Williams (Cubs), lf	4	1	1	1	0	0
fPepitone (Yankees), 1b	0	0	0	1	0	1	Mays (Giants), cf	3	1	0	7	0	0
Robinson (Orioles), 3b	4	0	2	1	2	0	Cepeda (Giants), 1b	4	0	1	6	0	0
Richardson (Yankees), 2b	4	0	1	0	4	0	hFlood (Cardinals)	0	1	0	0	0	0
Howard (Yankees), c	3	1	0	9	0	0	Boyer (Cardinals), 3b	4	1	2	0	2	0
Chance (Angels), p	1	0	0	0	1	0	Torre (Braves), c	2	0	0	5	0	0
Wyatt (Athletics), p	0	0	0	0	1	0	Edwards (Reds), c	1	1	0	5	0	0
bSiebern (Orioles)	1	0	0	0	0	0	Hunt (Mets), 2b	3	0	1	1	0	0
Pascual (Twins), p	0	0	0	0	1	0	iAaron (Braves)	1	0	0	0	0	0
eColavito (Athletics), rf	2	0	1	0	0	0	Drysdale (Dodgers), p	0	0	0	0	3	0
Totals	35	4	9	26	10	1	aStargell (Pirates)	1	0	0	0	0	0
							Bunning (Phillies), p	0	0	0	0	0	0
							cCallison (Phillies), rf	3	1	1	0	0	0
							Totals	34	7	8	27	6	0

American League	1	0	0	0	0	2	1	0	0	0—4
National League	0	0	0	2	1	0	0	0	4—7	

Two out when winning run scored.

Americans	IP.	H.	R.	ER.	BB.	SO.	Nationals	IP.	H.	R.	ER.	BB.	SO.
Chance (Angels)	3	2	0	0	0	2	Drysdale (Dodgers)	3	2	1	0	0	3
Wyatt (Athletics)	1	2	2	2	0	0	Bunning (Phillies)	2	2	0	0	0	4
Pascual (Twins)	2	2	1	1	0	1	Short (Phillies)	1	3	2	2	0	1
Radatz (Red Sox)	2⅔	2	4	4	2	5	Farrell (Colts)	2	2	1	1	1	1
							Marichal (Giants)	1	0	0	0	0	1

Winning pitcher—Marichal. Losing pitcher—Radatz.

aGrounded out for Drysdale in third. bFlied out for Wyatt in fifth. cPopped out for Bunning in fifth. dRan for Groat in fifth. eDoubled for Pascual in seventh. fRan for Allison in eighth. gStruck out for Farrell in eighth. hRan for Cepeda in ninth. iStruck out for Hunt in ninth. Runs batted in—Killebrew, Williams, Boyer, Groat, Robinson 2, Fregosi, Callison 3. Two-base hits—Groat, Colavito. Three-base hit—Robinson. Home runs—Williams, Boyer, Callison. Stolen base—Mays. Sacrifice fly—Fregosi. Left on bases—Americans 7, Nationals 3. Hit by pitcher—By Farrell (Howard). Wild pitch—Drysdale. Passed ball—Torre. Umpires—Sudol, Secory and Harvey (N. L.), Paparella, Chylak and Salerno (A. L.). Time of game—2:37. Attendance—50,844.

Game of 1965

Metropolitan Stadium, Minnesota, July 13

For the first time since the All-Star Game was launched in 1933, the National League gained the lead in the series when it defeated the American League, 6-5. In posting its seventh victory in the last eight decisions, the senior circuit took an 18-17 edge.

Willie Mays and Juan Marichal were the National League standouts. Mays hit a homer, drew two walks and scored the winning run. Marichal breezed through the first three innings, permitting only one hit and facing the minimum of nine batters.

The Nationals jumped on Milt Pappas for three quick runs in the opening inning. Mays led off with a 415-foot homer and Joe Torre connected with a mate aboard.

The old loop then made it 5-0 at the expense of Mudcat Grant in the second inning when Willie Stargell homered with Marichal aboard via a single.

After picking up one run in the fourth, the Americans exploded for four runs against Jim Maloney with two away in the fifth to knot the score. Both Dick McAuliffe and Harmon Killebrew homered with one on.

The N. L. broke the tie in the seventh inning against Sam McDowell. Mays worked him for a walk, raced to third on Hank Aaron's single and scored on Ron Santo's nubber to shortstop Zoilo Versalles, who was unable to make a play. The box score:

National League 6, American League 5

(National League Leads Series, 18-17-1)

NATIONALS	AB.	R.	H.	PO.	A.	E.	AMERICANS	AB.	R.	H.	PO.	A.	E.
Mays (Giants), cf	3	2	1	4	0	0	McAuliffe (Tigers), ss	3	2	2	3	0	0
Aaron (Braves), rf	5	0	1	0	0	0	McDowell (Indians), p	0	0	0	0	1	0
Stargell (Pirates), lf	3	2	2	1	0	0	eOliva (Twins), rf	2	0	1	0	0	0
fClemente (Pirates), lf	2	0	0	0	0	0	B. Robinson (Orioles), 3b	4	1	1	1	2	0
Allen (Phillies), 3b	3	0	1	0	1	0	Alvis (Indians), 3b	1	0	0	0	0	0
Santo (Cubs), 3b	2	0	1	2	0	0	Killebrew (Twins), 1b	3	1	1	7	1	0
Torre (Braves), c	4	1	1	5	1	0	Colavito (Indians), rf	4	0	1	1	0	0
Banks (Cubs), 1b	4	0	2	11	0	0	Fisher (White Sox), p	0	0	0	1	1	0
Rose (Reds), 2b	2	0	0	1	5	0	hPepitone (Yankees)	1	0	0	0	0	0
Wills (Dodgers), ss	4	0	1	2	3	0	Horton (Tigers), lf	3	0	0	2	0	0
Cardenas (Reds), ss	0	0	0	0	0	0	Mantilla (Red Sox), 2b	2	0	0	1	1	0
Marichal (Giants), p	1	1	1	0	0	0	Richardson (Yankees), 2b	2	0	0	2	1	0
bRojas (Phillies)	1	0	0	0	0	0	Davalillo (Indians), cf	2	0	1	1	0	0
Maloney (Reds), p	0	0	0	0	0	0	Versalles (Twins), ss	1	0	0	2	2	0
Drysdale (Dodgers), p	0	0	0	0	0	0	Battey (Twins), c	2	0	0	4	1	0
dF. Robinson (Reds)	1	0	0	0	0	0	Freehan (Tigers), c	1	0	1	4	0	0
Koufax (Dodgers), p	0	0	0	0	0	0	Pappas (Orioles), p	0	0	0	0	1	0
Farrell (Astros), p	0	0	0	0	0	0	Grant (Twins), p	0	0	0	0	0	0
gWilliams (Cubs)	1	0	0	0	0	0	aKaline (Tigers)	1	0	0	0	0	0
Gibson (Cardinals), p	0	0	0	1	0	0	Richert (Senators), p	0	0	0	0	0	0
							cHall (Twins), cf	2	1	0	0	0	0
Totals	36	6	11	27	10	0	Totals	34	5	8	27	11	0

National League	3	2	0	0	0	0	1	0	0 — 6
American League	0	0	0	1	4	0	0	0	0 — 5

Nationals	IP.	H.	R.	ER.	BB.	SO.	Americans	IP.	H.	R.	ER.	BB.	SO.
Marichal (Giants)	3	1	0	0	0	0	Pappas (Orioles)	1	4	3	3	1	0
Maloney (Reds)	1⅔	5	5	5	2	1	Grant (Twins)	2	2	2	2	1	3
Drysdale (Dodgers)	⅓	0	0	0	0	0	Richert (Senators)	2	1	0	0	0	2
Koufax (Dodgers)	1	0	0	0	2	1	McDowell (Indians)	2	3	1	1	1	2
Farrell (Astros)	1	0	0	0	1	0	Fisher (White Sox)	2	1	0	0	0	0
Gibson (Cardinals)	2	2	0	0	1	3							

Winning pitcher—Koufax. Losing pitcher—McDowell.

aGrounded out for Grant in third. bFlied out for Marichal in fourth. cWalked for Richert in fifth. dStruck out for Drysdale in sixth. eGrounded out for McDowell in seventh. fHit into force play for Stargell in seventh. gGrounded out for Farrell in eighth. hStruck out for Fisher in ninth. Runs batted in—Mays, Stargell 2. Santo, Torre 2. McAuliffe 2, Killebrew 2, Colavito. Home runs—Mays, Torre, Stargell, McAuliffe, Killebrew. Sacrifice hit—Rose. Two-base hit—Oliva. Home runs—Mays, Torre, Stargell, McAuliffe, Killebrew. Sacrifice hit—Rose. Double plays—B. Robinson, Mantilla and Killebrew; Wills, Rose and Banks; McDowell, Richardson and Killebrew. Left on bases—Nationals 7, Americans 8. Wild pitch—Maloney. Umpires—Stevens, DiMuro and Valentine (A. L.), Weyer, Williams and Kibler (N. L.). Time of game—2:45. Attendance—46,706.

*St. Louis catcher Tim McCarver gets a warm reception after
scoring the winning run in the 10th inning of the 1966 All-Star
Game at St. Louis' Busch Stadium.*

Game of 1966

Busch Memorial Stadium, St. Louis, July 12

Most of the 49,936 fans who attended the 1966 contest will best remember the occasion for the searing 105-degree temperature, but they also have memories of a sparkling 2-1 National League victory in 10 innings. The game was played out of turn in St. Louis to, help commemorate the city's bicentennial and to celebrate the opening of the new riverfront stadium.

The contest marked only the fourth in the midsummer series to go extra innings, and as on two previous occasions, a member of the Cardinals played a decisive role.

Tim McCarver, a St. Louis catcher, scored the winning run on a single by Maury Wills after opening the 10th inning with a hit and advancing to second on a sacrifice. Pete Richert, who took the mound in the 10th, was the victim.

Although allowing just one hit in three innings, Sandy Koufax permitted the lone A. L. run.

With one out in the second, Brooks Robinson smashed a liner to left field and wound up with a triple when Hank Aaron lost sight of the ball momentarily in the background of white shirts and it skipped past him to the wall. Robinson scored when Koufax uncorked a wild pitch.

The Nationals tied the game against Jim Kaat in the fourth frame. Willie Mays and Roberto Clemente led off with singles, and after Willie McCovey forced Clemente, Ron Santo beat out a slow roller as Mays raced across the plate. The box score:

National League 2, American League 1

(National League Leads Series, 19-17-1)

AMERICANS	AB.	R.	H.	PO.	A.	E.	NATIONALS	AB.	R.	H.	PO.	A.	E.
McAuliffe (Tigers), ss	3	0	0	1	1	0	Mays (Giants), cf	4	1	1	3	0	0
Stottlemyre (Yankees), p	0	0	0	0	0	0	Clemente (Pirates), rf	4	0	2	2	0	0
hColavito (Indians)	1	0	0	0	0	0	Aaron (Braves), lf	4	0	0	2	0	0
Siebert (Indians), p	0	0	0	0	0	0	McCovey (Giants), 1b	3	0	0	10	1	0
Richert (Senators), p	0	0	0	0	1	0	Santo (Cubs), 3b	4	0	1	2	2	0
Kaline (Tigers), cf	4	0	1	3	0	0	Torre (Braves), c	3	0	0	5	0	0
Agee (White Sox), cf	0	0	0	1	0	0	McCarver (Cardinals), c	1	1	1	1	0	0
F. Robinson (Orioles), lf	4	0	0	2	0	0	Lefebvre (Dodgers), 2b	2	0	0	2	0	0
Oliva (Twins), rf	4	0	0	0	0	0	Hunt (Mets), 2b	1	0	0	0	1	0
B. Robinson (Orioles), 3b	4	1	3	4	4	0	Cardenas (Reds), ss	2	0	0	2	2	0
Scott (Red Sox), 1b	2	0	0	4	1	0	fStargell (Pirates)	1	0	0	0	0	0
eCash (Tigers), 1b	2	0	0	4	0	0	Wills (Dodgers), ss	1	0	1	1	1	0
Freehan (Tigers), c	2	0	1	4	0	0	Koufax (Dodgers), p	0	0	0	0	0	0
Battey (Twins), c	1	0	0	1	0	0	aFlood (Cardinals)	1	0	0	0	0	0
Knoop (Angels), 2b	2	0	0	3	1	0	Bunning (Phillies), p	0	0	0	0	0	0
gRichardson (Yanks), 2b	2	0	0	1	1	0	bAllen (Phillies)	1	0	0	0	0	0
McLain (Tigers), p	1	0	0	0	1	0	Marichal (Giants), p	0	0	0	0	0	0
Kaat (Twins), p	0	0	0	0	0	0	iHart (Giants)	1	0	0	0	0	0
cKillebrew (Twins)	1	0	1	0	0	0	Perry (Giants), p	0	0	0	0	0	0
dFregosi (Angels), ss	2	0	0	0	1	0	Totals	33	2	6	30	7	0
Totals	35	1	6	28	11	0							

American League .... 0 1 0   0 0 0   0 0 0   0—1
National League .... 0 0 0   1 0 0   0 0 0   1—2

One out when winning run scored.

Americans	IP.	H.	R.	ER.	BB.	SO.	Nationals	IP.	H.	R.	ER.	BB.	SO.
McLain (Tigers)	3	0	0	0	0	3	Koufax (Dodgers)	3	1	1	1	0	1
Kaat (Twins)	2	3	1	1	0	1	Bunning (Phillies)	2	1	0	0	0	2
Stottlemyre (Yankees)	2	1	0	0	1	0	Marichal (Giants)	3	3	0	0	0	2
Siebert (Indians)	2	0	0	0	0	1	Perry (Giants)	2	1	0	0	1	1
Richert (Senators)	1/3	2	1	1	0	0							

Winning pitcher—Perry. Losing pitcher—Richert.

aGrounded out for Koufax in third. bStruck out for Bunning in fifth. cSingled for Kaat in sixth. dRan for Killebrew in sixth. eGrounded into double play for Scott in seventh. fFouled out for Cardenas in seventh. gGrounded out for Knoop in eighth. hFlied out for Stottlemyre in eighth. iStruck out for Marichal in eighth. Runs batted in—Santo, Wills. Two-base hit—Clemente. Three-base hit—B. Robinson. Double play—McCovey, Cardenas and McCovey. Left on bases—Americans 5, Nationals 5. Wild pitches— Koufax, Perry. Umpires—Barlick, Vargo and Engel (N. L.), Umont, Honochick and Neudecker (A. L.). Time of game—2:19. Attendance—49,936.

Game of 1967

Anaheim Stadium, California, July 11

The longest of the mid-season classics took place in the California Angels' 1-year-old park, Anaheim Stadium, before 46,309 fans, many of whom weren't around at the finish, three hours and 41 minutes after the beginning. The National League finally won, 2-1, in the 15th inning.

The contest was noteworthy because of the 30 strikeouts registered by the 12 pitchers who appeared in the game and because home runs accounted for all the scoring.

Philadelphia's Richie Allen put the N.L. one up in the second inning when he homered off A.L. starter Dean Chance of Minnesota. Baltimore's Brooks Robinson evened the score in the sixth when he banged a four-bagger off Chicago Cubs' righthander Ferguson Jenkins.

Finally, in the top of the 15th, Cincinnati's Tony Perez separated Kansas City hurler Jim (Catfish) Hunter's one-strike fast ball from the gathering gloom and hit it out of the park.

National League 2, American League 1

(National League Leads Series, 20-17-1)

NATIONALS	AB.	R.	H.	PO.	A.	E.	AMERICANS	AB.	R.	H.	PO.	A.	E.
Brock (Cardinals), lf	2	0	0	1	0	0	B. Robinson (Orioles), 3b	6	1	1	0	6	0
cMays (Giants), cf	4	0	0	3	0	0	Carew (Twins), 2b	3	0	0	2	3	0
Clemente (Pirates), rf	6	0	1	6	0	0	McAuliffe (Tigers), 2b	3	0	0	3	2	0
Aaron (Braves), cf-lf	6	0	1	2	0	0	Oliva (Twins), cf	6	0	2	4	0	0
Cepeda (Cardinals), 1b	6	0	0	6	0	0	Killebrew (Twins), 1b	6	0	0	15	1	0
Allen (Phillies), 3b	4	1	1	0	2	0	Conigliaro (Red Sox), rf	6	0	0	4	0	0
Perez (Reds), 3b	2	1	1	0	3	0	Yastrzemski (Red Sox), lf	4	0	3	2	0	0
Torre (Braves), c	2	0	0	4	1	0	Freehan (Tigers), c	5	0	0	13	0	0
Haller (Giants), c	1	0	0	7	0	0	Petrocelli (Red Sox), ss	1	0	0	0	1	0
gBanks (Cubs)	1	0	1	0	0	0	McGlothlin (Angels), p	0	0	0	0	0	0
McCarver (Cardinals), c	2	0	2	7	1	0	bMantle (Yankees)	1	0	0	0	0	0
Mazeroski (Pirates), 2b	4	0	0	7	1	0	Peters (White Sox), p	0	0	0	0	1	0
Drysdale (Dodgers), p	0	0	0	0	0	0	dMincher (Angels)	1	0	1	0	0	0
kHelms (Reds)	1	0	0	0	0	0	eAgee (White Sox)	0	0	0	0	0	0
Seaver (Mets), p	0	0	0	0	0	0	Downing (Yankees), p	0	0	0	0	0	0
Alley (Pirates), ss	5	0	0	1	3	0	hAlvis (Indians)	1	0	0	0	0	0
Marichal (Giants), p	1	0	0	0	0	0	Hunter (Athletics), p	1	0	0	0	0	0
Jenkins (Cubs), p	1	0	0	0	0	0	lBerry (White Sox)	1	0	0	0	0	0
Gibson (Cardinals), p	0	0	0	0	1	0	Chance (Twins), p	0	0	0	0	0	0
fWynn (Astros)	1	0	1	0	0	0	aFregosi (Angels), ss	4	0	1	2	3	0
Short (Phillies), p	0	0	0	0	1	0	Totals	49	1	8	45	17	0
iStaub (Astros)	1	0	1	0	0	0							
Cuellar (Astros), p	0	0	0	0	0	0							
jRose (Reds), 2b	1	0	0	1	0	0							
Totals	51	2	9	45	13	0							

Nationals	0	1	0	0	0	0	0	0	0	0	0	0	0	1—2				
Americans	0	0	0	0	0	1	0	0	0	0	0	0	0	0—1				

Nationals	IP.	H.	R.	ER.	BB.	SO.	Americans	IP.	H.	R.	ER.	BB.	SO.
Marichal (Giants)	3	1	0	0	0	3	Chance (Twins)	3	2	1	1	0	1
Jenkins (Cubs)	3	3	1	1	0	6	McGlothlin (Angels)	2	1	0	0	0	2
Gibson (Cardinals)	2	2	0	0	0	2	Peters (White Sox)	3	0	0	0	0	4
Short (Phillies)	2	0	0	0	1	1	Downing (Yankees)	2	2	0	0	0	2
Cuellar (Astros)	2	1	0	0	0	2	Hunter (Athletics)	5	4	1	1	0	4
Drysdale (Dodgers)	2	1	0	0	0	2							
Seaver (Mets)	1	0	0	0	1	1							

Winning pitcher—Drysdale. Losing pitcher—Hunter.

aSingled for Chance in third inning. bStruck out for McGlothlin in fifth inning. cStruck out for Brock in sixth inning. dSingled for Peters in eighth inning. eRan for Mincher in eighth inning. fSingled for Gibson in ninth inning. gSingled for Haller in tenth inning. hGrounded into fielder's choice for Downing in tenth inning. iSingled for Short in eleventh inning. jFlied out for Cuellar in thirteenth inning. kLined into double play for Drysdale in 15th inning. lStruck out for Hunter in 15th inning. Runs batted in—Allen, Perez, B. Robinson. Two-base hits—Yastrzemski, McCarver. Home runs—Allen, B. Robinson, Perez. Double plays—B. Robinson, Carew and Killebrew; McAuliffe and Killebrew. Stolen base—Aaron. Sacrifice hits—Fregosi, Freehan, Mazeroski. Left on bases—Nationals 5, Americans 7. Bases on balls—Off Short (Yastrzemski), off Seaver (Yastrzemski). Strikeouts—By Marichal 3 (Oliva, Yastrzemski, Freehan), by Jenkins 6 (Killebrew, Conigliaro, Mantle, Fregosi, Carew, Oliva), by Gibson 2 (Conigliaro, Freehan), by Short (Fregosi), by Cuellar 2 (B. Robinson, Oliva), by Drysdale 2 (Hunter, Killebrew), by Seaver (Berry), by Chance (Clemente), by McGlothlin 2 (Allen, Alley), by Peters 4 (Mays, Clemente, Cepeda, Allen), by Downing 2 (Clemente, Allen), by Hunter 4 (Alley 2, Clemente, Perez). Umpires—Runge (A.L.) at plate; Secory (N.L.); DiMuro (A.L.) second base; Burkhart (N.L.) third base; Ashford (A.L.) left field line; Pelekoudas (N.L.) right field line. Time of game—3:41. Attendance—46,309. Gross receipts—$324,428. Official scorers—Bob Addie, Washington Post; Ross Newhan, Long Beach Independent Press-Telegram, and Bob Hunter, Los Angeles Herald-Examiner.

Game of 1968
Astrodome, Houston, July 9

In the first 1-0 game in the 36-year history of All-Star competition, the National League scored an unearned run in the first inning and defeated the American League for the sixth straight time. The game, first in the classic series to be played indoors, packed the Astrodome with a crowd of 48,321 fans, who paid a record total of $383,733 at the gate.

Willie Mays, San Francisco's veteran star, was not scheduled to be in the N.L.'s starting lineup, but drew the assignment because of an injury to Pete Rose of Cincinnati. Batting in the leadoff spot, Mays grounded a single to left field. Cleveland's Luis Tiant, the A.L.'s starting pitcher, attempted to pick Mays off first, but his throw got by Harmon Killebrew, allowing Willie to reach second. Curt Flood of St. Louis walked, the fourth ball being a wild pitch that sent Mays to third. From this point, Mays was able to score the game's only run when his San Francisco teammate, Willie McCovey, grounded into a double play.

The Nationals collected only five hits and the A.L. just three. The total of eight tied the previous low set in the five-inning, rain-curtailed game at Philadelphia in 1952.

National League 1, American League 0

(National League Leads Series, 21-17-1)

AMERICANS	AB.	R.	H.	RBI.	PO.	A.
Fregosi (Angels), ss	3	0	1	0	1	6
Campaneris (Athletics), ss	1	0	0	0	1	0
Carew (Twins), 2b	3	0	0	0	2	2
Johnson (Orioles), 2b	1	0	0	0	1	1
Yastr'ski (Red Sox), cf-lf	4	0	0	0	0	0
Howard (Senators), rf	2	0	0	0	0	0
Oliva (Twins), rf	1	0	1	0	2	0
Horton (Tigers), lf	2	0	0	0	1	0
Azcue (Indians), c	1	0	0	0	5	0
Josephson (White Sox), c	0	0	0	0	0	0
Killebrew (Twins), 1b	1	0	0	0	4	0
Powell (Orioles), 1b	2	0	0	0	2	0
Freehan (Tigers), c	2	0	0	0	4	0
McLain (Tigers), p	0	0	0	0	0	0
McDowell (Indians), p	0	0	0	0	0	0
eMantle (Yankees)	1	0	0	0	0	0
Stottlemyre (Yankees), p	0	0	0	0	0	0
John (White Sox), p	0	0	0	0	0	0
Robinson (Orioles), 3b	2	0	0	0	0	1
Wert (Tigers), 3b	1	0	1	0	1	0
Tiant (Indians), p	0	0	0	0	0	0
aHarrelson (Red Sox)	1	0	0	0	0	0
Odom (Athletics), p	0	0	0	0	0	0
Monday (Athletics), cf	2	0	0	0	0	0
Totals	30	0	3	0	24	10

NATIONALS	AB.	R.	H.	RBI.	PO.	A.
Mays (Giants), cf	4	1	1	0	0	0
Flood (Cardinals), lf	1	0	0	0	1	0
M. Alou (Pirates), lf	1	0	1	0	1	0
Javier (Cardinals), 2b	0	0	0	0	0	0
McCovey (Giants), 1b	4	0	0	0	10	0
Aaron (Braves), rf	3	0	1	0	1	0
Santo (Cubs), 3b	2	0	1	0	1	1
Perez (Reds), 3b	0	0	0	0	0	1
Helms (Reds), 2b	3	0	1	0	1	2
Reed (Braves), p	0	0	0	0	0	0
Koosman (Mets), p	0	0	0	0	0	0
Grote (Mets), c	2	0	0	0	3	0
Carlton (Cardinals), p	0	0	0	0	0	1
cStaub (Astros)	1	0	0	0	0	0
Seaver (Mets), p	0	0	0	0	0	0
F. Alou (Braves), lf	0	0	0	0	0	0
Kessinger (Cubs), ss	2	0	0	1	1	2
dWilliams (Cubs)	1	0	0	0	0	0
Cardenas (Reds), ss	0	0	0	0	0	1
Drysdale (Dodgers), p	1	0	0	0	0	1
Marichal (Giants), p	0	0	0	0	0	0
bHaller (Dodgers), c	2	0	0	0	6	0
Bench (Reds), c	0	0	0	0	2	0
Totals	27	1	5	0	27	9

Americans	0	0	0	0	0	0	0	0	0—0
Nationals	1	0	0	0	0	0	0	0	x — 1

Americans	IP.	H.	R.	ER.	BB.	SO.
Tiant (Indians)	2	2	1	0	2	2
Odom (Athletics)	2	0	0	0	2	2
McLain (Tigers)	2	1	0	0	2	1
McDowell (Indians)	1	1	0	0	0	3
Stottlemyre (Yankees)	⅓	0	0	0	0	1
John (White Sox)	⅔	1	0	0	0	0

Nationals	IP.	H.	R.	ER.	BB.	SO.
Drysdale (Dodgers)	3	1	0	0	0	0
Marichal (Giants)	2	0	0	0	0	3
Carlton (Cardinals)	1	0	0	0	0	1
Seaver (Mets)	2	2	0	0	0	5
Reed (Braves)	⅔	0	0	0	0	1
Koosman (Mets)	⅓	0	0	0	0	1

Winning pitcher—Drysdale.   Losing pitcher—Tiant.

aFlied out for Tiant in third. bFlied out for Marichal in fifth. cPopped out for Carlton in sixth. dFlied out for Kessinger in sixth. eStruck out for McDowell in eighth. Error—Killebrew. Double plays—Carew, Fregosi and Killebrew; Johnson and Powell. Left on bases—Americans 3, Nationals 8. Two-base hits—Fregosi, Helms, Oliva, Wert. Stolen base—Aaron. Bases on balls—Off Tiant 2 (Flood, Aaron), off Odom 2 (Santo, Helms), off McLain 2 (Flood, Santo). Struck out—By Tiant 2 (Grote, Kessinger), by Odom 2 (McCovey, Aaron), by McLain 1 (McCovey), by McDowell 3 (Haller, Mays, McCovey), by Stottlemyre 1 (Aaron), by Marichal 3 (Howard, Powell, Freehan), by Carlton 1 (Fregosi), by Seaver 5 (Yastrzemski, Azcue, Powell, Mantle, Monday), by Reed 1 (Johnson), by Koosman 1 (Yastrzemski). Wild pitch—Tiant. Umpires—Crawford (N.L.), at plate; Napp (A.L.), first base; Steiner (N.L.), second base; Kinnamon (A.L.), third base; Wendelstedt (N.L.), right field line; Odom (A.L.), left field line. Time of game—2:10. Attendance—48,321.

Game of 1969

Robert F. Kennedy Memorial Stadium, Washington, July 23

The National League battered the American League, 9-3, for their seventh consecutive All-Star victory as 45,259 paid $417,832, a new record gate. The win gave the N. L. a margin of 22 victories to the A. L.'s 17, with one game ending in a tie.

The game had been scheduled for Tuesday evening, July 22, but a torrential rain forced postponement until the following day. Willie McCovey of the Giants was the hitting star with two homers, only the fourth player in All-Star history to accomplish the feat.

The issue was decided early as the N. L. scored an unearned run in the first, added two in the second on Johnny Bench's homer and sent nine men to the plate in the third as they tallied five times, two runs scoring on McCovey's first homer. Willie hit for the circuit again in the fourth to complete his club's scoring. Frank Howard of the host Senators homered in the second and Bill Freehan of the Tigers duplicated in the third. Freehan singled in another run in the fourth for the A. L.'s last tally.

National League 9, American League 3

(National League Leads Series, 22-17-1)

NATIONALS	AB.	R.	H.	RBI.	PO.	A.	AMERICANS	AB.	R.	H.	RBI.	PO.	A.
Alou (Pirates), cf	4	1	2	0	5	0	Carew (Twins), 2b	3	0	0	0	0	2
Kessinger (Cubs), ss	3	0	0	0	0	0	Andrews (Red Sox), 2b	1	0	0	0	0	0
eMays (Giants)	1	0	0	0	0	0	Jackson (Athletics), cf-rf	2	0	0	0	2	0
Menke (Astros), ss	1	0	0	0	1	0	Yastrzemski (Red Sox), lf	1	0	0	0	1	0
Aaron (Braves), rf	4	1	1	0	0	0	F. Robinson (Orioles), rf	2	0	0	0	0	0
Singer (Dodgers), p	0	0	0	0	0	0	Blair (Orioles), cf	2	0	0	0	2	0
Beckert (Cubs), 2b	1	0	0	0	0	0	Powell (Orioles), 1b	4	0	1	0	9	1
McCovey (Giants), 1b	4	2	2	3	2	0	Howard (Senators), lf	1	1	1	1	0	0
L. May (Reds), 1b	1	0	0	0	3	0	bSmith (Red Sox), lf-rf	2	1	0	0	0	0
Santo (Reds), 3b	3	0	0	0	2	1	Bando (Athletics), 3b	3	0	1	0	0	1
Perez (Reds), 3b	1	0	0	0	1	1	McDowell (Indians), p	0	0	0	0	0	0
Jones (Mets), lf	4	2	2	0	3	0	Culp (Red Sox), p	0	0	0	0	0	0
Rose (Reds), lf	1	0	0	0	2	0	fWhite (Yankees)	1	0	0	0	0	0
Bench (Reds), c	3	2	2	2	4	0	Petrocelli (Red Sox), ss	3	0	1	0	1	3
Hundley (Cubs), c	1	0	0	0	3	0	Fregosi (Angels), ss	1	0	0	0	0	0
Millan (Braves), 2b	4	1	1	2	1	1	Freehan (Tigers), c	2	1	2	2	4	0
Koosman (Mets), p	0	0	0	0	0	0	Roseboro (Twins), c	1	0	0	0	6	0
Dierker (Astros), p	0	0	0	0	0	0	gC. May (White Sox)	1	0	0	0	0	0
Niekro (Braves), p	0	0	0	0	0	1	Stottlemyre (Yankees), p	0	0	0	0	1	0
Carlton (Cardinals), p	2	0	1	1	0	1	Odom (Athletics), p	0	0	0	0	0	0
Gibson (Cardinals), p	0	0	0	0	0	0	Knowles (Senators), p	0	0	0	0	0	0
dBanks (Cubs)	1	0	0	0	0	0	aKillebrew (Twins)	1	0	0	0	0	0
Clemente (Pirates), rf	1	0	0	0	0	0	McLain (Tigers), p	0	0	0	0	0	0
Totals	40	9	11	8	27	5	cMincher (Pilots)	1	0	0	0	0	0
							McNally (Orioles), p	0	0	0	0	0	0
							B. Robinson (Orioles), 3b	1	0	0	0	1	1
							Totals	33	3	6	3	27	8

Nationals	1	2	5	1	0	0	0	0	0—9
Americans	0	1	1	1	0	0	0	0	0—3

Nationals	IP.	H.	R.	ER.	BB.	SO.	American	IP.	H.	R.	ER.	BB.	SO.
Carlton (Cardinals)	3	2	2	2	1	2	Stottlemyre (Yankees)	2	4	3	2	0	1
Gibson (Cardinals)	1	2	1	1	1	2	Odom (Athletics)	½	5	5	4	0	0
Singer (Dodgers)	2	0	0	0	0	0	Knowles (Senators)	⅔	0	0	0	0	0
Koosman (Mets)	1⅔	1	0	0	0	1	McLain (Tigers)	1	1	1	1	2	2
Dierker (Astros)	⅓	1	0	0	0	0	McNally (Orioles)	2	1	0	0	1	1
Niekro (Braves)	1	0	0	0	0	2	McDowell (Indians)	2	0	0	0	0	4
							Culp (Red Sox)	1	0	0	0	0	2

Winning pitcher—Carlton. Losing pitcher—Stottlemyre.

aFlied out for Knowles in third. bRan for Howard in fourth. cStruck out for McLain in fourth. dLined out for Gibson in fifth. eFlied out for Kessinger in fifth. fStruck out for Culp in ninth. gStruck out for Roseboro in ninth. Errors—Howard, Petrocelli. Left on bases—Nationals 7, Americans 5. Two-base hits—Millan, Carlton, Petrocelli. Home runs—Bench, Howard, McCovey 2, Freehan. Bases on balls—Off Carlton 1 (Jackson), off Gibson 1 (Howard), off McLain 2 (Santo, Bench), off McNally 1 (Alou). Struck out—By Carlton 2 (F. Robinson, Petrocelli), by Gibson 2 (Powell, Mincher), by Koosman 1 (B. Robinson), by Niekro 2 (White, C. May), by Stottlemyre 1 (Carlton), by McLain 2 (Aaron, Millan), by McNally 1 (McCovey), by McDowell 4 (Clemente, Alou, Menke, L. May), by Culp 2 (Perez, Hundley). Wild pitch—Stottlemyre. Umpires—Flaherty (AL) plate, Donatelli (NL) first base, Stewart (AL) second base, Gorman (NL) third base, Springstead (AL) left field line, Venzon (NL) right field line. Time of game—2:38. Attendance—45,259.

Game of 1970
Riverfront Stadium, Cincinnati, July 14

The 1970 All-Star game was one inning too long as far as the American League was concerned and the Nationals scored their eighth straight win of the series, 5-4, in 12 innings.

The Americans held a 4-1 lead going into the last half of the ninth inning, but a home run by San Francisco's Dick Dietz, singles by New York's Bud Harrelson, Houston's Joe Morgan and San Francisco's Willie McCovey and a sacrifice fly by Pittsburgh's Roberto Clemente tied the score.

The decisive run came across in the 12th on successive two-out singles by Cincinnati's Pete Rose, Los Angeles' Bill Grabarkewitz and Chicago's Jim Hickman.

Carl Yastrzemski of the Boston Red Sox, with four hits, was selected as the outstanding player of the game.

National League 5, American League 4

(National League Leads Series, 23-17-1)

AMERICANS	AB	R	H	RBI	PO	A
Aparicio (White Sox), ss	6	0	0	0	1	4
Yastrzemski (R. Sox), cf-1b	6	1	4	1	8	0
F. Robinson (O's), rf-lf	3	0	0	0	1	0
Horton (Tigers), lf	2	1	2	0	1	0
Powell (Orioles), 1b	3	0	0	0	5	0
Otis (Royals), cf	3	0	0	0	2	0
Killebrew (Twins), 3b	2	0	1	0	0	0
bHarper (Brewers)	0	0	0	0	0	0
B. Robinson (Orioles), 3b	3	1	2	2	1	1
Howard (Senators), lf	2	0	0	0	0	0
Oliva (Twins), rf	2	0	1	0	0	0
D. Johnson (Orioles), 2b	5	0	1	0	5	1
Wright (Angels), p	0	0	0	0	0	0
Freehan (Tigers), c	1	0	0	0	4	0
Fosse (Indians), c	2	1	1	1	7	0
Palmer (Orioles), p	1	0	0	0	0	0
McDowell (Indians), p	0	0	0	0	0	3
dA. Johnson (Angels)	1	0	0	0	0	0
J. Perry (Twins), p	0	0	0	0	0	0
fFregosi (Angels)	1	0	0	0	0	0
Hunter (Athletics), p	0	0	0	0	0	0
Peterson (Yankees), p	0	0	0	0	0	0
Stottlemyre (Yankees), p	0	0	0	0	0	0
Alomar (Angels), 2b	1	0	0	0	0	2
Totals	44	4	12	4	35	11

NATIONALS	AB	R	H	RBI	PO	A
Mays (Giants), cf	3	0	0	0	3	0
G. Perry (Giants), p	0	0	0	0	0	2
eMcCovey (Giants), 1b	2	0	1	1	1	0
gOsteen (Dodgers), p	0	0	0	0	1	0
iTorre (Cardinals)	1	0	0	0	0	0
Allen (Cardinals), 1b	3	0	0	0	4	0
Gibson (Cardinals), p	0	0	0	0	0	0
hClemente (Pirates), rf	1	0	0	1	2	0
Aaron (Braves), rf	2	0	0	0	1	0
Rose (Reds), rf-lf	3	1	1	0	3	0
Perez (Reds), 3b	3	0	0	0	1	1
Grabarkewitz (Dod.), 3b	3	0	1	0	0	1
Carty (Braves), lf	1	0	0	0	0	0
Hickman (Cubs), lf-1b	4	0	1	1	6	1
Bench (Reds), c	3	0	0	0	5	0
Dietz (Giants), c	2	1	1	1	2	0
Kessinger (Cubs), ss	2	0	2	0	0	0
Harrelson (Mets), ss	3	2	2	0	0	4
Beckert (Cubs), 2b	2	0	0	0	2	1
Gaston (Padres), cf	2	0	0	0	2	0
Seaver (Mets), p	0	0	0	0	0	0
aStaub (Expos)	1	0	0	0	0	0
Merritt (Reds), p	0	0	0	0	0	0
cMenke (Astros), 2b	0	0	0	0	2	1
Morgan (Astros), 2b	2	1	1	0	1	2
Totals	43	5	10	4	36	14

```
Americans   0   0 0 0 0 1   1 2 0   0 0 — 4
Nationals   0   0 0 0 0 1   0 3 0   1 — 5
```
†Two out when winning run scored.

Americans	IP	H	R	ER	BB	SO
Palmer (Orioles)	3	1	0	0	1	3
McDowell (Indians)	3	1	0	0	3	3
J. Perry (Twins)	2	1	1	1	1	3
Hunter (Athletics)	1/3	3	3	3	0	0
Peterson (Yankees)	0*	1	0	0	0	0
Stottlemyre (Yankees)	1 2/3	0	0	0	0	2
Wright (Angels)	1 2/3	3	1	1	0	0

Nationals	IP	H	R	ER	BB	SO
Seaver (Mets)	3	1	0	0	0	4
Merritt (Reds)	2	1	0	0	0	1
G. Perry (Giants)	2	4	2	2	1	0
Gibson (Cardinals)	2	3	2	2	1	0
Osteen (Dodgers)	3	3	0	0	1	0

*Pitched to one batter in ninth.

Winning pitcher—Osteen. Losing pitcher—Wright.

aFlied out for Seaver in third. bRan for Killebrew in fifth. cWalked for Merritt in fifth. dHit into force play for McDowell in seventh. eGrounded into double play for G. Perry in seventh. fFlied out for J. Perry in ninth. gRan for McCovey in ninth. hHit sacrifice fly for Gibson in ninth. iGrounded out for Osteen in twelfth. Errors—None. Double plays—Aparicio and Yastrzemski; Harrelson, Morgan and Hickman. Left on bases—Americans 9, Nationals 10. Two-base hits—Oliva, Yastrzemski. Three-base hit—B. Robinson. Home run—Dietz. Sacrifice hit—McDowell. Sacrifice flies—Fosse, Clemente. Caught stealing—Harper. Struck out—By Palmer 3 (Mays, Bench, Perez), by McDowell 3 (Perez, Bench 2), by J. Perry 3 (Allen, Rose, Hickman), by Stottlemyre 2 (Rose, Hickman), by Seaver 4 (Aparicio, F. Robinson, Killebrew, Howard), by Merritt 1 (F. Robinson), by Gibson 2 (D. Johnson, Aparicio). Bases on balls—Off Palmer 1 (Carty), off McDowell 3 (Menke, Allen, Rose), off J. Perry 1 (Gaston), off G. Perry 1 (Oliva), off Gibson 1 (Fosse), off Osteen 1 (Horton). Hit by pitcher—J. Perry (Menke). Umpires—Barlick (NL) plate, Rice (AL) first base, Secory (NL) second base, Haller (AL) third base, Dezelan (NL) left field, Goetz (AL) right field. Official scorers—Bob Hunter, Los Angeles Herald Examiner; Earl Lawson, Cincinnati Post and Times-Star; Si Burick, Dayton News. Time of game—3:19. Attendance—51,838.

One of the more famous and controversial plays in All-Star history occurred in the 12th inning of the 1970 game in Cincinnati when the Reds' Pete Rose crashed into A.L. catcher Ray Fosse to score the winning run.

Game of 1971
Tiger Stadium, Detroit, July 13

In a contest that featured six home runs, three for each side, the American League finally snapped the National League's All-Star Game winning streak at eight with a 6-4 triumph that pleased the majority of the crowd of 53,559 that paid a record All-Star Game gate of $435,134.

For a while, though, it seemed that the senior circuit would add another notch to its string as homers by Cincinnati's Johnny Bench and Atlanta's Hank Aaron off of Oakland's young lefty, Vida Blue, gave the Nationals an early 3-0 lead. But the Americans jumped on Pittsburgh's voluble Dock Ellis in the third inning when Baltimore's Frank Robinson and Oakland's Reggie Jackson connected for homers, each coming with a man on base. This gave the Americans a one-run lead and they were never headed thereafter.

The lead was increased when the Minnesota bomber, Harmon Killebrew, hit a circuit clout with a mate aboard in the sixth inning. Roberto Clemente, the Pittsburgh Pirates' great star, closed out the scoring with a home run in the eighth.

As a result of the victory, the American League, which once led the series, 12 games to four, closed the gap to 23-18, with one tie.

Frank Robinson won the Arch Ward Trophy as the game's most valuable player.

American League 6, National League 4
(National League Leads Series, 23-18-1)

NATIONALS	AB.	R.	H.	RBI.	PO.	A.	AMERICANS	AB.	R.	H.	RBI.	PO.	A.
Mays (Giants), cf	2	0	0	0	0	0	Carew (Twins), 2b	1	1	0	0	1	2
Clemente (Pirates), rf	2	1	1	1	1	0	Rojas (Royals), 2b	1	0	0	0	1	1
Millan (Braves), 2b	0	0	0	1	1	1	Murcer (Yankees), cf	3	0	1	0	1	0
Aaron (Braves), rf	2	1	1	1	0	0	Cuellar (Orioles), p	0	0	0	0	0	0
May (Reds), 1b	1	0	0	0	6	0	dBuford (Orioles)	1	0	0	0	0	0
Torre (Cardinals), 3b	3	0	0	0	1	0	Lolich (Tigers), p	0	0	0	0	0	3
fSanto (Cubs), 3b	1	0	0	0	0	1	Yastrzemski (Red Sox), lf	3	0	0	0	0	0
Stargell (Pirates), lf	2	1	0	0	2	0	F. Robinson (Orioles), rf	2	1	1	2	2	0
gBrock (Cardinals)	1	0	0	0	0	0	Kaline (Tigers), rf	2	1	1	0	2	0
McCovey (Giants), 1b	2	0	0	0	4	0	Cash (Tigers), 1b	2	0	0	0	7	0
Marichal (Giants), p	0	0	0	0	0	1	Killebrew (Twins), 1b	2	1	1	2	4	0
Kessinger (Cubs), ss	2	0	0	0	1	1	B. Robinson (Orioles), 3b	3	0	1	0	1	3
Bench (Reds), c	4	1	2	2	5	0	Freehan (Tigers), c	3	0	0	0	6	1
Beckert (Cubs), 2b	3	0	0	0	0	5	Munson (Yankees), c	0	0	0	0	1	0
Rose (Reds), rf	0	0	0	0	0	0	Aparicio (Red Sox), ss	3	1	1	0	1	2
Harrelson (Mets), ss	2	0	0	0	1	2	Blue (Athletics), p	0	0	0	0	0	0
Jenkins (Cubs), p	0	0	0	0	0	0	aJackson (Athletics)	1	1	1	2	0	0
cColbert (Padres)	1	0	0	0	0	0	Palmer (Orioles), p	0	0	0	0	0	0
Wilson (Astros), p	0	0	0	0	0	0	bHoward (Senators)	1	0	0	0	0	0
Ellis (Pirates), p	1	0	0	0	0	0	Otis (Royals), cf	1	0	0	0	0	0
Davis (Dodgers), cf	1	0	1	0	2	0	Totals	29	6	7	6	27	12
eBonds (Giants), cf	1	0	0	0	0	0							
Totals	31	4	5	4	24	11							

Nationals	0	2	1	0	0	0	0	1	0 — 4
Americans	0	0	4	0	0	2	0	0	x — 6

Nationals	IP.	H.	R.	ER.	BB.	SO.	Americans	IP.	H.	R.	ER.	BB.	SO.
Ellis (Pirates)	3	4	4	4	1	2	Blue (Athletics)	3	2	3	3	0	3
Marichal (Giants)	2	0	0	0	1	1	Palmer (Orioles)	2	1	0	0	0	2
Jenkins (Cubs)	1	3	2	2	0	0	Cuellar (Orioles)	2	1	0	0	1	2
Wilson (Astros)	2	0	0	0	1	2	Lolich (Tigers)	2	1	1	1	0	1

Winning pitcher—Blue. Losing pitcher—Ellis.

aHomered for Blue in third. bGrounded out for Palmer in fifth. cStruck out for Jenkins in seventh. dStruck out for Cuellar in seventh. eStruck out for Davis in eighth. fGrounded out for Torre in eighth. gBunted and was thrown out for Stargell in ninth. Errors—None. Double plays—B. Robinson, Rojas and Killebrew; Beckert, Kessinger and May; Santo, Millan and May. Left on bases—Nationals 2, Americans 2. Home runs—Bench, Aaron, Jackson, F. Robinson, Killebrew, Clemente. Bases on balls—Off Ellis 1 (Carew), off Marichal 1 (Carew), off Wilson 1 (Yastrzemski), off Cuellar 1 (May). Strikeouts—By Ellis 2 (Cash 2), by Marichal 1 (Murcer), by Wilson 2 (Buford, Kaline), by Blue 3 (McCovey, Ellis, Torre), by Palmer 2 (Stargell, Clemente), by Cuellar 2 (Stargell, Colbert), by Lolich 1 (Bonds). Hit by pitcher—By Blue (Stargell). Umpires—Umont (AL) plate, Pryor (NL) first base, O'Donnell (AL) second base, Harvey (NL) third base, Denkinger (AL) right field, Colosi (NL) left field. Time—2:05. Attendance—53,559.

Game of 1972

Atlanta Stadium, Atlanta, July 25

Late-inning tallies by the National League gave it a 4-3, 10-inning victory over the American League and enabled the senior circuit to resume its winning ways in the annual All-Star Game.

The triumph gave the Nationals a 24-18 margin in the series (there was one tie) and their ninth win in the last 10 games.

A home run with a man on by Kansas City's Cookie Rojas in the eighth inning had given the Americans a 3-2 lead going into the last of the ninth. Rojas' blast, which added to an American run scored earlier in the contest, had offset Atlanta's Henry Aaron's home run with a mate aboard in the sixth frame.

But in the bottom of the ninth, singles by the Cubs' Billy Williams and the Pirates' Manny Sanguillen opened the door for the run that tied the game. It came while a forceout was being made at second base on a grounder by the Astros' Lee May.

San Diego's Nate Colbert drew a walk to start the lower half of the 10th inning and was sacrificed to second by San Francisco's Chris Speier. Cincinnati's Joe Morgan, who was voted the Arch Ward Trophy as the game's most valuable player, then shot a line single to right-center field and Colbert scored easily with the winning run.

National League 4, American League 3

(National League Leads Series, 24-18-1)

NATIONALS	AB.	R.	H.	RBI.	PO.	A.	AMERICANS	AB.	R.	H.	RBI.	PO.	A.
Morgan (Reds), 2b	4	0	1	1	3	5	Carew (Twins), 2b	2	0	1	1	2	3
Mays (Mets), cf	2	0	0	0	2	0	cRojas (Royals), 2b	1	1	1	2	3	1
Cedeno (Astros), cf	2	1	1	0	0	0	Murcer (Yankees), cf	3	0	0	0	1	0
Aaron (Braves), rf	3	1	1	2	0	0	Scheinblum (Royals), rf	1	0	0	0	1	0
Oliver (Pirates), rf	1	0	0	0	0	0	Jackson (Athletics), rf-cf	4	0	2	0	5	0
Stargell (Pirates), lf	1	0	0	0	0	0	Allen (White Sox), 1b	3	0	0	0	4	0
Williams (Cubs), lf	2	1	1	0	0	0	Cash (Tigers), 1b	1	0	0	0	3	0
Bench (Reds), c	2	0	1	0	3	0	Yastrzemski (Red Sox), lf	3	0	0	0	3	0
Sanguillen (Pirates), c	2	0	1	0	6	0	Rudi (Athletics), lf	1	0	1	0	0	0
May (Astros), 1b	4	0	1	1	13	2	Grich (Orioles), ss	4	0	0	0	0	3
Torre (Cardinals), 3b	3	0	1	0	1	2	Robinson (Orioles), rf	2	0	0	0	0	1
Santo (Cubs), 3b	1	0	0	0	0	0	Bando (Athletics), 3b	2	0	0	0	1	1
Kessinger (Cubs), ss	2	0	0	0	0	0	Freehan (Tigers), c	1	1	0	0	3	0
Carlton (Phillies), p	0	0	0	0	0	0	Fisk (Red Sox), c	2	1	1	0	2	0
Stoneman (Expos), p	1	0	0	0	0	0	Palmer (Orioles), p	0	0	0	0	0	0
McGraw (Mets), p	0	0	0	0	0	0	Lolich (Tigers), p	1	0	0	0	0	0
eColbert (Padres)	0	1	0	0	0	0	Perry (Indians), p	0	0	0	0	0	0
Gibson (Cardinals), p	0	0	0	0	1	0	bSmith (Red Sox)	1	0	0	0	0	0
Blass (Pirates), p	0	0	0	0	0	0	Wood (White Sox), p	0	0	0	0	0	0
aBeckert (Cubs)	1	0	0	0	0	0	dPiniella (Royals)	1	0	0	0	0	0
Sutton (Dodgers), p	0	0	0	0	0	0	McNally (Orioles), p	0	0	0	0	0	1
Speier (Giants), ss	2	0	0	0	1	5	Totals	33	3	6	3	28	10
Totals	33	4	8	4	30	14							

```
Americans...................................... 0   0   1     0   0   0     0   2   0       0 — 3
Nationals...................................... 0   0   0     0   0   0     0   0   1       1 — 4
```

One out when winning run scored.

Nationals	IP.	H.	R.	ER.	BB.	SO.	Americans	IP.	H.	R.	ER.	BB.	SO.
Gibson (Cardinals)	2	1	0	0	0	0	Palmer (Orioles)	3	1	0	0	1	2
Blass (Pittsburgh)	1	1	1	1	1	0	Lolich (Tigers)	2	1	0	0	0	1
Sutton (Dodgers)	2	1	0	0	0	2	Perry (Indians)	2	3	2	2	0	1
Carlton (Phillies)	1	0	0	1	0	0	Wood (White Sox)	2	2	1	1	1	1
Stoneman (Expos)	2	2	2	2	0	2	McNally (Orioles)	⅓	1	1	1	1	0
McGraw (Mets)	2	1	0	0	4								

Winning pitcher—McGraw. Losing pitcher—McNally.

aFlied out for Blass in third. bStruck out for Perry in eighth. cHomered for Carew in eighth. dGrounded out for Wood in tenth. eWalked for McGraw in tenth. Errors—None. Double plays—Carew and Allen; May unassisted; May, Speier and May; Bando, Rojas and Cash. Left on bases—Americans 3, Nationals 5. Two-base hits—Jackson, Rudi. Home runs—Aaron, Rojas. Sacrifice hits—Palmer, Speier. Stolen base—Morgan. Bases on balls—Off Palmer 1 (Stargell), off Wood 1 (Morgan), off McNally 1 (Colbert), off Blass 1 (Freehan), off Carlton 1 (Carew). Strikeouts—By Palmer 2 (Aaron, Torre), by Lolich 1 (Mays), by Perry 1 (Stoneman), by Wood 1 (Cedeno), by Sutton 2 (Grich, Lolich), by Stoneman 2 (Yastrzemski, Smith), by McGraw 4 (Jackson, Cash, Grich, Fisk). Umpires—Landes (NL) plate, DiMuro (AL) first base, Weyer (NL) second base, Neudecker (AL) third base, Dale (NL) left field, Kunkel (AL) right field. Time—2:26. Attendance—53,107.

Game of 1973

Royals Stadium, Kansas City, July 24

The 1973 All-Star Game was generally agreed to be one of the least exciting as the National League, paced by San Francisco's Bobby Bonds, posted a lopsided 7-1 win, its 10th in the last 11 games.

Bonds entered the game in the fourth inning and, on his first at-bat in the fifth, belted a home run off California's Bill Singer. Then, in the seventh frame, the Giants' super star cracked a line drive to center and stretched what should have been a single into a double.

The batting display earned Bonds the game's Most Valuable Player designation in the form of the Commissioner's Award presented by THE SPORTING NEWS in memory of Arch Ward, originator of the All-Star Game. The box score:

National League 7, American League 1

(National League Leads Series, 25-18-1)

NATIONALS	AB.	R.	H.	RBI.	PO.	A.	AMERICANS	AB.	R.	H.	RBI.	PO.	A.
Rose (Reds), lf	3	1	0	0	1	0	Campaneris (Athletics), ss	3	0	0	0	1	2
Twitchell (Phillies), p	0	0	0	0	0	0	Brinkman (Tigers), ss	1	0	0	0	1	1
Giusti (Pirates), p	0	0	0	0	0	0	Carew (Twins), 2b	3	0	0	0	5	1
jMota (Dodgers), lf	1	0	0	0	0	0	Rojas (Royals), 2b	0	0	0	0	1	1
Brewer (Dodgers), p	0	0	0	0	0	0	Mayberry (Royals), 1b	3	0	1	0	8	0
Morgan (Reds), 2b	3	2	1	0	2	2	Jackson (Athletics), rf	4	1	1	0	0	0
Johnson (Braves), 2b	1	0	0	0	1	1	Blair (Orioles), cf	0	0	0	0	1	0
Cedeno (Astros), cf	3	0	1	1	3	0	Otis (Royals), cf	2	0	2	1	0	0
Russell (Dodgers), ss	2	0	0	0	0	2	May (Brewers), cf-rf	2	0	0	0	0	0
Aaron (Braves), 1b	2	0	1	1	3	1	Murcer (Yankees), lf	3	0	0	0	0	1
Torre (Cards), 1b-3b	3	0	0	0	5	0	Fisk (Red Sox), c	2	0	0	0	3	0
Williams (Cubs), rf	2	0	1	0	0	0	Munson (Yankees), c	2	0	0	0	5	1
Bonds (Giants), rf	2	1	2	2	0	0	Robinson (Orioles), 3b	2	0	0	0	1	3
Bench (Reds), c	3	1	1	1	3	0	Bando (Athletics), 3b	1	0	0	0	0	1
fSimmons (Cards), c	1	0	0	0	1	1	Nelson (Rangers), 3b	0	0	0	0	1	0
Santo (Cubs), 3b	1	1	1	0	0	1	kHorton (Tigers)	1	0	0	0	0	0
hColbert (Padres)	1	0	0	0	0	0	Hunter (Athletics), p	0	0	0	0	0	0
Fairly (Expos), 1b	0	0	0	0	4	0	Holtzman (Athletics), p	0	0	0	0	0	0
Speier (Giants), ss	2	0	0	0	1	1	Blyleven (Twins), p	0	0	0	0	0	1
dStargell (Pirates), lf	1	0	0	0	1	0	bBell (Indians)	1	0	1	0	0	0
iMays (Mets)	1	0	0	0	0	0	Singer (Angels), p	0	0	0	0	0	1
Seaver (Mets), p	0	0	0	0	0	0	cKelly (White Sox)	1	0	0	0	0	0
Watson (Astros), lf	0	0	0	0	0	0	Ryan (Angels), p	0	0	0	0	0	0
Wise (Cardinals), p	0	0	0	0	1	0	gSpencer (Rangers)	1	0	0	0	0	0
aEvans (Braves)	0	0	0	0	0	0	Lyle (Yankees), p	0	0	0	0	0	0
Osteen (Dodgers), p	0	0	0	0	0	1	Fingers (Athletics), p	0	0	0	0	0	0
Sutton (Dodgers), p	0	0	0	0	0	1	Totals	32	1	5	1	27	12
eDavis (Dodgers), cf	2	1	2	2	1	0							
Totals	34	7	10	7	27	12							

Nationals									
Nationals	0	0	2	1	2	2	0	0	0 — 7
Americans	0	1	0	0	0	0	0	0	0 — 1

Nationals	IP.	H.	R.	ER.	BB.	SO.	Americans	IP.	H.	R.	ER.	BB.	SO.
Wise (Cardinals)	2	2	1	1	0	1	Hunter (Athletics)	1⅓	1	0	0	0	1
Osteen (Dodgers)	2	2	0	0	1	1	Holtzman (Athletics)	⅔	0	0	0	0	0
Sutton (Dodgers)	1	0	0	0	0	0	Blyleven (Twins)	1	2	2	2	2	0
Twitchell (Phillies)	1	1	0	0	0	1	Singer (Angels)	2	3	3	3	1	2
Giusti (Pirates)	1	0	0	0	1	0	Ryan (Angels)	2	2	2	2	2	2
Seaver (Mets)	1	0	0	0	1	0	Lyle (Yankees)	1	1	0	0	0	1
Brewer (Dodgers)	1	0	0	0	1	2	Fingers (Athletics)	1	1	0	0	0	0

Winning pitcher—Wise. Losing pitcher—Blyleven.

aWalked for Wise in third. bTripled for Blyleven in third. cPopped out for Singer in fifth. dStruck out for Speier in sixth. eHomered for Sutton in sixth. fCalled out on strikes for Bench in seventh. gFlied out for Ryan in seventh. hFouled out for Santo in eighth. iStruck out for Stargell in eighth. jHit into force play for Giusti in eighth. kStruck out for Nelson in ninth. Errors—None. Double play—Rojas, Brinkman and Mayberry, Bonds. Left on bases—Nationals 6, Americans 7. Two-base hits—Jackson, Morgan, Mayberry, Bonds. Three-base hit—Bell. Home runs—Bench, Bonds, Davis. Sacrifice hit—Osteen. Stolen base—Otis. Passed ball—Fisk. Bases on balls—Off Blyleven 2 (Evans, Morgan), off Singer 1 (Santo), off Ryan 2 (Santo, Rose), off Osteen 1 (Mayberry), off Brewer 1 (Rojas), off Seaver 1 (Murcer). Strikeouts—By Hunter 1 (Cedeno), by Singer 2 (Speier, Cedeno), by Ryan 2 (Stargell, Simmons), by Lyle 1 (Mays), by Wise 1 (Campaneris), by Osteen 1 (Campaneris), by Twitchell 1 (Jackson), by Brewer 2 (Munson, Horton). Umpires—Chylak (AL) plate, Burkhart (NL) first base, Barnett (AL) second base, W. Williams (NL) third base, Luciano (AL) left field, Engel (NL) right field. Time—2:45. Attendance—40,849.

Official scorers—Sid Bordman, Kansas City Star; Russell Schneider, Cleveland Plain Dealer; Dick Young, New York Daily News.

Game of 1974

Three Rivers Stadium, Pittsburgh, July 23

The National League captured its 11th victory out of the last 12 All-Star engagements by posting an easy 7-2 win. The triumph gave the Nationals a 26-18 margin in the series, with one tie.

Los Angeles first baseman Steve Garvey, who wasn't even listed on the official All-Star ballot but had been voted in as a write-in candidate, justified the fans' confidence in him by emerging as the star of the game. The Dodger first baseman collected a single and a double, drove in a run, scored another and sparkled in the field.

St. Louis' Reggie Smith homered for the Nationals. Four hurlers appeared for the American League and none escaped unscathed.

The Americans scored two runs in the third inning for a 2-1 lead and threatened to put together a big inning. However, with two runners on base and two out, Garvey took Bobby Murcer's smash and threw to pitcher Andy Messersmith for the out.

Garvey's double keyed a two-run fourth inning, giving the Nationals the lead for keeps. The box score:

National League 7, American League 2

(National League Leads Series, 26-18-1)

AMERICANS	AB.	R.	H.	RBI.	PO.	A.
Carew (Twins), 2b	1	1	0	0	0	1
Grich (Orioles), 2b	3	0	1	0	0	2
Campaneris (Athletics), ss	4	0	0	0	2	3
Jackson (Athletics), rf	3	0	0	0	3	0
Allen (White Sox), 1b	2	0	1	1	2	0
Yastrz'ski (Red Sox), 1b	1	0	0	0	5	0
Murcer (Yankees), cf	2	0	0	0	0	0
Hendrick (Indians), cf	2	0	1	0	3	0
Burroughs (Rangers), lf	0	0	0	0	1	0
Rudi (Athletics), lf	2	0	0	0	1	0
B. Robinson (Orioles), 3b	3	0	0	0	0	0
hMayberry (Royals)	1	0	0	0	0	0
Fingers (Athletics), p	0	0	0	0	0	0
Munson (Yankees), c	3	1	1	0	7	0
Perry (Indians), p	0	0	0	0	0	0
bKaline (Tigers)	1	0	0	0	0	0
Tiant (Red Sox), p	0	0	0	0	0	0
dF. Robinson (Angels)	1	0	0	0	0	0
Hunter (Athletics), p	0	0	0	0	0	0
Chalk (Angels), 3b	1	0	0	0	0	0
Totals	30	2	4	1	24	6

NATIONALS	AB.	R.	H.	RBI.	PO.	A.
Rose (Reds), lf	2	0	0	0	1	0
Brett (Pirates), p	0	0	0	0	0	0
cBrock (Cardinals)	1	1	1	0	0	0
Smith (Cardinals), rf	2	1	1	1	2	0
Morgan (Reds), 2b	2	0	1	1	3	4
gCash (Phillies), 2b	1	0	0	0	0	1
Aaron (Braves), rf	2	0	0	0	0	0
Cedeno (Astros), cf	2	0	0	0	2	0
Bench (Reds), c	3	1	2	0	7	0
Grote (Mets), c	0	0	0	0	1	0
Wynn (Dodgers), cf-rf	3	1	1	0	0	0
Matlack (Mets), p	0	0	0	0	0	0
Grubb (Padres), lf	1	0	0	0	0	0
Garvey (Dodgers), 1b	4	1	2	1	6	2
Cey (Dodgers), 3b	2	0	1	2	0	0
eSchmidt (Phillies), 3b	0	1	0	0	0	1
Bowa (Phillies), ss	2	0	0	0	2	0
fPerez (Reds)	1	0	0	0	0	0
Kessinger (Cubs), ss	1	1	1	1	1	0
Messersmith (Dodgers), p	0	0	0	0	2	1
aGarr (Braves), lf	3	0	0	0	0	0
McGlothen (Cardinals), p	0	0	0	0	0	0
Marshall (Dodgers), p	1	0	0	0	0	1
Totals	33	7	10	6	27	10

Americans	0	0	2	0	0	0	0	0	0	—2
Nationals	0	1	0	2	1	0	1	2	x	—7

Americans	IP.	H.	R.	ER.	BB.	SO.
Perry (Indians)	3	3	1	1	0	4
Tiant (Red Sox)	2	4	3	2	1	0
Hunter (Athletics)	2	2	1	1	1	3
Fingers (Athletics)	1	1	2	2	1	0

Nationals	IP.	H.	R.	ER.	BB.	SO.
Messersmith (Dodgers)	3	2	2	2	3	4
Brett (Pirates)	2	1	0	0	1	0
Matlack (Mets)	1	1	0	0	1	0
McGlothen (Cardinals)	1	0	0	0	0	1
Marshall (Dodgers)	2	0	0	0	1	2

Winning pitcher—Brett. Losing pitcher—Tiant.

aStruck out for Messersmith in third. bFouled out for Perry in fourth. cSingled for Brett in fifth. dHit into force play for Tiant in sixth. eWalked for Cey in sixth. fStruck out for Bowa in sixth. gFlied out for Morgan in seventh. hGrounded out for B. Robinson in eighth. Errors—Bench, Munson. Double plays—None. Left on bases—Americans 8, Nationals 6. Two-base hits—Cey, Munson, Morgan, Garvey. Three-base hit—Kessinger. Home run—Smith. Stolen bases—Carew, Brock. Sacrifice hit—Perry. Sacrifice fly—Morgan. Wild pitch—Fingers. Bases on balls—Off Tiant 1 (Bench), off Hunter 1 (Schmidt), off Fingers 1 (Schmidt), off Messersmith 3 (Burroughs, Carew, Jackson), off Brett 1 (Burroughs), off Matlack 1 (Munson), off Marshall 1 (Yastrzemski). Strikeouts—By Perry 4 (Rose, Morgan, Bench, Garr), by Hunter 3 (Garvey, Perez, Cedeno), by Messersmith 4 (Campaneris 2, Jackson, Allen), by McGlothen 1 (Jackson), by Marshall 2 (Rudi, Chalk). Umpires—Sudol (NL) plate, Frantz (AL) first base, Vargo (NL) second base, Anthony (AL) third base, Kibler (NL) left field, Maloney (AL) right field. Time—2:37. Attendance—50,706.

Official scorers—Joe Heiling, Houston Post; Charley Feeney, Pittsburgh Post-Gazette; Luke Quay, McKeesport Daily News.

Game of 1975
County Stadium, Milwaukee, July 15

Chicago Cub third baseman Bill Madlock's bases-loaded single in the ninth snapped a 3-3 tie and sent the National League on to a 6-3 victory over the American League in the 46th All-Star Game.

Carl Yastrzemski's three-run homer in the sixth inning had enabled the Americans to overcome an early 3-0 National lead. The Red Sox veteran's blast came off the New York Mets Tom Seaver.

Madlock and Mets pitcher Jon Matlack were voted the outstanding players of the game.

The result gave the Nationals a 27-18 margin in the series, with one game ending in a tie.

Reggie Smith opened the National League ninth with a bloop single. After Al Oliver had doubled, Larry Bowa was hit by a pitch from reliever Rich Gossage.

Madlock grounded a single past third for two runs and Pete Rose hit a sacrifice fly, scoring Bowa to complete the uprising.

National League 6, American League 3

(National League Leads Series, 27-18-1)

NATIONALS	AB.	R.	H.	RBI.	PO.	A.	AMERICANS	AB.	R.	H.	RBI.	PO.	A.
Rose (Reds), rf-lf	4	0	2	1	4	0	Bonds (Yankees), cf	3	0	0	0	0	1
Carter (Expos), lf	0	0	0	0	1	0	Scott (Brewers), 1b	2	0	0	0	5	0
Brock (Cardinals), lf	3	1	1	0	2	0	Carew (Twins), 2b	5	0	1	0	3	1
Murcer (Giants), rf	2	0	0	0	1	0	Munson (Yankees), c	2	0	1	0	1	1
Jones (Padres), p	0	0	0	0	0	1	dWashington (Ath.), cf-lf	1	0	1	0	1	0
Morgan (Reds), 2b	4	0	1	0	0	1	Jackson (Athletics), rf	3	0	1	0	2	0
Cash (Phillies), 2b	1	0	0	0	0	0	Dent (White Sox), ss	1	0	0	0	0	1
Bench (Reds), c	4	0	1	1	10	1	Rudi (Athletics), lf	3	0	1	0	5	0
Garvey (Dodgers), 1b	3	1	2	1	4	1	eHendrick (Indians), rf	1	1	1	0	0	0
iPerez (Reds), 1b	1	0	0	0	1	1	Nettles (Yankees), 3b	4	0	1	0	2	2
Wynn (Dodgers), cf	2	1	1	1	1	0	Tenace (Athletics), 1b-c	3	1	0	0	4	0
Smith (Cardinals), cf-rf	2	1	1	0	0	0	Campaneris (Ath.), ss	2	0	2	0	3	2
Cey (Dodgers), 3b	3	0	1	0	0	1	fLynn (Red Sox), cf	2	0	0	0	1	0
Seaver (Mets), p	0	0	0	0	0	0	Blue (Athletics), p	0	0	0	0	0	1
Matlack (Mets), p	0	0	0	0	0	1	aAaron (Brewers)	1	0	0	0	0	0
jOliver (Pirates), cf	1	1	1	0	0	0	Busby (Royals), p	0	0	0	0	0	0
Concepcion (Reds), ss	2	0	1	0	1	1	cHargrove (Rangers)	1	0	0	0	0	0
hLuzinski (Phillies)	1	0	0	0	0	0	Kaat (White Sox), p	0	0	0	0	0	0
Bowa (Phillies), ss	0	1	0	0	2	0	gYastrzemski (Red Sox)	1	1	1	3	0	0
Reuss (Pirates), p	1	0	0	0	0	0	Hunter (Yankees), p	0	0	0	0	0	0
bWatson (Astros)	1	0	0	0	0	0	Gossage (White Sox), p	0	0	0	0	0	0
Sutton (Dodgers), p	0	0	0	0	0	0	kMcRae (Royals)	1	0	0	0	0	0
Madlock (Cubs), 3b	2	0	1	2	0	0	Totals	36	3	10	3	27	9
Totals	37	6	13	6	27	8							

Nationals	0	2	1	0	0	0	0	0	3—6
Americans	0	0	0	0	0	3	0	0	0—3

Nationals	IP.	H.	R.	ER.	BB.	SO.	Americans	IP.	H.	R.	ER.	BB.	SO.
Reuss (Pirates)	3	3	0	0	0	2	Blue (Athletics)	2	5	2	2	0	1
Sutton (Dodgers)	2	3	0	0	0	1	Busby (Royals)	2	4	1	1	0	0
Seaver (Mets)	1	2	3	3	1	2	Kaat (White Sox)	2	0	0	0	0	0
Matlack (Mets)	2	2	0	0	0	4	Hunter (Yankees)	2*	3	2	2	0	2
Jones (Padres)	1	0	0	0	0	1	Gossage (White Sox)	1	1	1	1	0	0

*Pitched to two batters in ninth.

Winning pitcher—Matlack. Losing pitcher—Hunter.

aLined out for Blue in second. bFlied out for Reuss in fourth. cFlied out for Busby in fourth. dRan for Munson in fifth. eRan for Rudi in sixth. fFlied out for Campaneris in sixth. gHomered for Kaat in sixth. hStruck out for Concepcion in seventh. iCalled out on strikes for Garvey in eighth. jDoubled for Matlack in ninth. kGrounded out for Gossage in ninth. Errors—Concepcion, Tenace. Double plays—None. Left on bases—Nationals 6, Americans 8. Two-base hit—Oliver. Home runs—Garvey, Wynn, Yastrzemski. Stolen bases—Brock, Washington, Hendrick, Nettles. Caught stealing — Concepcion, Washington. Sacrifice fly—Rose. Hit by pitcher—By Reuss (Munson), by Gossage (Bowa). Balk—Busby. Passed ball—Bench. Bases on balls—Off Seaver 1 (Tenace). Strikeouts—By Blue 1 (Concepcion), by Hunter 2 (Luzinski, Perez), by Reuss 2 (Jackson, Bonds), by Sutton 1 (Jackson), by Seaver 2 (Nettles, Scott), by Matlack 4 (Carew, Dent, Tenace, Lynn), by Jones 1 (Scott). Umpires—Haller (AL) plate, Pelekoudas (NL) first base, Springstead (AL) second base, Froemming (NL) third base, Goetz (AL) left field, McSherry (NL) right field. Time— 2:35. Attendance—51,480.

Official scorers—Charley Feeney, Pittsburgh Post-Gazette; Jerome Holtzman, Chicago Sun-Times; Tom Briere, Minneapolis Tribune.

Game of 1976
Veterans Stadium, Philadelphia, July 13

The National League continued its mastery over the American League, thumping the junior circuit's All-Stars, 7-1, in a game witnessed by 63,974 fans—third largest crowd in All-Star Game history—and which produced gate receipts of $772,346, a record for the mid-summer classic.

The game was held in Philadelphia to help celebrate the American Bicentennial, but the only celebrating was done by the National Leaguers.

Five N. L. pitchers throttled the Americans on five hits. The lone A. L. tally came on a homer by Boston's Fred Lynn.

George Foster of Cincinnati and Cesar Cedeno of Houston hit homers for the Nationals and Foster, who drove in three runs, was voted the game's Most Valuable Player.

The victory was the Nationals' 13th out of the last 14 games played and stretched their current winning streak in All-Star competition to five. The N. L. leads the overall standings, 28-18, with one tie.

The National League stars reached Detroit rookie Mark Fidrych for two runs in the first inning and Foster put the game on ice with his two-run clout in the third.

National League 7, American League 1

(National League Leads Series, 28-18-1)

AMERICANS	AB	R	H	RBI	PO	A
LeFlore (Tigers), lf	2	0	1	0	2	0
Yastrzemski (Red Sox), lf	2	0	0	0	0	0
Carew (Twins), 1b	3	0	0	0	9	2
Brett (Royals), 3b	2	0	0	0	0	1
Money (Brewers), 3b	1	0	0	0	0	1
Munson (Yankees), c	2	0	0	0	4	0
Fisk (Red Sox), c	1	0	0	0	1	0
dChambliss (Yankees)	1	0	0	0	0	0
Lynn (Red Sox), cf	3	1	1	1	0	0
eOtis (Royals)	1	0	0	0	0	0
Harrah (Rangers), ss	2	0	0	0	0	0
Belanger (Orioles), ss	1	0	0	0	1	1
Patek (Royals), ss	0	0	0	0	0	1
Staub (Tigers), rf	2	0	2	0	1	0
Tiant (Red Sox), p	0	0	0	0	0	0
cWynegar (Twins)	0	0	0	0	0	0
Tanana (Angels), p	0	0	0	0	1	0
Grich (Orioles), 2b	2	0	0	0	1	1
Garner (Athletics), 2b	1	0	0	0	1	1
Fidrych (Tigers), p	0	0	0	0	1	0
aMcRae (Royals)	1	0	0	0	0	0
Hunter (Yankees), p	0	0	0	0	0	0
bRivers (Yankees), rf	2	0	1	0	2	0
Totals	29	1	5	1	24	8

NATIONALS	AB	R	H	RBI	PO	A
Rose (Reds), 3b	3	1	2	0	0	1
Oliver (Pirates), rf-lf	1	0	0	0	1	0
Garvey (Dodgers), 1b	3	1	1	1	6	0
Cash (Phillies), 2b	1	1	1	0	1	1
Morgan (Reds), 2b	3	1	1	0	2	3
Perez (Reds), 1b	0	0	0	0	2	0
Foster (Reds), cf-rf	3	1	1	3	0	0
Montefusco (Giants), p	0	0	0	0	0	0
Russell (Dodgers), ss	1	0	0	0	1	2
Luzinski (Phillies), lf	3	0	0	0	0	0
Griffey (Reds), rf	1	1	1	1	0	0
Bench (Reds), c	2	0	1	0	1	0
Cedeno (Astros), cf	2	1	1	2	1	0
Kingman (Mets), rf	2	0	0	0	1	0
Boone (Phillies), c	2	0	0	0	5	0
Concepcion (Reds), ss	2	0	1	0	2	3
Bowa (Phillies), ss	1	0	0	0	2	1
Rhoden (Dodgers), p	0	0	0	0	0	0
Cey (Dodgers), 3b	0	0	0	0	0	0
Jones (Padres), p	1	0	0	0	1	1
Seaver (Mets), p	1	0	0	0	0	0
Schmidt (Phillies), 3b	1	0	0	0	0	0
Forsch (Astros), p	0	0	0	0	0	0
Totals	33	7	10	7	27	12

	1	2	3	4	5	6	7	8	9		
Americans	0	0	0	1	0	0	0	0	0	—	1
Nationals	2	0	2	0	0	0	0	3	x	—	7

Americans	IP	H	R	ER	BB	SO
Fidrych (Tigers)	2	4	2	2	0	1
Hunter (Yankees)	2	2	2	2	0	3
Tiant (Red Sox)	2	1	0	0	0	0
Tanana (Angels)	2	3	3	3	1	0

Nationals	IP	H	R	ER	BB	SO
Jones (Padres)	3	2	0	0	1	1
Seaver (Mets)	2	1	1	0	1	1
Montefusco (Giants)	2	0	0	0	2	2
Rhoden (Dodgers)	1	1	0	0	0	0
Forsch (Astros)	1	0	0	0	0	1

Winning pitcher—Jones. Losing pitcher—Fidrych.

aGrounded out for Fidrych in third. bStruck out for Hunter in fifth. cWalked for Tiant in seventh. dGrounded out for Fisk in ninth. eStruck out for Lynn in ninth. Errors—None. Double plays—Morgan, Concepcion and Garvey; Morgan, Bowa and Garvey; Cash, Russell and Perez; Money, Garner and Carew. Left on bases—Americans 4, Nationals 3. Three-base hits—Garvey, Rose. Home runs—Foster, Lynn, Cedeno. Stolen bases—Carew. Passed ball—Munson. Bases on balls—Off Jones 1 (Brett), off Montefusco 2 (Carew, Wynegar), off Tanana 1 (Perez). Strikeouts—By Jones 1 (LeFlore), by Seaver 1 (Rivers), by Montefusco 2 (Lynn, Garner), by Forsch 1 (Otis), by Fidrych 1 (Jones), by Hunter 3 (Bench, Kingman, Seaver), by Tiant 1 (Cedeno). Umpires—Wendelstedt (NL) plate, Neudecker (AL) first base, Olsen (NL) second base, Denkinger (AL) third base, Davidson (NL) left field, Evans (AL) right field. Time—2:12. Attendance—63,974. Official scorers—Richard Dozer, Chicago Tribune; Ray Kelly, Philadelphia Bulletin, and Bill Liston, Boston Herald-American.

Game of 1977
Yankee Stadium, New York, July 19

Cincinnati's Joe Morgan and Greg Luzinski of Philadelphia belted home runs in the first inning as the National League struck for four runs in their 7-5 verdict over the Americans.

Los Angeles righthander Don Sutton and San Francisco reliever Gary Lavelle each allowed one hit over the first five innings. Sutton, the winning pitcher, was selected to receive the Arch Ward Trophy as MVP of the game.

Morgan became the fourth player in All-Star history to lead off with a homer. Cincinnati's George Foster doubled home Dave Parker of Pittsburgh, before Luzinski connected off Jim Palmer, capping the opening-inning outburst against the Baltimore hurler. Steve Garvey of Los Angeles added a solo homer in the third and Boston's George Scott had the only A.L. homer. The game was played before a sellout crowd of 56,683.

National League 7, American League 5

(National League Leads Series, 29-18-1)

NATIONALS	AB.	R.	H.	RBI.	PO.	A.	AMERICANS	AB.	R.	H.	RBI.	PO.	A.
Morgan (Reds), 2b	4	1	1	1	0	0	Carew (Twins), 1b	3	1	1	0	7	0
Trillo (Cubs), 2b	1	0	0	0	0	1	Scott (Red Sox), 1b	2	1	1	2	4	0
Garvey (Dodgers), 1b	3	1	1	1	1	0	Randolph (Yankees), 2b	5	0	1	1	2	6
Montanez (Braves), 1b	2	0	0	0	6	1	Brett (Royals), 3b	2	0	0	0	2	1
Parker (Pirates), rf	3	1	1	0	2	0	Campbell (Red Sox), p	0	0	0	0	0	0
Templeton (Cardinals), ss	1	1	1	0	1	2	dFairly (Blue Jays)	1	0	0	0	0	0
Foster (Reds), cf	3	1	1	1	2	0	Lyle (Yankees), p	0	0	0	0	0	0
Morales (Cubs), cf	0	1	0	0	1	0	gMunson (Yankees)	1	0	0	0	0	0
Luzinski (Phillies), lf	2	1	1	2	0	0	Yastrzemski (Red Sox), cf	2	0	0	0	0	0
Winfield (Padres), lf	2	0	2	2	1	0	Lynn (Red Sox), cf	1	1	0	0	2	0
Cey (Dodgers), 3b	2	0	0	0	0	0	Zisk (White Sox), lf	3	0	2	2	0	0
Seaver (Reds), p	0	0	0	0	0	1	Singleton (Orioles), rf	0	0	0	0	0	0
eSmith (Dodgers)	1	0	1	0	0	0	Jackson (Yankees), rf	2	0	1	0	0	0
fSchmidt (Phillies)	0	0	0	0	0	0	Rice (Red Sox), rf-lf	2	0	1	0	1	0
R. Reuschel (Cubs), p	0	0	0	0	0	0	Fisk (Red Sox), c	2	0	0	0	6	1
Stearns (Mets), c	0	0	0	0	2	0	Wynegar (Twins), c	2	1	1	0	3	0
Bench (Reds), c	2	0	0	0	4	0	Burleson (Red Sox), ss	2	0	0	0	0	0
Lavelle (Giants), p	0	0	0	0	0	0	Campaneris (Rangers), ss	1	1	0	0	0	1
cRose (Reds), 3b	2	0	0	0	0	1	Palmer (Orioles), p	0	0	0	0	0	0
Concepcion (Reds), ss	1	0	0	0	1	1	Kern (Indians), p	0	0	0	0	0	0
Valentine (Expos), rf	1	0	0	0	0	0	aJones (Mariners)	1	0	0	0	0	0
Sutton (Dodgers), p	0	0	0	0	0	1	Eckersley (Indians), p	0	0	0	0	0	1
Simmons (Cardinals), c	3	0	0	0	5	0	bHisle (Twins)	1	0	0	0	0	0
Gossage (Pirates), p	0	0	0	0	0	0	LaRoche (Angels), p	0	0	0	0	0	0
Totals	33	7	9	7	27	8	Nettles (Yankees), 3b	2	0	0	0	0	1
							Totals	35	5	8	5	27	11

Nationals	4	0	1	0	0	0	0	2	0 — 7		
Americans	0	0	0	0	0	2	1	0	2 — 5		

Nationals	IP.	H.	R.	ER.	BB.	SO.	Americans	IP.	H.	R.	ER.	BB.	SO.
Sutton (Dodgers)	3	1	0	0	1	4	Palmer (Orioles)	2*	5	5	5	1	3
Lavelle (Giants)	2	1	0	0	0	2	Kern (Indians)	1	0	0	0	0	2
Seaver (Reds)	2	4	3	2	1	2	Eckersley (Indians)	2	0	0	0	0	1
R. Reuschel (Cubs)	1	0	0	0	0	0	LaRoche (Angels)	1	1	0	0	1	0
Gossage (Pirates)	1	1	2	2	1	2	Campbell (Red Sox)	1	0	0	0	1	2
							Lyle (Yankees)	2	3	2	2	0	1

*Pitched to one batter in third.
Winning pitcher—Sutton. Losing pitcher—Palmer.

aFlied out for Kern in third. bFlied out for Eckersley in fifth. cFlied out for Lavelle in sixth. dStruck out for Campbell in seventh. eSingled for Seaver in eighth. fRan for Smith in eighth. gStruck out for Lyle in ninth. Error—Templeton. Double plays—Randolph and Scott; Montanez, Templeton and Montanez. Left on bases—Nationals 4, Americans 7. Two-base hits—Foster, Winfield, Zisk, Templeton. Home runs—Morgan, Luzinski, Garvey, Scott. Caught stealing—Concepcion. Sacrifice hit—Sutton. Wild pitches—Palmer, Lyle. Hit by pitch—By Lyle (Morales), by R. Reuschel (Singleton). Bases on balls—Off Palmer 1 (Concepcion), off LaRoche 1 (Cey), off Campbell 1 (Valentine), off Sutton 1 (Brett), off Seaver 1 (Lynn), off Gossage 1 (Campaneris). Strikeouts—By Palmer 3 (Garvey, Cey, Bench), by Kern 2 (Parker, Foster), by Eckersley 1 (Garvey), by Campbell 2 (Morgan, Montanez), by Lyle 1 (Trillo), by Sutton 4 (Randolph 2, Zisk, Fisk), by Lavelle 2 (Yastrzemski, Jackson), by Seaver 2 (Campaneris, Fairly), by Gossage 2 (Nettles, Munson). Umpires —Kunkel (A.L.) plate, Harvey (N.L.) first base, Phillips (A.L.) second base, Stello (N.L.) third base, Pulli (N.L.) left field, Brinkman (A.L.) right field. Time—2:34. Attendance—56,683. Official scorers—Earl Lawson, Cincinnati Post Times & Star; Red Foley, New York Daily News and Ken Nigro, Baltimore Morning Sun.

Game of 1978

San Diego Stadium, San Diego, July 11

For the first time in history, the Most Valuable Player of the All-Star Game was a repeat winner, as the Dodgers' Steve Garvey, who won the honor in 1974, singled home two runs to tie the game and then tripled in the eighth inning to trigger a four-run outburst which carried the National League to a 7-3 triumph over the Americans.

It was the seventh N.L. victory in a row and their 15th in the last 16 games. The Nationals lead the overall standings, 30-18, with one tie.

The A.L. bolted to a 3-0 lead thanks in large part to a record-setting pair of triples by Rod Carew of the Twins.

However, a bases-loaded walk to the Phillies' Greg Luzinski and Garvey's two-run single tied the contest in the third.

Garvey's opposite-field triple was followed by a wild pitch by losing hurler Rich Gossage. Bob Boone later stroked a two-run single and Dave Lopes plated Boone. Ace reliever Bruce Sutter of the Cubs retired five straight batters to gain the victory.

National League 7, American League 3

(National League Leads Series, 30-18-1)

AMERICANS	AB.	R.	H.	RBI.	PO.	A.
Carew (Twins), 1b	4	2	2	0	6	1
Brett (Royals), 3b	3	1	2	2	0	2
Gossage (Yankees), p	0	0	0	0	0	0
Rice (Red Sox), lf	4	0	0	0	2	0
Lemon (White Sox), lf	0	0	0	0	0	0
Zisk (Rangers), rf	2	0	1	0	0	0
Evans (Red Sox), rf	1	0	0	0	3	0
Fisk (Red Sox), c	2	0	0	1	4	0
Sundberg (Rangers), c	0	0	0	0	2	1
fThompson (Tigers)	1	0	0	0	0	0
Lynn (Red Sox), cf	4	0	1	0	3	0
Money (Brewers), 2b	2	0	0	0	1	1
White (Royals), 2b	1	0	0	0	1	2
gPorter (Royals)	1	0	0	0	0	0
Patek (Royals), ss	3	0	1	0	1	1
Palmer (Orioles), p	1	0	0	0	1	0
Keough (A's), p	0	0	0	0	0	0
bHowell (Blue Jays)	1	0	0	0	0	0
Sorensen (Brewers), p	0	0	0	0	0	1
cHisle (Brewers)	1	0	1	0	0	0
Kern (Indians), p	0	0	0	0	0	0
Guidry (Yankees), p	0	0	0	0	0	0
Nettles (Yankees), 3b	0	0	0	0	0	1
Totals	31	3	8	3	24	10

NATIONALS	AB.	R.	H.	RBI.	PO.	A.
Rose (Reds), 3b	4	0	1	0	1	0
dLopes (Dodgers), 2b	1	0	1	1	0	1
Morgan (Reds), 2b	3	1	0	0	2	1
Clark (Giants), rf	1	0	0	0	0	0
Foster (Reds), cf	2	1	0	0	2	0
Luzinski (Phillies), lf	2	0	1	1	0	0
Fingers (Padres), p	0	0	0	0	0	1
eStargell (Pirates)	1	0	0	0	0	0
Sutter (Cubs), p	0	0	0	0	0	0
Niekro (Braves), p	0	0	0	0	0	0
Garvey (Dodgers), 1b	3	1	2	2	7	1
Simmons (Cardinals), c	3	0	1	0	4	1
Concepcion (Reds), ss	0	1	0	0	2	0
Monday (Dodgers), rf	2	0	0	0	1	0
Rogers (Expos), p	0	0	0	0	0	0
Winfield (Padres), lf	2	1	1	0	1	0
Bowa (Phillies), ss	3	1	2	0	2	4
Boone (Phillies), c	1	1	1	2	3	1
Pocoroba (Braves), c	0	0	0	0	0	0
Blue (Giants), p	0	0	0	0	0	1
aSmith (Dodgers), rf	3	0	0	0	1	0
Cey (Dodgers), 3b	1	0	0	0	1	0
Totals	32	7	10	6	27	11

Americans	2	0	1	0	0	0	0	0	0 — 3
Nationals	0	0	3	0	0	0	0	4	x — 7

Americans	IP.	H.	R.	ER.	BB.	SO.
Palmer (Orioles)	2⅔	3	3	3	4	4
Keough (A's)	⅓	1	0	0	0	0
Sorensen (Brewers)	3	1	0	0	0	0
Kern (Indians)	⅔	1	0	0	1	1
Guidry (Yankees)	⅓	0	0	0	0	0
Gossage (Yankees)	1	4	4	4	1	1

Nationals	IP.	H.	R.	ER.	BB.	SO.
Blue (Giants)	3	5	3	3	1	2
Rogers (Expos)	2	2	0	0	0	2
Fingers (Padres)	2	1	0	0	0	1
Sutter (Cubs)	1⅔	0	0	0	0	2
Niekro (Braves)	⅓	0	0	0	0	0

Winning pitcher—Sutter. Losing pitcher—Gossage.

aStruck out for Blue in third. bGrounded out for Keough in fourth. cSingled for Sorensen in seventh. dRan for Rose in seventh. eFlied out for Fingers in seventh. fFlied out for Sundberg in ninth. gFouled out for White in ninth. Error—Lemon. Double play—Brett, Money and Carew. Left on bases—Americans 4, Nationals 7. Two-base hits—Brett, Rose. Three-base hits—Carew 2, Garvey. Stolen bases—Bowa, Brett. Caught stealing—Zisk, Carew, Lopes. Sacrifice flies—Fisk, Brett. Wild pitches—Rogers, Gossage. Passed ball—Sundberg. Bases on balls—Off Palmer 4 (Garvey, Morgan, Foster, Luzinski), off Kern 1 (Foster), off Gossage 1 (Concepcion), off Blue 1 (Zisk). Strikeouts—By Palmer 4 (Morgan, Foster, Simmons, Smith), by Kern 1 (Smith), by Gossage 1 (Clark), by Blue 2 (Lynn, Money), by Rogers 2 (Rice, Zisk), by Fingers 1 (Patek), by Sutter 2 (Rice, Evans). Umpires—Pryor (N.L.) plate, Chylak (A.L.) first base, Tata (N.L.) second base, Deegan (A.L.) third base, Runge (N.L.) left field, McCoy (A.L.) right field. Time—2:37. Attendance—51,549. Official scorers—Bill Liston, Boston Herald American; Phil Collier, San Diego Union; Dick Miller, Los Angeles Herald-Examiner.

Game of 1979
Kingdome, Seattle, July 17

Lee Mazzilli of the Mets produced an eighth-inning pinch-homer to tie the game and an inning later coaxed a walk with the bases loaded to give the Nationals a 7-6 victory in the majors' All-Star Game.

In addition to going 1-for-3 with an RBI, Pittsburgh's Dave Parker took MVP honors by throwing out two runners, including Brian Downing at the plate in the eighth with the score tied, 6-6.

It was the eighth National League victory in a row and the N.L.'s 16th in the last 17 games. The box score:

National League 7, American League 6
(National League Leads Series, 31-18-1)

NATIONALS	AB.	R.	H.	RBI.	PO.	A	AMERICANS	AB.	R.	H.	RBI.	PO.	A.
Lopes (Dodgers), 2b	3	0	1	0	4	1	Smalley (Twins), ss	3	0	0	0	2	2
iMorgan (Reds), 2b	1	1	0	0	1	1	Grich (Angels), 2b	1	0	0	0	2	0
Parker (Pirates), rf	3	0	1	1	0	2	Brett (Royals), 3b	3	1	0	0	1	2
Garvey (Dodgers), 1b	2	1	0	0	5	0	Nettles (Yankees), 3b	1	0	1	0	0	0
Perry (Padres), p	0	0	0	0	0	0	Baylor (Angels), lf	4	2	2	1	1	0
Sambito (Astros), p	0	0	0	0	0	0	Kern (Rangers), p	0	0	0	0	0	0
Reynolds (Astros), ss	2	0	0	0	0	1	Guidry (Yankees), p	0	0	0	0	0	0
Schmidt (Phillies), 3b	3	2	2	1	1	1	lSingleton (Orioles)	1	0	0	0	0	0
Cey (Dodgers), 3b	1	0	0	0	2	1	Rice (Red Sox), rf-lf	5	0	1	0	3	0
Parrish (Expos), 3b	0	0	0	0	0	0	Lynn (Red Sox), cf	1	1	1	2	0	0
Foster (Reds), lf	1	0	1	1	0	0	Lemon (White Sox), cf	2	1	0	0	2	0
Matthews (Braves), lf	2	0	0	0	2	0	Yastrzemski (Red Sox), 1b	3	0	2	1	5	1
jMazzilli (Mets), cf	1	1	1	2	0	0	fBurleson (Red Sox), ss	2	1	0	0	0	1
Winfield (Padres), cf-lf	5	1	1	1	3	0	Porter (Royals), c	3	0	1	0	2	0
Boone (Phillies), c	2	1	1	0	0	0	Downing (Angels), c	1	0	1	0	3	0
Carter (Expos), c	2	0	1	1	6	1	White (Royals), 2b	2	0	0	0	2	2
Bowa (Phillies), ss	2	0	0	0	1	3	gBochte (Mariners), 1b	1	0	1	1	2	0
LaCoss (Reds), p	0	0	0	0	0	0	Ryan (Angels), p	0	0	0	0	0	0
kHernandez (Cardinals)	1	0	0	0	0	0	bCooper (Brewers)	0	0	0	0	0	0
Sutter (Cubs), p	0	0	0	0	0	1	Stanley (Red Sox), p	0	0	0	0	1	0
Carlton (Phillies), p	0	0	0	0	0	0	dKemp (Tigers)	1	0	0	0	0	0
aBrock (Cardinals)	1	0	1	0	0	0	Clear (Angels), p	0	0	0	0	0	0
Andujar (Astros), p	0	0	0	0	0	0	hJackson (Yankees), rf	1	0	0	0	0	0
cClark (Giants)	1	0	0	0	0	0	Totals	35	6	10	5	27	10
Rogers (Expos), p	0	0	0	0	0	0							
eRose (Phillies), 1b	2	0	0	0	2	0							
Totals	35	7	10	7	27	12							

Nationals .... 2 1 1 0 0 1 0 1 1—7
Americans .... 3 0 2 0 0 1 0 0 0—6

Nationals	IP.	H.	R.	ER.	BB.	SO.	Americans	IP.	H.	R.	ER.	BB.	SO.
Carlton (Phillies)	1	2	3	3	1	0	Ryan (Angels)	2	5	3	3	1	2
Andujar (Astros)	2	2	2	1	1	0	Stanley (Red Sox)	2	1	1	1	0	0
Rogers (Expos)	2	0	0	0	0	2	Clear (Angels)	2	1	1	1	1	0
Perry (Padres)	0*	3	1	1	0	0	Kern (Rangers)	2⅔	2	2	2	3	3
Sambito (Astros)	⅔	0	0	0	1	0	Guidry (Yankees)	⅓	0	0	0	1	0
LaCoss (Reds)	1⅓	1	0	0	0	0							
Sutter (Cubs)	2	0	0	0	2	3							

*Pitched to three batters in sixth.

Winning pitcher—Sutter. Losing pitcher—Kern.

aSingled for Carlton in second. bWalked for Ryan in second. cGrounded out for Andujar in fourth. dLined out for Stanley in fourth. eGrounded into double play for Rogers in sixth. fRan for Yastrzemski in sixth. gSingled for White in sixth. hGrounded into force play for Clear in sixth. iStruck out for Lopes in seventh. jHomered for Matthews in eighth. kStruck out for LaCoss in eighth. lSingled for Guidry in ninth. Error—Schmidt. Double plays—Brett, White and Yastrzemski; White, Smalley and Yastrzemski. Left on bases—Nationals 8, Americans 9. Two-base hits—Foster, Baylor, Schmidt, Winfield, Porter, Rice. Three-base hit—Schmidt. Home runs—Lynn, Mazzilli. Sacrifice hit—Bochte. Sacrifice fly—Parker. Wild pitch—Andujar. Hit by pitcher—By Andujar (Lemon). Balk—Kern. Bases on balls—Off Carlton 1 (Brett), off Andujar 1 (Cooper), off Sambito 1 (Smalley), off Sutter 2 (Jackson, Lemon), off Ryan 1 (Garvey), off Clear 1 (Bowa), off Kern 3 (Morgan, Parker, Cey), off Guidry 1 (Mazzilli). Strikeouts—By Rogers 2 (Rice, Lemon), by Sutter 3 (Grich, Rice, Burleson), by Ryan 2 (Lopes, Parker), by Kern 3 (Morgan, Winfield, Hernandez). Umpires—Maloney (A.L.) plate, Weyer (N.L.) first base, Bremigan (A.L.) second base, W. Williams (N.L.) third base, Cooney (A.L.) left field, Rennert (N.L.) right field. Time—3:11. Attendance—58,905. Official scorers—Jean-Paul Sarault, Montreal Metro-Matin; Dick Dozer, Chicago Tribune; Mike Kenyon, Seattle Post-Intelligencer.

Game of 1980
Dodger Stadium, Los Angeles, July 8

American League Cy Young winner Steve Stone had become the first pitcher since Denny McLain in 1966 to toss three perfect innings, Fred Lynn had hit a two-run homer for his third career All-Star Game home run and Tommy John had continued the A. L.'s perfect game until two were out in the fifth inning when Cincinnati's Ken Griffey belted a home run. That round-tripper sparked the National League to a 4-2 victory—their ninth consecutive victory—for a 32-18-1 series advantage.

Consecutive singles by Ray Knight, Phil Garner and George Hendrick produced the first of two N. L. tallies in the sixth. Garner then scored the go-ahead run when Dave Winfield's one-hopper handcuffed second baseman Willie Randolph for an error. Dave Concepcion scored an insurance run on a wild pitch in the seventh. Griffey, the game's MVP, started the inning with a single.

Jerry Reuss of the Dodgers struck out the side in the sixth inning and was credited with the victory. His strikeouts, along with three by J.R. Richard, four by Bob Welch and one by Bruce Sutter, were one short of the record (12). The box score:

National League 4, American League 2
(National League Leads Series, 32-18-1)

AMERICANS	AB.	R.	H.	RBI.	PO.	A.
Randolph (Yankees), 2b	4	0	2	0	0	3
Stieb (Blue Jays), p	0	0	0	0	0	0
Trammell (Tigers), ss	0	0	0	0	0	0
Carew (Angels), 1b	2	1	2	0	4	0
Cooper (Brewers), 1b	1	0	0	0	6	0
Lynn (Red Sox), cf	3	1	1	2	2	0
Bumbry (Orioles), cf	1	0	0	0	2	0
Jackson (Yankees), rf	2	0	1	0	0	0
aLandreaux (Twins), rf	1	0	0	1	0	0
Oglivie (Brewers), lf	2	0	0	0	1	0
Oliver (Rangers), lf	1	0	0	0	0	0
Gossage (Yankees), p	0	0	0	0	0	0
Fisk (Red Sox), c	2	0	0	0	5	0
Porter (Royals), c	1	0	0	0	0	1
Henderson (A's), lf	1	0	0	0	0	0
Nettles (Yankees), 3b	2	0	0	0	0	1
Bell (Rangers), 3b	2	0	0	0	0	2
Dent (Yankees), ss	2	0	1	0	0	1
John (Yankees), p	1	0	0	0	0	1
Farmer (White Sox), p	0	0	0	0	0	0
Grich (Angels), 2b	0	0	0	0	0	1
Stone (Orioles), p	1	0	0	0	0	0
Yount (Brewers), ss	2	0	0	0	3	2
Parrish (Tigers), c	1	0	0	0	0	0
Totals	32	2	7	2	24	12

NATIONALS	AB.	R.	H.	RBI.	PO.	A.
Lopes (Dodgers), 2b	1	0	0	0	0	2
Garner (Pirates), 2b	2	1	1	0	1	3
Smith (Dodgers), cf	2	0	0	0	0	0
Hendrick (Cardinals), cf	2	0	1	1	0	0
Sutter (Cubs), p	0	0	0	0	0	0
Parker (Pirates), rf	2	0	0	0	0	0
Winfield (Padres), rf	2	0	0	1	2	0
Garvey (Dodgers), 1b	2	0	0	0	7	0
bHernandez (Cards), 1b	2	0	2	0	5	0
Bench (Reds), c	1	0	0	0	5	0
Stearns (Mets), c	1	0	0	0	5	0
cRose (Phillies)	1	0	0	0	0	0
Bibby (Pirates), p	0	0	0	0	0	0
Murphy (Braves), cf	1	0	0	0	0	0
Kingman (Cubs), lf	1	0	0	0	0	0
Griffey (Reds), lf	3	1	2	1	0	0
Reitz (Cardinals), 3b	2	0	0	0	1	0
Reuss (Dodgers), p	0	0	0	0	0	0
Concepcion (Reds), ss	1	1	0	0	0	2
Russell (Dodgers), ss	2	0	0	0	0	2
Carter (Expos), c	1	0	0	0	1	0
Richard (Astros), p	0	0	0	0	0	0
Welch (Dodgers), p	1	0	0	0	0	1
Knight (Reds), 3b	1	1	1	0	0	1
Totals	31	4	7	3	27	11

Americans	0	0	0	0	2	0	0	0	0 — 2
Nationals	0	0	0	0	1	2	1	0	x — 4

Americans	IP.	H.	R.	ER.	BB.	SO.
Stone (Orioles)	3	0	0	0	0	3
John (Yankees)	2⅓	4	3	3	0	1
Farmer (White Sox)	⅔	1	0	0	0	0
Stieb (Blue Jays)	1	1	1	0	2	0
Gossage (Yankees)	1	1	0	0	0	0

Nationals	IP.	H.	R.	ER.	BB.	SO.
Richard (Astros)	2	1	0	0	2	3
Welch (Dodgers)	3	5	2	2	1	4
Reuss (Dodgers)	1	0	0	0	0	3
Bibby (Pirates)	1	1	0	0	0	0
Sutter (Cubs)	2	0	0	0	1	1

Winning pitcher—Reuss. Losing pitcher—John. Save—Sutter.

aRan for Jackson in fifth. bSingled for Garvey in sixth. cGrounded into double play for Stearns in sixth. Errors—Randolph 2. Double plays—Randolph, Yount and Cooper; Concepcion, Garner and Hernandez. Left on bases—Americans 7, Nationals 5. Two-base hit—Carew. Home runs—Lynn, Griffey. Stolen bases—Carew, Knight, Garner. Caught stealing—None. Wild pitches—Welch, Stieb 2. Passed ball—Porter. Bases on balls—Off Stieb 2 (Knight, Garner), off Richard 2 (Carew, Oglivie), off Welch 1 (Jackson), off Sutter 1 (Grich). Strikeouts—By Stone 3 (Parker, Kingman, Welch), by John 1 (Garner), by Richard 3 (Jackson, Fisk, Stone), by Welch 4 (Lynn, Oglivie, Fisk, Dent), by Reuss 3 (Porter, Bell, John), by Sutter 1 (Parrish). Umpires—Kibler (NL) plate, Barnett (AL) first base, Colosi (NL) second base, McKean (AL) third base, Dale (NL) left field, Garcia (AL) right field. Time—2:33. Attendance—56,088. Official scorers—Phil Collier, San Diego Union; Ed Browalski, Polish News; Bob Hunter, Valley News.

Game of 1981
Municipal Stadium, Cleveland, August 9

After a 50-day players strike, baseball was welcomed back with the 52nd All-Star Game, before a record crowd of 72,086. Montreal's Gary Carter belted a record-tying two home runs while Philadelphia's Mike Schmidt clouted a two-run homer off Milwaukee ace reliever Rollie Fingers in the eighth inning, giving the National League a 5-4 triumph.

The smash made a winner of San Francisco lefthander Vida Blue, whose only previous All-Star decision was also the A.L.'s last victory in the 1971 All-Star Classic, when he was with Oakland. St. Louis' Bruce Sutter came on to pick up the save and run his record to two wins and two saves in the last four midsummer games. The box score:

National League 5, American League 4
(National League Leads Series, 33-18-1)

NATIONALS	AB	R	H	RBI	PO	A		AMERICANS	AB	R	H	RBI	PO	A
Rose (Phillies), 1b	3	0	1	0	5	0		Carew (Angels), 1b	3	0	1	0	12	0
Hooton (Dodgers), p	0	0	0	0	0	0		gMurray (Orioles), 1b	2	0	0	0	2	1
Ruthven (Phillies), p	0	0	0	0	0	0		Randolph (Yankees), 2b	3	0	1	0	0	5
kGuerrero (Dodgers)	1	0	0	0	0	0		hSimmons (Brewers)	1	0	1	1	0	0
Blue (Giants), p	0	0	0	0	0	0		iWhite (Royals), 2b	1	0	0	0	1	0
Madlock (Pirates), 3b	1	0	0	0	0	1		Brett (Royals), 3b	3	0	0	0	0	1
Concepcion (Reds), ss	3	0	0	0	0	0		Norris (A's), p	0	0	0	0	0	0
Smith (Padres), ss	0	0	0	0	1	0		jOliver (Rangers)	1	0	0	0	0	0
Parker (Pirates), rf	3	1	1	1	1	0		Davis (Yankees), p	0	0	0	0	0	0
Easler (Pirates), rf	1	1	0	0	0	0		Fingers (Brewers), p	0	0	0	0	1	0
Schmidt (Phillies), 3b	4	1	2	2	0	2		Stieb (Blue Jays), p	1	0	0	0	1	1
Ryan (Astros), p	0	0	0	0	0	0		Winfield (Yankees), cf	4	0	0	0	1	0
Garner (Pirates), 2b	0	0	0	0	0	0		Singleton (Orioles), lf	3	2	2	1	0	0
Foster (Reds), lf	2	0	0	0	0	0		Burleson (Angels), ss	1	0	0	0	1	3
Baker (Dodgers), lf	2	0	1	0	2	0		Jackson (Yankees), rf	1	0	0	0	0	0
lRaines (Expos), lf	0	0	0	0	1	0		cEvans (Red Sox), rf	2	1	1	0	2	0
Dawson (Expos), cf	4	0	1	0	4	0		Fisk (White Sox), c	3	1	1	0	4	0
Carter (Expos), c	3	2	2	2	5	1		Diaz (Indians), c	1	0	0	0	2	0
Benedict (Braves), c	1	0	0	0	3	0		Dent (Yankees), ss	2	0	2	0	0	2
Lopes (Dodgers), 2b	0	0	0	0	1	0		fLynn (Angels)	1	0	1	1	0	0
Trillo (Phillies), 2b	2	0	0	0	1	1		Armas (A's), lf	1	0	0	0	0	0
mBuckner (Cubs)	1	0	0	0	0	0		Morris (Tigers), p	0	0	0	0	0	0
Sutter (Cardinals), p	0	0	0	0	0	0		bPaciorek (Mariners)	1	0	1	0	0	0
Valenzuela (Dodgers), p	0	0	0	0	0	1		Barker (Indians), p	0	0	0	0	0	0
aYoungblood (Mets)	1	0	0	0	0	0		dThomas (Brewers)	1	0	0	0	0	0
Seaver (Reds), p	0	0	0	0	0	2		Forsch (Angels), p	0	0	0	0	0	0
Knepper (Astros), p	0	0	0	0	0	1		Bell (Rangers), 3b	1	0	0	1	1	2
eKennedy (Padres)	1	0	0	0	0	0								
Garvey (Dodgers), 1b	2	0	1	0	3	1		Totals	37	4	11	4	27	16
Totals	35	5	9	5	27	10								

```
Nationals ...........  0   0  0   0  1  1   1  2  0 — 5
Americans ...........  0   1  0   0  0  3   0  0  0 — 4
```

Nationals	IP	H	R	ER	BB	SO		Americans	IP	H	R	ER	BB	SO
Valenzuela (Dodgers)	1	2	0	0	0	0		Morris (Tigers)	2	2	0	0	1	2
Seaver (Reds)	1	3	1	1	0	1		Barker (Indians)	2	0	0	0	0	1
Knepper (Astros)	2	1	0	0	2	3		Forsch (Angels)	1	1	1	1	0	0
Hooton (Dodgers)	1⅔	5	3	3	0	1		Norris (A's)	1	2	1	1	0	1
Ruthven (Phillies)	⅓	0	0	0	0	0		Davis (Yankees)	1	1	1	1	0	1
Blue (Giants)	1	0	0	0	0	1		Fingers (Brewers)	⅓	2	2	2	2	0
Ryan (Astros)	1	0	0	0	0	1		Stieb (Blue Jays)	1⅔	1	0	0	1	1
Sutter (Cardinals)	1	0	0	0	0	1								

Winning pitcher—Blue. Losing pitcher—Fingers. Save—Sutter.

Game-winning RBI—Schmidt.

aFouled out for Valenzuela in second. bSingled for Morris in second. cWalked for Jackson in fourth. dPopped out for Barker in fourth. eGrounded out for Knepper in fifth. fSingled home one run for Dent in sixth. gGrounded out for Carew in sixth. hSingled home one run for Randolph in sixth. iRan for Simmons in sixth. jFlied out for Norris in sixth. kStruck out for Ruthven in seventh. lRan for Baker in eighth. mGrounded out for Trillo in ninth. Errors—Schmidt, Fingers. Double plays—None. Left on bases—Nationals 7, Americans 9. Two-base hits—Dent, Schmidt, Garvey. Home runs—Singleton, Carter 2, Parker, Schmidt. Stolen bases—Dawson, Smith. Caught stealing—Carew. Sacrifice fly—Bell. Wild pitch—Blue. Bases on balls—Off Morris 1 (Lopes), off Fingers 2 (Smith, Easler), off Stieb 1 (Smith), off Knepper 2 (Winfield, Evans). Strikeouts—By Morris 2 (Concepcion, Schmidt), by Barker 1 (Parker), by Norris 1 (Dawson), by Davis 1 (Guerrero), by Stieb 1 (Benedict), by Seaver 1 (Fisk), by Knepper 3 (Randolph, Brett, Carew), by Hooton 1 (Brett), by Blue 1 (Diaz), by Ryan 1 (Armas), by Sutter 1 (Stieb). Umpires—Haller (A.L.) plate, Vargo (N.L.) first base, DiMuro (A.L.) second base, Engel (N.L.) third base, Kosc (A.L.) left field, Quick (N.L.) right field. Time—2:59. Attendance—72,086. Official scorers—Ray Kelly Jr., Camden (N.J.) Courier Post; Dave Nightingale, The Sporting News; Hank Kozloski, Horvitz Newspapers Inc. (Lorain, O.). Players listed on rosters but not used: N.L.—Carlton; A.L.—Burns, Corbett, McGregor.

Game of 1982
Olympic Stadium, Montreal, July 13

The 53rd All-Star Game ended just like the previous 10 contests—with a National League victory. The 4-1 final score represented the National League's 11th win in a row.

The American Leaguers wasted little time getting on the scoreboard, touching Montreal ace Steve Rogers for a first-inning run on singles by Oakland's Rickey Henderson and Kansas City's George Brett, a wild pitch and a sacrifice fly by California's Reggie Jackson.

But Cincinnati shortstop Dave Concepcion gave the Nationals all the runs they needed an inning later when he drilled a pitch from Boston's Dennis Eckersley into the left-field seats, just inside the foul pole.

The All-Star Game, the first played outside the United States, was witnessed by a crowd of 59,057.

The box score:

National League 4, American League 1

(National League Leads Series, 34-18-1)

AMERICANS	AB.	R.	H.	RBI.	PO.	A.	NATIONALS	AB.	R.	H.	RBI.	PO.	A.
Henderson (A's), lf	4	1	3	0	3	0	Raines (Expos), lf	1	0	0	0	0	0
Lynn (Angels), cf	2	0	0	0	0	0	Carlton (Phillies), p	0	0	0	0	0	1
Wilson (Royals), cf	2	0	0	0	1	0	eHorner (Braves)	1	0	0	0	0	0
mHrbek (Twins)	1	0	0	0	0	0	Soto (Reds), p	0	0	0	0	0	0
Brett (Royals), 3b	2	0	2	0	0	0	jThompson (Pirates)	1	0	0	0	0	0
cBell (Rangers), 3b	3	0	0	0	0	1	Valenzuela, (Dodgers), p	0	0	0	0	0	0
Jackson (Angels), rf	1	0	0	1	3	0	Minton (Giants), p	0	0	0	0	0	0
Winfield (Yankees), rf	2	0	1	0	0	0	Howe (Dodgers), p	0	0	0	0	0	0
Cooper (Brewers), 1b	2	0	1	0	5	0	Hume (Reds), p	0	0	0	0	0	0
fMurray (Orioles), 1b	1	0	0	0	4	0	Rose (Phillies), 1b	1	0	0	1	4	0
Yount (Brewers), ss	3	0	0	0	0	2	Oliver (Expos), 1b	2	1	2	0	2	0
Grich (Angels), 2b	1	0	0	0	2	2	Dawson (Expos), cf	4	0	1	0	4	0
gYastrzemski (Red Sox)	1	0	0	0	0	0	Schmidt (Phillies), 3b	1	0	0	0	0	0
Quisenberry (Royals), p	0	0	0	0	0	0	Knight (Astros), 3b	3	0	0	0	1	4
kMcRae (Royals)	0	0	0	0	0	0	Carter (Expos), c	3	0	1	1	7	0
Fingers (Brewers), p	0	0	0	0	0	0	hPena (Pirates), c	1	0	0	0	3	0
Fisk (White Sox), c	2	0	0	0	2	0	Stearns (Mets), c	0	0	0	0	0	0
Parrish (Tigers), c	2	0	1	0	2	3	Murphy (Braves), rf	2	1	0	0	2	0
Eckersley (Red Sox), p	1	0	0	0	0	0	Concepcion (Reds), ss	3	1	1	2	1	1
bThornton (Indians)	1	0	0	0	0	0	iO. Smith (Cardinals), ss	0	0	0	0	0	1
Clancy (Blue Jays), p	0	0	0	0	0	0	Trillo (Phillies), 2b	2	0	1	0	0	1
Bannister (Mariners), p	0	0	0	0	0	0	dSax (Dodgers), 2b	1	0	1	0	2	0
White (Royals), 2b	1	0	0	0	2	1	Rogers (Expos), p	0	0	0	0	0	0
lOglivie (Brewers)	1	0	0	0	0	0	aJones (Padres)	1	1	1	0	0	0
Totals	33	1	8	1	24	9	Baker (Dodgers), lf	2	0	0	0	2	0
							L. Smith (Cardinals), lf	0	0	0	0	1	0
							Totals	29	4	8	4	27	8

Americans	1	0	0	0	0	0	0	0	0—1
Nationals	0	2	1	0	0	1	0	x—4

Americans	IP.	H.	R.	ER.	BB.	SO.	Nationals	IP.	H.	R.	ER.	BB.	SO.
Eckersley (Red Sox)	3	2	3	3	2	1	Rogers (Expos)	3	4	1	1	0	2
Clancy (Blue Jays)	1	0	0	0	0	0	Carlton (Phillies)	2	1	0	0	2	4
Bannister (Mariners)	1	1	0	0	0	0	Soto (Reds)	2	3	0	0	0	4
Quisenberry (Royals)	2	3	1	1	0	1	Valenzuela (Dodgers)	⅔	0	0	0	2	0
Fingers (Brewers)	1	2	0	0	0	0	Minton (Giants)	⅔	0	0	0	1	0
							Howe (Dodgers)	⅓	0	0	0	0	0
							Hume (Reds)	⅓	0	0	0	0	0

Winning pitcher—Rogers. Losing pitcher—Eckersley. Save—Hume.

Game-winning RBI—Concepcion.

aTripled for Rogers in third. bStruck out for Eckersley in fourth. cStruck out for Brett in fifth. dRan for Trillo in fifth. eFlied out for Carlton in fifth. fFlied out for Cooper in sixth. gStruck out for Grich in sixth. hRan for Carter in sixth. iRan for Concepcion in seventh. jGrounded out for Soto in seventh. kWalked for Quisenberry in eighth. lFlied out for White in ninth. mFlied out for Wilson in ninth. Errors—Sax, Henderson, Bell. Double play—Carlton, Concepcion and Rose. Left on bases—Americans 11, Nationals 4. Two-base hits—Oliver, Parrish. Three-base hit—Jones. Home run—Concepcion. Stolen bases—Raines, Pena, Henderson. Caught stealing—Sax, O. Smith, Oliver. Sacrifice flies—Jackson, Rose. Wild pitch—Rogers. Bases on balls—Off Carlton 2 (Yount, Grich), off Valenzuela 2 (Murray, McRae), off Minton 1 (Henderson), off Eckersley 2 (Murphy, Raines). Strikeouts—By Rogers 2 (Yount, Grich), by Carlton 4 (Cooper, Fisk, Thornton, Bell), by Soto 4 (Yastrzemski, White, Wilson, Bell), by Eckersley 1 (Raines), by Quisenberry 1 (Knight). Umpires—Harvey (N.L.) plate, Springstead (A.L.) first base, McSherry (N.L.) second base, McKeon (A.L.) third base, Montague (N.L.) left field, Reilly (A.L.) right field. Time—2:53. Attendance—59,057. Official scorers—Ian MacDonald, Montreal Gazette; Dick O'Connor, Peninsula Times Tribune (Palo Alto, Calif.); Charlie Scoggins, Lowell (Mass.) Sun. Players listed on rosters but not used: A.L.—Clear, Gossage, Guidry, Harrah; N.L.—Durham, Niekro.

Game of 1983

Comiskey Park, Chicago, July 6

On the 50th anniversary of baseball's mid-summer classic, the American League bombed the National League, 13-3, to put an end to the senior league's winning streak and recent domination of the event. The National Leaguers had won 19 of the last 20 games played, including 11 in a row.

The A.L. ran away with the game, scoring seven runs in the third inning, capped by Fred Lynn's grand slam—the first such hit in the classic's history.

American League 13, National League 3
(National League Leads Series, 34-19-1)

NATIONALS	AB.	R.	H.	RBI.	PO.	A.
Sax, (Dodgers), 2b	3	1	1	1	2	0
Hubbard, (Braves), 2b	1	0	1	0	0	0
Raines, (Expos), lf	3	0	0	0	2	0
dMadlock, (Pirates), 3b	1	0	0	0	0	0
Dawson, (Expos), cf	3	0	0	0	3	0
Dravecky, (Padres), p	0	0	0	0	0	1
Perez, (Braves), p	0	0	0	0	0	0
Orosco, (Mets), p	0	0	0	0	0	0
gBench, (Reds)	1	0	0	0	0	0
L. Smith, (Cubs), p	0	0	0	0	1	0
Oliver, (Expos), 1b	2	1	1	0	2	1
Evans, (Giants), 1b	1	0	0	0	2	1
Murphy, (Braves), rf	3	0	1	1	0	0
Guerrero, (Dodgers), 3b-lf	1	0	0	0	0	0
Schmidt, (Phillies), 3b	3	0	0	0	0	0
Benedict, (Braves), c	1	0	1	0	5	0
Carter, (Expos), c	2	0	0	0	3	0
Durham, (Cubs), rf	2	0	0	0	0	0
O. Smith, (Cardinals), ss	2	1	1	0	0	0
McGee, (Cardinals), cf	2	0	1	0	2	0
Soto, (Reds), p	1	0	0	0	2	0
Hammaker, (Giants), p	0	0	0	0	0	0
Dawley, (Astros), p	0	0	0	0	0	0
bThon, (Astros), ss	3	0	1	0	0	2
Totals	35	3	8	2	24	5

AMERICANS	AB.	R.	H.	RBI.	PO.	A.
Carew, (Angels), 1b	3	2	2	1	3	0
Murray, (Orioles), 1b	2	0	0	0	4	0
Yount, (Brewers), ss	2	1	0	1	0	1
Ripken, (Orioles), ss	0	0	0	0	1	0
Lynn, (Angels), cf	3	1	1	4	1	0
Wilson, (Royals), cf	1	0	1	1	2	0
Rice, (Red Sox), lf	4	1	2	1	1	0
Oglivie, (Brewers), rf	1	0	0	0	0	0
Young, (Mariners), p	0	0	0	0	0	0
Quisenberry, (Royals), p	0	0	0	0	0	0
Brett, (Royals), 3b	4	2	2	1	1	5
Simmons, (Brewers), c	2	0	0	0	4	0
Parrish, (Tigers), c	2	0	0	0	1	0
hCooper, (Brewers)	1	1	1	0	0	0
Boone, (Angels), c	0	0	0	0	1	0
Winfield, (Yankees), rf	3	2	3	1	3	0
Kittle, (White Sox), lf-rf	2	1	1	0	1	0
Trillo, (Indians), 2b	3	1	1	0	3	1
eWhitaker, (Tigers), 2b	1	1	1	2	1	0
Stieb, (Blue Jays), p	0	0	0	0	0	2
aDeCinces (Angels)	1	0	0	0	0	0
Honeycutt, (Rangers), p	0	0	0	0	0	0
cWard, (Twins)	1	0	0	0	0	0
Stanley, (Red Sox), p	0	0	0	0	0	1
fYastrzemski, (Red Sox)	1	0	0	0	0	0
Henderson, (A's), lf	1	0	0	1	0	0
Totals	38	13	15	13	27	10

Nationals	1	0	0	1	1	0	0	0	0	— 3
Americans	1	1	7	0	0	0	2	2	x	— 13

Nationals	IP.	H.	R.	ER.	BB.	SO.
Soto (Reds)	2	2	2	0	2	2
Hammaker (Giants)	2/3	6	7	7	1	0
Dawley (Astros)	1 1/3	1	0	0	0	1
Dravecky (Padres)	2	1	0	0	0	2
Perez (Braves)	2/3	3	2	2	1	1
Orosco (Mets)	1/3	0	0	0	0	0
L. Smith (Cubs)	1	2	2	1	0	1

Americans	IP.	H.	R.	ER.	BB.	SO.
Stieb (Blue Jays)	3	0	1	0	1	4
Honeycutt (Rangers)	2	5	2	2	0	0
Stanley (Red Sox)	2	2	0	0	0	0
Young (Mariners)	1	0	0	0	0	1
Quisenberry (Royals)	1	1	0	0	0	1

Winning pitcher—Stieb. Losing pitcher—Soto.

Game-winning RBI—Yount.

aFlied out for Stieb in third. bSingled for Dawley in fifth. cFlied out for Honeycutt in fifth. dFlied out for Raines in seventh. eTripled one run home for Trillo in seventh. fCalled out on strikes for Stanley in seventh. gPopped out for Orosco in eighth. hSingled for Parrish in eighth. Errors—Stieb, Carew, Schmidt, Sax, Guerrero. Double plays—Yount, Trillo and Carew; Brett and Trillo. Left on bases—Nationals 6, Americans 9. Two-base hits—Winfield, Oliver, Wilson, Brett. Three-base hits—Brett, Whitaker. Home runs—Rice, Lynn. Stolen bases—Sax, Raines. Caught stealing—None. Sacrifice hit—Stieb. Sacrifice flies—Brett, Yount, Whitaker. Passed ball—Benedict. Bases on balls—Off Stieb 1 (Oliver), off Soto 2 (Lynn, Carew), off Hammaker 1 (Yount), off Perez 1 (Ripken). Strikeouts—By Stieb 4 (Dawson, Murphy, Schmidt, Raines), by Young 1 (Guerrero), by Quisenberry 1 (Durham), by Soto 2 (Yount, Lynn), by Dawley 1 (Parrish), by Dravecky 2 (Lynn, Brett), by Perez 1 (Yastrzemski), by Orosco 1 (Oglivie), by L. Smith 1 (Kittle). Umpires—Maloney (A.L.) plate, Wendelstedt (N.L.) first base, Hendry (A.L.) second base, Quick (N.L.) third base, Shulock (A.L.) left field, Pallone (N.L.) right field. Time—3:05. Attendance—43,801. Official scorers—Jerome Holtzman, Chicago Tribune; Joe Giuliotti, Boston Herald-American; Randy Minkoff, United Press International (Chicago). Players listed on rosters but not used: N.L.—Hendrick, Kennedy, Lavelle, Rogers, Valenzuela; A.L.—Lopez, T. Martinez, Sutcliffe.

California's Fred Lynn triumphantly circles the bases after hitting the first grand slam in All-Star history. Lynn's 1983 blast capped a seven-run third inning and sparked the 13-3 A.L. victory that snapped the N.L.'s All-Star winning streak at 11.

Game of 1984

Candlestick Park, San Francisco, July 10

In a game featuring a nine-inning record 21 strikeouts, the National League captured the 55th All-Star classic, 3-1.

American League pitchers struck out 10 batters and were paced by Oakland's Bill Caudill, who struck out all three batters he faced. However, the dramatics were supplied by Los Angeles lefty Fernando Valenzuela and New York's Dwight Gooden, a pair of National Leaguers. Valenzuela and Gooden, who at age 19 became the youngest performer in All-Star Game history, struck out three batters each and combined to whiff six straight batters during the fourth and fifth innings. That broke the team record of five registered 50 years to the day earlier when Carl Hubbell fanned five straight A.L. sluggers. Ironically, the 81-year-old Hubbell attended the '84 contest and watched his record get shattered.

The Nationals broke out on top in the first inning. With two out, San Diego's Steve Garvey singled and went to second when the ball skipped past California right

National League 3, American League 1

(National League Leads Series, 35-19-1)

AMERICANS	AB.	R.	H.	RBI.	PO.	A.	NATIONALS	AB.	R.	H.	RBI.	PO.	A.
Whitaker (Tigers), 2b	3	0	2	0	0	5	Gwynn (Padres), lf	3	0	1	0	0	0
Garcia (Blue Jays), 2b	1	0	0	0	1	0	Raines (Expos), lf	1	0	0	0	4	0
Carew (Angels), 1b	2	0	0	0	5	0	Sandberg (Cubs), 2b	4	0	1	0	0	0
Murray (Orioles), 1b	2	0	1	0	3	0	Garvey (Padres), 1b	3	1	1	0	5	1
Ripken (Orioles), ss	3	0	0	0	0	0	K. Hernandez (Mets), 1b	1	0	0	0	1	0
Griffin (Blue Jays), ss	0	0	0	0	0	1	Murphy (Braves), cf	3	1	2	1	0	0
gMattingly (Yankees)	1	0	0	0	0	0	Schmidt (Phillies), 3b	3	0	0	0	0	4
Winfield (Yankees), lf-rf	4	0	1	0	2	1	Wallach (Expos), 3b	1	0	0	0	0	0
Re. Jackson (Angels), rf	2	0	0	0	0	0	Strawberry (Mets), rf	2	0	1	0	0	0
Henderson (A's), lf-cf	2	0	0	0	0	0	Washington (Braves), rf	2	0	1	0	1	0
Brett (Royals), 3b	3	1	1	1	3	0	Carter (Expos), c	2	1	1	1	9	0
Caudill (A's), p	0	0	0	0	0	0	J. Davis (Cubs), c	1	0	0	0	1	0
W. Hernandez (Tigers), p	0	0	0	0	0	0	Gossage (Padres), p	0	0	0	0	0	0
Parrish (Tigers), c	2	0	0	0	3	1	O. Smith (Cardinals), ss	3	0	0	0	3	0
Sundberg (Brewers), c	1	0	0	0	6	0	Lea (Expos), p	0	0	0	0	0	1
Lemon (Tigers), cf	2	0	1	0	0	0	aC. Davis (Giants)	1	0	0	0	0	0
fRice (Red Sox), lf	1	0	0	0	1	0	Valenzuela (Dodgers), p	0	0	0	0	0	0
Stieb (Blue Jays), p	0	0	0	0	0	0	cMumphrey (Astros)	1	0	0	0	0	0
bThornton (Indians)	1	0	1	0	0	0	Gooden (Mets), p	0	0	0	0	1	0
Morris (Tigers), p	0	0	0	0	0	1	eBrenly (Giants)	1	0	0	0	0	0
dA. Davis (Mariners)	1	0	0	0	0	0	Soto (Reds), p	0	0	0	0	0	0
Dotson (White Sox), p	0	0	0	0	0	0	Pena (Pirates), c	0	0	0	0	2	0
Bell (Rangers), 3b	1	0	0	0	0	1	Totals	32	3	8	2	27	6
Totals	32	1	7	1	24	10							

Americans	0	1	0	0	0	0	0	0	0 — 1
Nationals	1	0	0	0	0	0	0	1	x — 3

AMERICANS	IP.	H.	R.	ER.	BB.	SO.	NATIONALS	IP.	H.	R.	ER.	BB.	SO.
Stieb (Blue Jays)	2	3	2	1	0	2	Lea (Expos)	2	3	1	1	0	2
Morris (Tigers)	2	2	0	0	1	2	Valenzuela (Dodgers)	2	2	0	0	0	3
Dotson (White Sox)	2	2	0	0	1	2	Gooden (Mets)	2	1	0	0	0	3
Caudill (A's)	1	0	0	0	0	3	Soto (Reds)	2	0	0	0	0	1
W. Hernandez (Tigers)	1	1	1	1	1	1	Gossage (Padres)	1	1	0	0	0	2

Winning pitcher—Lea. Losing pitcher—Stieb. Save—Gossage.

Game-winning RBI—Carter.

aLined out for Lea in second. bSingled for Stieb in third. cStruck out for Valenzuela in fourth. dStruck out for Morris in fifth. eStruck out for Gooden in sixth. fStruck out for Lemon in eighth. gFlied out for Griffin in ninth. Errors—Jackson, Parrish. Double play—Garvey and Carter. Left on bases—Americans 4, Nationals 7. Two-base hits—Whitaker, Murray, Washington, Winfield. Home runs—Brett, Carter, Murphy. Stolen bases—Sandberg, Strawberry, Gwynn, O. Smith. Bases on balls—Off Morris 1 (Murphy), off Dotson 1 (Carter). Strikeouts—By Stieb 2 (Schmidt, Strawberry), by Morris 2 (Gwynn, Mumphrey), by Dotson 2 (Schmidt, Brenly), by Caudill 3 (Raines, Sandberg, K. Hernandez), by W. Hernandez 1 (Washington), by Lea 2 (Carew, Parrish), by Valenzuela 3 (Winfield, Jackson, Brett), by Gooden 3 (Parrish, Lemon, A. Davis), by Soto 1 (Rice), by Gossage 2 (Murray, Henderson). Umpires—Weyer (N.L.) plate, Clark (A.L.) first base, Rennert (N.L.) second base, Merrill (A.L.) third base, Brocklander (N.L.) left field, Roe (A.L.) right field. T—2:29. Attendance—57,756. Official scorers—Jim Henneman, Baltimore Evening Sun, Bob Stevens (retired writer from San Francisco Chronicle) and Nick Peters, Oakland Tribune. Players listed on roster but not used: A.L.—Armas, Boddicker, Engle, Niekro, Quisenberry; N.L.—Holland, Marshall, Orosco, Ramirez, Samuel, Sutter.

One of the highlights of the 1984 All-Star Game at San Francisco's Candlestick Park was the record six consecutive strikeouts posted by two N.L. pitchers. Mets' 19-year-old rookie Dwight Gooden (above) struck out the first three A.L. batters he faced to complete the string.

fielder Reggie Jackson. Atlanta's Dale Murphy followed with a single and Garvey scored when Yankee left fielder Dave Winfield's one-hop throw to the plate was bobbled by Detroit catcher Lance Parrish.

The rest of the game's scoring came on home runs. Kansas City's George Brett tied the game with a solo homer in the top of the second, but Montreal's Gary Carter, who was voted the game's MVP, put the Nationals ahead to stay with a solo homer in the bottom of the second. The final run came in the eighth on Murphy's blast.

All-Star Game Squads

When the All-Star Game first was introduced in 1933, each squad included 18 players. The size of the teams was increased to 20 the following year and then to 21 in 1936, to 23 in 1937 and to 25 in 1939. With the expansion to 24 clubs in 1969 the squad size was hiked to 28. In 1981, because of the two-month players strike, each squad was permitted 30 players.

Each club now must be represented by at least one player. This wasn't true in the early years. As a result, several teams did not have a single player on the All-Star team. In 1983, the rosters were expanded to 29 to make room for A.L. star Carl Yastrzemski and N.L. star Johnny Bench, two players who were to retire at the end of the season.

The procedure of selecting the eight starting players for each team—all but the pitchers—in a poll was begun in 1947. At first, this was done in a fan poll. However, beginning in 1958 the league's managers, coaches and players voted to choose the eight starters for each team. This continued until 1970 when the fan voting was resumed.

Following are the yearly All-Star squads, with those players who were voted to the starting team each year since 1947 being designated by a black dot before their names:

1933

AMERICAN LEAGUE—Connie Mack, Philadelphia, manager; Edward Collins, Boston, and Arthur Fletcher, New York, coaches. **Boston (1)**—Richard Ferrell, c. **Chicago (2)**—James Dykes, 3b; Aloysius Simmons, of. **Cleveland (3)**—H. Earl Averill, of; Wesley Ferrell, p; Oral Hildebrand, p. **Detroit (1)**—Charles Gehringer, 2b. **New York (6)**—W. Benjamin Chapman, of; William Dickey, c; H. Louis Gehrig, 1b; Vernon Gomez, p; Anthony Lazzeri, 2b; George Ruth, of. **Philadelphia (2)**—James Foxx, 1b; Robert Grove, p. **St. Louis (1)**—Samuel West, of. **Washington (2)**—Joseph Cronin, ss; Alvin Crowder, p.
NATIONAL LEAGUE—John McGraw, New York, manager; William McKechnie, Boston, and Max Carey, Brooklyn, coaches. **Boston (1)**—Walter Berger, of. **Brooklyn (1)**—Anthony Cuccinello, 2b. **Chicago (3)**—Elwood English, ss; Charles Hartnett, c; Lonnie Warneke, p. **Cincinnati (1)**—Charles Hafey, of. **New York (4)**—Carl Hubbell, p; Frank O'Doul, of; Harold Schumacher, p; William Terry, 1b. **Philadelphia (2)**—Richard Bartell, ss; Charles Klein, of. **Pittsburgh (2)**—Harold Traynor, 3b; Paul Waner, of. **St. Louis (4)**—Frank Frisch, 2b; William Hallahan, p; John Martin, 3b; James Wilson, c.

1934

AMERICAN LEAGUE—Joseph Cronin, Washington, manager; Walter Johnson, Cleveland, and Albertus Schacht, Washington, coaches. **Boston (1)**—Richard Ferrell, c. **Chicago (2)**—James Dykes, 3b; Aloysius Simmons, of. **Cleveland (2)**—H. Earl Averill, of; Melvin Harder, p. **Detroit (3)**—Thomas Bridges, p; Gordon Cochrane, c; Charles Gehringer, 2b. **New York (6)**—W. Benjamin Chapman, of; William Dickey, c; H. Louis Gehrig, 1b; Vernon Gomez, p; Charles Ruffing, p; George Ruth, of. **Philadelphia (2)**—James Foxx, 1b; Michael Higgins, 3b. **St. Louis (1)**—Samuel West, of. **Washington (3)**—Joseph Cronin, ss; Henry Manush, of; Jack Russell, p.
NATIONAL LEAGUE—William Terry, manager; Charles Stengel, Brooklyn and William McKechnie, Boston, coaches. **Boston (2)**—Walter Berger, of; Frederick Frankhouse, p. **Brooklyn (2)**—Alfonso Lopez, c; Van Mungo, p. **Chicago (4)**—Charles Hartnett, c; William Herman, 2b; Charles Klein, of; Lonnie Warneke, p. **Cincinnati**—None. **New York (5)**—Carl Hubbell, p; Travis Jackson, ss; Joseph Moore, of; Melvin Ott, of; William Terry, 1b. (Moore replaced by Hazen Cuyler, of, Chicago). **Philadelphia**—None. **Pittsburgh (3)**—Harold Traynor, 3b; J. Floyd Vaughan, ss; Paul Waner, of. **St. Louis (4)**—Jerome Dean, p; Frank Frisch, 2b; John Martin, 3b; Joseph Medwick, of.

1935

AMERICAN LEAGUE—Gordon Cochrane, Detroit, manager; Delmer Baker, Detroit, and Rogers Hornsby, St. Louis, coaches. **Boston (3)**—Joseph Cronin, ss; Richard Ferrell, c;Robert Grove, p. **Chicago (1)**—Aloysius Simmons, of. **Cleveland (3)**—H. Earl Averill, of; Melvin Harder, p; Joseph Vosmik, of (Averill replaced by Roger Cramer, of, Philadelphia). **Detroit (4)**—Thomas Bridges, p; Gordon Cochrane, c; Charles Gehringer, 2b; Lynwood Rowe, p. **New York (3)**—W. Benjamin Chapman, of; H. Louis Gehrig, 1b; Vernon Gomez, p. **Philadelphia (2)**—James Foxx, 1b; Robert Johnson, of. **St. Louis (2)**— Ralston Hemsley, c; Samuel West, of. **Washington (2)**—Oswald Bluege, 3b; Charles Myer, 2b.
NATIONAL LEAGUE—Frank Frisch, St. Louis, manager; Charles Grimm, Chicago, and Charles Dressen, Cincinnati, coaches. **Boston (1)**—Walter Berger, of. **Brooklyn**—None. **Chicago (2)**—Charles Hartnett, c; William Herman, 2b. **Cincinnati (1)**—Paul Derringer, p. **New York (6)**—Carl Hubbell, p; August Mancuso, c; Joseph Moore, of; Melvin Ott, of; Harold Schumacher, p; William Terry, 1b. **Philadelphia (1)**—James Wilson, c. **Pittsburgh (2)**—J. Floyd Vaughan, ss; Paul Waner, of. **St. Louis (7)**—James Collins, 1b; Jerome Dean, p; Frank Frisch, 2b; John Martin, 3b; Joseph Medwick, of; William Walker, p; Burgess Whitehead, 2b.

1936

AMERICAN LEAGUE—Joseph McCarthy, New York, manager; Joseph Cronin, Boston, and Arthur Fletcher, New York, coaches. **Boston (3)**—Richard Ferrell, c; James Foxx, 3b; Robert Grove, p. **Chicago (2)**—Lucius Appling, ss; Raymond Radcliff, of. **Cleveland (2)**—H. Earl Averill, of; Melvin Harder, p. **Detroit (4)**—Thomas Bridges, p; Charles Gehringer, 2b; Leon Goslin, of; Lynwood Rowe, p (Bridges replaced by L. Vernon Kennedy, p, Chicago). **New York (7)**—Frank Crosetti, ss; William Dickey, c; Joseph DiMaggio, of; H. Louis Gehrig, 1b; Vernon Gomez, p; M. Monte Pearson, p; George Selkirk, of. **Philadelphia (1)**—Michael Higgins, 3b. **St. Louis (1)**—Ralston Hemsley, c. **Washington (1)**—W. Benjamin Chapman, of.

NATIONAL LEAGUE—Charles Grimm, Chicago, manager; Harold Traynor, Pittsburgh, and William McKechnie, Boston, coaches. **Boston (1)**—Walter Berger, of. **Brooklyn (1)**—Van Mungo, p. **Chicago (6)**—Curtis Davis, p; J. Frank Demaree, of; August Galan, of; Charles Hartnett, c; William Herman, 2b; Lonnie Warneke, p. **Cincinnati (2)**—Ernest Lombardi, c; Lewis Riggs, 3b. **New York (3)**—Carl Hubbell, p; Joseph Moore, of; Melvin Ott, of. **Philadelphia (1)**—Arthur Whitney, 3b. **Pittsburgh (2)**—August Suhr, 1b; J. Floyd Vaughan, ss. **St. Louis (5)**—James Collins, 1b; Jerome Dean, p; Leo Durocher, ss; Stuart Martin, 2b; Joseph Medwick, of.

1937

AMERICAN LEAGUE—Joseph McCarthy, New York, manager; Delmar Baker, Detroit, and Arthur Fletcher, New York, coaches. **Boston (4)**—Roger Cramer, of; Joseph Cronin, ss; James Foxx, 1b; Robert Grove, p. **Chicago (2)**—J. Luther Sewell, c; Monty Stratton, p (Stratton replaced by John Murphy, p, New York). **Cleveland (2)**—H. Earl Averill, of; Melvin Harder, p. **Detroit (4)**—Thomas Bridges, p; Charles Gehringer, 2b; Henry Greenberg, 1b; Gerald Walker, of (Walker replaced by Samuel West, of, St. Louis). **New York (5)**—William Dickey, c; Joseph DiMaggio, of; H. Louis Gehrig, 1b; Vernon Gomez, p; Robert Rolfe, 3b. **Philadelphia (1)**—Wallace Moses, of. **St. Louis (2)**— Roy Bell, of; Harlond Clift, 3b. **Washington (3)**—Richard Ferrell, c; Wesley Ferrell, p; Charles Myer, 2b.

NATIONAL LEAGUE—William Terry, New York, manager; Charles Dressen, Cincinnati; Frank Frisch, St. Louis, and Jesse Haines, St. Louis, coaches. **Boston (1)**—Eugene Moore, of. **Brooklyn (1)**—Van Mungo, p. **Chicago (5)**—James Collins, 1b; J. Frank Demaree, of; Charles Hartnett, c; William Herman, 2b; William Jurges, ss. **Cincinnati (2)**—Lee Grissom, p; Ernesto Lombardi, c. **New York (6)**—Richard Bartell, ss; Carl Hubbell, p; August Mancuso, c; Joseph Moore, of; Melvin Ott, of; Burgess Whitehead, 2b. **Philadelphia (1)**—William Walters, p. **Pittsburgh (3)**—Darrell Blanton, p; J. Floyd Vaughan, 3b; Paul Waner, of. **St. Louis (4)**—Jerome Dean, p; John Martin, of; Joseph Medwick, of; John Mize, 1b

1938

AMERICAN LEAGUE—Joseph McCarthy, New York, manager; Delmer Baker, Detroit, and Arthur Fletcher, New York, coaches. **Boston (4)**—Roger Cramer, of; Joseph Cronin, ss; James Foxx, 1b-3b; Robert Grove, p. **Chicago (1)**—Michael Kreevich, of. **Cleveland (3)**—John Allen, p; Robert Feller, p; H. Earl Averill, of. **Detroit (4)**—Charles Gehringer, 2b; Henry Greenberg, 1b; L. Vernon Kennedy, p; Rudolph York, c (Greenberg replaced by John Murphy, p, New York). **New York (6)**—William Dickey, c; Joseph DiMaggio, of; H. Louis Gehrig, 1b; Vernon Gomez, p; Robert Rolfe, 3b; Charles Ruffing, p. **Philadelphia (1)**—Robert Johnson, of. **St. Louis (1)**—Louis Newsom, p. **Washington (3)**—Richard Ferrell, c; John Lewis, 3b; Cecil Travis, ss.

NATIONAL LEAGUE—William Terry, New York, manager; William McKechnie, Cincinnati, and Frank Frisch, St. Louis, coaches. **Boston (2)**—Anthony Cuccinello, 2b; James Turner, p. **Brooklyn (3)**—Leo Durocher, ss; Harry Lavagetto, 3b; E. Gordon Phelps, c (Phelps replaced by Harry Danning, c, New York). **Chicago (4)**—Stanley Hack, 3b; Charles Hartnett, c; William Herman, 2b; William Lee, p. **Cincinnati (5)**—Paul Derringer, p; Ival Goodman, of; Ernesto Lombardi, c; Frank McCormick, 1b; John Vander Meer, p. **New York (4)**—Carl Hubbell, p; Henry Leiber, of; Joseph Moore, of; Melvin Ott, of. **Philadelphia (1)**—Hershel Martin, of. **Pittsburgh (3)**—Mace Brown, p; J. Floyd Vaughan, ss; Lloyd Waner, of. **St. Louis (1)**—Joseph Medwick, of.

1939

AMERICAN LEAGUE—Joseph McCarthy, New York, manager; Arthur Fletcher, New York, and Russell Blackburne, Philadelphia, coaches. **Boston (4)**—Roger Cramer, of; Joseph Cronin, ss; James Foxx, 1b; Robert Grove, p. **Chicago (2)**—Lucius Appling, ss; Theodore Lyons, p. **Cleveland (2)**—Robert Feller, p; Ralston Hemsley, c. **Detroit (3)**—Thomas Bridges, p; Henry Greenberg, 1b; Louis Newsom, p. **New York (9)**— Frank Crosetti, ss; William Dickey, c; Joseph DiMaggio, of; Vernon Gomez, p; Joseph Gordon, 2b; John Murphy, p; Robert Rolfe, 3b; Charles Ruffing, p; George Selkirk, of. **Philadelphia (2)**—Frank Hayes, c; Robert Johnson, of. **St. Louis (2)**—Myril Hoag, of; George McQuinn, 1b. **Washington (1)**—George Case, of. (NOTE—H. Louis Gehrig, 1b, New York, who retired as an active player in May because of illness, was named an honorary member of squad.)

NATIONAL LEAGUE—Charles Hartnett, Chicago, manager; Jonn Corriden, Chicago, and William Terry, New York, coaches. **Boston (1)**—Louis Fette, p. **Brooklyn (4)**—Adolph Camilli, 1b; Harry Lavagetto, 3b; Ernest Phelps, c; Whitlow Wyatt, p. **Chicago (3)**—Stanley Hack, 3b; William Herman, 2b; William Lee, p. **Cincinnati (7)**—Paul Derringer, p; Linus Frey, 2b; Ival Goodman, of; Ernesto Lombardi, c; Frank McCormick, 1b; John Vander Meer, p; William Walters, p. **New York (3)**—Harry Danning, c; William Jurges, ss; Melvin Ott, of. **Philadelphia (1)**—Morris Arnovich, of. **Pittsburgh (1)**—J. Floyd Vaughan, ss. **St. Louis (5)**—Curtis Davis, p; Joseph Medwick, of; John Mize, 1b; Terry Moore, of; Lonnie Warneke, p.

1940

AMERICAN LEAGUE—Joseph Cronin, Boston, manager; Thomas Daly, Boston, and Delmer Baker, Detroit, coaches. **Boston (4)**—Roger Cramer, of; Louis Finney, of; James Foxx, 1b; Theodore Williams, of. **Chicago (1)**—Lucius Appling, ss. **Cleveland (6)**—Louis Boudreau, ss; Robert Feller, p; Ralston Hemsley, c; Kenneth Keltner, 3b; Raymond Mack, 2b; Albert Milnar, p. **Detroit (3)**—Thomas Bridges, p; Henry Greenberg, of; Louis Newsom, p. **New York (7)**—William Dickey, c; Joseph DiMaggio, of; Joseph Gordon, 2b; Charles Keller, of; M. Monte Pearson, p; Robert Rolfe, 3b; Charles Ruffing, p (Rolfe replaced by Cecil Travis, 3b, Washington). **Philadelphia (2)**—Frank Hayes, c; Robert Johnson, of. **St. Louis (1)**—George McQuinn, 1b. **Washington (1)**—Emil Leonard, p.

NATIONAL LEAGUE—William McKechnie, Cincinnati, manager; Charles Stengel, Boston, and James Prothro, Philadelphia, coaches. **Boston (1)**—Max West, of. **Brooklyn (6)**—Peter Coscarart, 2b; Leo Durocher, ss; Harry Lavagetto, 3b; Joseph Medwick, of; Ernest Phelps, c; Whitlow Wyatt, p. **Chicago (3)**—Lawrence French, p; William Herman, 2b; Henry Leiber, of (Leiber replaced by William Nicholson, of, Chicago). **Cincinnati (4)**—Paul Derringer, p; Ernesto Lombardi, c; Frank McCormick, 1b; William Walters, p. **New York (5)**—Harry Danning, c; Carl Hubbell, p; William Jurges, ss; Joseph Moore, of; Melvin Ott, of (Jurges replaced by Edward Miller, ss, Boston). **Philadelphia (3)**—W. Kirby Higbe, p; Merrill May. 3b; Hugh Mulcahy, p. **Pittsburgh (1)**—J. Floyd Vaughan, ss. **St. Louis (2)**—John Mize, 1b; Terry Moore, of.

1941

AMERICAN LEAGUE—Delmer Baker, Detroit, manager; Mervyn Shea, Detroit, and Arthur Fletcher, New York, coaches. **Boston (5)**—Joseph Cronin, ss; Dominic DiMaggio, of; Robert Doerr, 2b; James Foxx, 1b; Theodore Williams, of. **Chicago (3)**—Lucius Appling, ss; Thornton Lee, p; Edgar Smith, p. **Cleveland (4)**—Louis Boudreau, ss; Robert Feller, p; J. Geoffrey Heath, of; Kenneth Keltner, 3b. **Detroit (3)**—J. Alton Benton, p; George Tebbetts, c; Rudolph York, 1b. **New York (6)**—William Dickey, c; Joseph DiMaggio, of; Joseph Gordon, 2b; Charles Keller, of; Charles Ruffing, p; Marius Russo, p. **Philadelphia (1)**—Frank Hayes, c. **St. Louis (1)**—Roy Cullenbine, of. **Washington (2)**—Sidney Hudson, p; Cecil Travis, 3b.

NATIONAL LEAGUE—William McKechnie, Cincinnati, manager; Leo Durocher, Brooklyn, and James Wilson, Chicago, coaches. **Boston (1)**—Edward Miller, ss. **Brooklyn (6)**—Adolph Camilli, 1b; William Herman, 2b; Harry Lavagetto, 3b; Arnold Owen, c; Harold Reiser, of; Whitlow Wyatt, p. (Camilli replaced by Frank McCormick, 1b, Cincinnati). **Chicago (4)**—Stanley Hack, 3b; Henry Leiber, of; William Nicholson, of; Claude Passeau, p. (Leiber replaced by Joseph Medwick, of, Brooklyn). **Cincinnati (3)**—Paul Derringer, p; Linus Frey, 2b; William Walters, p. **New York (3)**—Harry Danning, c; Carl Hubbell, p; Melvin Ott, of. **Philadelphia (1)**—Darrell Blanton, p. **Pittsburgh (3)**—Robert Elliott, of; Alfonso Lopez, c; J. Floyd Vaughan, ss. **St. Louis (4)**—John Mize, 1b; Terry Moore, of; Enos Slaughter, of; Lonnie Warneke, p.

1942

AMERICAN LEAGUE—Joseph McCarthy, New York, manager; Arthur Fletcher, New York, and Stanley Harris, Washington, coaches. **Boston (4)**—Dominic DiMaggio, of; Robert Doerr, 2b; Cecil Hughson, p; Theodore Williams, of. **Chicago (1)**—Edgar Smith, p. **Cleveland (3)**—James Bagby, p; Louis Boudreau, ss; Kenneth Keltner, 3b. **Detroit (4)**—J. Alton Benton, p; Harold Newhouser, p; George Tebbetts, c; Rudolph York, 1b. **New York (9)**—Ernest Bonham, p; Spurgeon Chandler, p; William Dickey, c; Joseph DiMaggio, of; Joseph Gordon, 2b; Thomas Henrich, of; Philip Rizzuto, ss; Warren Rosar, c; Charles Ruffing, p. (Dickey replaced by Harold Wagner, c, Philadelphia). **Philadelphia (1)**—Robert Johnson, of. **St. Louis (1)**—George McQuinn, 1b. **Washington (2)**—Sidney Hudson, p; Stanley Spence, of.

NATIONAL LEAGUE—Leo Durocher, Brooklyn, manager; William McKechnie, Cincinnati, and Frank Frisch, Pittsburgh, coaches. **Boston (2)**—Ernesto Lombardi, c; Edward Miller, ss. **Brooklyn (7)**—William Herman, 2b; Joseph Medwick, of; Arnold Owen, c; Harold Reese, ss; Harold Reiser, of; J. Floyd Vaughan, 3b; Whitlow Wyatt, p. **Chicago (1)**—Claude Passeau, p. **Cincinnati (4)**—Paul Derringer, p; Frank McCormick, 1b; John Vander Meer, p; William Walters, p. (Derringer replaced by Raymond Starr, p, Cincinnati). **New York (5)**—Carl Hubbell, p; Willard Marshall, of; Clifford Melton, p; John Mize, 1b; Melvin Ott, of. **Philadelphia (1)**—Daniel Litwhiler, of. **Pittsburgh (1)**—Robert Elliott, 3b. **St. Louis (5)**—James Brown, 2b; Morton Cooper, p; W. Walker Cooper, c; Terry Moore, of; Enos Slaughter, of.

1943

AMERICAN LEAGUE—Joseph McCarthy, New York, manager; Arthur Fletcher, New York, and Russell Blackburne, Philadelphia, coaches. **Boston (3)**—Robert Doerr, 2b; Cecil Hughson, p; Oscar Judd, p. **Chicago (1)**—Lucius Appling, ss. **Cleveland (6)**—James Bagby, p; Louis Boudreau, ss; J. Geoffrey Heath, of; Kenneth Keltner, 3b; Warren Rosar, c; Alfred Smith, p. **Detroit (2)**—Harold Newhouser, p; Rudolph York, 1b. **New York (6)**—Ernest Bonham, p; Spurgeon Chandler, p; William Dickey, c; Joseph Gordon, 2b; Charles Keller, of; John Lindell, of. (Keller replaced by Richard Wakefield, of, Detroit.) **Philadelphia (1)**—Richard Siebert, 1b. **St. Louis (2)**—Chester Laabs, of; Vernon Stephens, ss. **Washington (4)**—George Case, of; Jacob Early, c; Robert Johnson, of; Emil Leonard, p.

NATIONAL LEAGUE—William Southworth, St. Louis, manager; Frank Frisch, Pittsburgh, and Miguel Gonzalez, St. Louis, coaches. **Boston (1)**—Alva Javery, p. **Brooklyn (4)**—August Galan, of; William Herman, 2b; Arnold Owen, c; Fred Walker, of. **Chicago (3)**—Stanley Hack, 3b; William Nicholson, of; Claude Passeau, p. **Cincinnati (4)**—Linus Frey, 2b; Frank McCormick, 1b; Edward Miller, ss; John Vander Meer, p. (McCormick replaced by Elburt Fletcher, 1b, Pittsburgh). **New York (2)**—Ernesto Lombardi, c; Melvin Ott, of. **Philadelphia (1)**—Ellsworth Dahlgren, 1b. **Pittsburgh (2)**—Vincent DiMaggio, of; Truett Sewell, p. **St. Louis (8)**—Morton Cooper, p; W. Walker Cooper, c; George Kurowski, 3b; H. Max Lanier, p; Martin Marion, ss; Stanley Musial, of; Howard Pollet, p; Harry Walker, of. (Pollet replaced by Ace Adams, p, New York).

1944

AMERICAN LEAGUE—Joseph McCarthy, New York, manager; Joseph Cronin, Boston, and Arthur Fletcher, New York, coaches. **Boston (3)**—Robert Doerr, 2b; Cecil Hughson, p; Robert Johnson, of. **Chicago (2)**—L. Orval Grove, p; Thurman Tucker, of. **Cleveland (4)**—Louis Boudreau, ss; Roy Cullenbine, of; Oris Hockett, of; Kenneth Keltner, 3b. **Detroit (4)**—Michael Higgins, 3b; Harold Newhouser, p;

Paul Trout, p; Rudolph York, 1b. **New York (3)**—Henry Borowy, p; Ralston Hemsley, c; Joseph Page, p. **Philadelphia (2)**—Frank Hayes, c; Louis Newsom, p. **St. Louis (3)**—George McQuinn, 1b; Robert Muncrief, p; Vernon Stephens, ss. **Washington (4)**—George Case, of; Richard Ferrell, c; Emil Leonard, p; Stanley Spence, of. (Case replaced by Ervin Fox, of, Boston).

NATIONAL LEAGUE—William Southworth, St. Louis, manager; Fred Fitzsimmons, Philadelphia; John Wagner, Pittsburgh, and Miguel Gonzalez, St. Louis, coaches. **Boston (3)**—Nathan Andrews, of; Alva Javery, p; Cornelius Ryan, 2b. **Brooklyn (3)**—August Galan, of; Arnold Owen, c; Fred Walker, of. **Chicago (3)**—Philip Cavarretta, 1b; Donald Johnson, 2b; William Nicholson, of. **Cincinnati (4)**—Frank McCormick, 1b; Edward Miller, ss; Raymond Mueller, c; William Walters, p. (Miller replaced by Frank Zak, ss, Pittsburgh). **New York (2)**—Joseph Medwick, of; Melvin Ott, of. **Philadelphia (1)**—Kenneth Raffensberger, p. **Pittsburgh (3)**—Vincent DiMaggio, of; Robert Elliott, 3b; Truett Sewell, p. **St. Louis (6)**—W. Walker Cooper, c; George Kurowski, 3b; H. Max Lanier, p; Martin Marion, ss; George Munger, p; Stanley Musial, of, (Lanier and Munger replaced by James Tobin, p, Boston, and William Voiselle, p, New York).

1945—No Game

1946

AMERICAN LEAGUE—Stephen O'Neill, Detroit manager; Arthur Mills, Detroit, and J. Luther Sewell, St. Louis, coaches. **Boston (8)**—Dominic DiMaggio, of; Robert Doerr, 2b; David Ferriss, p; Maurice Harris, p; John Pesky, ss; Harold Wagner, c; Theodore Williams, of; Rudolph York, 1b. **Chicago (1)**—Lucius Appling, ss. **Cleveland (3)**—Robert Feller, p; Frank Hayes, c; Kenneth Keltner, 3b. **Detroit (1)**—Harold Newhouser, p. **New York (6)**—Spurgeon Chandler, p; William Dickey, c; Joseph DiMaggio, of; Joseph Gordon, 2b; Charles Keller, of; George Stirnweiss, 3b. **Philadelphia (2)**—Samuel Chapman, of; Warren Rosar, c. **St. Louis (2)**—John Kramer, p; Vernon Stephens, ss. **Washington (2)**—Stanley Spence, of; James Vernon, 1b.

NATIONAL LEAGUE—Charles Grimm, Chicago, manager; William Southworth, Boston, and William McKechnie, Cincinnati, coaches. **Boston (3)**—Morton Cooper, p; John Hopp, of; Philip Masi, c. **Brooklyn (4)**—W. Kirby Higbe, p; Harold Reese, ss; Harold Reiser, of; Fred Walker, of. (Reese replaced by Frank McCormick, 1b, Philadelphia). **Chicago (4)**—Philip Cavarretta, of; Harry Lowrey, of; Claude Passeau, p; John Schmitz, p. **Cincinnati (3)**—Ewell Blackwell, p; Raymond Lamanno, c; Edward Miller, ss. (Miller replaced by Emil Verban, 2b, Philadelphia). **New York (2)**—W. Walker Cooper, c; John Mize, 1b. **Philadelphia (1)**—Delmer Ennis, of. **Pittsburgh (2)**—Frank Gustine, 2b; Truett Sewell, p. **St. Louis (6)**—George Kurowski, 3b; Martin Marion, ss; Stanley Musial, of; Howard Pollet, p; Albert Schoendienst, 2b; Enos Slaughter, of

1947

AMERICAN LEAGUE—Joseph Cronin, Boston, manager; Delmer Baker, Boston, and Stephen O'Neill, Detroit, coaches. **Boston (2)**—Robert Doerr, 2b; ●Theodore Williams, of. **Chicago (2)**—Lucius Appling, ss; Rudolph York, 1b. **Cleveland (4)**—●Louis Boudreau, ss; ●Joseph Gordon, 2b; Robert Feller, p; James Hegan, c. (Feller replaced by Early Wynn, p, Washington). **Detroit (4)**—●George Kell, 3b; Patrick Mullin, of; Harold Newhouser, p; Paul Trout, p. **New York (8)**—Spurgeon Chandler, p; ●Joseph DiMaggio, of; Charles Keller, of; William Johnson, 3b; ●George McQuinn, 1b; Joseph Page, p; Aaron Robinson, c; Francis Shea, p. (Keller replaced by Thomas Henrich, of, New York). **Philadelphia (1)**—Warren Rosar, c. **St. Louis (1)**—John Kramer, p. **Washington (3)**—●John Lewis, of; Walter Masterson, p; Stanley Spence, of.

NATIONAL LEAGUE—Edwin Dyer, St. Louis, manager; Melvin Ott, New York, and W. Benjamin Chapman, Philadelphia, coaches. **Boston (4)**—●Robert Elliott, 3b; Philip Masi, c; John Sain, p; Warren Spahn, p. (Elliott replaced by George Kurowski, 3b, St. Louis). **Brooklyn (4)**—Ralph Branca, p; C. Bruce Edwards, c; Edward Stanky, 2b; ●Fred Walker, of. **Chicago (2)**—Philip Cavarretta, of; Andrew Pafko, of. **Cincinnati (3)**—Ewell Blackwell, p; Berthold Haas, of; ●Edward Miller, ss (Miller replaced by Harold Reese, ss, Brooklyn). **New York (3)**—●W. Walker Cooper, c; Willard Marshall, of; ●John Mize, 1b. **Philadelphia (3)**—Lynwood Rowe, p; ●Emil Verban, 2b; ●Harry Walker, of. **Pittsburgh (1)**—Frank Gustine, 3b. **St. Louis (5)**—Harry Brecheen, p; Martin Marion, ss; George Munger, p; Stanley Musial, 1b; ●Enos Slaughter, of.

1948

AMERICAN LEAGUE—Stanley Harris, New York manager; John Corriden, New York, and Charles Dressen, New York, coaches. **Boston (4)**—Robert Doerr, 2b; Vernon Stephens, ss; George Tebbetts, c; ●Theodore Williams, of. **Chicago (1)**—Joseph Haynes, p. **Cleveland (5)**—●Louis Boudreau, ss; Robert Feller, p; ●Joseph Gordon, 2b; Kenneth Keltner, 3b; Robert Lemon, p. (Feller replaced by Joseph Dobson, p, Boston). **Detroit (4)**—Walter Evers, of; ●George Kell, 3b; ●Patrick Mullin, of; Harold Newhouser, p. **New York (6)**—Lawrence Berra, c; ●Joseph DiMaggio, of; Thomas Henrich, of; ●George McQuinn, 1b; Joseph Page, p; Victor Raschi, p. **Philadelphia (2)**—Joseph Coleman, p; ●Warren Rosar, c. **St. Louis (1)**—Allen Zarilla, of. **Washington (2)**—Walter Masterson, p; James Vernon, 1b.

NATIONAL LEAGUE—Leo Durocher, Brooklyn, manager; Melvin Ott, New York, and Edwin Dyer, St. Louis, coaches. **Boston (5)**—Robert Elliott, 3b; Thomas Holmes, of; Philip Masi, c; John Sain, p; ●Edward Stanky, 2b. (Stanky replaced by William Rigney, 2b, New York). **Brooklyn (2)**—Ralph Branca, p; ●Harold Reese, ss. **Chicago (4)**—Clyde McCullough, c; ●Andrew Pafko, 3b; John Schmitz, p; Edward Waitkus, 1b. **Cincinnati (3)**—Ewell Blackwell, p. **New York (4)**—●W. Walker Cooper, c; Sidney Gordon, 3b; ●John Mize, 1b; Robert Thomson, of. **Philadelphia (1)**—●Richie Ashburn, of. **Pittsburgh (3)**—Frank Gustine, 3b; Ralph Kiner, of; Elmer Riddle, p. **St. Louis (5)**—Harry Brecheen, p; Martin Marion, ss; ●Stanley Musial, of; Albert Schoendienst, 2b; ●Enos Slaughter, of. (Marion replaced by John Kerr, ss, New York).

1949

AMERICAN LEAGUE—Louis Boudreau, Cleveland, manager; William McKechnie, Cleveland, and Herold Ruel, Cleveland, coaches. **Boston (6)**—●Dominic DiMaggio, of; William Goodman, 1b; Melvin Parnell, p; Vernon Stephens, ss; ●George Tebbetts, c; ●Theodore Williams, of. **Chicago (1)**—●Casimer Michaels, 2b. **Cleveland (5)**—Lawrence Doby, of; Joseph Gordon, 2b; James Hegan, c; Robert Lemon, p; L. Dale Mitchell, of. **Detroit (3)**—●George Kell, 3b; Virgil Trucks, p; Victor Wertz, of. **New York (5)**—Lawrence Berra, c; Joseph DiMaggio, of; ●Thomas Henrich, of; Victor Raschi, p; Allie Reynolds, p. **Philadelphia (3)**—Leland Brissie, p. ●Edwin Joost, ss; Alexander Kellner, p. **St. Louis (1)**—Robert Dillinger, 3b. **Washington (1)**—●W. Edward Robinson, 1b.

NATIONAL LEAGUE—William Southworth, Boston, manager; Burton Shotton, Brooklyn, and William Walters, Cincinnati, coaches. **Boston (2)**—Vernon Bickford, p; Warren Spahn, p. **Brooklyn (7)**—Ralph Branca, p; Roy Campanella, c; Gilbert Hodges, 1b; Donald Newcombe, p; ●Harold Reese, ss; ●Jack Robinson, 2b; Elwin Roe, p. **Chicago (1)**—Andrew Pafko, of. **Cincinnati (2)**—Ewell Blackwell, p; W. Walker Cooper, c. **New York (4)**—Sidney Gordon, 3b; ●Willard Marshall, of; ●John Mize, 1b; Robert Thomson, of. **Philadelphia (1)**—●Andrew Seminick, c. **Pittsburgh (1)**—●Ralph Kiner, of. **St. Louis (7)**—●Edward Kazak, 3b; Martin Marion, ss; George Munger, p; ●Stanley Musial, of; Howard Pollet, p; Albert Schoendienst, 2b; Enos Slaughter, of. (NOTE—Edward Waitkus, 1b, Philadelphia, sidelined by gunshot wound, was named honorary member of squad).

1950

AMERICAN LEAGUE—Charles Stengel, New York, manager; Frank Crosetti, New York, and William Dickey, New York, coaches. **Boston (5)**—Dominic DiMaggio, of; ●Robert Doerr, 2b; ●Walter Dropo, 1b; Vernon Stephens, ss; ●Theodore Williams, of. **Chicago (1)**—Ray Scarborough, p. **Cleveland (4)**—●Lawrence Doby, of; Robert Feller, p; James Hegan, c; Robert Lemon, p. **Detroit (4)**—●Walter Evers, of; Theodore Gray, p; Arthur Houtteman, p; ●George Kell, 3b. **New York (8)**—●Lawrence Berra, c; Thomas Byrne, p; Gerald Coleman, 2b; Joseph DiMaggio, of; Thomas Henrich, 1b; Victor Raschi, of; Allie Reynolds, p; ●Philip Rizzuto, ss. **Philadelphia (1)**—Ferris Fain, 1b. **St. Louis (1)**—J. Sherman Lollar, c. **Washington (1)**—Casimer Michaels, 2b.

NATIONAL LEAGUE—Burton Shotton, Brooklyn, manager; Jacob Pitler, Brooklyn, and Milton Stock, Brooklyn, coaches. **Boston (2)**—W. Walker Cooper, c; Warren Spahn, p. **Brooklyn (7)**—●Roy Campanella, c; Gilbert Hodges, 1b; Donald Newcombe, p; Harold Reese, ss; ●Jack Robinson, 2b; Elwin Roe, p; Edwin Snider, of. **Chicago (3)**—Andrew Pafko, of; Robert Rush, p; ●Henry Sauer, of. **Cincinnati (2)**—Ewell Blackwell, p; John Wyrostek, of. **New York (2)**—Lawrence Jansen, p; Edward Stanky, 2b. **Philadelphia (4)**—●Willie Jones, 3b; James Konstanty, p; Robin Roberts, p; Richard Sisler, of. **Pittsburgh (1)**—●Ralph Kiner, of. **St. Louis (4)**—Martin Marion, ss; ●Stanley Musial, 1b; Albert Schoendienst, 2b; ●Enos Slaughter, of.

1951

AMERICAN LEAGUE—Charles Stengel, New York, manager; William Dickey, New York, and Thomas Henrich, New York, coaches. **Boston (5)**—●Dominic DiMaggio, of; Robert Doerr, 2b; Melvin Parnell, p; Vernon Stephens, 3b; ●Theodore Williams, of. **Chicago (6)**—James Busby, of; ●Alfonso Carrasquel, ss; ●J. Nelson Fox, 2b; Randall Gumpert, p; Orestes Minoso, of; W. Edward Robinson, 1b. **Cleveland (3)**—Lawrence Doby, of; James Hegan, c; Robert Lemon, p. **Detroit (3)**—Frederick Hutchinson, p; ●George Kell, 3b; ●Victor Wertz, of. **New York (4)**—Lawrence Berra, c; Joseph DiMaggio, of; Edmund Lopat, p; Philip Rizzuto, ss. **Philadelphia (2)**—●Ferris Fain, 1b; Robert Shantz, p. **St. Louis (1)**—Ned Garver, p. **Washington (1)**—Conrado Marrero, p.

NATIONAL LEAGUE—Edwin Sawyer, Philadelphia, manager; Bernard Bengough, Allen Cooke and Ralph Perkins, all of Philadelphia, coaches. **Boston (2)**—●Robert Elliott, 3b; Warren Spahn, p. **Brooklyn (7)**—●Roy Campanella, c; ●Gilbert Hodges, 1b; Donald Newcombe, p; Harold Reese, ss; ●Jack Robinson, 2b; Elwin Roe, p; Edwin Snider, of. **Chicago (2)**—C. Bruce Edwards, c; Emil Leonard, p. **Cincinnati (2)**—Ewell Blackwell, p; John Wyrostek, of. **New York (3)**—●Alvin Dark, ss; Lawrence Jansen, p; Salvatore Maglie, p. **Philadelphia (4)**—●Richie Ashburn, of; ●Delmer Ennis, of; Willie Jones, 3b; Robin Roberts, p. **Pittsburgh (1)**—Ralph Kiner, of. **St. Louis (4)**—●Stanley Musial, of; Albert Schoendienst, 2b; Enos Slaughter, of; Waldon Westlake, of.

1952

AMERICAN LEAGUE—Charles Stengel, New York, manager; Anthony Cuccinello, Cleveland, and Alfonso Lopez, Cleveland, coaches. **Boston (2)**—●Dominic DiMaggio, of; George Kell, 3b (Kell replaced by Gil McDougald, 2b, New York). **Chicago (3)**—J. Nelson Fox, 2b; Orestes Minoso, of; ●W. Edward Robinson, 1b. **Cleveland (7)**—●Roberto Avila, 2b; Lawrence Doby, of; E. Mike Garcia, p; James Hegan, c; Robert Lemon, p; ●L. Dale Mitchell, of; ●Albert Rosen, 3b. **Detroit (1)**—Victor Wertz, of. **New York (6)**—●Henry Bauer, of; ●Lawrence Berra, c; Mickey Mantle, of; Victor Raschi, p; Allie Reynolds, p; ●Philip Rizzuto, ss. **Philadelphia (3)**—Ferris Fain, 1b; Edwin Joost, ss; Robert Shantz, p. **St. Louis (1)**—Leroy Paige, p. **Washington (2)**—Jack Jensen, of; Edward Yost, 3b.

NATIONAL LEAGUE—Leo Durocher, New York, manager; Frank Shellenback, New York, and Edward Stanky, St. Louis, coaches. **Boston (1)**—Warren Spahn, p. **Brooklyn (7)**—●Roy Campanella, c; Carl Furillo, of; Gilbert Hodges, 1b; Harold Reese, ss; Jack Robinson, 2b; Elwin Roe, p; Edwin Snider, of (Roe replaced by James Hearn, p, New York). **Chicago (3)**—Maurice Atwell, c; Robert Rush, p; ●Henry Sauer, of. **Cincinnati (1)**—Grady Hatton, 3b. **New York (6)**—Alvin Dark, ss; Monford Irvin, of (injured); ●Carroll Lockman, 1b; Salvatore Maglie, p; ●Robert Thomson, 3b; Wesley Westrum, c. **Philadelphia (3)**—●Granville Hamner, ss; Robin Roberts, p; Curtis Simmons, p. **Pittsburgh (1)**—Ralph Kiner, of. **St. Louis (4)**—●Stanley Musial, of; Albert Schoendienst, 2b; ●Enos Slaughter, of; Gerald Staley, p.

1953

AMERICAN LEAGUE—Charles Stengel, New York, manager; Louis Boudreau, Boston, and James Turner, New York, coaches. **Boston (3)**—●William Goodman, 2b; George Kell, 3b; Samuel White, c. **Chicago (5)**—●Alfonso Carrasquel, ss; Ferris Fain, 1b; J. Nelson Fox, 2b; Orestes Minoso, of; W. William Pierce, p. **Cleveland (4)**—Lawrence Doby, of; E. Mike Garcia, p; Robert Lemon, p; ●Albert Rosen, 3b. **Detroit (1)**—Harvey Kuenn, ss. **New York (7)**—●Henry Bauer, of; ●Lawrence Berra, c; ●Mickey Mantle, of; John Mize, 1b; Allie Reynolds, p; Philip Rizzuto, ss; John Sain, p. **Philadelphia (2)**—W. Edward Robinson, 1b; ●Gus Zernial, of. **St. Louis (2)**—G. William Hunter, ss; Leroy Paige, p. **Washington (1)**—●James Vernon, 1b. (NOTE—Theodore Williams, of, Boston, just released from military service, was named honorary member of squad.)

NATIONAL LEAGUE—Charles Dressen, Brooklyn, manager; William Herman, Harry Lavagetto and Jacob Pitler, all of Brooklyn, coaches. **Brooklyn (6)**—●Roy Campanella, c; Carl Furillo, of; Gilbert Hodges, 1b; ●Harold Reese, ss; Jack Robinson, 3b; Edwin Snider, of. **Chicago (1)**—Ralph Kiner, of. **Cincinnati (2)**—●David Bell, of; ●Theodore Kluszewski, 1b. **Milwaukee (3)**—Delmar Crandall, c; ●Edwin Mathews, 3b; Warren Spahn, p (Crandall replaced by Clyde McCullough, c, Chicago). **New York (2)**—J. Hoyt Wilhelm, p; David Williams, 2b. **Philadelphia (4)**—Richie Ashburn, of; Granville Hamner, ss; Robin Roberts, p; Curtis Simmons, p. **Pittsburgh (1)**—Murry Dickson, p. **St. Louis (6)**—Harvey Haddix, p; ●Stanley Musial, of; Delbert Rice, c; ●Albert Schoendienst, 2b; ●Enos Slaughter, of; Gerald Staley, p (Rice replaced by Wesley Westrum, c, New York.)

1954

AMERICAN LEAGUE—Charles Stengel, New York, manager; Martin Marion, Chicago, and Frederick Hutchinson, Detroit, coaches. **Baltimore (1)**—Robert Turley, p. **Boston (2)**—James Piersall, of; Theodore Williams, of. **Chicago (8)**—●Alfonso Carrasquel, ss; Ferris Fain, 1b; J. Nelson Fox, 2b; Robert Keegan, p; George Kell, 3b; J. Sherman Lollar, c; ●Orestes Minoso, of; Virgil Trucks, p (Fain replaced by D. Dean Stone, p, Washington, and Kell by James Vernon, 1b, Washington). **Cleveland (5)**—●Roberto Avila, 2b; Lawrence Doby, of; E. Mike Garcia, p; Robert Lemon, p; ●Albert Rosen, 1b (Garcia replaced by Sandalio Consuegra, p, Chicago). **Detroit (2)**—●Raymond Boone, 3b; Harvey Kuenn, ss. **New York (5)**—●Henry Bauer, of; ●Lawrence Berra, c; Edward Ford, p; ●Mickey Mantle, of; Allie Reynolds, p (Reynolds replaced by Irving Noren, of, New York). **Philadelphia (1)**—James Finigan, 3b. **Washington (1)**—Erwin Porterfield, p.

NATIONAL LEAGUE—Walter Alston, Brooklyn, manager; Charles Grimm, Milwaukee, and Leo Durocher, New York, coaches. **Brooklyn (6)**—●Roy Campanella, c; Carl Erskine, p; Gilbert Hodges, 1b; Harold Reese, ss; ●Jack Robinson, of; ●Edwin Snider, of. **Chicago (1)**—Ransom Jackson, 3b. **Cincinnati (2)**—David Bell, of; ●Theodore Kluszewski, 1b. **Milwaukee (3)**—Delmar Crandall, c; D. Eugene Conley, p; Warren Spahn, p. **New York (5)**—John Antonelli, p; ●Alvin Dark, ss; Marvin Grissom, p; Willie Mays, of; Donald Mueller, of. **Philadelphia (3)**—Forrest Burgess, c; ●Granville Hamner, 2b; Robin Roberts, p. **Pittsburgh (1)**—Frank Thomas, of. **St. Louis (4)**—Harvey Haddix, p; ●Raymond Jablonski, 3b; ●Stanley Musial, of; Albert Schoendienst, 2b (Haddix replaced by James Wilson, p, Milwaukee).

1955

AMERICAN LEAGUE—Alfonso Lopez, Cleveland, manager; Donald Gutteridge, Chicago, and Anthony Cuccinello, Cleveland, coaches. **Baltimore (1)**—James Wilson, p. **Boston (3)**—Jack Jensen, of; Franklin Sullivan, p; ●Theodore Williams, of. **Chicago (5)**—Alfonso Carrasquel, ss; ●J. Nelson Fox, 2b; Richard Donovan, p; J. Sherman Lollar, c; W. William Pierce, p. **Cleveland (6)**—Roberto Avila, 2b; Lawrence Doby, of; Albert Rosen, 3b; Alphonse Smith, of; Herbert Score, p; Early Wynn, p. **Detroit (3)**—William Hoeft, p; ●Albert Kaline, of; ●Harvey Kuenn, ss. **Kansas City (2)**—●James Finigan, 3b; Victor Power, 1b. **New York (4)**—●Lawrence Berra, c; Edward Ford, p; ●Mickey Mantle, of; Robert Turley, p. **Washington (1)**—●James Vernon, 1b.

NATIONAL LEAGUE—Leo Durocher, New York, manager; E. Mayo Smith, Philadelphia, and Fred Haney, Pittsburgh, coaches. **Brooklyn (4)**—●Roy Campanella, c; Gilbert Hodges, 1b; Donald Newcombe, p; ●Edwin Snider, of (Campanella replaced by Stanley Lopata, c, Philadelphia). **Chicago (4)**—Eugene Baker, 2b; ●Ernest Banks, ss; Ransom Jackson, 3b; Samuel Jones, p. **Cincinnati (3)**—Forrest Burgess, c; ●Theodore Kluszewski, 1b; Joseph Nuxhall, p. **Milwaukee (5)**—D. Eugene Conley, p; Delmar Crandall, c; John Logan, ss; ●Edwin Mathews, 3b; Henry Aaron, of. **New York (2)**—Willie Mays, of; ●Donald Mueller, of. **Philadelphia (2)**—●Delmer Ennis, of; Robin Roberts, p. **Pittsburgh (1)**—Frank Thomas, of. **St. Louis (4)**—Luis Arroyo, p; Harvey Haddix, p; Stanley Musial, 1b; ●Albert Schoendienst, 2b.

1956

AMERICAN LEAGUE—Charles Stengel, New York, manager; James Turner, New York, and Charles Dressen, Washington, coaches. **Baltimore (1)**—●George Kell, 3b. **Boston (5)**—Thomas Brewer, p; James Piersall, of; ●James Vernon, 1b; Franklin Sullivan, p; ●Theodore Williams, of. **Chicago (4)**—●J. Nelson Fox, 2b; J. Sherman Lollar, c; W. William Pierce, p; James Wilson, p. **Cleveland (2)**—Raymond Narleski, p; Early Wynn, p (Narleski replaced by Herbert Score, p, Cleveland). **Detroit (4)**—Raymond Boone, 3b; ●Albert Kaline, of; ●Harvey Kuenn, ss; Charles Maxwell, of. **Kansas City (2)**—Victor Power, 1b; Harry Simpson, of. **New York (6)**—●Lawrence Berra, c; Edward Ford, p; John Kucks, p; ●Mickey Mantle, of; Alfred Martin, 2b; Gilbert McDougald, ss. **Washington (1)**—Roy Sievers.

NATIONAL LEAGUE—Walter Alston, Brooklyn, manager; George Tebbetts, Cincinnati, and Frederick Hutchinson, St. Louis, coaches. **Brooklyn (4)**—Roy Campanella, c; James Gilliam, 2b; Clement Labine, p; Edwin Snider, of. **Chicago (1)**—Ernest Banks, ss. **Cincinnati (8)**—●L. Edgar Bailey, c; ●David Bell, of; Theodore Kluszewski, 1b; Brooks Lawrence, p; ●Roy McMillan, ss; Joseph Nuxhall, p; ●Frank Robinson, of; ●John Temple, 2b. **Milwaukee (4)**—Henry Aaron, of; Delmar Crandall, c; Edwin

Mathews, 3b; Warren Spahn, p (Crandall replaced by Stanley Lopata, c, Philadelphia). **New York (2)**—John Antonelli, p; Willie Mays, of. **Philadelphia (1)**—Robin Roberts, p. **Pittsburgh (2)**—Robert Friend, p; ●R. Dale Long, 1b. **St. Louis (3)**—●Kenton Boyer, 3b; ●Stanley Musial, of; Eldon Repulski, of.

1957

AMERICAN LEAGUE—Charles Stengel, New York, manager; Frank Crosetti, New York, and James Turner, New York, coaches. **Baltimore (3)**—●George Kell, 3b; William Loes, p; Augustus Triandos, c. **Boston (2)**—Frank Malzone, 3b; ●Theodore Williams, of. **Chicago (3)**—●J. Nelson Fox, 2b; Orestes Minoso, of; W. William Pierce, p. **Cleveland (3)**—Donald Mossi, p; ●Victor Wertz, 1b; Early Wynn, p. **Detroit (4)**—James Bunning, p; ●Albert Kaline, of; ●Harvey Kuenn, ss; Charles Maxwell, of. **Kansas City (1)**—Joseph DeMaestri, ss. **New York (8)**—●Lawrence Berra, c; Robert Grim, p; Elston Howard, c; ●Mickey Mantle, of; Gilbert McDougald, ss; Robert Richardson, 2b; Robert Shantz, p; William Skowron, 1b. **Washington (1)**—Roy Sievers, of.

NATIONAL LEAGUE—Walter Alston, Brooklyn, manager; Robert Scheffing, Chicago, and Robert Bragan, Pittsburgh, coaches. **Brooklyn (3)**—Gino Cimoli, of; Gilbert Hodges, 1b; Clement Labine, p. **Chicago (1)**—Ernest Banks, ss. **Cincinnati (6)**—●L. Edgar Bailey, c; David Bell, of; ●Donald Hoak, 3b; ●Roy McMillan, ss; ●Frank Robinson, of; ●John Temple, 2b. **Milwaukee (6)**—●Henry Aaron, of; S. Lewis Burdette, p; John Logan, ss; Edwin Mathews, 3b; Albert Schoendienst, 2b; Warren Spahn, p. **New York (2)**—John Antonelli, p; ●Willie Mays, of. **Philadelphia (2)**—John Sanford, p; Curtis Simmons, p. **Pittsburgh (1)**—Henry Foiles, c. **St. Louis (4)**—Lawrence Jackson, p; Wallace Moon, of; ●Stanley Musial, 1b; Harold Smith, c. (NOTE—David Bell and Wally Post of Cincinnati led voting for center and right field positions, respectively, but because of avalanche of Cincinnati votes, Commissioner Ford Frick arbitrarily named Mays and Aaron to starting lineup at those positions.)

1958

AMERICAN LEAGUE—Charles Stengel, manager; C. Luman Harris, Baltimore, and James Turner, New York, coaches. **Baltimore (2)**—William O'Dell, p; ●Augustus Triandos, c. **Boston (3)**—Jack Jensen, of; ●Frank Malzone, 3b; Theodore Williams, of. **Chicago (5)**—●Luis Aparicio, ss; ●J. Nelson Fox, 2b; J. Sherman Lollar, c; W. William Pierce, p; Early Wynn, p. **Cleveland (2)**—Raymond Narleski, p; James Vernon, 1b. **Detroit (2)**—Albert Kaline, of; Harvey Kuenn, of. **Kansas City (1)**—●Robert Cerv, of. **New York (9)**—Lawrence Berra, c; Rinold Duren, p; Edward Ford, p; Elston Howard, of; Anthony Kubek, ss; ●Mickey Mantle, of; Gilbert McDougald, 2b; ●William Skowron, 1b; Robert Turley p. **Washington (1)**—Everett Bridges, ss.

NATIONAL LEAGUE—Fred Haney, Milwaukee, manager; William Rigney, San Francisco and E. Mayo Smith, Philadelphia, coaches. **Chicago (3)**—●Ernest Banks, ss; Walter Moryn, of; R. Lee Walls, of. **Cincinnati (2)**—George Crowe, 1b; Robert Purkey, p. **Los Angeles (2)**—John Podres, p; John Roseboro, c. **Milwaukee (6)**—●Henry Aaron, of; John Logan, ss; Edwin Mathews, 3b; Donald McMahon, p; Warren Spahn, p. **Philadelphia (2)**—Richie Ashburn, of; Richard Farrell, p. **Pittsburgh (4)**—Robert Friend, p; ●William Mazeroski, 2b; ●Robert Skinner, of; ●Frank Thomas, 3b. **St. Louis (3)**—Donald Blasingame, 2b; Lawrence Jackson, p; ●Stanley Musial, 1b. **San Francisco (3)**—John Antonelli, p; ●Willie Mays, of; Robert Schmidt, c.

1959

AMERICAN LEAGUE—Charles Stengel, New York, manager; Anthony Cuccinello, White Sox, and Harry Craft, Kansas City, coaches. **Baltimore (2)**—Augustus Triandos, c; J. Hoyt Wilhelm, p. **Boston (3)**—Frank Malzone, 3b; James Runnels, 2b; Theodore Williams, of. **Chicago (5)**—●Luis Aparicio, ss; ●J. Nelson Fox, 2b; J. Sherman Lollar, c; W. William Pierce, p; Early Wynn, p. **Cleveland (3)**—●Rocco Colavito, of; ●Orestes Minoso, of; Victor Power, 1b. **Detroit (3)**—James Bunning, p; ●Albert Kaline, of; Harvey Kuenn, of. **Kansas City (1)**—Buddy Daley, p. **New York (6)**—Lawrence Berra, c; Rinold Duren, p; Edward Ford, p; Mickey Mantle, of; Gilbert McDougald, ss; ●William Skowron, 1b. **Washington (2)**—●Harmon Killebrew, 3b; Roy Sievers, 1b. SECOND GAME CHANGES: Players Replaced—Bunning, Ford, Kuenn, McDougald, Pierce, Skowron, Triandos. Additions—Frank Crosetti, New York, and Harry Lavagetto, Washington, coaches; William O'Dell, p; Jerry Walker, p, and Eugene Woodling, of, Baltimore; Calvin McLish, p, Cleveland; Roger Maris, of, Kansas City; Elston Howard, c-of, Anthony Kubek, ss, and Robert Richardson, 2b, New York; Camilo Pascual, p, and W. Robert Allison, of, Washington (Pascual replaced by Pedro Ramos, p, Washington).

NATIONAL LEAGUE—Fred Haney, Milwaukee, manager; Edwin Sawyer, Philadelphia, and Daniel Murtaugh, Pittsburgh, coaches. **Chicago (1)**—●Ernest Banks, ss. **Cincinnati (3)**—Vada Pinson, of; Frank Robinson, 1b; ●John Temple, 2b. **Los Angeles (2)**—Donald Drysdale, p; ●Wallace Moon, of. **Milwaukee (5)**—●Henry Aaron, of; S. Lewis Burdette, p; ●Delmar Crandall, c; ●Edwin Mathews, 3b; Warren Spahn, p. **Philadelphia (1)**—D. Eugene Conley, p. **Pittsburgh (4)**—Forrest Burgess, c; El Roy Face, p; Richard Groat, ss; William Mazeroski, 2b. **St. Louis (6)**—Kenton Boyer, 3b; Joseph Cunningham, of; Wilmer Mizell, p; Stanley Musial, 1b; Harold Smith, c; William White, of (Mizell replaced by Donald Elston, p, Chicago.) **San Francisco (3)**—John Antonelli, p; ●Orlando Cepeda, 1b; ●Willie Mays, of. SECOND GAME CHANGES: Players Replaced—White. Additions—William Herman, Milwaukee, and John Fitzpatrick, Milwaukee, coaches; James Gilliam, inf-of and Charles Neal, ss, Los Angeles; John Logan, ss, Milwaukee; Samuel Jones, p, San Francisco.

1960

AMERICAN LEAGUE—Alfonso Lopez, Chicago, manager; Anthony Cuccinello, Chicago, and Donald Gutteridge, Chicago, coaches. **Baltimore (4)**—Charles Estrada, p; James Gentile, 1b; ●Ronald Hansen, ss; Brooks Robinson, 3b. **Boston (4)**—●Frank Malzone, 3b; William Monbouquette, p; ●James Runnels, 2b; Theodore Williams, of. **Chicago (7)**—Luis Aparicio, ss; J. Nelson Fox, 2b; J. Sherman

Lollar, c; ●Orestes Minoso, of; Alphonse Smith, of; Gerald Staley, p; Early Wynn, p. **Cleveland (4)**—Gary Bell, p; Harvey Kuenn, of; Victor Power, 1b; Richard Stigman, p. **Detroit (2)**—Albert Kaline, of; Frank Lary, p; **Kansas City (1)**—Buddy Daley, p. **New York (7)**—●Lawrence Berra, c; James Coates, p; Edward Ford, p; Elston Howard, c; ●Mickey Mantle, of; ●Roger Maris, of; ●William Skowron, 1b. **Washington (1)**—Camilo Pascual, p (replaced by James Lemon, of, Washington). **SECOND GAME CHANGES:** None.

NATIONAL LEAGUE—Walter Alston, Los Angeles, manager; Frederick Hutchinson, Cincinnati, and Solly Hemus, St. Louis, coaches. **Chicago (1)**—●Ernest Banks, ss. **Cincinnati (3)**—L. Edgar Bailey, c; William Henry, p; ●Vada Pinson, of. **Los Angeles (4)** Norman Larker, 1b; Charles Neal, 2b; John Podres, p; Stanley Williams, p. **Milwaukee (5)**—●Henry Aaron, of; ●Joseph Adcock, 1b; Robert Buhl, p; ●Delmar Crandall, c; ●Edwin Mathews, 3b. **Philadelphia (1)**—Antonio Taylor, 2b. **Pittsburgh (8)**—Forrest Burgess, c; Roberto Clemente, of; El Roy Face, p; Robert Friend, p; Richard Groat, ss; Vernon Law, p; ●William Mazeroski, 2b; Robert Skinner, of. **St. Louis (5)**—Kenton Boyer, 3b; Lawrence Jackson, p; Lyndall McDaniel, p; Stanley Musial, of; William White, 1b. **San Francisco (3)**—Orlando Cepeda, of; ●Willie Mays, of; Michael McCormick, p. **SECOND GAME CHANGES:** None.

1961

AMERICAN LEAGUE—Paul Richards, Baltimore, manager; Frank Crosetti, New York, and James Vernon, Washington, coaches. **Baltimore (4)**—John Brandt, of; James Gentile, 1b; ●Brooks Robinson, 3b; J. Hoyt Wilhelm, p. **Boston (1)**—J. Miguel Fornieles, p. **Chicago (2)**—J. Nelson Fox, 2b; W. William Pierce, p. **Cleveland (3)**—James Perry, p; ●John Romano, c; ●John Temple, 2b. **Detroit (5)**—●Norman Cash, 1b; ●Rocco Colavito, of; Albert Kaline, of; Frank Lary, p; James Bunning, p. **Kansas City (1)**—Richard Howser, ss. **Los Angeles (1)**—Rinold Duren, p. **Minnesota (1)**—Harmon Killebrew, 3b. **New York (6)**—Lawrence, Berra, of-c; Edward Ford, p; Elston Howard, c; ●Anthony Kubek, ss; ●Mickey Mantle, of; ●Roger Maris, of. **Washington (1)**—Richard Donovan, p. **SECOND GAME CHANGES: Players Replaced**—Duren, Fornieles, Lary, Perry, Pierce. **Additions**—James Adair, Baltimore, and Michael Higgins, Boston, coaches; Donald Schwall, p, Boston; Roy Sievers, 1b, and Luis Aparicio, ss, Chicago; John Francona, of-1b, and A. Barry Latman, p, Cleveland; Kenneth McBride, p, Los Angeles; Camilo Pascual, p, Minnesota; Luis Arroyo, p, and William Skowron, 1b, New York.

NATIONAL LEAGUE—Daniel Murtaugh, Pittsburgh, manager; Gene Mauch, Philadelphia, and Alvin Dark, San Francisco, coaches. **Chicago (2)**—George Altman, of; Donald Zimmer, 2b. **Cincinnati (4)**—Joseph Jay, p; Edward Kasko, ss; Robert Purkey, p; Frank Robinson, of. **Los Angeles (3)**—Sanford Koufax, p; John Roseboro, c; ●Maurice Wills, ss. **Milwaukee (4)**—Henry Aaron, of; ●Frank Bolling, 2b; ●Edwin Mathews, 3b; Warren Spahn, p. **Philadelphia (1)**—Art Mahaffey, p. **Pittsburgh (4)**—●Forrest Burgess, c; ●Roberto Clemente, of; El Roy Face, p; Richard Stuart, 1b. **St. Louis (3)**—Kenton Boyer, 3b; Stanley Musial, of; ●William White, 1b. **San Francisco (4)**—●Orlando Cepeda, of; ●Willie Mays, of; Michael McCormick, p; Stuart Miller, p. **SECOND GAME CHANGES: Players Replaced**—None. **Additions**—Elvin Tappe, Chicago, and Charles Dressen, Milwaukee, coaches; Ernest Banks, ss, Chicago; Donald Drysdale, p, Los Angeles; L. Edgar Bailey, c, San Francisco.

1962

AMERICAN LEAGUE—Ralph Houk, New York, manager; William Hitchcock, Baltimore, and James Vernon, Washington, coaches. **Baltimore (3)**—●James Gentile, 1b; Brooks Robinson, 3b; J. Hoyt Wilhelm, p (Wilhelm replaced by Milton Pappas, p, Baltimore). **Boston (1)**—William Monbouquette, p. **Chicago (2)**—●Luis Aparicio, ss; James Landis, of. **Cleveland (2)**—Richard Donovan, p; John Romano, c. **Detroit (3)**—Henry Aguirre, p; James Bunning, p; Rocco Colavito, of. **Kansas City (1)**—Norman Siebern, 1b. **Los Angeles (3)**—●William Moran, 2b; J. LeRoy Thomas, of; ●Leon Wagner, of. **Minnesota (3)**—●Earl Battey, c; Camilo Pascual, p; ●Richard Rollins, 3b. **New York (6)**—Elston Howard, c; ●Mickey Mantle, of; ●Roger Maris, of; Robert Richardson, 2b; Ralph Terry, p; Thomas Tresh, ss. **Washington (1)**—David Stenhouse, p. **SECOND GAME CHANGES: Players Replaced**—Monbouquette, Landis. **Additions**—Henry Bauer, Kansas City, and William Rigney, Los Angeles, coaches; James Runnels, 1b, Boston; Al Kaline, of, Detroit; Kenneth McBride, p, Los Angeles; James Kaat, p, Minnesota; Lawrence Berra, c, New York. (McBride replaced by Ray Herbert, p, Chicago).

NATIONAL LEAGUE—Frederick Hutchinson, Cincinnati, manager; Charles Stengel, New York, and John Keane, St. Louis, coaches. **Chicago (1)**—Ernest Banks, 1b. **Cincinnati (1)**—Robert Purkey, p. **Houston (1)**—Richard Farrell, p. **Los Angeles (5)**—●H. Thomas Davis, of; Donald Drysdale, p; Sanford Koufax, p; John Roseboro, c; Maurice Wills, ss. **Milwaukee (4)**—Henry Aaron, of; Frank Bolling, 2b; ●Delmar Crandall, c; Robert Shaw, p (Aaron replaced by Warren Spahn, p, Milwaukee). **New York (1)**—Richie Ashburn, of. **Philadelphia (1)**—John Callison, of. **Pittsburgh (3)**—●Roberto Clemente, of; ●Richard Groat, ss; ●William Mazeroski, 2b. **St. Louis (3)**—●Kenton Boyer, 3b; Robert Gibson, p; Stanley Musial, of. **San Francisco (5)**—Felipe Alou, of; ●Orlando Cepeda, 1b; James Davenport, 3b; Juan Marichal, p; ●Willie Mays, of. **SECOND GAME CHANGES: Players Replaced**—Koufax, Shaw, Drysdale, Alou. **Additions**—Harry Craft, Houston, and George Tebbetts, Milwaukee, coaches; Billy Williams, of, and George Altman, of, Chicago; Frank Robinson, of, Cincinnati; John Podres, p, Los Angeles; Henry Aaron, of, and Edwin Mathews, 3b, Milwaukee; Arthur Mahaffey, p, Philadelphia.

1963

AMERICAN LEAGUE—Ralph Houk, New York, manager; John Pesky, Boston, and Sabath Mele, Minnesota, coaches. **Baltimore (3)**—Luis Aparicio, ss; Stephen Barber, p; Brooks Robinson, 3b (Barber replaced by William Monbouquette, p, Boston). **Boston (3)**—●Frank Malzone, 3b; Richard Radatz, p; Carl Yastrzemski, of. **Chicago (2)**—●J. Nelson Fox, 2b; Juan Pizarro, p. **Cleveland (1)**—James Grant, p. **Detroit (2)**—James Bunning, p; ●Albert Kaline, of. **Kansas City (1)**—Norman Siebern, 1b-of. **Los Angeles (3)**—Kenneth McBride, p; ●Albert Pearson, of; ●Leon Wagner, of. **Minnesota (4)**—W. Robert

Allison, of; ●Earl Battey, c; Harmon Killebrew, of; ●Zoilo Versalles, ss. **New York (6)**—James Bouton, p; Elston Howard, c; ●Mickey Mantle, of; ●Joseph Pepitone, 1b; Robert Richardson, 2b; Thomas Tresh, of. **Washington (1)**—Donald Leppert, c. **NOTE**—Mantle was sidelined with fracture of left foot when he was voted on team and was not included in squad.

NATIONAL LEAGUE—Alvin Dark, San Francisco, manager; Robert Kennedy, Chicago, and Gene Mauch, Philadelphia, coaches. **Chicago (2)**—Lawrence Jackson, p; Ronald Santo, 3b. **Cincinnati (2)**—John Edwards, c; James O'Toole, p. **Houston (1)**—Harold Woodeshick, p. **Los Angeles (4)**—●H. Thomas Davis, of; Donald Drysdale, p; Sanford Koufax, p; Maurice Wills, ss. **Milwaukee (3)**—●Henry Aaron, of; Warren Spahn, p; Joseph Torre, c. **New York (1)**—Edwin Snider, of. **Philadelphia (1)**—Raymond Culp, p. **Pittsburgh (2)**—Roberto Clemente, of; ●William Mazeroski, 2b (Mazeroski replaced by Julian Javier, 2b, St. Louis). **St. Louis (4)**—●Kenton Boyer, 3b; ●Richard Groat, ss; Stanley Musial, of; ●William White, 1b. **San Francisco (5)**—●L. Edgar Bailey, c; Orlando Cepeda, 1b; Juan Marichal, p; ●Willie Mays, of; Willie McCovey, of.

1964

AMERICAN LEAGUE—Alfonso Lopez, Chicago, manager; Anthony Cuccinello, Chicago, and Gilbert Hodges, Washington, coaches. **Baltimore (3)**—Luis Aparicio, ss; ●Brooks Robinson, 3b; Norman Siebern, 1b (Aparicio replaced by Edward Bressoud, ss, Boston). **Boston (2)**—Frank Malzone, 3b; Richard Radatz, p. **Chicago (2)**—Gary Peters, p; Juan Pizarro, p. **Cleveland (1)**—John Kralick, p. **Detroit (3)**—William Freehan, c; Albert Kaline, of; Jerry Lumpe, 2b (Kaline replaced by Rocco Colavito, of, Kansas City). **Kansas City (1)**—Jonathan Wyatt, p. **Los Angeles (2)**—W. Dean Chance, p; ●James Fregosi, ss. **Minnesota (5)**—●W. Robert Allison, 1b; Jimmie Hall, of; ●Harmon Killebrew, of; ●Pedro Oliva, of; Camilo Pascual, p. **New York (5)**—Edward Ford, p; ●Elston Howard, c; ●Mickey Mantle, of; Joseph Pepitone, 1b; ●Robert Richardson, 2b. **Washington (1)**—Charles Hinton, of.

NATIONAL LEAGUE—Walter Alston, Los Angeles, manager; Frederick Hutchinson, Cincinnati, and Charles Stengel, New York, coaches. **Chicago (3)**—Richard Ellsworth, p; Ronald Santo, 3b; ●Billy Williams, of. **Cincinnati (2)**—Leonardo Cardenas, ss; John Edwards, c **Houston (1)**—Richard Farrell, p. **Los Angeles (2)**—Donald Drysdale, p; Sanford Koufax, p. **Milwaukee (2)**—Henry Aaron, of; ●Joseph Torre, c. **New York (1)**—●Ronald Hunt, 2b. **Philadelphia (3)**—James Bunning, p; John Callison, of; Christopher Short, p. **Pittsburgh (4)**—Forrest Burgess, c; ●Roberto Clemente, of; William Mazeroski, 2b; Wilver Stargell, of. **St. Louis (4)**—●Kenton Boyer, 3b; Curtis Flood, of; ●Richard Groat, ss; William White, 1b. **San Francisco (3)**—●Orlando Cepeda, 1b; Juan Marichal, p; ●Willie Mays, of.

1965

AMERICAN LEAGUE—Alfonso Lopez, Chicago, manager; Donald Gutteridge, Chicago, and Sabath Mele, Minnesota, coaches. **Baltimore (2)**—Milton Pappas, p; ●Brooks Robinson, 3b. **Boston (2)**—●Felix Mantilla, 2b; Carl Yastrzemski, of (Yastrzemski replaced by William Freehan, c, Detroit). **Chicago (2)**—Eddie Fisher, p; ●William Skowron, 1b (Skowron replaced by Joe Pepitone, 1b, New York). **Cleveland (4)**—R. Maxwell Alvis, 3b; ●Rocco Colavito, of; ●Victor Davalillo, of; Samuel McDowell, p. **Detroit (3)**— ●Willie Horton, of; Albert Kaline, of; ●Richard McAuliffe, ss. **Kansas City (1)**—John O'Donoghue, p. **Los Angeles (1)**—Robert Lee, p. **Minnesota (5)**—●Earl Battey, c; James Grant, p; Jimmie Hall, of; Harmon Killebrew, 3b; Zoilo Versalles, ss. **New York (4)**—Elston Howard, c; Mickey Mantle, of; Robert Richardson, 2b; Melvin Stottlemyre, p (Mantle replaced by Pedro Oliva, of, Minnesota). **Washington (1)**—Pete Richert, p.

NATIONAL LEAGUE—Gene Mauch, Philadelphia, manager; Richard Sisler, Cincinnati, and Robert Bragan, Milwaukee, coaches. **Chicago (3)**—●Ernest Banks, 1b; Ronald Santo, 3b; Billy Williams, of. **Cincinnati (6)**—Leonardo Cardenas, ss; John Edwards, c; Samuel Ellis, p; James Maloney, p; Frank Robinson, of; ●Peter Rose, 2b. **Houston (1)**—Richard Farrell, p. **Los Angeles (2)**—Donald Drysdale, p; Sanford Koufax, p; ●Maurice Wills, ss. **Milwaukee (2)**—●Henry Aaron, of; ●Joseph Torre, c. **New York (1)**—Edward Kranepool, 1b. **Philadelphia (3)**—●Richard Allen, 3b; John Callison, of; Octavio Rojas, 2b. **Pittsburgh (3)**—Roberto Clemente, of; ●Wilver Stargell, of; Robert Veale, p. **St. Louis (1)**—Robert Gibson, p. **San Francisco (2)**—Juan Marichal, p; ●Willie Mays, of.

1966

AMERICAN LEAGUE—Sabath Mele, Minnesota, manager; Henry Bauer, Baltimore, and George Tebbetts, Cleveland, coaches. **Baltimore (4)**—Stephen Barber, p; Andrew Etchebarren, c; ●Brooks Robinson, 3b; ●Frank Robinson, of. **Boston (2)**—●George Scott, 1b; Carl Yastrzemski, of. **California (2)**—James Fregosi, ss; ●Robert Knoop, 2b. **Chicago (1)**—Tommie Agee, of. **Cleveland (3)**—Gary Bell, p; Rocco Colavito, of; Samuel McDowell, p (McDowell replaced by Wilfred Siebert, p, Cleveland). **Detroit (5)**—Norman Cash, 1b; ●William Freehan, c; ●Albert Kaline, of; ●Richard McAuliffe, ss; Dennis McLain, p. **Kansas City (1)**—James Hunter, p. **Minnesota (4)**—Earl Battey, c; James Kaat, p; Harmon Killebrew, 3b; ●Pedro Oliva, of. **New York (2)**—Robert Richardson, 2b; Melvin Stottlemyre, p. **Washington (1)**—Peter Richert, p.

NATIONAL LEAGUE—Walter Alston, Los Angeles, manager; Herman Franks, San Francisco, and Harry Walker, Pittsburgh, coaches. **Atlanta (3)**—●Henry Aaron, of; Felipe Alou, 1b; ●Joseph Torre, c. **Chicago (1)**—Ronald Santo, 3b. **Cincinnati (2)**—●Leonardo Cardenas, ss; William McCool, p. **Houston (2)**—●Joe Morgan, 2b; J. Claude Raymond, p. **Los Angeles (3)**—Sanford Koufax, p; James Lefebvre, 2b; Maurice Wills, ss. **New York (1)**—Ronald Hunt, 2b. **Philadelphia (2)**—Richard Allen, of; James Bunning, p. **Pittsburgh (3)**—●Roberto Clemente, of; Wilver Stargell, of; Robert Veale, p. **St. Louis (3)**—Curtis Flood, of; Robert Gibson, p; J. Timothy McCarver, c (Gibson replaced by Philip Regan, p, Los Angeles). **San Francisco (6)**—Thomas Haller, c; James Hart, 3b; Juan Marichal, p; ●Willie Mays, of; ●Willie McCovey, 1b; Gaylord Perry, p. (NOTE—Morgan was sidelined with fractured kneecap after being named to starting lineup and was not included on squad.)

1967

AMERICAN LEAGUE—Henry Bauer, Baltimore, manager; William Rigney, California, and Edward Stanky, Chicago, coaches. **Baltimore (3)**—●Brooks Robinson, 3b; Andrew Etchebarren, c; ●Frank Robinson, of (Frank Robinson replaced by A. Kenneth Berry, of, Chicago). **Boston (4)**—Anthony Conigliaro, of; James Lonborg, p; ●Americo Petrocelli, ss; ●Carl Yastrzemski, of. **California (3)**—James Fregosi, ss; James McGlothlin, p; Donald Mincher, 1b. **Chicago (3)**—Tommie Agee, of, Joel Horlen, p; Gary Peters, p. **Cleveland (2)**—R. Maxwell Alvis, 3b; Steve Hargan, p. **Detroit (3)**—●William Freehan, c; ●Albert Kaline, of; Richard McAuliffe, ss (Kaline replaced by Pedro Oliva, of, Minnesota). **Kansas City (1)**—James Hunter, p. **Minnesota (3)**—●Rodney Carew, 2b; W. Dean Chance, p; ●Harmon Killebrew, 1b. **New York (2)**—Alphonso Downing, p; Mickey Mantle, 1b. **Washington (1)**—Paulino Casanova, c.

NATIONAL LEAGUE—Walter Alston, Los Angeles, manager; Herman Franks, San Francisco, and Harry Walker, Pittsburgh, coaches. **Atlanta (3)**—●Henry Aaron, of; ●Joseph Torre, c; Denver Lemaster, p (Lemaster replaced by Chris Short, p, Philadelphia). **Chicago (3)**—Ernest Banks, 1b; Ferguson Jenkins, p. **Cincinnati (3)**—Tommy Helms, 2b; Atanasio Perez, 3b; Peter Rose, of. **Houston (3)**—Miguel Cuellar, p; Daniel Staub, of; James Wynn, of. **Los Angeles (2)**—Donald Drysdale, p; Claude Osteen, p. **New York (1)**—G. Thomas Seaver, p. **Philadelphia (1)**—●Richard Allen, 3b. **Pittsburgh (3)**—●L. Eugene Alley, ss; ●Roberto Clemente, of; ●William Mazeroski, 2b. **St. Louis (4)**—●Louis Brock, of; ●Orlando Cepeda, 1b; Robert Gibson, p; J. Timothy McCarver, c. **San Francisco (3)**—Thomas Haller, c; Juan Marichal, p; Willie Mays, of.

1968

AMERICAN LEAGUE—Richard Williams, Boston, manager; Calvin Ermer, Minnesota, and E. Mayo Smith, Detroit, coaches. **Baltimore (3)**—David Johnson, 2b; John Powell, 1b; ●Brooks Robinson, 3b. **Boston (3)**—Kenneth Harrelson, of; Jose Santiago, p; ●Carl Yastrzemski, of (Santiago replaced by Gary Bell, p, Boston). **California (1)**—●James Fregosi, ss. **Chicago (2)**—Thomas John, p; Duane Josephson, c. **Cleveland (3)**—Jose Azcue, c; Samuel McDowell, p; Luis Tiant, p. **Detroit (4)**—●William Freehan, c; ●Willie Horton, of; Dennis McLain, p; Donald Wert, 3b. **Minnesota (3)**—●Rodney Carew, 2b; ●Harmon Killebrew, 1b; Pedro Oliva, of. **New York (2)**—Mickey Mantle, of; Melvin Stottlemyre, p. **Oakland (3)**—Dagoberto Campaneris, ss; Robert Monday, of; Johnny Odom, p. **Washington (1)**—●Frank Howard, of.

NATIONAL LEAGUE—Albert Schoendienst, St. Louis, manager; J. David Bristol, Cincinnati, and Herman Franks, San Francisco, coaches. **Atlanta (3)**—●Henry Aaron, of; Felipe Alou, of; Ronald Reed, p. **Chicago (2)**—●Donald Kessinger, ss; ●Ronald Santo, 3b. **Cincinnati (4)**—Johnny Bench, c; ●Tommy Helms, 2b; Atanasio Perez, 3b; ●Peter Rose, of (Rose replaced by Billy Williams, of, Chicago). **Houston (1)**—Daniel Staub, 1b. **Los Angeles (2)**—Donald Drysdale, p; Thomas Haller, c. **New York (3)**—●Gerald Grote, c; Jerry Koosman, p; G. Thomas Seaver, p. **Philadelphia (1)**—Woodrow Fryman, p. **Pittsburgh (2)**—L. Eugene Alley, ss; Mateo Alou, of (Alley replaced by Leonardo Cardenas, ss, Cincinnati). **St. Louis (4)**—Steven Carlton, p; ●Curtis Flood, of; Robert Gibson, p; M. Julian Javier, 2b. **San Francisco (3)**—Juan Marichal, p; Willie Mays, of; ●Willie McCovey, 1b.

1969

AMERICAN LEAGUE—E. Mayo Smith, Detroit, manager; Alvin Dark, Cleveland, Earl Weaver, Baltimore, and Theodore Williams, Washington, coaches. **Baltimore (6)**—Paul Blair, of; David Johnson, 2b; David McNally, p; ●John Powell, 1b; Brooks Robinson, 3b; ●Frank Robinson, of (Johnson replaced by Michael Andrews, 2b, Boston). **Boston (4)**—Raymond Culp, p; ●Americo Petrocelli, ss; C. Reginald Smith, of; Carl Yastrzemski, of. **California (1)**—James Fregosi, ss. **Chicago (1)**—Carlos May, of. **Cleveland (1)**—Samuel McDowell, p. **Detroit (3)**—●William Freehan, c; Michael Lolich, p; Dennis McLain, p. **Kansas City (1)**—Eliseo Rodriguez, c. **Minnesota (4)**—●Rodney Carew, 2b; Harmon Killebrew, 1b; Pedro Oliva, of; John Roseboro, c (Oliva replaced by Roy White, of, New York). **New York (1)**—Melvin Stottlemyre, p. **Oakland (3)**—●Salvatore Bando, 3b; ●Reginald Jackson, of; Johnny Odom, p. **Seattle (1)**—J. Michael Hegan, of-1b (Hegan replaced by Donald Mincher, 1b, Seattle). **Washington (2)**—●Frank Howard, of; Darold Knowles, p.

NATIONAL LEAGUE—Albert Schoendienst, St. Louis, manager; Leo Durocher, Chicago, and J. David Bristol, Cincinnati, coaches. **Atlanta (3)**—●Henry Aaron, of; ●Felix Millan, 2b; Philip Niekro, p. **Chicago (5)**—Ernest Banks, 1b; Glenn Beckert, 2b; C. Randolph Hundley, c; ●Donald Kessinger, ss; ●Ronald Santo, 3b. **Cincinnati (4)**—●Johnny Bench, c; Lee May, 1b; Atanasio Perez, 3b; Peter Rose, of. **Houston (2)**—Lawrence Dierker, p; Denis Menke, ss. **Los Angeles (1)**—William Singer, p. **Montreal (1)**—Daniel Staub, of. **New York (3)**—●Cleon Jones, of; Jerry Koosman, p; G. Thomas Seaver, p. **Philadelphia (1)**—Grant Jackson, p. **Pittsburgh (2)**—●Mateo Alou, of; Roberto Clemente, of. **St. Louis (2)**—Steven Carlton, p; Robert Gibson, p. **San Diego (1)**—Christopher Cannizzaro, c. **San Francisco (3)**—Juan Marichal, p; Willie Mays, of; ●Willie McCovey, 1b.

1970

AMERICAN LEAGUE—Earl Weaver, Baltimore, manager; Ralph Houk, New York, Harold (Lefty) Phillips, California, coaches. **Baltimore (6)**—Miguel Cuellar, p; David McNally, p; James Palmer, p; ●John Powell, 1b; Brooks Robinson, 3b; ●Frank Robinson, of. **Boston (2)**—Gerald Moses, c; ●Carl Yastrzemski, of. **California (4)**—Santos Alomar, 2b; James Fregosi, ss; Alexander Johnson, of; Clyde Wright, p. **Chicago (1)**—●Luis Aparicio, ss. **Cleveland (2)**—Raymond Fosse, c; Samuel McDowell, p. **Detroit (2)**—●William Freehan, c; Willie Horton, of. **Kansas City (1)**—Amos Otis, of. **Milwaukee (1)**—Tommy Harper, 3b. **Minnesota (4)**—●Rodney Carew, 2b; ●Harmon Killebrew, 3b; Pedro Oliva, of; James Perry, p (Carew replaced by David Johnson, 2b, Baltimore). **New York (3)**—Fred Peterson, p; Melvin Stottlemyre, p; Roy White, of. **Oakland (1)**—James Hunter, p. **Washington (1)**—●Frank Howard, of.

NATIONAL LEAGUE—Gilbert Hodges, New York, manager; Leo Durocher, Chicago, Luman Harris, Atlanta, coaches. **Atlanta (4)**—●Henry Aaron, of; ●Ricardo Carty, of; Felix Millan, 2b; J. Hoyt Wilhelm, p (Millan replaced by Joe Morgan, 2b, Houston). **Chicago (3)**—●Glenn Beckert, 2b; James Hickman, of; ●Donald Kessinger, ss. **Cincinnati (5)**—●Johnny Bench, c; James Merritt, p; ●Atanasio Perez, 3b; Peter Rose, of; Wayne Simpson, p. **Houston (1)**—Denis Menke, ss. **Los Angeles (2)**—Billy Grabarkewitz, 3b; Claude Osteen, p. **Montreal (1)**—Daniel Staub, of. **New York (2)**—Derrel Harrelson, ss; G. Thomas Seaver, p. **Philadelphia (1)**—Joseph Hoerner, p. **Pittsburgh (1)**—Roberto Clemente, of. **St. Louis (3)**—●Richard Allen, 1b; Robert Gibson, p; Joseph Torre, c. **San Diego (1)**—Clarence Gaston, of. **San Francisco (4)**—Richard Dietz, c; ●Willie Mays, of; Willie McCovey, 1b; Gaylord Perry, p.

1971

AMERICAN LEAGUE—Earl Weaver, Baltimore, manager; G. William Hunter, Baltimore, Alfred (Billy) Martin, Detroit, coaches. **Baltimore (6)**—Donald Buford, of; Miguel Cuellar, p; James Palmer, p; ●John Powell, 1b; ●Brooks Robinson, 3b; ●Frank Robinson, of (Powell replaced by Norman Cash, 1b, Detroit). **Boston (3)**—Luis Aparicio, ss; Wilfred Siebert, p; ●Carl Yastrzemski, of. **California (1)**—John Messersmith, p. **Chicago (1)**—William Melton, 3b. **Cleveland (2)**—●Raymond Fosse, c; Samuel McDowell, p (Fosse replaced by David Duncan, c, Oakland and McDowell replaced by Wilbur Wood, p, Chicago). **Detroit (3)**—William Freehan, c; Albert Kaline, of; Michael Lolich, p. **Kansas City (2)**—Amos Otis, of; Octavio Rojas, 2b. **Milwaukee (1)**—Martin Pattin, p. **Minnesota (5)**—Leo Cardenas, ss; ●Rodney Carew, 2b; Harmon Killebrew, 3b; ●Pedro Oliva, of; James Perry, p (Oliva replaced by Reginald Jackson, of, Oakland). **New York (2)**—Thurman Munson, c; Bobby Murcer, of. **Oakland (1)**—Vida Blue, p. **Washington (1)**—Frank Howard, of.

NATIONAL LEAGUE—George (Sparky) Anderson, Cincinnati, manager; Walter Alston, Los Angeles, Pedro (Preston) Gomez, San Diego, Daniel Murtaugh, Pittsburgh, coaches. **Atlanta (2)**—●Henry Aaron, of; Felix Millan, 2b. **Chicago (4)**—●Glenn Beckert, 2b; Ferguson Jenkins, p; Donald Kessinger, ss; Ronald Santo, 3b. **Cincinnati (4)**—●Johnny Bench, c; Clay Carroll, p; Lee May, 1b; Peter Rose, of. **Houston (1)**—Lawrence Dierker, p (Dierker replaced by Donald Wilson, p, Houston). **Los Angeles (1)**—William Davis, of. **Montreal (1)**—Daniel Staub, of. **New York (2)**—●Derrel Harrelson, ss; G. Thomas Seaver, p. **Philadelphia (1)**—Richard Wise, p. **Pittsburgh (4)**—Roberto Clemente, of; Dock Ellis, p; Manuel Sanguillen, c; ●Wilver Stargell, of. **St. Louis (3)**—Louis Brock, of; Steven Carlton, p; ●Joseph Torre, 3b. **San Diego (1)**—Nathan Colbert, 1b. **San Francisco (4)**—Bobby Bonds, of; Juan Marichal, p; ●Willie Mays, of; ●Willie McCovey, 1b.

1972

AMERICAN LEAGUE—Earl Weaver, Baltimore, manager; Robert Lemon, Kansas City, Richard Williams, Oakland, coaches. **Baltimore (4)**—Patrick Dobson, p; David McNally, p; James Palmer, p; ●Brooks Robinson, 3b. **Boston (3)**—●Luis Aparicio, ss; Carlton Fisk, c; ●Carl Yastrzemski, of (Aparicio replaced by Toby Harrah, ss, Texas, who was replaced by Robert Grich, ss, Baltimore). **California (1)**—L. Nolan Ryan, p. **Chicago (3)**—●Richard Allen, 1b; Carlos May, of; Wilbur Wood, p. **Cleveland (1)**—Gaylord Perry, p. **Detroit (4)**—Norman Cash, 1b; Joseph Coleman, p; ●William Freehan, c; Michael Lolich, p (Coleman replaced by Kenneth Holtzman, p, Oakland). **Kansas City (5)**—Amos Otis, of; Freddie Patek, ss; Louis Piniella, of; Octavio Rojas, 2b; Richard Scheinblum, of (Patek replaced by Dagoberto Campaneris, ss, Oakland and Otis replaced by C. Reginald Smith, of, Boston). **Milwaukee (1)**—Eliseo Rodriguez, c. **Minnesota (1)**—●Rodney Carew, 2b. **New York (1)**—Bobby Murcer, of. **Oakland (4)**—Salvatore Bando, 3b; James Hunter, p; ●Reginald Jackson, of; Joseph Rudi, of. **Texas (0).**

NATIONAL LEAGUE—Daniel Murtaugh, Pittsburgh, manager; Charles Fox, San Francisco, Albert Schoendienst, St. Louis, coaches. **Atlanta (1)**—●Henry Aaron, of. **Chicago (4)**—●Glenn Beckert, 2b; ●Donald Kessinger, ss; Ronald Santo, 3b; Billy Williams, of. **Cincinnati (4)**—●Johnny Bench, c; Clay Carroll, p; ●Joe Morgan, 2b; Gary Nolan, p (Nolan replaced by Ferguson Jenkins, p, Chicago). **Houston (2)**—Cesar Cedeno, of; ●Lee May, 1b. **Los Angeles (1)**—Donald Sutton, p. **Montreal (1)**—William Stoneman, p. **New York (3)**—Willie Mays, of; Frank McGraw, p; G. Thomas Seaver, p. **Philadelphia (1)**—Steven Carlton, p. **Pittsburgh (5)**—Stephen Blass, p; ●Roberto Clemente, of; Albert Oliver, of; Manuel Sanguillen, c; ●Wilver Stargell, of. **St. Louis (4)**—Louis Brock, of; Robert Gibson, p; Ted Simmons, c; ●Joseph Torre, 3b. **San Diego (1)**—Nathan Colbert, 1b. **San Francisco (1)**—Chris Speier, ss.

1973

AMERICAN LEAGUE—Richard Williams, Oakland, manager; Charles Tanner, Chicago, Dorrel Herzog, Texas, coaches. **Baltimore (2)**—Paul Blair, of; ●Brooks Robinson, 3b; **Boston (3)**—●Carlton Fisk, c; William Lee, p; Carl Yastrzemski, 1b (Yastrzemski replaced by James Spencer, 1b, Texas). **California (2)**—L. Nolan Ryan, p; William Singer, p. **Chicago (1)**—●Richard Allen, 1b (Allen replaced by H. Patrick Kelly, of, Chicago). **Cleveland (1)**—David Bell, 3b. **Detroit (3)**—Edwin Brinkman, ss; William Freehan, c; Willie Horton, of. **Kansas City (3)**—John Mayberry, 1b; ●Amos Otis, of; Octavio Rojas, 2b. **Milwaukee (2)**—James Colborn, p; David May, of. **Minnesota (2)**—Rikalbert Blyleven, p; ●Rodney Carew, 2b. **New York (3)**—Albert Lyle, p; Thurman Munson, c; ●Bobby Murcer, of. **Oakland (6)**—Salvatore Bando, 3b; ●Dagoberto Campaneris, ss; Roland Fingers, p; Kenneth Holtzman, p; James Hunter, p; ●Reginald Jackson, of. **Texas (1)**—David Nelson, 2b.

NATIONAL LEAGUE—George (Sparky) Anderson, Cincinnati, manager; Gene Mauch, Montreal, William Virdon, Pittsburgh, coaches. **Atlanta (3)**—●Henry Aaron, of; Darrell Evans, 3b; David Johnson, 2b. **Chicago (2)**—●Ronald Santo, 3b; ●Billy Williams, of. **Cincinnati (5)**—●Johnny Bench, c; John Billingham, p; David Concepcion, ss; ●Joe Morgan, 2b; ●Pete Rose, of (Concepcion replaced by William Russell, ss, Los Angeles). **Houston (2)**—Cesar Cedeno, of; Robert Watson, of. **Los Angeles (5)**—James Brewer, p; William Davis, of; Manuel Mota, of; Claude Osteen, p; Donald Sutton, p. **Montreal (1)**—Ronald Fairly, 1b. **New York (2)**—Willie Mays, of; G. Thomas Seaver, p. **Philadelphia (1)**—Wayne Twitchell, p. **Pittsburgh (2)**—J. David Giusti, p; Wilver Stargell, of. **St. Louis (3)**—Ted Simmons, c; Joseph Torre, 3b; Richard Wise, p. **San Diego (1)**—Nathan Colbert, 1b. **San Francisco (2)**—Bobby Bonds, of; ●Chris Speier, ss.

1974

AMERICAN LEAGUE—Richard Williams, manager; Earl Weaver, Baltimore, honorary manager; Dorrel Herzog, California, John McKeon, Kansas City, coaches. **Baltimore (3)**—Miguel Cuellar, p; Robert Grich, 2b; ●Brooks Robinson, 3b. **Boston (3)**—●Carlton Fisk, c; Luis Tiant, p; Carl Yastrzemski, 1b (Fisk replaced by Edward Herrmann, c, Chicago, who was later replaced by James Sundberg, c, Texas). **California (2)**—David Chalk, 3b; Frank Robinson, of. **Chicago (2)**—●Richard Allen, 1b; Wilbur Wood, p. **Cleveland (2)**—George Hendrick, of; Gaylord Perry, p. **Detroit (2)**—John Hiller, p; Albert Kaline, of. **Kansas City (3)**—Steven Busby, p; John Mayberry, 1b; Octavio Rojas, 2b. **Milwaukee (1)**—Darrell Porter, c. **Minnesota (1)**—●Rodney Carew, 2b. **New York (2)**—Thurman Munson, c; ●Bobby Murcer, of. **Oakland (6)**—Salvatore Bando, 3b; ●Dagoberto Campaneris, ss; Roland Fingers, p; James Hunter, p; ●Reginald Jackson, of; Joseph Rudi, of (Bando replaced by Donald Money, 3b, Milwaukee). **Texas (1)**—●Jeffrey Burroughs, of.

Earl Weaver stepped down as manager of the A.L. in favor of Richard Williams, manager of the 1973 A.L. champion Oakland Athletics, who was inactive at the time of the All-Star Game.

NATIONAL LEAGUE—Lawrence (Yogi) Berra, New York, manager; George (Sparky) Anderson, Cincinnati, Albert (Red) Schoendienst, St. Louis, coaches. **Atlanta (3)**—●Henry Aaron, of; Lee Capra, p; Ralph Garr, of. **Chicago (1)**—Donald Kessinger, ss. **Cincinnati (4)**—●Johnny Bench, c; ●Joseph Morgan, 2b; Atanasio Perez, 1b; ●Pete Rose, of. **Houston (1)**—Cesar Cedeno, of. **Los Angeles (5)**—●Ronald Cey, 3b; ●Steven Garvey, 1b; Michael Marshall, p; John Messersmith, p; ●James Wynn, of. **Montreal (1)**—Stephen Rogers, p. **New York (2)**—Gerald Grote, c; Jonathan Matlack, p. **Philadelphia (4)**—●Lawrence Bowa, ss; Steven Carlton, p; David Cash, 2b; Michael Schmidt, 3b. **Pittsburgh (1)**—Kenneth Brett, p. **St. Louis (4)**—Louis Brock, of; Lynn McGlothen, p; Ted Simmons, c; Reginald Smith, of. **San Diego (1)**—John Grubb, of. **San Francisco (1)**—Chris Speier, ss.

1975

AMERICAN LEAGUE—Alvin Dark, Oakland, manager; Delmar Crandall, Milwaukee, Alfred Martin, Texas, coaches. **Baltimore (1)**—James Palmer, p. **Boston (2)**—Fredric Lynn, of; Carl Yastrzemski, of. **California (2)**—David Chalk, 3b; L. Nolan Ryan, p. **Chicago (4)**—Russell Dent, ss; Richard Gossage, p; James Kaat, p; Jorge Orta, 2b (Orta replaced by Colbert Harrah, ss, Texas). **Cleveland (1)**—George Hendrick, of. **Detroit (1)**—William Freehan, c. **Kansas City (2)**—Steven Busby, p; Harold McRae, of. **Milwaukee (2)**—Henry Aaron, of; George Scott, 1b. **Minnesota (1)**—●Rodney Carew, 2b. **New York (4)**—●Bobby Bonds, of; James Hunter, p; ●Thurman Munson, c; ●Graig Nettles, 3b. **Oakland (7)**—Vida Blue, p; ●Dagoberto Campaneris, ss; Roland Fingers, p; ●Reginald Jackson, of; Joseph Rudi, of; ●F. Gene Tenace, 1b; Claudell Washington, of. **Texas (1)**—D. Michael Hargrove, 1b.

NATIONAL LEAGUE—Walter Alston, Los Angeles, manager; Daniel Murtaugh, Pittsburgh, Albert Schoendienst, St. Louis, coaches. **Atlanta (1)**—Philip Niekro, p. **Chicago (1)**—Bill Madlock, 3b. **Cincinnati (5)**—●Johnny Bench, c; ●David Concepcion, ss; ●Joe Morgan, 2b; Atanasio Perez, 1b; ●Peter Rose, 3b. **Houston (1)**—Robert Watson, 1b. **Los Angeles (6)**—●Ronald Cey, 3b; ●Steven Garvey, 1b; Michael Marshall, p; John Messersmith, p; Donald Sutton, p; ●James Wynn, of. **Montreal (1)**—Gary Carter, of. **New York (2)**—Jonathan Matlack, p; G. Thomas Seaver, p. **Philadelphia (4)**—Lawrence Bowa, ss; David Cash, 2b; Gregory Luzinski, of; Frank McGraw, p. **Pittsburgh (3)**—Albert Oliver, of; Jerry Reuss, p; Manuel Sanguillen, c. **St. Louis (2)**—●Louis Brock, of; C. Reginald Smith, of. **San Diego (1)**—Randall Jones, p. **San Francisco (1)**—Bobby Murcer, of.

1976

AMERICAN LEAGUE—Darrell Johnson, Boston, manager; Gene Mauch, Minnesota, Frank Robinson, Cleveland, coaches. **Baltimore (2)**—Mark Belanger, ss; ●Robert Grich, 2b. **Boston (4)**—Carlton Fisk, c; ●Fredric Lynn, of; Luis Tiant, p; Carl Yastrzemski, 1b. **California (1)**—Frank Tanana, p. **Chicago (1)**—Richard Gossage, p. **Cleveland (1)**—David LaRoche, p. **Detroit (3)**—Mark Fidrych, p; ●Ronald LeFlore, of; ●Daniel Staub, of. **Kansas City (4)**—●George Brett, 3b; Harold McRae, of; Amos Otis, of; Freddie Patek, ss. **Milwaukee (2)**—Donald Money, 3b; William Travers, p. **Minnesota (2)**—●Rodney Carew, 1b; Harold Wynegar, c. **New York (6)**—C. Christopher Chambliss, 1b; James Hunter, p; Albert Lyle, p; ●Thurman Munson, c; William Randolph, 2b (replaced by Philip Garner, 2b, Oakland); John Rivers, of. **Oakland (1)**—Roland Fingers, p. **Texas (1)**—●Colbert Harrah, ss.

NATIONAL LEAGUE—George (Sparky) Anderson, Cincinnati, manager; John McNamara, San Diego, Daniel Ozark, Philadelphia, coaches. **Atlanta (1)**—John Messersmith, p (replaced by Richard Ruthven, p, Atlanta). **Chicago (1)**—Steven Swisher, c. **Cincinnati (7)**—●Johnny Bench, c; ●David Concepcion, ss; ●George Foster, of; G. Kenneth Griffey, of; ●Joe Morgan, 2b; Atanasio Perez, 1b; ●Peter Rose, 3b. **Houston (2)**—Cesar Cedeno, of; Kenneth Forsch, p. **Los Angeles (4)**—Ronald Cey, 3b; ●Steven Garvey, 1b; Richard Rhoden, p; William Russell, ss. **Montreal (1)**—Woodrow Fryman, p. **New York (3)**—●David Kingman, of; Jonathan Matlack, p; G. Thomas Seaver, p. **Philadelphia (5)**—Robert Boone, c; Lawrence Bowa, ss; David Cash, 2b; ●Gregory Luzinski, of; Michael Schmidt, 3b. **Pittsburgh (1)**—Albert Oliver, of. **St. Louis (1)**—Arnold McBride, of. **San Diego (1)**—Randall Jones, p. **San Francisco (1)**—John Montefusco, p.

1977

AMERICAN LEAGUE—Alfred (Billy) Martin, New York, manager; Alexander Grammas, Milwaukee, Robert Lemon, Chicago, coaches. **Baltimore (2)**—James Palmer, p; Kenneth Singleton, of. **Boston (7)**—●Richard Burleson, ss; William Campbell, p; ●Carlton Fisk, c; Fredric Lynn, of; James Rice, of; George Scott, 1b; ●Carl Yastrzemski, of. **California (1)**—Frank Tanana, p (replaced by David

LaRoche, p, California, who replaced L. Nolan Ryan, p, California). **Chicago (1)**—●Richard Zisk, of. **Cleveland (1)**—Dennis Eckersley, p. **Detroit (2)**—Mark Fidrych, p (replaced by James Kern, p, Cleveland); Jason Thompson, 1b. **Kansas City (1)**—●George Brett, 3b. **Milwaukee (1)**—Donald Money, 2b (replaced by James Slaton, p, Milwaukee). **Minnesota (3)**—●Rodney Carew, 1b; Larry Hisle, of; Harold Wynegar, c. **New York (5)**—●Reginald Jackson, of; Albert Lyle, p; Thurman Munson, c; Graig Nettles, 3b; ●William Randolph, 2b. **Oakland (1)**—Vida Blue, p (replaced by Wayne Gross, 3b, Oakland). **Seattle (1)**—Ruppert Jones, of. **Texas (1)**—Dagoberto Campaneris,.ss. **Toronto (1)**—Ron Fairly, 1b.

NATIONAL LEAGUE—George (Sparky) Anderson, Cincinnati, manager; Thomas Lasorda, Los Angeles, Daniel Ozark, Philadelphia, coaches. **Atlanta (1)**—Guillermo Montanez, 1b. **Chicago (4)**—Julio Morales, of; Ricky Reuschel, p; H. Bruce Sutter, p (replaced by Richard Gossage, p, Pittsburgh); J. Manuel Trillo, 2b. **Cincinnati (7)**—●Johnny Bench, c; ●David Concepcion, ss; ●George Foster, of; G. Kenneth Griffey, of; ●Joe Morgan, 2b; Peter Rose, 3b; G. Thomas Seaver, p. **Houston (1)**—Joaquin Andujar, p. **Los Angeles (4)**—●Ronald Cey, 3b; ●Steve Garvey, 1b; C. Reginald Smith, of; Donald Sutton, p. **Montreal (1)**—Ellis Valentine, of. **New York (1)**—John Stearns, c. **Philadelphia (3)**—Steven Carlton, p; ●Gregory Luzinski, of; Michael Schmidt, 3b. **Pittsburgh (2)**—John Candelaria, p; ●David Parker, of. **St. Louis (2)**—Ted Simmons, c; Garry Templeton, ss. **San Diego (1)**—David Winfield, of. **San Francisco (1)**—Gary Lavelle, p.

1978

AMERICAN LEAGUE—Alfred (Billy) Martin, New York, manager; Dorrel Herzog, Kansas City, Donald Zimmer, Boston, coaches. **Baltimore (3)**—Michael Flanagan, p; Eddie Murray, 1b; James Palmer, p. **Boston (5)**—Richard Burleson, ss (replaced by Gerald Remy, 2b, Boston); ●Carlton Fisk, c; Fredric Lynn, of; ●James Rice, of; Carl Yastrzemski, of (replaced by Dwight Evans, of, Boston). **California (1)**—Frank Tanana, p. **Chicago (1)**—Chester Lemon, of. **Cleveland (1)**—James Kern, p. **Detroit (1)**—Jason Thompson, 1b. **Kansas City (3)**—●George Brett, 3b; ●Freddie Patek, ss; Frank White, 2b. **Milwaukee (2)**—●Donald Money, 2b; Lary Sorensen, p. **Minnesota (1)**—●Rodney Carew, 1b. **New York (5)**—Richard Gossage, p; Ronald Guidry, p; ●Reginald Jackson, of (replaced by Graig Nettles, 3b, New York, who in turn was replaced by Larry Hisle, of, Milwaukee); Thurman Munson, c (replaced by Darrell Porter, c, Kansas City). **Oakland (1)**—Matthew Keough, p. **Seattle (1)**—G. Craig Reynolds, ss. **Texas (2)**—James Sundberg, c; ●Richard Zisk, of. **Toronto (1)**—Roy Howell, 3b.

NATIONAL LEAGUE—Thomas Lasorda, Los Angeles, manager; Charles Tanner, Pittsburgh, Daniel Ozark, Philadelphia, coaches. **Atlanta (2)**—Jeffrey Burroughs, of; Philip Niekro, p. **Chicago (1)**—H. Bruce Sutter, p. **Cincinnati (6)**—●Johnny Bench, c (replaced by Biff Pocoroba, c, Atlanta); David Concepcion, ss; ●George Foster, of; ●Joe Morgan, 2b; ●Peter Rose, 3b; G. Thomas Seaver, p. **Houston (1)**—Terry Puhl, of. **Los Angeles (6)**—Ronald Cey, 3b; ●Steven Garvey, 1b; Thomas John, p; David Lopes, 2b; ●Robert Monday, of; C. Reginald Smith, of. **Montreal (2)**—Ross Grimsley, p; Stephen Rogers, p. **New York (1)**—Patrick Zachry, p. **Philadelphia (3)**—Robert Boone, c; ●Lawrence Bowa, ss; ●Gregory Luzinski, of. **Pittsburgh (1)**—Wilver Stargell, 1b. **St. Louis (1)**—Ted Simmons, c. **San Diego (2)**—Roland Fingers, p; David Winfield, of. **San Francisco (2)**—Vida Blue, p; Jack Clark, of.

1979

AMERICAN LEAGUE—Robert Lemon, New York, manager; Patrick Corrales, Texas, Roy Hartsfield, Toronto, Darrell Johnson, Seattle, coaches. **Baltimore (2)**—Kenneth Singleton, of; Donald Stanhouse, p. **Boston (5)**—Richard Burleson, ss; ●Fredric Lynn, of; ●James Rice, of; Robert Stanley, p; ●Carl Yastrzemski, of. **California (6)**—Donald Baylor, of; ●Rodney Carew, 1b (replaced by Cecil Cooper, 1b, Milwaukee); Mark Clear, p; Brian Downing, c; Robert Grich, 2b; L. Nolan Ryan, p. **Chicago (1)**—Chester Lemon, of. **Cleveland (1)**—Isidro Monge, p. **Detroit (1)**—Steven Kemp, of. **Kansas City (3)**—●George Brett, 3b; ●Darrell Porter, c; ●Frank White, 2b. **Minnesota (1)**—●Roy Smalley, ss. **New York (4)**—Ronald Guidry, p; Reginald Jackson, of; Thomas John, p; Graig Nettles, 3b. **Oakland (1)**—Jeffrey Newman, c. **Seattle (1)**—Bruce Bochte, 1b. **Texas (1)**—James Kern, p. **Toronto (1)**—David Lemanczyk, p.

NATIONAL LEAGUE—Thomas Lasorda, Los Angeles, manager; Daniel Ozark, Philadelphia, Charles Tanner, Pittsburgh, coaches. **Atlanta (1)**—Gary Matthews, of. **Chicago (2)**—David Kingman, of (replaced by Keith Hernandez, 1b, St. Louis); H. Bruce Sutter, p. **Cincinnati (3)**—David Concepcion, ss (replaced by Larry Parrish, 3b, Montreal); ●George Foster, of; Michael LaCoss, p; Joe Morgan, 2b. **Houston (3)**—Joaquin Andujar, p; Joseph Niekro, p; Joseph Sambito, p. **Los Angeles (3)**—Ronald Cey, 3b; ●Steven Garvey, 1b; ●David Lopes, 2b. **Montreal (2)**—Gary Carter, c; Stephen Rogers, p. **New York (1)**—Lee Mazzilli, of. **Philadelphia (5)**—Robert Boone, c; ●Lawrence Bowa, ss; Steven Carlton, p; Peter Rose, 1b; ●Michael Schmidt, 3b. **Pittsburgh (1)**—●David Parker, of. **St. Louis (3)**—Louis Brock, of; ●Ted Simmons, c (replaced by Johnny Bench, c, Cincinnati, who in turn was replaced by John Stearns, c, New York); Garry Templeton, ss (replaced by G. Craig Reynolds, ss, Houston). **San Diego (2)**—Gaylord Perry, p; ●David Winfield, of. **San Francisco (1)**—Jack Clark, of.

1980

AMERICAN LEAGUE—Earl Weaver, Baltimore, manager; Frank Robinson, Baltimore, James Frey, Kansas City, coaches. **Baltimore (2)**—Alonza Bumbry, of; Steven Stone, p. **Boston (4)**—Thomas Burgmeier, p; ●Carlton Fisk, c; ●Fredric Lynn, of; ●James Rice, of (replaced due to injury). **California (2)**—●Rodney Carew, 1b; Robert Grich, 2b. **Chicago (1)**—Edward Farmer, p. **Cleveland (1)**—Jorge Orta, of. **Detroit (2)**—Lance Parrish, c; Alan Trammell, ss. **Kansas City (3)**—●George Brett, 3b (replaced due to injury); Lawrence Gura, p; Darrell Porter, c. **Milwaukee (4)**—Cecil Cooper, 1b; ●Paul Molitor, 2b (replaced due to injury); Benjamin Oglivie, of; Robin Yount, ss. **Minnesota (1)**—Kenneth Landreaux, of. **New York (6)**—●Russell Dent, ss; Richard Gossage, p; ●Reginald Jackson, of; Thomas John, p; Graig Nettles, 3b; William Randolph, 2b. **Oakland (1)**—Rickey Henderson, of. **Seattle (1)**—Frederick Honeycutt, p. **Texas (2)**—David Bell, 3b; Albert Oliver, of. **Toronto (1)**—David Stieb, p.

NATIONAL LEAGUE—Charles Tanner, Pittsburgh, manager; John McNamara, Cincinnati, William Virdon, Houston, coaches. **Atlanta (1)**—Dale Murphy, of. **Chicago (2)**—●David Kingman, of; H. Bruce Sutter, p. **Cincinnati (3)**—●Johnny Bench, c; David Concepcion, ss; G. Kenneth Griffey, of. **Houston (2)**—Jose Cruz, of; J. Rodney Richard, p. **Los Angeles (6)**—●Steven Garvey, 1b; ●David Lopes, 2b; Jerry Reuss, p; ●William Russell, ss; ●C. Reginald Smith, of; Robert Welch, p. **Montreal (1)**—Gary Carter, c. **New York (1)**—John Stearns, c. **Philadelphia (3)**—Steven Carlton, p; Peter Rose, 1b; ●Michael Schmidt, 3b (replaced by C. Ray Knight, 3b, Cincinnati). **Pittsburgh (4)**—James Bibby, p; Philip Garner, 2b; ●David Parker, of; Kenton Tekulve, p. **St. Louis (3)**—George Hendrick, of; Keith Hernandez, 1b; Kenneth Reitz, 3b. **San Diego (1)**—David Winfield, of. **San Francisco (1)**—Vida Blue, p (replaced by Eddie Whitson, p, San Francisco).

1981

AMERICAN LEAGUE—James Frey, Kansas City, manager; David Garcia, Cleveland, Donald Zimmer, Texas, coaches. **Baltimore (3)**—Scott McGregor, p; Eddie Murray, 1b; ●Kenneth Singleton, of. **Boston (1)**—Dwight Evans, of. **California (4)**—Richard Burleson, ss; ●Rodney Carew, 1b; Kenneth Forsch, p; Fredric Lynn, of. **Chicago (2)**—Robert Burns, p; Carlton Fisk, c. **Cleveland (2)**—Leonard Barker, p; Baudilio Diaz, c. **Detroit (1)**—●John Morris, p. **Kansas City (2)**—●George Brett, 3b; Frank White, 2b. **Milwaukee (3)**—Roland Fingers, p; Ted Simmons, c; Gorman Thomas, of. **Minnesota (1)**—Douglas Corbett, p. **New York (5)**—●Russell Dent, ss; Richard Gossage, p (replaced by Ronald Davis, p, New York); ●Reginald Jackson, of; ●William Randolph, 2b; ●David Winfield, of. **Oakland (2)**—Antonio Armas, of; Michael Norris, p. **Seattle (1)**—Thomas Paciorek, of. Texas (2)—David Bell, 3b, Albert Oliver, of. **Toronto (1)**—David Stieb, p.

NATIONAL LEAGUE—G. Dallas Green, Philadelphia, manager; William Virdon, Houston, Richard Williams, Montreal, coaches. **Atlanta (1)**—Bruce Benedict, c. **Chicago (1)**—William Buckner, 1b. **Cincinnati (3)**—●David Concepcion, ss; ●George Foster, of; G. Thomas Seaver, p. **Houston (2)**—L. Nolan Ryan, p; Robert Knepper, p. **Los Angeles (6)**—Johnnie Baker, of; Steven Garvey, 1b; Pedro Guerrero, of; Burt Hooton, p; ●David Lopes, 2b; ●Fernando Valenzuela, p. **Montreal (3)**—●Gary Carter, c; ●Andre Dawson, of; Timothy, Raines, of. **New York (1)**—Joel Youngblood, 3b. **Philadelphia (5)**—Steven Carlton, p; ●Peter Rose, 1b; Richard Ruthven, p; ●Michael Schmidt, 3b; Jesus Trillo, 2b. **Pittsburgh (4)**—Michael Easler, of; Philip Garner, 2b; Bill Madlock, 3b; ●David Parker, of. **St. Louis (1)**—H. Bruce Sutter, p. **San Diego (2)**—Terrence Kennedy, c; Osborne Smith, ss. **San Francisco (1)**—Vida Blue, p.

1982

AMERICAN LEAGUE—Alfred (Billy) Martin, Oakland, manager; George (Sparky) Anderson, Detroit, Richard Howser, Kansas City, coaches. **Baltimore (1)**—Eddie Murray, 1b. **Boston (3)**—Mark Clear, p; Dennis Eckersley, p; Carl Yastrzemski, 1b. **California (3)**—●Robert Grich, 2b; ●Reginald Jackson, of; ●Fredric Lynn, of. **Chicago (1)**—●Carlton Fisk, c. **Cleveland (2)**—Colbert Harrah, 3b; Andre Thornton, 1b. **Detroit (1)**—Lance Parrish, c. **Kansas City (5)**—●George Brett, 3b; Harold McRae, of; Daniel Quisenberry, p; Frank White, 2b; Willie Wilson, of. **Milwaukee (4)**—●Cecil Cooper, 1b; Roland Fingers, p; Benjamin Oglivie, of; ●Robin Yount, ss. **Minnesota (1)**—Kent Hrbek, 1b. **New York (3)**—Richard Gossage, p; Ronald Guidry, p; David Winfield, of. **Oakland (1)**—●Rickey Henderson, of. **Seattle (1)**—Floyd Bannister, p. **Texas (1)**—David Bell, 3b. **Toronto (1)**—James Clancy, p.

NATIONAL LEAGUE—Thomas Lasorda, Los Angeles, manager; John McNamara, Cincinnati, Charles Tanner, Pittsburgh, W. James Fanning, Montreal, coaches. **Atlanta (3)**—J. Robert Horner, 3b; ●Dale Murphy, of; Philip Niekro, p. **Chicago (1)**—Leon Durham, of. **Cincinnati (3)**—●David Concepcion, ss; Thomas Hume, p; Mario Soto, p. **Houston (1)**—C. Ray Knight, 3b. **Los Angeles (4)**—Johnnie Baker, of; Steven Howe, p; Stephen Sax, 2b; Fernando Valenzuela, p. **Montreal (5)**—●Gary Carter, c; ●Andre Dawson, of; Albert Oliver, 1b; ●Timothy Raines, of; Stephen Rogers, p. **New York (1)**—John Stearns, c. **Philadelphia (4)**—Steven Carlton, p; ●Peter Rose, 1b; ●Michael Schmidt, 3b; ●J. Manuel Trillo, 2b. **Pittsburgh (2)**—Antonio Pena, c; Jason Thompson, 1b. **St. Louis (2)**—Lonnie Smith, of; Osborne Smith, ss. **San Diego (1)**—Ruppert Jones, of. San Francisco (1)—Gregory Minton, p.

1983

AMERICAN LEAGUE—Harvey Kuenn, Milwaukee, manager; Joseph Altobelli, Baltimore, William Gardner, Minnesota, coaches. **Baltimore (2)**—Eddie Murray, 1b; Calvin Ripken, ss. **Boston (3)**—James Rice, of; Robert Stanley, p; Carl Yastrzemski, 1b. **California (5)**—Robert Boone, c; ●Rodney Carew, 1b; Douglas DeCinces, 3b; ●Reginald Jackson, of (replaced by Benjamin Oglivie, of, Milwaukee); ●Fredric Lynn, of. **Chicago (1)**—Ronald Kittle, of. **Cleveland (2)**—Richard Sutcliffe, p; ●J. Manuel Trillo, 2b. **Detroit (3)**—Aurelio Lopez, p; Lance Parrish, c; Louis Whitaker, 2b. **Kansas City (3)**—●George Brett, 3b; Daniel Quisenberry, p; Willie Wilson, of. **Milwaukee (3)**—Cecil Cooper, 1b; ●Ted Simmons, c; ●Robin Yount, ss. **Minnesota (1)**—Gary Ward, of. **New York (2)**—Ronald Guidry, p (replaced by Felix Martinez, p, Baltimore); ●David Winfield, of. **Oakland (1)**—Rickey Henderson, of. **Seattle (1)**—Matthew Young, p. **Texas (1)**—Frederick Honeycutt, p. **Toronto (1)**—David Stieb, p.

NATIONAL LEAGUE—Dorrel (Whitey) Herzog, St. Louis, manager; Patrick Corrales, Philadelphia, Thomas Lasorda, Los Angeles, Joseph Torre, Atlanta, coaches. **Atlanta (4)**—Bruce Benedict, c; Glenn Hubbard, 2b; ●Dale Murphy, of; Pascual Perez, p. **Chicago (2)**—Leon Durham, of; Lee Smith, p. **Cincinnati (2)**—Johnny Bench, c; Mario Soto, p. **Houston (2)**—William Dawley, p; Richard Thon, ss. **Los Angeles (3)**—Pedro Guerrero, 3b-of; ●Stephen Sax, 2b; Fernando Valenzuela, p. **Montreal (5)**—●Gary Carter, c; ●Andre Dawson, of; ●Albert Oliver, 1b; ●Timothy Raines, of; Stephen Rogers, p. **New York (1)**—Jesse Orosco, p. **Philadelphia (1)**—●Michael Schmidt, 3b. **Pittsburgh (1)**—Bill Madlock, 3b. **St. Louis (3)**—George Hendrick, of; Willie McGee, of; ●Ozzie Smith, ss. **San Diego (1)**—David Dravecky, p; Terrence Kennedy, c. **San Francisco (3)**—Darrell Evans, 1b; C. Atlee Hammaker, p; Gary Lavelle, p.

Montreal catcher Gary Carter hit his third All-Star home run in 1984 and captured MVP honors for the second time.

1984

AMERICAN LEAGUE—Joseph Altobelli, Baltimore, manager; George (Sparky) Anderson, Detroit, Anthony LaRussa, Chicago, coaches. **Baltimore (3)**—Michael Boddicker, p; Eddie Murray, 1b; ●Calvin Ripken, ss. **Boston (2)**—Antonio Armas, of; James Rice, of. **California (2)**—●Rodney Carew, 1b; ●Reginald Jackson, of. **Chicago (1)**—Richard Dotson, p. **Cleveland (1)**—Andre Thornton, 1b. **Detroit (6)**—Guillermo Hernandez, p; ●Chester Lemon, of; John Morris, p; ●Lance Parrish, c; Alan Trammell, ss (replaced by Alfredo Griffin, ss, Toronto); ●Louis Whitaker, 2b. **Kansas City (2)**—●George Brett, 3b; Daniel Quisenberry, p. **Milwaukee (1)**—James Sundberg, c. **Minnesota (1)**—R. David Engle, c. **New York (3)**—Donald Mattingly, 1b-of; Philip Niekro, p; ●David Winfield, of. **Oakland (2)**—William Caudill, p; Rickey Henderson, of. **Seattle (1)**—Alvin Davis, of. **Texas (1)**—David Bell, 3b. **Toronto (2)**—Damaso Garcia, 2b; David Stieb, p.

NATIONAL LEAGUE—Paul Owens, Philadelphia, manager; Thomas Lasorda, Los Angeles, Charles Tanner, Pittsburgh, coaches. **Atlanta (3)**—●Dale Murphy, of; Rafael Ramirez, ss; Claudell Washington, of. **Chicago (2)**—Jody Davis, c; ●Ryne Sandberg, 2b. **Cincinnati (1)**—Mario Soto, p. **Houston (1)**—Jerry Mumphrey, of. **Los Angeles (1)**—Michael Marshall, 1b-of. **Montreal (4)**—●Gary Carter, c; Charles Lea, p; Timothy Raines, of; Timothy Wallach, 3b. **New York (4)**—Dwight Gooden, p; Keith Hernandez, 1b; Jesse Orosco, p; ●Darryl Strawberry, of. **Philadelphia (3)**—Alfred Holland, p; Juan Samuel, 2b; ●Michael Schmidt, 3b. **Pittsburgh (1)**—Antonio Pena, c. **St. Louis (3)**—Joaquin Andujar, p (replaced by Fernando Valenzuela, p, Los Angeles); ●Osborne Smith, ss; H. Bruce Sutter, p. **San Diego (3)**—●Steven Garvey, 1b; Richard Gossage, p; ●Anthony Gwynn, of. **San Francisco (2)**—Robert Brenly, c; Charles Davis, of.

ALL-STAR HOME RUNS (123)

Player	Date	Inning	On	Pitcher
George Ruth, A. L.	July 6, 1933	3	1	William Hallahan
Frank Frisch, N. L.	July 6, 1933	6	0	Alvin Crowder
Frank Frisch, N. L.	July 10, 1934	1	0	Vernon Gomez
Joseph Medwick, N. L.	July 10, 1934	3	2	Vernon Gomez
James Foxx, A. L.	July 8, 1935	1	1	William Walker
August Galan, N. L.	July 7, 1936	5	0	Lynwood Rowe
H. Louis Gehrig, A. L.	July 7, 1936	7	0	Curtis Davis
H. Louis Gehrig, A. L.	July 7, 1937	3	1	Jerome Dean
Joseph DiMaggio, A. L.	July 11, 1939	5	0	William Lee
Max West, N. L.	July 9, 1940	1	2	Charles Ruffing
J. Floyd Vaughan, N. L.	July 8, 1941	7	1	Sidney Hudson
J. Floyd Vaughan, N. L.	July 8, 1941	8	1	Edgar Smith
Theodore Williams, A. L.	July 8, 1941	9	2	Claude Passeau
Louis Boudreau, A. L.	July 6, 1942	1	0	Morton Cooper
Rudolph York, A. L.	July 6, 1942	1	1	Morton Cooper
Arnold Owen, N. L.	July 6, 1942	8	0	J. Alton Benton
Robert Doerr, A. L.	July 13, 1943	2	2	Morton Cooper
Vincent DiMaggio, N. L.	July 13, 1943	9	0	Cecil Hughson
Charles Keller, A. L.	July 9, 1946	1	1	Claude Passeau
Theodore Williams, A. L.	July 9, 1946	4	0	W. Kirby Higbe
Theodore Williams, A. L.	July 9, 1946	8	2	Truett Sewell
John Mize, N. L.	July 8, 1947	4	0	Francis Shea
Stanley Musial, N. L.	July 13, 1948	1	1	Walter Masterson
Walter Evers, A. L.	July 13, 1948	2	0	Ralph Branca
Stanley Musial, N. L.	July 12, 1949	1	1	Melvin Parnell
Ralph Kiner, N. L.	July 12, 1949	6	1	Louis Brissie
Ralph Kiner, N. L.	July 11, 1950	9	0	Arthur Houtteman
Albert Schoendienst, N. L.	July 11, 1950	14	0	Theodore Gray
Stanley Musial, N. L.	July 10, 1951	4	0	Edmund Lopat
Robert Elliott, N. L.	July 10, 1951	4	1	Edmund Lopat
Victor Wertz, A. L.	July 10, 1951	4	0	Salvatore Maglie
George Kell, A. L.	July 10, 1951	5	0	Salvatore Maglie
Gilbert Hodges, N. L.	July 10, 1951	6	1	Fred Hutchinson
Ralph Kiner, N. L.	July 10, 1951	8	0	Melvin Parnell
Jack Robinson, N. L.	July 8, 1952	1	0	Victor Raschi
Henry Sauer, N. L.	July 8, 1952	4	1	Robert Lemon
Albert Rosen, A. L.	July 13, 1954	3	2	Robin Roberts
Raymond Boone, A. L.	July 13, 1954	3	0	Robin Roberts
Theodore Kluszewski, N. L.	July 13, 1954	5	1	Ervin Porterfield
Albert Rosen, A. L.	July 13, 1954	5	1	John Antonelli
David (Gus) Bell, N. L.	July 13, 1954	8	1	Robert Keegan
Lawrence Doby, A. L.	July 13, 1954	8	0	D. Eugene Conley
Mickey Mantle, A. L.	July 12, 1955	1	2	Robin Roberts
Stanley Musial, N. L.	July 12, 1955	12	0	Franklin Sullivan
Willie Mays, N. L.	July 10, 1956	4	1	Edward Ford
Theodore Williams, A. L.	July 10, 1956	6	1	Warren Spahn
Mickey Mantle, A. L.	July 10, 1956	6	0	Warren Spahn
Stanley Musial, N. L.	July 10, 1956	7	0	Thomas Brewer
Edwin Mathews, N. L.	July 7, 1959	1	0	Early Wynn
Albert Kaline, A. L.	July 7, 1959	4	0	Lewis Burdette
Frank Malzone, A. L.	Aug. 3, 1959	2	0	Donald Drysdale
Lawrence Berra, A. L.	Aug. 3, 1959	3	1	Donald Drysdale
Frank Robinson, N. L.	Aug. 3, 1959	5	0	Early Wynn
James Gilliam, N. L.	Aug. 3, 1959	7	0	William O'Dell
Rocco Colavito, A. L.	Aug. 3, 1959	8	0	ElRoy Face
Ernest Banks, N. L.	July 11, 1960	1	1	Bill Monbouquette
Delmar Crandall, N. L.	July 11, 1960	2	0	Bill Monbouquette
Albert Kaline, A. L.	July 11, 1960	8	0	Robert Buhl
Edwin Mathews, N. L.	July 13, 1960	2	1	Edward Ford
Willie Mays, N. L.	July 13, 1960	3	0	Edward Ford
Stanley Musial, N. L.	July 13, 1960	7	0	Gerald Staley
Kenton Boyer, N. L.	July 13, 1960	9	1	Gary Bell
Harmon Killebrew, A. L.	July 11, 1961	6	0	Michael McCormick
George Altman, N. L.	July 11, 1961	8	0	J. Miguel Fornieles
Rocco Colavito, A. L.	July 31, 1961	1	0	Robert Purkey
James Runnels, A. L.	July 30, 1962	3	0	Arthur Mahaffey
Leon Wagner, A. L.	July 30, 1962	4	1	Arthur Mahaffey
Rocco Colavito, A. L.	July 30, 1962	7	2	Richard Farrell
John Roseboro, N. L.	July 30, 1962	9	0	Milton Pappas
Billy Williams, N. L.	July 7, 1964	4	0	Johnathan Wyatt
Kenton Boyer, N. L.	July 7, 1964	4	0	Johnathan Wyatt
John Callison, N. L.	July 7, 1964	9	2	Richard Radatz
Willie Mays, N. L.	July 13, 1965	1	0	Milton Pappas
Joseph Torre, N. L.	July 13, 1965	1	1	Milton Pappas
Wilver Stargell, N. L.	July 13, 1965	2	1	James Grant
Richard McAuliffe, A. L.	July 13, 1965	5	0	James Maloney
Harmon Killebrew, A. L.	July 13, 1965	5	1	James Maloney
Richard Allen, N. L.	July 11, 1967	2	0	Dean Chance
Brooks Robinson, A. L.	July 11, 1967	6	0	Ferguson Jenkins
Atanasio (Tony) Perez, N. L.	July 11, 1967	15	0	James Hunter
Johnny Bench, N. L.	July 23, 1969	2	1	Melvin Stottlemyre

*The big bat of Atlanta slugger Dale Murphy produced its first
All-Star home run during the eighth inning of the 1984 game at
San Francisco's Candlestick Park.*

ALL-STAR HOME RUNS (123)—Continued

Player	Date	Inning	On	Pitcher
Frank Howard, A. L.	July 23, 1969	2	0	Steven Carlton
Willie McCovey, N. L.	July 23, 1969	3	1	Johnny Odom
William Freehan, A. L.	July 23, 1969	3	0	Steven Carlton
Willie McCovey, N. L.	July 23, 1969	4	0	Dennis McLain
Richard Dietz, N. L.	July 14, 1970	9	0	James Hunter
Johnny Bench, N. L.	July 13, 1971	2	1	Vida Blue
Henry Aaron, N. L.	July 13, 1971	3	0	Vida Blue
Reginald Jackson, A. L.	July 13, 1971	3	1	Dock Ellis
Frank Robinson, A. L.	July 13, 1971	3	1	Dock Ellis
Harmon Killebrew, A. L.	July 13, 1971	6	1	Ferguson Jenkins
Roberto Clemente, N. L.	July 13, 1971	8	0	Michael Lolich
Henry Aaron, N. L.	July 23, 1972	6	1	Gaylord Perry
Octavio Rojas, A. L.	July 25, 1972	8	1	William Stoneman
Johnny Bench, N. L.	July 24, 1973	4	0	William Singer
Bobby Bonds, N. L.	July 24, 1973	5	1	William Singer
William Davis, N. L.	July 24, 1973	6	1	L. Nolan Ryan
C. Reginald Smith, N. L.	July 23, 1974	7	0	James Hunter
Steven Garvey, N. L.	July 15, 1975	2	0	Vida Blue
James Wynn, N. L.	July 15, 1975	2	0	Vida Blue
Carl Yastrzemski, A. L.	July 15, 1975	6	2	G. Thomas Seaver
George Foster, N. L.	July 13, 1976	3	1	James Hunter
Fredric Lynn, A. L.	July 13, 1976	4	0	G. Thomas Seaver
Cesar Cedeno, N. L.	July 13, 1976	8	1	Frank Tanana
Joe Morgan, N. L.	July 19, 1977	1	0	James Palmer
Gregory Luzinski, N. L.	July 19, 1977	1	1	James Palmer
Steven Garvey, N. L.	July 19, 1977	3	0	James Palmer
George Scott, A. L.	July 19, 1977	9	1	Richard Gossage
Fredric Lynn, A. L.	July 17 1979	1	1	Steven Carlton
Lee Mazzilli, N. L.	July 17 1979	8	0	James Kern
Fredric Lynn, A. L.	July 8, 1980	5	1	Robert Welch
G. Kenneth Griffey, N. L.	July 8, 1980	5	0	Thomas John
Kenneth Singleton, A. L.	Aug. 9, 1981	2	0	G. Thomas Seaver
Gary Carter, N. L.	Aug. 9, 1981	5	0	Kenneth Forsch
David Parker, N. L.	Aug. 9, 1981	6	0	Michael Norris
Gary Carter, N. L.	Aug. 9, 1981	7	0	Ronald Davis
Michael Schmidt, N. L.	Aug. 9, 1981	8	1	Roland Fingers
David Concepcion, N. L.	July 13, 1982	2	1	Dennis Eckersley
James Rice, A. L.	July 6, 1983	3	0	C. Atlee Hammaker
Fredric Lynn, A. L.	July 6, 1983	3	3	C. Atlee Hammaker
George Brett, A. L.	July 10, 1984	2	0	Charles Lea
Gary Carter, N. L.	July 10, 1984	2	0	David Stieb
Dale Murphy, N. L.	July 10, 1984	8	0	Willie Hernandez

All-Star Game Records

INDIVIDUAL BATTING, BASE-RUNNING—GAME, INNING

Most At-Bats, Nine-Inning Game

5—28 times—Held by 27 players.
Last Players—David M. Winfield, N. L., July 17, 1979.
James E. Rice, A. L., July 17, 1979.

Most At-Bats, Extra-Inning Game

7—Willie E. Jones, N. L., July 11, 1950, 14 innings.

Most Times Faced Pitcher, Inning

2—George H. Ruth, A. L., July 10, 1934, fifth inning.
H. Louis Gehrig, A. L., July 10, 1934, fifth inning.
James E. Rice, A.L., July 6, 1983, third inning.

Most Runs, Game

4—Theodore S. Williams, A. L., July 9, 1946.

Most Runs, Inning

1—Held by many players.

Most Runs Batted In, Game

5—Theodore S. Williams, A. L., July 9, 1946.
Albert L. Rosen, A. L., July 13, 1954.

Most Runs Batted In, Inning

4—Fredric M. Lynn, A.L., July 6, 1983, third inning.

Most Hits, Game

4—Joseph M. Medwick, N. L., July 7, 1937 (5 at bats, 2 singles, 2 doubles), consecutive on last four plate appearances.
Theodore S. Williams, A. L., July 9, 1946 (4 at bats, 2 singles, 2 homers, also one base on balls), consecutive on last four plate appearances.
Carl M. Yastrzemski, A. L., July 14, 1970, night game, 12 innings, (6 at bats, 3 singles, 1 double).

Most Times Reached First Base Safely, Game

5—Philip J. Cavarretta, N. L., July 11, 1944 (3 bases on balls, one single, one triple).
Theodore S. Williams, A. L., July 9, 1946 (2 singles, 2 homers, one base on balls).

Most Hits, Inning

1—Held by many players.

Most One-Base Hits, Game (8 times)

3—Charles L. Gehringer, A. L., July 7, 1937.
William J. Herman, N. L., July 9, 1940.
Stanley C. Hack, N. L., July 13, 1943.
Roberto F. Avila, A. L., July 13, 1954.
Kenton L. Boyer, N. L., July 10, 1956.
Harmon Killebrew, A. L., July 7, 1964.
Carl M. Yastrzemski, A. L., July 14, 1970, night game, 12 innings.
Rickey H. Henderson, A. L., July 13, 1982, night game.

Most One-Base Hits, Inning

1—Held by many players.

Most Two-Base Hits, Game

2—Joseph M. Medwick, N. L., July 7, 1937.
Aloysius H. Simmons, A. L., July 10, 1934.
Theodore B. Kluszewski, N. L., July 10, 1956.
Ernest Banks, N. L., July 7, 1959.

Most Two-Base Hits, Inning

1—Held by many players.

Two-Base Hit, Inning, Batting in Three Runs

Never accomplished.

Most Three-Base Hits, Game

2—Rodney C. Carew, A. L., July 11, 1978.

Most Three-Base Hits, Inning
1—Held by many players.

Three-Base Hit, Inning, Batting in Three Runs
Never accomplished.

Most Home Runs, Game
2—J. Floyd Vaughan, N. L., July 8, 1941 (consecutive).
Theodore S. Williams, A. L., July 9, 1946.
Albert L. Rosen, A. L., July 13, 1954 (consecutive).
Willie L. McCovey, N. L., July 23, 1969 (consecutive).
Gary E. Carter, N. L., August 9, 1981 (consecutive).

Most Home Runs, Inning
1—Held by many players. Accomplished 123 times. 73 by N. L., 50 by A. L.

Hitting Home Run in First At-Bat (7)
Max West, N. L., July 9, 1940, first inning, two on base.
Walter Evers, A. L., July 13, 1948, second inning, none on base.
James Gilliam, N. L., Aug. 3, 1959, seventh inning, none on base.
George Altman, N. L., July 11, 1961, eighth inning, none on base.
Johnny Bench, N. L., July 23, 1969, second inning, one on base.
Richard Dietz, N. L., July 14, 1970, ninth inning, none on base.
Lee Mazzilli, N. L., July 17, 1979, eighth inning, none on base.

Hitting Home Run With Bases Loaded
Fredric M. Lynn, A.L., July 6, 1983, third inning.

Most Home Runs, Inning or Game, Pinch-Hitter (13)
1—Arnold M. Owen, N. L., July 6, 1942, eighth inning, none on base.
David R. Bell, N. L., July 13, 1954, eighth inning, one on base.
Lawrence E. Doby, A. L., July 13, 1954, eighth inning, none on base.
Willie H. Mays, N. L., July 10, 1956, fourth inning, one on base.
Stanley F. Musial, N. L., July 13, 1960, seventh inning, none on base.
Harmon C. Killebrew, A. L., July 11, 1961, sixth inning, none on base.
George L. Altman, N. L., July 11, 1961, eighth inning, none on base.
James E. Runnels, A. L., July 30, 1962, third inning, none on base.
Reginald M. Jackson, A. L., July 13, 1971, third inning, one on base.
Octavio V. Rojas, A. L., July 25, 1972, eighth inning, one on base.
William H. Davis, N. L., July 24, 1973, sixth inning, one on base.
Carl M. Yastrzemski, A. L., July 15, 1975, sixth inning, two on base.
Lee L. Mazzilli, N. L., July 17, 1979, eighth inning, none on base.

Most Times Home Run as Leadoff Batter, Start of Game
1—Frank F. Frisch, N. L., July 10, 1934.
Louis Boudreau, A. L., July 6, 1942.
Willie H. Mays, N. L., July 13, 1965.
Joe Leonard Morgan, N. L., July 19, 1977.

Most Long Hits, Game
2—Held by many players.

Most Long Hits, Inning
1—Held by many players.

Most Total Bases, Game
10—Theodore S. Williams, A. L., July 9, 1946.

Most Total Bases, Inning
4—Held by many players.

Most Sacrifice Hits, Game or Inning
1—Held by many players.

Most Sacrifice Flies, Game or Inning
1—Held by many players.

Most Bases on Balls, Game
3—Charles L. Gehringer, A. L., July 10, 1934.
Philip J. Cavarretta, N. L., July 11, 1944 (also one single, one triple; 5 plate appearances).

Most Bases on Balls, Inning
1—Held by many players.

Most Strikeouts, Nine-Inning Game
3—H. Louis Gehrig, A. L., July 10, 1934.
Robert L. Johnson, A. L., July 8, 1935.
Stanley C. Hack, N. L., July 11, 1939.
Joseph L. Gordon, A. L., July 6, 1942.
Kenneth F. Keltner, A. L., July 13, 1943.
James E. Hegan, A. L., July 11, 1950.
Mickey C. Mantle, A. L., July 10, 1956.
John Roseboro, N. L., July 31, 1961.
Willie L. McCovey, N. L., July 9, 1968.
Johnny L. Bench, N. L., July 14, 1970, night game; caught first six innings.

Most Strikeouts, Extra-Inning Game
4—Roberto W. Clemente, N. L., July 11, 1967 (consecutive).

Most Strikeouts, Inning
1—Held by many players.

Most Stolen Bases, Inning or Game
2—Willie H. Mays, N. L., July 9, 1963.

Stealing Home, Game
1—Harold J. Traynor, N. L., July 10, 1934, fifth inning (front end of a double steal with Mel Ott).

Most Times Caught Stealing, Nine-Inning Game
1—Held by many players

Most Times Caught Stealing, Extra-Inning Game
2—Pedro (Tony) Oliva, A. L., July 11, 1967, 15 innings.

Most Hit by Pitch, Inning or Game
1—Accomplished 24 times. (Held by 24 players.)

Most Grounded Into Double Plays, Game
2—Robert C. Richardson, A. L., July 9, 1963

INDIVIDUAL BATTING, BASE-RUNNING—TOTAL GAMES

Most Games
24—Stanley F. Musial, N. L., 1943, 1944, 1946, 1947, 1948, 1949, 1950, 1951, 1952, 1953, 1954, 1955, 1956, 1957, 1958, 1959, 1959, 1960, 1960, 1961, 1961, 1962, 1962, 1963 (consecutive).
Willie H. Mays, N. L., 1954, 1955, 1956, 1957, 1958, 1959, 1959, 1960, 1960, 1961, 1961, 1962, 1962, 1963, 1964, 1965, 1966, 1967, 1968, 1969, 1970, 1971, 1972, 1973 (consecutive).
Henry L. Aaron, N. L., 1955, 1956, 1957, 1958, 1959, 1959, 1960, 1960, 1961, 1961, 1962, 1963, 1964, 1965, 1966, 1967, 1968, 1969, 1970, 1971, 1972, 1973, 1974 (23 games), A. L., 1975, (1 game).

Most Games, Pinch-Hitter
10—Stanley F. Musial, 1947, 1955, 1959, first game, 1960, 1960, 1961, 1961, 1962, 1962, 1963 10 pinch-hit at-bats.

Highest Batting Average, Five or More Games
.500—Charles L. Gehringer, A. L., 1933, 1934, 1935, 1936, 1937, 1938 (6 games, 20 at-bats).

Most At-Bats, Total Games
75—Willie H. Mays, N. L., 1954, 1955, 1956, 1957, 1958, 1959, 1959, 1960, 1960, 1961, 1961, 1962, 1962, 1963, 1964, 1965, 1966, 1967, 1968, 1969, 1970, 1971, 1972, 1973 (24 games).

Most At-Bats, Total Games, Without a Hit
10—Terry B. Moore, N. L., 1939, 1940, 1941, 1942 (4 games).

Most Runs, Total Games

20—Willie H. Mays, N. L., 1954, 1955, 1956, 1957, 1958, 1959, 1959, 1960, 1960, 1961, 1961, 1962, 1962, 1963, 1964, 1965, 1966, 1967, 1968, 1969, 1970, 1971, 1972, 1973 (24 games).

Most Runs Batted In, Total Games

12—Theodore S. Williams, A. L., 1940, 1941, 1942, 1946, 1947, 1948, 1949, 1950, 1951, 1954, 1955, 1956, 1957, 1958, 1959, 1959, 1960, 1960 (18 games).

Most Hits, Total Games

23—Willie H. Mays, N. L., 1954, 1955, 1956, 1957, 1958, 1959, 1959, 1960, 1960, 1961, 1961, 1962, 1962, 1963, 1964, 1965, 1966, 1967, 1968, 1969, 1970, 1971, 1972, 1973 (24 games).

Most Consecutive Games Batted Safely, Total Games

7—Mickey C. Mantle, A. L., 1954, 1955, 1956, 1957, 1958, 1959 (second game), 1960 (second game). 1959, first game, pinch runner; 1960, first game, two bases on balls.

Joe L. Morgan, N. L., 1970, 1972, 1973, 1974, 1975, 1976, 1977 (was not on team in 1971).

6—Stanley F. Musial, N. L., 1953, 1954, 1955, 1956, 1957, 1958.
Willie H. Mays, N. L., 1954, 1955, 1956, 1957, 1958, 1959, first game.
Johnny Bench, N. L., 1971, 1972, 1973, 1974, 1975, 1976.

Most Hits, Total Games, as Pinch-Hitter

3—Stanley F. Musial, N. L., 1943, 1944, 1946, 1947, 1948, 1949, 1950, 1951, 1952, 1953, 1954, 1955, 1956, 1957, 1958, 1959, 1959, 1960, 1960, 1961, 1961, 1962, 1962, 1963 (24 games).

Most Two-Base Hits, Total Games

4—David M. Winfield, N. L., 1977, 1978, 1979, 1980; A. L., 1981, 1982, 1983, 1984 (8 games).

Most Three-Base Hits, Total Games

3—Willie H. Mays, N. L., 1954, 1955, 1956, 1957, 1958, 1959, 1959, 1960, 1960, 1961, 1961, 1962, 1962, 1963, 1964, 1965, 1966, 1967, 1968, 1969, 1970, 1971, 1972, 1973 (24 games).
Brooks C. Robinson, A. L., 1960, 1960, 1961, 1961, 1962, 1962, 1963, 1964, 1965, 1966, 1967, 1968, 1969, 1970, 1971, 1972, 1973, 1974 (18 games).

Most Home Runs, Total Games

6—Stanley F. Musial, N. L., 1943, 1944, 1946, 1947, 1948, 1949, 1950, 1951, 1952, 1953, 1954, 1955, 1956, 1957, 1958, 1959, 1959, 1960, 1960, 1961, 1961, 1962, 1962, 1963 (24 games).

Most Total Bases, Total Games

40—Stanley F. Musial, N. L., 1943, 1944, 1946, 1947, 1948, 1949, 1950, 1951, 1952, 1953, 1954, 1955, 1956, 1957, 1958, 1959, 1959, 1960, 1960, 1961, 1961, 1962, 1962, 1963 (24 games).
Willie H. Mays, N. L., 1954, 1955, 1956, 1957, 1958, 1959, 1959, 1960, 1960, 1961, 1961, 1962, 1962, 1963, 1964, 1965, 1966, 1967, 1968, 1969, 1970, 1971, 1972, 1973 (24 games).

Most Long Hits, Total Games

8—Stanley F. Musial, N. L., 1943, 1944, 1946, 1947, 1948, 1949, 1950, 1951, 1952, 1953, 1954, 1955, 1956, 1957, 1958, 1959, 1959, 1960, 1960, 1961, 1961, 1962, 1962, 1963 (24 games, two doubles, six home runs).
Willie H. Mays, N. L., 1954, 1955, 1956, 1957, 1958, 1959, 1959, 1960, 1960, 1961, 1961, 1962, 1962, 1963, 1964, 1965, 1966, 1967, 1968, 1969, 1970, 1971, 1972, 1973 (24 games, two doubles, three triples, three home runs.)

Most Extra Bases on Long Hits, Total Games

20—Stanley F. Musial, N. L., 1943, 1944, 1946, 1947, 1948, 1949, 1950, 1951, 1952, 1953, 1954, 1955, 1956, 1957, 1958, 1959, 1959, 1960, 1960, 1961, 1961, 1962, 1962, 1963 (24 games).

Most Sacrifice Hits, Total Games

1—Held by many players.

Most Sacrifice Flies, Total Games

2—Henry L. Aaron, N. L., 1955, 1956, 1957, 1958, 1959 (2), 1960 (2), 1961 (2), 1962, 1963, 1964, 1965, 1966, 1967, 1968, 1969, 1970, 1971, 1972, 1973, 1974 (23 games). A. L., 1975, (one game).

Roberto W. Clemente, N. L., 1960, 1960, 1961, 1961, 1962, 1962, 1963, 1964, 1965, 1966, 1967, 1969, 1970, 1971 (14 games).

Peter E. Rose, N. L., 1965, 1967, 1969, 1970, 1971, 1973, 1974, 1975, 1976, 1977, 1978, 1979, 1980, 1981, 1982 (15 games).

George H. Brett, A.L., 1976, 1977, 1978, 1979, 1981, 1982, 1983 (7 games).

Most Bases on Balls, Total Games

11—Theodore S. Williams, A. L., 1940, 1941, 1942, 1946, 1947, 1948, 1949, 1950, 1951, 1954, 1955, 1956, 1957, 1958, 1959, 1959, 1960, 1960 (18 games).

Most Strikeouts, Total Games

17—Mickey C. Mantle, A. L., 1953, 1954, 1955, 1956, 1957, 1958, 1959, 1959, 1960, 1960, 1961, 1961, 1962, 1964, 1967, 1968 (16 games).

Most Stolen Bases, Total Games

6—Willie H. Mays, N. L., 1954, 1955, 1956, 1957, 1958, 1959, 1959, 1960, 1960, 1961, 1961, 1962, 1962, 1963, 1964, 1965, 1966, 1967, 1968, 1969, 1970, 1971, 1972, 1973 (24 games).

Most Hit by Pitch, Total Games

1—Held by many players.

Most Times Grounded Into Double Plays, Total Games

3—Joseph P. DiMaggio, A. L., 1936, 1937, 1938, 1939, 1940, 1941, 1942, 1947, 1948, 1949, 1950 (11 games).

Peter E. Rose, N. L., 1965, 1967, 1969, 1970, 1971, 1973, 1974, 1975, 1976, 1977, 1978, 1979, 1980, 1981 (14 games).

Most Times Playing on Winning Club

17—Willie H. Mays, N. L., 1955, 1956, 1959 first game, 1960, 1960, 1961 first game, 1962 first game, 1963, 1964, 1965, 1966, 1967, 1968, 1969, 1970, 1972, 1973 (1 tie—1961 second game). (8 consecutive).

Henry L. Aaron, N. L., 1955, 1956, 1959 first game, 1960, 1960, 1961 first game, 1963, 1964, 1965, 1966, 1967, 1968, 1969, 1970, 1972, 1973, 1974 (1 tie—1961 second game). (8 consecutive).

Most Times Playing on Losing Club

15—Brooks C. Robinson, A. L., 1960, 1960, 1961 first game, 1962 first game, 1963, 1964, 1965, 1966, 1967, 1968, 1969, 1970, 1972, 1973, 1974 (1 tie—1961 second game). (8 consecutive).

Most Fielding Positions Played, Game

2—Held by many players.

Most Fielding Positions Played, Total Games

5—Peter E. Rose, N. L., Second base, left field, right field, third base, first base, 15 games.

CLUB BATTING, BASE-RUNNING—GAME, INNING

Most Official At-Bats, Nine-Inning Game, One Club

41—N. L., July 7, 1937.
A. L., July 12, 1949.

Most Official At-Bats, Nine-Inning Game, Both Clubs

79—N. L., (40), A. L. (39), July 13, 1954.

Fewest Official At-Bats, Nine-Inning Game, One Club

27—N. L., July 9, 1968 (8 innings).
29—N. L., July 9, 1940 (8 innings).
A. L., July 9, 1940 (9 innings).
A. L., July 13, 1943 (8 innings).
A. L., July 13, 1948 (8 innings).
A. L., July 10, 1962 (9 innings).
A. L., July 13, 1976 (9 innings).
N. L., July 13, 1982 (8 innings).

Fewest Official At-Bats, Nine-Inning Game, Both Clubs
57—A. L. (30), N. L. (27), July 9, 1968.

Most Runs, Game, One Club
13—A. L., July 6, 1983.

Most Runs, Game, Both Clubs
20—A. L. (11), N. L. (9), July 13, 1954.

Most Batters Facing Pitcher, Inning, One Club
11—A. L., July 10, 1934, fifth inning.

Most Batters Facing Pitcher, Inning, Both Clubs
19—A. L. (11), N. L. (8), July 10, 1934, fifth inning.

Most Consecutive Batters Facing Pitcher, Game, One Club, None Reaching Base
20—A. L., July 9, 1968. (James L. Fregosi, doubled, start of game, then 20 consecutive batters were retired until Pedro (Tony) Oliva doubled in seventh inning).

Most Runs, Inning, One Club
7—A. L., July 6, 1983, third inning.

Most Runs, Inning, Both Clubs
9—A. L. (6), N. L. (3), July 10, 1934, fifth inning.

Most Innings Scored, Game, One Club
5—A. L., July 9, 1946.
N. L., July 10, 1951.
A. L., July 13, 1954.
N. L., July 10, 1956.
A. L., July 30, 1962.
N. L., July 23, 1974.
A. L., July 6, 1983.

Most Innings Scored, Game, Both Clubs
9—A. L. (5), N. L. (4), July 30, 1962.

Most Consecutive Scoreless Innings, Total Games, One League
19—American League; Last 9 innings 1967; all 9 innings, 1968, first inning, 1969.

Most Hits, Game, One Club
17—A. L., July 13, 1954.

Most Hits, Game, Both Clubs
31—A. L. (17), N. L. (14), July 13, 1954.

Fewest Hits, Game, One Club
3—A. L., July 9, 1940.
N. L., July 9, 1946.
A. L., July 9, 1968.

Fewest Hits, Game, Both Clubs
8—N. L. (5), A. L. (3), July 9, 1968.

Highest Batting Average, Game, One Club
.436—A. L., July 13, 1954, 39 at-bats, 17 hits.

Lowest Batting Average, Game, One Club
.097—N. L., July 9, 1946, 31 at-bats, 3 hits.

Most One-Base Hits, Game, One Club
13—A. L., July 13, 1954.

Most One-Base Hits, Game, Both Clubs
22—A. L. (13), N. L. (9), July 13, 1954.

Fewest One-Base Hits, Game, One Club
0—A. L., July 9, 1968.

Fewest One-Base Hits, Game, Both Clubs
4—N. L. (4), A. L. (0), July 9, 1968.

Most Two-Base Hits, Game, One Club

5—A. L., July 10, 1934.
A. L., July 12, 1949.

Most Two-Base Hits, Game, Both Clubs

7—A. L. (5), N. L. (2), July 12, 1949.

Fewest Two-Base Hits, Game, One Club

0—Made in many games.

Fewest Two-Base Hits, Game, Both Clubs

0—July 6, 1942; July 9, 1946; July 13, 1948; July 8, 1958; July 13, 1976.

Most Three-Base Hits, Game, One Club

2—A. L., July 10, 1934.
A. L., July 10, 1951.
N. L., July 13, 1976.
A. L., July 11, 1978.
A. L., July 6, 1983.

Most Three-Base Hits, Game, Both Clubs

3—A. L. (2), N. L. (1), July 11, 1978.

Fewest Three-Base Hits, Game, One Club

0—Made in many games.

Fewest Three-Base Hits, Game, Both Clubs

0—Made in many games.

Most Home Runs, Game, One Club

4—N. L., July 10, 1951.
A. L., July 13, 1954.
N. L., July 13, 1960.
N. L., August 9, 1981.

Most Home Runs, Game, Both Clubs

6—N. L. (4), A. L. (2), July 10, 1951.
A. L. (4), N. L. (2), July 13, 1954.
A. L. (3), N. L. (3), July 13, 1971.

Most Home Runs, Extra-Inning Game, Both Clubs, No Other Runs

3—N. L. (2), A. L. (1), July 11, 1967.

Fewest Home Runs, Game, One Club

0—Made in many games.

Fewest Home Runs, Game, Both Clubs

0—July 6, 1938; July 11, 1944; July 14, 1953; July 9, 1957; July 8, 1958; July 10, 1962; July 9, 1963; July 12, 1966; July 9, 1968, July 11, 1978.

Most Home Runs, Inning, One Club (11 times)

2—A. L., July 6, 1942, first inning (Boudreau, York).
N. L., July 10, 1951, fourth inning (Musial, Elliott).
A. L., July 13, 1954, third inning (Rosen, Boone) (consecutive).
A. L., July 10, 1956, sixth inning (Williams, Mantle) (consecutive).
N. L., July 7, 1964, fourth inning (Williams, Boyer).
N. L., July 13, 1965, first inning (Mays, Torre).
A. L., July 13, 1965, fifth inning (McAuliffe, Killebrew).
A. L., July 13, 1971, third inning (Jackson, F. Robinson).
N. L., July 15, 1975, second inning (Garvey, Wynn) (consecutive).
N. L., July 19, 1977, first inning (Morgan, Luzinski).
A. L., July 6, 1983, third inning (Rice, Lynn).

Most Home Runs, Inning, Both Clubs

3—N. L., 2 (Musial, Elliott), A. L., 1 (Wertz), July 10, 1951, fourth inning.
A. L., 2 (Jackson, F. Robinson), N. L., 1 (Aaron), July 13, 1971, third inning.

Most Consecutive Games, One or More Home Runs

9—N. L.—1969, 1970, 1971, 1972, 1973, 1974, 1975, 1976, 1977.

Most Total Bases, Game, One Club

29—A. L., July 13, 1954.

Most Total Bases, Game, Both Clubs
52—A. L. (29), N. L. (23), July 13, 1954.

Fewest Total Bases, Game, One Club
3—N. L., July 9, 1946.

Fewest Total Bases, Game, Both Clubs
12—A. L. (6), N. L. (6), 1968.

Most Long Hits, Game, One Club
7—A. L., July 10, 1934, five doubles, two triples.
A. L., July 6, 1983, three doubles, two triples, two home runs.

Most Long Hits, Game, Both Clubs
10—N. L. (5), one double, four home runs; A. L. (5), one double, two triples, two home runs, July 10, 1951.

Fewest Long Hits, Game, One Club
0—A. L., July 11, 1944.
N. L., July 9, 1946.
A. L., July 14, 1953.
N. L., July 8, 1958.
A. L., July 8, 1958.
N. L., July 9, 1963.

Fewest Long Hits, Game, Both Clubs
0—July 8, 1958.

Most Extra Bases on Long Hits, Game, One Club
14—N. L., August 9, 1981.

Most Extra Bases on Long Hits, Game, Both Clubs
24—N. L. (13), A. L. (11), July 10, 1951.

Fewest Extra Bases on Long Hits, Game, One Club
0—A. L., July 11, 1944.
N. L., July 9, 1946.
A. L., July 14, 1953.
N. L., July 8, 1958.
A. L., July 8, 1958.
N. L., July 9, 1963.

Fewest Extra Bases on Long Hits, Game, Both Clubs
0—July 8, 1958.

Most Sacrifice Hits, Nine-Inning Game, One Club
3—N. L., July 11, 1944.

Most Sacrifice Hits, Nine-Inning Game, Both Clubs
3—N. L. (3), A. L. (0), July 11, 1944.

Fewest Sacrifice Hits, Game, One Club
0—Made in many games.

Fewest Sacrifice Hits, Game, Both Clubs
0—Made in many games.

Most Stolen Bases, Game, One Club
4—N. L., July 10, 1984.

Most Stolen Bases, Game, Both Clubs
4—N. L. (2), A. L. (2), July 10, 1934.
A. L. (3), N. L. (1), July 15, 1975.
N. L. (4), A. L. (0), July 10, 1984.

Fewest Stolen Bases, Game, One Club
0—Made in many games.

Fewest Stolen Bases, Game, Both Clubs
0—Made in many games.

Most Bases on Balls, Game, One Club
9—A. L., July 10, 1934.

Most Bases on Balls, Game, Both Clubs
   13—N. L. (8), A. L. (5), July 12, 1949.

Fewest Bases on Balls, Nine-Inning Game, One Club (7 times)
   0—N. L., July 6, 1933.
      N. L., July 7, 1937.
      N. L., July 6, 1938.
      A. L., July 6, 1942.
      A. L., July 10, 1956.
      A. L., July 9, 1968.
      N. L., July 15, 1975.
      A. L., July 10, 1984.

Fewest Bases on Balls, Extra-Inning Game, One Club
   0—N. L., July 11, 1967 (15 innings).

Fewest Bases on Balls, Nine-Inning Game, Both Clubs
   1—A. L. (1), N. L. (0), July 15, 1975.

Fewest Bases on Balls Extra-Inning Game, Both Clubs
   2—A. L. (2), N. L. (0), July 11, 1967 (15 innings).

Most Strikeouts, Game, One Club
   17—A. L., July 11, 1967 (15 innings).
   13—N. L., July 11, 1967 (15 innings).
   12—A. L., July 10, 1934.
      A. L., July 11, 1950 (14 innings).
      A. L., July 12, 1955 (12 innings).
      N. L., July 10, 1956.
      A. L., August 3, 1959.
      A. L., July 11, 1961 (ten innings).

Most Strikeouts, Nine-Inning Game, Both Clubs
   21—A. L. (11), N. L. (10), July 10, 1984.

Most Strikeouts, Extra-Inning Game, Both Clubs
   30—A. L. (17), N. L. (13), July 11, 1967 (15 innings).

Fewest Strikeouts, Game, One Club
   0—N. L., July 7, 1937.

Fewest Strikeouts, Game, Both Clubs
   6—A. L. (4), N. L. (2), July 8, 1958.

Most Runs Batted In, Game, One Club
   13—A. L., July 6, 1983.

Most Runs Batted In, Game, Both Clubs
   20—A. L. (11), N. L. (9), July 13, 1954.

Fewest Runs Batted in, Game, One Club
   0—A. L., July 9, 1940.
      N. L., July 9, 1946.
      A. L., July 13, 1960.
      A. L., July 12, 1966.
      A. L., July 9, 1968.
      N. L., July 9, 1968.

Fewest Runs Batted In, Game, Both Clubs
   0—A. L. (0), N. L. (0), July 9, 1968.

Most Left on Bases, Game, One Club
   12—A. L., July 10, 1934.
      N. L., July 12, 1949.
      A. L., July 13, 1960.

Most Left on Bases, Game, Both Clubs
   20—N. L. (12), A. L. (8), July 12, 1949.

Fewest Left on Bases, Game, One Club
   2—N. L., July 13, 1971 (Batted 9 innings).
      A. L., July 13, 1971 (Batted 8 innings).

Fewest Left on Bases, Game, Both Clubs
>   4—N. L. (2), A. L. (2), July 13, 1971.

Most Hit by Pitch, Game, One Club
>   2—A. L., July 10, 1962.

Most Hit by Pitch, Game, Both Clubs
>   2—A. L. (2), N. L. (0), July 10, 1962.
>   A. L. (1), N. L. (1), July 15, 1975.
>   A. L. (1), N. L. (1), July 19, 1977.

Fewest Hit by Pitch, Game, One Club
>   0—Made in many games.

Fewest Hit by Pitch, Game, Both Clubs
>   0—Made in many games.

Most Earned Runs, Game, One Club
>   12—A. L., July 9, 1946.

Most Earned Runs, Game, Both Clubs
>   20—A. L. (11), N. L. (9), July 13, 1954.

Fewest Earned Runs, Game, One Club
>   0—N. L., July 11, 1939.
>   A. L., July 9, 1940.
>   N. L., July 9, 1946.
>   A. L., July 13, 1960.
>   A. L., July 9, 1968.
>   N. L., July 9, 1968.

Fewest Earned Runs, Game, Both Clubs
>   0—A. L. (0), N. L. (0), July 9, 1968.

INDIVIDUAL FIELDING

FIRST BASEMEN'S FIELDING RECORDS

Most Games Played
>   9—Steven P. Garvey, N. L., 1974, 1975, 1976, 1977, 1978, 1979, 1980, 1981, 1984.

Most Putouts, Total Games
>   53—H. Louis Gehrig, A. L., 1933, 1934, 1935, 1936, 1937, 1938.

Most Assists, Total Games
>   6—Steven P. Garvey, N. L., 1974, 1975, 1976, 1977, 1978, 1979, 1980, 1981, 1984.

Most Chances Accepted, Total Games
>   55—H. Louis Gehrig, A. L., 1933, 1934, 1935, 1936, 1937, 1938.

Most Errors, Total Games
>   2—H. Louis Gehrig, A. L., 1933, 1934, 1935, 1936, 1937, 1938.

Most Double Plays, Total Games
>   6—William D. White, N. L., 1960 (2), 1961 (2), 1963.
>   Harmon C. Killebrew, A. L., 1965, 1967, 1968, 1971.

Most Putouts, Nine-Inning Game
>   14—George H. McQuinn, A. L., July 13, 1948.

Most Putouts, Extra-Inning Game
>   15—Harmon C. Killebrew, A. L., July 11, 1967.

Most Assists, Nine-Inning Game
>   3—P. Rudolph York, A. L., July 6, 1942.
>   William D. White, N. L., July 9, 1963.

Most Chances Accepted, Nine-Inning Game
>   14—P. Rudolph York, A. L., July 6, 1942, 11 putouts, 3 assists.
>   George H. McQuinn, A. L., July 13, 1948, 14 putouts.

Most Chances Accepted, Extra-Inning Game

16—Harmon C. Killebrew, A. L., July 11, 1967, 15 putouts, 1 assist.

Most Errors, Game

1—Held by many players.

Most Double Plays, Game

3—Stanley F. Musial, N. L., July 8, 1958.

Most Unassisted Double Plays, Game

1—James E. Runnels, A. L., August 3, 1959, second inning.
Lee A. May, N. L., July 25, 1972, third inning.

SECOND BASEMEN'S FIELDING RECORDS

Most Games Played

13—J. Nelson Fox, A. L., 1951, 1953, 1954, 1955, 1956, 1957, 1958, 1959 (2), 1960 (2), 1961, 1963.

Most Putouts, Total Games

25—J. Nelson Fox, A. L., 1951, 1953, 1954, 1955, 1956, 1957, 1958, 1959 (2), 1960 (2), 1961, 1963.

Most Assists, Total Games

23—William J. Herman, N. L., 1934, 1935, 1936, 1937, 1938, 1940, 1941, 1942, 1943.

Most Chances Accepted, Total Games

39—J. Nelson Fox, A. L., 1951, 1953, 1954, 1955, 1956, 1957, 1958, 1959 (2), 1960 (2), 1961, 1963 (25 putouts, 14 assists).

Most Errors, Total Games

2—William J. Herman, N. L., 1934, 1935, 1936, 1937, 1938, 1940, 1941, 1942, 1943.
J. Nelson Fox, A. L., 1951, 1953, 1954, 1955, 1956, 1957, 1958, 1959 (2), 1960 (2), 1961, 1963.
William L. Randolph, A. L., 1977, 1980, 1981.
Stephen L. Sax, N.L., 1982, 1983.

Most Double Plays, Total Games

4—William J. Herman, N. L., 1934, 1935, 1936, 1937, 1938, 1940, 1941, 1942, 1943.
William S. Mazeroski, N. L., 1958, 1959, 1960 (2).

Most Putouts, Nine-Inning Game

5—Frank F. Frisch, N. L., July 6, 1933.

Most Assists, Nine-Inning Game

6—William L. Randolph, A. L., July 19, 1977.

Most Chances Accepted, Nine-Inning Game

9—William S. Mazeroski, N. L., July 8, 1958.

Most Errors, Game

2—William J. Herman, N. L., July 13, 1943.
William L. Randolph, A. L., July 8, 1980.

Most Double Plays, Game

3—William J. Herman, N. L., July 13, 1943.
William S. Mazeroski, N. L., July 8, 1958.

Most Unassisted Double Plays, Game

Never accomplished.

THIRD BASEMEN'S FIELDING RECORDS

Most Games Played

18—Brooks C. Robinson, A. L., 1960, 1960, 1961, 1961, 1962, 1962, 1963, 1964, 1965, 1966, 1967, 1968, 1969, 1970, 1971, 1972, 1973, 1974 (consecutive).

Most Putouts, Total Games

11—Brooks C. Robinson, A. L., 1960, 1960, 1961, 1961, 1962, 1962, 1963, 1964, 1965, 1966, 1967, 1968, 1969, 1970, 1971, 1972, 1973, 1974 (18 games).

Most Assists, Total Games

 32—Brooks C. Robinson, A. L., 1960, 1960, 1961, 1961, 1962, 1962, 1963, 1964, 1965, 1966, 1967, 1968, 1969, 1970, 1971, 1972, 1973, 1974 (18 games).

Most Chances Accepted, Total Games

 43—Brooks C. Robinson, A. L., 1960, 1960, 1961, 1961, 1962, 1962, 1963, 1964, 1965, 1966, 1967, 1968, 1969, 1970, 1971, 1972, 1973, 1974 (18 games), 11 putouts (32 assists).

Most Errors, Total Games

 6—Edwin L. Mathews, N. L., 1953, 1955, 1957, 1959, 1960, 1960, 1961, 1961, 1962 second game.

Most Double Plays, Total Games

 3—Frank J. Malzone, A. L., 1957, 1958, 1959, 1959, 1960, 1960, 1963.
  Brooks C. Robinson, A. L., 1960, 1960, 1961, 1961, 1962, 1962, 1963, 1964, 1965, 1966, 1967, 1968, 1969, 1970, 1971, 1972, 1973, 1974 (18 games).
  George H. Brett, A.L., 1976, 1977, 1978, 1979, 1981, 1982, 1983 (7 games).

Most Putouts, Nine-Inning Game

 4—George C. Kell, A. L., July 10, 1951.

Most Putouts, Extra-Inning Game

 4—Brooks C. Robinson, A. L., July 12, 1966, 9⅓ innings.

Most Assists, Nine-Inning Game

 6—Kenneth F. Keltner, A. L., July 13, 1948.
  Frank J. Malzone, A. L., August 3, 1959.

Most Chances Accepted, Nine-Inning Game

 7—Kenneth F. Keltner, A. L., July 13, 1948, 1 putout, 6 assists.
  Frank J. Malzone, A. L., August 3, 1959, 1 putout, 6 assists.

Most Chances Accepted, Extra-Inning Game

 8—Brooks C. Robinson, A. L., July 12, 1966, 9⅓ innings, 4 putouts, 4 assists.

Most Errors, Game

 2—Robert A. Rolfe, A. L., July 7, 1937.
  Edwin L. Mathews, N. L., July 11, 1960; July 30, 1962.
  Kenton L. Boyer, N. L., July 11, 1961 (ten innings).

Most Errors, Inning

 2—Edwin L. Mathews, N. L., July 30, 1962, ninth inning.

Most Double Plays, Game

 1—Held by many players.

Most Unassisted Double Plays, Game

Never accomplished.

SHORTSTOPS' FIELDING RECORDS

Most Games Played

 10—Luis E. Aparicio, A. L., 1958, 1959, 1959, 1960 first game, 1961 second game, 1962, 1962, 1963, 1970, 1971.

Most Putouts, Total Games

 15—Luis E. Aparicio, A. L., 1958, 1959, 1959, 1960 first game, 1961 second game, 1962, 1962, 1963, 1970, 1971.

Most Assists, Total Games

 24—Joseph E. Cronin, A. L., 1933, 1934, 1935, 1937, 1938, 1939, 1941.

Most Chances Accepted, Total Games

 38—Joseph E. Cronin, A. L., 1933, 1934, 1935, 1937, 1938, 1939, 1941.

Most Errors, Total Games

 2—Joseph E. Cronin, A. L., 1933, 1934, 1935, 1937, 1938, 1939, 1941.
  Ernest Banks, N. L., 1955, 1957, 1958, 1959, 1959, 1960, 1960, 1961.

Most Double Plays, Total Games

 6—Ernest Banks, N. L., 1955, 1957, 1958, 1959, 1959, 1960, 1960, 1961.

Most Putouts, Nine-Inning Game

> 5—Alfonso Carrasquel, A. L., July 13, 1954.

Most Assists, Nine-Inning Game

> 8—Joseph E. Cronin, A. L., July 10, 1934.

Most Chances Accepted, Nine-Inning Game

> 10—Joseph E. Cronin, A. L., July 10, 1934, 2 putouts, 8 assists.
> Martin W. Marion, N. L., July 9, 1946, 4 putouts, 6 assists.

Most Errors, Game

> 1—Held by many players.

Most Double Plays, Game

> 2—Louis Boudreau, A. L., July 6, 1942.
> Martin W. Marion, N. L., July 9, 1946.
> Edwin J. Joost, A. L., July 12, 1949.
> Ernest Banks, N. L., July 8, 1958.
> Ernest Banks, N. L., July 13, 1960.
> Edward Kasko, N. L., July 31, 1961.
> Luis E. Aparicio, A. L., July 30, 1962.
> Richard M. Groat, N. L., July 9, 1963.

Most Unassisted Double Plays, Game

> Never accomplished.

OUTFIELDERS' FIELDING RECORDS

Most Games Played

> 22—Willie H. Mays, N. L., 1954, 1955, 1956, 1957, 1958, 1959, 1959, 1960, 1960, 1961, 1961, 1962, 1962, 1963, 1964, 1965, 1966, 1967, 1968, 1970, 1971, 1972 (19 consecutive).

Most Putouts, Total Games

> 55—Willie H. Mays, N. L., 1954, 1955, 1956, 1957, 1958, 1959, 1959, 1960, 1960, 1961, 1961, 1962, 1962, 1963, 1964, 1965, 1966, 1967, 1968, 1970, 1971, 1972 (22 games).

Most Assists, Total Games

> 3—Stanley F. Musial, N. L., 1943, 1944, 1946, 1948, 1949, 1951, 1952, 1953, 1954, 1955, 1956, 1962 second game (1947, 1959 first game, 1960 and 1961 both games, 1962 first game and 1963, pinch-hitter; 1950, 1957, 1958, 1959 second game, first base).

Most Chances Accepted, Total Games

> 55—Willie H. Mays, N. L., 1954, 1955, 1956, 1957, 1958, 1959, 1959, 1960, 1960, 1961, 1961, 1962, 1962, 1963, 1964, 1965, 1966, 1967, 1968, 1970, 1971, 1972 (22 games).

Most Errors, Total Games

> 2—Harold H. Reiser, N. L., 1941, 1942.
> Joseph P. DiMaggio, A. L., 1936, 1937, 1938, 1939, 1940, 1941, 1942, 1947, 1949, 1950.

Most Double Plays, Total Games

> 1—Stanley O. Spence, A. L., 1944, 1946, 1947.
> H. Thomas Davis, N. L., 1962 (2), 1963.

Most Putouts, Center Field, Nine-Inning Game

> 7—Chester P. Laabs, A. L., July 13, 1943.
> Willie H. Mays, N. L., July 7, 1964.

Most Putouts, Center Field, Fourteen-Inning Game

> 9—Lawrence E. Doby, A. L., July 11, 1950.

Most Putouts, Left Field, Nine-Inning Game

> 5—Samuel F. West, A. L., July 7, 1937.
> Frank Robinson, N. L., July 9, 1957.
> Joseph O. Rudi, A. L., July 15, 1975.

Most Putouts, Right Field, Nine-Inning Game

> 4—Charles E. Keller, A. L., July 9, 1940.
> Enos Slaughter, N. L., July 14, 1953.

Most Putouts, Right Field, Extra-Inning Game
    6—Roberto W. Clemente, N. L., July 11, 1967 (15 innings).

Most Assists, Game, Center Field
    1—Held by many players.

Most Assists, Game, Left Field
    1—Held by many players.

Most Assists, Game, Right Field
    2—David G. Parker, N. L., July 17, 1979.

Most Chances Accepted, Center Field, Nine-Inning Game
    7—Chester P. Laabs, A. L., July 13, 1943, 7 putouts.
      Willie H. Mays, N. L., July 7, 1964, 7 putouts.

Most Chances Accepted, Center Field, Fourteen-Inning Game
    9—Lawrence E. Doby, A. L., July 11, 1950, 9 putouts.

Most Chances Accepted, Left Field, Nine-Inning Game
    5—Samuel F. West, A. L., July 7, 1937, 5 putouts.
      Joseph O. Rudi, A. L., July 15, 1975.

Most Chances Accepted, Right Field, Nine-Inning Game
    4—Charles E. Keller, A. L., July 9, 1940, 4 putouts.

Most Errors, Game, Center Field
    2—Harold P. Reiser, N. L., July 8, 1941.

Most Errors, Game, Left Field
    1—Held by many players.

Most Errors, Game, Right Field
    1—Held by many players.

Most Double Plays, Game, Center Field
    Never accomplished.

Most Double Plays, Game, Left Field
    1—H. Thomas Davis, N. L., July 9, 1963.

Most Double Plays, Game, Right Field
    1—Stanley O. Spence, A. L., July 11, 1944.

Most Unassisted Double Plays, Game, Center Field, Left Field, Right Field
    Never accomplished.

CATCHER'S FIELDING RECORDS

Most Games Played
    14—Lawrence P. Berra, A. L., 1949, 1950, 1951, 1952, 1953, 1954, 1955, 1956, 1957, 1958,
      1959, 1960, 1960, 1961.

Most Putouts, Total Games
    61—Lawrence P. Berra, A. L., 1949, 1950, 1951, 1952, 1953, 1954, 1955, 1956, 1957, 1958,
      1959, 1960, 1960, 1961.

Most Assists, Total Games
    7—Lawrence P. Berra, A. L., 1949, 1950, 1951, 1952, 1953, 1954, 1955, 1956, 1957, 1958,
      1959, 1960, 1960, 1961.

Most Chances Accepted, Total Games
    68—Lawrence P. Berra, A. L., 1949, 1950, 1951, 1952, 1953, 1954, 1955, 1956, 1957, 1958,
      1959, 1960, 1960, 1961.

Most Errors, Total Games
    2—Forrest H. Burgess, N. L., 1954, 1955, 1960, 1960, 1961, 1961, (pinch-hitter only in
      1959, second game).

Most Double Plays, Total Games
    1—Held by many catchers.

Most Passed Balls, Total Games

1—Held by many players.

Most Putouts, Nine-Inning Game

10—William M. Dickey, A. L., July 11, 1939 (9 strikeouts).
Lawrence P. Berra, A. L., July 10, 1956 (9 strikeouts).
Delmar W. Crandall, N. L., July 7, 1959 (9 strikeouts).
Johnny L. Bench, N. L., July 15, 1975 (10 strikeouts).

Most Putouts, Extra-Inning Game

13—Roy Campanella, N. L., July 11, 1950 (14 innings—12 strikeouts).
Forrest H. Burgess, N. L., July 11, 1961 (10 innings—12 strikeouts).
William A. Freehan, A. L., July 11, 1967 (15 innings—13 strikeouts).

Most Assists, Game

3—Lance M. Parrish, A. L., July 13, 1982.

Most Chances Accepted, Nine-Inning Game

11—Lawrence P. Berra, A. L., July 10, 1956 (10 putouts, 1 assist).
Johnny L. Bench, N. L., July 15, 1975 (10 putouts, 1 assist).

Most Chances Accepted, Extra-Inning Game

15—Roy Campanella, N. L., July 11, 1950 (14 innings—13 putouts, 2 assists).

Most Errors, Game

1—Held by many players.

Most Double Plays, Game

1—Held by many players.

Most Unassisted Double Plays, Game

Never accomplished.

Most Passed Balls, Game

1—Held by many players.

Most Innings Caught, Game

15—William A. Freehan, A. L. July 11, 1967 (complete game).

PITCHERS' FIELDING RECORDS

Most Games Played

8—James P. Bunning, A. L., 1957, 1959 (first game), 1961 (2), 1962 (first game),
1963; N. L., 1964, 1966.
Donald S. Drysdale, N. L., 1959 (2), 1962 (first game), 1963, 1964, 1965, 1967, 1968.
Juan A. Marichal, N. L., 1962 (2), 1964, 1965, 1966, 1967, 1968, 1971.
G. Thomas Seaver, N. L., 1967, 1968, 1970, 1973, 1975, 1976, 1977, 1981.

Most Putouts, Total Games

3—Spurgeon F. Chandler, A. L., 1942.

Most Assists, Total Games

5—John S. Vander Meer, N. L., 1938, 1942, 1943.

Most Chances Accepted, Total Games

5—Melvin L. Harder, A. L., 1934, 1935, 1936, 1937 (2 putouts, 3 assists).
John S. Vander Meer, N. L., 1938, 1942, 1943 (5 assists).
Donald S. Drysdale, N. L., 1959 (2), 1962, (first game), 1963, 1964, 1965, 1967, 1968
(1 putout, 4 assists).

Most Errors, Total Games

1—Edgar Smith, A. L., 1941.
John F. Sain, N. L., 1947, 1948.
Samuel Jones, N. L., 1955, 1959.
Buddy L. Daley, A. L., 1960.
Roland G. Fingers, A. L., 1973, 1974, 1981; N. L., 1978.

Most Double Plays, Total Games

1—Held by many pitchers.

Most Putouts, Game
   3—Spurgeon F. Chandler, A. L., July 6, 1942.

Most Assists, Game
   3—John S. Vander Meer, N. L., July 6, 1938.
      Donald S. Drysdale, N. L., July 7, 1964.
      Michael S. Lolich, A. L., July 13, 1971.

Most Chances Accepted, Game
   4—Spurgeon F. Chandler, A. L., July 6, 1942 (3 putouts, 1 assist).

Most Errors, Game
   1—Held by many pitchers.

Most Double Plays, Game
   1—Held by many pitchers.

Most Unassisted Double Plays, Game
   Never accomplished.

CLUB FIELDING

Most Assists, Nine-Inning Game, One Club
   16—A. L., July 6, 1942.
      A. L., August 9, 1981.

Most Assists, Nine-Inning Game, Both Clubs
   26—A. L. (15), N. L. (11), July 12, 1949.
      A. L. (16), N. L. (10), August 9, 1981.

Fewest Assists, Eight-Inning Game, One Club
   4—A. L., July 9, 1940.
      N. L., July 13, 1948.

Fewest Assists, Nine-Inning Game, One Club
   5—N. L., July 10, 1934.
      N. L., July 9, 1957.
      N. L., July 23, 1969.

Fewest Assists, Nine-Inning Game, Both Clubs
   11—N. L. (6), A. L. (5), July 7, 1959.

Most Errors, Game, One Club
   5—N. L., July 12, 1949.
      N. L., July 11, 1961.

Most Errors, Nine-Inning Game, Both Clubs
   6—N. L. (5), A. L. (1), July 12, 1949.

Most Errors, Extra-Inning Game, Both Clubs
   7—N. L. (5), A. L. (2), July 11, 1961 (ten innings).

Fewest Errors, Game, One Club
   0—Made in many games.

Fewest Errors, Nine-Inning Game, Both Clubs
   0—July 13, 1948; July 14, 1953; July 10, 1956; July 13, 1960; July 10, 1962; July 13,
      1971; July 24, 1973, July 13, 1976.

Fewest Errors, Extra-Inning Game, Both Clubs
   0—July 11, 1967, 15 innings.
      July 14, 1970, 12 innings.
      July 12, 1966, 10 innings.
      July 25, 1972, 10 innings.

Most Consecutive Errorless Games, One Club
   11—N. L., July 9, 1963; July 7, 1964; July 13, 1965; July 12, 1966; July 11, 1967; July 9,
      1968; July 23, 1969; July 14, 1970; July 13, 1971; July 25, 1972; July 24, 1973.

Most Double Plays, Game, One Club

    3—N. L., July 13, 1943.
       N. L., July 8, 1958.
       N. L., July 9, 1963.
       N. L., July 13, 1976.

Most Double Plays, Game, Both Clubs

    4—N. L. (3), A. L. (1), July 13, 1943.
       N. L. (3), A. L. (1), July 8, 1958.
       N. L. (2), A. L. (2), July 25, 1972, 10 innings.
       N. L. (3), A. L. (1), July 13, 1976.

Fewest Double Plays, Game, One Club

    0—Made in many games.

Fewest Double Plays, Game, Both Clubs

    0—July 8, 1935; July 6, 1938; July 13, 1948; July 11, 1961 (ten innings); July 7, 1964;
       July 23, 1969; July 23, 1974; July 15, 1975; August 9, 1981.

Most Players One or More Putouts, Game, Nine Innings, One Club

    14—N. L., July 13, 1976; A. L., July 6, 1983.

Most Players One or More Putouts, Game, Nine Innings, Both Clubs

    25—N. L. (14), A. L. (11), July 13, 1976.

Most Players One or More Assists, Game, Nine Innings, One Club

    10—N. L., July 24, 1973.

Most Players One or More Assists, Game, Nine Innings, Both Clubs

    19—N. L. (10), A. L. (9), July 24, 1973.

INDIVIDUAL PITCHING RECORDS

Most Games Pitched

    8—James P. Bunning, A. L., 1957, 1959 (first game), 1961 (2), 1962 (first game),
       1963; N. L., 1964, 1966.
       Donald S. Drysdale, N. L., 1959 (2), 1962 (first game), 1963, 1964, 1965, 1967, 1968.
       Juan A. Marichal, N. L., 1962 (2), 1964, 1965, 1966, 1967, 1968, 1971.
       G. Thomas Seaver, N. L., 1967, 1968, 1970, 1973, 1975, 1976, 1977, 1981.

Most Consecutive Games Pitched

    6—Ewell Blackwell, N. L., 1946, 1947, 1948, 1949, 1950, 1951.
       Early Wynn, A. L., 1955, 1956, 1957, 1958, 1959 (2).

Most Games Started

    5—Vernon Gomez, A. L., 1933, 1934, 1935, 1937, 1938.
       Robin E. Roberts, N. L., 1950, 1951, 1953, 1954, 1955.
       Donald S. Drysdale, N. L., 1959 (2), 1962 (first game), 1964, 1968.

Most Games Finished

    5—Richard M. Gossage, A. L., 1975, 1978, 1980; N. L., 1977, 1984.

Most Games Won

    3—Vernon Gomez, A. L., 1933, 1935, 1937.

Most Games Lost

    2—Morton C. Cooper, N. L., 1942, 1943.
       Claude W. Passeau, N. L., 1941, 1946.
       Edward C. Ford, A. L., 1959 (first game), 1960 (second game).
       Luis C. Tiant, A. L., 1968, 1974.
       James A. Hunter, A. L., 1967, 1975.

Most Innings Pitched, Total Games

    19⅓—Donald S. Drysdale, N. L., 1959 (2), 1962 (first game), 1963, 1964, 1965, 1967, 1968
       (8 games).

Most Innings, Game

    6—Vernon Gomez, A. L., July 8, 1935.

Most Runs Allowed, Total Games

    13—Edward C. Ford, A. L., 1954, 1955, 1956, 1959, 1960, 1961.

Most Earned Runs Allowed, Total Games
  11—Edward C. Ford, A. L., 1954, 1955, 1956, 1959, 1960, 1961.

Most Runs Allowed, Game
  7—C. Atlee Hammaker, N. L., July 6, 1983.

Most Earned Runs Allowed, Game
  7—C. Atlee Hammaker, N. L., July 6, 1983.

Most Runs Allowed, Inning
  7—C. Atlee Hammaker, N. L., July 6, 1983, third inning.

Most Earned Runs Allowed, Inning
  7—C. Atlee Hammaker, N. L., July 6, 1983, third inning.

Most Hits Allowed, Total Games
  19—Edward C. Ford, A. L., 1954, 1955, 1956, 1959, 1960, 1961.

Most Hits Allowed, Inning
  6—C. Atlee Hammaker, N.L., July 6, 1983, third inning.

Most Hits Allowed, Game
  7—Thomas D. Bridges, A. L., July 7, 1937.

Most Home Runs Allowed, Total Games
  4—Vida Blue, A. L., 1971 (2), 1975 (2).
     James A. Hunter, A. L., 1967, 1970, 1974, 1976.

Most Home Runs Allowed, Game
  3—James A. Palmer, A. L., July 19, 1977.

Most Home Runs Allowed, Inning (11)
  2—Morton C. Cooper, N. L., July 6, 1942, first inning.
     Edmund W. Lopat, A. L., July 10, 1951, fourth inning.
     Robin E. Roberts, N. L., July 13, 1954, third inning (consecutive).
     Warren E. Spahn, N. L., July 10, 1956, sixth inning (consecutive).
     John T. Wyatt, A. L., July 7, 1964, fourth inning.
     Milton S. Pappas, A. L., July 13, 1965, first inning.
     James W. Maloney, N. L., July 13, 1965, fifth inning.
     Dock P. Ellis, N. L., July 13, 1971, third inning.
     Vida Blue, A. L., July 15, 1975, second inning (consecutive).
     James A. Palmer, A. L., July 19, 1977, first inning.
     C. Atlee Hammaker, A.L., July 6, 1983, third inning.

Most Bases on Balls, Total Games
  7—James A. Palmer, A. L., 1970 (1), 1972 (1), 1977 (1), 1978 (4).

Most Bases on Balls, Game
  5—William A. Hallahan, N. L., July 6, 1933, 2 innings.

Most Strikeouts, Total Games
  19—Donald S. Drysdale, N. L., 1959, 1959, 1962, 1963, 1964, 1965, 1967, 1968 (8 games).

Most Strikeouts, Game
  6—Carl O. Hubbell, N. L., July 10, 1934, 3 innings.
     John S. Vander Meer, N. L., July 13, 1943, 2⅔ innings.
     Lawrence J. Jansen, N. L., July 11, 1950, 5 innings.
     Ferguson A. Jenkins, N. L., July 11, 1967, 3 innings.

Most Consecutive Strikeouts, Game
  5—Carl O. Hubbell, N. L., July 10, 1934; 3 in first inning, 2 in second inning (Ruth, Gehrig, Foxx, Simmons, Cronin). Then Dickey singled, Gomez struck out.

Most Wild Pitches, Total Games
  2—Ewell Blackwell, N. L., 1946, 1947, 1948, 1949, 1950, 1951.
     Robin E. Roberts, N. L., 1950, 1951, 1953, 1954, 1955,
     Thomas A. Brewer, A. L., 1956.
     Juan A. Marichal, N. L., 1962, 1962, 1964, 1965, 1966, 1967, 1968, 1971.
     David A. Stieb, A. L., 1980, 1981.
     Stephen D. Rogers, N. L., 1978, 1979, 1982.

Most Wild Pitches, Game

2—Thomas A. Brewer, A. L., July 10, 1956, sixth and seventh innings.
Juan A. Marichal, N. L., July 30, 1962, ninth inning.
David A. Stieb, A. L., July 8, 1980, seventh inning.

Most Wild Pitches, Inning

2—Juan A. Marichal, N. L., July 30, 1962, ninth inning.
David A. Stieb, A. L., July 8, 1980, seventh inning.

Most Hit Batsmen, Inning or Game

1—Held by many pitchers.

Most Balks, Inning or Game

1—Robert B. Friend, N. L., July 11, 1960.
Stuart L. Miller, N. L., July 11, 1961.
Steven L. Busby, A. L., July 15, 1975.
James L. Kern, A. L., July 17, 1979.

GENERAL RECORDS

Earliest Date for All-Star Game

July 6, 1933 at Comiskey Park, Chicago.
July 6, 1938 at Crosley Field, Cincinnati.
July 6, 1942 at Polo Grounds, New York.
July 6, 1983 at Comiskey Park, Chicago.

Latest Date for All-Star Game

August 9, 1981 at Municipal Stadium, Cleveland.

All-Star Night Games

July 13, 1943 at Shibe Park, Philadelphia.
July 11, 1944 at Forbes Field, Pittsburgh.
July 9, 1968 at The Astrodome, Houston.
July 14, 1970 at Riverfront Stadium, Cincinnati.
July 13, 1971 at Tiger Stadium, Detroit.
July 25, 1972 at Atlanta Stadium, Atlanta.
July 24, 1973 at Royals Stadium, Kansas City.
July 23, 1974 at Three Rivers Stadium, Pittsburgh.
July 15, 1975 at County Stadium, Milwaukee.
July 13, 1976 at Veterans Stadium, Philadelphia.
July 19, 1977 at Yankee Stadium, New York.
July 11, 1978 at San Diego Stadium, San Diego.
August 9, 1981 at Municipal Stadium, Cleveland.
July 13, 1982 at Olympic Stadium, Montreal.
July 6, 1983 at Comiskey Park, Chicago.
July 10, 1984 at Candlestick Park, San Francisco.

Largest Attendance, Game

72,086 at Municipal Stadium, Cleveland, August 9, 1981.

Smallest Attendance, Game

25,556 at Braves Field, Boston, July 7, 1936.

Longest Game, by Innings

15 innings—at Anaheim Stadium, California, July 11, 1967. National League 2, American League 1.
14 innings—at Comiskey Park, Chicago, July 11, 1950. National League 4, American League 3.

Shortest Game, by Innings

5 innings—at Shibe Park, Philadelphia, July 8, 1952 (rain). National League 3, American League 2.

Longest Nine-Inning Game, by Time

3 hours, 10 minutes, at Municipal Stadium, Cleveland, July 13, 1954. American League 11, National League 9.

Shortest Nine-Inning Game, by Time

1 hour, 53 minutes, at Sportsman's Park, St. Louis, July 9, 1940. National League 4, American League 0.

Longest Extra-Inning Game, by Time

3 hours, 41 minutes, at Anaheim Stadium, California, July 11, 1967. National League 2, American League 1, 15 innings.

3 hours, 19 minutes, at Comiskey Park, Chicago, July 11, 1950. National League 4, American League 3, 14 innings.

3 hours, 19 minutes, at Riverfront Stadium, Cincinnati, July 14, 1970, night game, National League 5, American League 4, 12 innings.

Most Players, Nine-Inning Game, One Club

29—N. L., August 9, 1981.

Most Players, Extra-Inning Game, One Club

25—N. L., July 14, 1970.

Most Players, Nine-Inning Game, Both Clubs

56—N. L. (29), A. L. (27), August 9, 1981.

Most Players, Extra-Inning Game, Both Clubs

49—N. L. (25), A. L. (24), July 14, 1970, night game, 12 innings.

Fewest Players, Game, One Club

11—A. L., July 6, 1942.

Fewest Players, Game, Both Clubs

27—A. L. (15), N. L. (12), July 1, 1938.

Most Pitchers, Nine-Inning Game, One Club

8—N. L., August 9, 1981.

Most Pitchers, Extra-Inning Game, One Club

7—N. L., July 11, 1967.
A. L., July 14, 1970.

Most Pitchers, Nine-Inning Game, Both Clubs

15—N. L. (8), A. L. (7), August 9, 1981.

Fewest Pitchers, Game, One Club

2—A. L., July 8, 1935.
A. L., July 6, 1942.

Fewest Pitchers, Game, Both Clubs

6—N. L. (3), A. L. (3), July 6, 1933.
N. L. (4), A. L. (2), July 8, 1935.
N. L. (3), A. L. (3), July 6, 1938.
N. L. (3), A. L. (3), July 11, 1939.

Most Catchers, Nine-Inning Game, One Club

3—10 games—N. L.—1940, 1941, 1947, 1955, 1960, second game; 1968, 1977, 1978, 1980, 1984.
6 games—A. L.—1940, 1946, 1961, first game; 1968, 1980, 1983.

Most Catchers, Nine-Inning Game, Both Clubs

6—N. L. (3), A. L. (3), July 9, 1940.
N. L. (3), A. L. (3), July 9, 1968.
N. L. (3), A. L. (3), July 8, 1980.

Most First Basemen, Nine-Inning Game, One Club

3—N. L., July 9, 1946.
N. L., July 13, 1960, second game.
N. L., July 24, 1973.

Most First Basemen, Nine-Inning Game, Both Clubs

5—N. L. (3), A. L. (2), July 9, 1946.
N. L. (3), A. L. (2), July 13, 1960, second game.

Most Second Basemen, Nine-Inning Game, One Club

3—N. L., July 13, 1960, second game.
N. L., August 9, 1981.

Most Second Basemen, Nine-Inning Game, Both Clubs

5—N. L. (3), A. L. (2), July 13, 1960, second game.
N. L. (3), A. L. (2), August 9, 1981.

Most Third Basemen, Nine-Inning Game, One Club

 3—A. L., July 11, 1961, first game.
  A. L., July 24, 1973.
  N. L., July 13, 1976.
  N. L., July 6, 1983.

Most Third Basemen, Nine-Inning Game, Both Clubs

 5—A. L. (3), N. L. (2), July 11, 1961, first game.
  A. L. (3), N. L. (2), July 24, 1973.
  N. L. (3), A. L. (2), July 13, 1976.

Most Shortstops, Nine-Inning Game, One Club

 3—A. L., July 13, 1976.
  N. L., July 13, 1976.
  A. L., July 8, 1980.

Most Shortstops, Nine-Inning Game, Both Clubs

 6—A. L. (3), N. L. (3), July 13, 1976.

Most Infielders, Game, One Club

 10—N. L., July 13, 1960, second game.
  N. L., July 14, 1970, 12 innings.
  N. L., July 13, 1976.

Most Infielders, Game, Both Clubs

 18—N. L. (10), A. L. (8), July 13, 1976.

Most Outfielders, Nine-Inning Game, One Club

 8—N. L., July 24, 1973.

Most Outfielders, Nine-Inning Game, Both Clubs

 14—N. L. (7), A. L. (7), July 8, 1980.

Most Outfielders, Extra-Inning Game, Both Clubs

 13—N. L. (7), A. L. (6), July 14, 1970, 12 innings.

Most Right Fielders, Nine-Inning Game, One Club

 4—N. L., July 13, 1976.

Most Right Fielders, Nine-Inning Game, Both Clubs

 6—N. L. (4), A. L. (2), July 13, 1976.

Most Center Fielders, Nine-Inning Game, One Club

 3—A. L., July 10, 1934; A. L., July 9, 1946; A. L., July 12, 1949; N. L., July 15, 1975.

Most Center Fielders, Nine-Inning Game, Both Clubs

 5—A. L. (3), N. L. (2), July 10, 1934; A. L. (3), N. L. (2), July 9, 1946; A. L. (3), N. L. (2), July 12, 1949; N. L. (3), A. L. (2), July 15, 1975.

Most Left Fielders, Nine-Inning Game, One Club

 3—N. L., July 10, 1951; A. L., July 13, 1954; N. L., August 3, 1959, second game; N. L., July 9, 1968; A. L., July 23, 1969; N. L., July 15, 1975; A. L., July 8, 1980; N. L., August 9, 1981; N. L., July 13, 1982; A. L., July 6, 1983.

Most Left Fielders, Nine-Inning Game, Both Clubs

 5—N. L. (3), A. L. (2), July 10, 1951; A. L. (3), N. L. (2), July 13, 1954; N. L. (3), A. L. (2), July 9, 1968; A. L. (3), N. L. (2), July 23, 1969; N. L. (3), A. L. (2), July 15, 1975; A. L. (3), N. L. (2), July 8, 1980; N. L. (3), A. L. (2), August 9, 1981.

Most Left Fielders, Extra-Inning Game, Both Clubs

 6—N. L. (3), A. L., (3), July 14, 1970, 12 innings.

Most Pinch-Hitters, Nine-Inning Game, One Club

 8—N. L., July 9, 1957.

Most Pinch-Hitters, Nine-Inning Game, Both Clubs

 11—N. L. (7), A. L. (4), July 24, 1973.
  N. L. (7), A. L. (4), August 9, 1981.

Most Pinch-Hitters, Extra-Inning Game, Both Clubs

 11—N. L. (6), A. L. (5), July 11, 1967, 15 innings.

Fewest Pinch-Hitters, Game, One Club

    0—A. L., July 8, 1935.
       N. L., July 9, 1940.
       A. L., July 8, 1980.

Fewest Pinch-Hitters, Game, Both Clubs

    1—A. L., (1), N. L. (0), July 9, 1940.

Youngest Player to Participate in All-Star Game

    Dwight E. Gooden, 1984; 19 years, 7 months, 24 days.

Oldest Player to Participate in All-Star Game

    Leroy Paige, 1953; 47 years, 7 days.

Players Participating in All-Star Game, Each League (35)

    Henry L. Aaron, National League, 1955, 1956, 1957, 1958, 1959 (2), 1960 (2), 1961 (2), 1962, 1963, 1964, 1965, 1966, 1967, 1968, 1969, 1970, 1971, 1972, 1973, 1974. American League, 1975.

    Richard A. Allen, National League, 1965, 1966, 1967, 1970. American League, 1972, 1974.

    Vida R. Blue, American League, 1971, 1975. National League, 1978, 1981.

    Bobby L. Bonds, National League, 1971, 1973. American League, 1975.

    Robert R. Boone, National League, 1976, 1978, 1979. American League, 1983.

    James P. Bunning, American League, 1957, 1959, 1961 (2), 1962, 1963. National League, 1964, 1966.

    Miguel Cuellar, National League, 1967. American League, 1971.

    Raymond L. Culp, National League, 1963. American League, 1969.

    Ronald R. Fairly, National League, 1973. American League, 1977.

    Roland G. Fingers, American League, 1973, 1974, 1981, 1982. National League, 1978.

    Kenneth R. Forsch, National League, 1976. American League, 1981.

    Philip M. Garner, American League, 1976. National League, 1980, 1981.

    Richard M. Gossage, American League, 1975, 1978, 1980. National League, 1977, 1984.

    George A. Hendrick, American League, 1974, 1975. National League, 1980.

    David A. Johnson, American League, 1968, 1970. National League, 1973.

    Ruppert S. Jones, American League, 1977. National League, 1982.

    John R. Mize, National League, 1937, 1939, 1940, 1941, 1942, 1946, 1947, 1948, 1949. American League, 1953.

    Robert J. Monday, American League, 1968. National League, 1978.

    Bobby R. Murcer, American League, 1971, 1972, 1973, 1974; National League, 1975.

    Albert Oliver, National League, 1972, 1975, 1976, 1982, 1983. American League, 1980, 1981.

    Gaylord J. Perry, National League, 1966, 1970, 1979. American League, 1972, 1974.

    Frank Robinson, National League, 1956, 1957, 1959, 1961, 1962, 1965. American League, 1966, 1969, 1970, 1971, 1974.

    Octavio V. Rojas, National League, 1965. American League, 1971, 1972, 1973.

    John Roseboro, National League, 1961, 1962. American League, 1969.

    Lynwood T. Rowe, American League, 1936. National League, 1947.

    L. Nolan Ryan, American League, 1973, 1979. National League, 1981.

    Ted L. Simmons, National League, 1973, 1977, 1978. American League, 1981, 1983.

    William R. Singer, National League, 1969. American League, 1973.

    C. Reginald Smith, American League, 1969, 1972. National League, 1974, 1975, 1977, 1978, 1980.

    Daniel J. Staub, National League, 1967, 1968, 1970. American League, 1976.

    John E. Temple, National League, 1956, 1957, 1959 (2). American League, 1961 (2).

    Jason D. Thompson, American League, 1978. National League, 1982.

    J. Manuel Trillo, National League, 1977, 1981, 1982. American League, 1983.

    Claudell Washington, American League, 1975. National League, 1984.

    David M. Winfield, National League, 1977, 1978, 1979, 1980. American League, 1981, 1982, 1983, 1984.

Pitchers Starting in All-Star Game, Each League (1)

    Vida R. Blue, American League, 1971. National League, 1978.

All-Star Games Won

    35—National League (one tie). (Lost 19).
    19—American League (one tie). (Lost 35).

Most Consecutive All-Star Games Won

    11—National League, 1972, 1973, 1974, 1975, 1976, 1977, 1978, 1979, 1980, 1981, 1982.

Most Consecutive All-Star Games Lost
　11—American League, 1972, 1973, 1974, 1975, 1976, 1977, 1978, 1979, 1980, 1981, 1982.

Most All-Star Games Managed
　10—Charles D. Stengel, A. L., 1950, 1951, 1952, 1953, 1954, 1956, 1957, 1958, 1959 (2) (won 4, lost 6).

Most Consecutive All-Star Games Managed
　5—Charles D. Stengel, A. L., 1950, 1951, 1952, 1953, 1954; also 1956, 1957, 1958, 1959 (2).

Most All-Star Games Won as Manager
　7—Walter E. Alston, N. L., 1956, 1960 (2), 1964, 1966, 1967, 1975, (lost 2).

Most All-Star Games Lost as Manager
　6—Charles D. Stengel, A. L., 1950, 1951, 1952, 1953, 1956, 1959 first game (won 4).

Most Consecutive Defeats as All-Star Manager
　5—Alfonso R. Lopez, A. L., 1955, 1960 (2), 1964, 1965.

Most Consecutive Years Managing All-Star Losers
　4—Charles D. Stengel, A. L., 1950, 1951, 1952, 1953.

All-Star Game Composite Averages

BATTING AVERAGES

American League

Player, Club and Years Played	Pos.	G.	AB.	R.	H.	2B.	3B.	HR.	RBI.	B.A.
Aaron, Henry, 1975 Milwaukee	PH	1	1	0	0	0	0	0	0	.000
Agee, Tommie, 1966-67 Chicago	OF-PR	2	0	0	0	0	0	0	0	.000
Aguirre, Henry, 1962 Detroit	P	1	2	0	0	0	0	0	0	.000
Allen, John, 1938 Cleveland	P	1	1	0	0	0	0	0	0	.000
Allen, Richard, 1972-74 Chicago	1B	2	5	0	1	0	0	0	1	.200
Allison, W. Robert, 1963-64 Minnesota	OF-1B	2	4	0	0	0	0	0	0	.000
Alomar, Santos, 1970 California	2B	1	1	0	0	0	0	0	0	.000
Alvis, R. Maxwell, 1965-67 Cleveland	3B-PH	2	2	0	0	0	0	0	0	.000
Andrews, Michael, 1969 Boston	2B	1	1	0	0	0	0	0	0	.000
Aparicio, Luis, 1958-59 (2) -60-61-62 (2) Chicago; 1963 Baltimore; 1970 Chicago; 1971 Boston	SS	10	28	2	2	0	1	0	0	.071
Appling, Lucius, 1936-40-46-47 Chicago	SS-PH	4	9	1	4	1	0	0	2	.444
Armas, Antonio, 1981 Oakland	OF	1	1	0	0	0	0	0	0	.000
Averill, Earl, 1933-34-36-37-38 Cleveland	OF-PH	5	15	1	4	1	1	0	4	.267
Avila, Roberto, 1952-54-55 Cleveland	2B	3	6	1	4	0	0	0	3	.667
Azcue, Jose, 1968 Cleveland	C	1	1	0	0	0	0	0	0	.000
Bando, Salvatore, 1969-72-73 Oakland	3B	3	6	0	1	0	0	0	0	.167
Bannister, Floyd, 1982 Seattle	P	1	0	0	0	0	0	0	0	.000
Barker, Leonard, 1981 Cleveland	P	1	0	0	0	0	0	0	0	.000
Battey, Earl, 1962 (2) -63-65-66 Minnesota	C	5	9	1	1	0	0	0	1	.111
Bauer, Henry, 1952-53-54 New York	OF	3	7	0	2	0	0	0	0	.286
Baylor, Donald, 1979 California	OF	1	4	2	2	1	0	0	1	.500
Belanger, Mark, 1976 Baltimore	SS	1	1	0	0	0	0	0	0	.000
Bell, David, 1973 Cleveland; 1980-81-82-84 Texas	PH-3B	5	8	0	1	0	1	0	1	.125
Bell, Gary, 1960 (2) Cleveland	P	2	0	0	0	0	0	0	0	.000
Benton, J. Alton, 1942 Detroit	P	1	1	0	0	0	0	0	0	.000
Berra, Lawrence, 1949-50-51-52-53-54-55-56-57-58-59-60 (2) -61-62 New York	C-PH	15	41	5	8	0	0	1	3	.195
Berry, A. Kenneth, 1967 Chicago	PH	1	1	0	0	0	0	0	0	.000
Blair, Paul, 1969-73 Baltimore	OF	2	2	0	0	0	0	0	0	.000
Blue, Vida, 1971-75 Oakland	P	2	0	0	0	0	0	0	0	.000
Bluege, Oswald, 1935 Washington	3B	1	0	0	0	0	0	0	0	.000
Blyleven, Rikalbert, 1973 Minnesota	P	1	0	0	0	0	0	0	0	.000
Bochte, Bruce, 1979 Seattle	PH-1B	1	1	0	1	0	0	0	1	1.000
Bonds, Bobby, 1975 New York	OF	1	3	0	0	0	0	0	0	.000
Boone, Raymond, 1954-56 Detroit	3B-PH	2	5	1	1	0	0	1	1	.200
Boone, Robert, 1983 California	C	1	0	0	0	0	0	0	0	.000
Borowy, Henry, 1944 New York	P	1	1	0	1	0	0	0	1	1.000
Boudreau, Louis, 1940-41-42-47-48 Cleveland	SS	5	12	1	4	0	0	1	3	.333
Bouton, James, 1963 New York	P	1	0	0	0	0	0	0	0	.000
Brandt, Jack, 1961 Baltimore	PH	1	1	0	0	0	0	0	0	.000
Brett, George, 1976-77-78-79-81-82-83-84 Kansas City	3B	8	22	5	7	2	1	1	4	.318
Brewer, Thomas, 1956 Boston	P	1	0	0	0	0	0	0	0	.000
Bridges, Thomas, 1937-39 Detroit	P	2	2	0	0	0	0	0	0	.000
Brinkman, Edwin, 1973 Detroit	SS	1	1	0	0	0	0	0	0	.000
Brissie, Leland, 1949 Philadelphia	P	1	1	0	0	0	0	0	0	.000
Buford, Donald, 1971 Baltimore	PH	1	1	0	0	0	0	0	0	.000
Bumbry, Alonza, 1980 Baltimore	OF	1	1	0	0	0	0	0	0	.000
Bunning, James, 1957-59-61 (2) -62-63 Detroit	P	6	2	0	0	0	0	0	0	.000
Burleson, Rick, 1977-79 Boston; 1981 California	SS-PR	3	5	1	0	0	0	0	0	.000
Burroughs, Jeffrey, 1974 Texas	OF	1	0	0	0	0	0	0	0	.000
Busby, James, 1951 Chicago	OF	1	0	0	0	0	0	0	0	.000
Busby, Steven, 1975 Kansas City	P	1	0	0	0	0	0	0	0	.000
Campaneris, Dagoberto, 1968-73-74-75 Oak.; 1977 Tex.	SS	5	11	1	2	0	0	0	0	.182
Campbell, William, 1977 Boston	P	1	0	0	0	0	0	0	0	.000
Carew, Rodney, 1967-68-69-71-72-73-74-75-76-77-78 Minn.; 1980-81-83-84 California	2B-1B	15	41	8	10	1	2	0	2	.244
Cash, Norman, 1961 (2) -66-71-72 Detroit	1B	5	13	0	1	1	0	0	0	.077
Carrasquel, Alfonso, 1951-53-54-55 Chicago	SS	4	12	1	4	0	0	0	0	.333
Case, George, 1943 Washington	OF	1	2	1	0	0	0	0	0	.000
Caudill, William, 1984 Oakland	P	1	0	0	0	0	0	0	0	.000
Cerv, Robert, 1958 Kansas City	OF	1	2	0	1	0	0	0	0	.500
Chalk, David, 1974 California	3B	1	0	0	0	0	0	0	0	.000
Chambliss, C. Christopher, 1976 New York	PH	1	1	0	0	0	0	0	0	.000
Chance, Dean, 1964 Los Angeles; 1967 Minnesota	P	2	1	0	0	0	0	0	0	.000
Chandler, Spurgeon, 1942 New York	P	1	0	0	0	0	0	0	0	.000
Chapman, Benjamin, 1933-34-35 N. Y.; 36 Wash.	OF	4	8	0	2	0	1	0	0	.250
Chapman, Samuel, 1946 Philadelphia	OF	1	2	0	0	0	0	0	1	.000
Clancy, James, 1982 Toronto	P	1	0	0	0	0	0	0	0	.000
Clear, Mark, 1979 California	P	1	0	0	0	0	0	0	0	.000
Coates, James, 1960 New York	P	1	0	0	0	0	0	0	0	.000
Cochrane, Gordon, 1934 Detroit	C	1	1	0	0	0	0	0	0	.000
Colavito, Rocco, 1959 Clev.; 1961 (2) -62 (2) Det.; 1964 K. C.; 1965-66 Cleve.	OF-PH	9	25	3	6	1	0	3	8	.240
Coleman, Gerald, 1950 New York	2B	1	2	0	0	0	0	0	0	.000
Coleman, Joseph, 1948 Philadelphia	P	1	0	0	0	0	0	0	0	.000
Conigliaro, Anthony, 1967 Boston	OF	1	6	0	0	0	0	0	0	.000
Consuegra, Sandalio, 1954 Chicago	P	1	0	0	0	0	0	0	0	.000
Cooper, Cecil, 1979-80-82-83 Milwaukee	PH-1B	4	4	1	2	0	0	0	0	.500

Player, Club and Years Played	Pos.	G.	AB.	R.	H.	2B.	3B.	HR.	RBI.	B.A.
Cramer, Roger, 1935 Philadelphia; 1938-39 Boston	OF	3	6	0	1	0	0	0	0	.167
Cronin, Joseph, 1933-34 Wash.; 1935-37-38-39-41 Bos	SS	7	25	3	7	3	0	0	4	.280
Crosetti, Frank, 1936 New York	PH	1	1	0	0	0	0	0	0	.000
Crowder, Alvin, 1933 Washington	P	1	0	0	0	0	0	0	0	.000
Cuellar, Miguel, 1971 Baltimore	P	1	0	0	0	0	0	0	0	.000
Cullenbine, Roy, 1941 St. Louis	PH	1	1	0	0	0	0	0	0	.000
Culp, Raymond, 1969 Boston	P	1	0	0	0	0	0	0	0	.000
Daley, Buddy, 1959-60 Kansas City	P	2	0	0	0	0	0	0	0	.000
Davalillo, Victor, 1965 Cleveland	OF	1	2	0	1	0	0	0	0	.500
Davis, Alvin, 1984 Seattle	PH	1	1	0	0	0	0	0	0	.000
Davis, Ronald, 1981 New York	P	1	0	0	0	0	0	0	0	.000
DeCinces, Douglas, 1983 California	PH	1	1	0	0	0	0	0	0	.000
Dent, Russell, 1975 Chicago; 1980-81 New York	SS	3	5	0	3	1	0	0	0	.600
Diaz, Baudilio, 1981 Cleveland	C	1	1	0	0	0	0	0	0	.000
Dickey, William, 1934-36-37-38-39-40-41-46 N.Y.	C-PH	8	19	3	5	2	0	0	1	.263
Dillinger, Robert, 1949 St. Louis	3B	1	2	1	2	1	0	0	1	1.000
DiMaggio, Dominic, 1941-46-49-50-51-52 Boston	OF	6	17	2	6	2	0	0	2	.353
DiMaggio, Joseph, 1936-37-38-39-40-41-42-47-48-49-50 New York	OF-PH	11	40	7	9	2	0	1	6	.225
Doby, Lawrence,1949-50-51-52-53-54 Cleveland	OF-PH	6	10	2	3	1	0	1	1	.300
Doerr, Robert, 1941-43-44-46-47-48-50-51 Boston	2B	8	20	2	4	0	0	1	3	.200
Donovan, Richard, 1961 Washington; 1962 Clev	P	2	0	0	0	0	0	0	0	.000
Dotson, Richard, 1984 Chicago	P	1	0	0	0	0	0	0	0	.000
Downing, Alphonso, 1967 New York	P	1	0	0	0	0	0	0	0	.000
Downing, Brian, 1979 California	C	1	1	0	1	0	0	0	1	1.000
Dropo, Walter, 1950 Boston	1B	1	3	0	1	0	1	0	0	.333
Duren, Ryne, 1959 New York	P	1	0	0	0	0	0	0	0	.000
Dykes, James, 1933 Chicago	3B	1	3	1	2	0	0	0	0	.667
Early, Jacob, 1948 Washington	C	1	2	1	0	0	0	0	0	.000
Eckersley, Dennis, 1977 Cleveland; 1982 Boston	P	2	1	0	0	0	0	0	0	.000
Estrada, Charles, 1960 Baltimore	P	1	0	0	0	0	0	0	0	.000
Evans, Dwight, 1978-81 Boston	OF-PH	2	3	1	1	0	0	0	0	.333
Evers, Walter, 1948-50 Detroit	OF	2	6	1	1	0	0	1	1	.167
Fain, Ferris, 1950-51 Philadelphia; 1953 Chicago	1B	3	7	1	3	0	1	0	1	.429
Fairly, Ronald, 1977 Toronto	PH	1	1	0	0	0	0	0	0	.000
Farmer, Edward 1980 Chicago	P	1	0	0	0	0	0	0	0	.000
Feller, Robert, 1939-40-41-46-50 Cleveland	P	5	2	0	0	0	0	0	0	.000
Ferrell, Richard, 1933-36 Boston	C	2	5	0	0	0	0	0	0	.000
Fidrych, Mark, 1976 Detroit	P	1	0	0	0	0	0	0	0	.000
Fingers, Roland, 1973-74 Oakland; 1981-82 Milwaukee	P	4	0	0	0	0	0	0	0	.000
Finigan, James, 1955 Kansas City	3B	1	3	0	0	0	0	0	0	.000
Finney, Louis, 1940 Boston	OF	1	0	0	0	0	0	0	0	.000
Fisher, Eddie, 1965 Chicago	P	1	0	0	0	0	0	0	0	.000
Fisk, Carlton, 1972-73-76-77-78-80 Bos.; 1981-82 Chi.	C	8	16	2	2	0	0	0	1	.125
Ford, Edward, 1954-55-56-59-60-61 New York	P	6	3	0	0	0	0	0	0	.000
Fornieles, J. Miguel, 1961 Boston	P	1	0	0	0	0	0	0	0	.000
Forsch, Kenneth, 1981 California	P	1	0	0	0	0	0	0	0	.000
Fosse, Raymond, 1970 Cleveland	C	1	2	1	1	0	0	0	1	.500
Fox, J. Nelson, 1951-53-54-55-56-57-58-59(2)-60(2)-61-63 Chicago	2B-PH	13	38	7	14	0	0	0	5	.368
Foxx, James, 1934-35 Phila.; 1936-37-38-40-41 Bos.	1B-3B	7	19	3	6	1	0	1	4	.316
Freehan, William, 1965-66-67-68-69-70-71-72 Detroit	C	8	17	2	4	0	0	1	2	.235
Fregosi, James, 1964 L.A.; 1966-67-68-69-70 Calif.	SS-PH	6	15	1	3	1	0	0	1	.200
Garcia, Damaso, 1984 Toronto	2B	1	1	0	0	0	0	0	0	.000
Garcia, E. Mike, 1953 Cleveland	P	1	0	0	0	0	0	0	0	.000
Garner, Philip, 1976 Oakland	2B	1	1	0	0	0	0	0	0	.000
Garver, Ned, 1951 St. Louis	P	1	0	0	0	0	0	0	0	.000
Gehrig, H. Louis, 1933-34-35-36-37-38 New York	1B	6	18	4	4	1	0	2	5	.222
Gehringer, Charles, 1933-34-35-36-37-38 Detroit	2B	6	20	2	10	2	0	0	1	.500
Gentile, James, 1960-61-62(2) Baltimore	PH-1B	4	11	0	2	0	0	0	0	.182
Gomez, Vernon, 1933-34-35-37-38 New York	P	5	6	0	1	0	0	0	1	.167
Goodman, William, 1949-53 Boston	1B-2B	2	2	0	0	0	0	0	0	.000
Gordon, Jos., 1939-40-41-42-46 N. Y.; 1947-48-49 Clev.	2B	8	20	2	4	3	0	0	2	.200
Goslin, Leon, 1936 Detroit	OF	1	1	1	1	0	0	0	1	1.000
Gossage, Richard, 1975 Chicago; 1978-80 New York	P	3	0	0	0	0	0	0	0	.000
Grant, James, 1965 Minnesota	P	1	0	0	0	0	0	0	0	.000
Gray, Theodore, 1950 Detroit	P	1	0	0	0	0	0	0	0	.000
Greenberg, Henry, 1939-40 Detroit	1B-OF	2	5	1	1	0	0	0	0	.200
Grich, Robert, 1972-74-76 Balt.; 1979-80-82 Calif.	SS-2B	6	11	0	1	0	0	0	0	.091
Griffin, Alfredo, 1984 Toronto	SS	1	0	0	0	0	0	0	0	.000
Grim, Robert, 1957 New York	P	1	0	0	0	0	0	0	0	.000
Grove, Robert, 1933 Philadelphia; 1936-38 Boston	P	3	2	0	0	0	0	0	0	.000
Guidry, Ronald, 1978-79 New York	P	2	0	0	0	0	0	0	0	.000
Hall, Jimmie, 1964-65 Minnesota	OF-PH	2	2	1	0	0	0	0	0	.000
Hansen, Ronald, 1960 (2) Baltimore	SS	2	6	0	3	0	0	0	0	.500
Harder, Melvin, 1934-35-36-37 Cleveland	P	4	4	0	0	0	0	0	0	.000
Hargrove, D. Michael, 1975 Texas	PH	1	1	0	0	0	0	0	0	.000
Harper, Tommy, 1970 Milwaukee	PR	1	0	0	0	0	0	0	0	.000
Harrah, Colbert, 1976 Texas	SS	1	2	0	0	0	0	0	0	.000
Harrelson, Kenneth, 1968 Boston	PH	1	1	0	0	0	0	0	0	.000
Hayes, Frank, 1940-41-44 Philadelphia; 1946 Cleveland	C	4	4	0	0	0	0	0	0	.000
Heath, J. Geoffrey, 1941-43 Cleveland	OF-PH	2	3	0	0	0	0	0	0	.000
Hegan, James, 1950-51 Cleveland	C-PH	2	4	0	1	1	0	0	0	.250
Hemsley, Ralston, 1935 St. Louis; 1940 Cleve.; 1944 N. Y.	C	3	7	1	1	0	1	0	0	.143

Player, Club and Years Played	Pos.	G.	AB.	R.	H.	2B.	3B.	HR.	RBI.	B.A.
Henderson, Rickey, 1980-82-83-84 Oakland	OF	4	8	1	3	0	0	0	1	.375
Hendrick, George, 1974-75 Cleveland	OF-PR	2	3	1	2	0	0	0	0	.667
Henrich, Thomas, 1942-47-48-50 New York	OF-PH	4	9	1	1	1	0	0	0	.111
Herbert, Raymond, 1962 Chicago	P	1	1	0	0	0	0	0	0	.000
Hernandez, Guillermo, 1984 Detroit	P	1	0	0	0	0	0	0	0	.000
Higgins, Michael, 1936 Philadelphia; 1944 Detroit	3B-PH	2	3	0	0	0	0	0	0	.000
Hinton, Charles, 1964 Washington	OF	1	0	0	0	0	0	0	0	.000
Hisle, Larry, 1977 Minnesota; 1978 Milwaukee	PH	2	2	0	1	0	0	0	0	.500
Hoag, Myril, 1939 St. Louis	PH	1	1	0	0	0	0	0	0	.000
Holtzman, Kenneth, 1973 Oakland	P	1	0	0	0	0	0	0	0	.000
Honeycutt, Frederick, 1983 Texas	P	1	0	0	0	0	0	0	0	.000
Horton, Willie, 1965-68-70-73 Detroit	OF-PH	4	8	1	2	0	0	0	0	.250
Houtteman, Arthur, 1950 Detroit	P	1	1	0	0	0	0	0	0	.000
Howard, Elston, 1960-61 (2) -62-63-64 New York	C	6	9	1	0	0	0	0	0	.000
Howard, Frank, 1968-69-70-71 Washington	PH-OF	4	6	1	1	0	0	1	1	.167
Howell, Roy, 1978 Toronto	PH	1	1	0	0	0	0	0	0	.000
Howser, Richard, 1961 Kansas City	3B	1	1	0	0	0	0	0	0	.000
Hrbek, Kent, 1982 Minnesota	PH	1	1	0	0	0	0	0	0	.000
Hudson, Sidney, 1941 Washington	P	1	0	0	0	0	0	0	0	.000
Hughson, Cecil, 1943-44 Boston	P	2	1	0	0	0	0	0	0	.000
Hunter, G. William, 1953 St. Louis	PR	1	0	0	0	0	0	0	0	.000
Hunter, James, 1967 Kansas City; 1970-73-74 Oakland; 1975-76 New York	P	6	1	0	0	0	0	0	0	.000
Hutchinson, Fred, 1951 Detroit	P	1	0	0	0	0	0	0	0	.000
Jackson, Reginald, 1969-71-72-73-74-75 Oak.; 1977-79-80-81 N. Y.; 1982-84 California	PH-OF	12	26	2	7	2	0	1	3	.269
Jensen, Jack, 1952 Washington; 1955-58 Boston	OF-PH	3	5	0	0	0	0	0	1	.000
John, Thomas, 1968 Chicago; 1980 New York	P	2	1	0	0	0	0	0	0	.000
Johnson, Alexander, 1970 California	PH	1	1	0	0	0	0	0	0	.000
Johnson, David, 1968-70 Baltimore	2B	2	6	0	1	0	0	0	0	.167
Johnson, Robert, 1935-38-42 Philadelphia; 1943 Washington; 1944 Boston	OF-PH	5	9	0	1	0	0	0	0	.111
Johnson, William, 1947 New York	3B	1	0	0	0	0	0	0	0	.000
Jones, Ruppert, 1977 Seattle	PH	1	1	0	0	0	0	0	0	.000
Joost, Edwin, 1949 Philadelphia	SS	1	2	1	1	0	0	0	2	.500
Josephson, Duane, 1968 Chicago	C	1	0	0	0	0	0	0	0	.000
Kaat, James, 1966 Minnesota; 1975 Chicago	P	2	0	0	0	0	0	0	0	.000
Kaline, Albert, 1955-56-57-58-59 (2) -60 (2) -61 (2) -62-63-65-66-71-74 Detroit	OF-PH-PR	16	37	7	12	1	0	2	6	.324
Keegan, Robert, 1954 Chicago	P	1	0	0	0	0	0	0	0	.000
Kell, George, 1947-49-50-51 Det.; 1953 Bos.; 1956-57 Balt.	3B-PH	7	23	3	4	0	0	1	3	.174
Keller, Charles, 1940-41-46 New York	OF	3	7	2	1	0	0	1	2	.143
Kelly, H. Patrick, 1973 Chicago	PH	1	1	0	0	0	0	0	0	.000
Keltner, Kenneth, 1940-41-42-43-44-46-48 Cleveland	3B-PH	7	17	4	4	1	0	0	0	.235
Kemp, Steven, 1979 Detroit	PH	1	1	0	0	0	0	0	0	.000
Keough, Matthew, 1978 Oakland	P	1	0	0	0	0	0	0	0	.000
Kern, James, 1977-78 Cleveland; 1979 Texas	P	3	0	0	0	0	0	0	0	.000
Killebrew, Harmon, 1959 Wash.; 1961-63-64-65-66-67-68-69-70-71 Minnesota	3B-PH-OF-1B	11	26	4	8	0	0	3	6	.308
Kittle, Ronald, 1983 Chicago	OF	1	2	1	1	0	0	0	0	.500
Knoop, Robert, 1966 California	2B	1	2	0	0	0	0	0	0	.000
Knowles, Darold, 1969 Washington	P	1	0	0	0	0	0	0	0	.000
Kramer, John, 1946 St. Louis	P	1	1	1	1	0	0	0	0	1.000
Kreevich, Michael, 1938 Chicago	OF	1	2	0	0	0	0	0	0	.000
Kubek, Anthony, 1959-61 New York	PH-SS	2	5	1	0	0	0	0	0	.000
Kuenn, Harvey, 1953-55-56-57-59 Det.; 1960 (2) Clev.	PH-SS-OF	7	16	3	3	0	0	0	1	.188
Laabs, Chester, 1943 St. Louis	OF	1	3	1	0	0	0	0	0	.000
Landis, James, 1962 Chicago	OF	1	1	0	0	0	0	0	0	.000
Landreaux, Kenneth, 1980 Minnesota	OF	1	1	0	0	0	0	0	0	.000
LaRoche, David, 1977 California	P	1	0	0	0	0	0	0	0	.000
Lary, Frank, 1960 (2) -61 Detroit	P	3	0	0	0	0	0	0	0	.000
Lee, Thornton, 1941 Chicago	P	1	1	0	0	0	0	0	0	.000
LeFlore, Ronald, 1976 Detroit	OF	1	2	0	1	0	0	0	0	.500
Lemon, Chester, 1978-79 Chicago; 1984 Detroit	OF	3	4	1	1	0	0	0	0	.250
Lemon, James, 1960 Washington	OF	1	1	0	0	0	0	0	0	.000
Lemon, Robert, 1950-51-52-54 Cleveland	P	4	1	1	0	0	0	0	0	.000
Leonard, Emil, 1943 Washington	P	1	1	0	1	0	0	0	0	1.000
Lewis, John, 1938-47 Washington	3B-OF	2	3	0	0	0	0	0	0	.000
Loes, William, 1957 Baltimore	P	1	1	0	0	0	0	0	0	.000
Lolich, Michael, 1971-72 Detroit	P	2	1	0	0	0	0	0	0	.000
Lollar, J. Sherman, 1956-59 (2) -60 (2) Chicago	C-PH	5	6	0	2	1	0	0	0	.333
Lopat, Edmund, 1951 New York	P	1	0	0	0	0	0	0	0	.000
Lyle, Albert, 1973-77 New York	P	2	0	0	0	0	0	0	0	.000
Lynn, Fredric, 1975-76-77-78-79-80 Boston; 1981-82-83 California	PH-OF	9	20	5	6	0	0	4	10	.300
Mack, Raymond, 1940 Cleveland	2B	1	1	0	0	0	0	0	0	.000
Malzone, Frank, 1957-58-59 (2) -60 (2) -63 Boston	3B	7	20	3	3	0	0	1	2	.150
Mantle, Mickey, 1953-54-55-56-57-58-59 (2) -60 (2) -61 (2) -62-64-67-68 New York	OF-PH	16	43	5	10	0	0	2	4	.233
Mantilla, Felix, 1965 Boston	2B	1	2	0	0	0	0	0	0	.000
Manush, Henry, 1934 Washington	OF	1	2	0	0	0	0	0	0	.000

Player, Club and Years Played	Pos.	G.	AB.	R.	H.	2B.	3B.	HR.	RBI.	B.A.
Maris, Roger, 1959 K. C.; 1960 (2)-61 (2)-62 (2) N. York	OF-PH	7	19	2	2	1	0	0	2	.105
Martin, Alfred, 1956 New York	PH	1	1	0	0	0	0	0	0	.000
Masterson, Walter, 1947-48 Washington	P	2	0	0	0	0	0	0	0	.000
Mattingly, Donald, 1984 New York	PH	1	1	0	0	0	0	0	0	.000
Maxwell, Charles, 1957 Detroit	PH	1	1	0	1	0	0	0	0	1.000
May, Carlos, 1969 Chicago	PH	1	1	0	0	0	0	0	0	.000
May, David, 1973 Milwaukee	OF	1	2	0	0	0	0	0	0	.000
Mayberry, John, 1973-74 Kansas City	1B-PH	2	4	0	1	1	0	0	0	.250
McAuliffe, Richard, 1965-66-67 Detroit	SS-2B	3	9	2	2	0	0	1	2	.222
McBride, Kenneth, 1963 Los Angeles	P	1	1	0	1	0	0	0	1	1.000
McDougald, Gilbert, 1952-57-58-59 N. York	PH-SS-PR	4	4	1	1	0	0	0	1	.250
McDowell, Samuel, 1965-68-69-70 Cleveland	P	4	0	0	0	0	0	0	0	.000
McGlothlin, James, 1967 California	P	1	0	0	0	0	0	0	0	.000
McLain, Dennis, 1966-68-69 Detroit	P	3	1	0	0	0	0	0	0	.000
McLish, Calvin, 1959 Cleveland	P	1	0	0	0	0	0	0	0	.000
McNally, David, 1969-72 Baltimore	P	2	0	0	0	0	0	0	0	.000
McQuinn, George, 1944 St. Louis; 1947-48 New York	1B	3	12	1	3	0	0	0	0	.250
McRae, Harold, 1975-76-82 Kansas City	PH	3	2	0	0	0	0	0	0	.000
Michaels, Casimer, 1949 Chi.; 1950 Wash.	2B-PH	2	3	1	1	1	0	0	0	.333
Mincher, Donald, 1967 California; 1969 Seattle	PH	2	2	0	1	0	0	0	0	.500
Minoso, Orestes, 1951-52-53-54-57-60 (2) Chi.; 1959 Clev.	OF	8	20	2	6	2	0	0	2	.300
Mitchell, L. Dale, 1949-52 Cleveland	OF	2	2	0	1	1	0	0	1	.500
Mize, John, 1953 New York	PH	1	1	0	1	0	0	0	0	1.000
Monbouquette, William, 1960 Boston	P	1	0	0	0	0	0	0	0	.000
Monday, Robert, 1968 Oakland	OF	1	2	0	0	0	0	0	0	.000
Money, Donald, 1976-78 Milwaukee	3B-2B	2	3	0	0	0	0	0	0	.000
Moran, William, 1962 (2) Los Angeles	2B	2	7	0	2	0	0	0	0	.286
Morris, John, 1981-84 Detroit	P	2	0	0	0	0	0	0	0	.000
Mossi, Donald, 1957 Cleveland	P	1	0	0	0	0	0	0	0	.000
Mullin, Patrick, 1948 Detroit	OF	1	1	0	0	0	0	0	0	.000
Muncrief, Robert, 1948 St. Louis	P	1	0	0	0	0	0	0	0	.000
Munson, Thurman, 1971-73-74-75-76-77 N. York	PH-C	6	10	1	2	1	0	0	0	.200
Murcer, Bobby, 1971-72-73-74 New York	OF	4	11	0	1	0	0	0	0	.091
Murray, Eddie, 1981-82-83-84 Baltimore	PH-1B	4	7	0	1	1	0	0	0	.143
Narleski, Raymond, 1958 Cleveland	P	1	1	0	1	0	0	0	1	1.000
Nelson, David, 1973 Texas	3B	1	0	0	0	0	0	0	0	.000
Nettles, Graig, 1975-77-78-79-80 New York	3B	5	9	0	2	0	0	0	0	.222
Newhouser, Harold 1943-44-46-47-48 Detroit	P-PR	5	3	1	1	0	0	0	0	.333
Newsom, Louis, 1940 Detroit; 1944 Philadelphia	P	2	1	0	1	0	0	0	0	1.000
Noren, Irving, 1954 New York	OF	1	0	0	0	0	0	0	0	.000
Norris, Michael, 1981 Oakland	P	1	0	0	0	0	0	0	0	.000
O'Dell, William, 1958-59 Baltimore	P	2	0	0	0	0	0	0	0	.000
Odom, Johnny, 1968-69 Oakland	P	2	0	0	0	0	0	0	0	.000
Oglivie, Benjamin, 1980-82-83 Milwaukee	OF-PH	3	4	0	0	0	0	0	0	.000
Oliva, Pedro (Tony) 1964-65-66-67-68-70 Minn.	OF-PH	6	19	0	5	3	0	0	0	.263
Oliver, Albert, 1980-81 Texas	OF-PH	2	2	0	0	0	0	0	0	.000
Otis, Amos, 1970-71-73-76 Kansas City	OF-PH	4	7	0	2	0	0	0	0	.286
Paciorek, Thomas, 1981 Seattle	PH	1	1	0	1	0	0	0	0	1.000
Page, Joseph, 1947 New York	P	1	0	0	0	0	0	0	0	.000
Paige, Leroy, 1953 St. Louis	P	1	0	0	0	0	0	0	0	.000
Palmer, James, 1970-71-72-77-78 Baltimore	P	5	2	0	0	0	0	0	0	.000
Pappas, Milton, 1962 (2)-65 Baltimore	P	3	0	0	0	0	0	0	0	.000
Parnell, Melvin, 1949-51 Boston	P	2	1	0	0	0	0	0	0	.000
Parrish, Lance, 1980-82-83-84 Detroit	C	4	7	0	1	1	0	0	0	.143
Pascual, Camilo, 1961-62-64 Minnesota	P	3	2	0	0	0	0	0	0	.000
Patek, Freddie, 1976-78 Kansas City	SS	2	3	0	1	0	0	0	0	.333
Pearson, Albert, 1963 Los Angeles	OF	1	4	1	2	1	0	0	0	.500
Pepitone, Joseph, 1963-64-65 New York	1B-PR-PH	3	5	0	0	0	0	0	0	.000
Perry, Gaylord, 1972-74 Cleveland	P	2	0	0	0	0	0	0	0	.000
Perry, James, 1970 Minnesota	P	1	0	0	0	0	0	0	0	.000
Pesky, John, 1946 Boston	SS	1	2	0	0	0	0	0	0	.000
Peters, Gary, 1967 Chicago	P	1	0	0	0	0	0	0	0	.000
Peterson, Fred, 1970 New York	P	1	0	0	0	0	0	0	0	.000
Petrocelli, Americo, 1967-69 Boston	SS	2	4	0	1	1	0	0	0	.250
Pierce, W. William, 1953-55-56-57 Chicago	P	4	1	1	1	0	0	0	0	1.000
Piersall, James, 1954-56 Boston	OF	2	1	0	0	0	0	0	0	.000
Piniella, Louis, 1972 Kansas City	PH	1	1	0	0	0	0	0	0	.000
Pizarro, Juan, 1963 Chicago	P	1	0	0	0	0	0	0	0	.000
Porter, Darrell, 1978-79-80 Kansas City	PH-C	3	5	0	1	1	0	0	0	.200
Porterfield, Ervin, 1954 Washington	P	1	0	0	0	0	0	0	0	.000
Powell, John, 1968-69-70 Baltimore	1B	3	9	0	1	0	0	0	0	.111
Power, Victor, 1955-56 K. C.; 1959 (2)-60 Clev.	PH-1B	5	7	1	2	0	0	0	1	.286
Quisenberry, Daniel, 1982-83 Kansas City	P	2	0	0	0	0	0	0	0	.000
Radcliff, Raymond, 1936 Chicago	OF	1	2	0	1	0	0	0	0	.500
Radatz, Richard, 1963-64 Boston	P	2	1	0	0	0	0	0	0	.000
Randolph, William, 1977-80-81 New York	2B	3	12	0	4	0	0	0	1	.333
Raschi, Victor, 1948-49-50-52 New York	P	4	2	0	1	0	0	0	0	.500
Reynolds, Allie, 1950-53 New York	P	2	1	0	0	0	0	0	0	.000
Rice, James, 1977-78-79-83-84 Boston	OF-PH	5	16	1	4	1	0	1	1	.250
Richardson, Robert, 1962 (2)-63-64-65-66 New York	2B-PR-PH	6	11	1	1	0	0	0	0	.091
Richert, Peter, 1965-66 Washington	P	2	0	0	0	0	0	0	0	.000

Player, Club and Years Played	Pos.	G.	AB.	R.	H.	2B.	3B.	HR.	RBI.	B.A.
Ripken, Calvin, 1983-84 Baltimore	SS	2	3	0	0	0	0	0	0	.000
Rivers, John, 1976 New York	PH-OF	1	2	0	1	0	0	0	0	.500
Rizzuto, Philip, 1950-51-52-53 New York	SS	4	9	0	2	0	0	0	0	.222
Robinson, Brooks, 1960 (2)-61 (2)-62 (2)-63-64-65-66-67-68-69-70-71-72-73-74 Baltimore	3B-PH	18	45	5	13	0	3	1	5	.289
Robinson, Frank, 1966-69-70-71 Balt.; 1974 Calif.	OF-PH	5	12	1	1	0	0	1	2	.083
Robinson, W. Edward, 1949 Wash.; 1951-52 Chi.; 1953 Philadelphia	1B-PH	4	9	1	2	0	0	0	2	.222
Rojas, Octavio, 1971-72-73 Kansas City	2B-PH	3	2	1	1	0	0	1	2	.500
Rolfe, Robert, 1937-39 New York	3B	2	8	2	3	0	1	0	2	.375
Rollins, Richard, 1962 (2) Minnesota	3B	2	5	1	2	0	0	0	0	.400
Romano, John, 1961 (2)-62 Cleveland	C	3	6	0	1	0	0	0	0	.167
Rosar, Warren, 1946-47-48 Philadelphia	C	3	7	1	1	0	0	0	0	.143
Roseboro, John, 1969 Minnesota	C	1	1	0	0	0	0	0	0	.000
Rosen, Albert, 1952-53-54-55 Cleveland	3B-1B	4	11	3	3	0	0	2	5	.273
Rowe, Lynwood, 1936 Detroit	P	1	1	0	0	0	0	0	0	.000
Rudi, Joseph, 1972-74-75 Oakland	OF	3	6	0	2	1	0	0	0	.333
Ruffing, Charles, 1934-39-40 New York	P	3	2	0	1	0	0	0	2	.500
Runnels, James, 1959 (2)-60 (2)-62 Boston	PH-1B	5	7	1	1	0	0	1	1	.143
Ruth, George, 1933-34 New York	Of	2	6	2	2	0	0	1	2	.333
Ryan, L. Nolan, 1973-79 California	P	2	0	0	0	0	0	0	0	.000
Scheinblum, Richard, 1972 Kansas City	OF	1	1	0	0	0	0	0	0	.000
Schwall, Donald, 1961 Boston	P	1	1	0	0	0	0	0	0	.000
Score, Herbert, 1956 Cleveland	P	1	0	0	0	0	0	0	0	.000
Scott, George, 1966-77 Boston; 1975 Milwaukee	1B	3	6	1	1	0	0	1	2	.167
Selkirk, George, 1936-39 New York	OF-PH	2	2	1	1	0	0	0	1	.500
Shantz, Robert, 1952 Philadelphia	P	1	0	0	0	0	0	0	0	.000
Shea, Francis, 1947 New York	P	1	1	0	0	0	0	0	0	.000
Siebern, Norman, 1962 K. C., 1964 Baltimore	PH	2	2	0	0	0	0	0	0	.000
Siebert, Richard, 1943 Philadelphia	1B	1	1	0	0	0	0	0	0	.000
Siebert, Wilfred, 1966 Cleveland	P	1	0	0	0	0	0	0	0	.000
Sievers, Roy, 1956-59 Wash.; 1961 Chicago	PH	3	2	0	0	0	0	0	0	.000
Simmons, Aloysius, 1933-34-35 Chicago	OF	3	13	3	6	3	0	0	1	.462
Simmons, Ted, 1981-83 Milwaukee	PH-C	2	3	0	1	0	0	0	1	.333
Simpson, Harry, 1956 Kansas City	PH	1	1	0	0	0	0	0	0	.000
Singer, William, 1973 California	P	1	0	0	0	0	0	0	0	.000
Singleton, Kenneth, 1977-79-81 Baltimore	OF-PH	3	4	2	2	0	0	1	1	.500
Skowron, William, 1957-58-59-60 (2) New York	1B	5	14	1	6	1	0	0	0	.429
Smalley, Roy F. III, 1979 Minnesota	SS	1	3	0	0	0	0	0	0	.000
Smith, Alphonse, 1955 Cleve.; 1960 (2) Chi.	OF-PH	3	3	0	0	0	0	0	0	.000
Smith, Edgar, 1941 Chicago	P	1	1	0	0	0	0	0	0	.000
Smith, C. Reginald, 1969-72 Boston	PH-PR-OF	2	3	1	0	0	0	0	0	.000
Sorensen, Lary, 1978 Milwaukee	P	1	0	0	0	0	0	0	0	.000
Spence, Stanley, 1944-46-47 Washington	OF	3	5	1	3	0	0	0	1	.600
Spencer, James, 1973 Texas	PH	1	1	0	0	0	0	0	0	.000
Staley, Gerald, 1960 Chicago	P	1	0	0	0	0	0	0	0	.000
Stanley, Robert, 1979-83 Boston	P	2	0	0	0	0	0	0	0	.000
Staub, Daniel, 1976 Detroit	OF	1	2	0	2	0	0	0	0	1.000
Stenhouse, David, 1962 Washington	P	1	0	0	0	0	0	0	0	.000
Stephens, Vernon, 1943-44-46 St. Louis; 1948-49-51 Boston	SS-PH	6	15	1	5	1	0	0	2	.333
Stieb, David, 1980-81-83-84 Toronto	P	4	1	0	0	0	0	0	0	.000
Stirnweiss, George, 1946 New York	2B	1	3	1	1	0	0	0	0	.333
Stone, D. Dean, 1954 Washington	P	1	0	0	0	0	0	0	0	.000
Stone, Steven, 1980 Baltimore	P	1	0	0	0	0	0	0	0	.000
Stottlemyre, Melvin, 1966-68-69-70 New York	P	4	0	0	0	0	0	0	0	.000
Sullivan, Franklin, 1955 Boston	P	1	1	0	0	0	0	0	0	.000
Sundberg, James, 1978 Texas; 1984 Milwaukee	C	2	1	0	0	0	0	0	0	.000
Tanana, Frank, 1976 California	P	1	0	0	0	0	0	0	0	.000
Tebbetts, George, 1942 Detroit; 1948-49 Boston	C	3	7	1	2	1	0	0	1	.286
Temple, John, 1961 (2) Cleveland	2B	2	5	0	0	0	0	0	0	.000
Tenace, F. Gene, 1975 Oakland	1B-C	1	3	1	0	0	0	0	0	.000
Thomas, J. Gorman, 1981 Milwaukee	PH	1	1	0	0	0	0	0	0	.000
Thomas, J. Leroy, 1962 (2) Los Angeles	PH-OF	2	1	0	0	0	0	0	0	.000
Thompson, Jason, 1978 Detroit	PH	1	1	0	0	0	0	0	0	.000
Thornton, Andre, 1982-84 Cleveland	PH	2	2	0	1	0	0	0	0	.500
Tiant, Luis, 1968 Cleveland; 1974-76 Boston	P	3	1	0	0	0	0	0	0	.000
Trammell, Alan, 1980 Detroit	SS	1	0	0	0	0	0	0	0	.000
Travis, Cecil, 1940-41 Washington	3B	2	7	1	1	1	0	0	0	.143
Tresh, Thomas, 1962-63 New York	SS-OF	2	2	0	1	1	0	0	1	.500
Triandos, Augustus, 1958-59 Baltimore	C	2	6	0	2	1	0	0	2	.333
Trillo, J. Manuel, 1983 Cleveland	2B	3	3	1	1	0	0	0	0	.333
Trucks, Virgil, 1949 Detroit; 1954 Chicago	P	2	1	0	0	0	0	0	0	.000
Tucker, Thurman, 1944 Chicago	OF	1	4	0	0	0	0	0	0	.000
Turley, Robert, 1958 New York	P	1	0	0	0	0	0	0	0	.000
Vernon, James, 1946-48-53-54-55 Washington; 1956 Boston; 1958 Cleveland	1B-PH	7	14	2	2	0	0	0	1	.143
Versalles, Zoilo, 1963-65 Minnesota	SS	2	2	0	1	0	0	0	0	.500
Vosmik, Joseph, 1935 Cleveland	OF	1	4	1	1	0	0	0	0	.250
Wagner, Harold, 1946 Boston	C	1	1	0	0	0	0	0	0	.000
Wagner, Leon, 1962 (2)-63 Los Angeles	OF	3	11	2	5	0	0	1	2	.455
Wakefield, Richard, 1943 Detroit	OF	1	4	0	2	1	0	0	1	.500
Walker, Jerry, 1959 Baltimore	P	1	1	0	0	0	0	0	0	.000
Ward, Gary, 1983 Minnesota	PH	1	1	0	0	0	0	0	0	.000

Player, Club and Years Played	Pos.	G.	AB.	R.	H.	2B.	3B.	HR.	RBI.	B.A.
Washington, Claudell, 1975 Oakland	PR-OF	1	1	0	1	0	0	0	0	1.000
Wert, Donald, 1968 Detroit	3B	1	1	0	1	1	0	0	0	1.000
Wertz, Victor, 1949-51 Detroit; 1957 Cleveland	OF-1B	3	7	1	2	0	0	1	2	.286
West, Samuel, 1933-34-37 St. Louis	OF	3	4	1	1	0	0	0	0	.250
Whitaker, Louis, 1983-84 Detroit	PH-2B	2	4	1	3	1	1	0	2	.750
White, Frank, 1978-79-81-82 Kansas City	2B-PR	4	5	0	0	0	0	0	0	.000
White, Roy, 1969 New York	PH	1	1	0	0	0	0	0	0	.000
Wilhelm, J. Hoyt, 1959-61 Baltimore	P	2	1	0	0	0	0	0	0	.000
Williams, Theodore, 1940-41-42-46-47-48-49-50-51-54-55-56-57-58-59 (2)-60 (2) Boston	OF-PH	18	46	10	14	2	1	4	12	.304
Wilson, James, 1956 Chicago	P	1	0	0	0	0	0	0	0	.000
Wilson, Willie, 1982-83 Kansas City	OF	2	3	0	1	1	0	0	1	.333
Winfield, David, 1981-82-83-84 New York	OF	4	13	2	5	2	0	0	1	.385
Wood, Wilbur, 1972 Chicago	P	1	0	0	0	0	0	0	0	.000
Woodling, Eugene, 1959 Baltimore	PH	1	1	0	0	0	0	0	0	.000
Wright, Clyde, 1970 California	P	1	0	0	0	0	0	0	0	.000
Wyatt, Johnathan, 1964 Kansas City	P	1	0	0	0	0	0	0	0	.000
Wynegar, Harold, 1976-77 Minnesota	PH-C	2	2	1	1	0	0	0	0	.500
Wynn, Early, 1955-56-57 Clev.; 1958-59 (2)-60 Chicago	P	7	1	0	0	0	0	0	0	.000
Yastrzemski, Carl, 1963-67-68-69-70-71-72-74-75-76-77-79-82-83 Boston	OF-1B-PH	14	34	2	10	2	0	1	5	.294
York, Rudolph, 1938-41-42-43 Detroit; 1946 Boston	1B-PH	5	13	1	4	0	0	1	2	.308
Young, Matthew, 1983 Seattle	P	1	0	0	0	0	0	0	0	.000
Yount, Robin, 1980-82-83 Milwaukee	SS	3	7	1	0	0	0	0	1	.000
Zarilla, Allen, 1948 St. Louis	OF	1	2	0	0	0	0	0	0	.000
Zisk, Richard, 1977 Chicago; 1978 Texas	OF	2	5	0	3	1	0	0	2	.600

PITCHING RECORDS

American League

Player, Club and Years Pitched	G.	IP.	H.	R.	BB.	SO.	W.	L.	Pct.
Aguirre, Henry, 1962 Detroit	1	3	3	2	0	2	0	0	.000
Allen, John, 1938 Cleveland	1	3	2	1	0	3	0	0	.000
Bannister, Floyd, 1982 Seattle	1	1	1	0	0	0	0	0	.000
Barker, Leonard, 1981 Cleveland	1	2	0	0	0	1	0	0	.000
Bell, Gary, 1960 (2) Cleveland	2	3	2	2	2	0	0	0	.000
Benton, J. Alton, 1942 Detroit	1	5	4	1	2	1	0	0	.000
Blue, Vida, 1971-75 Oakland	2	5	7	5	0	4	1	0	1.000
Blyleven, Rikalbert, 1973 Minnesota	1	2	2	2	0	0	0	1	.000
Borowy, Henry, 1944 New York	1	3	3	0	1	0	0	0	.000
Bouton, James, 1963 New York	1	1	0	0	0	0	0	0	.000
Brewer, Thomas, 1956 Boston	1	2	4	3	1	2	0	0	.000
Bridges, Thomas, 1937-39 Detroit	2	5⅓	9	3	1	3	1	0	1.000
Brissie, Leland, 1949 Philadelphia	1	3	5	2	2	1	0	0	.000
Busby, Steven, 1975 Kansas City	1	2	4	1	0	0	0	0	.000
Bunning, James, 1957-59-61 (2)-62-63 Detroit	6	14	4	3	1	7	1	1	.500
Campbell, William, 1977 Boston	1	1	0	0	1	2	0	0	.000
Caudill, William, 1984 Oakland	1	1	0	0	0	3	0	0	.000
Chance, Dean, 1964 Los Angeles; 1967 Minnesota	2	6	4	1	0	3	0	0	.000
Chandler, Spurgeon, 1942 New York	1	4	2	0	0	2	1	0	1.000
Clancy, James, 1982 Toronto	1	1	0	0	0	0	0	0	.000
Clear, Mark, 1979 California	1	2	2	1	1	0	0	0	.000
Coates, James, 1960 New York	1	2	2	0	0	0	0	0	.000
Coleman, Joseph, 1948 Philadelphia	1	3	0	0	2	3	0	0	.000
Consuegra, Sandalio, 1954 Chicago	1	⅓	5	5	0	0	0	0	.000
Crowder, Alvin, 1933 Washington	1	3	3	2	0	0	0	0	.000
Cuellar, Miguel, 1971 Baltimore	1	2	1	0	1	2	0	0	.000
Culp, Raymond, 1969 Boston	1	1	0	0	0	2	0	0	.000
Daley, Buddy, 1959-60 Kansas City	2	1⅔	0	0	1	3	0	0	.000
Davis, Ronald, 1981 New York	1	1	1	1	0	1	0	0	.000
Donovan, Richard, 1961 Washington; 1962 Cleveland	2	4	7	1	0	1	0	0	.000
Dotson, Richard, 1984 Chicago	1	2	2	0	1	2	0	0	.000
Downing, Alphonso, 1967 New York	1	2	2	0	0	2	0	0	.000
Duren, Ryne, 1959 New York	1	3	1	0	1	4	0	0	.000
Eckersley, Dennis, 1977 Cleveland; 1982 Boston	2	5	2	3	2	2	0	1	.000
Estrada, Charles, 1960 Baltimore	1	1	4	1	0	1	0	0	.000
Farmer, Edward, 1980 Chicago	1	⅔	1	0	0	0	0	0	.000
Feller, Robert, 1939-40-41-46-50 Cleveland	5	12⅓	5	1	4	13	1	0	1.000
Fidrych, Mark, 1976 Detroit	2	4	4	2	0	1	0	1	.000
Fingers, Roland, 1973-74 Oakland; 1981-82 Milwaukee	4	3⅓	5	4	3	0	0	1	.000
Fisher, Eddie, 1965 Chicago	1	2	1	0	0	0	0	0	.000
Ford, Edward, 1954-55-56-59-60-61 New York	6	12	19	13	3	5	0	2	.000
Fornieles, J. Miguel, 1961 Boston	1	⅓	2	1	0	0	0	0	.000
Forsch, Kenneth, 1981 California	1	1	1	0	0	0	0	0	.000
Garcia, E. Mike, 1953 Cleveland	1	2	4	1	1	2	0	0	.000
Garver, Ned, 1951 St. Louis	1	3	1	1	1	1	0	0	.000
Gomez, Vernon, 1933-34-35-37-38 New York	5	18	11	6	3	9	3	1	.750
Gossage, Richard, 1975 Chicago; 1978-80 New York	3	3	6	5	1	1	0	1	.000
Grant, James, 1965 Minnesota	1	2	2	2	1	3	0	0	.000
Gray, Theodore, 1950 Detroit	1	1⅓	3	1	0	1	0	1	.000
Grim, Robert, 1957 New York	1	⅓	0	0	0	0	0	0	.000
Grove, Robert, 1933 Philadelphia; 1936-38 Boston	3	8	10	4	2	8	0	1	.000
Guidry, Ronald, 1978-79 New York	2	⅔	0	0	1	0	0	0	.000

Player, Club and Years Pitched	G.	IP.	H.	R.	BB.	SO.	W.	L.	Pct.
Harder, Melvin, 1934-35-36-37 Cleveland	4	13	9	0	1	5	1	0	1.000
Herbert, Raymond, 1962 Chicago	1	3	3	0	0	0	1	0	1.000
Hernandez, Guillermo, 1984 Detroit	1	1	1	1	0	1	0	0	.000
Holtzman, Kenneth, 1973 Oakland	1	⅔	1	0	0	0	0	0	.000
Honeycutt, Richard, 1983 Texas	1	2	5	2	0	0	0	0	.000
Houtteman, Arthur, 1960 Detroit	1	3	3	1	1	0	0	0	.000
Hudson, Sidney, 1941 Washington	1	1	3	2	1	1	0	0	.000
Hughson, Cecil, 1943-44 Boston	2	4⅔	10	6	1	4	0	1	.000
Hunter, James, 1967 Kansas City; 1970-73-74 Oakland; 1975-76 New York	6	12⅔	15	9	1	13	0	2	.000
Hutchinson, Frederick, 1951 Detroit	1	3	3	3	2	0	0	0	.000
John, Thomas, 1968 Chicago; 1980 New York	2	3	5	3	0	1	0	1	.000
Kaat, James, 1966 Minnesota; 1975 Chicago	2	4	3	1	0	1	0	0	.000
Keegan, Robert, 1954 Chicago	1	1⅔	3	2	0	1	0	0	.000
Keough, Matthew, 1978 Oakland	1	⅓	1	0	0	0	0	0	.000
Kern, James, 1977-78 Cleveland; 1979 Texas	3	4⅓	3	2	4	6	0	1	.000
Knowles, Darold, 1969 Washington	1	⅔	0	0	0	0	0	0	.000
Kramer, John, 1946 St. Louis	1	3	0	0	1	3	0	0	.000
LaRoche, David, 1977 California	1	1	1	0	1	0	0	0	.000
Lary, Frank, 1960 (2)-61 Detroit	3	2	2	1	1	1	0	0	.000
Lee, Thornton, 1941 Chicago	1	3	4	1	0	0	0	0	.000
Lemon, Robert, 1950-51-52-54 Cleveland	4	6⅔	6	2	3	3	0	1	.000
Leonard, Emil, 1943 Washington	1	3	2	1	0	0	1	0	1.000
Loes, William, 1957 Baltimore	1	3	3	0	0	1	0	0	.000
Lolich, Michael, 1971-72 Detroit	2	4	2	1	0	2	0	0	.000
Lopat, Edmund, 1951 New York	1	1	3	3	0	0	0	1	.000
Lyle, Albert, 1973-77 New York	2	3	4	2	0	2	0	0	.000
Masterson, Walter, 1947-48 Washington	2	4⅔	5	2	2	3	0	0	.000
McBride, Kenneth, 1963 Los Angeles	1	3	4	3	2	1	0	0	.000
McDowell, Samuel, 1965-68-69-70 Cleveland	4	8	5	1	4	12	0	1	.000
McGlothlin, James, 1967 California	1	2	1	0	0	2	0	0	.000
McLain, Dennis, 1966-68-69 Detroit	3	6	2	1	4	6	0	0	.000
McLish, Calvin, 1959 Cleveland	1	2	1	0	1	2	0	0	.000
McNally, David, 1969-72 Baltimore	2	2⅓	2	1	2	1	0	1	.000
Monbouquette, William, 1960 Boston	1	2	5	4	0	2	0	1	.000
Morris, John, 1981-84 Detroit	2	4	4	0	2	4	0	0	.000
Mossi, Donald, 1957 Cleveland	1	⅔	1	0	0	1	0	0	.000
Muncrief, Robert, 1944 St. Louis	1	1⅓	0	0	0	1	0	0	.000
Narleski, Raymond, 1958 Cleveland	1	3⅓	1	0	1	0	0	0	.000
Newhouser, Harold, 1943-44-46-47 Detroit	4	10⅓	8	3	3	8	0	0	.000
Newsom, Louis, 1940 Detroit; 1944 Philadelphia	2	3⅓	1	0	1	1	0	0	.000
Norris, Michael, 1981 Oakland	1	1	2	1	0	1	0	0	.000
O'Dell, William, 1958-59 Baltimore	2	4	1	1	0	2	0	0	.000
Odom, Johnny, 1968-69 Oakland	2	2⅓	5	5	2	2	0	0	.000
Page, Joseph, 1947 New York	1	1⅓	1	0	1	0	0	0	.000
Paige, Leroy, 1953 St. Louis	1	1	3	2	1	0	0	0	.000
Palmer, James, 1970-71-72-77-78 Baltimore	5	12⅔	11	8	7	14	0	1	.000
Pappas, Milton, 1962 (2)-65 Baltimore	3	3	5	4	2	0	0	0	.000
Parnell, Melvin, 1949-51 Boston	2	2	6	4	1	2	0	0	.000
Pascual, Camilo, 1961-62-64 Minnesota	3	8	6	3	2	6	0	1	.000
Perry, Gaylord, 1972-74 Cleveland	2	5	6	3	0	5	0	0	.000
Perry, James, 1970 Minnesota	1	2	1	1	1	3	0	0	.000
Peters, Gary, 1967 Chicago	1	3	0	0	0	4	0	0	.000
Peterson, Fred, 1970 New York	1	0	1	0	0	0	0	0	.000
Pierce, W. William, 1953-55-56-57 Chicago	4	10⅔	6	4	3	12	0	1	.000
Pizarro, Juan, 1963 Chicago	1	1	0	0	0	0	0	0	.000
Porterfield, Erwin, 1954 Washington	1	3	4	2	0	1	0	0	.000
Quisenberry, Daniel, 1982-83 Kansas City	2	3	4	1	0	2	0	0	.000
Radatz, Richard, 1963-64 Boston	2	4⅔	4	5	2	10	0	1	.000
Raschi, Victor, 1948-49-50-52 New York	4	11	7	3	4	8	1	0	1.000
Reynolds, Allie, 1950-53 New York	2	5	3	2	2	2	0	1	.000
Richert, Peter, 1965-66 Washington	2	2⅓	3	1	0	2	0	1	.000
Rowe, Lynwood, 1936 Detroit	1	3	4	2	1	2	0	0	.000
Ruffing, Charles, 1934-39-40 New York	3	7	13	7	2	6	0	1	.000
Ryan, L. Nolan, 1973-79 California	2	4	7	5	3	4	0	0	.000
Schwall, Donald, 1961 Boston	1	3	5	1	1	2	0	0	.000
Score, Herbert, 1956 Cleveland	1	1	0	0	1	1	0	0	.000
Shantz, Robert, 1952 Philadelphia	1	1	0	0	0	3	0	0	.000
Shea, Francis, 1947 New York	1	3	3	1	2	2	1	0	1.000
Siebert, Wilfred, 1966 Cleveland	1	2	0	0	0	1	0	0	.000
Singer, William, 1973 California	1	2	3	3	1	2	0	0	.000
Smith, Edgar, 1941 Chicago	1	2	2	2	0	2	1	0	1.000
Sorensen, Lary, 1978 Milwaukee	1	3	1	0	0	0	0	0	.000
Stanley, Robert, 1979-83 Boston	2	4	3	1	0	0	0	0	.000
Stenhouse, David, 1962 Washington	1	2	3	1	1	1	0	0	.000
Stieb, David, 1980-81-83-84 Toronto	4	7⅔	5	4	4	7	1	1	.500
Stone, D. Dean, 1954 Washington	1	⅓	0	0	0	0	1	0	1.000
Stone, Steven, 1980 Baltimore	1	3	0	0	0	3	0	0	.000
Stottlemyre, Melvin, 1966-68-69-70 New York	4	6	5	3	1	4	0	1	.000
Sullivan, Franklin, 1955 Boston	1	3⅓	4	1	1	4	0	0	.000
Staley, Gerald, 1960 Chicago	1	2	2	1	0	0	0	0	.000
Tanana, Frank, 1976 California	1	2	3	3	1	0	0	0	.000
Tiant, Luis, 1968 Cleveland; 1974-76 Boston	3	6	7	4	3	3	0	2	.000
Trucks, Virgil, 1949 Detroit; 1954 Chicago	2	3	3	2	3	0	1	0	1.000

Player, Club and Years Pitched	G.	IP.	H.	R.	BB.	SO.	W.	L.	Pct.
Turley, Robert, 1958 New York	1	1⅔	3	3	2	0	0	0	.000
Walker, Jerry, 1959 Baltimore	1	3	2	1	1	1	1	0	1.000
Wilhelm, J. Hoyt, 1959-61 Baltimore	2	2⅔	4	2	1	1	0	1	.000
Wyatt, Johnathan, 1964 Kansas City	1	1	2	2	0	0	0	0	.000
Wilson, James, 1956 Chicago	1	1	2	1	0	1	0	0	.000
Wood, Wilbur, 1972 Chicago	1	2	2	1	1	1	0	0	.000
Wright, Clyde, 1970 California	1	1⅓	3	1	0	0	0	1	.000
Wynn, Early, 1955-56-57 Clev.; 1958-59 (2)-60 Chicago	7	12⅓	9	4	4	8	1	0	1.000
Young, Matthew, 1983 Seattle	1	1	0	0	0	1	0	0	.000

BATTING AVERAGES

National League

Player, Club and Years Played	Pos.	G.	AB.	R.	H.	2B.	3B.	HR.	RBI.	B.A.
Aaron, Henry, 1955-56-57-58-59 (2)-60 (2)-61 (2)-62-63-64-65-66-67-68-69-70-71-72-73-74 Atlanta	1B-OF-PH	23	66	7	13	0	0	2	8	.197
Adcock, Joseph, 1960 (2) Milwaukee	1B	2	5	1	3	1	0	0	0	.600
Allen, Richard, 1965-66-67 Phila.; 1970 St. Louis	3B-PH-1B	4	11	1	2	0	0	1	1	.182
Alley, L. Eugene, 1967 Pittsburgh	SS	1	5	0	0	0	0	0	0	.000
Alou, Felipe, 1962 San Francisco, 1968 Atlanta	OF	2	0	0	0	0	0	0	1	.000
Alou, Mateo, 1968-69 Pittsburgh	OF	2	5	1	3	0	0	0	0	.600
Altman, George A., 1961 (2)-62 Chicago	PH-OF	3	3	1	1	0	0	1	1	.333
Andujar, Joaquin, 1979 Houston	P	1	0	0	0	0	0	0	0	.000
Antonelli, John A., 1954-56, N. Y.; 1959 San Francisco	P	3	1	0	0	0	0	0	0	.000
Ashburn, Richie, 1948-51-53 Phil.; 1962 New York	OF-PH	4	10	4	6	1	0	0	1	.600
Bailey, L. Edgar, 1956-57-60 Cinn.; 63 San Francisco	C	4	8	1	2	0	0	0	1	.250
Baker, Eugene, 1955 Chicago	PH	1	1	0	0	0	0	0	0	.000
Baker, Johnnie, 1981-82 Los Angeles	OF	2	4	0	1	0	0	0	0	.250
Banks, Ernest, 1955-57-58-59 (2)-60 (2)-61-62 (2)-65-67-69 Chicago	PH-SS-1B	13	33	4	10	3	1	1	3	.303
Bartell, Richard, 1933 Philadelphia; 1937 New York	SS	2	6	0	1	0	0	0	0	.167
Beckert, Glenn, 1969-70-71-72 Chicago	2B-PH	4	7	0	0	0	0	0	0	.000
Bell, David (Gus), 1953-54-56-57 Cincinnati	OF-PH	4	6	1	2	1	0	1	4	.333
Bench, Johnny, 1968-69-70-71-72-73-74-75-76-77-80-83 Cincinnati	C-PH	12	28	5	10	0	0	3	6	.357
Benedict, Bruce, 1981-83 Atlanta	C	2	2	0	1	0	0	0	0	.500
Berger, Walter, 1933-34-35 Boston	OF	3	8	0	0	0	0	0	0	.000
Bibby, James, 1980 Pittsburgh	P	1	0	0	0	0	0	0	0	.000
Bickford, Vernon, 1949 Boston	P	1	0	0	0	0	0	0	0	.000
Blackwell, Ewell, 1946-47-48-49-50-51 Cincinnati	P	6	1	0	0	0	0	0	0	.000
Blanton, Darrell, 1937 Pittsburgh	P	1	0	0	0	0	0	0	0	.000
Blasingame, Donald, 1958 St. Louis	PH	1	1	0	0	0	0	0	0	.000
Blass, Stephen, 1972 Pittsburgh	P	1	0	0	0	0	0	0	0	.000
Blue, Vida, 1978-81 San Francisco	P	2	0	0	0	0	0	0	0	.000
Bolling, Frank, 1961 (2)-62 (2) Milwaukee	2B	4	12	0	1	1	0	0	0	.083
Bonds, Bobby, 1971-73 San Francisco	PH-OF	2	3	1	2	1	0	1	2	.667
Boone, Robert, 1976-78-79 Philadelphia	C	3	5	2	2	0	0	0	0	.400
Bowa, Lawrence, 1974-75-76-78-79 Philadelphia	SS	5	8	2	2	0	0	0	0	.250
Boyer, Kenton, 1956-59(2)-60(2)-61-62(2)-63-64 St.L.	3B-PH	10	23	4	8	0	0	2	4	.348
Branca, Ralph, 1948 Brooklyn	P	1	1	0	0	0	0	0	0	.000
Brecheen, Harry, 1947 St. Louis	P	1	1	0	0	0	0	0	0	.000
Brenly, Robert, 1984 San Francisco	PH	1	1	0	0	0	0	0	0	.000
Brett, Kenneth, 1974 Pittsburgh	P	1	0	0	0	0	0	0	0	.000
Brewer, James, 1973 Los Angeles	P	1	0	0	0	0	0	0	0	.000
Brock, Louis, 1967-71-74-75-79 St. Louis	OF-PH	5	8	2	3	0	0	0	0	.375
Brown, James, 1942 St. Louis	2B	1	2	0	0	0	0	0	0	.000
Brown, Mace, 1938 Pittsburgh	P	1	0	0	0	0	0	0	0	.000
Buckner, William, 1981 Chicago	PH	1	1	0	0	0	0	0	0	.000
Buhl, Robert, 1960 Milwaukee	P	1	0	0	0	0	0	0	0	.000
Burdette, S. Lewis, 1957-59 Milwaukee	P	2	2	0	0	0	0	0	0	.000
Bunning, James, 1964-66 Philadelphia	P	2	0	0	0	0	0	0	0	.000
Burgess, Forrest, 1954 Philadelphia; 1955 Cincinnati; 1959-60 (2)-61 (2) Pittsburgh	C-PH	7	10	0	1	0	0	0	0	.100
Callison, John, 1962 (2)-64 Philadelphia	PH-OF	3	4	1	2	0	0	1	3	.500
Camilli, Adolph, 1939 Brooklyn	PH	1	1	0	0	0	0	0	0	.000
Campanella, Roy, 1949-50-51-52-53-54-56 Brooklyn	C	7	20	1	2	0	0	0	0	.100
Cardenas, Leonardo, 1964-65-66-68 Cincinnati	PR-SS	4	3	0	0	0	0	0	0	.000
Carlton, Steven, 1968-69 St. Louis; 1972-79-82 Philadelphia	P	5	2	0	1	1	0	0	1	.500
Carter, Gary, 1975-79-80-81-82-83-84 Montreal	OF-C	7	13	3	5	0	0	3	5	.385
Carty, Ricardo, 1970 Atlanta	OF	1	1	0	0	0	0	0	0	.000
Cash, David, 1974-75-76 Philadelphia	PH-2B	3	3	1	1	0	0	0	0	.333
Cavarretta, Philip, 1944-46-47 Chicago	2B-PH	3	4	1	2	0	1	0	0	.500
Cedeno, Cesar, 1972-73-74-76 Houston	OF	4	9	2	3	0	0	1	3	.333
Cepeda, Orlando, 1959-60 (2)-61 (2)-62 (2)-64 S. F.; 1967 St. Louis	1B-OF	9	27	0	1	0	0	0	1	.037
Cey, Ronald, 1974-75-76-77-78-79 Los Angeles	3B	6	9	0	2	1	0	0	2	.222
Cimoli, Gino, 1957 Brooklyn	PH	1	1	0	0	0	0	0	0	.000
Clark, Jack, 1978-79 San Francisco	PH	2	2	0	0	0	0	0	0	.000
Clemente, Roberto, 1960(2)-61(2)-62(2)-63-64-65-66-67-69-70-71 Pittsburgh	OF-PH	14	31	3	10	2	1	1	4	.323
Colbert, Nathan, 1971-72-73 San Diego	PH	3	2	1	0	0	0	0	0	.000

Player, Club and Years Played	Pos.	G.	AB.	R.	H.	2B.	3B.	HR.	RBI.	B.A.
Collins, James, 1935-36 St. Louis; 1937 Chicago	1B	3	4	0	1	0	0	0	0	.250
Concepcion, David, 1975-76-77-78-80-81-82 Cincinnati	SS	7	12	3	3	0	0	1	2	.250
Conley, D. Eugene, 1954-55 Milw.; 1959 Phila	P	3	0	0	0	0	0	0	0	.000
Cooper, Morton, 1942-43 St. Louis	P	2	1	0	0	0	0	0	0	.000
Cooper, Walker, 1942-43-44 St. L.; 1946-47-48 New York	C	6	15	1	5	0	0	0	1	.333
Coscarart, Peter, 1940 Brooklyn	2B	1	1	0	0	0	0	0	0	.000
Crandall, Delmar, 1955-58-59(2)-60(2)-62(2) Milw.	C	8	20	2	4	0	0	1	2	.200
Cuccinello, Anthony, 1933 Brooklyn	PH	1	1	0	0	0	0	0	0	.000
Cuellar, Miguel, 1967 Houston	P	1	0	0	0	0	0	0	0	.000
Culp, Raymond, 1963 Philadelphia	P	1	0	0	0	0	0	0	0	.000
Cunningham, Joseph, 1959 St. Louis	PH	1	1	0	0	0	0	0	0	.000
Cuyler, Hazen, 1934 Chicago	OF	1	2	0	0	0	0	0	0	.000
Dahlgren, Ellsworth, 1943 Philadelphia	1B	1	2	0	0	0	0	0	0	.000
Danning, Harry, 1940-41 New York	C	2	2	0	1	0	0	0	1	.500
Dark, Alvin, 1951-54 New York	SS	3	10	0	2	0	0	0	0	.200
Davenport, James, 1962 San Francisco	3B	1	1	0	1	0	0	0	0	1.000
Davis, Charles, 1984 San Francisco	PH	1	1	0	0	0	0	0	0	.000
Davis, Curtis, 1936 Chicago	P	1	0	0	0	0	0	0	0	.000
Davis, H. Thomas, 1962(2)-63 Los Angeles	OF	3	8	1	1	0	0	0	0	.125
Davis, Jody, 1984 Chicago	C	1	1	0	0	0	0	0	0	.000
Davis, William, 1971-73 Los Angeles	PH-OF	2	3	1	3	0	0	1	2	1.000
Dawley, William, 1983 Houston	P	1	0	0	0	0	0	0	0	.000
Dawson, Andre, 1981-82-83 Montreal	OF	3	11	0	2	0	0	0	0	.182
Dean, Jerome, 1934-35-36-37 St. Louis	P	4	3	0	0	0	0	0	0	.000
Demaree, Frank, 1936-37 Chicago	OF	2	8	1	2	0	0	0	0	.250
Derringer, Paul, 1935-39-40-41 Cincinnati	P	4	2	0	0	0	0	0	0	.000
Dickson, Murry, 1953 Pittsburgh	P	1	1	0	1	0	0	0	1	1.000
Dierker, Lawrence, 1969 Houston	P	1	0	0	0	0	0	0	0	.000
Dietz, Richard, 1970 San Francisco	C	1	2	1	1	0	0	1	1	.500
DiMaggio, Vincent, 1943-44 Pittsburgh	OF-PH	2	3	2	3	0	1	1	1	1.000
Dravecky, David, 1983 San Diego	P	1	0	0	0	0	0	0	0	.000
Drysdale, Donald, 1959(2)-62-63-64-65-67-68 Los Angeles	P	8	3	0	0	0	0	0	0	.000
Durham, Leon, 1983 Chicago	OF	1	2	0	0	0	0	0	0	.000
Durocher, Leo, 1936 St. Louis; 1938 Brooklyn	SS	2	6	1	2	0	0	0	0	.333
Easler, Michael, 1981 Pittsburgh	OF	1	1	0	0	0	0	0	0	.000
Edwards, Bruce, 1947 Brooklyn	C	1	0	0	0	0	0	0	0	.000
Edwards, John, 1963-64 Cincinnati	C	2	3	1	0	0	0	0	0	.000
Elliott, Robert, 1941-42-44 Pitts.; 1948-51 Boston	3B-OF	5	9	1	3	0	0	1	2	.333
Ellis, Dock, 1971 Pittsburgh	P	1	1	0	0	0	0	0	0	.000
Elston, Donald, 1959 Chicago	P	1	0	0	0	0	0	0	0	.000
English, Elwood, 1933 Chicago	SS	1	1	0	0	0	0	0	0	.000
Ennis, Delmer, 1946-51-55 Philadelphia	OF	3	5	0	0	0	0	0	0	.000
Erskine, Carl, 1954 Brooklyn	P	1	0	0	0	0	0	0	0	.000
Evans, Darrell, 1973 Atlanta; 1983 San Francisco	PH-1B	2	1	0	0	0	0	0	0	.000
Face, ElRoy, 1959(2)-60-61 Pittsburgh	P	4	0	0	0	0	0	0	0	.000
Fairly, Ronald, 1973 Montreal	1B	1	0	0	0	0	0	0	0	.000
Farrell, Richard, 1958 Phila.; 1962-64-65 Houston	P	4	0	0	0	0	0	0	0	.000
Fette, Louis, 1939 Boston	P	1	0	0	0	0	0	0	0	.000
Fingers, Roland, 1978 San Diego	P	1	0	0	0	0	0	0	0	.000
Fletcher, Elburt, 1943 Pittsburgh	1B	1	2	0	0	0	0	0	0	.000
Flood, Curtis, 1964-66-68 St. Louis	PR-PH	3	2	1	0	0	0	0	0	.000
Foiles, Henry, 1957 Pittsburgh	PH	1	1	1	1	0	0	0	0	1.000
Foster, George, 1976-77-78-79-81 Cincinnati	OF	5	11	3	3	2	0	1	5	.273
Forsch, Kenneth, 1976 Houston	P	1	0	0	0	0	0	0	0	.000
Frankhouse, Fred, 1934 Boston	P	1	1	0	0	0	0	0	0	.000
French, Lawrence, 1940 Chicago	P	1	0	0	0	0	0	0	0	.000
Friend, Robert, 1956-58-60 Pittsburgh	P	3	2	0	0	0	0	0	0	.000
Frey, Linus, 1939-41-43 Cincinnati	2B-PH	3	6	0	2	1	0	0	1	.333
Frisch, Frank, 1933-34 St. Louis	2B	2	7	4	4	0	0	2	2	.571
Galan, August, 1936 Chicago; 1943-44 Brooklyn	OF	3	9	2	2	0	0	1	2	.222
Garner, Philip, 1980-81 Pittsburgh	2B	2	2	1	1	0	0	0	0	.500
Garr, Ralph, 1974 Atlanta	PH-OF	1	3	0	0	0	0	0	0	.000
Garvey, Steven, 1974-75-76-77-78-79-80-81 Los Angeles; 1984 San Diego	1B	9	25	7	10	2	2	2	6	.400
Gaston, Clarence, 1970 San Diego	OF	1	2	0	0	0	0	0	0	.000
Gibson, Robert, 1962-65-67-69-70-72 St. Louis	P	6	0	0	0	0	0	0	0	.000
Gilliam, James, 1959 Los Angeles	3B	1	2	1	1	0	0	1	1	.500
Giusti, J. David, 1973 Pittsburgh	P	1	0	0	0	0	0	0	0	.000
Gooden, Dwight, 1984 New York	P	1	0	0	0	0	0	0	0	.000
Goodman, Ival, 1938-39 Cincinnati	OF	2	4	0	0	0	0	0	0	.000
Gordon, Sidney, 1949 New York	3B	1	2	0	1	1	0	0	0	.500
Gossage, Richard, 1977 Pittsburgh; 1984 San Diego	P	2	0	0	0	0	0	0	0	.000
Grabarkewitz, Billy, 1970 Los Angeles	3B	1	3	0	1	0	0	0	0	.333
Griffey, G. Kenneth, 1976-80 Cincinnati	OF	2	4	2	3	0	0	1	2	.750
Grissom, Lee, 1937 Cincinnati	P	1	0	0	0	0	0	0	0	.000
Grissom, Marvin, 1954 New York	P	1	0	0	0	0	0	0	0	.000
Groat, Richard, 1959(2)-60(2)-62(2) Pitts.; 1963-64 St. Louis	PH-SS	8	15	1	5	1	0	0	5	.333
Grote, Gerald, 1968-74 New York	C	2	2	0	0	0	0	0	0	.000
Grubb, John, 1974 San Diego	OF	1	1	0	0	0	0	0	0	.000
Guerrero, Pedro, 1981-83 Los Angeles	PH-3B-LF	2	2	0	0	0	0	0	0	.000
Gustine, Frank, 1946-47-48 Pittsburgh	2B-3B-PR	3	4	0	0	0	0	0	0	.000
Gwynn, Anthony, 1984 San Diego	OF	1	3	0	1	0	0	0	0	.333
Haas, Berthold, 1947 Cincinnati	PH	1	1	0	1	0	0	0	0	1.000

Player, Club and Years Played	Pos.	G.	AB.	R.	H.	2B.	3B.	HR.	RBI.	B.A.
Hack, Stanley, 1938-39-41-43 Chicago	3B	4	15	2	6	0	0	0	0	.400
Haddix, Harvey, 1955 St. Louis	P	1	0	0	0	0	0	0	0	.000
Hafey, Charles, 1933 Cincinnati	OF	1	4	0	1	0	0	0	0	.250
Hallahan, William, 1933 St. Louis	P	1	1	0	0	0	0	0	0	.000
Haller, Thomas, 1967 San Fran.; 1968 Los Angeles	C-PH	2	3	0	0	0	0	0	0	.000
Hammaker, C. Atlee, 1983 San Francisco	P	1	0	0	0	0	0	0	0	.000
Hamner, Granville, 1952-53-54 Philadelphia	SS-2B	3	4	0	0	0	0	0	0	.000
Harrelson, Derrel, 1970-71 New York	SS	2	5	2	2	0	0	0	0	.400
Hart, James, 1966 San Francisco	PH	1	1	0	0	0	0	0	0	.000
Hartnett, Charles, 1933-34-35-36-37 Chicago	C	5	10	2	2	0	1	0	1	.200
Helms, Tommy, 1967-68 Cincinnati	PH-2B	2	3	0	1	1	0	0	0	.333
Hendrick, George, 1980 St. Louis	OF	1	2	0	1	0	0	0	1	.500
Henry, William, 1960 Cincinnati	P	1	0	0	0	0	0	0	0	.000
Herman, William, 1934-35-36-37-38-39-40 Chicago; 1941-42-43 Brooklyn	2B-PH	10	30	3	13	2	0	0	0	.433
Hernandez, Keith, 1979-80 St. Louis; 1984 New York	PH-1B	3	4	0	2	0	0	0	0	.500
Hickman, James, 1970 Chicago	OF-1B	1	4	0	1	0	0	0	1	.250
Higbe, W. Kirby, 1946 Brooklyn	P	1	1	0	0	0	0	0	0	.000
Hoak, Donald, 1957 Cincinnati	3B	1	1	0	0	0	0	0	0	.000
Hodges, Gilbert, 1949-51-53-54-55-57 Brooklyn	1B-PR-PH	6	12	3	4	0	0	1	2	.333
Holmes, Thomas, 1948 Boston	OF	1	1	0	0	0	0	0	0	.000
Hooton, Burt, 1981 Los Angeles	P	1	0	0	0	0	0	0	0	.000
Hopp, John, 1946 Boston	OF	1	2	0	1	0	0	0	0	.500
Horner, J. Robert, 1982 Atlanta	PH	1	1	0	0	0	0	0	0	.000
Howe, Steven, 1982 Los Angeles	P	1	0	0	0	0	0	0	0	.000
Hubbard, Glenn, 1983 Atlanta	2B	1	1	0	1	0	0	0	0	1.000
Hubbell, Carl, 1933-34-36-37-40 New York	P	5	1	0	0	0	0	0	0	.000
Hume, Thomas, 1982 Cincinnati	P	1	0	0	0	0	0	0	0	.000
Hundley, C. Randolph, 1969 Chicago	C	1	1	0	0	0	0	0	0	.000
Hunt, Ronald, 1964-66 New York	2B	2	4	0	1	0	0	0	0	.250
Jablonski, Raymond, 1954 St. Louis	3B	1	3	1	1	0	0	1	1	.333
Jackson, Lawrence, 1957-58-60 St. L.; 1963 Chicago	P	4	1	0	0	0	0	0	0	.000
Jackson, Ransom, 1954-55 Chicago	3B	2	5	1	1	0	0	0	1	.200
Jackson, Travis, 1934 New York	SS	1	2	0	0	0	0	0	0	.000
Javery, Alva, 1943 Boston	P	1	0	0	0	0	0	0	0	.000
Javier, Julian, 1963-68 St. Louis	2B	2	4	0	0	0	0	0	0	.000
Jenkins, Ferguson, 1967-71 Chicago	P	2	1	0	0	0	0	0	0	.000
Johnson, David, 1973 Atlanta	2B	1	1	0	0	0	0	0	0	.000
Jones, Cleon, 1969 New York	OF	1	4	2	2	0	0	0	0	.500
Jones, Randall, 1975-76 San Diego	P	2	1	0	0	0	0	0	0	.000
Jones, Ruppert, 1982 San Diego	PH	1	1	1	1	0	1	0	0	1.000
Jones, Samuel, 1955 Chicago; 1959 San Francisco	P	2	0	0	0	0	0	0	0	.000
Jones, Willie, 1950-51 Philadelphia	3B	2	9	0	1	0	0	0	0	.111
Kasko, Edward, 1961 Cincinnati	SS	1	1	0	1	0	0	0	0	1.000
Kazak, Edward, 1949 St. Louis	3B	1	2	0	2	0	0	0	1	1.000
Kennedy, Terrence, 1981 San Diego	PH	1	1	0	0	0	0	0	0	.000
Kerr, John, 1948 New York	SS	1	2	0	0	0	0	0	0	.000
Kessinger, Donald, 1968-69-70-71-72-74 Chicago	SS	6	12	1	3	0	1	0	1	.250
Kiner, Ralph, 1948-49-50-51 Pitts.; 1953 Chicago	OF-PH	5	15	3	4	1	0	3	4	.267
Kingman, David, 1976 San Francisco; 1980 Chicago	OF	2	3	0	0	0	0	0	0	.000
Klein, Charles, 1933 Philadelphia; 1934 Chicago	OF	2	7	0	2	0	0	0	1	.286
Kluszewski, Theodore, 1953-54-55-56 Cincinnati	1B	4	14	4	7	3	0	1	4	.500
Knepper, Robert, 1981 Houston	P	1	0	0	0	0	0	0	0	.000
Knight, C. Ray, 1980 Cincinnati; 1982 Houston	3B	2	4	1	1	0	0	0	0	.250
Konstanty, C. James, 1950 Philadelphia	P	1	0	0	0	0	0	0	0	.000
Koosman, Jerry, 1968-69 New York	P	2	0	0	0	0	0	0	0	.000
Koufax, Sanford, 1961(2) -65-66 Los Angeles	P	4	0	0	0	0	0	0	0	.000
Kurowski, George, 1944-46-47 St. Louis	3B	3	6	0	1	1	0	0	2	.167
Labine, Clement, 1957 Brooklyn	P	1	0	0	0	0	0	0	0	.000
LaCoss, Michael, 1979 Cincinnati	P	1	0	0	0	0	0	0	0	.000
Lamanno, Raymond, 1946 Cincinnati	PH	1	1	0	0	0	0	0	0	.000
Larker, Norman, 1960(2) Los Angeles	PH	2	1	1	0	0	0	0	0	.000
Lavagetto, Harry, 1940-41 Brooklyn	3B	2	3	0	0	0	0	0	0	.000
Lavelle, Gary, 1977 San Francisco	P	1	0	0	0	0	0	0	0	.000
Law, Vernon, 1960(2) Pittsburgh	P	2	1	0	0	0	0	0	0	.000
Lea, Charles, 1984 Montreal	P	1	0	0	0	0	0	0	0	.000
Lee, William, 1938-39 Chicago	P	2	1	0	0	0	0	0	0	.000
Lefebvre, James, 1966 Los Angeles	2B	1	2	0	0	0	0	0	0	.000
Leiber, Henry, 1938 New York	PH	1	1	0	0	0	0	0	0	.000
Litwhiler, Daniel, 1942 Philadelphia	PH	1	1	0	1	0	0	0	0	1.000
Lockman, Carroll, 1952 New York	1B	1	3	0	0	0	0	0	0	.000
Logan, John, 1955-58 Milwaukee	SS-PH	2	4	0	1	0	0	0	1	.250
Lombardi, Ernest, 1938-39-40 Cin.; 1942 Bos.; 1943 N.Y.	C	5	13	0	5	0	0	0	1	.385
Long, R. Dale, 1956 Pittsburgh	1B	1	2	0	0	0	0	0	0	.000
Lopata, Stanley, 1955 Philadelphia	C	1	3	0	0	0	0	0	0	.000
Lopes, David, 1978-79-80-81 Los Angeles	PR-2B	4	5	0	2	0	0	0	1	.400
Lopez, Alfonso, 1934 Brooklyn; 1941 Pittsburgh	C	2	3	0	0	0	0	0	0	.000
Lowrey, Harry, 1946 Chicago	OF	1	2	0	1	0	0	0	0	.500
Luzinski, Gregory, 1975-76-77-78 Philadelphia	PH-OF	4	8	1	2	0	0	1	3	.250
Madlock, Bill, 1975 Chicago; 1981-83 Pittsburgh	3B-PH	3	4	0	1	0	0	0	2	.250
Maglie, Salvatore, 1951 New York	P	1	1	0	0	0	0	0	0	.000
Mahaffey, Arthur, 1961-62 Philadelphia	P	2	0	0	0	0	0	0	0	.000
Maloney, James, 1965 Cincinnati	P	1	0	0	0	0	0	0	0	.000
Mancuso, August, 1935-37 New York	PH-C	2	2	0	0	0	0	0	0	.000

Player, Club and Years Played	Pos.	G.	AB.	R.	H.	2B.	3B.	HR.	RBI.	B.A.
Marichal, Juan, 1962(2)-64-65-66-67-68-71 San Francisco......	P	8	2	1	1	0	0	0	0	.500
Marion, Martin, 1943-44-46-47-50 St. Louis	SS	5	12	1	1	0	0	0	0	.083
Marshall, Michael, 1974 Los Angeles	P	1	1	0	0	0	0	0	0	.000
Marshall, Willard, 1942-47-49 New York..................	OF-PH	3	3	1	0	0	0	0	0	.000
Martin, John, 1933-34-35 St. Louis..................	3B	3	8	1	1	0	0	0	1	.125
Masi, Philip, 1946-47-48 Boston	C-PR	3	4	0	1	0	0	0	0	.250
Mathews, Edwin, 1953-55-57-59(2)-60(2)-61(2)-62 Mil.	PH-3B	10	25	4	2	0	0	2	3	.080
Matlack, Jonathan, 1974-75 New York.................	P	2	0	0	0	0	0	0	0	.000
Matthews, Gary, 1979 Atlanta.................	OF	1	2	0	0	0	0	0	0	.000
May, Lee, 1969-71 Cincinnati; 1972 Houston	1B	3	6	0	1	0	0	0	1	.167
May, Merrill, 1940 Philadelphia	3B	1	1	0	0	0	0	0	0	.000
Mays, Willie, 1954-55-56-57 N.Y.; 1958-59(2)-60(2)-61(2)-62(2)-63-64-65-66-67-68-69-70-71 S.F.; 1972-73 N.Y............	OF-PH	24	75	20	23	2	3	3	9	.307
Mazeroski, William, 1958-59-60(2)-62(2)-67 Pittsburgh........	2B	7	16	0	2	0	0	0	0	.125
Mazzilli, Lee, 1979 New York	PH-OF	1	1	1	1	0	0	1	2	1.000
McCarver, J. Timothy, 1966-67 St. Louis..................	C	2	3	0	3	1	0	0	0	1.000
McCormick, Frank, 1938-39-40-41-42 Cinn.; 1946 Phila.	1B	6	12	1	1	0	0	0	0	.083
McCormick, Michael, 1960-61 San Francisco...............	P	2	1	0	0	0	0	0	0	.000
McCovey, Willie, 1963-66-68-69-70-71 San Fran...............	1B-PH	6	16	2	3	0	0	2	4	.188
McDaniel, Lyndall, 1960 St. Louis.................	P	1	0	0	0	0	0	0	0	.000
McGee, Willie, 1983 St. Louis.................	OF	1	2	0	1	0	0	0	0	.500
McGlothen, Lynn, 1974 St. Louis	P	1	0	0	0	0	0	0	0	.000
McGraw, Frank, 1972 New York.................	P	1	0	0	0	0	0	0	0	.000
McMillan, Roy, 1956-57 Cincinnati.................	SS	2	4	1	2	0	0	0	0	.500
Medwick, Joseph, 1934-35-36-37-38-39 St. Louis; 1940-41-42 Brooklyn; 1944 New York.................	OF-PH	10	27	2	7	2	0	1	6	.259
Menke, Denis, 1969-70 Houston	SS-PH-2B	2	1	0	0	0	0	0	0	.000
Merritt, James, 1970 Cincinnati	P	1	0	0	0	0	0	0	0	.000
Messersmith, John, 1974 Los Angeles	P	1	0	0	0	0	0	0	0	.000
Millan, Felix, 1969-71 Atlanta.................	2B	2	4	1	1	1	0	0	2	.250
Miller, Edward, 1940-41-42 Boston; 1943 Cincinnati	SS	4	4	0	0	0	0	0	0	.000
Miller, Stuart, 1961(2) San Francisco.................	P	2	0	0	0	0	0	0	0	.000
Minton, Gregory, 1982 San Francisco.................	P	1	0	0	0	0	0	0	0	.000
Mize, John, 1937-39-40-41 St. L.; 1942-46-47-48-49 N.Y...	1B-PH	9	23	2	5	1	0	1	2	.217
Monday, Robert, 1978 Los Angeles	OF	1	2	0	0	0	0	0	0	.000
Montanez, Guillermo, 1977 Atlanta.................	1B	1	2	0	0	0	0	0	0	.000
Montefusco, John, 1976 San Francisco.................	P	1	0	0	0	0	0	0	0	.000
Moon, Wallace, 1957 St. Louis; 1959(2) Los Angeles........	PH-OF	3	5	0	0	0	0	0	0	.000
Moore, Joseph, 1935-37-40 New York.................	OF	3	5	0	0	0	0	0	0	.000
Moore, Terry, 1939-40-41-42 St. Louis.................	OF	4	10	0	0	0	0	0	1	.000
Morales, Julio, 1977 Chicago.................	OF	1	0	1	0	0	0	0	0	.000
Morgan, Joe, 1970 Hous.; 1972-73-74-75-76-77-78-79 Cincinnati.................	2B-PH	9	26	7	7	2	0	1	3	.269
Mota, Manuel, 1973 Los Angeles.................	PH-OF	1	1	0	0	0	0	0	0	.000
Mueller, Donald, 1954-55 New York.................	PH-OF	2	3	0	2	1	0	0	1	.667
Mueller, Raymond, 1944 Cincinnati.................	C	2	0	0	0	0	0	0	0	.000
Mumphrey, Jerry, 1984 Houston.................	PH	1	1	0	0	0	0	0	0	.000
Munger, George, 1949 St. Louis.................	P	1	0	0	0	0	0	0	0	.000
Mungo, Van, 1934-37 Brooklyn.................	P	2	0	0	0	0	0	0	0	.000
Murcer, Bobby, 1975 San Francisco.................	OF	1	2	0	0	0	0	0	0	.000
Murphy, Dale, 1980-82-83-84 Atlanta.................	OF	4	9	2	3	0	0	1	2	.333
Musial, Stanley, 1943-44-46-47-48-49-50-51-52-53-54-55-56-57-58-59(2)-60(2)-61(2)-62(2)-63 St. Louis.......	OF-PH-1B	24	63	11	20	2	0	6	10	.317
Neal, Charles, 1959-60(2) Los Angeles.................	2B	3	2	0	0	0	0	0	0	.000
Newcombe, Donald, 1949-50-51-55 Brooklyn	P	4	3	0	1	0	0	0	1	.333
Nicholson, William, 1940-41-43-44 Chicago	OF-PH	4	6	1	1	1	0	0	1	.167
Niekro, Philip, 1969-78 Atlanta.................	P	2	0	0	0	0	0	0	0	.000
Nuxhall, Joseph, 1955 Cincinnati	P	1	2	0	0	0	0	0	0	.000
O'Doul, Francis, 1933 New York.................	PH	1	1	0	0	0	0	0	0	.000
Oliver, Albert, 1972-75-76 Pitts.; 1982-83 Mon..........	OF-PH-1B	5	7	3	4	3	0	0	0	.571
Orosco, Jesse, 1983 New York	P	1	0	0	0	0	0	0	0	.000
Osteen, Claude, 1970-73 Los Angeles.................	PR-P	2	0	0	0	0	0	0	0	.000
O'Toole, James, 1963 Cincinnati.................	P	1	1	0	0	0	0	0	0	.000
Ott, Melvin, 1934-35-36-37-38-39-40-41-42-43-44 N.Y....	OF-PH	11	23	2	5	1	1	0	0	.217
Owen, Arnold, 1941-42 Brooklyn.................	C	2	2	1	1	0	0	1	1	.500
Pafko, Andrew, 1947-48-49-50 Chicago	OF-3B	4	10	0	4	0	0	0	0	.400
Parker, David, 1977-79-80-81 Pittsburgh.................	OF	4	11	2	3	0	0	1	2	.273
Parrish, Larry, 1979 Montreal.................	3B	1	0	0	0	0	0	0	0	.000
Passeau, Claude, 1941-42-46 Chicago.................	P	3	2	0	0	0	0	0	0	.000
Pena, Antonio, 1982-84 Pittsburgh.................	PR-C	2	1	0	0	0	0	0	0	.000
Perez, Atanasio, 1967-68-69-70-74-75-76 Cin..............	3B-PH-1B	7	8	1	1	0	0	1	1	.125
Perez, Pascual, 1983 Atlanta.................	P	1	0	0	0	0	0	0	0	.000
Perry, Gaylord, 1966-70 San Francisco; 1979 San Diego	P	3	0	0	0	0	0	0	0	.000
Phelps, Ernest, 1939-40 Brooklyn.................	C	2	1	0	0	0	0	0	0	.000
Pinson, Vada, 1959-60(2) Cincinnati	PR-OF	3	1	0	0	0	0	0	0	.000
Pocoroba, Biff, 1978 Atlanta.................	C	1	0	0	0	0	0	0	0	.000
Podres, John, 1960-62 Los Angeles.................	P	2	1	1	1	1	0	0	0	1.000
Pollet, Howard, 1949 St. Louis.................	P	1	0	0	0	0	0	0	0	.000
Purkey, Robert, 1961(2)-62 Cincinnati.................	P	3	0	0	0	0	0	0	0	.000
Raffensberger, Kenneth, 1944 Philadelphia.................	P	1	0	0	0	0	0	0	0	.000
Raines, Timothy, 1981-82-83-84 Montreal.................	PR-OF	4	5	0	0	0	0	0	0	.000
Reed, Ronald, 1968 Atlanta.................	P	1	0	0	0	0	0	0	0	.000
Reese, Harold, 1942-47-48-49-50-51-52-53 Brooklyn	SS-PH	8	17	0	2	1	0	0	2	.118

Player, Club and Years Played	Pos.	G.	AB.	R.	H.	2B.	3B.	HR.	RBI.	B.A.
Reiser, Harold, 1941-42 Brooklyn	OF	2	7	0	1	0	0	0	0	.143
Reitz, Kenneth, 1980 St. Louis	3B	1	2	0	0	0	0	0	0	.000
Reuschel, Rick, 1977 Chicago	P	1	0	0	0	0	0	0	0	.000
Reuss, Jerry, 1975 Pittsburgh; 1980 Los Angeles	P	2	1	0	0	0	0	0	0	.000
Repulski, Eldon, 1956 St. Louis	PH	1	1	0	0	0	0	0	0	.000
Reynolds, G. Craig, 1979 Houston	SS	1	2	0	0	0	0	0	0	.000
Rhoden, Richard, 1976 Los Angeles	P	1	0	0	0	0	0	0	0	.000
Richard, J. R., 1980 Houston	P	1	0	0	0	0	0	0	0	.000
Riggs, Lewis, 1936 Cincinnati	PH-3B	1	1	0	0	0	0	0	0	.000
Rigney, William, 1948 New York	2B	1	0	0	0	0	0	0	0	.000
Roberts, Robin, 1950-51-53-54-55 Philadelphia	P	5	2	0	0	0	0	0	0	.000
Robinson, Frank, 1956-57-59-61-62-65 Cinn.	OF-1B-PH	6	12	1	5	0	0	1	1	.417
Robinson, Jack, 1949-50-51-52-53-54 Brooklyn	2B-PH-OF	6	18	7	6	2	0	1	4	.333
Roe, Elwin, 1949 Brooklyn	P	1	0	0	0	0	0	0	0	.000
Rogers, Stephen, 1978-79-82 Montreal	P	3	0	0	0	0	0	0	0	.000
Rojas, Octavio, 1965 Philadelphia	PH	1	1	0	0	0	0	0	0	.000
Rose, Peter, 1965-67-69-70-71-73-74-75-76-77-78 Cin.; 79-80-81-82 Philadelphia	PH-2B-OF-3B-1B	15	32	3	7	1	1	0	2	.219
Roseboro, John, 1961-62 Los Angeles	C	2	6	1	1	0	0	1	1	.167
Rowe, Lynwood, 1947 Philadelphia	PH	1	1	0	0	0	0	0	0	.000
Rush, Robert, 1952 Chicago	P	1	1	0	0	0	0	0	0	.000
Russell, William, 1973-76-80 Los Angeles	SS	3	5	0	0	0	0	0	0	.000
Ruthven, Richard, 1981 Philadelphia	P	1	0	0	0	0	0	0	0	.000
Ryan, Cornelius, 1944 Boston	2B	1	4	1	2	0	0	0	0	.500
Ryan, L. Nolan, 1981 Houston	P	1	0	0	0	0	0	0	0	.000
Sain, John, 1947-48 Boston	P	2	0	0	0	0	0	0	0	.000
Sambito, Joseph, 1979 Houston	P	1	0	0	0	0	0	0	0	.000
Sandberg, Ryne, 1984 Chicago	2B	1	4	0	1	0	0	0	0	.250
Sanford, John, 1957 Philadelphia	P	1	0	0	0	0	0	0	0	.000
Sanguillen, Manuel, 1972 Pittsburgh	C	1	2	0	1	0	0	0	0	.500
Santo, Ronald, 1963-65-66-68-69-71-72-73 Chicago	PH-3B	8	15	1	5	0	0	0	3	.333
Sauer, Henry, 1950-52 Chicago	OF	2	4	1	1	0	0	1	3	.250
Sax, Stephen, 1982-83 Los Angeles	PR-2B	2	4	1	2	0	0	0	1	.500
Schmidt, Michael, 1974-76-77-79-81-82-83-84 Philadelphia	PR-PH-3B	8	15	4	4	2	1	1	3	.267
Schmitz, John, 1948 Chicago	P	1	0	0	0	0	0	0	0	.000
Schoendienst, Albert, 1946-48-49-50-51-53-54-55 St. Louis; 1957 Milwaukee	2B-PH	9	21	1	4	0	0	1	1	.190
Schumacher, Harold, 1935 New York	P	1	1	0	0	0	0	0	0	.000
Seaver, G. Thomas, 1967-68-70-73-75-76 N.Y.; 1977-81 Cin.	P	8	1	0	0	0	0	0	0	.000
Seminick, Andrew, 1949 Philadelphia	C	1	1	0	0	0	0	0	0	.000
Sewell, Truett, 1943-44-46 Pittsburgh	P	3	1	0	0	0	0	0	0	.000
Shaw, Robert, 1962 Milwaukee	P	1	0	0	0	0	0	0	0	.000
Short, Christopher, 1964-67 Philadelphia	P	2	0	0	0	0	0	0	0	.000
Simmons, Curtis, 1952-53-57 Philadelphia	P	3	0	0	0	0	0	0	0	.000
Simmons, Ted, 1973-77-78 St. Louis	C	3	7	0	1	0	0	0	0	.143
Singer, William, 1969 Los Angeles	P	1	0	0	0	0	0	0	0	.000
Sisler, Richard, 1950 Philadelphia	PH	1	1	0	1	0	0	0	0	1.000
Skinner, Robert, 1958-60 (2) Pittsburgh	OF	3	10	1	3	0	0	0	2	.300
Slaughter, Enos, 1941-42-46-47-48-49-50-51-52-53 St. Louis	OF-PH	10	21	4	8	1	1	0	2	.381
Smith, C. Reginald, 1974-75 St.L.; 1977-78-80 L.A.	PH-OF	5	10	2	3	0	0	1	1	.300
Smith, Harold, 1959 St. Louis	C	1	2	0	0	0	0	0	0	.000
Smith, Lee, 1983 Chicago	P	1	0	0	0	0	0	0	0	.000
Smith, Lonnie, 1982 St. Louis	OF	1	0	0	0	0	0	0	0	.000
Smith, Osborne, 1981 San Diego; 1982-83-84 St. Louis	SS-PR	4	5	1	1	0	0	0	0	.200
Snider, Edwin, 1950-51-53-54-55-56 Brkn.; 1963 N. Y.	PH-OF	7	11	3	3	1	0	0	0	.273
Soto, Mario, 1982-83-84 Cincinnati	P	3	1	0	0	0	0	0	0	.000
Spahn, Warren, 1947-49 Bos.; 1953-54-56-58-61 Milw.	P	7	1	0	0	0	0	0	0	.000
Speier, Chris, 1972-73 San Francisco	SS	2	4	0	0	0	0	0	0	.000
Stanky, Edward, 1947 Brooklyn	2B	1	2	0	0	0	0	0	0	.000
Stargell, Wilver, 1964-65-66-71-72-73-78 Pittsburgh	PH-OF	7	10	3	2	0	0	1	2	.200
Staub, Daniel, 1967-68 Hous.; 1970 Montreal	PH	3	3	0	1	0	0	0	0	.333
Stearns, John, 1977-80-82 New York	C	3	1	0	0	0	0	0	0	.000
Strawberry, Darryl, 1984 New York	OF	1	2	0	1	0	0	0	0	.500
Stuart, Richard, 1961 (2) Pittsburgh	PH	2	2	0	1	1	0	0	0	.500
Stoneman, William, 1972 Montreal	P	1	1	0	0	0	0	0	0	.000
Sutter, H. Bruce, 1978-79-80 Chicago; 1981 St. Louis	P	4	0	0	0	0	0	0	0	.000
Sutton, Donald, 1972-73-75-77 Los Angeles	P	4	0	0	0	0	0	0	0	.000
Taylor, Antonio, 1960 (2) Philadelphia	PR-2B	2	1	0	1	0	0	0	0	1.000
Temple, John, 1956-57-59 (2) Cincinnati	2B	4	10	2	3	1	0	0	1	.300
Templeton, Garry, 1977 St. Louis	SS	1	1	1	1	1	0	0	0	1.000
Terry, William, 1933-34-35 New York	1B	3	10	0	4	0	0	0	1	.400
Thomas, Frank, 1954-55-58 Pittsburgh	PH-3B	3	5	0	1	0	0	0	0	.200
Thompson, Jason, 1982 Pittsburgh	PH	1	1	0	0	0	0	0	0	.000
Thomson, Robert, 1948-49-52 New York	PH-3B	3	4	0	0	0	0	0	0	.000
Thon, Richard, 1983 Houston	SS	1	3	0	1	0	0	0	0	.333
Tobin, James, 1944 Boston	P	1	0	0	0	0	0	0	0	.000
Torre, Joseph, 1964-65 Milw.; 1966-67 Atlanta; 1970-71-72-73 St. Louis	PH-C-3B-1B	8	21	1	2	0	0	1	2	.095
Traynor, Harold, 1933-34 Pittsburgh	3B	2	6	2	3	1	0	0	1	.500
Trillo, Jesus, 1977 Chicago; 1981-82 Philadelphia	2B	3	5	0	1	0	0	0	0	.200
Twitchell, Wayne, 1973 Pittsburgh	P	1	0	0	0	0	0	0	0	.000
Valentine, Ellis, 1977 Montreal	OF	1	1	0	0	0	0	0	0	.000

Player, Club and Years Played	Pos.	G.	AB.	R.	H.	2B.	3B.	HR.	RBI.	B.A.
Valenzuela, Fernando, 1981-82-84 Los Angeles	P	3	0	0	0	0	0	0	0	.000
Vander Meer, John, 1938-42-43 Cincinnati	P	3	1	0	0	0	0	0	0	.000
Vaughan, Floyd, 1934-35-37-39-40-41 Pitts.; 1942 Brkn	3B-SS	7	22	5	8	1	0	2	4	.364
Verban, Emil, 1946-47 Philadelphia	2B-PH	2	3	0	0	0	0	0	0	.000
Waitkus, Edward, 1948 Chicago	PH	1	0	0	0	0	0	0	0	.000
Walker, Fred, 1943-44-46-47 Brooklyn	OF-PH	4	10	0	2	0	0	0	2	.200
Walker, Harry, 1943 St. Louis; 1947 Philadelphia	OF	2	3	0	0	0	0	0	0	.000
Walker, William, 1935 St. Louis	P	1	0	0	0	0	0	0	0	.000
Wallach, Timothy, 1984 Montreal	3B	1	1	0	0	0	0	0	0	.000
Walls, Lee, 1958 Chicago	PH-OF	1	1	0	0	0	0	0	0	.000
Walters, William, 1937 Phila.; 1940-41-42-44 Cinn.	P	5	1	1	1	1	0	0	1	1.000
Waner, Paul, 1933-34-35-37 Pittsburgh	OF	4	8	0	0	0	0	0	0	.000
Warneke, Lonnie, 1933-34-36 Chicago	P	3	2	1	1	0	1	0	0	.500
Washington, Claudell, 1984 Atlanta	OF	1	2	0	1	1	0	0	0	.500
Watson, Robert, 1973-75 Houston	OF-PH	2	1	0	0	0	0	0	0	.000
Welch, Robert, 1980 Los Angeles	P	1	1	0	0	0	0	0	0	.000
West, Max, 1940 Boston	OF	1	1	1	1	0	0	1	3	1.000
Westlake, Waldon, 1951 St. Louis	OF	1	0	0	0	0	0	0	0	.000
White, William, 1960(2)-61(2)-63-64 St. Louis	PR-1B	6	14	1	4	1	0	0	2	.286
Whitehead, Burgess, 1935 St. Louis; 1938 New York	PR	2	0	0	0	0	0	0	0	.000
Whitney, Arthur, 1936 Philadelphia	3B	1	3	0	1	0	0	0	1	.333
Williams, Billy, 1962-64-65-68-72-73 Chicago	OF-PH	6	11	2	3	0	0	1	2	.273
Williams, David, 1954 New York	2B	1	0	0	0	0	0	0	0	.000
Williams, Stanley, 1960 Los Angeles	P	1	0	0	0	0	0	0	0	.000
Wills, Maurice, 1961(2)-62(2)-65-66 Los Angeles	SS-PR	6	14	2	5	0	0	0	1	.357
Wilson, Donald, 1971 Houston	P	1	0	0	0	0	0	0	0	.000
Wilson, James, 1933 St. Louis; 1935 Philadelphia	C	2	4	0	1	1	0	0	0	.250
Winfield, David, 1977-78-79-80 San Diego	OF	4	11	2	4	2	0	0	4	.364
Wise, Richard, 1973 St. Louis	P	1	0	0	0	0	0	0	0	.000
Woodeshick, Harold, 1963 Houston	P	1	0	0	0	0	0	0	0	.000
Wyatt, Whitlow, 1940-41 Brooklyn	P	2	1	0	0	0	0	0	0	.000
Wynn, James, 1967 Houston; 1974-75 Los Angeles	PH-OF	3	6	2	3	0	0	1	1	.500
Wyrostek, John, 1950-51 Cincinnati	OF	2	3	0	0	0	0	0	0	.000
Youngblood, Joel, 1981 New York	PH	1	1	0	0	0	0	0	0	.000
Zimmer, Donald, 1961 Chicago	2B	1	1	0	0	0	0	0	0	.000

PITCHING RECORDS

National League

Player, Club and Years Pitched	G.	IP.	H.	R.	BB.	SO.	W.	L.	Pct.
Andujar, Joaquin, 1979 Houston	1	2	2	2	1	0	0	0	.000
Antonelli, John, 1954-56 New York; 1959 San Francisco	3	6⅓	8	3	1	3	1	0	1.000
Bibby, James, 1980 Pittsburgh	1	1	1	0	0	0	0	0	.000
Bickford, Vernon, 1949 Boston	1	1	2	2	1	0	0	0	.000
Blackwell, Ewell, 1946-47-48-49-50-51 Cincinnati	6	13⅔	8	2	5	12	1	0	1.000
Blanton, Darrell, 1937 Pittsburgh	1	⅓	0	0	0	1	0	0	.000
Blass, Stephen, 1972 Pittsburgh	1	1	1	1	1	0	0	0	.000
Blue, Vida, 1978-81 San Francisco	2	4	5	3	1	3	1	0	1.000
Branca, Ralph, 1948 Brooklyn	1	3	1	2	3	3	0	0	.000
Brecheen, Harry, 1947 St. Louis	1	3	5	1	0	2	0	0	.000
Brett, Kenneth, 1974 Pittsburgh	1	2	1	0	1	0	1	0	1.000
Brewer, James, 1973 Los Angeles	1	1	0	0	1	2	0	0	.000
Brown, Mace, 1938 Pittsburgh	1	3	5	1	1	2	0	0	.000
Buhl, Robert, 1960 Milwaukee	1	1⅓	2	2	1	1	0	0	.000
Bunning, James, 1964-66 Philadelphia	2	4	3	1	0	6	0	0	.000
Burdette, S. Lewis, 1957-59 Milwaukee	2	7	6	1	1	2	0	0	.000
Carlton, Steven, 1968-69 St. Louis; 1972-79-82 Phila.	5	8	5	5	5	7	1	0	1.000
Conley, D. Eugene, 1954-55 Milwaukee; 1959 Phila.	3	3⅓	3	3	2	5	1	1	.500
Cooper, Morton, 1942-43 St. Louis	2	5⅓	8	7	2	3	0	2	.000
Cuellar, Miguel, 1967 Houston	1	2	1	0	0	2	0	0	.000
Culp, Raymond, 1963 Philadelphia	1	1	1	0	0	0	0	0	.000
Davis, Curtis, 1936 Chicago	1	⅔	4	3	1	0	0	0	.000
Dawley, William, 1983 Houston	1	1⅓	1	0	0	1	0	0	.000
Dean, Jerome, 1934-35-36-37 St. Louis	4	10	10	3	5	10	1	1	.500
Derringer, Paul, 1935-39-40-41 Cincinnati	4	8	6	1	1	6	1	0	1.000
Dickson, Murry, 1953 Pittsburgh	1	2	3	1	0	0	0	0	.000
Dierker, Lawrence, 1969 Houston	1	⅓	1	0	0	0	0	0	.000
Dravecky, David, 1983 San Diego	1	2	1	0	0	2	0	0	.000
Drysdale, Donald, 1959(2)-62-63-64-65-67-68 Los Ang.	8	19⅓	10	4	4	19	2	1	.667
Ellis, Dock, 1971 Pittsburgh	1	3	4	4	1	2	0	1	.000
Elston, Donald, 1959 Chicago	1	1	1	0	0	1	0	0	.000
Erskine, Carl, 1954 Brooklyn	1	⅔	1	0	0	1	0	0	.000
Face, ElRoy, 1959(2)-60-61 Pittsburgh	4	5⅔	6	6	2	7	0	0	.000
Farrell, Richard, 1958 Phila.; 1962-64-65 Houston	4	6	5	4	4	7	0	0	.000
Fette, Louis, 1939 Boston	1	2	1	0	1	1	0	0	.000
Fingers, Roland, 1978 San Diego	1	2	1	0	0	1	0	0	.000
Forsch, Kenneth, 1976 Houston	1	1	0	0	0	1	0	0	.000
Frankhouse, Fred, 1934 Boston	1	1	0	0	1	0	0	0	.000
French, Lawrence, 1940 Chicago	1	2	1	0	0	2	0	0	.000
Friend, Robert, 1956-58-60 Pittsburgh	3	8⅓	8	2	3	5	2	1	.667
Gibson, Robert, 1962-65-67-69-70-72 St. Louis	6	11	11	4	5	10	0	0	.000
Giusti, J. David, 1973 Pittsburgh	1	1	0	0	0	0	0	0	.000
Gooden, Dwight, 1984 New York	1	2	1	0	0	3	0	0	.000

Player, Club and Years Pitched	G.	IP.	H.	R.	BB.	SO.	W.	L.	Pct.
Gossage, Richard, 1977 Pittsburgh; 1984 San Diego	2	2	2	2	1	4	0	0	.000
Grissom, Lee, 1937 Cincinnati	1	1	2	1	0	2	0	0	.000
Grissom, Marvin, 1954 New York	1	1⅓	0	0	0	2	0	0	.000
Haddix, Harvey, 1955 St. Louis	1	3	3	1	0	2	0	0	.000
Hallahan, William, 1933 St. Louis	1	2	2	3	5	1	0	1	.000
Hammaker, C. Atlee, 1983 San Francisco	1	⅔	6	7	1	0	0	0	.000
Henry, William, 1960 Cincinnati	1	1	2	0	0	0	0	0	.000
Higbe, W. Kirby, 1946 Brooklyn	1	1⅓	5	4	1	2	0	0	.000
Hooton, Burt, 1981 Los Angeles	1	1⅔	5	3	0	1	0	0	.000
Howe, Steven, 1982 Los Angeles	1	⅓	0	0	0	0	0	0	.000
Hubbell, Carl, 1933-34-36-37-40 New York	5	9⅔	8	3	6	11	0	0	.000
Hume, Thomas, 1982 Cincinnati	1	⅓	0	0	0	0	0	0	.000
Jackson, Lawrence, 1957-58-60 St. Louis; 1963 Chicago	4	5⅔	6	2	3	3	1	0	1.000
Jansen, Lawrence, 1950 New York	1	5	1	0	0	6	0	0	.000
Javery, Alva, 1943 Boston	1	2	2	0	0	3	0	0	.000
Jenkins, Ferguson, 1971 Chicago	2	4	6	3	0	6	0	0	.000
Jones, Randall, 1975-76 San Diego	2	4	2	0	1	2	1	0	1.000
Jones, Samuel, 1955 Chicago; 1959 San Francisco	2	2⅔	1	1	4	4	0	0	.000
Knepper, Robert, 1981 Houston	1	2	1	0	2	3	0	0	.000
Konstanty, C. James, 1950 Philadelphia	1	1	0	0	0	2	0	0	.000
Koosman, Jerry, 1968-69 New York	2	2	1	0	0	2	0	0	.000
Koufax, Sanford 1961 (2) -65-66 Los Angeles	4	6	4	1	2	3	1	0	1.000
Labine, Clement, 1957 Brooklyn	1	1	3	3	0	1	0	0	.000
LaCoss, Michael, 1979 Cincinnati	1	1⅓	1	0	0	0	0	0	.000
Lavelle, Gary, 1977 San Francisco	1	2	1	0	0	2	0	0	.000
Law, Vernon, 1960 (2) Pittsburgh	2	2⅔	1	0	0	1	1	0	1.000
Lea, Charles, 1984 Montreal	1	2	3	1	0	2	1	0	1.000
Lee, William, 1938-39 Chicago	2	6	4	3	4	6	0	1	.000
Maglie, Salvatore, 1951 New York	1	3	3	2	1	1	1	0	1.000
Mahaffey, Arthur, 1961-62 Philadelphia	2	4	3	2	2	1	0	1	.000
Maloney, James, 1965 Cincinnati	1	1⅔	5	5	2	1	0	0	.000
Marichal, Juan, 1962 (2) -64-65-66-67-68-71 San Fran.	8	18	7	2	2	12	2	0	1.000
Marshall, Michael, 1974 Los Angeles	2	2	0	0	1	2	0	0	.000
Matlack, Jonathan, 1974-75 New York	2	3	3	0	1	4	1	0	1.000
McCormick, Michael, 1960-61 San Francisco	2	5⅓	4	2	4	5	0	0	.000
McDaniel, Lyndall, 1960 St. Louis	1	1	1	0	0	0	0	0	.000
McGlothen, Lynn, 1974 St. Louis	1	1	0	0	0	1	0	0	.000
McGraw, Frank, 1972 New York	1	2	1	0	0	4	1	0	1.000
Merritt, James, 1970 Cincinnati	1	2	1	0	0	1	0	0	.000
Messersmith, John, 1974 Los Angeles	1	3	2	2	3	4	0	0	.000
Miller, Stuart, 1961 (2) San Francisco	2	4⅔	1	1	1	9	1	0	1.000
Minton, Gregory, 1982 San Francisco	1	⅔	0	0	1	0	0	0	.000
Montefusco, John, 1976 San Francisco	1	2	0	0	2	2	0	0	.000
Munger, George, 1949 St. Louis	1	1	0	0	1	0	0	0	.000
Mungo, Van, 1934-37 Brooklyn	2	3	6	6	4	2	0	1	.000
Newcombe, Donald, 1949-50-51-55 Brooklyn	4	8⅔	9	4	2	5	0	1	.000
Niekro, Philip, 1969-78 Atlanta	2	1⅓	0	0	0	2	0	0	.000
Nuxhall, Joseph, 1955 Cincinnati	1	3⅓	2	0	3	5	0	0	.000
Orosco, Jesse, 1983 New York	1	⅓	0	0	0	1	0	0	.000
Osteen, Claude, 1970-73 Los Angeles	2	5	5	0	2	1	1	0	1.000
O'Toole, James, 1963 Cincinnati	2	4	1	0	1	0	0	0	.000
Passeau, Claude, 1941-42-46 Chicago	3	7⅔	9	7	3	4	0	2	.000
Perez, Pascual, 1983 Atlanta	1	⅔	3	2	1	1	0	0	.000
Perry, Gaylord, 1966-70 San Francisco; 1979 San Diego	3	4	8	3	2	1	1	0	1.000
Podres, John, 1960-62 Los Angeles	2	4	3	0	3	3	0	0	.000
Pollet, Howard, 1949 St. Louis	1	1	4	3	0	0	0	0	.000
Purkey, Robert, 1961 (2) -62 Cincinnati	3	6	3	2	2	4	0	0	.000
Raffensberger, Kenneth, 1944 Philadelphia	2	2	1	0	0	2	1	0	1.000
Reed, Ronald, 1968 Atlanta	1	⅔	0	0	0	1	0	0	.000
Reuschel, Rick, 1977 Chicago	1	1	1	0	0	0	0	0	.000
Reuss, Jerry, 1975 Pittsburgh; 1980 Los Angeles	2	4	3	0	0	5	1	0	1.000
Rhoden, Richard, 1976 Los Angeles	1	1	1	0	0	0	0	0	.000
Richard, J. R., 1980 Houston	1	2	1	0	2	3	0	0	.000
Roberts, Robin, 1950-51-53-54-55 Philadelphia	5	14	17	10	6	9	0	0	.000
Roe, Elwin, 1949 Brooklyn	1	1	0	0	0	0	0	0	.000
Rogers, Stephen, 1978-79-82 Montreal	3	7	6	1	0	6	1	0	1.000
Rush, Robert, 1952 Chicago	2	4	4	2	1	1	1	0	1.000
Ruthven, Richard, 1981 Philadelphia	1	⅓	0	0	0	0	0	0	.000
Ryan, L. Nolan, 1981 Houston	1	1	0	0	0	1	0	0	.000
Sain, John, 1947-48 Boston	2	2⅓	2	1	0	4	0	1	.000
Sambito, Joseph, 1979 Houston	1	⅔	0	0	1	0	0	0	.000
Sanford, John, 1957 Philadelphia	1	2	1	0	0	0	0	0	.000
Schmitz, John, 1948 Chicago	1	⅓	3	3	1	0	0	1	.000
Schumacher, Harold, 1935 New York	1	4	4	1	1	5	0	0	.000
Seaver, G. Thomas, 1967-68-70-73-75-76 N.Y.; 1977-81 Cincinnati	8	13	14	8	4	16	0	0	.000
Sewell, Truett, 1943-44-46 Pittsburgh	3	5	4	4	1	2	0	0	.000
Shaw, Robert, 1962 Milwaukee	1	2	1	0	1	1	0	0	.000
Short, Christopher, 1964-67 Philadelphia	2	3	3	2	1	2	0	0	.000
Simmons, Curtis, 1952-53-57 Philadelphia	3	6	4	4	2	4	0	1	.000
Smith, Lee, 1983 Chicago	1	1	2	2	0	1	0	0	.000
Singer, William, 1969 Los Angeles	1	2	0	0	0	0	0	0	.000
Smith, Lee, 1983 Chicago	1	1	2	2	0	1	0	0	.000
Soto, Mario, 1982-83-84 Cincinnati	3	6	5	2	2	7	0	1	.000

Player, Club and Years Pitched	G.	IP.	H.	R.	BB.	SO.	W.	L.	Pct.
Spahn, Warren, 1947-49 Boston; 1953-54-56-58-61									
Milwaukee	7	14	17	10	5	10	1	0	1.000
Stoneman, William, 1972 Montreal	1	2	2	2	0	2	0	0	.000
Sutter, H. Bruce, 1978-79-80 Chicago; 1981 St. Louis	4	6⅔	2	0	3	7	2	0	1.000
Sutton, Donald, 1972-73-75-77 Los Angeles	4	8	5	0	1	7	1	0	1.000
Tobin, James, 1944 Boston	1	1	0	0	0	0	0	0	.000
Twitchell, Wayne, 1973 Philadelphia	1	1	1	0	0	1	0	0	.000
Valenzuela, Fernando, 1981-82-84 Los Angeles	3	3⅔	4	0	2	3	0	0	.000
Vander Meer, John, 1938-42-43 Cincinnati	3	8⅔	5	1	1	11	1	0	1.000
Walker, William, 1935 St. Louis	1	2	2	3	1	2	0	1	.000
Walters, William, 1937 Phila.; 1940-41-42-44 Cincinnati	5	9	10	2	2	4	0	0	.000
Warneke, Lonnie, 1933-34-36 Chicago	3	7⅓	10	5	6	5	0	0	.000
Welch, Robert, 1980 Los Angeles	1	3	5	2	1	4	0	0	.000
Williams, Stanley, 1960 Los Angeles	1	2	2	0	1	2	0	0	.000
Wilson, Donald, 1971 Houston	1	2	0	0	1	2	0	0	.000
Wise, Richard, 1973 St. Louis	1	2	2	1	0	1	1	0	1.000
Woodeshick, Harold, 1963 Houston	1	2	1	0	1	3	0	0	.000
Wyatt, J. Whitlow, 1940-41 Brooklyn	2	4	1	0	1	1	0	0	.000

Championship Series Results, Records

Detroit's Milt Wilcox capped the Tigers' 1984 Championship Series victory over Kansas City by shutting out the Royals through eight innings.

AMERICAN LEAGUE

Year-Winner   **Loser**

1969—Baltimore (East), 3 games; Minnesota (West), 0 games.
1970—Baltimore (East), 3 games; Minnesota (West), 0 games.
1971—Baltimore (East), 3 games; Oakland (West), 0 games.
1972—Oakland (West), 3 games; Detroit (East), 2 games.
1973—Oakland (West), 3 games; Baltimore (East), 2 games.
1974—Oakland (West), 3 games; Baltimore (East), 1 game.
1975—Boston (East), 3 games; Oakland (West), 0 games.
1976—New York (East), 3 games; Kansas City (West), 2 games.
1977—New York (East), 3 games; Kansas City (West), 2 games.
1978—New York (East), 3 games; Kansas City (West), 1 game.
1979—Baltimore (East), 3 games; California (West), 1 game.
1980—Kansas City (West), 3 games; New York (East), 0 games.
1981—New York (East), 3 games; Oakland (West), 0 games.
1982—Milwaukee (East), 3 games; California (West), 2 games.
1983—Baltimore (East), 3 games; Chicago (West), 1 game.
1984—Detroit (East), 3 games; Kansas City (West), 0 games.

NATIONAL LEAGUE

Year-Winner   **Loser**

1969—New York (East), 3 games; Atlanta (West), 0 games.
1970—Cincinnati (West), 3 games; Pittsburgh (East), 0 games.
1971—Pittsburgh (East), 3 games; San Francisco (West), 1 game.
1972—Cincinnati (West), 3 games; Pittsburgh (East), 2 games.
1973—New York (East), 3 games; Cincinnati (West), 2 games.
1974—Los Angeles (West), 3 games; Pittsburgh (East), 1 game.
1975—Cincinnati (West), 3 games; Pittsburgh (East), 0 games.
1976—Cincinnati (West), 3 games; Philadelphia (East), 0 games.
1977—Los Angeles (West), 3 games; Philadelphia (East), 1 game.
1978—Los Angeles (West), 3 games; Philadelphia (East), 1 game.
1979—Pittsburgh (East), 3 games; Cincinnati (West), 0 games.
1980—Philadelphia (East), 3 games; Houston (West), 2 games.
1981—Los Angeles (West), 3 games; Montreal (East), 2 games.
1982—St. Louis (East), 3 games; Atlanta (West), 0 games.
1983—Philadelphia (East), 3 games; Los Angeles (West), 1 game.
1984—San Diego (West), 3 games; Chicago (East) 2 games.

AMERICAN LEAGUE
Championship Series of 1969

	W.	L.	Pct.
Baltimore (East)	3	0	1.000
Minnesota (West)	0	3	.000

Baltimore was the belle of the American League ball in 1969. The Orioles over-whelmed the opposition in winning the East Division title by 19 games. They were equally devastating in their treatment of the West Division champion Minnesota Twins in the A. L. Championship Series.

The Orioles disposed of the Twins in three straight games, vindicating those who had crowed that Baltimore was the best team to represent the American League since the New York Yankees' halcyon days.

The Twins were stubborn foes in the first two matches, played in Baltimore. The Orioles had to go 12 innings in taking the opener, 4-3, on October 4. Next day, Baltimore prevailed in 11 innings, 1-0. That was the Twins' last gasp. When the series moved to the Twin Cities October 6, the Orioles lowered the boom in an 11-2 romp.

Mike Cuellar and Dave McNally were Baltimore's 20-game winners. Cuellar performed satisfactorily in the playoff opener, though failing to receive credit for a victory. McNally pitched brilliantly in blanking Minnesota in the second game. Jim Palmer, author of a no-hitter against Oakland during the regular season, coasted to victory behind Baltimore's 18-hit attack in the playoff finale.

Oriole bats were impressive, too. Frank Robinson, Mark Belanger and Boog Powell rapped homers in the opener. The winning hit, however, was a perfectly executed bunt by Paul Blair, who squeezed Belanger home from third in the 12th inning.

Blair, the swift center fielder who enjoyed a banner season, whacked five hits and drove in five runs in the third-game rout. Left fielder Don Buford contributed four hits after going 0-for-9 in the first two games.

Oriole Manager Earl Weaver employed simple strategy to deal with Minneso-ta's Harmon Killebrew, A. L. home run and RBI champ: Walk him in any danger-ous situation. The Killer got nothing to swing at until the third game was on ice. Baltimore pitchers walked him five times in the first two games and pitched to him only when he could not wreck them with one swing.

Rod Carew and Tony Oliva were the Twins' other top hitters during the season. Carew, A. L. batting champ, was a dud in the playoffs, going 1-for-14. Oliva hit safely in each of the three games, including a homer in the opener, but was guilty of some shoddy fielding in the third game.

In the opener, 20-game winner Jim Perry held a 3-2 lead over the Orioles enter-ing the ninth inning. Powell tied the score with a smash over the right-field fence. Reliever Ron Perranoski, who worked in all three games, shut off Baltimore's offense at that point.

Then, with two down in the 12th and Belanger on third, Blair stepped to the plate. Acting on his own, he bunted toward third. Neither third sacker Killebrew nor catcher John Roseboro could make a play as Belanger sped across the plate with the winning run. Dick Hall, who pitched two-thirds of an inning, was the winner. Perranoski didn't allow a ball to leave the infield in the 12th, but was the loser nevertheless.

Winner of 15 games in a row during the season, McNally was saddled with a "lucky" tag because Baltimore frequently rallied to win after McNally had left on the short end of the score. He won the second game of the playoffs on his own exceptional pitching and Curt Motton's 11th-inning pinch-single. It scored Powell from second base with the only run of the game. McNally's victim was Dave Bos-well, who was a mighty tough opponent. McNally yielded only three hits, none after the fourth inning.

Twins' Manager Billy Martin, confronted with a pitching shortage, started Bob Miller, normally a reliever, in the third game. Miller lasted less than two innings, and his six successors fared no better. Every Oriole except pitcher Palmer hit safely in an assault that eliminated Minnesota and sent Baltimore into the World Series.

GAME OF SATURDAY, OCTOBER 4, AT BALTIMORE

Minnesota	AB.	R.	H.	RBI.	PO.	A.	Baltimore	AB.	R.	H.	RBI.	PO.	A.
Tovar, cf	4	0	0	0	3	0	Buford, lf	6	0	0	0	3	0
Carew, 2b	5	0	1	0	3	1	Blair, cf	5	0	1	1	1	0
Killebrew, 3b	2	1	0	0	3	2	F. Robinson, rf	3	1	1	1	1	0
Oliva, rf	5	2	2	2	3	0	Powell, 1b	5	1	2	1	13	0
Allison, lf	3	0	0	1	3	0	B. Robinson, 3b	5	0	4	0	2	4
Uhlaender, lf	1	0	1	0	0	0	Hendricks, c	3	0	0	0	9	0
Reese, 1b	4	0	0	0	10	1	Motton, ph	1	0	0	0	0	0
Cardenas, ss	5	0	0	0	5	3	Watt, p	0	0	0	0	0	0
Mitterwald, c	4	0	0	0	5	2	Salmon, ph	1	0	0	0	0	0
Roseboro, c	1	0	0	0	0	0	Lopez, p	0	0	0	0	0	0
Perry, p	3	0	0	0	0	1	Hall, p	0	0	0	0	0	0
Perranoski, p	1	0	0	0	0	0	Johnson, 2b	5	0	0	0	3	3
Totals	38	3	4	3	35	10	Belanger, ss	5	2	2	1	1	2
							Cuellar, p	2	0	0	0	0	0
							May, ph	1	0	0	0	0	0
							Richert, p	0	0	0	0	0	0
							Rettenmund, ph	0	0	0	0	0	0
							Etchebarren, c	1	0	0	0	3	0
							Totals	43	4	10	4	36	9

Minnesota	0	0	0		0	1	0		2	0	0	0 0 0 – 3
Baltimore	0	0	0		1	1	0		0	0	1	0 0 1 – 4

Two out when winning run scored.

Minnesota	IP.	H.	R.	ER.	BB.	SO.
Perry	8*	6	3	3	3	3
Perranoski (Loser)	3⅔	4	1	1	0	1

Baltimore	IP.	H.	R.	ER.	BB.	SO.
Cuellar	8	3	3	2	1	7
Richert	1	0	0	0	2	2
Watt	2	0	0	0	0	2
Lopez	⅓	1	0	0	2	0
Hall (Winner)	⅔	0	0	0	0	1

*Pitched to two batters in ninth.

Errors—F. Robinson. Uhlaender. Carew. Double play—Baltimore 1. Left on bases—Minnesota 5. Baltimore 8. Two-base hit—Oliva. Home runs—F. Robinson, Belanger, Oliva, Powell. Stolen base—Tovar. Sacrifice hit—Etchebarren. Sacrifice fly—Allison. Wild pitch—Lopez. Umpires—Chylak, Runge, Umont, Stewart. Rice and Flaherty. Time of game—3:29. Attendance—39,324.

GAME OF SUNDAY, OCTOBER 5, AT BALTIMORE

Minnesota	AB.	R.	H.	RBI.	PO.	A.	Baltimore	AB.	R.	H.	RBI.	PO.	A.
Tovar, cf	5	0	1	0	2	0	Buford, lf	3	0	0	0	1	0
Carew, 2b	4	0	0	0	2	1	Blair, cf	4	0	0	0	6	0
Killebrew, 3b	3	0	0	0	1	0	F. Robinson, rf	5	0	2	0	1	0
Oliva, rf	4	0	1	0	1	0	Powell, 1b	3	1	1	0	10	0
Allison, lf	5	0	0	0	3	0	B. Robinson, 3b	4	0	2	0	3	3
Reese, 1b	4	0	0	0	11	3	Johnson, 2b	4	0	2	0	1	2
Mitterwald, c	3	0	1	0	5	2	Belanger, ss	5	0	0	0	0	4
Cardenas, ss	4	0	0	0	6	5	Etchebarren, c	3	0	0	0	8	0
Boswell, p	4	0	0	0	1	4	Hendricks, ph-c	0	0	0	0	3	0
Perranoski, p	0	0	0	0	0	0	Motton, ph	1	0	1	1	0	0
Totals	36	0	3	0	32	15	McNally, p	4	0	0	0	0	0
							Totals	36	1	8	1	33	9

Minnesota	0	0	0	0	0	0	0	0	0 0 – 0
Baltimore	0	0	0	0	0	0	0	0	0 1 – 1

Two out when winning run scored.

Minnesota	IP.	H.	R.	ER.	BB.	SO.
Boswell (Loser)	10⅔	7	1	1	7	4
Perranoski	0*	1	0	0	0	0
Baltimore	IP.	H.	R.	ER.	BB.	SO.
McNally (Winner)	11	3	0	0	5	11

*Pitched to one batter in eleventh.

Error—Cardenas. Double plays—Minnesota 2. Left on bases—Minnesota 8, Baltimore 11. Two base hits—F. Robinson 2. Stolen base—Oliva. Sacrifice hit—B. Robinson. Wild pitch—Boswell. Umpires—Runge, Umont, Stewart, Rice, Flaherty and Chylak. Time of game—3:17. Attendance—41,704.

GAME OF MONDAY, OCTOBER 6, AT MINNESOTA

Baltimore	AB.	R.	H.	RBI.	PO.	A.
Buford, lf	5	3	4	1	4	0
Blair, cf	6	1	5	5	1	0
F. Robinson, rf	4	0	1	1	0	0
Powell, 1b	5	0	2	0	11	0
B. Robinson, 3b	5	1	1	0	1	3
Johnson, 2b	4	2	1	0	1	6
Hendricks, c	5	2	2	3	6	0
Belanger, ss	5	2	2	0	3	3
Palmer, p	5	0	0	0	0	1
Totals	44	11	18	10	27	13

Minnesota	AB.	R.	H.	RBI.	PO.	A.
Uhlaender, lf	5	0	0	0	4	0
Carew, 2b	5	0	0	0	1	1
Oliva, rf	4	1	2	0	2	1
Killebrew, 3b	3	1	1	0	2	1
Reese, 1b	4	0	2	2	5	1
Tovar, cf	4	0	0	0	5	0
Roseboro, c	4	0	1	0	6	1
Cardenas, ss	4	0	2	0	2	4
Miller, p	0	0	0	0	0	0
Woodson, p	1	0	1	0	0	0
Hall, p	0	0	0	0	0	0
Manuel, ph	0	0	0	0	0	0
Worthington, p	0	0	0	0	0	0
Grzenda, p	0	0	0	0	0	0
Renick, ph	1	0	0	0	0	0
Chance, p	0	0	0	0	0	0
Perranoski, p	0	0	0	0	0	0
Nettles, ph	1	0	1	0	0	0
Totals	36	2	10	2	27	9

Baltimore	0	3	0	2	0	1	0	2	3 — 11
Minnesota	1	0	0	0	1	0	0	0	0 — 2

Baltimore	IP.	H.	R.	ER.	BB.	SO.
Palmer (Winner)	9	10	2	2	2	4

Minnesota	IP.	H.	R.	ER.	BB.	SO.
Miller (Loser)	1⅔	5	3	1	0	0
Woodson	1⅔	3	2	2	3	2
Hall	⅔	0	0	0	0	0
Worthington	1⅓	3	1	1	0	1
Grzenda	⅔	0	0	0	0	0
Chance	2*	4	3	3	0	2
Perranoski	1	3	2	2	0	1

*Pitched to one batter in ninth.

Errors—Oliva 2. Double plays—Baltimore 1, Minnesota 1. Left on base—Baltimore 9, Minnesota 9. Two-base hits—Oliva, B. Robinson, Hendricks 2, Blair 2, Killebrew, Buford. Three-base hits—Belanger, Cardenas. Home run—Blair. Wild pitch—Palmer. Umpires—Umont, Stewart, Rice, Flaherty, Chylak and Runge. Time of game—2:48. Attendance—32,735.

BALTIMORE ORIOLES' BATTING AND FIELDING AVERAGES

Player—Position	G.	AB.	R.	H.	TB.	2B.	3B.	HR.	RBI.	B.A.	PO.	A.	E.	F.A.
B. Robinson, 3b	3	14	1	7	8	1	0	0	0	.500	6	10	0	1.000
Motton, ph	2	2	0	1	1	0	0	0	1	.500	0	0	0	.000
Blair, cf	3	15	1	6	11	2	0	1	6	.400	8	0	0	1.000
Powell, 1b	3	13	2	5	8	0	0	1	1	.385	34	0	0	.667
F. Robinson, rf	3	12	1	4	9	2	0	1	2	.333	2	0	1	.667
Buford, lf	3	14	3	4	5	1	0	0	1	.286	8	0	0	1.000
Belanger, ss	3	15	4	4	9	0	1	1	1	.267	4	9	0	1.000
Hendricks, ph-c	3	8	2	2	4	2	0	0	3	.250	18	0	0	1.000
Johnson, 2b	3	13	2	3	3	0	0	0	0	.231	5	11	0	1.000
Watt, p	1	0	0	0	0	0	0	0	0	.000	0	0	0	.000
Lopez, p	1	0	0	0	0	0	0	0	0	.000	0	0	0	.000
R. Hall, p	1	0	0	0	0	0	0	0	0	.000	0	0	0	.000
Richert, p	1	0	0	0	0	0	0	0	0	.000	0	0	0	.000
Rettenmund, ph	1	0	0	0	0	0	0	0	0	.000	0	0	0	.000
Salmon, p	1	1	0	0	0	0	0	0	0	.000	0	0	0	.000
May, ph	1	1	0	0	0	0	0	0	0	.000	0	0	0	.000
Cuellar, p	1	2	0	0	0	0	0	0	0	.000	0	0	0	.000
Etchebarren, c	2	4	0	0	0	0	0	0	0	.000	11	0	0	1.000
McNally, p	1	4	0	0	0	0	0	0	0	.000	0	0	0	.000
Palmer, p	1	5	0	0	0	0	0	0	0	.000	0	1	0	1.000
Totals	3	123	16	36	58	8	1	4	15	.293	96	31	1	.992

MINNESOTA TWINS' BATTING AND FIELDING AVERAGES

Player—Position	G.	AB.	R.	H.	TB.	2B.	3B.	HR.	RBI.	B.A.	PO.	A.	E.	F.A.
Nettles, ph	1	1	0	1	1	0	0	0	0	1.000	0	0	0	.000
Woodson, p	1	1	0	1	1	0	0	0	0	1.000	0	0	0	.000
Oliva, rf	3	13	3	5	10	2	0	0	2	.385	6	1	2	.778
Roseboro, c	2	5	0	1	1	0	0	0	0	.200	6	1	0	1.000
Reese, 1b	3	12	0	2	2	0	0	0	2	.167	26	5	0	1.000
Uhlaender, lf	2	6	0	1	1	0	0	0	0	.167	4	0	1	.800
Cardenas, ss	3	13	0	2	4	0	1	0	0	.154	13	12	1	.962
Mitterwald, c	2	7	0	1	1	0	0	0	0	.143	10	4	0	1.000
Killebrew, 3b	3	8	2	1	2	1	0	0	0	.125	6	3	0	1.000
Tovar, cf	3	13	0	1	1	0	0	0	0	.077	10	0	0	1.000
Carew, 2b	3	14	0	1	1	0	0	0	0	.071	6	3	1	.900
Chance, p	1	0	0	0	0	0	0	0	0	.000	0	0	0	.000
Miller, p	1	0	0	0	0	0	0	0	0	.000	0	0	0	.000
T. Hall, p	1	0	0	0	0	0	0	0	0	.000	0	0	0	.000
Manuel, ph	1	0	0	0	0	0	0	0	0	.000	0	0	0	.000
Worthington, p	1	0	0	0	0	0	0	0	0	.000	0	0	0	.000
Grzenda, p	1	0	0	0	0	0	0	0	0	.000	0	0	0	.000

Player—Position	G.	AB.	R.	H.	TB.	2B.	3B.	HR.	RBI.	B.A	PO.	A.	E.	F.A.
Renick, ph	1	1	0	0	0	0	0	0	0	.000	0	0	0	.000
Perranoski, p	3	1	0	0	0	0	0	0	0	.000	0	0	0	.000
Perry, p	1	3	0	0	0	0	0	0	0	.000	0	1	0	1.000
Boswell, p	1	4	0	0	0	0	0	0	0	.000	1	4	0	1.000
Allison, lf	2	8	0	0	0	0	0	0	1	.000	6	0	0	1.000
Totals	3	110	5	17	25	3	1	1	5	.155	94	34	5	.962

BALTIMORE ORIOLES' PITCHING RECORDS

Pitcher	G.	GS.	CG.	IP.	H.	R.	ER.	BB.	SO.	HB.	WP.	W.	L.	Pct.	ERA.
McNally	1	1	1	11	3	0	0	5	11	0	0	1	0	1.000	0.00
Watt	1	0	0	2	0	0	0	0	2	0	0	0	0	.000	0.00
Richert	1	0	0	1	0	0	0	2	2	0	0	0	0	.000	0.00
R. Hall	1	0	0	⅔	0	0	0	0	1	0	0	1	0	1.000	0.00
Lopez	1	0	0	⅓	1	0	0	2	0	0	1	0	0	.000	0.00
Palmer	1	1	1	9	10	2	2	2	4	0	1	1	0	1.000	2.00
Cuellar	1	1	0	8	3	3	2	1	7	0	0	0	0	.000	2.25
Totals	3	3	2	32	17	5	4	12	27	0	2	3	0	1.000	1.13

Shutout—McNally. No saves.

MINNESOTA TWINS' PITCHING RECORDS

Pitcher	G.	GS.	CG.	IP.	H.	R.	ER.	BB.	SO.	HB.	WP.	W.	L.	Pct.	ERA.
Grzenda	1	0	0	⅔	0	0	0	0	0	0	0	0	0	.000	0.00
T. Hall	1	0	0	⅔	0	0	0	0	0	0	0	0	0	.000	0.00
Boswell	1	1	0	10⅔	7	1	1	7	4	0	1	0	1	.000	0.84
Perry	1	1	0	8	6	3	3	3	3	0	0	0	0	.000	3.38
Miller	1	1	0	1⅔	5	3	1	0	0	0	0	0	1	.000	5.40
Perranoski	3	0	0	4⅔	8	3	3	0	2	0	0	0	1	.000	5.79
Worthington	1	0	0	1⅓	3	1	1	0	1	0	0	0	0	.000	6.75
Woodson	1	0	0	1⅔	3	2	2	3	2	0	0	0	0	.000	10.80
Chance	1	0	0	2	4	3	3	0	2	0	0	0	0	.000	13.50
Totals	3	3	0	31⅓	36	16	14	13	14	0	1	0	3	.000	4.02

No shutouts or saves.

COMPOSITE SCORE BY INNINGS

Baltimore	0	3	0	3	1	1	0	2	4	0	1	1—16
Minnesota	1	0	0	0	2	0	2	0	0	0	0	0— 5

Sacrifice hits—Etchebarren, B. Robinson.
Sacrifice fly—Allison.
Stolen bases—Oliva, Tovar.
Caught stealing—B. Robinson 2, Buford, Blair.
Double plays—Johnson and Powell; Belanger, Johnson and Powell; Cardenas and Reese; Boswell, Cardenas and Reese; Carew, Cardenas and Reese.
Hit by pitcher—None.
Passed balls—None.
Balks—None.
Left on bases—Baltimore 28—8, 11, 9; Minnesota 22—5, 8, 9.
Time of games—First game, 3:29; second game, 3:17; third game, 2:48.
Attendance—First game, 39,324; second game, 41,704; third game, 32,735.
Umpires—Chylak, Runge, Umont, Stewart, Rice and Flaherty.
Official scorers—Arno Goethel, St. Paul Pioneer Press; Neal Eskridge, Baltimore News-Post.

NATIONAL LEAGUE
Championship Series of 1969

	W.	L.	Pct.
New York (East)	3	0	1.000
Atlanta (West)	0	3	.000

Thirty-to-one shots do come through occasionally. And the National League's first experience with the two-division playoff system provided one of those rare instances. Note the East Division playoff.

Adding another lustrous chapter, the New York Mets swept the Atlanta Braves into oblivion in three Championship Series games to win their first league title after five 10th-place and two ninth-place finishes.

In the first game, played before 50,122 at Atlanta October 4, Tom Seaver, the Mets' 25-game winner, hooked up with Phil Niekro, winner of 23 decisions for the Braves.

Neither righthander finished. Niekro lasted eight innings, including the five-run eighth by which the Mets sewed up the verdict. Seaver departed for a pinch-hitter in the same decisive inning.

Wayne Garrett opened the tell-tale frame with a double and tied the score at 5-5 when Cleon Jones singled. Art Shamsky's third hit sent Jones to second. When Ken Boswell missed an attempted sacrifice, Jones was trapped off second. Catcher Bob Didier committed the cardinal sin of throwing behind the runner and Jones beat the relay throw to third base.

When Boswell bounced to the mound, the Braves retired only one runner, Al Weis, who ran for Shamsky at second base. On Ed Kranepool's grounder to first base, Orlando Cepeda fired wildly to the plate, Jones scoring the go-ahead run.

After Jerry Grote was retired, Bud Harrelson was walked intentionally, loading the bases. With Seaver due to bat, Hodges went to his bench and found just what he wanted. J. C. Martin pinch-singled three runs across the plate, providing the final nail in a 9-5 victory.

In the second game, witnessed by 50,270 October 5, Jerry Koosman, New York's 17-game winner, was staked to leads of 8-0 and 9-1, yet failed to survive the fifth inning.

The Mets tagged Ron Reed for four runs in one and two-thirds innings, added two off Paul Doyle and three off Milt Pappas before the Atlanta guns went to work.

A homer by Hank Aaron, who hit for the circuit in each of the three games, provided three runs. A single by Felix Millan, a double by Cepeda and a single by Clete Boyer accounted for two more tallies and shelled Koosman, then leading by only 9-6.

Ron Taylor and Tug McGraw shut out the Braves on two hits the rest of the way. The Mets picked up their final runs in the seventh when Jones homered with Tommie Agee on base, making the score 11-6.

With the series switched to New York, the Mets applied the clincher before 53,195 delirious devotees on October 6.

This game belonged to Nolan Ryan, who replaced Gary Gentry with none out in the third inning, runners on second and third and the Braves leading, 2-0.

Ryan fanned Rico Carty as a starter, walked Cepeda intentionally, whiffed Boyer and got Didier on a fly to left to escape damage.

The hard-throwing righthander made his only mistake in the fifth, when he grooved a two-run homer pitch to Cepeda, that gave the Braves a 4-3 margin.

Ryan quickly made amends for that boner, leading off the home portion of the inning with a single. Agee was retired, but Garrett, who had hit his last homer on May 6, exactly five months earlier, clouted Jarvis' first pitch into the upper stands in right and the Mets were in front to stay.

Ryan, who had appeared in only 89 innings during the regular season, allowed three hits in his seven innings, walked two and fanned seven, in addition to collecting a second hit in the 7-4 victory.

GAME OF SATURDAY, OCTOBER 4, AT ATLANTA

New York	AB.	R.	H.	RBI.	PO.	A.	Atlanta	AB.	R.	H.	RBI.	PO.	A.
Agee, cf	5	0	0	0	2	0	Millan, 2b	5	1	2	0	3	2
Garrett, 3b	4	1	2	0	1	2	Gonzalez, cf	5	2	2	0	1	0
Jones, lf	5	1	1	1	5	0	H. Aaron, rf	5	1	2	2	1	0
Shamsky, rf	4	1	3	0	2	0	Carty, lf	3	1	1	0	0	0
Weis, pr-2b	0	0	0	0	1	1	Lum, lf	1	0	1	0	0	0
Boswell, 2b	3	2	0	0	0	1	Cepeda, 1b	4	0	1	0	14	0
Gaspar, rf	0	0	0	0	0	0	Boyer, 3b	1	0	0	0	2	5
Kranepool, 1b	4	2	1	0	7	2	Didier, c	4	0	0	0	5	0
Grote, c	3	1	1	1	5	1	Garrido, ss	4	0	1	0	2	7
Harrelson, ss	3	1	1	2	2	1	Niekro, p	3	0	0	0	0	3
Seaver, p	3	0	0	0	1	1	Aspromonte, ph	1	0	0	0	0	0
Martin, ph	1	0	1	2	0	0	Upshaw, p	0	0	0	0	0	0
Taylor, p	0	0	0	0	1	0							
Totals	35	9	10	6	27	9	Totals	36	5	10	5	27	19

New York 0   2   0   2   0   0   0   5   0 — 9
Atlanta 0   1   2   0   1   0   1   0   0 — 5

New York	IP.	H.	R.	ER.	BB.	SO.
Seaver (Winner)	7	8	5	5	3	2
Taylor (Save)	2	2	0	0	0	0

Atlanta	IP.	H.	R.	ER.	BB.	SO.
Niekro (Loser)	8	9	9	4	4	4
Upshaw	1	1	0	0	0	1

Errors—Boswell, Cepeda, Gonzalez. Double plays—Atlanta 2. Left on bases—New York 3, Atlanta 9. Two-base hits—Carty, Millan, Gonzalez, H. Aaron, Garrett, Lum. Three-base hit—Harrelson. Home runs—Gonzalez, H. Aaron. Stolen bases—Cepeda, Jones. Sacrifice fly—Boyer. Hit by pitcher—By Seaver (Cepeda). Passed balls —Didier, Grote. Umpires—Barlick, Donatelli, Sudol, Vargo, Pelekoudas and Steiner. Time of game—2:37. Attendance—50,122.

GAME OF SUNDAY, OCTOBER 5, AT ATLANTA

New York	AB.	R.	H.	RBI.	PO.	A.	Atlanta	AB.	R.	H.	RBI.	PO.	A.
Agee, cf	4	3	2	2	3	0	Millan, 2b	2	1	2	0	0	5
Garrett, 3b	5	1	2	1	0	1	Gonzalez, cf	4	1	1	0	2	0
Jones, lf	5	2	3	3	3	0	H. Aaron, rf	5	1	1	3	3	0
Shamsky, rf	5	1	3	1	0	0	Carty, lf	4	2	1	0	1	0
Gaspar, pr-rf	0	0	0	0	2	0	Cepeda, 1b	4	1	2	1	8	0
Boswell, 2b	5	1	1	2	2	1	Boyer, 3b	4	0	1	2	1	2
McGraw, p	0	0	0	0	0	0	Dider, c	4	0	0	0	12	1
Kranepool, 1b	4	0	1	1	6	0	Garrido, ss	4	0	1	0	0	0
Grote, c	5	1	0	0	9	0	Reed, p	0	0	0	0	0	1
Harrelson, ss	5	1	1	1	2	2	Doyle, p	0	0	0	0	0	0
Koosman, p	2	1	0	0	0	1	Pappas, p	1	0	0	0	0	0
Taylor, p	0	0	0	0	0	0	T. Aaron, ph	1	0	0	0	0	0
Martin, ph	1	0	0	0	0	0	Britton, p	0	0	0	0	0	0
Weis, 2b	1	0	0	0	0	2	Upshaw, p	1	0	0	0	0	0
Totals	42	11	13	11	27	7	Aspromonte, ph	1	0	0	0	0	0
							Neibauer, p	0	0	0	0	0	0
							Totals	35	6	9	6	27	9

New York	1	3	2	2	1	0	2	0	0 – 11
Atlanta	0	0	0	1	5	0	0	0	0 – 6

New York	IP.	H.	R.	ER.	BB.	SO.
Koosman	4⅔	7	6	6	4	5
Taylor (Winner)	1⅓	1	0	0	0	2
McGraw (Save)	3	1	0	0	1	1

Atlanta	IP.	H.	R.	ER.	BB.	SO.
Reed (Loser)	1⅔	5	4	4	3	3
Doyle	1	2	2	0	1	3
Pappas	2⅓	4	3	3	0	4
Britton	⅓	0	0	0	1	0
Upshaw	2⅔	2	2	2	1	1
Neibauer	1	0	0	0	0	0

Errors—H. Aaron, Cepeda, Harrelson, Boyer. Double plays—New York 2, Atlanta 1. Left on bases—New York 10, Atlanta 7. Two-base hits—Jones, Harrelson, Carty, Garrett, Cepeda. Home runs—Agee, Boswell, H. Aaron, Jones. Stolen bases—Agee 2, Garrett, Jones. Umpires—Donatelli, Sudol, Vargo, Pelekoudas, Steiner and Barlick. Time of game—3:10. Attendance—50,270.

GAME OF MONDAY, OCTOBER 6, AT NEW YORK

Atlanta	AB.	R.	H.	RBI.	PO.	A.	New York	AB.	R.	H.	RBI.	PO.	A.
Millan, 2b	5	0	0	0	0	2	Agee, cf	5	1	3	2	4	0
Gonzalez, cf	5	1	2	0	1	0	Garrett, 3b	4	1	1	2	0	3
H. Aaron, rf	4	1	2	2	0	1	Jones, lf	4	1	2	0	3	0
Carty, lf	3	1	1	0	2	0	Shamsky, rf	4	1	1	0	1	0
Cepeda, 1b	3	1	2	2	7	1	Gaspar, pr-rf	0	0	0	0	0	0
Boyer, 3b	4	0	0	0	1	1	Boswell, 2b	4	1	3	3	1	0
Didier, c	3	0	0	0	7	0	Weis, 2b	0	0	0	0	0	0
Lum, ph	1	0	1	0	0	0	Kranepool, 1b	4	0	1	0	7	1
Jackson, ss	0	0	0	0	0	0	Grote, c	4	1	1	0	8	0
Garrido, ss	2	0	0	0	2	1	Harrelson, ss	3	0	0	0	2	3
Alou, ph	1	0	0	0	0	0	Gentry, p	0	0	0	0	0	0
Tillman, c	0	0	0	0	2	0	Ryan, p	4	1	2	0	1	0
Jarvis, p	2	0	0	0	1	2	Totals	36	7	14	7	27	7
Stone, p	1	0	0	0	1	1							
Upshaw, p	0	0	0	0	0	0							
Aspromonte, ph	1	0	0	0	0	0							
Totals	35	4	8	4	24	9							

Atlanta	2	0	0	0	2	0	0	0	0 – 4
New York	0	0	1	2	3	1	0	0	x – 7

Atlanta	IP.	H.	R.	ER.	BB.	SO.
Jarvis (Loser)	4⅓	10	6	6	0	6
Stone	1	2	1	1	0	0
Upshaw	2⅔	2	0	0	0	2

New York	IP.	H.	R.	ER.	BB.	SO.
Gentry	2*	5	2	2	1	1
Ryan (Winner)	7	3	2	2	2	7

*Pitched to three batters in third.

Error—Millan. Double play—Atlanta 1. Left on bases—Atlanta 7, New York 6. Two-base hits—Cepeda, Agee, H. Aaron, Kranepool, Jones, Grote. Home runs—H. Aaron, Agee, Boswell, Cepeda, Garrett. Sacrifice hit—Harrelson. Umpires—Sudol, Vargo, Pelekoudas, Steiner, Barlick and Donatelli. Time of game—2:24. Attendance—53,195.

NEW YORK METS' BATTING AND FIELDING AVERAGES

Player–Position	G.	AB.	R.	H.	TB.	2B.	3B.	HR.	RBI.	B.A.	PO.	A.	E.	F.A.
Shamsky, rf	3	13	3	7	7	0	0	0	1	.538	3	0	0	1.000
Ryan, p	1	4	1	2	2	0	0	0	0	.500	1	0	0	1.000
Martin, ph	2	2	0	1	1	0	0	0	2	.500	0	0	0	.000
Jones, lf	3	14	4	6	11	2	0	1	4	.429	11	0	0	1.000
Garrett, 3b	3	13	3	5	10	2	0	1	3	.385	1	6	0	1.000
Agee, cf	3	14	4	5	12	1	0	2	4	.357	9	0	0	1.000
Boswell, 2b	3	12	4	4	10	0	0	2	5	.333	3	2	1	.833
Kranepool, 1b	3	12	2	3	4	1	0	0	1	.250	20	3	0	1.000
Harrelson, ss	3	11	2	2	5	1	1	0	3	.182	6	6	1	.923
Grote, c	3	12	3	2	3	1	0	0	1	.167	22	1	0	1.000
Gaspar, rf-pr	3	0	0	0	0	0	0	0	0	.000	2	0	0	1.000
McGraw, p	1	0	0	0	0	0	0	0	0	.000	0	0	0	.000
Gentry, p	1	0	0	0	0	0	0	0	0	.000	0	0	0	.000
Taylor, p	2	0	0	0	0	0	0	0	0	.000	1	0	0	1.000
Weis, pr-2b	3	1	0	0	0	0	0	0	0	.000	1	3	0	1.000
Koosman, p	1	2	1	0	0	0	0	0	0	.000	0	1	0	1.000
Seaver, p	1	3	0	0	0	0	0	0	0	.000	1	1	0	1.000
Totals	3	113	27	37	65	8	1	6	24	.327	81	23	2	.981

ATLANTA BRAVES' BATTING AND FIELDING AVERAGES

Player–Position	G.	AB.	R.	H.	TB.	2B.	3B.	HR.	RBI.	B.A.	PO.	A.	E.	F.A.
Lum, lf-ph	2	2	0	2	3	1	0	0	0	1.000	0	0	0	.000
Cepeda, 1b	3	11	2	5	10	2	0	1	3	.455	29	1	2	.938
H. Aaron, rf	3	14	3	5	16	2	0	3	7	.357	4	1	1	.833
Gonzalez, cf	3	14	4	5	9	1	0	1	2	.357	3	1	1	.800
Millan, 2b	3	12	2	4	5	1	0	0	0	.333	3	9	1	.923
Carty, lf	3	10	4	3	5	2	0	0	0	.300	3	0	0	1.000
Garrido, ss	3	10	0	2	2	0	0	0	0	.200	4	8	0	1.000
Boyer, 3b	3	9	0	1	1	0	0	0	3	.111	4	8	1	.923
Tillman, c	1	0	0	0	0	0	0	0	0	.000	2	0	0	1.000
Reed, p	1	0	0	0	0	0	0	0	0	.000	0	1	0	1.000
Jackson, ss	1	0	0	0	0	0	0	0	0	.000	0	0	0	.000
Doyle, p	1	0	0	0	0	0	0	0	0	.000	0	0	0	.000
Britton, p	1	0	0	0	0	0	0	0	0	.000	0	0	0	.000
Neibauer, p	1	0	0	0	0	0	0	0	0	.000	0	0	0	.000
Stone, p	1	1	0	0	0	0	0	0	0	.000	1	1	0	1.000
Upshaw, p	1	1	0	0	0	0	0	0	0	.000	0	1	0	1.000
T. Aaron, ph	1	1	0	0	0	0	0	0	0	.000	0	0	0	.000
Alou, ph	1	1	0	0	0	0	0	0	0	.000	0	0	0	.000
Pappas, p	1	1	0	0	0	0	0	0	0	.000	0	0	0	.000
Jarvis, p	1	2	0	0	0	0	0	0	0	.000	1	2	0	1.000
Aspromonte, ph	3	3	0	0	0	0	0	0	0	.000	0	0	0	.000
Niekro, p	1	3	0	0	0	0	0	0	0	.000	0	3	0	1.000
Didier, c	3	11	0	0	0	0	0	0	0	.000	24	1	0	1.000
Totals	3	106	15	27	51	9	0	5	15	.255	78	37	6	.950

NEW YORK METS' PITCHING RECORDS

Pitcher	G.	GS.	CG.	IP.	H.	R.	ER.	BB.	SO.	HB.	WP.	W.	L.	Pct.	ERA.
Taylor	2	0	0	3⅓	3	0	0	0	4	0	0	1	0	1.000	0.00
McGraw	1	0	0	3	1	0	0	1	1	0	0	0	0	.000	0.00
Ryan	1	0	0	7	3	2	2	2	7	0	0	1	0	1.000	2.57
Seaver	1	1	0	7	8	5	5	3	2	1	0	1	0	1.000	6.43
Gentry	1	1	0	2	5	2	2	1	1	0	0	0	0	.000	9.00
Koosman	1	1	0	4⅔	7	6	6	4	5	0	0	0	0	.000	11.57
Totals	3	3	0	27	27	15	15	11	20	1	0	3	0	1.000	5.00

Saves–Taylor, McGraw. No shutouts.

ATLANTA BRAVES' PITCHING RECORDS

Pitcher	G.	GS.	CG.	IP.	H.	R.	ER.	BB.	SO.	HB.	WP.	W.	L.	Pct.	ERA.
Neibauer	1	0	0	1	0	0	0	0	1	0	0	0	0	.000	0.00
Doyle	1	0	0	1	2	2	0	1	3	0	0	0	0	.000	0.00
Britton	1	0	0	⅓	0	0	0	1	0	0	0	0	0	.000	0.00
Upshaw	3	0	0	6⅓	5	2	2	1	4	0	0	0	0	.000	2.84
Niekro	1	1	0	8	9	9	4	4	4	0	0	0	1	.000	4.50
Stone	1	0	0	1	2	1	1	0	4	0	0	0	0	.000	9.00
Pappas	1	0	0	2⅓	4	3	3	0	4	0	0	0	0	.000	11.57
Jarvis	1	1	0	4½	10	6	6	0	6	0	0	0	1	.000	12.46
Reed	1	1	0	1⅔	5	4	4	3	3	0	0	0	1	.000	21.60
Totals	3	3	0	26	37	27	20	10	25	0	0	0	3	.000	6.92

No shutouts or saves.

COMPOSITE SCORE BY INNINGS

	1	2	3	4	5	6	7	8	9	
New York	1	5	3	6	4	1	2	5	0	– 27
Atlanta	2	1	2	1	8	0	1	0	0	– 15

Sacrifice hit–Harrelson.
Sacrifice fly–Boyer.
Stolen bases–Cepeda, Jones 2, Garrett, Agee 2.
Caught stealing–Kranepool.

Double plays—Garrido, Millan and Cepeda; Upshaw, Garrido and Cepeda; Didier and Boyer; Javis and Garrido; Harrelson, Boswell and Kranepool; Weis, Harrelson and Kranepool.
Hit by pitcher—By Seaver (Cepeda).
Passed balls—Didier, Grote.
Balks—None.
Left on bases—New York 19–3, 10, 6; Atlanta 23–9, 7, 7.
Time of games—First game, 2:37; second game, 3:10; third game, 2:24.
Attendance—First game, 50,122; second game, 50,270; third game, 53,195.
Umpires—Barlick, Donatelli, Sudol, Vargo, Pelekoudas, and Steiner.
Official scorers—Jack Lang, Long Island Press; Wayne Minshew, Atlanta Consititution.

AMERICAN LEAGUE
Championship Series of 1970

	W.	L.	Pct.
Baltimore (East)	3	0	1.000
Minnesota (West)	0	3	.000

Sweeping success was once more the name of the game for the Baltimore Orioles in the 1970 American League Championship Series.

And for the Minnesota Twins, it was again dismal defeat in three games.

For Manager Earl Weaver's Baltimore brigade, which won a total of 217 games in two seasons, the playoff sweep was a continuation of their winning ways in the regular A. L. campaign, which finished with 11 consecutive victories.

The Twins enjoyed the lead only once, a 1-0 edge in the first inning of the opening game. Their only tie was forged one inning later. At all other points, the Baltimore behemoths dominated action.

Mike Cuellar, half of Baltimore's 24-win duo, received the Oriole opening game assignment in the Twin Cities. Although staked to an early 9-3 lead, the Cuban lefthander was unable to attain maximum efficiency on the cool and windy afternoon and departed in the fifth inning. Dick Hall, 40-year-old relief specialist, allowed only one hit in the final 4⅔ innings to pick up the victory.

With the teams deadlocked, 2-2, the Orioles put the game beyond Minnesota's reach in the fourth inning, aided considerably by Cuellar's bat and the lusty blasts of a strong wind blowing across Metropolitan Stadium from right field.

Two singles and Brooks Robinson's sacrifice fly produced one fourth-inning run off Jim Perry, the Twins' 24-game winner, and the Orioles then loaded the bases with one out.

The lefthanded-hitting Cuellar, with an .089 batting average and seven RBIs to show for his season's efforts, then pulled a Perry pitch toward foul territory in right field. As the ball passed first base it was patently foul, maybe as much as 15 feet. Cuellar himself stood transfixed at the plate, watching the pellet transcribe a high parabola in the direction of the right-field seats.

As the ball soared into the 29-mile-an-hour current, however, it started drifting toward fair territory. Cuellar started jogging from the plate. By the time he arrived at first base, the wind had worked its deviltry against the home forces, depositing the ball over the fence in fair territory, and giving Cuellar a grand-slam homer.

Before the inning was completed, Don Buford cuffed Perry for a knock-out homer and Bill Zepp yielded a left-field round-tripper to southpaw-swinging Boog Powell to complete the seven-run outburst.

Dave McNally, who registered a ten-inning, 1-0 three-hitter in the second game of the 1969 playoffs, received the second-game assignment again and once more responded with victory, although with considerably more ease.

The Birds handed McNally a four-run cushion. Powell doubled home Mark Belanger in the first inning, Frank Robinson homered with Belanger aboard in the third and McNally himself singled home Andy Etchebarren in the fourth.

The Twins nearly erased that lead with two swings of the bat in their turn, Killebrew connecting for a homer after a pass to Leo Cardenas and Tony Oliva hitting a solo smash.

Stan Williams, following Tom Hall and Bill Zepp to the mound, blanked Baltimore the next three frames and Ron Perranoski zeroed the visitors in the eighth before the East Division champs erupted for their second seven-run rally in the series.

McNally's bat ignited the conflagration with a wrong-field double and Dave Johnson concluded it with a three-run homer. All the Birds except Blair participated in the 13-hit feast, Belanger and Powell accounting for three apiece.

When the series shifted to Baltimore on October 5, Weaver called on his workhorse, Jim Palmer, to wrap it all up.

The big righthander, just ten days short of his twenty-fifth birthday and two years removed from an arm ailment that threatened his career, was razor-sharp, scattering seven hits.

In fairness, Palmer was entitled to a shutout. A brilliant sun blinded Frank Robinson while he was tracking down Cesar Tovar's fifth-inning fly that fell for a single. Cardenas' single produced a run, but that was all for the Twins.

A 20-game winner with a 2.71 ERA in regular play, Palmer set a personal career high of 12 strikeouts and issued only three walks.

He also laced a double and figured prominently in the second-inning Oriole run when his looper to short center field was misplayed for a two-base error. Palmer subsequently scored on Buford's double.

The Minnesota starting assignment went to Jim Kaat, a 14-game winner who had been handicapped by late-season arm miseries. The lefthander departed with none out in the third after yielding six hits. By that time the trend of the game had been established and three successors, while more effective, were helpless to change the outcome, the Birds cruising to an easy 6-1 victory.

Two singles, around a sacrifice, netted one Oriole run in the opening frame and Palmer made the score 2-0 in the second. A double by Brooks Robinson and Johnson's single shelled Kaat in the third. With 19-year-old Bert Blyleven on duty, Etchebarren grounded to Cardenas. The shortstop's throw to the plate was in time, but Robbie's crunching slide dislodged the ball from Paul Ratliff's mitt. Palmer's double made the score, 4-0, and Buford's sacrifice fly plated a fifth run.

Johnson's second homer of the series concluded the scoring in the seventh inning.

GAME OF SATURDAY, OCTOBER 3, AT MINNESOTA

Baltimore	AB.	R.	H.	RBI.	PO.	A.	Minnesota	AB.	R.	H.	RBI.	PO.	A.
Buford, lf	3	1	1	1	0	0	Tovar, cf-2b	5	1	2	1	1	0
Blair, cf	5	0	0	0	3	0	Cardenas, ss	4	0	0	0	2	5
Powell, 1b	5	1	2	2	10	1	Killebrew, 3b	5	1	2	2	1	1
F. Robinson, rf	4	1	1	0	0	0	Oliva, rf	4	1	3	0	3	0
B. Robinson, 3b	3	1	3	1	2	1	Alyea, lf	3	1	0	0	0	0
Johnson, 2b	3	1	1	0	4	2	Reese, 1b	4	0	0	0	10	1
Belanger, ss	4	1	1	1	2	5	Mitterwald, c	4	2	3	2	7	1
Cuellar, p	2	1	1	4	1	3	Thompson, 2b	3	0	1	0	1	3
Hall, p	2	1	1	0	0	0	Williams, p	0	0	0	0	0	0
Hendricks, c	5	2	2	0	5	0	Holt, ph-cf	1	0	0	0	0	0
							Perry, p	1	0	0	1	1	0
							Zepp, p	0	0	0	0	0	0
							Allison, ph	1	0	0	0	0	0
							Woodson, p	0	0	0	0	0	0
							Quilici, 2b	1	0	0	0	1	1
							Carew, ph	1	0	0	0	0	0
							Perranoski, p	0	0	0	0	0	0
Totals	36	10	13	9	27	12	Totals	37	6	11	6	27	12

```
Baltimore ..................................... 0   2   0   7   0   1   0   0   0 – 10
Minnesota ..................................... 1   1   0   1   3   0   0   0   0 –  6
```

Baltimore	IP.	H.	R.	ER.	BB.	SO.
Cuellar	4⅓	10	6	6	1	2
Hall (Winner)	4⅔	1	0	0	0	3

Minnesota	IP.	H.	R.	ER.	BB.	SO.
Perry (Loser)	3⅓	8	8	7	1	1
Zepp	⅔	1	1	1	0	2
Woodson	1*	2	1	1	1	0
Williams	3	2	0	0	1	1
Perranoski	1	0	0	0	0	2

*Pitched to two batters in sixth.

Errors—Thompson, Killebrew. Double plays—Baltimore 1, Minnesota 3. Left on bases—Baltimore 4, Minnesota 6. Two-base hits—Thompson, Oliva 2, B. Robinson. Home runs—Cuellar, Buford, Powell, Killebrew. Sacrifice hit—Cardenas. Sacrifice fly—B. Robinson. Hit by pitcher—By Perry (Johnson). Umpires—Stevens, Deegan, Satchell and Berry. Time—2:36. Attendance—26,847.

GAME OF SUNDAY, OCTOBER 4, AT MINNESOTA

Baltimore	AB.	R.	H.	RBI.	PO.	A.	Minnesota	AB.	R.	H.	RBI.	PO.	A.
Belanger, ss	4	3	3	0	1	5	Tovar, cf-lf	4	0	1	0	2	0
Blair, cf	4	0	0	0	0	0	Cardenas, ss	3	1	1	0	4	3
F. Robinson, rf	3	2	1	2	1	0	Killebrew, 1b	3	1	1	2	7	0
Powell, 1b	5	1	3	3	9	0	Oliva, rf	4	1	1	1	4	2
Rettenmund, lf	3	1	1	1	3	1	Alyea, lf	3	0	0	0	0	0
B. Robinson, 3b	5	1	1	0	1	4	Holt, pr-cf	0	0	0	0	0	0
Johnson, 2b	5	1	1	3	5	1	Mitterwald, c	4	0	1	0	9	0
Etchebarren, c	5	1	1	0	7	0	Renick, 3b	4	0	1	0	1	3
McNally, p	5	1	2	1	0	0	Thompson, 2b	4	0	0	0	0	0
Totals	39	11	13	10	27	11	Hall, p	1	0	0	0	0	0
							Zepp, p	0	0	0	0	0	0
							Williams, p	0	0	0	0	0	0
							Allison, ph	0	0	0	0	0	0
							Perranoski, p	0	0	0	0	0	1
							Tiant, p	0	0	0	0	0	0
							Quilici, ph	1	0	0	0	0	0
							Totals	31	3	6	3	27	9

Baltimore	1	0	2	1	0	0	0	0	7 – 11
Minnesota	0	0	0	3	0	0	0	0	0 – 3

Baltimore	IP.	H.	R.	ER.	BB.	SO.
McNally (Winner)	9	6	3	3	5	5

Minnesota	IP.	H.	R.	ER.	BB.	SO.
Hall (Loser)	3⅓	6	4	4	3	4
Zepp	⅔*	1	0	0	2	0
Williams	3	0	0	0	0	1
Perranoski	1⅓	5	5	5	1	1
Tiant	⅔	1	2	1	0	0

*Pitched to three batters in fifth.

Errors—Cardenas 2. Double plays—Baltimore 1, Minnesota 2. Left on bases—Baltimore 7, Minnesota 6. Two-base hits—Powell 2, Mitterwald, McNally. Home runs—F. Robinson, Killebrew, Oliva, Johnson. Stolen base—Rettenmund. Umpires—Haller, Odom, Neudecker, Honochick, Goetz and Springstead. Time—2:59. Attendance—27,490.

GAME OF MONDAY, OCTOBER 5, AT BALTIMORE

Minnesota	AB.	R.	H.	RBI.	PO.	A.	Baltimore	AB.	R.	H.	RBI.	PO.	A.
Tovar, lf	4	1	2	0	3	0	Buford, lf	4	1	2	2	2	0
Cardenas, ss	4	0	1	1	0	3	Blair, cf	4	0	1	0	1	0
Oliva, rf	4	0	2	0	3	0	F. Robinson, rf	3	0	0	0	1	0
Killebrew, 3b	3	0	0	0	0	3	Powell, 1b	4	0	1	1	5	0
Holt, cf	4	0	0	0	3	0	B. Robinson, 3b	4	1	3	0	0	0
Ratliff, c	4	0	1	0	7	0	Johnson, 2b	3	2	2	1	2	1
Reese, 1b	3	0	1	0	6	1	Etchebarren, c	4	0	0	0	12	0
Tiant, pr	0	0	0	0	0	0	Belanger, ss	4	1	0	0	3	4
Thompson, 2b	1	0	0	0	1	0	Palmer, p	4	1	1	1	1	1
Allison, ph	1	0	0	0	0	0	Totals	34	6	10	5	27	6
Quilici, 2b	0	0	0	0	0	0							
Alyea, ph	1	0	0	0	0	0							
Kaat, p	1	0	0	0	0	0							
Blyleven, p	0	0	0	0	1	0							
Manuel, ph	1	0	0	0	0	0							
Hall, p	0	0	0	0	0	0							
Carew, ph	1	0	0	0	0	0							
Perry, p	0	0	0	0	0	0							
Renick, ph	1	0	0	0	0	0							
Totals	33	1	7	1	24	7							

Minnesota	0	0	0	0	1	0	0	0	0 – 1
Baltimore	1	1	3	0	0	0	1	0	x – 6

Minnesota	IP.	H.	R.	ER.	BB.	SO.
Kaat (Loser)	2*	6	4	2	2	1
Blyleven	2	2	1	0	0	2
Hall	2	0	0	0	1	2
Perry	2	2	1	1	0	2

Baltimore	IP.	H.	R.	ER.	BB.	SO.
Palmer (Winner)	9	7	1	1	3	12

*Pitched to two batters in third.

Errors—Holt, Ratliff. Double play—Baltimore 1. Left on bases—Minnesota 8, Baltimore 9. Two-base hits—Buford, B. Robinson, Palmer. Three-base hit—Tovar. Home run—Johnson. Sacrifice hit—Blair. Sacrifice fly—Buford. Umpires—Odom, Neudecker, Springstead, Honochick, Haller and Goetz. Time—2:20. Attendance—27,608.

BALTIMORE ORIOLES' BATTING AND FIELDING AVERAGES

Player–Position	G.	AB.	R.	H.	TB.	2B.	3B.	HR.	RBI.	B.A.	PO.	A.	E.	F.A.
B. Robinson, 3b	3	12	3	7	9	2	0	0	1	.583	3	5	0	1.000
Cuellar, p	1	2	1	1	4	0	0	1	4	.500	1	3	0	1.000
R. Hall, p	1	2	1	1	1	0	0	0	0	.500	0	0	0	.000
Powell, 1b	3	14	2	6	11	2	0	1	6	.429	24	1	0	1.000
Buford, lf	2	7	2	3	7	1	0	1	3	.429	2	0	0	1.000
Hendricks, c	1	5	2	2	2	0	0	0	0	.400	5	0	0	1.000
McNally, p	1	5	1	2	3	1	0	0	1	.400	0	0	0	.000
Johnson, 2b	3	11	4	4	10	0	0	2	4	.364	11	4	0	1.000
Belanger, ss	3	12	5	4	4	0	0	0	1	.333	6	14	0	1.000
Rettenmund, lf	1	3	1	1	1	0	0	0	1	.333	3	1	0	1.000
Palmer, p	1	4	1	1	2	1	0	0	1	.250	1	1	0	1.000
F. Robinson, rf	3	10	3	2	5	0	0	1	2	.200	2	0	0	1.000
Etchebarren, c	2	9	1	1	1	0	0	0	0	.111	19	0	0	1.000
Blair, cf	3	13	0	1	1	0	0	0	0	.077	4	0	0	1.000
Totals	3	109	27	36	61	7	0	6	24	.330	81	29	0	1.000

MINNESOTA TWINS' BATTING AND FIELDING AVERAGES

Player–Position	G.	AB.	R.	H.	TB.	2B.	3B.	HR.	RBI.	B.A.	PO.	A.	E.	F.A.
Oliva, rf	3	12	2	6	11	2	0	1	1	.500	10	2	0	1.000
Mitterwald, c	2	8	2	4	5	1	0	0	2	.500	16	1	0	1.000
Tovar, cf-2b-lf	3	13	2	5	7	0	1	0	1	.385	6	0	0	1.000
Killebrew, 3b-1b	3	11	2	3	9	0	0	2	4	.273	8	4	1	.923
Ratliff, c	1	4	0	1	1	0	0	0	0	.250	7	0	1	.875
Renick, 3b-ph	2	5	0	1	1	0	0	0	0	.200	1	3	0	1.000
Cardenas, ss	3	11	1	2	2	0	0	0	1	.182	6	11	2	.895
Reese, 1b	2	7	0	1	1	0	0	0	0	.143	16	2	0	1.000
Thompson, 2b	3	8	0	1	2	1	0	0	0	.125	2	3	1	.833
Blyleven, p	1	0	0	0	0	0	0	0	0	.000	1	0	0	1.000
Perranoski, p	2	0	0	0	0	0	0	0	0	.000	0	1	0	1.000
Tiant, p-pr	2	0	0	0	0	0	0	0	0	.000	0	0	0	.000
Williams, p	2	0	0	0	0	0	0	0	0	.000	0	0	0	.000
Woodson, p	1	0	0	0	0	0	0	0	0	.000	0	0	0	.000
Zepp, p	2	0	0	0	0	0	0	0	0	.000	0	0	0	.000
T. Hall, p	2	1	0	0	0	0	0	0	0	.000	0	0	0	.000
Kaat, p	1	1	0	0	0	0	0	0	0	.000	0	0	0	.000
Manuel, ph	1	1	0	0	0	0	0	0	0	.000	0	0	0	.000
Perry, p	2	1	0	0	0	0	0	0	1	.000	1	0	0	1.000
Allison, ph	3	2	0	0	0	0	0	0	0	.000	0	0	0	.000
Carew, ph	2	2	0	0	0	0	0	0	0	.000	0	0	0	.000
Quilici, 2b-ph	3	2	0	0	0	0	0	0	0	.000	1	1	0	1.000
Holt, ph-cf-pr	3	5	0	0	0	0	0	0	0	.000	3	0	1	.750
Alyea, lf-ph	3	7	1	0	0	0	0	0	0	.000	0	0	0	.000
Totals	3	101	10	24	39	4	1	3	10	.238	78	28	6	.946

BALTIMORE ORIOLES' PITCHING RECORDS

Pitcher	G.	GS.	CG.	IP.	H.	R.	ER.	BB.	SO.	HB.	WP.	W.	L.	Pct.	ERA.
R. Hall	1	0	0	4⅔	1	0	0	0	3	0	0	1	0	1.000	0.00
Palmer	1	1	1	9	7	1	1	3	12	0	0	1	0	1.000	1.00
McNally	1	1	1	9	6	3	3	5	5	0	0	1	0	1.000	3.00
Cuellar	1	1	0	4⅓	10	6	6	1	2	0	0	0	0	.000	12.46
Totals	3	3	2	27	24	10	10	9	22	0	0	3	0	1.000	3.33

No shutouts or saves.

MINNESOTA TWINS' PITCHING RECORDS

Pitcher	G.	GS.	CG.	IP.	H.	R.	ER.	BB.	SO.	HB.	WP.	W.	L.	Pct.	ERA.
Williams	2	0	0	6	2	0	0	1	2	0	0	0	0	.000	0.00
Blyleven	1	0	0	2	2	1	0	0	2	0	0	0	0	.000	0.00
T. Hall	2	1	0	5⅓	6	4	4	4	6	0	0	0	1	.000	6.75
Zepp	2	0	0	1⅓	2	1	1	2	2	0	0	0	0	.000	6.75
Kaat	1	1	0	2	6	4	2	2	1	0	0	0	1	.000	9.00
Woodson	1	0	0	1	2	1	1	1	0	0	0	0	0	.000	9.00
Perry	2	1	0	5⅓	10	9	8	1	3	1	0	0	1	.000	13.50
Tiant	1	0	0	⅔	1	2	1	0	0	0	0	0	0	.000	13.50
Perranoski	2	0	0	2⅓	5	5	5	1	3	0	0	0	0	.000	19.29
Totals	3	3	0	26	36	27	22	12	19	1	0	0	3	.000	7.62

No shutouts or saves.

COMPOSITE SCORE BY INNINGS

Baltimore	2	3	5	8	0	1	1	0	7 – 27
Minnesota	1	1	0	4	4	0	0	0	0 – 10

Sacrifice hits–Cardenas, Blair.
Sacrifice flies–B. Robinson, Buford.
Stolen base–Rettenmund.
Caught stealing–None.
Double plays–Johnson, Belanger and Powell 2; Belanger, Johnson and Powell; Thompson, Cardenas and Reese; Reese, Mitterwald and Reese; Cardenas, Quilici and Reese; Oliva and Mitterwald; Perranoski, Cardenas and Killebrew.
Hit by pitcher–By Perry (Johnson).
Passed balls–None.
Balks–None.

Left on bases—Baltimore 20—4, 7, 9; Minnesota 20—6, 6, 8.
Time of games—First game, 2:36; second game, 2:59; third game, 2:20.
Attendance—First game, 26,847; second game, 27,490; third game, 27,608.
Umpires—Stevens, Deegan, Satchell and Berry (first game); Haller, Odom, Neudecker, Honochick, Goetz and Springstead (second and third games).
Official scorers—Tom Briere, Minneapolis Tribune; Phil Jackman, Baltimore Evening Sun.

NATIONAL LEAGUE
Championship Series of 1970

	W.	L.	Pct.
Cincinnati (West)	3	0	1.000
Pittsburgh (East)	0	3	.000

A potent attack and a question-mark pitching staff. That was the consensus view of the Cincnnati Reds as the 1970 National League Championship Series began in Pittsburgh's Three Rivers Stadium October 3. Two days later, it was all over. The Reds reigned as National League champions, but not because of their menacing bats. It was that shaky pitching staff which carried the Reds to three successive victories over the Pirates.

Cincinnati sluggers had whacked 191 home runs in cruising to the West Division title by 14½ games. East Division champ Pittsburgh wasn't that easy for the Reds, despite their three-game sweep. The Reds had all they could handle in each conquest, particularly the finale, in which the Pirates repeatedly threatened but could not deliver.

Cincinnati boasted dual heroes in subduing the Pirates, 3-0, in 10 innings in the playoff opener. Gary Nolan, an 18-game winner during the regular season, pitched nine shutout innings to edge Dock Ellis. Nolan departed for pinch-hitter Ty Cline in the 10th, which turned out to be a stroke of genius by Reds Manager Sparky Anderson. Cline socked a triple to lead off the inning. He scored the decisive run on Pete Rose's single, and Lee May doubled to provide two insurance tallies, sealing Ellis' fate. Reliever Clay Carroll protected Nolan's victory by holding Pittsburgh hitless in the 10th.

Another key contributor to the Reds' opening triumph was second baseman Tommy Helms. With Pirate runners on second and third and two out in the third inning, Dave Cash rifled a shot to Helms' right. Helms' diving stop and quick throw to first prevented two Buc runs.

Four minor league umpires worked the opener while the regularly assigned arbiters (and several others) picketed the Pittsburgh park. The umps were striking for higher pay in the pennant playoffs and World Series. An hour before game two was scheduled to start, the striking umps reached an agreement with the major leagues and returned to work.

The Reds didn't cut it quite as close in game two. They led from the third inning on, but never by much, in posting a 3-1 victory. Pittsburgh's chief tormentors in this one were Bobby Tolan, the swift center fielder, and Don Gullett, 19-year-old fireballing reliever.

Tolan was a complete mystery to Buc starter Luke Walker. Bobby began his three-hit salvo with a single in the third inning. He stole second base and wound up at third on catcher Manny Sanguillen's wild peg into center field. Walker's wild pitch permitted Tolan to score. Bobby delivered his kayo punch in the fifth, belting a home run over the wall in right-center, and capped his big day with a single off reliever Dave Giusti in the eighth.

Lefty Jim Merritt, Cincinnati's lone 20-game winner, was the second-game starter. Arm trouble had kept Merritt on the shelf in the closing weeks of the regular season, but Manager Anderson had precedent going for him in this case. Merritt had beaten the Pirates six times in six starts over a two-year period. He made it seven for seven by lasting 5⅓ innings this time. Carroll relieved Merritt in the sixth, but gave up two hits and had retired only one batter when Anderson signaled for Gullett.

That did it. Gullett shut off the Pirate threat immediately, striking out the side in the seventh and finishing with 3⅓ hitless rounds.

When the scene shifted to Cincinnati for game three, the Reds wrapped it up, 3-2, but not without a struggle. The Pirates scored a run in the first inning off Tony Cloninger, who averted disaster three times before Anderson finally yanked him for a pinch-hitter in the fifth with the score 2-2.

The slugging Reds uncorked their only power show of the playoffs in the first inning, Tony Perez and Bench smacking successive homers off Bob Moose. Pirate starter Moose showed more courage than stuff in the early going. But he hung on and proceeded to halt the Reds until he had two out in the eighth. Then he walked pinch-hitter Cline and gave up a single to Rose.

With Tolan coming up, Pirate Manager Danny Murtaugh brought in lefty Joe Gibbon. Tolan whacked a single to left. Cline took off from second and sped for the plate. He arrived just a hair ahead of Willie Stargell's peg, and the Reds had a 3-2 lead.

The Reds had a pitching star in this one, too, young Milt Wilcox, who worked three shutout innings in relief of Cloninger and earned the victory. Wilcox vanished for pinch-hitter Cline in the eighth. Wayne Granger tried to protect the Reds' 3-2 lead in the ninth, but was removed with two down and a runner on first. Gullett was Anderson's choice to wrap it up. The teen-ager wasn't invincible this time, yielding a single to Stargell. But with runners on first and third, Al Oliver swung at Gullett's first pitch and grounded to Helms.

GAME OF SATURDAY, OCTOBER 3, AT PITTSBURGH

Cincinnati	AB.	R.	H.	RBI.	PO.	A.
Rose, rf	5	1	2	1	1	0
Tolan, cf	5	0	1	0	2	0
Perez, 3b-1b	4	0	1	0	1	1
Bench, c	3	1	0	0	8	3
May, 1b	5	0	1	2	9	0
Concepcion, pr-ss	0	0	0	0	0	0
Carbo, lf	3	0	0	0	0	0
McRae, ph	1	0	0	0	0	0
Carroll, p	0	0	0	0	0	0
Helms, 2b	4	0	2	0	5	5
Woodward, ss-3b	4	0	0	0	4	4
Nolan, p	3	0	1	0	0	2
Cline, ph-lf	1	1	1	0	0	0
Totals	38	3	9	3	30	15

Pittsburgh	AB.	R.	H.	RBI.	PO.	A.
Alou, cf	3	0	2	0	4	0
Cash, 2b	5	0	0	0	3	3
Clemente, rf	5	0	0	0	3	0
Stargell, lf	4	0	3	0	2	0
Jeter, pr-lf	1	0	0	0	2	0
Oliver, 1b	3	0	0	0	10	0
Sanguillen, c	4	0	1	0	2	0
Hebner, 3b	4	0	2	0	0	2
Alley, ss	3	0	0	0	4	3
Ellis, p	2	0	0	0	0	3
Gibbon, p	0	0	0	0	0	0
Totals	34	0	8	0	30	11

Cincinnati	0	0	0	0	0	0	0	0	0	3 – 3
Pittsburgh	0	0	0	0	0	0	0	0	0	0 – 0

Cincinnati	IP.	H.	R.	ER.	BB.	SO.
Nolan (Winner)	9	8	0	0	4	6
Carroll (Save)	1	0	0	0	0	2

Pittsburgh	IP.	H.	R.	ER.	BB.	SO.
Ellis (Loser)	9⅔	9	3	3	4	1
Gibbon	⅓	0	0	0	0	1

Errors—None. Double play—Pittsburgh 1. Left on bases—Cincinnati 9, Pittsburgh 10. Two-base hits—Alou, Perez, Stargell, May. Three-base hit—Cline. Sacrifice hits—Ellis 2. Umpires—Grimsley. Blandford, Morgenweck and Grygiel. Time—2:23. Attendance—33,088.

GAME OF SUNDAY, OCTOBER 4, AT PITTSBURGH

Cincinnati	AB.	R.	H.	RBI.	PO.	A.
Rose, rf	4	0	0	0	2	0
Tolan, cf	4	3	3	1	2	0
Perez, 3b	4	0	2	1	2	3
Concepcion, ss	0	0	0	0	1	1
Bench, c	3	0	0	0	5	0
May, 1b	4	0	1	0	10	0
McRae, ph	3	0	0	0	2	0
Carroll, p	0	0	0	0	0	0
Gullett, p	1	0	0	0	0	0
Helms, 2b	4	0	1	0	3	3
Woodward, ss-3b	3	0	1	0	0	2
Merritt, p	2	0	0	0	0	2
Stewart, lf	2	0	0	0	0	0
Totals	34	3	8	2	27	11

Pittsburgh	AB.	R.	H.	RBI.	PO.	A.
Alou, cf	4	0	0	0	1	0
Cash, 2b	3	1	1	0	3	5
Clemente, rf	4	0	1	1	2	0
Sanguillen, c	4	0	1	0	6	0
Robertson, 1b	4	0	1	0	11	1
Stargell, lf	4	0	0	0	1	0
Pagan, 3b	3	0	1	0	0	4
Alley, ss	4	0	0	0	2	4
Walker, p	2	0	0	0	0	0
Jeter, ph	1	0	0	0	0	0
Giusti, p	0	0	0	0	1	0
Totals	33	1	5	1	27	14

| Cincinnati | 0 | 0 | 1 | 0 | 1 | 0 | 0 | 1 | 0 – 3 |
| Pittsburgh | 0 | 0 | 0 | 0 | 0 | 1 | 0 | 0 | 0 – 1 |

Cincinnati	IP.	H.	R.	ER.	BB.	SO.
Merritt (Winner)	5⅓	3	1	1	0	2
Carroll	⅓	2	0	0	0	0
Gullett (Save)	3⅓	0	0	0	2	3

Pittsburgh	IP.	H.	R.	ER.	BB.	SO.
Walker (Loser)	7	5	2	1	1	5
Giusti	2	3	1	1	1	0

Errors—Walker, Perez, Sanguillen. Double plays—Pittsburgh 2. Left on bases—Cincinnati 6, Pittsburgh 7. Two-base hits—Robertson, Cash, Perez. Home run—Tolan. Stolen base—Tolan. Wild pitch—Walker. Umpires—Landes, Pryor, Harvey, Engel, Wendelstedt and Colosi. Time—2:10. Attendance—39,317.

GAME OF MONDAY, OCTOBER 5, AT CINCINNATI

Pittsburgh	AB.	R.	H.	RBI.	PO.	A.	Cincinnati	AB.	R.	H.	RBI.	PO.	A.
Patek, ss	3	0	0	0	1	2	Rose, rf	4	0	1	0	0	0
Robertson, ph	1	0	0	0	0	0	Tolan, cf	3	0	1	1	1	0
Alou, cf	5	1	1	0	1	0	Perez, 3b	4	1	1	1	3	2
Clemente, rf	5	1	2	0	2	0	Granger, p	0	0	0	0	0	0
Stargell, lf	4	0	3	1	1	0	Gullett, p	0	0	0	0	0	0
Jeter, pr	0	0	0	0	0	0	Bench, c	3	1	2	1	7	0
Oliver, 1b	5	0	2	1	12	1	May, 1b	3	0	0	0	12	1
Sanguillen, c	4	0	0	0	5	1	Carbo, lf	3	0	0	0	0	0
Hebner, 3b	2	0	2	0	0	2	Helms, 2b	3	0	0	0	3	4
Mazeroski, 2b	2	0	0	0	1	4	Woodward, ss-3b	3	0	0	0	1	3
Moose, p	4	0	0	0	1	2	Cloninger, p	1	0	0	0	0	2
Gibbon, p	0	0	0	0	0	0	Bravo, ph	1	0	0	0	0	0
Giusti, p	0	0	0	0	0	0	Wilcox, p	0	0	0	0	0	1
							Cline, ph	0	1	0	0	0	0
Totals	35	2	10	2	24	12	Concepcion, ss	0	0	0	0	0	0
							Totals	28	3	5	3	27	13

| Pittsburgh | 1 | 0 | 0 | 0 | 1 | 0 | 0 | 0 | 0 – 2 |
| Cincinnati | 2 | 0 | 0 | 0 | 0 | 0 | 0 | 1 | x – 3 |

Pittsburgh	IP.	H.	R.	ER.	BB.	SO.
Moose (Loser)	7⅔	4	3	3	2	4
Gibbon	0*	1	0	0	0	0
Giusti	⅓	0	0	0	0	1

Cincinnati	IP.	H.	R.	ER.	BB.	SO.
Cloninger	5	7	2	2	4	1
Wilcox (Winner)	3	1	0	0	2	5
Granger	⅔	1	0	0	0	0
Gullett (Save)	⅓	1	0	0	0	0

*Pitched to one batter in eighth.

Errors—None. Double play—Cincinnati 1. Left on bases—Pittsburgh 12, Cincinnati 3. Two-base hits—Hebner 2. Home runs—Perez, Bench. Wild pitch—Cloninger. Umpires—Pryor, Harvey, Engel, Wendelstedt, Colosi and Landes. Time—2:38. Attendance—40,538.

CINCINNATI REDS' BATTING AND FIELDING AVERAGES

Player–Position	G.	AB.	R.	H.	TB.	2B.	3B.	HR.	RBI.	B.A.	PO.	A.	E.	F.A.
Cline, ph-lf	2	1	2	1	3	0	1	0	0	1.000	0	0	0	.000
Tolan, cf	3	12	3	5	8	0	0	1	2	.417	5	0	0	1.000
Perez, 3b-1b	3	12	1	4	9	2	0	1	2	.333	6	6	1	.923
Nolan, p	1	3	0	1	1	0	0	0	0	.333	0	2	0	1.000
Helms, 2b	3	11	0	3	3	0	0	0	0	.273	11	12	0	1.000
Rose, rf	3	13	1	3	3	0	0	0	1	.231	3	0	0	1.000
Bench, c	3	9	2	2	5	0	0	1	1	.222	20	3	0	1.000
May, 1b	3	12	0	2	3	1	0	0	2	.167	31	1	0	1.000
Woodward, ss-3b	3	10	0	1	1	0	0	0	0	.100	5	9	0	1.000
Carroll, p	2	0	0	0	0	0	0	0	0	.000	0	0	0	.000
Concepcion, pr-ss	3	0	0	0	0	0	0	0	0	.000	1	1	0	1.000
Granger, p	1	0	0	0	0	0	0	0	0	.000	0	0	0	.000
Wilcox, p	1	0	0	0	0	0	0	0	0	.000	0	1	0	1.000
Bravo, ph	1	1	0	0	0	0	0	0	0	.000	0	0	0	.000
Cloninger, p	1	1	0	0	0	0	0	0	0	.000	0	2	0	1.000
Gullett, p	2	1	0	0	0	0	0	0	0	.000	0	0	0	.000
Merritt, p	1	2	0	0	0	0	0	0	0	.000	0	2	0	1.000
Stewart, lf	1	2	0	0	0	0	0	0	0	.000	0	0	0	.000
McRae, ph-lf	2	4	0	0	0	0	0	0	0	.000	2	0	0	1.000
Carbo, lf	2	6	0	0	0	0	0	0	0	.000	0	0	0	.000
Totals	3	100	9	22	36	3	1	3	8	.220	84	39	1	.992

PITTSBURGH PIRATES' BATTING AND FIELDING AVERAGES

Player–Position	G.	AB.	R.	H.	TB.	2B.	3B.	HR.	RBI.	B.A.	PO.	A.	E.	F.A.
Hebner, 3b	2	6	0	4	6	2	0	0	0	.667	0	4	0	1.000
Stargell, lf	3	12	0	6	7	1	0	0	1	.500	4	0	0	1.000
Pagan, 3b	1	3	0	1	1	0	0	0	0	.333	0	4	0	1.000
Alou, cf	3	12	1	3	4	1	0	0	0	.250	6	0	0	1.000
Oliver, 1b	2	8	0	2	2	0	0	0	1	.250	22	1	0	1.000
Clemente, rf	3	14	1	3	3	0	0	0	1	.214	7	0	0	1.000

Player—Position	G.	AB.	R.	H.	TB.	2B.	3B.	HR.	RBI.	B.A.	PO.	A.	E.	F.A.
Robertson, 1b-ph	2	5	0	1	2	1	0	0	0	.200	11	1	0	1.000
Sanguillen, c	3	12	0	2	2	0	0	0	0	.167	13	1	1	.933
Cash, 2b	2	8	1	1	2	1	0	0	0	.125	6	8	0	1.000
Gibbon, p	2	0	0	0	0	0	0	0	0	.000	0	0	0	.000
Giusti, p	2	0	0	0	0	0	0	0	0	.000	1	0	0	1.000
Ellis, p	1	2	0	0	0	0	0	0	0	.000	0	3	0	1.000
Jeter, pr-lf-ph	3	2	0	0	0	0	0	0	0	.000	2	0	0	1.000
Mazeroski, 2b	1	2	0	0	0	0	0	0	0	.000	1	4	0	1.000
Walker, p	1	2	0	0	0	0	0	0	0	.000	0	0	1	.000
Patek, ss	1	3	0	0	0	0	0	0	0	.000	1	2	0	1.000
Moose, p	1	4	0	0	0	0	0	0	0	.000	1	2	0	1.000
Alley, ss	2	7	0	0	0	0	0	0	0	.000	6	7	0	1.000
Totals	3	102	3	23	29	6	0	0	3	.225	81	37	2	.983

CINCINNATI REDS' PITCHING RECORDS

Pitcher	G.	GS.	CG.	IP.	H.	R.	ER.	BB.	SO.	HB.	WP.	W.	L.	Pct.	ERA.
Nolan	1	1	0	9	8	0	0	4	6	0	0	1	0	1.000	0.00
Gullett	2	0	0	3⅔	1	0	0	2	3	0	0	0	0	.000	0.00
Wilcox	1	0	0	3	1	0	0	2	5	0	0	1	0	1.000	0.00
Carroll	2	0	0	1⅓	2	0	0	0	2	0	0	0	0	.000	0.00
Granger	1	0	0	⅔	1	0	0	0	0	0	0	0	0	.000	0.00
Merritt	1	1	0	5⅓	3	1	1	0	2	0	0	1	0	1.000	1.69
Cloninger	1	1	0	5	7	2	2	4	1	0	1	0	0	.000	3.60
Totals	3	3	0	28	23	3	3	12	19	0	1	3	0	1.000	0.96

Shutout—Nolan-Carroll (combined). Saves—Carroll, Gullett.

PITTSBURGH PIRATES' PITCHING RECORDS

Pitcher	G.	GS.	CG.	IP.	H.	R.	ER.	BB.	SO.	HB.	WP.	W.	L.	Pct.	ERA.
Gibbon	2	0	0	⅓	1	0	0	1	0	0	0	0	0	.000	0.00
Walker	1	1	0	7	5	2	1	1	5	0	1	0	1	.000	1.29
Ellis	1	1	0	9⅔	9	3	3	4	1	0	0	0	1	.000	2.79
Moose	1	1	0	7⅔	4	3	3	2	4	0	0	0	1	.000	3.52
Giusti	2	0	0	2⅓	3	1	1	1	1	0	0	0	0	.000	3.86
Totals	3	3	0	27	22	9	8	8	12	0	1	0	3	.000	2.67

No shutouts or saves.

COMPOSITE SCORE BY INNINGS

Cincinnati	2	0	1	0	1	0	0	2	0	3 – 9
Pittsburgh	1	0	0	0	1	1	0	0	0	0 – 3

Sacrifice hits—Ellis 2.
Stolen base—Tolan.
Caught stealing—Alou, Patek, Tolan.
Double plays—Alley, Cash and Oliver; Alley and Cash; Alley, Cash and Robertson; Perez, Helms and May.
Hit by pitchers—None.
Passed balls—None.
Balks—None.
Left on bases—Cincinnati 18—9, 6, 3; Pittsburgh 29—10, 7, 12.
Time of games—First game, 2:23; second game, 2:10; third game, 2:38.
Attendance—First game, 33,088; second game, 39,317; third game, 40,538.
Umpires—Grimsley, Blandford, Morgenweck and Grygiel (first game); Landes, Pryor, Harvey, Engel, Wendelstedt and Colosi (second and third games).
Official scorers—Charles Feeney, Pittsburgh Post-Gazette; Earl Lawson, Cincinnati Post and Times-Star.

AMERICAN LEAGUE
Championship Series of 1971

	W.	L.	Pct.
Baltimore (East)	3	0	1.000
Oakland (West)	0	3	.000

In 1971, the Orioles' victims were the Oakland A's, who had cruised to the West Division crown as impressively as the Orioles had shattered their Eastern rivals.

Oakland never was in it after seeing ace Vida Blue clubbed for four runs in the seventh inning of the opener October 3 in Baltimore. Blue went into that frame with a 3-1 lead. He emerged a 5-3 loser, and the A's might as well have capitulated then and there. They fell before Mike Cuellar, 5-1, the next day, and the day after that Jim Palmer killed them off, 5-3, in Oakland.

That made it nine victories in nine playoff games for the Orioles, starting in 1969, when they flattened the Minnesota Twins. The Twins came back for another dose of the same in 1970.

Baltimore entered the '71 playoffs with a pitching staff bristling with aces—four 20-game winners. The Orioles were the first to boast that kind of pitching firepower since the 1920 White Sox.

Dave McNally, Cuellar, Palmer and Pat Dobson were Manager Earl Weaver's 20-win artists. McNally defeated Blue in the playoff opener, Cuellar won the second game and Palmer the third. Dobson, despite his 20-8 record, delivered not a single pitch in the playoffs.

The Orioles fired a four-homer salvo, including two by Boog Powell, off Catfish Hunter in game two. Aside from that, Baltimore's noted sluggers were not devastating. Frank Robinson, longtime kingpin of the Oriole offense, made only one hit in 12 trips off Oakland pitching.

McNally, a 20-game winner for the fourth season in a row, survived a rocky start to win the opener. He trailed, 3-0, after 3½ innings, giving up three doubles and a triple. The A's had McNally tottering in the second. With two runs home, a runner on second and none out, second baseman Dick Green came to bat.

It was at this point that A's Manager Dick Williams made the first of several ultra-cautious moves which were to fuel criticism of his playoff strategy. He ordered Green to sacrifice, which put runner Dave Duncan on third with one out.

The next batter was Blue, whose bunting ability is well known. Vida tried to squeeze the run home, but the O's had guessed correctly on what was coming. McNally pitched out and Duncan was nailed in a rundown. Blue proceeded to strike out, and the A's splurge was over.

McNally gave up another run in the fourth, but that ended the A's scoring forays. Meanwhile, 24-game winner Blue yielded just one run and three hits the first six innings.

However, disaster overtook Vida in the very next frame. Frank Robinson led off with a walk and Powell struck out. Brooks Robinson's single sent F. Robby to second, after which Andy Etchebarren's fly to right advanced F. Robby to third.

Now there were runners on first and third with two down, and Blue appeared likely to quell the flurry without damage. After all, he'd beaten the O's twice in two tries during the season. And the next hitter was shortstop Mark Belanger, hardly a nemesis to any pitcher. But Belanger rifled a single to center to score F. Robby and ignite thunderous cheering from the crowd of 42,621.

Then Curt Motton, pinch-hitter hero of a '69 Oriole playoff victory over Minnesota, stepped up to bat for McNally. Curt slammed a double to the left-field corner, plating B. Robby and tying the score. Center fielder Paul Blair followed with the blow that doomed Blue, a two-run double to left.

Reliever Eddie Watt blanked the A's the last two innings and Oakland was one game down. Skipper Williams was subjected to further sharpshooting for his failure to remove Blue, or even visit the mound, during the seventh-inning barrage.

Next day, the A's put it to 20-game winner Hunter to stop the crafty Cuellar, who had won 20 for the third consecutive year.

The Catfish held Baltimore to seven hits, but unfortunately for him, four of them were home runs. Powell walloped two, Brooks Robinson and Ellie Hendricks the others.

Cuellar displayed his usual pitching artistry, a baffling assortment of curves and change-ups which the A's solved for a mere six hits.

Typical of the A's super-cautious approach to their task was an incident in the sixth inning when they were trailing, 2-1. Reggie Jackson led off against Cuellar with a double. Cleanup hitter Tommy Davis was up next and to the surprise of everyone in the park, he bunted. The next two hitters were easy outs. Davis' sacrifice, it turned out, was not ordered by Williams.

Now one game from oblivion, the A's had to send Diego Segui against Palmer in Oakland October 5. Segui got the call in place of Chuck Dobson, Oakland's No. 3 starter, who had a sore elbow.

Palmer's performance was not among his most noteworthy—he permitted three home runs, two of them by the slugging Jackson and the other by Sal Bando. But all three shots were struck with the bases empty, and Palmer had more than enough to pitch Baltimore's pennant clincher for the third straight year.

Loser of his only two starts against Baltimore during the season, Segui reached the fifth inning October 5 with the score 1-1. Then he met his Waterloo. The crusher was Brooks Robinson's two-run single. It came after Williams ordered an intentional pass to Hendricks, loading the bases.

Bando's homer cut the A's deficit to 3-2 in the sixth; but, in the seventh, F. Robby's double and Darold Knowles' wild pitch scored two runs and put Baltimore out of danger.

GAME OF SUNDAY, OCTOBER 3, AT BALTIMORE

Oakland	AB.	R.	H.	RBI.	PO.	A.	Baltimore	AB.	R.	H.	RBI.	PO.	A.
Campaneris, ss	4	0	1	0	0	0	Blair, cf	4	0	1	2	2	0
Rudi, lf	4	0	1	0	2	0	Johnson, 2b	4	1	1	0	1	3
Jackson, rf	4	0	0	0	3	0	Rettenmund, lf	4	0	1	1	3	0
Davis, 1b	4	1	1	0	4	0	F. Robinson, rf	3	1	0	0	2	0
Bando, 3b	4	1	2	0	2	1	Powell, 1b	4	0	1	0	9	1
Mangual, cf	4	1	2	2	2	0	B. Robinson, 3b	3	1	1	0	0	2
Duncan, c	3	0	2	1	9	0	Etchebarren, c	3	0	0	0	7	0
Epstein, ph	1	0	0	0	0	0	Belanger, ss	2	1	1	1	3	4
Green, 2b	1	0	0	0	2	3	McNally, p	2	0	0	0	0	2
Blue, p	3	0	0	0	0	1	Motton, ph	1	0	1	1	0	0
Fingers, p	0	0	0	0	0	0	Palmer, pr	0	1	0	0	0	0
							Watt, p	0	0	0	0	0	1
Totals	32	3	9	3	24	5	Totals	30	5	7	5	27	13

Oakland	0	2	0	1	0	0	0	0	0 – 3
Baltimore	0	0	0	1	0	0	4	0	x – 5

Oakland	IP.	H.	R.	ER.	BB.	SO.
Blue (Loser)	7	7	5	5	2	8
Fingers	1	0	0	0	0	1

Baltimore	IP.	H.	R.	ER.	BB.	SO.
McNally (Winner)	7	7	3	3	1	5
Watt (Save)	2	2	0	0	0	1

Error–Johnson. Double plays–Oakland 1, Baltimore 2. Left on base–Oakland 4, Baltimore 3. Two-base hits–Rudi, Bando, Duncan, Mangual, Johnson, Rettenmund, Motton, Blair, Campaneris. Three-base hit–Mangual. Sacrifice hit–Green. Umpires–Soar, Napp, DiMuro, O'Donnell, Luciano and Kunkel. Time–2:23. Attendance–42,621.

GAME OF MONDAY, OCTOBER 4, AT BALTIMORE

Oakland	AB.	R.	H.	RBI.	PO.	A.	Baltimore	AB.	R.	H.	RBI.	PO.	A.
Campaneris, ss	4	0	1	0	2	3	Buford, lf	3	0	0	0	1	0
Rudi, lf	3	0	0	0	2	0	Blair, cf	0	0	0	0	0	0
Jackson, rf	4	0	1	0	4	1	Johnson, 2b	3	1	0	0	1	1
Davis, 1b	3	0	1	0	4	0	Powell, 1b	4	2	2	3	12	0
Bando, 3b	4	1	1	0	2	0	F. Robinson, rf	4	0	0	0	4	0
Mangual, cf	4	0	0	0	2	0	Rettenmund, cf-lf	4	0	1	0	4	0
Duncan, c	3	0	1	1	6	0	B. Robinson, 3b	3	1	1	1	1	3
Green, 2b	3	0	1	0	2	0	Hendricks, c	3	1	2	1	2	0
Hunter, p	3	0	0	0	0	0	Belanger, ss	3	0	0	0	2	4
Totals	31	1	6	1	24	4	Cuellar, p	3	0	1	0	0	2
							Totals	30	5	7	5	27	10

Oakland	0	0	0	1	0	0	0	0	0 – 1
Baltimore	0	1	1	0	0	0	1	2	x – 5

Oakland	IP.	H.	R.	ER.	BB.	SO.
Hunter (Loser)	8	7	5	5	2	6

Baltimore	IP.	H.	R.	ER.	BB.	SO.
Cuellar (Winner)	9	6	1	1	2	2

Errors–None. Left on base–Oakland 5, Baltimore 3. Two-base hits–Davis, Bando, Jackson. Home runs–B. Robinson, Powell 2, Hendricks. Sacrifice hit–Davis. Umpires–Napp, O'Donnell, Luciano, DiMuro, Kunkel and Soar. Time–2:04. Attendance–35,003.

GAME OF TUESDAY, OCTOBER 5, AT OAKLAND

Baltimore	AB.	R.	H.	RBI.	PO.	A.	Oakland	AB.	R.	H.	RBI.	PO.	A.
Buford, lf	4	1	3	0	0	0	Campaneris, ss	4	0	0	0	1	3
Rettenmund, pr-lf	0	0	0	0	0	0	Monday, cf	3	0	0	0	4	0
Blair, cf	5	1	2	0	3	0	Jackson, rf	4	2	3	2	2	0
Powell, 1b	2	2	0	0	7	1	Epstein, 1b	4	0	1	0	4	0
F. Robinson, rf	5	1	1	1	1	0	Bando, 3b	3	1	1	1	2	1
Hendricks, c	1	0	0	1	4	0	Mangual, lf	4	0	0	0	2	0
Etchebarren, ph-c	2	0	0	0	4	0	Tenace, c	3	0	0	0	8	0
B. Robinson, 3b	5	0	2	2	3	2	Green, 2b	3	0	1	0	4	1
Johnson, 2b	3	0	2	0	3	2	Hegan, ph	1	0	0	0	0	0
Belanger, ss	3	0	1	0	1	3	Segui, p	2	0	0	0	0	0
Palmer, p	5	0	1	0	1	0	Fingers, p	0	0	0	0	0	0
Totals	35	5	12	4	27	8	Knowles, p	0	0	0	0	0	0
							Locker, p	0	0	0	0	0	0
							Davis, ph	1	0	1	0	0	0
							Grant, p	0	0	0	0	0	1
							Blefary, ph	1	0	0	0	0	0
							Totals	33	3	7	3	27	6

| Baltimore | 1 | 0 | 0 | 0 | 2 | 0 | 2 | 0 | 0 – 5 |
| Oakland | 0 | 0 | 1 | 0 | 0 | 1 | 0 | 1 | 0 – 3 |

Baltimore	IP.	H.	R.	ER.	BB.	SO.
Palmer (Winner)	9	7	3	3	3	8

Oakland	IP.	H.	R.	ER.	BB.	SO.
Segui (Loser)	4⅔	6	3	3	6	4
Fingers	1⅓*	2	2	2	1	1
Knowles	⅓	1	0	0	0	0
Locker	⅔	0	0	0	2	0
Grant	2	3	0	0	0	2

*Pitched on two batters in seventh.

Errors–None. Double plays–Baltimore 1, Oakland 3. Left on base–Baltimore 13, Oakland 6. Two-base hits–Johnson, F. Robinson, B. Robinson. Three-base hit–Buford. Home runs–Jackson 2, Bando. Sacrifice fly–Hendricks. Wild pitches–Palmer, Knowles. Umpires–DiMuro, Luciano, Soar, Kunkel, O'Donnell and Napp. Time–2:49. Attendance–33,176.

BALTIMORE ORIOLES' BATTING AND FIELDING AVERAGES

Player–Position	G.	AB.	R.	H.	TB.	2B.	3B.	HR.	RBI.	B.A.	PO.	A.	E.	F.A.
Motton, ph	1	1	0	1	2	1	0	0	1	1.000	0	0	0	.000
Hendricks, c	2	4	1	2	5	0	0	1	2	.500	6	0	0	1.000
Buford, lf	2	7	1	3	5	0	1	0	0	.429	1	0	0	1.000
B. Robinson, 3b	3	11	2	4	8	1	0	1	3	.364	4	7	0	1.000
Blair, cf	3	9	1	3	4	1	0	0	2	.333	5	0	0	1.000
Cuellar, p	1	3	0	1	1	0	0	0	0	.333	0	2	0	1.000
Johnson, 2b	3	10	2	3	5	2	0	0	0	.300	5	6	1	.917
Powell, 1b	3	10	4	3	9	0	0	2	3	.300	28	2	0	1.000
Belanger, ss	3	8	1	2	2	0	0	0	1	.250	6	11	0	1.000
Rettenmund, lf-cf-pr	3	8	0	2	3	1	0	0	1	.250	7	0	0	1.000
Palmer, pr-p	2	5	1	1	1	0	0	0	0	.200	1	0	0	1.000
F. Robinson, rf	3	12	2	1	2	1	0	0	1	.083	7	0	0	1.000
Watt, p	1	0	0	0	0	0	0	0	0	.000	0	1	0	1.000
McNally, p	1	0	0	0	0	0	0	0	0	.000	0	2	0	1.000
Etchebarren, c-ph	2	5	0	0	0	0	0	0	0	.000	11	0	0	1.000
Totals	3	95	15	26	47	7	1	4	14	.274	81	31	1	.991

OAKLAND ATHLETICS' BATTING AND FIELDING AVERAGES

Player–Position	G.	AB.	R.	H.	TB.	2B.	3B.	HR.	RBI.	B.A.	PO.	A.	E.	F.A.
Duncan, c	2	6	3	4	1	0	0	2	.500	15	0	0	1.000	
Davis, 1b-ph	3	8	1	3	4	1	0	0	0	.375	8	0	0	1.000
Bando, 3b	3	11	3	4	9	2	0	1	1	.364	6	2	0	1.000
Jackson, rf	3	12	2	4	11	1	0	2	2	.333	9	1	0	1.000
Green, 2b	3	7	0	2	2	0	0	0	0	.286	8	4	0	1.000
Epstein, ph-1b	2	5	0	1	1	0	0	0	0	.200	4	0	0	1.000
Campaneris, ss	3	12	0	2	3	1	0	0	0	.167	3	6	0	1.000
Mangual, cf-lf	3	12	1	2	5	1	1	0	2	.167	6	0	0	1.000
Rudi, lf	2	7	0	1	2	1	0	0	0	.143	4	0	0	1.000
Fingers, p	2	0	0	0	0	0	0	0	0	.000	0	0	0	.000
Grant, p	1	0	0	0	0	0	0	0	0	.000	0	1	0	1.000
Knowles, p	1	0	0	0	0	0	0	0	0	.000	0	0	0	.000
Locker, p	1	0	0	0	0	0	0	0	0	.000	0	0	0	.000
Blefary, ph	1	1	0	0	0	0	0	0	0	.000	0	0	0	.000
Hegan, ph	1	1	0	0	0	0	0	0	0	.000	0	0	0	.000
Segui, p	1	2	0	0	0	0	0	0	0	.000	0	0	0	.000
Blue, p	1	3	0	0	0	0	0	0	0	.000	0	1	0	1.000
Hunter, p	1	3	0	0	0	0	0	0	0	.000	0	0	0	.000
Monday, cf	1	3	0	0	0	0	0	0	0	.000	4	0	0	1.000
Tenace, c	1	3	0	0	0	0	0	0	0	.000	8	0	0	1.000
Totals	3	96	7	22	41	8	1	3	7	.229	75	15	0	1.000

BALTIMORE ORIOLES' PITCHING RECORDS

Pitcher	G.	GS.	CG.	IP.	H.	R.	ER.	BB.	SO.	HB.	WP.	W.	L.	Pct.	ERA.
Watt	1	0	0	2	2	0	0	0	1	0	0	0	0	.000	0.00
Cuellar	1	1	1	9	6	1	1	1	2	0	0	1	0	1.000	1.00
Palmer	1	1	1	9	7	3	3	3	8	0	1	1	0	1.000	3.00
McNally	1	1	0	7	7	3	3	1	5	0	0	1	0	1.000	3.86
Totals	3	3	2	27	22	7	7	5	16	0	1	3	0	1.000	2.33

No shutouts. Save–Watt.

OAKLAND ATHLETICS' PITCHING RECORDS

Pitcher	G.	GS.	CG.	IP.	H.	R.	ER.	BB.	SO.	HB.	WP.	W.	L.	Pct.	ERA.
Grant	1	0	0	2	3	0	0	0	2	0	0	0	0	.000	0.00
Locker	1	0	0	⅔	0	0	0	2	0	0	0	0	0	.000	0.00
Knowles	1	0	0	⅓	1	0	0	0	0	0	1	0	0	.000	0.00
Hunter	1	1	1	8	7	5	5	2	6	0	0	0	1	.000	5.63
Segui	1	1	0	4⅔	6	3	3	6	4	0	0	0	1	.000	5.79
Blue	1	1	0	7	7	5	5	2	8	0	0	0	1	.000	6.43
Fingers	2	0	0	2½	2	2	2	1	2	0	0	0	0	.000	7.71
Totals	3	3	1	25	26	15	15	13	22	0	1	0	3	.000	5.40

No shutouts or saves.

COMPOSITE SCORE BY INNINGS

Baltimore 1   1   1   1   2   0   7   2   0 – 15
Oakland.. 0   2   1   2   0   1   0   1   0 – 7

Sacrifice hits–Green, Davis.
Sacrifice fly–Hendricks.
Stolen bases–None.
Caught stealing–Davis, Duncan.
Double plays–Bando, Green and Davis; Johnson, Belanger and Powell; Belanger, Johnson and Powell 2;
Campaneris and Green; Green and Epstein; Bando and Epstein.
Hit by pitcher–None.
Passed balls–None.
Balks–None.
Left on bases–Baltimore 19–3, 3, 13; Oakland 15–4, 5, 6.
Time of games–First game, 2:23; second game, 2:04; third game, 2:49.
Attendance–First game, 42,621; second game, 35,003; third game, 33,176.
Umpires–Soar, Napp, DiMuro, O'Donnell, Luciano and Kunkel.
Official scorers–Dick O'Connor, Palo Alto Times; Lou Hatter, Baltimore Morning Sun.

NATIONAL LEAGUE
Championship Series of 1971

	W.	L.	Pct.
Pittsburgh (East)	3	1	.750
San Francisco (West)	1	3	.250

The big bat that led all major league home run hitters in 1971 was strangely silent during the National League Championship Series.

But another bat, swung by Bob Robertson, produced at a frenzied pace and the Pittsburgh Pirates defeated the San Francisco Giants, three games to one, to capture their first pennant since 1960.

While Willie Stargell drew a complete blank in the four games, going 0-for-14, Robertson collected seven hits in 16 trips to the plate, cracked four home runs and drove in six runs.

The big first baseman, who was inactivated by a kidney ailment for the entire 1968 season and by a knee condition for 31 games in 1971, enjoyed his most productive performance in the second contest, at Candlestick Park in San Francisco.

The Pirates, who lost the opening game, 5-4, although outhitting the Giants, 9 to 7, trailed, 2-1, after three innings of the second encounter. At this point, Robertson, who had doubled and scored in the second inning, hit a John Cumberland pitch into the right field seats for a home run.

In the seventh inning, Robertson poled a three-run shot to left field off Ron Bryant and, in the ninth, he connected off Steve Hamilton, driving the ball over the left-center field fence.

The 9-4 victory, credited to Dock Ellis, first of three Pittsburgh pitchers, was the Pirates' first at Candlestick Park after six consecutive defeats.

When the series shifted to Pittsburgh, Manager Danny Murtaugh nominated Nelson Briles (8-4 for the season) as the Pirates' starting pitcher.

In warming up however, the righthander suffered a recurrence of a hamstring pull and Bob Johnson, who compiled a 9-10 regular-season record, was tabbed as a replacement.

The 28-year-old righthander, who was allowed extra time to warm up, dueled Juan Marichal, the Giants' 18-game winner, on equal terms for seven innings and was returned a 2-1 winner when Richie Hebner poled a right-field home run in the last of the eighth.

Marichal, with a 25-10 lifetime record against the Pirates, yielded only three hits in the first seven innings, including a no-harm single to Roberto Clemente in the first inning, Robertson's second-inning homer, his third in as many consecutive trips, and Hebner's non-productive single in the sixth.

In the eighth, Hebner drilled "a screwball out over the plate" to deep right field where Bonds missed a leaping catch by about five inches, the ball falling into home run territory for the deciding tally.

With the Pirates just one victory away from the pennant that eluded them in 1970 via three consecutive losses to the Cincinnati Reds, Murtaugh called on Steve Blass to face his first-game opponent, Perry.

Blass, who lasted five innings in the opener, was less a mystery in his second try. In two innings, the righthander yielded eight hits and five runs, two of the blows being homers by Chris Speier and Willie McCovey.

Trailing, 5-2, the Pirates tagged Perry for three second-inning runs.

Perry, touched for 10 of the Pirates' 11 hits, blanked the N. L. East champions for the next three innings.

In the sixth stanza, however, the Bucs tagged him for one run on singles by Dave Cash and Clemente, around an infield out.

After Jerry Johnson relieved Perry, a passed ball permitted Cash to score and Clemente to go to second base. An intentional walk to Stargell was followed by Al Oliver's home run, giving the Pirates a 9-5 edge.

Bruce Kison, 20-year-old righthander who took over Pittsburgh mound duties in the third inning and allowed only two hits in 4⅔ innings, ran into trouble in the seventh inning when the Giants placed two runners on base.

Dave Giusti, who saved 30 Pittsburgh wins in the regular season and appeared in the first three championship contests, responded again and turned back the Giants without a run.

GAME OF SATURDAY, OCTOBER 2, AT SAN FRANCISCO

Pittsburgh	AB.	R.	H.	RBI.	PO.	A.	San Francisco	AB.	R.	H.	RBI.	PO.	A.
Cash, 2b	5	2	2	1	3	2	Henderson, lf	4	0	2	1	2	0
Hebner, 3b	5	0	1	0	0	0	Fuentes, 2b	4	1	1	2	2	3
Clemente, rf	4	0	0	3	0		Mays, cf	2	1	1	0	0	0
Stargell, lf	4	0	0	0	1	0	McCovey, 1b	3	1	1	2	12	0
Oliver, cf	4	0	1	2	3	0	Kingman, rf	3	0	0	0	3	0
Robertson, 1b	4	0	2	0	1	1	Bonds, rf	1	0	0	0	1	0
Sanguillen, c	4	0	1	0	10	0	Dietz, c	4	0	0	0	5	1
Hernandez, ss	2	1	1	0	1	0	Gallagher, 3b	2	0	0	0	0	0
Davalillo, ph	1	0	0	0	0	0	Lanier, 3b	1	0	0	0	1	0
Moose, p	0	0	0	0	0	0	Speier, ss	3	2	2	1	5	
May, ph	1	0	0	0	0	0	Perry, p	1	0	0	0	0	2
Giusti, p	0	0	0	0	0	0	Totals	28	5	7	5	27	12
Blass, p	1	0	0	0	1	1							
Alley, ss	2	1	1	0	1	1							
Totals	37	4	9	3	24	5							

Pittsburgh	0	0	2	0	0	0	2	0	0 – 4
San Francisco	0	0	1	0	4	0	0	0	x – 5

Pittsburgh	IP.	H.	R.	ER.	BB.	SO.
Blass (Loser)	5	6	5	5	2	9
Moose	2	0	0	0	0	0
Giusti	1	1	0	0	1	1

San Francisco	IP.	H.	R.	ER.	BB.	SO.
Perry (Winner)	9	9	4	3	1	5

Errors—McCovey, Speier. Double play—Pittsburgh 1. Left on base—Pittsburgh 9, San Francisco 4. Two-base hits—Cash, Henderson, Mays. Home runs—Fuentes, McCovey. Sacrifice hits—Blass, Perry 2. Hit by pitcher—By Perry (Stargell). Umpires—Gorman, Crawford, Weyer, Olsen, Stello and Davidson. Time—2:44. Attendance—40,977.

GAME OF SUNDAY, OCTOBER 3, AT SAN FRANCISCO

Pittsburgh	AB.	R.	H.	RBI.	PO.	A.	San Francisco	AB.	R.	H.	RBI.	PO.	A.
Cash, 2b	5	1	3	0	3	3	Henderson, lf	3	0	1	1	0	0
Clines, cf	3	1	1	1	1	0	Fuentes, 2b	5	2	2	0	4	0
Oliver, ph-cf	1	1	1	0	0	0	Mays, cf	5	1	2	3	2	0
Clemente, rf	5	1	3	1	3	0	McCovey, 1b	3	0	1	0	4	0
Stargell, lf	5	0	0	0	1	0	Rosario, pr	0	0	0	0	0	0
Robertson, 1b	5	4	4	5	9	1	Kingman, rf	4	0	1	0	2	0
Sanguillen, c	5	1	2	1	5	0	Dietz, c	4	0	0	0	14	1
Pagan, 3b	1	0	0	0	1	2	Gallagher, 3b	4	0	0	0	0	0
Hebner, ph-3b	3	0	0	0	1	1	Speier, ss	3	1	2	0	1	5
Hernandez, ss	4	0	1	1	2	2	Cumberland, p	0	0	0	0	0	0
Ellis, p	3	0	0	0	0	0	Barr, p	1	0	0	0	0	0
Miller, p	1	0	0	0	1	0	McMahon, p	0	0	0	0	0	0
Giusti, p	0	0	0	0	0	0	Duffy, ph	1	0	0	0	0	0
Totals	41	9	15	9	27	9	Carrithers, p	0	0	0	0	0	0
							Bryant, p	0	0	0	0	0	0
							Hart, ph	1	0	0	0	0	0
							Hamilton, p	0	0	0	0	0	0
							Totals	34	4	9	4	27	6

Pittsburgh	0	1	0	2	1	0	4	0	1 – 9
San Francisco	1	1	0	0	0	0	0	0	2 – 4

Pittsburgh	IP.	H.	R.	ER.	BB.	SO.
Ellis (Winner)	5‡	6	2	2	4	1
Miller	3x	3	2	2	3	3
Giusti (Save)	1	0	0	0	0	0

San Francisco	IP.	H.	R.	ER.	BB.	SO.
Cumberland (Loser)	3*	7	3	3	0	4
Barr	1†	3	1	1	0	2
McMahon	2	0	0	0	0	2
Carrithers	0§	3	3	3	0	0
Bryant	2	1	1	1	1	2
Hamilton	1	1	1	1	0	3

*Pitched to two batters in fourth.
†Pitched to two batters in fifth.
‡Pitched to two batters in sixth.
§Pitched to three batters in seventh.
xPitched to three batters in ninth.

Errors–None. Double plays–Pittsburgh 1, San Francisco 1. Left on base–Pittsburgh 7, San Francisco 12. Two-base hits–Mays, Robertson, Speier, Cash, Fuentes. Home runs–Robertson 3, Clines, Mays. Sacrifice hit–Cumberland. Stolen bases–Henderson, Sanguillen. Hit by pitcher–By Ellis (Gallagher), by Bryant (Hebner). Passed ball–Sanguillen. Umpires–Crawford, Weyer, Olsen, Stello, Davidson and Gorman. Time–3:23. Attendance–42,562.

GAME OF TUESDAY, OCTOBER 5, AT PITTSBURGH

San Francisco	AB.	R.	H.	RBI.	PO.	A.	Pittsburgh	AB.	R.	H.	RBI.	PO.	A.
Henderson, lf	4	1	1	0	2	0	Cash, 2b	4	0	0	2	4
Fuentes, 2b	3	0	0	0	1	2	Hebner, 3b	4	1	2	1	1	1
Mays, cf	4	0	1	0	0	0	Clemente, rf	4	0	1	0	5	0
McCovey, 1b	3	0	1	0	11	2	Stargell, lf	3	0	0	0	2	0
Bonds, rf	3	0	1	0	1	0	Oliver, cf	3	0	0	0	0	0
Dietz, c	3	0	0	0	7	0	Robertson, 1b	3	1	1	1	8	0
Gallagher, 3b	3	0	1	0	0	3	Sanguillen, c	3	0	0	0	7	1
Hart, ph	1	0	0	0	0	0	Hernandez, ss	3	0	0	0	2	5
Speier, ss	4	0	0	0	0	2	Johnson, p	2	0	0	0	0	0
Marichal, p	3	0	0	0	2	4	Davalillo, ph	1	0	0	0	0	0
Kingman, ph	1	0	0	0	0	0	Giusti, p	0	0	0	0	0	0
Totals	32	1	5	0	24	13	Totals	30	2	4	2	27	11

San Francisco	0	0	0	0	0	1	0	0	0 – 1
Pittsburgh	0	1	0	0	0	0	0	1	x – 2

San Francisco	IP.	H.	R.	ER.	BB.	SO.
Marichal (Loser)	8	4	2	2	0	6

Pittsburgh	IP.	H.	R.	ER.	BB.	SO.
Johnson (Winner)	8	5	1	0	3	7
Giusti (Save)	1	0	0	0	0	0

Errors–Bonds, Hebner, Fuentes. Left on base–San Francisco 8, Pittsburgh 4. Home runs–Robertson, Hebner. Sacrifice hit–Fuentes. Stolen base–Mays. Wild pitches–Marichal 2. Umpires–Weyer, Olsen, Stello, Davidson, Gorman and Crawford. Time–2:26. Attendance–38,322.

GAME OF WEDNESDAY, OCTOBER 6, AT PITTSBURGH

San Francisco	AB.	R.	H.	RBI.	PO.	A.	Pittsburgh	AB.	R.	H.	RBI.	PO.	A.
Henderson, lf	5	2	1	0	0	0	Cash, 2b	5	2	3	0	3	2
Fuentes, 2b	4	1	2	0	2	0	Hebner, 3b	5	2	3	2	1
Mays, cf	4	0	0	3	0	Clemente, rf	5	1	2	3	1	0
McCovey, 1b	5	1	3	4	7	1	Stargell, lf	2	1	0	0	2	0
Bonds, rf	4	0	1	0	1	0	Oliver, cf	4	1	1	3	2	0
Dietz, c	4	0	1	0	8	0	Robertson, 1b	4	0	0	0	7	0
Hart, 3b	3	0	0	0	0	2	Sanguillen, c	3	0	1	0	8	0
Gallagher, 3b	1	0	0	0	0	0	Hernandez, ss	4	1	1	0	2	2
Speier, ss	4	1	1	1	1	2	Blass, p	0	0	0	0	0	0
Perry, p	3	0	1	0	1	0	Mazeroski, ph	1	1	1	0	0	0
Johnson, p	0	0	0	0	0	0	Kison, p	2	0	0	0	0	1
Kingman, ph	1	0	0	0	0	0	Giusti, p	1	0	0	0	0	1
McMahon, p	0	0	0	0	1	1	Totals	36	9	11	9	27	7
Totals	38	5	10	5	24	6							

San Francisco	1	4	0	0	0	0	0	0	0 – 5
Pittsburgh	2	3	0	0	0	4	0	0	x – 9

San Francisco	IP.	H.	R.	ER.	BB.	SO.
Perry (Loser)	5⅔	10	7	7	2	6
Johnson	1⅓	1	2	2	1	2
McMahon	1	0	0	0	0	1

Pittsburgh	IP.	H.	R.	ER.	BB.	SO.
Blass	2	8	5	4	0	2
Kison (Winner)	4⅔	2	0	0	2	3
Giusti (Save)	2⅓	0	0	0	1	2

Errors–Cash, Hernandez. Double play–Pittsburgh 1. Left on base–San Francisco 9, Pittsburgh 6. Two-base hit–Hebner. Home runs–Speier, McCovey, Hebner, Oliver. Stolen base–Cash. Wild pitches–Perry, Kison. Passed ball–Dietz. Umpires–Olsen, Stello, Davidson, Gorman, Crawford and Weyer. Time–3:00. Attendance–35,487.

PITTSBURGH PIRATES' BATTING AND FIELDING AVERAGES

Player–Position	G.	AB.	R.	H.	TB.	2B.	3B.	HR.	RBI.	B.A.	PO.	A.	E.	F.A.
Mazeroski, ph	1	1	1	1	1	0	0	0	0	1.000	0	0	0	.000
Alley, ss	1	2	1	1	1	0	0	0	0	.500	1	1	0	1.000
Robertson, 1b	4	16	5	7	20	1	0	4	6	.438	25	2	0	1.000
Cash, 2b	4	19	5	8	10	2	0	0	1	.421	11	11	1	.957
Clemente, rf	4	18	2	6	6	0	0	0	4	.333	12	0	0	1.000
Clines, cf	1	3	1	1	4	0	0	1	1	.333	1	0	0	1.000
Hebner, 3b-ph	4	17	3	5	12	1	0	2	4	.294	4	3	1	.875
Sanguillen, c	4	15	1	4	4	0	0	0	1	.267	30	1	0	1.000
Oliver, cf-ph	4	12	2	3	6	0	0	1	5	.250	5	0	0	1.000
Hernandez, ss	4	13	2	3	3	0	0	0	1	.231	7	9	1	.941
Moose, p	1	0	0	0	0	0	0	0	0	.000	0	0	0	.000
Blass, p	2	1	0	0	0	0	0	0	0	.000	1	1	0	1.000
Giusti, p	4	1	0	0	0	0	0	0	0	.000	0	1	0	1.000
May, ph	1	1	0	0	0	0	0	0	0	.000	0	0	0	.000
Miller, p	1	1	0	0	0	0	0	0	0	.000	1	0	0	1.000
Pagan, 3b	1	0	0	0	0	0	0	0	0	.000	1	2	0	1.000
Davalillo, ph	2	2	0	0	0	0	0	0	0	.000	0	0	0	.000
R. Johnson, p	1	2	0	0	0	0	0	0	0	.000	0	0	0	.000
Kison, p	1	2	0	0	0	0	0	0	0	.000	0	1	0	1.000
Ellis, p	1	3	0	0	0	0	0	0	0	.000	0	0	0	.000
Stargell, lf	4	14	1	0	0	0	0	0	0	.000	6	0	0	1.000
Totals	4	144	24	39	67	4	0	8	23	.271	105	32	3	.979

SAN FRANCISCO GIANTS' BATTING AND FIELDING AVERAGES

Player–Position	G.	AB.	R.	H.	TB.	2B.	3B.	HR.	RBI.	B.A.	PO.	A.	E.	F.A.
McCovey, 1b	4	14	2	6	12	0	0	2	6	.429	34	3	1	.974
Speier, ss	4	14	4	5	9	1	0	1	1	.357	3	14	1	.944
Fuentes, 2b	4	16	4	5	9	1	0	1	2	.313	9	5	1	.933
Henderson, lf	4	16	3	5	6	1	0	0	2	.313	4	0	0	1.000
Mays, cf	4	15	2	4	9	2	0	1	3	.267	5	0	0	1.000
Bonds, rf	3	8	0	2	2	0	0	0	0	.250	3	0	1	.750
Perry, p	2	4	0	1	1	0	0	0	0	.250	1	2	0	1.000
Kingman, rf-ph	4	9	0	1	1	0	0	0	0	.111	5	0	0	1.000
Gallagher, 3b	4	10	0	1	1	0	0	0	0	.100	0	4	0	1.000
Dietz, c	4	15	0	1	1	0	0	0	5	.067	34	2	0	1.000
Bryant, p	1	0	0	0	0	0	0	0	0	.000	0	0	0	.000
Carrithers, p	1	0	0	0	0	0	0	0	0	.000	0	0	0	.000
Cumberland, p	1	0	0	0	0	0	0	0	0	.000	0	0	0	.000
Hamilton, p	1	0	0	0	0	0	0	0	0	.000	0	0	0	.000
J. Johnson, p	1	0	0	0	0	0	0	0	0	.000	0	0	0	.000
McMahon, p	2	0	0	0	0	0	0	0	0	.000	1	1	0	1.000
Rosario, pr	1	0	0	0	0	0	0	0	0	.000	0	0	0	.000
Barr, p	1	1	0	0	0	0	0	0	0	.000	0	0	0	.000
Duffy, ph	1	1	0	0	0	0	0	0	0	.000	0	0	0	.000
Lanier, 3b	1	1	0	0	0	0	0	0	0	.000	1	0	0	1.000
Marichal, p	1	3	0	0	0	0	0	0	0	.000	2	4	0	1.000
Hart, ph-3b	3	5	0	0	0	0	0	0	0	.000	0	2	0	1.000
Totals	4	132	15	31	51	5	0	5	14	.235	102	37	4	.972

PITTSBURGH PIRATES' PITCHING RECORDS

Pitcher	G.	GS.	CG.	IP.	H.	R.	ER.	BB.	SO.	HB.	WP.	W.	L.	Pct.	ERA.
R. Johnson	1	1	0	8	5	1	0	3	7	0	0	1	0	1.000	0.00
Giusti	4	0	0	5⅓	1	0	0	2	3	0	0	0	0	.000	0.00
Kison	1	0	0	4⅔	2	0	0	2	3	0	1	1	0	1.000	0.00
Moose	1	0	0	2	0	0	0	0	0	0	0	0	0	.000	0.00
Ellis	1	1	0	5	6	2	2	4	1	1	0	1	0	1.000	3.60
Miller	1	0	0	3	3	2	2	3	3	0	0	0	0	.000	6.00
Blass	2	2	0	7	14	10	9	2	11	0	0	0	1	.000	11.57
Totals	4	4	0	35	31	15	13	16	28	1	1	3	1	.750	3.34

No shutouts. Saves–Giusti 3.

SAN FRANCISCO GIANTS' PITCHING RECORDS

Pitcher	G.	GS.	CG.	IP.	H.	R.	ER.	BB.	SO.	HB.	WP.	W.	L.	Pct.	ERA.
McMahon	2	0	0	3	0	0	0	0	3	0	0	0	0	.000	0.00
Marichal	1	1	1	8	4	2	2	0	6	0	2	0	1	.000	2.25
Bryant	1	0	0	2	1	1	1	1	2	1	0	0	0	.000	4.50
Perry	2	2	1	14⅔	19	11	10	3	11	1	1	1	1	.500	6.14
Cumberland	1	1	0	3	7	3	3	0	4	0	0	0	1	.000	9.00
Barr	1	0	0	1	3	1	1	0	2	0	0	0	0	.000	9.00
Hamilton	1	0	0	1	1	1	1	0	3	0	0	0	0	.000	9.00
J. Johnson	1	0	0	1⅓	1	2	2	1	2	0	0	0	0	.000	13.50
Carrithers	1	0	0	0*	3	3	3	0	0	0	0	0	0	.000	......
Totals	4	4	2	34	39	24	23	5	33	2	3	1	3	.250	6.09

*Pitched to three batters in seventh inning of second game.

No shutouts or saves.

COMPOSITE SCORE BY INNINGS

Pittsburgh	2	5	2	2	1	4	6	1	1 – 24
San Francisco	2	5	1	0	4	1	0	0	2 – 15

Sacrifice hits—Perry 2, Blass, Cumberland, Fuentes.
Stolen bases—Henderson, Sanguillen, Mays, Cash.
Caught stealing—Cash.
Double plays—Alley, Cash and Robertson; Dietz and Fuentes; Hernandez, Cash and Robertson; Cash,
Hernandez and Robertson.
Left on bases—Pittsburgh 26—9, 7, 4, 6; San Francisco 33—4, 12, 8, 9.
Hit by pitchers—By Perry (Stargell), by Ellis (Gallagher), by Bryant (Hebner).
Passed balls—Sanguillen, Dietz.
Balks—None.
Time of games—First game, 2:44; second game, 3:23; third game, 2:26; fourth game, 3:00.
Attendance—First game, 40,977; second game, 42,562; third game, 38,322; fourth game, 35,487.
Umpires—Gorman, Crawford, Weyer, Olsen, Stello and Davidson.
Official scorers—Bill Christine, Pittsburgh Press; Jack Hanley, San Jose Mercury-News and Charles Fee-
ney, Pittsburgh Post-Gazette.

AMERICAN LEAGUE
Championship Series of 1972

	W.	L.	Pct.
Oakland (West)	3	2	.600
Detroit (East)	2	3	.400

Back in 1931, the Philadelphia A's won their third straight American League pennant. The A's were to wait 41 years for their next. When it finally came in 1972, the A's were long gone from Philadelphia, having traipsed across the country to Oakland after a stop in Kansas City.

Retaining their West Division crown in a breeze in '72, the A's outfought the East champion Detroit Tigers in a memorable pennant playoff, three games to two. It was the first A. L. Championship Series in the four-year history of the event that did not end in a three-game sweep.

The A's scored only 13 runs and logged just 38 hits, including one homer, in five playoff games, two of which were extra-inning struggles. Their eight-man pitching staff was equal to the task, granting the Tigers a mere 10 runs and 32 hits.

Blue Moon Odom, who pitched a shutout in winning game two, 5-0, was the only Oakland pitcher to go the route in the playoffs. That was no indictment of the A's starters. Rather, it was indicative of the superb relief pitching Manager Dick Williams could and did call upon at the first hint of trouble. Reliever Rollie Fingers appeared in three playoff games and was credited with the A's 3-2 victory in the 11-inning opener October 7 in Oakland.

Vida Blue nursed a season-long grudge against Owner Charlie Finley, the aftermath of Blue's holdout well into May. Nevertheless, the griping Blue was a brilliant fireman in the playoffs, blanking the Tigers for 5⅓ innings in four appearances. He saved the best for last, rescuing Odom in the sixth inning of game five and saving Oakland's pennant-clinching 2-1 triumph with four shutout rounds.

The playoffs dripped with drama and suspense from start to finish. Tiger ace Mickey Lolich carried a 2-1 lead into the last of the 11th in the opener. The A's thereupon scored twice to win it. The hero was Gonzalo Marquez, an obscure late addition to the A's roster. He lashed a pinch-single off Chuck Seelbach with one out and two aboard to score the tying run. On the same play, right fielder Al Kaline's throw shot past third sacker Aurelio Rodriguez, enabling Gene Tenace to cross the plate the winning tally.

Kaline was charged with an error, which rubbed out his hero halo in a hurry. Kaline had belted a homer off Fingers in the top of the 11th to give Detroit a 2-1 edge. Catfish Hunter pitched well for the A's, leaving in the ninth with the score tied, 1-1.

Buoyed by their opening-game success, the A's came on strong the next day, handing the Tigers a 5-0 beating behind Odom's three-hitter. Shortstop Campy Campaneris, with three singles, two runs and two stolen bases, was the Tigers' No. 1 nemesis. He also precipitated a near riot in the seventh inning when he threw his bat at Lerrin LaGrow, who had plunked Campy on the ankle with a pitch.

Tiger Manager Billy Martin, noted for his fistic conquests, dashed from the dugout, along with his players. Three umpires managed to keep Martin from Campaneris, a feat which nipped a budding brawl. Plate umpire Nestor Chylak banished both Campy and LaGrow. Later, A. L. President Joe Cronin fined Campaneris $500 and suspended him from the remaining playoff games. He was allowed to play in the World Series, but sat out the first seven games of the 1973 season by order of the Commissioner.

Needing one more win to kill off the Tigers, the A's proceeded to swoon, 3-0, before Joe Coleman's 14-strikeout job October 10 as the scene shifted to Detroit. Coleman's whiff total surpassed the old playoff record of 12 set by Baltimore's Jim Palmer against Minnesota in 1970.

Nobody could brand the Tigers quitters. Still one game from oblivion, they tied the series the next day in a 10-inning thriller, 4-3. It was a crushing defeat for the A's, who had taken a 3-1 lead with two runs in the top of the 10th, only to see the Tigers score three to win it.

Lolich pitched creditably for Detroit, as he had in the opener, but left for a pinch-hitter in the ninth with the score 1-1. The A's appeared to have the pennant wrapped up when they rocked Seelbach, Lolich's successor, for two runs in the 10th.

Then came Detroit's remarkable rally at the expense of Oakland relievers Bob Locker, Joe Horlen and Dave Hamilton. The carnage began with singles by Dick McAuliffe and Kaline, Horlen's wild pitch and a walk to Gates Brown. It continued with Tenace's muff of a throw on a force-play attempt while he was trying to play second base, Hamilton's bases-loaded walk to Norm Cash and Jim Northrup's winning hit to right field.

Next day, with a chill wind blowing and Detroit fans in one of their boisterous, destructive moods, the A's put it all together. Behind Odom and Blue, they turned back the Tigers and Woodie Fryman, 2-1, to hoist the pennant.

GAME OF SATURDAY, OCTOBER 7, AT OAKLAND

Detroit	AB.	R.	H.	RBI.	PO.	A.	Oakland	AB.	R.	H.	RBI.	PO.	A.
McAuliffe, 2b	5	0	0	0	2	3	Campaneris, ss	4	1	0	0	3	5
Kaline, rf	5	1	1	1	2	0	Alou, rf	5	0	1	0	0	0
Sims, c	5	0	2	0	4	0	Rudi, lf	4	0	0	1	4	0
Cash, 1b	3	1	1	1	12	0	Jackson, cf	5	0	2	0	4	0
Horton, lf	3	0	0	0	3	0	Bando, 3b	4	0	2	0	2	4
G. Brown, ph	1	0	0	0	0	0	Odom, pr	0	0	0	0	0	0
Stanley, cf	1	0	0	0	1	0	Epstein, 1b	3	0	2	0	14	0
Northrup, cf-lf	3	0	1	0	5	0	Hegan, pr	0	1	0	0	0	0
Rodriguez, 3b	4	0	0	0	1	4	Tenace, c	5	1	0	0	5	0
Brinkman, ss	4	0	1	0	1	2	Green, 2b	0	0	0	0	1	0
Lolich, p	4	0	0	0	3	0	Mangual, ph	1	0	0	0	0	0
Seelbach, p	0	0	0	0	0	0	Kubiak, 2b	2	0	1	0	0	5
Totals	38	2	6	2	31	12	Hendrick, ph	1	0	0	0	0	0
							Maxvill, 2b	0	0	0	0	0	1
							Marquez, ph	1	0	1	1	0	0
							Hunter, p	3	0	1	0	0	0
							Blue, p	0	0	0	0	0	0
							Fingers, p	1	0	0	0	0	0
							Totals	39	3	10	2	33	15

Detroit	0	1	0	0	0	0	0	0	0	0	1 — 2
Oakland	0	0	1	0	0	0	0	0	0	0	2 — 3

One out when winning run scored.

Detroit	IP.	H.	R.	ER.	BB.	SO.
Lolich (Loser)	10‡	9	3	2	3	4
Seelbach	⅓	1	0	0	0	0
Oakland	IP.	H.	R.	ER.	BB.	SO.
Hunter	8*	4	1	1	2	4
Blue	0†	0	0	0	0	0
Fingers (Winner)	3	2	1	1	0	1

*Pitched to one batter in ninth.
†Pitched to one batter in ninth.
‡Pitched to two batters in eleventh.

Errors—McAuliffe, Kubiak, Kaline. Double plays—Detroit 1, Oakland 1. Left on base—Detroit 6, Oakland 10. Two-base hits—Brinkman, Sims. Three-base hit—Sims. Home runs—Cash, Kaline. Sacrifice hits—Bando, Cash. Sacrifice fly—Rudi. Umpires—Flaherty, Chylak, Rice, Denkinger, Barnett and Frantz. Time—3:09. Attendance —29,536.

GAME OF SUNDAY, OCTOBER 8, AT OAKLAND

Detroit	AB.	R.	H.	RBI.	PO.	A.
McAuliffe, ss	4	0	0	0	4	1
Kaline, rf	4	0	1	0	3	0
Sims, c	3	0	0	0	9	1
Cash, 1b	3	0	1	0	2	2
Horton, lf	3	0	0	0	3	0
Northrup, cf	3	0	1	0	1	0
Taylor, 2b	3	0	0	0	1	1
Rodriguez, 3b	3	0	0	0	1	0
Fryman, p	1	0	0	0	0	1
Zachary, p	0	0	0	0	0	0
Scherman, p	0	0	0	0	0	0
Haller, ph	1	0	0	0	0	0
LaGrow, p	0	0	0	0	0	0
Hiller, p	0	0	0	0	0	0
G. Brown, ph	1	0	0	0	0	0
Totals	29	0	3	0	24	6

Oakland	AB.	R.	H.	RBI.	PO.	A.
Campaneris, ss	3	2	3	0	0	2
Maxvill, pr-ss	0	0	0	0	0	0
Alou, rf	4	1	1	1	3	0
Rudi, lf	3	1	2	1	0	0
Jackson, cf	4	0	1	2	3	0
Bando, 3b	4	0	0	0	1	6
Epstein, 1b	3	0	0	0	13	2
Hegan, 1b	0	0	0	0	1	0
Tenace, c	3	0	0	0	2	2
Green, 2b	1	0	0	0	1	2
Hendrick, ph	1	1	1	0	0	0
Kubiak, 2b	1	0	0	0	1	1
Odom, p	2	0	0	0	2	0
Totals	29	5	8	4	27	15

Detroit	0	0	0	0	0	0	0	0	0	– 0
Oakland	1	0	0	0	4	0	0	0	x	– 5

Detroit	IP.	H.	R.	ER.	BB.	SO.
Fryman (Loser)	4⅓	7	4	4	1	5
Zachary	0*	0	1	1	1	0
Scherman	⅔	1	0	0	0	1
LaGrow	1†	0	0	0	0	1
Hiller	2	0	0	0	0	1

Oakland	IP.	H.	R.	ER.	BB.	SO.
Odom (Winner)	9	3	0	0	0	2

*Pitched to one batter in fifth.
†Pitched to one batter in seventh.

Error—McAuliffe. Double play—Detroit 1. Left on base—Detroit 2, Oakland 4. Two-base hits—Rudi, Jackson. Stolen bases—Campaneris 2. Sacrifice hit—Odom. Hit by pitch—By LaGrow (Campaneris). Wild pitches—Zachary 2. Umpires—Chylak, Rice, Frantz, Barnett, Denkinger and Flaherty. Time—2:37. Attendance—31,088.

GAME OF TUESDAY, OCTOBER 10, AT DETROIT

Oakland	AB.	R.	H.	RBI.	PO.	A.
Alou, rf	5	0	3	0	1	0
Maxvill, ss	2	0	0	0	1	2
Duncan, ph-c	1	0	0	0	1	0
Rudi, lf	4	0	3	0	2	0
Jackson, cf	4	0	0	0	4	0
Epstein, 1b	4	0	0	0	9	0
Bando, 3b	4	0	1	0	0	3
Tenace, c-2b	2	0	0	0	3	3
Green, 2b	1	0	0	0	1	0
Mincher, ph	1	0	0	0	0	0
Kubiak, 2b	0	0	0	0	2	2
Marquez, ph	1	0	0	0	0	0
Cullen, ss	1	0	0	0	0	0
Holtzman, p	1	0	0	0	0	1
Mangual, ph	1	0	0	0	0	0
Fingers, p	0	0	0	0	0	0
Blue, p	0	0	0	0	0	0
Hegan, ph	1	0	0	0	0	0
Locker, p	0	0	0	0	0	0
Hendrick, ph	1	0	0	0	0	0
Totals	34	0	7	0	24	11

Detroit	AB.	R.	H.	RBI.	PO.	A.
Taylor, 2b	4	0	0	0	2	3
Rodriguez, 3b	4	0	0	0	0	0
Kaline, rf	3	1	2	0	0	0
Freehan, c	3	2	2	1	14	1
Horton, lf	2	0	0	0	1	0
Northrup, lf	1	0	0	0	1	0
Stanley, cf	3	0	1	0	3	0
I. Brown, 1b	2	0	1	2	2	0
Cash, ph-1b	1	0	0	0	0	1
McAuliffe, ss	3	0	1	0	5	2
Coleman, p	2	0	1	0	0	0
Totals	28	3	8	3	27	7

Oakland	0	0	0	0	0	0	0	0	0	– 0
Detroit	0	0	0	2	0	0	0	1	x	– 3

Oakland	IP.	H.	R.	ER.	BB.	SO.
Holtzman (Loser)	4	4	2	2	2	2
Fingers	1⅔	2	0	0	1	1
Blue	⅓	0	0	0	0	0
Locker	2	2	1	1	0	1

Detroit	IP.	H.	R.	ER.	BB.	SO.
Coleman (Winner)	9	7	0	0	3	14

Error—McAuliffe. Double plays—Oakland 3, Detroit 1. Left on base—Oakland 10, Detroit 5. Two-base hits—Alou 2, Freehan. Home run—Freehan. Stolen bases—Alou, Maxvill. Sacrifice hit—Freehan. Umpires—Rice, Denkinger, Chylak, Frantz, Flaherty and Barnett. Time—2:27. Attendance—41,156.

GAME OF WEDNESDAY, OCTOBER 11, AT DETROIT

Oakland	AB.	R.	H.	RBI.	PO.	A.	Detroit	AB.	R.	H.	RBI.	PO.	A.
Alou, rf	5	1	2	1	1	0	McAuliffe, ss	4	2	2	1	1	1
Maxvill, ss	2	0	1	0	0	1	Kaline, rf	3	1	1	0	1	0
Hendrick, ph	1	0	0	0	0	0	Sims, lf	3	0	1	0	2	0
Cullen, ss	0	0	0	0	0	2	Stanley, cf	1	0	1	0	3	0
Mangual, ph	1	0	0	0	0	0	G. Brown, ph	0	1	0	0	0	0
Kubiak, ss	1	0	1	0	0	0	Freehan, c	5	0	1	1	7	0
Rudi, lf	5	0	0	0	3	0	Cash, 1b	4	0	1	1	12	0
Jackson, cf	5	0	2	0	3	0	Northrup, cf-lf	5	0	1	1	2	0
Bando, 3b	5	0	0	0	1	2	Taylor, 2b	4	0	2	0	1	2
Epstein, 1b	3	1	1	1	9	0	Rodriguez, 3b	2	0	0	0	0	7
Tenace, c-2b	4	0	0	0	5	0	Lolich, p	3	0	0	0	1	0
Green, 2b	2	0	1	0	1	3	Horton, ph	1	0	0	0	0	0
Duncan, ph-c	1	0	0	0	4	1	Seelbach, p	0	0	0	0	0	0
Hunter, p	3	0	0	0	0	0	Hiller, p	0	0	0	0	0	0
Fingers, p	0	0	0	0	0	0	Totals	35	4	10	4	30	10
Blue, p	0	0	0	0	0	0							
Marquez, ph	1	1	1	0	0	0							
Locker, p	0	0	0	0	0	0							
Horlen, p	0	0	0	0	0	0							
Hamilton, p	0	0	0	0	0	0							
Totals	39	3	9	3	27	9							

Oakland	0	0	0	0	0	0	1	0	0	2 – 3
Detroit	0	0	1	0	0	0	0	0	0	3 – 4

None out when winning run scored.

Oakland	IP.	H.	R.	ER.	BB.	SO.
Hunter	7⅓	6	1	1	3	5
Fingers	⅔	0	0	0	0	1
Blue	1	1	0	0	1	2
Locker	0*	2	2	2	0	0
Horlen (Loser)	0†	0	1	1	1	0
Hamilton	0‡	1	0	0	1	0

Detroit	IP.	H.	R.	ER.	BB.	SO.
Lolich	9	5	1	1	2	6
Seelbach	⅔	3	2	2	0	0
Hiller (Winner)	⅓	1	0	0	0	0

*Pitched to two batters in tenth.
†Pitched to two batters in tenth.
‡Pitched to two batters in tenth.

Errors—Jackson, Rodriguez, Tenace. Double play—Oakland 1. Left on base—Oakland 8, Detroit 11. Two-base hits—Sims, Green, Taylor 2, Alou 2. Home runs—McAuliffe, Epstein. Sacrifice hit—Kaline. Wild pitch—Horlen. Umpires—Denkinger, Chylak, Rice, Flaherty, Barnett and Frantz. Time—3:04. Attendance—37,615.

GAME OF THURSDAY, OCTOBER 12, AT DETROIT

Oakland	AB.	R.	H.	RBI.	PO.	A.	Detroit	AB.	R.	H.	RBI.	PO.	A.
Alou, rf	2	0	1	0	3	0	McAuliffe, ss	4	1	1	0	0	3
Maxvill, ss	4	0	0	0	2	4	Kaline, rf	4	0	0	0	6	0
Rudi, lf	4	0	0	0	2	0	Sims, lf	3	0	0	0	1	0
Jackson, cf	0	1	0	0	0	0	Freehan, c	4	0	0	1	3	2
Hendrick, cf	3	1	0	0	1	0	Cash, 1b	4	0	1	0	13	0
Bando, 3b	3	0	1	0	2	1	Niekro, pr	0	0	0	0	0	0
Epstein, 1b	3	0	0	0	10	0	Northrup, cf	2	0	2	0	3	0
Tenace, c	3	0	1	1	6	0	Stanley, ph	1	0	0	0	0	0
Green, 2b	4	0	0	0	1	2	Taylor, 2b	4	0	0	0	1	3
Odom, p	2	0	1	0	0	1	Rodriguez, 3b	3	0	0	0	0	3
Blue, p	1	0	0	0	0	1	Fryman, p	2	0	0	0	0	2
Totals	29	2	4	1	27	9	Horton, ph	1	0	1	0	0	0
							Knox, pr	0	0	0	0	0	0
							Hiller, p	0	0	0	0	0	0
							Totals	32	1	5	1	27	13

Oakland	0	1	0	1	0	0	0	0	0 – 2
Detroit	1	0	0	0	0	0	0	0	0 – 1

Oakland	IP.	H.	R.	ER.	BB.	SO.
Odom (Winner)	5	2	1	0	2	3
Blue (Save)	4	3	0	0	0	3

Detroit	IP.	H.	R.	ER.	BB.	SO.
Fryman (Loser)	8	4	2	1	1	3
Hiller	1	0	0	0	1	0

Errors—McAuliffe, Sims. Double play—Detroit 1. Left on base—Oakland 6, Detroit 6. Two-base hit—Odom. Stolen bases—Jackson 2, Epstein. Sacrifice hits—Bando, Alou. Hit by pitch—By Fryman (Epstein, Alou). Wild pitch—Odom. Balk—Fryman. Passed ball—Tenace. Umpires—Chylak, Rice, Barnett, Flaherty, Frantz and Denkinger. Time—2:48. Attendance—50,276.

OAKLAND ATHLETICS' BATTING AND FIELDING AVERAGES

Player–Position	G.	AB.	R.	H.	TB.	2B.	3B.	HR.	RBI.	B.A.	PO.	A.	E.	F.A.
Marquez, ph	3	3	1	2	2	0	0	0	1	.667	0	0	0	.000
Kubiak, 2b-ss	4	4	0	2	2	0	0	0	1	.500	3	8	1	.917
Campaneris, ss	2	7	3	3	3	0	0	0	0	.429	3	7	0	1.000
Alou, rf	5	21	2	8	12	4	0	0	2	.381	8	0	0	1.000
Jackson, cf	5	18	1	5	6	1	0	0	2	.278	14	0	1	.933
Rudi, lf	5	20	1	5	6	1	0	0	2	.250	11	0	0	1.000
Odom, pr-p	3	4	0	1	2	1	0	0	0	.250	2	1	0	1.000
Bando, 3b	5	20	0	4	4	0	0	0	0	.200	6	16	0	1.000
Epstein, 1b	5	16	1	3	6	0	0	1	1	.188	55	2	0	1.000
Hunter, p	2	6	0	1	1	0	0	0	0	.167	0	0	0	.000
Hendrick, ph-cf	5	7	2	1	1	0	0	0	0	.143	1	0	0	1.000
Green, 2b	5	8	0	1	2	1	0	0	0	.125	5	7	0	1.000
Maxvill, 2b-pr-ss	5	8	0	1	1	0	0	0	0	.125	3	8	0	1.000
Tenace, c-2b	5	17	1	1	1	0	0	0	1	.059	21	5	1	.963
Hamilton, p	1	0	0	0	0	0	0	0	0	.000	0	0	0	.000
Horlen, p	1	0	0	0	0	0	0	0	0	.000	0	0	0	.000
Locker, p	2	0	0	0	0	0	0	0	0	.000	0	0	0	.000
Holtzman, p	1	1	0	0	0	0	0	0	0	.000	0	1	0	1.000
Mincher, ph	1	1	0	0	0	0	0	0	0	.000	0	0	0	.000
Cullen, ss	2	1	0	0	0	0	0	0	0	.000	0	2	0	1.000
Fingers, p	3	1	0	0	0	0	0	0	0	.000	0	0	0	.000
Hegan, pr-1b-ph	3	1	1	0	0	0	0	0	0	.000	1	0	0	1.000
Blue, p	4	1	0	0	0	0	0	0	0	.000	0	1	0	1.000
Duncan, ph-c	2	2	0	0	0	0	0	0	0	.000	5	1	0	1.000
Mangual, ph	3	3	0	0	0	0	0	0	0	.000	0	0	0	.000
Totals	5	170	13	38	49	8	0	1	10	.224	138	59	3	.985

DETROIT TIGERS' BATTING AND FIELDING AVERAGES

Player–Position	G.	AB.	R.	H.	TB.	2B.	3B.	HR.	RBI.	B.A.	PO.	A.	E.	F.A.
I. Brown, 1b	1	2	0	1	1	0	0	0	2	.500	2	0	0	1.000
Coleman, p	1	2	0	1	1	0	0	0	0	.500	0	0	0	.000
Northrup, cf-lf	5	14	0	5	5	0	0	0	1	.357	12	0	0	1.000
Stanley, cf-ph	4	6	0	2	2	0	0	0	0	.333	7	0	0	1.000
Cash, 1b-ph	5	15	1	4	7	0	0	1	2	.267	39	3	0	1.000
Kaline, rf	5	19	3	5	8	0	0	1	1	.263	12	0	1	.923
Freehan, c	3	12	2	3	7	1	0	1	3	.250	24	3	0	1.000
Brinkman, ss	1	4	0	1	2	1	0	0	0	.250	1	2	0	1.000
Sims, c-lf	4	14	0	3	7	2	1	0	0	.214	16	1	1	.944
McAuliffe, 2b-ss	5	20	3	4	7	0	0	1	1	.200	12	10	4	.846
Taylor, 3b	4	15	0	2	4	2	0	0	0	.133	5	9	0	1.000
Horton, lf-ph	5	10	0	1	1	0	0	0	0	.100	6	0	0	1.000
Knox, pr	1	0	0	0	0	0	0	0	0	.000	0	0	0	.000
LaGrow, p	1	0	0	0	0	0	0	0	0	.000	0	0	0	.000
Niekro, pr	1	0	0	0	0	0	0	0	0	.000	0	0	0	.000
Scherman, p	1	0	0	0	0	0	0	0	0	.000	0	0	0	.000
Zachary, p	1	0	0	0	0	0	0	0	0	.000	0	0	0	.000
Seelbach, p	2	0	0	0	0	0	0	0	0	.000	0	0	0	.000
Hiller, p	3	0	0	0	0	0	0	0	0	.000	0	0	0	.000
Haller, ph	1	1	0	0	0	0	0	0	0	.000	0	0	0	.000
G. Brown, ph	3	2	1	0	0	0	0	0	0	.000	0	0	0	.000
Fryman, p	2	3	0	0	0	0	0	0	0	.000	0	3	0	1.000
Lolich, p	2	7	0	0	0	0	0	0	0	.000	1	3	0	1.000
Rodriguez, 3b	5	16	0	0	0	0	0	0	0	.000	2	14	1	.941
Totals	5	162	10	32	52	6	1	4	10	.198	139	48	7	.964

OAKLAND ATHLETICS' PITCHING RECORDS

Pitcher	G.	GS.	CG.	IP.	H.	R.	ER.	BB.	SO.	HB.	WP.	W.	L.	Pct.	ERA.
Odom	2	2	1	14	5	1	0	2	5	0	1	2	0	1.000	0.00
Blue	4	0	0	5⅓	4	0	0	1	5	0	0	0	0	.000	0.00
Hamilton	1	0	0	0*	1	0	0	1	0	0	0	0	0	.000	0.00
Hunter	2	2	0	15⅓	10	2	2	5	9	0	0	0	0	.000	1.17
Fingers	3	0	0	5⅓	4	1	1	1	3	0	0	1	0	1.000	1.69
Holtzman	1	1	0	4	4	2	2	2	2	0	0	0	1	.000	4.50
Locker	2	0	0	2	4	3	3	0	1	0	0	0	0	.000	13.50
Horlen	1	0	0	0*	0	1	1	1	0	0	1	0	1	.000	....
Totals	5	5	1	46	32	10	9	13	25	0	2	3	2	.600	1.76

Shutout–Odom. Save–Blue.

DETROIT TIGERS' PITCHING RECORDS

Pitcher	G.	GS.	CG.	IP.	H.	R.	ER.	BB.	SO.	HB.	WP.	W.	L.	Pct.	ERA.
Coleman	1	1	1	9	7	0	0	3	14	0	0	1	0	1.000	0.00
Hiller	3	0	0	3⅓	1	0	0	1	1	0	0	1	0	1.000	0.00
LaGrow	1	0	0	1	0	0	0	0	1	1	0	0	0	.000	0.00
Scherman	1	0	0	⅔	1	0	0	0	1	0	0	0	0	.000	0.00
Lolich	2	2	0	19	14	4	3	5	10	0	0	0	1	.000	1.42
Fryman	2	2	0	12⅓	11	6	5	2	8	2	0	0	2	.000	3.65
Seelbach	2	0	0	1	4	2	2	0	0	0	0	0	0	.000	18.00
Zachary	1	0	0	0†	0	1	1	1	0	0	2	0	0	.000	....
Totals	5	5	1	46⅓	38	13	11	12	35	3	2	2	3	.400	2.11

*Pitched to two batters in tenth inning of fourth game. †Pitched to one batter in fifth inning of second game.
Shutout–Coleman. No saves.

COMPOSITE SCORE BY INNINGS

Oakland.......................... 1 1 1   1 4 0   1 0 0   2   2 – 13
Detroit............................ 1 1 1   2 0 0   0 1 0   3   1 – 10

Sacrifice hits—Cash, Bando 2, Odom, Freehan, Kaline, Alou.
Sacrifice fly—Rudi.
Stolen bases—Campaneris 2, Alou, Maxvill, Jackson 2, Epstein.
Caught stealing—Northrup, Alou, Tenace, McAuliffe.
Double plays—Rodriguez and McAuliffe; Kubiak, Campaneris and Epstein; Taylor, McAuliffe and Cash; Maxvill and Epstein; Maxvill, Kubiak and Epstein; Bando, Tenace and Epstein; Freehan and McAuliffe; Cullen, Green and Epstein; Rodriguez, Taylor and Cash.
Left on bases—Oakland 38–10, 4, 10, 8, 6; Detroit 30–6, 2, 5, 11, 6.
Hit by pitchers—By LaGrow (Campaneris), by Fryman (Alou, Epstein).
Passed ball—Tenace.
Balk—Fryman.
Time of games—First game, 3:09; second game, 2:37; third game, 2:27; fourth game, 3:04; fifth game, 2:48.
Attendance—First game, 29,536; second game, 31,088; third game, 41,156; fourth game, 37,615; fifth game, 50,276.
Umpires—Flaherty, Chylak, Rice, Denkinger, Barnett and Frantz.
Official scorers—Watson Spoelstra, Detroit News; Dick O'Connor, Palo Alto Times.

NATIONAL LEAGUE
Championship Series of 1972

	W.	L.	Pct.
Cincinnati (West)	3	2	.600
Pittsburgh (East)	2	3	.400

You're ahead by one run in the last of the ninth and the other team has its righthanded power hitters coming up. So whom do you want to pitch?

That was the situation facing Pittsburgh Pirate Manager Bill Virdon in the final game of the 1972 National League Championship Series.

And the Buc skipper brought in his best—righthander Dave Giusti, who had saved 22 games and won seven others during the regular season. But, unfortunately for the Pirates, Virdon went to the well and came up dry.

The first batter Giusti faced was Johnny Bench, home run king of the senior circuit during the regular season. Bench unloaded one of his specialties over the right-field fence and the score was tied at 3-3.

When Tony Perez and Denis Menke followed with singles, Virdon came to the mound and led Giusti away, replacing him with another righthander, Bob Moose.

Cesar Geronimo flied out deep to right, sending George Foster, running for Perez, to third. Darrel Chaney popped out for the second out.

With Hal McRae, batting for pitcher Clay Carroll, at bat, Moose uncorked a pitch that bounced in front of the plate and skipped past catcher Manny Sanguillen. Foster raced home with the run that gave the Reds the National League pennant.

Up to the fifth game, the two teams had staged a series which had held the interest of fans throughout the country and put to rest speculation that the Championship Series had failed to catch on.

Joe Morgan, second man up in the opener, hit a home run off Steve Blass.

But that was just a prelude to the Pirate outburst. Rennie Stennett singled, Al Oliver tripled, Willie Stargell doubled and Hebner singled. It all added up to three runs, more than enough, as events proved, to win the game.

But Pittsburgh got two more in the fifth on another single by Stennett and a homer by Oliver. All of the Buc runs came off Don Gullett.

The Reds returned the favor the next day with their own big first inning as starter Moose failed to retire a batter. Pete Rose and Morgan singled and Bobby Tolan, Bench and Perez hit successive doubles to plate a total of four runs.

The Pirates picked up single runs in the fourth, fifth and sixth and actually were in good position to get much more in the fifth. They had two men on with two out and a two-ball, no-strike count on Stargell when Tom Hall replaced starter Jack Billingham on the hill for the Reds. He got Stargell on a called third strike.

The scene shifted to Cincinnati's Riverfront Stadium for the third game and the Pirates won it, 3-2. But only after a tense struggle.

Cincinnati jumped off to a lead with two runs in the third on singles by Chaney, Morgan and Tolan. A stolen base by Morgan had set up the second run.

Sanguillen's homer off starter Gary Nolan gave the Bucs a counter in the fifth. Nolan left the game after hurling six innings when his arm tightened.

Pedro Borbon took the mound for the Reds in the seventh and hit Hebner with a pitch. Sanguillen singled and Gene Alley's sacrifice moved the runners along. Carroll relieved Borbon and issued an intentional pass to Vic Davalillo, pinch-hitting for Nelson Briles. A run came in on a hit by Stennett which bounced over the head of Perez at first. A double play got the Reds out of the inning with the score tied.

But Pittsburgh was not to be denied in the eighth. With one out, Stargell walked, Oliver doubled and Hebner was purposely passed to load the bases. Sanguillen forced Hebner at second, Chaney to Morgan, but the Pirates' catcher beat the relay to first and the winning run scored.

Pittsburgh was in a position at that stage to clinch its second successive flag, but the Pirates never came close the next day. Lefty Ross Grimsley set them down with just two hits, both by Roberto Clemente, as his teammates battered four Pirate pitchers for 11 hits and seven runs.

That brought the teams to the climactic fifth game.

GAME OF SATURDAY, OCTOBER 7, AT PITTSBURGH

Cincinnati	AB.	R.	H.	RBI.	PO.	A.	Pittsburgh	AB.	R.	H.	RBI.	PO.	A.
Rose, lf	5	0	2	0	1	0	Stennett, lf	4	2	2	0	7	0
Morgan, 2b	4	1	1	1	0	6	Oliver, cf	4	2	2	3	8	0
Tolan, cf	5	0	1	0	4	0	Clemente, rf	4	0	0	0	3	0
Bench, c	3	0	0	0	3	0	Stargell, 1b	3	1	1	1	2	0
Perez, 1b	4	0	1	0	14	0	Robertson, 1b	0	0	0	0	1	0
Menke, 3b	3	0	1	0	0	1	Sanguillen, c	3	0	0	0	2	0
Geronimo, rf	4	0	0	0	2	0	Hebner, 3b	3	0	1	1	0	0
Chaney, ss	4	0	0	0	0	4	Cash, 2b	3	0	0	0	0	2
Gullett, p	2	0	1	0	0	0	Alley, ss	3	0	0	0	3	0
Uhlaender, ph	1	0	1	0	0	0	Blass, p	3	0	0	0	1	0
Borbon, p	0	0	0	0	0	0	R. Hernandez, p	0	0	0	0	0	0
Hague, ph	0	0	0	0	0	0	Totals	30	5	6	5	27	2
Totals	35	1	8	1	24	11							

Cincinnati	1	0	0	0	0	0	0	0	0 – 1
Pittsburgh	3	0	0	0	2	0	0	0	x – 5

Cincinnati	IP.	H.	R.	ER.	BB.	SO.
Gullett (Loser)	6	6	5	5	0	3
Borbon	2	0	0	0	0	0

Pittsburgh	IP.	H.	R.	ER.	BB.	SO.
Blass (Winner)	8⅓	8	1	1	4	1
B. Hernandez (Save)	⅔	0	0	0	0	1

Errors—None. Left on base—Cincinnati 11, Pittsburgh 1. Two-base hits—Stargell, Rose. Three-base hit—Oliver. Home runs—Morgan, Oliver. Passed ball—Bench. Umpires—Donatelli, Burkhart, Harvey, Williams, Kibler and Wendelstedt. Time—1:57. Attendance—50,476.

GAME OF SUNDAY, OCTOBER 8, AT PITTSBURGH

Cincinnati	AB.	R.	H.	RBI.	PO.	A.	Pittsburgh	AB.	R.	H.	RBI.	PO.	A.
Rose, lf	4	1	1	0	2	0	Stennett, lf-2b	4	0	1	0	2	0
Morgan, 2b	4	2	2	1	3	4	Oliver, cf	5	1	2	0	3	0
Tolan, cf	4	1	2	2	1	0	Clemente, rf	3	0	0	1	1	0
Bench, c	4	1	1	0	8	0	Stargell, 1b-lf	3	0	0	0	6	0
Perez, 1b	4	0	1	2	7	2	Hebner, 3b	4	0	0	0	0	3
Menke, 3b	3	0	0	0	1	2	May, c	2	0	1	1	8	1
Geronimo, rf	4	0	1	0	1	0	Sanguillen, ph-c	2	1	1	0	2	0
Chaney, ss	2	0	0	0	2	2	Cash, 2b	4	0	1	1	2	1
Concepcion, ph-ss	2	0	0	0	0	0	Giusti, p	0	0	0	0	0	0
Billingham, p	2	0	0	0	1	0	Alley, ss	3	1	0	0	1	1
Hall, p	1	0	0	0	1	0	Moose, p	0	0	0	0	0	0
Totals	34	5	8	5	27	10	Johnson, p	1	0	0	0	0	0
							Mazeroski, ph	1	0	1	0	0	0
							Ellis, pr	0	0	0	0	0	0
							Kison, p	0	0	0	0	0	0
							Clines, ph	1	0	0	0	0	0
							R. Hernandez, p	0	0	0	0	0	2
							Robertson, 1b	0	0	0	0	1	0
							Totals	33	3	7	3	27	8

Cincinnati	4	0	0	0	0	0	0	1	0 – 5
Pittsburgh	0	0	0	1	1	1	0	0	0 – 3

Cincinnati	IP.	H.	R.	ER.	BB.	SO.
Billingham	4⅔	5	2	2	2	4
Hall (Winner)	4⅓	2	1	1	2	4

Pittsburgh	IP.	H.	R.	ER.	BB.	SO.
Moose (Loser)	0*	5	4	4	0	0
Johnson	5	1	0	0	1	6
Kison	1	0	0	0	0	2
R. Hernandez	2	1	1	1	0	1
Giusti	1	1	0	0	0	1

*Pitched to five batters in first.

Errors—Bench, Cash. Double plays—Cincinnati 1, Pittsburgh 2. Left on base—Cincinnati 3, Pittsburgh 8. Two-base hits—Tolan, Bench, Perez, Oliver, Sanguillen. Home run—Morgan. Hit by pitcher—By Billingham (Alley). Wild pitch—Johnson. Umpires—Burkhart, Harvey, Williams, Kibler, Wendelstedt and Donatelli. Time —2:43. Attendance—50,584.

GAME OF MONDAY, OCTOBER 9, AT CINCINNATI

Pittsburgh	AB.	R.	H.	RBI.	PO.	A.	Cincinnati	AB.	R.	H.	RBI.	PO.	A.
Stennett, lf	5	0	2	1	4	1	Rose, lf	4	0	3	0	3	0
Cash, 2b	5	0	1	0	1	0	Morgan, 2b	4	1	1	1	5	1
Clemente, rf	3	0	1	0	2	0	Tolan, cf	4	0	1	1	2	0
Stargell, 1b	3	0	0	0	4	2	Bench, c	4	0	1	0	5	2
Clines, pr	0	1	0	0	0	0	Perez, 1b	4	0	1	0	5	0
Robertson, 1b	0	0	0	0	0	1	Concepcion, pr	0	0	0	0	0	0
Oliver, cf	4	0	1	0	1	1	Menke, 3b	3	0	0	0	1	3
Hebner, 3b	2	1	0	0	1	1	Geronimo, rf	4	0	0	0	4	1
Sanguillen, c	4	1	2	2	8	0	Chaney, ss	3	1	1	0	2	3
Alley, ss	3	0	0	0	4	1	Nolan, p	2	0	0	0	0	0
Briles, p	2	0	0	0	1	1	Borbon, p	0	0	0	0	0	0
Davalillo, ph	0	0	0	0	0	0	Carroll, p	0	0	0	0	0	1
Kison, p	0	0	0	0	0	0	Hague, ph	1	0	0	0	0	0
Giusti, p	1	0	0	0	1	0	McGlothlin, p	0	0	0	0	0	0
Totals	32	3	7	3	27	8	Totals	33	2	8	2	27	11

Pittsburgh	0	0	0	0	1	0	1	1	0 – 3
Cincinnati	0	0	2	0	0	0	0	0	0 – 2

Pittsburgh	IP.	H.	R.	ER.	BB.	SO.
Briles	6	6	2	2	1	3
Kison (Winner)	1⅓	1	0	0	0	1
Giusti (Save)	1⅔	1	0	0	0	2

Cincinnati	IP.	H.	R.	ER.	BB.	SO.
Nolan	6	4	1	1	1	4
Borbon	⅓	1	1	1	0	0
Carroll (Loser)	1⅔	2	1	1	3	0
McGlothlin	1	0	0	0	0	0

Error—Chaney. Double plays—Pittsburgh 1, Cincinnati 1. Left on base—Pittsburgh 8, Cincinnati 5. Two-base hits—Rose 2, Clemente, Oliver. Three-base hit—Bench. Home run—Sanguillen. Stolen base—Morgan. Sacrifice hit—Alley. Hit by pitcher—By Borbon (Hebner). Wild pitch—Nolan. Umpires—Harvey, Williams, Kibler, Wendelstedt, Donatelli and Burkhart. Time—2:33. Attendance—52,420.

GAME OF TUESDAY, OCTOBER 10, AT CINCINNATI

Pittsburgh	AB.	R.	H.	RBI.	PO.	A.	Cincinnati	AB.	R.	H.	RBI.	PO.	A.
Stennett, lf	4	0	0	0	3	0	Rose, lf	4	0	2	1	1	0
Oliver, cf	4	0	0	0	4	0	Morgan, 2b	3	1	1	0	1	4
Clemente, rf	4	1	2	1	1	0	Tolan, cf	4	2	1	1	4	0
Stargell, 1b	3	0	0	0	7	1	Bench, c	3	1	2	1	5	0
Sanguillen, c	3	0	0	0	5	0	Perez, 1b	4	0	0	0	11	0
Cash, 2b	3	0	0	0	0	2	Menke, 3b	4	1	2	0	0	1
Hebner, 3b	3	0	0	0	3	5	Geronimo, rf	4	1	0	0	2	0
Alley, ss	3	0	0	0	1	1	Chaney, ss	3	1	1	1	3	6
Ellis, p	1	0	0	0	0	0	Grimsley, p	4	0	2	1	0	0
Mazeroski, ph	1	0	0	0	0	0	Totals	33	7	11	5	27	11
Johnson, p	0	0	0	0	0	0							
Walker, p	0	0	0	0	0	0							
Clines, ph	1	0	0	0	0	0							
Miller, p	0	0	0	0	0	0							
Totals	30	1	2	1	24	9							

Pittsburgh	0	0	0	0	0	0	1	0	0 – 1
Cincinnati	1	0	0	2	0	2	2	0	x – 7

Pittsburgh	IP.	H.	R.	ER.	BB.	SO.
Ellis (Loser)	5	5	3	0	1	3
Johnson	1	3	2	2	1	1
Walker	1	3	2	2	0	0
Miller	1	0	0	0	0	1

Cincinnati	IP.	H.	R.	ER.	BB.	SO.
Grimsley (Winner)	9	2	1	1	0	5

Errors—Sanguillen, Chaney, Alley 2. Left on base—Pittsburgh 2, Cincinnati 6. Two-base hits—Grimsley, Menke. Three-base hit—Tolan. Home run—Clemente. Stolen bases—Bench 2, Chaney. Sacrifice hit—Morgan. Sacrifice fly—Bench. Umpires—Williams, Kibler, Wendelstedt, Donatelli, Burkhart and Harvey. Time—1:58. Attendance—39,447.

GAME OF WEDNESDAY, OCTOBER 11, AT CINCINNATI

Pittsburgh	AB.	R.	H.	RBI.	PO.	A.	Cincinnati	AB.	R.	H.	RBI.	PO.	A.
Stennett, lf	4	0	1	0	1	0	Rose, lf	3	0	1	1	3	0
Oliver, cf	3	0	0	0	1	0	Morgan, 2b	4	0	0	0	2	3
Clemente, rf	3	0	1	0	3	0	Tolan, cf	4	0	0	0	2	0
Stargell, 1b	4	0	0	0	13	0	Bench, c	4	1	2	1	7	1
Robertson, 1b	0	0	0	0	0	0	Perez, 1b	4	0	1	0	8	1
Sanguillen, c	4	2	2	0	5	0	Foster, pr	0	1	0	0	0	0
Hebner, 3b	4	1	2	0	0	2	Menke, 3b	3	0	1	0	1	4
Cash, 2b	4	0	2	2	2	5	Geronimo, rf	4	1	1	1	2	0
Alley, ss	4	0	0	0	1	1	Chaney, ss	4	1	1	0	1	1
Blass, p	3	0	0	0	0	3	Gullett, p	0	0	0	0	0	0
R. Hernandez, p	0	0	0	0	0	0	Borbon, p	0	0	0	0	1	0
Giusti, p	0	0	0	0	0	0	Uhlaender, ph	1	0	0	0	0	0
Moose, p	0	0	0	0	0	0	Hall, p	0	0	0	0	0	0
Totals	33	3	8	2	26	11	Hague, ph	0	0	0	0	0	0
							Concepcion, pr	0	0	0	0	0	0
							Carroll, p	0	0	0	0	0	0
							McRae, ph	0	0	0	0	0	0
							Totals	31	4	7	3	27	10

Pittsburgh	0	2	0	1	0	0	0	0	0 – 3
Cincinnati	0	0	1	0	1	0	0	0	2 – 4

Two out when winning run scored.

Pittsburgh	IP.	H.	R.	ER.	BB.	SO.
Blass	7⅓	4	2	2	2	4
R. Hernandez	⅔	0	0	0	0	1
Giusti (Loser)	0†	3	2	2	0	0
Moose	⅔	0	0	0	0	0

Cincinnati	IP.	H.	R.	ER.	BB.	SO.
Gullett	3*	6	3	3	0	2
Borbon	2	1	0	0	0	1
Hall	3	1	0	0	1	4
Carroll (Winner)	1	0	0	0	0	0

*Pitched to two batters in fourth.
†Pitched to three batters in ninth.

Error—Chaney. Double play—Cincinnati 1. Left on base—Pittsburgh 5, Cincinnati 5. Two-base hits—Hebner, Rose. Home runs—Geronimo, Bench. Sacrifice hits—Gullett, Oliver, Rose. Wild pitches—Gullett, Moose. Umpires—Donatelli, Kibler, Wendelstedt, Burkhart, Harvey and Williams. Time—2:19. Attendance—41,887.

CINCINNATI REDS' BATTING AND FIELDING AVERAGES

Player—Position	G.	AB.	R.	H.	TB.	2B.	3B.	HR.	RBI.	B.A.	PO.	A.	E.	F.A.
Grimsley, p	1	4	0	2	3	1	0	0	1	.500	0	0	0	.000
Gullett, p	2	2	0	1	1	0	0	0	0	.500	0	0	0	.000
Uhlaender, ph	2	2	0	1	1	0	0	0	0	.500	0	0	0	.000
Rose, lf	5	20	1	9	13	4	0	0	2	.450	10	0	0	1.000
Bench, c	5	18	3	6	12	1	1	1	2	.333	28	3	1	.969
Morgan, 2b	5	19	5	5	11	0	0	2	3	.263	11	18	0	1.000
Menke, 3b	5	16	1	4	5	1	0	0	0	.250	3	11	0	1.000
Tolan, cf	5	21	3	5	8	1	1	0	4	.238	13	0	0	1.000
Perez, 1b	5	20	0	4	5	1	0	0	2	.200	45	3	0	1.000
Chaney, ss	5	16	3	3	3	0	0	0	1	.188	8	16	3	.889
Geronimo, rf	5	20	2	2	5	0	0	1	1	.100	11	1	0	1.000
Foster, pr	1	0	1	0	0	0	0	0	0	.000	0	0	0	.000
McGlothlin, p	1	0	0	0	0	0	0	0	0	.000	0	0	0	.000
McRae, ph	1	0	0	0	0	0	0	0	0	.000	0	0	0	.000
Carroll, p	2	0	0	0	0	0	0	0	0	.000	0	1	0	1.000
Borbon, p	3	0	0	0	0	0	0	0	0	.000	0	1	0	1.000
Hague, ph	3	1	0	0	0	0	0	0	0	.000	0	0	0	.000
Hall, p	2	1	0	0	0	0	0	0	0	.000	0	1	0	1.000
Billingham, p	1	2	0	0	0	0	0	0	0	.000	1	0	0	1.000
Nolan, p	1	2	0	0	0	0	0	0	0	.000	0	0	0	.000
Concepcion, ph-ss-pr	3	2	0	0	0	0	0	0	0	.000	0	0	0	.000
Totals	5	166	19	42	67	9	2	4	16	.253	132	53	4	.979

PITTSBURGH PIRATES' BATTING AND FIELDING AVERAGES

Player—Position	G.	AB.	R.	H.	TB.	2B.	3B.	HR.	RBI.	B.A.	PO.	A.	E.	F.A.
May, c	1	2	0	1	1	0	0	0	1	.500	8	1	0	1.000
Mazeroski, ph	2	2	0	1	1	0	0	0	0	.500	0	0	0	.000
Sanguillen, c-ph	5	16	4	5	9	1	0	1	2	.313	22	0	1	.957
Stennett, lf-2b	5	21	2	6	6	0	0	0	1	.286	17	1	0	1.000
Oliver, cf	5	20	3	5	12	2	1	1	3	.250	17	1	0	1.000
Clemente, rf	5	17	1	4	8	1	0	1	2	.235	10	0	0	1.000
Cash, 2b	5	19	0	4	4	0	0	0	3	.211	5	10	1	.938
Hebner, 3b	5	16	2	3	4	1	0	0	1	.188	5	11	0	1.000
Stargell, 1b-lf	5	16	1	1	2	1	0	0	1	.063	32	3	0	1.000
Davalillo, ph	1	0	0	0	0	0	0	0	0	.000	0	0	0	.000
Miller, p	1	0	0	0	0	0	0	0	0	.000	0	0	0	.000
Walker, p	1	0	0	0	0	0	0	0	0	.000	0	0	0	.000
Kison, p	2	0	0	0	0	0	0	0	0	.000	0	0	0	.000
Moose, p	2	0	0	0	0	0	0	0	0	.000	0	0	0	.000
R. Hernandez, p	3	0	0	0	0	0	0	0	0	.000	0	2	0	1.000

Player—Position	G.	AB.	R.	H.	TB.	2B.	3B.	HR.	RBI.	B.A.	PO.	A.	E.	F.A.
Robertson, 1b	4	0	0	0	0	0	0	0	0	.000	2	1	0	1.000
Ellis, pr-p	2	1	0	0	0	0	0	0	0	.000	0	0	0	.000
Johnson, p	2	1	0	0	0	0	0	0	0	.000	0	0	0	.000
Giusti, p	3	1	0	0	0	0	0	0	0	.000	1	0	0	1.000
Briles, p	1	2	0	0	0	0	0	0	0	.000	1	1	0	1.000
Clines, ph-pr	3	2	1	0	0	0	0	0	0	.000	0	0	0	.000
Blass, p	2	6	0	0	0	0	0	0	0	.000	1	3	0	1.000
Alley, ss	5	16	1	0	0	0	0	0	0	.000	10	4	2	.875
Totals	5	158	15	30	47	6	1	3	14	.190	131	38	4	.977

CINCINNATI REDS' PITCHING RECORDS

Pitcher	G.	GS.	CG.	IP.	H.	R.	ER.	BB.	SO.	HB.	WP.	W.	L.	Pct.	ERA.
McGlothlin	1	0	0	1	0	0	0	0	0	0	0	0	0	.000	0.00
Grimsley	1	1	1	9	2	1	1	0	5	0	0	1	0	1.000	1.00
Hall	2	0	0	7⅓	3	1	1	3	8	0	0	1	0	1.000	1.23
Nolan	1	1	0	6	4	1	1	1	4	0	1	0	0	.000	1.50
Borbon	3	0	0	4⅓	2	1	1	0	1	1	0	0	0	.000	2.08
Carroll	2	0	0	2⅔	2	1	1	3	0	0	0	1	1	.500	3.38
Billingham	1	1	0	4⅔	5	2	2	2	4	1	0	0	0	.000	3.86
Gullett	2	2	0	9	12	8	8	0	5	0	1	0	1	.000	8.00
Totals	5	5	1	44	30	15	15	9	27	2	2	3	2	.600	3.07

No shutouts or saves.

PITTSBURGH PIRATES' PITCHING RECORDS

Pitcher	G.	GS.	CG.	IP.	H.	R.	ER.	BB.	SO.	HB.	WP.	W.	L.	Pct.	ERA.
Ellis	1	1	0	5	5	3	0	1	3	0	0	0	1	.000	0.00
Kison	2	0	0	2⅓	1	0	0	0	3	0	0	1	0	1.000	0.00
Miller	1	0	0	1	0	0	0	1	0	0	0	0	0	.000	0.00
Blass	2	2	0	15⅔	12	3	3	6	5	0	0	1	0	1.000	1.72
R. Hernandez	3	0	0	3⅓	1	1	1	0	3	0	0	0	0	.000	2.70
Briles	1	1	0	6	6	2	2	1	3	0	0	0	0	.000	3.00
Johnson	2	0	0	6	4	2	2	7	0	1	0	0	0	.000	3.00
Giusti	3	0	0	2⅔	5	2	2	0	3	0	0	0	1	.000	6.75
Walker	1	0	0	1	3	2	2	0	0	0	0	0	0	.000	18.00
Moose	2	1	0	⅔	5	4	4	0	0	0	1	0	1	.000	54.00
Totals	5	5	0	43⅔	42	19	16	10	28	0	2	2	3	.400	3.30

No shutouts. Saves—R. Hernandez, Giusti.

COMPOSITE SCORE BY INNINGS

Cincinnati	6	0	3	2	1	2	2	1	2 – 19
Pittsburgh	3	2	0	2	4	1	2	1	0 – 15

Sacrifice hits—Alley, Morgan, Oliver, Rose, Gullett.
Sacrifice fly—Bench.
Stolen bases—Morgan, Bench 2, Chaney.
Caught stealing—Tolan, Stennett.
Double plays—Morgan, Chaney and Perez 2; Hebner and Stargell; May and Cash; Stennett and Sanguillen; Geronimo, Bench and Morgan.
Left on bases—Cincinnati 30—11, 3, 5, 6, 5; Pittsburgh 24—1, 8, 8, 2, 5.
Hit by pitcher—By Billingham (Alley); by Borbon (Hebner).
Passed ball—Bench.
Balks—None.
Time of games—First game, 1:57; second game, 2:43; third game, 2:33; fourth game, 1:58; fifth game, 2:19.
Attendance—First game, 50,476; second game, 50,584; third game, 52,420; fourth game, 39,447; fifth game, 41,887.
Umpires—Donatelli, Burkhart, Harvey, Williams, Kibler and Wendelstedt.
Official scorers—Jim Ferguson, Dayton Daily News; Luke Quay, McKeesport Daily News.

AMERICAN LEAGUE
Championship Series of 1973

	W.	L.	Pct.
Oakland (West)	3	2	.600
Baltimore (East)	2	3	.400

The Oakland A's won their second straight American League pennant when they downed the Baltimore Orioles in a five-game Championship Series.

They almost won it in four games, but a last-ditch Baltimore rally sent the series to a climactic fifth game.

The Orioles, who had been in three previous Championship Series (1969, 1970, 1971) and had never lost a game, continued their winning ways in the opening contest, played at Memorial Stadium in Baltimore.

Jim Palmer spent 16 minutes retiring the side in the top of the first inning. He walked the first two batters and struck out the next three.

The Orioles went to work against lefty Vida Blue and his successor, Horacio Pina. During that time, Merv Rettenmund singled, Paul Blair walked, Tommie Davis doubled, Don Baylor walked, Earl Williams singled, Andy Etchebarren was hit by a pitch and Mark Belanger singled. When the carnage was over, the Orioles had four runs. It was much more than they needed as Palmer proceeded to hurl a five-hit shutout, striking out 12 A's along the way. The final score was 6-0.

The Orioles' playoff winning streak was snapped at 10 the next day when Sal Bando hit two home runs off Dave McNally while Campy Campaneris and Joe Rudi hit one apiece. Catfish Hunter, who served up so many during the season that he threatened an A.L. record, didn't allow any, and the A's won the game, 6-3.

The third game, postponed a day by rain—the postponement triggered a rhubarb between A. L. President Joe Cronin and A's President Charlie Finley—was played at the Oakland-Alameda County Coliseum and produced a brilliant pitching battle between a pair of southpaws, Mike Cuellar of Baltimore and Ken Holtzman. It was decided in favor of the A's when Campaneris, first man up in the bottom of the 11th, snapped a 1-1 tie by hitting Cuellar's second pitch over the left-field fence for a home run.

Up to that point, Cuellar had allowed only three hits. He had a one-hit shutout for the first seven innings as he carefully nursed a 1-0 lead given him by Earl Williams' homer in the second inning. But in the eighth, pinch-hitter Jesus Alou singled and pinch-runner Allan Lewis was sacrificed to second by Mike Andrews. The play was controversial in that Cuellar appeared to have a force out at second base, but he ignored catcher Etchebarren's yells and took the safe out at first. This proved costly as, one out later, Joe Rudi singled home Lewis to tie the score.

The Oakland club appeared to have the flag safely tucked away in the fourth contest but it escaped them.

The A's knocked out Palmer with a three-run outburst in the second inning and, going into the top of the seventh, Blue was breezing along with a 4-0 bulge when he suddenly came apart at the seams. Williams drew a base on balls and Baylor followed with a single. Brooks Robinson came through with a run-producing single and Etchebarren hit the next pitch for a home run, making the score 4-4.

The tie didn't last long. The next inning Bobby Grich hit a home run off Rollie Fingers and that, coupled with Grant Jackson's stout relief pitching, gave the game to the Orioles and set up the contest for all the money the next afternoon.

A surprisingly small crowd of 24,265 showed up for the final game and they saw Hunter pitch a five-hit shutout, winning 3-0. Righthander Doyle Alexander was the Baltimore starter but he lasted only until the fourth inning. In that frame he was the victim of singles by Gene Tenace and Alou wrapped around a triple by Vic Davalillo. He was relieved by Palmer, who shut out Oakland the rest of the way, but the Orioles were helpless against Hunter's powerful pitching.

The A's first run in the game had come in the third inning on an error by Robinson, a sacrifice, and a single by Rudi.

GAME OF SATURDAY, OCTOBER 6, AT BALTIMORE

Oakland	AB.	R.	H.	RBI.	PO.	A.
Campaneris, ss	3	0	1	0	0	2
Rudi, lf	2	0	0	0	4	0
Bando, 3b	3	0	0	0	2	2
Jackson, rf	4	0	1	0	1	0
Johnson, dh	2	0	0	0	0	0
Bourque, dh	1	0	0	0	0	0
Tenace, 1b-c	4	0	1	0	5	0
Mangual, cf	4	0	0	0	1	0
Fosse, c	2	0	0	0	8	1
Davalillo, ph-1b	2	0	2	0	1	0
Green, 2b	2	0	0	0	2	0
Alou, ph	1	0	0	0	0	0
Kubiak, 2b	1	0	0	0	0	0
Blue, p	0	0	0	0	0	0
Pina, p	0	0	0	0	0	0
Odom, p	0	0	0	0	0	1
Fingers, p	0	0	0	0	0	0
Totals	31	0	5	0	24	6

Baltimore	AB.	R.	H.	RBI.	PO.	A.
Rettenmund, rf	4	1	1	0	0	0
Grich, 2b	5	0	0	0	3	0
Blair, cf	4	2	1	0	2	0
Davis, dh	5	1	3	1	0	0
Baylor, lf	3	2	2	1	4	0
Robinson, 3b	5	0	0	0	0	2
Williams, 1b	4	0	2	2	3	1
Etchebarren, c	3	0	2	1	12	0
Belanger, ss	3	0	1	1	2	2
Palmer, p	0	0	0	0	1	0
Totals	36	6	12	6	27	5

Oakland	0	0	0	0	0	0	0	0	0 – 0
Baltimore	4	0	0	0	0	0	1	1	x – 6

Oakland	IP.	H.	R.	ER.	BB.	SO.
Blue (Loser)	⅔	3	4	4	2	2
Pina	2	3	0	0	1	1
Odom	5	6	2	1	2	4
Fingers	⅓	0	0	0	0	0
Baltimore	IP.	H.	R.	ER.	BB.	SO.
Palmer (Winner)	9	5	0	0	5	12

Error—Campaneris. Double plays—Oakland 1, Baltimore 1. Left on base—Oakland 9, Baltimore 12. Two-base hits—Davis, Williams, Davalillo. Stolen base—Campaneris. Hit by pitch—By Pina (Etchebarren). Wild pitch—Blue. Umpires—Chylak, Haller, Maloney, Odom, Anthony and McCoy. Time—2:51. Attendance—41,279.

GAME OF SUNDAY, OCTOBER 7, AT BALTIMORE

Oakland	AB.	R.	H.	RBI.	PO.	A.	Baltimore	AB.	R.	H.	RBI.	PO.	A.
Campaneris, ss	5	2	3	2	5	3	Bumbry, lf	4	1	0	0	2	0
Rudi, lf	4	1	2	1	2	0	Coggins, rf-cf	5	1	2	0	2	0
Bando, 3b	4	2	2	3	1	1	Davis, dh	5	0	2	1	0	0
R. Jackson, rf	5	0	0	0	3	0	Powell, 1b	4	1	0	0	7	0
Tenace, 1b	3	0	0	0	6	1	Williams, c	4	0	2	1	8	0
Johnson, dh	4	0	1	0	0	0	Blair, cf	3	0	0	0	4	0
Mangual, cf	4	1	1	0	1	0	Crowley, ph-rf	1	0	0	0	1	0
Fosse, c	3	0	0	0	7	0	Robinson, 3b	3	0	1	1	0	2
Green, 2b	4	0	0	1	1	4	Hood, pr	0	0	0	0	0	0
Hunter, p	0	0	0	0	1	0	Baker, ss	0	0	0	0	0	0
Fingers, p	0	0	0	0	0	0	Grich, 2b	2	0	0	0	2	0
Totals	36	6	9	6	27	9	Belanger, ss	3	0	1	0	0	6
							Baylor, ph	1	0	0	0	0	0
							Brown, 3b	0	0	0	0	0	0
							McNally, p	0	0	0	0	0	0
							Reynolds, p	0	0	0	0	1	0
							G. Jackson, p	0	0	0	0	0	0
							Totals	35	3	8	3	27	8

Oakland	1	0	0	0	0	2	0	2	1 – 6
Baltimore	1	0	0	0	0	1	0	1	0 – 3

Oakland	IP.	H.	R.	ER.	BB.	SO.
Hunter (Winner)	7⅓	7	3	3	3	5
Fingers (Save)	1⅔	1	0	0	1	1
Baltimore	IP.	H.	R.	ER.	BB.	SO.
McNally (Loser)	7⅔	7	5	5	2	7
Reynolds	1	2	1	1	1	2
G. Jackson	⅓	0	0	0	0	0

Errors—None. Left on base—Oakland 7, Baltimore 9. Two-base hit—Williams. Home runs—Campaneris, Rudi, Bando 2. Stolen bases—Campaneris 2. Sacrifice hit—Fosse. Wild pitch—McNally. Passed ball—Williams. Umpires—Haller, Chylak, Maloney, Odom, Anthony and McCoy. Time—2:42. Attendance—48,425.

GAME OF TUESDAY, OCTOBER 9, AT OAKLAND

Baltimore	AB.	R.	H.	RBI.	PO.	A.	Oakland	AB.	R.	H.	RBI.	PO.	A.
Rettenmund, rf	5	0	0	0	2	0	Campaneris, ss	5	1	1	1	1	3
Grich, 2b	5	0	1	0	1	4	Rudi, lf	4	0	1	1	1	0
Blair, cf	4	0	1	0	1	0	Bando, 3b	4	0	0	0	2	2
Davis, dh	3	0	0	0	0	0	Jackson, rf	4	0	0	0	4	0
Baylor, lf	4	0	0	1	0	0	Tenace, 1b-c	4	0	1	0	9	1
Robinson, 3b	4	0	0	0	4	0	Johnson, dh	2	0	0	0	0	0
Williams, 1b	4	1	1	1	13	0	Conigliaro, cf	4	0	0	0	5	0
Etchebarren, c	4	0	0	0	10	1	Fosse, c	1	0	0	0	6	0
Belanger, ss	4	0	0	0	2	2	Alou, ph	1	0	1	0	0	0
Cuellar, p	0	0	0	0	0	2	Lewis, pr	0	1	0	0	0	0
Totals	37	1	3	1	30	13	Davalillo, 1b	1	0	0	0	2	0
							Green, 2b	2	0	0	0	2	2
							Andrews, ph	0	0	0	0	0	0
							Kubiak, 2b	1	0	0	0	0	1
							Holtzman, p	0	0	0	0	1	2
							Totals	33	2	4	2	33	11

Baltimore	0	1	0	0	0	0	0	0	0	0 – 1
Oakland	0	0	0	0	0	1	0	0	1 – 2

None out when winning run scored.

Baltimore	IP.*	H.	R.	ER.	BB.	SO.
Cuellar (Loser)	10*	4	2	2	3	11
Oakland	IP.	H.	R.	ER.	BB.	SO.
Holtzman (Winner)	11	3	1	1	1	7

*Pitched to one batter in eleventh.

Errors—Green 2, Davalillo. Double play—Oakland 1. Left on base—Baltimore 4, Oakland 5. Home runs—Williams, Campaneris. Sacrifice hit—Andrews. Umpires—Maloney, Haller, Anthony, Chylak, McCoy and Odom. Time—2:23. Attendance—34,367.

GAME OF WEDNESDAY, OCTOBER 10, AT OAKLAND

Baltimore	AB.	R.	H.	RBI.	PO.	A.
Rettenmund, rf	2	0	0	0	1	0
Grich, 2b	4	1	1	1	4	3
Blair, cf	4	0	1	0	0	0
Davis, dh	4	0	1	0	0	0
Williams, 1b	3	1	0	0	9	0
Baylor, lf	3	1	1	0	2	0
Robinson, 3b	4	1	2	1	1	3
Etchebarren, c	4	1	2	3	6	1
Belanger, ss	4	0	0	0	4	2
Palmer, p	0	0	0	0	0	0
Reynolds, p	0	0	0	0	0	0
Watt, p.	0	0	0	0	0	1
G. Jackson, p	0	0	0	0	0	0
Totals	32	5	8	5	27	10

Oakland	AB.	R.	H.	RBI.	PO.	A.
Campaneris, ss	4	0	1	0	0	3
Rudi, lf	4	0	0	0	2	0
Bando, 3b	3	0	0	0	0	1
R. Jackson, rf	4	0	1	0	7	0
Tenace, 1b-c	3	2	1	0	7	1
Davalillo, cf	3	1	2	0	1	0
Mangual, ph-cf	1	0	0	0	0	0
Johnson, dh	2	0	0	0	0	0
Bourque, ph-dh	0	0	0	0	0	0
Andrews, ph-1b	1	0	0	0	1	0
Fosse, c	2	1	1	3	3	2
Lewis, pr	0	0	0	0	0	0
Kubiak, 2b	0	0	0	0	0	0
Green, 2b	3	0	1	1	5	3
Alou, ph	1	0	0	0	0	0
Fingers, p	0	0	0	0	0	0
Blue, p	0	0	0	0	1	0
Totals	31	4	7	4	27	10

Baltimore	0	0	0	0	0	0	4	1	0	– 5
Oakland	0	3	0	0	0	1	0	0	0	– 4

Baltimore	IP.	H.	R.	ER.	BB.	SO.
Palmer	1⅓	4	3	3	2	2
Reynolds	4⅔*	3	1	1	2	3
Watt	⅓	0	0	0	0	0
G. Jackson (Winner)	2⅔	0	0	0	1	0

Oakland	IP.	H.	R.	ER.	BB.	SO.
Blue	6⅓	5	4	4	3	1
Fingers (Loser)	2⅔	3	1	1	1	3

*Pitched to one batter in seventh.

Errors–None. Double plays–Oakland 2. Left on base–Baltimore 4, Oakland 8. Two-base hits–Tenace, Fosse, Green, Robinson. Home runs–Etchebarren, Grich. Sacrifice hit–Rudi. Sacrifice fly–Fosse. Hit by pitch–By Watt (Bando). Umpires–Chylak, Haller, Maloney, Odom, Anthony and McCoy. Time–2:31. Attendance–27,497.

GAME OF THURSDAY, OCTOBER 11, AT OAKLAND

Baltimore	AB.	R.	H.	RBI.	PO.	A.
Bumbry, lf	3	0	0	0	2	1
Coggins, rf	4	0	2	0	2	0
Davis, dh	4	0	0	0	0	0
Williams, 1b	3	0	0	0	10	1
Blair, cf	3	0	0	0	1	0
Robinson, 3b	4	0	2	0	1	3
Grich, 2b	4	0	0	0	6	2
Etchebarren, c	3	0	1	0	2	0
Belanger, ss	2	0	0	0	0	5
Crowley, ph	1	0	0	0	0	0
Baker, ss	0	0	0	0	0	0
Alexander, p	0	0	0	0	0	2
Palmer, p	0	0	0	0	0	1
Totals	31	0	5	0	24	15

Oakland	AB.	R.	H.	RBI.	PO.	A.
Campaneris, ss	4	0	1	0	0	4
Rudi, lf	4	0	1	1	2	0
Bando, 3b	4	0	1	0	2	4
Jackson, rf	4	0	1	0	4	0
Tenace, 1b	3	1	1	0	13	0
Davalillo, cf	2	1	1	1	3	0
Alou, dh	3	0	1	1	0	0
Fosse, c	3	1	0	0	1	1
Green, 2b	2	0	0	0	2	2
Hunter, p	0	0	0	0	0	0
Totals	29	3	7	3	27	11

Baltimore	0	0	0	0	0	0	0	0	0	– 0
Oakland	0	0	1	2	0	0	0	0	x	– 3

Baltimore	IP.	H.	R.	ER.	BB.	SO.
Alexander (Loser)	3⅔	5	3	2	0	1
Palmer	4⅓	2	0	0	1	1

Oakland	IP.	H.	R.	ER.	BB.	SO.
Hunter (Winner)	9	5	0	0	2	1

Errors–Robinson, Bumbry. Double play–Baltimore 1. Left on base–Baltimore 7, Oakland 5. Two-base hits–Etchebarren, Coggins, Campaneris, Robinson. Three-base hit–Davalillo. Stolen base–Bumbry. Sacrifice hit–Green. Hit by pitch–By Hunter (Blair), by Alexander (Tenace). Umpires–Haller, Chylak, Maloney, Odom, Anthony and McCoy. Time–2:11. Attendance–24,265.

OAKLAND ATHLETICS' BATTING AND FIELDING AVERAGES

Player–Position	G.	AB.	R.	H.	TB.	2B.	3B.	HR.	RBI.	B.A.	PO.	A.	E.	F.A.
Davalillo, ph-1b-cf	4	8	2	5	8	1	1	0	1	.625	7	0	1	.875
Campaneris, ss	5	21	3	7	14	1	0	2	3	.333	6	15	1	.955
Alou, ph-dh	4	6	0	2	2	0	0	0	1	.333	0	0	0	.000
Tenace, 1b-c	5	17	3	4	5	1	0	0	0	.235	40	3	0	1.000
Rudi, lf	5	18	1	4	7	0	0	1	3	.222	11	0	0	1.000
Bando, 3b	5	18	2	3	9	0	0	2	3	.167	7	10	0	1.000
R. Jackson, rf	5	21	0	3	3	0	0	0	0	.143	19	0	0	1.000
Mangual, cf-ph	3	9	1	1	1	0	0	0	0	.111	2	0	0	1.000
Johnson, dh	4	10	0	1	1	0	0	0	0	.100	0	0	0	.000
Fosse, c	5	11	2	1	2	1	0	0	3	.091	25	4	0	1.000
Green, 2b	5	13	0	1	2	1	0	0	1	.077	12	11	2	.920

Player—Position	G.	AB.	R.	H.	TB.	2B.	3B.	HR.	RBI.	B.A.	PO.	A.	E.	F.A.
Lewis, pr	2	0	1	0	0	0	0	0	0	.000	0	0	0	.000
Blue, p	2	0	0	0	0	0	0	0	0	.000	1	0	0	1.000
Fingers, p	3	0	0	0	0	0	0	0	0	.000	0	0	0	.000
Holtzman, p	1	0	0	0	0	0	0	0	0	.000	1	2	0	1.000
Hunter, p	2	0	0	0	0	0	0	0	0	.000	1	0	0	1.000
Odom, p	1	0	0	0	0	0	0	0	0	.000	0	1	0	1.000
Pina, p	1	0	0	0	0	0	0	0	0	.000	0	0	0	.000
Andrews, ph-1b	2	1	0	0	0	0	0	0	0	.000	1	0	0	1.000
Bourque, ph-dh	2	1	0	0	0	0	0	0	0	.000	0	0	0	.000
Kubiak, 2b	3	2	0	0	0	0	0	0	0	.000	0	1	0	1.000
Conigliaro, cf	1	4	0	0	0	0	0	0	0	.000	5	0	0	1.000
Totals	5	160	15	32	54	5	1	5	15	.200	138	47	4	.979

BALTIMORE ORIOLES' BATTING AND FIELDING AVERAGES

Player—Position	G.	AB.	R.	H.	TB.	2B.	3B.	HR.	RBI.	B.A.	PO.	A.	E.	F.A.
Coggins, rf-cf	2	9	1	4	5	1	0	0	0	.444	4	0	0	1.000
Etchebarren, c	4	14	1	5	9	1	0	1	4	.357	30	2	0	1.000
Davis, dh	5	21	1	6	7	1	0	0	2	.286	0	0	0	.000
Williams, 1b-c	5	18	2	5	10	2	0	1	4	.278	43	2	0	1.000
Baylor, lf-ph	4	11	3	3	3	0	0	0	1	.273	7	0	0	1.000
Robinson, 3b	5	20	1	5	7	2	0	0	2	.250	2	14	1	.941
Blair, cf	5	18	2	3	3	0	0	0	0	.167	8	0	0	1.000
Belanger, ss	5	16	0	2	2	0	0	0	1	.125	8	17	0	1.000
Grich, 2b	5	20	1	2	5	0	0	1	1	.100	16	9	0	1.000
Rettenmund, rf	3	11	1	1	1	0	0	0	0	.091	3	0	0	1.000
Alexander, p	1	0	0	0	0	0	0	0	0	.000	0	2	0	1.000
Baker, ss	2	0	0	0	0	0	0	0	0	.000	0	0	0	.000
Brown, 3b	1	0	0	0	0	0	0	0	0	.000	0	0	0	.000
Cuellar, p	1	0	0	0	0	0	0	0	0	.000	0	2	0	1.000
Hood, pr	1	0	0	0	0	0	0	0	0	.000	0	0	0	.000
G. Jackson, p	2	0	0	0	0	0	0	0	0	.000	0	0	0	.000
McNally, p	1	0	0	0	0	0	0	0	0	.000	0	0	0	.000
Palmer, p	3	0	0	0	0	0	0	0	0	.000	1	1	0	1.000
Reynolds, p	2	0	0	0	0	0	0	0	0	.000	1	0	0	1.000
Watt, p	1	0	0	0	0	0	0	0	0	.000	0	1	0	1.000
Crowley, ph-rf	2	2	0	0	0	0	0	0	0	.000	1	0	0	1.000
Powell, 1b	1	4	1	0	0	0	0	0	0	.000	7	0	0	1.000
Bumbry, lf	2	7	1	0	0	0	0	0	0	.000	4	1	1	.833
Totals	5	171	15	36	52	7	0	3	15	.211	135	51	2	.989

OAKLAND ATHLETICS' PITCHING RECORDS

Pitcher	G.	GS.	CG.	IP.	H.	R.	ER.	BB.	SO.	HB.	WP.	W.	L.	Pct.	ERA.
Pina	1	0	0	2	3	0	0	1	1	1	0	0	0	.000	0.00
Holtzman	1	1	1	11	3	1	1	1	7	0	0	1	0	1.000	0.82
Hunter	2	2	1	16⅓	12	3	3	5	6	1	0	2	0	1.000	1.65
Odom	1	0	0	5	6	2	1	2	4	0	0	0	0	.000	1.80
Fingers	3	0	0	4⅔	4	1	1	2	4	0	0	0	1	.000	1.93
Blue	2	2	0	7	8	8	8	5	3	0	1	0	1	.000	10.29
Totals	5	5	2	46	36	15	14	16	25	2	1	3	2	.600	2.74

Shutout—Hunter. Save—Fingers.

BALTIMORE ORIOLES' PITCHING RECORDS

Pitcher	G.	GS.	CG.	IP.	H.	R.	ER.	BB.	SO.	HB.	WP.	W.	L.	Pct.	ERA.
G. Jackson	2	0	0	3	0	0	0	1	0	0	0	1	0	1.000	0.00
Watt	1	0	0	⅓	0	0	0	0	0	1	0	0	0	.000	0.00
Cuellar	1	1	1	10	4	2	2	3	11	0	0	0	1	.000	1.80
Palmer	3	2	1	14⅔	11	3	3	8	15	0	0	1	0	1.000	1.84
Reynolds	2	0	0	5⅔	5	2	2	3	5	0	0	0	0	.000	3.18
Alexander	1	1	0	3⅔	5	3	2	0	1	1	0	0	1	.000	4.91
McNally	1	1	0	7⅔	7	5	5	2	7	0	1	0	1	.000	5.87
Totals	5	5	2	45	32	15	14	17	39	2	1	2	3	.400	2.80

Shutout—Palmer. No Saves.

COMPOSITE SCORE BY INNINGS

Oakland	1	3	1	2	0	3	0	3	1	0	1 — 15
Baltimore	5	1	0	0	0	1	5	3	0	0	0 — 15

Sacrifice hits—Fosse, Andrews, Rudi, Green.
Sacrifice fly—Fosse.
Stolen bases—Campaneris 3, Bumbry.
Caught stealing—Rettenmund 2, Davis, R. Jackson, Blair.
Double plays—Fosse and Green 2; Williams, Belanger and Palmer; Holtzman, Green and Tenace; Campaneris, Green and Tenace; Alexander, Grich and Williams.
Left on bases—Oakland 34—9, 7, 5, 8, 5; Baltimore 36—12, 9, 4, 4, 7.
Hit by pitcher—By Pina (Etchebarren); by Watt (Bando); by Alexander (Tenace); by Hunter (Blair).
Passed ball—Williams.
Balks—None.

Time of games—First game, 2:51; second game, 2:42; third game, 2:23; fourth game, 2:31; fifth game, 2:11.
Attendance—First game, 41,279; second game, 48,425; third game, 34,367; fourth game, 27,497; fifth game, 24,265.
Umpires—Chylak, Haller, Maloney, Odom, Anthony and McCoy.
Official scorers—Jim Elliott, Baltimore Morning Sun; Herb Michelson, Sacramento Bee.

NATIONAL LEAGUE
Championship Series of 1973

	W.	L.	Pct.
New York (East)	3	2	.600
Cincinnati (West)	2	3	.400

The New York Mets dethroned the Cincinnati Reds in a five-game Championship Series in 1973 marked by riotous scenes unparalleled in baseball history.

The New Yorkers pinned their hopes in the Championship Series on pitching and to that end they sent their big ace, Tom Seaver, to the mound in the opening game, played at Cincinnati's Riverfront Stadium.

Seaver almost staged a personal tour de force. His double drove in his team's lone run in the second inning and the lead held up until the eighth inning when Pete Rose, later to become a storm center in the series, hit a home run. Johnny Bench hit a home run in the ninth inning and so Seaver, who had walked none and struck out 13, came out on the losing end.

While Seaver had come close to a shutout in the opener, teammate Jon Matlack did post a shutout the next afternoon. He yielded but two singles while the Mets collected five runs and seven hits off four Cincinnati pitchers.

Paced by Rusty Staub's two home runs and the steady pitching of lefty Jerry Koosman, the Mets had an easy win in the third game, played at Shea Stadium. Easy, that is, if only the box score is considered. For it was in this game that the fireworks were ignited.

In the ninth inning, Rose slid hard into Bud Harrelson in an attempt to break up a double play.

Harrelson completed the play and then he and Rose began pushing and shoving and finally fell to the ground flailing away at each other. Players from both benches and bullpens raced onto the field.

It took several minutes to restore peace, but neither Rose nor Harrelson was ejected.

When Rose returned to left field, the fans began throwing bottles, garbage and other assorted debris at him. The barrage became so intense that Manager Sparky Anderson pulled the Reds off the field.

Finally, Yogi Berra, Willie Mays, Staub, Cleon Jones and Seaver walked out to left field and pleaded with the fans to cease and desist. The appeal was heeded and the game proceeded to its finish.

Game No. 4 could be aptly entitled "Rose's Revenge." The peppery Cincinnati outfielder hit a home run in the 12th inning to give his team a 2-1 victory and square the series at two games apiece. Earlier in the contest, while out in the field, Rose had been given a beer shower by a Mets "fan."

The New York club salted the final game away in the fifth inning. With the score tied at 2-2, Wayne Garrett opened the frame with a double. Then Reds rookie third baseman Dan Driessen made a grievous mental blunder. When Felix Millan laid down a sacrifice bunt, pitcher Jack Billingham fielded the ball and threw to third, apparently in plenty of time to get the runner. But Driessen, thinking (or not thinking) he had a force play, stepped on the bag but neglected to tag the runner. Jones then doubled, and Milner walked. Mays got a pinch-hit single to score another run and still another scored on a fielder's choice before Harrelson's single plated the fourth and final tally of the inning.

Seaver, pitching for the Mets, protected his lead with the help of Tug McGraw's relief and the Mets were National League Champions for 1973.

After Cincinnati's Pete Rose and New York's Bud Harrelson fought during the ninth inning of Game 3 in the 1973 N.L. Championship Series, left fielder Rose became the target for irate Mets fans when he returned to his position.

GAME OF SATURDAY, OCTOBER 6, AT CINCINNATI

New York	AB.	R.	H.	RBI.	PO.	A.
Garrett, 3b	4	0	1	0	2	1
Millan, 2b	3	0	0	0	1	1
Staub, rf	2	0	0	0	2	0
Milner, 1b	3	0	1	0	3	1
Jones, lf	4	0	0	0	2	0
Grote, c	4	0	0	0	13	0
Hahn, cf	3	0	0	0	0	0
Harrelson, ss	2	1	0	0	2	1
Seaver, p	3	0	1	1	0	0
Totals	28	1	3	1	25	4

Cincinnati	AB.	R.	H.	RBI.	PO.	A.
Rose, lf	4	1	1	1	2	0
Morgan, 2b	4	0	0	0	2	6
Driessen, 3b	4	0	1	0	0	0
Perez, 1b	4	0	0	0	11	1
Bench, c	4	1	3	1	6	0
Griffey, rf	2	0	0	0	1	0
Geronimo, cf	3	0	1	0	5	0
Chaney, ss	2	0	0	0	0	2
Stahl, ph	1	0	0	0	0	0
Crosby, ss	0	0	0	0	0	2
Billingham, p	1	0	0	0	0	1
King, ph	1	0	0	0	0	0
Hall, p	0	0	0	0	0	0
Borbon, p	0	0	0	0	0	0
Totals	30	2	6	2	27	12

New York .... 0 1 0   0 0 0   0 0 0 – 1
Cincinnati ...... 0 0 0   0 0 0   0 1 1 – 2
One out when winning run scored.

New York	IP.	H.	R.	ER.	BB.	SO.
Seaver (Loser)	8⅓	6	2	2	0	13

Cincinnati	IP.	H.	R.	ER.	BB.	SO.
Billingham	8	3	1	1	3	6
Hall	0*	0	0	0	1	0
Borbon (Winner)	1	0	0	0	0	0

*Pitched to one batter in ninth.

Errors—None. Double play—Cincinnati 1. Left on base—New York 5, Cincinnati 5. Two-base hits—Seaver, Bench, Driessen. Home runs—Rose, Bench. Sacrifice hits—Millan, Billingham. Hit by pitch—By Seaver (Griffey). Umpires—Sudol, Vargo, Pelekoudas, Engel, Froemming and Dale. Time—2:00. Attendance—53,431.

GAME OF SUNDAY, OCTOBER 7, AT CINCINNATI

New York	AB.	R.	H.	RBI.	PO.	A.
Garrett, 3b	5	0	0	0	0	3
Millan, 2b	4	1	1	0	1	0
Staub, rf	3	2	1	1	3	0
Jones, lf	3	1	1	1	2	0
Milner, 1b	3	1	0	0	6	2
Grote, c	4	0	1	2	9	0
Hahn, cf	3	0	2	0	3	0
Harrelson, ss	4	0	1	1	3	4
Matlack, p	2	0	0	0	0	1
Totals	31	5	7	5	27	10

Cincinnati	AB.	R.	H.	RBI.	PO.	A.
Rose, lf	4	0	0	0	2	0
Morgan, 2b	4	0	0	0	3	3
Perez, 1b	4	0	0	0	5	1
Bench, c	4	0	0	0	7	2
Kosco, rf	2	0	2	0	4	0
Driessen, 3b	3	0	0	0	1	1
Geronimo, cf	3	0	0	0	3	0
Chaney, ss	0	0	0	0	1	1
Armbrister, ph	1	0	0	0	0	0
Hall, p	0	0	0	0	1	0
Borbon, p	0	0	0	0	0	0
Gullett, p	0	0	0	0	0	0
Gagliano, ph	1	0	0	0	0	0
Carroll, p	0	0	0	0	0	1
Menke, ph-ss	1	0	0	0	0	0
Totals	27	0	2	0	27	9

New York .... 0 0 0   1 0 0   0 0 4 – 5
Cincinnati ...... 0 0 0   0 0 0   0 0 0 – 0

New York	IP.	H.	R.	ER.	BB.	SO.
Matlack (Winner)	9	2	0	0	3	9

Cincinnati	IP.	H.	R.	ER.	BB.	SO.
Gullett (Loser)	5	2	1	1	2	3
Carroll	3	0	0	0	1	2
Hall	⅓	2	4	4	2	0
Borbon	⅔	3	0	0	0	1

Errors—None. Double play—Cincinnati 1. Left on base—New York 5, Cincinnati 4. Home run—Staub. Sacrifice hits—Gullett, Matlack. Umpires—Vargo, Pelekoudas, Engel, Froemming, Dale and Sudol. Time—2:19. Attendance—54,041.

GAME OF MONDAY, OCTOBER 8, AT NEW YORK

Cincinnati	AB.	R.	H.	RBI.	PO.	A.
Rose, lf	4	0	2	0	3	0
Morgan, 2b	4	0	1	1	0	5
Perez, 1b	4	0	0	0	8	0
Bench, c	4	0	1	0	6	0
Kosco, rf	4	0	0	0	4	0
Armbrister, cf	4	0	1	0	3	0
Menke, 3b	4	1	1	1	0	1
Chaney, ss	3	0	0	0	0	1
Gagliano, ph	1	0	0	0	0	0
Grimsley, p	0	0	0	0	0	0
Hall, p	0	0	0	0	0	0
Stahl, ph	1	1	1	0	0	0
Tomlin, p	0	0	0	0	0	0
Nelson, p	1	0	0	0	0	0
King, ph	1	0	1	0	0	0
Borbon, p	0	0	0	0	0	1
Totals	35	2	8	2	24	8

New York	AB.	R.	H.	RBI.	PO.	A.
Garrett, 3b	4	0	0	1	1	0
Millan, 2b	3	2	1	1	2	0
Staub, rf	5	2	2	4	0	0
Jones, lf	3	1	2	0	1	0
Milner, 1b	4	0	1	1	4	1
Grote, c	3	2	1	0	9	0
Hahn, cf	4	1	2	0	8	0
Harrelson, ss	4	0	0	0	2	3
Koosman, p	4	1	2	1	0	0
Totals	34	9	11	8	27	4

Cincinnati	0	0	2		0	0	0		0	0	0 – 2
New York	1	5	1		2	0	0		0	0	x – 9

Cincinnati	IP.	H.	R.	ER.	BB.	SO.
Grimsley (Loser)	1⅔	5	5	5	1	2
Hall	⅔	1	1	1	1	1
Tomlin	1⅔	5	3	3	1	1
Nelson	2⅓	0	0	0	1	0
Borbon	2	0	0	0.	0	2

New York	IP.	H.	R.	ER.	BB.	SO.
Koosman (Winner)	9	8	2	2	0	9

Errors–Kosco, Garrett. Double play–New York 1. Left on base–Cincinnati 6, New York 6. Two-base hits–Jones, Bench. Home runs–Staub 2, Menke. Sacrifice fly–Garrett. Umpires– Pelekoudas, Engel, Froemming, Dale, Sudol and Vargo. Time–2:48. Attendance–53,967.

GAME OF TUESDAY, OCTOBER 9, AT NEW YORK

Cincinnati	AB.	R.	H.	RBI.	PO.	A.	New York	AB.	R.	H.	RBI.	PO.	A.
Rose, lf	5	1	3	1	3	0	Garrett, 3b	5	0	0	0	1	1
Morgan, 2b	4	0	0	0	4	7	Millan, 2b	5	0	2	1	4	3
Perez, 1b	6	1	1	1	13	1	Staub, rf	5	0	0	0	5	0
Bench, c	4	0	1	0	7	0	Jones, lf	5	0	0	0	5	0
Kosco, rf	4	0	1	0	4	0	Milner, 1b	4	0	0	0	10	1
Menke, 3b-ss	4	0	1	0	0	3	Grote, c	4	0	1	0	7	1
Geronimo, cf	5	0	0	0	2	0	Hahn, cf	3	1	0	0	0	0
Chaney, ss	2	0	0	0	0	3	Harrelson, ss	4	0	0	0	2	5
Armbrister, ph	1	0	0	0	0	0	Stone, p	1	0	0	0	1	2
Crosby, ss	1	0	1	0	1	0	McGraw, p	1	0	0	0	1	0
Driessen, pr-3b	1	0	0	0	0	0	Boswell, ph	1	0	0	0	0	0
Norman, p	1	0	0	0	1	0	Parker, p	0	0	0	0	0	0
Stahl, ph	1	0	0	0	0	0	Totals	38	1	3	1	36	13
Gullett, p	1	0	0	0	1	0							
Gagliano, ph	1	0	0	0	0	0							
Carroll, p	0	0	0	0	0	0							
Griffey, ph	1	0	0	0	0	0							
Borbon, p	0	0	0	0	0	1							
Totals	42	2	8	2	36	15							

Cincinnati	0	0	0		0	0	0		1	0	0		0	0	1 – 2
New York	0	0	1		0	0	0		0	0	0		0	0	0 – 1

Cincinnati	IP.	H.	R.	ER.	BB.	SO.
Norman	5	1	1	1	3	3
Gullett	4	2	0	0	0	3
Carroll (Winner)	2	0	0	0	0	0
Borbon (Save)	1	0	0	0	0	0

New York	IP.	H.	R.	ER.	BB.	SO.
Stone	6⅔	3	1	1	2	4
McGraw	4⅓	4	0	0	3	3
Parker (Loser)	1	1	1	1	0	0

Errors–McGraw, Grote. Double plays–Cincinnati 1, New York 2. Left on base–Cincinnati 10, New York 4. Home runs–Perez, Rose. Sacrifice hit–Morgan. Wild pitch–McGraw. Umpires–Engel, Froemming, Dale, Sudol, Vargo and Pelekoudas. Time–3:07. Attendance–50,786.

GAME OF WEDNESDAY, OCTOBER 10, AT NEW YORK

Cincinnati	AB.	R.	H.	RBI.	PO.	A.	New York	AB.	R.	H.	RBI.	PO.	A.
Rose, lf	4	1	2	0	0	1	Garrett, 3b	5	1	1	0	0	1
Morgan, 2b	4	1	1	0	3	6	Millan, 2b	4	2	2	0	1	7
Driessen, 3b	4	0	1	1	2	0	Jones, rf-lf	5	1	3	2	0	0
Perez, 1b	4	0	1	1	10	1	Milner, 1b	3	1	1	0	14	1
Bench, c	3	0	0	0	5	0	Kranepool, lf	2	0	1	2	2	0
Griffey, rf	4	0	1	0	1	0	Mays, ph-cf	3	1	1	1	1	0
Geronimo, cf	4	0	0	1	1	0	Grote, c	4	0	1	0	4	0
Chaney, ss	2	0	0	0	1	3	Hahn, cf-rf	4	0	0	1	1	0
Stahl, ph	1	0	1	0	0	0	Harrelson, ss	4	0	2	1	3	1
Billingham, p	2	0	0	0	0	1	Seaver, p	3	1	1	0	0	3
Gullett, p	0	0	0	0	0	0	McGraw, p	0	0	0	0	1	0
Carroll, p	0	0	0	0	0	1	Totals	37	7	13	7	27	13
Crosby, ph	1	0	0	0	0	0							
Grimsley, p	0	0	0	0	1	0							
King, ph	0	0	0	0	0	0							
Totals	33	2	7	2	24	15							

Cincinnati	0	0	1		0	1	0		0	0	0 – 2
New York	2	0	0		0	4	1		0	0	x – 7

Cincinnati	IP.	H.	R.	ER.	BB.	SO.
Billingham (Loser)	4*	6	5	5	1	3
Gullett	0†	0	1	1	1	0
Carroll	2	5	1	1	0	0
Grimsley	2	2	0	0	1	1

New York	IP.	H.	R.	ER.	BB.	SO.
Seaver (Winner)	8⅓	7	2	1	5	4
McGraw (Save)	⅔	0	0	0	0	0

*Pitched to three batters in fifth.
†Pitched to one batter in fifth.

Errors—Jones, Driessen. Left on base—Cincinnati 10, New York 10. Two-base hits—Morgan, Griffey, Rose, Garrett, Jones, Seaver. Sacrifice hit—Millan. Sacrifice fly—Driessen. Wild pitch—Seaver. Umpires—Froemming, Dale, Sudol, Vargo, Pelekoudas and Engel. Time—2:40. Attendance—50,323.

NEW YORK METS' BATTING AND FIELDING AVERAGES

Player—Position	G.	AB.	R.	H.	TB.	2B.	3B.	HR.	RBI.	B.A.	PO.	A.	E.	F.A.
Koosman, p	1	4	1	2	2	0	0	0	1	.500	0	0	0	.000
Kranepool, lf	1	2	0	1	1	0	0	0	2	.500	2	0	0	1.000
Seaver, p	2	6	1	2	4	2	0	0	1	.333	0	3	0	1.000
Mays, ph-cf	1	3	1	1	1	0	0	0	1	.333	1	0	0	1.000
Millan, 2b	5	19	5	6	6	0	0	0	2	.316	9	11	0	1.000
Jones, lf-rf	5	20	3	6	8	2	0	0	3	.300	10	0	1	.909
Hahn, cf-rf	5	17	2	4	4	0	0	0	1	.235	2	0	0	1.000
Grote, c	5	19	2	4	4	0	0	0	2	.211	42	1	1	.977
Staub, rf	4	15	4	3	12	0	0	3	5	.200	10	0	0	1.000
Milner, 1b	5	17	2	3	3	0	0	0	1	.176	37	6	0	1.000
Harrelson, ss	5	18	1	3	3	0	0	0	2	.167	12	14	0	1.000
Garrett, 3b	5	23	1	2	3	1	0	0	1	.087	4	6	1	.909
Parker, p	1	0	0	0	0	0	0	0	0	.000	0	0	0	.000
Boswell, ph	1	1	0	0	0	0	0	0	0	.000	0	0	0	.000
McGraw, p	2	1	0	0	0	0	0	0	0	.000	2	0	1	.667
Stone, p	1	1	0	0	0	0	0	0	0	.000	1	2	0	1.000
Matlack, p	1	2	0	0	0	0	0	0	0	.000	0	1	0	1.000
Totals	5	168	23	37	51	5	0	3	22	.220	142	44	4	.979

CINCINNATI REDS' BATTING AND FIELDING AVERAGES

Player—Position	G.	AB.	R.	H.	TB.	2B.	3B.	HR.	RBI.	B.A.	PO.	A.	E.	F.A.
Stahl, ph	4	4	1	2	2	0	0	0	0	.500	0	0	0	.000
Crosby, ss-ph	3	2	0	1	1	0	0	0	0	.500	1	2	0	1.000
King, ph	3	2	0	1	1	0	0	0	0	.500	0	0	0	.000
Rose, lf	5	21	3	8	15	1	0	2	2	.381	10	1	0	1.000
Kosco, rf	3	10	0	3	3	0	0	0	0	.300	12	0	1	.923
Bench, c	5	19	1	5	10	2	0	1	1	.263	31	2	0	1.000
Menke, ph-ss-1b	3	9	1	2	5	0	0	1	1	.222	0	4	0	1.000
Driessen, 3b-pr	4	12	0	2	3	1	0	0	1	.167	3	2	1	.833
Armbrister, ph-cf	3	6	0	1	1	0	0	0	0	.167	3	0	0	1.000
Griffey, rf-ph	3	7	0	1	2	1	0	0	0	.143	2	0	0	1.000
Morgan, 2b	5	20	1	2	3	1	0	0	0	.100	12	27	0	1.000
Perez, 1b	5	22	1	2	5	0	0	1	2	.091	47	4	0	1.000
Geronimo, cf	4	15	0	1	1	0	0	0	0	.067	11	1	0	1.000
Borbon, p	4	0	0	0	0	0	0	0	0	.000	0	2	0	1.000
Carroll, p	3	0	0	0	0	0	0	0	0	.000	0	2	0	1.000
Grimsley, p	2	0	0	0	0	0	0	0	0	.000	1	0	0	1.000
Hall, p	3	0	0	0	0	0	0	0	0	.000	1	0	0	1.000
Tomlin, p	1	0	0	0	0	0	0	0	0	.000	0	0	0	.000
Gullett, p	3	1	0	0	0	0	0	0	0	.000	1	0	0	1.000
Nelson, p	1	1	0	0	0	0	0	0	0	.000	0	0	0	.000
Norman, p	1	1	0	0	0	0	0	0	0	.000	0	2	0	1.000
Billingham, p	2	3	0	0	0	0	0	0	0	.000	0	0	0	.000
Gagliano, ph	3	3	0	0	0	0	0	0	0	.000	2	0	0	.000
Chaney, ss	5	9	0	0	0	0	0	0	0	.000	2	10	0	1.000
Totals	5	167	8	31	52	6	0	5	8	.186	138	59	2	.990

NEW YORK METS' PITCHING RECORDS

Pitcher	G.	GS.	CG.	IP.	H.	R.	ER.	BB.	SO.	HB.	WP.	W.	L.	Pct.	ERA.
Matlack	1	1	1	9	2	0	0	3	9	0	0	1	0	1.000	0.00
McGraw	2	0	0	5	4	0	0	3	3	0	1	0	0	.000	0.00
Stone	1	1	0	6⅔	3	1	1	2	4	0	0	0	0	.000	1.35
Seaver	2	2	1	16⅔	13	4	3	5	17	1	1	1	1	.500	1.62
Koosman	1	1	1	9	8	2	2	0	9	0	0	1	0	1.000	2.00
Parker	1	0	0	1	1	1	1	0	0	0	0	0	1	.000	9.00
Totals	5	5	3	47⅓	31	8	7	13	42	1	2	3	2	.600	1.33

Shutout—Matlack. Save—McGraw.

CINCINNATI REDS' PITCHING RECORDS

Pitcher	G.	GS.	CG.	IP.	H.	R.	ER.	BB.	SO.	HB.	WP.	W.	L.	Pct.	ERA.
Borbon	4	0	0	4⅔	3	0	0	3	0	0	0	1	0	1.000	0.00
Nelson	1	0	0	2⅓	0	0	0	1	0	0	0	0	0	.000	0.00
Carroll	3	0	0	7	5	1	1	1	2	0	0	1	0	1.000	1.29
Norman	1	1	0	5	1	1	1	3	3	0	0	0	0	.000	1.80
Gullett	3	1	0	9	4	2	2	3	6	0	0	0	1	.000	2.00
Billingham	2	2	0	12	9	6	6	4	9	0	0	0	1	.000	4.50
Grimsley	2	1	0	3⅔	7	5	5	2	3	0	0	0	1	.000	12.27
Tomlin	1	0	0	1⅔	5	3	3	1	1	0	0	0	0	.000	16.20
Hall	3	0	0	⅔	3	5	5	4	1	0	0	0	0	.000	67.50
Totals	5	5	0	46	37	23	23	19	28	0	0	2	3	.400	4.50

No shutouts. Save—Borbon.

COMPOSITE SCORE BY INNINGS

New York	3	6	2	3	4	1	0	0	4	0	0	0 – 23
Cincinnati	0	0	3	0	1	0	1	1	1	0	0	1 – 8

Sacrifice hits—Millan 2, Billingham, Matlack, Gullett, Morgan.
Sacrifice flies—Garrett, Driessen.
Stolen bases—None.
Caught stealing—Driessen.
Double plays—Chaney, Morgan and Perez 2; Morgan, Chaney and Perez; Milner, Harrelson and Milner; Millan, Harrelson and Milner; Harrelson, Millan and Milner.
Left on bases—New York 30—5, 5, 6, 4, 10; Cincinnati 35—5, 4, 6, 10, 10.
Hit by pitcher—By Seaver (Griffey).
Passed balls—None.
Balks—None.
Time of games—First game, 2:00; second game, 2:19; third game, 2:48; fourth game, 3:07; fifth game, 2:40.
Attendance—First game, 53,431; second game, 54,041; third game, 53,967; fourth game, 50,786; fifth game, 50,323.
Umpires—Sudol, Vargo, Pelekoudas, Engel, Froemming and Dale.
Official scorers—Jack Lang, Long Island Press; Bob Hertzel, Cincinnati Enquirer.

AMERICAN LEAGUE
Championship Series of 1974

	W.	L.	Pct.
Oakland (West)	3	1	.750
Baltimore (East)	1	3	.250

The Oakland A's won their third consecutive American League pennant when they downed the Baltimore Orioles, three games to one, in the Championship Series.

The Orioles, who came into their fifth playoff in the last six years on the impetus of nine straight victories and 28 wins in their last 34 games of the regular season, carried their momentum into the Championship Series opener, played at Oakland.

The Birds jumped all over the ace of the Oakland staff, Jim Hunter, pounding him for six runs and eight hits, including three homers, in less than five innings. Hunter had a skein of seven straight decisions over the Birds going into the game. Southpaw Mike Cuellar pitched steady ball for the winners and got the decision with relief help in the ninth inning from Ross Grimsley.

A portent of things to happen came in the first inning when Paul Blair, second man in the batting order, hit a Hunter pitch for a home run. Bert Campaneris' single that followed a fielder's choice and a stolen base by Bill North gave the A's a temporary tie in the third inning. But a double by Bobby Grich and Tommy Davis' single put the Orioles ahead to stay in the fourth. A four-run outburst in the fifth, featuring homers by Brooks Robinson and Bobby Grich, locked up the game and sent Hunter to the showers.

When Cuellar yielded a single to Jesus Alou and a double to Claudell Washington, both pinch-hitters, to open the last of the ninth, he was pulled in favor of Grimsley, who got the last three outs without trouble. The final score was 6-3.

The A's assumed command the next day when Ken Holtzman permitted the Orioles only five hits en route to a 5-0 triumph. The Oakland club got an unearned run in the fourth when Bobby Grich dropped a foul pop by Sal Bando for an error. Two pitches later, Bando drove a Dave McNally pitch over the left-field fence for a homer. Joe Rudi tripled home North in the sixth for the second run. In the eighth inning, with two men on—the result of a walk and an error—Ray Fosse hit a home run off reliever Grant Jackson to put the game on ice.

The third game of the set, played in Baltimore, produced a brilliant pitching duel between A's lefty Vida Blue and Jim Palmer. Blue hurled a two-hitter and Palmer a four-hitter. But one of the four safe blows yielded by the Oriole righthander was a home run by Bando in the fourth inning. It was the only run of the game.

The fourth game saw the A's capture a 2-1 verdict, although their batting order was able to produce only one safe hit for the afternoon. Cuellar pitched a no-hitter for four and two-thirds innings but walked four consecutive batters to give Oakland a run. During his stint on the mound, the Oriole lefty walked no less than nine batters and was removed while yet to give up a hit.

The run that was to prove decisive came in the seventh off reliever Grimsley.

Bando walked and Reggie Jackson stroked a double off the left-field wall to plate Bando.

The Orioles almost pulled the game out of the bag in their last turn at bat. With one out and Rollie Fingers pitching in relief of Hunter, Blair walked and Grich singled. A force play provided the second out of the inning but Boog Powell's single drove in one run. Fingers, however, was equal to the occasion, striking out Baylor on a fast ball to clinch the league crown for Oakland.

The triumph of the A's was notable in a couple of ways. Besides marking Oakland's third straight pennant, it placed Manager Alvin Dark in the company of only two other managers who have won pennants in both major leagues. Joe McCarthy did it with the Cubs and the Yankees and Yogi Berra did it with the Yankees and the Mets.

GAME OF SATURDAY, OCTOBER 5, AT OAKLAND

Baltimore	AB.	R.	H.	RBI.	PO.	A.	Oakland	AB.	R.	H.	RBI.	PO.	A.
Coggins, rf	4	0	0	0	3	0	North, cf	5	2	1	0	3	0
Blair, cf	4	2	2	2	2	0	Campaneris, ss	4	0	3	3	0	5
Grich, 2b	4	2	2	2	1	2	Jackson, rf	4	0	0	0	0	0
Davis, dh	4	0	2	1	0	0	Bando, 2b	4	0	1	0	1	2
Powell, 1b	4	0	0	0	8	1	Rudi, lf	4	0	0	0	2	0
Baylor, lf	4	0	2	0	2	0	Tenace, 1b	3	0	0	0	12	1
Robinson, 3b	4	1	1	1	0	5	Mangual, dh	4	0	1	0	0	0
Hendricks, c	4	1	1	0	5	0	Fosse, c	2	0	1	0	6	0
Belanger, ss	3	0	0	0	6	2	Alou, ph	1	0	1	0	0	0
Cuellar, p	0	0	0	0	0	3	Trillo, pr	0	1	0	0	0	0
Grimsley, p	0	0	0	0	0	0	Green, 2b	2	0	0	0	2	3
Totals	35	6	10	6	27	13	C. Washington, ph	1	0	1	0	0	0
							Hunter, p	0	0	0	0	1	1
							Odom, p	0	0	0	0	0	0
							Fingers, p	0	0	0	0	0	0
							Totals	34	3	9	3	27	12

```
Baltimore ..................................... 1   0   0     1   4   0     0   0   0 — 6
Oakland ....................................... 0   0   1     0   1   0     0   0   1 — 3
```

Baltimore	IP.	H.	R.	ER.	BB.	SO.
Cuellar (Winner)	8*	9	3	3	4	4
Grimsley	1	0	0	0	0	0

Oakland	IP.	H.	R.	ER.	BB.	SO.
Hunter (Loser)	4⅔	8	6	6	0	3
Odom	3⅓	1	0	0	0	1
Fingers	1	1	0	0	0	1

*Pitched to two batters in ninth.

Errors—None. Double play—Oakland 1. Left on base—Baltimore 3, Oakland 9. Two-base hits—Grich, North, C. Washington. Home runs— Blair, Robinson, Grich. Stolen bases—North, Campaneris. Sacrifice hit—Belanger. Sacrifice fly—Campaneris. Passed ball—Fosse. Umpires—Napp, Neudecker, Goetz, Phillips, Springstead and Deegan. Time—2:29. Attendance—41,609.

GAME OF SUNDAY, OCTOBER 6, AT OAKLAND

Baltimore	AB.	R.	H.	RBI.	PO.	A.	Oakland	AB.	R.	H.	RBI.	PO.	A.
Belanger, ss	3	0	0	0	0	1	Campaneris, ss	4	0	0	0	0	6
Motton, ph	1	0	0	0	0	0	North, cf	2	1	0	0	6	0
Baker, ss	0	0	0	0	1	0	Bando, 3b	3	1	1	1	1	4
Blair, cf	3	0	1	0	0	0	R. Jackson, dh	3	0	0	0	0	0
Grich, 2b	4	0	0	0	7	5	H. Washington, pr	0	0	0	0	0	0
Davis, dh	4	0	1	0	0	0	Rudi, lf	4	0	2	1	1	0
Baylor, lf	4	0	0	0	2	0	Tenace, 1b	3	1	0	0	13	0
Robinson, 3b	2	0	0	0	1	3	C. Washington, rf	4	1	1	0	0	0
Williams, 1b	3	0	0	0	7	1	Fosse, c	4	1	3	3	3	1
Cabell, rf	3	0	1	0	2	0	Green, 2b	1	0	1	0	1	2
Etchebarren, c	3	0	2	0	3	0	Holt, ph	1	0	0	0	0	0
Bumbry, pr	0	0	0	0	0	0	Odom, pr	0	0	0	0	0	0
Hendricks, c	0	0	0	0	1	1	Maxvill, 2b	1	0	0	0	2	1
McNally, p	0	0	0	0	0	0	Holtzman, p	0	0	0	0	0	1
Garland, p	0	0	0	0	0	0	Totals	29	5	8	5	27	15
Reynolds, p	0	0	0	0	0	0							
G. Jackson, p	0	0	0	0	0	0							
Totals	30	0	5	0	24	11							

```
Baltimore ..................................... 0   0   0     0   0   0     0   0   0 — 0
Oakland ....................................... 0   0   0     1   0   1     0   3   x — 5
```

Baltimore	IP.	H.	R.	ER.	BB.	SO.
McNally (Loser)	5⅔	6	2	1	2	2
Garland	⅔	1	0	0	1	0
Reynolds	1⅓	0	1	0	3	1
G. Jackson	⅓	1	2	0	0	1

Oakland	IP.	H.	R.	ER.	BB.	SO.
Holtzman (Winner)	9	5	0	0	2	3

Errors—Grich, Baker. Double plays—Baltimore 2, Oakland 2. Left on base—Baltimore 5, Oakland 7. Two-base hit—Fosse. Three-base hit—Rudi. Home runs—Bando, Fosse. Stolen base—Tenace. Sacrifice hit—Green. Wild pitch—McNally. Umpires—Neudecker, Goetz, Phillips, Springstead, Deegan and Napp. Time—2:23. Attendance—42,810.

GAME OF TUESDAY, OCTOBER 8, AT BALTIMORE

Oakland	AB.	R.	H.	RBI.	PO.	A.	Baltimore	AB.	R.	H.	RBI.	PO.	A.
Campaneris, ss	4	0	0	0	1	2	Coggins, rf	3	0	0	0	2	0
North, cf	4	0	0	0	2	0	Cabell, ph	1	0	0	0	0	0
Bando, 3b	4	1	1	1	0	1	Blair, cf	4	0	0	0	2	0
Jackson, dh	4	0	1	0	0	0	Grich, 2b	4	0	1	0	3	2
Rudi, lf	4	0	0	0	2	0	Davis, dh	3	0	0	0	0	0
Tenace, 1b	2	0	0	0	6	0	Baylor, lf	3	0	1	0	4	0
H. Washington, pr	0	0	0	0	0	0	Robinson, 3b	3	0	0	0	2	3
Holt, 1b	0	0	0	0	1	0	Williams, 1b	3	0	0	0	9	0
C. Washington, rf	2	0	1	0	4	0	Etchebarren, c	3	0	0	0	4	1
Fosse, c	2	0	0	0	7	1	Belanger, ss	3	0	0	0	1	3
Green, 2b	3	0	1	0	4	2	Palmer, p	0	0	0	0	0	2
Blue, p	0	0	0	0	0	1	Totals	30	0	2	0	27	11
Totals	29	1	4	1	27	7							

Oakland	0	0	0	1	0	0	0	0	0 – 1
Baltimore	0	0	0	0	0	0	0	0	0 – 0

Oakland	IP.	H.	R.	ER.	BB.	SO.
Blue (Winner)	9	2	0	0	0	7

Baltimore	IP.	H.	R.	ER.	BB.	SO.
Palmer (Loser)	9	4	1	1	1	4

Errors—Williams, Green 2. Double play—Baltimore 1. Left on base—Oakland 4, Baltimore 3. Home run—Bando. Sacrifice hit—Fosse. Hit by Pitch—By Palmer (C. Washington). Umpires—Goetz, Phillips, Springstead, Deegan, Napp and Neudecker. Time—1:57. Attendance—32,060.

GAME OF WEDNESDAY, OCTOBER 9, AT BALTIMORE

Oakland	AB.	R.	H.	RBI.	PO.	A.	Baltimore	AB.	R.	H.	RBI.	PO.	A.
Campaneris, ss	5	0	0	0	2	4	Coggins, rf	4	0	0	0	1	0
North, cf	5	0	0	0	3	0	Blair, cf	3	1	1	0	3	0
Bando, 3b	2	2	0	0	1	1	Grich, 2b	4	0	1	0	2	3
Jackson, dh	1	0	1	1	0	0	Davis, dh	4	0	1	0	0	0
Odom, pr	0	0	0	0	0	0	Cabell, pr	0	0	0	0	0	0
Rudi, lf	1	0	0	0	0	0	Powell, 1b	4	0	1	1	14	0
Tenace, 1b	3	0	0	1	4	0	Palmer, pr	0	0	0	0	0	0
C. Washington, rf	4	0	0	0	7	0	Baylor, lf	4	0	1	0	1	0
Fosse, c	4	0	0	0	5	1	Robinson, 3b	3	0	0	1	2	2
Green, 2b	3	0	0	0	3	1	Hendricks, c	2	0	0	0	5	0
Hunter, p	0	0	0	0	2	1	Belanger, ss	0	0	0	0	0	6
Fingers, p	0	0	0	0	0	0	Bumbry, ph	1	0	0	0	0	0
Totals	28	2	1	2	27	9	Baker, ss	0	0	0	0	0	1
							Cuellar, p	0	0	0	0	0	2
							Grimsley, p	0	0	0	0	0	1
							Totals	29	1	5	1	27	15

Oakland	0	0	0	0	1	0	1	0	0 – 2
Baltimore	0	0	0	0	0	0	0	0	1 – 1

Oakland	IP.	H.	R.	ER.	BB.	SO.
Hunter (Winner)	7*	3	0	0	2	3
Fingers (Save)	2	2	1	1	1	2

Baltimore	IP.	H.	R.	ER.	BB.	SO.
Cuellar (Loser)	4⅔	0	1	1	9	2
Grimsley	4⅓	1	1	1	2	2

*Pitched to one batter in eighth.

Error—Belanger. Double plays—Oakland 1, Baltimore 1. Left on base—Oakland 10, Baltimore 5. Two-base hit—Jackson. Sacrifice hit—Belanger. Wild pitch—Cuellar. Umpires—Phillips, Springstead, Deegan, Napp, Neudecker and Goetz. Time—2:46. Attendance—28,136.

OAKLAND ATHLETICS' BATTING AND FIELDING AVERAGES

Player—Position	G.	AB.	R.	H.	TB.	2B.	3B.	HR.	RBI.	B.A.	PO.	A.	E.	F.A.
Alou, ph	1	1	0	1	1	0	0	0	0	1.000	0	0	0	.000
Fosse, c	4	12	1	4	8	1	0	1	3	.333	21	3	0	1.000
C. Washington, ph-rf	4	11	3	4	4	1	0	0	0	.273	11	0	0	1.000
Mangual, dh	1	4	0	1	1	0	0	0	0	.250	0	0	0	.000
Bando, 3b	4	13	4	3	9	0	0	2	2	.231	3	8	0	1.000
Green, 2b	4	9	0	2	2	0	0	0	0	.222	10	8	2	.900
Campaneris, ss	4	17	0	3	3	0	0	0	3	.176	3	17	0	1.000
R. Jackson, rf-dh	4	12	0	2	3	1	0	0	1	.167	0	0	0	.000
Rudi, lf	4	13	0	2	4	0	1	0	1	.154	5	0	0	1.000
North, cf	4	16	3	1	2	1	0	0	0	.063	14	0	0	1.000
Blue, p	1	0	0	0	0	0	0	0	0	.000	0	1	0	1.000
Fingers, p	2	0	0	0	0	0	0	0	0	.000	0	0	0	.000

Player–Position	G.	AB.	R.	H.	TB.	2B.	3B.	HR.	RBI.	B.A.	PO.	A.	E.	F.A.
Holt, ph-1b	2	0	0	0	0	0	0	0	0	.000	1	0	0	1.000
Holtzman, p	1	0	0	0	0	0	0	0	0	.000	0	1	0	1.000
Hunter, p	2	0	0	0	0	0	0	0	0	.000	3	2	0	1.000
Odom, p-pr	3	0	0	0	0	0	0	0	0	.000	0	0	0	.000
Trillo, pr	1	0	1	0	0	0	0	0	0	.000	0	0	0	.000
H. Washington, pr	2	0	0	0	0	0	0	0	0	.000	0	0	0	.000
Maxvill, 2b	1	1	0	0	0	0	0	0	0	.000	2	1	0	1.000
Tenace, 1b	4	11	1	0	0	0	0	0	1	.000	35	2	0	1.000
Totals	4	120	11	22	37	4	1	3	11	.183	108	43	2	.987

BALTIMORE ORIOLES' BATTING AND FIELDING AVERAGES

Player–Position	G.	AB.	R.	H.	TB.	2B.	3B.	HR.	RBI.	B.A.	PO.	A.	E.	F.A.
Etchebarren, c	2	6	0	2	2	0	0	0	0	.333	7	1	0	1.000
Blair, cf	4	14	3	4	7	0	0	1	2	.268	7	0	0	1.000
Baylor, lf	4	15	0	4	4	0	0	0	0	.267	9	0	0	1.000
Davis, dh	4	15	0	4	4	0	0	0	1	.267	0	0	0	.000
Grich, 2b	4	16	2	4	8	1	0	1	2	.250	13	12	1	.962
Cabell, rf-ph-pr	3	4	0	1	1	0	0	0	0	.250	2	0	0	1.000
Hendricks, c	3	6	1	1	1	0	0	0	0	.167	11	1	0	1.000
Powell, 1b	2	8	0	1	1	0	0	0	1	.125	22	1	0	1.000
Robinson, 3b	4	12	1	1	4	0	0	1	1	.083	4	13	0	1.000
Baker, ss	2	0	0	0	0	0	0	0	0	.000	1	1	1	.667
Cuellar, p	2	0	0	0	0	0	0	0	0	.000	0	5	0	1.000
Garland, p	1	0	0	0	0	0	0	0	0	.000	0	0	0	.000
Grimsley, p	2	0	0	0	0	0	0	0	0	.000	0	1	0	1.000
G. Jackson, p	1	0	0	0	0	0	0	0	0	.000	0	0	0	.000
McNally, p	1	0	0	0	0	0	0	0	0	.000	0	0	0	.000
Palmer, p-pr	2	0	0	0	0	0	0	0	0	.000	0	2	0	1.000
Reynolds, p	1	0	0	0	0	0	0	0	0	.000	0	0	0	.000
Bumbry, pr-ph	2	1	0	0	0	0	0	0	0	.000	0	0	0	.000
Motton, ph	1	1	0	0	0	0	0	0	0	.000	0	0	0	.000
Williams, 1b	2	6	0	0	0	0	0	0	0	.000	16	1	1	.944
Belanger, ss	4	9	0	0	0	0	0	0	0	.000	7	12	1	.950
Coggins, rf	3	11	0	0	0	0	0	0	0	.000	6	0	0	1.000
Totals	4	124	7	22	32	1	0	3	7	.177	105	50	4	.975

OAKLAND ATHLETICS' PITCHING RECORDS

Pitcher	G.	GS.	CG.	IP.	H.	R.	ER.	BB.	SO.	HB.	WP.	W.	L.	Pct.	ERA.
Blue	1	1	1	9	2	0	0	0	7	0	0	1	0	1.000	0.00
Holtzman	1	1	1	9	5	0	0	2	3	0	0	1	0	1.000	0.00
Odom	1	0	0	3⅓	1	0	0	1	1	0	0	0	0	.000	0.00
Fingers	2	0	0	3	3	1	1	1	3	0	0	0	0	.000	3.00
Hunter	2	2	0	11⅔	11	6	6	2	6	0	0	1	1	.500	4.63
Totals	4	4	2	36	22	7	7	5	20	0	0	3	1	.750	1.75

Shutouts–Blue, Holtzman. Save–Fingers.

BALTIMORE ORIOLES' PITCHING RECORDS

Pitcher	G.	GS.	CG.	IP.	H.	R.	ER.	BB.	SO.	HB.	WP.	W.	L.	Pct.	ERA.
Reynolds	1	0	0	1⅓	0	1	0	3	1	0	0	0	0	.000	0.00
Garland	1	0	0	⅔	1	0	0	1	0	0	0	0	0	.000	0.00
G. Jackson	1	0	0	⅓	1	2	0	1	0	0	0	0	0	.000	0.00
Palmer	1	1	1	9	4	1	1	1	4	1	0	0	1	.000	1.00
McNally	1	1	0	5⅔	6	2	1	2	2	0	1	0	1	.000	1.59
Grimsley	2	0	0	5⅓	1	1	1	2	2	0	0	0	0	.000	1.69
Cuellar	2	2	0	12⅔	9	4	4	13	6	0	1	1	1	.500	2.84
Totals	4	4	1	35	22	11	7	22	16	1	2	1	3	.250	1.80

No shutouts or saves.

COMPOSITE SCORE BY INNINGS

Oakland	0	0	1	2	2	1	1	3	1 – 11
Baltimore	1	0	0	1	4	0	0	0	1 – 7

Sacrifice hits–Belanger 2, Green, Fosse.
Sacrifice fly–Campaneris.
Stolen bases–North, Campaneris, Tenace.
Caught stealing–Campaneris, Blair 2, H. Washington 2, Baylor.
Double plays–Bando, Green and Tenace; Fosse and Green; Bando, Maxvill and Tenace; Green, Campaneris and Tenace; Grich and Williams; Belanger, Grich and Williams; Robinson and Williams; Belanger, Grich and Powell.
Left on bases–Oakland 30–9, 7, 4, 10; Baltimore 16–3, 5, 3, 5.
Hit by pitcher–By Palmer (C. Washington).
Passed ball–Fosse.
Balks–None.
Time of games–First game, 2:29; second game, 2:23; third game, 1:57; fourth game, 2:46.
Attendance–First game, 41,609; second game, 42,810; third game, 32,060; fourth game, 28,136.
Umpires–Napp, Neudecker, Goetz, Phillips, Springstead and Deegan.
Official scorers–Jim Henneman, Baltimore News-American; Jim Street, San Jose Mercury-News.

NATIONAL LEAGUE
Championship Series of 1974

	W.	L.	Pct.
Los Angeles (West)	3	1	.750
Pittsburgh (East)	1	3	.250

With Don Sutton giving up only one run in 17 innings of pitching in two starting assignments, the Los Angeles Dodgers subdued the Pittsburgh Pirates in the National League Championship Series, three games to one, in 1974.

The Dodgers had been winless in six games played at Pittsburgh's Three Rivers Stadium during the regular season but they remedied that situation in post-season play. In the opening game, Sutton was opposed by Jerry Reuss. The Pirate lefty yielded just one run in seven innings of work but left the game in favor of an ineffectual pinch-hitter. Dave Giusti came on in the eighth inning and gave up two insurance tallies. Meanwhile, Sutton set the Pittsburgh club down on four hits and no runs while striking out six and walking only one.

The Pittsburgh string of scoreless innings was extended to 15 before the Bucs finally got on the board in the seventh inning of the second game. But when they did score, there were no big base hits. One run came in on a groundout and the other on a high bouncer that escaped an infielder's glove and was scored as a single. But those two runs were enough to enable the Pirates to equalize the two runs that Los Angeles had scored earlier off starter Jim Rooker.

With the game tied going into the eighth stanza, it was a battle between ace relievers Mike Marshall, of Los Angeles, and Giusti. It was, however, strictly no contest.

Marshall retired six straight batters in the last two innings but Giusti couldn't retire even one. He was clubbed for three runs and four hits before getting the hook. An error by his catcher, Manny Sanguillen, didn't help matters. The final score was 5-2, and on the plane trip to Los Angeles, the Pirates had time to think about getting only a dozen singles in 18 innings and failing to score in 17 innings.

A record crowd for Dodger Stadium—55,953—showed up for the third game, confidently expecting the local nine to apply the coup de grace. But the home partisans were sorely disappointed.

Dodger starter Doug Rau lingered on the premises for barely 10 minutes, during which time he was bombed for five runs. With Bruce Kison pitching effectively for Pittsburgh and the Dodgers contributing five errors, the game was, for all practical purposes, over early. Kison gave up only two hits in the six and two-thirds innings he worked and his reliever, Ramon Hernandez, slammed the door on the Dodgers the rest of the way. The big blows for the Bucs were home runs by Willie Stargell and Richie Hebner. At game's end the Pirates had seven runs and the Dodgers had none.

Sutton and Reuss, as in the opener, were the opposing pitchers in the fourth game.

Sutton was just as good as he ever was, permitting but one run and three hits and striking out seven in eight innings of work before allowing the ubiquitous Marshall to mop up. Reuss simply didn't have his best stuff and was kayoed in the third inning.

His successors didn't fare much better. The unfortunate Giusti made his third appearance of the series and was just as ineffective as he had been in the first two, being charged with three runs in an inning and a third of toil. The biggest thunder came off the bat of Dodger first baseman Steve Garvey. He had four hits, including two homers, and drove in four runs. The final score was 12-1, a decisive margin by any standard and the largest in any game previously played in a Championship Series.

GAME OF SATURDAY, OCTOBER 5, AT PITTSBURGH

Los Angeles	AB.	R.	H.	RBI.	PO.	A.
Lopes, 2b	4	1	0	1	2	4
Buckner, lf	5	0	1	0	3	0
Wynn, cf	3	1	1	1	2	0
Garvey, 1b	4	0	2	0	9	1
Ferguson, rf	4	1	2	1	1	0
Cey, 3b	3	0	0	0	0	3
Russell, ss	5	0	2	0	3	2
Yeager, c	4	0	0	0	6	1
Sutton, p	3	0	1	0	1	0
Totals	35	3	9	3	27	11

Pittsburgh	AB.	R.	H.	RBI.	PO.	A.
Stennett, 2b	4	0	0	0	5	1
Hebner, 3b	3	0	0	0	1	3
Oliver, cf	4	0	0	0	5	0
Stargell, lf	4	0	2	0	5	0
Zisk, rf	4	0	0	0	0	0
Sanguillen, c	4	0	1	0	3	0
Kirkpatrick, 1b	3	0	0	0	5	0
Taveras, ss	2	0	0	0	2	1
Popovich, ph-ss	1	0	1	0	1	0
Reuss, p	2	0	0	0	0	0
Parker, ph	1	0	0	0	0	0
Giusti, p	0	0	0	0	0	2
Totals	32	0	4	0	27	7

Los Angeles	0	1	0	0	0	0	0	0	2 – 3
Pittsburgh	0	0	0	0	0	0	0	0	0 – 0

Los Angeles	IP.	H.	R.	ER.	BB.	SO.
Sutton (Winner)	9	4	0	0	1	6

Pittsburgh	IP.	H.	R.	ER.	BB.	SO.
Reuss (Loser)	7	5	1	1	4	3
Giusti	2	4	2	2	3	0

Errors—Cey 2. Double play—Los Angeles 1. Left on base—Los Angeles 13, Pittsburgh 7. Two-base hits—Garvey, Buckner, Wynn. Stolen base—Lopes. Sacrifice hit—Ferguson. Hit by pitch—By Sutton (Hebner). Umpires—Colosi, Pryor, Weyer, McSherry, Crawford and Davidson. Time—2:25. Attendance—40,638.

GAME OF SUNDAY, OCTOBER 6, AT PITTSBURGH

Los Angeles	AB.	R.	H.	RBI.	PO.	A.
Lopes, 2b	4	1	2	1	3	7
Buckner, lf	5	0	2	0	2	0
Wynn, cf	2	0	0	0	3	0
Garvey, 1b	5	0	1	1	13	1
Ferguson, rf-c	4	0	0	0	2	0
Cey, 3b	5	2	4	1	0	0
Russell, ss	4	1	1	0	3	3
Yeager, c	3	0	0	0	0	0
Crawford, ph-rf	2	1	1	1	0	0
Messersmith, p	3	0	0	0	1	2
Mota, ph	1	0	1	1	0	0
Lacy, cf	0	0	0	0	0	0
Marshall, p	0	0	0	0	0	0
Totals	38	5	12	5	27	13

Pittsburgh	AB.	R.	H.	RBI.	PO.	A.
Stennett, 2b	3	0	0	0	2	0
Hebner, 3b	3	0	1	1	2	1
Oliver, cf	4	0	1	1	3	0
Stargell, lf	3	0	1	0	0	0
Giusti, p	0	0	0	0	0	0
Demery, p	0	0	0	0	0	0
Hernandez, p	0	0	0	0	0	1
Parker, rf	4	0	0	0	3	0
Sanguillen, c	4	0	2	0	7	1
Kirkpatrick, 1b	4	0	0	0	9	0
Taveras, ss	0	0	0	0	0	0
Mendoza, ss	1	0	0	0	0	1
Popovich, ph-ss	2	1	1	0	1	0
Rooker, p	2	0	1	0	0	3
Zisk, ph	1	0	1	0	0	0
Clines, pr-lf	1	1	0	0	0	0
Totals	32	2	8	2	27	7

Los Angeles	1	0	0	1	0	0	0	3	0 – 5
Pittsburgh	0	0	0	0	0	0	2	0	0 – 2

Los Angeles	IP.	H.	R.	ER.	BB.	SO.
Messersmith (Winner)	7	8	2	2	3	0
Marshall	2	0	0	0	0	0

Pittsburgh	IP.	H.	R.	ER.	BB.	SO.
Rooker	7	6	2	2	5	4
Giusti (Loser)	0*	4	3	3	0	0
Demery	0†	1	0	0	0	0
Hernandez	2	1	0	0	1	1

*Pitched to four batters in eighth. †Pitched to one batter in eighth.

Errors—Sanguillen 2, Rooker. Double plays—Los Angeles 2, Pittsburgh 1. Left on base—Los Angeles 12, Pittsburgh 8. Two-base hits—Cey 2. Home run—Cey 2. Stolen bases—Taveras, Wynn, Lopes. Sacrifice hit—Stennett. Hit by pitch—By Messersmith (Taveras). Wild pitch—Demery. Umpires—Pryor, Weyer, McSherry, Crawford, Davidson and Colosi. Time—2:44. Attendance 49,247.

GAME OF TUESDAY, OCTOBER 8, AT LOS ANGELES

Pittsburgh	AB.	R.	H.	RBI.	PO.	A.
Stennett, 2b	5	1	1	0	1	4
Sanguillen, c	5	0	1	0	6	1
Oliver, cf	3	1	1	0	1	0
Stargell, lf	5	2	2	3	3	0
Zisk, rf	5	1	2	0	2	0
Clines, rf	0	0	0	0	0	0
Robertson, 1b	5	1	0	0	11	0
xHebner, 3b	3	1	2	3	1	0
Mendoza, ss	3	0	1	1	1	5
Kison, p	3	0	0	0	1	1
Hernandez, p	1	0	0	0	0	0
Totals	38	7	10	7	27	11

Los Angeles	AB.	R.	H.	RBI.	PO.	A.
Lopes, 2b	3	0	0	0	3	5
Buckner, lf	3	0	0	0	0	0
Mota, ph-lf	1	0	0	0	1	0
Wynn, cf	3	0	0	0	4	0
Garvey, 1b	4	0	0	0	9	0
Crawford, rf	2	0	0	0	0	0
Paciorek, ph-rf	1	0	1	0	0	0
Cey, 3b	4	0	0	0	1	0
Ferguson, c	3	0	0	0	3	0
Russell, ss	4	0	2	0	6	7
Rau, p	0	0	0	0	0	0
Hough, p	0	0	0	0	0	0
Joshua, ph	0	0	0	0	0	0
Downing, p	1	0	0	0	0	0
McMullen, ph	1	0	0	0	0	0
Solomon, p	0	0	0	0	0	0
Auerbach, ph	1	0	1	0	0	0
Totals	31	0	4	0	27	12

Dodgers pitcher Don Sutton tips his hat to Los Angeles fans after completing his eight-inning stint in Game 4 of the 1974 N.L. Championship Series. The Dodgers wrapped up the pennant with a 12-1 victory over the Pirates.

Pittsburgh	5	0	2	0	0	0	0	0	0 – 7
Los Angeles	0	0	0	0	0	0	0	0	0 – 0

Pittsburgh	IP.	H.	R.	ER.	BB.	SO.
Kison (Winner)	6⅔	2	0	0	6	5
Hernandez	2⅓	2	0	0	0	1

Los Angeles	IP.	H.	R.	ER.	BB.	SO.
Rau (Loser)	⅔	3	5	3	1	0
Hough	2⅓	4	2	2	0	2
Downing	4	1	0	0	1	0
Solomon	2	0	0	0	1	1

xAwarded first base on catcher's interference. Errors–Garvey, Hough, Lopes, Ferguson, Downing. Double plays–Los Angeles 3. Left on bases–Pittsburgh 8, Los Angeles 10. Two-base hits–Sanguillen, Auerbach. Home runs–Stargell, Hebner. Passed balls–Ferguson, Sanguillen. Umpires–Weyer, McSherry, Crawford, Davidson, Colosi and Pryor. Time–2:41. Attendance–55,953.

GAME OF WEDNESDAY, OCTOBER 9, AT LOS ANGELES

Pittsburgh	AB.	R.	H.	RBI.	PO.	A.
Stennett, 2b	4	0	0	0	2	5
Hebner, 3b	4	0	0	0	1	3
Oliver, cf	3	0	0	0	0	0
Stargell, lf	3	1	1	1	5	0
Parker, rf	3	0	1	0	1	1
Sanguillen, c	3	0	0	0	3	0
Kirkpatrick, 1b	2	0	0	0	8	0
Mendoza, ss	1	0	0	0	3	1
Popovich, ph-ss	2	0	1	0	0	0
Reuss, p	0	0	0	0	0	0
Brett, p	1	0	0	0	0	1
Demery, p	0	0	0	0	0	1
Giusti, p	0	0	0	0	1	0
Pizarro, p	0	0	0	0	0	0
Howe, ph	1	0	0	0	0	0
Totals	27	1	3	1	24	12

Los Angeles	AB.	R.	H.	RBI.	PO.	A.
Lopes, 2b	4	2	1	1	1	2
Buckner, lf	5	0	0	0	1	0
Wynn, cf	2	3	1	1	2	0
Garvey, 1b	5	4	4	4	9	0
Ferguson, rf	2	2	1	1	3	0
Cey, 3b	4	0	1	0	1	1
Russell, ss	5	0	2	3	1	4
Yeager, c	2	1	0	0	8	0
Sutton, p	4	0	1	1	1	3
Mota, ph	1	0	0	0	0	0
Marshall, p	0	0	0	0	0	0
Totals	34	12	12	11	27	10

Pittsburgh	0	0	0	0	0	0	1	0	0 – 1
Los Angeles	1	0	2	0	2	2	2	3	x – 12

Pittsburgh	IP.	H.	R.	ER.	BB.	SO.
Reuss (Loser)	2⅔	2	3	3	4	0
Brett	2⅓	3	2	2	2	1
Demery	1*	2	4	4	2	0
Giusti	1⅓	5	3	3	2	1
Pizarro	⅔	0	0	0	1	0

Los Angeles	IP.	H.	R.	ER.	BB.	SO.
Sutton (Winner)	8	3	1	1	1	7
Marshall	1	0	0	0	0	1

*Pitched to two batters in seventh.

Error–Stennett. Double plays–Pittsburgh 1, Los Angeles 2. Left on bases–Pittsburgh 1, Los Angeles 9. Two-base hits–Wynn, Cey. Three-base hit–Lopes. Home runs–Garvey 2, Stargell. Stolen bases–Lopes, Yeager. Sacrifice hit–Reuss. Umpires–McSherry, Crawford, Davidson, Colosi, Pryor and Weyer. Time–2:36. Attendance–54,424.

LOS ANGELES DODGERS' BATTING AND FIELDING AVERAGES

Player–Position	G.	AB.	R.	H.	TB.	2B.	3B.	HR.	RBI.	B.A.	PO.	A.	E.	F.A.
Auerbach, ph	1	1	0	1	2	1	0	0	0	1.000	0	0	0	.000
Paciorek, ph-rf	1	1	0	1	1	0	0	0	0	1.000	0	0	0	.000
Garvey, 1b	4	18	4	7	14	1	0	2	5	.389	40	2	1	.977
Russell, ss	4	18	1	7	7	0	0	0	3	.389	13	16	0	1.000
Mota, ph-lf	3	3	0	1	1	0	0	0	1	.333	1	0	0	1.000
Cey, 3b	4	16	2	5	11	3	0	1	1	.313	2	4	2	.750
Sutton, p	2	7	0	2	2	0	0	0	1	.286	2	3	0	1.000
Lopes, 2b	4	15	4	4	6	0	1	0	3	.267	9	18	1	.964
Crawford, ph-rf	2	4	1	1	1	0	0	0	0	.250	0	0	1	.000
Ferguson, rf-c	4	13	3	3	3	0	0	0	2	.231	9	0	1	.900
Wynn, cf	4	10	4	2	4	2	0	0	2	.200	11	0	0	1.000
Buckner, lf	4	18	0	3	4	1	0	0	0	.167	6	0	0	1.000
Hough, p	1	0	0	0	0	0	0	0	0	.000	0	0	1	.000
Joshua, ph	1	0	0	0	0	0	0	0	0	.000	0	0	0	.000
Lacy, pr	1	0	0	0	0	0	0	0	0	.000	0	0	0	.000
Marshall, p	2	0	0	0	0	0	0	0	0	.000	0	0	0	.000
Rau, p	1	0	0	0	0	0	0	0	0	.000	0	0	0	.000
Solomon, p	1	0	0	0	0	0	0	0	0	.000	0	0	0	.000
Downing, p	1	1	0	0	0	0	0	0	0	.000	0	0	1	.000
McMullen, ph	1	1	0	0	0	0	0	0	0	.000	0	0	0	.000
Messersmith, p	1	3	0	0	0	0	0	0	0	.000	1	2	0	1.000
Yeager, c	3	9	1	0	0	0	0	0	0	.000	14	1	0	1.000
Totals	4	138	20	37	56	8	1	3	19	.268	108	46	7	.957

PITTSBURGH PIRATES' BATTING AND FIELDING AVERAGES

Player–Position	G.	AB.	R.	H.	TB.	2B.	3B.	HR.	RBI.	B.A.	PO.	A.	E.	F.A.
Popovich, ph-ss	3	5	1	3	3	0	0	0	0	.600	2	0	0	1.000
Rooker, p	1	2	0	1	1	0	0	0	0	.500	0	3	1	.750
Stargell, lf	4	15	3	6	12	0	0	2	4	.400	13	0	0	1.000
Zisk, rf-ph	3	10	1	3	3	0	0	0	0	.300	2	0	0	1.000
Sanguillen, c	4	16	0	4	5	1	0	0	0	.250	19	2	2	.913
Hebner, 3b	4	13	1	3	6	0	0	1	4	.231	5	7	0	1.000
Mendoza, ss	3	5	0	1	1	0	0	0	1	.200	4	7	0	1.000
Oliver, cf	4	14	1	2	2	0	0	0	1	.143	9	0	0	1.000
Parker, ph-rf	3	8	0	1	1	0	0	0	0	.125	4	1	0	1.000
Stennett, 2b	4	16	1	1	1	0	0	0	0	.063	10	10	1	.952
Demery, p	2	0	0	0	0	0	0	0	0	.000	0	1	0	1.000
Giusti, p	3	0	0	0	0	0	0	0	0	.000	1	2	0	1.000
Pizarro, p	1	0	0	0	0	0	0	0	0	.000	0	0	0	.000
Brett, p	1	1	0	0	0	0	0	0	0	.000	0	1	0	1.000
Clines, pr-lf-rf	2	1	1	0	0	0	0	0	0	.000	0	0	0	.000
Hernandez, p	2	1	0	0	0	0	0	0	0	.000	0	1	0	1.000
Howe, ph	1	1	0	0	0	0	0	0	0	.000	0	0	0	.000
Reuss, p	2	2	0	0	0	0	0	0	0	.000	0	0	0	.000
Taveras, ss	2	2	0	0	0	0	0	0	0	.000	2	1	0	1.000
Kison, p	1	3	0	0	0	0	0	0	0	.000	1	1	0	1.000
Robertson, 1b	1	5	1	0	0	0	0	0	0	.000	11	0	0	1.000
Kirkpatrick, 1b	3	9	0	0	0	0	0	0	0	.000	22	0	0	1.000
Totals	4	129	10	25	35	1	0	3	10	.194	105	37	4	.973

LOS ANGELES DODGERS' PITCHING RECORDS

Pitcher	G.	GS.	CG.	IP.	H.	R.	ER.	BB.	SO.	HB.	WP.	W.	L.	Pct.	ERA.
Downing	1	0	0	4	1	0	0	1	0	0	0	0	0	.000	0.00
Marshall	2	0	0	3	0	0	0	0	1	0	0	0	0	.000	0.00
Solomon	1	0	0	2	2	0	0	1	1	0	0	0	0	.000	0.00
Sutton	2	2	1	17	7	1	1	2	13	1	0	2	0	1.000	0.53
Messersmith	1	1	0	7	8	2	2	3	0	1	0	1	0	1.000	2.57
Hough	1	0	0	2⅓	4	2	2	0	2	0	0	0	0	.000	7.71
Rau	1	1	0	⅔	3	5	3	1	0	0	0	0	1	.000	40.50
Totals	4	4	1	36	25	10	8	8	17	2	0	3	1	.750	2.00

Shutout—Sutton. No saves.

PITTSBURGH PIRATES' PITCHING RECORDS

Pitcher	G.	GS.	CG.	IP.	H.	R.	ER.	BB.	SO.	HB.	WP.	W.	L.	Pct.	ERA.
Kison	1	1	0	6⅔	2	0	0	6	5	0	0	1	0	1.000	0.00
Hernandez	2	0	0	4⅓	3	0	0	1	2	0	0	0	0	.000	0.00
Pizarro	1	0	0	⅔	0	0	0	1	0	0	0	0	0	.000	0.00
Rooker	1	1	0	7	6	2	2	5	4	0	0	0	0	.000	2.57
Reuss	2	2	0	9⅔	7	4	4	8	3	0	0	0	2	.000	3.72
Brett	1	0	0	2⅓	3	2	2	2	1	0	0	0	0	.000	7.71
Giusti	3	0	0	3⅓	13	8	8	5	1	0	0	0	1	.000	21.60
Demery	2	0	0	1	3	4	4	2	0	0	1	0	0	.000	36.00
Totals	4	4	0	35	37	20	20	30	16	0	1	1	3	.250	5.14

Shutouts—Kison-Hernandez (combined). Saves—None.

COMPOSITE SCORE BY INNINGS

Los Angeles	2	1	2	1	2	2	2	6	2	– 20
Pittsburgh	5	0	2	0	0	0	3	0	0	– 10

Catcher's interference–Hebner awarded first base on interference by Ferguson.
Sacrifice hits–Ferguson, Stennett, Reuss.
Sacrifice flies–None.
Stolen bases–Lopes 3, Wynn, Taveras, Yeager.
Caught stealing–None.
Double plays–Cey, Lopes and Garvey; Messersmith, Russell and Garvey; Lopes, Russell and Garvey 2; Russell and Lopes; Russell (unassisted); Russell and Garvey; Sutton and Garvey; Hernandez, Sanguillen and Kirkpatrick; Hebner, Stennett and Kirkpatrick.
Left on bases–Los Angeles 44–13, 12, 10, 9; Pittsburgh 24–7, 8, 8, 1.
Hit by pitcher–By Sutton (Hebner); by Messersmith (Taveras).
Passed balls–Ferguson, Sanguillen.
Balks–None.
Time of games–First game, 2:25; second game, 2:44; third game, 2:41; fourth game, 2:36.
Attendance–First game, 40,638; second game, 49,247; third game, 55,953; fourth game, 54,424.
Umpires–Colosi, Pryor, Weyer, McSherry, Crawford and Davidson.
Official scorers–Bob Hunter, Los Angeles Herald-Examiner; Bob Smizik, Pittsburgh Press.

AMERICAN LEAGUE
Championship Series of 1975

	W.	L.	Pct.
Boston (East)	3	0	1.000
Oakland (West)	0	3	.000

The Boston Red Sox captured their first pennant since 1967 and stopped the Oakland A's bid for their fourth straight American League title by sweeping the Championship Series in three straight games.

Many observers had felt before the playoffs that the A's might be at a disadvantage because the first two games of the set were slated for Boston's Fenway Park, a nightmare arena for lefthanders. But the A's were still rated favorites on the strength of their championship experience.

In the opener, Luis Tiant pitched a three-hitter as the Bosox batted out lefty Ken Holtzman in less than seven innings. Holtzman's cause wasn't helped at all by four errors behind him, three of the miscues coming on two consecutive first-inning plays.

The tone of the series was set in the opening inning when, with two out and Carl Yastrzemski on first, Bando let Carlton Fisk's grounder go through him. A's outfielder Claudell Washington threw over the cutoff man's head, off Bando's glove. As Yastrzemski scored, Fisk moved to second, from where he immediately scored on an error by second baseman Phil Garner.

The Sox added five more tallies in the seventh frame as a dropped fly by Bill North and Washington's problems at the wall added to the A's troubles.

The A's jumped off to a three-run lead in the second game, Reggie Jackson's two-run homer in the first being the big blow. But the Sox chased lefty Vida Blue in the fourth inning on the strength of Yastrzemski's two-run homer, Fisk's double, Fred Lynn's single and a double play grounder.

Fisk's single plated Yastrzemski, who had doubled, with the go-ahead run in the sixth. Rico Petrocelli's homer in the seventh and an RBI single by Lynn in the eighth added to the margin.

The A's, going down to the wire with resolute obstinacy, tried in the third game with another lefthander. It was again Holtzman, this time with just two days' rest.

The lefty left the game in the fifth inning with four runs charged against him, enough for the Boston victory. Once more, Holtzman received less than decent support from his teammates, an error by Washington giving the Red Sox their first run of the game.

As a matter of fact, the difference in outfield play between the two clubs was startling. The Boston outfielders, especially Yastrzemski, time and again thwarted A's rallies with great catches and throws.

GAME OF SATURDAY, OCTOBER 4, AT BOSTON

Oakland	AB.	R.	H.	RBI.	PO.	A.	Boston	AB.	R.	H.	RBI.	PO.	A.
North, cf	3	0	0	1	2	0	Beniquez, dh	4	1	2	1	0	0
Washington, lf	4	0	0	1	1	0	Doyle, 2b	3	1	0	1	0	1
Bando, 3b	4	0	0	0	1	4	Yastrzemski, lf	4	1	1	0	3	0
Jackson, rf	4	0	1	0	2	0	Fisk, c	4	2	1	0	9	0
Tenace, c	3	0	0	0	4	0	Lynn, cf	4	0	1	2	7	0
Rudi, 1b	4	0	1	0	10	1	Petrocelli, 3b	4	0	0	0	1	0
Williams, dh	3	0	0	0	0	0	Evans, rf	4	1	1	0	4	0
Hopkins, pr-dh	0	0	0	0	0	0	Cooper, 1b	3	0	1	0	2	0
Campaneris, ss	4	1	0	0	1	2	Burleson, ss	3	1	1	1	1	0
Garner, 2b	2	0	0	0	2	1	Tiant, p	0	0	0	0	0	1
Holt, ph	1	0	1	0	0	0	Totals	33	7	8	5	27	2
Martinez, pr-2b	0	0	0	0	0	1							
Holtzman, p	0	0	0	0	1	1							
Todd, p	0	0	0	0	0	0							
Lindblad, p	0	0	0	0	0	0							
Bosman, p	0	0	0	0	0	0							
Abbott, p	0	0	0	0	0	0							
Totals	32	1	3	1	24	10							

Oakland									
Oakland	0	0	0	0	0	0	0	1	0 – 1
Boston	2	0	0	0	0	0	5	0	x – 7

Oakland	IP.	H.	R.	ER.	BB.	SO.
Holtzman (Loser)	6⅓	5	4	2	1	4
Todd	0*	1	1	1	0	0
Lindblad	⅓	2	2	0	0	0
Bosman	⅓	0	0	0	0	0
Abbott	1	0	0	0	0	0

Boston	IP.	H.	R.	ER.	BB.	SO.
Tiant (Winner)	9	3	1	0	3	8

*Pitched to one batter in seventh.

Errors—Bando, Washington, Garner, Lynn, North, Burleson, Cooper. Left on bases—Oakland 7, Boston 5. Two-base hits—Evans, Burleson, Lynn, Holt. Stolen bases—Beniquez 2. Sacrifice hit—Cooper. Sacrifice fly—Doyle. Umpires—Denkinger, DiMuro, Kunkel, Luciano, Evans and Morgenweck. Time—2:40. Attendance—35,578.

GAME OF SUNDAY, OCTOBER 5, AT BOSTON

Oakland	AB.	R.	H.	RBI.	PO.	A.	Boston	AB.	R.	H.	RBI.	PO.	A.
North, cf	4	0	0	0	0	0	Beniquez, dh	4	1	1	0	0	0
Campaneris, ss	3	0	0	1	6		Doyle, 2b	3	1	1	0	2	1
Bando, 3b	4	1	4	0	0	3	Yastrzemski, lf	3	2	2	2	2	1
Jackson, rf	4	1	2	2	1	1	Fisk, c	4	1	2	1	4	0
Tenace, 1b-c	4	0	0	0	11	1	Lynn, cf	4	0	2	1	4	1
Rudi, lf	4	1	2	0	1	0	Petrocelli, 3b	4	1	1	1	2	3
Washington, dh	4	0	2	1	0	0	Evans, rf	3	0	0	0	1	0
Garner, 2b	2	0	0	0	4	2	Cooper, 1b	3	0	2	0	11	0
Harper, ph	0	0	0	0	0	0	Burleson, ss	2	0	1	0	1	6
Holt, 1b	1	0	0	0	1	2	Cleveland, p	0	0	0	0	0	1
Fosse, c	2	0	0	0	3	0	Moret, p	0	0	0	0	0	0
Williams, ph	1	0	0	0	0	0	Drago, p	0	0	0	0	0	0
Martinez, 2b	0	0	0	0	1	0	Totals	30	6	12	5	27	13
Tovar, ph	1	0	0	0	0	0							
Blue, p	0	0	0	0	0	0							
Todd, p	0	0	0	0	0	0							
Fingers, p	0	0	0	0	1	0							
Totals	34	3	10	3	24	15							

Oakland									
Oakland	2	0	0	1	0	0	0	0	0 – 3
Boston	0	0	0	3	0	1	1	1	x – 6

Oakland	IP.	H.	R.	ER.	BB.	SO.
Blue	3*	6	3	3	0	2
Todd	1†	1	0	0	0	0
Fingers (Loser)	4	5	3	3	1	3

Boston	IP.	H.	R.	ER.	BB.	SO.
Cleveland	5‡	7	3	3	1	2
Moret (Winner)	1§	1	0	0	1	0
Drago (Save)	3	2	0	0	0	2

*Pitched to four batters in fourth.
†Pitched to one batter in fifth.
‡Pitched to one batter in sixth.
§Pitched to one batter in seventh.

Errors—None. Double plays—Oakland 4, Boston 2. Left on bases—Oakland 6, Boston 3. Two-base hits—Bando 2, Rudi 2, Washington. Fisk, Cooper 2, Yastrzemski. Home runs—Jackson. Yastrzemski, Petrocelli. Sacrifice hits—Burleson, Doyle. Wild pitch—Drago. Umpires—DiMuro, Kunkel, Luciano, Evans, Morgenweck and Denkinger. Time—2:27. Attendance—35,578.

GAME OF TUESDAY, OCTOBER 7, AT OAKLAND

Boston	AB.	R.	H.	RBI.	PO.	A.	Oakland	AB.	R.	H.	RBI.	PO.	A.
Beniquez, dh	4	0	0	0	0	0	Campaneris, ss	4	0	0	0	0	2
Doyle, 2b	5	1	2	1	3	6	Washington, lf	4	1	1	0	0	0
Yastrzemski, lf	4	1	2	0	2	1	Bando, 3b	4	0	2	2	2	4
Fisk, c	4	1	2	1	2	0	Jackson, rf	4	0	2	1	2	0
Lynn, cf	3	1	1	0	1	0	Rudi, 1b	4	0	0	0	11	1
Petrocelli, 3b	4	0	1	1	1	0	Williams, dh	4	0	0	0	0	0
Evans, rf	3	0	0	0	2	0	Tenace, c	2	0	0	0	4	0
Cooper, 1b	4	0	1	1	11	1	North, cf	3	0	0	0	4	1
Burleson, ss	4	1	2	0	2	6	Garner, 2b	1	0	0	0	1	1
Wise, p	0	0	0	0	2	3	Tovar, ph-2b	1	2	1	0	2	2
Drago, p	0	0	0	0	1	1	Martinez, 2b	0	0	0	0	0	0
Totals	35	5	11	4	27	18	Holt, ph	1	0	0	0	0	0
							Holtzman, p	0	0	0	0	0	0
							Todd, p	0	0	0	0	0	0
							Lindblad, p	0	0	0	0	1	4
							Totals	32	3	6	3	27	15

Boston									
Boston	0	0	0	1	3	0	0	1	0 – 5
Oakland	0	0	0	0	0	1	0	2	0 – 3

Boston	IP.	H.	R.	ER.	BB.	SO.
Wise (Winner)	7⅓	6	3	2	3	2
Drago (Save)	1⅔	0	0	0	1	0

Oakland	IP.	H.	R.	ER.	BB.	SO.
Holtzman (Loser)	4⅔	7	4	3	0	3
Todd	0*	1	0	0	0	0
Lindblad	4⅓	3	1	0	1	0

*Pitched to one batter in fifth.

Errors—Washington. Tovar, Doyle. Double play—Boston 1. Left on bases—Boston 6, Oakland 6. Two-base hit—Burleson. Stolen base—Fisk. Sacrifice hits—Beniquez, Lynn. Wild pitch—Lindblad. Umpires—Kunkel, Luciano, Evans, Morgenweck, Denkinger and DiMuro. Time—2:30. Attendance—49,358.

BOSTON RED SOX' BATTING AND FIELDING AVERAGES

Player—Position	G.	AB.	R.	H.	TB.	2B.	3B.	HR.	RBI.	B.A.	PO.	A.	E.	F.A.
Yastrzemski, lf	3	11	4	5	9	1	0	1	2	.455	7	2	0	1.000
Burleson, ss	3	9	2	4	6	2	0	0	1	.444	4	12	1	.941
Fisk, c	3	12	4	5	6	1	0	0	2	.417	15	0	0	1.000
Cooper, 1b	3	10	0	4	6	2	0	0	1	.400	24	1	1	.962
Lynn, cf	3	11	1	4	5	1	0	0	3	.364	12	1	1	.929
Doyle, 2b	3	11	3	3	3	0	0	0	2	.273	5	8	1	.929
Beniquez, dh	3	12	2	3	3	0	0	0	1	.250	0	0	0	.000
Petrocelli, 3b	3	12	1	2	5	0	0	1	2	.167	4	3	0	1.000
Evans, rf	3	10	1	1	2	1	0	0	0	.100	7	0	0	1.000
Cleveland, p	1	0	0	0	0	0	0	0	0	.000	0	1	0	1.000
Drago, p	2	0	0	0	0	0	0	0	0	.000	1	1	0	1.000
Moret, p	1	0	0	0	0	0	0	0	0	.000	0	0	0	.000
Tiant, p	1	0	0	0	0	0	0	0	0	.000	0	1	0	1.000
Wise, p	1	0	0	0	0	0	0	0	0	.000	2	3	0	1.000
Totals	3	98	18	31	45	8	0	2	14	.316	81	33	4	.966

OAKLAND ATHLETICS' BATTING AND FIELDING AVERAGES

Player—Position	G.	AB.	R.	H.	TB.	2B.	3B.	HR.	RBI.	B.A.	PO.	A.	E.	F.A.
Bando, 3b	3	12	1	6	8	2	0	0	2	.500	3	11	1	.933
Tovar, ph-2b	2	2	2	1	1	0	0	0	0	.500	2	2	1	.800
Jackson, rf	3	12	1	5	8	0	0	1	3	.417	5	1	0	1.000
Holt, ph-1b	3	3	0	1	2	1	0	0	0	.333	1	2	0	1.000
Rudi, 1b-lf	3	12	1	3	5	2	0	0	0	.250	22	2	0	1.000
Washington, lf-dh	3	12	1	3	4	1	0	0	1	.250	1	0	2	.333
Fosse, c	1	2	0	0	0	0	0	0	0	.000	3	0	0	1.000
Garner, 2b	3	5	0	0	0	0	0	0	0	.000	7	4	1	.917
Williams, dh-ph	3	8	0	0	0	0	0	0	0	.000	0	0	0	.000
Tenace, c-1b	3	9	0	0	0	0	0	0	0	.000	19	1	0	1.000
North, cf	3	10	0	0	0	0	0	0	1	.000	6	1	1	.875
Campaneris, ss	3	11	1	0	0	0	0	0	0	.000	2	10	0	1.000
Abbott, p	1	0	0	0	0	0	0	0	0	.000	0	0	0	.000
Blue, p	1	0	0	0	0	0	0	0	0	.000	0	0	0	.000
Bosman, p	1	0	0	0	0	0	0	0	0	.000	1	0	0	1.000
Fingers, p	1	0	0	0	0	0	0	0	0	.000	0	0	0	.000
Harper, ph	1	0	0	0	0	0	0	0	0	.000	0	0	0	.000
Holtzman, p	2	0	0	0	0	0	0	0	0	.000	1	1	0	1.000
Hopkins, pr-dh	1	0	0	0	0	0	0	0	0	.000	0	0	0	.000
Lindblad, p	2	0	0	0	0	0	0	0	0	.000	1	4	0	1.000
Martinez, pr-2b	3	0	0	0	0	0	0	0	0	.000	1	1	0	1.000
Todd, p	3	0	0	0	0	0	0	0	0	.000	0	0	0	.000
Totals	3	98	7	19	28	6	0	1	7	.194	75	40	6	.950

BOSTON RED SOX' PITCHING RECORDS

Pitcher	G.	GS.	CG.	IP.	H.	R.	ER.	BB.	SO.	HB.	WP.	W.	L.	Pct.	ERA.
Tiant	1	1	1	9	3	1	0	3	8	0	0	1	0	1.000	0.00
Drago	2	0	0	4⅔	2	0	0	1	2	0	1	0	0	.000	0.00
Moret	1	0	0	1	1	0	0	1	0	0	0	1	0	1.000	0.00
Wise	1	1	0	7⅓	6	3	2	3	2	0	0	1	0	1.000	2.45
Cleveland	1	1	0	5	7	3	3	1	2	0	0	0	0	.000	5.40
Totals	3	3	1	27	19	7	5	9	14	0	1	3	0	1.000	1.67

No shutouts. Saves—Drago 2.

OAKLAND ATHLETICS' PITCHING RECORDS

Pitcher	G.	GS.	CG.	IP.	H.	R.	ER.	BB.	SO.	HB.	WP.	W.	L.	Pct.	ERA.
Lindblad	2	0	0	4⅔	5	3	0	1	0	0	1	0	0	.000	0.00
Abbott	1	0	0	1	0	0	0	0	0	0	0	0	0	.000	0.00
Bosman	1	0	0	⅓	0	0	0	0	0	0	0	0	0	.000	0.00
Holtzman	2	2	0	11	12	8	5	1	7	0	0	0	2	.000	4.09
Fingers	1	0	0	4	5	3	3	1	3	0	0	0	1	.000	6.75
Blue	1	1	0	3	6	3	3	0	2	0	0	0	0	.000	9.00
Todd	3	0	0	1	3	1	1	0	0	0	0	0	0	.000	9.00
Totals	3	3	0	25	31	18	12	3	12	0	1	0	3	.000	4.32

No shutouts or saves.

COMPOSITE SCORE BY INNINGS

Boston	2	0	0	4	3	1	6	2	0 – 18
Oakland	2	0	0	1	0	1	0	3	0 – 7

Sacrifice hits—Cooper, Doyle, Burleson, Beniquez, Lynn.
Sacrifice fly—Doyle.
Stolen bass—Beniquez 2, Fisk.

Caught stealing—None.
Double plays—Campaneris, Garner and Tenace 2; Jackson and Fosse; Tenace, Campaneris and Tenace; Petrocelli, Doyle and Cooper; Lynn and Cooper; Burleson, Doyle and Cooper.
Left on bases—Boston 14–5, 3, 6; Oakland 19–7, 6, 6.
Hit by pitcher—None.
Passed balls—None.
Balks—None.
Time of games—First game, 2:40; second game, 2:27; third game, 2:30.
Attendance—First game, 35,578; second game, 35,578; third game, 49,358.
Umpires—Denkinger, DiMuro, Kunkel, Luciano, Evans and Morgenweck.
Official scorers—Glenn Schwarz, San Francisco Examiner; George Bankert, Quincy Patriot Ledger.

NATIONAL LEAGUE
Championship Series of 1975

	W.	L.	Pct.
Cincinnati (West)	3	0	1.000
Pittsburgh (East)	0	3	.000

The Cincinnati Reds, easy winners of the National League's West Division, were expected to have little trouble with their Championship Series rivals, the Pittsburgh Pirates. And that's just the way things turned out.

The Rhinelanders cuffed four Bucco hurlers for 11 hits in the opener, breezing to an 8-3 triumph. Even Reds pitcher Don Gullett got into the act, getting two hits, one a home run, and driving in three runs.

The Cincinnati regulars took batting practice in the second game, banging out 12 hits as four more Pirate hurlers trudged to the mound. Tony Perez was the big cannon in the Reds' artillery, getting three hits, one a homer, as he drove in three runs. The final score was 6-1.

The high drama of the series came in the third game, played at Pittsburgh's Three Rivers Stadium.

The home team sent lefthander John Candelaria to the hill to try and stem the Red tide and the 21-year-old rookie responded magnificently. He yielded a solo homer to Concepcion in the second inning, but going into the eighth had a 2-1 lead, the result of Al Oliver's two-run homer in the Pirate sixth.

Candelaria struck out the first two batters in the eighth. That gave him a total of 14 for the game, a new playoff record. Concepcion's circuit clout had been the only Reds hit to that point.

But, inexplicably, he lost his control and walked the weak-hitting Merv Rettenmund, a pinch-hitter. Pete Rose then blasted a home run to put the Reds ahead, 3-2. When Joe Morgan followed Rose's homer with a double, Candelaria left the game.

The Pirates tied the game in the ninth when Reds relief pitcher Rawly Eastwick walked the tying run with two out.

But it all served to merely delay the inevitable.

The Reds got three hits and two runs off veteran Ramon Hernandez, the third Pittsburgh hurler, in the top of the 10th and so clinched the pennant.

GAME OF SATURDAY, OCTOBER 4, AT CINCINNATI

Pittsburgh	AB.	R.	H.	RBI.	PO.	A.	Cincinnati	AB.	R.	H.	RBI.	PO.	A.
Stennett, 2b	5	0	1	0	1	5	Rose, 3b	5	0	2	0	0	0
Sanguillen, c	4	0	1	0	5	1	Morgan, 2b	3	1	0	0	1	2
Oliver, cf	4	0	1	0	3	0	Bench, c	4	1	1	0	5	0
Stargell, 1b	4	0	0	0	8	0	Perez, 1b	4	2	2	1	6	3
Zisk, lf	4	0	1	0	2	0	Foster, lf	4	2	2	0	2	0
Parker, rf	2	2	0	0	4	0	Concepcion, ss	3	0	1	0	0	3
Hebner, 3b	4	1	2	1	0	1	Griffey, rf	4	1	1	3	2	1
Taveras, ss	3	0	1	1	1	2	Geronimo, cf	3	0	0	1	7	0
Reuss, p	1	0	0	0	0	1	Gullett, p	4	1	2	3	4	1
Brett, p	0	0	0	0	0	0	Totals	34	8	11	8	27	10
Robinson, ph	1	0	0	0	0	0							
Demery, p	0	0	0	0	0	0							
Randolph, ph	1	0	0	0	0	0							
Ellis, p	0	0	0	0	0	0							
Robertson, ph	1	0	1	1	0	0							
Reynolds, pr	0	0	0	0	0	0							
Totals	34	3	8	3	24	10							

Pittsburgh									
Pittsburgh	0	2	0	0	0	0	0	0	1 — 3
Cincinnati	0	1	3	0	4	0	0	0	x — 8

Pittsburgh	IP.	H.	R.	ER.	BB.	SO.
Reuss (Loser)	2⅔	4	4	4	4	1
Brett	1⅓	1	0	0	0	1
Demery	2	4	4	4	1	1
Ellis	2	2	0	0	0	2

Cincinnati	IP.	H.	R.	ER.	BB.	SO.
Gullett (Winner)	9	8	3	3	2	5

Errors—None. Left on bases—Pittsburgh 7, Cincinnati 8. Two-base hits—Hebner, Griffey. Home run—Gullett. Stolen bases—Morgan 3. Sacrifice fly—Geronimo. Hit by pitch—By Gullett (Parker). Wild pitch—Gullett. Passed balls—Sanguillen 2. Umpires—Kibler, Olsen, Pulli, W. Williams, Gorman and A. Williams. Time—3:00. Attendance—54,633.

GAME OF SUNDAY, OCTOBER 5, AT CINCINNATI

Pittsburgh	AB.	R.	H.	RBI.	PO.	A.	Cincinnati	AB.	R.	H.	RBI.	PO.	A.
Stennett, 2b	4	0	2	0	0	3	Rose, 3b	4	1	1	0	0	1
Sanguillen, c	4	0	0	0	9	0	Morgan, 2b	3	1	1	0	1	2
Oliver, cf	2	0	0	0	0	0	Bench, c	4	0	0	0	5	3
Stargell, 1b	3	1	1	0	6	0	Perez, 1b	4	1	3	3	12	2
Zisk, lf	3	0	2	0	2	0	Foster, lf	4	1	2	0	2	0
Parker, rf	4	0	0	0	4	1	Concepcion, ss	4	1	3	0	5	4
Hebner, 3b	3	0	0	1	0	1	Griffey, rf	4	1	2	1	0	0
Taveras, ss	3	0	0	0	3	3	Geronimo, cf	3	0	0	0	1	0
Robertson, ph	1	0	0	0	0	0	Norman, p	1	0	0	1	0	1
Rooker, p	1	0	0	0	0	0	Armbrister, ph	0	0	0	0	0	0
Robinson, ph	1	0	0	0	0	0	Crowley, ph	0	0	0	0	0	0
Tekulve, p	0	0	0	0	0	0	Rettenmund, ph	1	0	0	0	0	0
Brett, p	0	0	0	0	0	0	Eastwick, p	0	0	0	0	1	0
Kirkpatrick, ph	1	0	0	0	0	0	Totals	32	6	12	5	27	13
Kison, p	0	0	0	0	0	0							
Totals	30	1	5	1	24	8							

Pittsburgh									
Pittsburgh	0	0	0	1	0	0	0	0	0 — 1
Cincinnati	2	0	0	2	0	1	1	0	x — 6

Pittsburgh	IP.	H.	R.	ER.	BB.	SO.
Rooker (Loser)	4	7	4	4	0	5
Tekulve	1*	3	1	1	1	2
Brett	1	0	0	0	0	0
Kison	2	2	1	1	1	1

Cincinnati	IP.	H.	R.	ER.	BB.	SO.
Norman (Winner)	6	4	1	1	5	4
Eastwick (Save)	3	1	0	0	0	1

*Pitched to two batters in sixth.

Error—Concepcion. Double plays—Pittsburgh 3, Cincinnati 2. Left on bases—Pittsburgh 7, Cincinnati 5. Two-base hits—Stargell, Zisk, Morgan. Home run—Perez. Stolen base—Foster, Concepcion 2, Griffey 3, Morgan. Sacrifice fly—Norman. Wild pitch—Norman. Balk—Brett. Umpires—Olsen, Pulli, W. Williams, Gorman, A. Williams and Kibler. Time—2:51. Attendance—54,752.

GAME OF TUESDAY, OCTOBER 7, AT PITTSBURGH (N)

Cincinnati	AB.	R.	H.	RBI.	PO.	A.	Pittsburgh	AB.	R.	H.	RBI.	PO.	A.
Rose, 3b	5	2	2	2	2	0	Stennett, 2b-ss	5	0	0	0	2	0
Morgan, 2b	5	0	2	1	0	5	Hebner, 3b	5	1	2	0	0	0
Bench, c	5	0	0	0	8	1	Oliver, cf	5	1	1	2	2	0
Perez, 1b	4	0	0	0	9	0	Stargell, 1b	4	0	1	0	1	0
Foster, lf	3	0	0	0	3	0	Randolph, pr-2b	1	1	0	0	0	1
Concepcion, ss	4	1	1	1	1	1	Parker, rf	4	0	0	0	5	0
Griffey, rf	4	1	1	0	2	0	Zisk, lf	3	0	2	0	4	0
Geronimo, cf	4	0	0	0	5	0	Sanguillen, c	4	0	1	0	15	0
Nolan, p	2	0	0	0	0	0	Taveras, ss	1	0	0	0	0	1
C. Carroll, p	0	0	0	0	0	1	Kirkpatrick, ph	1	0	0	0	0	0
Rettenmund, ph	0	1	0	0	0	0	Reynolds, ss	1	0	0	0	0	0
McEnaney, p	0	0	0	0	0	0	Robertson, ph-1b	0	0	0	0	1	0
Eastwick, p	0	0	0	0	0	0	Candelaria, p	3	0	0	0	0	0
Armbrister, ph	0	0	0	1	0	0	Giusti, p	0	0	0	0	0	0
Borbon, p	0	0	0	0	0	0	Dyer, ph	0	0	0	1	0	0
Totals	36	5	6	5	30	8	Hernandez, p	0	0	0	0	0	0
							Tekulve, p	0	0	0	0	0	0
							Totals	37	3	7	3	30	2

Cincinnati									
Cincinnati	0	1	0	0	0	0	0	2	0	2 — 5
Pittsburgh	0	0	0	0	0	2	0	0	1	0 — 3

Cincinnati	IP.	H.	R.	ER.	BB.	SO.
Nolan	6	5	2	2	0	5
C. Carroll	1	0	0	0	1	1
McEnaney	1⅓	1	1	1	0	1
Eastwick (Winner)	⅔	1	0	0	2	0
Borbon (Save)	1	0	0	0	0	1

Pittsburgh	IP.	H.	R.	ER.	BB.	SO.
Candelaria	7⅔	3	3	3	2	14
Giusti	1⅓	0	0	0	0	1
Hernandez (Loser)	⅔	3	2	2	0	0
Tekulve	⅓	0	0	0	0	0

Errors—Reynolds, Sanguillen. Left on bases—Cincinnati 4, Pittsburgh 7. Two-base hits—Morgan 2. Home runs—Concepcion, Oliver, Rose. Stolen base—Bench. Sacrifice fly—Armbrister. Balk—Hernandez. Umpires—Pulli, W. Williams, Gorman, A. Williams, Kibler and Olsen. Time—2:47. Attendance—46,355.

CINCINNATI REDS' BATTING AND FIELDING AVERAGES

Player—Position	G.	AB.	R.	H.	TB.	2B.	3B.	HR.	RBI.	B.A.	PO.	A.	E.	F.A.
Gullett, p	1	4	1	2	5	0	0	1	3	.500	4	1	0	1.000
Concepcion, ss	3	11	2	5	8	0	0	1	1	.455	6	8	1	.933
Perez, 1b	3	12	3	5	8	0	0	1	4	.417	27	5	0	1.000
Foster, lf	3	11	3	4	4	0	0	0	0	.364	7	0	0	1.000
Rose, 3b	3	14	3	5	8	0	0	1	2	.357	2	1	0	1.000
Griffey, rf	3	12	3	4	5	1	0	0	4	.333	4	1	0	1.000
Morgan, 2b	3	11	2	3	6	3	0	0	1	.273	2	9	0	1.000
Bench, c	3	13	1	1	1	0	0	0	0	.077	18	4	0	1.000
Norman, p	1	1	0	0	0	0	0	0	1	.000	0	1	0	1.000
Rettenmund, ph	2	1	1	0	0	0	0	0	0	.000	0	0	0	.000
Nolan, p	1	2	0	0	0	0	0	0	0	.000	0	0	0	.000
Geronimo, cf	3	10	0	0	0	0	0	0	1	.000	13	0	0	1.000
Armbrister, ph	2	0	0	0	0	0	0	0	1	.000	0	0	0	.000
Borbon, p	1	0	0	0	0	0	0	0	0	.000	0	0	0	.000
Carroll, p	1	0	0	0	0	0	0	0	0	.000	0	1	0	1.000
Crowley, ph	1	0	0	0	0	0	0	0	0	.000	0	0	0	.000
Eastwick, p	2	0	0	0	0	0	0	0	0	.000	1	0	0	1.000
McEnaney, p	1	0	0	0	0	0	0	0	0	.000	0	0	0	.000
Totals	3	102	19	29	45	4	0	4	18	.284	84	31	1	.991

PITTSBURGH PIRATES' BATTING AND FIELDING AVERAGES

Player—Position	G.	AB.	R.	H.	TB.	2B.	3B.	HR.	RBI.	B.A.	PO.	A.	E.	F.A.
Zisk, lf	3	10	0	5	6	1	0	0	0	.500	8	0	0	1.000
Robertson, ph-1b	3	2	0	1	1	0	0	0	1	.500	1	0	0	1.000
Hebner, 3b	3	12	2	4	5	1	0	0	2	.333	0	2	0	1.000
Stennett, 2b-ss	3	14	0	3	3	0	0	0	0	.214	3	8	0	1.000
Oliver, cf	3	11	1	2	5	0	0	1	2	.182	5	0	0	1.000
Stargell, 1b	3	11	1	2	3	1	0	0	0	.182	15	0	0	1.000
Sanguillen, c	3	12	0	2	2	0	0	0	0	.167	29	1	1	.968
Taveras, ss	3	7	0	1	1	0	0	0	1	.143	4	6	0	1.000
Reuss, p	1	1	0	0	0	0	0	0	0	.000	0	1	0	1.000
Reynolds, pr-ss	2	1	0	0	0	0	0	0	0	.000	0	0	1	.000
Rooker, p	1	1	0	0	0	0	0	0	0	.000	0	0	0	.000
Kirkpatrick, ph	2	2	0	0	0	0	0	0	0	.000	0	0	0	.000
Randolph, ph-pr-2b	2	2	1	0	0	0	0	0	0	.000	0	1	0	1.000
Robinson, ph	2	2	0	0	0	0	0	0	0	.000	0	0	0	.000
Candelaria, p	1	3	0	0	0	0	0	0	0	.000	0	0	0	.000
Parker, rf	3	10	2	0	0	0	0	0	0	.000	13	1	0	1.000
Brett, p	2	0	0	0	0	0	0	0	0	.000	0	0	0	.000
Demery, p	1	0	0	0	0	0	0	0	0	.000	0	0	0	.000
Dyer, ph	1	0	0	0	0	0	0	0	1	.000	0	0	0	.000
Ellis, p	1	0	0	0	0	0	0	0	0	.000	0	0	0	.000
Giusti, p	1	0	0	0	0	0	0	0	0	.000	0	0	0	.000
Hernandez, p	1	0	0	0	0	0	0	0	0	.000	0	0	0	.000
Kison, p	1	0	0	0	0	0	0	0	0	.000	0	0	0	.000
Tekulve, p	2	0	0	0	0	0	0	0	0	.000	0	0	0	.000
Totals	3	101	7	20	26	3	0	1	7	.198	78	20	2	.980

CINCINNATI REDS' PITCHING RECORDS

Pitcher	G.	GS.	CG.	IP.	H.	R.	ER.	BB.	SO.	HB.	WP.	W.	L.	Pct.	ERA.
Eastwick	2	0	0	3⅔	2	0	0	2	1	0	0	1	0	1.000	0.00
Borbon	1	0	0	1	0	0	0	0	1	0	0	0	0	.000	0.00
Carroll	1	0	0	1	0	0	0	1	1	0	0	0	0	.000	0.00
Norman	1	1	0	6	4	1	1	5	4	0	1	1	0	1.000	1.50
Gullett	1	1	1	9	8	3	3	2	5	1	1	1	0	1.000	3.00
Nolan	1	1	0	6	5	2	2	0	5	0	0	0	0	.000	3.00
McEnaney	1	0	0	1⅓	1	1	1	0	1	0	0	0	0	.000	6.75
Totals	3	3	1	28	20	7	7	10	18	1	2	3	0	1.000	2.25

No shutouts. Saves—Eastwick, Borbon.

PITTSBURGH PIRATES' PITCHING RECORDS

Pitcher	G.	GS.	CG.	IP.	.	R.	ER.	BB.	SO.	HB.	WP.	W.	L.	Pct.	ERA.
Brett	2	0	0	2⅓	1	0	0	0	1	0	0	0	0	.000	0.00
Ellis	1	0	0	2	2	0	0	0	2	0	0	0	0	.000	0.00
Giusti	1	0	0	1⅓	0	0	0	1	1	0	0	0	0	.000	0.00
Candelaria	1	1	0	7⅔	3	3	3	2	14	0	0	0	0	.000	3.52
Kison	1	0	0	2	2	1	1	1	1	0	0	0	0	.000	4.50
Tekulve	2	0	0	1⅓	3	1	1	1	2	0	0	0	0	.000	6.75
Rooker	1	1	0	4	7	4	4	0	5	0	0	0	1	.000	9.00
Reuss	1	1	0	2⅔	4	4	4	4	1	0	0	0	1	.000	13.50

Pitcher	G.	GS.	CG.	IP.	H.	R.	ER.	BB.	SO.	HB.	WP.	W.	L.	Pct.	ERA.
Demery	1	0	0	2	4	4	4	1	1	0	0	0	0	.000	18.00
Hernandez	1	0	0	⅔	3	2	2	0	0	0	0	0	1	.000	27.00
Totals	3	3	0	26	29	19	19	9	28	0	0	0	3	.000	6.58

No shutouts or saves.

COMPOSITE SCORE BY INNINGS

Cincinnati..............................	2	2	3		2	4	1		1	2	0	2 — 19
Pittsburgh	0	2	0		1	0	2		0	0	2	0 — 7

Sacrifice hits—None.
Sacrifice flies—Ambrister, Geronimo, Norman.
Stolen bases—Morgan 4, Griffey 3. Concepcion 2, Bench, Foster.
Caught stealing—None.
Double plays—Concepcion and Perez; Morgan, Concepcion and Perez; Parker and Sanguillen; Stennett, Taveras and Stargell 2.
Left on bases—Cincinnati 17—8, 5, 4; Pittsburgh 21—7, 7, 7.
Hit by pitcher—By Gullett (Parker).
Passed balls—Sanguillen 2.
Balks—Brett, Hernandez.
Time of games—First game, 3:00; second game, 2:51; third game, 2:47.
Attendance—First game 54,633; second game, 54,752; third game, 46,355.
Umpires—Kibler, Olsen, Pulli, W. Williams, Gorman and A. Williams.
Official scorers—Earl Lawson, Cincinnati Post; Luke Quay, McKeesport Daily News.

AMERICAN LEAGUE
Championship Series of 1976

	W.	L.	Pct.
New York (East)...	3	2	.600
Kansas City (West)...	2	3	.400

With one swing of the bat, New York Yankee first baseman Chris Chambliss propelled his team to its first American League pennant since 1964 and touched off one of the wildest mob scenes in the history of American sports.

With the score tied, 6-6, in the bottom of the ninth inning in the fifth game of the Championship Series, Chambliss sent the first pitch from the Kansas City Royals' fireballing righthander, Mark Littell, over the right-field fence. Littell had yielded only one homer during the regular season.

As soon as it was clear that the 1976 American League season was over and the Yankees were winners, Yankee fans, who had been wandering in a desert of pennantless seasons—something to which they were not accustomed—rushed onto the field.

By the time Chambliss reached first base, he was surrounded by spectators. When he reached second, the bag had already been removed by a souvenir collector and Chambliss had to reach out to touch it. He never did reach third and came nowhere near home, although his teammates brought him out later to stamp his feet in the general vicinity of home plate.

The hero of the evening was fortune to escape without serious injury, as were his teammates. The fans' victory "celebration" turned into an orgy of hoodlumism and looting and resulted in about $100,000 worth of damage being done to Yankee Stadium.

Chambliss' homer was the climax of an exciting game. After the lead seesawed back and forth in the early going, the Yankees finally managed to carry a 6-3 bulge into the eighth frame. But the Royals' third baseman, George Brett, tied the game with a three-run home run. That set the stage for the pulsating finish.

The Yankees had been substantial favorites to win the playoff but the Royals, even after losing ace center fielder Amos Otis because of a leg injury in the first game, battled right down to the wire.

The Series opened in Kansas City and the Royals showed their nervousness by handing the Yanks two runs in the first inning with Brett committing a pair of misplays. Catfish Hunter subdued the home team easily, giving up only five hits, and the New Yorkers captured the game, 4-1.

In the second contest, the Royals found Yankee 19-game winner Ed Figueroa no puzzle and pounded out a 7-3 triumph.

The Yankees won the third engagement, 5-3, as Chambliss got two hits, including a home run, and drove in three runs.

The Royals knocked Hunter out of the box in the fourth inning of the fourth game, and copped a 7-4 decision to deadlock the Series.

That set up the climactic game of the 1976 American League season wherein Chambliss' big blow was the hit of the year.

GAME OF SATURDAY, OCTOBER 9, AT KANSAS CITY

New York	AB.	R.	H.	RBI.	PO.	A.	Kansas City	AB.	R.	H.	RBI.	PO.	A.
Rivers, cf	5	2	2	0	0	0	Otis, cf	1	0	0	0	0	0
R. White, lf	4	0	1	2	4	0	Wohlford, lf	3	0	0	0	2	0
Munson, c	5	1	1	0	5	2	Brett, 3b	4	0	3	0	1	3
Piniella, dh	4	0	2	0	0	0	McRae, dh	4	0	0	0	0	0
Chambliss, 1b	4	0	2	1	7	0	Mayberry, 1b	3	0	0	0	10	0
Nettles, 3b	4	0	0	0	3	3	Cowens, rf-cf	3	1	1	0	3	0
Maddox, rf	4	0	1	0	4	0	Poquette, lf-rf	3	0	0	1	4	0
Randolph, 2b	4	0	0	0	2	2	F. White, 2b	2	0	0	0	2	3
Stanley, ss	4	1	3	0	2	1	Rojas, ph-2b	1	0	0	0	0	0
Hunter, p	0	0	0	0	0	2	Patek, ss	3	0	1	0	1	3
Totals	38	4	12	3	27	10	Martinez, c	2	0	0	0	4	0
							Quirk, ph	0	0	0	0	0	0
							Wathan, c	0	0	0	0	0	0
							Stinson, ph	1	0	0	0	0	0
							Gura, p	0	0	0	0	0	0
							Littell, p	0	0	0	0	0	0
							Totals	30	1	5	1	27	9

New York	2	0	0	0	0	0	0	0	2 — 4
Kansas City	0	0	0	0	0	0	0	1	0 — 1

New York	IP.	H.	R.	ER.	BB.	SO.
Hunter (Winner)	9	5	1	1	0	5

Kansas City	IP.	H.	R.	ER.	BB.	SO.
Gura (Loser)	8⅔	12	4	3	1	4
Littell	⅓	0	0	0	0	0

Errors—Brett 2. Double play—Kansas City 1. Left on base—New York 8, Kansas City 2. Two-base hits—Stanley, R. White. Three-base hits—Chambliss, Cowens. Umpires—Brinkman, Haller, Maloney, Barnett, Franz and McCoy. Time—2:06. Attendance—41,077.

GAME OF SUNDAY, OCTOBER 10, AT KANSAS CITY (N)

New York	AB.	R.	H.	RBI.	PO.	A.	Kansas City	AB.	R.	H.	RBI.	PO.	A.
Rivers, cf	4	0	0	0	3	0	Wohlford, lf	4	1	1	0	2	0
R. White, lf	4	1	2	0	2	0	Cowens, cf	5	1	1	0	5	0
Munson, c	5	1	2	1	2	1	Brett, 3b	3	1	1	1	0	1
Chambliss, 1b	5	0	3	1	9	1	Mayberry, 1b	4	1	1	1	12	0
May, dh	5	1	2	0	0	0	McRae, dh	3	0	0	0	0	0
Nettles, 3b	3	0	1	0	2	5	Poquette, rf	3	1	2	2	2	0
Gamble, rf	4	0	1	1	3	0	F. White, 2b	4	1	1	0	3	5
Randolph, 2b	3	0	0	0	1	3	Patek, ss	4	1	1	1	1	6
Stanley, ss	3	0	1	0	0	4	Martinez, c	4	0	1	2	2	0
Piniella, ph	1	0	0	0	0	0	Leonard, p	0	0	0	0	0	0
Mason, ss	0	0	0	0	1	0	Splittorff, p	0	0	0	0	0	1
Figueroa, p	0	0	0	0	0	0	Mingori, p	0	0	0	0	0	0
Tidrow, p	0	0	0	0	1	0	Totals	34	7	9	7	27	13
Totals	37	3	12	3	24	14							

New York	0	1	2	0	0	0	0	0	0 — 3
Kansas City	2	0	0	0	0	2	0	3	x — 7

New York	IP.	H.	R.	ER.	BB.	SO.
Figueroa (Loser)	5⅓	6	4	4	2	2
Tidrow	2⅔	3	3	2	1	0

Kansas City	IP.	H.	R.	ER.	BB.	SO.
Leonard	2⅓	6	3	3	2	0
Splittorff (Winner)	5⅔	4	0	0	2	1
Mingori	1	2	0	0	0	1

Errors—Munson 2, Chambliss, Stanley, Gamble. Double plays—Kansas City 2. Left on base—New York 11, Kansas City 7. Two-base hits—May, R. White, Munson, Stanley, Nettles, Poquette. Three-base hit—Brett. Stolen bases—Cowens 2, Wohlford. Sacrifice fly—Brett. Umpires—Barnett, Maloney, Haller, Frantz, McCoy and Brinkman. Time—2:45. Attendance—41,091.

GAME OF TUESDAY, OCTOBER 12, AT NEW YORK (N)

Kansas City	AB.	R.	H.	RBI.	PO.	A.	New York	AB.	R.	H.	RBI.	PO.	A.
Wohlford, lf	2	1	0	0	0	0	Rivers, cf	5	0	1	0	1	0
Cowens, cf	4	0	1	0	1	0	R. White, lf	3	1	0	0	0	0
Brett, 3b	3	1	2	1	1	0	Munson, c	4	1	2	0	5	2
Mayberry, 1b	4	1	1	0	11	0	Piniella, dh	2	1	1	0	0	0
McRae, dh	2	0	0	1	0	0	May, ph-dh	1	0	0	0	0	0
Poquette, rf	3	0	1	1	2	0	Chambliss, 1b	4	2	2	3	10	2
Nelson, ph	1	0	0	0	0	0	Nettles, 3b	3	0	1	1	0	3
F. White, 2b	2	0	0	0	1	3	Maddox, rf	4	0	1	1	4	0
Rojas, ph-2b	1	0	0	0	0	1	Randolph, 2b	3	0	1	0	3	3
Patek, ss	3	0	1	0	3	5	Stanley, ss	3	0	0	0	3	4
Martinez, c	2	0	0	0	5	1	Ellis, p	0	0	0	0	1	0
Quirk, ph	1	0	0	0	0	0	Lyle, p	0	0	0	0	0	0
Stinson, c	0	0	0	0	0	0	Totals	32	5	9	5	27	14
Hassler, p	0	0	0	0	0	0							
Pattin, p	0	0	0	0	0	0							
Hall, p	0	0	0	0	0	0							
Mingori, p	0	0	0	0	0	0							
Littell, p	0	0	0	0	0	1							
Totals	28	3	6	3	24	11							

Kansas City	3	0	0	0	0	0	0	0	0 – 3
New York	0	0	0	2	0	3	0	0	x – 5

Kansas City	IP.	H.	R.	ER.	BB.	SO.
Hassler (Loser)	5*	4	4	4	3	3
Pattin	0†	0	1	1	1	0
Hall	⅓	1	0	0	0	0
Mingori	0‡	1	0	0	0	0
Littell	2⅔	3	0	0	1	2

New York	IP.	H.	R.	ER.	BB.	SO.
Ellis (Winner)	8	6	3	3	2	5
Lyle (Save)	1	0	0	0	1	0

*Pitched to two batters in sixth.
†Pitched to one batter in sixth.
‡Pitched to one batter in sixth.

Errors—None. Double plays—Kansas City 1, New York 2. Left on base—Kansas City 3, New York 8. Two-base hits—Poquette, Piniella, Munson, Maddox. Home run—Chambliss. Stolen bases—Wohlford, Chambliss, Randolph. Sacrifice fly—McRae. Hit by Pitcher—By Ellis (McRae). Passed ball—Munson. Umpires—Maloney, Haller, Frantz, McCoy, Brinkman and Barnett. Time—3:00. Attendance—56,808.

GAME OF WEDNESDAY, OCTOBER 13, AT NEW YORK

Kansas City	AB.	R.	H.	RBI.	PO.	A.	New York	AB.	R.	H.	RBI.	PO.	A.
Cowens, cf	5	0	0	0	4	0	Rivers, cf	4	0	1	0	5	0
Poquette, lf-rf	4	0	0	0	3	0	R. White, lf	4	0	1	0	7	0
Brett, 3b	4	0	0	0	1	2	Munson, c	4	0	2	0	2	1
Mayberry, 1b	3	1	0	0	9	0	Piniella, dh	4	0	0	0	0	0
McRae, rf	4	2	2	0	2	0	Chambliss, 1b	4	1	1	0	9	0
Wohlford, lf	0	0	0	0	3	0	Nettles, 3b	4	2	2	3	0	2
Quirk, dh	2	1	1	2	0	0	Maddox, rf	1	0	0	0	1	0
Nelson, ph-dh	1	0	0	0	0	0	Gamble, ph-rf	2	1	1	0	1	0
Rojas, 2b	3	1	2	1	1	3	Velez, ph	1	0	0	0	0	0
F. White, pr-2b	0	1	0	0	0	0	Randolph, 2b	4	0	1	1	1	1
Patek, ss	4	1	3	3	3	3	Stanley, ss	2	0	1	0	1	1
Martinez, c	3	0	1	1	1	1	Hendricks, ph	1	0	1	0	0	0
Gura, p	0	0	0	0	0	0	Guidry, pr	0	0	0	0	0	0
Bird, p	0	0	0	0	0	1	Mason, ss	0	0	0	0	0	2
Mingori, p	0	0	0	0	0	0	Alomar, ph	1	0	0	0	0	0
Totals	33	7	9	7	27	10	Hunter, p	0	0	0	0	0	1
							Tidrow, p	0	0	0	0	0	0
							Jackson, p	0	0	0	0	0	1
							Totals	36	4	11	4	27	9

Kansas City	0	3	0	2	0	1	0	1	0 – 7
New York	0	2	0	0	0	0	1	0	1 – 4

Kansas City	IP.	H.	R.	ER.	BB.	SO.
Gura	2*	6	2	2	0	0
Bird (Winner)	4⅔	4	1	1	0	1
Mingori (Save)	2⅓	1	1	1	1	0

New York	IP.	H.	R.	ER.	BB.	SO.
Hunter (Loser)	3†	5	5	5	1	0
Tidrow	3⅔	2	1	1	2	0
Jackson	2⅓	2	1	1	1	2

*Pitched to one batter in third.
†Pitched to two batters in fourth.

Error—Bird. Double play—Kansas City 1. Left on base—Kansas City 5, New York 5. Two-base hits—R. White, Patek 2, McRae, Gamble. Three-base hits—Quirk, McRae. Home runs—Nettles 2. Sacrifice flies—Rojas, Quirk. Umpires—Haller, Frantz, McCoy, Brinkman, Barnett and Maloney. Time—2:50. Attendance—56,355.

GAME OF THURSDAY, OCTOBER 14, AT NEW YORK (N)

Kansas City	AB.	R.	H.	RBI.	PO.	A.
Cowens, cf	4	1	1	0	2	0
Poquette, lf	3	0	0	0	2	0
Wohlford, ph-lf	2	1	1	0	0	0
Brett, 3b	4	2	2	3	0	1
Mayberry, 1b	4	1	2	2	6	1
McRae, rf	4	0	0	0	3	1
Quirk, dh	4	0	0	0	0	0
Rojas, 2b	4	1	1	0	3	2
Patek, ss	4	0	1	0	5	1
Martinez, c	4	0	3	1	3	2
Leonard, p	0	0	0	0	0	0
Splittorff, p	0	0	0	0	0	0
Pattin, p	0	0	0	0	0	0
Hassler, p	0	0	0	0	0	0
Littell, p	0	0	0	0	0	0
Totals	37	6	11	6	24	8

New York	AB.	R.	H.	RBI.	PO.	A.
Rivers, cf	5	3	4	0	2	0
R. White, lf	2	2	1	1	4	0
Munson, c	5	0	3	2	4	0
Chambliss, 1b	4	2	3	3	15	0
May, dh	4	0	0	0	0	0
Alomar, pr-dh	0	0	0	0	0	0
Nettles, 3b	3	0	0	0	0	1
Gamble, rf	2	0	0	0	0	0
Randolph, 2b	3	0	0	0	1	5
Stanley, ss	3	0	0	0	1	5
Figueroa, p	0	0	0	0	0	2
Jackson, p	0	0	0	0	0	0
Tidrow, p	0	0	0	0	0	0
Totals	31	7	11	6	27	13

Kansas City	2	1	0	0	0	0	0	3	0	6
New York	2	0	2	0	0	2	0	0	1	7

None out when winning run scored.

Kansas City	IP.	H.	R.	ER.	BB.	SO.
Leonard	0*	3	2	2	0	0
Splittorff	3⅔	3	2	2	3	1
Pattin	⅓	0	0	0	0	0
Hassler	2⅓	4	2	1	3	1
Littell (Loser)	1⅔‡	1	1	1	0	1

New York	IP.	H.	R.	ER.	BB.	SO.
Figueroa	7†	8	4	4	0	3
Jackson	1	2	2	2	0	1
Tidrow (Winner)	1	1	0	0	1	0

*Pitched to three batters in first.
†Pitched to one batter in eighth.
‡Pitched to one batter in ninth.

Errors—Gamble, Brett. Double play—New York 1. Left on bases—Kansas City 5, New York 9. Two-base hits—Brett, Chambliss. Three-base hit—Rivers. Home runs—Mayberry, Brett, Chambliss. Stolen bases—R. White, Rojas, Chambliss. Sacrifice hits—R. White, Gamble. Sacrifice fly—Chambliss. Umpires—Frantz, McCoy, Brinkman, Barnett, Maloney and Haller. Time—3:13. Attendance—56,821.

NEW YORK YANKEES' BATTING AND FIELDING AVERAGES

Player—Position	G.	AB.	R.	H.	TB.	2B.	3B.	HR.	RBI.	B.A.	PO.	A.	E.	F.A.
Hendricks, ph	1	1	0	1	1	0	0	0	0	1.000	0	0	0	.000
Chambliss, 1b	5	21	5	11	20	1	1	2	8	.524	50	3	1	.981
Munson, c	5	23	3	10	12	2	0	0	3	.435	18	6	2	.923
Rivers, cf	5	23	5	8	10	0	1	0	0	.348	11	0	0	1.000
Stanley, ss	5	15	1	5	7	2	0	0	0	.333	7	15	1	.957
R. White, lf	5	17	4	5	8	3	0	0	3	.294	17	0	0	1.000
Piniella, dh-ph	4	11	1	3	4	1	0	0	0	.273	0	0	0	.000
Gamble, rf-ph	3	8	1	2	3	1	0	0	1	.250	4	0	2	.667
Nettles, 3b	5	17	2	4	11	0	0	2	4	.235	5	14	0	1.000
Maddox, rf	3	9	0	2	3	1	0	0	1	.222	9	0	0	1.000
May, dh-ph	3	10	1	2	3	1	0	0	0	.200	0	0	0	.000
Randolph, 2b	5	17	0	2	2	0	0	0	1	.118	8	14	0	1.000
Ellis, p	1	0	0	0	0	0	0	0	0	.000	1	0	0	1.000
Guidry, pr	1	0	0	0	0	0	0	0	0	.000	0	0	0	.000
Lyle, p	1	0	0	0	0	0	0	0	0	.000	0	0	0	.000
Figueroa, p	2	0	0	0	0	0	0	0	0	.000	0	2	0	1.000
Hunter, p	2	0	0	0	0	0	0	0	0	.000	0	3	0	1.000
Jackson, p	2	0	0	0	0	0	0	0	0	.000	0	1	0	1.000
Mason, ss	2	0	0	0	0	0	0	0	0	.000	1	2	0	1.000
Tidrow, p	3	0	0	0	0	0	0	0	0	.000	1	0	0	1.000
Alomar, ph-pr-dh	2	1	0	0	0	0	0	0	0	.000	0	0	0	.000
Velez, ph	1	1	0	0	0	0	0	0	0	.000	0	0	0	.000
Totals	5	174	23	55	84	13	2	4	21	.316	132	60	6	.970

KANSAS CITY ROYALS' BATTING AND FIELDING AVERAGES

Player—Position	G.	AB.	R.	H.	TB.	2B.	3B.	HR.	RBI.	B.A.	PO.	A.	E.	F.A.
Brett, 3b	5	18	4	8	14	1	1	1	5	.444	3	7	3	.769
Patek, ss	5	18	2	7	9	2	0	0	4	.389	13	18	0	1.000
Martinez, c	5	15	0	5	5	0	0	0	4	.333	15	4	0	1.000
Rojas, ph-2b	4	9	2	3	3	0	0	0	1	.333	4	6	0	1.000
Mayberry, 1b	5	18	4	4	7	0	0	1	3	.222	48	1	0	1.000
Cowens, rf-cf	5	21	3	4	6	0	1	0	0	.190	15	0	0	1.000
Poquette, lf-cf	5	16	1	3	5	2	0	0	4	.188	13	0	0	1.000
Wohlford, lf-ph	5	11	3	2	2	0	0	0	0	.182	7	0	0	1.000
Quirk, ph-dh	4	7	1	1	3	0	1	0	2	.143	0	0	0	.000
F. White, 2b-pr	4	8	2	1	1	0	0	0	0	.125	6	11	0	1.000
McRae, dh-rf	5	17	2	2	5	1	1	0	1	.118	5	1	0	1.000
Bird, p	1	0	0	0	0	0	0	0	0	.000	0	1	1	.500
Hall, p	1	0	0	0	0	0	0	0	0	.000	0	0	0	.000
Wathan, c	1	0	0	0	0	0	0	0	0	.000	0	0	0	.000

Player—Position	G.	AB.	R.	H.	TB.	2B.	3B.	HR.	RBI.	B.A.	PO.	A.	E.	F.A.
Gura, p	2	0	0	0	0	0	0	0	0	.000	0	0	0	.000
Hassler, p	2	0	0	0	0	0	0	0	0	.000	0	0	0	.000
Leonard, p	2	0	0	0	0	0	0	0	0	.000	0	0	0	.000
Pattin, p	2	0	0	0	0	0	0	0	0	.000	0	0	0	.000
Splittorff, p	2	0	0	0	0	0	0	0	0	.000	0	1	0	1.000
Littell, p	3	0	0	0	0	0	0	0	0	.000	0	1	0	1.000
Mingori, p	3	0	0	0	0	0	0	0	0	.000	0	0	0	.000
Otis, cf	1	1	0	0	0	0	0	0	0	.000	0	0	0	.000
Stinson, ph-c	2	1	0	0	0	0	0	0	0	.000	0	0	0	.000
Nelson, ph-dh	2	2	0	0	0	0	0	0	0	.000	0	0	0	.000
Totals	5	162	24	40	60	6	4	2	24	.247	129	51	4	.978

NEW YORK YANKEES' PITCHING RECORDS

Pitcher	G.	GS.	CG.	IP.	H.	R.	ER.	BB.	SO.	HB.	WP.	W.	L.	Pct.	ERA.
Lyle	1	0	0	1	0	0	0	1	0	0	0	0	0	.000	0.00
Ellis	1	1	0	8	6	3	3	2	5	1	0	1	0	1.000	3.38
Tidrow	3	0	0	7⅓	6	4	3	4	0	0	0	1	0	1.000	3.68
Hunter	2	2	1	12	10	6	6	1	5	0	0	1	1	.500	4.50
Figueroa	2	2	0	12⅓	14	8	8	2	5	0	0	0	1	.000	5.84
Jackson	2	0	0	3⅓	4	3	3	1	3	0	0	0	0	.000	8.10
Totals	5	5	1	44	40	24	23	11	18	1	0	3	2	.600	4.70

No shutouts. Save—Lyle.

KANSAS CITY ROYALS' PITCHING RECORDS

Pitcher	G.	GS.	CG.	IP.	H.	R.	ER.	BB.	SO.	HB.	WP.	W.	L.	Pct.	ERA.
Hall	1	0	0	⅓	1	0	0	0	0	0	0	0	0	.000	0.00
Splittorff	2	0	0	9⅓	7	2	2	5	2	0	0	1	0	1.000	1.93
Bird	1	0	0	4⅔	4	1	1	0	1	0	0	1	0	1.000	1.93
Littell	3	0	0	4⅔	4	1	1	1	3	0	0	0	1	.000	1.93
Mingori	3	0	0	3⅓	4	1	1	0	1	0	0	0	0	.000	2.70
Gura	2	2	0	10⅔	18	6	5	1	4	0	0	0	1	.000	4.22
Hassler	2	1	0	7⅓	8	6	5	6	4	0	0	0	0	.000	6.14
Leonard	2	2	0	2⅓	9	5	5	2	0	0	0	0	0	.000	19.29
Pattin	2	0	0	⅓	0	1	1	1	0	0	0	0	0	.000	27.00
Totals	5	5	0	43	55	23	21	16	15	0	0	2	3	.400	4.40

No shutouts. Save—Mingori.

COMPOSITE SCORE BY INNINGS

New York	4	3	4		2	0	5	1	0	4 — 23
Kansas City	7	4	0		2	0	3	0	8	0 — 24

Sacrifice hits—Gamble, R. White.

Sacrifice flies—Brett, Chambliss, McRae, Quirk, Rojas.

Stolen bases—Chambliss 2, Cowens 2, Wohlford 2, Randolph, Rojas, R. White.

Caught stealing—Patek 3, Alomar, Brett, McRae, Munson, Rivers.

Double plays—Randolph and Chambliss; Chambliss, Stanley and Randolph; Stanley and Chambliss; Brett, F. White and Mayberry; Patek, F. White and Mayberry; Patek and Mayberry; Martinez and F. White; Rojas, Patek and Mayberry.

Left on bases—New York 41—8, 11, 8, 5, 9; Kansas City 22—2, 7, 3, 5, 5.

Hit by pitcher—By Ellis (McRae).

Passed ball—Munson.

Balks—None.

Time of games—First game, 2:06; second game, 2:45; third game, 3:00; fourth game, 2:50; fifth game, 3:13.

Attendance—First game, 41,077; second game, 41,091; third game, 56,808; fourth game, 56,355; fifth game, 56,821.

Umpires—Brinkman, Haller, Maloney, Barnett, Frantz and McCoy.

Official scorers—Sid Bordman, Kansas City Star; Phil Pepe, New York Daily News.

NATIONAL LEAGUE
Championship Series of 1976

	W.	L.	Pct.
Cincinnati (West)	3	0	1.000
Philadelphia (East)	0	3	.000

For most of the summer of 1976, baseball fans had been looking forward to what promised to be a great Championship Series between two fine teams, the Cincinnati Reds and the Philadelphia Phillies, each of whom had been impressive winners in their respective divisions.

The Series began in Philadelphia with each club sending its ace lefthander to the mound, Don Gullett for the Reds and Steve Carlton for the Phils. It was no contest. After a spate of first-inning wildness, Gullett was in command all the way, finishing an eight-inning stint with only one run and two hits against his record.

Carlton, meanwhile, was the victim of some shoddy support. A liner by Pete Rose was misplayed into a triple by right fielder Ollie Brown and that gave Cincinnati one of its runs. The Reds got another of their tallies when Phillies third sacker Mike Schmidt passed up an easy throw to first base and attempted, unsuccessfully, to tag a runner off third. Carlton was finally kayoed in the eighth frame and his successor, Tug McGraw, was rapped for a couple of hits that resulted in three runs to put the game out of reach for the home team.

After Gullett left the game with an injury to his left leg, the Phils managed to score a pair of runs off reliever Rawly Eastwick. But it was a meaningless gesture and served only to make the final score a respectable 6-3.

The largest crowd ever to see a Championship Series game—62,651—saw Phillies righthander Jim Lonborg ride a 2-0 lead and a no-hitter into the sixth inning of the second contest.

But in the sixth he walked leadoff batter Dave Concepcion, who moved to second on a groundout. Rose then got the first hit off Lonborg, a single to right that plated Concepcion. Ken Griffey followed with a single sending Rose to third and took second on the futile throw to third base. Lonborg was given the hook and replaced by Gene Garber. Joe Morgan drew an intentional walk to load the bases and Tony Perez then rammed a hot liner down the first-base line. Dick Allen was unable to handle it, two runs scored and the sun had begun to set on the Phillies' season.

Cincinnati added another run before the inning was over and again pounded McGraw in the next inning to walk away with a 6-2 victory.

The third game, played at Cincinnati's Riverfront Stadium, was the most exciting. The Phils carried a 6-4 into the bottom of the ninth but were hit by lightning in the form of successive home runs by the first two batters of the inning, George Foster and Johnny Bench. Both blows came off reliever Ron Reed.

After Bench's homer, Garber relieved and stayed only long enough to give up a single to Concepcion. Lefty Tom Underwood came on and loaded the bases on a walk, a sacrifice and another walk. Griffey then ended the 1976 National League season by chopping a high bounding hit off the glove of first baseman Bobby Tolan. Concepcion raced home with the run that gave the Reds a 7-6 triumph and their second straight flag.

GAME OF SATURDAY, OCTOBER 9, AT PHILADELPHIA (N)

Cincinnati	AB.	R.	H.	RBI.	PO.	A.	Philadelphia	AB.	R.	H.	RBI.	PO.	A.
Rose, 3b	5	1	3	1	1	2	Cash, 2b	4	1	1	0	2	0
Griffey, rf	4	0	1	0	5	0	Maddox, cf	4	1	2	0	2	0
Morgan, 2b	2	0	0	0	1	1	Schmidt, 3b	3	0	0	1	3	3
Eastwick, p	0	0	0	0	0	1	Luzinski, lf	3	1	1	1	2	0
Perez, 1b	3	0	0	1	8	0	Allen, 1b	3	0	1	0	5	0
Foster, lf	5	1	1	1	4	0	Brown, rf	2	0	0	0	2	0
Bench, c	5	1	2	0	4	2	Johnstone, ph	1	0	1	1	0	0
Concepcion, ss	3	2	1	0	0	2	McCarver, c	3	0	0	0	6	0
Geronimo, cf	4	0	0	0	4	0	McGraw, p	0	0	0	0	0	0
Gullett, p	4	1	2	3	0	0	Tolan, ph	1	0	0	0	0	0
Flynn, 2b	0	0	0	0	0	0	Bowa, ss	3	0	0	1	1	4
Totals	35	6	10	6	27	8	Hutton, ph	1	0	0	0	0	0
							Carlton, p	2	0	0	0	0	0
							Boone, c	1	0	0	0	4	0
							Totals	31	3	6	3	27	7

Cincinnati	0	0	1	0	0	2	0	3	0 – 6	
Philadelphia	1	0	0	0	0	0	0	0	2 – 3	

Cincinnati	IP.	H.	R.	ER.	BB.	SO.
Gullett (Winner)	8	2	1	1	3	4
Eastwick	1	4	2	2	0	0

Philadelphia	IP.	H.	R.	ER.	BB.	SO.
Carlton (Loser)	7*	8	5	4	5	6
McGraw	2	2	1	1	1	4

*Pitched to two batters in eighth.

Error—Schmidt. Double plays—Philadelphia 2. Left on bases—Cincinnati 9, Philadelphia 5. Two-base hits—Rose 2, Concepcion, Bench, Gullett, Cash, Luzinski. Three-base hits—Rose, Griffey. Home run—Foster. Stolen bases—Griffey, Bench, Morgan 2. Sacrifice flies—Schmidt, Perez. Wild pitches—McGraw, Eastwick. Umpires—Sudol, Dale, Stello, Vargo, Harvey and Tata. Time—2:39. Attendance—62,640.

GAME OF SUNDAY, OCTOBER 10, AT PHILADELPHIA

Cincinnati	AB.	R.	H.	RBI.	PO.	A.
Rose, 3b	5	2	2	1	1	2
Griffey, rf	4	1	2	1	4	0
Morgan, 2b	2	1	0	0	5	1
Perez, 1b	3	0	0	1	10	1
Foster, lf	4	0	0	1	0	0
Bench, c	4	0	1	0	4	1
Geronimo, cf	4	0	1	0	1	0
Concepcion, ss	3	1	0	0	1	5
Zachry, p	1	0	0	0	1	3
Driessen, ph	1	0	0	0	0	0
Borbon, p	2	1	0	0	0	0
Totals	33	6	6	4	27	13

Philadelphia	AB.	R.	H.	RBI.	PO.	A.
Cash, 2b	5	0	2	0	0	3
Maddox, cf	4	0	0	0	6	0
Schmidt, 3b	5	0	1	0	0	2
Luzinski, lf	4	1	1	1	4	0
Allen, 1b	3	1	1	0	12	0
Johnstone, rf	4	0	3	0	1	0
Boone, c	3	0	2	1	3	2
Bowa, ss	2	0	0	0	1	4
Lonborg, p	1	0	0	0	0	2
Garber, p	0	0	0	0	0	0
Tolan, ph	1	0	0	0	0	0
McGraw, p	0	0	0	0	0	1
Reed, p	0	0	0	0	0	0
McCarver, ph	1	0	0	0	0	0
Totals	33	2	10	2	27	14

Cincinnati									
Cincinnati	0	0	0	0	0	4	2	0	0 – 6
Philadelphia	0	1	0	0	1	0	0	0	0 – 2

Cincinnati	IP.	H.	R.	ER.	BB.	SO.
Zachry (Winner)	5	6	2	2	3	3
Borbon (Save)	4	4	0	0	1	0

Philadelphia	IP.	H.	R.	ER.	BB.	SO.
Lonborg (Loser)	5⅓	2	3	1	2	2
Garber	⅔	1	1	0	1	0
McGraw	⅓	2	2	2	0	1
Reed	2⅔	1	0	0	1	1

Error—Allen. Double plays—Cincinnati 2. Left on bases—Cincinnati 5, Philadelphia 10. Home run—Luzinski. Stolen base—Griffey. Sacrifice hits—Boone, Lonborg. Sacrifice fly—Perez. Wild pitch—McGraw. Umpires—Dale, Stello, Vargo, Harvey, Tata and Sudol. Time—2:24. Attendance—62,651.

GAME OF TUESDAY, OCTOBER 12, AT CINCINNATI

Philadelphia	AB.	R.	H.	RBI.	PO.	A.
Cash, 2b	4	0	1	1	6	5
Maddox, cf	5	1	1	1	1	0
Schmidt, 3b	5	1	3	1	1	4
Luzinski, lf	4	0	1	1	0	0
Reed, p	1	0	0	0	0	0
Garber, p	0	0	0	0	0	0
Underwood, p	0	0	0	0	0	0
Allen, 1b	3	0	0	0	11	0
Martin, lf	1	1	0	0	1	0
Johnstone, rf	4	1	3	1	2	0
Boone, c	3	0	0	0	1	0
Harmon, pr	0	1	0	0	0	0
Oates, c	1	0	0	0	1	0
Bowa, ss	3	1	1	1	0	3
Kaat, p	2	0	1	0	0	1
Tolan, lf-1b	0	0	0	0	1	0
Totals	36	6	11	6	25	13

Cincinnati	AB.	R.	H.	RBI.	PO.	A.
Rose, 3b	4	0	1	0	0	1
Griffey, rf	5	1	2	1	2	0
Morgan, 2b	3	1	0	0	3	3
Perez, 1b	4	1	2	1	9	1
Foster, lf	3	1	1	2	3	0
Bench, c	3	2	1	1	3	1
Concepcion, ss	4	1	1	0	1	5
Geronimo, cf	3	0	1	2	5	0
Nolan, p	0	0	0	0	1	0
Sarmiento, p	1	0	0	0	0	0
Borbon, p	0	0	0	0	0	0
Lum, ph	1	0	0	0	0	0
Eastwick, p	0	0	0	0	0	0
Armbrister, ph	0	0	0	0	0	0
Totals	31	7	9	7	27	11

Philadelphia									
Philadelphia	0	0	0	1	0	0	2	2	1 – 6
Cincinnati	0	0	0	0	0	0	4	0	3 – 7

One out when winning run scored.

Philadelphia	IP.	H.	R.	ER.	BB.	SO.
Kaat	6*	2	2	2	2	1
Reed	2†	5	4	4	1	1
Garber (Loser)	0‡	1	1	1	0	0
Underwood	⅓	1	0	0	2	0

Cincinnati	IP.	H.	R.	ER.	BB.	SO.
Nolan	5⅔	6	1	1	2	1
Sarmiento	1	2	2	2	1	0
Borbon	⅓	0	0	0	0	0
Eastwick (Winner)	2	3	3	2	2	1

*Pitched to two batters in seventh.
†Pitched to two batters in ninth.
‡Pitched to one batter in ninth.

Errors—Rose, Perez. Double plays—Philadelphia 1, Cincinnati 1. Left on bases—Philadelphia 10, Cincinnati 6. Two-base hits—Maddox, Schmidt 2, Luzinski, Johnstone, Bowa. Three-base hits—Johnstone, Geronimo. Home runs—Foster, Bench. Sacrifice hits—Kaat, Armbrister. Sacrifice flies—Cash, Foster. Wild pitch—Eastwick. Umpires—Stello, Vargo, Harvey, Tata, Sudol and Dale. Time—2:43. Attendance—55,047.

CINCINNATI REDS' BATTING AND FIELDING AVERAGES

Player—Position	G.	AB.	R.	H.	TB.	2B.	3B.	HR.	RBI.	B.A.	PO.	A.	E.	F.A.
Gullett, p	1	4	1	2	3	1	0	0	3	.500	0	0	0	.000
Rose, 3b	3	14	3	6	10	2	1	0	2	.429	2	5	1	.875
Griffey, rf	3	13	2	5	7	0	1	0	2	.385	11	0	0	1.000
Bench, c	3	12	3	4	8	1	0	1	1	.333	11	4	0	1.000
Concepcion, ss	3	10	4	2	3	1	0	0	0	.200	2	12	0	1.000

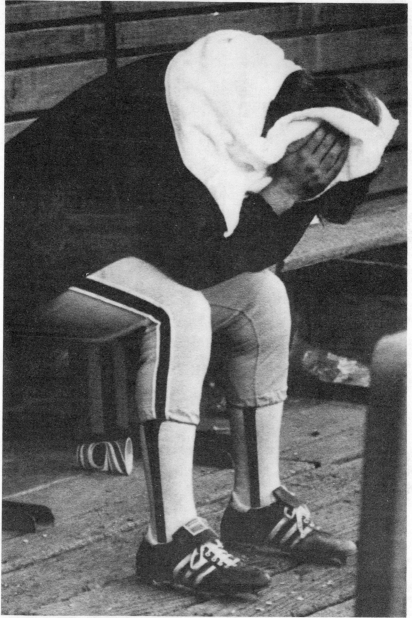

Philadelphia pitcher Tom Underwood shows his disappointment after the third and final game of the 1976 N.L. Championship Series. A three-run, ninth-inning rally by the Reds ended the Phillies' hopes.

Player–Position	G.	AB.	R.	H.	TB.	2B.	3B.	HR.	RBI.	B.A.	PO.	A.	E.	F.A.
Perez, 1b	3	10	1	2	2	0	0	0	3	.200	27	2	1	.967
Geronimo, cf	3	11	0	2	4	0	1	0	2	.182	10	0	0	1.000
Foster, lf	3	12	2	2	8	0	0	2	4	.167	7	0	0	1.000
Armbrister, ph	1	0	0	0	0	0	0	0	0	.000	0	0	0	.000
Eastwick, p	2	0	0	0	0	0	0	0	0	.000	0	1	0	1.000
Flynn, 2b	1	0	0	0	0	0	0	0	0	.000	0	0	0	.000
Nolan, p	1	0	0	0	0	0	0	0	0	.000	1	0	0	1.000
Driessen, ph	1	1	0	0	0	0	0	0	0	.000	0	0	0	.000
Lum, ph	1	1	0	0	0	0	0	0	0	.000	0	0	0	.000
Sarmiento, p	1	1	0	0	0	0	0	0	0	.000	0	0	0	.000
Zachry, p	1	1	0	0	0	0	0	0	0	.000	1	3	0	1.000
Borbon, p	2	2	1	0	0	0	0	0	0	.000	0	0	0	.000
Morgan, 2b	3	7	2	0	0	0	0	0	0	.000	9	5	0	1.000
Totals	3	99	19	25	45	5	3	3	17	.253	81	32	2	.983

PHILADELPHIA PHILLIES' BATTING AND FIELDING AVERAGES

Player–Position	G.	AB.	R.	H.	TB.	2B.	3B.	HR.	RBI.	B.A.	PO.	A.	E.	F.A.
Johnstone, ph-rf	3	9	1	7	10	1	1	0	2	.778	3	0	0	1.000
Kaat, p	1	2	0	1	1	0	0	0	0	.500	0	1	0	1.000
Cash, 2b	3	13	1	4	5	1	0	0	1	.308	8	8	0	1.000
Schmidt, 3b	3	13	1	4	6	2	0	0	2	.308	4	9	1	.929
Boone, c	3	7	0	2	2	0	0	0	1	.286	8	2	0	1.000
Luzinski, lf	3	11	2	3	8	2	0	1	3	.273	6	0	0	1.000
Maddox, cf	3	13	2	3	4	1	0	0	1	.231	9	0	0	1.000
Allen, 1b	3	9	1	2	2	0	0	0	0	.222	28	0	1	.966
Bowa, ss	3	8	1	1	2	1	0	0	0	.125	2	11	0	1.000
Garber, p	2	0	0	0	0	0	0	0	0	.000	0	0	0	.000
Harmon, pr	1	0	1	0	0	0	0	0	0	.000	0	0	0	.000
McGraw, p	2	0	0	0	0	0	0	0	0	.000	0	1	0	1.000
Underwood, p	1	0	0	0	0	0	0	0	0	.000	0	0	0	.000
Hutton, ph	1	1	0	0	0	0	0	0	0	.000	0	0	0	.000
Lonborg, p	1	1	0	0	0	0	0	0	0	.000	0	2	0	1.000
Martin, lf	1	1	1	0	0	0	0	0	0	.000	1	0	0	1.000
Oates, c	1	1	0	0	0	0	0	0	0	.000	1	0	0	1.000
Reed, p	2	1	0	0	0	0	0	0	0	.000	0	0	0	.000
Brown, rf	1	2	0	0	0	0	0	0	0	.000	2	0	0	1.000
Carlton, p	1	2	0	0	0	0	0	0	0	.000	0	0	0	.000
Tolan, ph-lf-1b	3	2	0	0	0	0	0	0	0	.000	1	0	0	1.000
McCarver, c-ph	2	4	0	0	0	0	0	0	0	.000	6	0	0	1.000
Totals	3	100	11	27	40	8	1	1	11	.270	79	34	2	.983

CINCINNATI REDS' PITCHING RECORDS

Pitcher	G.	GS.	CG.	IP.	H.	R.	ER.	BB.	SO.	HB.	WP.	W.	L.	Pct.	ERA.
Borbon	2	0	0	4⅓	4	0	0	1	0	0	0	0	0	.000	0.00
Gullett	1	1	0	8	2	1	1	3	4	0	0	1	0	1.000	1.13
Nolan	1	1	0	5⅔	6	1	1	2	1	0	0	0	0	.000	1.59
Zachry	1	1	0	5	6	2	2	3	3	0	0	1	0	1.000	3.60
Eastwick	2	0	0	3	7	5	4	2	1	0	2	1	0	1.000	12.00
Sarmiento	1	0	0	1	2	2	2	1	0	0	0	0	0	.000	18.00
Totals	3	3	0	27	27	11	10	12	9	0	2	3	0	1.000	3.33

No shutouts.   Save—Borbon.

PHILADELPHIA PHILLIES' PITCHING RECORDS

Pitcher	G.	GS.	CG.	IP.	H.	R.	ER.	BB.	SO.	HB.	WP.	W.	L.	Pct.	ERA.
Underwood	1	0	0	⅓	1	0	0	2	0	0	0	0	0	.000	0.00
Lonborg	1	1	0	5⅓	2	3	1	2	2	0	0	0	1	.000	1.69
Kaat	1	1	0	6	8	2	2	2	1	0	0	0	0	.000	3.00
Carlton	1	1	0	7	8	5	4	5	6	0	0	0	1	.000	5.14
Reed	2	0	0	4⅔	4	4	4	2	2	0	0	0	0	.000	7.71
McGraw	2	0	0	2⅓	4	3	3	1	5	0	2	0	0	.000	11.57
Garber	2	0	0	⅔	2	2	1	1	0	0	0	0	1	.000	13.50
Totals	3	3	0	26⅓	25	19	15	15	16	0	2	0	3	.000	5.13

No shutouts or saves.

COMPOSITE SCORE BY INNINGS

Cincinnati	0	0	1	0	0	6	6	3	3 – 19
Philadelphia	1	1	0	1	1	0	2	2	3 – 11

Sacrifice hits—Armbrister, Boone, Kaat, Lonborg.
Sacrifice flies—Perez 2, Foster, Cash, Schmidt.
Stolen bases—Griffey 2, Morgan 2, Bench.
Caught stealing—Geronimo, Maddox.
Double plays—Morgan (unassisted); Rose, Bench and Perez; Concepcion, Morgan and Perez; Schmidt (unassisted); Schmidt and Cash; Bowa, Cash and Allen.
Left on bases—Cincinnati 20—9, 5, 6; Philadelphia 25—5, 10, 10.
Hit by pitcher—None.
Passed balls—None.
Balks—None.
Time of games—First game, 2:39; second game, 2:24; third game, 2:43.
Attendance—First game, 62,640; second game, 62,651; third game, 55,047.
Umpires—Sudol, Dale, Stello, Vargo, Harvey and Tata.
Official scorers—Bob Hertzel, Cincinnati Enquirer; Bob Kenney, Camden Courier-Post.

AMERICAN LEAGUE
Championship Series of 1977

	W.	L.	Pct.
New York (East)...	3	2	.600
Kansas City (West)..	2	3	.400

There they were, Yankee Manager Billy Martin and his boss, George Steinbrenner, shaking hands and embracing in their mutual joy after the Bronx Bombers had disposed of the Kansas City Royals in five games of the American League Championship Series.

The joy expressed in that setting was pure ecstasy. The Yankees, billed as "the best club money can buy," had to score three runs in the ninth inning to overtake the Royals in the final game, 5-3.

It was the second straight year the Yankees had conquered the Royals for the A.L. pennant.

Pitchers Mike Torrez and Sparky Lyle were the key men in the final-game triumph. They held the Royals off the scoreboard on only four hits for the last 6⅔ innings, while the Yankees fought back from a 3-1 deficit.

The evening started in what had become typical Yankee high drama when Martin benched star outfielder Reggie Jackson, a 1-for-14 performer in the first four games.

Kansas City aggressively took a 2-0 lead in the first inning. With one out, Hal McRae got an infield single. George Brett followed with a triple to right-center. When he came up from his hard slide, Brett fired a right hand in the direction of the New York third baseman Graig Nettles and the two wrestled to the ground. Both benches emptied. (In game two, McRae had set the fierce tempo in bowling over Yankee second baseman Willie Randolph on a force play in the sixth inning.)

After order was restored, Al Cowens' grounder scored Brett. A run-scoring single by Cowens in the third made the score 3-1. Enter third-game loser Torrez for a 5⅓-inning scoreless stint. Lyle, who hurled 5⅓ innings of scoreless ball to win the fourth game, followed with his second straight victory by setting down the Royals for the final 1⅓ innings.

The Yanks struck for one run in the eighth, with Jackson's pinch-single being a key blow. Kansas City Manager Whitey Herzog, who had already called on three pitchers—excusing starter Paul Splittorff after an impressive seven-inning performance—went to his ace starter and 20-game winner Dennis Leonard in the ninth.

Paul Blair, who started in right field in place of Jackson, opened with a single. Pinch-hitter Roy White drew a walk. Lefthander Larry Gura, who had been routed for six hits and four runs in two innings a day earlier, was summoned by Herzog to face Mickey Rivers.

Rivers, who had gone 2-for-2 against Gura's deliveries in Game 4, slapped a single to right, scoring Blair and sending White to third. Mark Littell then took the mound and surrendered a sacrifice fly to Randolph for the go-ahead run. An insurance run followed on Brett's error.

Kansas City and New York had split their 10-game series during the 1977 season, but it was the Royals who showed no timidity, waltzing right into Yankee Stadium for a stunning 7-2 first-game victory.

The Royals flexed their muscles with three home runs and almost pulled off a triple play to end the game.

Lefthander Splittorff stifled the Yankees' bats, before being relieved by Doug Bird after surrendering his first walk of the game to Chambliss, leading off the ninth inning.

McRae's previously mentioned bodyblock of second baseman Randolph was the cause celebre in the second game.

Aroused by what they considered violent tactics by McRae, the Yankees broke a 2-2 tie with three runs in their half of the sixth. And lefty Ron Guidry held Kansas

City to three hits in a 6-2 victory.

Thus, the scene shifted to Royals Stadium for Game 3 and Kansas City right-hander Dennis Leonard was in complete control, limiting New York to four hits in a 6-2 triumph.

The Yankees pulled away to a 4-0 lead in three innings against Larry Gura in Game 4.

But Yankee starter Ed Figueroa couldn't stand prosperity and departed in the fourth with a 5-3 lead. Reliever Dick Tidrow yielded a run-producing double by Frank White.

Then Lyle entered with runners on first and third and two out in a one-run ball game. He quickly enticed Brett to fly out. For the next five innings, Sparky faced 16 batters, one over the minimum, while permitting only two hits.

Meanwhile, Mickey Rivers, who had 4-for-5, scored an insurance run in the ninth for the 6-4 final score.

GAME OF WEDNESDAY, OCTOBER 5, AT NEW YORK

Kansas City	AB.	R.	H.	RBI.	PO.	A.	New York	AB.	R.	H.	RBI.	PO.	A.
Patek, ss	4	1	2	2	6	0	Rivers, cf	4	1	3	0	4	0
McRae, dh	5	1	1	2	0	0	Nettles, 3b	4	0	0	0	0	2
Brett, 3b	5	0	0	0	2	2	Munson, c	4	1	1	2	4	1
Cowens, rf	4	2	3	1	4	0	Jackson, rf	4	0	0	0	1	0
Otis, cf	4	0	0	0	2	0	Piniella, lf	4	0	1	0	2	0
Mayberry, 1b	3	1	1	2	3	0	Chambliss, 1b	3	0	1	0	5	2
Zdeb, lf	4	0	0	0	3	0	Johnson, dh	4	0	2	0	0	0
Porter, c	2	1	1	0	3	0	Randolph, 2b	4	0	1	0	4	1
F. White, 2b	4	1	1	0	4	0	Dent, ss	3	0	0	0	6	3
Splittorff, p	0	0	0	0	0	2	R. White, ph	1	0	0	0	0	0
Bird, p	0	0	0	0	0	0	Gullett, p	0	0	0	0	0	0
Totals	35	7	9	7	27	4	Tidrow, p	0	0	0	0	1	2
							Lyle, p	0	0	0	0	0	0
							Totals	35	2	9	2	27	11

Kansas City	2	2	2	0	0	0	0	1	0 – 7
New York	0	0	2	0	0	0	0	0	0 – 2

Kansas City	IP.	H.	R.	ER.	BB.	SO.
Splittorff (Winner)	8*	8	2	2	1	2
Bird	1	1	0	0	0	0
New York	IP.	H.	R.	ER.	BB.	SO.
Gullett (Loser)	2	4	4	4	2	0
Tidrow	6⅔	5	3	3	2	3
Lyle	⅓	0	0	0	0	0

*Pitched to one batter in ninth.

Errors—None. Double play—Kansas City 1. Left on base—Kansas City 5, New York 7. Two-base hits—Patek, Randolph, Rivers. Home runs—McRae, Mayberry, Munson, Cowens. Stolen base—Zdeb. Umpires—Neudecker, Goetz, McKean, Springstead, Bremigan and Deegan. Time—2:40. Attendance—54,930.

GAME OF THURSDAY, OCTOBER 6, AT NEW YORK (N)

Kansas City	AB.	R.	H.	RBI.	PO.	A.	New York	AB.	R.	H.	RBI.	PO.	A.
Patek, ss	3	1	1	1	1	3	Rivers, cf	5	0	0	0	7	0
McRae, dh	2	0	0	0	0	0	Nettles, 3b	4	0	0	0	0	1
Brett, 3b	4	0	1	0	0	3	Munson, c	4	1	3	0	7	2
Cowens, rf	4	0	0	0	0	0	Jackson, rf	4	1	1	0	3	0
Otis, cf	4	0	0	0	3	1	Blair, rf	0	0	0	0	0	0
Mayberry, 1b	3	0	0	0	9	1	Piniella, lf	4	1	1	0	1	0
Zdeb, lf	3	0	0	0	1	0	Johnson, dh	4	2	2	2	0	0
Porter, c	1	1	0	0	3	0	Chambliss, 1b	2	0	0	0	3	1
Wathan, ph-c	1	0	0	0	2	0	Randolph, 2b	4	1	2	1	3	1
White, 2b	3	0	1	0	4	3	Dent, ss	3	0	1	1	2	2
Hassler, p	0	0	0	0	1	0	Guidry, p	0	0	0	0	1	0
Littell, p	0	0	0	0	0	0	Totals	34	6	10	4	27	7
Mingori, p	0	0	0	0	0	0							
Totals	28	2	3	1	24	11							

Kansas City	0	0	1	0	0	1	0	0	0 – 2
New York	0	0	0	0	2	3	0	1	x – 6

Kansas City	IP.	H.	R.	ER.	BB.	SO.
Hassler (Loser)	5⅔	5	3	3	0	3
Littell	2	5	3	1	3	1
Mingori	⅓	0	0	0	0	1
New York	IP.	H.	R.	ER.	BB.	SO.
Guidry (Winner)	9	3	2	2	3	7

Errors—Dent, Brett. Left on base—Kansas City 3, New York 7. Two-base hits—Patek, Johnson. Home run—Johnson. Stolen base—Jackson. Sacrifice fly—Patek. Balk—Hassler. Umpires—Goetz, McKean, Springstead, Bremigan, Deegan and Neudecker. Time—2:58. Attendance—56,230.

*When the Yankees and Royals squared off in Game 5 of the 1977
A.L. Championship Series, the tempo was set in the first inning.
Kansas City's George Brett, believing that New York third
baseman Graig Nettles had kicked him when he slid into third
with a triple, jumped up and started swinging.*

GAME OF FRIDAY, OCTOBER 7, AT KANSAS CITY (N)

New York	AB.	R.	H.	RBI.	PO.	A.	Kansas City	AB.	R.	H.	RBI.	PO.	A.
Rivers, cf	4	0	0	0	2	0	Poquette, rf	3	0	1	0	3	0
R. White, lf	4	1	2	0	2	0	Otis, ph-cf	2	0	1	2	1	0
Munson, c	4	0	0	0	2	0	McRae, lf	4	2	2	0	2	1
Jackson, rf	3	0	0	0	4	1	Zdeb, lf	0	0	0	0	0	0
Chambliss, 1b	4	0	0	0	9	3	Brett, 3b	4	1	2	0	1	1
Nettles, 3b	3	1	1	0	2	2	Cowens, cf-rf	4	0	0	2	2	0
Piniella, dh	3	0	1	1	0	0	Mayberry, 1b	4	0	1	1	12	0
Randolph, 2b	3	0	0	0	1	3	Lahoud, ph	1	2	0	0	0	0
Dent, ss	2	0	0	0	0	2	Wathan, ph-dh	1	0	0	0	0	0
Johnson, ph	1	0	0	0	0	0	Porter, c	4	1	3	0	6	0
Stanley, ss	0	0	0	0	0	0	Patek, ss	2	0	1	1	0	5
Torrez, p	0	0	0	0	2	1	F. White, 2b	4	0	1	0	0	3
Lyle, p	0	0	0	0	0	0	Leonard, p	0	0	0	0	0	0
Totals	31	2	4	1	24	12	Totals	33	6	12	6	27	10

New York	0	0	0	0	1	0	0	0	1 - 2
Kansas City	0	1	1	0	1	2	1	0	x - 6

New York	IP.	H.	R.	ER.	BB.	SO.
Torrez (Loser)	5⅔	8	5	5	2	1
Lyle	2⅓	4	1	1	0	1

Kansas City	IP.	H.	R.	ER.	BB.	SO.
Leonard (Winner)	9	4	2	1	1	4

Errors—R. White, Mayberry. Left on base—New York 3, Kansas City 7. Two-base hits—R. White 2, McRae 2, Piniella, Otis, Mayberry. Stolen bases—F. White, Otis. Sacrifice hits—Patek 2. Umpires—McKean, Springstead, Bremigan, Deegan, Neudecker and Goetz. Time—2:19. Attendance—41,285.

GAME OF SATURDAY, OCTOBER 8, AT KANSAS CITY

New York	AB.	R.	H.	RBI.	PO.	A.	Kansas City	AB.	R.	H.	RBI.	PO.	A.
Rivers, cf	5	2	4	1	4	0	Poquette, lf	3	0	0	0	0	0
Nettles, 3b	5	0	2	1	0	3	Zdeb, ph-lf	2	0	0	0	0	0
Munson, c	4	1	1	2	4	0	McRae, dh	3	1	2	0	0	0
Jackson, rf	3	0	0	2	0	0	Brett, 3b	4	0	2	1	1	3
Blair, rf	1	0	1	0	1	0	Cowens, rf	3	0	0	0	3	0
Piniella, lf	5	0	2	1	3	0	Mayberry, 1b	2	0	0	0	5	0
Johnson, dh	4	0	1	0	0	0	Wathan, 1b	2	0	0	0	6	0
R. White, pr-dh	0	0	0	0	0	0	Porter, c	4	0	0	0	3	0
Chambliss, 1b	4	0	0	0	10	0	Otis, cf	3	1	0	0	4	0
Randolph, 2b	4	2	1	0	2	2	Patek, ss	4	2	3	1	0	4
Dent, ss	3	1	1	1	1	4	F. White, 2b	3	0	1	2	4	4
Figueroa, p	0	0	0	0	0	0	Gura, p	0	0	0	0	0	0
Tidrow, p	0	0	0	0	0	0	Pattin, p	0	0	0	0	1	2
Lyle, p	0	0	0	0	0	0	Mingori, p	0	0	0	0	0	0
Totals	38	6	13	6	27	9	Bird, p	0	0	0	0	0	0
							Totals	33	4	8	4	27	13

New York	1	2	1	1	0	0	0	0	1 - 6
Kansas City	0	0	2	2	0	0	0	0	0 - 4

New York	IP.	H.	R.	ER.	BB.	SO.
Figueroa	3⅓	5	4	4	2	3
Tidrow	⅓	1	0	0	1	0
Lyle (Winner)	5⅓	2	0	0	0	1

Kansas City	IP.	H.	R.	ER.	BB.	SO.
Gura (Loser)	2*	6	4	4	1	2
Pattin	6†	6	2	1	0	0
Mingori	⅓	0	0	0	0	0
Bird	⅔	1	0	0	0	0

*Pitched to two batters in third. †Pitched to one batter in ninth.

Errors—Patek, Mayberry. Double plays—New York 1, Kansas City 1. Left on base—New York 8, Kansas City 6. Two-base hits—Rivers, Dent, Munson, Patek, F. White, Piniella. Three-base hits—Patek, Brett. Sacrifice hit—Dent. Sacrifice flies—F. White, Munson. Wild pitch—Mingori. Umpires—Springstead, Bremigan, Deegan, Neudecker, Goetz and McKean. Time—3:08. Attendance 41,135.

GAME OF SUNDAY, OCTOBER 9, AT KANSAS CITY (N)

New York	AB.	R.	H.	RBI.	PO.	A.	Kansas City	AB.	R.	H.	RBI.	PO.	A.
Rivers, cf	5	2	2	1	2	0	Patek, ss	5	0	0	0	1	6
Randolph, 2b	3	1	1	1	3	2	McRae, lf	4	2	3	0	0	0
Munson, c	5	0	1	1	7	1	Brett, 3b	3	1	1	1	1	3
Piniella, lf	5	0	2	0	3	1	Cowens, rf	4	0	2	2	5	0
Johnson, dh	2	0	1	0	0	0	Otis, cf	3	0	1	0	1	0
Jackson, ph-dh	2	0	1	1	0	0	Wathan, 1b	2	0	0	0	11	0
Nettles, 3b	4	0	0	0	0	4	LaCock, ph-1b	1	0	0	0	4	0
Chambliss, 1b	4	0	0	0	8	1	Rojas, dh	4	0	1	0	0	0
Blair, rf	4	1	1	0	1	0	Porter, c	4	0	1	0	3	0
Dent, ss	3	0	1	0	1	3	F. White, 2b	4	0	1	0	1	6
R. White, ph	0	1	0	0	0	0	Splittorff, p	0	0	0	0	0	1
Stanley, ss	0	0	0	0	1	0	Bird, p	0	0	0	0	0	0
Guidry, p	0	0	0	0	1	0	Mingori, p	0	0	0	0	0	0
Torrez, p	0	0	0	0	0	0	Leonard, p	0	0	0	0	0	0
Lyle, p	0	0	0	0	0	0	Gura, p	0	0	0	0	0	0
Totals	37	5	10	4	27	12	Littell, p	0	0	0	0	0	0
							Totals	34	3	10	3	27	16

New York	0	0	1	0	0	0	0	1	3 – 5	
Kansas City	2	0	1	0	0	0	0	0	0 – 3	

New York	IP.	H.	R.	ER.	BB.	SO.
Guidry	2⅓	6	3	3	0	1
Torrez	5⅓	3	0	0	3	4
Lyle (Winner)	1⅓	1	0	0	0	1

Kansas City	IP.	H.	R.	ER.	BB.	SO.
Splittorff	7*	6	2	2	2	2
Bird	⅓	2	0	0	0	1
Mingori	⅔	0	0	0	0	0
Leonard (Loser)	0†	1	2	2	1	0
Gura	0‡	1	1	0	0	0
Littell	1	0	0	0	0	0

*Pitched to one batter in eighth.
†Pitched to two batters in ninth.
‡Pitched to one batter in ninth.

Error–Brett. Double play–New York 1. Left on base–New York 9, Kansas City 7. Two-base hits–Piniella, McRae, Johnson. Three-base hit–Brett. Stolen bases–Rivers, Rojas, Otis. Sacrifice fly–Randolph. Umpires–Bremigan, Deegan, Neudecker, Springstead, Goetz and McKean. Time–3:04. Attendance–41,133.

NEW YORK YANKEES' BATTING AND FIELDING AVERAGES

Player–Position	G.	AB.	R.	H.	TB.	2B.	3B.	HR.	RBI.	B.A.	PO.	A.	E.	F.A.
Johnson, dh-ph	5	15	2	6	11	2	0	1	2	.400	0	0	0	.000
Blair, rf	3	5	1	2	2	0	0	0	0	.400	2	0	0	1.000
R. White, ph-lf-pr-dh	4	5	2	2	4	2	0	0	0	.400	2	0	1	.667
Rivers, cf	5	23	5	9	11	2	0	0	2	.391	19	0	0	1.000
Piniella, lf-dh	5	21	1	7	10	3	0	0	2	.333	9	1	0	1.000
Munson, c	5	21	3	6	10	1	0	1	5	.286	24	4	0	1.000
Randolph, 2b	5	18	4	5	6	1	0	0	2	.278	13	9	0	1.000
Dent, ss	5	14	1	3	4	1	0	0	2	.214	10	14	1	.960
Nettles, 3b	5	20	1	3	3	0	0	0	1	.150	2	12	0	1.000
Jackson, rf-ph-dh	5	16	1	2	2	0	0	0	1	.125	10	1	0	1.000
Chambliss, 1b	5	17	0	1	1	0	0	0	0	.059	35	7	0	1.000
Figueroa, p	1	0	0	0	0	0	0	0	0	.000	0	0	0	.000
Guidry, p	2	0	0	0	0	0	0	0	0	.000	2	0	0	1.000
Gullett, p	1	0	0	0	0	0	0	0	0	.000	0	0	0	.000
Lyle, p	4	0	0	0	0	0	0	0	0	.000	0	0	0	.000
Stanley, ss	2	0	0	0	0	0	0	0	0	.000	1	0	0	1.000
Tidrow, p	2	0	0	0	0	0	0	0	0	.000	1	2	0	1.000
Torrez, p	2	0	0	0	0	0	0	0	0	.000	2	1	0	1.000
Totals	5	175	21	46	64	12	0	2	17	.263	132	51	2	.989

KANSAS CITY ROYALS' BATTING AND FIELDING AVERAGES

Player–Position	G.	AB.	R.	H.	TB.	2B.	3B.	HR.	RBI.	B.A.	PO.	A.	E.	F.A.
McRae, dh-lf	5	18	6	8	14	3	0	1	2	.444	2	1	0	1.000
Patek, ss	5	18	4	7	12	3	1	0	5	.389	8	18	1	.963
Porter, c	5	15	3	5	5	0	0	0	0	.333	18	0	0	1.000
Brett, 3b	5	20	2	6	10	0	2	0	2	.300	5	12	2	.895
F. White, dh	5	18	1	5	6	1	0	0	2	.278	13	16	0	1.000
Cowens, rf-cf	5	19	2	5	8	0	0	1	5	.263	14	0	0	1.000
Rojas, dh	1	4	0	1	1	0	0	0	0	.250	0	0	0	.000
Mayberry, 1b	4	12	1	2	6	1	0	1	3	.167	29	1	2	.938
Poquette, rf-lf	2	6	0	1	1	0	0	0	0	.167	3	0	0	1.000
Otis, cf-ph	5	16	1	2	3	1	0	0	2	.125	11	1	0	1.000
Bird, p	3	0	0	0	0	0	0	0	0	.000	0	0	0	.000
Gura, p	2	0	0	0	0	0	0	0	0	.000	0	0	0	.000
Hassler, p	1	0	0	0	0	0	0	0	0	.000	1	0	0	1.000
Leonard, p	2	0	0	0	0	0	0	0	0	.000	0	0	0	.000
Littell, p	2	0	0	0	0	0	0	0	0	.000	0	0	0	.000
Mingori, p	3	0	0	0	0	0	0	0	0	.000	0	0	0	.000
Pattin, p	1	0	0	0	0	0	0	0	0	.000	1	2	0	1.000
Splittorff, p	2	0	0	0	0	0	0	0	0	.000	0	3	0	1.000
LaCock, ph-1b	1	1	0	0	0	0	0	0	0	.000	4	0	0	1.000
Lahoud, dh	1	1	2	0	0	0	0	0	0	.000	0	0	0	.000
Wathan, ph-c-dh-1b	4	6	0	0	0	0	0	0	0	.000	19	0	0	1.000
Zdeb, lf-ph	4	9	0	0	0	0	0	0	0	.000	4	0	0	1.000
Totals	5	163	22	42	66	9	3	3	21	.258	132	54	5	.974

NEW YORK YANKEES' PITCHING RECORDS

Pitcher	G.	GS.	CG.	IP.	H.	R.	ER.	BB.	SO.	HB.	WP.	W.	L.	Pct.	ERA.
Lyle	4	0	0	9⅓	7	1	1	0	3	0	0	2	0	1.000	0.96
Tidrow	2	0	0	7	6	3	3	3	0	0	0	0	0	.000	3.86
Guidry	2	2	0	11⅓	9	5	5	3	8	0	0	1	0	1.000	3.97
Torrez	2	1	0	11	11	5	5	5	5	0	0	0	1	.000	4.09
Figueroa	1	1	0	3⅓	5	4	4	2	3	0	0	0	0	.000	10.80
Gullett	1	1	0	2	4	4	4	2	0	0	0	0	1	.000	18.00
Totals	5	5	1	44	42	22	22	15	22	0	0	3	2	.600	4.50

No shutouts or saves.

KANSAS CITY ROYALS' PITCHING RECORDS

Pitcher	G.	GS.	CG.	IP.	H.	R.	ER.	BB.	SO.	HB.	WP.	W.	L.	Pct.	ERA.
Bird	3	0	0	2	4	0	0	0	1	0	0	0	0	.000	0.00
Mingori	3	0	0	1⅓	0	0	0	0	1	0	1	0	0	.000	0.00
Pattin	1	0	0	6	6	2	1	0	0	0	0	0	0	.000	1.50
Splittorff	2	2	0	15	14	4	4	3	4	0	0	1	0	1.000	2.40
Leonard	2	1	1	9	5	4	3	2	4	0	0	1	1	.500	3.00
Littell	2	0	0	3	5	3	1	3	1	0	0	0	0	.000	3.00
Hassler	1	1	0	5⅔	5	3	3	0	3	0	0	0	1	.000	4.76
Gura	2	1	0	2	7	5	4	1	2	0	0	0	1	.000	18.00
Totals	5	5	1	44	46	21	16	9	16	0	1	2	3	.400	3.27

No shutouts or saves.

COMPOSITE SCORE BY INNINGS

New York	1	2	4	1	3	3	0	2	5 – 21
Kansas City	4	3	7	2	1	3	1	1	0 – 22

Sacrifice hits—Dent, Patek 2.
Sacrifice flies—Munson, Randolph, Patek, F. White.
Stolen bases—Jackson, Rivers, Otis 2, Rojas, F. White, Zdeb.
Caught stealing—Brett, Cowens, McRae, F. White.
Double plays—Nettles, Randolph and Chambliss 2; Brett and F. White; Pattin and Brett.
Left on bases—New York 7, 7, 3, 8, 9—34; Kansas City 5, 3, 7, 6, 7—28.
Hit by pitcher—None.
Passed balls—None.
Balk—Hassler.
Time of games—First game, 2:40; second game, 2:58; third game, 2:19; fourth game, 3:08; fifth game, 3:04.
Attendance—First game, 54,930; second game, 56,230; third game, 41,285; fourth game, 41,135; fifth game, 41,133.
Umpires—Neudecker, Goetz, McKean, Springstead, Bremigan and Deegan.
Official scorers—Maury Allen, New York Post; Del Black, Kansas City Star.

NATIONAL LEAGUE
Championship Series of 1977

	W.	L.	Pct.
Los Angeles (West)	3	1	.750
Philadelphia (East)	1	3	.250

The Los Angeles Dodgers returned to their second World Series in four seasons after subduing the repeating East Division champions, the Philadelphia Phillies, in four games, one of which pivoted on a controversial call—a decision which, accurate or not, heavily influenced the outcome of an entire season.

In winning the title, the Dodgers became the first club in the nine-year history of the Championship Series to lose the first game at home and then come back to win the series. That initial game featured a pitching matchup of two of the league's outstanding lefthanders, Steve Carlton and Tommy John, each a prominent contender for the Cy Young Award later won by Carlton. Neither fared well, however. John, in large part due to poor defensive play, and Carlton, because of control problems.

John exited in the fifth inning after allowing four runs, all unearned. With two out in the first inning a poor throw by shortstop Bill Russell allowed Mike Schmidt to reach base. Greg Luzinski capitalized on the miscue, driving a 1-2 pitch over the center-field wall for a 2-0 Philadelphia lead. In the fourth inning, it was again a Russell mistake, this time a failure to touch second on a forceout, that opened the gates for two more runs. A tally off reliever Elias Sosa an inning later brought the count to 5-1 going into the home seventh.

In that inning, walks to pinch-hitter Jerry Grote and Reggie Smith, sandwiched around a Davey Lopes single, loaded the bases. After fouling away three full-count deliveries, Ron Cey, one of four Dodgers to hit thirty or more home runs in 1977, belted a game-tying grand slam.

But Gene Garber and Tug McGraw blanked the Dodgers the rest of the way, and when Bake McBride, Larry Bowa and Schmidt singled in the ninth, the Phillies had captured at least a split at Dodger Stadium.

Los Angeles prevailed in game two, 7-1, on the strength of the second Dodger grand slam in as many nights. This time it was Dusty Baker, also a member of the thirty-home run club. The fourth-inning blast broke a 1-1 tie.

Righthander Don Sutton scattered nine hits and did not walk a batter in going the route.

The season had come down to a best-of-three series, and the Phillies had ample reason for their swagger. They had won 60 of 81 games at the Vet during the regular season. Four of the six encounters with their playoff opponent had gone their way. And for a time it did seem that this advantage might tip the scales. Dodger starter Burt Hooton was visibly unnerved by the crowd's incessant hooting which accompanied his every delivery. With the bases loaded, plate umpire Harry Wendelstedt waved Larry Christenson, McBride, and Bowa to first with free passes. What had been a 2-0 deficit had become a 3-2 lead. After eight innings, the Phils had stretched their lead to 5-3.

With two outs in the ninth inning, no one on base and the dependable Garber having retired on ground balls all eight batters he had faced, Dodger Manager Tommy Lasorda was but one out from falling into a Dodger Blue trance.

But then it happened. In the space of a few short minutes, the Phillies' season unraveled. Ironically, it was the Dodgers' bench, considered inferior in pre-series analyses, that did the damage. Aging Vic Davalillo, obtained from the Mexican League in August, beat out a drag bunt. Then Manny Mota, a Davalillo contemporary, sent a two-strike pitch to deep left field. Luzinski, oddly unreplaced by Jerry Martin, a more capable fielder, got his glove on it but could not hang on as he bulled into the wall. Mota had a double, scoring Davalillo, and when the relay escaped second baseman Sizemore, Mota took third.

Lopes followed with a shot off the glove of third baseman Schmidt that Larry Bowa alertly rebounded and threw to first. Bruce Froemming ruled Lopes safe and the game was tied. The Phillies insisted otherwise.

Lopes became the game-winning run when, after moving up a base on an errant Garber pickoff attempt, he scored on a Bill Russell bouncer through the middle.

If the Dodgers were relaxed and assured before the fourth and what proved to be the final game, the Phillies could be excused for being less than that. Lopes had indeed appeared to be out on television replays but not by so great a margin that Froemming could be castigated or reproached with any fairness. Nevertheless, but for that call, it would have been the Phils and not the Dodgers who would be trying to wrap up the series before the largest crowd in Pennsylvania baseball history, 64,924.

In a game played almost entirely in a steady downpour of rain, Los Angeles took a third straight win and with it the title. Baker's two-run homer in the second inning was more than enough for Tommy John. Stranding nine runners, he bested Carlton, 4-1.

GAME OF TUESDAY, OCTOBER 4, AT LOS ANGELES (N)

Philadelphia	AB.	R.	H.	RBI.	PO.	A.	Los Angeles	AB.	R.	H.	RBI.	PO.	A.
McBride, cf	5	1	2	0	3	0	Lopes, 2b	5	1	2	1	3	3
Bowa, ss	5	2	1	0	0	5	Russell, ss	5	1	0	0	2	3
Schmidt, 3b	5	2	1	1	1	5	Smith, rf	4	0	0	0	1	0
Luzinski, lf	3	1	1	2	1	0	Cey, 3b	4	1	2	4	2	4
Johnson, 1b	4	0	1	0	8	0	Garvey, 1b	4	0	3	0	12	0
Hutton, 1b	1	0	0	0	5	0	Baker, lf	3	1	0	0	0	0
Martin, rf	3	0	0	0	1	0	Burke, cf	3	0	0	1	0	0
Johnstone, ph-rf	1	0	0	0	0	0	Monday, ph-cf	1	0	0	0	0	0
McCarver, c	3	1	1	0	2	0	Yeager, c	4	0	0	0	6	1
Boone, c	0	0	0	0	1	0	John, p	1	0	0	0	0	1
Sizemore, 2b	3	0	0	0	3	2	Garman, p	0	0	0	0	0	0
Carlton, p	2	0	2	1	0	0	Lacy, ph	1	1	1	0	0	0
Garber, p	0	0	0	0	0	1	Hough, p	0	0	0	0	0	1
Hebner, ph	1	0	0	0	0	0	Grote, ph	0	0	0	0	0	0
McGraw, p	0	0	0	0	0	0	Sosa, p	1	0	0	0	0	0
Totals	36	7	9	6	27	13	Totals	36	5	9	5	27	13

Philadelphia .... 2 0   0   0   2 1   0   0   2 – 7
Los Angeles .... 0 0   0   0   0 1   0   4   0 – 5

Philadelphia	IP.	H.	R.	ER.	BB.	SO.
Carlton	6⅔	9	5	5	3	3
Garber (Winner)	1⅓	0	0	0	0	2
McGraw (Save)	1	0	0	0	0	0

Los Angeles	IP.	H.	R.	ER.	BB.	SO.
John	4⅔	4	4	0	3	3
Garman	⅓	0	0	0	0	1
Hough	2	2	1	1	0	3
Sosa (Loser)	2	3	2	2	0	0

Errors—Russell 2. Double play—Los Angeles 1. Left on bases—Philadelphia 7, Los Angeles 7. Home runs—Luzinski, Cey. Stolen bases—Luzinski, Garvey. Sacrifice hit—Sizemore. Hit by pitcher—By John (Carlton). Balks—Carlton, Sosa. Umpires—Pryor, Engel, Wendelstedt, Froemming, Rennert and Runge. Time—2:35. Attendance—55,968.

GAME OF WEDNESDAY, OCTOBER 5, AT LOS ANGELES (N)

Philadelphia	AB.	R.	H.	RBI.	PO.	A.	Los Angeles	AB.	R.	H.	RBI.	PO.	A.
McBride, cf	4	1	2	1	0	1	Lopes, 2b	4	0	1	1	2	1
Bowa, ss	4	0	1	0	0	5	Russell, ss	4	2	2	0	3	2
Schmidt, 3b	4	0	0	0	1	1	Smith, rf	4	1	2	1	2	0
Luzinski, lf	4	0	1	0	1	0	Cey, 3b	3	1	1	0	2	1
Hebner, 1b	4	0	2	0	11	0	Garvey, 1b	3	1	0	0	7	1
Johnstone, rf	4	0	1	0	4	0	Baker, lf	4	1	1	4	3	0
Boone, c	4	0	1	0	6	1	Monday, cf	3	1	1	0	3	0
Sizemore, 2b	4	0	1	0	2	1	Burke, c	0	0	0	0	0	0
Lonborg, p	1	0	0	0	0	2	Yeager, c	3	0	1	1	5	0
Hutton, ph	1	0	0	0	0	0	Sutton, p	3	0	0	0	0	2
Reed, p	0	0	0	0	0	0	Totals	31	7	9	7	27	7
Brown, ph	1	0	0	0	0	0							
Brusstar, p	0	0	0	0	0	0							
Totals	35	1	9	1	24	11							

Philadelphia	0	0	1	0	0	0	0	0	0 – 1
Los Angeles	0	0	1	4	0	1	1	0	x – 7

Philadelphia	IP.	H.	R.	ER.	BB.	SO.
Lonborg (Loser)	4	5	5	5	1	1
Reed	2	2	1	1	1	2
Brusstar	2	2	1	1	0	2

Los Angeles	IP.	H.	R.	ER.	BB.	SO.
Sutton (Winner)	9	9	1	1	0	4

Errors—Sizemore, Lopes. Double plays—Los Angeles 2. Left on bases—Philadelphia 7, Los Angeles 3. Two-base hits—Luzinski, Monday. Three-bat hit—Smith. Home runs—McBride, Baker. Stolen base—Cey. Sacrifice hit—Cey. Umpires—Engel, Wendelstedt, Froemming, Rennert, Runge and Pryor. Time—2:14. Attendance—55,973.

GAME OF FRIDAY, OCTOBER 7, AT PHILADELPHIA

Los Angeles	AB.	R.	H.	RBI.	PO.	A.	Philadelphia	AB.	R.	H.	RBI.	PO.	A.
Lopes, 2b	5	1	1	1	3	3	McBride, rf	4	0	0	1	1	1
Russell, ss	5	0	2	1	5	2	Bowa, ss	4	0	0	1	0	5
Smith, rf	5	0	0	0	2	0	Schmidt, 3b	4	0	0	0	1	6
Cey, 3b	4	1	1	0	1	4	Luzinski, lf	3	0	1	0	0	1
Garvey, 1b	4	1	1	0	9	0	Martin, pr	0	0	0	0	0	0
Baker, lf	4	1	2	2	0	0	Hebner, 1b	5	2	1	0	14	0
Monday, cf	3	0	1	0	3	0	Maddox, cf	4	1	1	1	3	0
Grote, c	0	0	0	0	0	0	Boone, c	4	1	2	0	6	0
Yeager, c	2	0	1	1	3	0	Sizemore, 2b	3	1	1	0	2	3
Davalillo, ph	1	1	1	0	0	0	Christenson, p	0	0	0	1	0	0
Burke, cf	0	0	0	0	1	0	Brusstar, p	0	0	0	0	0	0
Hooton, p	1	0	1	0	0	1	Hutton, ph	1	0	0	0	0	0
Rhoden, p	1	0	0	0	0	0	Reed, p	0	0	0	0	0	0
Goodson, ph	1	0	0	0	0	0	McCarver, ph	1	0	0	0	0	0
Rau, p	0	0	0	0	0	0	Garber, p	0	0	0	0	0	1
Sosa, p	0	0	0	0	0	1	Totals	33	5	6	4	27	17
Rautzhan, p	0	0	0	0	0	0							
Mota, ph	1	1	1	0	0	0							
Garman, p	0	0	0	0	0	0							
Totals	37	6	12	5	27	11							

Los Angeles	0	2	0	1	0	0	0	0	3 – 6
Philadelphia	0	3	0	0	0	0	2	0	0 – 5

Los Angeles	IP.	H.	R.	ER.	BB.	SO.
Hooton	1⅔	2	3	3	4	1
Rhoden	4⅓	2	0	0	2	0
Rau	1	0	0	0	0	1
Sosa	⅔	2	2	1	0	0
Rautzhan (Winner)	⅓	0	0	0	0	0
Garman (Save)	1	0	0	0	0	0

Philadelphia	IP.	H.	R.	ER.	BB.	SO.
Christenson	3⅓	7	3	3	0	2
Brusstar	⅔	0	0	0	1	0
Reed	2	1	0	0	1	2
Garber (Loser)	3	4	3	2	0	4

Errors—Cey, Sizemore, Garber, Smith. Double play—Philadelphia 1. Left on bases—Los Angeles 6, Philadelphia 9. Two-base hits—Baker, Hooton, Cey, Russell, Hebner, Mota. Sacrifice hit—Garber. Hit by pitcher—By Garman (Luzinski). Passed ball—Boone. Umpires—Wendelstedt, Froemming, Rennert, Runge, Pryor and Engel. Time—2:51. Attendance—63,719.

GAME OF SATURDAY, OCTOBER 8, AT PHILADELPHIA (N)

Los Angeles	AB.	R.	H.	RBI.	PO.	A.
Lopes, 2b	3	0	0	0	1	3
Russell, ss	4	0	1	1	1	5
Smith, rf	3	0	1	0	2	0
Cey, 3b	2	1	0	0	2	5
Garvey, 1b	2	0	0	0	12	0
Baker, lf	3	2	1	2	0	0
Burke, cf	4	0	0	0	1	0
Yeager, c	4	1	1	0	8	0
John, p	4	0	1	0	0	0
Totals	29	4	5	3	27	13

Philadelphia	AB.	R.	H.	RBI.	PO.	A.
McBride, rf	5	0	0	0	2	0
Bowa, ss	4	0	0	0	0	2
Schmidt, 3b	3	0	0	0	1	3
Luzinski, lf	4	1	1	0	3	0
Hebner, 1b	4	0	2	0	7	0
Maddox, cf	3	0	2	1	3	0
McCarver, c	2	0	0	0	3	0
Reed, p	0	0	0	0	0	0
Brown, ph	1	0	0	0	0	0
McGraw, p	0	0	0	0	0	0
Martin, ph	1	0	0	0	0	0
Garber, p	0	0	0	0	0	0
Sizemore, 2b	3	0	1	0	3	2
Carlton, p	2	0	0	0	0	0
Boone, c	2	0	1	0	5	1
Totals	34	1	7	1	27	8

Los Angeles	0	2	0	0	2	0	0	0	0	– 4
Philadelphia	0	0	0	1	0	0	0	0	0	– 1

Los Angeles	IP.	H.	R.	ER.	BB.	SO.
John (Winner)	9	7	1	1	2	8

Philadelphia	IP.	H.	R.	ER.	BB.	SO.
Carlton (Loser)	5*	4	4	4	5	3
Reed	1	0	0	0	0	1
McGraw	2	1	0	0	2	3
Garber	1	0	0	0	0	1

*Pitched to on batter in sixth.

Errors—None. Double plays—Philadelphia 2. Left on bases—Los Angeles 6, Philadelphia 9. Two-base hit—Hebner. Home run—Baker. Stolen base—Smith. Sacrifice hit—Garvey. Hit by pitcher—By John (Maddox). Wild pitch—Carlton. Umpires—Froemming, Rennert, Runge, Pryor, Engel and Wendelstedt. Time—2:39. Attendance —64,924.

LOS ANGELES DODGERS' BATTING AND FIELDING AVERAGES

Player—Position	G.	AB.	R.	H.	TB.	2B.	3B.	HR.	RBI.	B.A.	PO.	A.	E.	F.A.
Davalillo, ph	1	1	1	1	1	0	0	0	0	1.000	0	0	0	.000
Hooton, p	1	1	0	1	2	1	0	0	0	1.000	0	1	0	1.000
Lacy, ph	1	1	1	1	1	0	0	0	0	1.000	0	0	0	.000
Mota, ph	1	1	1	1	2	1	0	0	0	1.000	0	0	0	.000
Baker, lf	4	14	4	5	12	1	0	2	8	.357	3	0	0	1.000
Cey, 3b	4	13	4	4	8	1	0	1	4	.308	7	14	1	.955
Garvey, 1b	4	13	2	4	4	0	0	0	0	.308	40	1	0	1.000
Monday, ph-cf	3	7	1	2	3	1	0	0	0	.286	6	0	0	1.000
Russell, ss	4	18	3	5	6	1	0	0	2	.278	11	12	2	.920
Lopes, 2b	4	17	2	4	4	0	0	0	3	.235	9	10	1	.950
Yeager, c	4	13	1	3	3	0	0	0	2	.231	22	1	0	1.000
John, p	2	5	0	1	1	0	0	0	0	.200	0	1	0	1.000
Smith, rf	4	16	2	3	5	0	1	0	1	.188	7	0	1	.875
Garman, p	2	0	0	0	0	0	0	0	0	.000	0	0	0	.000
Grote, ph-c	2	0	0	0	0	0	0	0	0	.000	0	0	0	.000
Hough, p	1	0	0	0	0	0	0	0	0	.000	0	1	0	1.000
Rau, p	1	0	0	0	0	0	0	0	0	.000	0	0	0	.000
Rautzhan, p	1	0	0	0	0	0	0	0	0	.000	0	0	0	.000
Goodson, ph	1	1	0	0	0	0	0	0	0	.000	0	0	0	.000
Rhoden, p	1	1	0	0	0	0	0	0	0	.000	0	0	0	.000
Sosa, p	2	1	0	0	0	0	0	0	0	.000	0	1	0	1.000
Sutton, p	1	3	0	0	0	0	0	0	0	.000	0	2	0	1.000
Burke, cf	4	7	0	0	0	0	0	0	0	.000	3	0	0	1.000
Totals	4	133	22	35	52	6	1	3	20	.263	108	44	5	.968

PHILADELPHIA PHILLIES' BATTING AND FIELDING AVERAGES

Player—Position	G.	AB.	R.	H.	TB.	2B.	3B.	HR.	RBI.	B.A.	PO.	A.	E.	F.A.
Carlton, p	2	4	0	2	2	0	0	0	1	.500	0	0	0	.000
Maddox, cf	2	7	1	3	3	0	0	0	2	.429	6	0	0	1.000
Boone, c	4	10	1	4	4	0	0	0	0	.400	18	2	0	1.000
Hebner, ph-1b	4	14	2	5	7	2	0	0	0	.357	32	0	0	1.000
Luzinski, lf	4	14	2	4	8	1	0	1	2	.286	4	1	0	1.000
Johnson, 1b	1	4	0	1	1	0	0	0	2	.250	8	0	0	1.000
Sizemore, 2b	4	13	1	3	3	0	0	0	0	.231	10	8	2	.900
McBride, cf-rf	4	18	2	4	7	0	0	1	2	.222	6	2	0	1.000
Johnstone, ph-rf	2	5	0	1	1	0	0	0	0	.200	4	0	0	1.000
McCarver, c-ph	3	6	1	1	1	0	0	0	0	.167	7	0	0	1.000
Bowa, ss	4	17	2	2	2	0	0	0	1	.118	4	17	0	1.000
Schmidt, 3b	4	16	2	1	1	0	0	0	1	.063	4	15	0	1.000
Brusstar, p	2	0	0	0	0	0	0	0	0	.000	0	0	0	.000
Christenson, p	1	0	0	0	0	0	0	0	1	.000	0	0	0	.000
Garber, p	3	0	0	0	0	0	0	0	0	.000	0	2	1	.667
McGraw, p	2	0	0	0	0	0	0	0	0	.000	0	0	0	.000
Reed, p	3	0	0	0	0	0	0	0	0	.000	0	0	0	.000

Player—Position	G.	AB.	R.	H.	TB.	2B.	3B.	HR.	RBI.	B.A.	PO.	A.	E.	F.A.
Lonborg, p	1	1	0	0	0	0	0	0	0	.000	0	2	0	1.000
Brown, ph	2	2	0	0	0	0	0	0	0	.000	0	0	0	.000
Hutton, 1b-ph	3	3	0	0	0	0	0	0	0	.000	5	0	0	1.000
Martin, rf-pr-ph	3	4	0	0	0	0	0	0	0	.000	1	0	0	1.000
Totals	4	138	14	31	40	3	0	2	12	.225	105	49	3	.981

LOS ANGELES DODGERS' PITCHING RECORDS

Pitcher	G.	GS.	CG.	IP.	H.	R.	ER.	BB.	SO.	HB.	WP.	W.	L.	Pct.	ERA.
Rhoden	1	0	0	4⅓	2	0	0	2	0	0	0	0	0	.000	0.00
Garman	2	0	0	1⅓	0	0	0	1	1	0	0	0	0	.000	0.00
Rau	1	0	0	1	0	0	0	1	0	0	0	0	0	.000	0.00
Rautzhan	1	0	0	⅓	0	0	0	0	0	0	0	1	0	1.000	0.00
John	2	2	1	13⅔	11	5	1	5	11	2	0	1	0	1.000	0.66
Sutton	1	1	1	9	9	1	1	0	4	0	0	1	0	1.000	1.00
Hough	1	0	0	2	2	1	1	0	3	0	0	0	0	.000	4.50
Sosa	2	0	0	2⅔	5	4	3	0	0	0	0	0	1	.000	10.13
Hooton	1	1	0	1⅔	2	3	3	4	1	0	0	0	0	.000	16.20
Totals	4	4	2	36	31	14	9	11	21	3	0	3	1	.750	2.25

No shutouts. Save—Garman.

PHILADELPHIA PHILLIES' PITCHING RECORDS

Pitcher	G.	GS.	CG.	IP.	H.	R.	ER.	BB.	SO.	HB.	WP.	W.	L.	Pct.	ERA.
McGraw	2	0	0	3	1	0	0	2	3	0	0	0	0	.000	0.00
Reed	3	0	0	5	3	1	1	2	5	0	0	0	0	.000	1.80
Garber	3	0	0	5⅓	4	3	2	0	3	0	0	1	1	.500	3.38
Brusstar	2	0	0	2⅔	2	1	1	1	2	0	0	0	0	.000	3.38
Carlton	2	2	0	11⅔	13	9	9	8	6	0	1	0	1	.000	6.94
Christenson	1	1	0	3⅓	7	3	3	0	2	0	0	0	0	.000	8.10
Lonborg	1	1	0	4	5	5	5	1	1	0	0	0	1	.000	11.25
Totals	4	4	0	35	35	22	21	14	22	0	1	1	3	.250	5.40

No shutouts. Save—McGraw.

COMPOSITE SCORE BY INNINGS

Los Angeles	0	4	1		5	3	1		5	0	3 – 22
Philadelphia	2	3	1		1	2	1		0	2	2 – 14

Sacrifice hits—Cey, Garvey, Garber, Sizemore.
Sacrifice flies—None.
Stolen bases—Cey, Garvey, Smith, Luzinski.
Caught stealing—Lopes.
Double plays—Russell, Lopes and Garvey; Garvey and Russell; Russell and Garvey; McBride and Boone; Bowa, Sizemore and Hebner 2.
Left on bases—Los Angeles 7, 3, 6, 6—22; Philadelphia 7, 7, 9, 9—32.
Hit by pitcher—By John 2 (Carlton, Maddox); by Garman (Luzinski).
Passed ball—Boone.
Balks—Sosa, Carlton.
Time of games—First game, 2:35; second game, 2:14; third game, 2:51; fourth game, 2:39.
Attendance—First game, 55,968; second game, 55,973; third game, 63,719; fourth game, 64,924.
Umpires—Pryor, Engel, Wendelstedt, Froemming, Rennert and Runge.
Official scorers—Gordon Verrell, Long Beach Independent Press-Telegram; Paul Giordano, Levittown Courier Times.

AMERICAN LEAGUE
Championship Series of 1978

	W.	L.	Pct.
New York (East)	3	1	.750
Kansas City (West)	1	3	.250

If you listened to the Royals, things had fallen just right for them in this third try at stopping the Yankees in the American League Championship Series. Kansas City would have its ace, Dennis Leonard, facing New York and virtually untested Jim Beattie, since Ron Guidry had been forced to pitch in the Yankees' one-game playoff against the Boston Red Sox. But as is often the case, things just didn't work out the way they were planned, with the Yankees winning the A.L. pennant three games to one.

New York ripped Leonard and three other Royals' pitchers for 16 hits and the 7-1 score could have been worse as the Yanks stranded 12 runners. While the Yankees were busy circling the base paths, Beattie, with help from Ken Clay, was limiting the Royals to just two hits.

New York went in front 1-0 in the second on a Bucky Dent single after a Roy White double. A double by Reggie Jackson and a triple by Graig Nettles increased the lead to 2-0 in the third. Leonard exited in the fifth after a leadoff single by Lou Piniella and was relieved by Steve Mingori. Jackson walked after a passed ball moved Piniella to second, and Chris Chambliss and Brian Doyle followed with run-scoring singles for a 4-0 Yankee lead.

In the Kansas City sixth, Beattie's control deserted him. After George Brett doubled to start the inning, Beattie walked Amos Otis and Pete LaCock to load the bases. Enter Clay with one out. He pitched out of trouble allowing one run on a sacrifice fly by Hal McRae and ending the inning on an Al Cowens ground out. Clay, in his relief role, did not allow a hit over the last 3⅔ innings.

Meanwhile, Jackson, who was on base five times, put the game out of reach in the eighth. Royals' reliever Al Hrabosky was summoned with two runners on. The "Mad Hungarian" went through his usual psyching routine but Jackson wasn't impressed. He blasted a three-run homer to right-center, clinching the verdict.

With the Yankees now relaxed entering Game Two, the Royals lowered the boom with a hitting barrage of their own. Kansas City jumped to a 5-0 lead after just two innings, knocking out New York starter Ed Figueroa. Singles by George Brett and Amos Otis and a sacrifice fly by Darrell Porter gave the Royals their run in the first, and four runs in the second came by way of five singles and a Bucky Dent error. The Yankees cut the lead to 5-2 off Royal starter Larry Gura in the seventh, knocking Gura out, but Freddie Patek enlisted some unexpected power in the bottom of the inning, crashing a two-run homer in the three-run inning as the Royals went on to a 10-4 win.

All George Brett did in game three was hit three homers, all off Catfish Hunter, but it was a Thurman Munson blow that decided the contest in favor of New York. Brett's first homer led off the game. But Jackson matched the clout in the New York second. No. 2 for Brett came in the third for a 2-1 Royal lead, but singles by Jackson and Pinella, following a Munson double, gave the Yankees a 3-2 lead in the fourth.

Brett's third homer tied the game leading off the fifth. But the Yankees went ahead again in the sixth on singles by White and Munson and a sacrifice fly by Jackson. In the eighth, Kansas City regained the lead, 5-4, and it was done without the aid of Brett. Porter scored Otis with a single, after Otis had doubled, and Porter scored the go-ahead run on a force out by Cowens. But the bottom of the eighth was the Royals' undoing. With one out, White singled off Royals' starter Paul Splittorff and with the righthanded-hitting Munson coming up, K. C. Manager Whitey Herzog called in reliever Doug Bird.

On the third delivery, Munson rocketed a home run into the left-center field bullpen. Rich Gossage stopped the Royals in the ninth.

With a 2-1 lead in the series, the Yankees now would be hard to beat. Guidry would be the pitcher in the crucial fourth game, while the Royals would come back with Leonard. It turned out to be a masterful pitching exhibition by both hurlers.

Brett greeted Guidry with a triple leading off the game and scored on a McRae single. McRae promptly stole second but was left there as Guidry retired the side. It was to be the only run yielded by Guidry in eight-plus innings.

Nettles tied the game for the Yankees with a leadoff homer in the second. Leonard then settled down to retire 10 consecutive batters, five on strikeouts, until one man was out in the sixth. It was then he made his final mistake, White hitting it for a homer and a 2-1 Yankee lead.

Guidry was also sailing along and escaped a two-out, first and third situation in the fourth by fanning Patek. However, when Otis led off the ninth with a double, Manager Bob Lemon called on Gossage. He didn't disappoint Lemon. Throwing nothing but bullets, Gossage struck out pinch-hitter Clint Hurdle and retired Porter and pinch-hitter Pete LaCock on fly balls to seal the New York victory.

Gossage capsuled the entire Yankee season after his fireman's effort. "We almost expected it to go to tomorrow," Gossage admitted. "We've done everything the hard way." But certainly the winning way.

GAME OF TUESDAY, OCTOBER 3, AT KANSAS CITY (N)

New York	AB.	R.	H.	RBI.	PO.	A.
Rivers, cf	5	0	2	0	3	0
Blair, pr-cf	1	1	0	0	2	0
Munson, c	5	0	1	0	6	0
Piniella, rf	5	2	2	0	6	0
Jackson, dh	3	2	3	3	0	0
Nettles, 3b	5	1	2	1	1	1
Chambliss, 1b	5	0	2	1	4	0
R. White, lf	4	1	1	0	1	0
Doyle, 2b	5	0	2	1	2	4
Dent, ss	5	0	1	1	0	1
Beattie, p	0	0	0	0	2	0
Clay, p	0	0	0	0	0	0
Totals	43	7	16	7	27	6

Kansas City	AB.	R.	H.	RBI.	PO.	A.
Braun, lf	4	0	0	0	5	0
Brett, 3b	4	1	1	0	2	4
Otis, cf	2	0	0	0	1	0
Porter, c	3	0	0	0	4	1
LaCock, 1b	2	0	0	0	9	0
McRae, dh	2	0	0	1	0	0
Cowens, rf	4	0	1	0	1	0
Patek, ss	3	0	0	0	4	3
Hurdle, ph	0	0	0	0	0	0
F. White, 2b	3	0	0	0	1	3
Poquette, ph	1	0	0	0	0	0
Leonard, p	0	0	0	0	0	0
Mingori, p	0	0	0	0	0	0
Hrabosky, p	0	0	0	0	0	0
Bird, p	0	0	0	0	0	1
Totals	28	1	2	1	27	12

New York	0	1	1	0	2	0	0	3	0 – 7
Kansas City	0	0	0	0	0	1	0	0	0 – 1

New York	IP.	H.	R.	ER.	BB.	SO.
Beattie (Winner)	5⅓	2	1	1	5	3
Clay (Save)	3⅔	0	0	0	3	2

Kansas City	IP.	H.	R.	ER.	BB.	SO.
Leonard (Loser)	4*	9	3	3	0	2
Mingori	3⅔	5	3	3	3	0
Hrabosky	⅓	1	1	1	0	0
Bird	1	1	0	0	0	1

*Pitched to one batter in fifth.

Errors—Otis, Brett. Left on bases—New York 12, Kansas City 9. Two-base hits—R. White, Jackson, Brett. Three-base hit—Nettles. Home run—Jackson. Stolen bases—LaCock, Otis. Sacrifice fly—McRae. Passed ball—Porter. Umpires—DiMuro, Garcia, Luciano, Kunkel, Phillips and Cooney. Time—2:57. Attendance—41,143.

GAME OF WEDNESDAY, OCTOBER 4, AT KANSAS CITY

New York	AB.	R.	H.	RBI.	PO.	A.
Rivers, cf	3	0	2	0	1	0
Thomasson, ph-cf	1	0	0	0	0	0
Munson, c	5	0	0	0	2	1
Piniella, lf	5	0	0	3	0	0
Jackson, rf	4	1	1	0	4	0
Nettles, 3b	4	1	1	0	1	2
Chambliss, 1b	4	1	4	1	10	1
R. White, dh	4	1	1	0	0	0
Stanley, 2b	2	0	1	0	1	2
Johnson, ph	1	0	0	0	0	0
Doyle, 2b	0	0	0	0	0	0
Blair, ph-2b	1	0	0	0	1	0
Dent, ss	4	0	2	3	0	4
Figueroa, p	0	0	0	0	0	0
Tidrow, p	0	0	0	0	0	2
Lyle, p	0	0	0	0	1	1
Totals	38	4	12	4	24	13

Kansas City	AB.	R.	H.	RBI.	PO.	A.
Brett, 3b	5	2	2	0	0	1
McRae, dh	3	0	2	0	0	0
Otis, cf	5	1	3	1	3	0
Porter, c	4	0	2	2	3	0
LaCock, 1b	5	1	2	1	11	1
Hurdle, lf	3	1	2	1	0	0
Wilson, pr-lf	1	0	0	0	1	0
Cowens, rf	4	2	1	0	0	0
Patek, ss	4	2	1	2	2	1
F. White, 2b	4	1	1	2	6	5
Gura, p	0	0	0	0	1	4
Pattin, p	0	0	0	0	0	0
Hrabosky, p	0	0	0	0	0	0
Totals	38	10	16	9	27	12

New York	0	0	0	0	0	0	2	2	0 – 4
Kansas City	1	4	0	0	0	0	3	2	x – 10

New York	IP.	H.	R.	ER.	BB.	SO.
Figueroa (Loser)	1*	5	5	3	0	0
Tidrow	5⅔	8	3	3	2	1
Lyle	1⅓	3	2	2	0	0

Kansas City	IP.	H.	R.	ER.	BB.	SO.
Gura (Winner)	6⅓	8	2	2	2	2
Pattin	⅔†	2	2	2	0	0
Hrabosky	2	2	0	0	0	1

*Pitched to four batters in second.
†Pitched to two batters in seventh.

Errors—Patek, Dent. Double plays—Kansas City 2. Left on bases—New York 9, Kansas City 8. Two-base hit—LaCock. Three-base hit—Hurdle. Home run—Patek. Stolen bases—Otis 2. Sacrifice hit—McRae. Sacrifice fly—Porter. Umpires—Garcia, Luciano, Kunkel, Phillips, Cooney and DiMuro. Time—2:42. A—41,158.

GAME OF FRIDAY, OCTOBER 6, AT NEW YORK

Kansas City	AB.	R.	H.	RBI.	PO.	A.	New York	AB.	R.	H.	RBI.	PO.	A.
Brett, 3b	5	3	3	0	0	1	Rivers, cf	1	0	1	0	2	1
McRae, dh	5	0	0	0	0	0	Blair, ph-cf	3	0	0	0	3	0
Otis, cf	3	1	2	0	2	0	R. White, lf	4	2	2	0	1	0
Porter, c	4	1	2	1	4	0	Thomasson, lf	0	0	0	0	1	0
LaCock, 1b	3	0	2	0	5	0	Munson, c	4	2	3	2	7	1
Hurdle, lf	4	0	1	0	6	1	Jackson, dh	3	2	2	3	0	0
Wilson, pr-lf	0	0	0	0	1	0	Piniella, rf	4	0	2	0	2	0
Cowens, rf	4	0	0	1	4	0	Nettles, 3b	3	0	0	0	1	1
Patek, ss	3	0	0	0	1	2	Chambliss, 1b	3	0	0	0	6	0
F. White, 2b	3	0	0	0	1	2	Stanley, 2b	3	0	0	0	2	1
Braun, ph	1	0	0	0	0	0	Dent, ss	3	0	0	0	2	2
Splittorff, p	0	0	0	0	0	0	Hunter, p	0	0	0	0	0	1
Bird, p	0	0	0	0	0	0	Gossage, p	0	0	0	0	0	1
Hrabosky, p	0	0	0	0	0	0							
Totals	35	5	10	5	24	6	Totals	31	6	10	5	27	8

Kansas City	1	0	1	0	1	0	0	2	0 – 5
New York	0	1	0	2	0	1	0	2	x – 6

Kansas City	IP.	H.	R.	ER.	BB.	SO.
Splittorff	7⅓	9	5	4	0	2
Bird (Loser)	0*	1	1	1	0	0
Hrabosky	⅔	0	0	0	0	1

New York	IP.	H.	R.	ER.	BB.	SO.
Hunter	6	7	3	3	3	5
Gossage (Winner)	3	3	2	2	0	2

*Pitched to one batter in eighth.

Error—Patek. Double plays—Kansas City 2, New York 1. Left on bases—Kansas City 6, New York 2. Two-base hits—LaCock, Porter, Munson, Otis. Three-base hit—LaCock. Home runs—Brett 3, Jackson, Munson. Stolen base—Otis. Sacrifice fly—Jackson. Passed ball—Munson. Umpires—Luciano, Kunkel, Phillips, Cooney, DiMuro and Garcia. Time—2:13. Attendance—55,535.

GAME OF SATURDAY, OCTOBER 7, AT NEW YORK (N)

Kansas City	AB.	R.	H.	RBI.	PO.	A.	New York	AB.	R.	H.	RBI.	PO.	A.
Brett, 3b	4	1	1	0	1	2	Rivers, cf	2	0	0	0	2	0
McRae, dh	4	0	1	1	0	0	Blair, cf	1	0	0	0	2	0
Otis, cf	4	0	1	0	2	0	R. White, lf	4	1	1	1	1	0
Cowens, rf	3	0	0	0	0	0	Thomasson, lf	0	0	0	0	1	0
Hurdle, ph	1	0	0	0	0	0	Munson, c	4	0	1	0	7	2
Porter, c	3	0	1	0	10	0	Jackson, dh	3	0	0	0	0	0
Wathan, 1b	3	0	0	0	7	0	Piniella, rf	3	0	0	0	2	0
LaCock, ph	1	0	0	0	0	0	Nettles, 3b	3	1	2	1	3	3
F. White, 2b	3	0	2	0	1	2	Chambliss, 1b	3	0	0	0	8	0
Patek, ss	3	0	0	0	2	2	Doyle, 2b	2	0	0	0	1	2
Wilson, lf	3	0	1	0	0	0	Dent, ss	3	0	0	0	0	1
Leonard, p	0	0	0	0	1	0	Guidry, p	0	0	0	0	0	0
							Gossage, p	0	0	0	0	0	0
Totals	32	1	7	1	24	6	Totals	28	2	4	2	27	8

Kansas City	1	0	0	0	0	0	0	0	0 – 1
New York	0	1	0	0	0	1	0	0	x – 2

Kansas City	IP.	H.	R.	ER.	BB.	SO.
Leonard (Loser)	8	4	2	2	2	9

New York	IP.	H.	R.	ER.	BB.	SO.
Guidry (Winner)	8*	7	1	1	1	7
Gossage (Save)	1	0	0	0	0	1

*Pitched to one batter in ninth.

Errors—None. Double play—New York 1. Left on bases—Kansas City 5, New York 4. Two-base hit—Otis. Three-base hit—Brett. Home runs—Nettles, R. White. Stolen base—McRae. Wild pitch—Leonard. Umpires—Kunkel, Phillips, Cooney, DiMuro, Garcia and Luciano. Time—2:20. Attendance—56,356.

NEW YORK YANKEES' BATTING AND FIELDING AVERAGES

Player—Position	G.	AB.	R.	H.	TB.	2B.	3B.	HR.	RBI.	B.A.	PO.	A.	E.	F.A.
Jackson, dh-rf	4	13	5	6	13	1	0	2	6	.462	4	0	0	1.000
Rivers, cf	4	11	0	5	5	0	0	0	0	.455	8	1	0	1.000
Chambliss, 1b	4	15	1	6	6	0	0	0	2	.400	28	1	0	1.000
Nettles, 3b	4	15	3	5	10	0	1	1	2	.333	6	7	0	1.000
R. White, lf-dh	4	16	5	5	9	1	0	1	1	.313	3	0	0	1.000
Doyle, 2b	3	7	0	2	2	0	0	0	1	.286	3	6	0	1.000
Munson, c	4	18	2	5	9	1	0	1	2	.278	22	4	0	1.000
Piniella, rf-lf	4	17	2	4	4	0	0	0	0	.235	13	0	0	1.000
Dent, ss	4	15	0	3	3	0	0	0	4	.200	2	8	1	.909
Stanley, 2b	2	5	0	1	1	0	0	0	0	.200	3	3	0	1.000
Beattie, p	1	0	0	0	0	0	0	0	0	.000	2	0	0	.000
Clay, p	1	0	0	0	0	0	0	0	0	.000	0	0	0	.000
Figueroa, p	1	0	0	0	0	0	0	0	0	.000	0	0	0	.000
Guidry, p	1	0	0	0	0	0	0	0	0	.000	0	0	0	.000
Hunter, p	1	0	0	0	0	0	0	0	0	.000	0	1	0	1.000
Lyle, p	1	0	0	0	0	0	0	0	0	.000	1	1	0	1.000

Player—Position	G.	AB.	R.	H.	TB.	2B.	3B.	HR.	RBI.	B.A.	PO.	A.	E.	F.A.
Tidrow, p	1	0	0	0	0	0	0	0	0	.000	0	2	0	1.000
Gossage, p	2	0	0	0	0	0	0	0	0	.000	0	1	0	1.000
Johnson, ph	1	1	0	0	0	0	0	0	0	.000	0	0	0	.000
Thomasson, ph-cf-lf	3	1	0	0	0	0	0	0	0	.000	2	0	0	1.000
Blair, pr-cf-ph-2b	4	6	1	0	0	0	0	0	0	.000	8	0	0	1.000
Totals	4	140	19	42	62	3	1	5	18	.300	105	35	1	.993

KANSAS CITY ROYALS' BATTING AND FIELDING AVERAGES

Player—Position	G.	AB.	R.	H.	TB.	2B.	3B.	HR.	RBI.	B.A.	PO.	A.	E.	F.A.
Otis, cf	4	14	2	6	8	2	0	0	1	.429	8	0	1	.889
Brett, 3b	4	18	7	7	19	1	1	3	3	.389	3	8	1	.917
Hurdle, ph-lf	4	8	1	3	5	0	1	0	1	.375	6	1	0	1.000
LaCock, 1b-ph	4	11	1	4	8	2	1	0	1	.364	25	1	0	1.000
Porter, c	4	14	1	5	6	1	0	0	3	.357	21	1	0	1.000
Wilson, pr-lf	3	4	0	1	1	0	0	0	0	.250	2	0	0	1.000
F. White, 2b	4	13	1	3	3	0	0	0	2	.231	9	12	0	1.000
McRae, dh	4	14	0	3	3	0	0	0	2	.214	0	0	0	.000
Cowens, rf	4	15	2	2	2	0	0	0	1	.133	5	0	0	1.000
Patek, ss	4	13	2	1	4	0	0	1	2	.077	9	8	2	.895
Gura, p	1	0	0	0	0	0	0	0	0	.000	1	4	0	1.000
Mingori, p	1	0	0	0	0	0	0	0	0	.000	0	0	0	.000
Pattin, p	1	0	0	0	0	0	0	0	0	.000	0	0	0	.000
Splittorff, p	1	0	0	0	0	0	0	0	0	.000	0	1	0	1.000
Bird, p	2	0	0	0	0	0	0	0	0	.000	1	0	0	1.000
Leonard, p	2	0	0	0	0	0	0	0	0	.000	0	0	0	.000
Hrabosky, p	3	0	0	0	0	0	0	0	0	.000	0	0	0	.000
Poquette, ph	1	1	0	0	0	0	0	0	0	.000	0	0	0	.000
Wathan, 1b	1	3	0	0	0	0	0	0	0	.000	7	0	0	1.000
Braun, lf-ph	2	5	0	0	0	0	0	0	0	.000	5	0	0	1.000
Totals	4	133	17	35	59	6	3	4	16	.263	102	36	4	.972

NEW YORK YANKEES' PITCHING RECORDS

Pitcher	G.	GS.	CG.	IP.	H.	R.	ER.	BB.	SO.	HB.	WP.	W.	L.	Pct.	ERA.
Clay	1	0	0	3⅔	0	0	0	3	2	0	0	0	0	.000	0.00
Guidry	1	1	0	8	7	1	1	1	7	0	0	1	0	1.000	1.13
Beattie	1	1	0	5⅓	2	1	1	5	3	0	0	1	0	1.000	1.69
Hunter	1	1	0	6	7	3	3	5	0	0	0	0	0	.000	4.50
Gossage	2	0	0	4	3	2	2	0	3	0	0	1	0	1.000	4.50
Tidrow	1	0	0	5⅔	8	3	3	2	1	0	0	0	0	.000	4.76
Lyle	1	0	0	1⅓	3	2	2	0	0	0	0	0	0	.000	13.50
Figueroa	1	1	0	1	5	5	3	0	0	0	0	0	1	.000	27.00
Totals	4	4	0	35	35	17	15	14	21	0	0	3	1	.750	3.86

Saves—Clay, Gossage. No shutouts.

KANSAS CITY ROYALS' PITCHING RECORDS

Pitcher	G.	GS.	CG.	IP.	H.	R.	ER.	BB.	SO.	HB.	WP.	W.	L.	Pct.	ERA.
Gura	1	1	0	6⅓	8	2	2	2	2	0	0	1	0	1.000	2.84
Hrabosky	3	0	0	3	3	1	1	0	2	0	0	0	0	.000	3.00
Leonard	2	2	1	12	13	5	5	2	11	0	1	0	2	.000	3.75
Splittorff	1	1	0	7⅓	9	5	4	0	2	0	0	0	0	.000	4.91
Mingori	1	0	0	3⅔	5	3	3	3	0	0	0	0	0	.000	7.36
Bird	2	0	0	⅔	1	2	1	1	0	0	0	0	1	.000	9.00
Pattin	1	0	0	⅔	2	2	2	0	0	0	0	0	0	.000	27.00
Totals	4	4	1	34	42	19	18	7	18	0	1	1	3	.250	4.76

No shutouts or saves.

COMPOSITE SCORE BY INNINGS

New York	0	3	1	2	2	2	2	7	0 — 19
Kansas City	3	4	1	0	1	1	3	4	0 — 17

Sacrifice hit—McRae.
Sacrifice flies—McRae, Porter, Jackson.
Stolen bases—LaCock, Otis 4, McRae.
Caught stealing—Jackson, McRae, Patek, Wilson.
Double plays—Brett, White and LaCock; Patek, White and LaCock; Rivers and Nettles; White, Patek and LaCock; Hurdle and Porter; Nettles and Chambliss.
Left on bases—Kansas City 28—9, 8, 6, 5; New York 27—12, 9, 4, 2.
Hit by pitchers—None.
Passed balls—Porter, Munson.
Balks—None.
Time of games—First game, 2:57; second game, 2:42; third game, 2:13; fourth game, 2:20.
Attendance—First game, 41,143; second game, 41,158; third game, 55,535; fourth game, 56,356.
Umpires—DiMuro, Garcia, Luciano, Kunkel, Phillips and Cooney.
Official scorers—Phil Pepe, New York Daily News; Del Black, Kansas City Star; Ken Leiker, Topeka Capital-Journal.

NATIONAL LEAGUE
Championship Series of 1978

	W.	L.	Pct.
Los Angeles (West)	3	1	.750
Philadelphia (East)	1	3	.250

As he made the long run from center field to the dugout, with Dodgers celebrating around him, Garry Maddox must have been in a daze. Two plays earlier, Maddox had dropped a two-out line drive off the bat of Dusty Baker, prolonging Los Angeles' 10th inning. And when Bill Russell followed with a single that scored Ron Cey from second base, the Dodgers had wrapped up their second consecutive National League title and handed the Phillies their third straight loss.

The series began in Philadelphia with Phils' manager Danny Ozark proclaiming a three-game sweep. However, after the Dodgers shelled four Phillies' pitchers for four home runs in the opener, Ozark amended his statement.

In the 9-5 Dodger victory, Steve Garvey's three-run homer followed a Davey Lopes double, a Mike Schmidt error on Russell's grounder and a run-scoring single by Reggie Smith. One inning later, Rick Monday blasted a triple to deep center field and Lopes cracked a two-run homer for a 6-1 Los Angeles lead against battered Phillies starter Larry Christenson.

In Game Two, the Phillies sent Dick Ruthven to face the Dodgers' Tommy John. Ruthven had been the ace of the staff during the second half of the season after being acquired from the Atlanta Braves, having won 11 of 15 decisions. And after pitching perfect ball against Los Angeles for the first three innings, it looked as though Ruthven and the Phillies might be ready to get back at the Dodgers.

But Los Angeles turned to the long ball once again. Lopes greeted Ruthven with a home run leading off the fourth and that was to be all John needed. The Dodger lefty allowed only four singles, induced hard-hitting Philadelphia to bounce into three double plays and watched as his fielders gobbled up the 18 ground balls that came weakly off the Phillies' bats.

Lopes continued to wreak havoc on Phillie pitching, driving in a run in the fifth on a single and another in the seventh with a triple. Steve Yeager knocked in the other Dodger run with a single in the 4-0 win and the teams traveled to Los Angeles with the Dodgers waiting to supply the knockout punch. But Steve Carlton had other thoughts in mind.

Carlton stopped the Dodgers in Game Three, more with his bat than with his arm. He staked the Phils to a 4-0 second-inning lead with a cannon-like three-run homer to center field off Don Sutton. The blast had followed a run-scoring single by Ted Sizemore. When the Dodgers crawled to within 4-3 after three innings, Carlton let his bat do the talking again.

Lopes opened the gates for the Phils' three-run sixth with a two-out error on Tim McCarver's grounder. Sizemore followed with a single and Carlton knocked in McCarver with another single. Sizemore scored when Smith's throw from right field sailed past third base, and Carlton then scored on Jerry Martin's pinch-double. That was to be all the Phillies needed, though Greg Luzinski added a homer in the ninth for good measure and a 9-4 victory, paving the way for Game Four and one of the most exciting games in Championship Series history.

Barring Maddox' error, the game was probably lost by the Phillies in the first inning. Schmidt doubled down the left-field line to start the game off Doug Rau. Larry Bowa walked and Maddox singled, loading the bases with none out. But Rau escaped with no runs scored. He struck out the dangerous Luzinski and retired Jose Cardenal on a liner to short and Martin on a foul pop to the catcher.

Los Angeles jumped to a 1-0 lead in the second when Baker scored Ron Cey with a single off Randy Lerch. But the Phillies came right back in the third, taking a 2-1 lead on a two-run homer by Luzinski. Cey evened matters with a homer of his own in the fourth, and Garvey gave the Dodgers the lead again with a homer in the sixth, knocking out Lerch.

Rau had given way to Rick Rhoden in the sixth and Bake McBride, hitting for Phillie reliever Warren Brusstar, tied the game again with a homer in the seventh. And that's the way it stayed until the memorable tenth. Tug McGraw had relieved Ron Reed in the ninth and appeared in command, retiring five straight batters. But with two down in the tenth, McGraw walked Cey on four pitches and Baker followed with the liner that Maddox mishandled, Cey stopping at second. It was now McGraw against Russell. And on the second pitch, Russell singled to center, scoring Cey and giving the Dodgers the game and series.

GAME OF WEDNESDAY, OCTOBER 4, AT PHILADELPHIA (N)

Los Angeles	AB.	R.	H.	RBI.	PO.	A.	Philadelphia	AB.	R.	H.	RBI.	PO.	A.
Lopes, 2b	5	2	3	2	3	3	McBride, rf	5	1	1	0	1	0
Russell, ss	5	1	1	0	1	2	Bowa, ss	5	1	3	0	0	4
Smith, rf	3	1	1	1	1	0	Maddox, cf	5	0	2	2	4	0
North, cf	1	0	0	0	0	0	Luzinski, lf	4	1	1	0	1	1
Garvey, 1b	5	3	3	4	6	1	Hebner, 1b	4	0	1	1	11	0
Cey, 3b	5	0	2	1	0	1	Schmidt, 3b	3	0	0	1	2	4
Baker, lf	3	0	1	0	1	0	Boone, c	4	0	1	0	6	1
Monday, cf-rf	4	1	1	0	4	0	Sizemore, 2b	4	1	2	0	2	3
Yeager, c	4	1	1	1	10	0	Christenson, p	1	0	0	0	0	0
Hooton, p	2	0	0	0	1	0	Brusstar, p	0	0	0	0	0	0
Welch, p	2	0	0	0	0	1	Gonzalez, ph	1	0	0	0	0	0
Totals	39	9	13	9	27	8	Eastwick, p	0	0	0	0	0	0
							McCarver, ph	1	0	0	0	0	0
							McGraw, p	0	0	0	0	0	0
							Martin, ph	1	1	1	1	0	0
							Totals	38	5	12	5	27	13

Los Angeles	0	0	4	2	1	1	0	0	1	1 — 9
Philadelphia	0	1	0	0	3	0	0	0	1	— 5

Los Angeles	IP.	H.	R.	ER.	BB.	SO.
Hooton	4⅔	10	4	4	0	5
Welch (Winner)	4⅓	2	1	1	0	5

Philadelphia	IP.	H.	R.	ER.	BB.	SO.
Christenson (Loser)	4½	7	7	6	1	3
Brusstar	⅔	1	0	0	0	0
Eastwick	1	3	1	1	0	1
McGraw	3	2	1	1	3	3

Errors—Lopes, Schmidt. Double plays—Los Angeles 1, Philadelphia 1. Left on bases—Los Angeles 8, Philadelphia 7. Two-base hit—Lopes. Three-base hits—Luzinski, Monday, Garvey. Home runs—Garvey 2, Lopes, Yeager, Martin. Sacrifice fly—Schmidt. Hit by pitcher—By Eastwick (Smith). Umpires—Weyer, Colosi, Olsen, Davidson, W. Williams and McSherry. Time—2:37. Attendance—63,460.

GAME OF THURSDAY, OCTOBER 5, AT PHILADELPHIA

Los Angeles	AB.	R.	H.	RBI.	PO.	A.	Philadelphia	AB.	R.	H.	RBI.	PO.	A.
Lopes, 2b	4	1	3	4	4	4	Schmidt, 3b	4	0	1	0	0	4
Russell, ss	4	0	1	0	1	9	Bowa, ss	4	0	1	0	1	4
Smith, rf	4	0	1	0	0	0	Maddox, cf	4	0	1	0	5	0
North, cf	0	0	0	0	0	0	Luzinski, lf	3	0	1	0	2	0
Garvey, 1b	4	0	0	0	16	0	Cardenal, 1b	2	0	0	0	10	0
Cey, 3b	4	0	0	0	0	7	Boone, c	3	0	1	0	5	0
Baker, lf	4	1	1	0	0	0	Martin, rf	2	0	0	0	1	0
Monday, cf-rf	4	1	1	0	2	0	Sizemore, 2b	3	0	0	0	3	1
Yeager, c	3	1	1	1	4	1	Ruthven, p	1	0	0	0	0	0
John, p	3	0	0	0	0	0	Brusstar, p	0	0	0	0	0	0
Totals	34	4	8	4	27	21	Morrison, ph	1	0	0	0	0	0
							Reed, p	0	0	0	0	0	0
							Foote, ph	1	0	0	0	0	0
							McGraw, p	0	0	0	0	0	0
							Totals	28	0	4	0	27	9

Los Angeles	0	0	0	1	2	0	1	0	0 — 4
Philadelphia	0	0	0	0	0	0	0	0	0 — 0

Los Angeles	IP.	H.	R.	ER.	BB.	SO.
John (Winner)	9	4	0	0	2	4

Philadelphia	IP.	H.	R.	ER.	BB.	SO.
Ruthven (Loser)	4⅔	6	3	3	0	3
Brusstar	1⅓	0	0	0	0	0
Reed	2	2	1	1	0	1
McGraw	1	0	0	0	1	0

Errors—None. Double plays—Los Angeles 3. Left on bases—Los Angeles 5, Philadelphia 3. Two-base hits—Smith, Baker. Three-base hit—Lopes. Home run—Lopes. Stolen base—Yeager. Sacrifice hit—John. Umpires—Colosi, Olsen, Davidson, W. Williams, McSherry and Weyer. Time—2:06. Attendance—60,642.

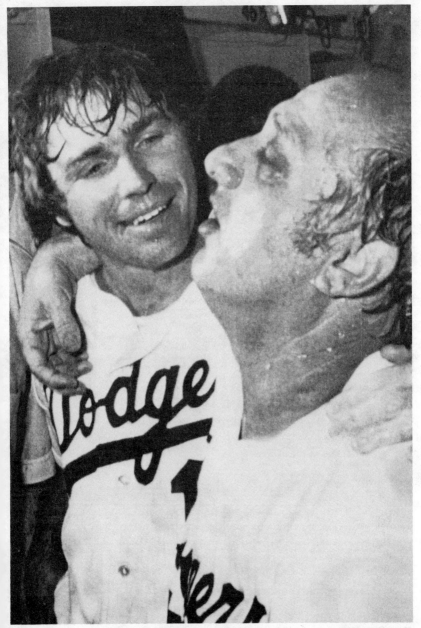

Emotional Dodgers Manager Tom Lasorda hugs Bill Russell after the shortstop had produced the game-winning hit against the Phillies in the 10th inning of the fourth and deciding game of the 1978 N.L. Championship Series.

GAME OF FRIDAY, OCTOBER 6, AT LOS ANGELES

Philadelphia	AB.	R.	H.	RBI.	PO.	A.		Los Angeles	AB.	R.	H.	RBI.	PO.	A.
McBride, rf	3	0	0	0	0	0		Lopes, 2b	4	0	0	0	2	2
Martin, ph-rf	2	0	1	1	1	0		North, cf	4	0	0	0	2	0
Bowa, ss	5	0	1	0	2	5		Smith, rf	4	1	1	0	2	0
Maddox, cf	5	1	1	0	3	0		Garvey, 1b	4	2	2	2	16	2
Luzinski, lf	5	1	3	1	1	0		Cey, 3b	3	1	1	1	2	3
Hebner, 1b	4	0	0	0	10	0		Baker, lf	3	0	1	0	0	0
Schmidt, 3b	4	1	1	0	1	5		Russell, ss	4	0	2	1	0	2
McCarver, c	3	2	0	1	8	0		Yeager, c	3	0	0	0	2	0
Sizemore, 2b	2	2	2	1	1	2		Lacy, ph	1	0	0	0	0	0
Carlton, p	4	2	2	4	0	0		Sutton, p	2	0	0	0	0	1
Totals	37	9	11	8	27	12		Rautzhan, p	0	0	0	0	0	1
								Mota, ph	1	0	1	0	0	0
								Hough, p	0	0	0	0	1	1
								Ferguson, ph	1	0	0	0	0	0
								Totals	34	4	8	4	27	12

Philadelphia	0	4	0	0	0	3	1	0	1	—	9
Los Angeles	0	1	2	0	0	0	0	1	0	—	4

Philadelphia	IP.	H.	R.	ER.	BB.	SO.
Carlton (Winner)	9	8	4	4	2	8

Los Angeles	IP.	H.	R.	ER.	BB.	SO.
Sutton (Loser)	5⅔	7	7	4	2	0
Rautzhan	1⅓	3	1	1	2	0
Hough	2	1	1	1	0	1

Errors—Lopes, Smith, Schmidt. Double plays—Philadelphia 2. Left on bases—Philadelphia 7, Los Angeles 5. Two-base hits—Schmidt, Martin, Russell, Garvey, Mota. Home runs—Carlton, Luzinski, Garvey. Sacrifice hits—Sizemore, Hebner. Umpires—Olsen, Davidson, W. Williams, McSherry, Weyer and Colosi. Time—2:18. Attendance—55,043.

GAME OF SATURDAY, OCTOBER 7, AT LOS ANGELES

Philadelphia	AB.	R.	H.	RBI.	PO.	A.		Los Angeles	AB.	R.	H.	RBI.	PO.	A.
Schmidt, 3b	4	0	1	0	0	5		Lopes, 2b	5	0	1	0	1	1
Bowa, ss	4	1	2	0	2	3		North, cf	3	0	0	0	7	0
Maddox, cf	5	0	1	0	4	0		Monday, ph-cf	2	0	0	0	0	0
Luzinski, lf	4	1	1	2	1	0		Smith, rf	5	0	0	0	2	0
Cardenal, 1b	4	0	1	0	11	0		Garvey, 1b	5	1	2	1	6	2
Martin, rf	4	0	0	0	5	0		Cey, 3b	4	3	2	1	0	2
Boone, c	4	0	0	0	5	1		Baker, lf	5	0	4	1	4	0
Sizemore, 2b	4	0	1	0	1	2		Russell, ss	4	0	3	1	2	1
Lerch, p	2	0	0	0	0	1		Yeager, c	3	0	1	0	5	1
Brusstar, p	0	0	0	0	0	0		Lacy, ph	1	0	0	0	0	0
McBride, ph	1	1	1	1	0	0		Grote, c	0	0	0	0	2	0
Reed, p	0	0	0	0	0	0		Rau, p	1	0	0	0	1	0
Hebner, ph	1	0	0	0	0	0		Mota, ph	1	0	0	0	0	0
McGraw, p	0	0	0	0	0	0		Rhoden, p	1	0	0	0	0	2
Totals	37	3	8	3	29	12		Ferguson, ph	1	0	0	0	0	0
								Forster, p	0	0	0	0	0	0
								Totals	40	4	13	4	30	9

Philadelphia	0	0	2	0	0	0	1	0	0	0	—	3
Los Angeles	0	1	0	1	0	1	0	0	0	1	—	4

Two out when winning run scored.

Philadelphia	IP.	H.	R.	ER.	BB.	SO.
Lerch	5⅓	7	3	3	0	0
Brusstar	⅔	1	0	0	1	0
Reed	2	4	0	0	0	1
McGraw (Loser)	1⅔	1	1	0	1	2

Los Angeles	IP.	H.	R.	ER.	BB.	SO.
Rau	5	5	2	2	2	1
Rhoden	4	2	1	1	1	3
Forster (Winner)	1	1	0	0	0	2

Errors—Boone, Maddox. Double play—Philadelphia 1. Left on bases—Philadelphia 7, Los Angeles 10. Two-base hits—Schmidt, Cey, Baker. Three-base hit—Sizemore. Home runs—Luzinski, Cey, Garvey, McBride. Stolen base—Lopes. Sacrifice hit—Mota. Umpires—Davidson, W. Williams, McSherry, Weyer, Colosi and Olsen. Time—2:53. Attendance—55,124.

LOS ANGELES DODGERS' BATTING AND FIELDING AVERAGES

Player—Position	G.	AB.	R.	H.	TB.	2B.	3B.	HR.	RBI.	B.A.	PO.	A.	E.	F.A.
Mota, ph	2	1	0	1	2	1	0	0	0	1.000	0	0	0	.000
Baker, lf	4	15	1	7	9	2	0	0	1	.467	5	0	0	1.000
Russell, ss	4	17	1	7	8	1	0	0	2	.412	4	14	0	1.000
Garvey, 1b	4	18	6	7	22	1	1	4	7	.389	44	5	0	1.000
Lopes, 2b	4	18	3	7	16	1	1	2	5	.389	10	10	2	.909
Cey, 3b	4	16	4	5	9	1	0	1	3	.313	2	13	0	1.000
Yeager, c	4	13	2	3	6	0	0	1	2	.231	21	2	0	1.000
Monday, cf-rf-ph	3	10	2	2	4	0	1	0	0	.200	6	0	0	1.000
Smith, rf	4	16	2	3	4	1	0	0	1	.188	5	0	1	.833
Grote, c	1	0	0	0	0	0	0	0	0	.000	2	0	0	1.000

Player–Position	G.	AB.	R.	H.	TB.	2B.	3B.	HR.	RBI.	B.A.	PO.	A.	E.	F.A.
Hough, p	1	0	0	0	0	0	0	0	0	.000	1	1	0	1.000
Forster, p	1	0	0	0	0	0	0	0	0	.000	0	0	0	.000
Rautzhan, p	1	0	0	0	0	0	0	0	0	.000	0	1	0	1.000
Rau, p	1	1	0	0	0	0	0	0	0	.000	1	0	0	1.000
Rhoden, p	1	1	0	0	0	0	0	0	0	.000	0	2	0	1.000
Hooton, p	1	2	0	0	0	0	0	0	0	.000	1	0	0	1.000
Sutton, p	1	2	0	0	0	0	0	0	0	.000	0	1	0	1.000
Welch, p	1	2	0	0	0	0	0	0	0	.000	0	1	0	1.000
Ferguson, ph	2	2	0	0	0	0	0	0	0	.000	0	0	0	.000
Lacy, ph	2	2	0	0	0	0	0	0	0	.000	0	0	0	.000
John, p	1	3	0	0	0	0	0	0	0	.000	0	0	0	.000
North, cf	4	8	0	0	0	0	0	0	0	.000	9	0	0	1.000
Totals	4	147	21	42	80	8	3	8	21	.286	111	50	3	.982

PHILADELPHIA PHILLIES' BATTING AND FIELDING AVERAGES

Player–Position	G.	AB.	R.	H.	TB.	2B.	3B.	HR.	RBI.	B.A.	PO.	A.	E.	F.A.
Carlton, p	1	4	2	2	5	0	0	1	4	.500	0	0	0	.000
Sizemore, 2b	4	13	3	5	7	0	1	0	1	.385	7	8	0	1.000
Luzinski, lf	4	16	3	6	14	0	1	2	3	.375	5	1	0	1.000
Bowa, ss	4	18	2	6	6	0	0	0	0	.333	5	16	0	1.000
Maddox, cf	4	19	1	5	5	0	0	0	2	.263	16	0	1	.941
McBride, rf-ph	3	9	2	2	5	0	0	1	1	.222	1	0	0	1.000
Martin, ph-rf	4	9	1	2	6	1	0	1	2	.222	7	0	0	1.000
Schmidt, 3b	4	15	1	3	5	2	0	0	1	.200	3	18	2	.913
Boone, c	3	11	0	2	2	0	0	0	0	.182	16	2	1	.947
Cardenal, 1b	2	6	0	1	1	0	0	0	0	.167	21	0	0	1.000
Hebner, 1b-ph	3	9	0	1	1	0	0	0	1	.111	21	0	0	1.000
Christenson, p	1	1	0	0	0	0	0	0	0	.000	0	0	0	.000
Eastwick, p	1	0	0	0	0	0	0	0	0	.000	0	0	0	.000
Reed, p	2	0	0	0	0	0	0	0	0	.000	0	0	0	.000
Brusstar, p	3	0	0	0	0	0	0	0	0	.000	0	0	0	.000
McGraw, p	3	0	0	0	0	0	0	0	0	.000	0	0	0	.000
Foote, ph	1	1	0	0	0	0	0	0	0	.000	0	0	0	.000
Gonzalez, ph	1	1	0	0	0	0	0	0	0	.000	0	0	0	.000
Morrison, ph	1	1	0	0	0	0	0	0	0	.000	0	0	0	.000
Ruthven, p	1	1	0	0	0	0	0	0	0	.000	0	0	0	.000
Lerch, p	1	2	0	0	0	0	0	0	0	.000	0	1	0	1.000
McCarver, ph-c	2	4	2	0	0	0	0	0	1	.000	8	0	0	1.000
Totals	4	140	17	35	57	3	2	5	16	.250	110	46	4	.975

LOS ANGELES DODGERS' PITCHING RECORDS

Pitcher	G.	GS.	CG.	IP.	H.	R.	ER.	BB.	SO.	HB.	WP.	W.	L.	Pct.	ERA.
John	1	1	1	9	4	0	0	2	4	0	0	1	0	1.000	0.00
Forster	1	0	0	1	1	0	0	0	2	0	0	1	0	1.000	0.00
Welch	1	0	0	4⅓	2	1	1	0	5	0	0	1	0	1.000	2.08
Rhoden	1	0	0	4	2	1	1	1	3	0	0	0	0	.000	2.25
Rau	1	1	0	5	5	2	2	2	1	0	0	0	0	.000	3.60
Hough	1	0	0	2	1	1	1	0	1	0	0	0	0	.000	4.50
Sutton	1	1	0	5⅔	7	7	4	2	0	0	0	0	1	.000	6.35
Rautzhan	1	0	0	1⅓	3	1	1	2	0	0	0	0	0	.000	6.75
Hooton	1	1	0	4⅔	10	4	4	0	5	0	0	0	0	.000	7.71
Totals	4	4	1	37	35	17	14	9	21	0	0	3	1	.750	3.41

Shutout–John. No saves.

PHILADELPHIA PHILLIES' PITCHING RECORDS

Pitcher	G.	GS.	CG.	IP.	H.	R.	ER.	BB.	SO.	HB.	WP.	W.	L.	Pct.	ERA.
Brusstar	3	0	0	2⅔	2	0	0	1	0	0	0	0	0	.000	0.00
McGraw	3	0	0	5⅔	3	2	1	5	5	0	0	0	1	.000	1.59
Reed	2	0	0	4	6	1	1	0	2	0	0	0	0	.000	2.25
Carlton	1	1	1	9	8	4	4	2	8	0	0	1	0	1.000	4.00
Lerch	1	1	0	5⅓	7	3	3	0	0	0	0	0	0	.000	5.06
Ruthven	1	1	0	4⅔	6	3	3	0	3	0	0	0	1	.000	5.79
Eastwick	1	0	0	1	3	1	1	0	1	1	0	0	0	.000	9.00
Christenson	1	1	0	4⅓	7	7	6	1	3	0	0	0	1	.000	12.46
Totals	4	4	1	36⅔	42	21	19	9	22	1	0	1	3	.250	4.66

No shutouts or saves.

COMPOSITE SCORE BY INNINGS

Los Angeles	0	2	6	4	3	2	1	1	1	1 – 21
Philadelphia	0	5	2	0	3	3	2	0	2	0 – 17

Sacrifice hits–John, Sizemore, Hebner, Mota.
Sacrifice fly–Schmidt.
Stolen bases–Yeager, Lopes.
Caught stealing–Schmidt, Garvey.
Double plays–Russell and Garvey; Bowa, Sizemore and Hebner; Russell, Lopes and Garvey; Lopes, Russell and Garvey; Cey, Lopes and Garvey; Sizemore, Bowa and Hebner 2; Sizemore, Bowa and Cardenal.
Left on bases–Los Angeles 28–8, 5, 5, 10; Philadelphia 24–7, 3, 7, 7.
Hit by pitcher–By Eastwick (Smith).
Passed balls–None.
Balks–None.

Time of games—First game, 2:37; second game, 2:06; third game, 2:18; fourth game, 2:53.
Attendance—First game, 63,460; second game, 60,642; third game, 55,043; fourth game, 55,124.
Umpires—Weyer, Colosi, Olsen, Davidson, W. Williams and McSherry.
Official scorers—Dick Robinson, Pasadena Star-News; Bob Kenney, Camden Courier-Post.

AMERICAN LEAGUE
Championship Series of 1979

	W.	L.	Pct.
Baltimore (East)	3	1	.750
California (West)	1	3	.250

"I've seen that play a hundred times before," said Baltimore shortstop Mark Belanger. "But by another third baseman."

"I thought of Brooks Robinson," said Brooks Robinson.

Memories. Of diving stops. Of World Series gems. Of Brooks Robinson.

But Brooks was retired and those sparkling plays were now only memories. . . . The California Angels had the bases loaded with one out in the fifth inning, trailing the Baltimore Orioles, 3-0, in the fourth game of the American League Championship Series. The Orioles led the Series two games to one, but the potential tying runs were on the bases.

Shortstop Jim Anderson was at the plate against Scott McGregor with 43,199 Anaheim Stadium fans on their feet, sensing their Angels were going to turn things around.

Anderson swung at the second pitch and hit a vicious one-hopper down the third base line. It looked like at least a double as the ball sped over the bag. Two runs would have scored for sure, maybe three. Doug DeCinces, who had never really escaped the shadow of Brooks Robinson at third base in the eyes of Orioles' rooters, dived to his right and somehow snared the ball. He recovered, straightened up and, while standing on third, threw to first to complete the double play and end the Angels' threat.

McGregor went on to hurl a six-hit shutout and the Orioles won 8-0 for a 3-1 Series triumph and their first visit to the World Series since 1971.

Pat Kelly's seventh-inning homer closed out the scoring and was the second three-run blast off California reliever John Montague. However, it was far less dramatic than the first one.

With two out in the 10th inning of the first game, the score deadlocked, 3-3, and DeCinces and Al Bumbry aboard via a single and intentional walk, respectively, pinch-hitter John Lowenstein strolled to the plate against Montague.

Lowenstein, sidelined for much of the latter part of the season because of a severely sprained ankle, sliced a two-strike pitch to the opposite field, just over the left-field wall to break up the game before 52,787 at Baltimore's Memorial Stadium.

Jim Palmer hurled the first nine innings, yielding seven hits, including a homer and double by Dan Ford, before Don Stanhouse pitched a perfect 10th inning to gain credit for the victory.

The Orioles sent 23-game winner Mike Flanagan to the mound in Game 2 and, after Ford connected off Flanagan in the first inning for his second homer in as many games, the AL Cy Young Award winner was given a 9-1 cushion in the first three innings, only to see it dwindle to one run before Stanhouse slowed the game down to his pace and saved a 9-8 victory.

The Orioles had scored four runs in their half of the first and added four more in the second, highlighted by first baseman Eddie Murray's 400-foot homer, before Kiko Garcia's RBI single in the third made the score 9-1.

After the Angels cuffed Flanagan for single runs in the sixth and seventh, they knocked the lefthander from the mound in the eighth, scoring three more runs, aided by a Murray error.

Stanhouse put gasoline on the fire for Flanagan in the eighth when he yielded a run-scoring single by Don Baylor and a sacrifice fly, reducing Baltimore's lead to 9-6.

In the ninth, Stanhouse permitted a walk, a pinch-double by Willie Davis, an infield out for one run and an RBI single by Carney Lansford, sending Baltimore skipper Earl Weaver to the mound.

"I was going to leave him (Stanhouse) in there until they tied the score," Weaver said later, after watching the Angels load the bases on a single by Ford and an intentional walk to Baylor, before Brian Downing grounded into a forceout to put a halt to the nail-biting.

With no days off for travel, the scene shifted to Anaheim Stadium for Game 3, where high drama once again dominated.

The Orioles were only two outs away from sweeping the series when the Angels struck back for a 4-3 victory.

Dennis Martinez spaced seven hits in the first eight innings prior to permitting a one-out double to Rod Carew in the ninth, bringing Stanhouse to the mound for the third straight game.

A walk to Downing preceded Bobby Grich's liner to center field where Al Bumbry, unable to hear the crack of the bat because of the roar of the crowd, got a late jump on the ball and dropped it for an error. Carew scored to tie the game, 3-3, with Downing stopping at second.

When Larry Harlow followed with a looping double down the left-field line, Downing raced home with the winning run.

The ecstasy was short-lived for the Angels, who finally made it to the playoffs after 19 years of trying.

GAME OF WEDNESDAY, OCTOBER 3, AT BALTIMORE (N)

California	AB.	R.	H.	RBI.	PO.	A.	Baltimore	AB.	R.	H.	RBI.	PO.	A.
Miller, cf	5	1	1	0	2	1	Bumbry, cf	4	1	0	0	3	0
Lansford, 3b	4	0	0	0	0	3	Belanger, ss	4	0	1	1	0	5
Ford, rf	4	1	2	2	3	0	Lowenstein, ph	1	1	1	3	0	0
Baylor, dh	4	0	0	0	0	0	Singleton, rf	3	0	0	0	1	0
Carew 1b	4	1	3	0	8	1	Murray, 1b	2	0	0	0	13	1
Downing, c	4	0	0	0	9	0	Kelly, lf	3	1	1	0	3	0
Grich, 2b	3	0	1	1	1	3	May, dh	4	0	0	0	0	0
Harlow, lf	4	0	0	0	4	0	DeCinces, 3b	3	2	1	1	2	3
Anderson, ss	3	0	0	0	1	2	Dauer, 2b	3	0	1	0	3	3
Davis, ph	1	0	0	0	0	0	Dempsey, c	3	1	1	1	4	1
Campaneris, ss	0	0	0	0	0	0	Crowley, ph	1	0	0	0	0	0
Ryan, p	0	0	0	0	0	0	Palmer, p	0	0	0	0	1	1
Montague, p	0	0	0	0	1	1	Stanhouse, p	0	0	0	0	0	0
Totals	36	3	7	3	29	11	Totals	31	6	6	6	30	14

```
California ............................. 1   0   1     0   0   1     0   0   0     0 – 3
Baltimore ............................. 0   0   2     1   0   0     0   0   0     3 – 6
```
Two out when winning run scored.

California	IP.	H.	R.	ER.	BB.	SO.
Ryan	7	4	3	1	3	8
Montague (Loser)	2⅔	2	3	3	2	1

Baltimore	IP.	H.	R.	ER.	BB.	SO.
Palmer	9	7	3	3	2	3
Stanhouse (Winner)	1	0	0	0	0	0

Error–Grich. Double plays–California 2. Left on bases–California 5, Baltimore 3. Two-base hits–Ford, Dempsey, Carew, Grich. Home runs–Ford, Lowenstein. Stolen base–Kelly. Caught stealing–Carew, Murray. Sacrifice hit–Dauer. Sacrifice fly–DeCinces. Wild pitch–Ryan. Passed ball–Dempsey. Umpires–Barnett, Ford, Evans, Denkinger, Clark and Kosc. Time–3:10. Attendance–52,787.

GAME OF THURSDAY, OCTOBER 4, AT BALTIMORE

California	AB.	R.	H.	RBI.	PO.	A.	Baltimore	AB.	R.	H.	RBI.	PO.	A.
Carew, 1b	5	2	1	1	10	0	Bumbry, cf	4	2	3	0	3	0
Lansford, 3b	5	1	3	3	0	1	Garcia, ss	3	1	2	2	2	9
Ford, rf	5	1	2	1	0	0	Singleton, rf	5	1	1	0	0	0
Baylor, dh	4	1	2	1	0	0	Murray, 1b	4	2	2	4	13	0
Downing, c	4	0	1	1	6	0	Lowenstein, lf	3	1	0	0	3	0
Grich, 2b	3	0	0	1	1	3	Kelly, dh	4	1	1	1	0	0
Clark, lf	3	0	0	0	3	0	DeCinces, 3b	3	1	1	1	1	2
Harlow, ph	0	0	0	0	0	0	Dauer, 2b	4	0	0	0	3	5
Miller, cf	4	1	0	0	2	0	Dempsey, c	4	0	1	0	2	0
Anderson, ss	2	0	0	0	2	3	Flanagan, p	0	0	0	0	0	0
Rettenmund, ph	0	0	0	0	0	0	Stanhouse, p	0	0	0	0	0	0
Thon, pr-ss	0	1	0	0	0	0	Totals	34	9	11	8	27	16
Davis, ph	1	1	1	0	0	0							
Frost, p	0	0	0	0	0	0							
Clear, p	0	0	0	0	0	0							
Aase, p	0	0	0	0	0	0							
Totals	36	8	10	8	24	7							

California	1	0	0	0	0	1	1	3	2 – 8
Baltimore	4	4	1	0	0	0	0	0	x – 9

California	IP.	H.	R.	ER.	BB.	SO.
Frost (Loser)	1⅓	5	6	5	3	0
Clear	5⅔	4	3	3	2	3
Aase	1	2	0	0	0	2

Baltimore	IP.	H.	R.	ER.	BB.	SO.
Flanagan (Winner)	7*	6	6	4	1	2
Stanhouse	2	4	2	2	2	0

*Pitched to three batters in eighth.

Errors—Ford, Murray. Double play—California 1. Left on bases—California 6, Baltimore 6. Two-base hits—Carew, Davis. Home runs—Ford, Murray. Stolen bases—Bumbry 2. Sacrifice flies—Grich, Downing. Wild pitch—Clear. Umpires—Ford, Evans, Denkinger, Clark, Kosc and Barnett. Time—2:51. Attendance—52,108.

GAME OF FRIDAY, OCTOBER 5, AT CALIFORNIA

Baltimore	AB.	R.	H.	RBI.	PO.	A.		California	AB.	R.	H.	RBI.	PO.	A.
Bumbry, cf	5	1	1	0	1	0		Miller, cf	4	0	1	0	7	1
Garcia, ss	3	0	0	0	2	2		Lansford, 3b	4	1	1	0	0	3
Crowley, ph	1	0	1	1	0	0		Ford, rf	4	0	1	1	2	0
Belanger, pr-ss	1	0	0	0	0	0		Baylor, dh	4	1	1	1	0	0
Singleton, rf	4	2	2	0	2	1		Carew, 1b	4	1	2	0	7	0
Murray, 1b	2	0	2	0	8	2		Downing, c	3	1	1	0	8	0
May, dh	3	0	1	1	0	0		Grich, 2b	4	0	0	0	1	1
DeCinces, 3b	3	0	0	1	0	1		Harlow, lf	4	0	1	1	2	0
Roenicke, lf	1	0	0	0	2	1		Anderson, ss	3	0	1	0	0	3
Lowenstein, ph-lf	1	0	0	0	2	0		Tanana, p	0	0	0	0	0	0
Dauer, 2b	4	0	1	0	3	4		Aase, p	0	0	0	0	0	1
Skaggs, c	4	0	0	0	3	1								
D. Martinez, p	0	0	0	0	2	0		Totals	34	4	9	3	27	9
Stanhouse, p	0	0	0	0	0	0								
Totals	32	3	8	3	25	12								

Baltimore	0	0	0	1	0	1	1	0	0 – 3
California	1	0	0	1	0	0	0	0	2 – 4

One out when winning run scored.

Baltimore	IP.	H.	R.	ER.	BB.	SO.
D. Martinez	8⅓	8	3	3	0	4
Stanhouse (Loser)	0†	1	1	0	1	0

California	IP.	H.	R.	ER.	BB.	SO.
Tanana	5*	6	2	2	2	3
Aase (Winner)	4	2	1	1	2	4

*Pitched to three batters in sixth.
†Pitched to three batters in ninth.

Errors—Garcia, Murray, Bumbry. Double plays—Baltimore 2, California 2. Left on bases—Baltimore 8, California 6. Two-base hits—Singleton, Carew, Harlow. Three-base hit—Bumbry. Home run—Baylor. Stolen bases—Lansford, Carew. Sacrifice fly—DeCinces. Hit by pitcher—By Tanana (Roenicke). Umpires—Evans, Denkinger, Clark, Kosc, Barnett and Ford. Time—2:59. Attendance—43, 199.

GAME OF SATURDAY, OCTOBER 6, AT CALIFORNIA

Baltimore	AB.	R.	H.	RBI.	PO.	A.		California	AB.	R.	H.	RBI.	PO.	A.
Bumbry, cf	3	1	0	0	3	0		Carew, 1b	4	0	1	0	9	0
Garcia, ss	5	0	1	0	2	5		Lansford, 3b	4	0	1	0	4	1
Belanger, ss	0	0	0	0	0	1		Ford, rf	4	0	0	0	1	0
Singleton, rf	4	1	3	2	2	0		Baylor, lf	4	0	0	0	4	0
Murray, 1b	4	1	1	1	10	0		Downing, c	4	0	1	0	4	0
Lowenstein, lf	1	0	0	0	1	0		Grich, 2b	3	0	1	0	1	5
Roenicke, ph-lf	4	1	1	1	1	0		Rettenmund, dh	2	0	0	0	0	0
Kelly, dh	4	1	2	3	0	0		Miller, cf	3	0	2	0	3	0
DeCinces, 3b	4	1	2	0	2	2		Anderson, ss	3	0	0	0	1	3
Smith, 2b	4	0	0	0	1	2		Knapp, p	0	0	0	0	0	0
Dauer, 2b	0	0	0	0	1	0		LaRoche, p	0	0	0	0	0	0
Dempsey, c	3	2	2	1	4	0		Frost, p	0	0	0	0	0	0
McGregor, p	0	0	0	0	0	0		Montague, p	0	0	0	0	0	1
Totals	36	8	12	8	27	10		Barlow, p	0	0	0	0	0	0
								Totals	31	0	6	0	27	10

Baltimore	0	0	2	1	0	0	5	0	0 – 8
California	0	0	0	0	0	0	0	0	0 – 0

Baltimore	IP.	H.	R.	ER.	BB.	SO.
McGregor (Winner)	9	6	0	0	1	4

California	IP.	H.	R.	ER.	BB.	SO.
Knapp (Loser)	2⅓	5	2	2	1	0
LaRoche	1⅓	2	1	1	1	1
Frost	3	3	4	4	2	1
Montague	1⅓	2	1	1	0	1
Barlow	1	0	0	0	1	0

Error—Garcia. Double plays—Baltimore 3, California 2. Left on bases—Baltimore 6, California 5. Two-base hits—DeCinces, Dempsey, Singleton. Home run—Kelly. Stolen bases—Kelly, Dempsey. Sacrifice fly—Singleton. Wild pitch—Frost. Umpires—Denkinger, Clark, Kosc, Barnett, Ford and Evans. Time—2:56. Attendance—43,199.

BALTIMORE ORIOLES' BATTING AND FIELDING AVERAGES

Player—Position	G.	AB.	R.	H.	TB.	2B.	3B.	HR.	RBI.	B.A.	PO.	A.	E.	F.A.
Crowley, ph	2	2	0	1	1	0	0	0	1	.500	0	0	0	.000
Murray, 1b	4	12	3	5	8	0	0	1	5	.417	44	3	2	.959
Dempsey, c	3	10	3	4	6	2	0	0	2	.400	10	1	0	1.000
Singleton, rf	4	16	4	6	8	2	0	0	2	.375	5	1	0	1.000
Kelly, lf-dh	3	11	3	4	7	0	0	1	4	.364	3	0	0	1.000
DeCinces, 3b	4	13	4	4	5	1	0	0	3	.308	5	8	0	1.000
Garcia, ss	3	11	1	3	3	0	0	0	2	.273	6	16	2	.917
Bumbry, cf	4	16	5	4	6	0	1	0	0	.250	10	0	1	.909
Roenicke, lf-ph	2	5	1	1	1	0	0	0	1	.200	3	1	0	1.000
Belanger, ss-pr	3	5	0	1	1	0	0	0	1	.200	0	6	0	1.000
Dauer, 2b	4	11	0	2	2	0	0	0	0	.182	10	12	0	1.000
Lowenstein, ph-lf	4	6	2	1	4	0	0	1	3	.167	6	0	0	1.000
May, dh	2	7	0	1	1	0	0	0	1	.143	0	0	0	.000
D. Martinez, p	1	0	0	0	0	0	0	0	0	.000	2	0	0	1.000
Palmer, p	1	0	0	0	0	0	0	0	0	.000	1	1	0	1.000
Flanagan, p	1	0	0	0	0	0	0	0	0	.000	0	0	0	.000
McGregor, p	1	0	0	0	0	0	0	0	0	.000	0	0	0	.000
Stanhouse, p	3	0	0	0	0	0	0	0	0	.000	0	0	0	.000
Skaggs, c	1	4	0	0	0	0	0	0	0	.000	3	1	0	1.000
Smith, 2b	1	4	0	0	0	0	0	0	0	.000	1	2	0	1.000
Totals	4	133	26	37	53	5	1	3	25	.278	109	52	5	.970

CALIFORNIA ANGELS' BATTING AND FIELDING AVERAGES

Player—Position	G.	AB.	R.	H.	TB.	2B.	3B.	HR.	RBI.	B.A.	PO.	A.	E.	F.A.
Davis, ph	2	2	1	1	2	1	0	0	0	.500	0	0	0	.000
Carew, 1b	4	17	4	7	10	3	0	0	1	.412	34	1	0	1.000
Ford, rf	4	17	2	5	12	1	0	2	4	.294	6	0	1	.857
Lansford, 3b	4	17	2	5	5	0	0	0	3	.294	4	8	0	1.000
Miller, cf	4	16	2	4	4	0	0	0	0	.250	14	2	0	1.000
Downing, c	4	15	1	3	3	0	0	0	1	.200	27	0	0	1.000
Baylor, dh-lf	4	16	2	3	6	0	0	1	2	.188	4	0	0	1.000
Grich, 2b	4	13	0	2	3	1	0	0	2	.154	4	12	1	.941
Harlow, lf-ph	3	8	0	1	2	1	0	0	1	.125	6	0	0	1.000
Anderson, ss	4	11	0	1	1	0	0	0	0	.091	4	11	0	1.000
Thon, pr-ss	1	0	1	0	0	0	0	0	0	.000	0	0	0	.000
Barlow, p	1	0	0	0	0	0	0	0	0	.000	0	0	0	.000
Campaneris, ss	1	0	0	0	0	0	0	0	0	.000	0	0	0	.000
Clear, p	1	0	0	0	0	0	0	0	0	.000	0	0	0	.000
Knapp, p	1	0	0	0	0	0	0	0	0	.000	0	0	0	.000
LaRoche, p	1	0	0	0	0	0	0	0	0	.000	0	0	0	.000
Ryan, p	1	0	0	0	0	0	0	0	0	.000	0	0	0	.000
Tanana, p	1	0	0	0	0	0	0	0	0	.000	0	0	0	.000
Montague, p	2	0	0	0	0	0	0	0	0	.000	1	2	0	1.000
Aase, p	2	0	0	0	0	0	0	0	0	.000	0	1	0	1.000
Frost, p	2	0	0	0	0	0	0	0	0	.000	0	0	0	.000
Rettenmund, ph-dh	2	2	0	0	0	0	0	0	0	.000	0	0	0	.000
Clark, lf	1	3	0	0	0	0	0	0	0	.000	3	0	0	1.000
Totals	4	137	15	32	48	7	0	3	14	.234	107	37	2	.986

BALTIMORE ORIOLES' PITCHING RECORDS

Pitcher	G.	GS.	CG.	IP.	H.	R.	ER.	BB.	SO.	HB.	WP.	W.	L.	Pct.	ERA.
McGregor	1	1	1	9	6	0	0	1	4	0	0	1	0	1.000	0.00
Palmer	1	1	0	9	7	3	3	2	3	0	0	0	0	.000	3.00
D. Martinez	1	1	0	8⅓	8	3	3	0	4	0	0	0	0	.000	3.24
Flanagan	1	1	0	7	6	6	4	1	2	0	0	1	0	1.000	5.14
Stanhouse	3	0	0	3	5	3	2	3	0	0	0	1	1	.500	6.00
Totals	4	4	1	36⅓	32	15	12	7	13	0	0	3	1	.750	2.97

Shutout—McGregor. No saves.

CALIFORNIA ANGELS' PITCHING RECORDS

Pitcher	G.	GS.	CG.	IP.	H.	R.	ER.	BB.	SO.	HB.	WP.	W.	L.	Pct.	ERA.
Barlow	1	0	0	1	0	0	0	0	0	0	0	0	0	.000	0.00
Ryan	1	1	0	7	4	3	1	3	8	0	1	0	0	.000	1.29
Aase	2	0	0	5	4	1	1	2	6	0	0	1	0	1.000	1.80
Tanana	1	1	0	5	6	2	2	2	3	1	0	0	0	.000	3.60
Clear	1	0	0	5⅔	4	3	3	2	3	0	1	0	0	.000	4.76
LaRoche	1	0	0	1⅓	2	1	1	1	1	0	0	0	0	.000	6.75
Knapp	1	1	0	2⅓	5	2	2	1	0	0	0	0	1	.000	7.71
Montague	2	0	0	4	4	4	4	2	2	0	0	0	1	.000	9.00
Frost	2	1	0	4⅓	8	10	9	5	1	0	1	0	1	.000	18.69
Totals	4	4	0	35⅔	37	26	23	18	24	1	3	1	3	.250	5.80

No shutouts or saves.

COMPOSITE SCORE BY INNINGS

Baltimore	4	4	5	3	0	1	6	0	0	3	— 26
California	3	0	1	1	0	2	1	3	4	0	— 15

Sacrifice hit—Dauer.
Sacrifice flies—DeCinces 2, Grich, Downing, Singleton.
Stolen bases—Bumbry 2, Kelley 2, Lansford, Carew, Dempsey.
Caught stealing—Carew, Murray.

Double plays—Lansford, Grich and Carew 2; Miller and Carew; Anderson, Grich and Carew 2; Roenicke, Garcia and Dauer; Dauer and Murray; Miller and Downing; Smith, Garcia and Murray; Lansford and Carew; DeCinces and Murray; Garcia, Smith and Murray.

Left on bases—Baltimore 3, 6, 8, 6—23; California 5, 6, 6, 5—22.

Hit by pitcher—By Tanana (Roenicke).

Passed ball—Dempsey.

Balks—None.

Time of games—First game, 3:10; second game, 2:51; third game, 2:59; fourth game, 2:56.

Attendance—First game, 52,787; second game, 52,108; third game, 43,199; fourth game, 43,199.

Umpires—Barnett, Ford, Evans, Denkinger, Clark and Kosc.

Official scorers—Jim Henneman, Baltimore News-American; Tracy Ringolsby, Long Beach Independent Press-Telegram.

NATIONAL LEAGUE
Championship Series of 1979

	W.	L.	Pct.
Pittsburgh (East)	3	0	1.000
Cincinnati (West)	0	3	.000

Can you picture Willie Stargell searching through his locker like a man possessed?

As Willie tells the story, while the Pirates were at Cincinnati for the first two games of their three-game sweep of the National League Championship Series, someone broke into his locker and swiped his final batch of 100 gold cloth stars—those stars he awarded to his teammates for various accomplishments during the season.

"The bag came up missing and still is," lamented Stargell, after he was unanimously selected the Most Valuable Player in the Series for batting .455 with 13 total bases and six RBIs. "It's a dirty trick for someone to pull on us now.

"When I found out they were missing, I ordered 3,000 more. If I have a choice, the entire squad will get a star for this one."

Stargell's contributions were headline material in papers across the country: A three-run, 11th-inning homer that decided a 5-2 win in the opener; a single and double in the Pirates' 10-inning 3-2 triumph in Game 2; a homer and two-run double in the 7-1 clinching victory.

It was sweet revenge for the Pirates' dauntless 38-year-old captain and main inspirational force, even if he couldn't celebrate the conquest of the Reds by awarding stars to his teammates. The Pirates had been swept by the Reds in the N.L. playoffs in 1970 and 1975.

After a 45-minute delay by rain at the start of Game 1, the Pirates, losers in eight of 12 games with the Reds in '79, bolted to a 2-0 lead in the third inning. Phil Garner sliced a homer to right field, Omar Moreno tripled on a drive that eluded the diving Dave Collins in right and Tim Foli contributed a sacrifice fly.

But the Reds rebounded with a pair in the fourth on a single by Dave Concepcion and a homer by George Foster off Pittsburgh starting pitcher John Candelaria.

The deadlock persisted until the top half of the 11th. For two innings in relief of starter Tom Seaver, righthander Tom Hume was in command. But Foli and Dave Parker singled before Stargell's first-pitch homer settled the issue and sent flocks of the 55,006 spectators streaming for the exits.

A single by Concepcion and walks to Foster and Johnny Bench gave Reds' diehards one last hope in their half, before Don Robinson fanned Ray Knight to end the threat.

After using five pitchers in the first game, Pittsburgh Manager Chuck Tanner came right back with six hurlers for a 3-2 verdict in 10 innings in Game 2.

Controversy surrounded the victory, however.

With the score tied 1-1 in the Pirates' half of the fifth, Garner lashed a liner to right field. The Reds' Collins dived for the ball, but second base umpire Frank Pulli ruled a trap. Television replays showed that Collins had made a clean grab.

Garner advanced on a sacrifice by pitcher Jim Bibby and scored on Foli's double, giving the Pirates a 2-1 lead.

The Pirates had plenty of reason to celebrate after dispatching the Cincinnati Reds in three straight games in the 1979 N.L. Championship Series.

The Reds knotted the score with one out in the ninth on a pinch-double by Hector Cruz and another two-bagger by Collins.

The rally continued when Dave Roberts walked Joe Morgan. Don Robinson was summoned by Tanner and proceeded to strike out Concepcion and retire Foster on a groundout.

Then Moreno and Parker singled around a Foli sacrifice in the 10th to make Robinson the winner and saddle Doug Bair with the loss.

A 30-minute rain delay preceded Game 3 as the scene shifted upriver to Pittsburgh on October 5.

Robinson, who saved Game 1, was extremely impressive as he set down five straight batters in the second game.

While Stargell was providing the slugging feats, the Pirates' pitching staff was limiting the once-feared Cincinnati offense to five runs in three games, climaxed by Bert Blyleven's route-going performance, only his fifth complete game of the year and first since August 15.

And the Bucs' bats went to work early, getting single runs in the first and second and two runs each in the third and fourth. Stargell and Bill Madlock socked homers in the third.

GAME OF TUESDAY, OCTOBER 2, AT CINCINNATI (N)

Pittsburgh	AB.	R.	H.	RBI.	PO.	A.	Cincinnati	AB.	R.	H.	RBI.	PO.	A.
Moreno, cf	5	1	1	0	2	0	Collins, rf	5	0	2	0	3	0
Foli, ss	4	0	2	1	1	6	Morgan, 2b	4	0	0	0	3	4
Alexander, pr	0	1	0	0	0	0	Concepcion, ss	5	1	2	0	1	6
B. Robinson, lf	0	0	0	0	0	0	Foster, lf	3	1	1	2	1	0
Parker, rf	4	1	1	0	2	0	Bench, c	3	0	2	0	7	0
Stargell, 1b	4	1	1	3	17	0	Knight, 3b	5	0	0	0	0	1
Milner, lf	5	0	0	1	0	0	Driessen, 1b	4	0	0	0	14	0
Stennett, 2b	0	0	0	0	1	0	Cruz, cf	4	0	0	0	3	0
Madlock, 3b	5	0	2	0	4	0	Seaver, p	2	0	0	0	0	0
Ott, c	5	0	1	0	7	2	Auerbach, ph	1	0	0	0	0	0
Garner, 2b-ss	4	1	2	1	3	5	Hume, p	1	0	0	0	0	2
Candelaria, p	3	0	0	0	0	0	Tomlin, p	0	0	0	0	1	0
Romo, p	0	0	0	0	0	0							
Tekulve, p	0	0	0	0	0	1	Totals	37	2	7	2	33	13
Easler, ph	1	0	0	0	0	0							
Jackson, p	1	0	0	0	0	0							
D. Robinson, p	0	0	0	0	0	0							
Totals	41	5	10	5	33	19							

Pittsburgh	0	0	2	0	0	0	0	0	0	0	3 — 5
Cincinnati	0	0	0	2	0	0	0	0	0	0	0 — 2

Pittsburgh	IP.	H.	R.	ER.	BB.	SO.
Candelaria	7	5	2	2	1	4
Romo	⅓	1	0	0	1	1
Tekulve	1⅔	0	0	0	1	0
Jackson (Winner)	1⅔	1	0	0	1	2
D. Robinson (Save)	⅓	0	0	0	1	1
Cincinnati	IP.	H.	R.	ER.	BB.	SO.
Seaver	8	5	2	2	2	5
Hume (Loser)	2⅓	5	3	3	0	1
Tomlin	⅔	0	0	0	1	1

Errors—None. Double plays—Pittsburgh 2, Cincinnati 1. Left on bases—Pittsburgh 7, Cincinnati 7. Three-base hits—Bench, Moreno. Home runs—Garner, Foster, Stargell. Stolen bases—Madlock 2, Collins. Caught stealing—Bench. Sacrifice fly—Foli. Umpires—Kibler, Montague, Dale, Pulli, Stello and Quick. Time—3:14. Attendance—55,006.

GAME OF WEDNESDAY, OCTOBER 3, AT CINCINNATI

Pittsburgh	AB.	R.	H.	RBI.	PO.	A.	Cincinnati	AB.	R.	H.	RBI.	PO.	A.
Moreno, cf	5	1	2	0	4	0	Collins, rf	5	0	1	1	0	0
Foli, ss	4	1	2	1	2	1	Morgan, 2b	3	0	0	0	6	6
Parker, rf	5	0	2	1	4	0	Concepcion, ss	5	0	2	0	1	8
Stargell, 1b	3	0	2	0	6	1	Foster, lf	3	0	1	0	3	2
Milner, lf	2	0	0	0	0	0	Bench, c	5	0	0	0	5	1
B. Robinson, lf	2	0	0	0	3	0	Driessen, 1b	4	1	1	0	12	0
Madlock, 3b	5	0	0	1	1	0	Knight, 3b	5	0	2	0	0	2
Ott, c	4	0	2	0	9	1	Geronimo, cf	3	0	0	0	3	0
Garner, 2b	4	1	1	0	1	3	Pastore, p	0	0	0	1	0	0
Bibby, p	0	0	0	0	0	1	Spilman, ph	1	0	0	0	0	0
Jackson, p	0	0	0	0	0	0	Tomlin, p	0	0	0	0	0	0
Romo, p	0	0	0	0	0	0	Hume, p	0	0	0	0	0	0
Tekulve, p	1	0	0	0	0	0	Cruz, ph	1	1	1	0	0	0
Roberts, p	0	0	0	0	0	0	Bair, p	0	0	0	0	0	1
D. Robinson, p	0	0	0	0	0	0	Totals	35	2	8	2	30	20
Totals	35	3	11	3	30	7							

Pittsburgh	0	0	0	1	1	0	0	0	0	1 – 3
Cincinnati	0	1	0	0	0	0	0	0	1	0 – 2

Pittsburgh	IP.	H.	R.	ER.	BB.	SO.
Bibby	7	4	1	1	4	5
Jackson	⅓	0	0	0	0	0
Romo	0*	2	0	0	0	0
Tekulve	1	2	1	1	1	2
Roberts	0†	0	0	0	1	0
D. Robinson (Winner)	1⅔	0	0	0	0	2

Cincinnati	IP.	H.	R.	ER.	BB.	SO.
Pastore	7	7	2	2	3	1
Tomlin	⅔	1	0	0	0	1
Hume	1⅓	1	0	0	0	1
Bair (Loser)	1	2	1	1	1	0

*Pitched to two batters in eighth.
†Pitched to one batter in ninth.

Errors—None. Double play—Cincinnati 1. Left on bases—Pittsburgh 9, Cincinnati 11. Two-base hits—Concepcion, Foli, Stargell, Cruz, Collins. Stolen bases—Morgan, Knight, Collins. Caught stealing—Concepcion. Sacrifice hits—Bibby 2, Geronimo, Foli. Sacrifice fly—Pastore. Wild pitch—Tekulve. Umpires—Montague, Dale, Pulli, Stello, Quick and Kibler. Time—3:24. Attendance—55,000.

GAME OF FRIDAY, OCTOBER 5, AT PITTSBURGH

Cincinnati	AB.	R.	H.	RBI.	PO.	A.
Collins, rf	4	0	2	0	2	0
Morgan, 2b	4	0	0	3	1
Concepcion, ss	4	0	2	0	1	0
Foster, lf	4	0	0	2	0
Bench, c	4	1	1	1	5	1
Driessen, 1b	4	0	0	0	6	0
Knight, 3b	4	0	2	0	2	0
Geronimo, cf	4	0	1	0	5	0
LaCoss, p	0	0	0	0	0	1
Norman, p	1	0	0	0	0	0
Leibrandt, p	0	0	0	0	0	0
Auerbach, ph	1	0	0	0	0	0
Soto, p	0	0	0	0	0	0
Spilman, ph	1	0	0	0	0	0
Tomlin, p	0	0	0	0	0	1
Hume, p	0	0	0	0	0	0
Totals	35	1	8	1	24	6

Pittsburgh	AB.	R.	H.	RBI.	PO.	A.
Moreno, cf	2	1	0	0	1	0
Foli, ss	4	0	0	1	0	2
Parker, rf	3	1	1	1	3	0
Stargell, 1b	4	1	2	3	9	1
Milner, lf	2	0	0	0	0	0
B. Robinson, lf	1	0	0	0	0	0
Madlock, 3b	2	1	1	1	0	3
Ott, c	4	0	0	0	9	0
Garner, 2b	4	2	2	0	4	1
Blyleven, p	3	1	1	0	1	1
Totals	29	7	7	6	27	8

Cincinnati	0	0	0	0	0	1	0	0	0 – 1
Pittsburgh	1	1	2	2	0	0	0	1	x – 7

Cincinnati	IP.	H.	R.	ER.	BB.	SO.
LaCoss (Loser)	1⅔	1	2	2	4	0
Norman	2	4	4	4	1	1
Leibrandt	⅓	0	0	0	0	0
Soto	2	0	0	0	0	1
Tomlin	1⅔	2	1	0	1	1
Hume	⅓	0	0	0	0	0

Pittsburgh	IP.	H.	R.	ER.	BB.	SO.
Blyleven (Winner)	9	8	1	1	0	9

Error—Geronimo. Left on bases—Cincinnati 7, Pittsburgh 8. Two-base hits—Knight, Stargell. Three-base hit—Garner. Home runs—Stargell, Madlock, Bench. Stolen bases—Moreno, Parker. Sacrifice hits—Moreno, Blyleven. Sacrifice flies—Parker, Foli. Balk—Leibrandt. Umpires—Dale, Pulli, Stello, Quick, Kibler and Montague. Time—2:45. Attendance—42,240.

PITTSBURGH PIRATES' BATTING AND FIELDING AVERAGES

Player—Position	G.	AB.	R.	H.	TB.	2B.	3B.	HR.	RBI.	B.A.	PO.	A.	E.	F.A.
Stargell, 1b	3	11	2	5	13	2	0	2	6	.455	32	2	0	1.000
Garner, 2b-ss	3	12	4	5	10	0	1	1	1	.417	8	9	0	1.000
Foli, ss	3	12	1	4	5	1	0	0	3	.333	3	9	0	1.000
Parker, rf	3	12	2	4	4	0	0	0	2	.333	9	0	0	1.000
Blyleven, p	1	3	1	1	1	0	0	0	0	.333	1	1	0	1.000
Madlock, 3b	3	12	1	3	6	0	0	1	2	.250	1	7	0	1.000
Moreno, cf	3	12	3	3	5	0	1	0	0	.250	7	0	0	1.000
Ott, c	3	13	0	3	3	0	0	0	0	.231	25	3	0	1.000
Alexander, pr	1	0	1	0	0	0	0	0	0	.000	0	0	0	.000
Bibby, p	1	0	0	0	0	0	0	0	0	.000	0	1	0	1.000
Stennett, 2b	1	0	0	0	0	0	0	0	0	.000	0	1	0	1.000
Roberts, p	1	0	0	0	0	0	0	0	0	.000	0	0	0	.000
D. Robinson, p	2	0	0	0	0	0	0	0	0	.000	0	0	0	.000
Romo, p	2	0	0	0	0	0	0	0	0	.000	0	0	0	.000
Easler, ph	1	1	0	0	0	0	0	0	0	.000	0	0	0	.000
Tekulve, p	2	1	0	0	0	0	0	0	0	.000	0	1	0	1.000
Jackson, p	2	1	0	0	0	0	0	0	0	.000	0	0	0	.000
Candelaria, p	1	3	0	0	0	0	0	0	0	.000	0	0	0	.000
B. Robinson, lf	3	3	0	0	0	0	0	0	0	.000	3	0	0	1.000
Milner, lf	3	9	0	0	0	0	0	0	0	.000	1	0	0	1.000
Totals	3	105	15	28	47	3	2	4	14	.267	90	34	0	1.000

CINCINNATI REDS' BATTING AND FIELDING AVERAGES

Player—Position	G.	AB.	R.	H.	TB.	2B.	3B.	HR.	RBI.	B.A.	PO.	A.	E.	F.A.
Concepcion, ss	3	14	1	6	7	1	0	0	0	.429	3	14	0	1.000
Collins, rf	3	14	0	5	6	1	0	0	1	.357	5	0	0	1.000
Knight, 3b	3	14	0	4	5	1	0	0	0	.286	0	5	0	1.000
Bench, c	3	12	1	3	8	0	1	1	1	.250	17	2	0	1.000
Foster, lf	3	10	1	2	5	0	0	1	2	.200	6	2	0	1.000
Cruz, cf-ph	2	5	1	1	2	1	0	0	0	.200	3	0	0	1.000
Geronimo, cf	2	7	0	1	1	0	0	0	0	.143	8	0	1	.889
Driessen, 1b	3	12	1	1	1	0	0	0	0	.083	32	0	0	1.000
Pastore, p	1	0	0	0	0	0	0	0	1	.000	0	0	0	.000
Bair, p	1	0	0	0	0	0	0	0	0	.000	0	1	0	1.000
LaCoss, p	1	0	0	0	0	0	0	0	0	.000	0	1	0	1.000
Leibrandt, p	1	0	0	0	0	0	0	0	0	.000	0	0	0	.000
Soto, p	1	0	0	0	0	0	0	0	0	.000	0	0	0	.000
Tomlin, p	3	0	0	0	0	0	0	0	0	.000	1	1	0	1.000
Norman, p	1	1	0	0	0	0	0	0	0	.000	0	0	0	.000
Hume, p	3	1	0	0	0	0	0	0	0	.000	0	2	0	1.000
Seaver, p	1	2	0	0	0	0	0	0	0	.000	0	0	0	.000
Auerbach, ph	2	2	0	0	0	0	0	0	0	.000	0	0	0	.000
Spilman, ph	2	2	0	0	0	0	0	0	0	.000	0	0	0	.000
Morgan, 2b	3	11	0	0	0	0	0	0	0	.000	12	11	0	1.000
Totals	3	107	5	23	35	4	1	2	5	.215	87	39	1	.992

PITTSBURGH PIRATES' PITCHING RECORDS

Pitcher	G.	GS.	CG.	IP.	H.	R.	ER.	BB.	SO.	HB.	WP.	W.	L.	Pct.	ERA.
D. Robinson	2	0	0	2	0	0	0	1	3	0	0	1	0	1.000	0.00
Jackson	2	0	0	2	1	0	0	1	2	0	0	1	0	1.000	0.00
Romo	2	0	0	⅓	3	0	0	1	1	0	0	0	0	.000	0.00
Roberts	1	0	0	0	0	0	0	1	0	0	0	0	0	.000	0.00
Blyleven	1	1	1	9	8	1	1	0	9	0	0	1	0	1.000	1.00
Bibby	1	1	0	7	4	1	1	4	5	0	0	0	0	.000	1.29
Candelaria	1	1	0	7	5	2	2	1	4	0	0	0	0	.000	2.57
Tekulve	2	0	0	2⅔	2	1	1	2	2	0	1	0	0	.000	3.38
Totals	3	3	1	30	23	5	5	11	26	0	1	3	0	1.000	1.50

No shutouts. Save—D. Robinson.

CINCINNATI REDS' PITCHING RECORDS

Pitcher	G.	GS.	CG.	IP.	H.	R.	ER.	BB.	SO.	HB.	WP.	W.	L.	Pct.	ERA.
Tomlin	3	0	0	3	3	1	0	2	3	0	0	0	0	.000	0.00
Soto	1	0	0	2	0	0	0	0	1	0	0	0	0	.000	0.00
Leibrandt	1	0	0	⅓	0	0	0	0	0	0	0	0	0	.000	0.00
Seaver	1	1	0	8	5	2	2	2	5	0	0	0	0	.000	2.25
Pastore	1	1	0	7	7	2	2	3	1	0	0	0	0	.000	2.57
Hume	3	0	0	4	6	3	3	0	2	0	0	0	1	.000	6.75
Bair	1	0	0	1	2	1	1	1	0	0	0	0	1	.000	9.00
LaCoss	1	1	0	1⅔	2	2	2	4	0	0	0	0	1	.000	10.80
Norman	1	0	0	2	4	4	4	1	1	0	0	0	0	.000	18.00
Totals	3	3	0	29	28	15	14	13	13	0	0	0	3	.000	4.34

No shutouts or saves.

COMPOSITE SCORE BY INNINGS

Pittsburgh	1	1	4	3	1	0	0	1	0	1	3 – 15
Cincinnati	0	1	0	2	0	1	0	0	1	0	0 – 5

Sacrifice hits—Bibby 2, Geronimo, Foli, Moreno, Blyleven.
Sacrifice flies—Foli 2, Pastore, Parker.
Stolen bases—Madlock 2, Collins 2, Morgan, Knight, Moreno, Parker.
Caught stealing—Bench, Concepcion.
Double plays—Concepcion, Morgan and Driessen 2; Garner, Foli and Stargell; Madlock, Garner, Stargell.
Left on bases—Pittsburgh 7, 9, 8—24; Cincinnati 7, 11, 7—25.
Hit by pitcher—None.
Passed balls—None.
Balk—Leibrandt.
Time of games—First game, 3:14; second game, 3:24; third game, 2:45.
Attendance—First game, 55,006; second game, 55,000; third game, 42,240.
Umpires—Kibler, Montague, Dale, Pulli, Stello and Quick.
Official scorers—Earl Lawson, Cincinnati Post; Dan Donovan, Pittsburgh Press.

AMERICAN LEAGUE
Championship Series of 1980

	W.	L.	Pct.
Kansas City (West)	3	0	1.000
New York (East)	0	3	.000

The Kansas City Royals were driven by the idea of beating the New York Yankees. Yes, beating those same Big Apple brutes who had sent the Royals away unhappy with playoff losses in 1976, '77 and '78.

The idea of beating the Yankees was almost haunting to the Royals, even to a player like THE SPORTING NEWS 1980 American League Fireman of the Year, Dan Quisenberry, who wasn't with Kansas City during those second-best seasons.

"I thought to myself, 'Hey, you know all the years the Royals had short relief problems and they blew leads—that's how they lost all those playoff games. You're the guy who is supposed to turn all that around this year. What are you walking all these guys for?' " Quisenberry commented before he set down the Yankees to extinguish an eighth-inning threat and preserve a 4-2 victory in Game 3, enabling the Royals to sweep the A.L. Championship Series from the Yanks.

"Our fans think we've already won the World Series by beating the Yankees," said George Brett, whose towering three-run homer into the third tier of seats at Yankee Stadium off ace reliever Rich Gossage erased a 2-1 deficit and provided the winning touch to the third game triumph.

Gossage, unhittable for the final eight weeks of the season, entered the contest after Tommy John yielded a two-out double by Willie Wilson. U.L. Washington greeted Gossage by beating out an infield chopper.

The stage was set. As Gossage put it: "It was power versus power."

In one classic swipe of the bat, Brett slayed the giants.

The Royals didn't begin the series with the glee that climaxed it. In fact, there was doubt in the mind of their starting pitcher, Larry Gura, after Rick Cerone and Lou Piniella hit back-to-back homers for a 2-0 lead in the second inning of Game 1.

Gura didn't exactly dazzle the Yanks but he did manage to scatter 10 hits and pitch the Royals to a 7-2 verdict and a one-game edge.

Frank White began the Kansas City comeback with a two-out, two-run double in the second and Willie Aikens sent two more runs home with a third-inning single. Brett blasted a homer in the seventh and Wilson doubled in the final two tallies in the eighth.

The Royals put together four straight hits for all their runs in the third inning and shaded the Yanks, 3-2, in Game 2. Darrell Porter and White singled before Wilson cleared the sacks with a triple and Washington completed the outburst with a two-base hit.

The Yankees had an inside-the-park homer by Graig Nettles and a run-scoring double by Willie Randolph for their only runs.

However, the most talked about New York play occurred in the eighth when Randolph was thrown out at the plate attempting to score from first on a two-out double by Bob Watson. Blustery Yankees Owner George Steinbrenner wanted third base coach Mike Ferraro fired. The consensus: when left fielder Wilson overthrew the relay man the runner had to score. Brett, backing up Washington, snared the throw and gunned Randolph out at the plate with a perfect peg.

White, who was voted MVP of the series with his 6-for-11 hitting and several outstanding plays in the field, staked the Royals to a 1-0 lead in Game 3 before the Yanks rallied for two runs in the sixth—one coming off starter Paul Splittorff and the other coming off Quisenberry.

Center stage was set for the Brett-Gossage confrontation.

"We all kept hollering, 'It's going to happen, it's going to happen,' " said White. "We just knew they couldn't keep getting George (0 for his last 7) out like that."

The rest is history.

GAME OF WEDNESDAY, OCTOBER 8, AT KANSAS CITY

New York	AB.	R.	H.	RBI.	PO.	A.	Kansas City	AB.	R.	H.	RBI.	PO.	A.
Randolph, 2b	5	0	2	0	0	5	Wilson, lf	5	0	1	2	2	0
Dent, ss	4	0	2	0	3	3	Washington, ss	4	0	1	0	1	3
Watson, 1b	4	0	2	0	11	2	G. Brett, 3b	3	2	2	1	1	2
Jackson, rf	4	0	0	1	0		McRae, dh	3	0	0	0	0	0
Soderholm, dh	4	0	1	0	0	0	Otis, cf	4	2	2	0	5	0
Cerone, c	4	1	1	1	6	1	Wathan, rf	1	1	0	0	4	0
Piniella, lf	3	1	1	1	1	0	Hurdle, rf	0	0	0	0	0	0
Rodriguez, 3b	4	0	1	0	1	2	Aikens, 1b	4	0	1	2	7	0
Brown, cf	4	0	0	0	1	0	LaCock, 1b	0	0	0	0	0	0
Guidry, p	0	0	0	0	0	1	Porter, c	4	1	0	0	5	0
Davis, p	0	0	0	0	0	2	White, 2b	4	1	3	2	2	3
Underwood, p	0	0	0	0	0	1	Gura, p	0	0	0	0	0	1
Totals	36	2	10	2	24	17	Totals	32	7	10	7	27	9

New York			0	2	0		0	0	0		0	0	0 – 2
Kansas City			0	2	2		0	0	0		1	2	x – 7

New York	IP.	H.	R.	ER.	BB.	SO.
Guidry (Loser)	3	5	4	4	4	2
Davis	4	3	1	1	1	3
Underwood	1	2	2	0	0	2

Kansas City	IP.	H.	R.	ER.	BB.	SO.
Gura (Winner)	9	10	2	2	1	4

Game-winning RBI–Aikens.

Error–Watson. Double play–New York 1. Left on bases–New York 9, Kansas City 7. Two-base hits–Randolph, G. Brett, Rodriguez, White, Watson, Otis, Wilson. Home runs–Cerone, Piniella, G. Brett. Stolen bases–Otis, White. Sacrifice hit–Dent. Hit by pitcher–By Davis (McRae). Wild pitch–Guidry. Umpires–Palermo, Brinkman, McCoy, Haller, Kaiser and Maloney. Time–3:00. Attendance–42,598.

GAME OF THURSDAY, OCTOBER 9, AT KANSAS CITY (N)

New York	AB.	R.	H.	RBI.	PO.	A.	Kansas City	AB.	R.	H.	RBI.	PO.	A.
Randolph, 2b	4	0	2	1	1	1	Wilson, lf	3	1	1	2	2	1
Murcer, dh	4	0	0	0	0	0	Washington, ss	3	0	1	1	3	1
Watson, 1b	4	0	1	0	6	2	G. Brett, 3b	4	0	0	0	0	3
Jackson, rf	4	0	2	0	2	0	McRae, dh	3	0	0	0	0	0
Gamble, lf	4	0	0	0	1	0	Otis, cf	4	0	1	0	3	0
Cerone, c	4	0	2	0	4	1	Wathan, rf	3	0	0	0	3	0
Nettles, 3b	4	1	1	1	0	1	Hurdle, rf	0	0	0	0	0	0
Dent, ss	3	0	0	0	3	2	Aikens, 1b	3	0	0	0	7	0
Brown, cf	2	1	0	0	5	0	Porter, c	3	1	1	0	8	1
May, p	0	0	0	0	2	2	White, 2b	3	1	2	0	1	2
							Leonard, p	0	0	0	0	0	0
Totals	33	2	8	2	24	9	Quisenberry, p	0	0	0	0	0	0
							Totals	29	3	6	3	27	8

New York			0	0	0		0	2	0		0	0	0 – 2
Kansas City			0	0	3		0	0	0		0	0	x – 3

New York	IP.	H.	R.	ER.	BB.	SO.
May (Loser)	8	6	3	3	3	4

Kansas City	IP.	H.	R.	ER.	BB.	SO.
Leonard (Winner)	8*	7	2	2	1	8
Quisenberry (Save)	1	1	0	0	0	0

*Pitched to one batter in ninth.

Game-winning RBI–Wilson.

Errors–None. Double play–Kansas City 1. Left on bases–New York 5, Kansas City 5. Two-base hits–Washington, Randolph, Watson. Three-base hit–Wilson. Home run–Nettles. Stolen base–Otis. Umpires–Brinkman, McCoy, Haller, Kaiser, Maloney and Palermo. Time–2:51. Attendance–42,633.

GAME OF FRIDAY, OCTOBER 10, AT NEW YORK (N)

Kansas City	AB.	R.	H.	RBI.	PO.	A.	New York	AB.	R.	H.	RBI.	PO.	A.
Wilson, lf	5	1	2	0	2	0	Randolph, 2b	4	0	1	0	1	3
Washington, ss	4	1	2	0	1	3	Dent, ss	4	0	0	0	3	7
G. Brett, 3b	4	1	1	3	1	2	Watson, 1b	4	0	3	0	11	1
McRae, dh	4	0	2	0	0	0	Jackson, rf	3	1	1	0	2	0
Otis, cf	4	0	1	0	3	0	Soderholm, dh	2	0	0	0	0	0
Aikens, 1b	4	0	3	0	8	1	Gamble, ph-dh	1	1	1	0	0	0
Porter, c	3	0	0	0	4	0	Cerone, c	4	0	1	1	4	2
Hurdle, rf	2	0	0	0	1	0	Piniella, lf	2	0	0	0	4	0
Wathan, ph-rf	2	0	0	0	0	0	Spencer, ph	1	0	0	0	0	0
White, 2b	4	1	1	1	6	5	Lefebvre, lf	0	0	0	0	0	0
Splittorff, p	0	0	0	0	0	0	Rodriguez, 3b	2	0	1	0	1	0
Quisenberry, p	0	0	0	0	1	0	Nettles, ph-3b	2	0	0	0	1	1
							Brown, cf	4	0	0	0	1	0
							John, p	0	0	0	0	0	1
							Gossage, p	0	0	0	0	0	0
							Underwood, p	0	0	0	0	0	1
Totals	36	4	12	4	27	12	Totals	33	2	8	1	27	16

Kansas City			0	0	0		0	1	0		3	0	0 – 4
New York			0	0	0		0	0	2		0	0	0 – 2

Kansas City	IP.	H.	R.	ER.	BB.	SO.
Splittorff	5⅓	5	1	1	2	3
Quisenberry (Winner)	3⅔	3	1	0	2	1

New York	IP.	H.	R.	ER.	BB.	SO.
John	6⅔	8	2	2	1	3
Gossage (Loser)	⅓	3	2	2	0	0
Underwood	2	1	0	0	0	1

Game-winning RBI–G. Brett.

Error–White. Double plays–Kansas City 2, New York 1. Left on bases–Kansas City 6, New York 8. Two-base hits–Watson, Jackson, Wilson. Three-base hit–Watson. Home runs–White, G. Brett. Wild pitch–John. Balk–Splittorff. Umpires–McCoy, Haller, Kaiser, Maloney, Palermo and Brinkman. Time–2:59. Attendance–56,588.

KANSAS CITY ROYALS' BATTING AND FIELDING AVERAGES

Player—Position	G.	AB.	R.	H.	TB.	2B.	3B.	HR.	RBI.	B.A.	PO.	A.	E.	F.A.
White, 2b	3	11	3	6	10	1	0	1	3	.545	9	10	1	.950
Washington, ss	3	11	1	4	5	1	0	0	1	.364	5	7	0	1.000
Aikens, 1b	3	11	0	4	4	0	0	0	2	.364	22	1	0	1.000
Otis, cf	3	12	2	4	5	1	0	0	0	.333	11	0	0	1.000
Wilson, lf	3	13	2	4	8	2	1	0	4	.308	6	1	0	1.000
G. Brett, 3b	3	11	3	3	10	1	0	2	4	.273	2	7	0	1.000
McRae, dh	3	10	0	2	2	0	0	0	0	.200	0	0	0	.000
Porter, c	3	10	2	1	1	0	0	0	0	.100	17	1	0	1.000
Quisenberry, p	2	0	0	0	0	0	0	0	0	.000	1	0	0	1.000
Gura, p	1	0	0	0	0	0	0	0	0	.000	0	1	0	1.000
LaCock, 1b	1	0	0	0	0	0	0	0	0	.000	0	0	0	.000
Leonard, p	1	0	0	0	0	0	0	0	0	.000	0	0	0	.000
Splittorff, p	1	0	0	0	0	0	0	0	0	.000	0	1	0	1.000
Hurdle, rf	3	2	0	0	0	0	0	0	0	.000	1	0	0	1.000
Wathan, rf-ph	3	6	1	0	0	0	0	0	0	.000	7	0	0	1.000
Totals	3	97	14	28	45	6	1	3	14	.289	81	29	1	.991

NEW YORK YANKEES' BATTING AND FIELDING AVERAGES

Player—Position	G.	AB.	R.	H.	TB.	2B.	3B.	HR.	RBI.	B.A.	PO.	A.	E.	F.A.
Watson, 1b	3	12	0	6	11	3	1	0	0	.500	28	5	1	.971
Randolph, 2b	3	13	0	5	7	2	0	0	1	.385	2	9	0	1.000
Cerone, c	3	12	1	4	7	0	0	1	2	.333	14	4	0	1.000
Rodriguez, 3b	2	6	0	2	3	1	0	0	0	.333	2	2	0	1.000
Jackson, rf	3	11	1	3	4	1	0	0	0	.273	5	0	0	1.000
Piniella, lf	2	5	1	1	4	0	0	1	1	.200	5	0	0	1.000
Gamble, lf-ph-dh	2	5	1	1	1	0	0	0	0	.200	1	0	0	1.000
Dent, ss	3	11	0	2	2	0	0	0	0	.182	9	12	0	1.000
Nettles, 3b-ph	2	6	1	1	4	0	0	1	1	.167	0	2	0	1.000
Soderholm, dh	2	6	0	1	1	0	0	0	0	.167	0	0	0	.000
Underwood, p	2	0	0	0	0	0	0	0	0	.000	0	2	0	1.000
Davis, p	1	0	0	0	0	0	0	0	0	.000	0	2	0	1.000
Gossage, p	1	0	0	0	0	0	0	0	0	.000	0	0	0	.000
Guidry, p	1	0	0	0	0	0	0	0	0	.000	0	1	0	1.000
John, p	1	0	0	0	0	0	0	0	0	.000	0	1	0	1.000
Lefebvre, lf	1	0	0	0	0	0	0	0	0	.000	0	0	0	.000
May, p	1	0	0	0	0	0	0	0	0	.000	2	2	0	1.000
Spencer, ph	1	1	0	0	0	0	0	0	0	.000	0	0	0	.000
Murcer, dh	1	4	0	0	0	0	0	0	0	.000	0	0	0	.000
Brown, cf	3	10	1	0	0	0	0	0	0	.000	7	0	0	1.000
Totals	3	102	6	26	44	7	1	3	5	.255	75	42	1	.992

KANSAS CITY ROYALS' PITCHING RECORDS

Pitcher	G.	GS.	CG.	IP.	H.	R.	ER.	BB.	SO.	HB.	WP.	W.	L.	Pct.	ERA.
Quisenberry	2	0	0	4⅔	4	1	0	2	1	0	0	1	0	1.000	0.00
Splittorff	1	1	0	5⅓	5	1	1	2	3	0	0	0	0	.000	1.69
Gura	1	1	1	9	10	2	2	1	4	0	0	1	0	1.000	2.00
Leonard	1	1	0	8	7	2	2	1	8	0	0	1	0	1.000	2.25
Totals	3	3	1	27	26	6	5	6	16	0	0	3	0	1.000	1.67

No shutouts. Save—Quisenberry.

NEW YORK YANKEES' PITCHING RECORDS

Pitcher	G.	GS.	CG.	IP.	H.	R.	ER.	BB.	SO.	HB.	WP.	W.	L.	Pct.	ERA.
Underwood	2	0	0	3	3	2	0	0	3	0	0	0	0	.000	0.00
Davis	1	0	0	4	3	1	1	1	3	1	0	0	0	.000	2.25
John	1	1	0	6⅔	8	2	2	1	3	0	1	0	0	.000	2.70
May	1	1	1	8	6	3	3	3	4	0	0	0	1	.000	3.38
Guidry	1	1	0	3	5	4	4	4	2	0	1	0	1	.000	12.00
Gossage	1	0	0	⅓	3	2	2	0	0	0	0	0	1	.000	54.00
Totals	3	3	1	25	28	14	12	9	15	1	2	0	3	.000	4.32

No shutouts or saves.

COMPOSITE SCORE BY INNINGS

Kansas City	0	2	5	0	1	0	4	2	0 – 14
New York	0	2	0	0	2	2	0	0	0 – 6

Game-winning RBIs—Aikens, Wilson, G. Brett.
Sacrifice hit—Dent.
Sacrifice flies—None.
Stolen bases—Otis 2, White.
Caught stealing—McRae 3, Washington, Otis.
Double plays—Randolph, Dent and Watson; White, Washington and Aikens; Dent, Randolph and Watson; Splittorff, White and Aikens; Washington and White.
Left on bases—Kansas City 7, 5, 6–18; New York 9, 5, 8–22.
Hit by pitcher—By Davis (McRae).
Passed balls—None.
Balk—Splittorff.
Time of games—First game, 3:00; second game, 2:51; third game, 2:59.
Attendance—First game, 42,598; second game, 42,633; third game, 56,588.
Umpires—Palermo, Brinkman, McCoy, Haller, Kaiser and Maloney.
Official scorers—Red Foley, New York Daily News; Don Pfannenstiel, Independence (Mo.) Examiner.

NATIONAL LEAGUE
Championship Series of 1980

	W.	L.	Pct.
Philadelphia (East)..	3	2	.600
Houston (West)	2	3	.400

The 1980 National League Championship Series had everything anyone could ever hope for. It had controversy. It had rallies. It had high-drama. It had more rallies. It had heartbreak. Most of all, it had two teams that wouldn't give up.

Not until Garry Maddox cradled that final fly ball by Enos Cabell in the 10th inning of the fifth game October 12 did the Philadelphia Phillies finally gain an edge for an 8-7 victory and a three games to two elimination of the West Division champion Houston Astros.

The Phillies rebounded from a 1-0 deficit in the first game when Greg Luzinski slammed a two-run homer to left field in the seventh inning and Greg Gross plated Maddox with a pinch-single in the eighth for a 3-1 verdict.

The Phils were on the threshold of a second consecutive victory at Veterans Stadium after Steve Carlton and Tug McGraw had collaborated in the opener. However, Bake McBride held up at third base on a single by Lonnie Smith, loading the bases, in a controversial play with the score tied, 3-3, in the ninth inning. Third base coach Lee Elia held up his arms to stop McBride and then motioned feverishly to send McBride when Smith's looper fell safely in right field. Houston reliever Frank LaCorte slammed the door by fanning Manny Trillo and getting Maddox on a foul pop.

The Astros rallied with a four-run outburst in the 10th inning to take a 7-4 decision, sending the series to Houston tied at one game apiece.

Terry Puhl opened the 10th with a single. After a sacrifice by Cabell and an intentional walk to Joe Morgan, Puhl scored on a single by Jose Cruz. Rafael Landestoy, running for Morgan, beat a throw home on a grounder to shortstop Larry Bowa by Cesar Cedeno before Dave Bergman capped the outburst with a two-run triple.

Joe Niekro, Houston's two-time 20-game winner, and injury-plagued Larry Christenson of the Phillies spun zeroes at one another in Game 3. The Phils fired 10 blanks at Niekro while Christenson was shutting out the Astros for six frames and McGraw for three more.

In the 11th, Morgan crashed a leadoff triple and Cruz and Art Howe were walked intentionally, before Dennis Walling's sacrifice fly scored pinch-runner Landestoy and made a winner of Dave Smith for one inning of work.

The victory was costly to the Astros, however, as outfielder Cedeno suffered a compound dislocation of the right ankle when he stepped awkwardly on first base while trying to beat a double-play relay in the sixth inning.

Game 4 abounded in controversy, was protested by both clubs and ended up in a 5-3, 10-inning triumph by the Phillies to tie the series at two games each.

McBride and Trillo started the confusion in the fourth inning with singles off Vern Ruhle. When Maddox stroked a soft liner back to the mound controversy turned to chaos.

Ruhle fielded the ball and threw to first base for an apparent double play. Philadelphia players streamed from the dugout, insisting that Ruhle had trapped the ball. Houston players maintained the ball had been caught. Slow-motion replays from numerous angles were inconclusive.

During the confusion, Houston first baseman Howe strolled over to second base and claimed a triple play.

Plate umpire Doug Harvey, with nearly two decades of National League experience, reset the play after conferring with fellow umpires and meeting with N.L. President Chub Feeney, who was in a first base box seat.

"Maddox hits the ball and steps in front of me," Harvey began. "There are

Houston catcher Luis Pujols reflects about what might have been after the Astros had lost in heart-breaking fashion to the Phillies in the 1980 N.L. Championship Series.

runners out there wondering if it's a catch or a trap. My first reaction is no catch and I put my hands down to signal fair ball in play. But I see the pitcher throw to first as though he's going for the double play.

"So I ask for help and they tell me the pitcher caught the ball, and that's good enough for me."

Inasmuch as time had been called before Howe tagged second base, Harvey disallowed the putout, returned McBride to second and ordered the game to go on. The rhubarb consumed 20 minutes and prompted an official protest by each club before the Phillies were retired without any scoring.

After the Astros had taken a 2-0 lead with single runs in the fourth and fifth, there was another argument in their half of the sixth when Gary Woods was called out for leaving base too soon while attempting to score on a fly ball by Luis Pujols.

The Phillies took a 3-2 lead in the eighth when Gross, pinch-hitting for Carlton, singled and scored on singles by Smith and Pete Rose. Schmidt's infield single scored Smith and Trillo followed with a sacrifice fly.

After the Astros once again tied the score in the ninth on a run-scoring single by Puhl, Rose singled and raced home bowling over catcher Bruce Bochy, when pinch-hitter Luzinski doubled. Trillo also doubled, driving in Luzinski.

Bochy was in the game only because Alan Ashby suffered a rib separation in the West Division playoff with Los Angeles and Pujols was sidelined with an ankle injury when struck by an eighth-inning foul tip.

The topsy-turvy fifth game saw the Astros' 5-2 lead evaporate into a 7-5 deficit before they staged a rally in the eighth inning to force extra innings.

GAME OF TUESDAY, OCTOBER 7, AT PHILADELPHIA (N)

Houston	AB.	R.	H.	RBI.	PO.	A.	Philadelphia	AB.	R.	H.	RBI.	PO.	A.
Landestoy, 2b	5	0	0	0	1	2	Rose, 1b	4	1	2	0	11	1
Cabell, 3b	4	0	1	0	0	2	McBride, rf	4	0	1	0	2	0
Cruz, lf	3	1	1	0	5	0	Schmidt, 3b	3	0	0	0	0	4
Cedeno, cf	3	0	1	0	1	0	Luzinski, lf	4	1	1	2	0	0
Howe, 1b	4	0	0	0	8	1	Unser, lf	0	0	0	0	1	0
Woods, rf	4	0	2	1	1	0	Trillo, 2b	4	0	0	0	5	8
Pujols, c	3	0	0	0	5	1	Maddox, cf	3	1	1	0	3	0
Bergman, pr	0	0	0	0	0	0	Bowa, ss	2	0	1	0	1	1
Reynolds, ss	2	0	0	0	2	4	Boone, c	3	0	1	0	4	1
Puhl, ph	1	0	0	0	0	0	Carlton, p	2	0	0	0	0	0
Forsch, p	2	0	2	0	1	0	Gross, ph	1	0	1	1	0	0
Leonard, ph	1	0	0	0	0	0	McGraw, p	0	0	0	0	0	0
Totals	32	1	7	1	24	10	Totals	30	3	8	3	27	15

Houston .... 0 0 1 0 0 0 0 0 0 – 1
Philadelphia .... 0 0 0 0 0 2 1 0 x – 3

Houston	IP.	H.	R.	ER.	BB.	SO.
Forsch (Loser)	8	8	3	3	1	5

Philadelphia	IP.	H.	R.	ER.	BB.	SO.
Carlton (Winner)	7	7	1	1	3	3
McGraw (Save)	2	0	0	0	1	1

Game-winning RBI—Luzinski.
Error—Bowa. Double play—Philadelphia 1. Left on bases—Houston 9, Philadelphia 5. Home run—Luzinski. Stolen bases—McBride, Maddox. Sacrifice hits—Forsch, Bowa. Umpires—Engel, Tata, Froemming, Harvey, Vargo and Crawford. Time—2:35. Attendance—65,277.

GAME OF WEDNESDAY, OCTOBER 8, AT PHILADELPHIA (N)

Houston	AB.	R.	H.	RBI.	PO.	A.	Philadelphia	AB.	R.	H.	RBI.	PO.	A.
Puhl, rf	5	1	3	2	3	0	Rose, 1b	4	0	2	0	14	2
Cabell, 3b	4	0	0	0	0	0	McBride, rf	5	0	1	0	2	0
Morgan, 2b	2	1	1	0	4	0	Schmidt, 3b	6	1	2	0	0	3
Landestoy, pr-2b	0	1	0	0	0	1	Luzinski, lf	4	1	2	1	3	0
Cruz, lf	4	1	2	2	4	0	L. Smith, pr-lf	1	1	0	0	0	0
Cedeno, cf	5	1	1	1	3	0	Trillo, 2b	3	0	1	0	2	7
Howe, 1b	4	0	0	0	5	1	Maddox, cf	5	0	2	2	2	0
Bergman, 1b	1	0	1	2	1	1	Bowa, ss	4	1	2	0	0	4
Ashby, c	5	0	0	0	9	2	Boone, c	4	0	1	0	5	0
Reynolds, ss	3	1	0	0	1	1	Ruthven, p	2	0	0	0	2	0
Ryan, p	1	1	0	0	0	2	Gross, ph	0	0	0	0	0	0
Sambito, p	0	0	0	0	0	0	McGraw, p	0	0	0	0	0	0
D. Smith, p	0	0	0	0	0	0	Unser, ph	1	0	0	0	0	0
Leonard, ph	1	0	0	0	0	0	Reed, p	0	0	0	0	0	0
LaCorte, p	1	0	0	0	0	0	Saucier, p	0	0	0	0	0	0
Andujar, p	0	0	0	0	0	0	G. Vukovich, ph	1	0	0	0	0	0
Totals	36	7	8	7	30	8	Totals	40	4	14	3	30	16

Houston	0	0	1	0	0	0	1	1	0	4 – 7
Philadelphia	0	0	0	2	0	0	0	1	0	1 – 4

Houston	IP.	H.	R.	ER.	BB.	SO.
Ryan	6⅓	8	2	2	1	6
Sambito	⅓	0	0	0	1	1
D. Smith	1⅓	2	1	1	1	2
LaCorte (Winner)	1*	4	1	0	1	1
Andujar (Save)	1	0	0	0	1	0

Philadelphia	IP.	H.	R.	ER.	BB.	SO.
Ruthven	7	3	2	2	5	4
McGraw	1	2	1	1	0	0
Reed (Loser)	1⅓	2	4	4	1	1
Saucier	⅔	1	0	0	1	0

*Pitched to two batters in tenth.

Game-winning RBI–Cruz.

Errors–Schmidt, McBride, Reynolds. Double play–Philadelphia 1. Left on bases–Houston 8, Philadelphia 14. Two-base hits–Schmidt, Luzinski, Puhl, Morgan. Three-base hit–Bergman. Sacrifice hits–Trillo 2, Ryan, Gross, Cabell. Umpires–Tata, Froemming, Harvey, Vargo, Crawford and Engel. Time–3:34. Attendance–65,476.

GAME OF FRIDAY, OCTOBER 10, AT HOUSTON

Philadelphia	AB.	R.	H.	RBI.	PO.	A.	Houston	AB.	R.	H.	RBI.	PO.	A.
Rose, 1b	5	0	1	0	13	0	Puhl, rf-cf	4	0	2	0	5	0
McBride, rf	5	0	1	0	1	0	Cabell, 3b	4	0	2	0	1	4
Schmidt, 3b	5	0	1	0	2	0	Morgan, 2b	4	0	1	0	0	2
Luzinski, lf	5	0	0	0	2	0	Landestoy, pr	0	1	0	0	0	0
Trillo, 2b	5	0	2	0	4	5	Cruz, lf	2	0	1	0	7	0
Maddox, cf	4	0	2	0	6	0	Cedeno, cf	3	0	0	0	1	0
Bowa, ss	3	0	0	0	2	4	Bergman, 1b	1	0	0	0	5	0
Boone, c	4	0	0	0	3	1	Howe, ph	0	0	0	0	0	0
Unser, ph	1	0	0	0	0	0	Walling, 1b-rf	3	0	0	1	5	0
Moreland, c	0	0	0	0	0	0	Pujols, c	3	0	0	0	5	0
Christenson, p	2	0	0	0	0	1	Reynolds, ss	3	0	0	0	3	5
G. Vukovich, ph	1	0	0	0	0	0	Niekro, p	3	0	0	0	1	0
Noles, p	0	0	0	0	0	1	Woods, ph	1	0	0	0	0	0
McGraw, p	1	0	0	0	0	0	Smith, p	0	0	0	0	0	0
Totals	41	0	7	0	31	14	Totals	31	1	6	1	33	11

Philadelphia	0	0	0	0	0	0	0	0	0	0	0 – 0
Houston	0	0	0	0	0	0	0	0	0	0	1 – 1

One out when winning run scored.

Philadelphia	IP.	H.	R.	ER.	BB.	SO.
Christenson	6	3	0	0	4	2
Noles	1⅓	1	0	0	1	0
McGraw (Loser)	3	2	1	1	3	1

Houston	IP.	H.	R.	ER.	BB.	SO.
Niekro	10	6	0	0	1	2
Smith (Winner)	1	1	0	0	1	2

Game-winning RBI–Walling.

Errors–Christenson, Bergman. Double plays–Philadelphia 2. Left on bases–Philadelphia 11, Houston 10. Two-base hits–Puhl, Trillo, Maddox. Three-base hits–Cruz, Morgan. Stolen bases–Schmidt, Maddox. Sacrifice hits–Reynolds, Cabell. Sacrifice fly–Walling. Hit by pitch–By Niekro (Maddox). Passed ball-Pujols. Umpires–Froemming, Harvey, Vargo, Crawford, Engel and Tata. Time–3:22. Attendance–44,443.

GAME OF SATURDAY, OCTOBER 11, AT HOUSTON

Philadelphia	AB.	R.	H.	RBI.	PO.	A.	Houston	AB.	R.	H.	RBI.	PO.	A.
L. Smith, lf	4	1	2	0	2	1	Puhl, cf	3	0	1	1	2	0
Unser, lf-rf	1	0	0	0	1	0	Cabell, 3b	4	1	1	0	0	2
Rose, 1b	4	2	2	1	6	2	Morgan, 2b	3	0	0	0	1	4
Schmidt, 3b	5	0	2	1	3	5	Woods, rf	2	0	0	0	0	0
McBride, rf	4	0	2	0	3	2	Walling, ph	1	0	0	0	0	0
Luzinski, ph	1	1	1	1	0	0	Leonard, rf	1	0	0	0	2	1
McGraw, p	0	0	0	0	0	0	Howe, 1b	3	0	1	1	12	1
Trillo, 2b	4	0	2	2	3	0	Cruz, lf	3	0	0	0	2	0
Maddox, cf	4	0	0	0	6	0	Pujols, c	3	1	1	0	3	0
Bowa, ss	5	0	1	0	0	0	Bochy, c	1	0	0	0	5	1
Boone, c	4	0	0	0	4	1	Landestoy, ss	3	1	1	1	2	4
Carlton, p	2	0	0	0	0	1	Ruhle, p	3	0	0	0	1	1
Noles, p	0	0	0	0	1	1	D. Smith, p	0	0	0	0	0	0
Saucier, p	0	0	0	0	0	0	Sambito, p	0	0	0	0	0	0
Reed, p	0	0	0	0	1	0	Totals	30	3	5	3	30	14
Gross, ph	1	1	1	0	0	0							
Brusstar, p	1	0	0	0	0	0							
G. Vukovich, lf	0	0	0	0	0	0							
Totals	40	5	13	5	30	13							

Philadelphia	0	0	0	0	0	0	0	3	0	2 – 5	
Houston	0	0	0	1	1	0	0	0	1	0 – 3	

Philadelphia	IP.	H.	R.	ER.	BB.	SO.
Carlton	5⅓	4	2	2	5	3
Noles	1⅓	0	0	0	2	0
Saucier	0*	0	0	0	1	0
Reed	⅓	0	0	0	0	0
Brusstar (Winner)	2	1	1	1	1	0
McGraw (Save)	1	0	0	0	0	1

Houston	IP.	H.	R.	ER.	BB.	SO.
Ruhle	7†	8	3	3	1	3
D. Smith	0‡	1	0	0	0	0
Sambito (Loser)	3	4	2	2	1	5

*Pitched to one batter in seventh.
†Pitched to three batters in eighth.
‡Pitched to one batter in eighth.

Game-winning RBI−Luzinski.
Error−Landestoy. Double plays−Philadelphia 3, Houston 2. Left on bases−Philadelphia 8, Houston 8. Two-base hits−Howe, Cabell, Luzinski, Trillo. Three-base hit−Pujols. Stolen bases−McBride, L. Smith, Landestoy, Woods, Puhl, Bowa. Sacrifice hit−Sambito. Sacrifice flies−Howe, Trillo. Umpires−Harvey, Vargo, Crawford, Engel, Tata and Froemming. Time−3:55. Attendance−44,952.

GAME OF SUNDAY, OCTOBER 12, AT HOUSTON (N)

Philadelphia	AB.	R.	H.	RBI.	PO.	A.	Houston	AB.	R.	H.	RBI.	PO.	A.
Rose, 1b	3	0	1	1	9	2	Puhl, cf	6	3	4	0	3	0
McBride, rf	3	0	0	0	3	1	Cabell, 3b	5	0	1	0	0	1
Moreland, ph	1	0	0	1	0	0	Morgan, 2b	4	0	0	0	4	2
Aviles, pr	0	1	0	0	0	0	Landestoy, 2b	1	0	1	1	2	1
McGraw, p	0	0	0	0	0	0	Cruz, lf	3	1	2	2	1	0
G. Vukovich, ph	1	0	0	0	0	0	Walling, rf	5	2	1	1	1	0
Ruthven, p	0	0	0	0	0	0	LaCorte, p	0	0	0	0	0	0
Schmidt, 3b	5	0	0	0	0	3	Howe, 1b	4	0	2	1	4	0
Luzinski, lf	3	0	1	0	0	0	Bergman, pr-1b	1	0	0	0	2	1
Smith, pr	0	0	0	0	0	0	Pujols, c	1	0	0	0	8	1
Christenson, p	0	0	0	0	0	0	Ashby, ph-c	3	0	1	1	2	0
Reed, p	0	0	0	0	0	0	Reynolds, ss	5	1	2	0	2	2
Unser, ph-rf	2	2	2	1	0	0	Ryan, p	3	0	0	0	1	1
Trillo, 2b	5	1	3	2	4	5	Sambito, p	0	0	0	0	0	0
Maddox, cf	4	1	1	1	6	0	Forsch, p	0	0	0	0	0	0
Bowa, ss	5	1	2	0	1	2	Woods, ph-rf	1	0	0	0	0	0
Boone, c	3	1	2	2	6	0	Heep, ph	1	0	0	0	0	0
Bystrom, p	2	0	0	0	0	0							
Brusstar, p	0	0	0	0	0	0	Totals	43	7	14	6	30	9
Gross, lf	2	1	1	0	1	0							
Totals	39	8	13	8	30	13							

Philadelphia	0	2	0	0	0	0	0	5	0	1 − 8
Houston	1	0	0	0	0	1	3	2	0	0 − 7

Philadelphia	IP.	H.	R.	ER.	BB.	SO.
Bystrom	5⅓	7	2	1	2	1
Brusstar	⅔	0	0	0	0	0
Christenson	⅔	2	3	3	1	0
Reed	⅓	1	0	0	0	0
McGraw	1	4	2	2	0	2
Ruthven (Winner)	2	0	0	0	0	0

Houston	IP.	H.	R.	ER.	BB.	SO.
Ryan	7*	8	6	6	2	8
Sambito	⅓	0	0	0	0	0
Forsch	⅔	2	1	1	0	1
LaCorte (Loser)	2	3	1	1	1	1

*Pitched to four batters in eighth.

Game-winning RBI−Maddox.
Errors−Trillo, Luzinski. Double plays−Houston 2. Left on bases−Philadelphia 5, Houston 10. Two-base hits−Cruz, Reynolds, Unser, Maddox. Three-base hits−Howe, Trillo. Stolen base−Puhl. Sacrifice hits−Cabell, Boone. Wild pitch−Christenson. Umpires−Vargo, Crawford, Engel, Tata, Froemming and Harvey. Time−3:38. Attendance−44,802.

PHILADELPHIA PHILLIES' BATTING AND FIELDING AVERAGES

Player−Position	G.	AB.	R.	H.	TB.	2B.	3B.	HR.	RBI.	B.A.	PO.	A.	E.	F.A.
Gross, ph-lf	4	4	2	3	3	0	0	0	1	.750	1	0	0	1.000
L. Smith, pr-lf	3	5	2	3	3	0	0	0	0	.600	2	1	0	1.000
Rose, 1b	5	20	3	8	8	0	0	0	2	.400	53	7	0	1.000
Unser, lf-ph-rf	5	5	2	2	3	1	0	0	1	.400	2	0	0	1.000
Trillo, 2b	5	21	1	8	12	2	1	0	4	.381	18	25	1	.977
Bowa, ss	5	19	2	6	6	0	0	0	0	.316	4	11	1	.938
Maddox, cf	5	20	2	6	8	2	0	0	3	.300	23	0	0	1.000
Luzinski, lf-ph	5	17	3	5	10	2	0	1	4	.294	5	0	1	.833
McBride, rf	5	21	0	5	5	0	0	0	0	.238	11	3	1	.933
Boone, c	5	18	1	4	4	0	0	0	2	.222	22	3	0	1.000
Schmidt, 3b	5	24	1	5	6	1	0	0	1	.208	3	17	1	.952
Reed, p	3	0	0	0	0	0	0	0	0	.000	1	0	0	1.000
Noles, p	2	0	0	0	0	0	0	0	0	.000	1	2	0	1.000
Saucier, p	2	0	0	0	0	0	0	0	0	.000	0	0	0	.000
Aviles, pr	1	0	1	0	0	0	0	0	0	.000	0	0	0	.000

Player–Position	G.	AB.	R.	H.	TB.	2B.	3B.	HR.	RBI.	B.A.	PO.	A.	E.	F.A.
McGraw, p	5	1	0	0	0	0	0	0	0	.000	0	0	0	.000
Brusstar, p	2	1	0	0	0	0	0	0	0	.000	0	0	0	.000
Moreland, c-ph	2	1	0	0	0	0	0	0	1	.000	0	0	0	.000
Christenson, p	2	2	0	0	0	0	0	0	0	.000	0	1	1	.500
Ruthven, p	2	2	0	0	0	0	0	0	0	.000	2	0	0	1.000
Bystrom, p	1	2	0	0	0	0	0	0	0	.000	0	0	0	.000
G. Vukovich, ph-lf	4	3	0	0	0	0	0	0	0	.000	0	0	0	.000
Carlton, p	2	4	0	0	0	0	0	0	0	.000	0	1	0	1.000
Totals	5	190	20	55	68	8	1	1	19	.290	148	71	6	.973

HOUSTON ASTROS' BATTING AND FIELDING AVERAGES

Player–Position	G.	AB.	R.	H.	TB.	2B.	3B.	HR.	RBI.	B.A.	PO.	A.	E.	F.A.
Forsch, p	2	2	0	2	2	0	0	0	0	1.000	1	0	0	1.000
Puhl, ph-rf-cf	5	19	4	10	12	2	0	0	3	.526	13	0	0	1.000
Cruz, lf	5	15	3	6	9	1	1	0	4	.400	19	0	0	1.000
Bergman, pr-1b	4	3	0	1	3	0	1	0	2	.333	8	2	1	.909
Woods, rf-ph	4	8	0	2	2	0	0	0	1	.250	1	0	0	1.000
Cabell, 3b	5	21	1	5	6	1	0	0	0	.238	1	9	0	1.000
Landestoy, 2b-pr-ss	5	9	3	2	2	0	0	0	2	.222	5	8	1	.929
Howe, 1b-ph	5	15	0	3	6	1	1	0	2	.200	29	3	0	1.000
Cedeno, cf	3	11	1	2	2	0	0	0	1	.182	5	0	0	1.000
Morgan, 2b	4	13	1	2	5	1	1	0	0	.154	9	8	0	1.000
Reynolds, ss	4	13	2	2	3	1	0	0	0	.154	8	12	1	.952
Ashby, c-ph	2	8	0	1	1	0	0	0	1	.125	11	2	0	1.000
Walling, 1b-rf-ph	3	9	2	1	1	0	0	0	0	.111	6	0	0	1.000
Pujols, c	4	10	1	1	3	0	1	0	0	.100	21	2	0	1.000
Sambito, p	3	0	0	0	0	0	0	0	0	.000	0	0	0	.000
D. Smith, p	3	0	0	0	0	0	0	0	0	.000	0	0	0	.000
Andujar, p	1	0	0	0	0	0	0	0	0	.000	0	0	0	.000
LaCorte, p	2	1	0	0	0	0	0	0	0	.000	0	0	0	.000
Bochy, c	1	1	0	0	0	0	0	0	0	.000	5	1	0	1.000
Heep, ph	1	1	0	0	0	0	0	0	0	.000	0	0	0	.000
Leonard, ph-rf	3	3	0	0	0	0	0	0	0	.000	2	1	0	1.000
Niekro, p	1	3	0	0	0	0	0	0	0	.000	1	0	0	1.000
Ruhle, p	1	3	0	0	0	0	0	0	0	.000	1	1	0	1.000
Ryan, p	2	4	1	0	0	0	0	0	0	.000	1	3	0	1.000
Totals	5	172	19	40	57	7	5	0	18	.233	147	52	3	.985

PHILADELPHIA PHILLIES' PITCHING RECORDS

Pitcher	G.	GS.	CG.	IP.	H.	R.	ER.	BB.	SO.	HB.	WP.	W.	L.	Pct.	ERA.
Noles	2	0	0	2⅔	1	0	0	3	0	0	0	0	0	.000	0.00
Saucier	2	0	0	⅔	1	0	0	2	0	0	0	0	0	.000	0.00
Bystrom	1	1	0	5⅓	7	2	1	2	1	0	0	0	0	.000	1.69
Ruthven	2	1	0	9	3	2	2	5	4	0	0	1	0	1.000	2.00
Carlton	2	2	0	12⅓	11	3	3	8	6	0	0	1	0	1.000	2.19
Brusstar	2	0	0	2⅔	1	1	1	1	0	0	0	1	0	1.000	3.38
Christenson	2	1	0	6⅔	5	3	3	5	2	0	1	0	0	.000	4.05
McGraw	5	0	0	8	8	4	4	4	5	0	0	0	1	.000	4.50
Reed	3	0	0	2	3	4	4	1	1	0	0	0	1	.000	18.00
Totals	5	5	0	49⅓	40	19	18	31	19	0	1	3	2	.600	3.28

No shutouts. Saves–McGraw 2.

HOUSTON ASTROS' PITCHING RECORDS

Pitcher	G.	GS.	CG.	IP.	H.	R.	ER.	BB.	SO.	HB.	WP.	W.	L.	Pct.	ERA.
Niekro	1	1	0	10	6	0	0	1	2	1	0	0	0	.000	0.00
Andujar	1	0	0	1	0	0	0	1	0	0	0	0	0	.000	0.00
LaCorte	2	0	0	3	7	2	1	2	2	0	0	1	1	.500	3.00
Ruhle	1	1	0	7	8	3	3	1	3	0	0	0	0	.000	3.86
D. Smith	3	0	0	2⅓	4	1	1	2	4	0	0	1	0	1.000	3.86
Forsch	2	1	1	8⅔	10	4	4	1	6	0	0	1	0	.000	4.15
Sambito	3	0	0	3⅔	4	2	2	2	6	0	0	0	1	.000	4.91
Ryan	2	2	0	13⅓	16	8	8	3	14	0	0	0	0	.000	5.40
Totals	5	5	1	49	55	20	19	13	37	1	0	2	3	.400	3.49

Shutout–Niekro-D. Smith (combined). Save–Andujar.

COMPOSITE SCORE BY INNINGS

Philadelphia	0	2	0	2	0	2	1	9	0	4	0 – 20
Houston	1	0	2	1	1	1	4	3	1	4	1 – 19

Game-winning RBIs–Luzinski 2, Cruz, Walling, Maddox.
Sacrifice hits–Cabell 3, Trillo 2, Forsch, Bowa, Ryan, Gross, Reynolds, Sambito, Boone.
Sacrifice flies–Walling, Howe, Trillo.
Stolen bases–Maddox 2, McBride 2, Puhl 2, Schmidt, L. Smith, Landestoy, Woods, Bowa.
Caught stealing–Rose 2, Maddox, Cabell.
Double plays–Bowa, Trillo and Rose 3; Trillo, Bowa and Rose; Ruhle and Howe; Leonard, Bochy and Morgan; L. Smith and Schmidt; McBride, Boone, Noles and Schmidt; McBride and Rose; Reynolds, Morgan and Howe; Cabell, Morgan and Howe.
Left on bases–Philadelphia 5, 14, 11, 8, 5–43; Houston–9, 8, 10, 8, 10–45.
Hit by pitcher–By Niekro (Maddox).
Passed ball–Pujols.
Balks–None.

Time of games—First game, 2:35; second game, 3:34; third game, 3:22; fourth game, 3:55; fifth game, 3:38.
Attendance—First game, 65,277; second game, 65,476; third game, 44,443; fourth game, 44,952; fifth game, 44,802.

Umpires—Engel, Tata, Froemming, Harvey, Vargo and Crawford.

Official scorers—John Black, Rosenberg (Tex.) Herald-Coaster; Paul Giordano, Bucks County (Pa.) Courier; Ivy McLemore, Houston Post.

AMERICAN LEAGUE
Championship Series of 1981

	W.	L.	Pct.
New York (East)	3	0	1.000
Oakland (West)	0	3	.000

While everyone was concentrating on the war of words between Billy Martin and George Steinbrenner as the Oakland A's and New York Yankees prepared to square off in the American League Championship Series, Graig Nettles quietly went about his business.

The 37-year-old Nettles started the series with a three-run double, keying the Yankees' 3-1 victory in Game 1. He went 4-for-4, including a three-run homer, to lead the Yanks in a 13-3 rout in Game 2. Then he ended the series the way he started it—with a three-run double that climaxed a 4-0 triumph and a three-game Yankee sweep.

"This series was a victory for the veterans," said Nettles. He added that it was an inside joke. But everyone knew Steinbrenner had issued a win-or-else ultimatum to the club during the A.L. East Division Series against Milwaukee. The "or else" meant that the veteran New York club would be broken up.

Nettles' 6-for-12 performance with a Championship Series-record nine RBIs was a dramatic contrast to his 1-for-17 batting mark in the division series against the Brewers.

"George made his big speech before we eliminated Milwaukee in the division series," Nettles said. "He said we'd better win or a lot of the veterans would be gone. We joked about it later."

Joke or no joke, the Yankees were laced with veteran players. Six of their eight starters were over 30 as were seven of their pitchers. Someone suggested in jest that the proud Yankee pinstripes had been erased and replaced by varicose veins.

Martin tried to pull a psyche job on the Yankees before the series, saying that his youthful A's were "awesome against lefthanders." He also pointed out that the Yanks had to use their top two pitchers, Ron Guidry and Dave Righetti, to finish off the Brewers.

"If I'm only the No. 3 man in the Yankee rotation, then we must be in pretty good shape because we still have No. 1 and No. 2 waiting to pitch," growled 35-year-old Tommy John after he, Ron Davis and Goose Gossage had stymied the A's on six hits in Game 1.

The victory was secured in the first inning when Larry Milbourne stroked a one-out single, Dave Winfield and Oscar Gamble walked, and Nettles drilled an 0-2 pitch into the left-center field gap to clear the bases.

The A's held a 3-1 lead in Game 2 behind Steve McCatty after they pushed across two runs in the top of the fourth inning. But the Yanks responded with seven runs in their half and rolled to a 13-3 win.

Nettles opened the inning with a single and later set another Championship Series record by becoming the first player to get two hits in one inning. After Bob Watson flied out, Cerone was hit by a pitch and Willie Randolph stroked an RBI single. Jerry Mumphrey walked to load the bases and Dave Beard replaced McCatty on the mound for Oakland. Milbourne tied the game with a single before Winfield provided a two-run double and Lou Piniella blasted a three-run homer.

George Frazier hurled 5⅔ innings of scoreless relief for the victory. The Yankees' 13 runs and 19 hits also were records.

Game 3 was a pitchers battle. Oakland's Matt Keough and Righetti of New York threw zeros for the first five innings. Then Randolph broke up the scoreless tie with a two-out homer in the sixth to back the five-hit pitching by Righetti, Davis and Gossage as the Yankees captured their 33rd A.L. pennant.

The Yanks had stranded nine runners in the first five innings before Randolph slugged his first homer since April 28 and his first in post-season play since 1977. New

York threw zeros for the first five innings. Then Randolph broke up the scoreless tie with a two-out homer in the sixth to back the five-hit pitching by Righetti, Davis and Gossage as the Yankees captured their 33rd A.L. pennant.

The Yanks had stranded nine runners in the first five innings before Randolph slugged his first homer since April 28 and his first in post-season play since 1977. New York put the game out of reach in the ninth on Nettles' three-run double.

The Yankees finished off the A's in three straight games, but to borrow a line from Yogi Berra, a coach for the Yankees, "It isn't over 'til it's over." Not when the Yanks are involved at least.

A team party was held at an Oakland restaurant the night of October 15. Friends and family were present and what was billed as a celebration turned into a shoving match when Nettles' family was allegedly mistreated by some of Reggie Jackson's friends. Before order could be restored, Nettles had popped Jackson with a right hand and Mr. October was seeing stars.

It was just another chapter in the wacky world of the Yankees.

GAME OF TUESDAY, OCTOBER 13, AT NEW YORK (N)

Oakland	AB.	R.	H.	RBI.	PO.	A.	New York	AB.	R.	H.	RBI.	PO.	A.
Henderson, lf	4	0	2	0	1	0	Mumphrey, cf	4	0	1	0	1	0
Murphy, cf	2	0	0	1	6	0	Milbourne, ss	4	1	3	0	2	4
Johnson, dh	3	0	0	0	0	0	Winfield, lf	3	0	0	0	2	0
Armas, rf	4	0	1	0	2	1	Jackson, rf	3	1	0	0	1	0
Klutts, 3b	3	0	2	0	1	1	Gamble, dh	2	1	0	0	0	0
Gross, ph-3b	1	0	0	0	0	0	Piniella, ph-dh	1	0	1	0	0	0
Moore, 1b	4	0	0	0	4	1	Nettles, 3b	3	0	1	3	0	2
Newman, c	2	0	0	0	4	1	Watson, 1b	3	0	1	0	8	0
Drumright, ph	1	0	0	0	0	0	Brown, pr	0	0	0	0	0	0
Heath, c	1	0	0	0	1	0	Revering, 1b	1	0	0	0	3	0
McKay, 2b	4	0	0	0	1	2	Cerone, c	2	0	0	0	6	0
Picciolo, ss	3	1	1	0	3	1	Randolph, 2b	3	0	0	0	4	7
Totals	32	1	6	1	23	7	Totals	29	3	7	3	27	13

Oakland	0	0	0	0	1	0	0	0	0 – 1
New York	3	0	0	0	0	0	0	0	x – 3

Oakland	IP.	H.	R.	ER.	BB.	SO.
Norris (Loser)	7⅓	6	3	3	2	4
Underwood	⅔	1	0	0	2	0

New York	IP.	H.	R.	ER.	BB.	SO.
John (Winner)	6	6	1	1	1	3
Davis	1⅓	0	0	0	2	3
Gossage (Save)	1⅔	0	0	0	0	0

Game-winning RBI–Nettles.

Errors–Nettles, Henderson. Double plays–New York 2. Left on base–Oakland 7, New York 7. Two-base hits–Nettles, Henderson 2. Stolen base–Jackson. Sacrifice hit–Cerone. Umpires–Bremigan, Goetz, Neudecker, Springstead, Merrill and Voltaggio. Time–2:52. Attendance–55,740.

GAME OF WEDNESDAY, OCTOBER 14, AT NEW YORK

Oakland	AB.	R.	H.	RBI.	PO.	A.	New York	AB.	R.	H.	RBI.	PO.	A.
Henderson, lf	5	0	1	1	3	0	Mumphrey, cf	5	2	4	0	3	0
Murphy, cf	5	0	2	0	3	0	Milbourne, ss	5	2	2	1	0	1
Moore, 1b	2	0	0	0	3	2	Robertson, ph-ss	1	0	0	0	2	1
Spencer, ph-1b	2	0	0	0	3	2	Winfield, lf	5	2	2	2	2	0
Armas, rf	4	0	0	0	1	1	Jackson, rf	1	0	0	1	0	0
Klutts, 3b	2	1	1	0	0	2	Piniella, rf	3	1	1	3	0	0
Gross, ph-3b	2	0	0	1	0	0	Brown, rf	1	1	1	0	0	0
Heath, c	4	1	2	0	2	0	Gamble, dh	3	1	1	1	0	0
McKay, 2b	4	0	2	1	2	3	Nettles, 3b	4	2	4	3	3	0
Bosetti, dh	1	1	1	0	0	0	Rodriguez, 3b	0	0	0	0	0	0
Drumright, ph-dh	2	0	0	0	0	0	Watson, 1b	4	0	1	1	2	0
Stanley, ss	3	0	1	1	4	2	Revering, 1b	1	0	1	0	3	1
Davis, ph	1	0	1	0	0	0	Cerone, c	4	1	0	0	10	2
							Foote, c	0	0	0	0	0	0
							Randolph, 2b	5	1	2	1	2	3
Totals	37	3	11	3	22	12	Totals	42	13	19	13	27	8

Oakland	0	0	1	2	0	0	0	0	0 – 3
New York	1	0	0	7	0	1	4	0	x – 13

Oakland	IP.	H.	R.	ER.	BB.	SO.
McCatty (Loser)	3⅓	6	5	5	2	2
Beard	⅔	5	3	3	0	0
Jones	2	2	1	1	1	0
Kingman	⅓	3	3	3	0	0
Owchinko	1⅔	3	1	1	0	0

New York	IP.	H.	R.	ER.	BB.	SO.
May	3⅓	6	3	3	0	5
Frazier (Winner)	5⅔	5	0	0	1	5

Game-winning RBI—Winfield.

Error—Klutts. Double plays—New York 2. Left on base—Oakland 8, New York 11. Two-base hits—Mumphrey, Bosetti, Winfield, Murphy. Three-base hit—Henderson. Home runs—Piniella, Nettles. Stolen base—Winfield. Sacrifice fly—Gamble. Hit by pitcher—By McCatty (Cerone), by Jones (Nettles). Wild pitch—Frazier. Passed ball—Cerone. Umpires—Goetz, Neudecker, Springstead, Merrill, Voltaggio and Bremigan. Time—3:08. Attendance—48,497.

GAME OF THURSDAY, OCTOBER 15, AT OAKLAND (N)

New York	AB.	R.	H.	RBI.	PO.	A.	Oakland	AB.	R.	H.	RBI.	PO.	A.
Mumphrey, cf	3	0	1	0	0	0	Henderson, lf	2	0	1	0	2	0
Milbourne, ss	4	1	1	0	0	2	Heath, lf	1	0	0	0	0	1
Winfield, lf	5	0	0	0	2	0	Murphy, cf	1	0	0	0	0	0
Murcer, dh	3	0	1	0	0	0	Bosetti, ph-cf	3	0	0	0	2	0
Piniella, ph-dh	1	1	1	0	0	0	Johnson, dh	3	0	0	0	0	0
Gamble, rf	1	0	0	0	4	0	Armas, rf	4	0	1	0	2	0
Foote, ph	1	0	1	0	0	0	Klutts, 3b	2	0	0	0	2	2
Brown, pr-rf	0	1	0	0	0	0	Gross, ph-3b	2	0	0	0	1	0
Nettles, 3b	5	0	1	3	1	2	Moore, 1b	2	0	2	0	6	0
Watson, 1b	5	0	1	0	7	0	Spencer, ph-1b	1	0	0	0	1	0
Cerone, c	4	0	1	0	7	0	McKay, 2b	3	0	1	0	4	1
Randolph, 2b	4	1	2	1	6	2	Newman, c	3	0	0	0	5	0
							Picciolo, ss	2	0	0	0	2	4
Totals	36	4	10	4	27	6	Drumright, ph	1	0	0	0	0	0
							Stanley, ss	0	0	0	0	0	0
							Totals	30	0	5	0	27	8

New York	0	0	0	0	0	1	0	0	3 – 4
Oakland	0	0	0	0	0	0	0	0	0 – 0

New York	IP.	H.	R.	ER.	BB.	SO.
Righetti (Winner)	6	4	0	0	2	4
Davis	2	0	0	0	0	1
Gossage	1	1	0	0	0	2

Oakland	IP.	H.	R.	ER.	BB.	SO.
Keough (Loser)	8⅓	7	2	1	6	4
Underwood	⅔	3	2	2	0	0

Game-winning RBI—Randolph.

Errors—Picciolo, McKay. Double plays—New York 2, Oakland 1. Left on base—New York 12, Oakland 5. Two-base hit—Nettles. Home run—Randolph. Stolen bases—Henderson 2. Sacrifice hit—Milbourne. Wild pitch—Keough. Umpires—Neudecker, Springstead, Merrill, Voltaggio, Bremigan and Goetz. Time—3:19. Attendance—47,302.

NEW YORK YANKEES' BATTING AND FIELDING AVERAGES

Player—Position	G.	AB.	R.	H.	TB.	2B.	3B.	HR.	RBI.	B.A.	PO.	A.	E.	F.A.
Brown, pr-rf	3	1	2	1	1	0	0	0	0	1.000	0	0	0	.000
Foote, c-ph	2	1	0	1	1	0	0	0	0	1.000	0	0	0	.000
Piniella, ph-dh-rf	3	5	2	3	6	0	0	1	3	.600	0	0	0	.000
Nettles, 3b	3	12	2	6	11	2	0	1	9	.500	4	4	1	.889
Mumphrey, cf	3	12	2	6	7	1	0	0	0	.500	4	0	0	1.000
Revering, 1b	2	2	0	1	1	0	0	0	0	.500	6	1	0	1.000
Milbourne, ss	3	13	4	6	6	0	0	0	1	.462	2	7	0	1.000
Randolph, 2b	3	12	2	4	7	0	0	1	2	.333	12	12	0	1.000
Murcer, dh	1	3	0	1	1	0	0	0	0	.333	0	0	0	.000
Watson, 1b	3	12	0	3	3	0	0	0	1	.250	17	0	0	1.000
Gamble, dh-rf	3	6	2	1	1	0	0	0	1	.167	4	0	0	1.000
Winfield, lf	3	13	2	2	3	1	0	0	2	.154	6	0	0	1.000
Cerone, c	3	10	1	1	1	0	0	0	0	.100	23	2	0	1.000
Davis, p	2	0	0	0	0	0	0	0	0	.000	0	0	0	.000
Gossage, p	2	0	0	0	0	0	0	0	0	.000	0	0	0	.000
Frazier, p	1	0	0	0	0	0	0	0	0	.000	0	2	0	1.000
John, p	1	0	0	0	0	0	0	0	0	.000	0	0	0	.000
May, p	1	0	0	0	0	0	0	0	0	.000	0	0	0	.000
Righetti, p	1	0	0	0	0	0	0	0	0	.000	0	1	0	1.000
Rodriguez, 3b	1	0	0	0	0	0	0	0	0	.000	0	0	0	.000
Robertson, ph-ss	1	1	0	0	0	0	0	0	0	.000	2	1	0	1.000
Jackson, rf	2	4	1	0	0	0	0	0	1	.000	1	0	0	1.000
Totals	3	107	20	36	49	4	0	3	20	.336	81	30	1	.991

OAKLAND ATHLETICS' BATTING AND FIELDING AVERAGES

Player—Position	G.	AB.	R.	H.	TB.	2B.	3B.	HR.	RBI.	B.A.	PO.	A.	E.	F.A.
Davis, ph	1	1	0	1	1	0	0	0	0	1.000	0	0	0	.000
Klutts, 3b	3	7	1	3	3	0	0	0	0	.429	3	5	1	.889
Henderson, lf	3	11	0	4	8	2	1	0	1	.364	6	0	1	.857
Heath, c-lf	3	6	1	2	2	0	0	0	0	.333	3	1	0	1.000
Stanley, ss	2	3	0	1	1	0	0	0	0	.333	4	2	0	1.000
McKay, 2b	3	11	0	3	3	0	0	0	1	.273	7	6	1	.929
Murphy, cf	3	8	0	2	3	1	0	0	1	.250	9	0	0	1.000
Moore, 1b	3	8	0	2	2	0	0	0	0	.250	13	3	0	1.000
Bosetti, dh-ph-cf	2	4	1	1	2	1	0	0	0	.250	2	0	0	1.000
Picciolo, ss	2	5	1	1	1	0	0	0	0	.200	5	5	1	.909
Armas, rf	3	12	0	2	2	0	0	0	0	.167	5	2	0	1.000

Player–Position	G.	AB.	R.	H.	TB.	2B.	3B.	HR.	RBI.	B.A.	PO.	A.	E.	F.A.
Underwood, p	2	0	0	0	0	0	0	0	0	.000	0	0	0	.000
Beard, p	1	0	0	0	0	0	0	0	0	.000	0	1	0	1.000
Jones, p	1	0	0	0	0	0	0	0	0	.000	1	0	0	1.000
Keough, p	1	0	0	0	0	0	0	0	0	.000	0	1	0	1.000
Kingman, p	1	0	0	0	0	0	0	0	0	.000	0	0	0	.000
McCatty, p	1	0	0	0	0	0	0	0	0	.000	1	1	0	1.000
Norris, p	1	0	0	0	0	0	0	0	0	.000	1	2	0	1.000
Owchinko, p	1	0	0	0	0	0	0	0	0	.000	0	1	0	1.000
Spencer, ph-1b	2	3	0	0	0	0	0	0	0	.000	4	2	0	1.000
Drumright, ph-dh	3	4	0	0	0	0	0	0	0	.000	0	0	0	.000
Gross, ph-3b	3	5	0	0	0	0	0	0	0	.000	2	0	0	1.000
Newman, c	2	5	0	0	0	0	0	0	0	.000	9	1	0	1.000
Johnson, dh	2	6	0	0	0	0	0	0	0	.000	0	0	0	.000
Totals	3	99	4	22	28	4	1	0	4	.222	75	33	4	.964

NEW YORK YANKEES' PITCHING RECORDS

Pitcher	G.	GS.	CG.	IP.	H.	R.	ER.	BB.	SO.	HB.	WP.	W.	L.	Pct.	ERA.
Righetti	1	1	0	6	4	0	0	2	4	0	1	1	0	1.000	0.00
Frazier	1	0	0	5⅔	5	0	0	1	5	0	1	1	0	1.000	0.00
Davis	2	0	0	3⅓	0	0	0	2	4	0	0	0	0*	.000	0.00
Gossage	2	0	0	2⅔	1	0	0	0	2	0	0	0	0	.000	0.00
John	1	1	0	6	6	1	1	1	3	0	0	1	0	1.000	1.50
May	1	1	0	3⅓	6	3	3	0	5	0	0	0	0	.000	8.10
Totals	3	3	0	27	22	4	4	6	23	0	1	3	0	1.000	1.33

Shutout—Righetti-Davis-Gossage (combined). Save—Gossage.

OAKLAND ATHLETICS' PITCHING RECORDS

Pitcher	G.	GS.	CG.	IP.	H.	R.	ER.	BB.	SO.	HB.	WP.	W.	L.	Pct.	ERA.
Keough	1	1	0	8⅓	7	2	1	6	4	0	1	0	1	.000	1.08
Norris	1	1	0	7⅓	6	3	3	2	4	0	0	0	1	.000	3.68
Jones	1	0	0	2	2	1	1	1	0	1	0	0	0	.000	4.50
Owchinko	1	0	0	1⅔	3	1	1	0	0	0	0	0	0	.000	5.40
McCatty	1	1	0	3⅓	6	5	5	2	2	1	0	0	1	.000	13.50
Underwood	2	0	0	1⅓	4	2	2	2	0	0	0	0	0	.000	13.50
Beard	1	0	0	⅔	5	3	3	0	0	0	0	0	0	.000	40.50
Kingman	1	0	0	⅓	3	3	3	0	0	0	0	0	0	.000	81.00
Totals	3	3	0	25	36	20	19	13	10	2	1	0	3	.000	6.84

No shutouts or saves.

COMPOSITE SCORE BY INNINGS

New York	4	0	0	7	0	2	4	0	3	— 20
Oakland	0	0	1	2	1	0	0	0	0	— 4

Game-winning RBIs—Nettles, Winfield, Randolph.
Sacrifice hits—Cerone, Milbourne.
Sacrifice fly—Gamble.
Stolen bases—Henderson 2, Jackson, Winfield.
Caught stealing—Mumphrey.
Double plays—Nettles, Randolph and Watson 2; Milbourne, Randolph and Watson 2; Frazier, Cerone and Watson; Revering, Robertson and Revering; Picciolo and Spencer.
Left on bases—New York 7, 11, 12—30; Oakland 7, 8, 5—20.
Hit by pitcher—By McCatty (Cerone), by Jones (Nettles).
Passed ball—Cerone.
Balks—None.
Time of games—First game, 2:52; second game, 3:08; third game, 3:19.
Attendance—First game, 55,740; second game, 48,497; third game, 47,302.
Umpires—Bremigan, Goetz, Neudecker, Springstead, Merrill and Voltaggio.
Official scorers—Red Foley, New York Daily News; Glenn Schwartz, San Francisco Examiner.

NATIONAL LEAGUE
Championship Series of 1981

	W.	L.	Pct.
Los Angeles (West)	3	2	.600
Montreal (East)	2	3	.400

"I don't know what to think. I'm just numb. I didn't make the pitch where I wanted. Mechanically, I made a mistake. I was called on to do the job and I came up one pitch short."

Montreal ace righthander Steve Rogers was being a little hard on himself October 19 after Rick Monday's two-out, ninth-inning home run had given the Los Angeles Dodgers a 2-1 victory over the Expos and a fifth-game triumph in the National League Championship Series.

"This wasn't supposed to be the last chapter of a book written for a sixth grader," Rogers said. "One pitch different and I could have written a fairy tale ending. Only this was reality."

There was a chill in the air. The rain that had postponed Game 5 one day earlier also had delayed the start of this game by some 26 minutes. Snow was even in the Montreal forecast.

But by mid-afternoon the sun had broken through and Montreal's Ray Burris and rookie sensation Fernando Valenzuela of the Dodgers had dueled on even terms for eight innings.

When Montreal Manager Jim Fanning summoned Rogers from his bullpen, he was calling on his late-season ace. Rogers had won four straight games and had permitted just two runs in 42 innings. But those statistics were compiled in starting roles.

The relief appearance was only the third in Rogers' nine-year major league career and the first since July 3, 1978. His fairy tale did not have a happy ending.

Lightning struck in the form of Monday. Monday's Monday Punch conjured visions of Bobby Thomson vs. Ralph Branca in 1951 and Chris Chambliss vs. Mark Littell in 1976.

"I knew I hit the ball well, but I couldn't see it because of the glare," Monday said. "I saw Andre Dawson racing to the wall in center field, so I thought he was going to catch it. When he didn't catch it, I knew it had cleared the fence. I couldn't control myself."

The 35-year-old Monday was finishing off the final year of a five-year contract with the Dodgers. The only questions he had been answering in recent weeks pertained to what he was going to do in the future—outside of baseball.

Monday batted .315 during the season, including a great month of September when he belted six home runs. He was on the bench when the Championship Series began. Though he started Game 4 in place of a slumping Ken Landreaux, Monday was 1-for-5 in the series. He had struck out four times—hardly the stats of a hero. But. . . .

After the Expos took a 1-0 lead in Game 5, it was Monday who started the Dodgers' fifth inning with a single and eventually came home on Valenzuela's groundout. Then, Monday's clout in the ninth turned the 40-degree chill into a warm wonderful day for Lasorda's Dodger Blue.

The victory kept the Dodgers' record in Championship Series play perfect—they've won all four N.L. series they've played, defeating Pittsburgh in 1974, Philadelphia in '77 and '78 and now the Expos. They had to do it the hard way, too, rebounding from a 2-1 deficit by winning two straight games on the road.

The series opened in warm, sunny Los Angeles, where the Dodgers had beaten the Expos in 18 of their previous 19 meetings. Game 1 of the Championship Series was no different.

The Dodgers were aided by the return of third baseman Ron Cey, while the Expos were boosted by the return of fleet left fielder Tim Raines, who broke a bone in his hand September 12 and was relegated to pinch-running activity.

Cey, who had missed 28 games with a broken bone in his left forearm, celebrated his return to action with a double into the right-field corner to drive home Steve Garvey for the game's first run in the second inning. Mike Scioscia's single moved Cey to third and he scored on Bill Russell's perfectly placed squeeze bunt.

With two out in the eighth, Cey singled and Pedro Guerrero and Scioscia hit back-to-back home runs to insure the verdict. The Dodgers turned four double plays behind the combined hurling of Burt Hooton, Bob Welch and Steve Howe.

Game 2 pitted Valenzuela for the Dodgers against Burris. Advantage Dodgers?

Burris proved differently, stopping the Dodgers, 3-0, on five singles to even the series at one game apiece. Burris, who said he tried to throw the ball by the Dodgers earlier in the season when he was shelled for six runs in one start and two in another, kept them off balance all night and was never in serious trouble.

With one out in the second inning, Larry Parrish and Jerry White reached Valenzuela for singles. Warren Cromartie followed with a double that scored Parrish. After Chris Speier walked to fill the bases and Burris struck out, Raines singled to left. Singles by Dawson and Gary Carter and Dusty Baker's throwing error provided the Expos with their third run in the sixth inning.

"From Burris to B-R-R-R!!!" read one headline as the series shifted to chilly Montreal for Game 3.

Rogers went the route on a seven-hitter, yielding only one run when the Dodgers put together singles by Baker and Garvey and a run-scoring groundout by Cey. The Dodgers' Jerry Reuss held a 1-0 lead going into the bottom of the sixth.

Dawson touched him for a seemingly harmless two-out single and the tall, blond lefthander walked Carter. Parrish tied the game with an RBI single and White turned from anonymous outfielder (.218 with three homers in '81) into a Canadian national hero when he sent one of Reuss' fastballs over the left-field wall for a 4-1 victory.

The script for Game 4 was similar. With the score knotted at 1-1 going into the eighth inning, it was Dodgers first baseman Garvey who stepped into the spotlight.

Baker opened the eighth with a single off Bill Gullickson and Garvey followed with a two-run homer. The Dodgers sent 10 men to the plate and added four runs in the ninth, coasting home with a 7-1 triumph.

GAME OF TUESDAY, OCTOBER 13, AT LOS ANGELES

Montreal	AB.	R.	H.	RBI.	PO.	A.
Raines, lf	4	0	1	0	5	0
Scott, 2b	3	0	2	0	1	1
Dawson, cf	4	0	0	0	1	0
Carter, c	3	1	2	0	7	1
Parrish, 3b	4	0	1	1	0	0
Cromartie, 1b	4	0	1	0	8	0
White, rf	4	0	2	0	0	0
Speier, ss	4	0	0	0	2	2
Gullickson, p	1	0	0	0	0	1
Francona, ph	1	0	0	0	0	0
Reardon, p	0	0	0	0	0	0
Totals	32	1	9	1	24	5

Los Angeles	AB.	R.	H.	RBI.	PO.	A.
Lopes, 2b	3	0	1	0	6	4
Landreaux, cf	4	0	1	0	0	0
Baker, lf	3	0	0	0	3	0
Garvey, 1b	4	1	1	0	9	0
Cey, 3b	4	1	2	1	2	2
Thomas, pr-3b	0	1	0	0	0	0
Guerrero, rf	4	1	1	2	2	1
Scioscia, c	3	1	2	1	4	1
Russell, ss	3	0	0	1	1	3
Hooton, p	3	0	0	0	0	0
Welch, p	0	0	0	0	0	0
Howe, p	0	0	0	0	0	0
Totals	31	5	8	5	27	11

```
Montreal.............................. 0   0   0    0   0   0    0   0   1 – 1
Los Angeles .......................... 0   2   0    0   0   0    0   3   x – 5
```

Montreal	IP.	H.	R.	ER.	BB.	SO.
Gullickson (Loser)	7	5	2	2	2	6
Reardon	1	3	3	3	0	0

Los Angeles	IP.	H.	R.	ER.	BB.	SO.
Hooton (Winner)	7⅓	6	0	0	3	2
Welch	⅔*	2	1	1	0	1
Howe	1	1	0	0	0	0

*Pitched to two batters in the ninth.

Game-winning RBI—Cey.

Errors—None. Double plays—Los Angeles 4. Left on base—Montreal 7, Los Angeles 6. Two-base hits—Carter, White, Cey, Landreaux, Parrish. Home runs—Guerrero, Scioscia. Stolen bases—White, Scott, Lopes 2. Sacrifice hit—Russell. Hit by pitcher—By Gullickson (Baker). Umpires—Pryor, Gregg, Runge, Rennert, Wendelstedt and West. Time—2:47. Attendance—51,273.

GAME OF WEDNESDAY, OCTOBER 14, AT LOS ANGELES (N)

Montreal	AB.	R.	H.	RBI.	PO.	A.
Raines, lf	5	0	3	1	1	0
Francona, lf	0	0	0	0	0	0
Scott, 2b	4	0	0	0	3	3
Dawson, cf	4	1	1	0	4	0
Carter, c	4	0	2	0	4	0
Parrish, 3b	4	1	1	0	0	3
White, rf	3	1	1	0	1	0
Cromartie, 1b	4	0	1	1	8	1
Speier, ss	3	0	1	0	6	3
Burris, p	4	0	0	0	0	0
Totals	35	3	10	2	27	10

Los Angeles	AB.	R.	H.	RBI.	PO.	A.
Lopes, 2b	3	0	0	0	0	3
Monday, ph	1	0	0	0	0	0
Castillo, p	0	0	0	0	0	1
Landreaux, cf	3	0	0	0	1	0
Baker, lf	4	0	2	0	2	0
Garvey, 1b	4	0	1	0	11	1
Cey, 3b	4	0	0	0	1	4
Guerrero, rf	3	0	0	0	1	1
Scioscia, c	3	0	0	0	7	0
Russell, ss	3	0	2	0	4	3
Valenzuela, p	2	0	0	0	0	1
Niedenfuer, p	0	0	0	0	0	1
Forster, p	0	0	0	0	0	0
Pena, p	0	0	0	0	0	0
Johnstone, ph	1	0	0	0	0	0
Sax, 2b	0	0	0	0	0	1
Totals	31	0	5	0	27	16

```
Montreal.............................. 0   2   0    0   0   1    0   0   0 – 3
Los Angeles .......................... 0   0   0    0   0   0    0   0   0 – 0
```

Montreal	IP.	H.	R.	ER.	BB.	SO.
Burris (Winner)	9	5	0	0	2	3

Los Angeles	IP.	H.	R.	ER.	BB.	SO.
Valenzuela (Loser)	6	7	3	3	2	4
Niedenfuer	⅓	2	0	0	0	0
Forster	⅓	0	0	0	0	1
Pena	1⅓	1	0	0	0	0
Castillo	1	0	0	0	0	1

Game-winning RBI—Cromartie.

Errors—Baker, Speier. Double plays—Montreal 2. Left on base—Montreal 7, Los Angeles 6. Two-base hits—Cromartie, Raines. Wild pitch—Valenzuela. Umpires—Gregg, Runge, Rennert, Wendelstedt, West and Pryor. Time—2:48. Attendance—53,463.

GAME OF FRIDAY, OCTOBER 16, AT MONTREAL (N)

Los Angeles	AB.	R.	H.	RBI.	PO.	A.	Montreal	AB.	R.	H.	RBI.	PO.	A.
Lopes, 2b	4	0	2	0	2	1	Raines, lf	4	0	0	0	1	0
Landreaux, cf	3	0	0	0	2	0	Scott, 2b	4	0	0	0	2	4
Baker, lf	4	1	1	0	1	0	Dawson, cf	4	1	2	0	0	0
Garvey, 1b	4	0	2	0	14	1	Carter, c	3	1	1	0	5	1
Cey, 3b	4	0	1	1	2	8	Parrish, 3b	4	1	2	1	1	6
Guerrero, rf	4	0	0	0	0	0	White, rf	3	1	1	3	0	0
Scioscia, c	4	0	0	0	2	0	Cromartie, 1b	3	0	0	0	15	0
Russell, ss	3	0	1	0	1	3	Speier, ss	3	0	1	0	3	4
Reuss, p	2	0	0	0	0	0	Rogers, p	2	0	0	0	0	1
Johnstone, ph	1	0	0	0	0	0							
Pena, p	0	0	0	0	0	0	Totals	30	4	7	4	27	16
Totals	33	1	7	1	24	13							

Los Angeles	0	0	0	1	0	0	0	0	0 – 1
Montreal	0	0	0	0	0	4	0	0	x – 4

Los Angeles	IP.	H.	R.	ER.	BB.	SO.
Reuss (Loser)	7	7	4	4	1	2
Pena	1	0	0	0	0	0

Montreal	IP.	H.	R.	ER.	BB.	SO.
Rogers (Winner)	9	7	1	1	1	5

Game-winning RBI—White.

Error—Scott. Double plays—Montreal 3. Left on base—Los Angeles 6, Montreal 4. Home run—White. Stolen base—Lopes. Sacrifice hit—Rogers. Wild pitch—Rogers. Passed ball—Scioscia. Umpires—Runge, Rennert, Wendelstedt, West, Pryor and Gregg. Time—2:27. Attendance—54,372.

GAME OF SATURDAY, OCTOBER 17, AT MONTREAL

Los Angeles	AB.	R.	H.	RBI.	PO.	A.	Montreal	AB.	R.	H.	RBI.	PO.	A.
Lopes, 2b	4	0	1	0	2	2	Raines, lf	4	0	0	0	0	0
Russell, ss	3	2	0	0	2	1	Scott, 2b	4	0	1	0	2	2
Baker, lf	4	2	3	3	4	0	Dawson, cf	4	0	0	0	3	0
Garvey, 1b	5	1	2	2	5	0	Carter, c	3	1	1	0	8	0
Cey, 3b	3	0	2	1	0	0	Parrish, 3b	4	0	0	0	2	3
Monday, rf	4	0	1	0	2	0	White, rf	3	0	1	0	3	0
Landreaux, cf	0	0	0	0	1	0	Cromartie, 1b	4	0	1	1	5	1
Guerrero, cf-rf	4	0	0	0	1	0	Speier, ss	3	0	1	0	4	2
Welch, p	0	0	0	0	0	0	Gullickson, p	2	0	0	0	0	1
Smith, ph	1	0	1	1	0	0	Fryman, p	0	0	0	0	0	0
Howe, p	0	0	0	0	0	0	Sosa, p	0	0	0	0	0	0
Scioscia	0	0	0	0	0	0	Lee, p	0	0	0	0	0	0
Yeager, ph-c	2	1	1	0	2	0	Milner, ph	1	0	0	0	0	0
Hooton, p	2	0	0	0	0	1							
Thomas, rf	1	1	1	0	1	0	Totals	32	1	5	1	27	9
Totals	35	7	12	7	27	4							

Los Angeles	0	0	1	0	0	0	0	2	4 – 7
Montreal	0	0	0	1	0	0	0	0	0 – 1

Los Angeles	IP.	H.	R.	ER.	BB.	SO.
Hooton (Winner)	7⅓	5	1	0	3	5
Welch	⅔	0	0	0	0	1
Howe	1	0	0	0	0	2

Montreal	IP.	H.	R.	ER.	BB.	SO.
Gullickson (Loser)	7⅓	7	3	2	4	6
Fryman	1	3	4	4	1	1
Sosa	⅓	1	0	0	1	0
Lee	⅓	1	0	0	0	0

Game-winning RBI—Garvey.

Errors—Parrish, Cey. Double plays—Montreal 2. Left on base—Los Angeles 10, Montreal 8. Two-base hit—Baker. Home run—Garvey. Stolen base—Lopes. Sacrifice hits—Russell, Gullickson, Hooton, Lopes. Umpires—Rennert, Wendelstedt, West, Pryor, Gregg and Runge. Time—3:14. Attendance—54,499.

GAME OF MONDAY, OCTOBER 19, AT MONTREAL

Los Angeles	AB.	R.	H.	RBI.	PO.	A.	Montreal	AB.	R.	H.	RBI.	PO.	A.
Lopes, 2b	4	0	1	0	3	3	Raines, lf	4	1	1	0	2	0
Russell, ss	4	0	2	0	2	3	Scott, 2b	3	0	0	0	4	4
Baker, lf	4	0	0	0	0	0	Dawson, cf	4	0	0	0	4	0
Garvey, 1b	4	0	0	0	10	0	Carter, c	3	0	1	0	3	1
Cey, 3b	3	0	0	0	0	2	Manuel, pr	0	0	0	0	0	0
Monday, rf	4	2	2	1	0	0	Parrish, 3b	3	0	1	0	0	1
Landreaux, cf	0	0	0	0	0	0	White, rf	3	0	0	0	2	0
Guerrero, cf-rf	4	0	1	0	5	0	Cromartie, 1b	3	0	0	0	12	0
Scioscia, c	3	0	0	0	7	0	Speier, ss	3	0	0	0	0	5
Valenzuela, p	3	0	0	1	0	1	Burris, p	2	0	0	0	0	1
Welch, p	0	0	0	0	0	0	Wallach, ph	1	0	0	0	0	0
							Rogers, p	0	0	0	0	0	0
Totals	33	2	6	2	27	9	Totals	29	1	3	0	27	12

Los Angeles	0	0	0	0	1	0	0	0	1 – 2
Montreal	1	0	0	0	0	0	0	0	0 – 1

Los Angeles	IP.	H.	R.	ER.	BB.	SO.
Valenzuela (Winner)	8⅔	3	1	1	3	6
Welch (Save)	⅓	0	0	0	0	0
Montreal	IP.	H.	R.	ER.	BB.	SO.
Burris	8	5	1	1	1	1
Rogers (Loser)	1	1	1	1	0	1

Game-winning RBI—Monday.

Error—Speier. Double plays—Los Angeles 1, Montreal 1. Left on base—Los Angeles 5, Montreal 5. Two-base hits—Raines, Parrish. Three-base hit—Russell. Home run—Monday. Stolen base—Lopes. Sacrifice hit—Scott. Wild pitch—Burris. Umpires—Wendelstedt, West, Pryor, Gregg, Runge and Rennert. Time—2:41. Attendance—36,491.

LOS ANGELES DODGERS' BATTING AND FIELDING AVERAGES

Player–Position	G.	AB.	R.	H.	TB.	2B.	3B.	HR.	RBI.	B.A.	PO.	A.	E.	F.A.
Thomas, pr-3b-rf	2	1	2	1	1	0	0	0	0	1.000	1	0	0	1.000
Smith, ph	1	1	0	1	1	0	0	0	1	1.000	0	0	0	.000
Yeager, ph-c	1	2	1	1	1	0	0	0	0	.500	2	0	0	1.000
Monday, ph-rf	3	9	2	3	6	0	0	1	1	.333	2	0	0	1.000
Baker, lf	5	19	3	6	7	1	0	0	3	.316	10	0	1	.909
Russell, ss	5	16	2	5	7	0	1	0	1	.313	10	13	0	1.000
Garvey, 1b	5	21	2	6	9	0	0	1	2	.286	49	2	0	1.000
Cey, 3b	5	18	1	5	6	1	0	0	3	.278	5	16	1	.955
Lopes, 2b	5	18	0	5	5	0	0	0	0	.278	13	13	0	1.000
Scioscia, c	5	15	1	2	5	0	0	1	1	.133	27	1	0	1.000
Guerrero, rf-cf	5	19	1	2	5	0	0	1	2	.105	9	2	0	1.000
Landreaux, cf	5	10	0	1	2	1	0	0	0	.100	4	0	0	1.000
Welch, p	3	0	0	0	0	0	0	0	0	.000	0	0	0	.000
Howe, p	2	0	0	0	0	0	0	0	0	.000	0	0	0	.000
Pena, p	2	0	0	0	0	0	0	0	0	.000	0	0	0	.000
Castillo, p	1	0	0	0	0	0	0	0	0	.000	0	1	0	1.000
Forster, p	1	0	0	0	0	0	0	0	0	.000	0	0	0	.000
Niedenfuer, p	1	0	0	0	0	0	0	0	0	.000	0	1	0	1.000
Sax, 2b	1	0	0	0	0	0	0	0	0	.000	0	1	0	1.000
Johnstone, ph	2	2	0	0	0	0	0	0	0	.000	0	0	0	.000
Reuss, p	1	2	0	0	0	0	0	0	0	.000	0	0	0	.000
Hooton, p	2	5	0	0	0	0	0	0	0	.000	0	1	0	1.000
Valenzuela, p	2	5	0	0	0	0	0	0	1	.000	0	2	0	1.000
Totals	5	163	15	38	55	3	1	4	15	.233	132	53	2	.989

MONTREAL EXPOS' BATTING AND FIELDING AVERAGES

Player–Position	G.	AB.	R.	H.	TB.	2B.	3B.	HR.	RBI.	B.A.	PO.	A.	E.	F.A.
Carter, c	5	16	3	7	8	1	0	0	0	.438	27	3	0	1.000
White, rf	5	16	2	5	9	1	0	1	3	.313	6	0	0	1.000
Parrish, 3b	5	19	2	5	7	2	0	0	2	.263	3	13	1	.941
Raines, lf	5	21	1	5	7	2	0	0	1	.238	9	0	0	1.000
Speier, ss	5	16	0	3	3	0	0	0	0	.188	15	16	2	.939
Cromartie, 1b	5	18	0	3	4	1	0	0	2	.167	48	2	0	1.000
Scott, 2b	5	18	0	3	3	0	0	0	0	.167	12	14	1	.963
Dawson, cf	5	20	2	3	3	0	0	0	0	.150	12	0	0	1.000
Fryman, p	1	0	0	0	0	0	0	0	0	.000	0	0	0	.000
Lee, p	1	0	0	0	0	0	0	0	0	.000	0	0	0	.000
Manuel, pr	1	0	0	0	0	0	0	0	0	.000	0	0	0	.000
Reardon, p	1	0	0	0	0	0	0	0	0	.000	0	0	0	.000
Sosa, p	1	0	0	0	0	0	0	0	0	.000	0	0	0	.000
Francona, ph-lf	2	1	0	0	0	0	0	0	0	.000	0	0	0	.000
Milner, ph	1	1	0	0	0	0	0	0	0	.000	0	0	0	.000
Wallach, ph	1	1	0	0	0	0	0	0	0	.000	0	0	0	.000
Rogers, p	2	2	0	0	0	0	0	0	0	.000	0	1	0	1.000
Gullickson, p	2	3	0	0	0	0	0	0	0	.000	0	2	0	1.000
Burris, p	2	6	0	0	0	0	0	0	0	.000	0	1	0	1.000
Totals	5	158	10	34	44	7	0	1	8	.215	132	52	4	.979

LOS ANGELES DODGERS' PITCHING RECORDS

Pitcher	G.	GS.	CG.	IP.	H.	R.	ER.	BB.	SO.	HB.	WP.	W.	L.	Pct.	ERA.
Hooton	2	2	0	14⅔	11	1	0	6	7	0	0	2	0	1.000	0.00
Pena	2	0	0	2⅓	1	0	0	0	0	0	0	0	0	.000	0.00
Howe	2	0	0	2	1	0	0	2	0	0	0	0	0	.000	0.00
Castillo	1	0	0	1	0	0	0	0	1	0	0	0	0	.000	0.00
Forster	1	0	0	⅓	0	0	0	0	1	0	0	0	0	.000	0.00
Niedenfuer	1	0	0	⅓	2	0	0	0	0	0	0	0	0	.000	0.00
Valenzuela	2	2	0	14⅔	10	4	4	5	10	0	1	1	1	.500	2.45
Reuss	1	1	0	7	7	4	4	1	2	0	0	0	1	.000	5.14
Welch	3	0	0	1⅔	2	1	1	0	2	0	0	0	0	.000	5.40
Totals	5	5	0	44	34	10	9	12	25	0	1	3	2	.600	1.84

No shutouts. Save—Welch.

MONTREAL EXPOS' PITCHING RECORDS

Pitcher	G.	GS.	CG.	IP.	H.	R.	ER.	BB.	SO.	HB.	WP.	W.	L.	Pct.	ERA.
Lee	1	0	0	⅓	1	0	0	0	0	0	0	0	0	.000	0.00
Sosa	1	0	0	⅓	1	0	0	1	0	0	0	0	0	.000	0.00
Burris	2	2	1	17	10	1	1	3	4	0	1	1	0	1.000	0.53
Rogers	2	1	1	10	8	2	2	1	6	0	1	1	1	.500	1.80
Gullickson	2	2	0	14⅓	12	5	4	6	12	1	0	0	2	.000	2.51
Reardon	1	0	0	1	3	3	3	0	0	0	0	0	0	.000	27.00
Fryman	1	0	0	1	3	4	4	1	1	0	0	0	0	.000	36.00
Totals	5	5	2	44	38	15	14	12	23	1	2	2	3	.400	2.86

Shutout—Burris. No saves.

COMPOSITE SCORE BY INNINGS

Los Angeles	0	2	1	1	1	0	0	5	5	— 15
Montreal	1	2	0	1	0	5	0	0	1	— 10

Game-winning RBIs—Cey, Cromartie, White, Garvey, Monday.
Sacrifice hits—Russell 2, Rogers, Gullickson, Hooton, Lopes, Scott.
Sacrifice flies—None.
Stolen bases—Lopes 5, White, Scott.
Caught stealing—Raines.
Double plays—Lopes, Russell and Garvey 2; Speier, Scott and Cromartie 2; Scott, Speier and Cromartie 2; Cey, Lopes and Garvey; Guerrero and Lopes; Russell, Lopes and Garvey; Parrish, Scott and Cromartie; Speier and Scott; Parrish, Speier and Scott; Parrish and Cromartie.
Left on bases—Los Angeles 6, 6, 6, 10, 5—33, Montreal 7, 7, 4, 8, 5—31.
Hit by pitcher—By Gullickson (Baker).
Passed ball—Scioscia.
Balks—None.
Time of games—First game, 2:47; second game, 2:48; third game, 2:27; fourth game, 3:14; fifth game, 2:41.
Attendance—First game, 51,273; second game, 53,463; third game, 54,372; fourth game, 54,499; fifth game, 36,491.
Umpires—Pryor, Gregg, Runge, Rennert, Wendelstedt and West.
Official scorers—Chris Mortensen, Torrance (Cal.) Daily Breeze; Michael Spinelli.

AMERICAN LEAGUE
Championship Series of 1982

	W.	L.	Pct.
Milwaukee (East)	3	2	.600
California (West)	2	3	.400

In many postseason games in the American League over the past decade, the man you expected to see celebrating was Reggie Jackson. But it didn't happen in 1982.

Jackson didn't have a chance to wave his magic wand in the ninth inning with California trailing Milwaukee, 4-3, in the fifth and decisive game of the A.L. Championship Series. Instead, he was left in the on-deck circle watching Peter Ladd retire Rod Carew for the final out as the Brewers captured the first A.L. pennant in the franchise's 14 years.

History confronted Manager Harvey Kuenn's Brewers with at least 15 good reasons why they should fail in their bid for a comeback triumph in the series. Entering the 1982 playoffs, 15 teams had fallen behind two games to none in Championship Series play and then dropped into oblivion.

But the Brewers had beaten the odds after losing the first two games of the series at Anaheim and then trailing late in Game 5. In Game 1, the Angels looked like the champions, devastating Mike Caldwell and the Brewers, 8-3, behind five runs batted in by Don Baylor and a complete-game effort by 39-year-old lefthander Tommy John.

Baylor drove home the game's first run with a sacrifice fly in the opening inning. But Milwaukee bolted to a 3-1 advantage on a towering two-run homer by Gorman Thomas in the second and a run-scoring groundout by Cecil Cooper in the third.

Baylor, who set a league record with 21 game-winning RBIs during the season, followed an RBI single by Bobby Grich with a two-run triple in the third to put the Angels ahead, 4-3. In the fourth, he singled home two more runs. The five RBIs matched a Championship Series record established by Paul Blair of Baltimore in 1969 and equaled by Bob Robertson of Pittsburgh in 1971.

California's Bruce Kison limited the Brewers to five hits in Game 2, struck out eight, issued no walks and induced 14 Milwaukee batters to ground out as the Angels gained a 2-0 cushion in the series with a 4-2 triumph.

Tim Foli drove home the game's first run with a single in the second inning. Bob Boone followed with a suicide squeeze bunt, giving California a 2-0 lead. In the third, Jackson performed some of his autumn magic with a long homer over the center-field wall. Boone produced the final California run with a sacrifice fly in the fourth.

The only runs the Brewers could muster came on a two-run, inside-the-park home run by Paul Molitor in the fifth inning.

The change of scenery seemed to agree with the Brewers when the series shifted to Milwaukee. The Brewers roared to a 5-0 cushion after seven innings in Game 3 and had veteran Don Sutton on the mound.

After Robin Yount walked to lead off the fourth inning, Cooper doubled him home. Ted Simmons singled Cooper to third before Thomas produced the second run with a sacrifice fly to center. A single by Ben Oglivie preceded another sacrifice fly, this one by Don Money. The Brewers added to that 3-0 lead when Molitor collected his second two-run homer in as many games in the seventh.

But then the Brewers got a scare.

Boone led off the California eighth with a long drive to left field. Oglivie leaped for the ball, but he had it snatched from his grasp by a fan who was leaning over the grandstand wall. Umpire Larry Barnett ruled that the fan caught the ball behind the fence (although an instant replay on television showed that the spectator leaned over the wall).

The controversial call gave the Angels new life. With one out, Carew singled. Then, with two outs, Fred Lynn and Baylor stroked run-scoring doubles to cut the Milwaukee lead to 5-3.

With the .300-hitting Doug DeCinces at the plate, Milwaukee's Kuenn chose Ladd to replace Sutton. The big hurler, who had been summoned by the Brewers from their Triple-A club at Vancouver in July, possessed a 90-miles-per-hour fastball.

Ladd got DeCinces to ground to third and then disposed of the Angels in order in the ninth, striking out two batters to preserve the victory.

The next afternoon, following a rain delay at the start, pitcher Moose Haas got the call for the Brewers and John was back for the Angels after only three days rest.

But the name to remember in Game 4 was Mark Brouhard, a substitute left fielder for Oglivie (who was bothered by a rib injury). Brouhard hadn't played since September 11 but scored four times, had a single, double and homer and drove in three runs to key the Brewers' 9-5 victory that evened the series at two games apiece.

Brouhard had been sent to the minors as late as August 12. He returned on August 30, just prior to the deadline for being eligible for the playoffs.

Walks to Simmons and Money preceded Brouhard's RBI single in the second inning. When Lynn made a poor throw from center field and DeCinces made another error on the same play, the Brewers had scored three runs. They scored three more in the fourth on a wild pitch, a run-scoring single by Jim Gantner and a groundout by Molitor.

When the rains came again in the fifth inning, Haas wondered whether he would make the record book; he had a no-hitter going. But when play resumed in the sixth, Lynn cracked a run-scoring double to cut the Milwaukee margin to 6-1.

Gantner provided another RBI single in the Milwaukee half of the sixth, but the Angels rallied for four runs in the eighth and knocked Haas from the mound when Baylor smashed a bases-loaded homer.

Jim Slaton took the mound and retired five straight batters, while Brouhard put the game out of reach with his two-run homer in the eighth.

The Angels opened Game 5 with a double by Brian Downing, who later scored on a single by Lynn. But the Brewers scored in their half of the first on a double by Molitor, a grounder and a sacrifice fly by Simmons.

Lynn, who had 11 hits in the playoffs and was the series' Most Valuable Player, drove home the second California run with a single in the third. Boone extended the Angels' lead to 3-1 in the fourth with an RBI single.

But Oglivie, back in the lineup, belted a long home run over the right-field wall in the Brewers' fourth.

With one out in the Angels' fifth, Jackson drew a walk from Milwaukee starter Pete Vuckovich. Lynn and Baylor followed with singles. But any threat of the Angels adding to their 3-2 lead was squelched when Brewers' catcher-turned-right fielder Charlie Moore nailed Jackson at third base with a perfect throw following Lynn's hit.

Kison, who had a lifetime September-October record of 32-8, pitched five innings before giving way to hard-throwing Luis Sanchez. Sanchez mowed down the Brewers in the sixth and then retired Money to lead off the seventh before running into trouble.

Moore's bloop hit dropped in the middle of the infield, just out of the reach of a diving Grich at second base. First-base umpire Al Clark ruled that Grich had caught the ball, but was overruled by home-plate umpire Don Denkinger.

Gantner followed with a single up the middle and, after Molitor fouled out for the second out, Yount coaxed a walk.

Cooper, who had gone 2-for-19 and was hitless in his previous nine at-bats, strolled to the plate. He had been a .313 hitter during the regular season. Nearly everyone expected California Manager Gene Mauch to bring in lefthander Andy Hassler, but the veteran skipper stayed with Sanchez.

Actually, Cooper was surprised that Mauch hadn't brought in Hassler. "Hassler is tough on lefthanders and he's been tough on me," Cooper said.

The 1-and-1 pitch to Cooper was a fastball, tailing away but slightly up in the strike zone, and Cooper stroked it to left field. Two runs scored and the Brewers had a 4-3 lead.

"I thought it might carry too far and be the third out," said Cooper. "When it didn't, I had the most satisfying hit of my life."

In the ninth, after a leadoff pinch single by Ron Jackson, Ladd was called on to make his third appearance of the series. Boone sacrificed pinch-runner Rob Wilfong to second base. Downing then grounded to third, before Carew bounced to Yount at shortstop.

"I saw every bounce going into Robin's glove," Ladd said. "And I saw every inch of his throw to first base."

So did Jackson, who was left waiting in the on-deck circle for an at-bat that never came.

GAME OF TUESDAY, OCTOBER 5, AT CALIFORNIA (N)

Milwaukee	AB.	R.	H.	RBI.	PO.	A.	California	AB.	R.	H.	RBI.	PO.	A.
Molitor, 3b	4	1	1	0	0	0	Downing, lf	4	2	1	0	1	0
Yount, ss	4	0	1	0	4	1	Beniquez, lf	0	0	0	0	1	0
Cooper, 1b	4	0	1	1	6	0	DeCinces, 3b	4	2	2	0	2	5
Simmons, c	4	1	2	0	7	0	Grich, 2b	3	1	2	1	1	3
Thomas, cf	4	1	1	2	3	0	Baylor, dh	3	1	2	5	0	0
Oglivie, lf	4	0	0	2	2	0	Re. Jackson, rf	0	0	0	0	1	0
Money, dh	3	0	0	0	0	0	Clark, rf	4	1	3	1	4	0
Moore, rf	3	0	1	0	1	0	Lynn, cf	4	0	0	0	8	2
Gantner, 2b	4	0	0	0	0	3	Carew, 1b	4	0	0	0	1	1
Caldwell, p	0	0	0	0	2	0	Foli, ss	4	0	0	0	1	1
Slaton, p	0	0	0	0	1	0	Boone, c	4	1	1	0	5	0
Ladd, p	0	0	0	0	0	0	John, p	0	0	0	0	3	1
Bernard, p	0	0	0	0	0	0	Totals	34	8	10	8	27	12
Totals	34	3	7	3	24	6							

Milwaukee	0	2	1	0	0	0	0	0	0 — 3			
California	1	0	4	2	1	0	0	0	x — 8			

Milwaukee	IP.	H.	R.	ER.	BB.	SO.
Caldwell (Loser)	3*	7	6	5	1	2
Slaton	3	3	2	1	1	2
Ladd	1	0	0	0	0	3
Bernard	1	0	0	0	0	0

California	IP.	H.	R.	ER.	BB.	SO.
John (Winner)	9	7	3	3	1	5

*Pitched to one batter in fourth.

Game-winning RBI—Baylor.
Errors—Caldwell, Molitor. Double play—Milwaukee 1. Left on bases—Milwaukee 6, California 5. Two-base hits—Cooper, Grich. Three-base hit—Baylor. Home runs— Thomas, Lynn. Sacrifice fly—Baylor. Hit by pitcher—By John (Moore). Wild pitch—Caldwell. Umpires—Barnett, Kunkel, Garcia, Palermo, Denkinger and Clark. Time—2:31. Attendance—64,406.

GAME OF WEDNESDAY, OCTOBER 6, AT CALIFORNIA (N)

Milwaukee	AB.	R.	H.	RBI.	PO.	A.	California	AB.	R.	H.	RBI.	PO.	A.
Molitor, 3b	4	1	2	2	1	1	Downing, lf	3	0	0	0	1	0
Yount, ss	4	0	1	0	2	3	Beniquez, lf	0	0	0	0	0	0
Cooper, 1b	4	0	0	0	5	1	Carew, 1b	4	0	0	0	14	0
Simmons, c	4	0	0	0	5	0	Re. Jackson, rf	3	1	1	1	1	0
Oglivie, lf	4	0	0	0	1	0	Clark, rf	0	0	0	0	0	0
Thomas, cf	3	0	0	0	3	0	Lynn, cf	4	1	2	0	1	0
Howell, dh	3	0	0	0	0	0	Baylor, dh	3	0	0	0	0	0
Moore, rf	3	1	2	0	3	0	DeCinces, 3b	3	2	1	0	1	1
Gantner, 2b	3	0	0	0	4	2	Grich, 2b	2	0	1	0	1	5
Vuckovich, p	0	0	0	0	0	1	Foli, ss	2	0	1	1	0	2
Totals	32	2	5	2	24	8	Boone, c	1	0	0	2	8	1
							Kison, p	0	0	0	0	0	0
							Totals	25	4	6	4	27	9

Milwaukee	0	0	0	0	2	0	0	0	0 — 2
California	0	2	1	1	0	0	0	0	x — 4

Milwaukee	IP.	H.	·R.	ER.	BB.	SO.
Vuckovich (Loser)	8	6	4	4	4	4

California	IP.	H.	R.	ER.	BB.	SO.
Kison (Winner)	9	5	2	2	0	8

Game-winning RBI—Foli.
Errors—None. Double plays—Milwaukee 2. Left on bases—Milwaukee 3, California 5. Two-base hit—DeCinces. Home runs—Re. Jackson, Molitor. Sacrifice hits—Boone, Foli. Sacrifice fly—Boone. Hit by pitcher—By Vuckovich (Grich). Umpires—Kunkel, Garcia, Palermo, Denkinger, Clark and Barnett. Time—2:06. Attendance—64,179.

GAME OF FRIDAY, OCTOBER 8, AT MILWAUKEE

California	AB.	R.	H.	RBI.	PO.	A.	Milwaukee	AB.	R.	H.	RBI.	PO.	A.
Downing, lf	4	0	0	0	2	0	Molitor, 3b	4	1	1	2	1	4
Carew, 1b	4	1	2	0	4	0	Yount, ss	2	1	1	0	0	4
Re. Jackson, rf	4	0	1	0	0	0	Cooper, 1b	4	1	1	1	12	0
Lynn, cf	3	1	2	1	4	0	Simmons, c	4	1	1	0	11	0
Baylor, dh	3	0	1	1	0	0	Thomas, cf	3	0	0	1	2	0
DeCinces, 3b	4	0	1	0	3	1	Oglivie, lf	3	0	1	0	0	0
Grich, 2b	4	0	0	0	2	2	Money, dh	1	0	0	1	0	0
Foli, ss	3	0	0	0	3	1	Edwards, pr-dh	0	1	0	0	0	0
Wilfong, ph	1	0	0	0	0	0	Moore, rf	2	0	1	0	0	0
Boone, c	4	1	1	1	6	0	Gantner, 2b	3	0	0	0	1	1
Zahn, p	0	0	0	0	0	0	Sutton, p	0	0	0	0	0	1
Witt, p	0	0	0	0	0	1	Ladd, p	0	0	0	0	0	0
Hassler, p	0	0	0	0	0	0	Totals	26	5	6	5	27	10
Totals	34	3	8	3	24	5							

California	0	0	0	0	0	0	0	3	0 — 3
Milwaukee	0	0	0	3	0	0	2	0	x — 5

California	IP.	H.	R.	ER.	BB.	SO.
Zahn (Loser)	3⅔	4	3	3	1	2
Witt	3	2	2	2	2	3
Hassler	1⅓	0	0	0	0	1

Milwaukee	IP.	H.	R.	ER.	BB.	SO.
Sutton (Winner)	7⅔	8	3	3	2	9
Ladd (Save)	1⅓	0	0	0	0	2

Game-winning RBI—Cooper.
Errors—None. Double plays—California 1, Milwaukee 1. Left on bases—California 6, Milwaukee 4. Two-base hits—Lynn, Baylor, Cooper. Home runs—Molitor, Boone. Stolen base—Carew. Sacrifice hit—Moore. Sacrifice flies—Thomas, Money. Hit by pitcher—By Zahn (Oglivie). Umpires—Garcia, Palermo, Denkinger, Clark, Barnett and Kunkel. Time—2:41. Attendance—50,135.

GAME OF SATURDAY, OCTOBER 9, AT MILWAUKEE

California	AB.	R.	H.	RBI.	PO.	A.	Milwaukee	AB.	R.	H.	RBI.	PO.	A.
Downing, lf	4	1	1	0	0	0	Molitor, 3b	4	0	0	1	0	3
Carew, 1b	2	1	1	0	10	2	Yount, ss	4	0	1	0	2	2
Re. Jackson, rf	4	1	0	0	0	0	Cooper, 1b	4	0	0	0	5	1
Lynn, cf	3	1	1	1	4	0	Simmons, c	3	1	0	0	9	1
Baylor, dh	4	1	1	4	0	0	Thomas, cf	2	0	0	0	5	0
DeCinces, 3b	4	0	0	0	1	3	Money, dh	3	2	2	0	0	0
Grich, 2b	3	0	0	0	3	5	Edwards, pr-dh	0	1	0	0	0	0
Foli, ss	4	0	1	0	2	3	Brouhard, lf	4	4	3	3	1	0
Boone, c	4	0	0	0	4	2	Moore, rf	2	1	1	0	2	0
John, p	0	0	0	0	0	0	Gantner, 2b	4	0	2	2	3	0
Goltz, p	0	0	0	0	0	0	Haas, p	0	0	0	0	0	0
Sanchez, p	0	0	0	0	0	0	Slaton, p	0	0	0	0	0	0
Totals	32	5	5	5	24	15	Totals	30	9	9	6	27	7

California	0	0	0	0	0	1	0	4	0 — 5
Milwaukee	0	3	0	3	0	1	0	2	x — 9

California	IP.	H.	R.	ER.	BB.	SO.
John (Loser)	3⅓	4	6	4	5	1
Goltz	3⅔	4	3	3	2	2
Sanchez	1	1	0	0	0	0
Milwaukee	IP.	H.	R.	ER.	BB.	SO.
Haas (Winner)	7⅓	5	5	4	5	7
Slaton (Save)	1⅔	0	0	0	0	1

*Pitched to two batters in eighth.
Game-winning RBI—Brouhard.
Errors—Lynn, DeCinces 2, Yount, Cooper. Double play—California 1. Left on bases—California 5, Milwaukee 5. Two-base hits—Lynn, Carew, Brouhard. Home runs—Baylor, Brouhard. Stolen base—Edwards. Caught stealing—Carew, Molitor, Thomas. Sacrifice hit—Moore. Wild pitches—John 3. Passed ball—Boone. Umpires—Palermo, Denkinger, Clark, Barnett, Kunkel and Garcia. Time—3:10. Attendance—51,003.

GAME OF SUNDAY, OCTOBER 10, AT MILWAUKEE

California	AB.	R.	H.	RBI.	PO.	A.	Milwaukee	AB.	R.	H.	RBI.	PO.	A.
Downing, lf	4	1	1	0	1	0	Molitor, 3b	3	1	2	0	2	3
Carew, 1b	3	0	0	0	7	0	Yount, ss	2	0	0	0	3	2
Re. Jackson, rf	3	0	0	0	1	0	Cooper, 1b	4	0	1	2	9	1
Lynn, cf	4	0	3	2	3	0	Simmons, c	3	0	0	1	4	2
Baylor, dh	4	0	1	0	0	0	Oglivie, lf	4	1	1	1	2	0
DeCinces, 3b	4	1	3	0	2	2	Thomas, cf	3	0	0	0	0	0
Grich, 2b	3	0	0	0	3	2	Edwards, cf	1	0	0	0	2	0
Foli, ss	3	0	0	0	0	0	Money, dh	4	0	0	0	0	0
Ro. Jackson, ph	1	0	1	0	0	0	Moore, rf	3	1	1	0	1	1
Wilfong, pr	0	0	0	0	0	0	Gantner, 2b	2	1	1	0	4	2
Boone, c	3	1	2	1	7	0	Vuckovich, p	0	0	0	0	0	2
Kison, p	0	0	0	0	0	0	McClure, p	0	0	0	0	0	0
Sanchez, p	0	0	0	0	0	0	Ladd, p	0	0	0	0	0	1
Hassler, p	0	0	0	0	0	1	Totals	29	4	6	4	27	14
Totals	32	3	11	3	24	5							

California	1	0	1	1	0	0	0	0	0 — 3
Milwaukee	1	0	0	1	0	0	2	0	x — 4

California	IP.	H.	R.	ER.	BB.	SO.
Kison	5	3	2	1	3	4
Sanchez (Loser)	1⅔	3	2	2	1	1
Hassler	1⅓	0	0	0	0	1
Milwaukee	IP.	H.	R.	ER.	BB.	SO.
Vuckovich	6⅓	9	3	3	3	4
McClure (Winner)	1⅔*	2	0	0	0	0
Ladd (Save)	1	0	0	0	0	0

*Pitched to one batter in ninth.
Game-winning RBI—Cooper.
Errors—Oglivie 2, Molitor, Cooper, DeCinces. Double plays—California 1, Milwaukee 2. Left on bases—California 8, Milwaukee 6. Two-base hits—Downing, DeCinces, Molitor. Home run—Oglivie. Stolen base—Molitor. Caught stealing—DeCinces. Sacrifice hits—Downing, Grich, Boone. Sacrifice fly—Simmons. Umpires—Denkinger, Clark, Barnett, Kunkel, Garcia and Palermo. Time—3:01. Attendance—54,968.

MILWAUKEE BREWERS' BATTING AND FIELDING AVERAGES

Player—Position	G.	AB.	R.	H.	TB.	2B.	3B.	HR.	RBI.	B.A.	PO.	A.	E.	F.A.
Brouhard, lf	1	4	4	3	7	1	0	1	3	.750	1	0	0	1.000
Moore, rf	5	13	3	6	6	0	0	0	0	.462	7	1	0	1.000
Molitor, 3b	5	19	4	6	13	1	0	2	5	.316	4	11	2	.882
Yount, ss	5	16	1	4	4	0	0	0	0	.250	11	12	1	.958
Gantner, 2b	5	16	1	3	3	0	0	0	2	.188	12	8	0	1.000
Money, dh	4	11	2	2	2	0	0	0	1	.182	0	0	0	.000
Simmons, c	5	18	3	3	3	0	0	0	1	.167	36	3	0	1.000
Cooper, 1b	5	20	1	3	5	2	0	0	4	.150	37	3	2	.952
Oglivie, lf	4	15	1	2	5	0	0	1	1	.133	5	0	2	.714
Thomas, cf	5	16	1	1	4	0	0	1	3	.063	13	0	0	1.000
Edwards, pr-dh-cf	3	0	2	0	0	0	0	0	0	.000	2	0	0	1.000
Ladd, p	3	0	0	0	0	0	0	0	0	.000	0	1	0	1.000
Slaton, p	2	0	0	0	0	0	0	0	0	.000	1	0	0	1.000
Vuckovich, p	2	0	0	0	0	0	0	0	0	.000	0	3	0	1.000
Bernard, p	1	0	0	0	0	0	0	0	0	.000	0	0	0	.000
Caldwell, p	1	0	0	0	0	0	0	0	0	.000	0	2	1	.667
Haas, p	1	0	0	0	0	0	0	0	0	.000	0	0	0	.000
McClure, p	1	0	0	0	0	0	0	0	0	.000	0	0	0	.000
Sutton, p	1	0	0	0	0	0	0	0	0	.000	0	1	0	1.000
Howell, dh	1	3	0	0	0	0	0	0	0	.000	0	0	0	.000
Totals	5	151	23	33	52	4	0	5	20	.219	129	45	8	.956

CALIFORNIA ANGELS' BATTING AND FIELDING AVERAGES

Player—Position	G.	AB.	R.	H.	TB.	2B.	3B.	HR.	RBI.	B.A.	PO.	A.	E.	F.A.
Ro. Jackson, ph	1	1	0	1	1	0	0	0	0	1.000	0	0	0	.000
Lynn, cf	5	18	5	11	16	2	0	1	5	.611	16	0	1	.941
DeCinces, 3b	5	19	5	6	8	2	0	0	0	.316	9	12	3	.875
Baylor, dh	5	17	2	5	11	1	1	1	10	.294	0	0	0	.000
Boone, c	5	16	3	4	7	0	0	1	4	.250	30	3	0	1.000
Grich, 2b	5	15	1	3	4	1	0	0	1	.200	10	17	0	1.000

Player—Position	G.	AB.	R.	H.	TB.	2B.	3B.	HR.	RBI.	B.A.	PO.	A.	E.	F.A.
Carew, 1b	5	17	2	3	4	1	0	0	0	.176	43	4	0	1.000
Downing, lf	5	19	3	3	4	1	0	0	0	.158	5	0	0	1.000
Foli, ss	5	16	0	2	2	0	0	0	1	.125	6	7	0	1.000
Re. Jackson, rf	5	18	2	2	5	0	0	1	2	.111	2	0	0	1.000
Beniquez, lf	2	0	0	0	0	0	0	0	0	.000	1	0	0	1.000
Clark, rf	2	0	0	0	0	0	0	0	0	.000	1	0	0	1.000
Hassler, p	2	0	0	0	0	0	0	0	0	.000	0	1	0	1.000
John, p	2	0	0	0	0	0	0	0	0	.000	3	1	0	1.000
Kison, p	2	0	0	0	0	0	0	0	0	.000	0	0	0	.000
Sanchez, p	2	0	0	0	0	0	0	0	0	.000	0	0	0	.000
Goltz, p	1	0	0	0	0	0	0	0	0	.000	0	0	0	.000
Witt, p	1	0	0	0	0	0	0	0	0	.000	0	1	0	1.000
Zahn, p	1	0	0	0	0	0	0	0	0	.000	0	0	0	.000
Wilfong, ph-pr	2	1	0	0	0	0	0	0	0	.000	0	0	0	.000
Totals	5	157	23	40	62	8	1	4	23	.255	126	46	4	.977

MILWAUKEE BREWERS' PITCHING RECORDS

Pitcher	G.	GS.	CG.	IP.	H.	R.	ER.	BB.	SO.	HB.	WP.	W.	L.	Pct.	ERA.
Ladd	3	0	0	3⅓	0	0	0	5	0	0	0	0	0	.000	0.00
McClure	1	0	0	1⅔	2	0	0	0	0	0	0	1	0	1.000	0.00
Bernard	1	0	0	1	0	0	0	0	0	0	0	0	0	.000	0.00
Slaton	2	0	0	4⅔	3	2	1	1	3	0	0	0	0	.000	1.93
Sutton	1	1	0	7⅔	8	3	3	2	9	0	1	1	0	1.000	3.52
Vuckovich	2	2	1	14⅓	15	7	7	7	8	0	0	0	1	.000	4.40
Haas	1	1	0	7⅓	5	5	4	5	7	0	0	1	0	1.000	4.91
Caldwell	1	1	0	3	7	6	5	1	2	0	1	0	1	.000	15.00
Totals	5	5	1	43	40	23	20	16	34	0	1	3	2	.600	4.19

No shutouts. Saves—Ladd 2, Slaton.

CALIFORNIA ANGELS' PITCHING RECORDS

Pitcher	G.	GS.	CG.	IP.	H.	R.	ER.	BB.	SO.	HB.	WP.	W.	L.	Pct.	ERA.
Hassler	2	0	0	2⅔	0	0	0	2	0	0	0	0	0	.000	0.00
Kison	2	2	1	14	8	4	3	3	12	0	0	1	0	1.000	1.93
John	2	2	1	12⅓	11	9	7	6	6	1	3	1	1	.500	5.11
Witt	1	0	0	3	2	2	2	2	3	0	0	0	0	.000	6.00
Sanchez	2	0	0	2⅔	4	2	2	1	1	0	0	0	1	.000	6.75
Goltz	1	0	0	3⅔	4	3	3	2	2	0	0	0	0	.000	7.36
Zahn	1	1	0	3⅔	4	3	3	1	2	1	0	0	1	.000	7.36
Totals	5	5	2	42	33	23	20	15	28	2	3	2	3	.400	4.29

No shutouts or saves.

COMPOSITE SCORE BY INNINGS

Milwaukee	1	5	1	7	2	1	4	2	0 — 23
California	2	2	6	4	1	1	0	7	0 — 23

Game-winning RBIs—Cooper 2, Baylor, Foli, Brouhard.
Sacrifice hits—Boone 2, Moore 2, Foli, Downing, Grich.
Sacrifice flies—Baylor, Boone, Thomas, Money, Simmons.
Stolen bases—Carew, Edwards, Molitor.
Caught stealing—Carew, Molitor, Thomas, DeCinces.
Double plays—Gantner, Yount and Cooper 2; Yount (unassisted); Yount, Gantner and Cooper; DeCinces, Grich and Carew; Molitor and Cooper; Grich, Carew, Foli, Carew and DeCinces; DeCinces and Grich; Molitor, Gantner and Cooper.
Left on bases—Milwaukee 6, 3, 4, 5, 6—24; California 5, 5, 6, 5, 8—29.
Hit by pitcher—By John (Moore), by Vuckovich (Grich), by Zahn (Oglivie).
Passed ball—Boone.
Balks—None.
Time of games—First game, 2:31; second game, 2:06; third game, 2:41; fourth game, 3:10; fifth game, 3:01.
Attendance—First game, 64,406; second game, 64,179; third game, 50,135; fourth game, 51,003; fifth game, 54,968.
Umpires—Barnett, Kunkel, Garcia, Palermo, Denkinger and Clark.
Official scorers—Ed Munson, Pancho Palesse.

NATIONAL LEAGUE
Championship Series of 1982

	W.	L.	Pct.
St. Louis (East)	3	0	1.000
Atlanta (West)	0	3	.000

Darrell Porter squirmed when a flock of reporters approached his spot in the locker room at Atlanta Stadium. The veteran catcher had just helped the St. Louis Cardinals sweep the Atlanta Braves in the 1982 National League Championship Series.

Porter had been an inspirational leader. The pitchers gave him credit for pulling together an otherwise questionable staff and making the unit a meaningful contributor to the Cardinals' success.

And, more importantly, Porter turned in his best offensive showing since leaving Kansas City following the 1980 season to sign a huge free-agent contract with the Cardinals. He reached base safely 10 times (five hits and five walks) in 14 plate appearances. He drove in a run, scored once in each of the three games and tied a Championship Series record (for a three-game series) with three doubles.

But Porter, who had set his life straight after years of alcohol and drug abuse, was reluctant to accept the fact that he had been chosen the series' Most Valuable Player.

"I'm a .230 hitter and no one should have to count on a .230 hitter," he said. "I used to be an awfully consistent player. But not anymore. But my life is on the upswing and has been since 1980 (when he entered a drug rehabilitation center)."

Actually, Porter batted .231 during the 1982 season after hitting .224 in 1981 for the Cardinals. But he was the driving force in the Cardinals' first Championship Series appearance.

"I went into this Championship Series totally relaxed," Porter continued. "I feel comfortable at the plate. But I don't even want to ask anyone what I'm doing differently up there, I'm just going to keep doing what I'm doing. I just want to have some fun. I want to relax."

However, there were other Cardinal players who did things right, too.

Rain aborted Game 1 in which the Braves, behind pitching ace Phil Niekro, were leading the Cardinals 1-0 after 4½ innings. The postponement erased Niekro and Joaquin Andujar of the Cardinals as the opening-game pitchers. Bob Forsch then treated the St. Louis fans to a dazzling three-hit shutout one night later as the Cardinals jumped in front in the series with a 7-0 victory.

Forsch, who struck out six batters and walked none, became the third man to pitch a shutout in the first game of a league Championship Series. The others were Baltimore's Jim Palmer in 1973 and Don Sutton of Los Angeles in 1974.

Forsch helped offensively, too. He had two singles, hit a sacrifice fly in a five-run sixth inning that spelled the exit of starter-loser Pascual Perez and scored the game's final run in the eighth.

Game 1 also brought attention to a spindly youngster named Willie McGee. McGee was a speedster who got away from New York Yankees Owner George Steinbrenner. He was frozen on the Yankees' Double A roster at Nashville (Southern League) before Steinbrenner dealt him to the Cardinals for pitcher Bob Sykes during the previous October.

McGee, the fastest of the Cardinals, made headlines for not coming home on what should have been an inside-the-park home run when his third-inning drive into the right-field corner skipped away from the Braves' Claudell Washington.

McGee admitted later that he got caught up in the excitement and forgot to look for third-base coach Chuck Hiller, who was waving the rookie home.

"The words I said can't be repeated," said a smiling McGee, who scored on Ozzie Smith's sacrifice fly. That was the only run Forsch needed.

However, the Cardinals broke it open in the sixth, setting a Championship Series record for most hits in an inning (six) and tying the mark for most runs (five). George Hendrick, McGee and Ozzie Smith produced run-scoring singles to highlight the outburst.

Prior to the series there hadn't been a rainout at Busch Memorial Stadium since August of 1976, but Game 2 also was delayed a day by more heavy thunderstorms.

Though the Cardinals scored a run off Niekro in the first inning of the second contest, the Braves took command in the third. Rafael Ramirez singled home Bruce Benedict, who had walked and advanced to second on a sacrifice, and then came all the way around himself when the ball got past McGee in center field and went to the wall for a three-base error.

With knuckleballer Niekro pitching well after his washed-out effort of three days earlier, the Braves increased their lead to 3-1 in the fifth on a single by Glenn Hubbard, Benedict's double and a sacrifice fly by Niekro.

The Cardinals pecked away at the lead, getting a sixth-inning run on Porter's second double of the game, which chased Keith Hernandez home from first base. And with Gene Garber pitching in the eighth for the Braves, Porter drew a one-out walk, went to third on a single by Hendrick and scored the tying run on McGee's high bounder up the middle. Atlanta shortstop Ramirez got to the ball, but the only man he could retire was Hendrick

A subdued Joe Torre watched helplessly as his Braves fell to the rampaging Cardinals in the 1982 N.L. Championship Series.

at second base.

Momentum seemingly had swung to the Cardinals.

David Green, who went into to play left field in the eighth inning, opened the ninth with a single to left. Tom Herr sacrificed Green to second, bringing Ken Oberkfell to the plate.

Oberkfell, who had a .289 average during the regular season but a .600 mark over his career against Garber (6 for 10), was given a chance to bat even though Cardinal reliever Bruce Sutter was scheduled to be the next hitter.

When Oberkfell lashed a liner just over the glove of a leaping Brett Butler in center field, the Cardinals had themselves a 4-3 victory and a 2-0 lead in the series.

If the come-from behind effort by the Cardinals in Game 2 hadn't finished off the Braves, then a four-run outburst in the second inning of Game 3 at Atlanta did.

Hernandez began the uprising with a single to left. Porter walked. Hendrick lined a single to right-center field to score Hernandez. McGee then split the gap in right-center for a triple, making the score 3-0. Ozzie Smith boosted the lead to four runs with a single to left-center. Exit Atlanta starter Rick Camp.

The Redbirds added a run in the fifth on a leadoff double by Herr and a two-out single by Hernandez. And McGee hit a bases-empty homer in the ninth.

The only runs the Braves could manage against Andujar came in the seventh when Atlanta had four singles, scoring on a double-play grounder by Chris Chambliss and a single by Hubbard. Sutter quelled that rally, and retired the last seven batters for a 6-2 triumph.

Sutter, who was the winning pitcher in Game 2, retired 13 men in succession in his 4⅓ innings of Championship Series work.

The St. Louis moundsmen limited the Braves to just five runs in three games. Atlanta, which had 146 homers in the regular season, had none in the series. In fact, the Braves had only one extra-base hit. More importantly, Cardinal pitchers held the Braves' three leading run-producers, Dale Murphy, Bob Horner and Chambliss, to four hits—all singles —and no RBIs in 32 at-bats.

It was the second visit to the N.L. Championship Series for the Braves, who were swept by the New York Mets in 1969.

The Cardinals, on the other hand, became the sixth team to sweep an N.L. series. Better yet, they had earned their first visit to the World Series since 1968, when they lost to the Detroit Tigers.

GAME OF THURSDAY, OCTOBER 7, AT ST. LOUIS (N)

Atlanta	AB.	R.	H.	RBI.	PO.	A.	St. Louis	AB.	R.	H.	RBI.	PO.	A.
Washington, rf	4	0	2	0	3	0	Herr, 2b	5	0	2	0	2	2
Ramirez, ss	4	0	0	0	1	2	Oberkfell, 3b	5	0	1	1	0	3
Murphy, cf	4	0	0	0	4	0	L. Smith, lf	3	1	1	1	0	0
Chambliss, 1b	3	0	0	0	8	1	Green, lf	0	0	0	0	0	0
Horner, 3b	3	0	0	0	0	2	Hernandez, 1b	4	1	1	0	10	0
Royster, lf	3	0	0	0	2	0	Hendrick, rf	4	1	1	1	3	0
Hubbard, 2b	3	0	0	0	0	3	Porter, c	4	1	2	0	6	1
Benedict, c	3	0	1	0	5	0	McGee, cf	4	2	2	1	3	0
Perez, p	2	0	0	0	0	1	O. Smith, ss	3	0	1	2	3	4
Bedrosian, p	0	0	0	0	0	0	Forsch, p	3	1	2	1	0	2
Moore, p	0	0	0	0	1	0	Totals	35	7	13	7	27	12
Whisenton, ph	1	0	0	0	0	0							
Walk, p	0	0	0	0	0	0							
Totals	30	0	3	0	24	9							

Atlanta	0	0	0	0	0	0	0	0	0 — 0
St. Louis	0	0	1	0	0	5	0	1	x — 7

Atlanta	IP.	H.	R.	ER.	BB.	SO.
Perez (Loser)	5*	7	4	4	1	2
Bedrosian	⅔	3	2	2	1	1
Moore	1⅓	1	0	0	0	1
Walk	1	2	1	1	1	1

St. Louis	IP.	H.	R.	ER.	BB.	SO.
Forsch (Winner)	9	3	0	0	0	6

*Pitched to three batters in sixth.

Game-winning RBI—O. Smith.

Error—Oberkfell. Left on bases—Atlanta 3, St. Louis 11. Two-base hit—Porter. Three-base hit—McGee. Caught stealing—Washington. Sacrifice flies—O. Smith, Forsch, L. Smith. Hit by pitcher—By Moore (L. Smith). Wild pitch—Bedrosian. Umpires—Williams, Engel, Wendelstedt, Froemming, Rennert and Runge. Time—2:25. Attendance—53,008.

GAME OF SATURDAY, OCTOBER 9, AT ST. LOUIS (N)

Atlanta	AB.	R.	H.	RBI.	PO.	A.	St. Louis	AB.	R.	H.	RBI.	PO.	A.
Washington, rf	3	0	0	0	2	1	Herr, 2b	3	0	0	0	2	2
Ramirez, ss	4	1	1	1	2	5	Oberkfell, 3b	5	1	1	1	1	0
Murphy, cf-lf	4	0	1	0	1	0	L. Smith, lf	4	0	1	0	1	0
Chambliss, 1b	3	0	0	0	12	1	Sutter, p	0	0	0	0	0	0
Horner, 3b	4	0	0	0	1	0	Hernandez, 1b	4	1	1	0	11	1
Butler, cf	0	0	0	0	0	0	Porter, c	2	1	2	1	5	1
Royster, lf-3b	4	0	2	0	0	0	Hendrick, rf	4	0	2	0	1	0
Hubbard, 2b	3	1	1	0	1	4	McGee, cf	4	0	0	1	6	0
Benedict, c	2	1	1	0	5	2	O. Smith, ss	2	0	1	0	0	3
Niekro, p	0	0	0	1	1	1	Stuper, p	1	0	0	0	0	0
Pocoroba, ph	1	0	0	0	0	0	Braun, ph	1	0	0	0	0	0
Garber, p	1	0	0	0	0	1	Bair, p	0	0	0	0	0	1
							Green, lf	1	1	1	0	0	0
Totals	29	3	6	2	25	15	Totals	31	4	9	3	27	10

```
Atlanta ..........................  0  0  2   0  1  0   0  0  0 — 3
St. Louis .......................  1  0  0   0  0  1   0  1  1 — 4
        One out when winning run scored.
```

Atlanta	IP.	H.	R.	ER.	BB.	SO.
Niekro	6	6	2	2	4	5
Garber (Loser)	2⅓	3	2	2	1	2

St. Louis	IP.	H.	R.	ER.	BB.	SO.
Stuper	6	4	3	2	1	4
Bair	1*	2	0	0	3	0
Sutter (Winner)	2	0	0	0	0	1

*Pitched to two batters in eighth.

Game-winning RBI—Oberkfell.

Error—McGee. Left on bases—Atlanta 6, St. Louis 9. Two-base hits—Porter 2, Benedict. Stolen bases—O. Smith, Murphy. Caught stealing—Murphy. Sacrifice hits—Stuper, Niekro, Hubbard, Herr. Sacrifice fly—Niekro. Wild pitch—Niekro. Passed ball—Benedict. Umpires—Engel, Wendelstedt, Froemming, Rennert, Runge and Williams. Time—2:46. Attendance—53,408.

GAME OF SUNDAY, OCTOBER 10, AT ATLANTA (N)

St. Louis	AB.	R.	H.	RBI.	PO.	A.	Atlanta	AB.	R.	H.	RBI.	PO.	A.
Herr, 2b	5	1	1	0	2	6	Ramirez, ss	3	0	1	0	2	4
Oberkfell, 3b	5	0	1	0	1	1	Royster, lf	4	0	0	0	2	0
L. Smith, lf	4	0	1	0	1	0	Washington, rf	2	0	1	0	0	0
Hernandez, 1b	4	1	2	1	14	0	Harper, pr-rf	1	1	0	0	0	0
Porter, c	3	1	1	0	4	1	Horner, 3b	4	0	1	0	1	3
Hendrick, rf	5	1	1	1	1	0	Chambliss, 1b	4	0	0	0	10	3
McGee, cf	5	2	2	3	3	0	Murphy, cf	3	1	2	0	3	0
O. Smith, ss	4	0	3	1	1	4	Hubbard, 2b	3	0	1	1	3	4
Andujar, p	1	0	0	0	0	1	Benedict, c	3	0	0	0	6	0
Sutter, p	1	0	0	0	0	0	Camp, p	0	0	0	0	0	0
							Perez, p	1	0	0	0	0	0
							Moore, p	0	0	0	0	0	0
							Whisenton, ph	1	0	0	0	0	0
							Mahler, p	0	0	0	0	0	1
							Bedrosian, p	0	0	0	0	0	0
							Butler, ph	1	0	0	0	0	0
							Garber, p	0	0	0	0	0	0
Totals	37	6	12	6	27	13	Totals	30	2	6	1	27	15

```
St. Louis .......................  0  4  0   0  1  0   0  0  1 — 6
Atlanta ..........................  0  0  0   0  0  0   2  0  0 — 2
```

St. Louis	IP.	H.	R.	ER.	BB.	SO.
Andujar (Winner)	6⅔	6	2	2	2	4
Sutter (Save)	2⅓	0	0	0	0	0

Atlanta	IP.	H.	R.	ER.	BB.	SO.
Camp (Loser)	1*	4	4	4	1	0
Perez	3⅔	3	1	1	1	2
Moore	1⅓	1	0	0	0	0
Mahler	1⅔	3	0	0	2	0
Bedrosian	⅓	0	0	0	0	1
Garber	1	1	1	1	0	1

*Pitched to five batters in second.

Game-winning RBI—Hendrick.

Error—Ramirez. Double plays—St. Louis 3. Left on bases—St. Louis 11, Atlanta 3. Two-base hit—Herr. Three-base hit—McGee. Home run—McGee. Sacrifice hits—Andujar 2, L. Smith. Wild pitches—Andujar 2. Balk—Andujar. Umpires—Wendelstedt, Froemming, Rennert, Runge, Williams and Engel. Time—2:51. Attendance—52,173.

ST. LOUIS CARDINALS' BATTING AND FIELDING AVERAGES

Player—Position	G.	AB.	R.	H.	TB.	2B.	3B.	HR.	RBI.	B.A.	PO.	A.	E.	F.A.
Green, lf	2	1	1	1	1	0	0	0	0	1.000	0	0	0	.000
Forsch, p	1	3	1	2	2	0	0	0	1	.667	0	2	0	1.000
Porter, c	3	9	3	5	8	3	0	0	0	.556	15	3	0	1.000

Player—Position	G.	AB.	R.	H.	TB.	2B.	3B.	HR.	RBI.	B.A.	PO.	A.	E.	F.A.
O. Smith, ss	3	9	0	5	5	0	0	0	3	.556	4	11	0	1.000
Hernandez, 1b	3	12	3	4	4	0	0	0	1	.333	35	1	0	1.000
McGee, cf	3	13	4	4	11	0	2	1	5	.308	12	0	1	.923
Hendrick, rf	3	13	2	4	4	0	0	0	2	.308	5	0	0	1.000
L. Smith, lf	3	11	1	3	3	0	0	0	1	.273	2	0	0	1.000
Herr, 2b	3	13	3	3	4	1	0	0	0	.231	6	10	0	1.000
Oberkfell, 3b	3	15	1	3	3	0	0	0	2	.200	2	4	1	.857
Bair, p	1	0	0	0	0	0	0	0	0	.000	0	1	0	1.000
Sutter, p	2	1	0	0	0	0	0	0	0	.000	0	2	0	1.000
Andujar, p	1	1	0	0	0	0	0	0	0	.000	0	1	0	1.000
Braun, ph	1	1	0	0	0	0	0	0	0	.000	0	0	0	.000
Stuper, p	1	1	0	0	0	0	0	0	0	.000	0	0	0	.000
Totals	3	103	17	34	45	4	2	1	16	.330	81	35	2	.983

ATLANTA BRAVES' BATTING AND FIELDING AVERAGES

Player—Position	G.	AB.	R.	H.	TB.	2B.	3B.	HR.	RBI.	B.A.	PO.	A.	E.	F.A.
Washington, rf	3	9	0	3	3	0	0	0	0	.333	5	1	0	1.000
Murphy, cf-lf	3	11	1	3	3	0	0	0	0	.273	8	0	0	1.000
Benedict, c	3	8	1	2	3	1	0	0	0	.250	16	2	0	1.000
Hubbard, 2b	3	9	1	2	2	0	0	0	1	.222	4	11	0	1.000
Ramirez, ss	3	11	1	2	2	0	0	0	1	.182	5	11	1	.941
Royster, lf-3b	3	11	0	2	2	0	0	0	0	.182	4	0	0	1.000
Horner, 3b	3	11	0	1	1	0	0	0	0	.091	2	5	0	1.000
Bedrosian, p	2	0	0	0	0	0	0	0	0	.000	0	0	0	.000
Moore, p	2	0	0	0	0	0	0	0	0	.000	1	0	0	1.000
Camp, p	1	0	0	0	0	0	0	0	0	.000	0	0	0	.000
Mahler, p	1	0	0	0	0	0	0	0	0	.000	0	1	0	1.000
Niekro, p	1	0	0	0	0	0	0	0	1	.000	1	1	0	1.000
Walk, p	1	0	0	0	0	0	0	0	0	.000	0	0	0	.000
Butler, cf-ph	2	1	0	0	0	0	0	0	0	.000	0	0	0	.000
Garber, p	2	1	0	0	0	0	0	0	0	.000	0	1	0	1.000
Pocoroba, ph	1	1	0	0	0	0	0	0	0	.000	0	0	0	.000
Harper, pr-rf	1	1	1	0	0	0	0	0	0	.000	0	0	0	.000
Whisenton, ph	2	2	0	0	0	0	0	0	0	.000	0	0	0	.000
Perez, p	2	3	0	0	0	0	0	0	0	.000	0	1	0	1.000
Chambliss, 1b	3	10	0	0	0	0	0	0	0	.000	30	5	0	1.000
Totals	3	89	5	15	16	1	0	0	3	.169	76	39	1	.991

ST. LOUIS CARDINALS' PITCHING RECORDS

Pitcher	G.	GS.	CG.	IP.	H.	R.	ER.	BB.	SO.	HB.	WP.	W.	L.	Pct.	ERA.
Forsch	1	1	1	9	3	0	0	0	6	0	0	1	0	1.000	0.00
Sutter	2	0	0	4⅓	0	0	0	0	1	0	0	1	0	1.000	0.00
Bair	1	0	0	1	2	0	0	3	0	0	0	0	0	.000	0.00
Andujar	1	1	0	6⅔	6	2	2	2	4	0	2	1	0	1.000	2.70
Stuper	1	1	0	6	4	3	2	1	4	0	0	0	0	.000	3.00
Totals	3	3	1	27	15	5	4	6	15	0	2	3	0	1.000	1.33

Shutout—Forsch. Save—Sutter.

ATLANTA BRAVES' PITCHING RECORDS

Pitcher	G.	GS.	CG.	IP.	H.	R.	ER.	BB.	SO.	HB.	WP.	W.	L.	Pct.	ERA.
Moore	2	0	0	2⅔	2	0	0	0	1	1	0	0	0	.000	0.00
Mahler	1	0	0	1⅔	3	0	0	2	0	0	0	0	0	.000	0.00
Niekro	1	1	0	6	6	2	2	4	5	0	1	0	0	.000	3.00
Perez	2	1	0	8⅔	10	5	5	2	4	0	0	0	1	.000	5.19
Garber	2	0	0	3⅓	4	3	3	1	3	0	0	0	1	.000	8.10
Walk	1	0	0	1	3	1	1	1	1	0	0	0	0	.000	9.00
Bedrosian	2	0	0	1	3	2	2	1	2	0	1	0	0	.000	18.00
Camp	1	1	0	1	4	4	4	1	0	0	0	0	1	.000	36.00
Totals	3	3	0	25⅓	35	17	17	12	16	1	2	0	3	.000	6.04

No shutouts or saves.

COMPOSITE SCORE BY INNINGS

St. Louis	1	4	1	0	1	6	0	2	2 — 17
Atlanta	0	0	2	0	1	0	2	0	0 — 5

Game-winning RBIs—O. Smith, Oberkfell, Hendrick.
Sacrifice hits—Andujar 2, Stuper, Niekro, Hubbard, Herr, L. Smith.
Sacrifice flies—O. Smith, Forsch, L. Smith, Niekro.
Stolen bases—O. Smith, Murphy.
Caught stealing—Washington, Murphy.
Double plays—Oberkfell, Herr and Hernandez; Herr and Hernandez; Herr, O. Smith and Hernandez.
Left on bases—St. Louis 11, 9, 11—31; Atlanta 3, 6, 3—12.
Hit by pitcher—By Moore (L. Smith).
Passed ball—Benedict.
Balk—Andujar.
Time of games—First game, 2:25; second game, 2:46; third game, 2:51.
Attendance—First game, 53,008; second game, 53,408; third game, 52,173.
Umpires—Williams, Engel, Wendelstedt, Froemming, Rennert and Runge.
Official scorers—Jack Herman, St. Louis Globe-Democrat; Randy Donaldson.

AMERICAN LEAGUE
Championship Series of 1983

	W.	L.	Pct.
Baltimore (East)	3	1	.750
Chicago (West)	1	3	.250

After watching Chicago righthander LaMarr Hoyt mow down his Baltimore teammates, 2-1, on five hits in Game 1 of the 1983 American League Championship Series, Orioles designated hitter Ken Singleton suggested: "We had better win the next three games, guys, because I don't think any of us wants to face Hoyt again in Game 5."

The Orioles took Singleton's suggestion to heart, prevailing by 4-0, 11-1 and 3-0 scores in the next three games to earn the right to face the Philadelphia Phillies in the World Series.

Baltimore pitchers made sure Hoyt wouldn't take the mound again, limiting the White Sox to one run in the final 31 innings of the playoff series. The Orioles' staff combined for a 0.49 earned-run average overall and stymied the heart of the Chicago batting order, holding Carlton Fisk, Greg Luzinski, Ron Kittle, Harold Baines and Tom Paciorek to a combined .183 average on 13 hits in 71 at-bats.

As dominant as Hoyt was in Game 1, Baltimore rookie righthander Mike Boddicker was even more masterful in the second game as he blanked the Sox on five hits and struck out a Championship Series record-tying 14 batters. Boddicker, who went 16-8 after being recalled from Rochester (International) in early May to replace the injured Jim Palmer, tied Detroit's Joe Coleman, who fanned 14 Oakland hitters in 1972, and Pittsburgh's John Candelaria, who had 14 strikeouts against Cincinnati in 1975. The performance led to Boddicker's selection as the A.L. playoffs' Most Valuable Player.

"Good hitters take advantage of pitchers' mistakes," Chicago Manager Tony LaRussa said with a sigh, "but Boddicker didn't make any mistakes."

Gary Roenicke was the offensive star in Game 2, scoring three runs and driving in two with a homer in the sixth inning. Half of Baltimore's left-field combination (he platooned with John Lowenstein), Roenicke doubled and scored on Julio Cruz's error in the second, walked and scored on Singleton's double in the fourth and then belted his homer to climax the scoring.

The scene shifted to Chicago for Game 3, and the Orioles brought out all of their artillery. The Orioles jumped on 22-game winner Richard Dotson in the first inning as Eddie Murray slugged a three-run homer. Murray, held hitless in his previous 29 postseason at-bats (21 in the 1979 World Series and eight in the first two games of this playoff), connected after a double by Jim Dwyer and a single by Cal Ripken.

Al Bumbry's double scored another run in the second, and there was no stopping the Orioles. Baltimore had only eight hits off four Chicago hurlers, but the Sox pitchers walked nine batters. Murray, who drew three bases on balls, scored four runs.

Mike Flanagan pitched five innings before his knee stiffened and Sammy Stewart came on to limit the Sox to one hit and no runs over the final four frames to record the save.

Flanagan was part of a full-blown brouhaha when he plunked Kittle on the left knee with a pitch in the fourth inning. Both benches emptied. One inning later, Dotson zinged Ripken in the left side. When Murray followed at the plate and a Dotson delivery buzzed the Baltimore batsman, Murray threatened Dotson and both benches emptied again. Peace was maintained, however.

Though the Orioles led the series, two games to one, the Sox figured they had the edge in the Britt Burns-Storm Davis pitching pairing in Game 4. The matchup turned out to be a dandy.

Davis hurled six innings of scoreless ball before Tippy Martinez took over after Greg Walker singled to open the Chicago seventh. Burns matched zeroes with both as the scoreless duel extended into the 10th inning.

When a game of such importance goes down to the wire, a player least expected to produce often becomes the hero. The name to go down in history this time was Tito Landrum.

Ticketed for the minor leagues in spring training by the St. Louis Cardinals but given a reprieve because of an injury to outfielder Willie McGee, Landrum had only five at-bats with the Cards when he finally was sent to Triple-A in late April. He batted .292 with 18 homers and 77 RBIs at Louisville (American Association), but was frozen in the minors until being obtained by the Orioles on August 31 to complete a June trade of utilityman Floyd Rayford. Landrum batted .310 the remainder of the season for the Orioles as a part-time player.

Landrum, 0-for-5 in the first three games of the playoffs, was in the starting lineup in Games 2 and 4 because right fielder Dan Ford had come up lame in Game 1. Having a 1-for-4 day when he strode to the plate in the 10th inning of the fourth game, the 28-year-old Landrum belted a home run against a brisk wind that had held up numerous long blasts earlier in the game.

"Pinch me a couple of times when I leave here," Landrum told reporters afterward, "to see if I'm really here."

As heartwarming as the story had become for Landrum, a veteran of 11 seasons in the Cardinals' organization, it had evolved into a nightmare for Burns, who was brilliant in holding the Orioles at bay while awaiting the one run that would have made him a winner. Instead, Burns' 147 pitches resulted only in a losing effort.

After Burns departed, the Orioles added two more runs against Salome Barojas. Ripken, Murray and Roenicke stroked successive singles and, after Juan Agosto replaced Barojas, pinch-hitter Benny Ayala scored Murray with a sacrifice fly.

In every big game, there are "what-if" situations. On this occasion, Chicago fans were wondering what would have happened if Sox shortstop Jerry Dybzinski hadn't blundered in the seventh inning. Walker and Vance Law had opened that inning with singles. Dybzinski was asked to bunt the runners along.

On a 3-and-1 count, Dybzinski forced pinch-runner Mike Squires at third base when Oriole catcher Rick Dempsey pounced on the bunt and retired the lead runner. Julio Cruz followed with a single to left, but Dybzinski rounded second base too far and got caught in a rundown. Law was gunned down at the plate on the play, snuffing out the rally.

"I made a big mistake," Dybzinski said. "I had the adrenaline flowing and, well, it was a big mistake."

While the Sox had missed on their first chance at making the World Series since 1959, the Orioles had evaded a second go-round with 24-game winner Hoyt and made it to the World Series for the second time in five years.

GAME OF WEDNESDAY, OCTOBER 5, AT BALTIMORE

Chicago	AB.	R.	H.	RBI.	PO.	A.
R. Law, cf	5	1	3	0	3	0
Fisk, c	5	0	1	0	5	0
Paciorek, 1b-lf	4	1	2	1	9	2
Luzinski, dh	3	0	1	0	0	0
Kittle, lf	3	0	0	0	1	0
Squires, 1b	1	0	0	0	2	0
Baines, rf	4	0	0	0	2	0
V. Law, 3b	3	0	0	0	2	2
Fletcher, ss	2	0	0	0	2	2
J. Cruz, 2b	2	0	0	0	1	6
Hoyt, p	0	0	0	0	2	1
Totals	32	2	7	1	27	13

Baltimore	AB.	R.	H.	RBI.	PO.	A.
Bumbry, cf	4	0	0	0	0	0
Ford, rf	4	0	1	0	1	0
Landrum, pr	0	1	0	0	0	0
Ripken, ss	4	0	1	1	2	2
Murray, 1b	4	0	0	0	10	1
Lowenstein, lf	3	0	0	0	1	0
Singleton, dh	3	0	1	0	0	0
Dauer, 2b	3	0	0	0	5	3
T. Cruz, 3b	3	0	1	0	3	6
Dempsey, c	2	0	1	0	4	2
Dwyer, ph	1	0	0	0	0	0
McGregor, p	0	0	0	0	1	1
Stewart, p	0	0	0	0	0	0
T. Martinez, p	0	0	0	0	0	1
Totals	31	1	5	1	27	16

Chicago	0	0	1	0	0	1	0	0	0 — 2
Baltimore	0	0	0	0	0	0	0	0	1 — 1

Chicago	IP.	H.	R.	ER.	BB.	SO.
Hoyt (Winner)	9	5	1	1	0	4

Baltimore	IP.	H.	R.	ER.	BB.	SO.
McGregor (Loser)	6⅔	6	2	1	3	2
Stewart	⅓*	1	0	0	1	1
T. Martinez	2	0	0	0	2	1

*Pitched to two batters in eighth.

Game-winning RBI—Paciorek.

Error—Murray. Double plays—Chicago 1, Baltimore 1. Left on bases—Chicago 10, Baltimore 3. Two-base hits—Luzinski, Singleton, R. Law, Ford. Sacrifice hit—Fletcher. Wild pitch—T. Martinez. Balk—McGregor. Umpires—McKean, Merrill, Bremigan, Evans, Phillips and Reilly. Time—2:38. Attendance—51,289.

Baltimore catcher Rick Dempsey gives relief ace Tippy Mar-
tinez a big lift after the Orioles' 1983 Championship Series-
clinching victory over the White Sox.

GAME OF THURSDAY, OCTOBER 6, AT BALTIMORE (N)

Chicago	AB.	R.	H.	RBI.	PO.	A.
R. Law, cf	4	0	2	0	2	0
Fisk, c	3	0	0	0	6	0
Baines, rf	4	0	0	0	1	0
Dybzinski, ss	0	0	0	0	1	1
Luzinski, dh	3	0	0	0	0	0
Paciorek, 1b	3	0	1	0	9	0
Kittle, lf	3	0	1	0	2	0
V. Law, 3b	2	0	0	0	0	3
Walker, ph	1	0	0	0	0	0
Rodriguez, 3b	0	0	0	0	0	0
Squires, ph	1	0	0	0	0	0
Fletcher, ss	2	0	0	0	1	3
Hairston, ph-rf	1	0	0	0	0	0
J. Cruz, 2b	4	0	1	0	2	1
Bannister, p	0	0	0	0	0	0
Barojas, p	0	0	0	0	0	1
Lamp, p	0	0	0	0	0	0
Totals	31	0	5	0	24	9

Baltimore	AB.	R.	H.	RBI.	PO.	A.
Shelby, cf	4	0	1	0	0	0
Landrum, rf	4	0	0	0	2	0
Ripken, ss	4	1	2	0	0	0
Murray, 1b	4	0	0	0	6	0
Roenicke, lf	2	3	2	2	1	0
Singleton, dh	4	0	1	1	0	0
Dauer, 2b	3	0	0	0	2	3
T. Cruz, 3b	3	0	0	0	1	3
Dempsey, c	3	0	0	0	15	1
Boddicker, p	0	0	0	0	0	1
Totals	31	4	6	3	27	8

Chicago	0	0	0	0	0	0	0	0	0 — 0
Baltimore	0	1	0	1	0	2	0	0	x — 4

Chicago	IP.	H.	R.	ER.	BB.	SO.
Bannister (Loser)	6	5	4	3	1	5
Barojas	1	1	0	0	0	0
Lamp	1	0	0	0	1	0

Baltimore	IP.	H.	R.	ER.	BB.	SO.
Boddicker (Winner)	9	5	0	0	3	14

Game-winning RBI—None.

Errors—V. Law, Rodriguez. Double plays—Chicago 1, Baltimore 1. Left on bases—Chicago 9, Baltimore 5. Two-base hits—Roenicke, Singleton, Ripken. Home run—Roenicke. Stolen bases—R. Law 2, Shelby. Caught stealing—Paciorek. Hit by pitcher—By Boddicker (Paciorek, Luzinski). Umpires—Merrill, Bremigan, Evans, Phillips, Reilly and McKean. Time—2:51. Attendance—52,347.

GAME OF FRIDAY, OCTOBER 7, AT CHICAGO (N)

Baltimore	AB.	R.	H.	RBI.	PO.	A.
Bumbry, cf	4	0	1	1	3	0
Shelby, ph-cf	0	1	0	0	0	0
Dwyer, rf	3	1	1	0	4	0
Landrum, ph-rf	1	0	0	0	2	0
Ripken, ss	4	3	2	0	2	4
Murray, 1b	2	4	1	3	7	2
Lowenstein, lf	3	0	1	2	3	0
Roenicke, ph-lf	0	1	0	1	0	0
Singleton, dh	3	0	1	0	0	0
Palmer, pr	0	0	0	0	0	0
Nolan, ph	0	0	0	1	0	0
Dauer, 2b	4	0	0	1	1	4
T. Cruz, 3b	5	0	1	1	1	1
Dempsey, c	3	1	0	0	2	0
Flanagan, p	0	0	0	0	0	0
Stewart, p	0	0	0	0	2	0
Totals	32	11	8	10	27	11

Chicago	AB.	R.	H.	RBI.	PO.	A.
R. Law, cf	4	0	2	0	3	0
Fisk, c	4	0	1	0	8	2
Paciorek, 1b	4	0	0	0	11	1
Luzinski, dh	4	0	1	0	0	0
Kittle, lf	1	1	1	0	0	0
Hairston, ph-lf	2	0	0	0	0	0
Baines, rf	4	0	0	0	2	1
V. Law, 3b	2	0	1	1	1	1
Squires, ph	1	0	0	0	0	0
Rodriguez, 3b	0	0	0	0	0	0
Fletcher, ss	3	0	0	0	1	3
J. Cruz, 2b	3	0	0	0	1	5
Dotson, p	0	0	0	0	1	1
Tidrow, p	0	0	0	0	0	0
Koosman, p	0	0	0	0	0	0
Lamp, p	0	0	0	0	0	0
Totals	32	1	6	1	27	14

Baltimore	3	1	0	0	2	0	0	1	4 — 11
Chicago	0	1	0	0	0	0	0	0	0 — 1

Baltimore	IP.	H.	R.	ER.	BB.	SO.
Flanagan (Winner)	5	5	1	1	0	1
Stewart (Save)	4	1	0	0	0	1

Chicago	IP.	H.	R.	ER.	BB.	SO.
Dotson (Loser)	5	6	6	6	3	3
Tidrow	3	1	1	1	3	3
Koosman	1/3	1	3	2	2	0
Lamp	2/3	0	1	0	1	1

Game-winning RBI—Murray.

Errors—Dempsey, Hairston. Double plays—Baltimore 1, Chicago 1. Left on bases—Baltimore 6, Chicago 5. Two-base hits—Dwyer, Bumbry, Kittle, Fisk, Lowenstein, Ripken. Home run—Murray. Stolen base—Murray. Sacrifice flies—Nolan, Dauer. Hit by pitcher—By Flanagan (Kittle); by Dotson (Ripken). Umpires—Bremigan, Evans, Phillips, Reilly, McKean and Merrill. Time—2:58. Attendance—46,635.

GAME OF SATURDAY, OCTOBER 8, AT CHICAGO

Baltimore	AB.	R.	H.	RBI.	PO.	A.
Shelby, cf	5	0	1	0	3	0
Landrum, rf	5	1	2	1	1	0
Ripken, ss	3	1	1	0	3	5
Murray, 1b	5	1	3	0	11	0
Roenicke, lf	2	0	1	1	3	1
Singleton, dh	2	0	0	0	0	0
Bumbry, pr	0	0	0	0	0	0
Ford, ph	1	0	0	0	0	0
Lowenstein, ph	0	0	0	0	0	0
Ayala, ph	0	0	0	1	0	0
Dauer, 2b	4	0	0	0	0	2
T. Cruz, 3b	4	0	0	0	1	3
Dempsey, c	4	0	1	0	8	2
Davis, p	0	0	0	0	0	0
T. Martinez, p	0	0	0	0	0	1
Totals	35	3	9	3	30	14

Chicago	AB.	R.	H.	RBI.	PO.	A.
R. Law, cf	5	0	0	0	2	0
Fisk, c	5	0	1	0	8	1
Baines, rf	4	0	2	0	0	0
Luzinski, dh	5	0	0	0	0	0
Paciorek, lf	5	0	1	0	1	0
Walker, 1b	2	0	1	0	7	1
Squires, pr-1b	1	0	0	0	4	0
V. Law, 3b	4	0	1	0	0	3
Dybzinski, ss	4	0	1	0	2	7
J. Cruz, 2b	3	0	3	0	6	2
Burns, p	0	0	0	0	0	1
Barojas, p	0	0	0	0	0	0
Agosto, p	0	0	0	0	0	0
Lamp, p	0	0	0	0	0	0
Totals	38	0	10	0	30	15

Baltimore	0	0	0	0	0	0	0	0	0	3 — 3
Chicago	0	0	0	0	0	0	0	0	0	0 — 0

Baltimore	IP.	H.	R.	ER.	BB.	SO.
Davis	6*	5	0	0	2	2
T. Martinez (Winner)	4	5	0	0	1	4

Chicago	IP.	H.	R.	ER.	BB.	SO.
Burns (Loser)	9⅓	6	1	1	5	8
Barojas	0†	3	2	2	0	0
Agosto	⅓	0	0	0	0	0
Lamp	⅓	0	0	0	0	0

*Pitched to one batter in seventh.
†Pitched to three batters in tenth.

Game-winning RBI—Landrum.

Errors—None. Double plays—Baltimore 1, Chicago 2. Left on bases—Baltimore 10, Chicago 11. Home run—Landrum. Stolen bases—J. Cruz 2. Sacrifice hit—Dauer. Sacrifice fly—Ayala. Hit by pitcher—By Burns (Roenicke). Balk—T. Martinez. Umpires—Evans, Phillips, Reilly, McKean, Merrill and Bremigan. Time—3:41. Attendance—45,477.

BALTIMORE ORIOLES' BATTING AND FIELDING AVERAGES

Player—Position	G.	AB.	R.	H.	TB.	2B.	3B.	HR.	RBI.	B.A.	PO.	A.	E.	F.A.
Roenicke, lf-ph	3	4	4	3	7	1	0	1	4	.750	4	1	0	1.000
Ripken, ss	4	15	5	6	8	2	0	0	1	.400	7	11	0	1.000
Murray, 1b	4	15	5	4	7	0	0	1	3	.267	34	3	1	.974
Singleton, dh	4	12	0	3	5	2	0	0	1	.250	0	0	0	.000
Dwyer, ph-rf	2	4	1	1	2	1	0	0	0	.250	4	0	0	1.000
Shelby, cf-ph	3	9	1	2	2	0	0	0	0	.222	3	0	0	1.000
Landrum, pr-rf-ph	4	10	2	2	5	0	0	1	1	.200	5	0	0	1.000
Ford, rf-ph	2	5	0	1	2	1	0	0	0	.200	1	0	0	1.000
Dempsey, c	4	12	1	2	2	0	0	0	0	.167	29	5	1	.971
Lowenstein, lf-ph	3	6	0	1	2	1	0	0	2	.167	4	0	0	1.000
T. Cruz, 3b	4	15	0	2	2	0	0	0	1	.133	6	13	0	1.000
Bumbry, cf-pr	3	8	0	1	2	1	0	0	1	.125	3	0	0	1.000
T. Martinez, p	2	0	0	0	0	0	0	0	0	.000	0	2	0	1.000
Stewart, p	2	0	0	0	0	0	0	0	0	.000	2	0	0	1.000
Ayala, ph	1	0	0	0	0	0	0	0	1	.000	0	0	0	.000
Boddicker, p	1	0	0	0	0	0	0	0	0	.000	0	1	0	1.000
Davis, p	1	0	0	0	0	0	0	0	0	.000	0	0	0	.000
Flanagan, p	1	0	0	0	0	0	0	0	0	.000	0	0	0	.000
McGregor, p	1	0	0	0	0	0	0	0	0	.000	1	1	0	1.000
Nolan, ph	1	0	0	0	0	0	0	0	1	.000	0	0	0	.000
Palmer, pr	1	0	0	0	0	0	0	0	0	.000	0	0	0	.000
Dauer, 2b	4	14	0	0	0	0	0	0	1	.000	8	12	0	1.000
Totals	4	129	19	28	46	9	0	3	17	.217	111	49	2	.988

CHICAGO WHITE SOX' BATTING AND FIELDING AVERAGES

Player—Position	G.	AB.	R.	H.	TB.	2B.	3B.	HR.	RBI.	B.A.	PO.	A.	E.	F.A.
R. Law, cf	4	18	1	7	8	1	0	0	0	.389	10	0	0	1.000
J. Cruz, 2b	4	12	0	4	4	0	0	0	0	.333	10	14	0	1.000
Walker, ph-1b	2	3	0	1	1	0	0	0	0	.333	7	1	0	1.000
Kittle, lf	3	7	1	2	3	1	0	0	0	.286	3	0	0	1.000
Paciorek, 1b-lf	4	16	1	4	4	0	0	0	1	.250	30	3	0	1.000
Dybzinski, ss	2	4	0	1	1	0	0	0	0	.250	3	8	0	1.000
V. Law, 3b	4	11	0	2	2	0	0	0	1	.182	1	9	1	.909
Fisk, c	4	17	0	3	4	1	0	0	0	.176	27	3	0	1.000
Luzinski, dh	4	15	0	2	3	1	0	0	0	.133	0	0	0	.000
Baines, rf	4	16	0	2	2	0	0	0	0	.125	5	1	0	1.000

BASEBALL DOPE BOOK

Player—Position	G.	AB.	R.	H.	TB.	2B.	3B.	HR.	RBI.	B.A.	PO.	A.	E.	F.A.
Lamp, p	3	0	0	0	0	0	0	0	0	.000	0	0	0	.000
Barojas, p	2	0	0	0	0	0	0	0	0	.000	0	1	0	1.000
Rodriguez, 3b	2	0	0	0	0	0	0	0	0	.000	0	0	1	.000
Agosto, p	1	0	0	0	0	0	0	0	0	.000	0	0	0	.000
Bannister, p	1	0	0	0	0	0	0	0	0	.000	0	0	0	.000
Burns, p	1	0	0	0	0	0	0	0	0	.000	0	1	0	1.000
Dotson, p	1	0	0	0	0	0	0	0	0	.000	1	1	0	1.000
Hoyt, p	1	0	0	0	0	0	0	0	0	.000	2	1	0	1.000
Koosman, p	1	0	0	0	0	0	0	0	0	.000	0	0	0	.000
Tidrow, p	1	0	0	0	0	0	0	0	0	.000	0	0	0	.000
Hairston, ph-rf-lf	2	3	0	0	0	0	0	0	0	.000	0	0	1	.000
Squires, 1b-ph-pr	4	4	0	0	0	0	0	0	0	.000	6	0	0	1.000
Fletcher, ss	3	7	0	0	0	0	0	0	0	.000	3	8	0	1.000
Totals	4	133	3	28	32	4	0	0	2	.211	108	51	3	.981

BALTIMORE ORIOLES' PITCHING RECORDS

Pitcher	G.	GS.	CG.	IP.	H.	R.	ER.	BB.	SO.	HB.	WP.	W.	L.	Pct.	ERA.
Boddicker	1	1	1	9	5	0	0	3	14	2	0	1	0	1.000	0.00
Davis	1	1	0	6	5	0	0	2	2	0	0	0	0	.000	0.00
T. Martinez	2	0	0	6	5	0	0	3	5	0	1	1	0	1.000	0.00
Stewart	2	0	0	4⅓	2	0	0	1	2	0	0	0	0	.000	0.00
McGregor	1	1	0	6⅔	6	2	1	3	2	0	0	0	1	.000	1.35
Flanagan	1	1	0	5	5	1	1	0	1	1	0	1	0	1.000	1.80
Totals	4	4	1	37	28	3	2	12	26	3	1	3	1	.750	0.49

Shutouts—Boddicker, Davis-T. Martinez (combined). Save—Stewart.

CHICAGO WHITE SOX' PITCHING RECORDS

Pitcher	G.	GS.	CG.	IP.	H.	R.	ER.	BB.	SO.	HB.	WP.	W.	L.	Pct.	ERA.
Lamp	3	0	0	2	0	1	0	2	1	0	0	0	0	.000	0.00
Agosto	1	0	0	⅓	0	0	0	0	0	0	0	0	0	.000	0.00
Burns	1	1	0	9⅓	6	1	1	5	8	1	0	0	1	.000	0.96
Hoyt	1	1	1	9	5	1	1	0	4	0	0	1	0	1.000	1.00
Tidrow	1	0	0	3	1	1	1	3	3	0	0	0	0	.000	3.00
Bannister	1	1	0	6	5	4	3	1	5	0	0	0	1	.000	4.50
Dotson	1	1	0	5	6	6	6	3	3	1	0	0	1	.000	10.80
Barojas	2	0	0	1	4	2	2	0	0	0	0	0	0	.000	18.00
Koosman	1	0	0	⅓	1	3	2	2	0	0	0	0	0	.000	54.00
Totals	4	4	1	36	28	19	16	16	24	2	0	1	3	.250	4.00

No shutouts or saves.

COMPOSITE SCORE BY INNINGS

Baltimore	3	2	0	1	2	2	0	1	5	3 — 19
Chicago	0	1	1	0	0	1	0	0	0	0 — 3

Game-winning RBIs—Paciorek, Murray, Landrum.
Sacrifice hits—Fletcher, Dauer.
Sacrifice flies—Nolan, Dauer, Ayala.
Stolen bases—R. Law 2, J. Cruz 2, Shelby, Murray.
Caught stealing—Paciorek.
Double plays—Fletcher, J. Cruz and Paciorek 2; Ripken, Dauer and Murray; Dempsey and T. Cruz; Dybzinski and Paciorek; Dauer, Ripken and Murray; Ripken and Murray; V. Law, J. Cruz and Walker.
Left on bases—Baltimore 3, 5, 6, 10—24; Chicago 10, 9, 5, 11—35.
Hit by pitcher—By Boddicker (Paciorek, Luzinski); by Flanagan (Kittle); by Dotson (Ripken); by Burns (Roenicke).
Passed balls—None.
Balks—McGregor, T. Martinez.
Time of games—First game, 2:38; second game, 2:51; third game, 2:58; fourth game, 3:41.
Attendance—First game, 51,289; second game, 52,347; third game, 46,635; fourth game, 45,477.
Umpires—McKean, Merrill, Bremigan, Evans, Phillips and Reilly.
Official scorers—Neal Eskridge; Dave Nightingale, The Sporting News.

NATIONAL LEAGUE
Championship Series of 1983

	W.	L.	Pct.
Philadelphia (East)	**3**	**1**	**.750**
Los Angeles (West)	**1**	**3**	**.250**

When he strolled to the plate in the second inning of the second game of the 1983 National League Championship Series, Gary Matthews did so with considerable trepidation.

Matthews, a .284 career hitter entering the 1983 season and a man who normally produced 15-20 homers and more than 70 runs batted in per year, had fallen off to a .258 average in '83 with only 10 homers and 50 RBIs. He had become a platoon player shortly after Phillies General Manager Paul Owens took over as field manager July 18, spending a lot of time on the bench in the waning months of the season.

Matthews, a righthanded batter, knew very well that many platoon players never become regulars again. And at age 33, he wasn't pleased with the outlook.

The Championship Series, Matthews figured, offered the perfect setting for regaining his starting left-field job. The fact that he was 0-for-4 in Game 1 against Los Angeles lefthander Jerry Reuss hadn't set well with Matthews. And he knew the Dodgers were talking about starting righthanders Bob Welch and Alejandro Pena in Games 3 and 4 when the playoffs shifted from Los Angeles to Philadelphia. If he was going to produce, now was the time.

To that end, Matthews ended a personal 1-for-25 slump in great fashion against lefthander Fernando Valenzuela by blasting a home run into the left-field seats. He wound up with a 2-for-4 game, and his homer was the only offense for the Phillies as they dropped a 4-1 decision to even the Championship Series at one game apiece.

When the playoff resumed two days later, Owens again had penciled Matthews' name into the lineup, even though Welch was on the mound. Gary responded with a 3-for-3 day, including another homer and four RBIs, as the Phillies downed the Dodgers, 7-2.

Now, Matthews was on a roll. There was no keeping him out of the lineup.

In the first inning of Game 4, he clubbed a three-run homer off Reuss (Pena had pitched in relief the day before) and, behind lefthander Steve Carlton, the Phillies won another 7-2 decision to advance to the World Series against the Baltimore Orioles.

"Not playing was the low point in my career," Matthews said solemnly after being named the Most Valuable Player of the N.L. title series. "But I didn't dwell on it or tear up the clubhouse or sulk. I knew I could still do it, that I wasn't washed up."

Matthews had five straight hits to set an N.L. Championship Series record. His eight RBIs tied a league playoff mark set by the Dodgers' Dusty Baker in 1977, and his homers in three consecutive games equalled Hank Aaron's Championship Series record established in 1969.

Matthews, whose RBI total surpassed his output in the final four weeks of the season and whose three homers were one more than he had hit since the All-Star break, was asked if his playoff success could erase the misfortunes of the regular season.

Matthews took a long sip of champagne as he pondered his answer.

"This doesn't make up for it, if that's what you mean," he said. "I would have rather had a good season and a good playoff. I'm not going to lie to you, this was a tough year.

"I feel I could have had this kind of streak if I had played regularly, but I'm not going to complain. Greg Gross and Joe Lefebvre added a lot to our ballclub. We wouldn't be here if it wasn't for them."

The Phillies also wouldn't have made it to the World Series without the strong pitching of Carlton and Al Holland, who combined for victories in the Championship Series opener and in the clincher. Reliever Ron Reed also helped out in the finale.

Mike Schmidt's first-inning homer was all the offense the Phillies needed behind Carlton and Holland in Game 1. When Carlton (who permitted only seven hits in 7⅔ innings) loaded the bases on singles by Steve Sax and Baker and a walk to Pedro Guerrero in the eighth inning, Holland bailed out the veteran by getting Mike Marshall to fly out. Holland then set down the Dodgers in the ninth to preserve the Phils' 1-0 victory.

The Phillies' bats were unproductive in Game 2 against Valenzuela and reliever Tom Niedenfuer, the Dodgers knotting the playoffs on the strength of Guerrero's two-run triple in the fifth inning and a run-scoring single by Jack Fimple in the eighth.

The Phillies got their first two runs in Game 3 without a hit, scoring on a passed ball and on a groundout by Ivan DeJesus in the second inning. They added another run in the third on Lefebvre's sacrifice fly. Then, after Marshall belted a two-run homer for the Dodgers in the fourth, Matthews took over. He hit a solo homer in the bottom of the fourth, drove in two more runs with a single in the fifth and climaxed the victory with another run-scoring single in the seventh. Meanwhile, rookie Charles Hudson shackled the Dodgers on four hits.

Schmidt and Sixto Lezcano had two-out singles preceding Matthews' three-run blast in the first inning of Game 4. Schmidt, who had three hits in the final game and batted .467

(7-for-15) in the four games, doubled home a run and scored on a groundout by Garry Maddox in the fifth, making the score 5-1. Lezcano increased the lead to 7-1 with a two-run homer in the sixth.

Carlton, Reed and Holland scattered 10 hits in the decisive triumph.

Matthews, Pete Rose, Joe Morgan and others may have been unhappy over some of Owens' strategy during the season, but no one was complaining after the Phillies had won their second N.L. pennant in four years.

GAME OF TUESDAY, OCTOBER 4, AT LOS ANGELES (N)

Philadelphia	AB.	R.	H.	RBI.	PO.	A.	Los Angeles	AB.	R.	H.	RBI.	PO.	A.
Morgan, 2b	4	0	0	0	3	1	Sax, 2b	4	0	3	0	1	5
Rose, 1b	4	0	1	0	8	1	Russell, ss	3	0	1	0	0	3
Schmidt, 3b	3	1	2	1	0	2	Baker, lf	4	0	1	0	3	0
Lezcano, rf	3	0	1	0	2	0	Guerrero, 3b	2	0	0	0	0	1
Matthews, lf	4	0	0	0	2	0	Marshall, 1b	4	0	0	0	11	0
Holland, p	0	0	0	0	0	0	Niedenfuer, p	0	0	0	0	0	1
Maddox, cf	4	0	1	0	4	0	Yeager, c	4	0	0	0	4	0
Diaz, c	3	0	0	0	6	0	Landreaux, cf	3	0	0	0	3	0
DeJesus, ss	3	0	0	0	1	2	Morales, ph	1	0	0	0	0	0
Carlton, p	3	0	0	0	1	3	Thomas, rf	4	0	2	0	4	0
G. Gross, lf	1	0	0	0	0	0	Reuss, p	1	0	0	0	0	1
							Maldonado, ph	1	0	0	0	0	0
							Brock, 1b	1	0	0	0	1	0
Totals	32	1	5	1	27	9	Totals	32	0	7	0	27	11

Philadelphia	1	0	0	0	0	0	0	0	0—1
Los Angeles	0	0	0	0	0	0	0	0	0—0

Philadelphia	IP.	H.	R.	ER.	BB.	SO.
Carlton (Winner)	7⅔	7	0	0	2	6
Holland (Save)	1⅓	0	0	0	0	0
Los Angeles	**IP.**	**H.**	**R.**	**ER.**	**BB.**	**SO.**
Reuss (Loser)	8	5	1	1	3	3
Niedenfuer	1	0	0	0	1	1

Game-winning RBI—Schmidt.

Error—Schmidt. Left on bases—Philadelphia 8, Los Angeles 9. Home run—Schmidt. Stolen base—Thomas. Sacrifice hits—Reuss, Russell. Wild pitches—Carlton, Reuss. Umpires—Tata, Stello, McSherry, Weyer, Harvey and Crawford. Time—2:17. Attendance—49,963.

GAME OF WEDNESDAY, OCTOBER 5, AT LOS ANGELES (N)

Philadelphia	AB.	R.	H.	RBI.	PO.	A.	Los Angeles	AB.	R.	H.	RBI.	PO.	A.
Morgan, 2b	3	0	0	0	4	3	Sax, 2b	4	0	0	0	4	4
Rose, 1b	3	0	0	0	7	0	Brock, 1b	4	1	0	0	7	0
Schmidt, 3b	4	0	1	0	1	3	Thomas, rf	0	0	0	0	0	0
Lezcano, rf	4	0	0	0	1	0	Baker, lf	3	2	0	0	3	0
Matthews, lf	4	1	2	1	1	0	Guerrero, 3b	3	0	1	2	0	2
Maddox, cf	3	0	2	0	4	0	Landreaux, cf	3	0	2	1	3	0
G. Gross, ph	0	0	0	0	0	0	Marshall, rf-1b	4	0	0	0	2	0
Diaz, c	3	0	0	0	5	1	Russell, ss	3	1	2	0	1	5
Lefebvre, ph	1	0	0	0	0	0	Fimple, c	4	0	1	1	6	1
DeJesus, ss	2	0	1	0	1	3	Valenzuela, p	3	0	0	1	1	0
Hayes, ph	1	0	0	0	0	0	Niedenfuer, p	0	0	0	0	0	0
Denny, p	1	0	0	0	0	0							
Perez, ph	1	0	1	0	0	0	Totals	31	4	6	4	27	12
Samuel, pr	0	0	0	0	0	0							
Reed, p	0	0	0	0	0	1							
Virgil, ph	1	0	0	0	0	0							
Totals	31	1	7	1	24	11							

Philadelphia	0	1	0	0	0	0	0	0	0—1
Los Angeles	1	0	0	0	2	0	0	1	x—4

Philadelphia	IP.	H.	R.	ER.	BB.	SO.
Denny (Loser)	6	5	3	0	3	3
Reed	2	1	1	1	1	1
Los Angeles	**IP.**	**H.**	**R.**	**ER.**	**BB.**	**SO.**
Valenzuela (Winner)	8*	7	1	1	4	5
Niedenfuer (Save)	1	0	0	0	0	2

*Pitched to two batters in ninth.

Game-winning RBI—Guerrero.

Errors—DeJesus, Maddox, Russell. Double plays—Los Angeles 3. Left on bases—Philadelphia 8, Los Angeles 8. Two-base hit—Maddox. Three-base hit—Guerrero. Home run—Matthews. Stolen bases—Rose, Russell. Sacrifice hit—Denny. Hit by pitcher—By Denny (Guerrero). Wild pitch—Valenzuela. Umpires—Stello, McSherry, Weyer, Harvey, Crawford and Tata. Time—2:44. Attendance—55,967.

GAME OF FRIDAY, OCTOBER 7, AT PHILADELPHIA

Los Angeles	AB.	R.	H.	RBI.	PO.	A.
Sax, 2b	3	0	0	0	1	0
Brock, 1b	4	0	0	0	5	0
Baker, lf	4	1	2	0	2	0
Guerrero, 3b	4	0	0	0	0	4
Landreaux, cf	4	0	0	0	5	0
Marshall, rf	3	1	1	2	4	0
Russell, ss	4	0	0	0	0	0
Fimple, c	3	0	0	0	7	1
Welch, p	0	0	0	0	0	0
Pena, p	1	0	1	0	0	0
Landestoy, ph	1	0	0	0	0	0
Honeycutt, p	0	0	0	0	0	0
Beckwith, p	0	0	0	0	0	0
Thomas, ph	1	0	0	0	0	0
Zachry, p	0	0	0	0	0	0
Totals	32	2	4	2	24	5

Philadelphia	AB.	R.	H.	RBI.	PO.	A.
Morgan, 2b	4	1	1	0	0	2
Rose, 1b	4	2	3	0	7	0
Schmidt, 3b	3	1	1	0	3	1
Lefebvre, rf	1	0	0	1	2	0
Lezcano, ph-rf	2	0	0	0	0	0
Matthews, lf	3	2	3	4	2	0
Dernier, cf	0	0	0	0	0	0
G. Gross, cf-lf	3	1	0	0	4	0
Diaz, c	3	0	0	0	9	0
DeJesus, ss	4	0	1	1	0	2
Hudson, p	4	0	0	0	0	0
Totals	31	7	9	6	27	5

Los Angeles	0	0	0	2	0	0	0	0	0	— 2
Philadelphia	0	2	1	1	2	0	1	0	x	— 7

Los Angeles	IP.	H.	R.	ER.	BB.	SO.
Welch (Loser)	1⅓	0	2	1	2	0
Pena	2⅔	4	2	2	1	3
Honeycutt	⅓	2	2	2	0	0
Beckwith	1⅔	1	0	0	0	3
Zachry	2	2	1	1	1	1

Philadelphia	IP.	H.	R.	ER.	BB.	SO.
Hudson (Winner)	9	4	2	2	2	9

Game-winning RBI—None.

Error—DeJesus. Left on bases—Los Angeles 5, Philadelphia 5. Two-base hits—Baker, Schmidt. Home runs—Marshall, Matthews. Stolen bases—Sax, Matthews. Caught stealing—Rose. Sacrifice flies—Lefebvre. Wild pitches—Pena 2. Passed ball—Fimple. Umpires—McSherry, Weyer, Harvey, Crawford, Tata and Stello. Time—2:51. Attendance—53,490.

GAME OF SATURDAY, OCTOBER 8, AT PHILADELPHIA (N)

Los Angeles	AB.	R.	H.	RBI.	PO.	A.
Sax, 2b	5	0	1	0	5	3
Russell, ss	4	0	1	0	3	2
Guerrero, 3b	3	1	2	0	0	2
Baker, 1b	3	1	2	1	1	0
Marshall, 1b	4	0	1	0	5	2
Yeager, c	2	0	1	0	3	1
Monday, ph	0	0	0	0	0	0
Morales, ph	1	0	0	0	0	0
Fimple, c	0	0	0	0	1	0
Landreaux, cf	4	0	0	0	1	0
Thomas, rf	4	0	2	0	3	0
Reuss, p	2	0	0	0	0	0
Beckwith, p	0	0	0	0	0	0
Honeycutt, p	0	0	0	0	1	0
Landestoy, ph	1	0	0	0	0	0
Zachry, p	0	0	0	0	1	0
Maldonado, ph	1	0	0	0	0	0
Totals	34	2	10	1	24	10

Philadelphia	AB.	R.	H.	RBI.	PO.	A.
Morgan, 2b	4	0	0	0	1	1
Rose, 1b	5	1	2	0	7	1
Schmidt, 3b	5	3	3	1	2	1
Lezcano, rf-lf	4	2	3	2	2	1
Matthews, lf	3	1	1	3	1	0
Reed, p	0	0	0	0	0	0
Hayes, rf	1	0	0	0	0	0
Maddox, cf	4	0	0	1	0	0
Diaz, c	4	0	2	0	12	1
DeJesus, ss	3	0	1	0	2	4
Carlton, p	2	0	1	0	0	2
G. Gross, lf	1	0	0	0	0	0
Holland, p	0	0	0	0	0	0
Totals	36	7	13	7	27	11

Los Angeles	0	0	0	1	0	0	0	1	0	— 2
Philadelphia	3	0	0	0	2	2	0	0	x	— 7

Los Angeles	IP.	H.	R.	ER.	BB.	SO.
Reuss (Loser)	4*	9	5	5	0	1
Beckwith	⅔	0	0	0	2	0
Honeycutt	1⅓	2	2	2	0	2
Zachry	2	2	0	0	1	1

Philadelphia	IP.	H.	R.	ER.	BB.	SO.
Carlton (Winner)	6	6	1	1	3	7
Reed	1⅓	3	1	0	0	2
Holland	1⅔	1	0	0	0	3

*Pitched to two batters in fifth.

Game-winning RBI—Matthews.

Error—Lezcano. Left on bases—Los Angeles 9, Philadelphia 10. Two-base hits—Guerrero, Marshall, Schmidt, Yeager, Diaz, Thomas. Home runs—Matthews, Baker, Lezcano. Caught stealing—Sax, Marshall. Sacrifice hits—Carlton, Lezcano. Hit by pitcher—By Carlton (Yeager). Wild pitches—Carlton. Umpires—Weyer, Harvey, Crawford, Tata, Stello and McSherry. Time—2:50. Attendance—64,494.

PHILADELPHIA PHILLIES' BATTING AND FIELDING AVERAGES

Player—Position	G.	AB.	R.	H.	TB.	2B.	3B.	HR.	RBI.	B.A.	PO.	A.	E.	F.A.
Perez, ph	1	1	0	1	1	0	0	0	0	1.000	0	0	0	.000
Schmidt, 3b	4	15	5	7	12	2	0	1	2	.467	6	7	1	.929
Matthews, lf	4	14	4	6	15	0	0	3	8	.429	6	0	0	1.000
Rose, 1b	4	16	3	6	6	0	0	0	0	.375	29	2	0	1.000
Lezcano, rf-ph-lf	4	13	2	4	7	0	0	1	2	.308	5	1	1	.857
Maddox, cf	3	11	0	3	4	1	0	0	1	.273	8	0	1	.889

Player—Position	G.	AB.	R.	H.	TB.	2B.	3B.	HR.	RBI.	B.A.	PO.	A.	E.	F.A.
DeJesus, ss	4	12	0	3	3	0	0	0	1	.250	4	11	2	.882
Carlton, p	2	5	0	1	1	0	0	0	0	.200	1	5	0	1.000
Diaz, c	4	13	0	2	3	1	0	0	0	.154	32	2	0	1.000
Morgan, 2b	4	15	1	1	1	0	0	0	0	.067	8	7	0	1.000
Dernier, cf	1	0	0	0	0	0	0	0	0	.000	0	0	0	.000
Holland, p	2	0	0	0	0	0	0	0	0	.000	0	0	0	.000
Reed, p	2	0	0	0	0	0	0	0	0	.000	0	1	0	1.000
Samuel, pr	1	0	0	0	0	0	0	0	0	.000	0	0	0	.000
Denny, p	1	1	0	0	0	0	0	0	0	.000	0	0	0	.000
Virgil, ph	1	1	0	0	0	0	0	0	0	.000	0	0	0	.000
Hayes, ph-rf	2	2	0	0	0	0	0	0	0	.000	0	0	0	.000
Lefebvre, ph-rf	2	2	0	0	0	0	0	0	1	.000	2	0	0	1.000
Hudson, p	1	4	0	0	0	0	0	0	0	.000	0	0	0	.000
G. Gross, lf-ph-cf	4	5	1	0	0	0	0	0	0	.000	4	0	0	1.000
Totals	4	130	16	34	53	4	0	5	15	.262	105	36	5	.966

LOS ANGELES DODGERS' BATTING AND FIELDING AVERAGES

Player—Position	G.	AB.	R.	H.	TB.	2B.	3B.	HR.	RBI.	B.A.	PO.	A.	E.	F.A.
Pena, p	1	1	0	1	1	0	0	0	0	1.000	0	0	0	.000
Thomas, rf-ph	4	9	0	4	5	1	0	0	0	.444	7	0	0	1.000
Baker, lf	4	14	4	5	9	1	0	1	1	.357	9	0	0	1.000
Russell, ss	4	14	1	4	4	0	0	0	0	.286	4	10	1	.933
S. Sax, 2b	4	16	0	4	4	0	0	0	0	.250	11	12	0	1.000
Guerrero, 3b	4	12	1	3	6	1	1	0	2	.250	0	9	0	1.000
Yeager, c	2	6	0	1	2	1	0	0	0	.167	7	1	0	1.000
Landreaux, cf	4	14	0	2	2	0	0	0	1	.143	12	0	0	1.000
Fimple, c	3	7	0	1	1	0	0	0	1	.143	14	2	0	1.000
Marshall, 1b-rf	4	15	1	2	6	1	0	1	2	.133	22	2	0	1.000
Beckwith, p	2	0	0	0	0	0	0	0	0	.000	0	0	0	.000
Honeycutt, p	2	0	0	0	0	0	0	0	0	.000	1	0	0	1.000
Niedenfuer, p	2	0	0	0	0	0	0	0	0	.000	0	1	0	1.000
Zachry, p	2	0	0	0	0	0	0	0	0	.000	1	0	0	1.000
Monday, ph	1	0	0	0	0	0	0	0	0	.000	0	0	0	.000
Welch, p	1	0	0	0	0	0	0	0	0	.000	0	0	0	.000
Landestoy, ph	2	2	0	0	0	0	0	0	0	.000	0	0	0	.000
Maldonado, ph	2	2	0	0	0	0	0	0	0	.000	0	0	0	.000
Morales, ph	2	2	0	0	0	0	0	0	0	.000	0	0	0	.000
Reuss, p	2	3	0	0	0	0	0	0	0	.000	0	1	0	1.000
Valenzuela, p	1	3	0	0	0	0	0	0	0	.000	1	0	0	1.000
Brock, 1b	3	9	1	0	0	0	0	0	0	.000	13	0	0	1.000
Totals	4	129	8	27	40	5	1	2	7	.209	102	38	1	.993

PHILADELPHIA PHILLIES' PITCHING RECORDS

Pitcher	G.	GS.	CG.	IP.	H.	R.	ER.	BB.	SO.	HB.	WP.	W.	L.	Pct.	ERA.
Denny	1	1	0	6	5	3	0	3	3	1	0	0	1	.000	0.00
Holland	2	0	0	3	1	0	0	0	3	0	0	0	0	.000	0.00
Carlton	2	2	0	13⅔	13	1	1	5	13	1	2	2	0	1.000	0.66
Hudson	1	1	1	9	4	2	2	2	9	0	0	1	0	1.000	2.00
Reed	2	0	0	3⅓	4	2	1	1	3	0	0	0	0	.000	2.70
Totals	4	4	1	35	27	8	4	11	31	2	2	3	1	.750	1.03

Shutout—Carlton-Holland (combined). Save—Holland.

LOS ANGELES DODGERS' PITCHING RECORDS

Pitcher	G.	GS.	CG.	IP.	H.	R.	ER.	BB.	SO.	HB.	WP.	W.	L.	Pct.	ERA.
Beckwith	2	0	0	2⅓	1	0	0	2	3	0	0	0	0	.000	0.00
Niedenfuer	2	0	0	2	0	0	0	1	3	0	0	0	0	.000	0.00
Valenzuela	1	1	0	8	7	1	1	4	5	0	1	1	0	1.000	1.13
Zachry	2	0	0	4	4	1	1	2	2	0	0	0	0	.000	2.25
Reuss	2	2	0	12	14	6	6	3	4	0	1	0	2	.000	4.50
Pena	1	0	0	2⅔	4	2	2	1	3	0	2	0	0	.000	6.75
Welch	1	1	0	1⅓	0	2	1	2	0	0	0	0	1	.000	6.75
Honeycutt	2	0	0	1⅔	4	4	4	0	2	0	0	0	0	.000	21.60
Totals	4	4	0	34	34	16	15	15	22	0	4	1	3	.250	3.97

No shutouts. Save—Niedenfuer.

COMPOSITE SCORE BY INNINGS

Philadelphia	4	3	1		1	4	2		1	0	0 — 16
Los Angeles	1	0	0		3	2	0		0	2	0 — 8

Game-winning RBIs—Schmidt, Guerrero, Matthews.
Sacrifice hits—Reuss, Russell, Denny, Carlton, Lezcano.
Sacrifice fly—Lefebvre.
Stolen bases—Thomas, Rose, Russell, Sax, Matthews.
Caught stealing—Rose, Sax, Marshall.
Double plays—Russell, Sax and Brock 2; Russell, Sax and Marshall.
Left on bases—Philadelphia 8, 8, 5, 10—31; Los Angeles 9, 8, 5, 9—31.
Hit by pitcher—By Denny (Guerrero), by Carlton (Yeager).
Passed ball—Fimple.
Balks—None.
Time of games—First game, 2:17; second game, 2:44; third game, 2:51; fourth game, 2:50.
Attendance—First game, 49,963; second game, 55,967; third game, 53,490; fourth game, 64,494.
Umpires—Tata, Stello, McSherry, Weyer, Harvey and Crawford.
Official scorers—Jay Dunn, Trentonian (N.J.); Terry Johnson, Torrance (Cal.) Daily Breeze; Wayne Monroe, Pasadena Star-News.

AMERICAN LEAGUE
Championship Series of 1984

	W.	L.	Pct.
Detroit (East)	3	0	1.000
Kansas City (West)	0	3	.000

When Milt Wilcox was a fuzzy-cheeked 20-year-old rookie with the Cincinnati Reds in 1970, he didn't often see eye to eye with Sparky Anderson, a rookie manager with the Reds that season. But in the intervening 14 years, the two have come closer together in their way of thinking.

"He did so much talking, I was never sure whether he knew what he was talking about," Wilcox said of his first impressions of Anderson, who went on to lead the Reds to five National League West titles and four visits to the World Series before being fired after the 1978 season. He was hired by the Detroit Tigers the next season.

"Now I know he handles his players well," Wilcox said. "He gets everyone into the game and makes everyone feel a part of the team."

The future didn't materialize quite as nicely for Wilcox as it did for Anderson following their days with the Reds. Wilcox was traded to Cleveland in December of 1971, then hurt his arm the next season. He was traded again in 1975, this time to the Chicago Cubs, and a year later he was sold to the Tigers. His fortune improved at that point, and he has won at least 11 games in seven of his eight seasons in Detroit since then. He fashioned his best record ever at 17-8 in 1984 and helped the Tigers win the American League East title.

Prior to starting Game 3 of the A.L. Championship Series against the Kansas City Royals, Wilcox said one of his first big thrills in baseball was when Anderson brought him in to pitch in the third game of the 1970 N.L. Championship Series. He hurled three shutout innings and was credited with a 3-2 victory over the Pittsburgh Pirates that clinched the pennant for the Reds.

On October 5, 1984, 14 years to the day after he had been summoned from the bullpen to help wrap up the Reds' title, Anderson again showed confidence in Wilcox, sending him to the mound against the Royals with a chance to clinch the A.L. pennant for the Tigers. When the results were in, Wilcox had become the first pitcher to record clinching victories in the Championship Series in each league.

Wilcox was the beneficiary of a single run that night in Detroit. Designated hitter Barbaro Garbey opened the second inning with a single up the middle. Center fielder Chet Lemon forced Garbey at second, but Lemon went to third on an ensuing single by Darrell Evans. Third baseman Marty Castillo then hit a two-hopper to Kansas City shortstop Onix Concepcion, who flipped to Frank White for the force on Evans at second. White's relay to first, however, was an instant late, and Castillo was safe as Lemon scored. That was to be the only run surrendered by Kansas City lefthander Charlie Leibrandt, who allowed the Tigers just three hits while starting and finishing for the Royals.

But Wilcox made that one run look monumental. He struck out eight batters, walked two and allowed only a single by third baseman George Brett in the fourth and another by catcher Don Slaught in the eighth. There were two outs in the eighth when first baseman Evans made a diving stop of center fielder Willie Wilson's hard-hit grounder in the hole, scrambled to his feet and narrowly beat a sliding Wilson at first.

Wilcox, who completed none of his 33 starts during the regular season, gave way to Willie Hernandez at the start of the ninth. The lefthander preserved the 1-0 decision that gave the Tigers a three-game sweep over the Royals.

Before the playoffs, Detroit had become the fourth team in major league history to be in first place from the start of its season to the end of the year, joining the 1923 New York Giants, 1927 New York Yankees and 1955 Brooklyn Dodgers in that category. The Tigers started the season at a 35-5 pace and finished with 104 regular-season victories.

The Tigers proved they were no fluke right from the start against the Royals. In the first inning of the opener in Kansas City, they exploded for two runs, the 62nd time in 1984 they had scored in the first inning. This time, second baseman Lou Whitaker stroked a leadoff single to right and shortstop Alan Trammell followed with a run-scoring triple over the head of left fielder Darryl Motley. Trammell scored one out later on a sacrifice fly by catcher Lance Parrish.

The Royals put in a serious bid to erase Detroit's 2-0 lead in their half of the third inning when George Brett sent a hard smash to right field with the bases loaded and two out, but Kirk Gibson made a diving catch to snuff out the threat.

"It was a great play by Gibson," Anderson said. "The ball was hooking and sinking, and he stayed with it. A year ago Brett would have been running for a while."

Brett, too, thought he had provided a key hit. "When I saw him start to dive, I said to myself, 'Oh, man. Beautiful. That's three runs and I'm on third.' When I saw him start to dive I thought he was crazy. It turned out I was crazy."

The Tigers slowly started to pull away as left fielder Larry Herndon hit a leadoff homer off loser Bud Black in the fourth inning. Trammell opened the fifth with a home run off Black and two innings later delivered a run-scoring single off reliever Mark Huismann to make the score 5-0. Evans and Castillo drove in one run each in the eighth before Parrish pounded out the Tigers' third homer (all leadoff shots) of the game in the ninth.

Kansas City's only run came in the seventh when designated hitter Jorge Orta smashed a leadoff triple and came home on a grounder by Motley. The Royals managed only five hits off winner Jack Morris and none off Hernandez, who worked the final two innings to wrap up Detroit's 8-1 victory.

In Game 2 of the playoffs, the Tigers were to win the eighth of eight games between the two clubs at Royals Stadium in '84, but not without a struggle.

In yet another first-inning explosion, the Tigers scored two runs. Whitaker opened the game by reaching first base on an error by Concepcion at short. One out later, Gibson and Parrish smacked back-to-back run-scoring doubles. Gibson made it 3-0 in the third when he slugged a home run over the center-field wall.

The Royals got to starter Dan Petry for a run in the fourth on a walk to right fielder Pat Sheridan, a single by Brett and a fielder's-choice grounder by Orta. Then they turned to their bench. Dane Iorg drove in a run with a two-out pinch-hit single in the seventh. Lynn Jones, batting for Sheridan, greeted Hernandez with another pinch single to open the eighth. After Brett struck out, Hal McRae ripped a pinch double into the left-field corner, scoring Jones and tying the game, 3-3.

Entering the ninth, Kansas City Manager Dick Howser removed starter Bret Saberhagen, a 20-year-old rookie. Saberhagen had gotten off to a shaky start and was behind, 3-0, after three innings, but he yielded only a pair of singles in the next five innings to keep the Royals in the game.

After Hernandez was touched for the tying run in the eighth, the game came down to a duel of relievers: Kansas City's Dan Quisenberry vs. Detroit's Aurelio Lopez.

Parrish singled sharply off the glove of third baseman Greg Pryor to open the winning uprising for the Tigers in the 11th. Evans sacrificed, but both runners were safe when catcher Slaught fumbled the ball. After left fielder Ruppert Jones failed in his bunt attempt and forced Parrish at third, designated hitter Johnny Grubb belted a high sinker from Quisenberry into right-center, scoring Evans and Jones and giving the Tigers a 5-3 margin.

Lopez was not overpowering, but he was tough when he had to be for the Tigers. He escaped from a 10th-inning jam by getting first baseman Steve Balboni to fly to center with two men on and two out, and he retired Lynn Jones on a fly to right with two on in the 11th to earn the victory and give Detroit a 2-0 edge in the playoffs.

After squeaking by the Royals with one run in Game 3, the Tigers captured their first A.L. pennant since 1968. Gibson, who blunted a rally with his diving catch in Game 1 and was 5 for 12 with a homer in the three games, was named the Most Valuable Player of the playoffs. But the Tigers' entire pitching staff, which held the Royals to a combined .170 batting average, shared in the credit.

Kansas City's leadoff hitter, Wilson, was 2 for 13. Balboni, who led the club in runs batted in during the regular season, was 1 for 11 with no RBIs. Brett, who also failed to drive in a run in the series, was 3 for 13. White was 1 for 11, while Concepcion and Sheridan, key Kansas City hitters down the stretch, were a combined 0 for 13. The Royals never led in any game, were outscored, 14-4, were outhomered, 4-0, and had only two extra-base hits. Defensively, the Royals committed seven errors in the three games.

Howser, now winless in nine postseason games as a manager, shook his head and said: "We weren't in the first game, but our pitching was good enough to win the last two, which is what makes it frustrating. We definitely didn't swing the bats real good, but you have to credit their pitching. I've said all along that improved pitching is what sets this Detroit team apart from others of recent years."

GAME OF TUESDAY, OCTOBER 2, AT KANSAS CITY (N)

Detroit	AB.	R.	H.	RBI.	PO.	A.	Kansas City	AB.	R.	H.	RBI.	PO.	A.
Whitaker, 2b	5	2	1	0	0	1	Wilson, cf	4	0	1	0	4	0
Brookens, 2b	0	0	0	0	0	0	Sheridan, rf	2	0	0	0	3	0
Trammell, ss	3	2	3	3	1	5	L. Jones, ph-rf	1	0	0	0	1	0
Baker, ss	0	0	0	0	0	0	Brett, 3b	4	0	0	0	2	1
Gibson, rf	5	0	2	0	3	0	Orta, dh	4	1	1	0	0	0
Parrish, c	4	1	1	2	6	0	Motley, lf	4	0	0	1	4	0
Herndon, lf	3	1	1	1	3	0	Balboni, 1b	4	0	0	6	1	
R. Jones, ph-lf	1	0	0	0	2	0	White, 2b	3	0	1	0	1	2
Kuntz, ph-lf	1	0	0	0	0	0	Slaught, c	3	0	2	0	5	0
Garbey, dh	5	1	2	0	0	0	Concepcion, ss	3	0	0	0	0	2
Lemon, cf	5	0	0	0	2	0	Black, p	0	0	0	0	1	1
Evans, 1b	4	0	2	1	8	1	Huismann, p	0	0	0	0	0	0
Bergman, pr-1b	0	1	0	0	1	0	M. Jones, p	0	0	0	0	0	0
Castillo, 3b	4	0	2	1	0	1							
Morris, p	0	0	0	0	1	1	Totals	32	1	5	1	27	7
Hernandez, p	0	0	0	0	0	0							
Totals	40	8	14	8	27	9							

Detroit	2	0	0	1	1	0	1	2	1—8
Kansas City	0	0	0	0	0	0	1	0	0—1

Detroit	IP.	H.	R.	ER.	BB.	SO.
Morris (Winner)	7	5	1	1	1	4
Hernandez	2	0	0	0	0	2

Kansas City	IP.	H.	R.	ER.	BB.	SO.
Black (Loser)	5	7	4	4	1	3
Huismann	2⅔	6	3	2	1	2
M. Jones	1⅓	1	1	1	0	0

Game-winning RBI—Trammell.

Error—Sheridan. Double play—Kansas City 1. Left on bases—Detroit 8, Kansas City 5. Two-base hit—Evans. Three-base hits—Trammell, Orta. Home runs—Herndon, Trammell, Parrish. Sacrifice fly—Parrish. Wild pitch—Huismann. Umpires—Deegan, Bible, Christal, Zirbel, Jordan and O'Dell. Time—2:42. Attendance—41,973.

GAME OF WEDNESDAY, OCTOBER 3, AT KANSAS CITY (N)

Detroit	AB.	R.	H.	RBI.	PO.	A.	Kansas City	AB.	R.	H.	RBI.	PO.	A.
Whitaker, 2b	5	1	1	0	5	5	Wilson, cf	5	0	1	0	4	0
Trammell, ss	5	0	1	0	0	2	Sheridan, rf	2	1	0	0	6	0
Gibson, rf	4	2	2	2	3	0	L. Jones, ph-rf	3	1	1	0	1	0
Parrish, c	5	0	2	1	7	2	Brett, 3b	5	0	2	0	0	2
Evans, 3b-1b	4	1	0	0	7	1	Pryor, pr-3b	0	0	0	0	1	0
R. Jones, lf	4	1	0	0	3	0	Orta, dh	3	0	0	0	0	0
Grubb, dh	4	0	1	2	0	0	McRae, ph	1	0	1	1	0	0
Lemon, cf	5	0	0	0	4	0	Wathan, pr-dh	1	0	0	0	0	0
Bergman, 1b	1	0	1	0	4	0	Motley, lf	4	0	2	0	4	0
Brookens, 3b	2	0	0	0	0	2	Balboni, 1b	5	0	1	0	7	1
Garbey, ph	1	0	0	0	0	0	White, 2b	5	1	0	0	1	0
Castillo, 3b	1	0	0	0	0	0	Slaught, c	5	0	1	0	6	0
Petry, p	0	0	0	0	0	0	Concepcion, ss	2	0	0	0	0	2
Hernandez, p	0	0	0	0	0	0	Iorg, ph	1	0	1	1	0	0
Lopez, p	0	0	0	0	0	0	Biancalana, pr-ss	1	0	0	0	1	2
Totals	41	5	8	5	33	12	Washington, ph	1	0	0	0	0	0
							Saberhagen, p	0	0	0	0	1	1
							Quisenberry, p	0	0	0	0	1	1
							Totals	44	3	10	3	33	9

Detroit	2	0	1	0	0	0	0	0	0	0	2—5
Kansas City	0	0	0	1	0	0	1	1	0	0	0—3

Detroit	IP.	H.	R.	ER.	BB.	SO.
Petry	7	4	2	2	1	4
Hernandez	1	2	1	1	1	1
Lopez (Winner)	3	4	0	0	1	2

Kansas City	IP.	H.	R.	ER.	BB.	SO.
Saberhagen	8	6	3	2	1	5
Quisenberry (Loser)	3	2	2	1	1	1

Game-winning RBI—Grubb.

Error—Concepcion, Saberhagen, Brookens, Slaught. Left on bases—Detroit 7, Kansas City 11. Two-base hits—Gibson, Parrish, McRae, Grubb. Home run—Gibson. Stolen base—Bergman. Caught stealing—Wilson. Sacrifice hits—Grubb, Evans. Umpires—Deegan, Bible, Christal, Jones, Denny and Nothnagel. Time—3:37. Attendance—42,019.

GAME OF FRIDAY, OCTOBER 5, AT DETROIT (N)

Kansas City	AB.	R.	H.	RBI.	PO.	A.
Wilson, cf	4	0	0	0	2	0
Sheridan, rf	2	0	0	0	0	0
L. Jones, ph	1	0	0	0	0	0
Brett, 3b	4	0	1	0	0	4
Orta, dh	3	0	0	0	0	0
McRae, ph	1	0	1	0	0	0
Washington, pr	0	0	0	0	0	0
Motley, lf	4	0	0	0	3	0
Balboni, 1b	2	0	0	0	7	1
White, 2b	3	0	0	0	5	1
Slaught, c	3	0	1	0	6	0
Concepcion, ss	2	0	0	0	0	2
Iorg, ph	1	0	0	0	0	0
Biancalana, ss	0	0	0	0	0	0
Leibrandt, p	0	0	0	0	1	2
Totals	30	0	3	0	24	10

Detroit	AB.	R.	H.	RBI.	PO.	A.
Whitaker, 2b	4	0	0	0	0	0
Trammell, ss	3	0	0	0	0	1
Gibson, rf	3	0	1	0	1	0
Parrish, c	3	0	0	0	8	0
Herndon, lf	2	0	0	0	3	0
Garbey, dh	3	0	1	0	0	0
Lemon, cf	3	1	0	0	3	0
Evans, 1b	2	0	1	0	7	2
Castillo, 3b	3	0	0	1	3	3
Wilcox, p	0	0	0	0	2	0
Hernandez, p	0	0	0	0	0	0
Totals	26	1	3	1	27	6

Kansas City	0	0	0	0	0	0	0	0	0 — 0
Detroit	0	1	0	0	0	0	0	0	x — 1

Kansas City	IP.	H.	R.	ER.	BB.	SO.
Leibrandt (Loser)	8	3	1	1	4	6

Detroit	IP.	H.	R.	ER.	BB.	SO.
Wilcox (Winner)	8	2	0	0	2	8
Hernandez (Save)	1	1	0	0	0	0

Game-winning RBI—Castillo.

Errors—Slaught 2, Balboni. Double play—Kansas City 1. Left on bases—Kansas City 5, Detroit 5. Stolen bases—Castillo, Gibson, Evans. Umpires—Deegan, Bible, Christal, Cossey, Runchey and Zivic. Time—2:39. Attendance—52,168.

DETROIT TIGERS' BATTING AND FIELDING AVERAGES

Player—Position	G.	AB.	R.	H.	TB.	2B.	3B.	HR.	RBI.	B.A.	PO.	A.	E.	F.A.
Bergman, pr-1b	2	1	1	1	1	0	0	0	0	1.000	5	0	0	1.000
Gibson, rf	3	12	2	5	9	1	0	1	2	.417	7	0	0	1.000
Trammell, ss	3	11	2	4	9	0	1	1	3	.364	1	8	0	1.000
Garbey, dh-ph	3	9	1	3	3	0	0	0	0	.333	0	0	0	.000
Evans, 1b-3b	3	10	1	3	4	1	0	0	1	.300	22	4	0	1.000
Parrish, c	3	12	1	3	7	1	0	1	3	.250	21	2	0	1.000
Castillo, 3b	3	8	0	2	2	0	0	0	2	.250	3	4	0	1.000
Grubb, dh	1	4	0	1	2	1	0	0	2	.250	0	0	0	.000
Herndon, lf	2	5	1	1	4	0	0	1	1	.200	6	0	0	1.000
Whitaker, 2b	3	14	3	2	2	0	0	0	0	.143	5	6	0	1.000
Hernandez, p	3	0	0	0	0	0	0	0	0	.000	0	0	0	.000
Baker, ss	1	0	0	0	0	0	0	0	0	.000	0	0	0	.000
Lopez, p	1	0	0	0	0	0	0	0	0	.000	0	0	0	.000
Morris, p	1	0	0	0	0	0	0	0	0	.000	1	1	0	1.000
Petry, p	1	0	0	0	0	0	0	0	0	.000	0	0	0	.000
Wilcox, p	1	0	0	0	0	0	0	0	0	.000	2	0	0	1.000
Kuntz, ph-lf	1	1	0	0	0	0	0	0	0	.000	0	0	0	.000
Brookens, 2b-3b	2	2	0	0	0	0	0	0	0	.000	0	2	1	.667
R. Jones, ph-lf	2	5	1	0	0	0	0	0	0	.000	5	0	0	1.000
Lemon, cf	3	13	1	0	0	0	0	0	0	.000	9	0	0	1.000
Totals	3	107	14	25	43	4	1	4	14	.234	87	27	1	.991

KANSAS CITY ROYALS' BATTING AND FIELDING AVERAGES

Player—Position	G.	AB.	R.	H.	TB.	2B.	3B.	HR.	RBI.	B.A.	PO.	A.	E.	F.A.
McRae, ph	2	2	0	2	3	1	0	0	1	1.000	0	0	0	.000
Iorg, ph	2	2	0	1	1	0	0	0	1	.500	0	0	0	.000
Slaught, c	3	11	0	4	4	0	0	0	0	.364	17	0	3	.850
Brett, 3b	3	13	0	3	3	0	0	0	0	.231	2	7	0	1.000
L. Jones, ph-rf	3	5	1	1	1	0	0	0	0	.200	2	0	0	1.000
Motley, lf	3	12	0	2	2	0	0	0	1	.167	11	0	0	1.000
Wilson, cf	3	13	0	2	2	0	0	0	0	.154	10	0	0	1.000
Orta, dh	3	10	1	1	3	0	1	0	1	.100	0	0	0	.000
Balboni, 1b	3	11	0	1	1	0	0	0	0	.091	20	3	1	.958
White, 2b	3	11	1	1	1	0	0	0	0	.091	7	3	0	1.000
Black, p	1	0	0	0	0	0	0	0	0	.000	1	1	0	1.000
Huismann, p	1	0	0	0	0	0	0	0	0	.000	0	0	0	.000
M. Jones, p	1	0	0	0	0	0	0	0	0	.000	0	0	0	.000
Leibrandt, p	1	0	0	0	0	0	0	0	0	.000	1	2	0	1.000
Pryor, pr-3b	1	0	0	0	0	0	0	0	0	.000	1	0	0	.000
Quisenberry, p	1	0	0	0	0	0	0	0	0	.000	1	1	0	1.000
Saberhagen, p	1	0	0	0	0	0	0	0	0	.000	1	1	1	.667
Biancalana, pr-ss	2	1	0	0	0	0	0	0	0	.000	1	2	0	1.000
Washington, ph-pr	2	1	0	0	0	0	0	0	0	.000	0	0	0	.000
Wathan, pr-dh	1	1	0	0	0	0	0	0	0	.000	0	0	0	.000
Sheridan, rf	3	6	1	0	0	0	0	0	0	.000	9	0	1	.900
Concepcion, ss	3	7	0	0	0	0	0	0	0	.000	0	6	1	.857
Totals	3	106	4	18	21	1	1	0	4	.170	84	26	7	.940

DETROIT TIGERS' PITCHING RECORDS

Pitcher	G.	GS.	CG.	IP.	H.	R.	ER.	BB.	SO.	HB.	WP.	W.	L.	Pct.	ERA.
Wilcox	1	1	0	8	2	0	0	2	8	0	0	1	0	1.000	0.00
Lopez	1	0	0	3	4	0	0	1	2	0	0	1	0	1.000	0.00
Morris	1	1	0	7	5	1	1	1	4	0	0	1	0	1.000	1.29
Hernandez	3	0	0	4	3	1	1	3	0	0	0	0	0	.000	2.25
Petry	1	1	0	7	4	2	2	1	4	0	0	0	0	.000	2.57
Totals	3	3	0	29	18	4	4	6	21	0	0	3	0	1.000	1.24

Shutout—Wilcox-Hernandez (combined). Save—Hernandez.

KANSAS CITY ROYALS' PITCHING RECORDS

Pitcher	G.	GS.	CG.	IP.	H.	R.	ER.	BB.	SO.	HB.	WP.	W.	L.	Pct.	ERA.
Leibrandt	1	1	1	8	3	1	1	4	6	0	0	0	1	.000	1.13
Saberhagen	1	1	0	8	6	3	2	1	5	0	0	0	0	.000	2.25
Quisenberry	1	0	0	3	2	2	1	1	1	0	0	0	1	.000	3.00
Huismann	1	0	0	2⅔	6	3	2	1	2	0	1	0	0	.000	6.75
M. Jones	1	0	0	1⅓	1	1	1	0	0	0	0	0	0	.000	6.75
Black	1	1	0	5	7	4	4	1	3	0	0	0	1	.000	7.20
Totals	3	3	1	28	25	14	11	8	17	0	1	0	3	.000	3.54

No shutouts or saves.

COMPOSITE SCORE BY INNINGS

Detroit	4	1	1	1	1	0	1	2	1	0	2 — 14
Kansas City	0	0	0	1	0	0	2	1	0	0	0 — 4

Game-winning RBIs—Trammell, Grubb, Castillo.
Sacrifice hits—Grubb, Evans.
Sacrifice fly—Parrish.
Stolen bases—Bergman, Castillo, Gibson, Evans.
Caught stealing—Wilson.
Double plays—Concepcion, White and Balboni; Brett, White and Balboni.
Left on bases—Detroit 8, 7, 5—20; Kansas City 5, 11, 5—21.
Hit by pitcher—None.
Passed balls—None.
Balks—None.
Time of games—First game, 2:42; second game, 3:37; third game, 2:39.
Attendance—First game, 41,973; second game, 42,019; third game, 52,168.
Umpires—Deegan, Bible, Christal (all three games); Zirbel, Jordan, O'Dell (first game); Jones, Denny, Nothnagel (second game); Cossey, Runchey, Zivic (third game).
Official scorers—Del Black, Kansas City official scorer; Ed Browalski, Polish News (Detroit).

NATIONAL LEAGUE
Championship Series of 1984

	W.	L.	Pct.
San Diego (West)	3	2	.600
Chicago (East)	2	3	.400

All of America, it seemed, was behind them. Two victories in two games—the first by a 13-0 score, the second a 4-2 margin—also were behind them. Needing just one more win, the Chicago Cubs appeared to be on their way to ending their 39-year World Series famine.

But a funny thing happened to the Cubs en route to the Fall Classic. The San Diego Padres, given up for dead after losing the first two games in Chicago, came back to life, won the next three games and became the first team ever to recover from a 2-0 deficit and win the National League Championship Series. Such a comeback had been achieved only once before, by the Milwaukee Brewers against the California Angels in the 1982 American League playoffs.

The beginning of the 1984 N.L. playoffs was almost as stunning as its improbable conclusion.

Numerous Championship Series batting records were broken or tied as the Cubs thrashed the Padres in the opener. They banged out 16 hits, including five home runs, and scored 13 runs, all N.L. playoff records. That cushion made it easy on starter Rick Sutcliffe, who allowed only two hits—a bunt single by first baseman Steve Garvey and a bloop single by shortstop Garry Templeton—while striking out eight and walking five over seven innings.

The outcome never really was in doubt. After the Padres went down in order in the top of the first, center fielder Bob Dernier, aided by a 20-mph wind, belted Eric Show's second pitch of the game into the left-field bleachers, making him the first player in an N.L. playoff game to hit a first-inning leadoff home run. After second baseman Ryne Sandberg struck out, left fielder Gary Matthews slugged another homer to left.

It got worse for San Diego.

Sutcliffe added insult to injury when he led off the third with a tremendous home run that cleared the right-field bleachers and landed outside Wrigley Field on Sheffield Avenue. The Cubs added two more runs in that inning on a run-scoring single by first baseman Leon Durham and a sacrifice fly by right fielder Keith Moreland.

Moreland also provided the Cubs with the play of the game defensively, snaring a sinking liner by left fielder Carmelo Martinez with the bases loaded and two out in the fourth.

"Moreland's play turned what could have been a close game into a runaway," said Sutcliffe, the winning pitcher.

The Cubs poured it on after that, exploding off Greg Harris, who had taken over for Show. They had six runs in the fifth, half of which came on Matthews' second homer of the game. Third baseman Ron Cey supplied the coup de grace with a solo shot in the two-run sixth.

Every player in the Cubs' starting lineup had at least one hit and one run batted in. Matthews' two home runs extended his streak of Championship Series homers to four (a major league record), having hit one in each of the last three games of the 1983 playoffs when he led the Philadelphia Phillies to the league pennant.

The Cubs showed a different side of their attack in Game 2, using speed and daring to defeat the Padres. Dernier and Sandberg were the architects of the 4-2 victory.

Dernier opened Chicago's half of the first with a single off Mark Thurmond and then caught the Padres napping on the next play, Sandberg's hit-and-run groundout to third baseman Luis Salazar. Dernier raced all the way to third on the play, beating a weak throw by Garvey. Dernier then scored on Matthews' grounder to short. It was the fifth straight Championship Series game in which Matthews had driven in a run, another record.

In the third, Moreland singled and scored on Cey's double to left-center as Templeton's relay throw to the plate skipped away from Padres catcher Terry Kennedy. Cey took third on the play and scored on catcher Jody Davis' sacrifice fly, giving Chicago a 3-0 lead.

After San Diego scored its first run of the series on a double by right fielder Tony Gwynn and a sacrifice fly by center fielder Kevin McReynolds in the fourth, the Cubs put the final nail in the Padres' coffin in their half of the inning. Starting pitcher Steve Trout hit a one-out single and was forced at second by Dernier, who promptly stole second and then scored on a double by Sandberg. That double knocked out Thurmond, who took the loss.

Trout yielded only a run-scoring single by Garvey in the sixth after that. The left-hander went 8⅓ innings to gain the victory, allowing just five hits while walking three and striking out two. Lee Smith relieved Trout and recorded the final two outs for the save.

When the Cubs took a 1-0 lead in the second inning of Game 3 on a double by Moreland and an RBI single by Cey, they appeared to be on the verge of a three-game sweep. But the Padres were to have none of that script.

Kennedy and McReynolds opened the Padres' fifth with singles, and one out later, Templeton came to the plate for the biggest hit of his career, a two-run double to the wall in left-center. That gave the Padres a 2-1 edge, their first lead of the series. Templeton scored the third run of the inning on a single by second baseman Alan Wiggins.

One inning later, third baseman Graig Nettles singled in Gwynn, who had led off with a single, and knocked out Cubs starter (and loser) Dennis Eckersley. Kennedy greeted reliever George Frazier with a single, setting the stage for a three-run homer by McReynolds.

That 7-1 lead was in the capable hands of starter Ed Whitson, a righthander who in 1984 went from a below-.500 pitcher to a 14-game winner thanks to his palmball, a pitch he developed when a cut on his index finger required him to hold the ball differently. With his palmball and his outstanding fastball, Whitson allowed only five hits before being

San Diego first baseman Steve Garvey was No. 1 among Padres fans after winning Game 4 of the 1984 N.L. Championship Series with a ninth-inning home run.

relieved in the ninth by Goose Gossage, who struck out two of the three batters he faced and preserved the win.

Game 4 was, by far, the most competitive and dramatic of the playoffs. It also was a showcase for San Diego's Garvey.

Garvey had four hits and five RBIs in Game 4, including a run-scoring double that capped a two-run third, marking the first time the Padres had scored first in the series. Garvey's hit followed a single and stolen base by Templeton, a single by Wiggins and a sacrifice fly by Gwynn.

But the Cubs came right back to take the lead with three runs in the fourth. Matthews led off with a walk, and two outs later, Davis and Durham—the latter breaking out of a 1-for-14 postseason slump—banged out back-to-back homers off Padres starter Tim Lollar.

That put the ball right back into Garvey's court. After Tim Flannery stroked a pinch-hit single to open the fifth and advanced to third on a bunt and a groundout, Garvey singled up the middle off Cubs starter Scott Sanderson to tie the score at 3-3. In the seventh, pinch-hitter Bobby Brown walked with one out and stole second before reliever Tim Stoddard was ordered to walk Gwynn and pitch to Garvey. The first baseman responded with a single to left, scoring Brown with the go-ahead run. Gwynn then scored on a passed ball to make it 5-3.

The seesaw battle continued, however, when the Cubs came to bat against Gossage in the eighth. Sandberg reached first on an infield hit and stole second as Matthews struck out. Moreland singled for one run, and one out later, Davis doubled off the center-field wall to even the score, 5-5.

It looked ominous for the Padres in the ninth when the Cubs loaded the bases with two out. Dernier doubled, Matthews was walked intentionally and Henry Cotto, who had entered the game as a pinch runner for Moreland in the eighth, was hit by a Craig Lefferts delivery. But Lefferts retired Cey on a weak grounder to second to thwart the rally.

Garvey had saved his best act of the day for the bottom of the ninth. After Wiggins struck out to open the inning, Gwynn singled, bringing Garvey to the plate. Smith, Chicago's ace reliever, challenged Garvey with a fastball, which the veteran crushed into the bleachers in right-center, making a winner of Lefferts and a loser of Smith.

"As soon as the ball went toward the fence, everything froze in time," Garvey said. "It was as if all sound stopped."

It was Garvey's first homer since August 15, and his five RBIs gave him 20 during his 21-game Championship Series career. (He added one more RBI in Game 5.) Reggie Jackson had held the major league record with 18 playoff RBIs.

The Padres had met the challenge of evening the series at two games each. But in the decisive fifth game, they still had to beat the Cy Young Award winner Sutcliffe, who finished the season with 15 straight victories (including Game 1 of the playoffs). The righthander had a 0.37 earned-run average in three of those games against San Diego.

The Padres managed just two weak infield hits in the first five innings against Sutcliffe, one by Kennedy in the second and one by Templeton in the fifth. Meanwhile, Durham had belted a two-run homer in the first inning and Davis had contributed a leadoff blast in the second for a 3-0 Chicago lead.

Two batters later, the San Diego bullpen took control. Righthander Andy Hawkins replaced Show with one out in the second and Dave Dravecky, Lefferts and Gossage followed to total 7⅔ innings of shutout relief.

The Padres began to whittle at Chicago's lead in the sixth. Wiggins laid down a bunt for a single. Gwynn followed with a single to left. Garvey then walked to load the bases. Nettles got Wiggins home with a sacrifice fly to center as Gwynn advanced to third. Kennedy then lined a Sutcliffe pitch to left, where Matthews made a diving catch. Gwynn tagged up and scored to make the score 3-2.

Sutcliffe was back in trouble in the seventh after he walked Martinez, the first batter of the inning, on four straight pitches. Templeton sacrificed Martinez to second, and pinch-hitter Flannery followed with a sharp grounder to Durham at first. The ball went between Durham's legs for an error, and Martinez scored to tie the game, 3-3.

The Cubs' only luck in that inning was bad luck. The next batter, Wiggins, punched a check-swing single into short left field. Gwynn then delivered the key blow, a smash at Sandberg that took a bad hop and rocketed over the second baseman's shoulder and into right-center for a double, scoring Flannery and Wiggins. Gwynn took third on the throw home and scored on Garvey's single, giving San Diego its final 6-3 edge.

"I knew we would find a way, but I also knew we'd have to scrap against Sutcliffe," Gwynn said. "He put his pitches where he wanted to for five innings—low, inside, on the corners. I knew he was getting tired in the seventh, though, when he threw me a high fastball."

The victory was the culmination of a dream for the Padres, an expansion team in 1969 that never had finished better than fourth in the N.L. West before 1984.

Though the Cubs failed in their bid to go to the World Series for the first time since 1945, they had a terrific season, only to fall one game short. "We had them by the throat," Cubs General Manager Dallas Green said, "and let them get away."

GAME OF TUESDAY, OCTOBER 2, AT CHICAGO

San Diego	AB.	R.	H.	RBI.	PO.	A.	Chicago	AB.	R.	H.	RBI.	PO.	A.
Wiggins, 2b	5	0	0	0	2	3	Dernier, cf	3	3	2	1	6	0
Gwynn, rf	4	0	0	0	1	0	Sandberg, 2b	4	2	2	1	2	3
Garvey, 1b	4	0	2	0	6	0	Matthews, lf	4	2	2	4	0	0
Nettles, 3b	4	0	1	0	1	1	Cotto, lf	1	0	1	0	0	0
Kennedy, c	3	0	0	0	6	0	Durham, 1b	5	0	1	1	4	0
McReynolds, cf	2	0	0	0	3	0	Moreland, rf	3	1	1	1	1	0
Martinez, lf	3	0	1	0	1	0	Woods, ph-rf	1	0	0	0	1	0
Templeton, ss	3	0	2	0	4	1	Cey, 3b	3	2	1	1	0	0
Show, p	1	0	0	0	0	0	Veryzer, 3b	0	0	0	0	0	0
Flannery, ph	0	0	0	0	0	0	Davis, c	4	1	2	1	8	0
Harris, p	0	0	0	0	0	0	Lake, c	1	0	1	0	0	0
Brown, ph	1	0	0	0	0	0	Bowa, ss	4	1	1	1	5	2
Booker, p	0	0	0	0	0	0	Sutcliffe, p	4	1	2	1	0	0
Summers, ph	1	0	0	0	0	0	Brusstar, p	1	0	0	0	0	0
Totals	31	0	6	0	24	5	Totals	38	13	16	12	27	5

San Diego	0	0	0	0	0	0	0	0	0 — 0
Chicago	2	0	3	0	6	2	0	0	x — 13

San Diego	IP.	H.	R.	ER.	BB.	SO.
Show (Loser)	4	5	5	5	2	2
Harris	2	9	8	7	3	2
Booker	2	2	0	0	1	2

Chicago	IP.	H.	R.	ER.	BB.	SO.
Sutcliffe (Winner)	7	2	0	0	5	8
Brusstar	2	4	0	0	0	0

Game-winning RBI—Dernier.

Error—Templeton. Double play—San Diego 1, Chicago 2. Left on bases—San Diego 10, Chicago 8. Two-base hits—Dernier, Davis, Lake. Home runs—Dernier, Matthews 2, Sutcliffe, Cey. Sacrifice fly—Moreland. Hit by pitcher—By Sutcliffe (Flannery). Umpires—Cavanaugh, Slickenmeyer, Pomponi and Maher. Time—2:49. Attendance—36,282.

GAME OF WEDNESDAY, OCTOBER 3, AT CHICAGO

San Diego	AB.	R.	H.	RBI.	PO.	A.	Chicago	AB.	R.	H.	RBI.	PO.	A.
Wiggins, 2b	3	1	1	0	3	1	Dernier, cf	3	2	1	0	0	0
Gwynn, rf	4	1	1	0	4	0	Sandberg, 2b	4	0	2	1	2	5
Garvey, 1b	4	0	1	1	9	2	Matthews, lf	3	0	0	1	3	0
McReynolds, cf	2	0	0	1	2	0	Cotto, lf	0	0	0	0	2	0
Martinez, lf	4	0	1	0	2	0	Moreland, rf	4	1	2	0	2	0
Kennedy, c	4	0	0	0	1	1	Smith, p	0	0	0	0	0	0
Salazar, 3b	3	0	0	0	1	3	Cey, 3b	3	1	1	1	0	2
Templeton, ss	2	0	0	0	1	3	Davis, c	3	0	0	1	3	0
Thurmond, p	1	0	1	0	0	1	Durham, 1b	4	0	0	0	14	0
Hawkins, p	0	0	0	0	0	0	Bowa, ss	3	0	1	0	1	7
Ramirez, ph	1	0	0	0	0	0	Trout, p	2	0	1	0	0	1
Dravecky, p	0	0	0	0	1	1	Lopes, lf	0	0	0	0	0	0
Bevacqua, ph	1	0	0	0	0	0	Totals	29	4	8	4	27	15
Lefferts, p	0	0	0	0	0	0							
Totals	29	2	5	2	24	12							

San Diego	0	0	0	1	0	1	0	0	0 — 2
Chicago	1	0	2	1	0	0	0	0	x — 4

San Diego	IP.	H.	R.	ER.	BB.	SO.
Thurmond (Loser)	3⅔	7	4	4	2	1
Hawkins	1⅓	0	0	0	1	0
Dravecky	2	1	0	0	0	1
Lefferts	1	0	0	0	0	0

Chicago	IP.	H.	R.	ER.	BB.	SO.
Trout (Winner)	8⅓	5	2	2	3	2
Smith (Save)	⅔	0	0	0	0	1

Game-winning RBI—Matthews.

Error—Trout. Double plays—Chicago 2. Left on bases—San Diego 4, Chicago 6. Two-base hits—Moreland, Cey, Gwynn, Sandberg. Stolen base—Dernier. Caught stealing—Sandberg. Sacrifice hit—Trout. Sacrifice flies—Davis, McReynolds. Umpires—Slickenmeyer, Pomponi, Maher and Cavanaugh. Time—2:18. Attendance—36,282.

GAME OF THURSDAY, OCTOBER 4, AT SAN DIEGO (N)

Chicago	AB.	R.	H.	RBI.	PO.	A.
Dernier, cf	3	0	0	0	3	1
Sandberg, 2b	4	0	1	0	4	5
Matthews, lf	3	0	1	0	2	0
Durham, 1b	4	0	0	0	11	2
Moreland, rf	4	1	1	0	0	0
Cey, 3b	4	0	1	1	0	1
Davis, c	3	0	1	0	2	2
Bowa, ss	3	0	0	0	1	2
Eckersley, p	2	0	0	0	0	0
Frazier, p	0	0	0	0	0	0
Bosley, ph	1	0	0	0	0	0
Stoddard, p	0	0	0	0	1	0
Totals	31	1	5	1	24	13

San Diego	AB.	R.	H.	RBI.	PO.	A.
Wiggins, 2b	4	0	2	1	0	4
Gwynn, rf	4	1	3	0	0	0
Garvey, 1b	4	0	0	0	8	0
Nettles, 3b	4	1	1	1	0	2
Kennedy, c	4	2	2	0	8	1
McReynolds, cf	3	2	2	3	3	0
Martinez, lf	3	0	0	0	0	0
Templeton, ss	3	1	1	2	7	2
Whitson, p	3	0	0	0	1	0
Gossage, p	0	0	0	0	0	0
Totals	32	7	11	7	27	9

Chicago	0	1	0	0	0	0	0	0	0 — 1	
San Diego	0	0	0	0	3	4	0	0	x — 7	

Chicago	IP.	H.	R.	ER.	BB.	SO.
Eckersley (Loser)	5⅓	9	5	5	0	0
Frazier	1⅔	2	2	2	0	1
Stoddard	1	0	0	0	0	2

San Diego	IP.	H.	R.	ER.	BB.	SO.
Whitson (Winner)	8	5	1	1	2	6
Gossage	1	0	0	0	0	2

Game-winning RBI—Templeton.

Errors—None. Double plays—Chicago 1, San Diego 1. Left on bases—Chicago 5, San Diego 1. Two-base hits—Gwynn, Moreland, Templeton, Sandberg. Home run—McReynolds. Stolen base—Sandberg. Caught stealing—Wiggins. Umpires—Bovey, Campagna, Fisher and Stewart. Time—2:19. Attendance—58,346.

GAME OF SATURDAY, OCTOBER 6, AT SAN DIEGO (N)

Chicago	AB.	R.	H.	RBI.	PO.	A.
Dernier, cf	4	0	1	0	0	0
Sandberg, 2b	3	1	1	0	3	2
Matthews, lf	3	1	0	0	3	0
Moreland, rf	4	0	1	1	4	0
Cotto, pr-rf	0	1	0	0	0	0
Cey, 3b	5	0	0	0	1	1
Davis, c	4	1	3	3	4	0
Durham, 1b	3	1	1	1	10	1
Bowa, ss	3	0	1	0	0	4
Hebner, ph	1	0	0	0	0	0
Smith, p	0	0	0	0	0	0
Sanderson, p	2	0	0	0	0	1
Brusstar, p	0	0	0	0	0	0
Lopes, ph	1	0	0	0	0	0
Stoddard, p	0	0	0	0	0	1
Veryzer, ss	1	0	0	0	0	0
Totals	34	5	8	5	25	10

San Diego	AB.	R.	H.	RBI.	PO.	A.
Wiggins, 2b	4	1	1	0	1	1
Gwynn, rf	3	2	1	1	2	0
Garvey, 1b	5	1	4	5	8	0
Nettles, 3b	3	0	0	0	3	3
Kennedy, c	4	0	1	0	7	0
McReynolds, cf	3	0	1	0	2	0
Salazar, ph-cf	1	0	0	0	0	0
Martinez, lf	4	0	1	0	0	0
Templeton, ss	4	1	1	0	4	3
Lollar, p	1	0	0	0	0	0
Hawkins, p	0	0	0	0	0	1
Flannery, ph	1	1	1	0	0	0
Dravecky, p	0	0	0	0	0	2
Brown, ph	0	1	0	0	0	0
Gossage, p	0	0	0	0	0	0
Summers, ph	1	0	0	0	0	0
Lefferts, p	0	0	0	0	0	0
Totals	34	7	11	6	27	8

Chicago	0	0	0	3	0	0	0	2	0 — 5	
San Diego	0	0	2	0	1	0	2	0	2 — 7	

One out when winning run scored.

Chicago	IP.	H.	R.	ER.	BB.	SO.
Sanderson	4⅔	6	3	3	1	2
Brusstar	1⅓	1	0	0	0	0
Stoddard	1	1	2	1	2	0
Smith (Loser)	1⅓	3	2	2	0	2

San Diego	IP.	H.	R.	ER.	BB.	SO.
Lollar	4⅓	3	3	3	4	3
Hawkins	⅔	0	0	0	0	0
Dravecky	2	1	0	0	0	2
Gossage	1	3	2	2	1	1
Lefferts (Winner)	1	1	0	0	1	0

Game-winning RBI—Garvey.

Error—Sandberg. Double plays—Chicago 1, San Diego 1. Left on bases—Chicago 9, San Diego 7. Two-base hits—Bowa, Garvey, Dernier, Davis. Home runs—Davis, Durham, Garvey. Stolen bases—Templeton, Dernier, Brown, Sandberg. Sacrifice hit—Wiggins. Sacrifice fly—Gwynn. Hit by pitch—By Lefferts (Cotto). Passed ball—Davis. Umpires—Bovey, Campagna, Fisher and Stewart. Time—3:13. Attendance—58,354.

GAME OF SUNDAY, OCTOBER 7, AT SAN DIEGO

Chicago	AB.	R.	H.	RBI.	PO.	A.
Dernier, cf	4	0	0	0	3	0
Sandberg, 2b	4	0	1	0	2	3
Matthews, lf	2	1	0	0	2	0
Durham, 1b	4	1	1	2	8	0
Moreland, lf	3	0	1	0	2	0
Cey, 3b	4	0	0	0	0	2
Davis, c	4	1	1	1	6	0
Bowa, ss	2	0	0	0	1	0
Bosley, ph	1	0	0	0	0	0
Veryzer, ss	0	0	0	0	0	0
Sutcliffe, p	2	0	1	0	0	0
Trout, p	0	0	0	0	0	0
Hebner, ph	0	0	0	0	0	0
Brusstar, p	0	0	0	0	0	1
Totals	30	3	5	3	24	6

San Diego	AB.	R.	H.	RBI.	PO.	A.
Wiggins, 2b	3	2	2	0	5	2
Gwynn, rf	4	2	2	2	2	0
Garvey, 1b	3	0	1	1	4	1
Nettles, 3b	3	0	0	1	1	2
Kennedy, c	3	0	1	1	6	2
Brown, cf	3	0	0	0	3	0
Salazar, cf	1	0	1	0	0	0
Martinez, lf	3	1	0	0	3	0
Templeton, ss	3	0	1	0	3	2
Show, p	0	0	0	0	0	0
Hawkins, p	0	0	0	0	0	0
Ramirez, ph	1	0	0	0	0	0
Dravecky, p	0	0	0	0	0	0
Bevacqua, ph	1	0	0	0	0	0
Lefferts, p	0	0	0	0	0	0
Flannery, ph	1	1	0	0	0	0
Gossage, p	0	0	0	0	0	0
Totals	29	6	8	5	27	9

Chicago	2	1	0	0	0	0	0	0	0 – 3
San Diego	0	0	0	0	0	2	4	0	x – 6

Chicago	IP.	H.	R.	ER.	BB.	SO.
Sutcliffe (Loser)	6⅓	7	6	5	3	2
Trout	⅔	0	0	0	0	1
Brusstar	1	1	0	0	0	1

San Diego	IP.	H.	R.	ER.	BB.	SO.
Show	1⅓	3	3	3	2	0
Hawkins	1⅔	0	0	0	1	1
Dravecky	2	0	0	0	0	2
Lefferts (Winner)	2	0	0	0	0	1
Gossage (Save)	2	2	0	0	0	2

Game-winning RBI—Gwynn.

Error—Durham. Double play—San Diego 1. Left on bases—Chicago 4, San Diego 5. Two-base hit—Gwynn. Three-base hit—Salazar. Home runs—Durham, Davis. Stolen bases—Matthews, Sandberg. Caught stealing—Dernier, Matthews, Salazar. Sacrifice hit—Templeton. Sacrifice fly—Nettles, Kennedy. Hit by pitch—by Gossage (Hebner). Umpires—Kibler, Runge, McSherry and Harvey. Time—2:41. Attendance—58,359.

SAN DIEGO PADRES' BATTING AND FIELDING AVERAGES

Player—Position	G.	AB.	R.	H.	TB.	2B.	3B.	HR.	RBI.	B.A.	PO.	A.	E.	F.A.
Thurmond, p	1	1	0	1	1	0	0	0	0	1.000	0	1	0	1.000
Flannery, ph	3	2	2	1	1	0	0	0	0	.500	0	0	0	.000
Garvey, 1b	5	20	1	8	12	1	0	1	7	.400	35	3	0	1.000
Gwynn, rf	5	19	6	7	10	3	0	0	3	.368	9	0	0	1.000
Templeton, ss	5	15	2	5	6	1	0	0	2	.333	19	11	1	.968
Wiggins, 2b	5	19	4	6	6	0	0	0	1	.316	11	11	0	1.000
McReynolds, cf	4	10	2	3	6	0	0	1	4	.300	10	0	0	1.000
Kennedy, c	5	18	2	4	4	0	0	0	1	.222	28	4	0	1.000
Salazar, 3b-ph-cf	3	5	0	1	3	0	1	0	0	.200	1	3	0	1.000
Martinez, lf	5	17	1	3	3	0	0	0	0	.176	6	0	0	1.000
Nettles, 3b	4	14	1	2	2	0	0	0	2	.143	5	8	0	1.000
Dravecky, p	3	0	0	0	0	0	0	0	0	.000	1	1	0	1.000
Gossage, p	3	0	0	0	0	0	0	0	0	.000	0	0	0	.000
Hawkins, p	3	0	0	0	0	0	0	0	0	.000	0	1	0	1.000
Lefferts, p	3	0	0	0	0	0	0	0	0	.000	0	0	0	.000
Booker, p	1	0	0	0	0	0	0	0	0	.000	0	0	0	.000
Harris, p	1	0	0	0	0	0	0	0	0	.000	0	0	0	.000
Show, p	2	1	0	0	0	0	0	0	0	.000	0	0	0	.000
Lollar, p	1	1	0	0	0	0	0	0	0	.000	0	0	0	.000
Bevacqua, ph	2	2	0	0	0	0	0	0	0	.000	0	0	0	.000
Ramirez, ph	2	2	0	0	0	0	0	0	0	.000	0	0	0	.000
Summers, ph	2	2	0	0	0	0	0	0	0	.000	0	0	0	.000
Whitson, p	1	3	0	0	0	0	0	0	0	.000	1	0	0	1.000
Brown, ph-cf	3	4	1	0	0	0	0	0	0	.000	3	0	0	1.000
Totals	5	155	22	41	54	5	1	2	20	.265	129	43	1	.994

CHICAGO CUBS' BATTING AND FIELDING AVERAGES

Player—Position	G.	AB.	R.	H.	TB.	2B.	3B.	HR.	RBI.	B.A.	PO.	A.	E.	F.A.
Cotto, lf-pr-rf	3	1	1	1	1	0	0	0	0	1.000	2	0	0	1.000
Lake, c	1	1	0	1	2	1	0	0	0	1.000	0	0	0	.000
Sutcliffe, p	2	6	1	3	6	0	0	1	1	.500	0	0	0	.000
Trout, p	2	2	0	1	1	0	0	0	0	.500	0	1	1	.500
Davis, c	5	18	3	7	15	2	0	2	6	.389	23	2	0	1.000
Sandberg, 2b	5	19	3	7	9	2	0	0	2	.368	13	18	1	.969
Moreland, rf	5	18	3	6	8	2	0	0	2	.333	9	0	0	1.000
Dernier, cf	5	17	5	4	9	2	0	1	1	.235	12	1	0	1.000
Bowa, ss	5	15	1	3	4	1	0	0	1	.200	8	15	0	1.000
Matthews, lf	5	15	4	3	9	0	0	2	5	.200	10	0	0	1.000

Player—Position	G.	AB.	R.	H.	TB.	2B.	3B.	HR.	RBI.	B.A.	PO.	A.	E.	F.A.
Cey, 3b	5	19	3	3	7	1	0	1	3	.158	1	6	0	1.000
Durham, 1b	5	20	2	3	9	0	0	2	4	.150	47	3	1	.980
Smith, p	2	0	0	0	0	0	0	0	0	.000	0	0	0	.000
Stoddard, p	2	0	0	0	0	0	0	0	0	.000	1	1	0	1.000
Frazier, p	1	0	0	0	0	0	0	0	0	.000	0	0	0	.000
Brusstar, p	3	1	0	0	0	0	0	0	0	.000	0	1	0	1.000
Veryzer, 3b-ss	3	1	0	0	0	0	0	0	0	.000	0	0	0	.000
Hebner, ph	2	1	0	0	0	0	0	0	0	.000	0	0	0	.000
Lopes, rf-ph	2	1	0	0	0	0	0	0	0	.000	0	0	0	.000
Woods, ph-rf	1	1	0	0	0	0	0	0	0	.000	1	0	0	1.000
Bosley, ph	2	2	0	0	0	0	0	0	0	.000	0	0	0	.000
Eckersley, p	1	2	0	0	0	0	0	0	0	.000	0	0	0	.000
Sanderson, p	1	2	0	0	0	0	0	0	0	.000	0	1	0	1.000
Totals	5	162	26	42	80	11	0	9	25	.259	127	49	3	.983

SAN DIEGO PADRES' PITCHING RECORDS

Pitcher	G.	GS.	CG.	IP.	H.	R.	ER.	BB.	SO.	HB.	WP.	W.	L.	Pct.	ERA.
Dravecky	3	0	0	6	2	0	0	0	5	0	0	0	0	.000	0.00
Lefferts	3	0	0	4	1	0	0	1	1	1	0	2	0	1.000	0.00
Hawkins	3	0	0	3⅔	0	0	0	2	1	0	0	0	0	.000	0.00
Booker	1	0	0	2	2	0	0	1	2	0	0	0	0	.000	0.00
Whitson	1	1	0	8	5	1	1	2	6	0	0	1	0	1.000	1.13
Gossage	3	0	0	4	5	2	2	1	5	1	0	0	0	.000	4.50
Lollar	1	1	0	4⅓	3	3	3	4	3	0	0	0	0	.000	6.23
Thurmond	1	1	0	3⅔	7	4	4	2	1	0	0	0	1	.000	9.82
Show	2	2	0	5⅓	8	8	8	4	2	0	0	0	1	.000	13.50
Harris	1	0	0	2	9	8	7	3	2	0	0	0	0	.000	31.50
Totals	5	5	0	43	42	26	25	20	28	2	0	3	2	.600	5.23

No shutouts. Save—Gossage.

CHICAGO CUBS' PITCHING RECORDS

Pitcher	G.	GS.	CG.	IP.	H.	R.	ER.	BB.	SO.	HB.	WP.	W.	L.	Pct.	ERA.
Brusstar	3	0	0	4⅓	6	0	0	0	1	0	0	0	0	.000	0.00
Trout	2	1	0	9	5	2	2	3	3	0	0	1	0	1.000	2.00
Sutcliffe	2	2	0	13⅓	9	6	5	8	10	1	0	1	1	.500	3.38
Stoddard	2	0	0	2	1	2	1	2	2	0	0	0	0	.000	4.50
Sanderson	1	1	0	4⅔	6	3	3	1	2	0	0	0	0	.000	5.79
Eckersley	1	1	0	5⅓	9	5	5	0	0	0	0	0	1	.000	8.44
Smith	2	0	0	2	3	2	2	0	3	0	0	0	1	.000	9.00
Frazier	1	0	0	1⅔	2	2	2	0	1	0	0	0	0	.000	10.80
Totals	5	5	0	42⅓	41	22	20	14	22	1	0	2	3	.400	4.25

No shutouts. Save—Smith.

COMPOSITE SCORE BY INNINGS

San Diego	0	0	2	1	4	7	6	0	2 — 22
Chicago	5	2	5	4	6	2	0	2	0 — 26

Game-winning RBIs—Dernier, Matthews, Templeton, Garvey, Gwynn.
Sacrifice hits—Trout, Wiggins, Templeton.
Sacrifice flies—Moreland, Davis, McReynolds, Gwynn, Nettles, Kennedy.
Stolen bases—Sandberg 3, Dernier 2, Templeton, Brown, Matthews.
Caught stealing—Sandberg, Wiggins, Dernier, Matthews, Salazar.
Double plays—Sandberg, Bowa and Durham 3; Bowa, Sandberg and Durham 3; Templeton and Garvey; Wiggins, Templeton and Garvey; Hawkins, Templeton and Garvey; Kennedy, Templeton, Garvey and Wiggins.
Left on bases—San Diego 10, 4, 1, 7, 5—27; Chicago 8, 6, 5, 9, 4—32.
Hit by pitcher—By Sutcliffe (Flannery); by Lefferts (Cotto), by Gossage (Hebner).
Passed ball—Davis.
Balks—None.
Time of games—First game, 2:49; second game, 2:18; third game, 2:19; fourth game, 3:13; fifth game, 2:41.
Attendance—First game, 36,282; second game, 36,282; third game, 58,346; fourth game, 58,354; fifth game, 58,359.
Umpires—Cavanaugh, Slickenmeyer, Pomponi, Maher (first and second games); Bovy, Campagna, Fisher, Stewart (third and fourth games); Kibler, Runge, McSherry, Harvey (fifth game).
Official scorers—John Cunningham, San Diego official scorer; Jay Dunn, Trentonian (N.J.); Randy Minkoff, United Press International (Chicago); Dave Nightingale, The Sporting News.

CHAMPIONSHIP SERIES STANDINGS
Series Won and Lost

American League—East Division

	W.	L.	Pct.
Boston	1	0	1.000
Milwaukee	1	0	1.000
New York	4	1	.800
Baltimore	5	2	.714
Detroit	1	1	.500
Totals	12	4	.750

American League—West Division

	W.	L.	Pct.
Oakland	3	3	.500
Kansas City	1	4	.200
Minnesota	0	2	.000
California	0	2	.000
Chicago	0	1	.000
Totals	4	12	.250

National League—East Division

	W.	L.	Pct.
New York	2	0	1.000
St. Louis	1	0	1.000
Philadelphia	2	3	.400
Pittsburgh	2	4	.333
Montreal	0	1	.000
Chicago	0	1	.000
Totals	7	9	.438

National League—West Division

	W.	L.	Pct.
San Diego	1	0	1.000
Los Angeles	4	1	.800
Cincinnati	4	2	.667
San Francisco	0	1	.000
Houston	0	1	.000
Atlanta	0	2	.000
Totals	9	7	.563

Games Won and Lost

American League—East Division

	W.	L.	Pct.
Boston	3	0	1.000
Baltimore	18	8	.692
Detroit	5	3	.625
New York	12	8	.600
Milwaukee	3	2	.600
Totals	41	21	.661

American League—West Division

	W.	L.	Pct.
Kansas City	8	12	.400
Oakland	9	14	.391
California	3	6	.333
Chicago	1	3	.250
Minnesota	0	6	.000
Totals	21	41	.339

National League—East Division

	W.	L.	Pct.
St. Louis	3	0	1.000
New York	6	2	.750
Pittsburgh	9	13	.409
Montreal	2	3	.400
Chicago	2	3	.400
Philadelphia	8	12	.400
Totals	30	33	.476

National League—West Division

	W.	L.	Pct.
Cincinnati	14	8	.636
Los Angeles	13	8	.619
San Diego	3	2	.600
Houston	2	3	.400
San Francisco	1	3	.250
Atlanta	0	6	.000
Totals	33	30	.524

Series, Games Played; Home Games, Away Games
AMERICAN LEAGUE

East Division

	Ser.	G.	Ho.	Abr.
Baltimore	7	26	13	13
New York	5	20	10	10
Detroit	2	8	4	4
Milwaukee	1	5	3	2
Boston	1	3	2	1
Totals	16	62	32	30

West Division

	Ser.	G.	Ho.	Abr.
Oakland	6	23	10	13
Kansas City	5	20	11	9
California	2	9	4	5
Minnesota	2	6	3	3
Chicago	1	4	2	2
Totals	16	62	30	32

NATIONAL LEAGUE

East Division

	Ser.	G.	Ho.	Abr.
Pittsburgh	6	22	10	12
Philadelphia	5	20	10	10
New York	2	8	4	4
Montreal	1	5	2	3
Chicago	1	5	2	3
St. Louis	1	3	2	1
Totals	16	63	30	33

West Division

	Ser.	G.	Ho.	Abr.
Cincinnati	6	22	11	11
Los Angeles	5	21	10	11
Atlanta	2	6	3	3
Houston	1	5	3	2
San Diego	1	5	3	2
San Francisco	1	4	2	2
Totals	16	63	32	31

GAMES PLAYED IN EACH CITY

AMERICAN LEAGUE (62)

Baltimore 13
Kansas City 11
Oakland 10
New York 10
California (Anaheim) 4
Detroit 4
Minnesota (Bloomington) 3
Milwaukee 3
Boston 2
Chicago 2

NATIONAL LEAGUE (63)

Cincinnati 11
Pittsburgh 10
Philadelphia 10
Los Angeles 10
New York 4
Houston 3
Montreal 3
Atlanta 3
San Diego 3
San Francisco 2
St. Louis 2
Chicago 2

CHAMPIONSHIP SERIES SHUTOUT GAMES

AMERICAN LEAGUE (12)

October   5, 1969—McNally, Baltimore 1, Minnesota 0; 3 hits (11 innings).
October   8, 1972—Odom, Oakland 5, Detroit 0; 3 hits.
October 10, 1972—Coleman, Detroit 3, Oakland 0; 7 hits.
October   6, 1973—Palmer, Baltimore 6, Oakland 0; 5 hits.
October 11, 1973—Hunter, Oakland 3, Baltimore 0; 5 hits.
October   6, 1974—Holtzman, Oakland 5, Baltimore 0; 5 hits.
October   8, 1974—Blue, Oakland 1, Baltimore 0; 2 hits.
October   6, 1979—McGregor, Baltimore 8, California 0; 6 hits.
October 15, 1981—Righetti, Davis and Gossage, New York 4, Oakland 0; 5 hits.
October   6, 1983—Boddicker, Baltimore 4, Chicago 0; 5 hits.
October   8, 1983—Davis and T. Martinez, Baltimore 3, Chicago 0; 10 hits (10 innings).
October   5, 1984—Wilcox and Hernandez, Detroit 1, Kansas City 0; 3 hits.

NATIONAL LEAGUE (9)

October   3, 1970—Nolan and Carroll, Cincinnati 3, Pittsburgh 0; 8 hits (10 innings).
October   7, 1973—Matlack, New York 5, Cincinnati 0; 2 hits.
October   5, 1974—Sutton, Los Angeles 3, Pittsburgh 0; 4 hits.
October   8, 1974—Kison and Hernandez, Pittsburgh 7, Los Angeles 0; 4 hits.
October   4, 1978—John, Los Angeles 4, Philadelphia 0; 4 hits.
October 10, 1980—Niekro and D. Smith, Houston 1, Philadelphia 0; 7 hits (11 innings).
October 14, 1981—Burris, Montreal 3, Los Angeles 0; 5 hits.
October   7, 1982—Forsch, St. Louis 7, Atlanta 0; 3 hits.
October   4, 1983—Carlton and Holland, Philadelphia 1, Los Angeles 0; 7 hits.

CHAMPIONSHIP SERIES EXTRA-INNING GAMES (18)

October   4, 1969—at Baltimore, 12 innings, Baltimore AL East 4, Minnesota AL West 3.
October   5, 1969—at Baltimore, 11 innings, Baltimore AL East 1, Minnesota AL West 0.
October   3, 1970—at Pittsburgh, 10 innings, Cincinnati NL West 3, Pittsburgh NL East 0.
October   7, 1972—at Oakland, 11 innings, Oakland AL West 3, Detroit AL East 2.
October 11, 1972—at Detroit, 10 innings, Detroit AL East 4, Oakland AL West 3.
October   9, 1973—at Oakland, 11 innings, Oakland AL West 2, Baltimore AL East 1.
October   9, 1973—at New York, 12 innings, Cincinnati NL West 2, New York NL East 1.
October   7, 1975—at Pittsburgh, 10 innings, Cincinnati NL West 5, Pittsburgh NL East 3.
October   7, 1978—at Los Angeles, 10 innings, Los Angeles NL West 4, Philadelphia NL East 3.
October   2, 1979—at Cincinnati, 11 innings, Pittsburgh NL East 5, Cincinnati NL West 2.
October   3, 1979—at Cincinnati, 10 innings, Pittsburgh NL East 3, Cincinnati NL West 2.
October   3, 1979—at Baltimore, 10 innings, Baltimore AL East 6, California AL West 2.
October   8, 1980—at Philadelphia, 10 innings, Houston NL West 7, Philadelphia NL East 4.
October 10, 1980—at Houston, 11 innings, Houston NL West 1, Philadelphia NL East 0.
October 11, 1980—at Houston, 10 innings, Philadelphia NL East 5, Houston NL West 3.
October 12, 1980—at Houston, 10 innings, Philadelphia NL East 8, Houston NL West 7.
October   8, 1983—at Chicago, 10 innings, Baltimore AL East 3, Chicago AL West 0.
October   3, 1984—at Kansas City, 11 innings, Detroit AL East 5, Kansas City AL West 3.

WINNING, LOSING CLUBS
AMERICAN LEAGUE WINNING CLUBS

Baltimore (East)	5—1969-70-71-79-83.
New York (East)	4—1976-77-78-81.
Oakland (West)	3—1972-73-74.
Boston (East)	1—1975.
Kansas City (West)	1—1980.
Milwaukee (East)	1—1982.
Detroit (East)	1—1984.

East Division Has Won 12, Lost 4

AMERICAN LEAGUE LOSING CLUBS

Kansas City (West)	4—1976-77-78-84.
Oakland (West)	3—1971-75-81.
Baltimore (East)	2—1973-74.
Minnesota (West)	2—1969-70.
California (West)	2—1979-82.
Detroit (East)	1—1972.
New York (East)	1—1980.
Chicago (West)	1—1983.

NATIONAL LEAGUE WINNING CLUBS

Cincinnati (West)	4—1970-72-75-76.
Los Angeles (West)	4—1974-77-78-81.
New York (East)	2—1969-73.
Pittsburgh (East)	2—1971-79.
Philadelphia (East)	2—1980-83.
St. Louis (East)	1—1982.
San Diego (West)	1—1984.

West Division Has Won 9, Lost 7

NATIONAL LEAGUE LOSING CLUBS

Pittsburgh (East)	4—1970-72-74-75.
Philadelphia (East)	3—1976-77-78.
Cincinnati (West)	2—1973-79.
Atlanta (West)	2—1969-82.
San Francisco (West)	1—1971.
Houston (West)	1—1980.
Montreal (East)	1—1981.
Los Angeles (West)	1—1983.
Chicago (East)	1—1984.

SERIES WON

3-game Series—3—Baltimore AL, 1969, 1970, 1971.
        3—Cincinnati NL, 1970, 1975, 1976.
        1—Boston AL, 1975.
        1—New York NL, 1969.
        1—Pittsburgh NL, 1979.
        1—Kansas City AL, 1980.
        1—New York AL, 1981.
        1—St. Louis NL, 1982.
        1—Detroit AL, 1984.

4-game Series—3—Los Angeles NL, 1974, 1977, 1978.
        2—Baltimore AL, 1979, 1983.
        1—Oakland AL, 1974.
        1—Pittsburgh NL, 1971.
        1—New York AL, 1978.
        1—Philadelphia NL, 1983.

5-game Series—2—New York AL, 1976, 1977.
        2—Oakland AL, 1972, 1973.
        1—Cincinnati NL, 1972.
        1—New York NL, 1973.
        1—Philadelphia NL, 1980.
        1—Los Angeles NL, 1981.
        1—Milwaukee AL, 1982.
        1—San Diego NL, 1984.

SERIES LOST

3-game Series—3—Oakland AL, 1971, 1975, 1981.
                   2—Minnesota AL, 1969, 1970.
                   2—Pittsburgh NL, 1970, 1975.
                   2—Atlanta NL, 1969, 1982.
                   1—Philadelphia NL, 1976.
                   1—Cincinnati NL, 1979.
                   1—New York AL, 1980.
                   1—Kansas City AL, 1984.

4-game Series—2—Philadelphia NL, 1977, 1978.
                   1—Baltimore AL, 1974.
                   1—Pittsburgh NL, 1974.
                   1—San Francisco NL, 1971.
                   1—Kansas City AL, 1978.
                   1—California AL, 1979.
                   1—Chicago AL, 1983.
                   1—Los Angeles NL, 1983.

5-game Series—2—Kansas City AL, 1976, 1977.
                   1—Baltimore AL, 1973.
                   1—Cincinnati NL, 1973.
                   1—Detroit AL, 1972.
                   1—Pittsburgh NL, 1972.
                   1—Houston NL, 1980.
                   1—Montreal NL, 1981.
                   1—California AL, 1982.
                   1—Chicago NL, 1984.

.400 Hitters Playing in All Games, Each Series
(9 or more at-bats)

AMERICAN LEAGUE (31)

Player and Club	Year	G.	AB.	R.	H.	2B.	3B.	HR.	TB.	B.A.
Lynn, Fredric M., California	1982	5	18	5	11	2	0	1	16	.611
Robinson, Brooks C., Baltimore	1970	3	12	3	7	2	0	0	9	.583
White, Frank, Kansas City	1980	3	11	3	6	1	0	1	10	.545
Chambliss, C. Christopher, N.Y.	1976	5	21	5	11	1	1	2	20	.524
Robinson, Brooks C., Baltimore	1969	3	14	1	7	1	0	0	8	.500
Oliva, Antonio, Minnesota	1970	3	12	2	6	2	0	1	11	.500
Bando, Salvatore L., Oakland	1975	3	12	1	6	2	0	0	8	.500
Watson, Robert J., New York	1980	3	12	0	6	3	1	0	11	.500
Nettles, Graig, New York	1981	3	12	2	6	2	0	1	11	.500
Mumphrey, Jerry W., New York	1981	3	12	2	6	1	0	0	7	.500
Jackson, Reginald M., New York	1978	4	13	5	6	1	0	2	13	.462
Milbourne, Lawrence, W., N.Y.	1981	3	13	4	6	0	0	0	6	.462
Moore, Charles W., Milwaukee	1982	5	13	3	6	0	0	0	6	.462
Yastrzemski, Carl M., Boston	1975	3	11	4	5	1	0	1	9	.455
Rivers, John M., New York	1978	4	11	0	5	0	0	0	5	.455
Burleson, Richard P., Boston	1975	3	9	2	4	2	0	0	6	.444
Brett, George H., Kansas City	1976	5	18	4	8	1	1	1	14	.444
McRae, Harold A., Kansas City	1977	5	18	6	8	3	0	1	14	.444
Munson, Thurman L., New York	1976	5	23	3	10	2	0	0	12	.435
Powell, John W., Baltimore	1970	3	14	2	6	2	0	1	11	.429
Otis, Amos J., Kansas City	1978	4	14	2	6	2	0	0	8	.429
Fisk, Carlton E., Boston	1975	3	12	4	5	1	0	0	6	.417
Jackson, Reginald M., Oakland	1975	3	12	1	5	0	0	1	8	.417
Murray, Eddie C., Baltimore	1979	4	12	3	5	0	0	1	8	.417
Gibson, Kirk H., Detroit	1984	3	12	2	5	1	0	1	9	.417
Carew, Rodney, C., California	1979	4	17	4	7	3	0	0	10	.412
Blair, Paul L., Baltimore	1969	3	15	1	6	2	0	1	11	.400
Johnson, Clifford, New York	1977	5	15	2	6	2	0	1	11	.400
Chambliss, C. Christopher, N.Y.	1978	4	15	1	6	0	0	0	6	.400
Ripken, Calvin E., Baltimore	1983	4	15	5	6	2	0	0	8	.400
Cooper, Cecil C., Boston	1975	3	10	0	4	2	0	0	6	.400

.400 Hitters Playing in All Games, Each Series
(9 or more at-bats)

NATIONAL LEAGUE (31)

Player and Club	Year	G.	AB.	R.	H.	2B.	3B.	HR.	TB.	B.A.
Johnstone, John W., Phila.	1976	3	9	1	7	1	1	0	10	.778
Porter, Darrell R., St. Louis	1982	3	9	3	5	3	0	0	8	.556
Smith, Osborne E., St. Louis	1982	3	9	0	5	0	0	0	5	.556
Shamsky, Arthur L., N.Y.	1969	3	13	3	7	0	0	0	7	.538
Puhl, Terry S., Houston	1980	5	19	4	10	2	0	0	12	.526
Stargell, Wilver D., Pitts.	1970	3	12	0	6	1	0	0	7	.500
Zisk, Richard W., Pittsburgh	1975	3	10	0	5	1	0	0	6	.500
Baker, Johnnie B., Los Angeles	1978	4	15	1	7	2	0	0	9	.467
Schmidt, Michael J., Phila.	1983	4	15	5	7	2	0	1	12	.467
Cepeda, Orlando M., Atlanta	1969	3	11	2	5	2	0	1	10	.455
Concepcion, David I., Cinc	1975	3	11	2	5	0	0	1	8	.455
Stargell, Wilver D., Pittsburgh	1979	3	11	2	5	2	0	2	13	.455
Rose, Peter E., Cincinnati	1972	5	20	1	9	4	0	0	13	.450
Thomas, Derrel O., Los Angeles	1983	4	9	0	4	1	0	0	5	.444
Robertson, Robert E., Pitts.	1971	4	16	5	7	1	0	4	20	.438
Carter, Gary E., Montreal	1981	5	16	3	7	1	0	0	8	.438
Jones, Cleon J., New York	1969	3	14	4	6	2	0	1	11	.429
McCovey, Willie L., San Fran.	1971	4	14	2	6	0	0	2	12	.429
Rose, Peter E., Cincinnati	1976	3	14	3	6	2	1	0	10	.429
Concepcion, David I., Cin.	1979	3	14	1	6	1	0	0	7	.429
Matthews, Gary N., Phila.	1983	4	14	4	6	0	0	3	15	.429
Cash, David, Pittsburgh	1971	4	19	5	8	2	0	0	10	.421
Tolan, Robert, Cincinnati	1970	3	12	3	5	0	0	1	8	.417
Perez, Atanasio R., Cincinnati	1975	3	12	3	5	0	0	1	8	.417
Garner, Philip M., Pittsburgh	1979	3	12	4	5	0	1	1	10	.417
Russell, William E., L.A.	1978	4	17	1	7	1	0	0	8	.412
Rose, Peter E., Philadelphia	1980	5	20	3	8	0	0	0	8	.400
Garvey, Steven P., San Diego	1984	5	20	1	8	1	0	1	12	.400
Stargell, Wilver D., Pittsburgh	1974	4	15	3	6	0	0	2	12	.400
Cruz, Jose D., Houston	1980	5	15	3	6	1	1	0	9	.400
Boone, Robert R., Philadelphia	1977	4	10	1	4	0	0	0	4	.400

LEADING BATSMEN, CHAMPIONSHIP SERIES
PLAYING IN ALL GAMES, EACH SERIES (4 or more hits)
AMERICAN LEAGUE

Year	Player and Club	G.	AB.	R.	H.	2B.	3B.	HR.	TB.	B.A.
1969—Brooks C. Robinson, Baltimore		3	14	1	7	1	0	0	8	.500
1970—Brooks C. Robinson, Baltimore		3	12	3	7	2	0	0	9	.583
1971—Brooks C. Robinson, Baltimore		3	11	2	4	1	0	1	8	.364
Salvatore L. Bando, Oakland		3	11	3	4	2	0	1	9	.364
1972—Mateo R. Alou, Oakland		5	21	2	8	4	0	0	12	.381
1973—Dagoberto B. Campaneris, Oakland		5	21	3	7	1	0	2	14	.333
1974—Raymond E. Fosse, Oakland		4	12	1	4	1	0	1	8	.333
1975—Salvatore L. Bando, Oakland		3	12	1	6	2	0	0	8	.500
1976—C. Christopher Chambliss, New York		5	21	5	11	1	1	2	20	.524
1977—Harold A. McRae, Kansas City		5	18	6	8	3	0	1	14	.444
1978—Reginald M. Jackson, New York		4	13	5	6	1	0	2	13	.462
1979—Eddie C. Murray, Baltimore		4	12	3	5	0	0	1	8	.417
1980—Frank White, Kansas City		3	11	3	6	1	0	1	10	.545
1981—Graig Nettles, New York		3	12	2	6	2	0	1	11	.500
Jerry W. Mumphrey, New York		3	12	2	6	1	0	0	7	.500
1982—Fredric M. Lynn, California		5	18	5	11	2	0	1	16	.611
1983—Calvin E. Ripken, Baltimore		4	15	5	6	2	0	0	8	.400
1984—Kirk H. Gibson, Detroit		3	12	2	5	1	0	1	9	.417

NATIONAL LEAGUE

Year	Player and Club	G.	AB.	R.	H.	2B.	3B.	HR.	TB.	B.A.
1969—Arthur L. Shamsky, New York		3	13	3	7	0	0	0	7	.538
1970—Wilver D. Stargell, Pittsburgh		3	12	0	6	1	0	0	7	.500
1971—Robert E. Robertson, Pittsburgh		4	16	5	7	1	0	4	20	.438
1972—Peter E. Rose, Cincinnati		5	20	1	9	4	0	0	13	.450
1973—Peter E. Rose, Cincinnati		5	21	3	8	1	0	2	15	.381
1974—Wilver D. Stargell, Pittsburgh		4	15	3	6	0	0	2	12	.400

BASEBALL DOPE BOOK

Year	Player and Club	G.	AB.	R.	H.	2B.	3B.	HR.	TB.	B.A.
1975—	Richard W. Zisk, Pittsburgh	3	10	0	5	1	0	0	6	.500
1976—	John W. Johnstone, Philadelphia	3	9	1	7	1	1	0	10	.778
1977—	Robert R. Boone, Philadelphia............	4	10	1	4	0	0	0	4	.400
1978—	Johnnie B. Baker, Los Angeles............	4	15	1	7	2	0	0	9	.467
1979—	Wilver D. Stargell, Pittsburgh	3	11	2	5	2	0	2	13	.455
1980—	Terry S. Puhl, Houston.........................	5	19	4	10	2	0	0	12	.526
1981—	Gary E. Carter, Montreal	5	16	3	7	1	0	0	8	.438
1982—	Darrell R. Porter, St. Louis	3	9	3	5	3	0	0	8	.556
	Osborne E. Smith, St. Louis.................	3	9	0	5	0	0	0	5	.556
1983—	Michael J. Schmidt, Philadelphia............	4	15	5	7	2	0	1	12	.467
1984—	Steven P. Garvey, San Diego.................	5	20	1	8	1	0	1	12	.400

CLUB BATTING

AMERICAN LEAGUE

Year—Club	G.	AB.	R.	H.	TB.	2B.	3B.	HR.	SH.	SF.	SB.	BB.	SO.	RBI.	B.A.
1969— Baltimore, East........	3	123	16	36	58	8	1	4	2	0	0	13	14	15	.293
Minnesota, West.......	3	110	5	17	25	3	1	1	0	1	2	12	27	5	.155
1970— Baltimore, East........	3	109	27	36	61	7	0	6	1	2	1	12	19	24	.330
Minnesota, West.......	3	101	10	24	39	4	1	3	1	0	0	9	22	10	.238
1971— Baltimore, East........	3	95	15	26	47	7	1	4	0	1	0	13	22	14	.274
Oakland, West	3	96	7	22	41	8	1	3	2	0	0	5	16	7	.229
1972— Detroit, East	5	162	10	32	52	6	1	4	3	0	0	13	25	10	.198
Oakland, West	5	170	13	38	49	8	0	1	4	1	7	12	35	10	.224
1973— Baltimore, East........	5	171	15	36	52	7	0	3	0	0	1	16	25	15	.211
Oakland, West	5	160	15	32	54	5	1	5	4	1	3	17	39	15	.200
1974— Baltimore, East........	4	124	7	22	32	1	0	3	2	0	0	5	20	7	.177
Oakland, West	4	120	11	22	37	4	1	3	2	1	3	22	16	11	.183
1975— Boston, East	3	98	18	31	45	8	0	2	5	1	3	3	12	14	.316
Oakland, West	3	98	7	19	28	6	0	1	0	0	0	9	14	7	.194
1976— New York, East........	3	174	23	55	84	13	2	4	2	1	4	16	15	21	.316
Kansas City, West....	5	162	24	40	60	6	4	2	0	4	5	11	18	24	.247
1977— New York, East........	5	175	21	46	64	12	0	2	1	2	2	9	16	17	.263
Kansas City, West....	5	163	22	42	66	9	3	3	2	2	5	15	22	21	.258
1978— New York, East........	4	140	19	42	62	3	1	5	0	1	0	7	18	18	.300
Kansas City, West....	4	133	17	35	59	6	3	4	1	2	6	14	21	16	.263
1979— Baltimore, East........	4	133	26	37	53	5	1	3	1	3	5	18	24	25	.278
California, West	4	137	15	32	48	7	0	3	0	2	2	7	13	14	.234
1980— New York, East........	3	102	6	26	44	7	1	3	1	0	0	6	16	5	.255
Kansas City, West....	3	97	14	28	45	6	1	3	0	0	3	9	15	14	.289
1981— New York, East........	3	107	20	36	49	4	0	3	2	1	2	13	10	20	.336
Oakland, West	3	99	4	22	28	4	1	0	0	0	2	6	23	4	.222
1982— Milwaukee, East........	5	151	23	33	52	4	0	5	2	3	2	15	28	20	.219
California, West	5	157	23	40	62	8	1	4	5	2	1	16	34	23	.255
1983— Baltimore, East........	4	129	19	28	46	9	0	3	1	3	2	16	24	17	.217
Chicago, West	4	133	3	28	32	4	0	0	1	0	4	12	26	2	.211
1984— Detroit, East	3	107	14	25	43	4	1	4	2	1	4	8	17	14	.234
Kansas City, West....	3	106	4	18	21	1	1	0	0	0	0	6	21	4	.170

NATIONAL LEAGUE

Year—Club	G.	AB.	R.	H.	TB.	2B.	3B.	HR.	SH.	SF.	SB.	BB.	SO.	RBI.	B.A.
1969— New York, East........	3	113	27	37	65	8	1	6	1	0	5	10	25	24	.327
Atlanta, West............	3	106	15	27	51	9	0	5	0	1	1	11	20	15	.255
1970— Pittsburgh, East........	3	102	3	23	29	6	0	0	2	0	0	12	19	3	.225
Cincinnati, West.......	3	100	9	22	36	3	1	3	0	0	1	8	12	8	.220
1971— Pittsburgh, East........	4	144	24	39	67	4	0	8	1	0	2	5	33	23	.271
San Francisco, West	4	132	25	31	51	5	0	5	4	0	2	16	28	14	.235
1972— Pittsburgh, East........	5	158	15	30	47	6	1	3	2	0	0	9	27	14	.190
Cincinnati, West.......	5	166	19	42	67	9	2	4	3	1	4	10	28	16	.253
1973— New York, East........	5	168	23	37	51	5	0	3	3	1	0	19	28	22	.220
Cincinnati, West.......	5	167	8	31	52	6	0	5	3	1	0	13	42	8	.186
1974— Pittsburgh, East........	4	129	10	25	35	1	0	3	2	0	1	8	17	10	.194
Los Angeles, West ...	4	138	20	37	56	8	1	3	1	0	5	30	16	19	.268
1975— Pittsburgh, East........	3	101	7	20	26	3	0	1	0	0	0	10	18	7	.198
Cincinnati, West.......	3	102	19	29	45	4	0	4	0	3	11	9	28	18	.284
1976— Philadelphia, East ...	3	100	11	27	40	8	1	1	3	2	0	12	9	11	.270
Cincinnati, West.......	3	99	19	25	45	5	3	3	1	3	5	15	16	17	.253
1977— Philadelphia, East ...	4	138	14	31	40	3	0	2	2	0	1	11	21	12	.225
Los Angeles, West ...	4	133	22	35	52	6	1	3	2	0	3	14	22	20	.263
1978— Philadelphia, East ...	4	140	17	35	57	3	2	5	2	1	0	9	21	16	.250
Los Angeles, West ...	4	147	21	42	80	8	3	8	2	0	2	9	22	21	.286
1979— Pittsburgh, East........	3	105	15	28	47	3	2	4	5	3	4	13	13	14	.267
Cincinnati, West.......	3	107	5	23	35	4	1	2	1	1	4	11	26	5	.215
1980— Philadelphia, East ...	5	190	20	55	68	8	1	1	5	1	7	13	37	19	.291
Houston, West...........	5	172	19	40	57	7	5	0	7	2	4	31	19	18	.233
1981— Montreal, East...........	5	158	10	34	44	7	0	1	3	0	2	12	25	8	.215
Los Angeles, West ...	5	163	15	38	55	3	1	4	4	0	5	12	23	15	.233
1982— St. Louis, East...........	3	103	17	34	45	4	2	1	5	3	1	12	16	16	.330
Atlanta, West............	3	89	5	15	16	1	0	0	2	1	1	6	15	3	.169
1983— Philadelphia, East ...	4	130	16	34	53	4	0	5	3	1	2	15	22	15	.262
Los Angeles, West ...	4	129	8	27	40	5	1	2	2	0	3	11	31	7	.209
1984— Chicago, East............	5	162	26	42	80	11	0	9	1	2	6	20	28	25	.259
San Diego, West........	5	155	22	41	54	5	1	2	2	4	2	14	22	20	.265

MISCELLANEOUS CLUB STATISTICS

CLUB FIELDING, LEFT ON BASES, PLAYERS, PITCHERS USED

AMERICAN LEAGUE

Year—Team, Division	G.	PO.	A.	E.	DP.	PB.	F.A.	LOB.	Pl.	Pi.
1969—Baltimore, East	3	96	31	1	2	0	.992	28	20	7
Minnesota, West	3	94	34	5	3	0	.962	22	22	9
1970—Baltimore, East	3	81	29	0	3	0	1.000	20	14	4
Minnesota, West	3	78	28	6	5	0	.946	20	24	9
1971—Baltimore, East	3	81	31	1	3	0	.991	19	15	4
Oakland, West	3	75	15	0	4	0	1.000	15	20	7
1972—Detroit, East	5	139	48	7	4	0	.964	30	24	8
Oakland, West	5	138	59	3	5	1	.985	38	25	8
1973—Baltimore, East	5	135	51	2	2	1	.989	36	23	7
Oakland, West	5	138	47	4	4	0	.979	34	22	6
1974—Baltimore, East	4	105	50	4	4	0	.975	16	22	7
Oakland, West	4	108	43	2	4	1	.987	30	20	5
1975—Boston, East	3	81	33	4	3	0	.966	14	14	5
Oakland, West	3	75	40	6	4	0	.950	19	22	7
1976—New York, East	5	132	60	6	3	1	.970	41	22	6
Kansas City, West	5	129	51	4	5	0	.978	22	24	9
1977—New York, East	5	132	51	2	2	0	.989	34	18	6
Kansas City, West	5	132	54	5	2	0	.974	28	22	8
1978—New York, East	4	105	35	1	2	1	.993	27	21	8
Kansas City, West	4	102	36	4	4	1	.972	28	20	7
1979—Baltimore, East	4	109	52	5	5	1	.970	23	20	5
California, West	4	107	37	2	7	0	.986	22	23	9
1980—New York, East	3	75	42	1	2	0	.991	22	20	6
Kansas City, West	3	81	29	1	3	0	.991	18	15	4
1981—New York, East	3	81	30	1	6	1	.991	30	22	6
Oakland, West	3	75	33	4	1	0	.964	20	24	8
1982—Milwaukee, East	5	129	45	8	5	0	.956	24	20	8
California, West	5	126	46	4	3	1	.977	29	20	7
1983—Baltimore, East	4	111	49	2	4	0	.988	24	22	6
Chicago, West	4	108	51	3	5	0	.981	35	23	9
1984—Detroit, East	3	87	27	1	0	0	.991	20	20	5
Kansas City, West	3	84	26	7	2	0	.940	21	22	6

NATIONAL LEAGUE

Year—Team, Division	G.	PO.	A.	E.	DP.	PB.	F.A.	LOB.	Pl.	Pi.
1969—New York, East	3	81	23	2	2	1	.981	19	17	6
Atlanta, West	3	78	37	6	4	1	.950	23	23	9
1970—Pittsburgh, East	3	81	37	2	3	0	.983	29	18	5
Cincinnati, West	3	84	39	1	1	0	.992	18	20	7
1971—Pittsburgh, East	4	105	32	3	3	1	.979	26	21	7
San Francisco, West	4	102	37	4	1	1	.972	33	22	9
1972—Pittsburgh, East	5	131	38	4	3	0	.977	24	23	10
Cincinnati, West	5	132	53	4	3	1	.979	30	21	8
1973—New York, East	5	142	44	4	3	0	.979	30	17	6
Cincinnati, West	5	138	59	2	3	0	.990	35	24	9
1974—Pittsburgh, East	4	105	37	4	2	1	.973	24	22	8
Los Angeles, West	4	108	46	7	8	1	.957	44	22	7
1975—Pittsburgh, East	3	78	20	2	3	2	.980	21	24	10
Cincinnati, West	3	84	31	1	2	0	.991	17	18	7
1976—Philadelphia, East	3	79	34	2	3	0	.983	25	22	7
Cincinnati, West	3	81	32	2	3	0	.983	20	18	6
1977—Philadelphia, East	4	105	49	3	3	1	.981	32	21	7
Los Angeles, West	4	108	44	5	3	0	.968	22	23	9
1978—Philadelphia, East	4	110	46	4	4	0	.975	24	22	8
Los Angeles, West	4	111	50	3	4	0	.982	28	22	9
1979—Pittsburgh, East	3	90	34	0	2	0	1.000	24	20	8
Cincinnati, West	3	87	39	1	2	0	.992	25	20	9
1980—Philadelphia, East	5	148	71	6	7	0	.973	43	23	9
Houston, West	5	147	52	3	4	1	.985	45	24	7
1981—Montreal, East	5	132	52	4	8	0	.979	31	19	7
Los Angeles, West	5	132	53	2	5	1	.989	33	23	9
1982—St. Louis, East	3	81	35	2	3	0	.983	31	15	5
Atlanta, West	3	76	39	1	0	1	.991	12	20	8
1983—Philadelphia, East	4	105	36	5	0	0	.966	31	20	5
Los Angeles, West	4	102	38	1	3	1	.993	31	22	8
1984—Chicago, East	5	127	49	3	6	1	.983	32	23	8
San Diego, West	5	129	43	1	4	0	.994	27	24	10

CHAMPIONSHIP SERIES HOME RUNS

AMERICAN LEAGUE (94)

1969—4—Baltimore (East), Frank Robinson (1), Mark H. Belanger (1), John W. Powell (1), Paul L. Blair (1).

1—Minnesota (West), Antonio Oliva (1).

1970—6—Baltimore (East), David A. Johnson (2), Miguel Cuellar (1), Donald A. Buford (1), John W. Powell (1), Frank Robinson (1).

        3—Minnesota (West), Harmon C. Killebrew (2), Antonio Oliva (1).
1971—4—Baltimore (East), John W. Powell (2), Brooks C. Robinson (1), Elrod J. Hendricks (1).
        3—Oakland (West), Reginald M. Jackson (2), Salvatore L. Bando (1).
1972—4—Detroit (East), Norman D. Cash (1), Albert W. Kaline (1), William A. Freehan (1), Richard J. McAuliffe (1).
        1—Oakland (West), Michael P. Epstein (1).
1973—5—Oakland (West), Salvatore L. Bando (2), Dagoberto B. Campaneris (2), Joseph O. Rudi (1).
        3—Baltimore (East), Earl C. Williams (1), Andrew A. Etchebarren (1), Robert A. Grich (1).
1974—3—Baltimore (East), Paul L. Blair (1), Brooks C. Robinson (1), Robert A. Grich (1).
        3—Oakland (West), Salvatore L. Bando (2), Raymond E. Fosse (1).
1975—2—Boston (East), Carl M. Yastrzemski (1), Americo P. Petrocelli (1).
        1—Oakland (West), Reginald M. Jackson (1).
1976—4—New York (East), Graig Nettles (2), C. Christopher Chambliss (2).
        2—Kansas City (West), John C. Mayberry (1), George H. Brett (1).
1977—3—Kansas City (West), Harold A. McRae (1), John C. Mayberry (1), Alfred E. Cowens (1).
        2—New York (East), Thurman L. Munson (1), Clifford Johnson (1).
1978—5—New York (East), Reginald M. Jackson (2), Thurman L. Munson (1), Graig Nettles (1), Roy H. White (1).
        4—Kansas City (West), George H. Brett (3), Freddie J. Patek (1).
1979—3—Baltimore (East), John L. Lowenstein (1), Eddie C. Murray (1), H. Patrick Kelly (1).
        3—California (West), Darnell G. Ford (2), Donald E. Baylor (1).
1980—3—New York (East), Richard A. Cerone (1), Louis V. Piniella (1), Graig Nettles (1).
        3—Kansas City (West), George H. Brett (2), Frank White (1).
1981—3—New York (East), Louis V. Piniella (1), Graig Nettles (1), William L. Randolph (1).
        0—Oakland (West).
1982—5—Milwaukee (East), Paul L. Molitor (2), J. Gorman Thomas (1), Mark S. Brouhard (1), Benjamin A. Oglivie (1).
        4—California (West), Fredric M. Lynn (1), Reginald M. Jackson (1), Robert R. Boone (1), Donald E. Baylor (1).
1983—3—Baltimore (East), Gary S. Roenicke (1), Eddie C. Murray (1), Terry L. Landrum (1).
        0—Chicago (West).
1984—4—Detroit (East), Kirk H. Gibson (1), Larry D. Herndon (1), Lance M. Parrish (1), Alan S. Trammell (1).
        0—Kansas City (West).

NATIONAL LEAGUE (106)

1969—6—New York (East), Tommie L. Agee (2), Kenneth G. Boswell (2), Cleon J. Jones (1), R. Wayne Garrett (1).
        5—Atlanta (West), Henry L. Aaron (3), A. Antonio Gonzalez (1), Orlando M. Cepeda (1).
1970—3—Cincinnati (West), Robert Tolan (1), Atanasio R. Perez (1), Johnny L. Bench (1).
        0—Pittsburgh (East).
1971—8—Pittsburgh (East), Robert E. Robertson (4), Richard J. Hebner (2), Eugene A. Clines (1), Albert Oliver (1).
        5—San Francisco (West), Willie L. McCovey (2), Rigoberto Fuentes (1), Willie H. Mays (1), Chris E. Speier (1).
1972—4—Cincinnati (West), Joe L. Morgan (2), Cesar F. Geronimo (1), Johnny L. Bench (1).
        3—Pittsburgh (East), Albert Oliver (1), Manuel D. Sanguillen (1), Roberto W. Clemente (1).
1973—5—Cincinnati (West), Peter E. Rose (2), Johnny L. Bench (1), Denis J. Menke (1), Atanasio R. Perez (1).
        3—New York (East), Daniel J. Staub (3).
1974—3—Los Angeles (West), Steven P. Garvey (2), Ronald C. Cey (1).
        3—Pittsburgh (East), Wilver D. Stargell (2), Richard J. Hebner (1).
1975—4—Cincinnati (West), Donald E. Gullett (1), Atanasio R. Perez (1), David I. Concepcion (1), Peter E. Rose (1).
        1—Pittsburgh (East), Albert Oliver (1).
1976—3—Cincinnati (West), George A. Foster (2), Johnny L. Bench (1).
        1—Philadelphia (East), Gregory M. Luzinski (1).
1977—3—Los Angeles (West), Johnnie B. Baker (2), Ronald C. Cey (1).
        2—Philadelphia (East), Gregory M. Luzinski (1), Arnold R. McBride (1).
1978—8—Los Angeles (West), Steven P. Garvey (4), David E. Lopes (2), Stephen W. Yeager (1), Ronald C. Cey (1).
        5—Philadelphia (East), Gregory M. Luzinski (2), Jerry L. Martin (1), Steven N. Carlton (1), Arnold R. McBride (1).
1979—4—Pittsburgh (East), Wilver D. Stargell (2), Philip M. Garner (1), Bill Madlock (1).
        2—Cincinnati (West), George A. Foster (1), Johnny L. Bench (1).
1980—1—Philadelphia (East), Gregory M. Luzinski (1).
        0—Houston (West).
1981—4—Los Angeles (West), Pedro Guerrero (1), Michael L. Scioscia (1), Steven P. Garvey (1), Robert J. Monday (1).
        1—Montreal (East), Jerome C. White (1).

Angels slugger Reggie Jackson holds the major league record for most Championship Series played (10) and shares the A.L. record for most home runs in Championship Series play (6) with Kansas City's George Brett.

1982—1—St. Louis (East), Willie D. McGee (1).
    0—Atlanta (West).
1983—5—Philadelphia (East), Gary N. Matthews (3), Michael J. Schmidt (1), Sixto Lezcano (1).
    2—Los Angeles (West), Michael A. Marshall (1), Johnnie B. Baker (1).
1984—9—Chicago (East), Jody R. Davis (2), Leon Durham (2), Gary N. Matthews (2), Ronald C. Cey (1), Robert E. Dernier (1), Richard L. Sutcliffe (1).
    2—San Diego (West), Steven P. Garvey (1), W. Kevin McReynolds (1).

CHAMPIONSHIP SERIES PLAYERS, 1969 THROUGH 1984
(Players Appearing in One or More Games)

— A —

Aaron, Henry L.—Atlanta NL 1969.
Aaron, Tommie L.—Atlanta NL 1969.
Aase, Donald W.—California AL 1979.
Abbott, W. Glenn—Oakland AL 1975.
Agee, Tommie L.—New York NL 1969.
Agosto, Juan R.—Chicago AL 1983.
Aikens, Willie M.—Kansas City AL 1980.
Alexander, Doyle L.—Baltimore AL 1973.
Alexander, Matthew—Pittsburgh NL 1979.
Allen, Richard A.—Philadelphia NL 1976.
Alley, L. Eugene—Pittsburgh NL 1970-71-72.
Allison, W. Robert—Minnesota AL 1969-70.
Alomar, Santos—New York AL 1976.
Alou, Felipe R.—Atlanta NL 1969.
Alou, Jesus M.—Oakland AL 1973-74.
Alou, Mateo R.—Pittsburgh NL 1970; Oakland AL 1972.
Alyea, Garrabrant R.—Minnesota AL 1970.
Anderson, James L.—California AL 1979.
Andrews, Michael J.—Oakland AL 1973.
Andujar, Joaquin—Houston NL 1980; St. Louis NL 1982.
Armas, Antonio R.—Oakland AL 1981.
Armbrister, Edison R.—Cincinnati NL 1973-75-76.
Ashby, Alan D.—Houston NL 1980.
Aspromonte, Robert T.—Atlanta NL 1969.
Auerbach, Frederick S.—Los Angeles NL 1974; Cincinnati NL 1979.
Aviles, Ramon A.A.—Philadelphia NL 1980.
Ayala, Benigno F.—Baltimore AL 1983.

— B —

Baines, Harold D.—Chicago AL 1983.
Bair, C. Douglas—Cincinnati NL 1979; St. Louis NL 1982.
Baker, Douglas L.—Detroit AL 1984.
Baker, Frank W.—Baltimore AL 1973-74.
Baker, Johnnie B.—Los Angeles NL 1977-78-81-83.
Balboni, Stephen C.—Kansas City AL 1984.
Bando, Salvatore L.—Oakland AL 1971-72-73-74-75.
Bannister, Floyd F.—Chicago AL 1983.
Barlow, Michael R.—California AL 1979.
Barojas, Salome—Chicago AL 1983.
Barr, James L.—San Francisco NL 1971.
Baylor, Donald E.—Baltimore AL 1973-74; California AL 1979-82.
Beard, C. David—Oakland AL 1981.
Beattie, James L.—New York AL 1978.
Beckwith, T. Joseph—Los Angeles NL 1983.
Bedrosian, Stephen W.—Atlanta NL 1982.
Belanger, Mark H.—Baltimore AL 1969-70-71-73-74-79.
Bench, Johnny L.—Cincinnati NL 1970-72-73-75-76-79.
Benedict, Bruce E.—Atlanta NL 1982.
Beniquez, Juan J.—Boston AL 1975; California AL 1982.
Bergman, David B.—Houston NL 1980; Detroit AL 1984.
Bernard, Dwight V.—Milwaukee AL 1982.
Bevacqua, Kurt A.—San Diego NL 1984.

Biancalana, Roland A.—Kansas City AL 1984.
Bibby, James B.—Pittsburgh NL 1979.
Billingham, John E.—Cincinnati NL 1972-73.
Bird, J. Douglas—Kansas City AL 1976-77-78.
Black, Harry R.—Kansas City AL 1984.
Blair, Paul L.—Baltimore AL 1969-70-71-73-74; New York AL 1977-78.
Blass, Stephen R.—Pittsburgh NL 1971-72.
Blefary, Curtis L.—Oakland AL 1971.
Blue, Vida R.—Oakland AL 1971-72-73-74-75.
Blyleven, Rikalbert—Minnesota AL 1970; Pittsburgh NL 1979.
Bochy, Bruce D.—Houston NL 1980.
Boddicker, Michael J.—Baltimore AL 1983.
Bonds, Bobby L.—San Francisco NL 1971.
Booker, Gregory S.—San Diego NL 1984.
Boone, Robert R.—Philadelphia NL 1976-77-78-80; California AL 1982.
Borbon, Pedro R.—Cincinnati NL 1972-73-75-76.
Bosetti, Richard A.—Oakland AL 1981.
Bosley, Thaddis—Chicago NL 1984.
Bosman, Richard A.—Oakland AL 1975.
Boswell, David W.—Minnesota AL 1969.
Boswell, Kenneth G.—New York NL 1969-73.
Bourque, Patrick D.—Oakland AL 1973.
Bowa, Lawrence R.—Philadelphia NL 1976-77-78-80; Chicago NL 1984.
Boyer, Cletis L.—Atlanta NL 1969.
Braun, Stephen R.—Kansas City AL 1978; St. Louis NL 1982.
Bravo, Angel A.—Cincinnati NL 1970.
Brett, George H.—Kansas City AL 1976-77-78-80-84.
Brett, Kenneth A.—Pittsburgh NL 1974-75.
Briles, Nelson K.—Pittsburgh NL 1972.
Brinkman, Edwin A.—Detroit AL 1972.
Britton, James A.—Atlanta NL 1969.
Brock, Gregory A.—Los Angeles NL 1983.
Brookens, Thomas D.—Detroit AL 1984.
Brouhard, Mark S.—Milwaukee AL 1982.
Brown, Isaac—Detroit AL 1972.
Brown, Larry L.—Baltimore AL 1973.
Brown, Ollie L.—Philadelphia NL 1976-77.
Brown, R.L. Bobby—New York AL 1980-81; San Diego NL 1984.
Brown, W. Gates—Detroit AL 1972.
Brusstar, Warren S.—Philadelphia NL 1977-78-80; Chicago NL 1984.
Bryant, Ronald R.—San Francisco NL 1971.
Buckner, William J.—Los Angeles NL 1974.
Buford, Donald A.—Baltimore AL 1969-70-71.
Bumbry, Alonza B.—Baltimore AL 1973-74-79-83.
Burke, Glenn L.—Los Angeles NL 1977.
Burleson, Richard P.—Boston AL 1975.
Burns, R. Britt—Chicago AL 1983.
Burris, B. Ray—Montreal NL 1981.
Butler, Brett M.—Atlanta NL 1982.
Bystrom, Martin E.—Philadelphia NL 1980.

– C –

Cabell, Enos M.—Baltimore AL 1974; Houston NL 1980.
Caldwell, R. Michael—Milwaukee AL 1982.
Camp, Rick L.—Atlanta NL 1982.
Campaneris, Dagoberto B.—Oakland AL 1971-72-73-74-75; California AL 1979.
Candelaria, John R.—Pittsburgh NL 1975-79.
Carbo, Bernardo—Cincinnati NL 1970.
Cardenal, Jose D.—Philadelphia NL 1978.
Cardenas, Leonardo A.—Minnesota AL 1969-70.
Carew, Rodney C.—Minnesota AL 1969-70; California AL 1979-82.
Carlton, Steven N.—Philadelphia NL 1976-77-78-80-83.
Carrithers, Donald G.—San Francisco NL 1971.
Carroll, Clay P.—Cincinnati NL 1970-72-73-75.
Carter, Gary E.—Montreal NL 1981.
Carty, Ricardo A. J.—Atlanta NL 1969.
Cash, David—Pittsburgh NL 1970-71-72; Philadelphia NL 1976.
Cash, Norman D.—Detroit AL 1972.
Castillo, Martin H.—Detroit AL 1984.
Castillo, Robert E.—Los Angeles NL 1981.
Cedeno, Cesar—Houston NL 1980.
Cepeda, Orlando M.—Atlanta NL 1969.
Cerone, Richard A.—New York AL 1980-81.
Cey, Ronald C.—Los Angeles NL 1974-77-78-81; Chicago NL 1984.
Chambliss, C. Christopher—New York AL 1976-77-78; Atlanta NL 1982.
Chance, W. Dean—Minnesota AL 1969.
Chaney, Darrel L.—Cincinnati NL 1972-73.
Christenson, Larry R.—Philadelphia NL 1977-78-80.
Clark, Robert C.—California AL 1979-82.
Clay, Kenneth E.—New York AL 1978.
Clear, Mark A.—California AL 1979.
Clemente, Roberto W.—Pittsburgh NL 1970-71-72.
Cleveland, Reginald L.—Boston AL 1975.
Cline, Tyrone A.—Cincinnati NL 1970.
Clines, Eugene A.—Pittsburgh NL 1971-72-74.
Cloninger, Tony L.—Cincinnati NL 1970.
Coggins, Richard A.—Baltimore AL 1973-74.
Coleman, Joseph H.—Detroit AL 1972.
Collins, David S.—Cincinnati NL 1979.
Concepcion, David I.—Cincinnati NL 1970-72-75-76-79.
Concepcion, Onix—Kansas City AL 1984.
Conigliaro, William M.—Oakland AL 1973.
Cooper, Cecil C.—Boston AL 1975; Milwaukee AL 1982.
Cotto, Henry—Chicago NL 1984.
Cowens, Alfred E.—Kansas City AL 1976-77-78.
Crawford, Willie M.—Los Angeles NL 1974.
Cromartie, Warren L.—Montreal NL 1981.
Crosby, Edward C.—Cincinnati NL 1973.
Crowley, Terrence M.—Baltimore AL 1973-79; Cincinnati NL 1975.
Cruz, Hector—Cincinnati NL 1979.
Cruz, Jose—Houston NL 1980.
Cruz, Julio L.—Chicago AL 1983.
Cruz, Todd R.—Baltimore AL 1983.

Cuellar, Miguel—Baltimore AL 1969-70-71-73-74.
Cullen Timothy L.—Oakland AL 1972.
Cumberland, John S.—San Francisco NL 1971.

– D –

Dauer, Richard F.—Baltimore AL 1979-83.
Davalillo, Victor J.—Pittsburgh NL 1971-72; Oakland AL 1973; Los Angeles NL 1977.
Davis, George E.—Baltimore AL 1983.
Davis, H. Thomas—Oakland AL 1971; Baltimore AL 1973-74.
Davis, Jody R.—Chicago NL 1984.
Davis, Michael D.—Oakland AL 1981.
Davis, Ronald G.—New York AL 1980-1981.
Davis, William H.—California AL 1979.
Dawson, Andre F.—Montreal NL 1981.
DeCinces, Douglas V.—Baltimore AL 1979; California AL 1982.
DeJesus, Ivan—Philadelphia NL 1983.
Demery, Lawrence C.—Pittsburgh NL 1974-75.
Dempsey, J. Rikard—Baltimore AL 1979-83.
Denny, John A.—Philadelphia NL 1983.
Dent, Russell E.—New York AL 1977-78-80.
Dernier, Robert E.—Philadelphia NL 1983; Chicago NL 1984.
Diaz, Baudilio J.—Philadelphia NL 1983.
Didier, Robert D.—Atlanta NL 1969.
Dietz, Richard A.—San Francisco NL 1971.
Dotson, Richard E.—Chicago AL 1983.
Downing, Alphonso E.—Los Angeles NL 1974.
Downing, Brian J.—California AL 1979-82.
Doyle, Brian R.—New York AL 1978.
Doyle, Paul S.—Atlanta NL 1969.
Doyle, R. Dennis—Boston AL 1975.
Drago, Richard A.—Boston AL 1975.
Dravecky, David F.—San Diego NL 1984.
Driessen, Daniel D.—Cincinnati NL 1973-76-79.
Drumright, Keith A.—Oakland AL 1981.
Duffy, Frank T.—San Francisco NL 1971.
Duncan, David E.—Oakland AL 1971-72.
Durham, Leon—Chicago NL 1984.
Dwyer, James E.—Baltimore AL 1983.
Dybzinski, Jerome M.—Chicago AL 1983.
Dyer, Don R.—Pittsburgh NL 1975.

– E –

Easler, Michael A.—Pittsburgh NL 1979.
Eastwick, Rawlins J.—Cincinnati NL 1975-76; Philadelphia NL 1978.
Eckersley, Dennis L.—Chicago NL 1984.
Edwards, Marshall L.—Milwaukee AL 1982.
Ellis, Dock P.—Pittsburgh NL 1970-71-72-75; New York AL 1976.
Epstein, Michael P.—Oakland AL 1971-72.
Etchebarren, Andrew A.—Baltimore AL 1969-70-71-73-74.
Evans, Darrell W.—Detroit AL 1984.
Evans, Dwight W.—Boston AL 1975.

– F –

Ferguson, Joseph V.—Los Angeles NL 1974-78.

Figueroa, Eduardo—New York AL 1976-77-78.

Fimple, John J.—Los Angeles NL 1983.

Fingers, Roland G.—Oakland AL 1971-72-73-74-75.

Fisk, Carlton E.—Boston AL 1975; Chicago AL 1983.

Flanagan, Michael K.—Baltimore AL 1979-83.

Flannery, Timothy E.—San Diego NL 1984.

Fletcher, Scott B.—Chicago AL 1983.

Flynn, R. Douglas—Cincinnati NL 1976.

Foli, Timothy J.—Pittsburgh NL 1979; California AL 1982.

Foote, Barry C.—Philadelphia NL 1978; New York AL 1981.

Ford, Darnell G.—California AL 1979; Baltimore AL 1983.

Forsch, Kenneth R.—Houston NL 1980.

Forsch, Robert H.—St. Louis NL 1982.

Forster, Terry J.—Los Angeles NL 1978-81.

Fosse, Raymond E.—Oakland AL 1973-74-75.

Foster, George A.—Cincinnati NL 1972-75-76-79.

Francona, Terry J.—Montreal NL 1981.

Frazier, George A.—New York AL 1981; Chicago NL 1984.

Freehan, William A.—Detroit AL 1972.

Frost, C. David—California AL 1979.

Fryman, Woodrow T.—Detroit AL 1972; Montreal NL 1981.

Fuentes, Rigoberto San Francisco NL 1971.

— G —

Gagliano, Philip J.—Cincinnati NL 1973.

Gallagher, Alan M.—San Francisco NL 1971.

Gamble, Oscar C.—New York AL 1976-80-81.

Gantner, James E.—Milwaukee AL 1982.

Garber, H. Eugene—Philadelphia NL 1976-77; Atlanta NL 1982.

Garbey, Barbaro G.—Detroit AL 1984.

Garcia, Alfonso R.—Baltimore AL 1979.

Garland, M. Wayne—Baltimore AL 1974.

Garman, Michael D.—Los Angeles NL 1977.

Garner, Philip M.—Oakland AL 1975; Pittsburgh NL 1979.

Garrett, R. Wayne—New York NL 1969-73.

Garrido, Gil G.—Atlanta NL 1969.

Garvey, Steven P.—Los Angeles NL 1974-77-78-81; San Diego NL 1984.

Gaspar, Rodney E.—New York NL 1969.

Gentry, Gary E.—New York NL 1969.

Geronimo, Cesar F.—Cincinnati NL 1972-73-75-76-79.

Gibbon, Joseph C.—Pittsburgh NL 1970.

Gibson, Kirk H.—Detroit AL 1984.

Giusti, J. David—Pittsburgh NL 1970-71-72-74-75.

Goltz, David A.—California AL 1982.

Gonzalez, A. Antonio—Atlanta NL 1969.

Gonzalez, Julio C.—Philadelphia NL 1978.

Goodson, J. Edward—Los Angeles NL 1977.

Gossage, Richard M.—New York AL 1978-80-81; San Diego NL 1984.

Granger, Wayne A.—Cincinnati NL 1970.

Grant, James T.—Oakland AL 1971.

Green, David A.—St. Louis NL 1982.

Green, Richard L.—Oakland AL 1971-72-73-74.

Grich, Robert A.—Baltimore AL 1973-74; California AL 1979-82.

Griffey, G. Kenneth—Cincinnati NL 1973-75-76.

Grimsley, Ross A.—Cincinnati NL 1972-73; Baltimore AL 1974.

Gross, Gregory E.—Philadelphia NL 1980-83.

Gross, Wayne D.—Oakland AL 1981.

Grote, Gerald W.—New York NL 1969-73; Los Angeles NL 1977-78.

Grubb, John M.—Detroit AL 1984.

Grzenda, Joseph C.—Minnesota AL 1969.

Guerrero, Pedro—Los Angeles NL 1981-83.

Guidry, Ronald A.—New York AL 1976-77-78-80.

Gullett, Donald E.—Cincinnati NL 1970-72-73-75-76; New York AL 1977.

Gullickson, William L.—Montreal NL 1981.

Gura, Lawrence C.—Kansas City AL 1976-77-78-80.

Gwynn, Anthony K.—San Diego NL 1984.

— H —

Haas, Bryan E.—Milwaukee AL 1982.

Hague, Joe C.—Cincinnati NL 1972.

Hahn, Donald A.—New York NL 1973.

Hairston, Jerry W.—Chicago AL 1983.

Hall, Richard W.—Baltimore AL 1969-70.

Hall, Thomas E.—Minnesota AL 1969-70; Cincinnati NL 1972-73; Kansas City AL 1976.

Haller, Thomas F.—Detroit AL 1972.

Hamilton, David E.—Oakland AL 1972.

Hamilton, Steve A.—San Francisco NL 1971.

Harlow, Larry D.—California AL 1979.

Harmon, Terry W.—Philadelphia NL 1976.

Harper, Terry J.—Atlanta NL 1982.

Harper, Tommy—Oakland AL 1975.

Harrelson, Derrel M.—New York NL 1969-73.

Harris, Greg A.—San Diego NL 1984.

Hart, James R.—San Francisco NL 1971.

Hassler, Andrew E.—Kansas City AL 1976-77; California AL 1982.

Hawkins, M. Andrew—San Diego NL 1984.

Hayes, Von F.—Philadelphia NL 1983.

Heath, Michael T.—Oakland AL 1981.

Hebner, Richard J.—Pittsburgh NL 1970-71-72-74-75; Philadelphia NL 1977-78; Chicago NL 1984.

Heep, Daniel W.—Houston NL 1980.

Hegan, J. Michael—Oakland AL 1971-72.

Helms, Tommy V.—Cincinnati NL 1970.

Henderson, Kenneth J.—San Francisco NL 1971.

Henderson, Rickey H.—Oakland AL 1981.

Hendrick, George A.—Oakland AL 1972; St. Louis NL 1982.

Hendricks, Elrod J.—Baltimore AL 1969-70-71-74; New York AL 1976.

Hernandez, Guillermo—Detroit AL 1984.

Hernandez, Jacinto—Pittsburgh NL 1971.

Hernandez, Keith—St. Louis NL 1982.

Hernandez, Ramon G.—Pittsburgh NL 1972-74-75.

Herndon, Larry D.—Detroit AL 1984.
Herr, Thomas M.—St. Louis NL 1982.
Hiller, John F.—Detroit AL 1972.
Holland, Alfred W.—Philadelphia NL 1983.
Holt, James W.—Minnesota AL 1970; Oakland AL 1974-75.
Holtzman, Kenneth D.—Oakland AL 1972-73-74-75.
Honeycutt, Frederick W.—Los Angeles NL 1983.
Hood, Donald H.—Baltimore AL 1973.
Hooton, Burt C.—Los Angeles NL 1977-78-81
Hopkins, Donald—Oakland AL 1975.
Horlen, Joel E.—Oakland AL 1972.
Horner, J. Robert—Atlanta NL 1982.
Horton, William W.—Detroit AL 1972.
Hough, Charles O.—Los Angeles NL 1974-77-78.
Howe, Arthur H.—Pittsburgh NL 1974; Houston NL 1980.
Howe, Steven R.—Los Angeles NL 1981.
Howell, Roy L.—Milwaukee AL 1982.
Hoyt, D. LaMarr—Chicago AL 1983.
Hrabosky, Alan T.—Kansas City AL 1978.
Hubbard, Glenn D.—Atlanta NL 1982.
Hudson, Charles L.—Philadelphia NL 1983.
Huismann, Mark L.—Kansas City AL 1984.
Hume, Thomas H.—Cincinnati NL 1979.
Hunter, James A.—Oakland AL 1971-72-73-74; New York AL 1976-78.
Hurdle, Clinton M.—Kansas City AL 1978-80.
Hutton, Thomas G.—Philadelphia NL 1976-77.

— I —

Iorg, Dane C.—Kansas City AL 1984.

— J —

Jackson, Grant D.—Baltimore AL 1973-74; New York AL 1976; Pittsburgh NL 1979.
Jackson, Reginald M.—Oakland AL 1971-72-73-74-75; New York AL 1977-78-80-81; California AL 1982.
Jackson, Ronnie D.—California AL 1982.
Jackson, R. Sonny—Atlanta NL 1969.
Jarvis, R. Patrick—Atlanta NL 1969.
Jeter, Johnny—Pittsburgh NL 1970.
John, Thomas E.—Los Angeles NL 1977-78; New York AL 1980-81; California AL 1982.
Johnson, Clifford—New York AL 1977-78; Oakland AL 1981.
Johnson, David A.—Baltimore AL 1969-70-71; Philadelphia NL 1977.
Johnson, Deron R.—Oakland AL 1973.
Johnson, Jerry M.—San Francisco NL 1971.
Johnson, Robert D.—Pittsburgh NL 1971-72.
Johnstone, John W.—Philadelphia NL 1976-77-81.
Jones, Cleon J.—New York NL 1969-73.
Jones, Jeffrey A.—Oakland AL 1981.
Jones, Lynn M.—Kansas City AL 1984.
Jones, Michael C.—Kansas City AL 1984.
Jones, Ruppert S.—Detroit AL 1984.
Joshua, Von E.—Los Angeles NL 1974.

— K —

Kaat, James L.—Minnesota AL 1970; Philadelphia NL 1976.
Kaline, Albert W.—Detroit AL 1972.
Kelly, Patrick H.—Baltimore AL 1979.
Kennedy, Terrence E.—San Diego NL 1984.
Keough, Matthew L.—Oakland AL 1981.
Killebrew, Harmon C.—Minnesota AL 1969-70.
King, Harold—Cincinnati NL 1973.
Kingman, Brian P.—Oakland AL 1981.
Kingman, David A.—San Francisco NL 1971.
Kirkpatrick, Edgar L.—Pittsburgh NL 1974-75.
Kison, Bruce E.—Pittsburgh NL 1971-72-74-75; California AL 1982.
Kittle, Ronald D.—Chicago AL 1983.
Klutts, Gene E.—Oakland AL 1981.
Knapp, Christian R.—California AL 1979.
Knight, C. Ray—Cincinnati NL 1979.
Knowles, Darold D.—Oakland AL 1971.
Knox, John C.—Detroit AL 1972.
Koosman, Jerry M.—New York NL 1969-73; Chicago AL 1983.
Kosco, Andrew J.—Cincinnati NL 1973.
Kranepool, Edward E.—New York NL 1969-73.
Kubiak, Theodore R.—Oakland AL 1972-73.
Kuntz, Russell J.—Detroit AL 1984.

— L —

LaCock, Ralph P.—Kansas City AL 1977-78-80.
LaCorte, Frank J.—Houston NL 1980.
LaCoss, Michael J.—Cincinnati NL 1979.
Lacy, Leondaus—Los Angeles NL 1974-77-78.
Ladd, Peter L.—Milwaukee AL 1982.
LaGrow, Lerrin H.—Detroit AL 1972.
Lahoud, Joseph M.—Kansas City AL 1977.
Lake, Steven M.—Chicago NL 1984.
Lamp, Dennis P.—Chicago AL 1983.
Landestoy, Rafael S.C.—Houston NL 1980; Los Angeles NL 1983.
Landreaux, Kenneth F.—Los Angeles NL 1981-83.
Landrum, Terry L.—Baltimore AL 1983.
Lanier, Harold C.—San Francisco NL 1971.
Lansford, Carney R.—California AL 1979.
LaRoche, David E.—California AL 1979.
Law, Rudy K.—Chicago AL 1983.
Law, Vance A.—Chicago AL 1983.
Lee, William F.—Montreal NL 1981.
Lefebvre, Joseph H.—New York AL 1980; Philadelphia NL 1983.
Lefferts, Craig L.—San Diego NL 1984.
Leibrandt, Charles L.—Cincinnati NL 1979; Kansas City AL 1984.
Lemon, Chester E.—Detroit AL 1984.
Leonard, Dennis P.—Kansas City AL 1976-77-78-80.
Leonard, Jeffrey N.—Houston NL 1980.
Lerch, Randy L.—Philadelphia NL 1978.
Lewis, Allan S.—Oakland AL 1973.
Lezcano, Sixto—Philadelphia NL 1983.
Lindblad, Paul A.—Oakland AL 1975.
Littell, Mark A.—Kansas City AL 1976-77.
Locker, Robert A.—Oakland AL 1971-72.
Lolich, Michael S.—Detroit AL 1972.
Lollar, W. Timothy—San Diego NL 1984.

Lonborg, James R.—Philadelphia NL 1976-77.

Lopes, David E.—Los Angeles NL 1974-77-78-81; Chicago NL 1984.

Lopez, Aurelio A.—Detroit AL 1984.

Lopez, Marcelino P.—Baltimore AL 1969.

Lowenstein, John L.—Baltimore AL 1979-83.

Lum, Michael K.—Atlanta NL 1969; Cincinnati NL 1976.

Luzinski, Gregory M.—Philadelphia NL 1976-77-78-80; Chicago AL 1983.

Lyle, Albert W.—New York AL 1976-77-78.

Lynn, Fredric M.—Boston AL 1975; California AL 1982.

— M —

Maddox, Elliott—New York AL 1976.

Maddox, Garry L.—Philadelphia NL 1976-77-78-80-83.

Madlock, Bill—Pittsburgh NL 1979.

Mahler, Richard K.—Atlanta NL 1982.

Maldonado, Candido—Los Angeles NL 1983.

Mangual, Angel L.—Oakland AL 1971-72-73-74.

Manuel, Charles F.—Minnesota AL 1969-70.

Manuel, Jerry—Montreal NL 1981.

Marichal, Juan A.—San Francisco NL 1971.

Marquez, Gonzalo—Oakland AL 1972.

Marshall, Michael A.—Los Angeles NL 1983.

Marshall, Michael G.—Los Angeles NL 1974.

Martin, Jerry L.—Philadelphia NL 1976-77-78.

Martin, Joseph C.—New York NL 1969.

Martinez, Carmelo—San Diego NL 1984.

Martinez, Felix A.—Baltimore AL 1983.

Martinez, J. Buck—Kansas City AL 1976.

Martinez, J. Dennis—Baltimore AL 1979.

Martinez, Teodoro N.—Oakland AL 1975.

Mason, James P.—New York AL 1976.

Matlack, Jonathan T.—New York NL 1973.

Matthews, Gary N.—Philadelphia NL 1983; Chicago NL 1984.

Maxvill, C. Dallan—Oakland AL 1972-74.

May, Carlos—New York AL 1976.

May, David L.—Baltimore AL 1969.

May, Lee A.—Cincinnati NL 1970; Baltimore AL 1979.

May, Milton S.—Pittsburgh NL 1971-72.

May, Rudolph—New York AL 1980-81.

Mayberry, John C.—Kansas City AL 1976-77.

Mays, Willie H.—San Francisco NL 1971; New York NL 1973.

Mazeroski, Williams S.—Pittsburgh NL 1970-71-72.

McAuliffe, Richard J.—Detroit AL 1972.

McBride, Arnold R.—Philadelphia NL 1977-78-80.

McCarver, J. Timothy—Philadelphia NL 1976-77-78.

McCatty, Steven E.—Oakland AL 1981.

McClure, Robert C.—Milwaukee AL 1982.

McCovey, Willie L.—San Francisco NL 1971.

McEnaney, William H.—Cincinnati NL 1975.

McGee, Willie D.—St. Louis NL 1982.

McGlothlin, James M.—Cincinnati NL 1972.

McGraw, Frank E.—New York NL 1969-73; Philadelphia NL 1976-77-78-80.

McGregor, Scott H.—Baltimore AL 1979-83.

McKay, David L.—Oakland AL 1981.

McMahon, Donald J.—San Francisco NL 1971.

McMullen, Kenneth L.—Los Angeles NL 1974.

McNally, David A.—Baltimore AL 1969-70-71-73-74.

McRae, Harold A.—Cincinnati NL 1970-72; Kansas City AL 1976-77-78-80-84.

McReynolds, W. Kevin—San Diego NL 1984.

Mendoza, Mario—Pittsburgh NL 1974.

Menke, Denis J.—Cincinnati NL 1972-73.

Merritt, James J.—Cincinnati NL 1970.

Messersmith, John A.—Los Angeles NL 1974.

Milbourne, Lawrence W.—New York AL 1981.

Millan, Felix B. M.—Atlanta NL 1969; New York NL 1973.

Miller, Richard A.—California AL 1979.

Miller, Robert L.—Minnesota AL 1969; Pittsburgh NL 1971-72.

Milner, John D.—New York NL 1973; Pittsburgh NL 1979; Montreal NL 1981.

Mincher, Donald R.—Oakland AL 1972.

Mingori, Stephen B.—Kansas City AL 1976-77-78.

Mitterwald, George E.—Minnesota AL 1969-70.

Molitor, Paul L.—Milwaukee AL 1982.

Monday, Robert J.—Oakland AL 1971; Los Angeles NL 1977-78-81-83.

Money, Donald W.—Milwaukee AL 1982.

Montague, John E.—California AL 1979.

Moore, Charles W.—Milwaukee AL 1982.

Moore, Donnie R.—Atlanta NL 1982.

Moore, Kelvin O.—Oakland AL 1981.

Moose, Robert R.—Pittsburgh NL 1970-71-72.

Morales, Jose M.—Los Angeles NL 1983.

Moreland, B. Keith—Philadelphia NL 1980; Chicago NL 1984.

Moreno, Omar R.—Pittsburgh NL 1979.

Moret, Rogelio—Boston AL 1975.

Morgan, Joe L.—Cincinnati NL 1972-73-75-76-79; Houston NL 1980; Philadelphia NL 1983.

Morris, John S.—Detroit AL 1984.

Morrison, James F.—Philadelphia NL 1978.

Mota, Manuel R.—Los Angeles NL 1974-77-78.

Motley, Darryl D.—Kansas City AL 1984.

Motton, Curtell H.—Baltimore AL 1969-71-74.

Mumphrey, Jerry W.—New York AL 1981.

Munson, Thurman, L.—New York AL 1976-77-78.

Murcer, Bobby R.—New York AL 1980-81.

Murphy, Dale B.—Atlanta NL 1982.

Murphy, Dwayne K.—Oakland AL 1981.

Murray, Eddie C.—Baltimore AL 1979-83.

— N —

Neibauer, Gary W.—Atlanta NL 1969.

Nelson, David E.—Kansas City AL 1976.
Nelson, Roger E.—Cincinnati NL 1973.
Nettles, Graig—Minnesota AL 1969; New York AL 1976-77-78-80-81; San Diego NL 1984.
Newman, Jeffrey L.—Oakland AL 1981.
Niedenfuer, Thomas E.—Los Angeles NL 1981-83.
Niekro, Joseph F.—Detroit AL 1972; Houston NL 1980.
Niekro, Philip H.—Atlanta NL 1969-82.
Nolan, Gary L.—Cincinnati NL 1970-72-75-76.
Nolan, Joseph W.—Baltimore AL 1983.
Noles, Dickie R.—Philadelphia NL 1980.
Norman, Fredie H.—Cincinnati NL 1973-75-79.
Norris, Michael K.—Oakland AL 1981.
North, William A.—Oakland AL 1974-75; Los Angeles NL 1978.
Northrup, James T.—Detroit AL 1972.

— O —

Oates, Johnny L.—Philadelphia NL 1976.
Oberkfell, Kenneth R.—St. Louis NL 1982.
Odom, Johnny L.—Oakland AL 1972-73-74.
Oglivie, Benjamin A.—Milwaukee AL 1982.
Oliva, Antonio—Minnesota AL 1969-70.
Oliver, Albert—Pittsburgh NL 1970-71-72-74-75.
Orta, Jorge—Kansas City AL 1984.
Otis, Amos J.—Kansas City AL 1976-77-78-80.
Ott, N. Edward—Pittsburgh NL 1979.
Owchinko, Robert D.—Oakland AL 1981.

— P —

Paciorek, Thomas M.—Los Angeles NL 1974; Chicago AL 1983.
Pagan, Jose A.—Pittsburgh NL 1970-71.
Palmer, James A.—Baltimore AL 1969-70-71-73-74-79-83.
Pappas, Milton S.—Atlanta NL 1969.
Parker, David G.—Pittsburgh NL 1974-75-79.
Parker, Harry W.—New York NL 1973.
Parrish, Lance M.—Detroit AL 1984.
Parrish, Larry A.—Montreal NL 1981.
Pastore, Frank E.—Cincinnati, NL 1979.
Patek, Freddie J.—Pittsburgh NL 1970; Kansas City AL 1976-77-78.
Pattin, Martin W.—Kansas City AL 1976-77-78.
Pena, Alejandro—Los Angeles NL 1981-83.
Perez, Atanasio R.—Cincinnati NL 1970-72-73-75-76; Philadelphia NL 1983.
Perez, Pascual—Atlanta NL 1982.
Perranoski, Ronald P.—Minnesota AL 1969-70.
Perry, Gaylord J.—San Francisco NL 1971.
Perry, James E.—Minnesota AL 1969-70.
Petrocelli, Americo P.—Boston AL 1975.
Petry, Daniel J.—Detroit AL 1984.
Picciolo, Robert M.—Oakland AL 1981.
Pina, Horacio—Oakland AL 1973.
Piniella, Louis V.—New York AL 1976-77-78-80-81.
Pizarro, Juan—Pittsburgh NL 1974.
Pocoroba, Biff—Atlanta NL 1982.
Popovich, Paul E.—Pittsburgh NL 1974.
Poquette, Thomas A.—Kansas City AL 1976-77-78.

Porter, Darrell R.—Kansas City AL 1977-78-80; St. Louis NL 1982.
Powell, John W.—Baltimore AL 1969-70-71-73-74.
Pryor, Gregory R.—Kansas City AL 1984.
Puhl, Terry S.—Houston NL 1980.
Pujols, Luis B.—Houston NL 1980.

— Q —

Quilici, Frank R.—Minnesota AL 1970.
Quirk, James P.—Kansas City AL 1976.
Quisenberry, Daniel R.—Kansas City AL 1980-84.

— R —

Raines, Timothy—Montreal NL 1981.
Ramirez, Mario—San Diego NL 1984.
Ramirez, Rafael E.—Atlanta NL 1982.
Randolph, William L.—Pittsburgh NL 1975; New York AL 1976-77-80-81.
Ratliff, Paul H.—Minnesota AL 1970.
Rau, Douglas J.—Los Angeles NL 1974-77-78.
Rautzhan, Clarence G.—Los Angeles NL 1977-78.
Reardon, Jeffrey J.—Montreal NL 1981.
Reed, Ronald L.—Atlanta NL 1969; Philadelphia NL 1976-77-78-80-83.
Reese, Richard B.—Minnesota AL 1969-70.
Renick, W. Richard—Minnesota AL 1969-70.
Rettenmund, Mervin W.—Baltimore AL 1969-70-71-73; Cincinnati NL 1975; California AL 1979.
Reuss, Jerry—Pittsburgh NL 1974-75; Los Angeles NL 1981-83.
Revering, David A.—New York AL 1981.
Reynolds, G. Craig—Pittsburgh NL 1975; Houston NL 1980.
Reynolds, Robert A.—Baltimore AL 1973-74.
Rhoden, Richard A.—Los Angeles NL 1977-78.
Richert, Peter G.—Baltimore AL 1969.
Righetti, David A.—New York AL 1981.
Ripken, Calvin E.—Baltimore AL 1983.
Rivers, John M.—New York AL 1976-77-78.
Roberts, David A.—Pittsburgh NL 1979.
Robertson, Andre L.—New York AL 1981.
Robertson, Robert E.—Pittsburgh NL 1970-71-72-74-75.
Robinson, Brooks C.—Baltimore AL 1969-70-71-73-74.
Robinson, Don A.—Pittsburgh NL 1979.
Robinson, Frank—Baltimore AL 1969-70-71.
Robinson, William H.—Pittsburgh NL 1975-79.
Rodriguez, Aurelio—Detroit AL 1972; New York AL 1980-81; Chicago AL 1983.
Roenicke, Gary S.—Baltimore AL 1979-83.
Rogers, Stephen D.—Montreal NL 1981.
Rojas, Octavio—Kansas City AL 1976-77.
Romo, Enrique—Pittsburgh NL 1979.
Rooker, James P.—Pittsburgh NL 1974-75.
Rosario, Angel—San Francisco NL 1971.
Rose, Peter E.—Cincinnati NL 1970-72-73-75-76; Philadelphia NL 1980-83.
Roseboro, John—Minnesota AL 1969.
Royster, Jeron K.—Atlanta NL 1982.
Rudi, Joseph O.—Oakland AL 1971-72-73-74-75.

Ruhle, Vernon G.—Houston NL 1980.
Russell, William E.—Los Angeles NL 1974-77-78-81-83.
Ruthven, Richard D.—Philadelphia NL 1978-80.
Ryan, L. Nolan—New York NL 1969; California AL 1979; Houston NL 1980.

— S —

Saberhagen, Bret W.—Kansas City AL 1984.
Salazar, Luis E.—San Diego NL 1984.
Salmon, Ruthford E.—Baltimore AL 1969.
Sambito, Joseph C.—Houston NL 1980.
Samuel, Juan M.—Philadelphia NL 1983.
Sanchez, Luis M.—California AL 1982.
Sandberg, Ryne D.—Chicago NL 1984.
Sanderson, Scott D.—Chicago NL 1984.
Sanguillen, Manuel de J.—Pittsburgh NL 1970-71-72-74-75.
Sarmiento, Manuel E.—Cincinnati NL 1976.
Saucier, Kevin A.—Philadelphia NL 1980.
Sax, Stephen L.—Los Angeles NL 1981-83.
Scherman, Frederick J.—Detroit AL 1972.
Schmidt, Michael J.—Philadelphia NL 1976-77-78-80-83.
Scioscia, Michael L.—Los Angeles NL 1981.
Scott, Rodney D.—Montreal NL 1981.
Seaver, G. Thomas—New York NL 1969-73; Cincinnati NL 1979.
Seelbach, Charles F.—Detroit AL 1972.
Segui, Diego P.—Oakland AL 1971.
Shamsky, Arthur L.—New York NL 1969.
Shelby, John T.—Baltimore AL 1983.
Sheridan, Patrick A.—Kansas City AL 1984.
Show, Eric V.—San Diego NL 1984.
Simmons, Ted L.—Milwaukee AL 1982.
Sims, Duane B.—Detroit AL 1972.
Singleton, Kenneth W.—Baltimore AL 1979-83.
Sizemore, Ted C.—Philadelphia NL 1977-78.
Skaggs, David L.—Baltimore AL 1979.
Slaton, James M.—Milwaukee AL 1982.
Slaught, Donald M.—Kansas City AL 1984.
Smith, Billy E.—Baltimore AL 1979.
Smith, C. Reginald—Los Angeles NL 1977-78-81.
Smith, David S.—Houston NL 1980.
Smith, Lee A.—Chicago NL 1984.
Smith, Lonnie—Philadelphia NL 1980; St. Louis NL 1982.
Smith, Osborne E.—St. Louis NL 1982.
Soderholm, Eric T.—New York AL 1980.
Solomon, Eddie—Los Angeles NL 1974.
Sosa, Elias—Los Angeles NL 1977; Montreal NL 1981.
Soto, Mario M.—Cincinnati NL 1979.
Speier, Chris E.—San Francisco NL 1971; Montreal NL 1981.
Spencer, James L.—New York AL 1980; Oakland AL 1981.
Spilman, Harry W.—Cincinnati NL 1979.
Splittorff, Paul W.—Kansas City AL 1976-77-78-80.
Squires, Michael L.—Chicago AL 1983.
Stahl, Larry F.—Cincinnati NL 1973.
Stanhouse, Donald J.—Baltimore AL 1979.
Stanley, Frederick B.—New York AL 1976-77-78; Oakland AL 1981.
Stanley, Mitchell J.—Detroit AL 1972.

Stargell, Wilver D.—Pittsburgh NL 1970-71-72-74-75-79.
Staub, Daniel J.—New York NL 1973.
Stennett, Renaldo A.—Pittsburgh NL 1972-74-75-79.
Stewart, James F.—Cincinnati NL 1970.
Stewart, Samuel L.—Baltimore AL 1983.
Stinson, G. Robert—Kansas City AL 1976.
Stoddard, Timothy P.—Chicago NL 1984.
Stone, George H.—Atlanta NL 1969; New York NL 1973.
Stuper, John A.—St. Louis NL 1982.
Summers, John J.—San Diego NL 1984.
Sutcliffe, Richard L.—Chicago NL 1984.
Sutter, H. Bruce—St. Louis NL 1982.
Sutton, Donald H.—Los Angeles NL 1974-77-78; Milwaukee AL 1982.

— T —

Tanana, Frank D.—California AL 1979.
Taveras, Franklin—Pittsburgh NL 1974-75.
Taylor, Antonio—Detroit AL 1972.
Taylor, Ronald W.—New York NL 1969.
Tekulve, Kenton C.—Pittsburgh NL 1975-79.
Templeton, Garry L.—San Diego NL 1984.
Tenace, F. Gene—Oakland AL 1971-72-73-74-75.
Thomas, Derrel O.—Los Angeles NL 1981-83.
Thomas, J. Gorman—Milwaukee AL 1982.
Thomasson, Gary L.—New York AL 1978.
Thompson, Danny L.—Minnesota AL 1970.
Thon, Richard W.—California AL 1979.
Thurmond, Mark A.—San Diego NL 1984.
Tiant, Luis C.—Minnesota AL 1970; Boston AL 1975.
Tidrow, Richard W.—New York AL 1976-77-78; Chicago AL 1983.
Tillman, J. Robert—Atlanta NL 1969.
Todd, James R.—Oakland AL 1975.
Tolan, Robert—Cincinnati NL 1970-72; Philadelphia NL 1976.
Tomlin, David A.—Cincinnati NL 1973-79.
Torrez, Michael A.—New York AL 1977.
Tovar, Cesar L.—Minnesota AL 1969-70; Oakland AL 1975.
Trammell, Alan S.—Detroit AL 1984.
Trillo, J. Manuel—Oakland AL 1974; Philadelphia NL 1980.
Trout, Steven R.—Chicago NL 1984.

— U —

Uhlaender, Theodore O.—Minnesota AL 1969; Cincinnati NL 1972.
Underwood, Thomas G.—Philadelphia NL 1976; New York AL 1980; Oakland AL 1981.
Unser, Delbert B.—Philadelphia NL 1980.
Upshaw, Cecil L.—Atlanta NL 1969.

— V —

Valenzuela, Fernando—Los Angeles NL 1981-83.
Velez, Otoniel—New York AL 1976.
Veryzer, Thomas M.—Chicago NL 1984.
Virgil, Osvaldo J.—Philadelphia NL 1983.
Vuckovich, Peter D.—Milwaukee AL 1982.
Vukovich, George S.—Philadelphia NL 1980.

— W —

Walk, Robert V.—Atlanta NL 1982.
Walker, Gregory L.—Chicago AL 1983.
Walker, J. Luke—Pittsburgh NL 1970-72.
Wallach, Timothy C.—Montreal NL 1981.
Walling, Dennis M.—Houston NL 1980.
Washington, Claudell—Oakland AL 1974-75; Atlanta NL 1982.
Washington, Herbert L.—Oakland AL 1974.
Washington, U. L.—Kansas City AL 1980-84.
Wathan, John D.—Kansas City AL 1976-77-78-80-84.
Watson, Robert J.—New York AL 1980-81.
Watt, Eddie D.—Baltimore AL 1969-71-73.
Weis, Albert J.—New York NL 1969.
Welch, Robert L.—Los Angeles NL 1978-81-83.
Whisenton, Larry—Atlanta NL 1982.
Whitaker, Louis R.—Detroit AL 1984.
White, Frank—Kansas City AL 1976-77-78-80-84.
White, Jerome C.—Montreal NL 1981.
White, Roy H.—New York AL 1976-77-78.
Whitson, Eddie L.—San Diego NL 1984.
Wiggins, Alan A.—San Diego NL 1984.
Wilcox, Milton E.—Cincinnati NL 1970; Detroit AL 1984.
Wilfong, Robert D.—California AL 1982.
Williams, Billy L.—Oakland AL 1975.
Williams, Earl C.—Baltimore AL 1973-74.

Williams, Stanley W.—Minnesota AL 1970.
Wilson, Willie J.—Kansas City AL 1978-80-84.
Winfield, David M.—New York AL 1981.
Wise, Richard C.—Boston AL 1975.
Witt, Michael A.—California AL 1982.
Wohlford, James E.—Kansas City AL 1976.
Woods, Gary L.—Houston NL 1980; Chicago NL 1984.
Woodson, Richard L.—Minnesota AL 1969-70.
Woodward, William F.—Cincinnati NL 1970.
Worthington, Allan F.—Minnesota AL 1969.
Wynn, James S.—Los Angeles NL 1974.

— Y —

Yastrzemski, Carl M.—Boston AL 1975.
Yeager, Stephen W.—Los Angeles NL 1974-77-78-81-83.
Yount, Robin R.—Milwaukee AL 1982.

— Z —

Zachary, W. Chris—Detroit AL 1972.
Zachry, Patrick P.—Cincinnati NL 1976; Los Angeles NL 1983.
Zahn, Geoffrey C.—California AL 1982.
Zdeb, Joseph E.—Kansas City AL 1977.
Zepp, William C.—Minnesota AL 1970.
Zisk, Richard W.—Pittsburgh NL 1974-75.

CHAMPIONSHIP SERIES MANAGERS (31)

Alston, Walter E.—Los Angeles NL 1974.
Altobelli, Joseph S.—Baltimore AL 1983.
Anderson, George L.—Cincinnati NL 1970-72-73-75-76; Detroit AL 1984.
Berra, Lawrence P.—New York NL 1973.
Dark, Alvin R.—Oakland AL 1974-75.
Fanning, W. James—Montreal NL 1981.
Fox, Charles F.—San Francisco NL 1971.
Fregosi, James L.—California AL 1979.
Frey, James G.—Kansas City AL 1980; Chicago NL 1984.
Green, G. Dallas—Philadelphia NL 1980.
Harris, C. Luman—Atlanta NL 1969.
Herzog, Dorrell N. E.—Kansas City AL 1976-77-78; St. Louis NL 1982.
Hodges, Gilbert R.—New York NL 1969.
Howser, Richard D.—New York AL 1980; Kansas City AL 1984.
Johnson, Darrell D.—Boston AL 1975.
Kuenn, Harvey E.—Milwaukee AL 1982.
LaRussa, Anthony—Chicago AL 1983.
Lasorda, Thomas C.—Los Angeles NL

1977-78-81-83.
Lemon, Robert G.—New York AL 1978-81.
Martin, Alfred M.—Minnesota AL 1969; Detroit AL 1972; New York AL 1976-77; Oakland AL 1981.
Mauch, Gene W.—California AL 1982.
McNamara, John F.—Cincinnati NL 1979.
Murtaugh, Daniel E.—Pittsburgh NL 1970-71-74-75.
Owens, Paul F.—Philadelphia NL 1983.
Ozark, Daniel L.—Philadelphia NL 1976-77-78.
Rigney, William J.—Minnesota AL 1970.
Tanner, Charles W.—Pittsburgh NL 1979.
Torre, Joseph P.—Atlanta NL 1982.
Virdon, William C.—Pittsburgh NL 1972; Houston NL 1980.
Weaver, Earl S.—Baltimore AL 1969-70-71-73-74-79.
Williams, Richard H.—Oakland AL 1971-72-73; San Diego NL 1984.

INDIVIDUAL SERIES SERVICE

Most Series Played

A. L.—10—Jackson, Reginald M., Oakland, 1971, 1972, 1973, 1974, 1975; New York, 1977, 1978, 1980, 1981; California, 1982.

N. L.— 8—Hebner, Richard J., Pittsburgh, 1970, 1971, 1972, 1974, 1975; Philadelphia, 1977, 1978; Chicago, 1984.

Most Series Played, One Club

A. L.—7—James A. Palmer, Baltimore, 1969, 1970, 1971, 1973, 1974, 1979, 1983.

N. L.—6—Johnny L. Bench, Cincinnati, 1970, 1972, 1973, 1975, 1976, 1979.
Wilver D. Stargell, Pittsburgh, 1970, 1971, 1972, 1974, 1975, 1979.

Most Clubs, Total Series

Both Leagues—3—Davalillo, Victor J., Pittsburgh NL, 1971, 1972; Oakland AL, 1973; Los Angeles NL, 1977.

Hall, Thomas E., Minnesota AL, 1969, 1970; Cincinnati NL 1972, 1973; Kansas City AL, 1976.

Rettenmund, Mervin W., Baltimore AL, 1969, 1970, 1971, 1973; Cincinnati NL, 1975; California AL, 1979.

Jackson, Grant D., Baltimore AL, 1973, 1974; New York AL, 1976; Pittsburgh NL, 1979.

Ryan, L. Nolan, New York NL, 1969; California AL, 1979; Houston NL, 1980.

Underwood, Thomas G., Philadelphia NL, 1976; New York AL, 1980; Oakland AL, 1981.

Nettles, Graig, Minnesota AL, 1969; New York AL, 1976, 1977, 1978, 1980, 1981; San Diego NL 1984.

N.L.—3—Milner, John D., New York, 1973; Pittsburgh, 1979; Montreal, 1981.

Morgan, Joe L., Cincinnati, 1972, 1973, 1975, 1976, 1979; Houston, 1980; Philadelphia, 1983.

Hebner, Richard J., Pittsburgh, 1970, 1971, 1972, 1974, 1975; Philadelphia, 1977, 1978; Chicago, 1984.

A.L.—3—Jackson, Reginald M., Oakland, 1971, 1972, 1973, 1974, 1975; New York, 1977, 1978, 1980, 1981; California, 1982.

Rodriguez, Aurelio, Detroit, 1972; New York, 1980, 1981; Chicago, 1983.

Most Consecutive Series Played

A. L.—5—Salvatore L. Bando, Vida R. Blue, Dagoberto B. Campaneris, Roland G. Fingers, Reginald M. Jackson, Joseph O. Rudi, F. Gene Tenace, Oakland, 1971 through 1975.

N. L.—3—Held by many players.

Most Series Playing in All Games

A. L.—9—Reginald M. Jackson, Oakland, 1971, 1972, 1973, 1974, 1975; New York, 1977, 1978, 1980; California, 1982; 37 games.

N. L.—7—Peter E. Rose, Cincinnati, 1970, 1972, 1973, 1975, 1976; Philadelphia, 1980, 1983; 28 games.

Most Games, Total Series

A. L.—39—Jackson, Reginald M., Oakland, 1971, 1972, 1973, 1974, 1975; New York, 1977, 1978, 1980, 1981; California, 1982; 10 Series, 34 consecutive games.

N. L.—28—Rose, Peter E., Cincinnati, 1970, 1972, 1973, 1975, 1976; Philadelphia, 1980, 1983; 7 Series, 28 consecutive games.

Most Games, Total Series, One Club

N. L.—22—Johnny L. Bench, Cincinnati, 1970, 1972, 1973, 1975, 1976, 1979; 6 Series.
Wilver D. Stargell, Pittsburgh, 1970, 1971, 1972, 1974, 1975, 1979; 6 Series.

A. L.—21—Mark H. Belanger, Baltimore, 1969, 1970, 1971, 1973, 1974, 1979; 6 Series.

Most Times on Winning Club, Playing One or More Games Each Series

A. L.—6—Reginald M. Jackson, Oakland, 1972, 1973, 1974; New York, 1977, 1978, 1981.

N. L.—6—Peter E. Rose, Cincinnati, 1970, 1972, 1975, 1976; Philadelphia, 1980, 1983.

Most Times on Losing Club, Playing One or More Games Each Series

N. L.—7—Hebner, Richard J., Pittsburgh, 1970, 1972, 1974, 1975; Philadelphia, 1977, 1978; Chicago, 1984.

A. L.—4—Baylor, Donald E., Baltimore, 1973, 1974; California, 1979, 1982.
Carew, Rodney C., Minnesota, 1969, 1970; California, 1979, 1982.
Grich, Robert A., Baltimore, 1973, 1974; California, 1979, 1982.
Jackson, Reginald M., Oakland, 1971, 1975; New York, 1980; California, 1982.
Brett, George H., Kansas City, 1976, 1977, 1978, 1984.
McRae, Harold A., Kansas City, 1976, 1977, 1978, 1984.
Wathan, John D., Kansas City, 1976, 1977, 1978, 1984.
Wilson, Willie J., Kansas City, 1976, 1977, 1978, 1984.

Most Positions Played, Total Series

N. L.—4—Rose, Peter E., Cincinnati, 1970, 1972, 1973, 1975, 1976; Philadelphia, 1980; 24 games, right field, left field, third base, first base.

A. L.—3—Tovar, Cesar L., Minnesota, 1969, 1970; Oakland, 1975; 8 games, center field, second base, left field.

Rettenmund, Mervin W., Baltimore, 1969, 1970, 1971, 1973; California, 1979; 10 games, left field, center field, right field.

Tenace, F. Gene, Oakland, 1971, 1972, 1973, 1974, 1975; 18 games, catcher, second base, first base.

Blair, Paul L., Baltimore, 1969, 1970, 1971, 1973, 1974; New York, 1977, 1978; 25 games, center field, right field, second base.

Wathan, John D., Kansas City, 1976, 1977, 1978, 1980, 1984; 8 games, catcher, first base, right field.

Most Positions Played, Series

A. L.—3—Tovar, Cesar L., Minnesota, 1970, center field, second base, left field; 3-game Series, 3 games.

N. L.—2—Held by many players.

Oldest Championship Series Player (Non-Pitcher)

N. L.—Rose, Peter E., Philadelphia; 42 years, 5 months, 24 days on October 8, 1983.

A. L.—Davis, William H., California; 39 years, 5 months, 19 days on October 4, 1979.

Oldest Championship Series Pitcher

N. L.—Niekro, Philip H., Atlanta; 43 years, 6 months, 8 days on October 9, 1982.

A. L.—Koosman, Jerry M., Chicago; 40 years, 9 months, 14 days on October 7, 1983.

Youngest Championship Series Player (Non-Pitcher)

A. L.—Washington, Claudell, Oakland; 20 years, 1 month, 5 days on October 5, 1974.

N. L.—Speier, Chris E., San Francisco; 21 years, 3 months, 4 days on October 2, 1971.

Youngest Championship Series Pitcher

A. L.—Blyleven, Rikalbert, Minnesota; 19 years, 5 months, 29 days on October 5, 1970.

N. L.—Gullett, Donald E., Cincinnati; 19 years, 8 months, 28 days on October 4, 1970.

Most Years Between First and Second Series

N. L.—13—Niekro, Philip H., Atlanta, 1969, 1982.

A. L.— 8—Rodriguez, Aurelio, Detroit, 1972; New York, 1980.

Fisk, Carlton E., Boston, 1975; Chicago, 1983.

Most Years Between First and Last Series

A. L.—14—Palmer, James A., Baltimore, 1969, 1983.

N. L.—14—Reed, Ronald L., Atlanta, 1969; Philadelphia, 1983.

Hebner, Richard J., Pittsburgh, 1970; Chicago, 1984.

Both Leagues—15—Nettles, Graig, Minnesota AL, 1969; San Diego NL, 1984.

INDIVIDUAL BATTING

Highest Batting Average, Total Series (10 or More Games and 30 or More At-Bats)

A. L.—.386—Rivers, John M., New York, 1976, 1977, 1978; 3 Series, 14 games, 57 at-bats, 22 hits.

N. L.—.381—Rose, Peter E., Cincinnati, 1970, 1972, 1973, 1975, 1976; Philadelphia, 1980, 1983; 7 Series, 28 games, 118 at-bats, 45 hits.

Highest Batting Average, Series (Playing All Games and 8 or More At-Bats)

3-game Series—N. L.—.778—Johnstone, John W., Philadelphia, 1976.

A. L.—.583—Robinson, Brooks C., Baltimore, 1970.

4-game Series—N. L.—.467—Baker, Johnnie B., Los Angeles, 1978.

Schmidt, Michael J., Philadelphia, 1983.

A. L.—.462—Jackson, Reginald M., New York, 1978.

5-game Series—A. L.—.611—Lynn, Fredric M., California, 1982.

N. L.—.526—Puhl, Terry S., Houston, 1980.

Highest Slugging Average, Total Series (10 or More Games and 30 or More At-Bats)

A. L.—.700—Brett, George H., Kansas City, 1976, 1977, 1978, 1980, 1984; 5 Series, 20 games, 80 at-bats, 27 hits, 3 doubles, 4 triples, 6 home runs, 56 total bases.

N. L.—.678—Garvey, Steven P., Los Angeles, 1974, 1977, 1978, 1981; San Diego, 1984; 5 Series, 22 games, 90 at-bats, 32 hits, 3 doubles, 1 triple, 8 home runs, 61 total bases.

Highest Slugging Average, Series (10 or More At-Bats)

3-game Series—N. L.—1.182—Stargell, Wilver D., Pittsburgh, 1979.
          A. L.— .917—Oliva, Antonio, Minnesota, 1970.
                     Jackson, Reginald M., Oakland, 1971.
                     Watson, Robert J., New York, 1980.
                     Nettles, Graig, New York, 1981.
4-game Series—N. L.—1.250—Robertson, Robert E., Pittsburgh, 1971.
          A. L.—1.056—Brett, George H., Kansas City, 1978.
5-game Series—A. L.— .952—Chambliss, C. Christopher, New York, 1976.
          N. L.— .833—Davis, Jody R., Chicago, 1984.

Most At-Bats, Total Series

A. L.— 137— Jackson, Reginald M., Oakland, 1971, 1972, 1973, 1974, 1975; New York, 1977, 1978, 1980, 1981; California, 1982; 10 Series, 39 games.
N. L.— 118— Rose, Peter E., Cincinnati, 1970, 1972, 1973, 1975, 1976; Philadelphia, 1980, 1983; 7 Series, 28 games.

Most At-Bats, Series

3-game Series—A. L.— 15—Belanger, Mark H., Baltimore, 1969.
                    Blair, Paul L., Baltimore, 1969.
          N. L.—15—Oberkfell, Kenneth R., St. Louis, 1982.
4-game Series—N. L.—19—Cash, David, Pittsburgh, 1978.
                    Maddox, Garry L., Philadelphia, 1978.
          A. L.—18—Brett, George H., Kansas City, 1978.
                    Munson, Thurman L., New York, 1978.
                    Law, Rudy K., Chicago, 1983.
5-game Series—N. L.—24—Schmidt, Michael J., Philadelphia, 1980.
          A. L.—23—Munson, Thurman L., New York, 1976.
                    Rivers, John M., New York, 1976, 1977.

Most Consecutive Hitless Times at Bat, Total Series

Both Leagues—31—North, William A., Oakland AL, 1974 (last 13 times at bat), 1975 (all 10 times at bat); Los Angeles NL, 1978 (all 8 times at bat).
N. L.—30—Geronimo, Cesar F., Cincinnati, 1973 (last 13 times at bat), 1975 (all 10 times at bat), 1976 (first 7 times at bat).
A. L.—24—Campaneris, Dagoberto B., Oakland, 1974 (last 13 times at bat), 1975 (all 11 times at bat); California, 1979 (0 times at bat).

Most At-Bats, Total Series, No Hits

A. L.—13—Lemon, Chester E., Detroit, 1984 (13).
N. L.—11—Didier, Robert D., Atlanta, 1969.
            Kirkpatrick, Edgar L., Pittsburgh, 1974 (9), 1975 (2).

Most At-Bats, Game, Nine Innings

A. L.—6—Blair, Paul L., Baltimore, October 6, 1969.
N. L.—5—Held by many players.

Most At-Bats, Extra-Inning Game

A. L.—6—Buford, Donald A., Baltimore, October 4, 1969; 12 innings.
N. L.—6—Perez, Atanasio R., Cincinnati, October 9, 1973; 12 innings.
           Schmidt, Michael J., Philadelphia, October 8, 1980; 10 innings.
           Puhl, Terry S., Houston, October 12, 1980; 10 innings.

Most At-Bats, Game, Nine Innings, No Hits

A. L.-N. L.—5—Held by many players.

Most At-Bats, Extra-Inning Game, No Hits

A. L.—6—Buford, Donald A., Baltimore, October 4, 1969; 12 innings.
N. L.—5—Held by many players.

Most At-Bats, Inning

N. L.—2—Garrett, R. Wayne, New York, October 7, 1973; ninth inning.
           Yeager, Stephen W., Los Angeles, October 17, 1981; ninth inning.
           Hernandez, Keith, St. Louis, October 7, 1982; sixth inning.
           Matthews, Gary N., Chicago, October 2, 1984; fifth inning.
A. L.—2—Robinson, Frank, Baltimore, October 3, 1970; fourth inning.
           McNally, David A., Baltimore, October 4, 1970; ninth inning.
           Rettenmund, Mervin W., Baltimore, October 6, 1973; first inning.
           Nettles, Graig, New York, October 14, 1981; fourth inning.
           Watson, Robert J., New York, October 14, 1981; fourth inning.

Most Times Faced Pitcher, Inning

N. L.—2—Garrett, R. Wayne, New York, October 7, 1973; ninth inning.
           Yeager, Stephen W., Los Angeles, October 17, 1981; ninth inning.

Smith, Lonnie, St. Louis, October 7, 1982; sixth inning.
Hernandez, Keith, St. Louis, October 7, 1982; sixth inning.
Dernier, Robert E., Chicago, October 2, 1984; fifth inning.
Sandberg, Ryne D., Chicago, October 2, 1984; fifth inning.
Matthews, Gary N., Chicago, October 2, 1984; fifth inning.
A. L.—2—Robinson, Frank, Baltimore, October 3, 1970; fourth inning.
McNally, David A., Baltimore, October 4, 1970; ninth inning.
Rettenmund, Mervin W., Baltimore, October 6, 1973; first inning.
Nettles, Graig, New York, October 14, 1981; fourth inning.
Watson, Robert J., New York, October 14, 1981; fourth inning.
Cerone, Richard A., New York, October 14, 1981; fourth inning.

Most Runs, Total Series

N. L.—17—Rose, Peter E., Cincinnati, 1970, 1972, 1973, 1975, 1976; Philadelphia, 1980, 1983; 7 Series, 28 games.
A. L.—16—Brett, George H., Kansas City, 1976, 1977, 1978, 1980, 1984; 5 Series, 20 games.

Most Runs, Series

3-game Series—A. L.— 5—Belanger, Mark H., Baltimore, 1970.
N. L.—4—Held by many players.
4-game Series—A. L.— 7—Brett, George H., Kansas City, 1978.
N. L.—6—Garvey, Steven P., Los Angeles, 1978.
5-game Series—A. L.— 6—McRae, Harold A., Kansas City, 1977.
N. L.—6—Gwynn, Anthony K., San Diego, 1984.

Most Runs, Game

N. L.—4—Robertson, Robert E., Pittsburgh, October 3, 1971.
Garvey, Steven P., Los Angeles, October 9, 1974.
A. L.—4—Brouhard, Mark S., Milwaukee, October 9, 1982.
Murray, Eddie C., Baltimore, October 7, 1983.

Most Runs, Inning

A. L.-N. L.—1—Held by many players.

Most Hits, Total Series

N. L.—45—Rose, Peter E., Cincinnati, 1970, 1972, 1973, 1975, 1976; Philadelphia, 1980, 1983; 7 Series, 28 games.
A. L.—32—Jackson, Reginald M., Oakland, 1971, 1972, 1973, 1974, 1975; New York, 1977, 1978, 1980, 1981; California, 1982; 10 Series, 39 games.

Most Hits, Series

3-game Series—A. L.— 7—Robinson, Brooks C., Baltimore, 1969, 1970.
N. L.— 7—Shamsky, Arthur L., New York, 1969.
Johnstone, John W., Philadelphia, 1976.
4-game Series—N. L.— 8—Cash, David, Pittsburgh, 1971.
A. L.— 7—Brett, George H., Kansas City, 1978.
Carew, Rodney C., California, 1979.
Law, Rudy K., Chicago, 1983.
5-game Series—A. L.—11—Chambliss, C. Christopher, New York, 1976.
Lynn, Fredric M., California, 1982.
N. L.—10—Puhl, Terry S., Houston, 1980.

Most Hits, Two Consecutive Series

N. L.—17—Rose, Peter E., Cincinnati, 1972 (9), 1973 (8).
A. L.—15—Lynn, Fredric M., Boston, 1975 (4); California, 1982 (11).

Most Series, One or More Hits

A. L.—9—Jackson, Reginald M., Oakland, 1971, 1972, 1973, 1974, 1975; New York, 1977, 1978, 1980; California, 1982.
N. L.—7—Hebner, Richard J., Pittsburgh, 1970, 1971, 1972, 1974, 1975; Philadelphia, 1977, 1978.
Rose, Peter E., Cincinnati, 1970, 1972, 1973, 1975, 1976; Philadelphia, 1980, 1983.

Most Consecutive Hits, Total Series

N. L.—6—Garvey, Steven P., Los Angeles, October 9, 1974 (4), October 4, 1977 (2).
A. L.—5—Bando, Salvatore L., Oakland, October 5 (4), October 7 (1), 1975.
Rivers, John M., New York, October 13 (1), October 14 (4), 1976.
Chambliss, C. Christopher, New York, October 3 (1), October 4 (4), 1978.

Most Consecutive Hits, One Series

A. L.—5—Bando, Salvatore L., Oakland, October 5 (4), October 7 (1), 1975.
Rivers, John M., New York, October 13 (1), October 14 (4), 1976.
Chambliss, C. Christopher, New York, October 3 (1), October 4 (4), 1978.

N. L.—5—Matthews, Gary N., Philadelphia, October 5 (1), October 7 (3), October 8 (1), 1983; one walk during streak.

Most Hits, Game

A. L.—5—Blair, Paul L., Baltimore, October 6, 1969.
N. L.—4—Robertson, Robert E., Pittsburgh, October 3, 1971.
     Cey, Ronald C., Los Angeles, October 6, 1974.
     Garvey, Steven P., Los Angeles, October 9, 1974.
     Baker, Johnnie B., Los Angeles, October 7, 1978; 10 innings.
     Puhl, Terry S., Houston, October 12, 1980.
     Garvey, Steven P., San Diego, October 6, 1984.

Most Times Reached First Base Safely, Nine-Inning Game (Batting 1.000)

A. L.—5—Jackson, Reginald M., New York, October 3, 1978; 2 bases on balls, 1 single, 1 double, 1 home run.
     Nettles, Graig, New York, October 14, 1981; 1 hit by pitcher, 3 singles, 1 home run.
N. L.—5—Millan, Felix B. M., Atlanta, October 5, 1969; 3 bases on balls, 2 singles.

Getting All Club's Hits, Game (Most)

N. L.—2—Clemente, Roberto W., Pittsburgh, October 10, 1972.
     Kosco, Andrew J., Cincinnati, October 7, 1973.
A. L.—1—Jackson, Reginald M., Oakland, October 9, 1974.

Most Consecutive Games, One or More Hits, Total Series

N. L.—15—Rose, Peter E., Cincinnati, 1973 (last 3), 1975 (3), 1976 (3); Philadelphia, 1980 (5), 1983 (first 1).
A. L.— 9—Robinson, Brooks C., Baltimore, 1969 (3), 1970 (3), 1971 (3).
     Patek, Freddie J., Kansas City, 1976 (5), 1977 (first 4).
     Brett, George H., Kansas City, 1977 (last 4), 1978 (4), 1980 (first 1).

Most Hits, Two Consecutive Games, One Series

A. L.—6—Robinson, Brooks C., Baltimore, October 4 (4), October 5 (2), 1969, first game 12 innings, second game 11 innings.
     Bando, Salvatore L., Oakland, October 5 (4), October 7 (2), 1975.
     Rivers, John M., New York, October 8 (4), October 9 (2), 1977.
     Chambliss, C. Christopher, New York, October 3 (2), October 4 (4), 1978.
N. L.—6—Shamsky, Arthur L., New York, October 4 (3), October 5 (3), 1969.
     Robertson, Robert E., Pittsburgh, October 2 (2), October 3 (4), 1971.
     Johnstone, John W., Philadelphia, October 10 (3), October 12 (3), 1976.
     Lopes, David E., Los Angeles, October 4 (3), October 5 (3), 1978.

Most Hits, Inning

A. L.—2—Nettles, Graig, New York, October 14, 1981; fourth inning.
N. L.—1—Held by many players.

Most One-Base Hits, Total Series

N. L.—34—Rose, Peter E., Cincinnati, 1970, 1972, 1973, 1975, 1976; Philadelphia, 1980, 1983; 7 Series, 28 games.
A. L.—21—Jackson, Reginald M., Oakland, 1971, 1972, 1973, 1974, 1975; New York, 1977, 1978, 1980, 1981; California 1982; 10 Series, 39 games.

Most One-Base Hits, Series

3-game Series—N. L.—7—Shamsky, Arthur L., New York, 1969.
          A. L.— 6—Robinson, Brooks C., Baltimore, 1969.
4-game Series—N. L.—7—Russell, William E., Los Angeles, 1974.
          A. L.— 6—Chambliss, C. Christopher, New York, 1978.
               Law, Rudy K., Chicago, 1983.
5-game Series—A. L.— 8—Munson, Thurman L., New York, 1976.
               Lynn, Fredric M., California, 1982.
          N. L.— 8—Rose, Peter E., Philadelphia, 1980.
               Puhl, Terry S., Houston, 1980.

Most One-Base Hits, Game

A. L.—4—Robinson, Brooks C., Baltimore, October 4, 1969; 12 innings.
     Chambliss, C. Christopher, New York, October 4, 1978.
N. L.—4—Puhl, Terry S., Houston, October 12, 1980; 10 innings.
N. L.—Nine-inning record—3—Held by many players.

Most One-Base Hits, Inning

A. L.—2—Nettles, Graig, New York, October 14, 1981; fourth inning.
N. L.—1—Held by many players.

Most Two-Base Hits, Total Series

N. L.—7—Rose, Peter E., Cincinnati, 1970, 1972, 1973, 1975, 1976; Philadelphia, 1980, 1983; 7 Series, 28 games.

Hebner, Richard J., Pittsburgh, 1970, 1971, 1972, 1974, 1975; Philadelphia, 1977, 1978; Chicago, 1984; 8 Series, 27 games.

Schmidt, Michael J., Philadelphia, 1976, 1977, 1978, 1980, 1983; 5 Series, 20 games.

Cey, Ronald C., Los Angeles, 1974, 1977, 1978, 1981; Chicago, 1984; 5 Series, 22 games.

A. L.—6—Robinson, Brooks C., Baltimore, 1969, 1970, 1971, 1973, 1974; 5 Series, 18 games.

White, Roy H., New York, 1976, 1977, 1978; 3 Series, 13 games.

Most Two-Base Hits, Series

3-game Series—N. L.—3— Morgan, Joe L., Cincinnati, 1975.
Porter, Darrell R., St. Louis, 1982.
A. L.— 3—Watson, Robert J., New York, 1980.
4-game Series—N. L.—3—Cey, Ronald C., Los Angeles, 1974.
A. L.— 3—Carew, Rodney C., California, 1979.
5-game Series—A. L.— 4—Alou, Mateo R., Oakland, 1972.
N. L.— 4—Rose, Peter E., Cincinnati, 1972.

Most Two-Base Hits, Game

A. L.-N. L.—2—Held by many players.

Most Two-Base Hits, Inning

A. L.-N. L.—1—Held by many players.

Most Three-Base Hits, Total Series

A. L.—4—Brett, George H., Kansas City, 1976, 1977, 1978, 1980, 1984; 5 Series, 20 games.

N. L.—2—Lopes, David E., Los Angeles, 1974, 1977, 1978, 1981; Chicago, 1984; 5 Series, 19 games.

Bench, Johnny L., Cincinnati, 1970, 1972, 1973, 1975, 1976, 1979; 6 Series, 22 games.

McGee, Willie D., St. Louis, 1982; 1 Series, 3 games.

Most Three-Base Hits, Series

A. L.—2—Brett, George H., Kansas City, 1977; 5-game Series.
N. L.—2—McGee, Willie D., St. Louis, 1982; 3-game Series.

Most Three-Base Hits, Game

A. L.-N. L.—1—Held by many players.

Most Three-Base Hits, Game, Batting in Three Runs

A. L.-N. L—Never accomplished.

Most Home Runs, Total Series

N. L.—8—Garvey, Steven P., Los Angeles, 1974, 1977, 1978, 1981; San Diego, 1984; 5 Series, 22 games.

A. L.—6—Brett, George H., Kansas City, 1976, 1977, 1978, 1980, 1984; 5 Series, 20 games.

Jackson, Reginald M., Oakland, 1971, 1972, 1973, 1974, 1975; New York, 1977, 1978, 1980, 1981; California, 1982; 10 Series, 39 games.

Three or More Home Runs, Total Series

National League			American League		
Player	Series	HR.	Player	Series	HR.
Garvey, Steven P.	5	8	Brett, George H.	5	6
Matthews, Gary N.	2	5	Jackson, Reginald M.	10	6
Luzinski, Gregory M.	5	5	Bando, Salvatore L.	5	5
Bench, Johnny L.	6	5	Nettles, Graig	6	5
Robertson, Robert E.	5	4	Powell, John W.	5	4
Cey, Ronald C.	5	4			
Stargell, Wilver D.	6	4			
Aaron, Henry L.	1	3			
Staub, Daniel J.	1	3			
Foster, George A.	4	3			
Oliver, Albert	5	3			
Perez, Atanasio R.	6	3			
Rose, Peter E.	7	3			
Hebner, Richard J.	8	3			

Most Home Runs, Series

3-game Series—N. L.— 3—Aaron, Henry L., Atlanta, 1969.
             A. L.— 2—Johnson, David A., Baltimore, 1970
                      Killebrew, Harmon C., Minnesota, 1970.
                      Powell, John W., Baltimore, 1971.
                      Jackson, Reginald M., Oakland, 1971.
                      Brett, George H., Kansas City, 1980.
4-game Series—N. L.— 4—Robertson, Robert E., Pittsburgh, 1971.
                      Garvey, Steven P., Los Angeles, 1978.
             A. L.— 3—Brett, George H., Kansas City, 1978.
5-game Series—N. L.— 3—Staub, Daniel J., New York, 1973.
             A. L.— 2—Campaneris, Dagoberto B., Oakland, 1973.
                      Bando, Salvatore L., Oakland, 1973.
                      Chambliss, C. Christopher, New York, 1976.
                      Nettles, Graig, New York, 1976.
                      Molitor, Paul L., Milwaukee, 1982.

Most Series, One or More Home Runs

N. L.—5—Bench, Johnny L., Cincinnati, 1970 (1), 1972 (1), 1973 (1), 1976 (1), 1979 (1).
A. L.—4—Nettles, Graig, New York, 1976 (2), 1978 (1), 1980 (1), 1981 (1).
           Jackson, Reginald M., Oakland, 1971 (2), 1975 (1); New York, 1978 (2); California, 1982 (1).

Most Series, Two or More Home Runs

N. L.—2—Garvey, Steven P., Los Angeles, 1974 (2), 1978 (4).
           Stargell, Wilver D., Pittsburgh, 1974 (2), 1979 (2).
           Matthews, Gary N., Philadelphia, 1983 (3); Chicago, 1984 (2).
A. L.—2—Bando, Salvatore L., Oakland, 1973 (2), 1974 (2).
           Jackson, Reginald M., Oakland, 1971 (2); New York, 1978 (2).
           Brett, George H., Kansas City, 1978 (3), 1980 (2).

Most Home Runs, Game

N. L.—3—Robertson, Robert E., Pittsburgh, October 3, 1971.
     2—Staub, Daniel J., New York, October 8, 1973.
           Garvey, Steven P., Los Angeles, October 9, 1974.
           Garvey, Steven P., Los Angeles, October 4, 1978.
           Matthews, Gary N., Chicago, October 2, 1984.
A. L.—3—Brett, George H., Kansas City, October 6, 1978.
     2—Powell, John W., Baltimore, October 4, 1971.
           Jackson, Reginald M., Oakland, October 5, 1971.
           Bando, Salvatore L., Oakland, October 7, 1973.
           Nettles, Graig, New York, October 13, 1976.

Most Home Runs with Bases Filled, Game

A. L.—1—Cuellar, Miguel, Baltimore, October 3, 1970; fourth inning.
           Baylor, Donald E., California, October 9, 1982; eighth inning.
N. L.—1—Cey, Ronald C., Los Angeles, October 4, 1977; seventh inning.
           Baker, Johnnie B., Los Angeles, October 5, 1977; fourth inning.

Inside-the-Park Home Runs

Nettles, Graig, New York, October 9, 1980; fifth inning, 0 on base.
Molitor, Paul L., Milwaukee, October 6, 1982; fifth inning, 1 on base.

Most Home Runs, Pinch-Hitter, Game

N. L.—1—Martin, Jerry L., Philadelphia, October 4, 1978; ninth inning.
           McBride, Arnold R., Philadelphia, October 7, 1978; seventh inning.
A. L.—1—Lowenstein, John L., Baltimore, October 3, 1979; tenth inning.

Hitting Home Run, Leadoff Batter, Start of Game

A. L.—Campaneris, Dagoberto B., Oakland, October 7, 1973; at Baltimore.
     Brett, George H., Kansas City, October 6, 1978; at New York.
N. L.—Dernier, Robert E., Chicago, October 2, 1984; at Chicago.

Home Runs Winning 1-0 Games

A. L.—Bando, Salvatore L., Oakland, October 8, 1974; fourth inning.
N. L.—Never accomplished.

Most Home Runs, Game, by Pitcher

A. L.—1—Cuellar, Miguel, Baltimore, October 3, 1970; 3 on base.
N. L.—1—Gullett, Donald E., Cincinnati, October 4, 1975; 1 on base.
           Carlton, Steven N., Philadelphia, October 6, 1978; 2 on base.
           Sutcliffe, Richard L., Chicago, October 2, 1984; 0 on base.

Most Home Runs, Game, by Rookie

N. L.—1—Garrett, R. Wayne, New York, October 6, 1969.
Clines, Eugene A., Pittsburgh, October 3, 1971.
Speier, Chris E., San Francisco, October 6, 1971.
McGee, Willie D., St. Louis, October 10, 1982.
A. L.—Never accomplished.

Most Consecutive Games, Series, Hitting One or More Home Runs

N. L.—3—Aaron, Henry L., Atlanta, October 4, 5, 6, 1969.
Matthews, Gary N., Philadelphia, October 5, 7, 8, 1983.
A. L.—2—Killebrew, Harmon C., Minnesota, October 3, 4, 1970.
Johnson, David A., Baltimore, October 4, 5, 1970.
Campaneris, Dagoberto B., Oakland, October 7, 9, 1973; second game 11 innings.
Bando, Salvatore L., Oakland, October 6, 8, 1974.
Ford, Darnell G., California, October 3, 4, 1979.
Molitor, Paul L., Milwaukee, October 6, 8, 1982.

Most Home Runs, Two Consecutive Games, One Series, Hitting Homer in Each Game

N. L.—4—Robertson, Robert E., Pittsburgh, October 3 (3), 5 (1), 1971.
A. L.—2—Killebrew, Harmon C., Minnesota, October 3, 4, 1970.
Johnson, David A., Baltimore, October 4, 5, 1970.
Campaneris, Dagoberto B., Oakland, October 7, 9, 1973; second game 11 innings.
Bando, Salvatore L., Oakland, October 6, 8, 1974.
Ford, Darnell G., California, October 3, 4, 1979.
Molitor, Paul L., Milwaukee, October 6, 8, 1982.

Hitting Home Run in First Championship Series At-Bat

A. L.—Robinson, Frank, Baltimore, October 4, 1969; fourth inning (walked in first inning).
Cash, Norman D., Detroit, October 7, 1972; second inning.
Ford, Darnell G., California, October 3, 1979; first inning.
Lowenstein, John L., Baltimore, October 3, 1979; tenth inning (pinch-hit).
Cerone, Richard A., New York, October 8, 1980; first inning.
Thomas, J. Gorman, Milwaukee, October 5, 1982; second inning.
N. L.—Morgan, Joe L., Cincinnati, October 7, 1972; first inning.
Sutcliffe, Richard L., Chicago, October 2, 1984; third inning.

Most Home Runs, Inning

A. L.-N. L.—1—Held by many players.

Most Home Runs, Two Consecutive Innings

N. L.—2—Staub, Daniel J., New York, October 8, 1973, first and second innings.
A. L.—Never accomplished.

Most Long Hits, Total Series

A. L.—13—Brett, George H., Kansas City, 1976, 1977, 1978, 1980, 1984; 5 Series, 20 games.
N. L.—12—Garvey, Steven P., Los Angeles, 1974, 1977, 1978, 1981; San Diego, 1984; 5 Series, 22 games.

Most Long Hits, Series

3-game Series—N. L.—5—Aaron, Henry L., Atlanta, 1969.
A. L.—4—Watson, Robert J., New York, 1980.
4-game Series—N. L.—6—Garvey, Steven P., Los Angeles, 1978.
A. L.—5—Brett, George H., Kansas City, 1978.
5-game Series—N. L.—4—Rose, Peter E., Cincinnati, 1972.
Oliver, Albert, Pittsburgh, 1972.
A. L.—4—Held by many players.

Most Long Hits, Game

N. L.—4—Robertson, Robert E., Pittsburgh, October 3, 1971; 3 home runs, 1 double.
A. L.—3—Blair, Paul L., Baltimore, October 6, 1969; 2 doubles, 1 home run.
Brett, George H., Kansas City, October 6, 1978; 3 home runs.

Most Long Hits, Two Consecutive Games, Series

N. L.—5—Robertson, Robert E., Pittsburgh, October 3 (4), 3 home runs, 1 double; October 5 (1), 1 home run, 1971.
A. L.—4—Brett, George H., Kansas City, October 6 (3), 3 home runs; October 7 (1), 1 triple, 1978.

Most Long Hits, Inning

A. L.-N. L.—1—Held by many players.

Most Total Bases, Total Series

   N. L.—63—Rose, Peter E., Cincinnati, 1970, 1972, 1973, 1975, 1976; Philadelphia, 1980, 1983; 7 Series, 28 games.
   A. L.—56—Brett, George H., Kansas City, 1976, 1977, 1978, 1980, 1984; 5 Series, 20 games.

Most Total Bases, Series

   3-game Series—N. L.—16—Aaron, Henry L., Atlanta, 1969.
              A. L.—11—Held by many players.
   4-game Series—N. L.—22—Garvey, Steven P., Los Angeles, 1978.
              A. L.—19—Brett, George H., Kansas City, 1978.
   5-game Series—A. L.—20—Chambliss, C. Christopher, New York, 1976.
              N. L.—15—Rose, Peter E., Cincinnati, 1973.
                     Davis, Jody R., Chicago, 1984.

Most Total Bases, Game

   N. L.—14—Robertson, Robert E., Pittsburgh, October 3, 1971; 3 home runs, 1 double.
   A. L.—12—Brett, George H., Kansas City, October 6, 1978; 3 home runs.

Most Total Bases, Inning

   A. L.-N. L.—4—Held by many players.

Most Runs Batted In, Total Series

   N. L.—21—Garvey, Steven P., Los Angeles, 1974, 1977, 1978, 1981; San Diego, 1984; 5 Series, 22 games.
   A. L.—18—Jackson, Reginald M., Oakland, 1971, 1972, 1973, 1974, 1975; New York, 1977, 1978, 1980, 1981; California, 1982; 10 Series, 39 games.

Most Runs Batted In, Series

   3-game Series—A. L.— 9—Nettles, Graig, New York, 1981.
              N. L.— 7—Aaron, Henry L., Atlanta, 1969.
   4-game Series—N. L.— 8—Baker, Johnnie B., Los Angeles, 1977.
                     Matthews, Gary N., Philadelphia, 1983.
              A. L.— 6— Jackson, Reginald M., New York, 1978.
   5-game Series—A. L.—10—Baylor, Donald E., California, 1982.
              N. L.— 7—Garvey, Steven P., San Diego, 1984.

Most Runs Batted In, Game

   A. L.—5—Blair, Paul L., Baltimore, October 6, 1969.
          Baylor, Donald E., California, October 5, 1982.
   N. L.—5—Robertson, Robert E., Pittsburgh, October 3, 1971.
          Garvey, Steven P., San Diego, October 6, 1984.

Most Runs Batted In, Inning

   A. L.—4—Cuellar, Miguel, Baltimore, October 3, 1970; bases-loaded home run in fourth inning.
          Baylor, Donald E., California, October 9, 1982; bases-loaded home run in eighth inning.
   N. L.—4—Cey, Ronald C., Los Angeles, October 4, 1977; bases-loaded home run in seventh inning.
          Baker, Johnnie B., Los Angeles, October 5, 1977; bases-loaded home run in fourth inning.

Most Consecutive Games, One or More Runs Batted In, Total Series

   A. L.—4—Patek, Freddie J., Kansas City, 1977 (first 4); 5 runs batted in.
          Roenicke, Gary S., Baltimore, 1979 (last 1), 1983 (first 3); 5 runs batted in.
   N. L.—4—Perez, Atanasio R., Cincinnati, 1973 (last 2), 1975 (first 2); 6 runs batted in.
          Lopes, David E., Los Angeles, 1974 (last 1), 1977 (first 3); 4 runs batted in.
          Luzinski, Gregory M., Philadelphia, 1976 (3), 1977 (first 1); 5 runs batted in.
          Maddox, Garry L., Philadelphia, 1976 (last 1), 1977 (2), 1978 (first 1); 5 runs batted in.
          Foster, George A., Cincinnati, 1976 (3), 1979 (first 1); 6 runs batted in.
          Luzinski, Gregory M., Philadelphia, 1978 (last 2), 1980 (first 2); 6 runs batted in.

Batting in All Club's Runs, Game (Most)

   A. L.—3—Campaneris, Dagoberto B., Oakland, October 5, 1974.
          Nettles, Graig, New York, October 13, 1981.
   N. L.—2—Foster, George A., Cincinnati, October 2, 1979; 11 innings.
          Marshall, Michael A., Los Angeles, October 7, 1983.

Most Game-Winning RBIs, Total Series (Since 1980)

   N. L.—2—Luzinski, Gregory M., Philadelphia, 1980.
          Matthews, Gary N., Philadelphia, 1983; Chicago, 1984.
   A. L.—2—Cooper, Cecil C., Milwaukee, 1982.

Most Game-Winning RBIs, Series (Since 1980)

N. L.—2—Luzinski, Gregory M., Philadelphia, 1980.
A. L.—2—Cooper, Cecil C., Milwaukee, 1982.

Most Bases on Balls, Total Series

N. L.—23—Morgan, Joe L., Cincinnati, 1972, 1973, 1975, 1976, 1979; Houston, 1980; Philadelphia, 1983; 7 Series, 27 games.
A. L.—15—Jackson, Reginald M., Oakland, 1971, 1972, 1973, 1974, 1975; New York, 1977, 1978, 1980, 1981; California, 1982; 10 Series, 39 games.

Most Bases on Balls, Series

3-game Series—A. L.— 6—Killebrew, Harmon C., Minnesota, 1969.
N. L.—6—Morgan, Joe L., Cincinnati, 1976.
4-game Series—N. L.— 9—Wynn, James S., Los Angeles, 1974.
A. L.— 5—Jackson, Reginald M., Oakland, 1974.
Murray, Eddie C., Baltimore, 1979.
Roenicke, Gary S., Baltimore 1983.
5-game Series—N. L.— 8—Cruz, Jose, Houston, 1980.
A. L.— 5—White, Roy H., New York, 1976.

Most Consecutive Bases on Balls, One Series

A. L.—4—Killebrew, Harmon C., Minnesota, October 4 (3), October 5 (1), 1969.
Roenicke, Gary S., Baltimore, October 6 (1), 7 (1), 8 (2), 1983.
N. L.—3—Foster, George A., Cincinnati, October 2 (1), October 3 (2), 1979.
Matthews, Gary N., Chicago, October 6 (1), October 7 (2), 1984.

Most Bases on Balls, Game

A. L.-N. L.—3—Held by many players.

Most Bases on Balls with Bases Filled, Game

A. L.—1—Cash, Norman D., Detroit, October 11, 1972; tenth inning.
Tenace, F. Gene, Oakland, October 9, 1974; fifth inning.
Roenicke, Gary S., Baltimore, October 7, 1983; ninth inning.
N. L.—1—Lopes, David E., Los Angeles, October 5, 1974; second inning.
Dyer, Don R., Pittsburgh, October 7, 1975; ninth inning.
Christenson, Larry R., Philadelphia, October 7, 1977; second inning.
McBride, Arnold R., Philadelphia, October 7, 1977; second inning.
Bowa, Lawrence R., Philadelphia, October 7, 1977; second inning.
Rose, Peter E., Philadelphia, October 12, 1980; eighth inning.

Most Bases on Balls, Two Consecutive Games

A. L.—5—Killebrew, Harmon C., Minnesota, October 4 (3), October 5 (2), 1969; first game 12 innings, second game 11 innings.
N. L.—5—Wynn, James S., Los Angeles, October 5 (2), October 6 (3), 1974.

Most Bases on Balls, Inning

A. L.-N. L.—1—Held by many players.

Most Strikeouts, Total Series

A. L.—34—Jackson, Reginald M., Oakland, 1971, 1972, 1973, 1974, 1975; New York, 1977, 1978, 1980, 1981; California, 1982; 10 Series, 39 games.
N. L.—24—Geronimo, Cesar F., Cincinnati, 1972, 1973, 1975, 1976, 1979; 5 Series, 17 games.

Most Strikeouts, Series

3-game Series—A. L.— 7—Cardenas, Leonardo A., Minnesota, 1969.
N. L.—7—Geronimo, Cesar F., Cincinnati, 1975.
4-game Series—N. L.— 6—Clemente, Roberto W., Pittsburgh, 1971.
Stargell, Wilver D., Pittsburgh, 1971.
Marshall, Michael A., Los Angeles, 1983.
A. L.— 5—Otis, Amos J., Kansas City, 1978.
Cruz, Todd R., Baltimore, 1983.
Luzinski, Gregory M., Chicago, 1983.
5-game Series—N. L.— 7—Perez, Atanasio R., Cincinnati, 1972.
Geronimo, Cesar F., Cincinnati, 1973.
A. L.— 7—Jackson, Reginald M., California, 1982.
Grich, Robert A., California, 1982.

Most Consecutive Strikeouts, One Series (Consecutive at-bats)

N. L.—7—Geronimo, Cesar F., Cincinnati, October 4 (1), October 5 (3), October 7 (3), 1975, third game 10 innings, one base on balls during streak.
A. L.—4—Cardenas, Leonardo A., Minnesota, October 4 (2), October 5 (2), 1969; first game 12 innings, second game 11 innings.
Boswell, David W., Minnesota, October 5, 1969; 11 innings.

Bando, Salvatore L., Oakland, October 9 (2), October 10 (2), 1973; first game 11 innings, one base on balls during streak.

Grich, Robert A., California, October 6 (1), October 8 (3), 1982.

Most Consecutive Strikeouts, One Series (Consecutive plate appearances)

N. L.—5—Geronimo, Cesar F., Cincinnati, October 6 (1), October 7 (3), October 9 (1), 1973; third game 12 innings.

A. L.—4—Cardenas, Leonardo A., Minnesota, October 4 (2), October 5 (2), 1969; first game 12 innings, second game 11 innings.

Boswell, David W., Minnesota, October 5, 1969; 11 innings.

Grich, Robert A., California, October 6 (1), October 8 (3), 1982.

Most Strikeouts, Game

A. L.—4—Boswell, David W., Minnesota, October 5, 1969; consecutive, 11 innings.

Nine-inning record—A. L.-N. L.—3—Held by many players.

Most Strikeouts, Inning

A. L.-N. L.—1—Held by many players.

Most Sacrifice Hits, Total Series

Both Leagues—4—Boone, Robert R., Philadelphia NL, 1976, 1977, 1978, 1980; California AL, 1982; 5 Series, 20 games.

A. L.—3—Green, Richard L., Oakland, 1971, 1972, 1973, 1974; 4 Series, 17 games.

N. L.—3—Cabell, Enos M., Houston, 1980; 1 Series, 5 games.

Russell, William E., Los Angeles, 1974, 1977, 1978, 1981, 1983; 5 Series, 21 games.

Most Sacrifice Hits, Series

3-game Series—N. L.— 2— Ellis, Dock P., Pittsburgh, 1970.

Bibby, James B., Pittsburgh, 1979.

Andujar, Joaquin, St. Louis, 1982.

A. L.— 1— Held by many players.

4-game Series—N. L.— 2— Perry, Gaylord J. San Francisco, 1971.

A. L.— 2— Belanger, Mark H., Baltimore, 1974.

5-game Series—N. L.— 3— Cabell, Enos M., Houston, 1980.

A. L.— 2— Bando, Salvatore L., Oakland, 1972.

Patek, Freddie J., Kansas City, 1977.

Boone, Robert R., California, 1982.

Moore, Charles W., Milwaukee, 1982.

Most Sacrifice Hits, Game

A. L.—2—Patek, Freddie J., Kansas City, October 7, 1977.

N. L.—2—Ellis, Dock P., Pittsburgh, October 3, 1970; 10 innings.

Perry, Gaylord J., San Francisco, October 2, 1971.

Bibby, James B., Pittsburgh, October 3, 1979.

Trillo, J. Manuel, Philadelphia, October 8, 1980; 10 innings.

Andujar, Joaquin, St. Louis, 1982.

Most Sacrifice Flies, Total Series

A. L.—2—McRae, Harold A., Kansas City, 1976, 1977, 1978, 1980, 1984; 5 Series, 19 games.

DeCinces, Douglas V., Baltimore, 1979; 1 Series, 4 games.

N. L.—2—Perez, Atanasio R., Cincinnati, 1970, 1972, 1973, 1975, 1976; 5 Series, 19 games.

Schmidt, Michael J., Philadelphia, 1976, 1977, 1978, 1980; 4 Series, 16 games.

Foli, Timothy J., Pittsburgh, 1979; 1 Series, 3 games.

Most Sacrifice Flies, Series

N. L.—2—Perez, Atanasio R., Cincinnati, 1976; 3-game Series.

Foli, Timothy J., Pittsburgh, 1979; 3-game Series.

A. L.—2—DeCinces, Douglas V., Baltimore, 1979; 4-game Series.

Most Sacrifice Flies, Game

A. L.-N. L.—1—Held by many players.

Most Hit by Pitch, Total Series

N. L.—4—Hebner, Richard J., Pittsburgh, 1971 (1), 1972 (1), 1974 (1); Chicago, 1984 (1).

A. L.—2—McRae, Harold A., Kansas City, 1976 (1), 1980 (1).

Roenicke, Gary S., Baltimore, 1979 (1), 1983 (1).

Most Hit by Pitch, Series

A. L.-N. L.—1—Held by many players.

Most Hit by Pitch, Game

A. L.-N. L.—1—Held by many players.

Most Times Awarded First Base on Catcher's Interference, Game

N. L.—1—Hebner, Richard J., Pittsburgh, October 8, 1974, fifth inning.
A. L.—Never accomplished.

Most Grounded Into Double Play, Total Series

N. L.—4—Guerrero, Pedro, Los Angeles, 1981, 1983; 2 Series, 9 games.
A. L.—4—Randolph, William L., New York, 1976, 1977, 1980, 1981; 4 Series, 16 games.

Most Grounded Into Double Play, Series

N. L.—4—Guerrero, Pedro, Los Angeles, 1981; 19 at-bats in 5 games of 5-game Series.
A. L.—3—Taylor, Antonio, Detroit, 1972; 15 at-bats in 4 games of 5-game Series.

Most Grounded Into Double Play, Game

A. L.—3—Taylor, Antonio, Detroit, October 10, 1972.
N. L.—2—Jones, Cleon J., New York, October 4, 1969.
        Guerrero, Pedro, Los Angeles, October 16, 1981.
        Royster, Jeron K., Atlanta, October 10, 1982.

INDIVIDUAL PINCH-HITTING

Most Series Appeared as Pinch-Hitter

Both Leagues—4—Davalillo, Victor J., Pittsburgh NL, 1971, 1972; Oakland AL, 1973;
        Los Angeles NL, 1977; 5 games.
N. L.—4—Monday, Robert J., Los Angeles, 1977, 1978, 1981, 1983; 4 games.
        Hebner, Richard J., Pittsburgh, 1971; Philadelphia, 1977, 1978; Chicago, 1984;
        5 games.
A. L.—3—Motton, Curtell H., Baltimore, 1969, 1971, 1974; 4 games.
        Holt, James W., Minnesota, 1970; Oakland, 1974, 1975; 4 games.

Most Games, Pinch-Hitter, Total Series

N. L.—6—Mota, Manuel R., Los Angeles, 1974 (3), 1977 (1), 1978 (2); 6 plate appear-
        ances, 5 at-bats.
A. L.—4—Held by many players.

Most Games, Pinch-Hitter, Series

A. L.—4—Hendrick, George A., Oakland, 1972.
N. L.—4—Stahl, Larry F., Cincinnati, 1973.

Most At-Bats, Pinch-Hitter, Total Series

N. L.—5—Mota, Manuel R., Los Angeles, 1974 (3), 1977 (1), 1978 (1).
A. L.—4—Hendrick, George A., Oakland, 1972.
        Mangual, Angel L., Oakland, 1972 (3), 1973 (1).
        Alou, Jesus M., Oakland, 1973 (3), 1974 (1).
        Motton, Curtell H., Baltimore, 1969 (2), 1971 (1), 1974 (1).
        Crowley, Terrence M., Baltimore, 1973 (2), 1979 (2).

Most At-Bats, Pinch-Hitter, Series

A. L.—4—Hendrick, George A., Oakland, 1972.
N. L.—4—Stahl, Larry F., Cincinnati, 1973.

Most Plate Appearances, Pinch-Hitter, Total Series

N. L.—6—Mota, Manuel R., Los Angeles, 1974 (3), 1977 (1), 1978 (2).
A. L.—4—Held by many players.

Most Runs, Pinch-Hitter, Total Series

N. L.—2—Cline, Tyrone A., Cincinnati, 1970; 1 Series, 2 games.
A. L.—1—Held by many players.

Most Runs, Pinch-Hitter, Series

N. L.—2—Cline, Tyrone A., Cincinnati, 1970; 2 games.
A. L.—1—Held by many players.

Most Hits, Pinch-Hitter, Total Series

N. L.—3—Popovich, Paul E., Pittsburgh, 1974; 1 Series, 3 games.
        Mota, Manuel R., Los Angeles, 1974, 1977, 1978; 3 Series, 6 games.
A. L.—2—Marquez, Gonzalo, Oakland, 1972; 1 Series, 3 games.
        Motton, Curtell H., Baltimore, 1969, 1971, 1974; 3 Series, 4 games.
        Alou, Jesus M., Oakland, 1973, 1974; 2 Series, 4 games.
        Piniella, Louis V., New York, 1976, 1981; 2 Series, 3 games.
        McRae, Harold A., Kansas City, 1984; 1 Series, 2 games.

Most Hits, Pinch-Hitter, Series

N. L.—3—Popovich, Paul E., Pittsburgh, 1974; 3 games.

A. L.—2—Marquez, Gonzalo, Oakland, 1972; 3 games.
Piniella, Louis V., New York, 1981; 2 games.
McRae, Harold A., Kansas City, 1984; 2 games.

Most Consecutive Hits, Pinch-Hitter

N. L.—3—Popovich, Paul E., Pittsburgh, October 5, 6, 9, 1974.
A. L.—2—Motton, Curtell H., Baltimore, October 5, 1969; October 3, 1971.
Piniella, Louis V., New York, October 13, 15, 1981.
McRae, Harold A., Kansas City, October 3, 5, 1984.

Most One-Base Hits, Pinch-Hitter, Total Series

N. L.—3—Popovich, Paul E., Pittsburgh, 1974; 1 Series, 3 games.
A. L.—2—Marquez, Gonzalo, Oakland, 1972; 1 Series, 3 games.
Alou, Jesus M., Oakland, 1973, 1974; 2 Series, 4 games.
Piniella, Louis V., New York, 1976, 1981; 2 Series, 3 games.

Most One-Base Hits, Pinch-Hitter, Series

N. L.—3—Popovich, Paul E., Pittsburgh, 1974; 3 games.
A. L.—2—Marquez, Gonzalo, Oakland, 1972; 3 games.
Piniella, Louis V., New York, 1981; 2 games.

Most Two-Base Hits, Pinch-Hitter, Total Series

N. L.—2—Mota, Manuel R., Los Angeles, 1974, 1977, 1978; 3 Series, 6 games.
A. L.—1—Held by many players.

Most Three-Base Hits, Pinch-Hitter, Total Series

N. L.—1—Cline, Tyrone A., Cincinnati, 1970; 1 Series, 2 games.
A. L.—Never accomplished.

Home Runs by Pinch-Hitters

N. L.—Martin, Jerry L., Philadelphia, October 4, 1978; ninth inning.
McBride, Arnold R., Philadelphia, October 7, 1978; seventh inning.
A. L.—Lowenstein, John L., Baltimore, October 3, 1979; tenth inning.

Most Total Bases, Pinch-Hitter, Total Series

N. L.—6—Martin, Jerry L., Philadelphia, 1977, 1978; 2 Series, 3 games.
A. L.—4—Lowenstein, John L., Baltimore, 1979; 1 Series, 2 games.

Most Total Bases, Pinch-Hitter, Series

N. L.—6—Martin, Jerry L., Philadelphia, 1978; 2 games.
A. L.—4—Lowenstein, John L., Baltimore, 1979; 2 games.

Most Total Bases, Pinch-Hitter, Game

N. L.—4—Martin, Jerry L., Philadelphia, October 4, 1978; home run in ninth inning.
McBride, Arnold R., Philadelphia, October 7, 1978; home run in seventh inning.
A. L.—4—Lowenstein, John L., Baltimore, October 3, 1979; home run in tenth inning.

Most Runs Batted In, Pinch-Hitter, Total Series

A. L.—3—Lowenstein, John L., Baltimore, 1979; 1 Series, 2 games.
N. L.—2—Martin, Joseph C., New York, 1969; 1 Series, 2 games.
Martin, Jerry L., Philadelphia, 1977, 1978; 2 Series, 3 games.

Most Runs Batted In, Pinch-Hitter, Series

A. L.—3—Lowenstein, John L., Baltimore, 1979; 2 games.
N. L.—2—Martin, Joseph C., New York, 1969; 2 games.
Martin, Jerry L., Philadelphia, 1978; 2 games.

Most Runs Batted In, Pinch-Hitter, Game

A. L.—3—Lowenstein, John L., Baltimore, 1979; tenth inning.
N. L.—2—Martin, Joseph C., New York, October 4, 1969; eighth inning.

Most Bases on Balls, Pinch-Hitter, Total Series

Both Leagues—2—Rettenmund, Mervin W., Baltimore AL, 1969; Cincinnati NL, 1975;
California AL, 1979; 3 Series, 4 games.
N. L.—2—Hague, Joe C., Cincinnati, 1972; 1 Series, 3 games.
A. L.—1—Held by many players.

Bases on Balls with Bases Filled by Pinch-Hitters, Game

N. L.—Dyer, Don R., Pittsburgh, October 7, 1975; ninth inning.
A. L.—Never accomplished.

Most Strikeouts, Pinch-Hitter, Total Series

N. L.—3—Monday, Robert J., Los Angeles, 1977, 1978, 1981; 3 Series, 3 games.
A. L.—1—Held by many players.

Most Strikeouts, Pinch-Hitter, Series

    N. L.—2—Armbrister, Edison R., Cincinnati, 1973; 2 games.
              Leonard, Jeffrey N., Houston, 1980; 2 games.
              Woods, Gary L., Houston, 1980; 2 games.
              Bosley, Thaddis, Chicago, 1980; 2 games.
    A. L.—1—Held by many players.

Sacrifice Hits by Pinch-Hitters, Game

    A. L.—Andrews, Michael J., Oakland, October 9, 1973; eighth inning.
    N. L.—Armbrister, Edison R., Cincinnati, October 12, 1976; ninth inning.
            Mota, Manuel R., Los Angeles, October 7, 1978; fifth inning.
            Gross, Gregory E., Philadelphia, October 8, 1980; seventh inning.

Sacrifice Flies by Pinch-Hitters, Game

    N. L.—Armbrister, Edison R., Cincinnati, October 7, 1975; tenth inning.
    A. L.—Nolan, Joseph W., Baltimore, October 7, 1983; ninth inning.
            Ayala, Benigno F., Baltimore, October 8, 1983; tenth inning.

Hit by Pitches by Pinch-Hitters, Game

    N. L.—Flannery, Timothy E., San Diego, October 2, 1984; fifth inning.
            Hebner, Richard J., Chicago, October 7, 1984; eighth inning.
    A. L.—Never accomplished.

Grounding into Double Play by Pinch-Hitters, Game

    A. L.—Renick, W. Richard, Minnesota, October 6, 1969; sixth inning.
            Roenicke, Gary S., Baltimore, October 6, 1979; third inning.
    N. L.—Hart, James R., San Francisco, October 3, 1971; eighth inning.
            Mota, Manuel R., Los Angeles, October 9, 1974; eighth inning.
            Ferguson, Joseph V., Los Angeles, October 6, 1978; ninth inning.
            Bevacqua, Kurt A., San Diego, October 3, 1984; eighth inning.

INDIVIDUAL BASE RUNNING

Most Stolen Bases, Total Series

    N. L.—9—Lopes, David E., Los Angeles, 1974, 1977, 1978, 1981; 4 Series, 17 games.
    A. L.—8—Otis, Amos J., Kansas City, 1976, 1977, 1978, 1980; 4 Series, 13 games.

Most Stolen Bases, Series

    3-game Series—N. L.—4—Morgan, Joe L., Cincinnati, 1975.
                   A. L.—2—Beniquez, Juan J., Boston, 1975.
                         Otis, Amos J., Kansas City, 1980.
                         Henderson, Rickey H., Oakland, 1981.
    4-game Series—A. L.—4—Otis, Amos J., Kansas City, 1978.
                   N. L.—3—Lopes, David E., Los Angeles, 1974.
    5-game Series—N. L.—5—Lopes, David E., Los Angeles, 1981.
                   A. L.—3—Campaneris, Dagoberto B., Oakland, 1973.

Most Stolen Bases, Game

    N. L.—3—Morgan, Joe L., Cincinnati, October 4, 1975.
            Griffey, G. Kenneth, Cincinnati, October 5, 1975.
    A. L.—2—Held by many players.

Most Times Stealing Home, Game

    A. L.—1—Jackson, Reginald M., Oakland, October 12, 1972; second inning (front end of
            double steal).
    N. L.—Never accomplished.

Most Stolen Bases, Inning

    N. L.—2—Morgan, Joe L., Cincinnati, October 4, 1975; third inning.
            Griffey, G. Kenneth, Cincinnati, October 5, 1975; sixth inning.
    A. L.—2—Campaneris, Dagoberto B., Oakland, October 8, 1972; first inning.
            Jackson, Reginald M., Oakland, October 12, 1972; second inning.
             Beniquez, Juan J., Boston, October 4, 1975; seventh inning.

Most Caught Stealing, Total Series

    A. L.—6—McRae, Harold A., Kansas City, 1976, 1977, 1978, 1980, 1984; 1 stolen base.
    N. L.—3—Rose, Peter E., Cincinnati, 1970, 1972, 1973, 1975, 1976; Philadelphia, 1980,
            1983; 7 Series, 28 games, 1 stolen base.

Most Caught Stealing, Series

    3-game Series—A. L.—3—McRae, Harold A., Kansas City, 1980; 0 stolen bases.
                   N. L.—1—Held by many players.

4-game Series—A. L.— 2—Blair, Paul L., Baltimore, 1974; 0 stolen bases.
          Washington, Herbert L., Oakland, 1974; 0 stolen bases.
      N. L.—2—Rose, Peter E., Philadelphia, 1980; 0 stolen bases.
5-game Series—A. L.— 3—Patek, Freddie J., Kansas City, 1976; 0 stolen bases.
      N. L.—2—Rose, Peter E., Philadelphia, 1980; 0 stolen bases.

Most Caught Stealing, Game

A. L.—2—Robinson, Brooks C., Baltimore, October 4, 1969; 12 innings.
Nine-inning record—A. L.-N. L.—1—Held by many players.

Most Caught Stealing, Inning

A. L.-N. L.—1—Held by many players.

INDIVIDUAL PINCH-RUNNING

Most Games, Pinch-Runner, Total Series

Both Leagues—3—Bergman, David B., Houston N.L., 1980; Detroit A.L., 1984; 2 Series, 0
          runs.
A. L.—3—Odom, Johnny L., Oakland, 1972, 1974; 2 Series, 0 runs.
N. L.—3—Concepcion, David I., Cincinnati, 1970, 1972; 2 Series, 0 runs.

Most Games, Pinch-Runner, Series

A. L.—2—Lewis, Allan S., Oakland, 1973.
      Odom, Johnny L., Oakland, 1974.
      Washington, Herbert L., Oakland, 1974.
      Wilson, Willie J., Kansas City, 1978.
      Brown, R. L. Bobby, New York, 1981.
      Edwards, Marshall L., Milwaukee, 1982.
N. L.—2—Gaspar, Rodney E., New York, 1969.
      Jeter, Johnny, Pittsburgh, 1970.
      Concepcion, David I., Cincinnati, 1972.
      Landestoy, Rafael S.C., Houston, 1980.
      Smith, Lonnie, Philadelphia, 1980.

Most Runs, Pinch-Runner, Total Series

N. L.—2—Clines, Eugene A., Pittsburgh, 1972, 1974; 2 Series, 2 games.
      Landestoy, Rafael S.C., Houston, 1980; 1 Series, 2 games.
A. L.—2—Edwards, Marshall L., Milwaukee, 1982; 1 Series, 2 games.

Most Runs, Pinch-Runner, Series

N. L.—2—Landestoy, Rafael S.C., Houston, 1980; 2 games.
A. L.—2—Edwards, Marshall L., Milwaukee, 1982; 2 games.

Most Stolen Bases, Pinch-Runner, Game

A. L.—1—Edwards, Marshall L., Milwaukee, October 9, 1982.
N. L.—Never accomplished.

Most Caught Stealing, Pinch-Runner, Total Series

A. L.—2—Washington, Herbert L., Oakland, 1974; 1 Series, 2 games.
N. L.—Never accomplished.

Most Caught Stealing, Pinch-Runner, Series

A. L.—2—Washington, Herbert L., Oakland, 1974; 2 games.
N. L.—Never accomplished.

Most Caught Stealing, Pinch-Runner, Game

A. L.—1—Washington, Herbert L., Oakland, October 6, 8, 1974.
      Alomar, Santos, New York, October 14, 1976.
N. L.—Never accomplished.

CLUB BATTING

Highest Batting Average, Series, One Club

3-game Series—A. L.— .336—New York vs. Oakland, 1981.
          N. L.— .330—St. Louis vs. Atlanta, 1982.
4-game Series—A. L.— .300—New York vs. Kansas City, 1978.
          N. L.— .286—Los Angeles vs. Philadelphia, 1978.
5-game Series—A. L.— .316—New York vs. Kansas City, 1976.
          N. L.— .291—Philadelphia vs. Houston, 1980.

Highest Batting Average, Series, Both Clubs

3-game Series—N. L.—.292—New York .327, Atlanta .255, 1969.
           A. L.—.286—Baltimore .330, Minnesota .238, 1970.
4-game Series—A. L.—.282—New York .300, Kansas City .263, 1978.
           N. L.—.268—Los Angeles .286, Philadelphia .250, 1978.
5-game Series—A. L.—.283—New York .316, Kansas City .247, 1976.
           N. L.—.263—Philadelphia .291, Houston .233, 1980.

Highest Batting Average, Series, Championship Series Loser

3-game Series—N. L.—.270—Philadelphia vs. Cincinnati, 1976.
           A. L.—.255—New York vs. Kansas City, 1980.
4-game Series—N. L.—.250—Philadelphia vs. Los Angeles, 1978.
           A. L.—.263—Kansas City vs. New York, 1978.
5-game Series—A. L.—.258—Kansas City vs. New York, 1977.
           N. L.—.259—Chicago vs. San Diego, 1984.

Lowest Batting Average, Series, One Club

3-game Series—A. L.—.155—Minnesota vs. Baltimore, 1969.
           N. L.—.169—Atlanta vs. St. Louis, 1982.
4-game Series—A. L.—.177—Baltimore vs. Oakland, 1974.
           N. L.—.194—Pittsburgh vs. Los Angeles, 1974.
5-game Series—N. L.—.186—Cincinnati vs. New York, 1973.
           A. L.—.198—Detroit vs. Oakland, 1972.

Lowest Batting Average, Series, Both Clubs

3-game Series—A. L.—.202—Detroit .234, Kansas City .170, 1984.
           N. L.—.223—Pittsburgh .225, Cincinnati .220, 1970.
4-game Series—A. L.—.180—Oakland .183, Baltimore .177, 1974.
           N. L.—.232—Los Angeles .268, Pittsburgh .194, 1974.
5-game Series—A. L.—.205—Baltimore .211, Oakland .200, 1973.
           N. L.—.203—New York .220, Cincinnati .186, 1973.

Lowest Batting Average, Series, Championship Series Winner

3-game Series—N. L.—.220—Cincinnati vs. Pittsburgh, 1970.
           A. L.—.234—Detroit vs. Kansas City, 1984.
4-game Series—A. L.—.183—Oakland vs. Baltimore, 1974.
           N. L.—.262—Philadelphia vs. Los Angeles, 1983.
5-game Series—A. L.—.200—Oakland vs. Baltimore, 1973.
           N. L.—.220—New York vs. Cincinnati, 1973.

Highest Slugging Average, Series, One Club

3-game Series—N. L.—.575 —New York vs. Atlanta, 1969.
           A. L.—.560 —Baltimore vs. Minnesota, 1970.
4-game Series—N. L.—.544 —Los Angeles vs. Philadelphia, 1978.
           A. L.—.4436—Kansas City vs. New York, 1978.
                   .4428—New York vs. Kansas City, 1978.
5-game Series—N. L.—.494 —Chicago vs. San Diego, 1984.
           A. L.—.483 —New York vs. Kansas City, 1976.

Highest Slugging Average, Series, Both Clubs

3-game Series—N. L.—.530—New York .575, Atlanta .481, 1969.
           A. L.—.476—Baltimore .560, Minnesota .386, 1970.
4-game Series—N. L.—.477—Los Angeles .544, Philadelphia .407, 1978.
           A. L.—.443—Kansas City .4436, New York .4428, 1978.
5-game Series—A. L.—.429—New York .483, Kansas City .370, 1976.
           N. L.—.423—Chicago .494, San Diego .348, 1984.

Lowest Slugging Average, Series, One Club

3-game Series—N. L.—.180—Atlanta vs. St. Louis, 1982.
           A. L.—.198—Kansas City vs. Detroit, 1984.
4-game Series—A. L.—.241—Chicago vs. Baltimore, 1983.
           N. L.—.271—Pittsburgh vs. Los Angeles, 1974.
5-game Series—A. L.—.288—Oakland vs. Detroit, 1972.
           N. L.—.278—Montreal vs. Los Angeles, 1981.

Lowest Slugging Average, Series, Both Clubs

3-game Series—A. L.—.300—Detroit .402, Kansas City .198, 1984.
           N. L.—.318—St. Louis .437, Atlanta .180, 1982.
4-game Series—A. L.—.283—Oakland .308, Baltimore .258, 1974.
           N. L.—.339—Los Angeles .391, Philadelphia .290, 1977.
5-game Series—A. L.—.304—Detroit .321, Oakland .288, 1972.
           N. L.—.307—Cincinnati .311, New York .304, 1973.

Most At-Bats, Total Series, One Club
A. L.— 884— Baltimore, 7 Series, 26 games.
N. L.— 741— Cincinnati; 6 Series, 22 games.

Most At-Bats, Series, One Club
3-game Series—A. L.— 123—Baltimore vs. Minnesota, 1969.
              N. L.—113—New York vs. Atlanta, 1969.
4-game Series—N. L.—147—Los Angeles vs. Philadelphia, 1978.
              A. L.—140—New York vs. Kansas City, 1978.
5-game Series—N. L.—190—Philadelphia vs. Houston, 1980.
              A. L.—175—New York vs. Kansas City, 1977.

Most At-Bats, Series, Both Clubs
3-game Series—A. L.— 233—Baltimore 123, Minnesota 110, 1969.
              N. L.—219—New York 113, Atlanta 106, 1969.
4-game Series—N. L.—287—Los Angeles 147, Philadelphia 140, 1978.
              A. L.—273—New York 140, Kansas City 133, 1978.
5-game Series—N. L.—362—Philadelphia 190, Houston 172, 1980.
              A. L.—338—New York 175, Kansas City 163, 1977.

Fewest At-Bats, Series, One Club
3-game Series—N. L.— 89—Atlanta vs. St. Louis, 1982.
              A. L.— 95—Baltimore vs. Oakland, 1971.
4-game Series—A. L.—120—Oakland vs. Baltimore, 1974.
              N. L.—129—Pittsburgh vs. Los Angeles, 1974.
                           Los Angeles vs. Philadelphia, 1983.
5-game Series—A. L.—151—Milwaukee vs. California, 1982.
              N. L.—155—San Diego vs. Chicago, 1984.

Fewest At-Bats, Series, Both Clubs
3-game Series—A. L.—191—Oakland 96, Baltimore 95, 1971.
              N. L.—192—St. Louis 103, Atlanta 89, 1982.
4-game Series—A. L.—244—Baltimore 124, Oakland 120, 1974.
              N. L.—259—Philadelphia 130, Los Angeles 129, 1983.
5-game Series—A. L.—308—California 157, Milwaukee 151, 1982.
              N. L.—317—Chicago 162, San Diego 155, 1984.

Most At-Bats, Game, One Club
A. L.—44—Baltimore vs. Minnesota, October 6, 1969.
          Kansas City vs. Detroit, October 3, 1984; 11 innings.
N. L.—43—Houston vs. Philadelphia, October 12, 1980; 10 innings.
N. L.—Nine-inning record—42—New York vs. Atlanta, October 5, 1969.

Most At-Bats, Game, Nine Innings, Both Clubs
A. L.—80—Baltimore 44, Minnesota 36, October 6, 1969.
N. L.—77—New York 42, Atlanta 35, October 5, 1969.
          Los Angeles 39, Philadelphia 38, October 4, 1978.

Most At-Bats, Extra-Inning Game, Both Clubs
A. L.—85—Kansas City 44, Detroit 41, October 3, 1984; 11 innings.
N. L.—82—Houston 43, Philadelphia 39, October 12, 1980; 10 innings.

Fewest Official At-Bats, Game, One Club
N. L.—27—Cincinnati vs. New York, October 7, 1973.
          Pittsburgh vs. Los Angeles, October 9, 1974.
A. L.—25—California vs. Milwaukee, October 6, 1982; batted 8 innings.

Fewest Official At-Bats, Game, Both Clubs
A. L.—56—Kansas City 30, Detroit 26, October 5, 1984.
N. L.—58—Cincinnati 30, New York 28, October 6, 1973.
          New York 31, Cincinnati 27, October 7, 1973.
          Chicago 29, San Diego 29, October 3, 1984.

Most At-Bats, Inning, One Club
A. L.—10—New York vs. Oakland, October 14, 1981; fourth inning.
N. L.— 9—Chicago vs. San Diego, October 2, 1984; fifth inning.

Most At-Bats, Inning, Both Clubs
A. L.—16—New York 10, Oakland 6, October 14, 1981; fourth inning.
N. L.—15—Philadelphia 8, Houston 7, October 12, 1980; eighth inning.

Most Men Facing Pitcher, Inning, One Club
A. L.—12—New York vs. Oakland, October 14, 1981; fourth inning.
N. L.—12—Chicago vs. San Diego, October 2, 1984; fifth inning.

Most Men Facing Pitcher, Inning, Both Clubs

A. L.—19—New York 12, Oakland 7, October 14, 1981; fourth inning.
N. L.—17—Chicago 12, San Diego 5, October 2, 1984; fifth inning.

Most Runs, Total Series, One Club

A. L.— 125— Baltimore; 7 Series, 26 games.
N. L.— 86— Los Angeles; 5 Series, 21 games.

Most Runs, Series, One Club

3-game Series—A. L.— 27—Baltimore vs. Minnesota, 1970.
            N. L.—27—New York vs. Atlanta, 1969.
4-game Series—A. L.— 26—Baltimore vs. California, 1979.
            N. L.—24—Pittsburgh vs. San Francisco, 1971.
5-game Series—N. L.— 26—Chicago vs. San Diego, 1984.
            A. L.—24—Kansas City vs. New York, 1976.

Most Runs, Series, Both Clubs

3-game Series—N. L.—42—New York 27, Atlanta 15, 1969.
            A. L.—37—Baltimore 27, Minnesota 10, 1970.
4-game Series—A. L.—41—Baltimore 26, California 15, 1979.
            N. L.—39—Pittsburgh 24, San Francisco 15, 1971.
5-game Series—N. L.—48—Chicago 26, San Diego 22, 1984.
            A. L.—47—Kansas City 24, New York 23, 1976.

Most Runs, Series, Championship Series Loser

3-game Series—N. L.—15—Atlanta vs. New York, 1969.
            A. L.—10—Minnesota vs. Baltimore, 1970.
4-game Series—N. L.—17—Philadelphia vs. Los Angeles, 1978.
            A. L.—17—Kansas City vs. New York, 1978.
5-game Series—N. L.—26—Chicago vs. San Diego, 1984.
            A. L.—24—Kansas City vs. New York, 1976.

Fewest Runs, Series, One Club

3-game Series—N. L.— 3—Pittsburgh vs. Cincinnati, 1970.
            A. L.— 4—Oakland vs. New York, 1981.
                   Kansas City vs. Detroit, 1984.
4-game Series—A. L.— 3—Chicago vs. Baltimore, 1983.
            N. L.—10—Pittsburgh vs. Los Angeles, 1974.
5-game Series—N. L.— 8—Cincinnati vs. New York, 1973.
            A. L.—10—Detroit vs. Oakland, 1972.

Fewest Runs, Series, Both Clubs

3-game Series—N. L.—12—Cincinnati 9, Pittsburgh 3, 1970.
            A. L.—18—Detroit 14, Kansas City 4, 1984.
4-game Series—A. L.—18—Oakland 11, Baltimore 7, 1974.
            N. L.—30—Los Angeles 20, Pittsburgh 10, 1974.
5-game Series—A. L.—23—Oakland 13, Detroit 10, 1972.
            N. L.—25—Los Angeles 15, Montreal 10, 1981.

Most Runs, Game, One Club

A. L.—13—New York vs. Oakland, October 14, 1981.
N. L.—13—Chicago vs. San Diego, October 2, 1984.

Largest Score, Shutout Game

N. L.—Chicago 13, San Diego 0, October 2, 1984.
A. L.—Baltimore 8, California 0, October 6, 1979.

Most Earned Runs, Game, One Club

A. L.—13—New York vs. Oakland, October 14, 1981.
N. L.—12—Los Angeles vs. Pittsburgh, October 9, 1974.
        Chicago vs. San Diego, October 2, 1984.

Most Runs, Game, Both Clubs

N. L.—17—New York 11, Atlanta 6, October 5, 1969.
A. L.—17—Baltimore 9, California 8, October 4, 1979.

Most Players, One or More Runs, Game, One Club

A. L.—9—Baltimore vs. Minnesota, October 3, 1970.
      New York vs. Oakland, October 14, 1981
N. L.—8—New York vs. Atlanta, October 5, 1969.
      Chicago vs. San Diego, October 2, 1984.

Most Players, One or More Runs, Game, Both Clubs

A. L.—14—Baltimore 9, Minnesota 5, October 3, 1970.
           Baltimore 7, California 7, October 4, 1979.
N. L.—13—New York 8, Atlanta 5, October 5, 1969.

Most Innings Scored, Game, One Club

N. L.—6—New York vs. Atlanta, October 5, 1969.
         Los Angeles vs. Pittsburgh, October 9, 1974.
A. L.—6—Detroit vs. Kansas City, October 2, 1984.

Most Innings Scored, Game, Both Clubs

A. L.—8—New York 4, Kansas City 4, October 6, 1978.
         Calforinia 5, Baltimore 3, October 4, 1979.
N. L.—8—New York 6, Atlanta 2, October 5, 1969.
         Pittsburgh 5, San Francisco 3, October 3, 1971.
         Los Angeles 5, Philadelphia 3, October 4, 1978.

Most Runs, Inning, One Club

A. L.—7—Baltimore vs. Minnesota, October 3, 1970; fourth inning.
         Baltimore vs. Minnesota, October 4, 1970; ninth inning.
         New York vs. Oakland, October 14, 1981; fourth inning.
N. L.—6—Chicago vs. San Diego, October 2, 1984; fifth inning.

Most Runs, Inning, Both Clubs

A. L.—9—New York 7, Oakland 2, October 14, 1981; fourth inning.
N. L.—7—San Francisco 4, Pittsburgh 3, October 6, 1971; second inning.
         Philadelphia 5, Houston 2, October 12, 1980; eighth inning.

Most Runs, First Inning, One Club

N. L.—5—Pittsburgh vs. Los Angeles, October 8, 1974.
A. L.—4—Baltimore vs. Oakland, October 6, 1973.
         Baltimore vs. California, October 4, 1979.

Most Runs, Second Inning, One Club

N. L.—5—New York vs. Cincinnati, October 8, 1973.
A. L.—4—Kansas City vs. New York, October 4, 1978.
         Baltimore vs. California, October 4, 1979.

Most Runs, Third Inning, One Club

N. L.—4—Los Angeles vs. Philadelphia, October 4, 1978.
A. L.—4—California vs. Milwaukee, October 5, 1982.

Most Runs, Fourth Inning, One Club

A. L.—7—Baltimore vs. Minnesota, October 3, 1970.
         New York vs. Oakland, October 14, 1981.
N. L.—4—Los Angeles vs. Philadelphia, October 5, 1977.

Most Runs, Fifth Inning, One Club

N. L.—6—Chicago vs. San Diego, October 2, 1984.
A. L.—4—Oakland vs. Detroit, October 8, 1972.
         Baltimore vs. Oakland, October 5, 1974.

Most Runs, Sixth Inning, One Club

N. L.—5—St. Louis vs. Atlanta, October 7, 1982.
A. L.—3—New York vs. Kansas City, October 12, 1976.
         New York vs. Kansas City, October 6, 1977.

Most Runs, Seventh Inning, One Club

A. L.—5—Boston vs. Oakland, October 4, 1975.
         Baltimore vs. California, October 6, 1979.
N. L.—4—Pittsburgh vs. San Francisco, October 3, 1971.
         Cincinnati vs. Philadelphia, October 12, 1976.
         Los Angeles vs. Philadelphia, October 4, 1977.

Most Runs, Eighth Inning, One Club

N. L.—5—New York vs. Atlanta, October 4, 1969.
         Philadelphia vs. Houston, October 12, 1980.
A. L.—4—California vs. Milwaukee, October 9, 1982.

Most Runs, Ninth Inning, One Club

A. L.—7—Baltimore vs. Minnesota, October 4, 1970.
N. L.—4—New York vs. Cincinnati, October 7, 1973.
         Los Angeles vs. Montreal, October 17, 1981.

Most Runs, Tenth Inning, One Club

N. L.—4—Houston vs. Philadelphia, October 8, 1980.
A. L.—3—Detroit vs. Oakland, October 11, 1972.
    Baltimore vs. California, October 3, 1979.
    Baltimore vs. Chicago, October 8, 1983.

Most Runs, Eleventh Inning, One Club

N. L.—3—Pittsburgh vs. Cincinnati, October 2, 1979.
A. L.—2—Oakland vs. Detroit, October 7, 1972.
    Detroit vs. Kansas City, October 3, 1984.

Most Runs, Twelfth Inning, One Club

A. L.—1—Baltimore vs. Minnesota, October 4, 1969.
N. L.—1—Cincinnati vs. New York, October 9, 1973.

Most Runs, Extra Inning, One Club

N. L.—4—Houston vs. Philadelphia, October 8, 1980; tenth inning.
A. L.—3—Detroit vs. Oakland, October 11, 1972; tenth inning.
    Baltimore vs. California, October 3, 1979; tenth inning.
    Baltimore vs. Chicago, October 8, 1983; tenth inning.

Most Runs, Extra Inning, Both Clubs

A. L.—5—Detroit 3, Oakland 2, October 11, 1972; tenth inning.
N. L.—5—Houston 4, Philadelphia 1, October 8, 1980; tenth inning.

Most Hits, Total Series, One Club

A. L.— 221— Baltimore; 7 Series, 26 games.
N. L.— 182— Philadelphia; 5 Series, 20 games.

Most Hits, Series, One Club

3-game Series—N. L.—37—New York vs. Atlanta, 1969.
              A. L.— 36—Baltimore vs. Minnesota, 1969, 1970.
                     New York vs. Oakland, 1981.
4-game Series—N. L.—42—Los Angeles vs. Philadelphia, 1978.
              A. L.—42—New York vs. Kansas City, 1978.
5-game Series—A. L.— 55—New York vs. Kansas City, 1976.
              N. L.—55—Philadelphia vs. Houston, 1980.

Most Hits, Series, Both Clubs

3-game Series—N. L.—64—New York 37, Atlanta 27, 1969.
              A. L.—60—Baltimore 36, Minnesota 24, 1970.
4-game Series—N. L.— 77—Los Angeles 42, Philadelphia 35, 1978.
              A. L.— 77—New York 42, Kansas City 35, 1978.
5-game Series—A. L.— 95—New York 55, Kansas City 40, 1976.
              N. L.— 95—Philadelphia 55, Houston 40, 1980.

Fewest Hits, Series, One Club

3-game Series—N. L.—15—Atlanta vs. St. Louis, 1982.
              A. L.—17—Minnesota vs. Baltimore, 1969.
4-game Series—A. L.— 22—Baltimore vs. Oakland, 1974.
                     Oakland vs. Baltimore, 1974.
              N. L.—25—Pittsburgh vs. Los Angeles, 1974.
5-game Series—N. L.—30—Pittsburgh vs. Cincinnati, 1972.
              A. L.— 32—Detroit vs. Oakland, 1972.
                     Oakland vs. Baltimore, 1973.

Fewest Hits, Series, Both Clubs

3-game Series—A. L.— 43—Detroit 25, Kansas City 18, 1984.
              N. L.—45—Pittsburgh 23, Cincinnati 22, 1970.
4-game Series—A. L.—44—Baltimore 22, Oakland 22, 1974.
              N. L.—62—Los Angeles 37, Pittsburgh 25, 1974.
5-game Series—A. L.—68—Baltimore 36, Oakland 32, 1973.
              N. L.—68—New York 37, Cincinnati 31, 1973.

Most Hits, Game, One Club

A. L.—19—New York vs. Oakland, October 14, 1981.
N. L.—16—Chicago vs. San Diego, October 2, 1984.

Most Hits, Game, Both Clubs

A. L.—30—New York 19, Oakland 10, October 14, 1981.
N. L.—27—Houston 14, Philadelphia 13, October 12, 1980; 10 innings.
N. L.—Nine-inning record—25—Los Angeles 13, Philadelphia 12, October 4, 1978.

Fewest Hits, Game, One Club

A. L.—1—Oakland vs. Baltimore, October 9, 1974.
N. L.—2—Pittsburgh vs. Cincinnati, October 10, 1972.
        Cincinnati vs. New York, October 7, 1973.

Fewest Hits, Game, Both Clubs

A. L.—6—Oakand 4, Baltimore 2, October 8, 1974.
        Baltimore 5, Oakland 1, October 9, 1974.
        Detroit 3, Kansas City 3, October 5, 1984.
N. L.—9—San Francisco 5, Pittsburgh 4, October 5, 1971.
        Cincinnati 6, New York 3, October 6, 1973.
        New York 7, Cincinnati 2, October 7, 1973.
        Los Angeles 6, Montreal 3, October 19, 1981.

Most Players, One or More Hits, Game, One Club

N. L.—11—Chicago vs. San Diego, October 2, 1984.
A. L.—10—New York vs. Oakland, October 14, 1981

Most Players, One or More Hits, Game, Both Clubs

A. L.—18—New York 10, Oakland 8, October 14, 1981.
N. L.—16—Los Angeles 8, Philadelphia 8, October 4, 1978.
        Houston 8, Philadelphia 8, October 12, 1980; 10 innings.

Most Hits, Inning, One Club

A. L.—7—Baltimore vs. Minnesota, October 3, 1970; fourth inning.
        New York vs. Oakland, October 14, 1981; fourth inning.
N. L.—6—St. Louis vs. Atlanta, October 7, 1982; sixth inning.
        Chicago vs. San Diego, October 2, 1984.

Most Hits, Inning, Both Clubs

A. L.—11—New York 7, Oakland 4, October 14, 1981; fourth inning.
N. L.— 9—Philadelphia 5, Houston 4, October 12, 1980; eighth inning.

Most Consecutive Hits, Inning, One Club (Consecutive at-bats)

A. L.—7—Baltimore vs. Minnesota, October 3, 1970; fourth inning; sacrifice fly during
        streak.
N. L.—6—St. Louis vs. Atlanta, October 7, 1982; sixth inning; walk during streak.

Most Consecutive Hits, Inning, One Club (Consecutive plate appearances)

N. L.—5—Cincinnati vs. Pittsburgh, October 8, 1972; first inning.
        Los Angeles vs. Pittsburgh, October 6, 1974; eighth inning.
A. L.—5—New York vs. Oakland, October 14, 1981; fourth inning.

Most One-Base Hits, Total Series, One Club

A. L.— 148— Baltimore; 7 Series, 26 games.
N. L.— 138— Philadelphia; 5 Series, 20 games.

Most One-Base Hits, Series, One Club

3-game Series—A. L.— 29—New York vs. Oakland, 1981.
              N. L.—27—St. Louis vs. Atlanta, 1982.
4-game Series—A. L.— 33—New York vs. Kansas City, 1978.
              N. L.—27—Pittsburgh vs. San Francisco, 1971.
5-game Series—N. L.—45—Philadelphia vs. Houston, 1980.
              A. L.—36—New York vs. Kansas City, 1976.

Most One-Base Hits, Series, Both Clubs

3-game Series—A. L.— 46—New York 29, Oakland 17, 1981.
              N. L.—41—St. Louis 27, Atlanta 14, 1982.
4-game Series—A. L.— 55—New York 33, Kansas City 22, 1978.
              N. L.—51—Philadelphia 26, Los Angeles 25, 1977.
5-game Series—N. L.—73—Philadelphia 45, Houston 28, 1980.
              A. L.—64—New York 36, Kansas City 28, 1976.

Fewest One-Base Hits, Series, One Club

3-game Series—A. L.— 10—Oakand vs. Baltimore, 1971.
              N. L.—13—Atlanta vs. New York, 1969.
4-game Series—A. L.— 14—Oakland vs. Baltimore, 1974.
              N. L.—19—Los Angeles vs. Philadelphia, 1983.
5-game Series—N. L.—20—Pittsburgh vs. Cincinnati, 1972.
              Cincinnati vs. New York, 1973.
              A. L.—21—Detroit vs. Oakland, 1972.
              Oakland vs. Baltimore, 1973.

Fewest One-Base Hits, Series, Both Clubs

3-game Series—A. L.— 24—Baltimore 14, Oakland 10, 1971.
             N. L.—31—Philadelphia 17, Cincinnati 14, 1976.
4-game Series—A. L.— 32—Baltimore 18, Oakland 14, 1974.
             N. L.—44—Philadelphia 25, Los Angeles 19, 1983.
5-game Series—A. L.— 47—Baltimore 26, Oakland 21, 1973.
             N. L.—47—Cincinnati 27, Pittsburgh 20, 1972.

Most One-Base Hits, Game, One Club

A. L.—15—New York vs. Oakland, October 14, 1981.
N. L.—12—Philadelphia vs. Houston, October 8, 1980; 10 innings.
N. L.—Nine-inning record—11—St. Louis vs. Atlanta, October 7, 1982.

Most One-Base Hits, Game, Both Clubs

A. L.—25—Kansas City 13, New York 12, October 4, 1978.
N. L.—17—Los Angeles 9, Pittsburgh 8, October 6, 1974.
        Philadelphia 12, Houston 5, October 8, 1980; 10 innings.

Fewest One-Base Hits, Game, One Club

A. L.—0—Oakland vs. Baltimore, October 9, 1974.
N. L.—1—Pittsburgh vs. Cincinnati, October 10, 1972.
     Montreal vs. Los Angeles, October 19, 1981.

Fewest One-Base Hits, Game, Both Clubs

N. L.—4—New York 2, Cincinnati 2, October 6, 1973.
A. L.—5—Oakland 3, Baltimore 2, October 9, 1973; 11 innings.
     Oakland 3, Baltimore 2, October 8, 1974.
     Baltimore 5, Oakland 0, October 9, 1974.

Most One-Base Hits, Inning, One Club

N. L.—6—St. Louis vs. Atlanta, October 7, 1982; sixth inning.
A. L.—5—Kansas City vs. New York, October 4, 1978; second inning.
     New York vs. Oakland, October 14, 1981; fourth inning.

Most One-Base Hits, Inning, Both Clubs

A. L.—9—New York 5, Oakland 4, October 14, 1981; fourth inning.
N. L.—8—Philadelphia 4, Houston 4, October 12, 1980; eighth inning.

Most Two-Base Hits, Total Series, One Club

A. L.—40—New York; 5 Series, 20 games.
N. L.—31—Cincinnati; 6 Series, 22 games.

Most Two-Base Hits, Series, One Club

3-game Series—N. L.— 9—Atlanta vs. New York, 1969.
             A. L.— 8—Baltimore vs. Minnesota, 1969.
                  Oakland vs. Baltimore, 1971.
                  Boston vs. Oakland, 1975.
4-game Series—A. L.— 9—Baltimore vs. Chicago, 1983.
             N. L.— 8—Los Angeles vs. Pittsburgh, 1974.
                  Los Angeles vs. Philadelphia, 1978.
5-game Series—A. L.—13—New York vs. Kansas City, 1976.
             N. L.—11—Chicago vs. San Diego, 1984.

Most Two-Base Hits, Series, Both Clubs

3-game Series—N. L.—17—Atlanta 9, New York 8, 1969.
             A. L.—15—Oakland 8, Baltimore 7, 1971.
4-game Series—A. L.—13—Baltimore 9, Chicago 4, 1983.
             N. L.—11—Los Angeles 8, Philadelphia 3, 1978.
5-game Series—A. L.—21—New York 12, Kansas City 9, 1977.
             N. L.—16—Chicago 11, San Diego 5, 1984.

Fewest Two-Base Hits, Series, One Club

3-game Series—N. L.— 1—Atlanta vs. St. Louis, 1982.
             A. L.— 1—Kansas City vs. Detroit, 1984.
4-game Series—A. L.— 1—Baltimore vs. Oakland, 1974.
             N. L.— 1—Pittsburgh vs. Los Angeles, 1974.
5-game Series—N. L.— 3—Los Angeles vs. Montreal, 1981.
             A. L.— 4—Milwaukee vs. California, 1982.

Fewest Two-Base Hits, Series, Both Clubs

3-game Series—N. L.— 5—St. Louis 4, Atlanta 1, 1982.
             A. L.— 5—Detroit 4, Kansas City 1, 1984.
4-game Series—A. L.— 5—Oakland 4, Baltimore 1, 1974.

N. L.— 9—San Francisco 5, Pittsburgh 4, 1971.
            Los Angeles 8, Pittsburgh 1, 1974.
            Los Angeles 6, Philadelphia 3, 1977.
            Los Angeles 5, Philadelphia 4, 1983.
5-game Series—N. L.—10—Montreal 7, Los Angeles 3, 1981.
            A. L.—12—Baltimore 7, Oakland 5, 1973.
            California 8, Milwaukee 4, 1982.

Most Two-Base Hits, Game, One Club

A. L.—6—Baltimore vs. Minnesota, October 6, 1969.
N. L.—6—Philadelphia vs. Cincinnati, October 12, 1976.

Most Two-Base Hits, Game, Both Clubs

A. L.—9—Oakland 5, Baltimore 4, October 3, 1971.
N. L.—7—Cincinnati 5, Philadelphia 2, October 9, 1976.

Most Two-Base Hits, Inning, One Club

A. L.—3—Oakland vs. Baltimore, October 10, 1973; second inning.
            Boston vs. Oakland, October 4, 1975; seventh inning.
N. L.—3—Atlanta vs. New York, October 4, 1969; third inning, consecutive.
            Cincinnati vs. Pittsburgh, October 8, 1972; first inning, consecutive.
            Cincinnati vs. Philadelphia, October 9, 1976; eighth inning.

Most Three-Base Hits, Total Series, One Club

A. L.—12—Kansas City; 5 Series, 20 games.
N. L.— 7—Cincinnati; 6 Series, 22 games.
            Los Angeles; 5 Series, 21 games.

Most Three-Base Hits, Series, One Club

3-game Series—N. L.—3—Cincinnati vs. Philadelphia, 1976.
            A. L.—1—Held by many clubs.
4-game Series—A. L.— 3—Kansas City vs. New York, 1978.
            N. L.—3—Los Angeles vs. Philadelphia, 1978.
5-game Series—N. L.—5—Houston vs. Philadelphia, 1980.
            A. L.— 4—Kansas City vs. New York, 1976.

Most Three-Base Hits, Series, Both Clubs

3-game Series—N. L.—4—Cincinnati 3, Philadelphia 1, 1976.
            A. L.— 2—Baltimore 1, Minnesota 1, 1969.
            Baltimore 1, Oakland 1, 1971.
            Kansas City 1, New York 1, 1980.
4-game Series—N. L.—5—Los Angeles 3, Philadelphia 2, 1978.
            A. L.— 4—Kansas City 3, New York 1, 1978.
5-game Series—A. L.— 6—Kansas City 4, New York 2, 1976.
            N. L.—6—Houston 5, Philadelphia 1, 1980.

Fewest Three-Base Hits, Series, One Club

A. L.-N. L.—0—Held by many clubs in Series of all lengths.

Fewest Three-Base Hits, Series, Both Clubs

3-game Series—N. L.—0—Cincinnati 0, Pittsburgh 0, 1975.
            A. L.— 0—Boston 0, Oakland 0, 1975.
4-game Series—N. L.—0—Pittsburgh 0, San Francisco 0, 1971.
            A. L.—0—Baltimore 0, Chicago 0, 1983.
5-game Series—N. L.—0—Cincinnati 0, New York 0, 1973.
            A. L.—1—Detroit 1, Oakland 0, 1972.
            Oakland 1, Baltimore 0, 1973.
            California 1, Milwaukee 0, 1982.

Most Three-Base Hits, Game, One Club

A. L.—2—Kansas City vs. New York, October 13, 1976.
            Kansas City vs. New York, October 8, 1977.
N. L.—2—Cincinnati vs. Philadelphia, October 9, 1976.
            Los Angeles vs. Philadelphia, October 4, 1978.
            Houston vs. Philadelphia, October 10, 1980; 11 innings.

Most Three-Base Hits, Game, Both Clubs

N. L.—3—Los Angeles 2, Philadelphia 1, October 4, 1978.
A. L.—2—Baltimore 1, Minnesota 1, October 6, 1969.
            Kansas City 1, New York 1, October 9, 1976.
            Kansas City 2, New York 0, October 13, 1976.
            Kansas City 2, New York 0, October 8, 1977.
            Detroit 1, Kansas City 1, October 2, 1984.

Most Three-Base Hits, Inning, One Club

A. L.—2—Kansas City vs. New York, October 8, 1977; third inning.
N. L.—1—Held by many clubs.

Most Home Runs, Total Series, One Club

A. L.—26—Baltimore; 7 Series, 26 games.
N. L.—21—Cincinnati; 6 Series, 22 games.

Most Home Runs, Series, One Club

3-game Series—N. L.— 6—New York vs. Atlanta, 1969.
              A. L.— 6—Baltimore vs. Minnesota, 1970.
4-game Series—N. L.— 8—Pittsburgh vs. San Francisco, 1971.
                      Los Angeles vs. Philadelphia, 1978.
              A. L.— 5—New York vs. Kansas City, 1978.
5-game Series—N. L.— 9—Chicago vs. San Diego, 1984.
              A. L.— 5—Oakland vs. Baltimore, 1973.
                      Milwaukee vs. California, 1982.

Most Home Runs, Series, Both Clubs

3-game Series—N. L.—11—New York 6, Atlanta 5, 1969.
             A.L.— 9—Baltimore 6, Minnesota 3, 1970.
4-game Series—N. L.—13—Pittsburgh 8, San Francisco 5, 1971.
                     Los Angeles 8, Philadelphia 5, 1978.
              A. L.— 9—New York 5, Kansas City 4, 1978.
5-game Series—N.L.— 11—Chicago 9, San Diego 2, 1984.
             A. L.— 9—Milwaukee 5, California 4, 1982.

Fewest Home Runs, Series, One Club

3-game Series—N. L.— 0—Pittsburgh vs. Cincinnati, 1970.
                      Atlanta vs. St. Louis, 1982.
              A. L.— 0—Oakland vs. New York, 1981.
                      Kansas City vs. Detroit, 1984.
4-game Series—N. L.— 2—Philadelphia vs. Los Angeles, 1977.
              A. L.— 0—Chicago vs. Baltimore, 1983.
5-game Series—N. L.— 0—Houston vs. Philadelphia, 1980.
              A. L.— 1—Oakland vs. Detroit, 1972.

Fewest Home Runs, Series, Both Clubs

3-game Series—N. L.— 1—St. Louis 1, Atlanta 0, 1982.
              A. L.— 2—New York 2, Oakland 0, 1981.
4-game Series—A. L.— 3—Baltimore 3, Chicago 0, 1983.
              N. L.— 5—Los Angeles 3, Philadelphia 2, 1977.
5-game Series—N. L.— 1—Philadelphia 1, Houston 0, 1980.
              A. L.— 5—Detroit 4, Oakland 1, 1972.
                      Kansas City 3, New York 2, 1977.

Most Consecutive Games, Total Series, One or More Home Runs

N. L.—6—Los Angeles, last game vs. Philadelphia, 1977 (1 home run), all four games vs.
      Philadelphia, 1978 (8 home runs), first game vs. Montreal, 1981 (2 home
      runs).
A. L.—5—New York, last three games vs. Kansas City, 1976 (4 home runs), first two
      games vs. Kansas City, 1977 (2 home runs).
      Milwaukee, all five games vs. California, 1982 (5 home runs).

Most Consecutive Games, Series, One or More Home Runs

A. L.—5—Milwaukee vs. California, October 5, 6, 8, 9, 10, 1982; 5 home runs.
N. L.—4—Los Angeles vs. Philadelphia, October 4, 5, 6, 7, 1978; 8 home runs.
      Philadelphia vs. Los Angeles, October 4, 5, 7, 8, 1983; 5 home runs.

Most Home Runs With Bases Filled, Total Series, One Club

N. L.—2—Los Angeles; 3 Series, 12 games.
A. L.—1—Baltimore; 7 Series, 26 games.
      California; 2 Series, 9 games.

Most Home Runs With Bases Filled, Series, One Club

N. L.—2—Los Angeles vs. Philadelphia, 1977.
A. L.—1—Baltimore vs. Minnesota, 1970.
      California vs. Milwaukee, 1982.

Most Home Runs, Game, One Club

N. L.—5—Chicago vs. San Diego, October 2, 1984.
A. L.—4—Baltimore vs. Oakland, October 4, 1971.
      Oakland vs. Baltimore, October 7, 1973.

Most Home Runs, Game, Both Clubs

A. L.—5—Kansas City 3, New York 2, October 6, 1978.
N. L.—5—New York 3, Atlanta 2, October 6, 1969.
      Pittsburgh 4, San Francisco 1, October 3, 1971.
      Los Angeles 4, Philadelphia 1, October 4, 1978.
      Chicago 5, San Diego 0, October 2, 1984.

Most Home Runs, Inning, One Club

   A. L.—3—Baltimore vs. Minnesota, October 3, 1970; fourth inning (first 2 consecutive).
   N. L.—2—Cincinnati vs. Pittsburgh, October 5, 1970; first inning (consecutive).
       San Francisco vs. Pittsburgh, October 2, 1971; fifth inning.
       San Francisco vs. Pittsburgh, October 6, 1971; second inning.
       Pittsburgh vs. Los Angeles, October 8, 1974; first inning.
       Cincinnati vs. Philadelphia, October 12, 1976; ninth inning (consecutive).
       Pittsburgh vs. Cincinnati, October 5, 1979; third inning.
       Los Angeles vs. Montreal, October 13, 1981, eighth inning (consecutive).
       Chicago vs. San Diego, October 2, 1984; first inning.
       Chicago vs. San Diego, October 6, 1984; fourth inning (consecutive).

Most Home Runs, Inning, Both Clubs

   A. L.—3—Baltimore 3, Minnesota 0, October 3, 1970, fourth inning.
   N. L.—3—San Francisco 2, Pittsburgh 1, October 6, 1971, second inning.

Most Consecutive Home Runs, Inning, One Club

   A. L.—2—Baltimore (Cuellar and Buford) vs. Minnesota, October 3, 1970; fourth inning.
       Minnesota (Killebrew and Oliva) vs. Baltimore, October 4, 1970; fourth inning.
       Oakland (Rudi and Bando) vs. Baltimore, October 7, 1973; sixth inning.
       New York (Cerone and Piniella) vs. Kansas City, October 8, 1980; second inning.
   N. L.—2—Cincinnati (Perez and Bench) vs. Pittsburgh, October 5, 1970; first inning.
       Cincinnati (Foster and Bench) vs. Philadelphia, October 12, 1976; ninth inning.
       Los Angeles (Guerrero and Scioscia) vs. Montreal, October 13, 1981; eighth inning.
       Chicago (Davis and Durham) vs. San Diego, October 6, 1984; fourth inning.

Most Long Hits, Total Series, One Club

   A. L.—73—Baltimore; 7 Series, 26 games.
   N. L.—59—Cincinnati; 6 Series, 22 games.

Most Long Hits, Series, One Club

   3-game Series—N. L.—15—New York vs. Atlanta, 1969.
              A. L.—13—Baltimore vs. Minnesota, 1969, 1970.
   4-game Series—N. L.—19—Los Angeles vs. Philadelphia, 1978.
              A. L.—13—Kansas City vs. New York, 1978.
   5-game Series—N. L.—20—Chicago vs. San Diego, 1984.
              A. L.—19—New York vs. Kansas City, 1976.

Most Long Hits, Series, Both Clubs

   3-game Series—N. L.—29—New York 15, Atlanta 14, 1969.
              A. L.—24—Baltimore 12, Oakland 12, 1971.
   4-game Series—N. L.—29—Los Angeles 19, Philadelphia 10, 1978.
              A. L.—22—Kansas City 13, New York 9, 1978.
   5-game Series—A. L.—31—New York 19, Kansas City 12, 1976.
              N. L.—28—Chicago 20, San Diego 8, 1984.

Fewest Long Hits, Series, One Club

   3-game Series—N. L.—1—Atlanta vs. St. Louis, 1982.
              A. L.—2—Kansas City vs. Detroit, 1984.
   4-game Series—N. L.—4—Pittsburgh vs. Los Angeles, 1974.
              A. L.—4—Baltimore vs. Oakland, 1974.
                    Chicago vs. Baltimore, 1983.
   5-game Series—N. L.—8—New York vs. Cincinnati, 1973.
                    Los Angeles vs. Montreal, 1981.
                    Montreal vs. Los Angeles, 1981.
                    San Diego vs. Chicago, 1984.
              A. L.—9—Oakland vs. Detroit, 1972.

Fewest Long Hits, Series, Both Clubs

   3-game Series—N. L.—8—St. Louis 7, Atlanta 1, 1982.
              A. L.—11—Detroit 9, Kansas City 2, 1984.
   4-game Series—A. L.—12—Oakland 8, Baltimore 4, 1974.
              N. L.—15—Los Angeles 10, Philadelphia 5, 1977.
   5-game Series—N. L.—16—Los Angeles 8, Montreal 8, 1981.
              A. L.—20—Detroit 11, Oakland 9, 1972.

Most Long Hits, Game, One Club

   A. L.—8—Baltimore vs. Minnesota, October 6, 1969; 6 doubles, 1 triple, 1 home run.
   N. L.—8—Cincinnati vs. Philadelphia, October 9, 1976; 5 doubles, 2 triples, 1 home run.
       Chicago vs. San Diego, October 2, 1984; 3 doubles, 5 home runs.

Most Long Hits, Game, Both Clubs

A. L.—12—Oakland 6 (5 doubles, 1 home run), Boston 6 (4 doubles, 2 home runs), October 5, 1975.

N. L.—11—New York 7 (4 doubles, 3 home runs), Atlanta 4 (2 doubles, 2 home runs), October 6, 1969.

Most Extra Bases on Long Hits, Total Series, One Club

A. L.— 128— Baltimore; 7 Series, 26 games (44 on doubles, 6 on triples, 78 on home runs).

N. L.— 108— Cincinnati; 6 Series, 22 games (31 on doubles, 14 on triples, 63 on home runs).

Most Extra Bases on Long Hits, Series, One Club

3-game Series—N. L.—28—New York vs. Atlanta, 1969.
              A. L.—25—Baltimore vs. Minnesota, 1970.
4-game Series—N. L.—38—Los Angeles vs. Philadelphia, 1978.
              A. L.—24—Kansas City vs. New York, 1978.
5-game Series—N. L.—38—Chicago vs. San Diego, 1984.
              A. L.—29—New York vs. Kansas City, 1976.

Most Extra Bases on Long Hits, Series, Both Clubs

3-game Series—N. L.—52—New York 28, Atlanta 24, 1969.
              A. L.—40—Baltimore 25, Minnesota 15, 1970.
                       Baltimore 21, Oakland 19, 1971.
4-game Series—N. L.—60—Los Angeles 38, Philadelphia 22, 1978.
              A. L.—44—Kansas City 24, New York 20, 1978.
5-game Series—N. L.—51—Chicago 38, San Diego 13, 1984.
              A. L.—49—New York 29, Kansas City 20, 1976.

Fewest Extra Bases on Long Hits, Series, One Club

3-game Series—N. L.— 1—Atlanta vs. St. Louis, 1982.
              A. L.— 3—Kansas City vs. Detroit, 1984.
4-game Series—A. L.— 4—Chicago vs. Baltimore, 1983.
              N. L.— 9—Philadelphia vs. Los Angeles, 1977.
5-game Series—N. L.—10—Montreal vs. Los Angeles, 1981.
              A. L.—11—Oakland vs. Detroit, 1972.

Fewest Extra Bases on Long Hits, Series, Both Clubs

3-game Series—N. L.—12—St. Louis 11, Atlanta 1, 1982.
              A. L.—17—New York 11, Oakland 6, 1981.
4-game Series—A. L.—22—Baltimore 18, Chicago 4, 1983.
              N. L.—26—Los Angeles 17, Philadelphia 9, 1977.
5-game Series—N. L.—27—Los Angeles 17, Montreal 10, 1981.
              A. L.—31—Detroit 20, Oakland 11, 1972.

Most Total Bases, Total Series, One Club

A. L.— 349— Baltimore; 7 Series, 26 games.

N. L.— 283— Los Angeles; 5 Series, 21 games.

Most Total Bases, Series, One Club

3-game Series—N. L.—65—New York vs. Atlanta, 1969.
              A. L.—61—Baltimore vs. Minnesota, 1970.
4-game Series—N. L.—80—Los Angeles vs. Philadelphia, 1978.
               A. L.—62—New York vs. Kansas City, 1978.
5-game Series—A. L.—84—New York vs. Kansas City, 1976.
              N. L.—80—Chicago vs. San Diego, 1984.

Most Total Bases, Series, Both Clubs

3-game Series—N. L.— 116—New York 65, Atlanta 51, 1969.
              A. L.— 100—Baltimore 61, Minnesota 39, 1970.
4-game Series—N. L.—137—Los Angeles 80, Philadelphia 57, 1978.
              A. L.—121—New York 62, Kansas City 59, 1978.
5-game Series—A. L.— 144—New York 84, Kansas City 60, 1976.
              N. L—134—Chicago 80, San Diego 54, 1984.

Fewest Total Bases, Series, One Club

3-game Series—N. L.—16—Atlanta vs. St. Louis, 1982.
              A. L.—21—Kansas City vs. Detroit, 1984.
4-game Series—A. L.—32—Baltimore vs. Oakland, 1974.
                       Chicago vs. Baltimore, 1983.
              N. L.—35—Pittsburgh vs. Los Angeles, 1974.
5-game Series—N. L.—44—Montreal vs. Los Angeles, 1981.
              A. L.—49—Oakland vs. Detroit, 1972.

Fewest Total Bases, Series, Both Clubs

3-game Series—N. L.— 61—St. Louis 45, Atlanta 16, 1982.
                     A. L.— 64—Detroit 43, Kansas City 21, 1984.
4-game Series—A. L.— 69—Oakland 37, Baltimore 32, 1974.
                     N. L.— 91—Los Angeles 56, Pittsburgh 35, 1974.
5-game Series—N. L.— 99—Los Angeles 55, Montreal 44, 1981.
                     A. L.—101—Detroit 52, Oakland 49, 1972.

Most Total Bases, Game, One Club

N. L.—34—Chicago vs. San Diego, October 2, 1984.
A. L.—29—Baltimore vs. Minnesota, October 6, 1969.

Most Total Bases, Game, Both Clubs

N. L.—47—Los Angeles 30, Philadelphia 17, October 4, 1978.
A. L.—43—Baltimore 29, Minnesota 14, October 6, 1969.

Fewest Total Bases, Game, One Club

N. L.—2—Cincinnati vs. New York, October 7, 1973.
A. L.—2—Baltimore vs. Oakland, October 8, 1974.
          Oakland vs. Baltimore, October 9, 1974.

Fewest Total Bases, Game, Both Clubs

A. L.— 6—Detroit 3, Kansas City 3, October 5, 1984.
N. L.—12—New York 10, Cincinnati 2, October 7, 1973.

Most Total Bases, Inning, One Club

A. L.—16—Baltimore vs. Minnesota, October 3, 1970; fourth inning.
N. L.—11—San Francisco vs. Pittsburgh, October 6, 1971; second inning.

Most Total Bases, Inning, Both Clubs

A. L.—18—Baltimore 16, Minnesota 2, October 3, 1970; fourth inning.
N. L.—17—San Francisco 11, Pittsburgh 6, October 6, 1971; second inning.

Most Runs Batted In, Total Series, One Club

A. L.— 117— Baltimore; 7 Series, 26 games.
N. L.— 82— Los Angeles; 5 Series, 21 games.

Most Runs Batted In, Series, One Club

3-game Series—A. L.— 24—Baltimore vs. Minnesota, 1970.
               N. L.— 24—New York vs. Atlanta, 1969.
4-game Series—A. L.— 25—Baltimore vs. California, 1979.
               N. L.— 23—Pittsburgh vs. San Francisco, 1971.
5-game Series—N. L.— 25—Chicago vs. San Diego, 1984.
               A. L.— 24—Kansas City vs. New York, 1976.

Most Runs Batted In, Series, Both Clubs

3-game Series—N. L.— 39—New York 24, Atlanta 15, 1969.
               A. L.— 34—Baltimore 24, Minnesota 10, 1970.
4-game Series—A. L.— 39—Baltimore 25, California 14, 1979.
               N. L.— 37—Pittsburgh 23, San Francisco 14, 1971.
                         Los Angeles 21, Philadelphia 16, 1978.
5-game Series—A. L.— 45—Kansas City 24, New York 21, 1976.
               N. L.— 45—Chicago 25, San Diego 20, 1984.

Fewest Runs Batted In, Series, One Club

3-game Series—N. L.— 3—Pittsburgh vs. Cincinnati, 1970.
                         Atlanta vs. St. Louis, 1982.
               A. L.— 4—Oakland vs. New York, 1981.
                         Kansas City vs. Detroit, 1984.
4-game Series—A. L.— 2—Chicago vs. Baltimore, 1983.
               N. L.— 7—Los Angeles vs. Philadelphia, 1983.
5-game Series—N. L.— 8—Cincinnati vs. New York, 1973.
                         Montreal vs. Los Angeles, 1981.
               A. L.—10—Oakland vs. Detroit, 1972.
                         Detroit vs. Oakland, 1972.

Fewest Runs Batted In, Series, Both Clubs

3-game Series—N. L.—11—Cincinnati 8, Pittsburgh 3, 1970.
               A. L.—18—Detroit 14, Kansas City 4, 1984.
4-game Series—A. L.—18—Oakland 11, Baltimore 7, 1974.
               N. L.—22—Philadelphia 15, Los Angeles 7, 1983.
5-game Series—A. L.—20—Oakland 10, Detroit 10, 1972.
               N. L.—23—Los Angeles 15, Montreal 8, 1981.

Most Runs Batted In, Game, One Club

A. L.—13—New York vs. Oakland, October 14, 1981.
N. L.—12—Chicago vs. San Diego, October 2, 1984.

Most Runs Batted In, Game, Both Clubs

N. L.—17—New York 11, Atlanta 6, October 5, 1969.
A. L.—16—Baltimore 8, California 8, October 4, 1979.
　　　　　New York 13, Oakland 3, 1981.

Most Runs Batted In, Inning, One Club

A. L.—7—Baltimore vs. Minnesota, October 3, 1970; fourth inning.
　　　　　New York vs. Oakland, October 14, 1981; fourth inning.
N. L.—6—Chicago vs. San Diego, October 2, 1984; fifth inning.

Most Runs Batted In, Inning, Both Clubs

A. L.—9—New York 7, Oakland 2, October 14, 1981; fourth inning.
N. L.—7—San Francisco 4, Pittsburgh 3, October 6, 1971; second inning.
　　　　　Philadelphia 5, Houston 2, October 12, 1980; eighth inning.

Fewest Runs Batted In, Game, Both Clubs

A. L.—1—Baltimore 1, Minnesota 0, October 5, 1969; 11 innings.
　　　　　Oakland 1, Baltimore 0, October 8, 1974.
　　　　　Detroit 1, Kansas City 0, October 5, 1984.
N. L.—1—Houston 1, Philadelphia 0, October 10, 1980; 11 innings.
　　　　　Philadelphia 1, Los Angeles 0, October 4, 1983.

Most Bases on Balls, Total Series, One Club

A. L.—93—Baltimore; 7 Series, 26 games.
N. L.—76—Los Angeles; 5 Series, 21 games.

Most Bases on Balls, Series, One Club

3-game Series—N. L.—15—Cincinnati vs. Philadelphia, 1976.
　　　　　　　A. L.—13—Baltimore vs. Minnesota, 1969.
　　　　　　　　　　　　Baltimore vs. Oakland, 1971.
4-game Series—N. L.—30—Los Angeles vs. Pittsburgh, 1974.
　　　　　　　A. L.—22—Oakland vs. Baltimore, 1974.
5-game Series—N. L.—31—Houston vs. Philadelphia, 1980.
　　　　　　　A. L.—17—Oakland vs. Baltimore, 1973.

Most Bases on Balls, Series, Both Clubs

3-game Series—N. L.—27—Cincinnati 15, Philadelphia 12, 1976.
　　　　　　　A. L.—25—Baltimore 13, Minnesota 12, 1969.
4-game Series—N. L.—38—Los Angeles 30, Pittsburgh 8, 1974.
　　　　　　　A. L.—28—Baltimore 16, Chicago 12, 1983.
5-game Series—N. L.—44—Houston 31, Philadelphia 13, 1980.
　　　　　　　A. L.—33—Oakland 17, Baltimore 16, 1973.

Fewest Bases on Balls, Series, One Club

3-game Series—A. L.— 3—Boston vs. Oakland, 1975.
　　　　　　　N. L.— 6—Atlanta vs. St. Louis, 1982.
4-game Series—A. L.— 5—Baltimore vs. Oakland, 1974.
　　　　　　　N. L.— 5—Pittsburgh vs. San Francisco, 1971.
5-game Series—A. L.— 9—New York vs. Kansas City, 1977.
　　　　　　　N. L.— 9—Pittsburgh vs. Cincinnati, 1972.

Fewest Bases on Balls, Series, Both Clubs

3-game Series—A. L.— 12—Oakland 9, Boston 3, 1975.
　　　　　　　N. L.—18—St. Louis 12, Atlanta 6, 1982.
4-game Series—N. L.—18—Los Angeles 9, Philadelphia 9, 1978.
　　　　　　　A. L.— 21—Kansas City 14, New York 7, 1978.
5-game Series—N. L.—19—Cincinnati 10, Pittsburgh 9, 1972.
　　　　　　　A. L.—24—Kansas City 15, New York 9, 1977.

Most Bases on Balls, Game, One Club

A. L.—11—Oakland vs. Baltimore, October 9, 1974.
N. L.—11—Los Angeles vs. Pittsburgh, October 9, 1974.

Most Bases on Balls, Game, Both Clubs

A. L.—14—Oakland 11, Baltimore 3, October 9, 1974.
N. L.—12—Los Angeles 11, Pittsburgh 1, October 9, 1974.
　　　　　Houston 7, Philadelphia 5, October 8, 1980; 10 innings.

Fewest Bases on Balls, Game, One Club

A. L.-N. L.—0—Held by many clubs.

Fewest Bases on Balls, Game, Both Clubs

A. L.—1—Oakland 1, Baltimore 0, October 8, 1974.
New York 1, Kansas City 0, October 9, 1976.
N. L.—2—Cincinnati 2, Pittsburgh 0, October 10, 1972.
Los Angeles 1, Montreal 1, October 16, 1981.
Chicago 2, San Diego 0, October 4, 1984.

Most Bases on Balls, Inning, One Club

A. L.—4—Oakland vs. Baltimore, October 9, 1974; fifth inning, consecutive.
N. L.—4—Philadelphia vs. Los Angeles, October 7, 1977; second inning, consecutive.

Most Bases on Balls, Inning, Both Clubs

N. L.—5—Philadelphia 3, Cincinnati 2, October 9, 1976; first inning.
A. L.—4—Made in many innings.

Most Strikeouts, Total Series, One Club

N. L.— 152— Cincinnati; 6 Series, 22 games.
A. L.— 143— Oakland; 6 Series, 23 games.

Most Strikeouts, Series, One Club

3-game Series—N. L.—28—Cincinnati vs. Pittsburgh, 1975.
A. L.—27—Minnesota vs. Baltimore, 1969.
4-game Series—N. L.—33—Pittsburgh vs. San Francisco, 1971.
A. L.—26—Chicago vs. Baltimore, 1983.
5-game Series—N. L.—42—Cincinnati vs. New York, 1973.
A. L.—39—Oakland vs. Baltimore, 1973.

Most Strikeouts, Series, Both Clubs

3-game Series—N. L.—46—Cincinnati 28, Pittsburgh 18, 1975.
A. L.—41—Minnesota 27, Baltimore 14, 1969.
Minnesota 22, Baltimore 19, 1970.
4-game Series—N. L.—61—Pittsburgh 33, San Francisco 28, 1971.
A. L.—50—Chicago 26, Baltimore 24, 1983.
5-game Series—N. L.—70—Cincinnati 42, New York 28, 1973.
A. L.—64—Oakland 39, Baltimore 25, 1973.

Fewest Strikeouts, Series, One Club

3-game Series—N. L.— 9—Philadelphia vs. Cincinnati, 1976.
A. L.—10—New York vs. Oakland, 1981.
4-game Series—A. L.—13—California vs. Baltimore, 1979.
N. L.—16—Los Angeles vs. Pittsburgh, 1974.
5-game Series—A. L.—15—New York vs. Kansas City, 1976.
N. L.—19—Houston vs. Philadelphia, 1980.

Fewest Strikeouts, Series, Both Clubs

3-game Series—N. L.—25—Cincinnati 16, Philadelphia 9, 1976.
A. L.—26—Oakland 14, Boston 12, 1975.
4-game Series—N. L.—33—Pittsburgh 17, Los Angeles 16, 1974.
A. L.—36—Baltimore 20, Oakland 16, 1974.
5-game Series—A. L.—33—Kansas City 18, New York 15, 1976.
N. L.—48—Montreal 25, Los Angeles 23, 1981.

Most Strikeouts, Game, Nine Innings, One Club

A. L.—14—Oakland vs. Detroit, October 10, 1972.
Chicago vs. Baltimore, October 6, 1983.
N. L.—13—Pittsburgh vs. San Francisco, October 3, 1971.
Cincinnati vs. New York, October 6, 1973.

Most Strikeouts, Extra-Inning Game, One Club

N. L.—15—Cincinnati vs. Pittsburgh, October 7, 1975; 10 innings.
A. L.—Less than nine-inning record.

Most Strikeouts, Game, Nine Innings, Both Clubs

N. L.—20—New York 12, Atlanta 8, October 5, 1969.
A. L.—19—Minnesota 12, Baltimore 7, October 5, 1970.
Oakland 12, Baltimore 7, October 6, 1973.

Most Strikeouts, Extra-Inning Game, Both Clubs

N. L.—23—Cincinnati 15, Pittsburgh 8, October 7, 1975; 10 innings.
A. L.—Less than nine-inning record.

Fewest Strikeouts, Game, One Club

N. L.—0—Pittsburgh vs. Los Angeles, October 6, 1974.

A. L.—1—Baltimore vs. Oakland, October 11, 1973.
 New York vs. Kansas City, October 13, 1976.
 Kansas City vs. New York, October 4, 1978.

Fewest Strikeouts, Game, Both Clubs

A. L.—3—Oakland 2, Baltimore 1, October 11, 1973.
 Kansas City 2, New York 1, October 13, 1976.
N. L.—4—Philadelphia 2, Cincinnati 2, October 12, 1976.

Most Consecutive Strikeouts, Game, One Club

A. L.—4—Oakland vs. Detroit, October 10, 1972; 1 in fourth inning, 3 in fifth inning.
 Baltimore vs. California, October 3, 1979; 3 in first inning, 1 in second inning.
 Kansas City vs. Detroit, October 5, 1984; 2 in fourth inning, 2 in fifth inning.
N. L.—4—Pittsburgh vs. Cincinnati, October 5, 1970; 2 in sixth inning, 2 in seventh inning.
 Cincinnati vs. Pittsburgh, October 7, 1975; 3 in first inning, 1 in second inning.

Most Strikeouts, Inning, One Club

A. L.-N. L.—3—Held by many clubs.

Most Strikeouts, Inning, Both Clubs

A. L.—5—Oakland 3, Baltimore 2, October 6, 1973; first inning.
 Boston 3, Oakland 2, October 4, 1975; second inning.
 Baltimore 3, Chicago 2, October 6, 1983; first inning.
N. L.—5—New York 3, Atlanta 2, October 5, 1969; third inning.
 New York 3, Atlanta 2, October 6, 1969; third inning.
 Philadelphia 3, Los Angeles 2, October 4, 1977; seventh inning.

Most Sacrifice Hits, Total Series, One Club

N. L.—15—Philadelphia; 5 Series, 20 games.
A. L.—12—Oakland; 6 Series, 23 games.

Most Sacrifice Hits, Series, One Club

3-game Series—A. L.— 5—Boston vs. Oakland, 1975.
 N. L.— 5—Pittsburgh vs. Cincinnati, 1979.
 St. Louis vs. Atlanta, 1982.
4-game Series—N. L.—4—San Francisco vs. Pittsburgh, 1971.
 A. L.— 2—Baltimore vs. Oakland, 1974.
 Oakland vs. Baltimore, 1974.
5-game Series—N. L.—7—Houston vs. Philadelphia, 1980.
 A. L.— 5—California vs. Milwaukee, 1982.

Most Sacrifice Hits, Series, Both Clubs

3-game Series—N. L.— 7—St. Louis 5, Atlanta 2, 1982.
 A. L.— 5—Boston 5, Oakland 0, 1975.
4-game Series—N. L.— 5—San Francisco 4, Pittsburgh 1, 1971.
 Philadelphia 3, Los Angeles 2, 1983.
 A. L.— 4—Baltimore 2, Oakland 2, 1974.
5-game Series—N. L.—12—Houston 7, Philadelphia 5, 1980.
 A. L.— 7—Oakland 4, Detroit 3, 1972.
 California 5, Milwaukee 2, 1982.

Fewest Sacrifice Hits, Series, One Club

3-game Series—A. L.-N. L.—0—Held by many clubs.
4-game Series—A. L.— 0—New York vs. Kansas City, 1978.
 California vs. Baltimore, 1979.
 N. L.—1—Pittsburgh vs. San Francisco, 1971.
 Los Angeles vs. Pittsburgh, 1974.
5-game Series—A. L.— 0—Baltimore vs. Oakland, 1973.
 Kansas City vs. New York, 1976.
 N. L.—1—Chicago vs. San Diego, 1984.

Fewest Sacrifice Hits, Series, Both Clubs

3-game Series—N. L.— 0—Cincinnati 0, Pittsburgh 0, 1975.
 A. L.— 1—New York 1, Kansas City 0, 1980.
4-game Series—A. L.— 1—Kansas City 1, New York 0, 1978.
 Baltimore 1, California 0, 1979.
 N. L.—3—Pittsburgh 2, Los Angeles 1, 1974.
5-game Series—A. L.— 2—New York 2, Kansas City 0, 1976.
 N. L.—3—San Diego 2, Chicago 1, 1984.

Most Sacrifice Hits, Game, One Club

N. L.—3—Pittsburgh vs. Cincinnati, October 3, 1979; 10 innings.
 Philadelphia vs. Houston, October 8, 1980; 10 innings.

Los Angeles vs. Montreal, October 17, 1981.
St. Louis vs. Atlanta, October 9, 1982.
A. L.—3—California vs. Milwaukee, October 10, 1982.

Most Sacrifice Hits, Game, Both Clubs

N. L.—4—Pittsburgh 3, Cincinnati 1, October 3, 1979; 10 innings.
Los Angeles 3, Montreal 1, October 17, 1981.
St. Louis 2, Atlanta 2, October 9, 1982.
A. L.—3—California 3, Milwaukee 0, October 10, 1982.

Most Sacrifice Hits, Inning, One Club

N. L.—2—Philadelphia vs. Cincinnati, October 10, 1976; fourth inning.
A. L.—1—Held by many clubs.

Most Sacrifice Flies, Total Series, One Club

N. L.—9—Cincinnati; 6 Series, 22 games.
A. L.—9—Baltimore; 7 Series, 26 games.

Most Sacrifice Flies, Series, One Club

3-game Series—N. L.— 3—Cincinnati vs. Pittsburgh, 1975.
Cincinnati vs. Philadelphia, 1976.
Pittsburgh vs. Cincinnati, 1979.
St. Louis vs. Atlanta, 1982.
A. L.— 2—Baltimore vs. Minnesota, 1970.
4-game Series—A. L.— 3—Baltimore vs. California, 1979.
Baltimore vs. Chicago, 1983.
N. L.—1—Philadelphia vs. Los Angeles, 1978, 1983.
5-game Series—A. L.— 4—Kansas City vs. New York, 1976.
N. L.—4—San Diego vs. Chicago, 1984.

Most Sacrifice Flies, Series, Both Clubs

3-game Series—N. L.— 5—Cincinnati 3, Philadelphia 2, 1976.
A. L.— 2—Baltimore 2, Minnesota 0, 1970.
4-game Series—A. L.— 5—Baltimore 3, California 2, 1979.
N. L.—1—Philadelphia 1, Los Angeles 0, 1978, 1983.
6-game Series—N. L.— 6—San Diego 4, Chicago 2, 1984.
A. L.— 5—Kansas City 4, New York 1, 1976.
Milwaukee 3, California 2, 1982.

Most Sacrifice Flies, Game, One Club

N. L.—3—St. Louis vs. Atlanta, October 7, 1982.
A. L.—2—Kansas City vs. New York, October 13, 1976.
California vs. Baltimore, October 4, 1979.
Milwaukee vs. California, October 8, 1982.
Baltimore vs. Chicago, October 7, 1983.

Most Sacrifice Flies, Game, Both Clubs

N. L.—3—St. Louis 3, Atlanta 0, October 7, 1982.
A. L.—2—Kansas City 2, New York 0, October 13, 1976.
Kansas City 1, New York 1, October 8, 1977.
California 2, Baltimore 0, October 4, 1979.
Milwaukee 2, California 0, October 8, 1982.
Baltimore 2, Chicago 0, October 7, 1983.

Most Sacrifice Flies, Inning, One Club

A. L.—2—Baltimore vs. Chicago, October 7, 1983; ninth inning.
N. L.—2—San Diego vs. Chicago, October 7, 1984; sixth inning.

Most Hit by Pitch, Total Series, One Club

N. L.—7—Pittsburgh; 6 Series, 22 games.
A. L.—6—Oakland; 6 Series, 23 games.
Baltimore; 7 Series, 26 games.

Most Hit by Pitch, Series, One Club

3-game Series—A. L.— 2—New York vs. Oakland, 1981.
N. L.—1—Atlanta vs. New York, 1969.
Pittsburgh vs. Cincinnati, 1975.
4-game Series—N. L.— 3—Philadelphia vs. Los Angeles, 1977.
A. L.— 3—Chicago vs. Baltimore, 1983.
5-game Series—A. L.— 3—Oakland vs. Detroit, 1972.
N. L.—2—Pittsburgh vs. Cincinnati, 1972.
Chicago vs. San Diego, 1984.

Most Hit by Pitch, Series, Both Clubs

3-game Series—A. L.— 2—New York 2, Oakland 0, 1981.

N. L.—1—Atlanta 1, New York 0, 1969.
Pittsburgh 1, Cincinnati 0, 1975.
4-game Series—A. L.— 5—Oakland 3, Baltimore 2, 1983.
N. L.— 3—Pittsburgh 2, San Francisco 1, 1971.
Philadelphia 3, Los Angeles 0, 1977.
5-game Series—A. L.— 4—Baltimore 2, Oakland 2, 1973.
N. L.—3—Chicago 2, San Diego 1, 1984.

Fewest Hit by Pitch, Series, One Club

A. L.-N. L.—0—Held by many clubs in Series of all lengths.

Fewest Hit by Pitch, Series, Both Clubs

3-game Series—N. L.— 0—Cincinnati 0, Pittsburgh 0, 1970, 1979.
Cincinnati 0, Philadelphia 0, 1976.
A. L.— 0—Baltimore 0, Minnesota 0, 1969.
Baltimore 0, Oakland 0, 1971.
Boston 0, Oakland 0, 1975.
Detroit 0, Kansas City 0, 1984.
4-game Series—A. L.— 0—Kansas City 0, New York 0, 1978.
N. L.—1—Los Angeles 1, Philadelphia 0, 1978.
5-game Series—A. L.— 0—New York 0, Kansas City 0, 1977.
N. L.—1—Cincinnati 1, New York 0, 1973.
Philadelphia 1, Houston 0, 1980.
Los Angeles 1, Montreal 0, 1981.

Most Hit by Pitch Game, One Club

A. L.—2—Oakland vs. Detroit, October 12, 1972.
New York vs. Oakland, October 14, 1981.
Chicago vs. Baltimore, October 6, 1983.
N. L.—1—Held by many clubs.

Most Hit by Pitch, Game, Both Clubs

N. L.—2—San Francisco 1, Pittsburgh 1, October 3, 1971.
A. L.—2—Oakland 2, Detroit 0, October 12, 1972.
Oakland 1, Baltimore 1, October 11, 1973.
New York 2, Oakland 0, October 14, 1981.
Chicago 2, Baltimore 0, October 6, 1983.

Most Hit by Pitch, Inning, One Club

A. L.-N. L.—1—Held by many clubs.

CLUB PINCH-HITTING

Most Times Pinch-Hitter Used, Series, One Club

3-game Series—A. L.— 10—Minnesota vs. Baltimore, 1970.
N. L.— 9—Pittsburgh vs. Cincinnati, 1975.
4-game Series—N. L.— 8—Los Angeles vs. Pittsburgh, 1974.
Philadelphia vs. Los Angeles, 1977, 1978.
Los Angeles vs. Philadelphia, 1983.
A. L.— 8—Baltimore vs. Chicago, 1983.
5-game Series—N. L.—15—Cincinnati vs. New York, 1973.
A. L.—14—Oakland vs. Detroit, 1972.

Most Times Pinch-Hitter Used, Series, Both Clubs

3-game Series—N. L.—14—Pittsburgh 9, Cincinnati 5, 1975.
A. L.—13—Oakland 8, New York 5, 1981.
4-game Series—N. L.—15—Philadelphia 8, Los Angeles 7, 1978.
A. L.—13—Baltimore 8, Chicago 5, 1983.
5-game Series—A. L.—22—Oakland 14, Detroit 8, 1972.
N. L.—20—Philadelphia 11, Houston 9, 1980.

Fewest Times Pinch-Hitter Used, Series, One Club

3-game Series—A. L.— 0—Baltimore vs. Minnesota, 1970.
Boston vs. Oakland, 1975.
N. L.—1—Pittsburgh vs. Cincinnati, 1979.
4-game Series—A. L.— 3—Oakland vs. Baltimore, 1974.
Baltimore vs. Oakland, 1974.
N. L.—5—San Francisco vs. Pittsburgh, 1971.
5-game Series—A. L.— 0—Milwaukee vs. California, 1982.
N. L.—1—New York vs. Cincinnati, 1973.

Fewest Times Pinch-Hitter Used, Series, Both Clubs

3-game Series—A. L.— 4—New York 3, Kansas City 1, 1980.
　　　　　　　 N. L.— 5—Atlanta 4, St. Louis 1, 1982.
4-game Series—A. L.— 6—Oakland 3, Baltimore 3, 1974.
　　　　　　　 N. L.—11—Pittsburgh 6, San Francisco 5, 1971.
5-game Series—A. L.— 2—California 2, Milwaukee 0, 1982.
　　　　　　　 N. L.— 8—Los Angeles 5, Montreal 3, 1981.

Most At-Bats, Pinch-Hitters, Total Series, One Club

A. L.—37—Oakland; 6 Series, 23 games.
N. L.—36—Philadelphia; 5 Series, 20 games.

Most At-Bats, Pinch-Hitters, Series, One Club

3-game Series—A. L.— 9—Minnesota vs. Baltimore, 1970.
　　　　　　　 N. L.— 7—Pittsburgh vs. Cincinnati, 1975.
4-game Series—N. L.— 8—Philadelphia vs. Los Angeles, 1977, 1978.
　　　　　　　 A. L.— 5—Chicago vs. Baltimore, 1983.
5-game Series—N. L.—14—Cincinnati vs. New York, 1973.
　　　　　　　 A. L.—13—Oakland vs. Detroit, 1972.

Most At-Bats, Pinch-Hitters, Series, Both Clubs

3-game Series—A. L.—11—Oakland 7, New York 4, 1981.
　　　　　　　 N. L.— 8—Atlanta 6, New York 2, 1969.
　　　　　　　　　　　　Pittsburgh 7, Cincinnati 1, 1975.
4-game Series—N. L.—14—Philadelphia 8, Los Angeles 6, 1978.
　　　　　　　 A. L.— 8—New York 4, Kansas City 4, 1978.
　　　　　　　　　　　　Chicago 5, Baltimore 3, 1983.
5-game Series—A. L.—20—Oakland 13, Detroit 7, 1972.
　　　　　　　 N. L.—18—Philadelphia 10, Houston 8, 1980.

Most Plate Appearances, Pinch-Hitters, Total Series, Club

A. L.—44—Oakland; 6 Series, 23 games.
N. L.—38—Philadelphia; 5 Series, 20 games.

Most Plate Appearances, Pinch-Hitters, Series, One Club

3-game Series—A. L.—10—Minnesota vs. Baltimore, 1970.
　　　　　　　 N. L.— 9—Pittsburgh vs. Cincinnati, 1975.
4-game Series—N. L.— 8—Los Angeles vs. Pittsburgh, 1974.
　　　　　　　　　　　　Philadelphia vs. Los Angeles, 1977, 1978.
　　　　　　　 A. L.— 7—Baltimore vs. Chicago, 1983.
5-game Series—N. L.—15—Cincinnati vs. New York, 1973.
　　　　　　　 A. L.—14—Oakland vs. Detroit, 1972.

Most Plate Appearances, Pinch-Hitters, Series, Both Clubs

3-game Series—A. L.—13—Oakland 8, New York 5, 1981.
　　　　　　　 N. L.—12—Pittsburgh 9, Cincinnati 3, 1975.
4-game Series—N. L.—15—Philadelphia 8, Los Angeles 7, 1978.
　　　　　　　 A. L.—12—Baltimore 7, Chicago 5, 1983.
5-game Series—A. L.—22—Oakland 14, Detroit 8, 1972.
　　　　　　　 N. L.—20—Philadelphia 11, Houston 9, 1980.

Most Pinch-Hitters, Game, One Club

A. L.—6—Oakland vs. Detroit, October 10, 1972.
N. L.—5—Los Angeles vs. Pittsburgh, October 8, 1974.
　　　　　Philadelphia vs. Los Angeles, October 5, 1983.

Most Pinch-Hitters, Game, Both Clubs

A. L.—7—Oakland 6, Detroit 1, October 10, 1972.
N. L.—6—Pittsburgh 3, Cincinnati 3, October 5, 1975.
　　　　　Los Angeles 4, Philadelphia 2, October 7, 1978; 10 innings.
　　　　　Philadelphia 3, Houston 3, October 12, 1980; 10 innings.
　　　　　San Diego 4, Chicago 2, October 6, 1984.

Most Plate Appearances, Pinch-Hitters, Game, One Club

A. L.—6—Oakland vs. Detroit, October 10, 1972.
N. L.—5—Los Angeles vs. Pittsburgh, October 8, 1974.
　　　　　Philadelphia vs. Los Angeles, October 5, 1983.

Most Plate Appearances, Pinch-Hitters, Game, Both Clubs

A. L.—7—Oakland 6, Detroit 1, October 10, 1972.
N. L.—6—Los Angeles 4, Philadelphia 2, October 7, 1978; 10 innings.
　　　　　Philadelphia 3, Houston 3, October 12, 1980; 10 innings.
　　　　　San Diego 4, Chicago 2, October 6, 1984.

Most At-Bats, Pinch-Hitters, Game, One Club

A. L.—6—Oakland vs. Detroit, October 10, 1972.
N. L.—4—Cincinnati vs. New York, October 9, 1973; 12 innings.
    Los Angeles vs. Pittsburgh, October 8, 1974.
    Philadelphia vs. Los Angeles, October 5, 1983.

Most At-Bats, Pinch-Hitters, Game, Both Clubs

A. L.—7—Oakland 6, Detroit 1, October 10, 1972.
N. L.—6—Philadelphia 3, Houston 3, October 12, 1980; 10 innings.
Nine-inning record—5—Los Angeles 3, Philadelphia 2, October 7, 1977.
    San Diego 3, Chicago 2, October 6, 1984.

Most Pinch-Hitters, Inning, One Club

A. L.—4—Baltimore vs. Chicago, October 7, 1983; ninth inning.
N. L.—4—Philadelphia vs. Los Angeles, October 5, 1983; ninth inning.

Most Runs, Pinch-Hitters, Series, One Club

N. L.—3—Los Angeles vs. Philadelphia, 1977; 4-game Series.
    Philadelphia vs. Houston, 1980; 5-game Series.
    San Diego vs. Chicago, 1984; 5-game Series.
A. L.—2—Oakland vs. Detroit, 1972; 5-game Series.
    Baltimore vs. Chicago, 1983; 4-game Series.

Most Runs, Pinch-Hitters, Series, Both Clubs

A. L.—3—Oakland 2, Detroit 1, 1972; 5-game Series.
N. L.—3—Los Angeles 3, Philadelphia 0, 1977; 4-game Series.

Most Runs, Pinch-Hitters, Game, One Club

N. L.—2—Los Angeles vs. Philadelphia, October 7, 1977.
    Philadelphia vs. Houston, October 11, 1980; 10 innings.
    San Diego vs. Chicago, October 6, 1984.
A. L.—2—Baltimore vs. Chicago, October 7, 1983.

Most Runs, Pinch-Hitters, Inning, One Club

N. L.—2—Los Angeles vs. Philadelphia, October 7, 1977; ninth inning.
A. L.—2—Baltimore vs. Chicago, October 7, 1983; ninth inning.

Most Hits, Pinch-Hitters, Series, One Club

N. L.—4—Pittsburgh vs. Los Angeles, 1974; 4-game Series.
    Los Angeles vs. Pittsburgh, 1974; 4-game Series.
    Philadelphia vs. Houston, 1980; 5-game Series.
A. L.—4—Kansas City vs. Detroit, 1974.

Most Hits, Pinch-Hitters, Series, Both Clubs

N. L.—8—Pittsburgh 4, Los Angeles 4, 1974; 4-game Series.
A. L.—4—Oakland 3, Detroit 1, 1972; 5-game Series.
    Kansas City 4, Detroit 0, 1984.

Most Hits, Pinch-Hitters, Game, One Club

A. L.—3—Kansas City vs. Detroit, October 3, 1984; 11 innings.
N. L.—2—Held by many clubs.

Most Hits, Pinch-Hitters, Game, Both Clubs

N. L.—4—Los Angeles 2, Pittsburgh 2, October 6, 1974.
A. L.—3—Kansas City 3, Detroit 0, October 3, 1984; 11 innings.
Nine-inning record—2—Oakland 2, Baltimore 0, October 5, 1974.
    New York 2, Oakland 0, October 15, 1981.

Most Consecutive Hits, Pinch-Hitters, Game, One Club

A. L.-N. L.—2—Occurred many times.

Most Hits, Pinch-Hitters, Inning, One Club

A. L.-N. L.—2—Occurred many times.

Most One-Base Hits, Pinch-Hitters, Series, One Club

N. L.—4—Pittsburgh vs. Los Angeles, 1974; 4-game Series.
A. L.—3—Oakland vs. Detroit, 1972; 5-game Series.
    New York vs. Oakland, 1981; 3-game Series.
    Kansas City vs. Detroit, 1984; 3-game Series.

Most One-Base Hits, Pinch-Hitters, Series, Both Clubs

N. L.—7—Pittsburgh 4, Los Angeles 3, 1974; 4-game Series.
A. L.—4—Oakland 3, Detroit 1, 1972; 5-game Series.

Most Two-Base Hits, Pinch-Hitters, Series, One Club

A. L.-N. L.—1—Held by many clubs.

Most Two-Base Hits, Pinch-Hitters, Series, Both Clubs

N. L.—2—Los Angeles 1, Philadelphia 1, 1978; 4-game Series.
A. L.—1—Made in many Series.

Most Three-Base Hits, Pinch-Hitters, Series, One Club

N. L.—1—Cincinnati vs. Pittsburgh, 1970; 3-game Series.
A. L.—Never accomplished.

Most Home Runs, Pinch-Hitters, Series, One Club

N. L.—2—Philadelphia vs. Los Angeles, 1978; 4-game Series.
A. L.—1—Baltimore vs. California, 1979; 4-game Series.

Most Total Bases, Pinch-Hitters, Series, One Club

N. L.—10—Philadelphia vs. Los Angeles, 1978; 4-game Series.
A. L.— 5—Baltimore vs. California, 1979; 4-game Series.
               Kansas City vs. Detroit, 1984; 3-game Series.

Most Total Bases, Pinch-Hitters, Series, Both Clubs

N. L.—12—Philadelphia 10, Los Angeles 2, 1978; 4-game Series.
A. L.— 7—Baltimore 5, California 2, 1979; 4-game Series.

Most Runs Batted In, Pinch-Hitters, Series, One Club

A. L.—4—Baltimore vs. California, 1979; 4-game Series.
N. L.—4—Philadelphia vs. Houston, 1980; 5-game Series.

Most Runs Batted In, Pinch-Hitters, Series, Both Clubs

N. L.—5—Philadelphia 4, Houston 1, 1980; 5-game Series.
A. L.—4—Baltimore 4, California 0, 1979; 4-game Series.

Most Runs Batted In, Pinch-Hitters, Game, One Club

A. L.—3—Baltimore vs. California, October 3, 1979; 10 innings.
         2—Kansas City vs. New York, October 7, 1977.
            Baltimore vs. Chicago, October 7, 1983.
            Kansas City vs. Detroit, October 3, 1984; 11 innings.
N. L.—2—New York vs. Atlanta, October 4, 1969.
            Los Angeles vs. Pittsburgh, October 6, 1974.

Most Runs Batted In, Pinch-Hitters, Game, Both Clubs

A. L.—3—Baltimore 3, California 0, October 3, 1979; 10 innings.
         2—Kansas City 2, New York 0, October 7, 1977.
            Baltimore 2, Chicago 0, October 7, 1983.
            Kansas City 2, Detroit 0, October 3, 1984; 11 innings.
N. L.—2—New York 2, Atlanta 0, October 4, 1969.
            Los Angeles 2, Pittsburgh 0, October 6, 1974.
            Cincinnati 1, Pittsburgh 1, October 7, 1975; 10 innings.
            Houston 1, Philadelphia 1, October 12, 1980; 10 innings.

Most Runs Batted In, Pinch-Hitters, Inning, One Club

A. L.—3—Baltimore vs. California, October 3, 1979; tenth inning.
N. L.—2—New York vs. Atlanta, October 4, 1969; eighth inning.
            Los Angeles vs. Pittsburgh, October 6, 1974; eighth inning.

Most Bases on Balls, Pinch-Hitters, Series, One Club

A. L.—2—Oakland vs. Boston, 1975; 3-game Series.
            California vs. Baltimore, 1979; 4-game Series.
            Baltimore vs. Chicago, 1983; 4-game Series.
N. L.—2—Cincinnati vs. Pittsburgh, 1972; 5-game Series.
            Pittsburgh vs. Cincinnati, 1975; 3-game Series.

Most Bases on Balls, Pinch-Hitters, Series, Both Clubs

N. L.—3—Cincinnati 2, Pittsburgh 1, 1972; 5-game Series.
            Pittsburgh 2, Cincinnati 1, 1975; 3-game Series.
A. L.—3—California 2, Baltimore 1, 1979; 4-game Series.

Most Bases on Balls, Pinch-Hitters, Game, One Club

N. L.—2—Pittsburgh vs. Cincinnati, October 7, 1975; 10 innings.
A. L.—2—California vs. Baltimore, October 4, 1979.
            Baltimore vs. Chicago, October 7, 1983.

Most Bases on Balls, Pinch-Hitters, Game, Both Clubs

N. L.—3—Pittsburgh 2, Cincinnati 1, October 7, 1975; 10 innings.

A. L.—2—Detroit 1, Oakland 1, October 11, 1972; 10 innings.
California 2, Baltimore 0, October 4, 1979.
Baltimore 2, Chicago 0, October 7, 1983.

Most Bases on Balls, Pinch-Hitters, Inning, One Club

N. L.—2—Pittsburgh vs. Cincinnati, October 7, 1975; ninth inning.
A. L.—2—Baltimore vs. Chicago, October 7, 1983; ninth inning.

Most Strikeouts, Pinch-Hitters, Series, One Club

N. L.—7—Cincinnati vs. New York, 1973; 5-game Series.
A. L.—4—Minnesota vs. Baltimore, 1970; 3-game Series.
Oakland vs. Detroit, 1972; 5-game Series.

Most Strikeouts, Pinch-Hitters, Series, Both Clubs

N. L.—7—Cincinnati 7, New York 0, 1973; 5-game Series.
A. L.—4—Minnesota 4, Baltimore 0, 1970; 3-game Series.
Oakland 4, Detroit 0, 1972; 5-game Series.

Most Strikeouts, Pinch-Hitters, Game, One Club

A. L.—4—Oakland vs. Detroit, October 10, 1972.
N. L.—3—Cincinnati vs. New York, October 7, 1973.
Los Angeles vs. Philadelphia, October 8, 1983.

Most Strikeouts, Pinch-Hitters, Inning, One Club

A. L.—2—Oakland vs. Baltimore, October 5, 1971; ninth inning, consecutive.
N. L.—2—Cincinnati vs. New York, October 7, 1973; eighth inning, consecutive.

Most Sacrifice Hits, Pinch-Hitters, Game, One Club

A. L.—1—Oakland vs. Baltimore, October 9, 1973; 11 innings.
N. L.—1—Cincinnati vs. Philadelphia, October 12, 1976.
Los Angeles vs. Philadelphia, October 7, 1978; 10 innings.
Philadelphia vs. Houston, October 8, 1980; 10 innings.

Most Sacrifice Flies, Pinch-Hitters, Game, One Club

N. L.—1—Cincinnati vs. Pittsburgh, October 7, 1975; 10 innings.
A. L.—1—Baltimore vs. Chicago, October 7, 1983.
Baltimore vs. Chicago, October 8, 1983; 10 innings.

Most Hit by Pitch, Pinch-Hitters, Game, One Club

N. L.—1—San Diego vs. Chicago, October 2, 1984.
Chicago vs. San Diego, October 7, 1984.
A. L.—Never accomplished.

Most Grounded into Double Plays, Pinch-Hitters, Game, One Club

A. L.—1—Minnesota vs. Baltimore, October 6, 1969.
Baltimore vs. California, October 6, 1979.
N. L.—1—San Francisco vs. Pittsburgh, October 3, 1971.
Los Angeles vs. Pittsburgh, October 9, 1974.
Los Angeles vs. Philadelphia, October 6, 1978.
San Diego vs. Chicago, October 3, 1984.

CLUB BASE RUNNING

Most Stolen Bases, Total Series, One Club

N. L.—25—Cincinnati; 6 Series, 22 games.
A. L.—19—Kansas City; 5 Series, 20 games.

Most Stolen Bases, Series, One Club

3-game Series—N. L.—11—Cincinnati vs. Pittsburgh, 1975.
             A. L.— 4—Detroit vs. Kansas City, 1984.
4-game Series—A. L.— 6—Kansas City vs. New York, 1978.
             N. L.— 5—Los Angeles vs. Pittsburgh, 1974.
5-game Series—A. L.— 7—Oakland vs. Detroit, 1972.
             N. L.— 7—Philadelphia vs. Houston, 1980.

Most Stolen Bases, Series, Both Clubs

3-game Series—N. L.—11—Cincinnati 11, Pittsburgh 0, 1975.
             A. L.— 4—New York 2, Oakland 2, 1981.
                 Detroit 4, Kansas City 0, 1984.
4-game Series—A. L.— 7—Baltimore 5, California 2, 1979.
             N. L.— 6—Los Angeles 5, Pittsburgh 1, 1974.
5-game Series—A. L.— 9—Kansas City 5, New York 4, 1976.
             N. L.—11—Philadelphia 7, Houston 4, 1980.

Fewest Stolen Bases, Series, One Club

A. L.-N. L.—0—Held by many clubs in Series of all lengths.

Fewest Stolen Bases, Series, Both Clubs

3-game Series—A. L.— 0— Baltimore 0, Oakland 0, 1971.
               N. L.—1—Cincinnati 1, Pittsburgh 0, 1970.
4-game Series—N. L.—2—Los Angeles 2, Philadelphia 0, 1978.
               A. L.— 3— Oakland 3, Baltimore 0, 1974.
5-game Series—N. L.— 0— Cincinnati 0, New York 0, 1973.
               A. L.— 3— Milwaukee 2, California 1, 1982.

Most Stolen Bases, Game, One Club

N. L.—7—Cincinnati vs. Pittsburgh, October 5, 1975.
A. L.—3—Oakland vs. Detroit, October 12, 1972.
       Kansas City vs. New York, October 10, 1976.
       Detroit vs. Kansas City, October 5, 1984.

Most Stolen Bases, Game, Both Clubs

N. L.—7—Cincinnati 7, Pittsburgh 0, October 5, 1975.
A. L.—3—Made in many games.

Longest Game, No Stolen Bases, One Club

A. L.—12 innings— Baltimore vs. Minnesota, October 4, 1969.
N. L.—12 innings— New York vs. Cincinnati, October 9, 1973.
              Cincinnati vs. New York, October 9, 1973.

Longest Game, No Stolen Bases, Both Clubs

N. L.—12 innings— New York 0, Cincinnati 0, October 9, 1973.
A. L.—11 innings— Detroit 0, Oakland 0, October 7, 1972.
              Baltimore 0, Oakland 0, October 9, 1973.

Most Stolen Bases, Inning, One Club

A. L.—3—Oakland vs. Detroit, October 12, 1972; second inning.
N. L.—2—New York vs. Atlanta, October 5, 1969; first inning.
       Cincinnati vs. Pittsburgh, October 4, 1975; third inning.
       Cincinnati vs. Pittsburgh, October 5, 1975; first inning, fourth inning, sixth
       inning.

Most Caught Stealing, Series, One Club

3-game Series—A. L.— 5— Kansas City vs. New York, 1980.
               N. L.— 2— Pittsburgh vs. Cincinnati, 1970.
                      Cincinnati vs. Pittsburgh, 1979.
                      Atlanta vs. St. Louis, 1982.
4-game Series—A. L.— 3— Oakland vs. Baltimore, 1974.
                      Baltimore vs. Oakland, 1974.
                      Kansas City vs. New York, 1978.
               N. L.— 2— Los Angeles vs. Philadelphia, 1983.
5-game Series—A. L.— 5— Kansas City vs. New York, 1976.
               N. L.— 3— Philadelphia vs. Houston, 1980.
                      Chicago vs. San Diego, 1984.

Most Caught Stealing, Series, Both Clubs

3-game Series—A. L.— 5— Kansas City 5, New York 0, 1980.
               N. L.— 3— Pittsburgh 2, Cincinnati 1, 1970.
4-game Series—A. L.— 6— Oakland 3, Baltimore 3, 1974.
               N. L.— 3— Los Angeles 2, Philadelphia 1, 1983.
5-game Series—A. L.— 8— Kansas City 5, New York 3, 1976.
               N. L.— 5— Chicago 3, San Diego 2, 1984.

Fewest Caught Stealing, Series, One Club

A. L.-N. L.—0—By many clubs in Series of all lengths.

Fewest Caught Stealing, Series, Both Clubs

3-game Series—N. L.— 0— Cincinnati 0, Pittsburgh 0, 1975.
               A. L.— 0— Baltimore 0, Minnesota 0, 1970.
                      Boston 0, Oakland 0, 1975.
4-game Series—N. L.— 0— Los Angeles 0, Pittsburgh 0, 1974.
               A. L.— 1— Chicago 1, Baltimore 0, 1983.
5-game Series—N. L.— 1— Cincinnati 1, New York 0, 1973.
                      Montreal 1, Los Angeles 0, 1981.
               A. L.— 4— Detroit 2, Oakland 2, 1972.
                      Kansas City 4, New York 0, 1977.
                      Milwaukee 2, California 2, 1982.

Most Caught Stealing, Game, One Club

A. L.-N. L.—2—Held by many clubs.

Most Caught Stealing, Game, Both Clubs

A. L.—3—Baltimore 2, Oakland 1, October 10, 1973.
        Kansas City 2, New York 1, October 12, 1976.
        Milwaukee 2, California 1, October 9, 1982.
N. L.—3—Chicago 2, San Diego 1, October 7, 1984.

Most Caught Stealing, Inning, One Club

A. L.-N. L.—1—Held by many clubs.

Most Left on Bases, Total Series, One Club

N. L.— 158— Los Angeles; 5 Series, 21 games.
A. L.— 166— Baltimore; 7 Series, 26 games.

Most Left on Bases, Series, One Club

3-game Series—N. L.—31—St. Louis vs. Atlanta, 1982.
             A. L.—30—New York vs. Oakland, 1981.
4-game Series—N. L.—44—Los Angeles vs. Pittsburgh, 1974.
             A. L.—35—Chicago vs. Baltimore, 1983.
5-game Series—N. L.—45—Houston vs. Philadelphia, 1980.
             A. L.—41—New York vs. Kansas City, 1976.

Most Left on Bases, Series, Both Clubs

3-game Series—A. L.— 50—Baltimore 28, Minnesota 22, 1969.
                      New York 30, Oakland 20, 1981.
             N. L.—49—Cincinnati 25, Pittsburgh 24, 1979.
4-game Series—N. L.—68—Los Angeles 44, Pittsburgh 24, 1974.
             A. L.—59—Chicago 35, Baltimore 24, 1983.
5-game Series—N. L.—88—Houston 45, Philadelphia 43, 1980.
             A. L.—70—Baltimore 36, Oakland 34, 1973.

Fewest Left on Bases, Series, One Club

3-game Series—N. L.—12—Atlanta vs. St. Louis, 1982.
             A. L.—14—Boston vs. Oakland, 1975.
4-game Series—A. L.— 16—Baltimore vs. Oakland, 1974.
             N. L.—22—Los Angeles vs. Philadelphia, 1977.
5-game Series—A. L.— 22—Kansas City vs. New York, 1976.
             N. L.—24—Pittsburgh vs. Cincinnati, 1972.

Fewest Left on Bases, Series, Both Clubs

3-game Series—A. L.— 33—Oakland 19, Boston 14, 1975.
             N. L.—38—Pittsburgh 21, Cincinnati 17, 1975.
4-game Series—A. L.— 45—Baltimore 23, California 22, 1979.
             N. L.—52—Los Angeles 28, Philadelphia 24, 1978.
5-game Series—N. L.—54—Cincinnati 30, Pittsburgh 24, 1972.
             A. L.—62—New York 34, Kansas City 28, 1977.

Most Left on Bases, Game, One Club

N. L.—14—Philadelphia vs. Houston, October 8, 1980; 10 innings.
N. L.—Nine-inning record—13—Los Angeles vs. Pittsburgh, October 5, 1974.
A. L.—13—Baltimore vs. Oakland, October 5, 1971.

Most Left on Bases, Two Consecutive Games, One Club

N. L.—25—Los Angeles vs. Pittsburgh, October 5 (13), October 6 (12), 1974.
A. L.—21—Baltimore vs. Oakland, October 6 (12), October 7 (9), 1973.
        New York vs. Kansas City, October 3 (12), October 4 (9), 1978.

Most Left on Bases, Shutout Defeat, One Club

A. L.—11—Chicago vs. Baltimore, October 8, 1983 (lost 3-0 in 10 innings).
A. L.—Nine-inning record—Oakland vs. Detroit, October 10, 1972 (lost 3-0).
N. L.—11—Philadelphia vs. Houston, October 10, 1980 (lost 1-0 in 11 innings).
N. L.—Nine-inning record—10—Los Angeles vs. Pittsburgh, October 8, 1974 (lost 7-0).
           San Diego vs. Chicago, October 2, 1984 (lost 13-0).

Most Left on Bases, Game, Both Clubs

N. L.—22—Philadelphia 14, Houston 8, October 8, 1980; 10 innings.
N. L.—Nine-inning record—20—Cincinnati 10, New York 10, October 10, 1973.
        Los Angeles 13, Pittsburgh 7, October 5, 1974.
        Los Angeles 12, Pittsburgh 8, October 6, 1974.
A. L.—21—Baltimore 12, Oakland 9, October 6, 1973.
        New York 12, Kansas City 9, October 3, 1978.
        Chicago 11, Baltimore 10, October 8, 1983; 10 innings.

Fewest Left on Bases, Game, One Club

N. L.—1—Pittsburgh vs. Cincinnati, October 7, 1972.
Pittsburgh vs. Los Angeles, October 9, 1974.
San Diego vs. Chicago, October 4, 1984.
A. L.—2—Detroit vs. Oakland, October 8, 1972.
Kansas City vs. New York, October 9, 1976.
New York vs. Kansas City, October 6, 1978.

Fewest Left on Bases, Game, Both Clubs

A. L.—6—Oakland 4, Detroit 2, October 8, 1972.
N. L.—6—Chicago 5, San Diego 1, October 4, 1984.

CLUB PINCH-RUNNING

Most Pinch-Runners Used, Total Series, One Club

A. L.—12—Oakland, 1971, 1972, 1973, 1974, 1975, 1981; 6 Series, 23 games.
N. L.— 7—Pittsburgh, 1970, 1971, 1972, 1974, 1975, 1979; 6 Series, 22 games.

Most Pinch-Runners Used, Series, One Club

A. L.—5—Oakland vs. Baltimore, 1974; 4-game Series.
N. L.—3—New York vs. Atlanta, 1969; 3-game Series.
Cincinnati vs. Pittsburgh, 1972; 5-game Series.
Houston vs. Philadelphia, 1980; 5-game Series.
Philadelphia vs. Houston, 1980; 5-game Series.

Most Pinch-Runners Used, Series, Both Clubs

A. L.—8—Oakland 5, Baltimore 3, 1974; 4-game Series.
N. L.—6—Houston 3, Philadelphia 3, 1980; 5-game Series.

Fewest Pinch-Runners Used, Series, One Club

A. L.-N. L.—0—Held by many clubs.

Fewest Pinch-Runners Used, Series, Both Clubs

A. L.—0—Baltimore 0, Minnesota 0, 1969; 3-game Series.
Kansas City 0, New York 0, 1980; 3-game Series.
N. L.—0—Philadelphia 0, Los Angeles 0, 1978; 4-game Series.

Most Pinch-Runners Used, Game, One Club

A. L.—3—Kansas City vs. Detroit, October 3, 1984; 11 innings.
Nine-inning record—2—Detroit vs. Oakland, October 12, 1972.
Oakland vs. Baltimore, October 6, 1974.
Baltimore vs. Oakland, October 9, 1974.
Oakland vs. Boston, October 4, 1975.
N. L.—2—Cincinnati vs. Pittsburgh, October 11, 1972.
Philadelphia vs. Houston, October 12, 1980; 10 innings.

Most Pinch-Runners Used, Game, Both Clubs

A. L.—3—Oakland 2, Baltimore 1, October 6, 1974.
Baltimore 2, Oakland 1, October 9, 1974.
Kansas City 3, Detroit 0, October 3, 1984; 11 innings.
N. L.—3—Philadelphia 2, Houston 1, October 12, 1980; 10 innings.

Most Pinch-Runners Used, Inning, One Club

A. L.—2—Oakland vs. Detroit, October 7, 1972; eleventh inning.
Baltimore vs. Oakland, October 9, 1974; ninth inning.
N. L.—1—Held by many clubs.

INDIVIDUAL FIELDING

FIRST BASEMEN'S FIELDING RECORDS

Most Series Played

A. L.—5—Powell, John W., Baltimore, 1969, 1970, 1971, 1973, 1974; 12 games.
N. L.—5—Perez, Atanasio R., Cincinnati, 1970, 1972, 1973, 1975, 1976; 17 games.
Robertson, Robert E., Pittsburgh, 1970, 1971, 1972, 1974, 1975; 11 games.
Garvey, Steven P., Los Angeles, 1974, 1977, 1978, 1981; San Diego, 1984; 22 games.

Most Games Played, Total Series

N. L.—22—Garvey, Steven P., Los Angeles, 1974, 1977, 1978, 1981; San Diego, 1984; 5 Series.
A. L.—14—Chambliss, C. Christopher, New York, 1976, 1977, 1978; 3 Series.

Highest Fielding Average, Series, With Most Chances Accepted

3-game Series—N. L.—1.000—Hernandez, Keith, St. Louis, 1982; 36 chances accepted.
               A. L.—1.000—Powell, John W., Baltimore, 1969; 34 chances accepted.
4-game Series—N. L.—1.000—Garvey, Steven P., Los Angeles, 1978; 49 chances accepted.
               A. L.—1.000—Tenace, F. Gene, Oakland, 1974; 37 chances accepted.
5-game Series—N. L.—1.000—Rose, Peter E., Philadelphia, 1980; 60 chances accepted.
               A. L.—1.000—Epstein, Michael P., Oakland, 1972; 57 chances accepted.

Most Consecutive Errorless Games, Total Series

N. L.—19—Garvey, Steven P., Los Angeles, San Diego, October 9, 1974 through October 7, 1984.
A. L.—12—Powell, John W., Baltimore, October 4, 1969 through October 9, 1974.
         Chambliss, C. Christopher, New York, October 12, 1976 through October 7, 1978.

Most Putouts, Total Series

N. L.—208—Garvey, Steven P., Los Angeles, 1974, 1977, 1978, 1981; San Diego, 1984; 5 Series, 22 games.
A. L.—115—Powell, John W., Baltimore, 1969, 1970, 1971, 1973, 1974; 5 Series, 12 games.

Most Putouts, Series

3-game Series—N. L.—35—Hernandez, Keith, St. Louis, 1982.
               A. L.—34—Powell, John W., Baltimore, 1969.
4-game Series—N. L.—44—Garvey, Steven P., Los Angeles, 1978.
               A. L.—44—Murray, Eddie C., Baltimore, 1979.
5-game Series—A. L.—55—Epstein, Michael P., Oakland, 1972.
               N. L.—53—Rose, Peter E., Philadelphia, 1980.

Most Putouts, Game

N. L.—17—Stargell, Wilver D., Pittsburgh, October 2, 1979; 11 innings.
      16—Garvey, Steven P., Los Angeles, October 5, 1978.
           Garvey, Steven P., Los Angeles, October 6, 1978.
A. L.—15—Chambliss, C. Christopher, New York, October 14, 1976.

Most Putouts, Inning

A. L.-N.L.—3—Held by many first basemen.

Fewest Putouts, Game, Nine Innings

N. L.—1—Robertson, Robert E., Pittsburgh, October 2, 1971.
A. L.—2—Cash, Norman D., Detroit, October 8, 1972.
         Cooper, Cecil C., Boston, October 4, 1975.

Most Assists, Total Series

Both Leagues—16—Chambliss, C. Christopher, New York AL, 1976, 1977, 1978; Atlanta NL, 1982; 4 Series, 17 games.
N. L.—14—Perez, Atanasio R., Cincinnati, 1970, 1972, 1973, 1975, 1976; 5 Series, 17 games.
A. L.—11—Chambliss, C. Christopher, New York, 1976, 1977, 1978; 3 Series, 14 games.

Most Assists, Series

3-game Series—A. L.— 5—Reese, Richard B., Minnesota, 1969.
                      Watson, Robert J., New York, 1980.
               N. L.— 5—Perez, Atanasio R., Cincinnati, 1975.
                      Chambliss, C. Christopher, Atlanta, 1982.
4-game Series—N. L.— 5—Garvey, Steven P., Los Angeles, 1978.
               A. L.— 3—Murray, Eddie C., Baltimore, 1979, 1983.
                      Paciorek, Thomas M., Chicago, 1983.
5-game Series—A. L.— 7—Chambliss, C. Christopher, New York, 1977.
               N. L.— 7—Rose, Peter E., Philadelphia, 1980.

Most Assists, Game

N. L.—3—Perez, Atanasio R., Cincinnati, October 4, 1975.
         Chambliss, C. Christopher, Atlanta, October 10, 1982.
A. L.—3—Reese, Richard B., Minnesota, October 5, 1969; 11 innings.
         Chambliss, C. Christopher, New York, October 7, 1977.

Most Assists, Inning

A. L.—2—Chambliss, C. Christopher, New York, October 5, 1977; sixth inning.
         Chambliss, C. Christopher, New York, October 7, 1977; second inning.
N. L.—2—Milner, John D., New York, October 7, 1973; second inning.
         Garvey, Steven P., Los Angeles, October 7, 1978; fifth inning.
         Rose, Peter E., Philadelphia, October 11, 1980; seventh inning.

Most Chances Accepted, Total Series

N. L.— 221— Garvey, Steven P., Los Angeles, 1974, 1977, 1978, 1981; San Diego, 1984; 5
Series, 22 games.
A. L.— 124— Chambliss, C. Christopher, New York, 1976, 1977, 1978; 3 Series, 14 games.

Most Chances Accepted, Series

3-game Series—N. L.—36—Hernandez, Keith, St. Louis, 1982.
A. L.—34—Powell, John W., Baltimore, 1969.
4-game Series—N. L.—49—Garvey, Steven P., Los Angeles, 1978.
A. L.—47—Murray, Eddie C., Baltimore, 1979.
5-game Series—N. L.—60—Rose, Peter E., Philadelphia, 1980.
A. L.—57—Epstein, Michael P., Oakland, 1972.

Most Chances Accepted, Game

N. L.—18—Garvey, Steven P., Los Angeles, October 6, 1978; 16 putouts, 2 assists, 0
errors.
A. L.—15—Epstein, Michael P., Oakland, October 8, 1972; 13 putouts, 2 assists, 0 errors.
Chambliss, C. Christopher, New York, October 14, 1976; 15 putouts, 0 assists,
0 errors.

Most Chances Accepted, Inning

A. L.-N. L.—3—Held by many first basemen.

Fewest Chances Offered, Game, Nine Innings

N. L.—2—Robertson, Robert E., Pittsburgh, October 2, 1971; 1 putout, 1 assist, 0 errors.
A. L.—3—Cooper, Cecil C., Boston, October 4, 1975; 2 putouts, 0 assists, 1 error.

Most Errors, Total Series

A. L.—3—Cooper, Cecil C., Boston, 1975; Milwaukee, 1982; 2 Series, 8 games.
N. L.—2—Cepeda, Orlando M., Atlanta, 1969; 1 Series, 3 games.

Most Errors, Series

3-game Series—N. L.— 2—Cepeda, Orlando M., Atlanta, 1969.
A. L.— 1—Cooper, Cecil C., Boston, 1975.
Balboni, Stephen C., Kansas City, 1984.
4-game Series—A. L.— 2—Murray, Eddie C., Baltimore, 1979.
N. L.—1—McCovey, Willie L., San Francisco, 1971.
Garvey, Steven P., Los Angeles, 1974.
5-game Series—A. L.— 2—Mayberry, John C., Kansas City, 1977.
Cooper, Cecil C., Milwaukee, 1982.
N. L.—1—Durham, Leon, Chicago, 1984.

Most Errors, Game

A. L.-N. L.—1—Held by many first basemen.

Most Double Plays, Total Series

N. L.—21—Garvey, Steven P., Los Angeles, 1974, 1977, 1978, 1981; San Diego, 1984; 5
Series, 22 games.
A. L.— 9—Powell, John W., Baltimore, 1969, 1970, 1971, 1973, 1974; 5 Series, 12 games.

Most Double Plays, Series

3-game Series—A. L.— 6—Watson, Robert J., New York, 1981.
N. L.— 3—Hernandez, Keith, St. Louis, 1982.
4-game Series—N. L.—6—Garvey, Steven P., Los Angeles, 1974.
A. L.— 6—Carew, Rodney C., California, 1979.
5-game Series—N. L.— 6—Cromartie, Warren L., Montreal, 1981.
A. L.—5—Epstein, Michael P., Oakland, 1972.
Cooper, Cecil C., Milwaukee, 1982.

Most Double Plays Started, Series

3-game Series—A. L.— 1—Held by many players.
N. L.—Never accomplished.
4-game Series—N. L.—1—Garvey, Steven P., Los Angeles, 1977.
A. L.—Never accomplished.
5-game Series—N. L.—1—Milner, John D., New York, 1973.
A. L.—1—Williams, Earl C., Baltimore, 1973.
Chambliss, C. Christopher, New York, 1976.

Most Double Plays, Game

N. L.—3—Garvey, Steven P., Los Angeles, October 5, 1978.
Garvey, Steven P., Los Angeles, October 13, 1981.
Hernandez, Keith, St. Louis, 1982.
A. L.—3—Reese, Richard B., Minnesota, October 3, 1970.
Epstein, Michael P., Oakland, October 10, 1972.

Tenace, F. Gene, Oakland, October 5, 1975.
Murray, Eddie C., Baltimore, October 6, 1979.

Most Double Plays Started, Game
A. L.-N. L.—1—Held by many first basemen.

Most Unassisted Double Plays, Game
A. L.-N. L.—1—Never accomplished.

SECOND BASEMEN'S FIELDING RECORDS

Most Series Played
N. L.—7—Morgan, Joe L., Cincinnati, 1972, 1973, 1975, 1976, 1979; Houston, 1980; Philadelphia, 1983; 27 games.
A. L.—5—White, Frank, Kansas City, 1976, 1977, 1978, 1980, 1984; 19 games.

Most Games Played, Total Series
N. L.—27—Morgan, Joe L., Cincinnati, 1972, 1973, 1975, 1976, 1979; Houston, 1980; Philadelphia, 1983; 7 Series.
A. L.—19—White, Frank, Kansas City, 1976, 1977, 1978, 1980, 1984; 5 Series.

Highest Fielding Average, Series, With Most Chances Accepted
3-game Series—N. L.—1.000—Helms, Tommy V., Cincinnati, 1970; 23 chances accepted.
Morgan, Joe L., Cincinnati, 1979; 23 chances accepted.
A. L.—1.000—Randolph, William L., New York, 1981; 24 chances accepted.
4-game Series—A. L.—1.000—Cruz, Julio L., Chicago, 1983; 24 chances accepted.
N. L.—1.000—Sax, Stephen L., Los Angeles, 1983; 23 chances accepted.
5-game Series—N. L.—1.000—Morgan, Joe L., Cincinnati, 1973; 39 chances accepted.
A. L.—1.000—White, Frank, Kansas City, 1977; 29 chances accepted.

Most Consecutive Errorless Games, Total Series
N. L.—27—Morgan, Joe L., Cincinnati, Houston, Philadelphia, October 7, 1972 through October 8, 1983.
A. L.—16—Randolph, William L., New York, October 9, 1976 through October 15, 1981.

Most Putouts, Total Series
N. L.—63—Morgan, Joe L., Cincinnati, 1972, 1973, 1975, 1976, 1979; Houston, 1980; Philadelphia, 1983; 7 Series, 27 games.
A. L.—44—White, Frank, Kansas City, 1976, 1977, 1978, 1980, 1984; 5 Series, 19 games.

Most Putouts, Series
3-game Series—N. L.—12—Morgan, Joe L., Cincinnati, 1979.
A. L.—12—Randolph, William L., New York, 1981.
4-game Series—A. L.—13—Grich, Robert A., Baltimore, 1974.
N. L.—11—Cash, David, Pittsburgh, 1971.
Sax, Stephen L., Los Angeles, 1983.
5-game Series—A. L.—16—Grich, Robert A., Baltimore, 1973.
N. L.—18—Trillo, J. Manuel, Philadelphia, 1980.

Most Putouts, Game
A. L.—7—Grich, Robert A., Baltimore, October 6, 1974.
N. L.—6—Cash, David, Philadelphia, October 12, 1976.
Morgan, Joe L., Cincinnati, October 3, 1979; 10 innings.
Lopes, David E., Los Angeles, October 13, 1981.

Most Putouts, Inning
N. L.—3—Morgan, Joe L., Cincinnati, October 10, 1976; eighth inning.
Sandberg, Ryne D., Chicago, October 4, 1984; fifth inning.
A. L.—3—Grich, Robert A., Baltimore, October 11, 1973; third inning.
Green, Richard L., Oakland, October 8, 1974; seventh inning.

Most Assists, Total Series
N. L.—85—Morgan, Joe L., Cincinnati, 1972, 1973, 1975, 1976, 1979; Houston, 1980; Philadelphia, 1983; 7 Series, 27 games.
A. L.—52—White, Frank, Kansas City, 1976, 1977, 1978, 1980, 1984; 5 Series, 19 games.

Most Assists, Series
3-game Series—N. L.—12—Helms, Tommy V., Cincinnati, 1970.
A. L.—12—Randolph, William L., New York, 1981.
4-game Series—N. L.—18—Lopes, David E., Los Angeles, 1974.
A. L.—14—Cruz, Julio L., Chicago, 1983.
5-game Series—N. L.—27—Morgan, Joe L., Cincinnati, 1973.
A. L.—17—Grich, Robert A., California, 1982.

Most Assists, Game

N. L.—8—Trillo, J. Manuel, Philadelphia, October 7, 1980.
A. L.—7—Randolph, William L., New York, October 13, 1981.

Most Assists, Inning

A. L.-N. L.—2—Held by many second basemen.

Most Chances Accepted, Total Series

N. L.— 148— Morgan, Joe L., Cincinnati, 1972, 1973, 1975, 1976, 1979; Houston, 1980;
         Philadelphia, 1983; 7 Series, 27 games.
A. L.— 96— White, Frank, Kansas City, 1976, 1977, 1978, 1980, 1984; 5 Series, 19 games.

Most Chances Accepted, Series

3-game Series—A. L.— 24—Randolph, William L., New York, 1981.
               N. L.—23—Helms, Tommy V., Cincinnati, 1970.
                        Morgan, Joe L., Cincinnati, 1979.
4-game Series—N. L.—27—Lopes, David E., Los Angeles, 1974.
               A. L.—25—Grich, Robert A., Baltimore, 1974.
5-game Series—N. L.—43—Trillo, J. Manuel, Philadelphia, 1980.
               A. L.—29—White, Frank, Kansas City, 1977.

Most Chances Accepted, Game

N. L.—13—Trillo, J. Manuel, Philadelphia, October 7, 1980; 5 putouts, 8 assists, 0 errors.
A. L.—12—Grich, Robert A., Baltimore, October 6, 1974; 7 putouts, 5 assists, 1 error.

Most Chances Accepted, Inning

A. L.-N. L.—3—Held by many second basemen.

Fewest Chances Offered, Game

A. L.—0—Thompson, Danny L., Minnesota, October 4, 1970.
N. L.—1—Cash, David, Pittsburgh, October 9, 1972.
         Millan, Felix B. M., New York, October 7, 1973.
         Sax, Stephen L., Los Angeles, October 7, 1983.

Most Errors, Total Series

A. L.—4—Green, Richard L., Oakland, 1971, 1972, 1973, 1974; 4 Series, 17 games.
N. L.—4—Lopes, David E., Los Angeles, 1974, 1977, 1978, 1981; 4 Series, 17 games.

Most Errors, Series

3-game Series—A. L.— N. L.—1—Held by many second basemen.
4-game Series—A. L.— 2—Green, Richard L., Oakland, 1974.
               N. L.— 2—Sizemore, Ted C., Philadelphia, 1977.
                        Lopes, David E., Los Angeles, 1978.
5-game Series—A. L.— 2—Green, Richard L., Oakland, 1973.
               N. L.—1—Held by many second basemen.

Most Errors, Game

A. L.—2—Green, Richard L., Oakland, October 9, 1973; 11 innings.
         Green, Richard L., Oakland, October 8, 1974.
N. L.—1—Held by many second basemen.

Most Errors, Inning

A. L.-N. L.—1—Held by many second basemen.

Most Double Plays, Total Series

N. L.—14—Morgan, Joe L., Cincinnati, 1972, 1973, 1975, 1976, 1979; Houston, 1980; 6
         Series, 23 games.
A. L.—12—White, Frank, Kansas City, 1976, 1977, 1978, 1980, 1984; 5 Series, 19 games.

Most Double Plays, Series

3-game Series—A. L.— 4—Randolph, William L., New York, 1981.
               N. L.—3—Cash, David, Pittsburgh, 1970.
                        Herr, Thomas M., St. Louis, 1982.
4-game Series—N. L.—4—Lopes, David E., Los Angeles, 1974.
                        Sizemore, Ted C., Philadelphia, 1978.
               A. L.— 4—Grich, Robert A., California, 1979.
5-game Series—N. L.—7—Scott, Rodney D., Montreal, 1981.
               A. L.— 4—Green, Richard L., Oakland, 1973.
                        Gantner, James E., Milwaukee, 1982.

Most Double Plays Started, Series

3-game Series—A. L.— 2—Johnson, David A., Baltimore, 1970.
               N. L.—2—Stennett, Renaldo A., Pittsburgh, 1975.
                        Herr, Thomas M., St. Louis, 1982.

4-game Series—N. L.—3—Sizemore, Ted C., Philadelphia, 1978.
    A. L.—1—Held by many second basemen.
5-game Series—N. L.—3—Sandberg, Ryne D., Chicago, 1984.
    A. L.—2—Gantner, James E., Milwaukee, 1982.

Most Double Plays, Game

N. L.—4—Lopes, David E., Los Angeles, October 13, 1981.
A. L.—2—Held by many second basemen.

Most Double Plays Started, Game

N. L.—2—Stennett, Renaldo A., Pittsburgh, October 5, 1975.
    Sizemore, Ted C., Philadelphia, October 6, 1978.
    Scott, Rodney D., Montreal, October 17, 1981.
    Herr, Thomas M., St. Louis, October 10, 1982.
    Sandberg, Ryne D., Chicago, October 2, 1984.
A. L.—1—Held by many second basemen.

Most Unassisted Double Plays, Game

N. L.—1—Morgan, Joe L., October 10, 1976.
A. L.—Never accomplished.

THIRD BASEMEN'S FIELDING RECORDS

Most Series Played

Both Leagues—6—Nettles, Graig, New York AL, 1976, 1977, 1978, 1980, 1981; San Diego
    NL, 1984; 23 games.
N. L.—5—Hebner, Richard J., Pittsburgh, 1970, 1971, 1972, 1974, 1975; 18 games.
    Schmidt, Michael J., Philadelphia, 1976, 1977, 1978, 1980, 1983; 20 games.
    Cey, Ronald C., Los Angeles, 1974, 1977, 1978, 1981; Chicago, 1984; 22 games.
A. L.—5—Robinson, Brooks C., Baltimore, 1969, 1970, 1971, 1973, 1974; 18 games.
    Bando, Salvatore L., Oakland, 1971, 1972, 1973, 1974, 1975; 20 games.
    Nettles, Graig, New York, 1976, 1977, 1978, 1980, 1981; 19 games.

Most Games Played, Total Series

Both Leagues—23—Nettles, Graig, New York AL, 1976, 1977, 1978, 1980, 1981; San Diego
    NL, 1984; 6 Series.
N. L.—22—Cey, Ronald C., Los Angeles, 1974, 1977, 1978, 1981; Chicago, 1984; 5 Series.
A. L.—20—Bando, Salvatore L., Oakland, 1971, 1972, 1973, 1974, 1975; 5 Series.
    Brett, George H., Kansas City, 1976, 1977, 1978, 1980, 1984; 5 Series.

Highest Fielding Average, Series, With Most Chances Accepted

3-game Series—A. L.—1.000—Robinson, Brooks C., Baltimore, 1969; 16 chances accept-
    ed.
    N. L.—1.000—Madlock, Bill, Pittsburgh, 1979; 8 chances accepted.
4-game Series—N. L.—1.000—Schmidt, Michael J., Philadelphia, 1977; 19 chances ac-
    cepted.
    A. L.—1.000—Cruz, Todd R., Baltimore, 1983; 19 chances accepted.
5-game Series—A. L.—1.000—Bando, Salvatore L., Oakland, 1972; 22 chances accepted.
    N. L.—1.000—Hebner, Richard J., Pittsburgh, 1972; 16 chances accept-
    ed.

Most Consecutive Errorless Games, Total Series

A. L.—17—Bando, Salvatore L., Oakland, October 3, 1971 through October 9, 1974.
N. L.—13—Hebner, Richard J., Pittsburgh, October 6, 1971 through October 7, 1975.

Most Putouts, Total Series

A. L.—25—Bando, Salvatore L., Oakland, 1971, 1972, 1973, 1974, 1975; 5 Series, 20 games.
N. L.—20—Schmidt, Michael J., Philadelphia, 1976, 1977, 1978, 1980, 1983; 5 Series, 20
    games.

Most Putouts, Series

3-game Series—A. L.— 6—Robinson, Brooks C., Baltimore, 1969.
    Killebrew, Harmon C., Minnesota, 1969.
    Bando, Salvatore L., Oakland, 1971.
    N. L.— 5—Perez, Atanasio R., Cincinnati, 1970.
4-game Series—N. L.— 7—Cey, Ronald C., Los Angeles, 1977.
    A. L.— 6—Nettles, Graig, New York, 1978.
    Cruz, Todd R., Baltimore, 1983.
5-game Series—A. L.— 9—DeCinces, Douglas V., California, 1982.
    N. L.— 5—Hebner, Richard J., Pittsburgh, 1972.
    Cey, Ronald C., Los Angeles, 1981.
    Nettles, Graig, San Diego, 1984.

Most Putouts, Game

    A. L.—4—Lansford, Carney R., California, October 6, 1979.
    N. L.—3—Perez, Atanasio R., Cincinnati, October 5, 1970.
            Hebner, Richard J., Pittsburgh, October 10, 1972.
            Schmidt, Michael J., Philadelphia, October 9, 1976.
            Schmidt, Michael J., Philadelphia, October 11, 1980; 10 innings.
            Schmidt, Michael J., Philadelphia, October 7, 1983.
            Nettles, Graig, San Diego, October 6, 1984.

Most Putouts, Inning

    A. L.-N. L.—2—Held by many third basemen.

Most Assists, Total Series

    N. L.—66—Schmidt, Michael J., Philadelphia, 1976, 1977, 1978, 1980, 1983; 5 Series, 20
            games.
    A. L.—49—Robinson, Brooks C., Baltimore, 1969, 1970, 1971, 1973, 1974; 5 Series, 18
            games.

Most Assists, Series

    3-game Series—A. L.— 11—Bando, Salvatore L., Oakland, 1975.
                  N. L.— 9—Schmidt, Michael J., Philadelphia, 1976.
    4-game Series—N. L.—18—Schmidt, Michael J., Philadelphia, 1978.
                  A. L.—13—Robinson, Brooks C., Baltimore, 1974.
                          Cruz, Todd R., Baltimore, 1983.
    5-game Series—N. L.—17—Schmidt, Michael J., Philadelphia, 1980.
                  A. L.—16—Bando, Salvatore L., Oakland, 1972.

Most Assists, Game, Nine Innings

    N. L.—8—Cey, Ronald C., Los Angeles, October 16, 1981.
    A. L.—6—Bando, Salvatore L., Oakland, October 8, 1972.
            Cruz, Todd R., Baltimore, October 5, 1983.

Most Assists, Extra-Inning Game

    A. L.—7—Rodriguez, Aurelio, Detroit, October 11, 1972; 10 innings.
    N. L.—Less than nine-inning record.

Most Assists, Inning

    N. L.—3—Cey, Ronald C., Los Angeles, October 4, 1977; fourth inning.
            Cey, Ronald C., Los Angeles, October 16, 1981; eighth inning.
    A. L.—2—Cruz, Todd R., Baltimore, October 5, 1983; fifth inning.

Most Chances Accepted, Total Series

    N. L.—86—Schmidt, Michael J., Philadelphia, 1976, 1977, 1978, 1980, 1983; 5 Series, 20
            games.
    A. L.—72—Bando, Salvatore L., Oakland, 1971, 1972, 1973, 1974, 1975; 5 Series, 20 games.

Most Chances Accepted, Series

    3-game Series—A. L.— 16—Robinson, Brooks C., Baltimore, 1969.
                  N. L.—13—Schmidt, Michael J., Philadelphia, 1976.
    4-game Series—N. L.—21—Cey, Ronald C., Los Angeles, 1977.
                          Schmidt, Michael J., Philadelphia, 1978.
                  A. L.—19—Cruz, Todd R., Baltimore, 1983.
    5-game Series—A. L.— 22—Bando, Salvatore L., Oakland, 1972.
                  N. L.—21—Cey, Ronald C., Los Angeles, 1981.

Most Chances Accepted, Game

    N. L.—10—Cey, Ronald C., Los Angeles, October 16, 1981; 2 putouts, 8 assists, 0 errors.
    A. L.— 9—Cruz, Todd R., Baltimore, October 5, 1983; 3 putouts, 6 assists, 0 errors.

Most Chances Accepted, Inning

    A. L.-N. L.—3—Held by many third basemen.

Fewest Chances Offered, Game

    A.L.-N.L.—0—Held by many players.

Most Errors, Total Series

    A. L.—6—Brett, George H., Kansas City, 1976, 1977, 1978, 1980, 1984; 5 Series, 20 games.
    N. L.—5—Schmidt, Michael J., Philadelphia, 1976, 1977, 1978, 1980, 1983; 5 Series, 20
            games.

Most Errors, Series

    3-game Series—A. L.-N. L.—1—Held by many third basemen.
    4-game Series—N. L.—2—Cey, Ronald C., Los Angeles, 1974.
                          Schmidt, Michael J., Philadelphia, 1978.
                  A. L.— 1—Brett, George H., Kansas City, 1978.

5-game Series—A. L.— 3—Brett, George H., Kansas City, 1976.
DeCinces, Douglas V., California, 1982.
N. L.—1—Held by many third basemen.

Most Errors, Game

A. L.—2—Brett, George H., Kansas City, October 9, 1976.
DeCinces, Douglas V., California, October 9, 1982.
N. L.—2—Cey, Ronald C., Los Angeles, October 5, 1974.

Most Errors, Inning

A. L.—2—Brett, George H., Kansas City, October 9, 1976; first inning.
N. L.—1—Held by many third basemen.

Most Double Plays, Total Series

A. L.—6—Nettles, Graig, New York, 1976, 1977, 1978, 1980, 1981; 5 Series, 19 games.
N. L.—4—Schmidt, Michael J., Philadelphia, 1976, 1977, 1978, 1980; 4 Series, 16 games.

Most Double Plays, Series

3-game Series—A. L.— 2—Bando, Salvatore L., Oakland, 1971.
Nettles, Graig, New York, 1981.
N. L.—2—Schmidt, Michael J., Philadelphia, 1976.
4-game Series—A. L.— 3—Lansford, Carney R. California, 1979.
N. L.—1—Cey, Ronald C., Los Angeles, 1974, 1978.
Hebner, Richard J., Pittsburgh, 1974.
5-game Series—N. L.— 3—Parrish, Larry A., Montreal, 1981.
A. L.— 3—DeCinces, Douglas V., California, 1982.

Most Double Plays Started, Series

3-game Series—A. L.— 2—Bando, Salvatore L., Oakland, 1971.
Nettles, Graig, New York, 1981.
N. L.—2—Schmidt, Michael J., Philadelphia, 1976.
4-game Series—A. L.— 3—Lansford, Carney R., California, 1979.
N. L.—1—Cey, Ronald C., Los Angeles, 1974, 1978.
Hebner, Richard J., Pittsburgh, 1974.
5-game Series—N. L.— 3—Parrish, Larry A., Montreal, 1981.
A. L.— 2—Rodriguez, Aurelio, Detroit, 1972.
Nettles, Graig, New York, 1977.
DeCinces, Douglas V., California, 1982.
Molitor, Paul L., Milwaukee, 1982.

Most Double Plays, Game

N. L.—2—Schmidt, Michael J., Philadelphia, October 9, 1976.
Schmidt, Michael J., Philadelphia, October 11, 1980; 10 innings.
Parrish, Larry A., Montreal, October 16, 1981.
A. L.—1—Held by many third basemen.

Most Double Plays Started, Game

N. L.—2—Schmidt, Michael J., Philadelphia, October 9, 1976.
Parrish, Larry A., Montreal, October 16, 1981.
A. L.—1—Held by many third basemen.

Most Unassisted Double Plays, Game

N. L.—1—Schmidt, Michael J., Philadelphia, October 9, 1976.
A. L.—Never accomplished.

SHORTSTOPS' FIELDING RECORDS

Most Series Played

A. L.—6—Belanger, Mark H., Baltimore, 1969, 1970, 1971, 1973, 1974, 1979; 21 games.
Campaneris, Dagoberto B., Oakland, 1971, 1972, 1973, 1974, 1975, California, 1979; 18 games.
N. L.—5—Concepcion, David I., Cincinnati, 1970, 1972, 1975, 1976, 1979; 13 games.
Russell, William E., Los Angeles, 1974, 1977, 1978, 1981, 1983; 21 games.
Bowa, Lawrence R., Philadelphia, 1976, 1977, 1978, 1980; Chicago, 1984; 21 games.

Most Games Played, Total Series

A. L.—21—Belanger, Mark H., Baltimore, 1969, 1970, 1971, 1973, 1974, 1979; 6 Series.
N. L.—21—Russell, William E., Los Angeles, 1974, 1977, 1978, 1981, 1983; 5 Series.
Bowa, Lawrence R., Philadelphia, 1976, 1977, 1978, 1980; Chicago, 1984; 5 Series.

Highest Fielding Average, Series, With Most Chances Accepted

3-game Series—A. L.—1.000—Dent, Russell E., New York, 1980; 21 chances accepted.
                N. L.—1.000—Concepcion, David I., Cincinnati, 1979; 17 chances accepted.
4-game Series—N. L.—1.000—Russell, William E., Los Angeles, 1974; 29 chances accepted.
                A. L.—1.000—Campaneris, Dagoberto B., Oakland, 1974; 20 chances accepted.
5-game Series—A. L.—1.000—Patek, Freddie J., Kansas City, 1976; 31 chances accepted.
                N. L.—1.000—Harrelson, Derrel M., New York, 1973; 26 chances accepted.

Most Consecutive Errorless Games, Total Series

A. L.—17—Belanger, Mark H., Baltimore, October 4, 1969 through October 8, 1974.
N. L.—13—Russell, William E., Los Angeles, October 5, 1977 through October 4, 1983.

Most Putouts, Total Series

N. L.—42—Russell, William E., Los Angeles, 1974, 1977, 1978, 1981, 1983; 5 Series, 21 games.
A. L.—31—Belanger, Mark H., Baltimore, 1969, 1970, 1971, 1973, 1974, 1979; 6 Series, 21 games.

Most Putouts, Series

3-game Series—A. L.—13—Cardenas, Leonardo A., Minnesota, 1969.
                N. L.— 6—Held by many shortstops.
4-game Series—N. L.—13—Russell, William E., Los Angeles, 1974.
                A. L.— 9—Patek, Freddie J., Kansas City, 1978.
5-game Series—N. L.—19—Templeton, Garry, L., San Diego, 1984.
                A. L.—13—Patek, Freddie J., Kansas City, 1976.

Most Putouts, Game

N. L.—7—Templeton, Garry L., San Diego, October 4, 1984.
A. L.—6—Belanger, Mark H., Baltimore, October 5, 1974.
      Dent, Russell E., New York, October 5, 1977.
      Patek, Freddie J., Kansas City, October 5, 1977.

Most Putouts, Inning

A. L.—3—Belanger, Mark H., Baltimore, October 5, 1974; third inning.
      Patek, Freddie J., Kansas City, October 5, 1977; second inning.
N. L.—3—Speier, Chris E., Montreal, October 14, 1981; fifth inning.

Most Assists, Total Series

N. L.—70—Bowa, Lawrence R., Philadelphia, 1976, 1977, 1978, 1980; Chicago, 1984; 5 Series, 21 games.
A. L.—69—Belanger, Mark H., Baltimore, 1969, 1970, 1971, 1973, 1974, 1979; 6 Series, 21 games.

Most Assists, Series

3-game Series—A. L.—14—Belanger, Mark H., Baltimore, 1970.
                N. L.—14—Concepcion, David I., Cincinnati, 1979.
4-game Series—A. L.—17—Campaneris, Dagoberto B., Oakland, 1974.
                N. L.—17—Bowa, Lawrence R., Philadelphia, 1977.
5-game Series—A. L.—18—Patek, Freddie J., Kansas City, 1976, 1977.
                N. L.—16—Chaney, Darrel L., Cincinnati, 1972.
                      Speier, Chris E., Montreal, 1981.

Most Assists, Game

N. L.—9—Russell, William E., Los Angeles, October 5, 1978.
A. L.—9—Garcia, Alfonso R., Baltimore, October 4, 1979.

Most Assists, Inning

A. L.—3—Belanger, Mark H., Baltimore, October 7, 1973; seventh inning.
N. L.—3—Concepcion, David I., Cincinnati, October 3, 1979; fourth inning.

Most Chances Accepted, Total Series

N. L.—107—Russell, William E., Los Angeles, 1974, 1977, 1978, 1981, 1983; 5 Series, 21 games.
A. L.—100—Belanger, Mark H., Baltimore, 1969, 1970, 1971, 1973, 1974, 1979; 6 Series, 21 games.

Most Chances Accepted, Series

3-game Series—A. L.—25—Cardenas, Leonardo A., Minnesota, 1969.
                N. L.—17—Concepcion, David I., Cincinnati, 1979.

4-game Series—N. L.—29—Russell, William E., Los Angeles, 1974.
              A. L.—22—Garcia, Alfonso R., Baltimore, 1979.
5-game Series—A. L.—31—Patek, Freddie J., Kansas City, 1976.
              N. L.—31—Speier, Chris E., Montreal, 1981.

Most Chances Accepted, Game

N. L.—13—Russell, William E., Los Angeles, October 8, 1974; 6 putouts, 7 assists, 0 errors.
A. L.—11—Cardenas, Leonardo A., Minnesota, October 5, 1969; 11 innings; 6 putouts, 5 assists, 1 error.
     Garcia, Alfonso R., Baltimore, October 4, 1979; 2 putouts, 9 assists, 0 errors.

Most Chances Accepted, Inning

A. L.-N. L.—3—Held by many shortstops.

Fewest Chances Offered, Game

A. L.—0—Campaneris, Dagoberto B., Oakland, October 3, 1971.
     Foli, Timothy J., California, October 10, 1982.
     Ripken, Calvin E., Baltimore, October 6, 1983.
N. L.—0—Garrido, Gil G., Atlanta, October 5, 1969.
     Bowa, Lawrence R., Philadelphia, October 11, 1980; 10 innings.
     Russell, William E., Los Angeles, October 7, 1983.

Most Errors, Total Series

N. L.—3—Chaney, Darrel L., Cincinnati, 1972, 1973; 2 Series, 10 games.
     Speier, Chris E., San Francisco, 1971; Montreal, 1981; 2 Series, 9 games.
     Russell, William E., Los Angeles, 1974, 1977, 1978, 1981, 1983; 5 Series, 21 games.
A. L.—3—Cardenas, Leonardo A., Minnesota, 1969, 1970; 2 Series; 6 games.
     McAuliffe, Richard J., Detroit, 1972; 1 Series, 4 games.
     Patek, Freddie J., Kansas City, 1976, 1977, 1978; 3 Series, 14 games.

Most Errors, Series

3-game Series—A. L.— 2—Cardenas, Leonardo A., Minnesota, 1970.
              N. L.— 1—Held by many shortstops.
4-game Series—A. L.— 2—Patek, Freddie J., Kansas City, 1978.
                  Garcia, Alfonso R., Baltimore, 1979.
              N. L.— 2—Russell, William E., Los Angeles, 1977.
                  DeJesus, Ivan, Philadelphia, 1983.
5-game Series—A. L.— 3—McAuliffe, Richard J., Detroit, 1972.
              N. L.— 3—Chaney, Darrel L., Cincinnati, 1972.

Most Errors, Game

A. L.—2—Cardenas, Leonardo A., Minnesota, October 4, 1970.
N. L.—2—Alley, L. Eugene, Pittsburgh, October 10, 1972.
     Russell, William E., Los Angeles, October 4, 1977.

Most Errors, Inning

N. L.—2—Alley, L. Eugene, Pittsburgh, October 10, 1972; fourth inning.
A. L.—1—Held by many shortstops.

Most Double Plays, Total Series

N. L.—17—Russell, William E., Los Angeles, 1974, 1977, 1978, 1981, 1983; 5 Series, 21 games.
      Bowa, Lawrence R., Philadelphia, 1976, 1977, 1978, 1980; Chicago, 1984; 5 Series, 21 games.
A. L.—10—Belanger, Mark H., Baltimore, 1969, 1970, 1971, 1973, 1974, 1979; 6 Series, 21 games.

Most Double Plays, Series

3-game Series—N. L.— 3—Garrido, Gil C., Atlanta, 1969.
                  Alley, L. Eugene, Pittsburgh, 1970.
              A. L.— 3—Held by many shortstops.
4-game Series—N. L.— 6—Russell, William E., Los Angeles, 1974.
              A. L.— 3—Garcia, Alfonso R., Baltimore, 1979.
                  Ripken, Calvin E., Baltimore, 1983.
5-game Series—N. L.— 6—Speier, Chris E., Montreal, 1981.
                  Bowa, Lawrence R., Chicago, 1984.
              A. L.— 4—Yount, Robin R., Milwaukee, 1982.

Most Double Plays Started, Series

3-game Series—N. L.— 3—Alley, L. Eugene, Pittsburgh, 1970.
              A. L.— 2—Belanger, Mark H., Baltimore, 1971.
                  Campaneris, Dagoberto B., Oakland, 1975.
                  Milbourne, Lawrence W., New York, 1981.

4-game Series—N. L.—3—Russell, William E., Los Angeles, 1974.
                A. L.—2—Belanger, Mark H., Baltimore, 1974.
                       Anderson, James L., California, 1979.
                       Ripken, Calvin E., Baltimore, 1983.
5-game Series—N. L.—3—Bowa, Lawrence R., Philadelphia, 1980.
                       Speier, Chris E., Montreal, 1981.
                       Bowa, Lawrence R., Chicago, 1984.
                A. L.—2—Maxvill, C. Dallan, Oakland, 1972.
                       Patek, Freddie J., Kansas City, 1976.
                       Yount, Robin R., Milwaukee, 1982.

Most Double Plays, Game

A. L.—3—Campaneris, Dagoberto B., Oakland, October 5, 1975.
N. L.—3—Russell, William E., Los Angeles, October 8, 1974.
           Russell, William E., Los Angeles, October 5, 1983.

Most Double Plays Started, Game

N. L.—3—Russell, William E., Los Angeles, October 5, 1983.
A. L.—2—Maxvill, C. Dallan, Oakland, October 10, 1972.
           Campaneris, Dagoberto B., Oakland, October 5, 1975.
           Patek, Freddie J., Kansas City, October 10, 1976.

Most Unassisted Double Plays, Game

N. L.—1—Russell, William E., Los Angeles, October 8, 1974.
A. L.—1—Yount, Robin R., Milwaukee, October 5, 1982.

OUTFIELDERS' FIELDING RECORDS

Most Series Played

A. L.—10—Jackson, Reginald M., Oakland, 1971, 1972, 1973, 1974, 1975; New York, 1977, 1978, 1980, 1981; California, 1982; 32 games.
N. L.— 5—Geronimo, Cesar F., Cincinnati, 1972, 1973, 1975, 1976, 1979; 17 games.
           Maddox, Garry L., Philadelphia, 1976, 1977, 1978, 1980, 1983; 17 games.

Most Games Played, Total Series

A. L.—32—Jackson, Reginald M., Oakland, 1971, 1972, 1973, 1974, 1975; New York, 1977, 1978, 1980, 1981; California, 1982, 10 Series.
N. L.—17—Geronimo, Cesar F., Cincinnati, 1972, 1973, 1975, 1976, 1979; 5 Series.
           Maddox, Garry L., Philadelphia, 1976, 1977, 1978, 1980, 1983; 5 Series.

Highest Fielding Average, Series, With Most Chances Accepted

3-game Series—N. L.—1.000—Parker, David G., Pittsburgh, 1975; 14 chances accepted.
                A. L.—1.000—Oliva, Antonio, Minnesota, 1970; 12 chances accepted.
4-game Series—A. L.—1.000—Miller, Richard A., California, 1979; 16 chances accepted.
                N. L.—1.000—Stargell, Wilver D., Pittsburgh, 1974, 13 chances accepted.
5-game Series—N.L.— 1.000—Maddox, Garry L., Philadelphia, 1980; 23 chances accepted.
                A. L.—1.000—Jackson, Reginald M., Oakland, 1973; 19 chances accepted.
                           Rivers, John M., New York, 1977; 19 chances accepted.

Most Consecutive Errorless Games, Total Series

A. L.—25—Jackson, Reginald M., Oakland, New York, California, October 12, 1972 through October 10, 1982; 48 chances accepted.
N. L.—16—Oliver, Albert, Pittsburgh, October 2, 1971 through October 7, 1975; 37 chances accepted.
           Geronimo, Cesar F., Cincinnati; October 7, 1972 through October 3, 1979; 50 chances accepted.

Most Putouts, Total Series

A. L.—69—Jackson, Reginald M., Oakland, 1971, 1972, 1973, 1974, 1975; New York, 1977, 1978, 1980, 1981; California, 1982; 10 Series, 32 games.
N. L.—62—Maddox, Garry L., Philadelphia, 1976, 1977, 1978, 1980, 1983; 5 Series, 17 games.

Most Putouts, Series

3-game Series—N. L.—13—Geronimo, Cesar F., Cincinnati, 1975.
                Parker, David G., Pittsburgh, 1975.
                A. L.—12—Lynn, Fredric M., Boston, 1975.
4-game Series—N. L.—16—Maddox, Garry L., Philadelphia, 1978.
                A. L.—14—North, William A., Oakland, 1974.
                Miller, Richard A., California, 1979.

5-game Series—N. L.—23—Maddox, Garry L., Philadelphia, 1980.
           A. L.—19—Jackson, Reginald M., Oakland, 1973.
                      Rivers, John M., New York, 1977.

Most Putouts, Game, Center Field

N. L.—8—Oliver, Albert, Pittsburgh, October 7, 1972.
        Hahn, Donald A., New York, October 8, 1973.
A. L.—7—Lynn, Fredric M., Boston, October 4, 1975.
        Rivers, John M., New York, October 6, 1977.
        Miller, Richard A., California, October 5, 1979.

Most Putouts, Game, Left Field

A. L.—7—White, Roy H., New York, October 13, 1976.
N. L.—7—Stennett, Renaldo A., Pittsburgh, October 7, 1972.
        Cruz, Jose, Houston, October 10, 1980; 11 innings.

Most Putouts, Game, Right Field

A. L.—7—Jackson, Reginald M., Oakland, October 10, 1973.
        Washington, Claudell, Oakland, October 9, 1974.
N. L.—5—Held by many right fielders.

Most Consecutive Putouts, Game

A. L.—4—Gamble, Oscar C., New York, October 15, 1981; 3 in sixth inning, 1 in seventh
         inning; right field.
N. L.—4—Dawson, Andre F., Montreal, October 19, 1981; 1 in sixth inning, 3 in seventh
         inning; center field.

Most Putouts, Inning, Outfielder

A. L.—3—Jackson, Reginald M., New York, October 7, 1977; right field, fourth inning.
        Hurdle, Clinton M., Kansas City, October 6, 1978; left field, seventh inning,
         consecutive.
        Gamble, Oscar C., New York, October 15, 1981; right field, sixth inning, con-
         secutive.
N. L.—3—Dawson, Andre F., Montreal, October 19, 1981; center field, seventh inning,
         consecutive.

Most Assists, Total Series

N. L.—5—McBride, Arnold R., Philadelphia, 1977, 1978, 1980; 3 Series, 11 games.
A. L.—3—Oliva, Antonio, Minnesota, 1969, 1970; 2 Series, 6 games.
        Jackson, Reginald M., Oakland, 1971, 1972, 1973, 1974, 1975; New York, 1977,
         1978, 1980, 1981; 9 Series, 27 games.

Fewest Assists, Total Series (Most Games)

A. L.—0—Blair, Paul L., Baltimore, 1969, 1970, 1971, 1973, 1974; New York, 1977, 1978; 7
         Series, 24 games.
N. L.—0—Maddox, Garry L., Philadelphia, 1976, 1977, 1978, 1980, 1983; 5 Series, 17
         games.

Most Assists, Series

3-game Series—A. L.— 2—Oliva, Antonio, Minnesota, 1970.
                       Yastrzemski, Carl M., Boston, 1975.
                       Armas, Antonio R., Oakland, 1981.
              N. L.—2—Foster, George A., Cincinnati. 1979.
4-game Series—N. L.—2—McBride, Arnold R., Philadelphia, 1977.
              A. L.— 2—Miller, Richard A., California, 1979.
5-game Series—N. L.—3—McBride, Arnold R., Philadelphia, 1980.
              A. L.—1—Held by many outfielders.

Most Assists, Game

A. L.—2—Oliva, Antonio, Minnesota, October 4, 1970.
N. L.—2—Foster, George A., Cincinnati, October 3, 1979; 10 innings.
        McBride, Arnold R., Philadelphia, October 11, 1980; 10 innings.

Most Chances Accepted, Total Series

A. L.—72—Jackson, Reginald M., Oakland, 1971, 1972, 1973, 1974, 1975; New York, 1977,
          1978, 1980, 1981; California, 1982; 10 Series, 32 games.
N. L.—62—Maddox, Garry L., Philadelphia, 1976, 1977, 1978, 1980, 1983; 5 Series, 17
          games.

Most Chances Accepted, Series

3-game Series—N. L.—14—Parker, David G., Pittsburgh, 1975.
              A. L.—13—Lynn, Fredric M., Boston, 1975.
4-game Series—N. L.—16—Maddox, Garry L., Philadelphia, 1978.
              A. L.—16—Miller, Richard A., California, 1979.

5-game Series—N. L.—23—Maddox, Garry L., Philadelphia, 1980.
　　　　　　　　A. L.—19—Jackson, Reginald M., Oakland, 1973.
　　　　　　　　　　Rivers, John M., New York, 1977.

Most Chances Accepted, Game, Center Field

N. L.—8—Oliver, Albert, Pittsburgh, October 7, 1972; 8 putouts, 0 assists, 0 errors.
　　　　Hahn, Donald A., New York, October 8, 1973; 8 putouts, 0 assists, 0 errors.
A. L.—8—Miller, Richard A., California, October 5, 1979; 7 putouts, 1 assist, 0 errors.

Most Chances Accepted, Game, Left Field

A. L.—7—White, Roy H., New York, October 13, 1976; 7 putouts, 0 assists, 0 errors.
　　　　Hurdle, Clinton M., Kansas City, October 6, 1978; 6 putouts, 1 assist, 0 errors.
N. L.—7—Stennett, Renaldo A., Pittsburgh, October 7, 1972; 7 putouts, 0 assists, 0 errors.
　　　　Cruz, Jose, Houston, October 10, 1980; 7 putouts, 0 assists, 0 errors.

Most Chances Accepted, Game, Right Field

A. D.—7—Jackson, Reginald M., Oakland, October 10, 1973; 7 putouts, 0 assists, 0 errors.
　　　　Washington, Claudell, Oakland, October 9, 1974; 7 putouts, 0 assists, 0 errors.
N. L.—5—Held by many right fielders.

Longest Game, No Chances Offered, Outfielder

N. L.—12 innings— Hahn, Donald A., New York, October 9, 1973.
A. L.—11 innings— Alou, Mateo R., Oakland, October 7, 1972.

Most Chances Accepted, Inning

A. L.-N. L.—3—Held by many players.

Most Errors, Total Series

N. L.—2—Smith, C. Reginald, Los Angeles, 1977, 1978; 2 Series, 8 games.
A. L.—2—Oliva, Antonio, Minnesota, 1969, 1970; 2 Series, 6 games.
　　　　Washington, Claudell, Oakland, 1974, 1975; 2 Series, 5 games.
　　　　Gamble, Oscar C., New York, 1976, 1980, 1981; 3 Series, 5 games.
　　　　Bumbry, Alonza B., Baltimore, 1973, 1979; 2 Series, 6 games.
　　　　Oglivie, Benjamin A., Milwaukee, 1982; 1 Series, 4 games.

Most Errors, Series

A. L.—2—Oliva, Antonio, Minnesota, 1969; 3-game Series.
　　　　Washington, Claudell, Oakland, 1975; 3-game Series.
　　　　Gamble, Oscar C., New York, 1976; 5-game Series.
　　　　Oglivie, Benjamin A., Milwaukee, 1982; 5-game Series.
N. L.—1—Held by many outfielders.

Most Errors, Game

A. L.—2—Oliva, Antonio, Minnesota, October 6, 1969.
　　　　Oglivie, Benjamin A., Milwaukee, October 10, 1982.
N. L.—1—Held by many outfielders.

Most Errors, Inning

A. L.-N. L.—1—Held by many outfielders.

Most Double Plays, Total Series

N. L.—3—McBride, Arnold R., Philadelphia, 1977, 1978, 1980; 3 Series, 11 games.
A. L.—2—Miller, Richard A., California, 1979; 1 Series, 4 games.

Most Double Plays, Game

N. L.—2—McBride, Arnold R., Philadelphia, October 11, 1980; 10 innings.
A. L.-N. L.—Nine-inning record—1—Held by many outfielders.

Most Double Plays Started, Game

N. L.—2—McBride, Arnold R., Philadelphia, October 11, 1980; 10 innings.
A. L.-N. L.—Nine-inning record—1—Held by many outfielders.

Most Unassisted Double Plays, Game

A. L.-N. L.—Never accomplished.

CATCHERS' FIELDING RECORDS

Most Series Played

N. L.—6—Bench, Johnny L., Cincinnati, 1970, 1972, 1973, 1975, 1976, 1979; 22 games.
A. L.—5—Etchebarren, Andrew A., Baltimore, 1969, 1970, 1971, 1973, 1974; 12 games.

Most Games Caught, Total Series

N. L.—22—Bench, Johnny L., Cincinnati, 1970, 1972, 1973, 1975, 1976, 1979; 6 Series.
A. L.—14—Munson, Thurman L., New York, 1976, 1977, 1978; 3 Series.

Highest Fielding Average, Series, With Most Chances Accepted

3-game Series—N. L.—1.000—Ott, N. Edward, Pittsburgh, 1979; 28 chances accepted.
　　　　　　　　A. L.—1.000—Cerone, Richard A., New York, 1981; 25 chances accepted.
4-game Series—N. L.—1.000—Dietz, Richard A., San Francisco, 1971; 36 chances accepted.
　　　　　　　　A. L.—1.000—Fisk, Carlton E., Chicago, 1983; 30 chances accepted.
5-game Series—A. L.—1.000—Simmons, Ted L., Milwaukee, 1982; 39 chances accepted.
　　　　　　　　N. L.—1.000—Bench, Johnny L., Cincinnati, 1973; 33 chances accepted.

Most Consecutive Errorless Games, Total Series

N. L.—17—Bench, Johnny L., Cincinnati, October 9, 1972 through October 5, 1979.
A. L.—12—Etchebarren, Andrew A., Baltimore, October 4, 1969 through October 8, 1974.
　　　　　Munson, Thurman L., New York, October 12, 1976 through October 7, 1978.
　　　　　Porter, Darrell R., Kansas City, October 5, 1977 through October 10, 1980.

Most Putouts, Total Series

N. L.— 125— Bench, Johnny L., Cincinnati, 1970, 1972, 1973, 1975, 1976, 1979; 6 Series, 22 games.
A. L.— 78— Etchebarren, Andrew A., Baltimore, 1969, 1970, 1971, 1973, 1974; 5 Series, 12 games.

Most Putouts, Series

3-game Series—N. L.—29—Sanguillen, Manuel D., Pittsburgh, 1975.
　　　　　　　　A. L.—23—Cerone, Richard A., New York, 1981.
4-game Series—N. L.—34—Dietz, Richard A., San Francisco, 1971.
　　　　　　　　A. L.—29—Dempsey, J. Rikard, Baltimore, 1983.
5-game Series—N. L.—42—Grote, Gerald W., New York, 1973.
　　　　　　　　A. L.—36—Simmons, Ted L., Milwaukee, 1982.

Most Putouts, Game, Nine Innings

A. L.—15—Dempsey, J. Rikard, Baltimore, October 6, 1983.
N. L.—14—Dietz, Richard A., San Francisco, October 3, 1971.

Most Putouts, Extra-Inning Game

N. L.—15—Sanguillen, Manuel D., Pittsburgh, October 7, 1975; 10 innings.
A. L.—Less than nine-inning record.

Fewest Putouts, Game

A. L.—1—Fosse, Raymond E., Oakland, October 11, 1973.
　　　　　Martinez, J. Buck, Kansas City, October 13, 1976.
N. L.—1—Kennedy, Terrence E., San Diego, October 3, 1984.

Most Putouts, Inning

A. L.-N. L.—3—Held by many catchers.

Most Assists, Total Series

N. L.—18—Bench, Johnny L., Cincinnati, 1970, 1972, 1973, 1975, 1976, 1979; 6 Series, 22 games.
A. L.—14—Munson, Thurman L., New York, 1976, 1977, 1978; 3 Series, 14 games.

Most Assists, Series

3-game Series—A. L.— 4—Mitterwald, George E., Minnesota, 1969.
　　　　　　　　　　　　Cerone, Richard A., New York, 1980.
　　　　　　　　N. L.— 4—Bench, Johnny L., Cincinnati, 1975, 1976.
4-game Series—A. L.— 5—Dempsey, J. Rikard, Baltimore, 1983.
　　　　　　　　N. L.— 2—Held by many catchers.
5-game Series—A. L.— 6—Munson, Thurman L., New York, 1976.
　　　　　　　　N. L.— 4—Kennedy, Terrence E., San Diego, 1984.

Most Assists, Game

N. L.—3—Bench, Johnny L., Cincinnati, October 3, 1970; 10 innings.
　　　　　Bench, Johnny L., Cincinnati, October 5, 1975.
A. L.—2—Held by many catchers.

Most Assists, Inning

N. L.—2—Bench, Johnny L., Cincinnati, October 7, 1973; eighth inning.
A. L.—1—Held by many catchers.

Most Chances Accepted, Total Series

N. L.— 143— Bench, Johnny L., Cincinnati, 1970, 1972, 1973, 1975, 1976, 1979; 6 Series, 22 games.
A. L.— 81— Etchebarren, Andrew A., Baltimore, 1969, 1970, 1971, 1973, 1974; 5 Series, 12 games.

Most Chances Accepted, Series

   3-game Series—N. L.—30—Sanguillen, Manuel D., Pittsburgh, 1975.
                 A. L.—25—Cerone, Richard A., New York, 1981.
   4-game Series—N. L.—36—Dietz, Richard A., San Francisco, 1971.
                 A. L.—34—Dempsey, J. Rikard, Baltimore, 1983.
   5-game Series—N. L.—43—Grote, Gerald W., New York, 1973.
                 A. L.—39—Simmons, Ted L., Milwaukee, 1982.

Most Chances Accepted, Game

   A. L.—16—Dempsey, J. Rikard, Baltimore, October 6, 1983; 15 putouts, 1 assist, 0 errors.
   N. L.—15—Dietz, Richard A., San Francisco, October 3, 1971; 14 putouts, 1 assist, 0 errors.
        Sanguillen, Manuel D., Pittsburgh, October 7, 1975; 10 innings; 15 putouts, 0 assists, 1 error.

Most Chances Accepted, Inning

   A. L.-N. L.—3—Held by many catchers.

Fewest Chances Offered, Game

   A. L.-N. L.—2—Held by many catchers.

Most Errors, Total Series

   N. L.—5—Sanguillen, Manuel D., Pittsburgh, 1970, 1971, 1972, 1974, 1975; 5 Series, 19 games.
   A. L.—3—Slaught, Donald M., Kansas City, 1984; 1 Series, 3 games.

Most Errors, Series

   3-game Series—A. L.— 3—Slaught, Donald M., Kansas City, 1984.
                 N. L.—1—Sanguillen, Manuel D., Pittsburgh, 1970, 1975.
   4-game Series—N. L.—2—Sanguillen, Manuel D., Pittsburgh, 1974.
                 A. L.— 1—Dempsey, J. Rikard, Baltimore, 1983.
   5-game Series—A. L.— 2—Munson, Thurman L., New York, 1976.
                 N. L.—1—Bench, Johnny L., Cincinnati, 1972.
                        Sanguillen, Manuel D., Pittsburgh, 1972.
                        Grote, Gerald W., New York, 1973.

Most Errors, Game

   A. L.—2—Munson, Thurman L., New York, October 10, 1976.
        Slaught, Donald M., Kansas City, October 5, 1984.
   N. L.—2—Sanguillen, Manuel D., Pittsburgh, October 6, 1974.

Most Errors, Inning

   A. L.-N. L.—1—Held by many catchers.

Most Passed Balls, Total Series

   N. L.—4—Sanguillen, Manuel D., Pittsburgh, 1970, 1971, 1972, 1974, 1975; 5 Series, 19 games.
   A. L.—2—Munson, Thurman L., New York, 1976, 1977, 1978; 3 Series, 14 games.

Most Passed Balls, Series

   N. L.—2—Sanguillen, Manuel D., Pittsburgh, 1975; 3-game Series.
   A. L.—1—Held by many catchers.

Most Passed Balls, Game

   N. L.—2—Sanguillen, Manuel D., Pittsburgh, October 4, 1975.
   A. L.—1—Held by many catchers.

Most Passed Balls, Inning

   A L.-N. L.—1—Held by many catchers.

Most Double Plays Total Series

   A. L.—4—Fosse, Raymond E., Oakland, 1973, 1974, 1975; 3 Series, 10 games.
   N. L.—3—Sanguillen, Manuel D., Pittsburgh, 1970, 1971, 1972, 1974, 1975; 5 Series, 19 games.

Most Double Plays, Series

   A. L.—2—Mitterwald, George E., Minnesota, 1970; 3-game Series.
        Fosse, Raymond E., Oakland, 1973; 5-game Series.
   N. L.—1—Held by many catchers.

Most Double Plays Started, Series

   A. L.—2—Fosse, Raymond E., Oakland, 1973; 5-game Series.
   N. L.—1—Held by many catchers.

Most Double Plays, Game
 A. L.-N. L.—1—Held by many catchers.

Most Double Plays Started, Game
 A. L.-N. L.—1—Held by many catchers.

Most Unassisted Double Plays, Game
 A. L.-N. L.—Never accomplished.

Most Players Caught Stealing, Total Series
 A. L.—12—Munson, Thurman L., New York, 1976, 1977, 1978; 3 Series, 14 games.
 N. L.— 3—Bench, Johnny L., Cincinnati, 1970, 1972, 1973, 1975, 1976, 1979; 6 Series, 22 games.
   Boone, Robert R., Philadelphia, 1976, 1977, 1978, 1980; 4 Series, 14 games.

Most Players Caught Stealing, Series
 3-game Series—A. L.— 4—Mitterwald, George E., Minnesota, 1969.
       N. L.—1—Held by many catchers.
 4-game Series—A. L.— 3—Fosse, Raymond E., Oakland, 1974.
         Munson, Thurman L., New York, 1978.
       N. L.—1—Held by many catchers.
 5-game Series—A. L.— 5—Munson, Thurman L., New York, 1976.
       N. L.—2—Kennedy, Terrence E., San Diego, 1984.
         Davis, Jody R., Chicago, 1984.

Most Players Caught Stealing, Inning
 A. L.-N. L.—1—Held by many catchers.

Most Players Caught Stealing, Game
 A. L.—2—Held by many catchers.
 N. L.—2—Kennedy, Terrence E., San Diego, 1984.

PITCHERS' FIELDING RECORDS

Most Series Pitched
 Both Leagues—6—Gullett, Donald E., Cincinnati NL, 1970, 1972, 1973, 1975, 1976; New York AL, 1977; 10 games.
 A. L.—6—Hunter, James A., Oakland, 1971, 1972, 1973, 1974; New York, 1976, 1978; 10 games.
   Palmer, James A., Baltimore, 1969, 1970, 1971, 1973, 1974, 1979; 8 games.
 N. L.—6—McGraw, Frank E., New York, 1969, 1973; Philadelphia, 1976, 1977, 1978, 1980; 15 games.
   Reed, Ronald L., Atlanta, 1969; Philadelphia, 1976, 1977, 1978, 1980, 1983; 13 games.

Most Games Pitched, Total Series
 N. L.—15—McGraw, Frank E., New York, 1969, 1973; Philadelphia, 1976, 1977, 1978, 1980; 6 Series.
 A. L.—11—Fingers, Roland G., Oakland, 1971, 1972, 1973, 1974, 1975; 5 Series.

Most Games Pitched, Series
 3-game Series—N. L.— 3—Upshaw, Cecil L., Atlanta, 1969; 6⅓ innings.
         Tomlin, David A., Cincinnati, 1979; 3 innings.
         Hume, Thomas H., Cincinnati, 1979; 4 innings.
       A. L.— 3—Perranoski, Ronald P., Minnesota, 1969; 4⅔ innings.
         Todd, James R., Oakland, 1975; 1 inning.
         Hernandez, Guillermo, Detroit, 1984; 4 innings.
 4-game Series—N. L.— 4—Giusti, J. David, Pittsburgh, 1971; 5⅓ innings.
       A. L.— 3—Hrabosky, Alan T., Kansas City, 1978; 3 innings.
         Stanhouse, Donald J., Baltimore, 1979; 3 innings.
         Lamp, Dennis P., Chicago, 1983; 2 innings.
 5-game Series—N. L.— 5—McGraw, Frank E., Philadelphia, 1980; 8 innings.
       A. L.— 4—Blue, Vida R., Oakland, 1972; 5⅓ innings.
         Lyle, Albert W., New York, 1977; 9⅓ innings.

Highest Fielding Average, Series, With Most Chances Accepted
 3-game Series—N. L.—1.000—Gullett, Donald E., Cincinnati, 1975; 5 chances accepted.
       A. L.—1.000—Boswell, David W., Minnesota, 1969; 5 chances accepted.
         Lindblad, Paul A., Oakland, 1975; 5 chances accepted.
         Wise, Richard C., Boston, 1975; 5 chances accepted.
 4-game Series—N. L.—1.000—Marichal, Juan A., San Francisco, 1971; 6 chances accepted.
         Carlton, Steven N., Philadelphia, 1983; 6 chances accepted.

A. L.—1.000—Cuellar, Miguel, Baltimore, 1974; 5 chances accepted.
Hunter, James A., Oakland, 1974; 5 chances accepted.
Gura, Lawrence C., Kansas City, 1978; 5 chances accepted.
5-game Series—N. L.—1.000—Blass, Stephen R., Pittsburgh, 1972; 4 chances accepted.
Ryan, L. Nolan, Houston, 1980; 4 chances accepted.
A. L.—1.000—Lolich, Michael S., Detroit, 1972; 4 chances accepted.
John, Thomas E., California, 1982; 4 chances accepted.

Most Consecutive Errorless Games, Total Series

N. L.—13—Giusti, J. David, Pittsburgh, October 4, 1970 through October 7, 1975.
McGraw, Frank E., New York, Philadelphia, October 10, 1973 through October 12, 1980.
Reed, Ronald L., Atlanta, Philadelphia, October 5, 1969 through October 8, 1983.
A. L.—11—Fingers, Roland G., Oakland, October 3, 1971 through October 5, 1975.

Most Putouts, Total Series

N. L.—5—Gullett, Donald E., Cincinnati, 1970, 1972, 1973, 1975, 1976; 5 Series, 9 games.
A. L.—4—Hunter, James A., Oakland, 1971, 1972, 1973, 1974; New York, 1976, 1978; 6 Series, 10 games.
Palmer James A., Baltimore, 1969, 1970, 1971, 1973, 1974, 1979; 6 Series, 8 games.

Most Putouts, Series

3-game Series—N. L.—4—Gullett, Donald E., Cincinnati, 1975.
A. L.—2—Wise, Richard, C., Boston, 1975.
Wilcox, Milton E., Detroit, 1984.
4-game Series—A. L.—3—Hunter, James A., Oakland, 1974.
N. L.—2—Marichal, Juan A., San Francisco, 1971.
Sutton, Donald H., Los Angeles, 1974.
5-game Series—A. L.—3—John, Thomas E., California, 1982.
N. L.—2—McGraw, Frank E., New York, 1973.
Ruthven, Richard D., Philadelphia, 1980.

Most Putouts, Game

N. L.—4—Gullett, Donald E., Cincinnati, October 4, 1975.
A. L.—3—John, Thomas E., California, October 5, 1982.

Most Putouts, Inning

A. L.—2—Torrez, Michael A., New York, October 7, 1977; second inning.
N. L.—2—Gullett, Donald E., Cincinnati, October 4, 1975; third inning.

Most Assists, Total Series

A. L.—12—Cuellar, Miguel, Baltimore, 1969, 1970, 1971, 1973, 1974; 5 Series, 6 games.
N. L.— 6—Sutton, Donald H., Los Angeles, 1974, 1977, 1978; 3 Series, 4 games.
Carlton, Steven N., Philadelphia, 1976, 1977, 1978, 1980, 1983; 5 Series, 8 games.

Most Assists, Series

3-game Series—A. L.—4—Boswell, David W., Minnesota, 1969.
Lindblad, Paul A., Oakland, 1975.
N. L.—3—Niekro, Philip H., Atlanta, 1969.
Ellis, Dock P., Pittsburgh, 1970.
Zachry, Patrick P., Cincinnati, 1976.
4-game Series—A. L.—5—Cuellar, Miguel, Baltimore, 1974.
N. L.—5—Carlton, Steven N., Philadelphia, 1983.
5-game Series—N. L.—3—Blass, Stephen R., Pittsburgh, 1972.
Seaver, G. Thomas, New York, 1973.
Ryan, L. Nolan, Houston, 1980.
A. L.—3—Held by many pitchers.

Most Assists, Game

N. L.—4—Marichal, Juan A., San Francisco, October 5, 1971.
A. L.—4—Boswell, David W., Minnesota, October 5, 1969; 11 innings.
Lindblad, Paul A., Oakland, October 7, 1975.
Gura, Lawrence C., Kansas City, October 4, 1978.

Most Assists, Inning

N. L.—3—Zachry, Patrick P., Cincinnati, October 10, 1976; fourth inning.
A. L.—2—Held by many pitchers.

Most Chances Accepted, Total Series

A. L.—13—Cuellar, Miguel, Baltimore, 1969, 1970, 1971, 1973, 1974; 5 Series, 6 games.
N. L.— 8—Sutton, Donald H., Los Angeles, 1974, 1977, 1978; 3 Series, 4 games.

Most Chances Accepted, Series

3-game Series—N. L.—5—Gullett, Donald E., Cincinnati, 1975.
          A. L.—5—Boswell, David W., Minnesota, 1969.
                  Wise, Richard C., Boston, 1975.
                  Lindblad, Paul A., Oakland, 1975.
4-game Series—N. L.—6—Marichal, Juan A., San Francisco, 1971.
                  Carlton, Steven N., Philadelphia, 1983.
          A. L.—5—Hunter, James A., Oakland, 1974.
                  Cuellar, Miguel, Baltimore, 1974.
                  Gura, Lawrence C., Kansas City, 1978.
5-game Series—N. L.—4—Blass, Stephen R., Pittsburgh, 1972.
                  Ryan, L. Nolan, Houston, 1980.
          A. L.—4—Lolich, Michael S., Detroit, 1972.
                  John, Thomas E., California, 1982.

Most Chances Accepted, Game

N. L.—6—Marichal, Juan A., San Francisco, October 5, 1971.
A. L.—5—Boswell, David W., Minnesota, October 5, 1969; 11 innings.
        Wise, Richard C., Boston, October 7, 1975.
        Lindblad, Paul A., Oakland, October 7, 1975.
        Gura, Lawrence C., Kansas City, October 4, 1978.

Most Chances Accepted, Inning

N. L.—3—Zachry, Patrick P., Cincinnati, October 10, 1976; fourth inning.
A. L.—2—Held by many pitchers.

Most Errors, Total Series

A. L.-N. L.—1—Held by many pitchers.

Most Errors, Series

A. L.-N. L.—1—Held by many pitchers.

Most Errors, Game

A. L.-N. L.—1—Held by many pitchers.

Most Double Plays, Total Series

A. L.-N. L.—1—Held by many pitchers.

Most Double Plays Started, Total Series

A. L.-N. L.—1—Held by many pitchers.

Most Unassisted Double Plays, Game

A. L.-N. L.—Never accomplished.

CLUB FIELDING

Highest Fielding Average, Series, One Club

3-game Series—A. L.—1.000—Baltimore vs. Minnesota, 1970.
                      Oakland vs. Baltimore, 1971.
          N. L.—1.000—Pittsburgh vs. Cincinnati, 1979.
4-game Series—A. L.— .993—New York vs. Kansas City, 1978.
          N. L.— .993—Los Angeles vs. Philadelphia, 1983.
5-game Series—N. L.— .994—San Diego vs. Chicago, 1984.
          A. L.— .989—Baltimore vs. Oakland, 1973.
                  New York vs. Kansas City, 1977.

Highest Fielding Average, Series, Both Clubs

3-game Series—N. L.—.996—Pittsburgh 1.000, Cincinnati .992, 1979.
          A. L.—.995—Oakland 1.000, Baltimore .991, 1971.
4-game Series—A. L.—.982—New York .993, Kansas City .972, 1978.
          N. L.—.979—Los Angeles .993, Philadelphia .966, 1983.
5-game Series—N. L.—.989—San Diego .994, Chicago .983, 1984.
          A. L.—.984—Baltimore .989, Oakland .979, 1973.

Lowest Fielding Average, Series, One Club

3-game Series—A. L.—.940—Kansas City vs. Detroit, 1984.
          N. L.—.950—Atlanta vs. New York, 1969.
4-game Series—N. L.—.957—Los Angeles vs. Pittsburgh, 1974.
          A. L.—.970—Baltimore vs. California, 1979.
5-game Series—A. L.—.956—Milwaukee vs. California, 1982.
          N. L.—.973—Philadelphia vs. Houston, 1980.

Lowest Fielding Average, Series, Both Clubs

3-game Series—A. L.— .958—Boston .966, Oakland .950, 1975.
　　　　　　　　N. L.— .965—New York .981, Atlanta .950, 1969.
4-game Series—N. L.— .964—Pittsburgh .973, Los Angeles .957, 1974.
　　　　　　　　A. L.— .978—California .986, Baltimore .970, 1979.
5-game Series—A. L.— .966—California .977, Milwaukee .956, 1982.
　　　　　　　　N. L.— .978—Cincinnati .979, Pittsburgh .977, 1972.

Most Putouts, Total Series

A. L.— 718— Baltimore; 7 Series, 26 games.
N. L.— 606— Cincinnati; 6 Series, 22 games.

Most Putouts, Series, One Club

3-game Series—A. L.— 96—Baltimore vs. Minnesota, 1969.
　　　　　　　　N. L.— 90—Pittsburgh vs. Cincinnati, 1979.
4-game Series—N. L.—111—Los Angeles vs. Philadelphia, 1978.
　　　　　　　　A. L.—111—Baltimore vs. Chicago, 1983.
5-game Series—N. L.—148—Philadelphia vs. Houston, 1980.
　　　　　　　　A. L.—139—Detroit vs. Oakland, 1972.

Most Putouts, Series, Both Clubs

3-game Series—A. L.— 190—Baltimore 96, Minnesota 94, 1969.
　　　　　　　　N. L.—177—Pittsburgh 90, Cincinnati 87, 1979.
4-game Series—N. L.—221—Los Angeles 111, Philadelphia 110, 1978.
　　　　　　　　A. L.—219—Baltimore 111, Chicago 108, 1983.
5-game Series—N. L.—295—Philadelphia 148, Houston 147, 1980.
　　　　　　　　A. L.—277—Detroit 139, Oakland 138, 1972.

Fewest Putouts, Series, One Club

3-game Series—A. L.— 75—Oakland vs. Baltimore, 1971.
　　　　　　　　　　　　Oakland vs. Boston, 1975.
　　　　　　　　　　　　New York vs. Kansas City, 1980.
　　　　　　　　　　　　Oakland vs. New York, 1981.
　　　　　　　　N. L.— 76—Atlanta vs. St. Louis, 1982.
4-game Series—A. L.—102—Kansas City vs. New York, 1978.
　　　　　　　　N. L.—102—San Francisco vs. Pittsburgh, 1971.
　　　　　　　　　　　　Los Angeles vs. Philadelphia, 1983.
5-game Series—A. L.—126—California vs. Milwaukee, 1982.
　　　　　　　　N. L.—127—Chicago vs. San Diego, 1984.

Fewest Putouts, Series, Both Clubs

3-game Series—A. L.— 156—Baltimore 81, Oakland 75, 1971.
　　　　　　　　　　　　Boston 81, Oakland 75, 1975.
　　　　　　　　　　　　Kansas City 81, New York 75, 1980.
　　　　　　　　　　　　New York 81, Oakland 75, 1981.
　　　　　　　　N. L.—157—St. Louis 81, Atlanta 76, 1982.
4-game Series—A. L.—207—New York 105, Kansas City 102, 1978.
　　　　　　　　　　　　Philadelphia 105, Los Angeles 102, 1983.
　　　　　　　　N. L.—207—Pittsburgh 105, San Francisco 102, 1971.
5-game Series—A. L.—255—Milwaukee 129, California 126, 1982.
　　　　　　　　N. L.—256—Chicago 129, San Diego 127, 1984.

Most Players, One or More Putouts, Game, One Club

N. L.—11—Houston vs. Philadelphia, October 12, 1980; 10 innings.
N. L.—Nine-inning record—10—Held by many clubs.
A. L.—11—Oakland vs. New York, October 14, 1981.
　　　　　　Kansas City vs. Detroit, October 3, 1984; 11 innings.

Most Players, One or More Putouts, Game, Both Clubs

N. L.—20—Cincinnati 10, Pittsburgh 10, October 8, 1972.
A. L.—19—Oakland 11, New York 8, October 14, 1981.

Most Putouts, Catchers, Inning, Both Clubs

A. L.—5—Baltimore 3, Oakland 2, October 6, 1973; first inning.
　　　　　　Oakland 3, Boston 2, October 4, 1975; second inning.
　　　　　　Chicago 3, Baltimore 2, October 6, 1983; first inning.
N. L.—5—Atlanta 3, New York 2, October 5, 1969; third inning.
　　　　　　Atlanta 3, New York 2, October 6, 1969; third inning.
　　　　　　Los Angeles 3, Philadelphia 2, October 4, 1977; seventh inning.

Most Putouts, Outfield, Game, One Club

N. L.—18—Pittsburgh vs. Cincinnati, October 7, 1972.
A. L.—14—Boston vs. Oakland, October 4, 1975.
　　　　　　New York vs. Kansas City, October 13, 1976.

Most Putouts, Outfield, Game, Both Clubs

    A. L.—26—New York 14, Kansas City 12, October 13, 1976.
    N. L.—25—Pittsburgh 18, Cincinnati 7, October 7, 1972.

Fewest Putouts, Outfield, Game, Nine Innings, One Club

    N. L.—1—Atlanta vs. New York, October 4, 1969.
           Cincinnati vs. Pittsburgh, October 5, 1970.
           Montreal vs. Los Angeles, October 16, 1981.
    A. L.—2—Oakland vs. Boston, October 5 1975; fielded 8 innings.
           Milwaukee vs. California, October 8, 1982.
           Baltimore vs. Chicago, October 5, 1983.

Fewest Putouts, Outfield, Extra-Inning Game, One Club

    N. L.—3—Cincinnati vs. Pittsburgh, October 3, 1970; 10 innings.
    A. L.—4—Baltimore vs. Oakland, October 9, 1973; fielded 10 innings of 11-inning game.

Fewest Putouts, Outfield, Game, Nine Innings, Both Clubs

    N. L.—5—Pittsburgh 4, Cincinnati 1, October 5, 1970.
    A. L.—7—Minnesota 4, Baltimore 3, October 3, 1970.

Fewest Putouts, Outfield, Extra-Inning Game, Both Clubs

    A. L.—10—Baltimore 7, Chicago 3, October 8, 1983; 10 innings.
    N. L.—12—Cincinnati 7, Pittsburgh 5, October 2, 1979; 11 innings.

Most Putouts, Outfield, Inning, One Club

    A. L.-N. L.—3—Held by many clubs.

Most Putouts, Outfield, Inning, Both Clubs

    A. L.—6—Baltimore 3, Oakland 3, October 11, 1973; seventh inning.
    N. L.—5—New York 3, Atlanta 2, October 5, 1969; seventh inning.
           Pittsburgh 3, Cincinnati 2, October 7, 1972; third inning.
           Los Angeles 3, Philadelphia 2, October 7, 1978; third inning.

Most Assists, Total Series

    A. L.— 293— Baltimore; 7 Series, 26 games.
    N. L.— 253— Cincinnati; 6 Series, 22 games.

Most Assists, Series, One Club

    3-game Series—A. L.— 41—New York vs. Kansas City, 1980.
                   N. L.—39—Cincinnati vs. Pittsburgh, 1970, 1979.
                           Atlanta vs. St. Louis, 1982.
    4-game Series—A. L.—52—Baltimore vs. California, 1979.
                   N. L.—50—Los Angeles vs. Philadelphia, 1978.
    5-game Series—N. L.—71—Philadelphia vs. Houston, 1980.
                   A. L.—60—New York vs. Kansas City, 1976.

Most Assists, Series, Both Clubs

    3-game Series—N. L.— 76—Cincinnati 39, Pittsburgh 37, 1970.
                   A. L.— 73—Oakland 40, Boston 33, 1975.
    4-game Series—A. L.— 100—Chicago 51, Baltimore 49, 1983.
                   N. L.— 96—Los Angeles 50, Philadelphia 46, 1978.
    5-game Series—A. L.— 111—New York 60, Kansas City 51, 1976.
                   N. L.—123—Philadelphia 71, Houston 52, 1980.

Fewest Assists, Series, One Club

    3-game Series—A. L.—15—Oakland vs. Baltimore, 1971.
                   N. L.—20—Pittsburgh vs. Cincinnati, 1975.
    4-game Series—N. L.—32—Pittsburgh vs. San Francisco, 1971.
                   A. L.—35—New York vs. Kansas City, 1978.
    5-game Series—N. L.—38—Pittsburgh vs. Cincinnati, 1972.
                   A. L.—45—Milwaukee vs. California, 1982.

Fewest Assists, Series, Both Clubs

    3-game Series—A. L.— 46—Baltimore 31, Oakland 15, 1971.
                   N. L.—51—Cincinnati 31, Pittsburgh 20, 1975.
    4-game Series—N. L.—69—San Francisco 37, Pittsburgh 32, 1971.
                   A. L.—71—Kansas City 36, New York 35, 1978.
    5-game Series—N. L.—91—Cincinnati 53, Pittsburgh 38, 1972.
                   A. L.—91—California 46, Milwaukee 45, 1982.

Most Assists, Game, One Club

    N. L.—21—Los Angeles vs. Philadelphia, October 5, 1978.
    A. L.—18—Boston vs. Oakland, October 7, 1975.

Most Assists, Game, Both Clubs

A. L.—33—Boston 18, Oakland 15, October 7, 1975.
N. L.—32—Pittsburgh 19, Cincinnati 13, October 2, 1979; 11 innings.
      30—Los Angeles 21, Philadelphia 9, October 5, 1978.

Most Players, One or More Assists, Game, One Club

N. L.—9—Los Angeles vs. Montreal, October 14, 1981.
A. L.—9—Oakland vs. New York, October 14, 1981.

Most Players, One or More Assists, Game, Both Clubs

A. L.—15—Oakland 9, New York 6, October 14, 1981.
N. L.—14—Philadelphia 7, Houston 7, October 11, 1980; 10 innings.
N. L.—Nine-inning record—13—New York 7, Atlanta 6, October 4, 1969.
      Pittsburgh 7, Cincinnati 6, October 9, 1972.
      Cincinnati 8, New York 5, October 10, 1973.
      Los Angeles 9, Montreal 4, October 14, 1981.
      Atlanta 7, St. Louis 6, October 9, 1982.

Fewest Assists, Game, One Club

A. L.—2—Boston vs. Oakland, October 4, 1975.
N. L.—2—Pittsburgh vs. Cincinnati, October 7, 1972.
      Pittsburgh vs. Cincinnati, October 7, 1975, 10 innings.

Fewest Assists, Game, Both Clubs

N. L.—10—Cincinnati 8, Pittsburgh 2, October 7, 1975; 10 innings.
      Los Angeles 5, Philadelphia 5, October 7, 1983.
      San Diego 5, Chicago 5, October 2, 1984.
A. L.—11—Oakland 6, Baltimore 5, October 6, 1973.

Most Assists, Outfield, Game, One Club

N. L.—3—Philadelphia vs. Houston, October 11, 1980; 10 innings.
N. L.—Nine-inning record—2—Pittsburgh vs. Cincinnati, October 9, 1972.
      Cincinnati vs. New York, October 10, 1973.
      Philadelphia vs. Los Angeles, October 7, 1977.
A. L.—2—Minnesota vs. Baltimore, October 4, 1970.
      Boston vs. Oakland, October 5, 1975.
      Baltimore vs. California, October 5, 1979.

Most Assists, Outfield, Game, Both Clubs

N. L.—4—Philadelphia 3, Houston 1, October 11, 1980; 10 innings.
N. L.—Nine-inning record—3—Pittsburgh 2, Cincinnati 1, October 9, 1972.
A. L.—3—Minnesota 2, Baltimore 1, October 4, 1970.
      Boston 2, Oakland 1, October 5, 1975.
      Baltimore 2, California 1, October 5, 1979.

Most Assists, Outfield, Inning, One Club

N. L.—2—Cincinnati vs. New York, October 10, 1973; fifth inning.
A. L.—1—Held by many clubs.

Fewest Chances Offered, Outfield, Game, Nine Innings, One Club

N. L.—1—Cincinnati vs. Pittsburgh, October 5, 1970.
      Montreal vs. Los Angeles, October 16, 1981.
A. L.—2—Kansas City vs. New York, October 7, 1978.
      Milwaukee vs. California, October 8, 1982.

Fewest Chances Offered, Outfield, Extra-Inning Game, One Club

N. L.—3—Cincinnati vs. Pittsburgh, October 3, 1970; 10 innings.
A. L.—4—Baltimore vs. Oakland, October 9, 1973; fielded 10 innings of 11-inning game.

Fewest Chances Offered, Outfield, Game, Nine Innings, Both Clubs

N. L.—5—Pittsburgh 4, Cincinnati 1, October 5, 1970.
A. L.—7—Minnesota 4, Baltimore 3, October 3, 1970.

Fewest Chances Offered, Outfield, Extra-Inning Game, Both Clubs

A. L.—10—Baltimore 7, Chicago 3, October 8, 1983; 10 innings.
N. L.—12—Cincinnati 7, Pittsburgh 5, October 2, 1979; 11 innings.

Most Errors, Outfield, Game, One Club

A. L.—2—Minnesota vs. Baltimore, October 6, 1969.
      Oakland vs. Boston, October 4, 1975.
      Milwaukee vs. California, October 10, 1982.
N. L.—1—Held by many clubs.

Most Errors, Outfield, Game, Both Clubs

A. L.—3—Oakland 2, Boston 1, October 4, 1975.

N. L.—1—Made in many games.

Most Errors, Total Series

A. L.—21—Kansas City; 5 Series, 20 games.

N. L.—20—Philadelphia; 5 Series, 20 games.

Most Errors, Series, One Club

3-game Series—A. L.— 7—Kansas City vs. Detroit, 1984.

   N. L.— 6—Atlanta vs. New York, 1969.

4-game Series—N. L.— 7—Los Angeles vs. Pittsburgh, 1974.

   A. L.— 5—Baltimore vs. California, 1979.

5-game Series—A. L.— 8—Milwaukee vs. California, 1982.

   N. L.— 6—Philadelphia vs. Houston, 1980.

Most Errors, Series, Both Clubs

3-game Series—A. L.— 10—Oakland 6, Boston 4, 1975.

   N. L.— 8—Atlanta 6, New York 2, 1969.

4-game Series—N. L.—11—Los Angeles 7, Pittsburgh 4, 1974.

   A. L.— 7—Baltimore 5, California 2, 1979.

5-game Series—A. L.—12—Milwaukee 8, California 4, 1982.

   N. L.— 9—Philadelphia 6, Houston 3, 1980.

Fewest Errors, Series, One Club

3-game Series—A. L.— 0—Baltimore vs. Minnesota, 1970.

   Oakland vs. Baltimore, 1971.

   N. L.—0—Pittsburgh vs. Cincinnati, 1979.

4-game Series—A. L.—1—New York vs. Kansas City, 1978.

   N. L.—1—Los Angeles vs. Philadelphia, 1983.

5-game Series—N. L.—1—San Diego vs. Chicago, 1984.

   A. L.—2—Baltimore vs. Oakland, 1973.

   New York vs. Kansas City, 1977.

Fewest Errors, Series, Both Clubs

3-game Series—A. L.—1—Baltimore 1, Oakland 0, 1971.

   N. L.—1—Cincinnati 1, Pittsburgh 0, 1979.

4-game Series—A. L.— 5—Kansas City 4, New York 1, 1978.

   N. L.— 6—Philadelphia 5, Los Angeles 1, 1983.

5-game Series—N. L.—4—Chicago 3, San Diego 1, 1984.

   A. L.— 6—Oakland 4, Baltimore 2, 1973.

Most Errorless Games, Total Series

N. L.—14—Pittsburgh; 6 Series, 22 games.

A. L.—15—Baltimore; 7 Series, 26 games.

Most Errors, Game, One Club

A. L.—5—New York vs. Kansas City, October 10, 1976.

N. L.—5—Los Angeles vs. Pittsburgh, October 8, 1974.

Most Errors, Game, Both Clubs

A. L.—7—Oakland 4, Boston 3, October 4, 1975.

N. L.—5—Los Angeles 5, Pittsburgh 0, October 8, 1974.

Most Errors, Infield, Game, One Club

A. L.—3—Oakland vs. Baltimore, October 9, 1973; 11 innings.

   Nine-inning record—2—Held by many clubs.

N. L.—2—Held by many clubs.

Most Errors, Infield, Game, Both Clubs

A. L.—4—Boston 2, Oakland 2, October 4, 1975.

N. L.—3—Atlanta 2, New York 1, October 5, 1969.

   Pittsburgh 2, Cincinnati 1, October 10, 1972.

Longest Errorless Game, One Club

N. L.—12 innings— Cincinnati vs. New York, October 9, 1973; fielded 12 complete innings.

A. L.—11 innings— Baltimore vs. Minnesota, October 5, 1969; fielded 11 complete innings.

   Baltimore vs. Oakland, October 9, 1973; fielded 10 complete innings of 11-inning game.

Longest Errorless Game, Both Clubs

N. L.—11 innings— Pittsburgh vs. Cincinnati, October 2, 1979; both clubs fielded 11 complete innings.

A. L.—10 innings— Baltimore vs. Chicago, October 8, 1983; both clubs fielded 10 complete innings.

Most Errors, Inning, One Club

A. L.—3—Oakland vs. Boston, October 4, 1975; first inning.
N. L.—2—Held by many clubs.

Most Passed Balls, Total Series

N. L.—4—Pittsburgh; 5 Series, 19 games.
A. L.—3—New York; 5 Series, 20 games.

Most Passed Balls, Series, One Club

N. L.—2—Pittsburgh vs. Cincinnati, 1975; 3-game Series.
A. L.—1—Held by many clubs.

Most Passed Balls, Series, Both Clubs

A. L.—2—Kansas City 1, New York 1, 1978.
N. L.—2—Made in many Series.

Most Passed Balls, Game, One Club

N. L.—2—Pittsburgh vs. Cincinnati, October 4, 1975.
A. L.—1—Held by many clubs.

Most Passed Balls, Inning, One Club

A. L.-N. L.—1—Held by many clubs.

Most Double Plays, Total Series

A. L.—27—Oakland; 6 Series, 23 games.
N. L.—23—Los Angeles; 5 Series, 21 games.

Most Double Plays, Series, One Club

3-game Series—A. L.— 6— New York vs. Oakland, 1981.
             N. L.— 4— Atlanta vs. New York, 1969.
4-game Series—N. L.— 8— Los Angeles vs. Pittsburgh, 1974.
             A. L.— 7— California vs. Baltimore, 1979.
5-game Series—N. L.— 8— Montreal vs. Los Angeles, 1981.
             A. L.— 5— Oakland vs. Detroit, 1972.
                     Kansas City vs. New York, 1976.
                     Milwaukee vs. California, 1982.

Most Double Plays, Series, Both Clubs

3-game Series—A. L.— 8—Minnesota 5, Baltimore 3, 1970.
             N. L.— 6—Atlanta 4, New York 2, 1969.
                     Cincinnati 3, Philadelphia 3, 1976.
4-game Series—A. L.—12—California 7, Baltimore 5, 1979.
             N. L.—10—Los Angeles 8, Pittsburgh 2, 1974.
5-game Series—N. L.—13—Montreal 8, Los Angeles 5, 1981.
             A. L.— 9—Oakland 5, Detroit 4, 1972.

Fewest Double Plays, Series, One Club

3-game Series—N. L.— 0—Atlanta vs. St. Louis, 1982.
             A. L.— 0— Detroit vs. Kansas City, 1984.
4-game Series—N. L.— 0—Philadelphia vs. Los Angeles, 1983.
             A. L.— 2—New York vs. Kansas City, 1978.
5-game Series—A. L.— 2—Held by many clubs.
             N. L.— 3—Held by many clubs.

Fewest Double Plays, Series, Both Clubs

3-game Series—A. L.— 2—Kansas City 2, Detroit 0, 1984.
             N. L.— 3—St. Louis 3, Atlanta 0, 1982.
4-game Series—N. L.— 3—Los Angeles 3, Philadelphia 0, 1983.
             A. L.— 6— Kansas City 4, New York 2, 1978.
5-game Series—A. L.— 4— Kansas City 2, New York 2, 1977.
             N. L.— 6—Cincinnati 3, Pittsburgh 3, 1972.
                     Cincinnati 3, New York 3, 1973.

Most Double Plays, Game, One Club

A. L.—4—Oakland vs. Boston, October 5, 1975.
N. L.—4—Los Angeles vs. Montreal, October 13, 1981.

Most Double Plays, Game, Both Clubs

A. L.—6—Oakland 4, Boston 2, October 5, 1975.
N. L.—5—Pittsburgh 3, Cincinnati 2, October 5, 1975.
       Philadelphia 3, Houston 2, October 11, 1980; 10 innings.

Most Triple Plays, Series, One Club
A. L.-N. L.—Never accomplished.

INDIVIDUAL PITCHING

Most Series Pitched
A. L.—6—Hunter, James, A., Oakland, 1971, 1972, 1973, 1974; New York, 1976, 1978; 10 games.
Palmer, James A., Baltimore, 1969, 1970, 1971, 1973, 1974, 1979; 8 games.
Both Leagues—6—Gullett, Donald E., Cincinnati NL, 1970, 1972, 1973, 1975, 1976, 9 games; New York AL, 1977; 1 game.
N. L.—6—McGraw, Frank E., New York, 1969, 1973; Philadelphia, 1976, 1977, 1978, 1980; 15 games.
Reed, Ronald L., Atlanta, 1969; Philadelphia, 1976, 1977, 1978, 1980, 1983; 13 games.

Most Games Pitched, Total Series
N. L.—15—McGraw, Frank E., New York, 1969, 1973; Philadelphia, 1976, 1977, 1978, 1980; 6 Series.
A. L.—11—Fingers, Roland G., Oakland, 1971, 1972, 1973, 1974, 1975; 5 Series.

Most Games Pitched, Series
3-game Series—N. L.— 3—Upshaw, Cecil L., Atlanta, 1969; 6⅓ innings.
Tomlin, David A., Cincinnati, 1979; 3 innings.
Hume, Thomas H., Cincinnati, 1979; 4 innings.
A. L.— 3—Perranoski, Ronald P., Minnesota, 1969; 4⅔ innings.
Todd, James, R., Oakland, 1975; 1 inning.
Hernandez, Guillermo, Detroit, 1984; 4 innings.
4-game Series—N. L.— 4—Giusti, J. David, Pittsburgh, 1971; 5⅓ innings.
A. L.— 3—Hrabosky, Alan T., Kansas City, 1978; 3 innings.
Stanhouse, Donald J., Baltimore, 1979; 3 innings.
Lamp, Dennis P., Chicago, 1983; 2 innings.
5-game Series—N. L.— 5—McGraw, Frank E., Philadelphia, 1980; 8 innings.
A. L.— 4—Blue, Vida R., Oakland, 1972; 5½ innings.
Lyle, Albert W., New York, 1977; 9 innings.

Most Consecutive Games Pitched, Series
N. L.—5—McGraw, Frank E., Philadelphia, October 7, 8, 10, 11, 12, 1980.
A. L.—3—Perranoski, Ronald P., Minnesota, October 4, 5, 6, 1969.
Blue, Vida R., Oakland, October 10, 11, 12, 1972.
Todd, James R., Oakland, October 4, 5, 7, 1975.
Lyle, Albert W., New York, October 7, 8, 9, 1977.
Hrabosky, Alan T., Kansas City, October 3, 4, 6, 1978.
Stanhouse, Donald J., Baltimore, October 3, 4, 5, 1979.
Lamp, Dennis P., Chicago, October 6, 7, 8, 1983.
Hernandez, Guillermo, Detroit, October 2, 3, 5, 1984.

Most Games Started, Total Series
A. L.—10—Hunter, James A., Oakland, 1971, 1972, 1973, 1974; New York, 1976, 1978; 6 Series.
N. L.— 8— Carlton, Steven N., Philadelphia, 1976, 1977, 1978, 1980, 1983; 5 Series.

Most Opening Games Started, Total Series
Both Leagues—4—Gullett, Donald E., Cincinnati NL, 1972, 1975, 1976; New York AL, 1977; won 2, lost 2.
N. L.—4—Carlton, Steven N., Philadelphia, 1976, 1977, 1980, 1983; won 2, lost 1, no decision 1.
A. L.—3—Cuellar, Miguel, Baltimore, 1969, 1970, 1974; won 1 lost 0, no decision 2.
Hunter, James A., Oakland, 1972, 1974; New York, 1976; won 1, lost 1, no decision 1.

Most Games Started, Series
3-game Series—A. L.— 2—Holtzman, Kenneth D., Oakland, 1975.
N. L.— 1—Held by many pitchers.
4-game Series—A. L.— N. L.—2—Held by many pitchers.
5-game Series—A. L.— N. L.—2—Held by many pitchers.

Most Games Finished, Total Series
N. L.—9—Giusti, J. David, Pittsburgh, 1970, 1971, 1972, 1974, 1975; 5 Series, 13 games.
McGraw, Frank E., New York, Philadelphia, 1969, 1973, 1976, 1977, 1978, 1980; 6 Series, 15 games.
A. L.—8—Fingers, Roland G., Oakland, 1971, 1972, 1973, 1974, 1975; 5 Series, 11 games.

Most Games Finished, Series

3-game Series—A. L.— 3—Perranoski, Ronald P., Minnesota, 1969.
            N. L.— 2—Held by many pitchers.
4-game Series—N. L.— 4—Giusti, J. David, Pittsburgh, 1971.
            A. L.— 3—Stanhouse, Donald J., Baltimore, 1979.
            Lamp, Dennis P., Chicago, 1983.
5-game Series—A. L.— 4—Lyle, Albert W., New York, 1977.
            N. L.— 4—Borbon, Pedro R., Cincinnati, 1973.

Most Complete Games Pitched, Total Series

A. L.—5—Palmer, James A., Baltimore, 1969, 1970, 1971, 1973, 1974.
N. L.—2—Sutton, Donald H., Los Angeles, 1974, 1977.
      John, Thomas E., Los Angeles, 1977, 1978.

Most Consecutive Complete Games Pitched, Total Series

A. L.—4—Palmer, James A., Baltimore, 1969 (1), 1970 (1), 1971 (1), 1973 (1); won 4,
      lost 0.
N. L.—2—John, Thomas E., Los Angeles, 1977 (1), 1978 (1); won 2, lost 0.

Most Complete Games, Series

A. L.-N. L.—1—Held by many pitchers in Series of all lengths.

Most Games, Total Series, Relief Pitcher

N. L.—15—McGraw, Frank E., New York, Philadelphia, 1969, 1973, 1976, 1977, 1978,
      1980; 27 innings.
A. L.—11—Fingers, Roland G., Oakland, 1971, 1972, 1973, 1974, 1975; 19⅓ innings.

Most Series, One or More Games as Relief Pitcher

N. L.—6—McGraw, Frank E., New York, Philadelphia, 1969, 1973, 1976, 1977, 1978,
      1980; 15 games as relief pitcher.
A. L.—5—Fingers, Roland G., Oakland, 1971, 1972, 1973, 1974, 1975, 11 games as relief
      pitcher.

Most Games, Series, Relief Pitcher

3-game Series—N. L.— 3—Upshaw, Cecil L., Atlana, 1969; 6⅓ innings.
            Tomlin, David A., Cincinnati, 1979; 3 innings.
            Hume, Thomas H., Cincinnati, 1979; 4 innings.
            A. L.— 3—Perranoski, Ronald P., Minnesota, 1969; 4⅔ innings.
            Todd, James R., Oakland, 1975; 1 inning.
            Hernandez, Guillermo, Detroit, 1984; 4 innings.
4-game Series—N. L.— 4—Giusti, J. David, Pittsburgh, 1971; 5⅓ innings.
            A. L.— 3—Hrabosky, Alan T., Kansas City, 1978; 3 innings.
            Stanhouse, Donald J., Baltimore, 1979; 3 innings.
            Lamp, Dennis P., Chicago, 1983; 2 innings.
5-game Series—N. L.— 5—McGraw, Frank E., Philadelphia, 1980; 8 innings.
            A. L.— 4—Blue, Vida R., Oakland, 1972; 5⅓ innings.
            Lyle, Albert W., New York, 1977; 9⅓ innings.

Most Games Won, Total Series

Both Leagues—4—Kison, Bruce E., Pittsburgh NL, 1971, 1972, 1974, 1975; California AL,
      1982; won 4, lost 0, 5 Series, 7 games.
      John, Thomas E., Los Angeles NL, 1977, 1978; New York AL, 1980,
      1981; California AL, 1982; won 4, lost 1, 5 Series, 7 games.
      Sutton, Donald H., Los Angeles NL, 1974, 1977, 1978; Milwaukee AL,
      1982; won 4, lost 1, 4 Series, 5 games.
A. L.—4—Palmer, James A., Baltimore, 1969, 1970, 1971, 1973, 1974, 1979; won 4, lost 1, 6
      Series, 8 games.
      Hunter, James A., Oakland, 1971, 1972, 1973, 1974; New York 1976, 1978; won
      4, lost 3, 6 Series, 10 games.
N. L.—4—Carlton, Steven N., Philadelphia, 1976, 1977, 1978, 1980, 1983; won 4, lost 2, 5
      Series, 8 games.

Pitchers Winning 3 or More Games, Total Series

Both Leagues

Pitcher and Club	Years	W.	L.
Kison, Bruce E., Pitts. NL, Cal. AL	1971-72-74-75-82	4	0
John, Thomas E., L.A. NL, N.Y. AL, Cal. AL	1977-78-80-81-82	4	1
Sutton, Donald H., L.A. NL, Mil. AL	1974-77-78-82	4	1

American League

Pitcher and Club	Years	W.	L.
Palmer, James A., Baltimore	1969-70-71-73-74-79	4	1
Hunter, James A., Oakland, New York	1971-72-73-74-76-78	4	3
McNally, David A., Baltimore	1969-70-71-73-74	3	2

National League

Pitcher and Club	Years	W.	L.
Carlton, Steven N., Philadelphia	1976-77-78-80-83	4	2
Kison, Bruce E., Pittsburgh	1971-72-74-75	3	0
Sutton, Donald H., Los Angeles	1974-77-78	3	1

Most Games Won, Total Series, No Defeats

Both Leagues—4—Kison, Bruce E., Pittsburgh NL, 1971, 1972, 1974, 1975; California AL, 1982.

N. L.—3—Kison, Bruce W., Pittsburgh, 1971, 1972, 1974.

A. L.—2—Hall, Richard W., Baltimore, 1969, 1970.
Odom, Johnny L., Oakland, 1972 (2).
Splittorff, Paul W., Kansas City, 1976, 1977.
Lyle, Albert W., New York, 1977 (2).
Flanagan, Michael K., Baltimore, 1979, 1983.

Most Games Won, Series

3-game Series—A. L.— N. L.—1—Held by many pitchers.
4-game Series—N. L.—2—Sutton, Donald H., Los Angeles, 1974 (one complete).
Carlton, Steven N., Philadelphia, 1983 (no complete).
A. L.—1—Held by many pitchers.
5-game Series—A. L.—2—Odom, Johnny L., Oakland, 1972 (one complete).
Hunter, James A., Oakland, 1973 (one complete).
Lyle, Albert W., New York, 1977 (no complete).
N. L.—2—Hooton, Burt C., Los Angeles, 1981 (no complete).
Lefferts, Craig L., San Diego, 1984 (no complete).

Most Consecutive Games Won, Total Series

Both Leagues—4—Kison, Bruce E., Pittsburgh NL, October 6, 1971; October 9, 1972; October 8, 1974; California AL, October 6, 1982; one complete, three incomplete.
John, Thomas E., Los Angeles NL, October 8, 1977; October 5, 1978; New York AL, October 13, 1981; California AL, October 5, 1982; three complete, one incomplete.

A. L.—4—Palmer, James A., Baltimore, October 6, 1969; October 5, 1970; October 5, 1971; October 6, 1973; all complete.

N. L.—4—Carlton, Steven N., Philadelphia, October 6, 1978; October 7, 1980; October 4, 1983; October 8, 1983; one complete, three incomplete.

Most Consecutive Complete Games Won, Total Series

A. L.—4—Palmer, James A., Baltimore, October 6, 1969; October 5, 1970; October 5, 1971; October 6, 1973.

N. L.—2—John, Thomas E., Los Angeles, October 8, 1977; October 5, 1978.

Most Games Won, Series, As Relief Pitcher

A. L.—2—Lyle, Albert W., New York, 1977; 5-game Series.
N. L.—2—Lefferts, Craig L., San Diego, 1984; 5-game Series.

Most Opening Games Won, Total Series

N. L.—2—Gullett, Donald E., Cincinnati, 1975, 1976.
Carlton, Steven N., Philadelphia, 1980, 1983.
A. L.—2—Hall, Richard W., Baltimore, 1969, 1970.
John, Thomas E., New York, 1981; California, 1982.

Most Games Lost, Total Series

N. L.—6—Reuss, Jerry, Pittsburgh, 1974, 1975; Los Angeles, 1981, 1983; won 0, 4 Series, 6 games.
A. L.—3—Holtzman, Kenneth D., Oakland, 1972, 1973, 1974, 1975; won 2, 4 Series, 5 games.
Hunter, James A., Oakland, 1971, 1972, 1973, 1974; New York, 1976, 1978; won 4, 6 Series, 10 games.
Leonard, Dennis P., Kansas City, 1976, 1977, 1978; won 1, 3 Series, 6 games.

Most Games Lost, Total Series, No Victories

N. L.—6—Reuss, Jerry, Pittsburgh, 1974 (2), 1975; Los Angeles, 1981, 1983 (2).
A. L.—2—Fryman, Woodrow T., Detroit, 1972 (2).
Hassler, Andrew E., Kansas City, 1976, 1977.
Figueroa, Eduardo, New York, 1976, 1978.

Most Consecutive Games Lost, Total Series

N. L.—6—Reuss, Jerry, Pittsburgh, 1974 (2), 1975; Los Angeles, 1981, 1983 (2).
A. L.—3—Leonard, Dennis P., Kansas City, 1977, 1978 (2).

Most Games Lost, Series

3-game Series—A. L.— 2—Holtzman, Kenneth D., Oakland, 1975.
            N. L.—1—Held by many pitchers.
4-game Series—A. L.— 2—Leonard, Dennis P., Kansas City, 1978.
            N. L.—2—Reuss, Jerry, Pittsburgh, 1974.
                    Reuss, Jerry, Los Angeles, 1983.
5-game Series—A. L.— 2—Fryman, Woodrow T., Detroit, 1972.
            N. L.—2—Gullickson, William L., Montreal, 1981.

Most Saves, Total Series

N. L.—5—McGraw, Frank E., New York, 1969, 1973; Philadelphia, 1977, 1980 (2).
A. L.—2—Fingers, Roland G., Oakland, 1973, 1974.
        Drago, Richard A., Boston, 1975 (2).
        Gossage, Richard M., New York, 1978, 1981.
        Ladd, Peter L., Milwaukee, 1982.

Most Saves, Series

3-game Series—A. L.— 2—Drago, Richard A., Boston, 1975.
            N. L.—2—Gullett, Donald E., Cincinnati, 1970.
4-game Series—N. L.—3—Giusti, J. David, Pittsburgh, 1971.
            A. L.—1—Held by many pitchers.
5-game Series—N. L.— 2—McGraw, Frank E., Philadelphia, 1980.
            A. L.— 2—Ladd, Peter L., Milwaukee, 1982.

Most Innings Pitched, Total Series

A. L.— 69⅓— Hunter, James A., Oakland, 1971, 1972, 1973, 1974; New York, 1976, 1978;
        6 Series, 10 games.
N. L.— 53⅔— Carlton, Steven N., Philadelphia, 1976, 1977, 1978, 1980, 1983; 5 Series, 8
        games.

Most Innings Pitched, Series

3-game Series—A. L.— 11 — McNally, David A., Baltimore, 1969.
                          Holtzman, Kenneth D., Oakland, 1975.
            N. L.— 9⅔—Ellis, Dock P., Pittsburgh, 1970.
4-game Series—N. L.—17 —Sutton, Donald H., Los Angeles, 1974.
            A. L.—12⅔—Cuellar, Miguel, Baltimore, 1974.
5-game Series—A. L.— 19 —Lolich, Michael S., Detroit, 1972.
            N. L.—17 —Burris, B. Ray, Montreal, 1981.

Most Innings Pitched, Game

A. L.—11—McNally, David A., Baltimore, October 5, 1969, complete game, won 1-0.
        Holtzman, Kenneth D., Oakland, October 9, 1973, complete game, won 2-1.
N. L.—10—Niekro, Joseph F., Houston, October 10, 1980, incomplete game, no decision.

Most Shutouts, Series

A. L.-N. L.—1—Held by many pitchers.

Most Consecutive Scoreless Innings, Total Series

A. L.— 19⅓— Holtzman, Kenneth D., Oakland, October 9, 1973 (9⅔ innings); October 6,
        1974 (9 innings); October 4, 1975 (⅔ innings).
N. L.— 15⅔— Sutton, Donald H., Los Angeles, October 5, 1974 (9 innings); October 9,
        1974 (6⅔ innings).

Most Consecutive Scoreless Innings, Series

N. L.— 15⅔— Sutton, Donald H., Los Angeles, October 5, 9, 1974.
A. L.— 11 — McNally, David A., Baltimore, October 5, 1969.

Most Consecutive Hitless Innings, Total Series

A. L.— 11 — McNally, David A., Baltimore, October 5 (8 innings), 1969; October 4 (3
        innings), 1970.
N. L.— 6⅔— Billingham, John E., Cincinnati, October 6 (6⅓ innings), October 10 (⅓
        inning), 1973.

Most Consecutive Hitless Innings, Game

A. L.— 8 — McNally, David A., Baltimore, October 5, 1969; 11-inning game.
N. L.— 6⅓— Billingham, John E., Cincinnati, October 6, 1973.

Most Runs Allowed, Total Series

A. L.—25—Hunter, James A., Oakland, 1971, 1972, 1973, 1974; New York, 1976, 1978; 6
        Series, 10 games.
N. L.—22—Carlton, Steven N., Philadelphia, 1976, 1977, 1978, 1980, 1983; 5 Series, 8
        games.

Most Earned Runs Allowed, Total Series

    A. L.—25—Hunter, James A., Oakland, 1971, 1972, 1973, 1974; New York, 1976, 1978; 6
         Series, 10 games.
    N. L.—21—Carlton, Steven N., Philadelphia, 1976, 1977, 1978, 1980, 1983; 5 Series, 8
         games.

Most Runs Allowed, Series

    3-game Series—A. L.— 9—Perry, James E., Minnesota, 1970.
               N. L.— 9—Niekro, Philip H., Atlanta, 1969.
    4-game Series—N. L.—11—Perry, Gaylord J., San Francisco, 1971.
               A. L.—10—Frost, C. David, California, 1979.
    5-game Series—A. L.— 9—John, Thomas E., California, 1982.
               N. L.— 8—Gullett, Donald E., Cincinnati, 1972.
                        Ryan, L. Nolan, Houston, 1980.
                        Harris, Greg A., San Diego, 1984.
                        Show, Eric V., San Diego, 1984.

Most Earned Runs Allowed, Series

    3-game Series—A. L.— 8—Perry, James E., Minnesota, 1970.
               N. L.— 6—Koosman, Jerry M., New York, 1969.
                        Jarvis, R. Patrick, Atlanta, 1969.
    4-game Series—N. L.—10—Perry, Gaylord J., San Francisco, 1971.
               A. L.— 9—Frost, C. David, California, 1979.
    5-game Series—N. L.— 8—Gullett, Donald E., Cincinnati, 1972.
                        Ryan, L. Nolan, Houston, 1980.
                        Show, Eric V., San Diego, 1984.
               A. L.— 8—Blue, Vida R., Oakland, 1973.
                        Figueroa, Eduardo, New York, 1976.

Most Runs Allowed, Game

    N. L.—9—Niekro, Philip H., Atlanta, October 4, 1969.
    A. L.—8—Perry, James E., Minnesota, October 3, 1970.

Most Earned Runs Allowed, Game

    A. L.—7—Perry, James E., Minnesota, October 3, 1970.
    N. L.—7—Perry, Gaylord J., San Francisco, October 6, 1971.
            Harris, Greg A., San Diego, October 2, 1984.

Most Runs Allowed, Inning

    A. L.—6—Perry, James E., Minnesota, October 3, 1970; fourth inning.
    N. L.—6—Harris, Greg A., San Diego, October 2, 1984; fifth inning.

Most Earned Runs Allowed, Inning

    A. L.—6—Perry, James E., Minnesota, October 3, 1970; fourth inning.
    N. L.—6—Harris, Greg A., San Diego, October 2, 1984; fifth inning.

Most Hits Allowed, Total Series

    A. L.—57—Hunter, James A., Oakland, 1971, 1972, 1973, 1974; New York, 1976, 1978; 6
         Series, 10 games.
    N. L.—53—Carlton, Steven N., Philadelphia, 1976, 1977, 1978, 1980, 1983; 5 Series, 8
         games.

Most Hits Allowed, Series

    3-game Series—A. L.—12—Holtzman, Kenneth D., Oakland, 1975.
               N. L.—10—Jarvis, R. Patrick, Atlanta, 1969.
    4-game Series—N. L.—19—Perry, Gaylord J., San Francisco, 1971.
               A. L.—13—Leonard, Dennis P., Kansas City, 1978.
    5-game Series—A. L.—18—Gura, Lawrence C., Kansas City, 1976.
               N. L.—16—Ryan, L. Nolan, Houston, 1980.

Most Hits Allowed, Game

    A. L.—12—Gura, Lawrence C., Kansas City, October 9, 1976.
    N. L.—10—Jarvis, R. Patrick, Atlanta, October 6, 1969.
             Perry, Gaylord J., San Francisco, October 6, 1971.
             Hooton, Burt C., Los Angeles, October 4, 1978.

Fewest Hits Allowed Game, Nine Innings

    A. L.—2—Blue, Vida R., Oakland, October 8, 1974.
    N. L.—2—Grimsley, Ross A., Cincinnati, October 10, 1972.
            Matlack, Jonathan T., New York, October 7, 1973.

Most Hits Allowed, Inning

    A. L.—6—Perry, James E., Minnesota, October 3, 1970; fourth inning.
    N. L.—6—Harris, Greg A., San Diego, October 2, 1984; fifth inning.

Most Consecutive Hits Allowed, Inning (Consecutive At-Bats)

A. L.—6—Perry, James E., Minnesota, October 3, 1970; fourth inning (sacrifice fly during streak).
N. L.—5—Moose, Robert R., Pittsburgh, October 8, 1972; first inning.

Most Consecutive Hits Allowed, Inning (Consecutive Plate Appearances)

N. L.—5—Moose, Robert R., Pittsburgh, October 8, 1972; first inning.
A. L.—5—Beard, C. David, Oakland, October 14, 1981; fourth inning.

Most Two-Base Hits Allowed, Game

N. L.—4—Seaver, G. Thomas, New York, October 4, 1969.
A. L.—4—McNally, David A., Baltimore, October 3, 1971.
               Blue, Vida R., Oakland, October 3, 1971.

Most Three-Base Hits Allowed, Game

A. L.—2—Figueroa, Eduardo, New York, October 8, 1977.
N. L.—2—Carlton, Steven N., Philadelphia, October 9, 1976.
               Christenson, Larry R., Philadelphia, October 4, 1978.

Most Home Runs Allowed, Total Series

A. L.—12—Hunter, James A., Oakland, 1971 (4), 1972 (2), 1974 (3), New York, 1978 (3).
N. L.— 6—Blass, Stephen R., Pittsburgh, 1971 (4), 1972 (2).

Most Home Runs Allowed, Series

3-game Series—A. L.— 4—Hunter, James A., Oakland, 1971.
                       N. L.— 3—Jarvis, R. Patrick, Atlanta, 1969.
4-game Series—N. L.— 4—Blass, Stephen R., Pittsburgh, 1971.
                       A. L.— 3—Hunter, James A., Oakland, 1974; New York, 1978.
5-game Series—N. L.— 5—Show, Eric V., San Diego, 1984.
                       A. L.— 4—McNally, David A., Baltimore, 1973.

Most Home Runs Allowed, Game

A. L.—4—Hunter, James A., Oakland, October 4, 1971.
               McNally, David A., Baltimore, October 7, 1973.
N. L.—3—Jarvis, R. Patrick, Atlanta, October 6, 1969.
               Show, Eric V., San Diego, October 2, 1984.

Most Home Runs With Bases Loaded Allowed, Game

A. L.—1—Perry, James E., Minnesota, October 3, 1970; fourth inning.
               Haas, Bryan E., Milwaukee, October 9, 1982; eighth inning.
N. L.—1—Carlton, Steven N., Philadelphia, October 4, 1977; seventh inning.
               Lonborg, James R., Philadelphia, October 5, 1977; fourth inning.

Most Home Runs Allowed, Inning

A. L.—2—Perry, James E., Minnesota, October 3, 1970; fourth inning.
               McNally, David A., Baltimore, October 4, 1970; fourth inning.
               McNally, David A., Baltimore, October 7, 1973; sixth inning.
               Hunter, James A., Oakland, October 5, 1974; fifth inning.
               Gura, Lawrence C., Kansas City, October 8, 1980; second inning.
N. L.—2—Moose, Robert R., Pittsburgh, October 5, 1970; first inning.
               Blass, Stephen R., Pittsburgh, October 2, 1971; fifth inning.
               Blass, Stephen R., Pittsburgh, October 6, 1971; second inning.
               Rau, Douglas J., Los Angeles, October 8, 1974; first inning.
               Reed, Ronald L., Philadelphia, October 12, 1976; ninth inning.
               Norman, Fredie H., Cincinnati, October 5, 1979; third inning.
               Reardon, Jeffrey J., Montreal, October 13, 1981; eighth inning.
               Show, Eric V., San Diego, October 2, 1984; first inning.
               Lollar, W. Timothy, San Diego, October 6, 1984; fourth inning.

Most Consecutive Home Runs Allowed, Inning

N. L.—2—Moose, Robert R., Pittsburgh, October 5, 1970; first inning.
               Reed, Ronald L., Philadelphia, October 12, 1976; ninth inning.
               Reardon, Jeffrey J., Montreal, October 13, 1981; eighth inning.
               Lollar, W. Timothy, San Diego, October 6, 1984; fourth inning.
A. L.—2—Perry, James E., Minnesota, October 3, 1970; fourth inning.
               McNally, David A., Baltimore, October 4, 1970; fourth inning.
               McNally, David A., Baltimore, October 7, 1973; sixth inning.
               Gura, Lawrence C., Kansas City, October 8, 1980; second inning.

Most Total Bases Allowed, Game

N. L.—22—Jarvis, R. Patrick, Atlanta, October 6, 1969.
A. L.—20—Hunter, James A., New York, October 6, 1978.

Most Bases on Balls, Total Series

N. L.—28—Carlton, Steven N., Philadelphia, 1976, 1977, 1978, 1980, 1983; 5 Series, 8 games.
A. L.—19—Cuellar, Miguel, Baltimore, 1969, 1970, 1971, 1973, 1974; 5 Series, 6 games.
Palmer, James A., Baltimore, 1969, 1970, 1971, 1973, 1974, 1979; 6 Series, 8 games.

Most Bases on Balls, Series

3-game Series—A. L.— 7—Boswell, David W., Minnesota, 1969.
N. L.— 5—Norman, Fredie H., Cincinnati, 1975.
Carlton, Steven N., Philadelphia, 1976.
4-game Series—A. L.—13—Cuellar, Miguel, Baltimore, 1974.
N. L.— 8—Reuss, Jerry, Pittsburgh, 1974.
Carlton, Steven N., Philadelphia, 1977.
5-game Series—A. L.— 8—Palmer, James A., Baltimore, 1973.
N. L.— 8—Carlton, Steven N., Philadelphia, 1980.
Sutcliffe, Richard L., Chicago, 1984.

Most Bases on Balls, Game

A. L.—9—Cuellar, Miguel, Baltimore, October 9, 1974.
N. L.—6—Kison, Bruce E., Pittsburgh, October 8, 1974.

Most Bases on Balls, Inning

A. L.—4—Cuellar, Miguel, Baltimore, October 9, 1974; fifth inning, consecutive.
N. L.—4—Hooton, Burt E., Los Angeles, October 7, 1977; second inning, consecutive.

Most Consecutive Bases on Balls, Inning

A. L.—4—Cuellar, Miguel, Baltimore, October 9, 1974; fifth inning.
N. L.—4—Hooton, Burt E., Los Angeles, October 7, 1977; second inning.

Most Strikeouts, Total Series

A. L.—46—Palmer, James A., Baltimore, 1969, 1970, 1971, 1973, 1974, 1979; 8 Series, 6 games.
N. L.—39—Carlton, Steven N., Philadelphia, 1976, 1977, 1978, 1980, 1983; 5 Series, 8 games.

Most Strikeouts, Series

3-game Series—N. L.—14—Candelaria, John R., Pittsburgh 1975.
A. L.—12—Palmer, James A., Baltimore, 1970.
4-game Series—A. L.—14—Boddicker, Michael J., Baltimore, 1983.
N. L.—13—Sutton, Donald H., Los Angeles, 1974.
Carlton, Steven N., Philadelphia, 1983.
5-game Series—N. L.—17—Seaver, G. Thomas, New York, 1973.
A. L.—15—Palmer, James A., Baltimore, 1973.

Most Strikeouts, Game

A. L.—14—Coleman, Joseph H., Detroit, October 10, 1972.
Boddicker, Michael J., Baltimore, October 6, 1983.
N. L.—14—Candelaria, John R., Pittsburgh, October 7, 1975 (pitched first 7⅔ innings of 10-inning game).

Ten or More Strikeouts by Pitchers in Championship Series Game

AMERICAN LEAGUE

Date	Pitcher and Club	SO.	Score
Oct. 5, 1969	McNally, Baltimore vs. Minnesota (11 inn.)	11	1-0
Oct. 5, 1970	Palmer, Baltimore vs. Minnesota	12	6-1
Oct. 10, 1972	Coleman, Detroit vs. Oakland	14	3-0
Oct. 6, 1973	Palmer, Baltimore, vs. Oakland	12	6-0
Oct. 9, 1973	Cuellar, Baltimore vs. Oakland (10 inn.)	11	1-2
Oct. 6, 1983	Boddicker, Baltimore vs. Chicago	14	4-0

NATIONAL LEAGUE

Date	Pitcher and Club	SO.	Score
Oct. 6, 1973	Seaver, New York vs. Cincinnati (8⅓ inn.)	13	1-2
Oct. 7, 1975	Candelaria, Pitts. vs. Cincinnati (7⅔ inn.)	14	3-5

Most Strikeouts, Game, Relief Pitcher

N. L.—7—Ryan, L. Nolan, New York, October 6, 1969; pitched 7 innings.
A. L.—5—Frazier, George A., New York, October 14, 1981; pitched 5⅔ innings.

Most Consecutive Strikeouts, Game

A. L.—4—Coleman, Joseph H., Detroit, October 10, 1972; 1 in fourth inning, 3 in fifth inning.

Ryan, L. Nolan, California, October 3, 1979; 3 in first inning, 1 in second inning.

Wilcox, Milton E., Detroit, October 5, 1984; 2 in fourth inning, 2 in fifth inning.

N. L.—4—Wilcox, Milton E., Cincinnati, October 5, 1970; 2 in sixth inning, 2 in seventh inning.

Candelaria, John R., Pittsburgh, October 7, 1975; 3 in first inning, 1 in second inning.

Most Consecutive Strikeouts, Start of Game

N. L.—4—Candelaria, John R., Pittsburgh, October 7, 1975.

A. L.—4—Ryan, L. Nolan, California, October 3, 1979.

Most Strikeouts, Inning

A. L.-N. L.—3—Held by many pitchers.

Most Hit Batsmen, Total Series

Both Leagues—3—John, Thomas E., Los Angeles NL, 1977 (2); California AL, 1982.

A. L.—2—Fryman, Woodrow T., Detroit, 1972 (2).

Boddicker, Michael J., Baltimore, 1983 (2).

N. L.—2—Seaver, G. Thomas, New York, 1969, 1973.

John, Thomas E., Los Angeles, 1977 (2).

Most Hit Batsmen, Series

A. L.—2—Fryman, Woodrow T., Detroit, 1972; 5-game Series.

Boddicker, Michael J., Baltimore, 1983; 4-game Series.

N. L.—2—John, Thomas E., Los Angeles, 1977; 4-game Series.

Most Hit Batsmen, Game

A. L.—2—Fryman, Woodrow T., Detroit, October 12, 1972.

Boddicker, Michael J., Baltimore, October 6, 1983.

N. L.—1—Held by many pitchers.

Most Hit Batsmen, Inning

A. L.-N. L.—1—Held by many pitchers.

Most Wild Pitches, Total Series

A. L.—4—John, Thomas E., New York, 1980; California, 1982.

N. L.—3—McGraw, Frank E., New York, 1973; Philadelphia, 1976 (2).

Carlton, Steven N., Philadelphia, 1977, 1983 (2).

Most Wild Pitches, Series

A. L.—3—John, Thomas E., California, 1982; 5-game Series.

N. L.—2—Held by many pitchers.

Most Wild Pitches, Game

A. L.—3—John, Thomas E., California, October 9, 1982.

N. L.—2—Marichal, Juan A., San Francisco, October 5, 1971.

Andujar, Joaquin, St. Louis, October 10, 1982.

Pena, Alejandro, Los Angeles, October 7, 1983.

Most Wild Pitches, Inning

A. L.—2—Zachary, W. Chris, Detroit, October 8, 1972; fifth inning.

John, Thomas E., California, October 9, 1982.

N. L.—1—Held by many pitchers.

Most Balks, Game

A. L.-N. L.—1—Held by many pitchers.

CLUB PITCHING

Most Pitchers, Series, One Club

3-game Series—N. L.—10—Pittsburgh vs. Cincinnati, 1975.

A. L.— 9—Minnesota vs. Baltimore, 1969, 1970.

4-game Series—N. L.— 9—San Francisco vs. Pittsburgh, 1971.

Los Angeles vs. Philadelphia, 1977, 1978.

A. L.— 9—California vs. Baltimore, 1979.

Chicago vs. Baltimore, 1983.

5-game Series—N. L.—10—Pittsburgh vs. Cincinnati, 1972.

San Diego vs. Chicago, 1984.

A. L.— 9—Kansas City vs. New York, 1976.

Most Pitchers, Series, Both Clubs

3-game Series—N. L.—17—Pittsburgh 10, Cincinnati 7, 1975.

Cincinnati 9, Pittsburgh 8, 1979.

A. L.—16—Minnesota 9, Baltimore 7, 1969.
4-game Series—N. L.—17—Los Angeles 9, Philadelphia 8, 1978.
A. L.—15—New York 8, Kansas City 7, 1978.
Chicago 9, Baltimore 6, 1983.
5-game Series—N. L.—18—Pittsburgh 10, Cincinnati 8, 1972.
San Diego 10, Chicago 8, 1984.
A. L.—16—Oakland 8, Detroit 8, 1972.

Fewest Pitchers, Series, One Club

3-game Series—A. L.— 4—Baltimore vs. Minnesota, 1970.
Baltimore vs. Oakland, 1971.
Kansas City vs. New York, 1980.
N. L.— 5—Pittsburgh vs. Cincinnati, 1970.
St. Louis vs. Atlanta, 1982.
4-game Series—A. L.— 5—Oakland vs. Baltimore, 1974.
Baltimore vs. California, 1979.
N. L.— 5—Philadelphia vs. Los Angeles, 1983.
5-game Series—N. L.— 6—New York vs. Cincinnati, 1973.
A. L.— 6—Oakland vs. Baltimore, 1973.
New York vs. Kansas City, 1976, 1977.

Fewest Pitchers, Series, Both Clubs

3-game Series—A. L.— 10—New York 6, Kansas City 4, 1980.
N. L.—12—Cincinnati 7, Pittsburgh 5, 1970.
4-game Series—A. L.—12—Baltimore 7, Oakland 5, 1974.
N. L.—13—Los Angeles 8, Philadelphia 5, 1983.
5-game Series—A. L.—13—Baltimore 7, Oakland 6, 1973.
N. L.—15—Cincinnati 9, New York 6 , 1973.

Most Appearances by Pitchers, Series, One Club

3-game Series—A. L.—14—Minnesota vs. Baltimore, 1970.
N. L.—13—Cincinnati vs. Pittsburgh, 1979.
4-game Series—N. L.—14—Philadelphia vs. Los Angeles, 1977.
A. L.—12—California vs. Baltimore, 1979.
Chicago vs. Baltimore, 1983.
5-game Series—N. L.—21—Philadelphia vs. Houston, 1980.
A. L.—18—Kansas City vs. New York, 1976.

Most Appearances by Pitchers, Series, Both Clubs

3-game Series—N. L.—25—Cincinnati 13, Pittsburgh 12, 1979.
A. L.—18—Minnesota 11, Baltimore 7, 1969.
Minnesota 14, Baltimore 4, 1970.
4-game Series—N. L.—26—Philadelphia 14, Los Angeles 12, 1977.
A. L.—20—Kansas City 11, New York 9, 1978.
Chicago 12, Baltimore 8, 1983.
5-game Series—N. L.—36—Philadelphia 21, Houston 15, 1980.
A. L.—29—Oakland 16, Detroit 13, 1972.
Kansas City 18, New York 11, 1976.

Most Pitchers, Game, One Club

A. L.—7—Minnesota vs. Baltimore, October 6, 1969.
N. L.—6—Atlanta vs. New York, October 5, 1969.
San Francisco vs. Pittsburgh, October 3, 1971.
Los Angeles vs. Philadelphia, October 7, 1977.
Pittsburgh vs. Cincinnati, October 3, 1979; 10 innings.
Cincinnati vs. Pittsburgh, October 5, 1979.
Philadelphia vs. Houston October 11, 1980; 10 innings.
Philadelphia vs. Houston, October 12, 1980; 10 innings.
Atlanta vs. St. Louis, October 10, 1982.

Most Pitchers, Game, Winning Club

N. L.—6—Los Angeles vs. Philadelphia, October 7, 1977.
Pittsburgh vs. Cincinnati, October 3, 1979; 10 innings.
Philadelphia vs. Houston, October 11, 1980; 10 innings.
Philadelphia vs. Houston, October 12, 1980; 10 innings.
A. L.—5—Baltimore vs. Minnesota, October 4, 1969; 12 innings.

Most Pitchers, Game, Losing Club

A. L.—7—Minnesota vs. Baltimore, October 6, 1969.
N. L.—6—Atlanta vs. New York, October 5, 1969.
San Francisco vs. Pittsburgh, October 3, 1971.
Cincinnati vs. Pittsburgh, October 5, 1979.

Most Pitchers, Game, Both Clubs

N. L.—10—Los Angeles 6, Philadelphia 4, October 7, 1977.
    Pittsburgh 6, Cincinnati 4, October 3, 1979; 10 innings.
    Philadelphia 6, Houston 4, October 12, 1980; 10 innings.
A. L.— 9—Oakland 6, Detroit 3, October 11, 1972; 10 innings.
    Kansas City 6, New York 3, October 9, 1977.

Most Pitchers, Inning, One Club

A. L.—5—Kansas City vs. New York, October 12, 1976; sixth inning.
N. L.—3—Made in many games.

Most Complete Games, Series, One Club

3-game Series—A. L.— 2—Baltimore vs. Minnesota, 1969, 1970.
          Baltimore vs. Oakland, 1971.
      N. L.—1—Cincinnati vs. Pittsburgh, 1975.
          Pittsburgh vs. Cincinnati, 1979.
          St. Louis vs. Atlanta, 1982.
4-game Series—A. L.— 2—Oakland vs. Baltimore, 1974.
      N. L.—2—San Francisco vs. Pittsburgh, 1971.
          Los Angeles vs. Philadelphia, 1977.
5-game Series—N. L.— 3—New York vs. Cincinnati, 1973.
      A. L.—2—Oakland vs. Baltimore, 1973.
          Baltimore vs. Oakland, 1973.
          California vs. Milwaukee, 1982.

Most Complete Games, Series, Both Clubs

3-game Series—A. L.— 3—Baltimore 2, Oakland 1, 1971.
      N. L.—1—Cincinnati 1, Pittsburgh 0, 1975.
          Pittsburgh 1, Cincinnati 0, 1979.
          St. Louis 1, Atlanta 0, 1982.
4-game Series—A. L.— 3—Oakland 2, Baltimore 1, 1974.
      N. L.—2—San Francisco 2, Pittsburgh 0, 1971.
          Los Angeles 2, Philadelphia 0, 1977.
          Los Angeles 1, Philadelphia 1, 1978.
5-game Series—A. L.— 4—Baltimore 2, Oakland 2, 1973.
      N. L.—3—New York 3, Cincinnati 0, 1973.

Most Saves, Series, One Club

3-game Series—N. L.— 3—Cincinnati vs. Pittsburgh, 1970.
      A. L.— 2—Boston vs. Oakland, 1975.
4-game Series—N. L.— 3—Pittsburgh vs. San Francisco, 1971.
      A. L.— 2—New York vs. Kansas City, 1978.
5-game Series—A. L.— 3—Milwaukee vs. California, 1982.
      N. L.— 2—Pittsburgh vs. Cincinnati, 1972.
          Philadelphia vs. Houston, 1980.

Most Saves, Series, Both Clubs

3-game Series—N. L.— 3—Cincinnati 3, Pittsburgh 0, 1970.
      A. L.— 2—Boston 2, Oakland 0, 1975.
4-game Series—N. L.— 3—Pittsburgh 3, San Francisco 0, 1971.
      A. L.— 2—New York 2, Kansas City 0, 1978.
5-game Series—N. L.— 5—Houston 3, Philadelphia 2, 1980.
      A. L.— 3—Milwaukee 3, California 0, 1982.

Fewest Saves, Series, One Club and Both Clubs

A. L.-N. L.—0—Held by many clubs in Series of all lengths.

Most Runs Allowed, Total Series, One Club

N. L.—89—Philadelphia; 5 Series, 20 games.
A. L.—85—Oakland; 6 Series, 23 games.

Most Shutouts Won, Total Series

A. L.—5—Baltimore, 1969, 1973, 1979, 1983 (2).
N. L.—2—Los Angeles, 1974, 1978.

Most Shutouts Lost, Total Series

A. L.—3—Baltimore, 1973, 1974 (2).
N. L.—3—Los Angeles, 1974, 1981, 1983.

Most Shutouts Won, Series, One Club

A. L.—2—Oakland vs. Baltimore, 1974; 4-game Series.
    Baltimore vs. Chicago, 1983; 4-game Series.
N. L.—1—Held by many clubs.

Most Consecutive Shutouts Won, Series, One Club
> A. L.—2—Oakland vs. Baltimore, October 6, 8, 1974.
> N. L.—1—Held by many clubs.

Most Shutouts, Series, Both Clubs
> N. L.—2—Los Angeles 1, Pittsburgh 1, 1974; 4-game Series.
> A. L.—2—Oakland 1, Detroit 1, 1972; 5-game Series.
> Oakland 1, Baltimore 1, 1973; 5-game Series.
> Oakland 2, Baltimore 0, 1974; 4-game Series.
> Baltimore 2, Chicago 0, 1983; 4-game Series.

Most Consecutive Games, Total Series, Without Being Shut Out
> A. L.—20—New York, October 9, 1976 through October 15, 1981.
> N. L.—12—Cincinnati, October 8, 1973 through October 5, 1979.

Most Consecutive Innings Shut Out Opponent, Total Series
> A. L.—31 —Oakland vs. Baltimore, October 5 (last one-third of fifth inning) to October 9, 1974 (first two-thirds of ninth inning).
> N. L.—18⅓—Houston vs. Philadelphia, October 8 (last one-third of tenth inning) to October 11 (through seven innings).

Most Consecutive Innings Shut Out Opponent, Series
> A. L.—31 —Oakland vs. Baltimore, October 5 (last one-third of fifth inning) to October 9, 1974 (first two-thirds of ninth inning).
> N. L.—18⅓—Houston vs. Philadelphia, October 8 (last one-third of tenth inning) to October 11 (through seven innings).

Largest Score, Shutout Game
> N. L.— 13-0— Chicago 13, San Diego 0, October 2, 1984.
> A. L.— 8-0— Baltimore 8, California 0, October 6, 1979.

Longest Shutout Game
> A. L.—11 innings— Baltimore 1, Minnesota 0, October 5, 1969.
> N. L.—11 innings— Houston 1, Philadelphia 0, October 10, 1980.

Championship Series 1-0 Games
> A. L.—Baltimore 1, Minnesota 0, October 5, 1969; 11 innings.
> Oakland 1, Baltimore 0, October 8, 1974.
> Detroit 1, Kansas City 0, October 5, 1984.
> N. L.—Houston 1, Philadelphia 0, October 10, 1980; 11 innings.
> Philadelphia 1, Los Angeles 0, October 4, 1983.

Most Wild Pitches, Series, One Club
> N. L.—4—Los Angeles vs. Philadelphia, 1983; 4-game Series.
> A. L.—3—California vs. Baltimore, 1979; 4-game Series.
> California vs. Milwaukee, 1982; 5-game Series.

Most Wild Pitches, Series, Both Clubs
> N. L.—6—Los Angeles 4, Philadelphia 2, 1983; 4-game Series.
> A. L.—4—Detroit 2, Oakland 2, 1972; 5-game Series.
> California 3, Milwaukee 1, 1982; 5-game Series.

Most Balks, Series, One Club
> N. L.—2—Pittsburgh vs. Cincinnati, 1975; 3-game Series.
> A. L.—2—Baltimore vs. Chicago, 1983; 4-game Series.

Most Balks, Series, Both Clubs
> N. L.—2—Pittsburgh 2, Cincinnati 0, 1975; 3-game Series.
> Philadelphia 1, Los Angeles 1, 1977; 4-game Series.
> A. L.—2—Baltimore 2, Chicago 0, 1983; 4-game Series.

Fewest Balks, Series, One Club and Both Clubs
> A. L.-N. L.—0—Held by many clubs in Series of all lengths.

GENERAL CLUB RECORDS

Most Series Played
> A. L.—7—Baltimore, 1969, 1970, 1971, 1973, 1974, 1979, 1983; won 5, lost 2.
> N. L.—6—Pittsburgh, 1970, 1971, 1972, 1974, 1975, 1979; won 2, lost 4.
> Cincinnati, 1970, 1972, 1973, 1975 1976, 1979; won 4, lost 2.

Most Series Won
> A. L.—5—Baltimore, 1969, 1970, 1971, 1979, 1983; lost 2.
> New York, 1976, 1977, 1978, 1981; lost 1.

N. L.—4—Cincinnati, 1970, 1972, 1975, 1976; lost 2.
Los Angeles, 1974, 1977, 1978, 1981; lost 1.

Most Consecutive Years Winning Series

A. L.—3—Baltimore, 1969, 1970, 1971.
Oakland, 1972, 1973, 1974.
New York, 1976, 1977, 1978.
N. L.—2—Cincinnati, 1975, 1976.
Los Angeles, 1977, 1978.

Most Series Lost

N. L.—4—Pittsburgh, 1970, 1972, 1974, 1975; won 2.
A. L.—4—Kansas City, 1976, 1977, 1978, 1984; won 1.

Most Consecutive Years Losing Series

A. L.—3—Kansas City, 1976, 1977, 1978.
N. L.—3—Philadelphia, 1976, 1977, 1978.

Most Times Winning Series in Three Consecutive Games

A. L.—3—Baltimore, 1969, 1970, 1971.
N. L.—3—Cincinnati, 1970, 1975, 1976.

Winning Series After Winning First Game

A. L.—Accomplished 11 times.
N. L.—Accomplished 11 times.

Winning Series After Losing First Game

N. L.—Accomplished 5 times.
A. L.—Accomplished 5 times.

Winning Series After Winning One Game and Losing Two

N. L.—Cincinnati vs. Pittsburgh, 1972.
Philadelphia vs. Houston, 1980.
Los Angeles vs. Montreal, 1981.
San Diego vs. Chicago, 1984.
A. L.—New York vs. Kansas City, 1977.
Milwaukee vs. California, 1982.

Winning Series After Losing First Two Games

A. L.—Milwaukee vs. California, 1982.
N. L.—San Diego vs. Chicago, 1984.

Most Games Played, Total Series

A. L.—26—Baltimore, 7 Series; won 18, lost 8.
N. L.—22—Pittsburgh, 6 Series; won 9, lost 13.
Cincinnati, 6 Series; won 14, lost 8.

Most Games Won, Total Series

A. L.—18—Baltimore, 7 Series; won 18, lost 8.
N. L.—14—Cincinnati, 6 Series; won 14, lost 8.

Most Games Lost, Total Series

N. L.—13—Pittsburgh, 6 Series; won 9, lost 13.
A. L.—14—Oakland, 6 Series; won 9, lost 14.

Most Extra-Inning Games, Total Series

N. L.—5—Cincinnati, 6 Series, 22 games; won 3 lost 2.
Philadelphia, 4 Series, 16 games; won 2, lost 3.
A. L.—5—Baltimore, 7 Series, 26 games; won 4, lost 1.

Most Extra-Inning Games Won, Total Series

A. L.—4—Baltimore, 7 Series, 26 games; won 4, lost 1.
N. L.—3—Cincinnati, 6 Series, 22 games; won 3, lost 1.

Most Extra-Inning Games Lost, Total Series

N. L.—3—Philadelphia, 4 Series, 16 games; won 2, lost 3.
A. L.—2—Minnesota, 2 Series, 6 games; won 0, lost 2.

Most Extra-Inning Games, Series

3-game Series—A. L.— 2—Baltimore vs. Minnesota, 1969.
N. L.— 2—Cincinnati vs. Pittsburgh, 1979.
4-game Series—N. L.—1—Los Angeles vs. Philadelphia, 1978.
A. L.—1—Baltimore vs. California, 1979.
Baltimore vs. Chicago, 1983.
5-game Series—N. L.—4—Philadelphia vs. Houston, 1980.
A. L.— 2—Detroit vs. Oakland, 1972.

Most Games Won by One Run, Series, One Club

3-game Series—A. L.— 2—Baltimore vs. Minnesota, 1969.
            N. L.—1—Occurred often.
4-game Series—A. L.— 2—Oakland vs. Baltimore, 1974.
                    New York vs. Kansas City, 1978.
            N. L.—1—Occurred often.
5-game Series—A. L.— 2—Oakland vs. Detroit, 1972.
            N. L.—2—Cincinnati vs. New York, 1973.

Most Games Decided by One Run, Series, Both Clubs

3-game Series—A. L.— 2—Baltimore (won 2) vs. Minnesota, 1969.
            N. L.—1—Occurred often.
4-game Series—A. L.— 2—Oakland (won 2) vs. Baltimore, 1974.
                    New York (won 2) vs. Kansas City, 1978.
                    Baltimore (won 1) vs. California (won 1), 1979.
            N. L.— 2—San Francisco (won 1) vs. Pittsburgh (won 1), 1971.
5-game Series—A. L.— 3—Oakland (won 2) vs. Detroit (won 1), 1972.
            N. L.—2—Pittsburgh (won 1) vs. Cincinnati (won 1), 1972.
                    Cincinnati (won 2) vs. New York, 1973.
                    Philadelphia (won 1) vs. Houston (won 1), 1980.

Most Consecutive Series Won, Division

N. L.—5—West Division, 1974, 1975, 1976, 1977, 1978.
A. L.—5—East Division, 1975, 1976, 1977, 1978, 1979.

Most Consecutive Games Won, League, Total Series

A. L.—10—Baltimore, 1969 (3), 1970 (3), 1971 (3), 1973 (first 1).
N. L.— 6—Cincinnati, 1975 (3), 1976 (3).

Most Consecutive Games Lost, League, Total Series

A. L.—6—Minnesota, 1969 (3), 1970 (3).
        Oakland, 1975 (3), 1981 (3).
N. L.—6—Atlanta, 1969 (3), 1982 (3).

Most Consecutive Games Won, Division

A. L.—9—East Division, 1969 (3), 1970 (3), 1971 (3).
N. L.—7—West Division, 1974 (last 1), 1975 (3), 1976 (3).

Earliest Date for Championship Series Game

N. L.—October 2, 1971, at San Francisco; San Francisco 5, Pittsburgh 4.
        October 2, 1979, at Cincinnati; Pittsburgh 5, Cincinnati 2; 11 innings.
        October 2, 1984, at Chicago; Chicago 13, San Diego 0.
A. L.—October 2, 1984, at Kansas City; Detroit 8, Kansas City 1.

Earliest Date for Championship Series Final Game

N. L.—October 5, 1970, at Cincinnati; Cincinnati 3, Pittsburgh 2; 3-game Series.
        October 5, 1979, at Pittsburgh; Pittsburgh 7, Cincinnati 1; 3-game Series.
A. L.—October 5, 1970, at Baltimore; Baltimore 6, Minnesota 1; 3-game Series.
        October 5, 1971, at Oakland; Baltimore 5, Oakland 3; 3-game Series.
        October 5, 1984, at Detroit; Detroit 1, Kansas City 0; 3-game Series.

Latest Date for Championship Series Start

N. L.—October 13, 1981, at Los Angeles; 5-game Series ended at Montreal on October 19, 1981.
A. L.—October 13, 1981, at New York; 3-game Series ended at Oakland on October 15, 1981.

Latest Date for Championship Series Finish

N. L.—October 19, 1981—Series started October 13, 1981 at Los Angeles; 5-game Series ended at Montreal.
A. L.—October 15, 1981—Series started October 13, 1981 at New York; 3-game Series ended at Oakland.

Longest Game

A. L.—12 innings— Baltimore 4, Minnesota 3, at Baltimore, October 4, 1969.
N. L.—12 innings— Cincinnati 2, New York 1, at New York, October 9, 1973.

Longest Game by Time, Nine Innings

N. L.—3 hours, 23 minutes—Pittsburgh 9, San Francisco 4, at San Francisco, October 3, 1971.
A. L.—3 hours, 19 minutes—New York 4, Oakland 0, at Oakland, October 15, 1981.

Longest Game by Time, Extra Innings

N. L.—3 hours, 55 minutes—Philadelphia 5, Houston 3, at Houston, October 11, 1980, 10 innings.

A. L.—3 hours, 41 minutes—Baltimore 3, Chicago 0, at Chicago, October 8, 1983, 10 innings.

Shortest Game by Time

    A. L.—1 hour, 57 minutes-Oakland 1, Baltimore 0, at Baltimore, October 8, 1974.
    N. L.—1 hour, 57 minutes-Pittsburgh 5, Cincinnati 1, at Pittsburgh, October 7, 1972.

MOST PLAYERS USED AT POSITIONS

Most Players, Series, One Club

    3-game Series—A. L.— 24—Minnesota vs. Baltimore, 1970.
                               Oakland vs. New York, 1981.
                 N. L.—24—Pittsburgh vs. Cincinnati, 1975.
    4-game Series—N. L.—23—Los Angeles vs. Philadelphia, 1977.
                 A. L.—23—California vs. Baltimore, 1979.
                                 Chicago vs. Baltimore, 1983.
    5-game Series—A. L.— 25—Oakland vs. Detroit, 1972.
                 N. L.—24—Cincinnati vs. New York, 1973.
                                 Houston vs. Philadelphia, 1980.
                                 San Diego vs. Chicago, 1984.

Most Players, Series, Both Clubs

    3-game Series—A. L.— 46—Oakland 24, New York 22, 1981.
                 N. L.—42—Pittsburgh 24, Cincinnati 18, 1975.
    4-game Series—A. L.— 45—Chicago 23, Baltimore 22, 1983.
                 N. L.—44—Los Angeles 22, Pittsburgh 22, 1974.
                                 Los Angeles 23, Philadelphia 21, 1977.
                                 Los Angeles 22, Philadelphia 22, 1978.
    5-game Series—A. L.— 49—Oakland 25, Detroit 24, 1972.
                 N. L.—47—Houston 24, Philadelphia 23, 1980.
                                 San Diego 24, Chicago 23, 1984.

Fewest Players, Series, One Club

    3-game Series—A. L.— 14—Baltimore vs. Minnesota, 1970.
                                   Boston vs. Oakland, 1975.
                 N. L.—15—St. Louis vs. Atlanta, 1982.
    4-game Series—A. L.— 20—Oakland vs. Baltimore, 1974.
                                   Kansas City vs. New York, 1978.
                                   Baltimore vs. California, 1979.
                 N. L.—20—Philadelphia vs. Los Angeles, 1983.
    5-game Series—N. L.—17—New York vs. Cincinnati, 1973.
                 A. L.—18—New York vs. Kansas City, 1977.

Fewest Players, Series, Both Clubs

    3-game Series—A. L.— 35—Oakland 20, Baltimore 15, 1971.
                                   New York 20, Kansas City 15, 1980.
                 N. L.—35—Atlanta 20, St. Louis 15, 1982.
    4-game Series—A. L.— 41—New York 21, Kansas City 20, 1978.
                 N. L.—42—Los Angeles 22, Philadelphia 20, 1983.
    5-game Series—A. L.— 40—Kansas City 22, New York 18, 1977.
                                   Milwaukee 20, California 20, 1982.
                 N. L.—41—Cincinnati 24, New York 17, 1973.

Most Times, One Club Using Only Nine Players in Game, Series

    3-game Series—A. L.— 2—Baltimore vs. Minnesota, 1970.
                 N. L.— 1—Cincinnati vs. Pittsburgh, 1975.
    4-game Series—N. L.— 1—Los Angeles vs. Pittsburgh, 1974.
                                   Los Angeles vs. Philadelphia, 1977.
                 A. L.— 0—Never accomplished.
    5-game Series—N. L.— 3—New York vs. Cincinnati, 1973.
                 A. L.— 0—Never accomplished.

Most Players, Game, One Club

    A. L.—20—Oakland vs. Detroit, October 10, 1972.
                   Oakland vs. Detroit, October 11, 1972; 10 innings.
    N. L.—20—Philadelphia vs. Houston, October 12, 1980; 10 innings.
    N. L.—Nine-inning record—19—Los Angeles vs. Philadelphia, October 7, 1977.

Most Players, Nine-Inning Game, Both Clubs

    A. L.—35—Oakland 18, New York 17, October 14, 1981.
    N. L.—34—Los Angeles, 19, Philadelphia 15, October 7, 1977.

Most Players, Extra-Inning Game, Both Clubs

N. L.—37—Philadelphia 20, Houston 17, October 12, 1980; 10 innings.
A. L.—Less than nine-inning record.

FIRST BASEMEN

Most First Basemen, Series, One Club

3-game Series—A. L.— 3—Oakland vs. Boston, 1975.
                N. L.— 2—Held by many clubs.
4-game Series—N. L.— 3—Philadelphia vs. Los Angeles, 1977.
                A. L.— 3—Chicago vs. Baltimore, 1983.
5-game Series—A. L.— 3—Oakland vs. Baltimore, 1973.
                       Kansas City vs. New York, 1977.
                N. L.— 3—Houston vs. Philadelphia, 1980.

Most First Basemen, Series, Both Clubs

3-game Series—A. L.— 4—Oakland 3, Boston 1, 1975.
                       Oakland 2, New York 2, 1981.
                N. L.— 4—Cincinnati 2, Pittsburgh 2, 1970.
4-game Series—A. L.— 4—Baltimore 2, Oakland 2, 1974.
                       Chicago 3, Baltimore 1, 1983.
                N. L.— 4—Philadelphia 3, Los Angeles 1, 1977.
5-game Series—A. L.— 5—Oakland 3, Baltimore 2, 1973.
                N. L.— 4—Houston 3, Philadelphia 1, 1980.

Most First Basemen, Game, One Club

A. L.-N. L.—2—Made in many games.

Most First Basemen, Game, Both Clubs

A. L.-N. L.—3—Made in many games.

SECOND BASEMEN

Most Second Basemen, Series, One Club

3-game Series—A. L.— 3—Minnesota vs. Baltimore, 1970.
                       Oakland vs. Boston, 1975.
                N. L.— 2—Held by many clubs.
4-game Series—A. L.— 3—New York vs. Kansas City, 1978.
                N. L.— 1—Held by many clubs.
5-game Series—A. L.— 4—Oakland vs. Detroit, 1972.
                N. L.— 2—Held by many clubs.

Most Second Basemen, Series, Both Clubs

3-game Series—A. L.— 4—Minnesota 3, Baltimore 1, 1970.
                       Oakland 3, Boston 1, 1975.
                N. L.— 3—Made in many Series.
4-game Series—A. L.— 4—New York 3, Kansas City 1, 1978.
                N. L.— 2—Made in many Series.
5-game Series—A. L.— 6—Oakland 4, Detroit 2, 1972.
                N. L.— 3—Made in many Series.

Most Second Basemen, Game, One Club

A. L.—3—Minnesota vs. Baltimore, October 3, 1970.
       Oakland vs. Detroit, October 7, 1972; 11 innings.
       Oakland vs. Detroit, October 10, 1972.
       Oakland vs. Boston, October 7, 1975.
       New York vs. Kansas City, October 4, 1978.
N. L.—2—Made in many games.

Most Second Basemen, Game, Both Clubs

A. L.—4—Minnesota 3, Baltimore 1, October 3, 1970.
       Oakland 3, Detroit 1, October 7, 1972; 11 innings.
       Oakland 3, Detroit 1, October 10, 1972.
       Oakland 3, Boston 1, October 7, 1975.
       New York 3, Kansas City 1, October 4, 1978.
N. L.—3—Made in many games.

THIRD BASEMEN

Most Third Basemen, Series, One Club

3-game Series—A. L.— 3—Detroit vs. Kansas City, 1984.
                N. L.—Held by many clubs.

4-game Series—N. L.—3—San Francisco vs. Pittsburgh, 1971.
                A. L.—2—Chicago vs. Baltimore, 1983.
5-game Series—A.L.-N.L.—2—Held by many clubs.

Most Third Basemen, Series, Both Clubs

3-game Series—A. L.— 5—Detroit 3, Kansas City 2, 1984.
                N. L.—4—Cincinnati 2, Pittsburgh 2, 1970.
                        San Diego 2, Chicago 2, 1984.
4-game Series—N. L.—5—San Francisco 3, Pittsburgh 2, 1971.
                A. L.—3—Chicago 2, Baltimore 1, 1983.
5-game Series—A. L.— 3—Baltimore 2, Oakland 1, 1973.
                N. L.—3—Cincinnati 2, New York 1, 1973.
                        Los Angeles 2, Montreal 1, 1981.

Most Third Basemen, Game, One Club

A. L.—3—Detroit vs. Kansas City, October 3, 1984; 11 innings.
Nine-inning record—A.L.-N.L.—2—Held by many clubs.

Most Third Basemen, Game, Both Clubs

A. L.—5—Detroit 3, Kansas City 2, October 3, 1984; 11 innings.
Nine-inning record—A. L.-N. L.—3—Made in many games.

SHORTSTOPS

Most Shortstops, Series, One Club

3-game Series—N. L.— 3—Pittsburgh vs. Cincinnati, 1975.
                A. L.— 2—Held by many clubs.
4-game Series—N. L.— 3—Pittsburgh vs. Los Angeles, 1974.
                A. L.— 3—California vs. Baltimore, 1979.
5-game Series—A. L.— 4—Oakland vs. Detroit, 1972.
                N. L.— 3—Cincinnati vs. New York, 1973.

Most Shortstops, Series, Both Clubs

3-game Series—N. L.— 4—Cincinnati 2, Pittsburgh 2, 1970.
                        Pittsburgh 3, Cincinnati 1, 1975.
                A. L.— 4—Oakland 2, New York 2, 1981.
4-game Series—A. L.— 5—California 3, Baltimore 2, 1979.
                N. L.—4—Pittsburgh 3, Los Angeles 1, 1974.
5-game Series—A. L.— 6—Oakland 4, Detroit 2, 1972.
                N. L.—4—Cincinnati 3, New York 1, 1973.

Most Shortstops, Game, One Club

N. L.—3—Cincinnati vs. New York, October 9, 1973; 12 innings.
         Pittsburgh vs. Los Angeles, October 6, 1974.
         Pittsburgh vs. Cincinnati, October 7, 1975; 10 innings.
A. L.—3—Oakland vs. Detroit, October 11, 1972; 10 innings.
         Nine-inning record—2—Held by many clubs.

Most Shortstops, Game, Both Clubs

A. L.—4—Oakland 3, Detroit 1, October 11, 1972; 10 innings.
         Nine-inning record—3—Made in many games.
N. L.—4—Cincinnati 3, New York 1, October 9, 1973; 12 innings.
         Pittsburgh 3, Los Angeles 1, October 6, 1974.
         Pittsburgh 3, Cincinnati 1, October 7, 1975; 10 innings.

LEFT FIELDERS

Most Left Fielders, Series, One Club

3-game Series—N. L.— 4—Cincinnati vs. Pittsburgh, 1970.
                A. L.— 3—New York vs. Kansas City, 1980.
                        Detroit vs. Kansas City, 1984.
4-game Series—A. L.— 3—Kansas City vs. New York, 1978.
                        New York vs. Kansas City, 1978.
                        Baltimore vs. California, 1979.
                        California vs. Baltimore, 1979.
                        Chicago vs. Baltimore, 1983.
                N. L.— 3—Philadelphia vs. Los Angeles, 1983.
5-game Series—A. L.— 3—Detroit vs. Oakland, 1972.
                        Kansas City vs. New York, 1977.
                N. L.— 5—Philadelphia vs. Houston, 1980.

Most Left Fielders, Series, Both Clubs

3-game Series—N. L.— 6—Cincinnati 4, Pittsburgh 2, 1970.

A. L.—4—Baltimore 2, Minnesota 2, 1970.
Baltimore 2, Oakland 2, 1971.
New York 3, Kansas City 1, 1980.
Detroit 3, Kansas City 1, 1984.
4-game Series—A. L.— 6—Kansas City 3, New York 3, 1978.
Baltimore 3, California 3, 1979.
N. L.—4—Los Angeles 2, Pittsburgh 2, 1974.
Philadelphia 3, Los Angeles 1, 1983.
5-game Series—A. L.— 5—Kansas City 3, New York 2, 1977.
N. L.—6—Philadelphia 5, Houston 1, 1980.

Most Left Fielders, Game, One Club

N. L.—3—Philadelphia vs. Cincinnati, October 12, 1976.
Philadelphia vs. Houston, October 11, 1980; 10 innings.
Philadelphia vs. Los Angeles, October 8, 1983.
A. L.—3—Detroit vs. Kansas City, October 2, 1984.

Most Left Fielders, Game, Both Clubs

A. L.—4—Kansas City 2, New York 2, October 6, 1978.
Detroit 3, Kansas City 1, October 2, 1984.
N. L.—4—Cincinnati 2, Pittsburgh 2, October 3, 1970; 10 innings.
Philadelphia 3, Cincinnati 1, October 12, 1976.
Philadelphia 3, Houston 1, October 11, 1980; 10 innings.
St. Louis 2, Atlanta 2, October 9, 1982.
Philadelphia 3, Los Angeles 1, October 8, 1983.

CENTER FIELDERS

Most Center Fielders, Series, One Club

3-game Series—A. L.— 2—Held by many clubs.
N. L.—2—Cincinnati vs. Pittsburgh, 1979.
4-game Series—A. L.— 3—New York vs. Kansas City, 1978.
N. L.—3—Philadelphia vs. Los Angeles, 1983.
5-game Series—A. L.— 3—Oakland vs. Baltimore, 1973.
N. L.—3—San Diego vs. Chicago 1984.

Most Center Fielders, Series, Both Clubs

3-game Series—A. L.— 4—Baltimore 2, Oakland 2. 1971.
N. L.—3—Cincinnati 2, Pittsburgh 1, 1979.
Atlanta 2, St. Louis 1, 1982.
4-game Series—A. L.— 4—New York 3, Kansas City 1, 1978.
N. L.—4—Los Angeles 2, Philadelphia 2, 1977.
Philadelphia 3, Los Angeles 1, 1983.
5-game Series—A. L.— 5—Oakland 3, Baltimore 2, 1973.
N. L.—4—Cincinnati 2, New York 2, 1973.
San Diego 3, Chicago 1, 1984.

Most Center Fielders, Game, One Club

A. L.-N. L.—2—Held by many clubs.

Most Center Fielders, Game, Both Clubs

A. L.-N. L.—3—Made in many games.

RIGHT FIELDERS

Most Right Fielders, Series, One Club

3-game Series—A. L.— 4—New York vs. Oakland, 1981.
N. L.— 2—New York vs. Atlanta, 1969.
Philadelphia vs. Cincinnati, 1976.
4-game Series—N. L.— 3—Held by many clubs.
A. L.— 3—Baltimore vs. Chicago, 1983.
5-game Series—N. L.— 4—Houston vs. Philadelphia, 1980.
Chicago vs. San Diego, 1984.
A. L.— 3—Baltimore vs. Oakland, 1973.
Kansas City vs. New York, 1976.

Most Right Fielders, Series, Both Clubs

3-game Series—A. L.— 5—New York 4, Oakland 1, 1981.
N. L.— 3—New York 2, Atlanta 1, 1969.
Philadelphia 2, Cincinnati 1, 1976.
4-game Series—N. L.— 6—Los Angeles 3, Pittsburgh 3, 1974.
A. L.— 5—Baltimore 3, Chicago 2, 1983.
5-game Series—N. L.— 6—Houston 4, Philadelphia 2, 1980.
A. L.— 5—Kansas City 3, New York 2, 1976.

Most Right Fielders, Game, One Club

    A. L.—3—New York vs. Oakland, October 14, 1981.
    N. L.—3—Los Angeles vs. Montreal, October 17, 1981.

Most Right Fielders, Game, Both Clubs

    A. L.—4—Kansas City 2, New York 2, October 13, 1976.
        New York 3, Oakland 1, October 14, 1981.
    N. L.—4—Pittsburgh 2, Los Angeles 2, October 8, 1974.
        Houston 2, Philadelphia 2, October 11, 1980; 10 innings.
        Los Angeles 3, Montreal 1, October 17, 1981.

CATCHERS

Most Catchers, Series, One Club

    3-game Series—N. L.— 3—Philadelphia vs. Cincinnati, 1976.
                A. L.— 2—Held by many clubs.
    4-game Series—A. L.— 2—Baltimore vs. Oakland, 1974.
                      Baltimore vs. California, 1979.
                N. L.— 2—Los Angeles vs. Pittsburgh, 1974.
                      Los Angeles vs. Philadelphia, 1977, 1978, 1983.
                      Philadelphia vs. Los Angeles, 1977, 1978.
    5-game Series—A. L.— 3—Kansas City vs. New York, 1976.
                N. L.— 3—Houston vs. Philadelphia, 1980.

Most Catchers, Series, Both Clubs

    3-game Series—N. L.— 4—Philadelphia 3, Cincinnati 1, 1976.
                A. L.— 4—Baltimore 2, Minnesota 2, 1969, 1970.
                      Baltimore 2, Oakland 2, 1971.
                      New York 2, Oakland 2, 1981.
    4-game Series—N. L.— 4—Los Angeles 2, Philadelphia 2, 1977, 1978.
                A. L.— 3—Baltimore 2, Oakland 1, 1974.
                      Baltimore 2, California 1, 1979.
    5-game Series—N. L.— 5—Houston 3, Philadelphia 2, 1980.
                A. L.— 4—Made in many Series.

Most Catchers, Game, One Club

    A. L.-N. L.—2—Held by many clubs.

Most Catchers, Game, Both Clubs

    A. L.—4—Baltimore 2, Minnesota 2, October 4, 1969; 12 innings.
    Nine-inning record—A. L.-N. L.—3—Made in many games.

PITCHERS

See CLUB PITCHING RECORDS on page 468.

RECORDS OF CHAMPIONSHIP SERIES MANAGERS
AMERICAN LEAGUE (16)

	Series	Series Won	Series Lost	Games Won	Games Lost
Altobelli, Joseph S., Baltimore (East)	1	1	0	3	1
Anderson, George L., Detroit (East)	1	1	0	3	0
Dark, Alvin R., Oakland (West)	2	1	1	3	4
Fregosi, James L., California (West)	1	0	1	1	3
Frey, James G., Kansas City (West)	1	1	0	3	0
Herzog, Dorrell N. E., Kansas City (West)	3	0	3	5	9
Howser, Richard D., New York (East), Kansas City (West)	2	0	2	0	6
Johnson, Darrell D., Boston (East)	1	1	0	3	0
Kuenn, Harvey E., Milwaukee (East)	1	1	0	3	2
LaRussa, Anthony, Chicago (West)	1	0	1	1	3
Lemon, Robert G., New York (East)	2	2	0	6	1
Martin, Alfred M., Minnesota (West), Detroit (East), New York (East), Oakland (West)	5	2	3	8	13
Mauch, Gene W., California (West)	1	0	1	2	3
Rigney, William J., Minnesota (West)	1	0	1	0	3
Weaver, Earl S., Baltimore (East)	6	4	2	15	7
Williams, Richard H., Oakland (West)	3	2	1	6	7

NATIONAL LEAGUE (19)

	Series	Series Won	Series Lost	Games Won	Games Lost
Alston, Walter E., Los Angeles (West)	1	1	0	3	1
Anderson, George L., Cincinnati (West)	5	4	1	14	5
Berra, Lawrence P., New York (East)	1	1	0	3	2
Fanning, W. James, Montreal (East)	1	0	1	2	3
Frey, James G., Chicago (East)	1	0	1	2	3
Fox, Charles F., San Francisco (West)	1	0	1	1	3
Green, G. Dallas, Philadelphia (East)	1	1	0	3	2
Harris, C. Luman, Atlanta (West)	1	0	1	0	3
Herzog, Dorrell N. E., St. Louis (East)	1	1	0	3	0
Hodges, Gilbert R., New York (East)	1	1	0	3	0
Lasorda, Thomas C., Los Angeles (West)	4	3	1	10	7
McNamara, John F., Cincinnati (West)	1	0	1	0	3
Murtaugh, Daniel E., Pittsburgh (East)	4	1	3	4	10
Owens, Paul F., Philadelphia (East)	1	1	0	3	1
Ozark, Daniel L., Philadelphia (East)	3	0	3	2	9
Tanner, Charles W., Pittsburgh (East)	1	1	0	3	0
Torre, Joseph P., Atlanta (West)	1	0	1	0	3
Virdon, William C., Pitts. (East), Hous. (West)	2	0	2	4	6
Williams, Richard H., San Diego (West)	1	1	0	3	2

Managers Representing Both Leagues

	Series	Series Won	Series Lost	Games Won	Games Lost
Combined record of Anderson, George L., Cincinnati N.L. and Detroit A.L.	6	5	1	17	5
Combined record of Frey, James G., Kansas City A.L. and Chicago N.L.	2	1	1	5	3
Combined record of Herzog, Dorrell N. E., Kansas City A.L. and St. Louis N.L.	4	1	3	8	9
Combined record of Williams, Richard H., Oakland A.L. and San Diego N.L.	4	3	1	9	9

Most Series, Manager

Both Leagues—6—Anderson, George L., Cincinnati N.L.; Detroit A.L.; won 5, lost 1.
A. L.—6—Weaver, Earl S., Baltimore, 1969, 1970, 1971, 1973, 1974, 1979; won 4, lost 2.
N. L.—5—Anderson, George L., Cincinnati, 1970, 1972, 1973, 1975, 1976; won 4, lost 1.

Most Championship Series Winners Managed

Both Leagues—5—Anderson, George L., Cincinnati N.L., 1970, 1972, 1975, 1976; Detroit A.L., 1984.
N. L.—4—Anderson, George L., Cincinnati, 1970, 1972, 1975, 1976.
A. L.—4—Weaver, Earl S., Baltimore, 1969, 1970, 1971, 1979.

Most Championship Series Losers Managed

A. L.—3—Herzog, Dorrell N. E., Kansas City, 1976, 1977, 1978.
　　　　　Martin, Alfred M., Minnesota, 1969; Detroit, 1972; Oakland, 1981.
N. L.—3—Murtaugh, Daniel E., Pittsburgh, 1970, 1974, 1975.
　　　　　Ozark, Daniel L., Philadelphia, 1976, 1977, 1978.

Most Different Clubs Managed, League

A. L.—4—Martin, Alfred M., Minnesota 1970, Detroit 1972, New York 1976, 1977, Oakland 1981.
N. L.—2—Virdon, William C., Pittsburgh 1972, Houston 1980.

CHAMPIONSHIP SERIES ATTENDANCE

AMERICAN LEAGUE

Year	G.	Game 1	Game 2	Game 3	Game 4	Game 5	Total
1969	3	39,324	41,704	32,735	....	....	113,763
1970	3	26,847	27,470	27,608	....	....	81,945
1971	3	42,621	35,003	33,176	....	....	110,800
1972	5	29,536	31,088	41,156	37,615	50,276	189,671
1973	5	41,279	48,425	34,367	27,497	24,265	175,833
1974	4	41,609	42,810	32,060	28,136	....	144,615
1975	3	35,578	35,578	49,358	....	....	120,514
1976	5	41,077	41,091	56,808	56,355	56,821	252,152
1977	5	54,930	56,230	41,285	41,135	41,133	234,713
1978	4	41,143	41,158	55,535	56,356	....	194,192
1979	4	52,787	52,108	43,199	43,199	....	191,293
1980	3	42,598	42,633	56,588	....	....	141,819
1981	3	55,740	48,497	47,302	....	....	151,539
1982	5	64,406	64,179	50,135	51,003	54,968	284,691
1983	4	51,289	52,347	46,635	45,477	....	195,748
1984	3	41,973	42,019	52,168	....	....	136,160

NATIONAL LEAGUE

Year	G.	Game 1	Game 2	Game 3	Game 4	Game 5	Total
1969	3	50,122	50,270	53,195	....	....	153,587
1970	3	33,088	39,317	40,538	....	....	112,943
1971	4	40,977	42,562	38,322	35,482	....	157,348
1972	5	50,476	50,584	52,420	39,447	41,887	234,814
1973	5	53,431	54,041	53,967	50,786	50,323	262,548
1974	4	40,638	49,247	55,953	54,424	....	200,262
1975	3	54,633	54,752	46,355	....	....	155,740
1976	3	62,640	62,651	55,047	....	....	180,338
1977	4	55,968	55,973	63,719	64,924	....	240,584
1978	4	63,460	60,642	55,043	55,124	....	234,269
1979	3	55,006	55,000	42,240	....	....	152,246
1980	5	65,277	65,476	44,443	44,952	44,802	264,950
1981	5	51,273	53,463	54,372	54,499	36,491	250,098
1982	3	53,008	53,408	52,173	....	....	158,589
1983	4	49,963	55,967	53,490	64,494	....	223,914
1984	5	36,282	36,282	58,346	58,354	58,359	247,623

Largest Attendance, Game

N. L.—64,924—At Philadelphia, October 8, 1977; Los Angeles 4, Philadelphia 1; fourth game.

A. L.—64,406—At California, October 5, 1982; California 8, Milwaukee 3; first game.

Smallest Attendance, Game

A. L.—24,265—At Oakland, October 11, 1973; Oakland 3, Baltimore 0; fifth game.

N. L.—33,088—At Pittsburgh, October 3, 1970; Cincinnati 3, Pittsburgh 0; first game.

Largest Attendance, Series

3-game Series—N. L.—180,338—Cincinnati vs. Philadelphia, 1976.

A. L.—151,539—Oakland vs. New York, 1981.

4-game Series—N. L.—240,584—Philadelphia vs. Los Angeles, 1977.

A. L.—195,748—Baltimore vs. Chicago, 1983.

5-game Series—A. L.—284,691—California vs. Milwaukee, 1982.

N. L.—264,950—Philadelphia vs. Houston, 1980.

Smallest Attendance, Series

3-game Series—A. L.— 81,945—Baltimore vs. Minnesota, 1970.

N. L.—112,943—Pittsburgh vs. Cincinnati, 1970.

4-game Series—A. L.—144,615—Baltimore vs. Oakland, 1974.

N. L.—157,348—San Francisco vs. Pittsburgh, 1971.

5-game Series—A. L.—175,833—Baltimore vs. Oakland, 1973.

N. L.—234,814—Pittsburgh vs. Cincinnati, 1972.